D1473829

PC Magazine Guide to Using Quattro Pro 3.0/4.0

PC Magazine
Guide to
Using Quattro
Pro 3.0/4.0

The LeBlond Group
Geoffrey T. LeBlond
Laura D. Mann
William B. LeBlond
Michael J. Francis
Nikhil Mirchandani
Cliff Fischbach
Charles J. LeBlond, Jr.

Ziff-Davis Press
Emeryville, California

Development Editor	Eric Stone
Copy Editor	Winnie Kelly
Editorial Assistant	Noelle Graney
Technical Reviewer	Bruce Gendron
Project Coordinator	Bill Cassel
Proofreader	Aidan Wylde
Cover Design	Blue Design, San Francisco
Book Design	Laura Lamar/MAX, San Francisco
Technical Illustration	Cherie Plumlee Computer Graphics & Illustration
Word Processing	Howard Blechman and Cat Haglund
Page Layout	Adrian Severynen and Anna L. Marks
Indexer	Anne Leach

This book was produced on a Macintosh IIfx, with the following applications: FrameMaker®, Microsoft® Word, MacLink®*Plus*, Aldus® FreeHand™, Adobe Photoshop™, and Collage Plus™.

Ziff-Davis Press
5903 Christie Avenue
Emeryville, CA 94608

Copyright © 1992 by The LeBlond Group. All rights reserved.

PC Magazine is a registered trademark of Ziff Communications Company. Ziff-Davis Press, ZD Press, and PC Magazine Guide to Using are trademarks of Ziff Communications Company.

All other product names and services identified throughout this book are trademarks or registered trademarks of their respective companies. They are used throughout this book in editorial fashion only and for the benefit of such companies. No such uses, or the use of any trade name, is intended to convey endorsement or other affiliation with the book.

No part of this publication may be reproduced in any form, or stored in a database or retrieval system, or transmitted or distributed in any form by any means, electronic, mechanical photocopying, recording, or otherwise, without the prior written permission of Ziff-Davis Press, except as permitted by the Copyright Act of 1976 and except that the program listings may be entered, stored, and executed in a computer system.

THE INFORMATION AND MATERIAL CONTAINED IN THIS BOOK ARE PROVIDED "AS IS," WITHOUT WARRANTY OF ANY KIND, EXPRESS OR IMPLIED, INCLUDING WITHOUT LIMITATION ANY WARRANTY CONCERNING THE ACCURACY, ADEQUACY OR COMPLETENESS OF SUCH INFORMATION OR MATERIAL OR THE RESULTS TO BE OBTAINED FROM USING SUCH INFORMATION OR MATERIAL. NEITHER ZIFF-DAVIS PRESS NOR THE AUTHOR SHALL BE RESPONSIBLE FOR ANY CLAIMS ATTRIBUTABLE TO ERRORS, OMISSIONS OR OTHER INACCURACIES IN THE INFORMATION OR MATERIAL CONTAINED IN THIS BOOK, AND IN NO EVENT SHALL ZIFF-DAVIS PRESS OR THE AUTHOR BE LIABLE FOR DIRECT, INDIRECT, SPECIAL, INCIDENTAL OR CONSEQUENTIAL DAMAGES ARISING OUT OF THE USE OF SUCH INFORMATION OR MATERIAL.

ISBN 1-56276-071-8
Manufactured in the United States of America
10 9 8 7 6 5 4 3 2

To Noel and John Mann

—L.D.M.

To Mom

—G.T.L. and W.B.L.

CONTENTS AT A GLANCE

TABLE OF CONTENTS

ACKNOWLEDGMENTS

We would like to thank the following people for their gracious assistance with this book:

Nan Borreson of Borland International for making sure we got all the software we needed, and for keeping us informed all along the way.

Michael Scott of Borland International for a technical edit *par excellence*, and for that Saturday morning phone call that meant so much to the accuracy of this book.

And Cindy Hudson and Harry Blake for asking us to be among the first Ziff-Davis Press authors.

INTRODUCTION

THE FIRST TIME I HEARD OF QUATTRO (OR WHAT WAS EVENTUALLY TO become Quattro) was at a Lotus Developer Conference in Cambridge, Massachusetts, in 1985. A small group of Borland officials was on hand to woo Lotus 1-2-3 add-in developers like ourselves to create enhancement products for a brand-new, top secret spreadsheet they promised would "take the market by storm." At the time, 1-2-3 had what seemed like an unbreakable stranglehold on the spreadsheet market—so much so that we dismissed Borland's claims as mere hyperbole.

Looking back, I'm surprised to see how accurate Borland's assertions were, though I'm sure they would be the first to admit that it took a bit longer than expected. Since its introduction in 1987, Quattro (now Quattro Pro) has made its way from a less-than-remarkable product to a bona fide contender for the spreadsheet crown. With its latest release, Quattro Pro 4.0, Borland has seized the initiative in innovation. Quattro Pro offers an extremely powerful spreadsheet at a remarkably reasonable price.

Why We Wrote This Book

At the LeBlond Group, we've been involved with spreadsheets for quite some time now. I wrote my first spreadsheet book in 1983. Since then, our company has written numerous other spreadsheet books and has developed enhancement software for spreadsheets, primarily for Lotus products.

This is an update of our first book about Quattro Pro. If I had to pick one reason why we wrote the original book in 1991, it would be the simple fact that we couldn't resist the topic any longer. Quattro Pro 3.0 was a truly compelling product that was a joy to use. Borland has taken a good thing and made it even better in version 4.0. But rather than redesign the product from the ground up, they've chosen to add some incremental improvements and a dozen or so new features. Still, the two versions remain quite similar. In response to this, we've updated the book to cover all the new features of 4.0, yet we've maintained the thorough coverage of version 3.0 that readers of the first edition have enjoyed so much. Regardless of which version of Quattro Pro you're using, you'll find all the information you need here.

Who Should Read This Book

PC Magazine Guide to Using Quattro Pro 3.0/4.0 is intended to be the definitive tutorial and reference on Quattro Pro versions 3.0 and 4.0. It is for all users wishing to quickly achieve maximum productivity with Quattro Pro. The guide provides a comprehensive, step-by-step tour of Quattro Pro's spreadsheet, graphics, database, and WYSIWYG (what you see is what you get) features. It is designed to work just as well for novices as for experienced users.

For new users, this guide offers

- An in-depth discussion of all Quattro Pro features, commands, and functions that is sure to make you a master at using the program.

- Highlighted tips and techniques that will help you make the maximum use of the program.

For experienced users, the book contains

- An complete discussion of Quattro Pro 4.0's new features.

- A review of Quattro Pro's networking capabilities.

- Complete coverage of macros and macro programming.

- An in-depth explanation of how to take advantage of Quattro Pro in Microsoft Windows.

- A thorough review of Quattro Pro's advanced math features.

And these are just some of the topics. Whatever your skill level, *PC Magazine Guide to Using Quattro Pro 3.0/4.0* is sure to be a book that you can turn to again and again as you learn to master Quattro Pro.

How This Book Is Organized

PC Magazine Guide to Using Quattro Pro 3.0/4.0 is organized into 15 chapters that cover almost every conceivable aspect of Quattro Pro.

Chapter 1: Quattro Pro Basics

This chapter discusses the major features of Quattro Pro. After reading this chapter, you'll have the fundamental understanding you need to begin making effective use of the program.

Chapter 2: Managing the Desktop

Although many of the chapters in this book discuss how to manage windows on the Quattro Pro desktop, this chapter deals with that subject in detail. You'll learn how to create multiple windows, stack and tile windows, move between files, and more.

Chapter 3: Changing the Appearance of Data

With its WYSIWYG feature, Quattro Pro lets you change the appearance of your data and immediately see the effect on your screen. This chapter shows you how to fine-tune the appearance of your data, including how to control fonts and formatting.

Chapter 4: Manipulating Data

This chapter describes all the commands that are available for editing your spreadsheet data. You'll learn how to copy, move, and erase data, as well as how to fill ranges with values and how to convert formulas to their underlying numbers.

Chapter 5: File Management

Quattro Pro's /File commands are among its most powerful, and this chapter teaches you how to use all of them. For example, you'll learn how to place multiple files on the desktop. You'll also learn how to save files in compressed format using SQZ!.

Chapter 6: Printing Spreadsheets

This chapter examines all the aspects of printing spreadsheets in Quattro Pro. For example, you'll discover how to send output to the printer and how to print files to disk so that you can use them with other programs or print them out later.

Chapter 7: Functions

Quattro Pro's numerous @*functions* can save you hours of work. This chapter serves as a guide to Quattro Pro's @functions and is organized for easy reference.

Chapter 8: Creating Graphs

Since Quattro Pro's inception, graphing has stood out as one of its most attractive features. This chapter covers a broad range of topics that will show you how to take advantage of Quattro Pro's graphs. For example, you will learn how to create and customize all the different graph types as well as how to print your graphs.

Chapter 9: Using the Graph Annotator

Quattro Pro's Graph Annotator compares favorably to stand-alone graphics programs, and this chapter will show you its numerous capabilities. For example, you'll find out how to add custom text and shapes to a graph, and how to create your own slide shows complete with visual transitions and sound effects.

Chapter 10: Database Management

This chapter describes how to create a database in Quattro Pro and how to use the /Database commands to sort and query it. Other topics include how to access external databases stored in Paradox and how to restrict data entry to a particular area of the spreadsheet.

Chapter 11: Analyzing Data

Quattro Pro can perform sophisticated mathematical analysis, but understanding its tools can be difficult without some help. We've taken the time and effort to pick apart Quattro Pro's mathematical analysis commands, and Chapter 11 will pass all this information on to you. Special emphasis is given to Quattro Pro 4.0's new Optimizer, a tool for solving complex nonlinear problems.

Chapter 12: Creating Macros

When you've reached the point where you want to take Quattro Pro to its limits, you're ready to begin creating macros. This chapter teaches you all the basics of creating and using macros in Quattro Pro and includes numerous examples to enhance your understanding.

Chapter 13: Programming with Macros

This chapter is a reference to Quattro Pro's macro programming commands. Here you'll learn how to use these commands to create custom applications of your own design.

Chapter 14: Networking Quattro Pro

Quattro Pro's built-in networking features make it easy to share data across a network. This chapter tells you how to install Quattro Pro on a network and how to take advantage of Quattro Pro 4.0's advanced Novell NetWare support features.

Chapter 15: Customizing Quattro Pro

This chapter describes the many ways you can customize Quattro Pro's appearance and settings. For example, you'll learn how to set up your printer, how to control Quattro Pro's display mode, and how to create custom menus. Other topics include how to set up an extended memory cache and how to use Quattro Pro in Microsoft Windows.

Conventions

To help make this guide easier to read, we've followed certain conventions throughout. An example of each one follows:

- All commands appear as they do on the screen, with a comma separating each command keyword in a sequence—for example, /Edit, Copy.

- Keys to be typed by the user are boldfaced when they appear within the body of a paragraph—for example, "type **3000** and press Enter." Longer inputs are placed on a separate line in a different type style, as in the following:

    ```
    +G2+F8*E13+G8*G13
    ```

- When two or more keys must be pressed together, they are separated by a hyphen—for example, Alt-F5.

In Conclusion

Quattro Pro brings a new level of sophistication to the spreadsheet arena. With this new offering, Borland has seized the initiative with the most reasonably priced, intelligently designed spreadsheet on the market today.

We wrote *PC Magazine Guide to Using Quattro Pro 3.0/4.0* to help you gain full mastery of the program, and to serve as a lasting resource as you build your knowledge of this unique program. We hope you find it a valuable addition to your computer library.

Geoffrey T. LeBlond

C H A P T E R

Quattro Pro Basics

WHEN QUATTRO WAS INTRODUCED IN 1987, IT OFFERED NO RADICAL new twists on the spreadsheet concept. In fact, it was viewed primarily as a clone of Lotus 1-2-3. It did perform some functions better than 1-2-3—for example, its business graphs and macro debugging were superior—and it had a compellingly economical price.

In the years that have followed, however, Quattro Pro has taken the lead in innovation and is now well on its way to setting a new standard for DOS-based spreadsheets. In version 3.0, Quattro Pro took on a completely new look. Its WYSIWYG (What You See Is What You Get) display mode provided many of the features of a graphical user interface, such as the ability to choose typeface styles and sizes on screen, and produce presentation-quality output. In its latest incarnation, version 4.0, Quattro Pro's display has been even further refined. It now includes a new SpeedBar feature for quick access to commonly used commands and functions. But this is just one of several new features you'll find in this product.

This first chapter teaches you the basics of Quattro Pro—how to interpret what you see on the screen and build functional spreadsheets. You'll learn how to move around in the spreadsheet using the keyboard and the mouse. You'll also explore Quattro Pro's menus and its help system.

Note. When you've completed this chapter, you'll have all the skills you need to go anywhere else in the book and learn more about what interests you.

A Tour of the Screen

In Quattro Pro, your work is displayed on the screen in an area known as the *desktop*. You can place multiple spreadsheets on the desktop, each in its own *window*. You can also save the current arrangement of spreadsheets in a workspace file.

The desktop has five areas: the menu bar, input line, status line, Speed-Bar (known as the mouse palette in Quattro Pro version 3.0), and spreadsheet area. Figure 1.1 illustrates each of these areas, and the following sections describe them.

NOTE. *This chapter assumes that you have an EGA, VGA, or Super VGA monitor and graphics adapter and are working with Quattro Pro in WYSIWYG display mode. If your screen doesn't look like the figures you see in the early part of this chapter, Quattro Pro is running in Character mode. See "Switching Between Character and WYSIWYG Display Modes" for a description of these two display modes and how to switch between them.*

The Spreadsheet Area

The spreadsheet area is divided into columns labeled with letters across the top, and rows labeled with numbers along the left side of the screen. The intersections of columns and rows form a matrix of small rectangles known as cells. Each cell starts out empty and fills when you place data in it.

Figure 1.1

The main areas of
the Quattro Pro
screen

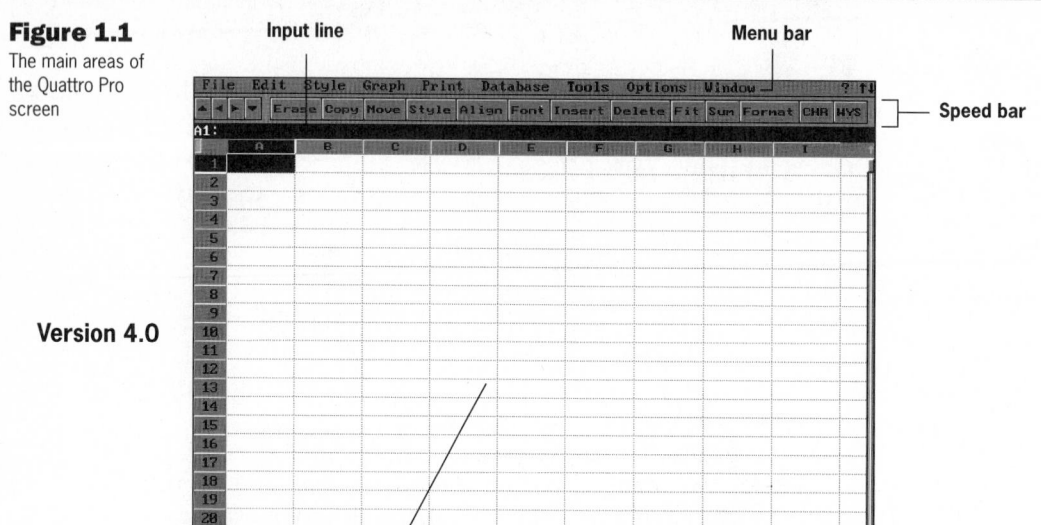

Input line

Menu bar

Speed bar

Version 4.0

Status line

Spreadsheet area

Input line

Mouse
palette

Version 3.0

The combination of a row number and a column letter forms the *cell address*—for example, C9 or AB199; notice that the column letter always comes first. The *cell selector* is the highlighted rectangle that identifies the *current cell*. This is the cell that will be affected by your next action, for example, typing a number into the spreadsheet. In Figure 1.1, the current cell is A1.

The spreadsheet area that you see on your screen is actually a window onto a much larger matrix of cells. In fact, the entire Quattro Pro spreadsheet is composed of 256 columns by 8,192 rows. (The address of the lower-rightmost cell in the matrix is IV8192.) The visible spreadsheet area is limited by two factors: the graphics display mode and the size of the spreadsheet window. Later on, you'll learn how to change both of these. But for now, assume that the size of the visible spreadsheet area is limited to what appears on the screen when you start Quattro Pro for the first time.

The Input Line

Note. The input line is the second line in Quattro Pro version 3.0.

Note. For the protection status to appear in the input line, global protection must be turned on with /Options, Protection, Enable; see Chapter 2.

The *input line* (sometimes called the *edit line*) is the third line on the screen. It serves as a window through which you enter and edit information for the spreadsheet. It is also the window through which you respond to Quattro Pro commands and prompts, for example, when you copy data from one cell to another or assign a special font (type style) to a cell.

Typically, the input line contains information about the current cell, starting with its cell address followed by a colon. (The cell address reflects the location of the cell selector.) Following the colon, you may see the cell's format, in parentheses. The format controls how a value (a number or formula) is displayed in the cell. The format only appears when you have changed from the default format (see Chapter 3). If the cell is protected, you may see the cell's protection status (PR or U). If a cell is protected, you cannot change its value.

The input line may next show the cell's column width (measured in characters), in brackets, if you have changed the width from the default. Any special font assignment for the cell appears next. Finally, you'll see the cell contents.

Here is a typical input line entry:

```
C9: (F2) U [W13] [F2] 1234
```

This line tells you that the current cell is at the intersection of column C and row 9; the cell contains a number that is displayed in Fixed format with two decimal places (F2); the cell is unprotected (U); the cell's column width is 13 (W13); and the cell contains the number 1234. Later on you will learn more about all the items that follow the colon and precede the cell contents, as well as how to enter numbers, labels, and formats.

When a cell is completely blank, the items following the colon generally do not appear. When you enter information into the cell, that information appears in the input line as well as in the spreadsheet area below. The section "Entering Data in Cells" in this chapter describes how to enter information into the spreadsheet.

The Status Line

Tip. You can have Quattro Pro display the date and time on the status line by using the /Options, Other, Clock command (Chapter 15).

The *status line* appears at the bottom of the screen and shows the file name on the left, followed by the window number in brackets. If you have not loaded or saved the spreadsheet, the file name appears as SHEET#.WQ1, where # is the number of the current window. In Figure 1.2, the current file name is SAMPLE.WQ1 and it is located in window 1. The rest of the status line contains a series of indicators, described in the next section.

Figure 1.2

Elements of the status line

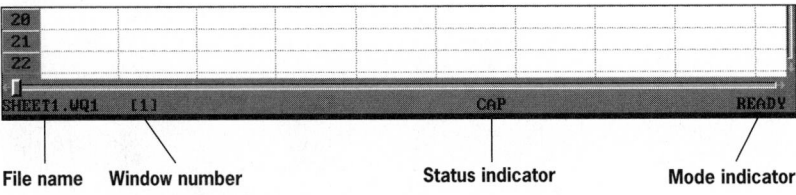

File name   Window number   Status indicator   Mode indicator

Mode and Status Indicators

Quattro Pro has two types of indicators—*mode indicators* and *status indicators*. Only one mode indicator appears at a time, always at the far right of the status line. Any number of status indicators may appear just to the left of the mode indicator. See Figure 1.2.

Mode indicators provide information about how Quattro Pro is functioning. For example, when it is waiting for your input, the mode indicator shows READY. While Quattro Pro is busy performing some task and cannot accept input, the mode indicator shows WAIT.

Status indicators are linked to a key that you have pressed to put the system in a particular state. For example, pressing End causes the END indicator to appear—you can then press another key to move the cell selector around the spreadsheet in large steps (see "The End Key" later in this chapter). Table 1.1 defines the mode and status indicators.

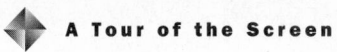

Table 1.1   **Quattro Pro's Spreadsheet Mode and Status Indicators**

Indicator	Description
CALC	The spreadsheet needs recalculating; press Calc (F9).
CAP	You pressed Caps Lock to turn on capitalization.
CIRC	Quattro Pro has detected a circular reference (a formula that refers to itself or to another formula that refers back to it).
DATE	You pressed Ctrl-D to enter a date or time number.
DEBUG	Quattro Pro is in Debug mode. When you execute a macro in Debug mode, the Debug Window lets you watch as Quattro Pro executes your macro one step at a time.
EDIT	You pressed Edit (F2) to edit a cell entry, or made an error entering a formula. (See Table 1.13 for special keys used in Edit mode.)
END	You pressed the End key and Quattro Pro is waiting for the next key. Press any cursor movement key (see Table 1.5) to move to the end of a continuous block of non-blank cells, or press End, Enter, or Esc to cancel.
ERROR	Quattro Pro has detected an error in the current spreadsheet. Press Esc to return to what you were doing before the error occurred or Edit (F2) to correct the error.
EXT	You are designating a cell block to be followed by a command that operates on that block.
FIND	You selected /Database, Query, Locate to find database records matching certain criteria, and Quattro Pro has located such a record. Or you pressed Query (F7) to repeat the latest /Database, Query command.
FRMT	You are editing a format line with Tools, Parse, Edit.
HELP	You pressed Help (F1) and a help screen is displayed; press Esc to return to the spreadsheet.
LABEL	You are entering a label (text).
MACRO	Quattro Pro is now running a macro.
MENU	You pressed either the / key, Choices (F3), Functions (Alt-F3), or Macros (Shift-F3) to activate Quattro Pro's command menus. To choose a menu item, use the arrow keys to highlight it and press Enter; or type the highlighted key letter for the command you want; or click on the command with your mouse. Press Esc to remove a menu display.
NUM	The Num Lock key is on.
OVLY	Quattro Pro is loading an overlay file.

Table 1.1	(Continued)	
Indicator	**Description**	
OVR	You pressed the Ins key; as you type, Quattro Pro overwrites existing characters. Press Ins again to return to Ready mode.	
POINT	You are being prompted to specify a cell or block in response to a command or formula you entered; you can also use Choices (F3) to view a list of block names.	
READY	Quattro Pro is waiting for input.	
REC	Quattro Pro is recording a macro.	
REP	The value you are entering in a menu command will be used to replace a current spreadsheet value.	
SCR	You pressed the Scroll Lock key. If you use any of the cell selector movement keys, Quattro Pro scrolls the entire window in the direction of the key.	
VALUE	You are entering a value (number or formula).	
WAIT	Quattro Pro is busy—it's either completing a command or recalculating the spreadsheet.	

Switching Between Character and WYSIWYG Display Modes

When you installed Quattro Pro, you undoubtedly noticed that the program senses the type of display you are using and adjusts itself accordingly. It uses the WYSIWYG (What You See Is What You Get) display mode if you have an EGA or VGA monitor. Otherwise, it uses Character mode.

WYSIWYG display is the mode used throughout this book. As its name implies, WYSIWYG's major advantage is that it displays on the screen what you will get when you print your output to a graphics printer. The display includes fonts, shading and line drawing, inserted graphs, and the like.

Character mode (also called text mode), on the other hand, uses the standard IBM character set. It does not show any of your custom fonts, nor does it give a very realistic picture of how your line drawing and shading will appear when you print. Figure 1.3 shows how your screen appears in Character mode in versions 3.0 and 4.0.

You can switch back and forth between WYSIWYG and Character mode using the keyboard or using *buttons* on the screen:

■ Using the keyboard, select the /Options, Display Mode command. To choose Character mode, select the A: 80x25 option. To choose WYSIWYG mode, select B: WYSIWYG.

Note. The WYSIWYG and Character modes are just two of the many display modes that Quattro Pro offers. When you select the /Options, Display Mode command, you'll see that there are many others. Chapter 15 tells you about the various display modes.

- Using the mouse, click on the CHR button in the SpeedBar (or mouse palette) to switch to Character mode. Click on the WYS button for WYSIWYG mode. (In Quattro Pro version 4.0's character mode, you'll need to click on the Bar button before the CHR and WYS buttons will appear.)

Figure 1.3
Character display
mode

Version 4.0

```
  File   Edit   Style   Graph   Print   Database   Tools   Options   Window          ? ↑↓
  C8: \-
    │      A        B         C        D        E        F        G        H       ↑End
   1                                          Business Plan 1992                      ▲
   2                                          Quarterly Proforma                    ◀ ↓ ▶
   3                                           Profit or Loss                         ▼
   4                                              (000's)
   5                                                                                 ■ERS
   6                                        6 months           9 months
   7                              1st Qtr  2nd Qtr   Y-T-D   3rd Qtr   Y-T-D  4th Qtr CPY
   8
   9  Sales                         1666     1691     3357     1770     5127    1867  MOV
  10
  11  Cost of Sales                  820      622     1442      650     2092     689  STY
  12
  13  Gross Margin                   846     1069     1915     1120     3035    1178  ALN
  14
  15  Admin Expenses                 688      692     1380      797     2177     869  FNT
  16
  17  Pre-Tax Profit                 158      377      535      323      858     309  INS
  18
  19                                                                                 BAR
  20
  PROFORMA.WQ1 [2]                                                              READY
```

Version 3.0

```
  File   Edit   Style   Graph   Print   Database   Tools   Options   Window          ↑↓
  C8: \-                                                                              ?
    │      A        B         C        D        E        F        G        H       End
   1                                          Business Plan 1992                      ▲
   2                                          Quarterly Proforma                    ◀ ▶
   3                                           Profit or Loss                         ▼
   4                                              (000's)
   5
   6                                        6 months           9 months             Esc
   7                              1st Qtr  2nd Qtr   Y-T-D   3rd Qtr   Y-T-D  4th Qtr
   8                                                                                 ↵
   9  Sales                         1666     1691     3357     1770     5127    1867
  10                                                                                 Del
  11  Cost of Sales                  820      622     1442      650     2092     689
  12                                                                                 @
  13  Gross Margin                   846     1069     1915     1120     3035    1178
  14                                                                                 5
  15  Admin Expenses                 688      692     1380      797     2177     869
  16                                                                                 WYS
  17  Pre-Tax Profit                 158      377      535      323      858     309
  18                                                                                 CHR
  19
  20
  PROFORMA.WQ1 [2]                                                              READY
```

One major advantage of Character mode is that Quattro Pro updates the screen more quickly than in WYSIWYG mode. The difference is particularly noticeable when you move the cell selector around the spreadsheet using the keyboard. Sometimes the delay in WYSIWYG mode can cause you to overshoot the mark.

Another advantage is that it is easier to work with multiple spreadsheet windows in Character mode than in WYSIWYG mode. Chapter 2 describes in detail the differences between these two display modes.

Function Keys

The *function keys* F1 through F10 are assigned to routine tasks that you want Quattro Pro to perform. Some are shortcuts to menu commands, and others perform unique tasks that you cannot accomplish in any other way. You can use the function keys alone or in combination with the Alt or Shift key. Table 1.2 is a summary of the names assigned to the various function key combinations, and Table 1.3 gives a detailed description of the various activities assigned to each key. Each of these keys is explained fully in appropriate chapters of this book. Whenever a function key is expressed in the text, you will see its name followed by its key assignment in parentheses, for example, Debug (Shift-F2).

Table 1.2   **Function Key Names**

Key	Alone	With Alt	With Shift
F1	Help		
F2	Edit	Macro Menu	Debug
F3	Choices	Functions	Macros
F4	Abs		
F5	GoTo	Undo	Pick Window
F6	Pane	Zoom	Next Window
F7	Query	All Select	Select
F8	Table		Move
F9	Calc		Copy
F10	Graph		Paste

Table 1.3   **Quattro Pro's Function Keys**

Key	Name	Description
F1	Help	Displays context-sensitive help screens. Press Esc to exit help.
F2	Edit	In Ready mode, switches to Edit mode and displays the current cell entry in the input line for you to edit. In File Manager, used to rename a file. In a file prompt box, F2 locates the first file beginning with the characters you type. In the Graph Annotator, after selecting a text element, F2 puts Quattro Pro in Edit mode.
F3	Choices	When Quattro Pro prompts you for a block or you're in Edit mode with your cursor positioned after an operator, F3 brings up a list of block names assigned in the current spreadsheet. You can also display the Choices list after typing +, *, or (and then F3. Press + on the numeric keypad to show the cell coordinates of the named blocks, and − to remove them. If you select a block name, Quattro Pro enters it on the input line. In the Graph Annotator, F3 activates the Property Sheet.
F4	Abs	Changes the cell address at the left of the cursor to an absolute reference. Press F4 repeatedly to cycle through the other possible mixed and relative reference combinations, and back to absolute.
F5	GoTo	Positions the cell selector in the cell address you specify, or in the upper-right corner cell of a named block.
F6	Pane	If you have two windows displayed, moves the cell selector to the inactive window. In File Manager, F6 moves between the control pane, file list pane, and tree pane.
F7	Query	Repeats last /Database, Query command. In the Graph Annotator, press F7 after selecting a group of objects to enter Proportional Resize mode.
F8	Table	Repeats the last executed /Tools, What-If command.
F9	Calc	Recalculates all formulas in the spreadsheet (in Ready mode); converts a formula to its current value (in Value and Edit modes). In a File Manager window, F9 rereads the current directory. If you're using manual recalculation in WYSIWYG display mode, F9 redraws the screen.
F10	Graph	Draws the current graph on the screen. Pressing Esc returns you to the spreadsheet. In Graph Annotator, press F10 to redraw the graph.
Alt-F2	Macro Menu	Displays the Macro Menu (a shortcut for /Tools, Macro).

Table 1.3   **(Continued)**

Key	Name	Description
Alt-F3	Functions	Displays the list of Quattro Pro functions. Selecting one enters it on the input line.
Alt-F5	Undo	When enabled, lets you reverse erasures, edits, deletions, and file retrievals (a shortcut for /Edit, Undo).
Alt-F6	Zoom	Expands the active window to full screen, or reduces expanded window to its previous size.
Alt-F7	All Select	Selects all active files in the File Manager list. Deselects selected files.
Shift-F2	Debug	Starts Debug mode so you can execute your macro step by step and pinpoint any problem areas.
Shift-F3	Macros	Displays a menu for Quattro Pro's Keyboard, Screen, Interactive, Program flow, Cells, Files, and / Command menu-equivalent macro commands.
Shift-F5	Pick Window	Displays a list of all open windows (like Alt-0). Select any window from the list to activate it.
Shift-F6	Next Window	Moves to the next open window, in the order that windows were created.
Shift-F7	Select	Starts Ext mode, so you can use arrow keys to preselect a block before using a command on that block. In File Manager, designates a highlighted file in the active file list for copying or moving.
Shift-F8	Move	In the File Manager, removes marked files from the active file list and stores them in a temporary memory buffer so you can insert them elsewhere.
Shift-F9	Copy	In File Manager, copies marked files in the active file list into temporary memory so you can insert them elsewhere.
Shift-F10	Paste	Inserts all files stored in temporary memory into the directory selected in the active File Manager list.

Getting Help

Quattro Pro provides a comprehensive, *context-sensitive* help facility that you can access by pressing Help (F1). Context-sensitive means that the help function makes a guess about what you are doing and displays an appropriate help screen. To return to the spreadsheet, press Esc.

Tip. To access help using the mouse, click on the question mark (?) at the end of the menu bar (in the mouse palette in version 3.0). To leave help, click anywhere outside of the help window.

Once you are in help, you can easily navigate between help topics. Each help screen displays a list of *keywords* in red, which when you choose them will take you to related topics. The keywords may appear within the body of the help text or at the bottom of the screen. Keywords at the bottom may include "Previous" and "Next," when there is more than one screen on the current topic, and "Help Topics." The Help Topics screen lists all the major topics for which you can get on-line help; this screen appears automatically when you access help from Ready mode.

To choose a help keyword, use the arrow keys to highlight the one you want and press Enter. (You can also click on a keyword with the mouse.) Pressing Home takes you to the first keyword on the screen; End takes you to the last keyword. Backspace returns you to the previous help screen.

Quattro Pro version 4.0 has a new feature for accessing an alphabetical list of help topics. When you press F1 and then F3, you'll see the help index in Figure 1.4. A title bar at the top of the list shows the name of the help screen that will appear when you select the highlighted item.

Figure 1.4

The alphabetical help index

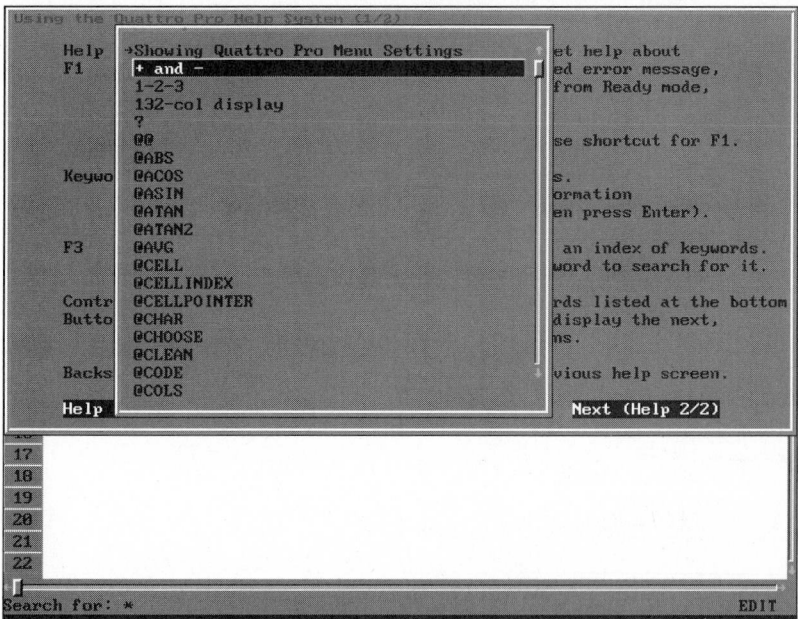

The quickest way to navigate to a help topic if it doesn't appear in the currently displayed list is to press the first letter of the topic. Quattro Pro will immediately skip to the first item that begins with that letter. If you want to get even closer to the topic, continue to type characters and Quattro Pro will shift the highlight accordingly.

Using the Mouse

If you have a mouse and you've loaded your mouse software (see Chapter 15) Quattro Pro will automatically detect its presence. You can tell when Quattro Pro is recognizing your mouse because it displays a variety of mouse-related elements on the screen, as illustrated in Figure 1.5. Here is a description of these elements:

- The *mouse pointer* appears as an arrow symbol in WYSIWYG and other graphics modes; in Character mode, it appears as a small rectangle. By moving the mouse pointer, you can focus Quattro Pro's attention on a particular area of the screen.

- The *SpeedBar* at the top of the screen includes several icons that serve as shortcuts for commonly used commands and functions.

- The *mouse palette* at the right of the screen in Quattro Pro version 3.0 is a trimmed-down version of the SpeedBar (see "Using the Mouse Palette in Quattro Pro Version 3.0," just below).

- The *scroll bars* let you scroll the screen horizontally and vertically (see "Scrolling with the Mouse," later in this chapter).

- When windows are tiled or stacked on the desktop in Character mode, the *zoom icon* lets you expand (zoom) a window to occupy the full screen. Conversely you can restore (unzoom) a window to its previous size.

- The *close box* lets you close a file and its window.

TIP. *If you are left-handed, you may want to have Quattro Pro recognize the right mouse button instead of the left. Use the /Options, Hardware, Mouse Button, Right command to do this.*

Figure 1.5
Mouse elements on
the Quattro Pro
screen

Version 4.0

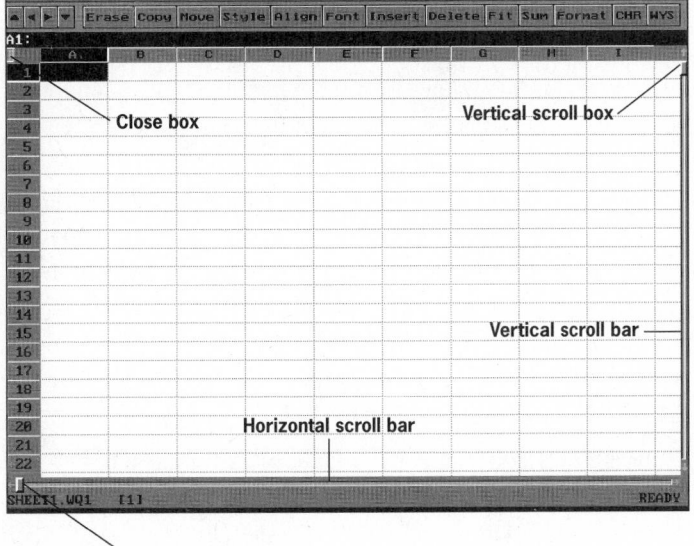

Close box

Vertical scroll box

Vertical scroll bar

Horizontal scroll bar

Horizontal scroll box

Zoom icon

Version 3.0

Mouse
palette

Using the SpeedBar

Note. The BAR icon that appears in Character mode allows you to access additional SpeedBar buttons.

The SpeedBar at the top of the screen (Figure 1.5) is one of Quattro Pro version 4.0's most highly touted new features. It has a series of buttons that you can click on to perform such things as cutting and pasting data, assigning styles, and summing adjacent cells. Here's a breakdown of the icons that appear in the SpeedBar when Quattro Pro is in READY mode:

▲◀▶▼   Each of these arrow buttons functions in the same way that a keyboard arrow does when you press End and then the arrow key. These mouse arrows let you move quickly around the spreadsheet in the direction of the arrow (see "The End Key" for more details).

`Erase`   Lets you erase a block of cells (shortcut for /Edit, Erase Block).

`Copy`   Lets you copy a block of cells (shortcut for /Edit, Copy).

`Move`   Lets you move a block of cells (shortcut for /Edit, Move).

`Style`   Lets you assign a named style to a block of cells (shortcut for /Style, Use Style).

`Align`   Lets you adjust the alignment of cell contents (shortcut for /Style, Alignment).

`Font`   Lets you change the typeface, style, color, and point size of a block of cells (shortcut for /Style, Font).

`Insert`   Lets you insert blank columns, rows, and blocks in a spreadsheet (shortcut for /Edit, Insert).

`Delete`   Lets you delete blank columns, rows, and blocks in a spreadsheet (shortcut for /Edit, Delete).

`Fit`   Lets you adjust the column width according to the length of the data that resides in a block or column (shortcut for /Style, Block Size, Auto Width).

`Sum`   Sums adjacent cells using @SUM.

`Format`   Lets you assign a numeric format to a cell (shortcut for /Style, Numeric Format).

`CHR`   Switches to Character mode.

`WYS`   Switches to WYSIWYG mode.

In EDIT mode, the Edit Speedbar displays these items:

▲ ◄ ► ▼	Same action as for READY mode (see above).
Name	Lets you select from a list of named blocks (same as pressing F3).
Abs	Cycles cell coordinates between relative, absolute, and mixed cell addressing (same as pressing F4).
Calc	Recalculates a formula and replaces it with its result on the input line (same as pressing F9).
Macro	Displays a menu from which you can see different lists of menu-equivalent macro commands (same as pressing Shift-F3).
@	Displays a list of @functions (same as pressing Alt-F3).
+	Enters a plus sign (+).
–	Enters a minus sign (–).
*	Enters a multiplication sign (*).
/	Enters a division sign (/).
(	Enters a left parenthesis.
,	Enters a comma.
)	Enters a right parenthesis.

TIP. *The SpeedBar is completely customizable in Quattro Pro version 4.0. To reassign the action of SpeedBar items, use the /Options, SpeedBar command (see Chapter 12).*

Using the Mouse Palette in Quattro Pro Version 3.0

The mouse palette at the right of the Quattro Pro version 3.0 screen (Figure 1.5) is the precursor of version 4.0's SpeedBar. Although it performs fewer actions than the SpeedBar and is only partially customizable, it is handy for performing certain actions without having to switch back to the keyboard.

`[ ? ]` This is the Help icon; it displays Quattro Pro's help system.

`[End]`
`[▲]`
`[◄|►]`
`[▼]`   Each of these arrow buttons functions in the same way that a keyboard arrow key does when you press End and then the arrow key (see "The End Key" for more details).

`[Esc]` The same as pressing the Esc key.

`[◄┘]` The same as pressing the Enter key.

`[Del]` The same as pressing the Del key.

`[ @ ]` Displays a list of @functions; the same as pressing Functions (Alt-F3).

`[ 5 ]` This button initially beeps, but you can reassign it to execute your own macro.

`[WYS]` Changes the display mode to WYSIWYG.

`[CHR]` Changes the display mode to character (80x25) mode

TIP. *You can customize the last seven buttons on the mouse palette to have them execute your own macros. Use the /Options, Mouse Palette, 1st Button through 7th Button commands. See Chapter 12.*

The sections that follow describe other ways you can take advantage of the mouse.

Moving Around the Spreadsheet

When you first start Quattro Pro, the cell selector is in cell A1 and you can enter data in that cell. Before you can enter data into another spreadsheet cell, however, you must move the cell selector to that cell. Quattro Pro offers a variety of ways to navigate within the spreadsheet, using the keyboard or the mouse.

Moving with the Keyboard

In Quattro Pro you use the calculator-style numeric keypad at the right of the keyboard to move the cell selector in the spreadsheet area, the cursor during data entry, and the command selector in Menu mode. If you have a 101-key-style keyboard, you also have separate gray arrow keys to use for movement.

Table 1.4 shows the cell selector movement keys and how they work. Note that sometimes two keys combine to perform a single action. In the sections that follow, you will see how to move around the spreadsheet with the most commonly used of these cell selector movement keys.

Table 1.4	**Cell Selector Movement Keys**
Key	**Cell Selector Movement**
←	One column to the left.
→	One column to the right.
↑	Up one row.
↓	Down one row.
Ctrl - ← or Shift-Tab	One windowful to the left.
Ctrl - → or Tab	One windowful to the right.
Home	To cell A1.
End	When followed by an arrow key, moves in the direction of the arrow to the next transition between blank and non-blank cells. End Home moves the cell selector to the lower-right corner of the active area.
PgDn	Down one windowful.
PgUp	Up one windowful.
F5 (GoTo)	To any cell address you specify.

Tip. If the NUM status indicator appears at the bottom of your screen, you will enter numbers into the input line when you press the arrow keys, instead of moving the cell selector around the spreadsheet. Press the Num Lock key once to turn off the NUM indicator and allow the cell selector to move.

The Arrow Keys

The arrow keys are the most basic keys for moving the cell selector around the spreadsheet—they let you move the cell selector one cell at a time in the direction of the arrow. For example, if the cell selector is sitting in cell A1, as in Figure 1.6, and you press →, the cell selector moves to cell B1. Pressing ↓ moves the cell selector to B2. If you then press ←, the cell selector moves to cell A2. Finally, pressing ↑ returns the cell selector to A1.

Moving the Window Around the Spreadsheet

Because of the vast size of the Quattro Pro spreadsheet (256 columns by 8,192 rows), there is no possible way to view all cells in the matrix at one time. In order to see a cell that does not currently appear within the spreadsheet area, you must *scroll* the window to it. Using the keyboard, all you have to do is move the cell selector beyond the edge of the window, and Quattro Pro scrolls the window contents to keep the cell selector in view.

The way that Quattro Pro scrolls the window depends on two factors: the size of the window and the number of columns and rows. Later on, you'll learn how to adjust these settings. For now, suppose your screen looks like Figure 1.6, with the cell selector in cell A1, and you press → until the cell selector is in I1. If you press → one more time to move beyond the edge of the window, Quattro Pro scrolls the screen to bring column J into view and moves the cell selector into J1—column A no longer appears on the screen, as shown in Figure 1.7. Now imagine that you press ↓ to move the cell selector to J22. If you press ↓ once again to move beyond the edge of the window, Quattro Pro scrolls the screen so that it looks like Figure 1.7.

Figure 1.6

A fresh spreadsheet

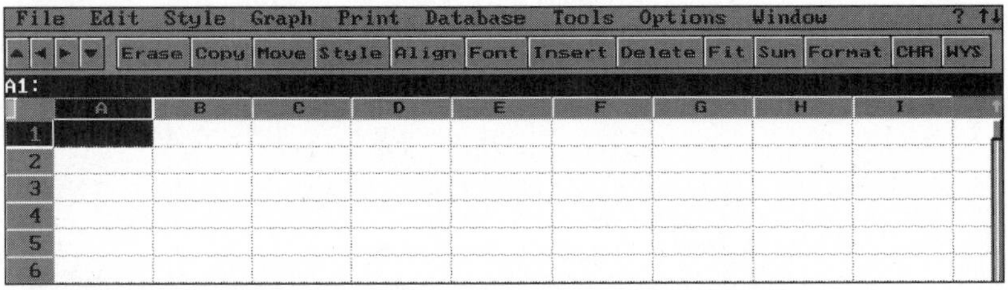

File	Edit	Style	Graph	Print	Database	Tools	Options	Window	? ↑↓

| ▲ ◄ ► ▼ | Erase | Copy | Move | Style | Align | Font | Insert | Delete | Fit | Sum | Format | CHR | WYS |

A1:

	A	B	C	D	E	F	G	H	I
1									
2									
3									
4									
5									
6									

Tip. You can use GoTo (F5) to look at another area of the spreadsheet without moving the cell selector from its original position. Just press GoTo (F5), and move to the area of the spreadsheet you want to see. To cancel the GoTo operation and return the cell selector to its original position, press Esc.

Moving the Cell Selector a Windowful at a Time

Quattro Pro has four keys for moving the cell selector around the spreadsheet a windowful at a time: Ctrl-→ (or Tab), Ctrl-← (or Shift-Tab), PgUp, and PgDn. These keys are helpful when you need to move in large segments.

The Ctrl-→ (or Tab) and Ctrl-← (or Shift-Tab) keys let you move laterally a windowful at a time. For example, if your screen looks like Figure 1.6 with the cell selector in A1, and you press Ctrl-→, the cell selector shifts nine columns to the right and displays J1 in the upper-left corner. Press Ctrl-←, and Quattro Pro shifts ten columns to the left, back to cell A1.

To move up and down a windowful at a time, you use the PgUp and PgDn keys. Suppose you have the first 22 rows showing on your screen, with the cell selector located in cell A1. Press PgDn, and the cell selector moves down 22 rows and displays cell A23 in the upper-left corner. Press PgDn again, and the cell selector moves to A45. Similarly, pressing PgUp moves the cell selector up 22 rows to cell A23. Press PgUp a second time, and the cell selector returns to its original position of cell A1.

Figure 1.7

Moving beyond the
edge of the window

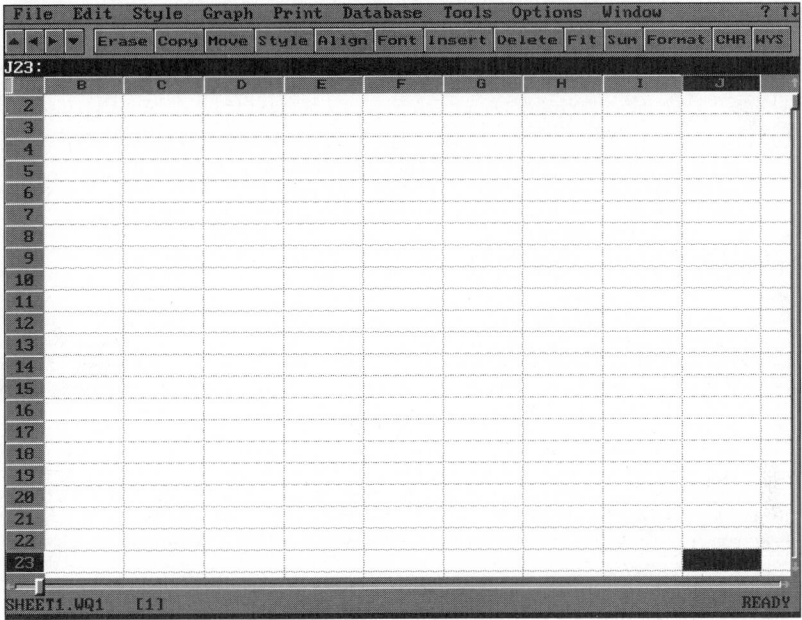

These are the factors that determine how Quattro Pro behaves when
you press a window movement key:

- The number of columns and rows that can appear on the screen. This depends on the display mode you've chosen. For example, WYSIWYG
  mode displays more columns and rows than Character mode. Other
  graphics modes show even more columns and rows.

- The width of each column and the height of each row. In Chapter 3,
  you'll learn how to change these settings to control the appearance of
  the spreadsheet.

- The number of columns and rows in a window. Quattro Pro has a variety
  of commands for managing the size and placement of windows on the
  desktop. Chapter 2 describes these commands in detail.

For example, if you are running Quattro Pro in Character mode, only 20
spreadsheet rows appear on the screen, and PgUp and PgDn move the cell
selector only that number of rows. By the same token, if you have adjusted
the column widths in the spreadsheet, pressing Ctrl-→ or Ctrl-← may move
the cell selector more or less than the ten columns normally displayed in
WYSIWYG mode. Irrespective of all these different factors, Quattro Pro

always moves the cell selector according to the size of the current window, whose size may or may not occupy the full screen.

The End Key

The End key lets you move the cell selector to the end of a block of cells. Pressing End by itself has no immediate effect. But when you press an arrow key after pressing End, the cell selector moves in the direction of the arrow to the next filled cell (a cell that contains data) that is followed or preceded by a blank cell. If there is no filled cell in the direction of the arrow, the cell selector moves to the spreadsheet boundary.

Suppose you have the spreadsheet in Figure 1.8, with the cell selector in cell A3. Press End-→, and Quattro Pro moves the cell selector to C3 (the next filled cell that is followed by a blank cell). Press End-→ again, and the cell selector moves to E3 (the next filled cell that is preceded by a blank cell). Press End-→ a third time, and the cell selector moves to H3 (again, the next filled cell followed by a blank cell). Press End-→ a final time, and the cell selector moves to the spreadsheet boundary, cell IV3.

Note. Clicking on the arrow buttons in the SpeedBar (and version 3.0's mouse palette) works the same as pressing an End-arrow key combination on the keyboard.

Figure 1.8
Using the End key with → to move the cell selector

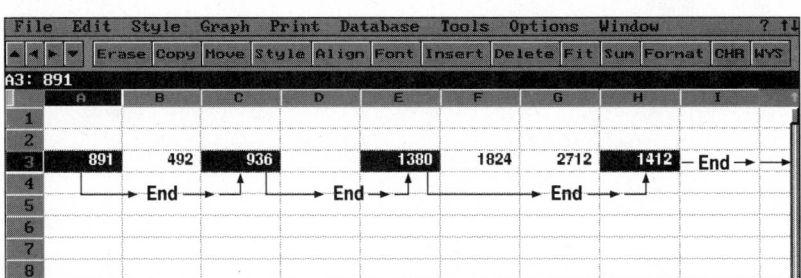

The Home Key

Pressing the Home key takes you to cell A1 in the spreadsheet. This cell is known as the *home position* in a spreadsheet.

The action of the Home key is quite helpful if your intent is in fact to move to the home position. If you press Home by mistake, however, it can be quite annoying, because there is no convenient way to return to your original location. Typically, you have to resort to some combination of arrow keys, PgDn, and Ctrl-→ to get back to where you were. If you happen to remember the original cell address, you can press GoTo (F5), type the address, and press Enter.

The End Home Combination

The End Home combination takes you to the lower-right corner of the *active area* of the spreadsheet. The active area is a rectangular block that encompasses every entry in the spreadsheet. When determining the active area, Quattro Pro includes any blank cells that have been formatted, assigned a font other than Font 1, or contain line drawing or shading (you'll learn more about these features in later chapters).

In Figure 1.9, notice that the cell selector is in cell A1. If you press End Home, Quattro Pro moves the cell selector to cell H14, the lower-right corner of the active area, as shown in Figure 1.10.

Figure 1.9

A sample spreadsheet

File	Edit	Style	Graph	Print	Database	Tools	Options	Window		? ↑↓

| ▲ ◄ ► ▼ | Erase | Copy | Move | Style | Align | Font | Insert | Delete | Fit | Sum | Format | CHR | WYS |

A1: [W13]

	A	B	C	D	E	F	G	H
1								
2								
3			EXPENSE REPORT FOR ALLISON SPRINGS					
4			WEEK ENDING JUNE 27, 1992					
5								
6	DAY OF WEEK	DATE	LOCATION	TRANSPORT	HOTEL	ENTERTAIN	MEALS	TOTAL
7	SUNDAY	06/21	SAN DIEGO	$89.00	$0.00	$10.00	$36.95	$135.95
8	MONDAY	06/22	SAN DIEGO	$9.00	$67.00	$32.50	$19.56	$128.06
9	TUESDAY	06/23	SAN DIEGO	$27.55	$67.00	$0.00	$35.00	$129.55
10	WEDNESDAY	06/24	SAN DIEGO	$12.50	$67.00	$98.10	$45.15	$222.75
11	THURSDAY	06/25	SAN DIEGO	$0.00	$67.00	$0.00	$24.25	$91.25
12	FRIDAY	06/26	SAN DIEGO	$0.00	$67.00	$0.00	$28.55	$95.55
13	SATURDAY	06/27	SAN JOSE	$133.00	$67.00	$0.00	$0.00	$200.00
14	TOTAL			$271.05	$402.00	$140.60	$189.46	$1,003.11
15								
16								
17								
18								
19								
20								
21								
22								

SAMPLE.WQ1   [2]   READY

The Scroll Lock Key

By pressing Scroll Lock, you can move the entire window around the spreadsheet yet keep the cell selector in place. In Figure 1.10, if you press Scroll Lock followed by →, Quattro Pro scrolls the window one column to the left. Figure 1.11 shows the results. Notice that the cell selector still resides in cell H14. In addition, an SCR indicator appears in the status line at the bottom of your screen.

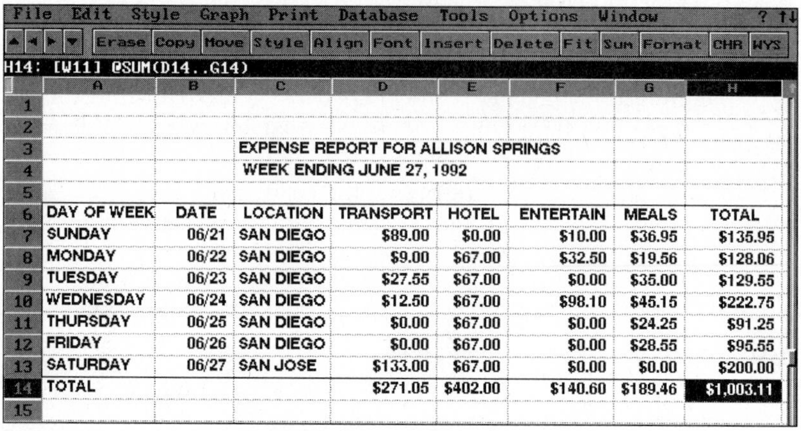

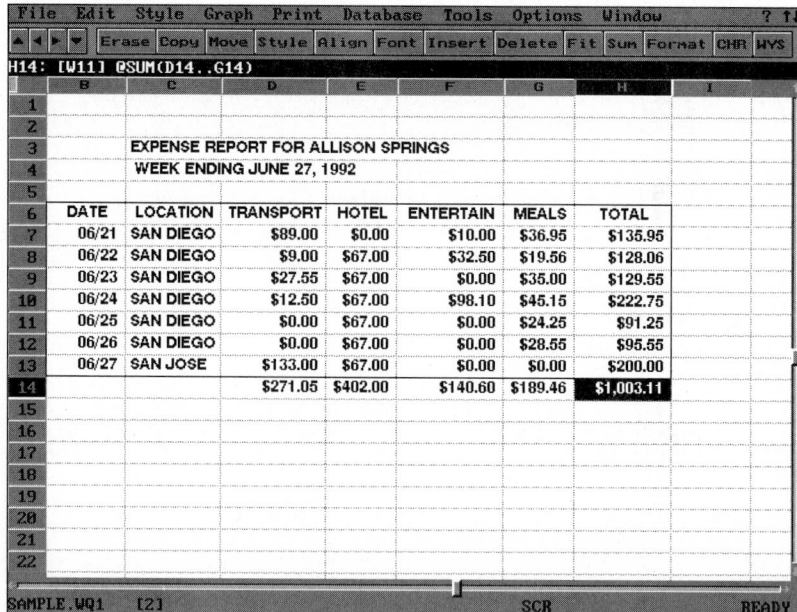

Figure 1.10
After pressing End Home

Figure 1.11
After pressing Scroll Lock→

Moving with the Mouse

You'll find that moving the cell selector with the mouse is especially easy, particularly if you are moving to a cell within the current window.

Moving to a Cell Within the Window

When a cell appears within the current window, the easiest way to move to that cell is to click on it with the mouse. Quattro Pro instantly moves the cell selector to that cell. You can then enter or edit data in the cell as you like.

Scrolling with the Mouse

Scrolling with the mouse involves using the vertical and horizontal scroll bars that border the window, as shown in Figure 1.12. You can scroll in any of the following ways with the mouse:

Note. You can also move around the spreadsheet using the arrow buttons in the SpeedBar (or version 3.0's mouse palette). These buttons have the same effect as pressing an End arrow key combination on the keyboard. See "The End Key" earlier in the chapter.

- To scroll up or down a row at a time, click on the top or bottom arrow in the vertical scroll bar. You can scroll continuously by pointing to the top or bottom arrow and holding down the mouse button.

- To scroll left or right a column at a time, click on the left or right arrow in the horizontal scroll bar. You can scroll continuously by pointing to the left or right arrow and holding down the mouse button.

Figure 1.12

Scroll bars and scroll boxes

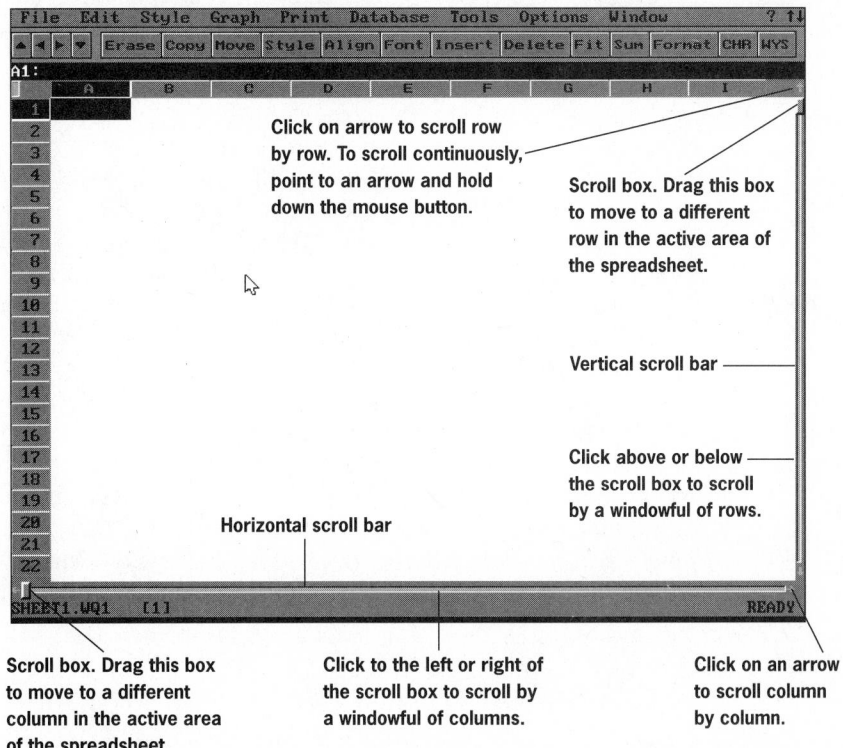

■ To scroll up or down a windowful of rows, click above or below the scroll box in the vertical scroll bar.

■ To scroll left or right a windowful of columns, click to the left or right of the scroll box in the horizontal scroll bar.

■ To move to a different column in the active area of the spreadsheet, drag the scroll box in the horizontal scroll bar to the left or right.

■ To move to a different row in the active area of the spreadsheet, drag the scroll box in the vertical scroll bar up or down.

Note. When you scroll with the mouse, the cell selector always remains in view.

■ To move to the home position (A1), drag the scroll box in the vertical scroll bar all the way to the top, and the one in the horizontal scroll bar all the way to the left.

In theory, the position of a scroll box within a scroll bar is relative to the cell selector's position in the active area of the spreadsheet. As you work with Quattro Pro, however, you'll find that the way it positions the scroll boxes within the scroll bars is not all that precise. Therefore, the only practical use for a scroll box is to drag it to one end of the scroll bar or the other, thus moving to the edge of the active area.

Jumping to Cells

Tip. You can also use GoTo (F5) to jump between open files. See Chapter 2.

If you have a complex spreadsheet with many cell entries, there is a faster way to move around within it than by using the mouse and selector movement keys: You can jump directly to a cell with GoTo (F5). When you press GoTo, Quattro Pro prompts you for an address and displays the current cell address after the prompt. Just type the cell address or block name you want to move to (block names are discussed later in this chapter). When you press Enter, Quattro Pro takes you directly to that cell.

For example, suppose the cell selector is in A1, and you want to jump to M5. Press GoTo (F5), type **M5**, and press Enter, and Quattro Pro shifts the screen to look like Figure 1.13. Notice that when the cell you are jumping to is not within the window, Quattro Pro positions that cell in the upper-left corner of the visible window. If the cell is within view, Quattro Pro merely jumps the cell selector to that cell without shifting the window contents.

Menus

As you know, whenever you start Quattro Pro, the menu bar appears on the first line of the screen. It is through this menu bar that you can copy and move cell contents, create graphs, print data, save files, and perform many other powerful operations for which Quattro Pro is well known.

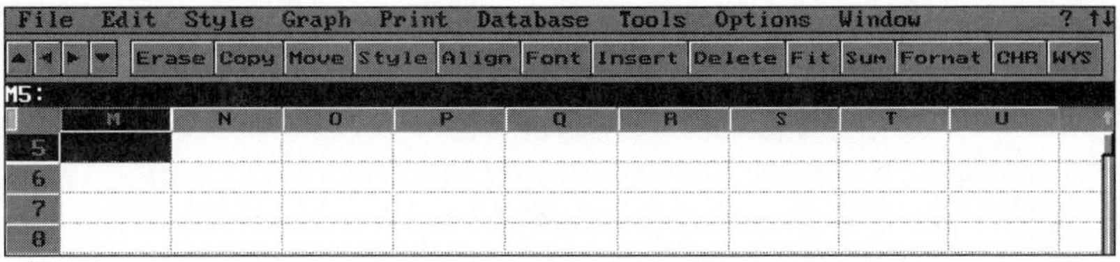

Figure 1.13
Using GoTo (F5) to
jump to cell M5

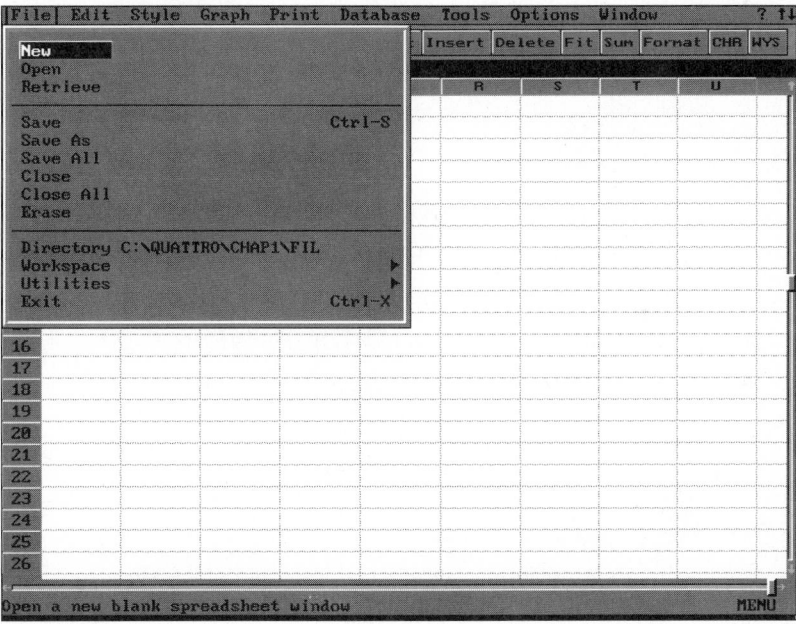

When you select a command from the menu bar, Quattro Pro typically offers the items related to that command in a *pull-down menu*. Figure 1.14 shows the /File pull-down menu. As with almost every operation in Quattro Pro, you can use either the keyboard or the mouse (or both) to access Quattro Pro's menus.

Figure 1.14
The /File pull-down
menu

Here are some conventions used in Quattro Pro's menus:

- **Arrow (▸)** If an option in a pull-down menu has related commands, an arrow appears to the right of that option. Select an option in the pull-down menu, and the related commands appear in a separate menu known as a *child menu*. Options in child menus may also have arrows indicating additional child menus are available.

- **Red or Bold Letters**   Each option in a menu has one red or boldfaced letter, indicating that you can select that option by typing the letter on the keyboard. For example, to select the /File option from the menu bar, type / (slash) followed by **F**. The / selects the main menu and F the File menu.

- **Shortcut Keys**   Next to many menu items you'll see a *shortcut* key sequence. Pressing this key sequence has the same effect as selecting the command. Figure 1.14 shows that Ctrl-S is a shortcut for selecting the /File, Save command.

- **Horizontal Lines**   These lines separate groups of related commands in a pull-down menu.

- **Command Settings**   For many commands, Quattro Pro shows the current command setting to the right of the menu option. In Figure 1.14, for example, you can see that the current /File, Directory setting is C:\QUATTRO\CHAP1\FILES. (Quattro Pro has actually truncated this setting to fit within the allotted space.)

TIP. *You can remove the command settings from a menu and shrink the menu's width by pressing the Contract key (the minus key on the numeric keypad). To have the settings reappear, use the Expand key (the plus key on the numeric keypad).*

Accessing Menus with the Keyboard

To select a menu item with the keyboard, press / (slash) or Menu (F3) to activate the menu bar. Then type the red (or bold) letter you see within the menu item, or use the arrow keys to highlight the menu item and press Enter. To leave the main menu and return to the spreadsheet, press Esc (or Ctrl-Break).

When you access the menu bar, a rectangular pointer called the *command selector* highlights a command, and a description of the highlighted command appears in the last line of the screen. Table 1.5 defines the keys that you can use within menus.

Accessing Menus with the Mouse

To access Quattro Pro's main menu with the mouse, simply click on any command in the menu bar. Once you've clicked on a command, that command is

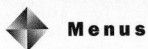

highlighted, its pull-down menu appears, and the first item in the pull-down menu is also highlighted. After you've accessed the menu, you can then select an item from within a pull-down menu by clicking on it as well.

Table 1.5 **Keys for Navigating the Menus**

Key	Result
/ (slash)	Activates the menu bar in a spreadsheet or in File Manager. Activates the Graph Annotator in a displayed graph or the Toolbox in the Annotator. Activates the Macro Debugger menu in a Macro Debugger window. Activates the Transcript menu in a Transcript window.
Ctrl-Break	Returns to the spreadsheet in Ready mode from any command level. Halts a running macro.
Ctrl-D	Press before entering a date or time in response to a menu prompt to have Quattro Pro convert your entry to a date or time number.
End	Moves selector to last command in menu.
Enter	Selects highlighted menu option. Ctrl-Enter stores a menu command as a shortcut key.
Esc	From menu bar, returns to spreadsheet in Ready mode. In menus, regresses one level in the command hierarchy.
Home	Moves selector to first command in menu.
←	On menu bar, moves one command to the left. From first item on menu bar, moves to last item on menu bar. In child menus, moves up one command, or from first item in menu to last item.
→	On menu bar, moves one command to the right. From last item on menu bar, moves to first item on menu bar. In a child menu, moves down one command, or from last item in menu to first item.
↑	On the menu bar, same as ←. In a child menu, moves up one command.
↓	On the menu bar, opens a pull-down menu. In a child menu, moves down one command.
Red or bold letters	Chooses a menu item.
Spacebar	Same as →.
+ on numeric keypad (Expand)	Displays the command settings, if any, for the menu you are in. In a Choices (F3) list, makes Quattro Pro display the block coordinates. Pressing F3 then expands the Choices (F3) list.
– on numeric keypad (Contract)	In a menu, shrinks the display so that command settings disappear. In a Choices (F3) list, removes displayed block coordinates.

Table 1.6 shows how you can use the mouse with menus.

When using the mouse to access Quattro Pro's menus, one of the easiest ways to see all the available first-level menu choices and their associated descriptions is to drag the mouse pointer from one menu item to the next. Hold down the left mouse button and keep it held down as you move the mouse. When you reach the item you want, release the button to select the menu choice and issue the command.

Table 1.6   **Mouse Clicks in Menus**

Click On	Result
A menu bar option	Activates the main menu
Highlighted menu option	Chooses that option
Elsewhere on the screen	Cancels the entire command
The ↵ button in the mouse palette (version 3.0 only)	Selects the highlighted option
The Esc button in the mouse palette (version 3.0 only)	Same as pressing the Esc key

---

To bail out of the menu without selecting a command, simply release the mouse button outside the menu area.

Canceling a Command

Tip. If you inadvertently enter the File Manager (/File, Utilities, File Manager), use /File, Close to exit it. Similarly, to exit the Annotator (/Graph, Annotate) use /Q.

If you select a command and then decide that you don't want to execute the command after all, you can cancel it with the mouse or the keyboard.

To cancel a command with the keyboard and return to the spreadsheet in Ready mode, press Ctrl-Break. You can use Ctrl-Break from anywhere within Quattro Pro's command hierarchy. For example, suppose you select the /Options, Hardware, Screen command, and when you see the command's child window, you decide you've chosen the wrong command. Press Ctrl-Break, and Quattro Pro removes all the menus from the screen and returns you to the spreadsheet.

To exit the current command level and return to the previous command level, press Esc. From the main menu bar, Esc returns you to the spreadsheet in Ready mode.

You can cancel a command by using the mouse in any of the following ways:

- Click anywhere outside the menu, and Quattro Pro returns you to the spreadsheet.

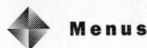 **Menus**

- Click on another command to select it instead. (This technique does not work when Quattro Pro is prompting you for input in the input line.)

- In version 3.0, click on the Esc button in the mouse palette. This is the same as pressing the Esc key.

Creating Your Own Shortcuts

Many Quattro Pro commands have shortcuts assigned to them—for example, Ctrl-X for /File, Exit. Table 1.7 lists Quattro Pro's preassigned shortcuts.

Table 1.7   **Preassigned Shortcut Keys**

Shortcut	Command
Ctrl-A	/Style, Alignment
Ctrl-C	/Edit, Copy
*Ctrl-D	Switches Quattro Pro to Date mode
Ctrl-E	/Edit, Erase Block
Ctrl-F	/Style, Numeric Format
Ctrl-G	/Graph, Fast Graph
Ctrl-I	/Edit, Insert
Ctrl-M	/Edit, Move
Ctrl-N	/Edit, Search & Replace, Next
Ctrl-P	/Edit, Search & Replace, Previous
Ctrl-R	/Window, Move/Size
Ctrl-S	/File, Save
Ctrl-T	/Window, Tile
Ctrl-W	/Style, Column Width
Ctrl-X	/File, Exit

*   This shortcut is used to enter dates or times directly into your spreadsheet and cannot be reassigned. All others can be reassigned.

As you work with Quattro Pro, you may decide you want to assign shortcuts to other commands. Fortunately, Quattro Pro makes it easy to define your own shortcuts. Suppose you want to assign the shortcut Ctrl-B to the /Style, Font command. To create this shortcut,

1. Activate the /Style pull-down menu and highlight the Font option.

2. Press Ctrl-Enter. Quattro Pro displays a prompt in the status line requesting that you hold down the Ctrl key and press any letter.

3. Press Ctrl-B. Quattro Pro instantly displays the new shortcut assignment in the menu to the right of the Font command.

4. Press Esc to return to the spreadsheet in Ready mode.

Note. If you try to assign a Ctrl-letter key sequence that is already assigned to a shortcut, Quattro Pro won't let you. You must first cancel the existing assignment before you can reassign the key sequence to another shortcut.

To test your new shortcut, simply press Ctrl-B. Interestingly, Quattro Pro displays the Font menu without its parent, the /Style menu. In addition, if you press Esc to cancel the command, Quattro Pro returns you to the spreadsheet in Ready mode; it does not return you to the /Style menu.

Quattro Pro saves the shortcut along with the current menu, in this case the Quattro Pro menu (QUATTRO.MU). If you use another menu—for example, the 1-2-3–compatible menu—you must reassign the shortcut key there. (See Chapter 15 for more on changing menus.)

To cancel a shortcut you've created, highlight the command in the menu, and press Ctrl-Enter followed by Del twice.

Remember that Quattro Pro also provides function key shortcuts, for example, Alt-F5 for /Edit, Undo. Function key shortcuts are not reassignable. (Table 1.3 gave you a list of these keys.)

Dialog Boxes

In version 4.0, several of Quattro Pro's multilayered menus have been converted to dialog boxes, making their settings much easier to find and use. For example, Figure 1.15 shows the new /Graph, Customize Series dialog box for stacked bar graphs, which replaces as many as four layers of menu items. Besides the /Graph menu, another place where you'll find a new dialog box is from the /Print, Layout command.

Entering Data in Cells

There are two types of cell entries you can make: *values* and *labels*. Values are numbers and formulas, and labels are text (also called *strings*). Quattro Pro changes the mode indicator to VALUE or LABEL to reflect the type of entry it thinks you are making.

Figure 1.15

The /Graph, Customize Series dialog box for stacked bar graphs

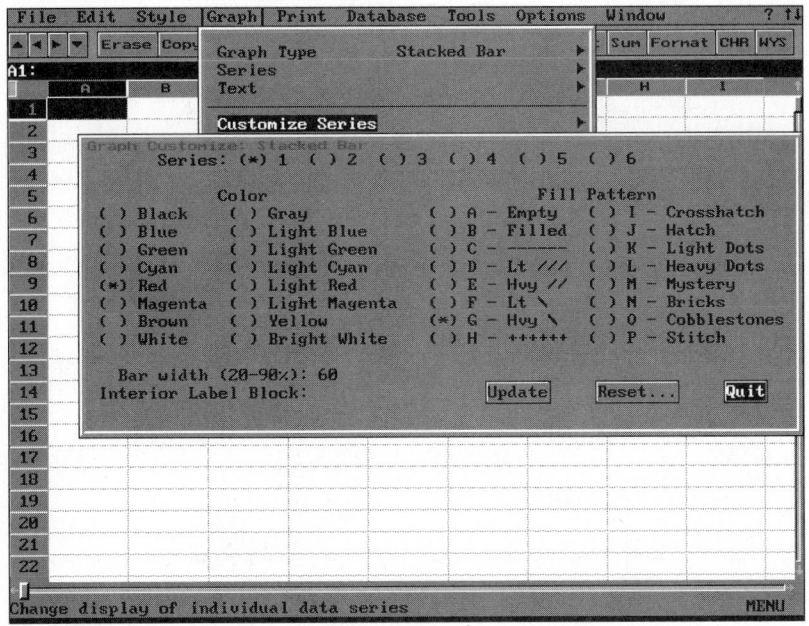

Quattro Pro determines the type of entry you are making based on the first character you type. If you type a number, Quattro Pro knows you are making a value entry; if you type a letter, Quattro Pro assumes you are entering a label.

Before you can enter data in a cell, you must first move the cell selector to that cell. You can then enter a number or label in the cell by simply typing it and pressing Enter. For example, to enter the number 456 in cell A1, type **456** and press Enter. Figure 1.16 shows the results.

Figure 1.16

Entering 456 in a cell

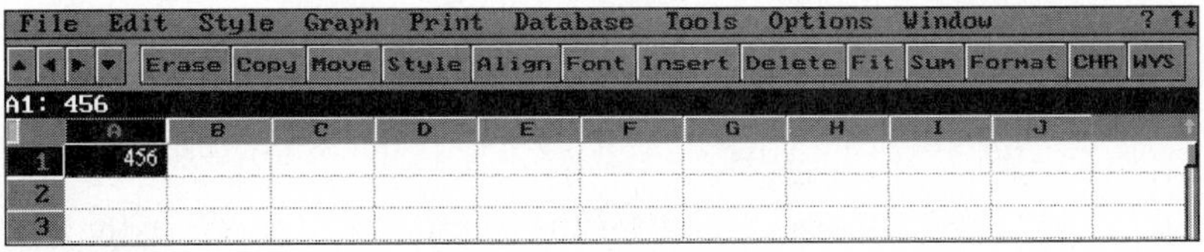

Confirming a Cell Entry

After you have finished typing an entry, you can *confirm* it in a variety of ways, depending on how you want the cell selector to move afterwards. When you confirm an entry, Quattro Pro transfers it from the input line to the current cell.

Note. If you make an error while entering data in a cell, Quattro Pro displays an error message and shifts to Edit mode. See "Editing Cell Entries" later in this chapter.

The simplest way to confirm an entry using the keyboard is to press Enter. The simplest way with the mouse is to click on [Enter] in the input line, or the ↵ button in the Quattro Pro 3.0 mouse palette. Confirming an entry in any of these ways leaves the cell selector in its original position.

You can also move the cell selector at the same time that you confirm an entry. Just use any of the movement keys, including ↑, ↓, →, ←, Ctrl-→, Ctrl-←, PgUp, PgDn, Home, and End, after typing your cell entry.

For example, suppose you want to enter a row of numbers and move the cell selector to the right as you go. Press → to confirm each entry, and you'll move the cell selector to the right cell. Figure 1.17 shows the position of the cell selector after you type 456 in cell A1, press →, type 567 in cell B1, and press → again.

Figure 1.17
Using the → key to confirm cell entries

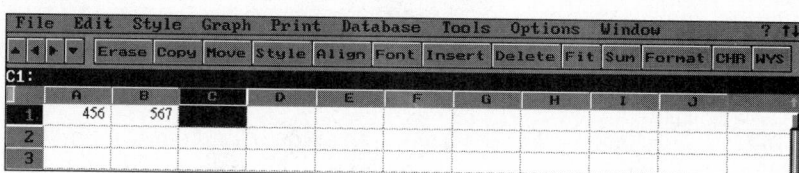

You can also use the mouse to confirm an entry and move the cell selector at the same time. For example, suppose you want to enter a number in cell B1, and then move to cell D1 to make another entry. After typing the entry in cell B1, all you have to do is click the mouse pointer in D1. Quattro Pro instantly enters the number in B1 and moves the cell selector to D1.

Changing Cell Entries Before Confirming Them

After typing a cell entry, if you decide that you want to change the entry before confirming it, you can use any of the following keys:

- **Backspace**   Removes the character to the left of the cursor.
- **Esc**   Cancels the entire entry and returns you to Ready mode.
- **Edit (F2)**   Switches to Edit mode (see "Editing Cell Entries," later).

If you are using the mouse, you can change a cell entry by clicking on:

■ The place in the entry where you want to make a change.

■ [Esc] in the input line to erase the current entry, yet remain in Value or Label mode.

Entering Labels

Labels are text entries. In Figure 1.18, for example, all the Selling and Administrative Expenses titles are entered as labels. The maximum length of a label is 254 characters (the same as the maximum cell entry length).

Figure 1.18

Sample labels

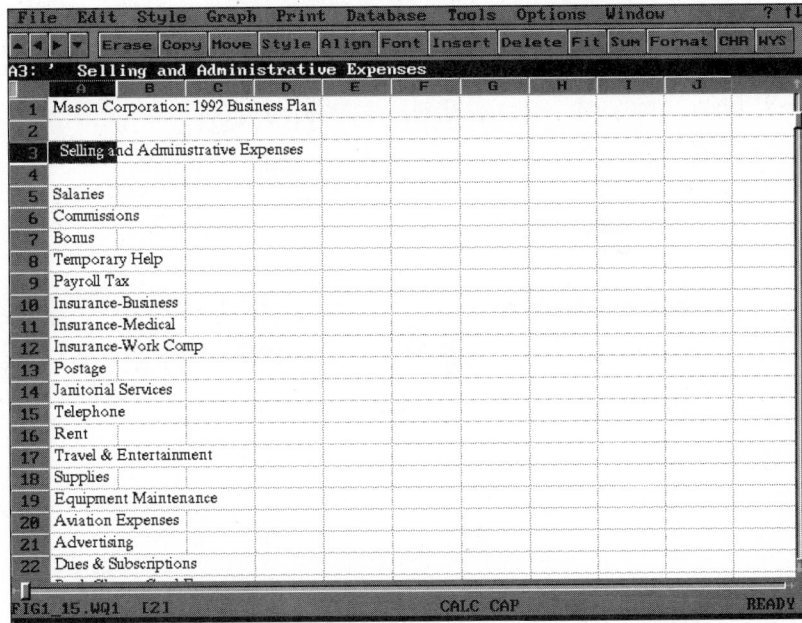

Label Prefixes and Alignment

A label always begins with a *label prefix*, which determines how the label is aligned in the cell. Table 1.8 lists Quattro Pro's label prefixes and how they affect alignment. Figure 1.19 shows how each type of label prefix affects the alignment of the label Salaries.

In most cases, when you enter a label in a cell, you don't need to bother entering a label prefix, because Quattro Pro provides one automatically. When you begin a cell entry with a letter (or a space), Quattro Pro assumes you are entering a label and provides the default label prefix, normally ' for left-alignment. For example, when you type Salaries in cell C1 (Figure 1.19) and press Enter, Quattro Pro automatically inserts the default label prefix in front of the entry. (To check the label prefix of any entry, simply move the cell selector to the cell and look in the input line at the character that precedes the entry.)

Table 1.8 **Label Prefixes**

Character	Effect
'	Aligns label at left edge of cell (default)
"	Aligns label at right edge of cell
^	Centers label in cell
\	Repeats characters in label to fill entire cell
|	Displays label on screen but doesn't print it

Figure 1.19
How label prefixes affect alignment

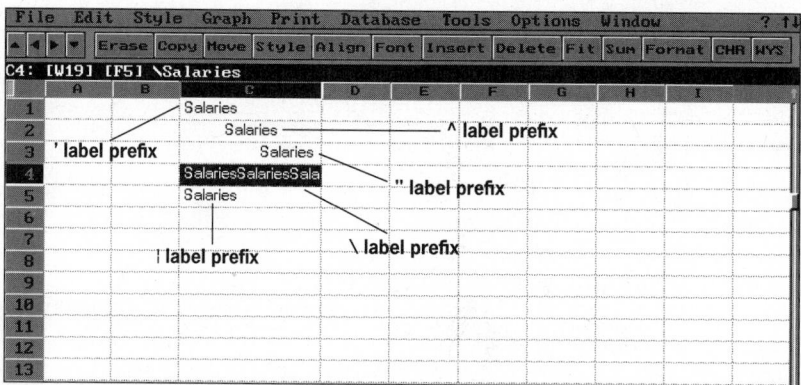

When you enter a label that begins with a number or numeric symbol (see "Entering Values") you must first enter a label prefix. If you don't, Quattro Pro issues the error message "Invalid cell or block address." For example, suppose you want to enter the label 92 Rate in a cell. If you type **92 Rate** and press Enter, Quattro Pro objects because it cannot determine whether you are entering a label or a value. Press Esc (or Enter) to clear the error message, and Quattro Pro shifts to Edit mode so that you can change your entry. To correct this error, you would press Home (or click on the 9) to move the cursor to the start of the entry, and then type a label prefix in front of the first character. For example, to have Quattro Pro align the label in the center of the cell, insert a caret (^) at the start of the entry. The label will then read ^92 Rate, and Quattro Pro will accept your entry.

Some entries for which you will want to explicitly enter label prefixes are street addresses, phone numbers, and Social Security numbers. For instance, if you enter the phone number 408-555-9824 in a cell without first typing a label prefix, Quattro Pro assumes you are entering a numeric formula and displays a negative number in the cell. To clarify your intent, precede the numbers with a label prefix.

TIP. *If you enter a label and then decide you want to change its alignment, the /Style, Alignment command (see Chapter 3) is much faster than Edit mode, and also works with numbers. In Quattro Pro 4.0,* Align *is a shortcut for /Style, Alignment.*

Changing the Global Label Alignment

Note. Chapter 3 discusses all the global options for controlling the appearance of the spreadsheet.

When you first start up Quattro Pro, some of its settings are already assigned. These settings are called *global settings* (or *global options*), because they affect the entire spreadsheet. Quattro Pro has global settings for such elements as the numeric format (how numbers appear), whether zeros are displayed, the width of columns, and the default label alignment. If you want to change the default label alignment from left-alignment to right-alignment, for example, you use the /Options, Formats, Align Labels, Right command. After you make this change, whenever you type a label Quattro Pro inserts a " (right-alignment) label prefix instead of a ' (left-alignment) label prefix.

Working with Long Labels

Note. In Quattro Pro 4.0, the global /Options, Formats, Align Labels setting is also controlled by the Alignment setting in the named style NORMAL. See "Creating Named Styles in Quattro Pro 4.0" in Chapter 3 for more details.

Sometimes a label entry is too long to fit within a column. When this happens, the label spills over into the next column to the right and is known as a *long label*. If you then make another entry in the cell to the right, the part of the long label that spills over from the previous column disappears from view. Move the cell selector back to the long label, however, and you can see that the entire entry is still there, even though it is not displayed in the spreadsheet.

For example, in Figure 1.20, cell A1 contains a long label. The same label appears in cell A3. However, Quattro Pro cuts off the long label in cell A3, because of the entry in cell B3. To show more of the long label, you can expand the width of column A. Chapter 3 describes how to do this, as well as how to change the global setting for all the column widths.

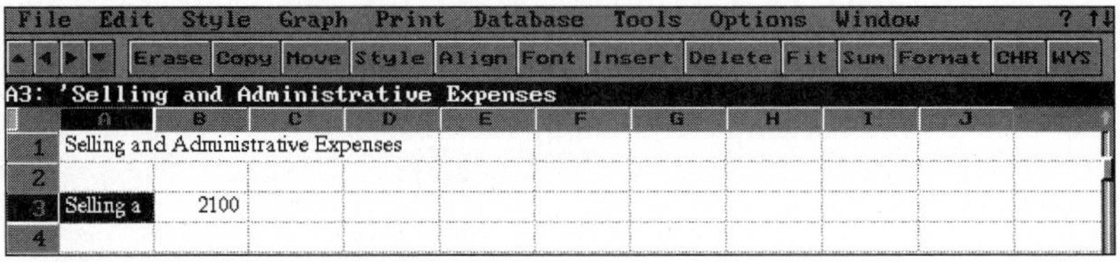

Figure 1.20
Working with long labels

Repeating Characters

The \ label prefix lets you fill a cell with the label that follows it. In other words, Quattro Pro repeats the characters in the label as many times as necessary to fill the cell. The two most common reasons for using repeating characters are to underline cells and to create dividers between sections of a spreadsheet. For example, if you type **\-** and press Enter, Quattro Pro repeats the hyphen character enough times to fill the cell. Figure 1.21 shows the result.

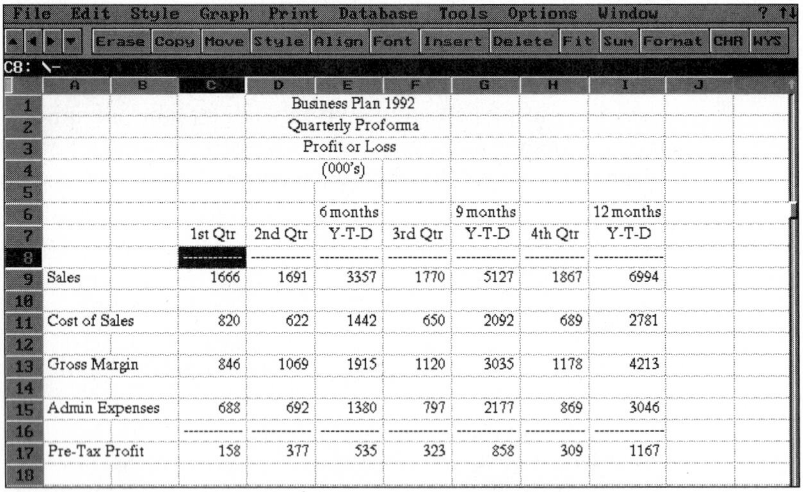

	A	B	C	D	E	F	G	H	I	J
1				Business Plan 1992						
2				Quarterly Proforma						
3				Profit or Loss						
4				(000's)						
5										
6					6 months		9 months		12 months	
7			1st Qtr	2nd Qtr	Y-T-D	3rd Qtr	Y-T-D	4th Qtr	Y-T-D	
8			----------	----------	----------	----------	----------	----------	----------	
9	Sales		1666	1691	3357	1770	5127	1867	6994	
10										
11	Cost of Sales		820	622	1442	650	2092	689	2781	
12										
13	Gross Margin		846	1069	1915	1120	3035	1178	4213	
14										
15	Admin Expenses		688	692	1380	797	2177	869	3046	
16			----------	----------	----------	----------	----------	----------	----------	
17	Pre-Tax Profit		158	377	535	323	858	309	1167	
18										

Figure 1.21
Using the \ label prefix to fill a cell

In Quattro's early days, about the only way to underline (or double-underline) a cell entry was to place repeating characters in the next cell down below the entry. Recent versions of the program, however, offer more elegant ways to underline. One way is to change the font of an entry to one with the Underline style attribute. Another way is to use Quattro Pro's line drawing feature to draw a line along the bottom edge of the cell. Chapter 3 discusses these techniques in detail.

Entering Values

A *value* is a number or formula. It always begins with one of the numbers 0 to 9 or one of these numeric symbols: + – (. @ # $. When you begin to enter a number or numeric symbol, the mode indicator changes to VALUE.

Numbers

In Quattro Pro, numbers have the following characteristics:

- They can range from 10^{-308} to 10^{308}.

- They cannot include spaces or commas.

- You can enter them in scientific notation (for example, 3.45E11 or 3.45E12).

- They cannot exceed 254 characters.

- They can begin with $, but Quattro Pro discards this symbol when you confirm the entry.

When you enter a number, Quattro Pro assumes it is positive. If you want to enter a negative number, precede the entry with a hyphen or a minus sign (typed on the numeric keypad).

By default, Quattro Pro right-aligns numbers. If you prefer a different alignment, you can use the /Style, Alignment command (see Chapter 3).

Working with Long Values

When a value exceeds its column width, it is known as a long value. In Quattro Pro, long values are not handled like long labels. Instead of allowing a long value to spill over into the adjacent blank cell, Quattro Pro displays a series of asterisks, as shown in Figure 1.22, in the cell that contains the long value.

Here are Quattro Pro's rules for displaying long values:

Note. Chapter 3 tells you how to change the numeric format of your cell entries.

- When the format of a cell is General (the default) and the column width is not wide enough to show the entire entry, Quattro Pro displays the integer portion, if it can. If even the integer portion is too wide, Quattro Pro displays the value in scientific notation. If the column width is insufficient to show scientific notation, Quattro Pro displays asterisks.

- If you've chosen a format other than General—for example, Currency (as in Figure 1.22)—Quattro Pro displays asterisks.

If you want to see the entire long value, you must change the column width (see Chapter 3). Move the cell selector to the column containing the long value, and select /Style, Column Width (or press Ctrl-W). When

Quattro Pro prompts you for a column width, press → to increase the number of places until the column looks wide enough (if you go too far, press ←). Press Enter to complete the command.

Figure 1.22
Long values are
displayed as
asterisks

File	Edit	Style	Graph	Print	Database	Tools	Options	Window	? ↑↓

| ▲ ◄ ► ▼ | Erase | Copy | Move | Style | Align | Font | Insert | Delete | Fit | Sum | Format | CHR | WYS |

B4: (C0) 1325421

	A	B	C	D	E	F	G	H	I
1	PROFIT AND LOSS PROJECTION - 1992								
2									
3	Revenues								
4	Product Sales	********							
5	Rentals	$81,335							
6	Maintenance Fees	$48,813							
7	Total	********							
8									
9	Cost of Sales								
10	Material Costs	$177,688							
11	Packaging Costs	$7,107							
12	Shipping Costs	$11,194							
13	Sales Commissions	$16,271							
14		$212,260							
15									

Entering Dates

Note. See Chapter
3 for more
information about
formatting dates.

Quattro Pro employs a special numbering system for dates. Each date from December 31, 1899, to December 31, 2099, is assigned a sequential number from 1 to 73050. These numbers are called *date-values*.

   The most convenient way to enter a date-value in a spreadsheet is to press Ctrl-D and then type the date in any of the date formats shown in Figure 1.23. (As you'll learn in Chapter 3, these formats correspond to the five available date formats that can be assigned to a cell.) Quattro Pro displays the date as you enter it, so you don't have to format it.

   For example, cell A3 of Figure 1.23 shows what happens when you press Ctrl-D, type **04-APR-94**, and press Enter. Although Quattro Pro converts this entry to the corresponding date-value, 34428, it appears as you entered it in—in this case, in the D1 DD-MMM-YY format.

   When you use the D2 or D5 formats, which don't include a year component, Quattro Pro takes the year from your computer's system clock, 1994 in this example, and returns the date-value 33698 corresponding to April 4, 1994. Similarly, because the D3 format doesn't include a day component, Quattro Pro assumes the first day of the month and returns a date-value of 34425 corresponding to April 1, 1994.

   You can also use the @DATE(*year,month,day*) function to return the corresponding date value for a date. For example @DATE(94,4,4) in row 11 also returns the date-value 34428, although you must then format the cell yourself. If you use /Style, Numeric Format, or the Format button in Quattro Pro 4.0, and then choose Date 1, this date-value appears as 04-Apr-94. (@DATE is discussed in Chapter 7.)

Figure 1.23
Using Ctrl-D to enter dates

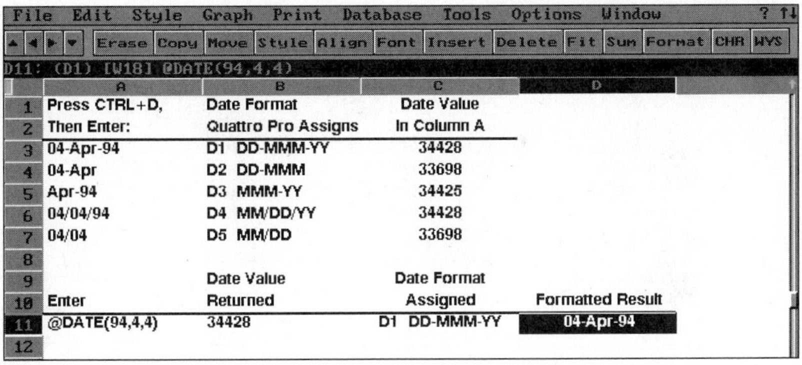

	A	B	C	D
1	Press CTRL+D,	Date Format	Date Value	
2	Then Enter:	Quattro Pro Assigns	In Column A	
3	04-Apr-94	D1 DD-MMM-YY	34428	
4	04-Apr	D2 DD-MMM	33698	
5	Apr-94	D3 MMM-YY	34425	
6	04/04/94	D4 MM/DD/YY	34428	
7	04/04	D5 MM/DD	33698	
8				
9		Date Value	Date Format	
10	Enter	Returned	Assigned	Formatted Result
11	@DATE(94,4,4)	34428	D1 DD-MMM-YY	04-Apr-94
12				

D11: (D1) [W18] @DATE(94,4,4)

TIP. *In Quattro Pro 4.0, you can create custom date formats to display a date almost any way you wish. For example, you can create a format that includes the day of the week that a date represents. See Chapter 3.*

Entering Times

Note. See Chapter 3 for more information about formatting times.

Quattro Pro also uses a sequential numbering system for times. Each time from midnight to 11:59:59 PM is assigned a decimal number from .000000 to .999999. These are known as *time-values*. This time numbering system is cyclical, however, and begins again every day. For example, .5 always represents noon.

Using Ctrl-D is also the easiest way to enter a time. Simply press Ctrl-D and type the time in any of the formats shown in Figure 1.24. (These formats correspond to the four available time formats discussed in Chapter 3.) Quattro Pro stores the result as a time-value, but displays the time as you entered it.

For example, if you press Ctrl-D, and then enter **01:55:25 PM**, you can see in row 3 of Figure 1.24 how Quattro Pro returns the time-value 0.580150 but displays the formatted result as you entered it. Quattro Pro uses the same time-value when you enter 13:55:25 in the D8 military time format. When you use the D7 or D9 time formats, which don't include a seconds component, Quattro Pro assumes 0 seconds and uses the time-value 0.579861.

Tip. In Quattro Pro 4.0, you can create custom time formats to display a time almost any way you want. See Chapter 3.

You can also use the more traditional @TIME(*hour,minutes,seconds*) function to return the corresponding time-value for a time. For example, @TIME(13,55,25) in row 10 returns the time-value 0.580150. Format it using

/Style, Numeric Format (or the Format button in Quattro Pro 4.0), and then choose Date, Time, 1 to make it appear as 01:55:25 PM. (@TIME is discussed in Chapter 7.)

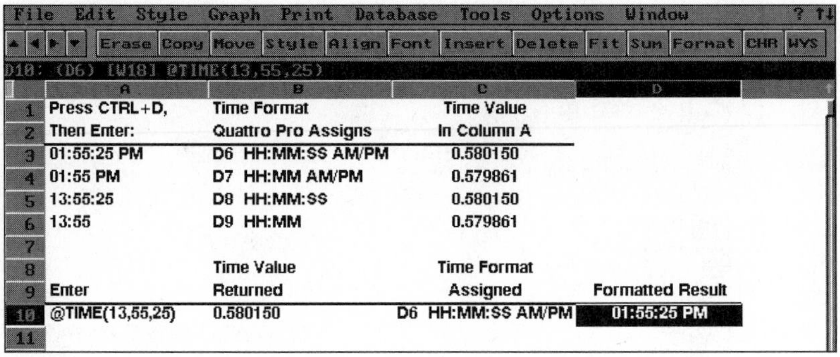

Figure 1.24
Using Ctrl-D to
enter times

Making Combined Date/Time Entries

Because date-values and time-values are part of the same sequential numbering system, you can create a combined date/time value. For example, at 1:55 PM on April 4, 1992, try entering **@NOW** in a cell. The @NOW function, discussed in Chapter 7, reads the current date and time from your computer's system clock and returns the combined date/time value 33698.579861.

In Quattro Pro 3.0, you can only format this value to show either the date, April 4, 1992, or the time, 1:55 PM. In Quattro Pro 4.0, however, you can create a custom numeric format that displays both the date and time this value represents. See Chapter 3.

Entering Formulas

Much of the power of Quattro Pro lies in its formulas. At its most basic level, a spreadsheet formula adds, subtracts, multiplies, or divides two numbers in the current spreadsheet, and displays the result in the cell in which the formula was entered. Beyond simple number crunching, though, Quattro Pro formulas offer you a broad range of data-calculating abilities, including label handling, logical testing, and built-in specialized formulas.

Formulas also let you take advantage of one of Quattro Pro's most important features: instant recalculation. When you enter a formula to add a column of numbers, for example, Quattro Pro displays the result in a spreadsheet cell, but also stores the formula in that cell. Later, if you change the underlying

data, Quattro Pro automatically recalculates the formula in the cell, and instantly displays the new results.

A Quattro Pro formula is like any basic algebraic formula: It combines values and operators to calculate a single result. Formulas can be up to 254 characters long and must begin with one of the following characters:

0 1 2 3 4 5 6 7 8 9 . + - (@ # $

To enter a formula that does not begin with one of these characters, you must precede it with a plus (+) sign, so that Quattro Pro knows the entry is a formula and not a label. On the other hand, if you want to enter text in a formula, you must convert whatever label you enter to a string by enclosing it in double quotation marks. For example, instead of entering 'TOTALS in a formula, you would enter "TOTALS".

Table 1.9 shows the special symbols you can use in formulas. Most of these symbols are mathematical operators, such as + or <; others convey special formula instructions to Quattro Pro. For example, & (ampersand) tells Quattro Pro to *concatenate*, or join together, two strings into one string. You'll see many examples of these symbols in the following sections.

Table 1.9   **Formula Symbols**

Symbol	Description
+	Positive number, or addition in a numeric formula
–	Negative value, or subtraction in a numeric formula
*	Multiplication in a numeric formula
/	Division in a numeric formula
@	String following this symbol is an @function name
.	Decimal point in a formula
(	Begins @function arguments, or changes order of precedence
)	Ends an @function, or changes order of precedence
#	Starts or ends certain logical operators (for example, #AND#)
>	Greater than
<	Less than
=	Equal to

Table 1.9   (Continued)

Symbol	Description
$	Starts absolute reference (for example, $B$5)
&	String concatenation

Numeric Formulas

Numeric formulas are the type you will probably find you use the most with Quattro Pro. Numeric formulas are useful for many tasks—from simple arithmetic calculations you can also do on a calculator, to more advanced financial calculations, such as internal rate of return or quantitative analysis.

Using mathematical operators, you can create numeric formulas that perform calculations with numbers, cell addresses, and specialized @functions. An operator precedes a number, cell address, or function, and tells Quattro Pro which mathematical operation to perform. Numeric formulas use these mathematical operators: + (plus) for addition, – (minus) for subtraction, / (forward slash) for division, * (asterisk) for multiplication, and ^ (caret) for exponentiation.

Let's begin by entering a simple numeric formula. For example, move your cell selector to C2 and enter **123+456**. (Although Quattro Pro accepts spaces between operators and values, it deletes them from the resulting formula.) When you press Enter to confirm the entry, Quattro Pro automatically calculates the formula's result and displays the number 579 in the cell. Examine the input line at the top of your screen, and you will notice that it contains your original formula, while the calculated value is displayed in the spreadsheet. Figure 1.25 shows examples of other simple numeric formulas.

TIP. *In Quattro Pro 4.0, the operators + – / *, (and) are represented by buttons in the Edit SpeedBar. When you're entering or editing a formula, these buttons are an efficient way to include operators. For instance, in the previous example you can enter* **123***, select* ⊞ *to add the + operator, and then enter* **456***.*

Figure 1.25 shows that when Quattro Pro uses the default column width of 9, it actually displays your results using only 8 significant places. However, if you widen the columns (see Chapter 3), you will see your results are actually stored in full decimal precision. In cell C7, for example, the result is carried out to ten decimal places.

TIP. *You can attach a note to a formula. See "Adding Cell Notes to Formulas and Values," later.*

Figure 1.25

Some simple numeric formulas

	A	B	C	D	E	F	G	H
	File Edit Style Graph Print Database Tools Options Window						? ↑↓	
	▲ ◄ ► ▼	Erase Copy Move Style Align Font Insert Delete Fit Sum Format CHR WYS						
	C7: [W9] 0.1234/567							
1	Formula Entered							
2	In Column C		Result					
3								
4	123+456		579					
5	0.123+456		456.123					
6	123-456		-333					
7	0.1234/567		0.000218					
8	123*456		56088					
9	123^0		1					
10								

Using Cell References

So far, you have only used literal numbers in your formulas. As you work more with formulas, however, you will find that many formulas refer to other cells using *cell references*. By referencing another cell, you can incorporate the value that cell contains into your numeric formula. You reference the other cell by specifying its cell address. Note, however, that Quattro Pro displays the cell address, but not its value content, within a numeric formula on the input line.

The advantage of using a cell reference in a formula, rather than a numeric value, becomes evident when you change the value in a referenced cell. Quattro Pro immediately uses this new value in the formula and updates the result. This gives you the advantage of being able to change values and thus explore various *what-if scenarios*, a fundamental tool of spreadsheet analysis.

NOTE. *When you create a formula that begins with a cell reference, remember to start your entry with one of these numeric operators: + − ($. This lets Quattro Pro know you are not entering a label.*

For example, say you are working on the spreadsheet in Figure 1.26, which contains the values 50, 100, and 1000 in cells A5, A6, and A7. In cell C5, enter the formula **+A5**. When you press Enter, Quattro Pro displays 50 in cell C5. Then move to cell C6 and enter the formula **+A6/A5**; you are instructing Quattro Pro to divide the value in A6 by the value in A5, and Quattro Pro displays the value 2 in C6. Next move to cell C7 and enter the formula **(A5+A6)*A7**. When you press Enter, Quattro Pro adds the values in A5 and A6 first, and then multiplies that result by the value in A7. The result, 150000, is displayed in C7. Of course, the input line at the top continues to display the formula just as you entered it.

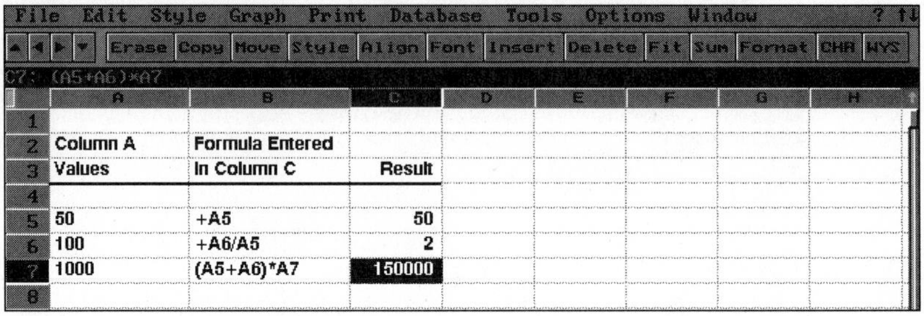

	A	B	C
1			
2	Column A	Formula Entered	
3	Values	In Column C	Result
4			
5	50	+A5	50
6	100	+A6/A5	2
7	1000	(A5+A6)*A7	150000
8			

Figure 1.26
Using cell references in formulas

To see how Quattro Pro updates your formulas, try changing the contents of cell A6 to, say, 1. Notice how Quattro Pro changes the displayed values in cells C6 and C7 to .02 and 51000, respectively. Although the displayed values change, notice that the underlying formulas displayed on the input line remain the same.

The numeric formula examples so far have been simple in comparison to the calculations Quattro Pro has the power to make. A numeric formula can employ many cell references and various operators within the same formula. The more you use Quattro Pro, however, the more you will discover that it is better to keep your formulas and cell references as simple as possible. It's better, when you can, to break one large formula down into several smaller components stored in various cells. That way, not only are the formulas easier to understand, but they are easier to diagnose and correct if errors occur.

Pointing to Cells

Using your cell selector or a mouse to specify cell references in a formula saves you the trouble of having to type their column and row addresses. Specifying cells with the cell selector or mouse is known as *pointing*. Pointing saves you time and eliminates a potential source of errors.

Before pointing to a cell, remember that you must first enter a +, –, /, ^, or (. Then, when you use any cell selector movement key or click the mouse on a cell, Quattro Pro shifts to Point mode. You can then designate the cell you want by pointing to it with the cell selector or the mouse. Quattro Pro records the coordinates of the cell you highlight.

Suppose, for example, you are using the spreadsheet shown in Figure 1.27, and you want to use your cell selector to enter the gas mileage formula +B2/B3 in cell C4.

1. Starting with the cell selector in C4, type **+** then press ← once. Quattro Pro shifts to Point mode.

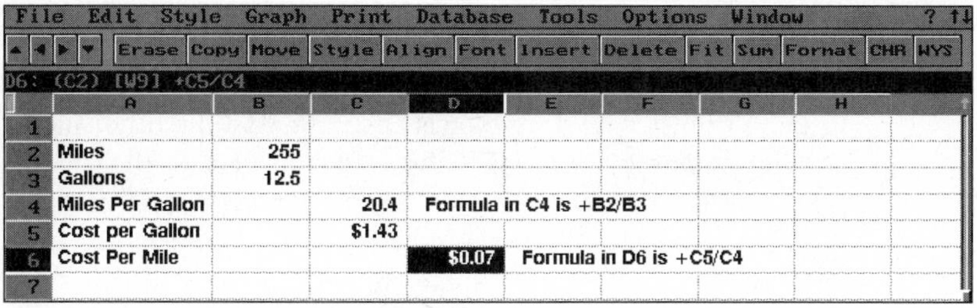

Figure 1.27

Entering formulas
by pointing

File Edit Style Graph Print Database Tools Options Window	? ↑↓

| ▲ ◀ ▶ ▼ | Erase | Copy | Move | Style | Align | Font | Insert | Delete | Fit | Sum | Format | CHR | WYS |

D6: (C2) [W9] +C5/C4

	A	B	C	D	E	F	G	H
1								
2	Miles	255						
3	Gallons	12.5						
4	Miles Per Gallon		20.4	Formula in C4 is +B2/B3				
5	Cost per Gallon		$1.43					
6	Cost Per Mile			$0.07	Formula in D6 is +C5/C4			
7								

2. Press ↑ twice to point to cell B2. Quattro Pro then displays +B2 on the input line.

3. Type the division operator **/**. Quattro Pro appends it to your formula and returns the cell selector to C4.

4. Press ← once again, and then press ↑ once, so the selector is highlighting cell B3.

5. Press Enter to complete the formula, and you'll see your mileage results, 20.4 miles per gallon, in C4.

An even more efficient pointing method is to use your mouse. Using Figure 1.27 again, suppose you want to determine your fuel cost per mile using the formula +C5/C4 in cell D6. First click on cell D6 to position the cell selector there. Then enter a **+** and select cell C5 to enter your cost per gallon value. Next, enter a **/** or select the / button in version 4.0, which locks in that cell address. Then select cell C4 to enter the cell address for your miles per gallon value, and select [Enter] in the input line. The result, .07, appears in D6.

In these examples, pointing appears to be a rather simple method for entering data. However, using pointing techniques to enter blocks of data presents another set of issues that are addressed in "Working with Blocks" later in this chapter.

Absolute and Relative References

There are three types of cell references you can use in a Quattro Pro formula: *relative*, *absolute*, and *mixed*. The type of reference you use affects how the /Edit, Copy command behaves when you copy the formula from one cell to another. Chapter 4 contains the comprehensive discussion of the /Edit, Copy command and cell referencing, but we will briefly define these types of cell references here to complete your introduction to formulas.

So far, the only cell references you've worked with have been relative. That is, if you copy any of the preceding formulas to other cells, Quattro Pro automatically compensates by changing the cell coordinates in the formula *relative to* their new position. An absolute reference, on the other hand, causes Quattro Pro to freeze the cell coordinates when you use the /Edit, Copy command. That is, the absolute cell reference remains the same no matter where it is copied in the spreadsheet. A mixed cell reference is a hybrid; half of the cell reference is absolute, and the other half is relative.

For example, $A$1 is an absolute reference to the first cell in a spreadsheet; A1 is a relative reference to the same cell. $A1 and A$1 are both mixed references, with the $ indicating which part of the address is fixed, or absolute. You can type in an absolute reference yourself, or you can press F4 (the ABS key) to cycle through the various combinations available. Many users at first find this concept difficult to grasp. This is why it receives special attention in Chapter 4.

TIP. *In Quattro Pro 4.0,* Abs *in the Edit Speedbar is the same as F4 (ABS).*

String Formulas

String formulas are any formulas that have a string result, including those created with string functions or the concatenation operator (&). For example, if cell A1 contains the string "For the Year Ended" and cell A2 contains the string "12/31/91", you can concatenate the two together in cell A3 using the string formula

```
+A1&" "&A2
```

The result displayed in cell A3 is the string "For the Year Ended 12/31/91." Chapter 7 examines string functions and concatenation in more detail.

Logical Formulas

You can use *logical formulas* to test whether a condition in the spreadsheet is true or false. If the condition defined in a logical formula evaluates to true, Quattro Pro returns the value 1; if the condition evaluates to false, Quattro Pro returns 0. A logical formula consists of a *conditional expression* that contains one of the logical operators listed in Table 1.10, and either values, cell addresses, labels or strings, functions, or some combination of these.

One way to use a logical formula is for checking the value contained in a cell. For example, to see if the value contained in cell B2 is greater than 1,000, you might use the logical formula in cell C2:

```
+B2>1000
```

Table 1.10	**Logical Operators**

Operator	Definition
=	Equal to
>	Greater than
<	Less than
>=	Greater than or equal to
<=	Less than or equal to
<>	Not equal to
#AND#	Both condition 1 and condition 2 are true
#OR#	Either condition 1 or condition 2 is true
#NOT#	Condition 1 is not true

Note. Logical formulas are also often used to specify criteria for querying a database. See Chapter 10.

In some cases, you can specify a result for Quattro Pro to return based on whether a condition is true or false. The logical formula in cell D2,

```
@IF(B2>1000,"","ADD FUNDS")
```

says for Quattro Pro to enter an empty string in cell D2 *if* the contents of cell B2 are greater than 1,000, but to enter the string "ADD FUNDS" in D2 *if* the contents of B2 are equal to or less than 1,000. Incidentally, since this logical formula results in a string value, it is also considered a string formula.

Functions

Note. See Chapter 7 for a complete discussion of Quattro Pro's functions.

Functions are built-in formulas that perform some type of calculation. You can access Quattro Pro 4.0's Edit SpeedBar or a list of all its functions if you press Alt-F3, or select the @ button in the mouse palette in Quattro Pro 3.0. For example, one of Quattro Pro's most frequently used mathematical functions is @SUM, which you can use to total a block of values. Figure 1.28 shows how you can enter the @SUM formula in cell B13 to add the office expenses contained in the block B5..B11. Imagine how much time you save by using this function, instead of having to enter the formula

```
+B5+B6+B7+B8+B9+B10+B11
```

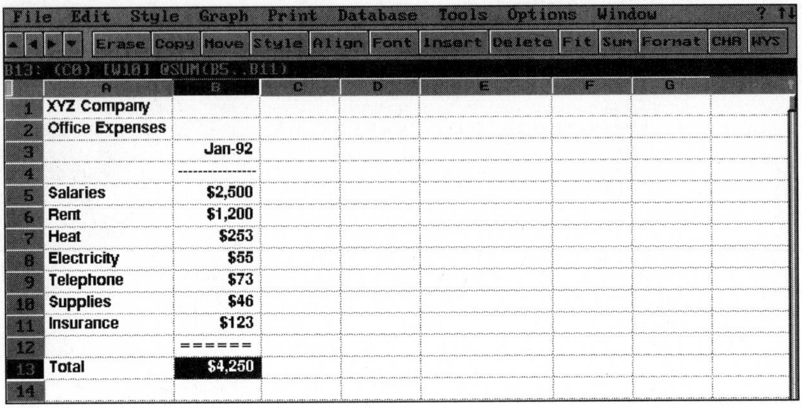

Figure 1.28
Using the @SUM
function

```
File  Edit  Style  Graph  Print  Database  Tools  Options  Window      ? ↑↓
▲ ◀ ▶ ▼  Erase Copy Move Style Align Font Insert Delete Fit Sum Format CHR WYS
B13:  (C0) [W10] @SUM(B5..B11)
         A              B          C       D       E       F       G
  1  XYZ Company
  2  Office Expenses
  3                   Jan-92
  4                 ------------
  5  Salaries        $2,500
  6  Rent            $1,200
  7  Heat            $253
  8  Electricity     $55
  9  Telephone       $73
 10  Supplies        $46
 11  Insurance       $123
 12                 ========
 13  Total           $4,250
 14
```

Error Values

Sooner or later you will enter a formula that will return ERR rather than the value or label you expected. This can happen for a variety of reasons, but here are some of the more common ones:

- You are dividing a value by zero. This often happens if the denominator is a blank cell or a label, both of which Quattro Pro evaluates as 0.

- When you moved a block of data, you wrote over a cell reference used in a formula. See Chapter 4.

Note. See Chapter 4 for more on using /Edit, Copy, Move, and Delete.

- When you deleted a row or column of data, you deleted a cell reference used in a formula. For example, suppose you have the formula +A2+A3+A4 in cell A5. If you delete row 2, 3, or 4, cell A5 will return ERR.

Order of Precedence

As discussed, operators perform mathematical, string, or logical operations in formulas. Often, however, formulas have more than one operator, as in the formula +A2–D3/C1. The result of this formula depends on the order in which Quattro Pro performs the arithmetic operations. Of course, Quattro Pro uses the conventional mathematical order of operator precedence; in addition, however, Quattro Pro assumes its own order of precedence for string and logical formulas.

Table 1.11 presents Quattro Pro's order of operator precedence. In this table, operations are performed in the order shown in the Order column. For operations with equal precedence, Quattro Pro moves from left to right in the formula. In the formula mentioned above, the division D3/C1 would be done first, and the result would then be subtracted from +A2.

Table 1.11

Order	Operator	Operation
1	^	Exponentiation
2	+	Formula or positive value
2	–	Negative value
3	*	Multiplication
3	/	Division
4	+	Addition
4	–	Subtraction
5	=	Equal to test
5	<>	Not equal to test
5	>	Greater than test
5	<	Less than test
5	>=	Greater than or equal to test
5	<=	Less than or equal to test
6	#NOT#	Logical NOT test
7	#AND#	Logical AND test
7	#OR#	Logical OR test
7	&	String concatenation

To override Quattro Pro's established order of precedence, designate the operation you want done first by enclosing it in parentheses. For example, the formula (A2–D3)/C1, tells Quattro Pro to do the subtraction before the division. Understanding Quattro Pro's order of precedence and when to use parentheses to change it helps you define your formulas so they perform exactly the operations you want them to perform.

Adding Cell Notes to Formulas and Values

Sometimes it's difficult to remember the assumptions that went into the formulas or values in a spreadsheet. Quattro Pro offers a solution: notes. You can add a note directly after a value or formula by using a semicolon.

For example, try entering **500;number of employees** in cell A2. As you can see in Figure 1.29, Quattro Pro evaluates 500 as a value and displays it in cell A2. It evaluates everything after the semicolon—number of employees—as a note. Although you can see this note in the input line, it isn't displayed in the spreadsheet. What's more, a note isn't printed.

Figure 1.29

Adding notes to values and formulas

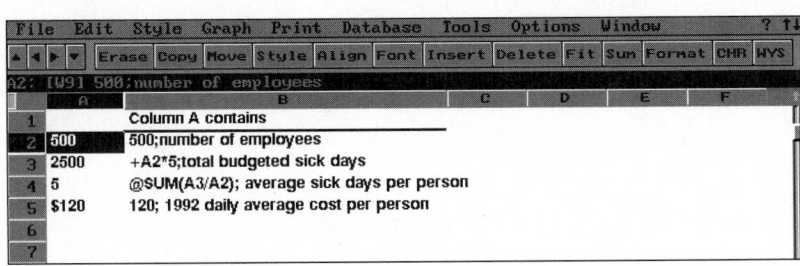

Column B of Figure 1.29 shows other notes that have been added to the formulas and values in column A. For example, cell A3 actually contains the formula and note

```
+A2*5;total budgeted sick days
```

Editing Cell Entries

Since we all make mistakes or change our minds about an entry sooner or later, knowing how to edit or alter entries already made is essential. Quattro Pro makes editing easy to do with either the keyboard or a mouse, or a combination of the two.

Before modifying a cell's contents, always consult the input line at the top of your screen. There Quattro Pro displays the entry as you entered it. As you are aware, this is not necessarily the same as how your entry is displayed in the cell. When a cell contains a formula that produces a value, you edit the formula on the input line, and the value result in the cell is automatically updated when you press Enter.

Editing with the Keyboard

To edit a cell entry with the keyboard, first position the cell selector on the cell you want to change. You can then enter entirely new cell contents or change the existing contents.

If you want to erase and replace the entire cell's contents, there are two ways. The simplest is to just type in a new entry, and when you press Enter or any of the cell selector movement keys, your new entry replaces the old one. Or you can erase the cell's contents by pressing Del, typing your new entry, and pressing Enter (or any of the cell selector movement keys).

On the other hand, if you want to alter the existing cell contents, press Edit (F2), and the Quattro Pro mode indicator changes from READY to EDIT. In Edit mode, you can insert or delete characters in any cell entry without having to retype the entry. Table 1.12 lists the roles of the cursor movement keys in Edit mode. The more familiar you become with the special Edit keys, the more time and keystrokes you will save.

Table 1.12 **Special Edit Mode Cursor Movement Keys**

Key	Action in Edit Mode
Backspace	Deletes the character to the left of the cursor.
Ctrl-\	Deletes all characters from the cursor to the end of the entry.
Ctrl-Backspace	Deletes the contents of the input line.
Del	Deletes the character at the cursor.
↑ and ↓	Enters data on the input line, exits Edit mode, and moves the cell selector up or down one cell. However, if the cursor follows an operator at the end of an entry and puts Quattro Pro in Point mode, you can input cell references by pointing to them.
End	Moves the cursor to the end of the entry on the input line.
Enter	Enters data and exits Edit mode.
Esc	Erases the entry and starts over. Press twice to exit Edit mode.
← and →	Moves the cursor left or right one character.
Shift-Tab or Ctrl - ←	Moves the cursor left five characters.
Tab or Ctrl - →	Moves the cursor right five characters.
Home	Moves the cursor to the start of the entry.

Tip. To convert a formula to its underlying (or literal) value, press Calc (F9) or the Calc button while in Edit mode. For example, this technique converts the formula @SUM(B5..B11) to the result it currently returns, the value 100 perhaps.

When you enter Edit mode, Quattro Pro displays your entry on the input line with the cursor at the end. To edit part of the entry, move the cursor to where you want to make the change; here is where the special Edit keys can make your life easier. For example, to move the cursor to the beginning of an entry, press Home and Quattro Pro moves your cursor there instantly. Similarly, if you have already edited part of the entry, and you want to add on to the end of it, press the End key. The cursor moves to the end of your entry, and you can just start typing. You can also delete any unwanted remainder of an edited entry by pressing Ctrl-\.

To erase a character, you can press the Del key when the cursor is directly on the character, or you can move to the character to the right and press Backspace.

Let's try using some of the Edit keys. Say you have tried to enter **1991 Income Staement** in cell D3, and Quattro Pro beeps at you and displays the error message "Invalid cell or block address." You actually have to correct two errors: You need to add a label prefix, and correct a spelling mistake. After you press Esc to clear the error message, Quattro Pro automatically enters Edit mode and even positions the cursor on the source of the error (but this time it won't help you in making your corrections). First press Home, so you can insert the ' prefix. Next, press End to move to the end of the entry. Then press Ctrl-← to move five spaces to the left, where you can type in the missing **t**. Finally, press Enter, and your corrected entry appears in the cell.

Editing with the Mouse

To edit a cell entry using the mouse, simply select the cell you want to edit, and then click on the input line. This shifts Quattro Pro to Edit mode, where you have your choice of combining mouse and keyboard editing techniques. The most efficient editing requires a combination of the two. Using the mouse, you click on the precise character you want to edit, and the cursor instantly skips there. From there you can use the keyboard techniques described above to make your edits. In Quattro Pro 3.0, you can also use the following mouse palette buttons:

- **Del**   Deletes the character at the cursor.

- **Esc**   To erase the entire entry on the input line, click on this button once. Click on it a second time to restore the original, unedited information and return to Ready mode.

- ↵   After completing your changes, click on this button to confirm your entry and return to Ready mode.

NOTE. *Editing with the mouse in Quattro Pro can take some getting used to. Typically, when you click on a precise character in the input line, the mouse* *pointer stays in the same position when Quattro Pro shifts to Edit mode. However, exactly where the cursor ends up within the entry is anybody's guess. You must again click on the character you want to edit to position the cursor there and continue editing.*

Working with Blocks

Formulas, and many menu commands, operate on blocks of data. A *block* is any rectangular group of contiguous cells. A block can be as small as a single cell or as large as the entire spreadsheet file.

You define a block in Quattro Pro by entering the cell addresses of its diagonally opposite corner cells. Usually these are the cells at the top-left and bottom-right corners of the block. You can also enter the other opposite set of corner cells, but Quattro Pro will immediately translate the addresses to the top-left and bottom-right cells.

Figure 1.30 presents examples of single- and multiple-cell blocks. To indicate a block, you first provide the cell address of the top-left cell, followed by one or two periods, and then the address of the bottom-right cell. For example, to specify the block of cells from C8 through E13, you would use C8..E13.

Figure 1.30
Single- and multiple-cell blocks

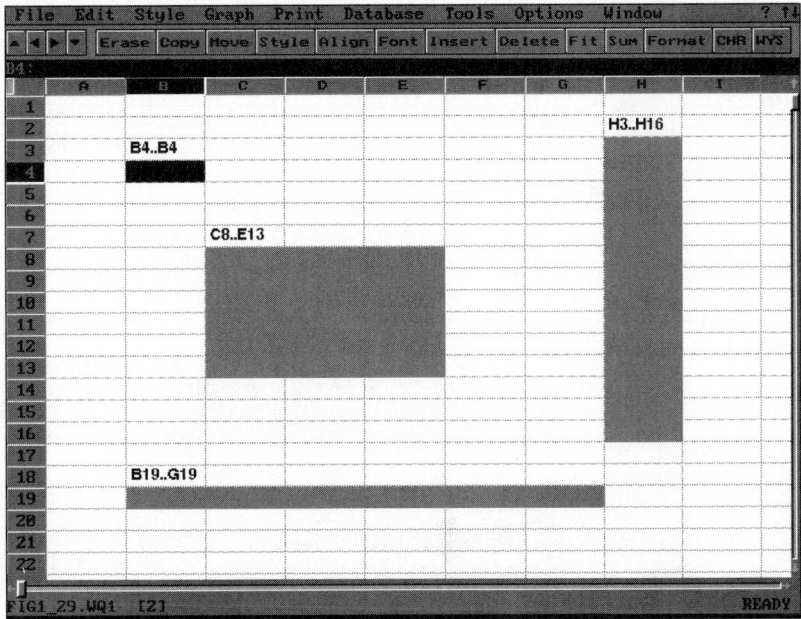

Selecting Blocks with the Keyboard

Suppose you have the spreadsheet in Figure 1.31, and you want to format the numbers in the entire block B4..E7 to show dollar signs. To do this, you use the /Style, Numeric Format command or the Format button in Quattro Pro 4.0. You have the option of selecting the block either before or after you choose the command.

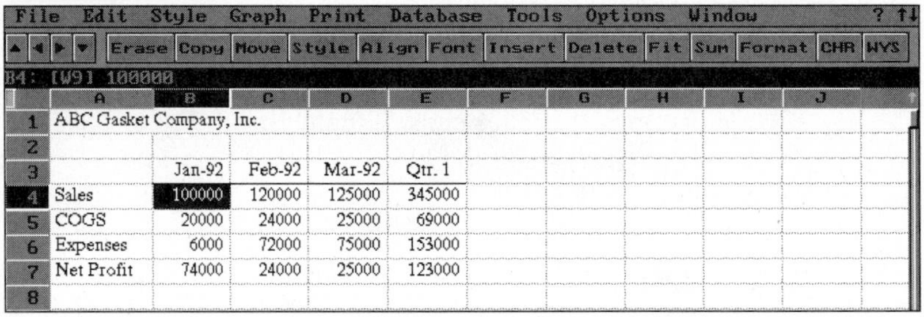

Figure 1.31

A spreadsheet for ABC Gasket Company, Inc.

Preselecting the Block Before Choosing the Command

To preselect the block with the keyboard before choosing the command,

1. Move the cell selector to B4.

2. Press Select (Shift-F7). Quattro Pro displays an EXT indicator in the status line, and *anchors* the cell selector in cell B4. This cell is said to be the *anchor cell* because it contains the anchored cell selector.

3. Press End then → followed by End then ↓. This moves the *free cell* (the cell diagonally opposite the anchor cell) to E7. Quattro Pro expands the cell selector to highlight the block B4..E7, as shown in Figure 1.32.

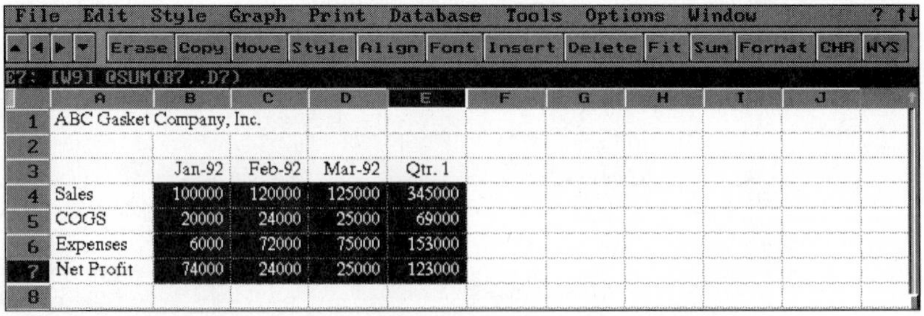

Figure 1.32

After selecting a block with the keyboard

4. Now select the /Style, Numeric Format command. (In Quattro Pro 4.0, the Format button also works.) Choose Currency, and then enter **0** for the number of decimal places. When you press Enter, Quattro Pro automatically applies these formatting settings to each cell in the block. Figure 1.33 shows the results.

NOTE. *In Quattro Pro 4.0, a preselected block usually remains selected after a command is completed. This lets you apply different commands without having to reselect the same block each time.*

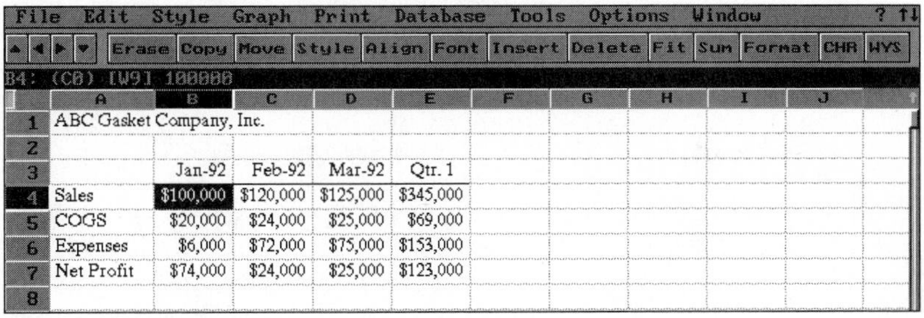

Figure 1.33
The results of
formatting B4..E7
for Currency, 0
places

File	Edit	Style	Graph	Print	Database	Tools	Options	Window		? ↑↓

| ▲ | ◀ | ▶ | ▼ | Erase | Copy | Move | Style | Align | Font | Insert | Delete | Fit | Sum | Format | CHR | WYS |

B4: (C0) [W9] 100000

	A	B	C	D	E	F	G	H	I	J
1	ABC Gasket Company, Inc.									
2										
3		Jan-92	Feb-92	Mar-92	Qtr. 1					
4	Sales	$100,000	$120,000	$125,000	$345,000					
5	COGS	$20,000	$24,000	$25,000	$69,000					
6	Expenses	$6,000	$72,000	$75,000	$153,000					
7	Net Profit	$74,000	$24,000	$25,000	$123,000					
8										

Selecting the Block after Choosing the Command

If you decide to specify the block after invoking the command, the procedure is slightly different, because Quattro Pro automatically shifts to Point mode when it prompts you to specify the block. Here are the steps:

1. Move the cell selector to B4.

2. Select the /Style, Numeric Format command or the Format button in Quattro Pro 4.0. Choose Currency, and then enter **0** for the number of decimal places. When you press Enter, Quattro Pro prompts you for the block to modify.

3. Press End, and then →. The cell selector expands horizontally to highlight the block B4..E4.

4. Press End, and then ↓. The cell selector expands vertically to include the entire block B4..E7.

5. Press Enter to complete the command.

Selecting a Block When Entering a Formula

Although the previous example shows how to select a block after entering a command, you can use the same technique any time Quattro Pro enters

Point mode. For example, here is how you would enter the @SUM function in cell E7 of Figure 1.32 and select the block B7..D7 in the process:

1. After locating the cell selector in cell E7, type **@SUM(.**

2. Press ← to switch to Point mode and locate the cell selector on cell D7.

3. Press period (.) to anchor the highlight on cell D7. The formula in the input line now reads @SUM(D7..D7.

4. Press ← twice to expand the highlight to D7..B7. The formula now reads @SUM(D7..B7.

5. Type) or choose the) button in Quattro Pro 4.0 to complete the formula. Press Enter to confirm.

Selecting a Block with the Mouse

When selecting a block with the mouse, the procedure is the same whether you select the block before or after choosing a command. Using the ABC Gasket Company example, you can use the mouse to highlight the block B4..E7 in Figure 1.31 before or after selecting the /Style, Numeric Format, Currency, 0 command. Use either of these methods:

- Select cell B4, and then drag the mouse pointer to cell E7. Then release the button.

- Click the mouse on cell B4, move the mouse pointer to cell E7, and while holding down the right mouse button, click the left one.

Changing Block Selections During a Command

Sometimes when you select a command, Quattro Pro displays the cell selector already anchored to a cell.

For example, try locating your cell selector in cell E7, and then select the /Edit, Erase Block command (which erases a block of cells). Quattro Pro displays the prompt, "Block to be modified: E7..E7." Here the cell selector is already anchored to cell E7. You can tell that it is anchored because E7 is displayed as a block address. If you now use the cell selector movement keys, Quattro Pro expands the highlight from that cell.

But suppose you want to erase another block, say D3..E5. Just press Esc to unanchor the cell selector. In the current example, the prompt now reads, "Block to be modified: E7." To reanchor the cell selector—this time in cell D3—move to that cell and press . (period). You can then expand the highlight to E5.

If you change your mind about the block you've selected when specifying a block during a command, you can press Esc to cancel it or Backspace to return to the cell that was current when you started the command.

The period, Backspace, and Esc keys have different roles when used with unanchored and anchored blocks, as shown in Table 1.13.

Table 1.13   Special Keys for Unanchored and Anchored Blocks

Key	Action in Unanchored Block	Action in Anchored Block
. (period)	Anchors block.	Rotates the anchor cell from one corner of the block to another in a clockwise (or counterclockwise) direction.
Backspace	Returns the cell selector to the current cell.	Unanchors the cell selector and returns it to the current cell.
Esc	If you're using a command, Esc unanchors the cell and returns you to the previous command menu or prompt. If you're entering a formula, Esc returns you to Value mode.	Unanchors the block.

Naming Blocks

Quattro Pro lets you assign a name, such as COSTS, to a block of cells, such as A1..A20. You can then refer to this *block name* in a command or formula, as in @SUM(COSTS).

Note. If you're a 1-2-3 convert, be aware that you can't use undefined block names in Quattro Pro.

Why would you want to use block names? There are two main advantages. First, you'll probably find it easier to remember a block name than to remember its block coordinates. Second, a block is "attached" to its block name. This means that if you change the block coordinates assigned to a block name, any formulas that use that block name automatically refer to the new block of cells.

Creating a Named Block

It's easy to assign a name to a block of cells, such as B2..D2 in Figure 1.34. First, preselect this block, and then select /Edit, Names, Create. In the text

box shown in Figure 1.35, enter a block name, such as SALES, that meets
these guidelines:

- A block name can be up to 15 characters long. When you enter a longer
  name, Quattro Pro truncates it to the first 15 characters. A name can be
  composed of any characters A to Z and any numbers 0 through 9, as well
  as special characters such as $ and %. You can even use a . (period), an
  underscore, or a blank space.

- Don't worry about capitalization; block names aren't case-sensitive. For
  example, "Totals", "totals", and "toTals" all refer to the same named
  block within a spreadsheet.

- Avoid characters like + − * / & > < @ # { and ?, especially at the end of a
  block name, and ! at the beginning of a block name. They can be easily
  misinterpreted by Quattro Pro as part of a formula.

- Avoid using a number as the first character; Quattro Pro won't let you
  use such a block name in a formula.

- Avoid a block name that resembles a cell address, row number, or column letter. In a formula, Quattro Pro won't consider AA, Q3, or 1994 as
  valid block names. It's okay, however, to include these as part of a block
  name, as in Q31994.

- Avoid a block name that is an @function name, such as AVG, or a
  macro key name, like GOTO.

- Avoid assigning more than one name to the same block. Trouble can
  arise when you change the coordinates of one block name—you also
  change the coordinates of the other block names. You may end up
  changing block references you didn't mean to change.

When a block name describes a multicell block, Quattro Pro immediately places that name into all existing formulas that use that block. Compare Figures 1.34 and 1.36, for instance, and you can see how Quattro Pro
converts @SUM(B2..D2) to @SUM(SALES). When you assign a block
name to a single cell, however, no substitution takes place.

Using a Block Name

Once you create a block name like SALES, you can use it in place of the
block coordinates in any formula or command. In Figure 1.36, for instance,
entering @SUM(SALES) is the same as entering @SUM(B2..D2). If you create a block name assigned to a single cell, you can use it just like a cell address, as in +NET_PRICE+COSTS*5.

Figure 1.34

Assigning a name
to a block

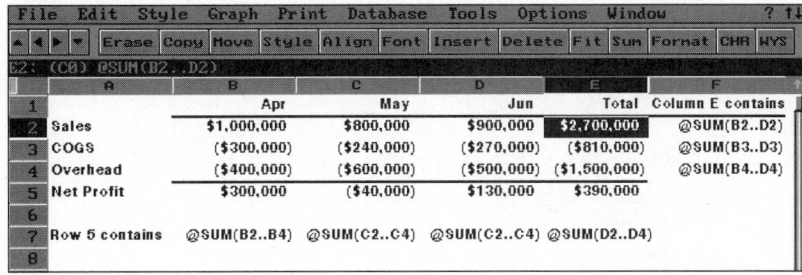

Figure 1.35

Before assigning a
name to a block

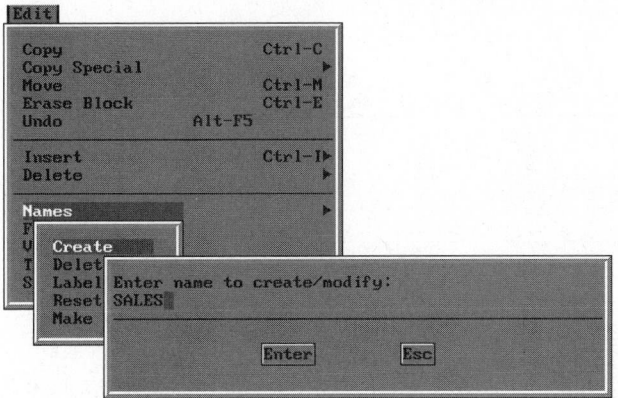

Figure 1.36

How Quattro Pro
uses assigned
block names

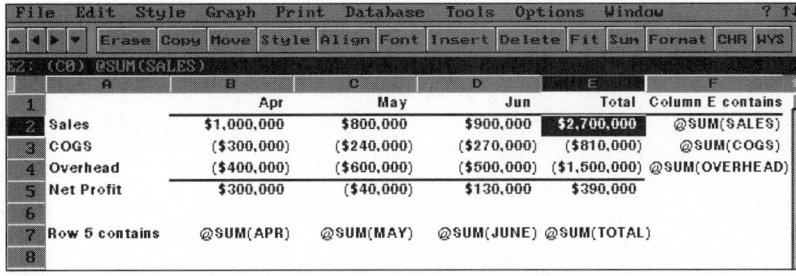

You can also use Quattro Pro's Choices (F3) feature to paste a block name into a formula or function. For example, suppose you're building a formula using @AVG. Type **@AVG(** and press F3. You'll see a list of all the block names for the spreadsheet file. Choose the block name you want, SALES for instance. (Pressing + adds the block coordinates that each block name represents to the list.) Press Enter and Quattro Pro pastes the name into your formula. Type **)** to complete @AVG(SALES).

To quickly move to the upper-left cell defining a block name, press F5 (GoTo) and then F3 (Choices). You can then choose the block name from the Choices list displayed, SALES for example. (As shown in Figure 1.37, pressing + adds the block coordinates to the list.) Quattro Pro then moves the cell selector to the upper-left cell of this block, in this case cell B2 in Figure 1.36.

Figure 1.37

Pressing F3 (Choices) then + in Quattro Pro 4.0

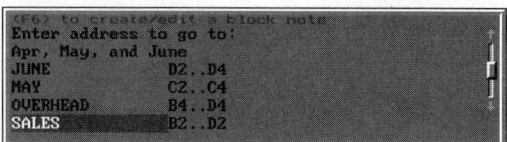

TIP. *In Quattro Pro 4.0, any note you've added to a block name is displayed in the Choices list whenever you highlight that name. In Figure 1.37, for instance, you can see that the block name SALES has the note "Apr, May, and June" attached to it.*

How Moving Affects Named Blocks

If you use Edit, Move to move the contents of a named block, Quattro Pro automatically adjusts the block name. For instance, imagine that you use /Edit, Move to move the data in B2..D2 of Figure 1.36 to B14..D14. The block name SALES then automatically refers to B14..D14.

When you work with named blocks, you should never move data into a named block's beginning or ending cell. To see why, imagine that you move data into cell B2 of Figure 1.36, which is the upper-left cell defining the named block SALES. When you do, the block name SALES becomes invalid, and any formulas that reference this block name display ERR. For example, @SUM(SALES) in cell E2 changes to @SUM(ERR) and returns ERR. To solve this problem, select /Edit, Names, Create, where SALES is still displayed in the list box. Choose it, and then respecify B2..D2 as the block you want it assigned to.

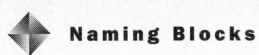

Attaching a Note to a Block Name in Quattro Pro 4.0

In Quattro Pro 4.0, you can add a note to a block name. You'll find that a note is a good way to easily identify what a block name represents at a later date. For example, to add the identifying note "Apr, May, and June" to the block name SALES in Figure 1.36, first select /Edit, Names, Create. In the list box displayed, highlight SALES (don't select it). Then press F6 to access the frontmost menu shown in Figure 1.38A. Enter this note, which can be up to 71 characters long. When you press Enter to confirm, you can see in Figure 1.38B how Quattro Pro 4.0 returns you to the Create list box, where this note is displayed whenever you highlight SALES.

Figure 1.38

Adding a note to the block name SALES

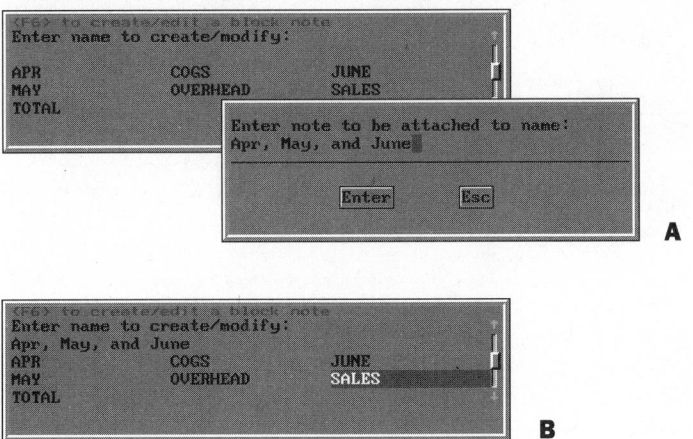

Although you can't see the block note you've added in the spreadsheet, there are two other ways you can. As you can see in Figure 1.37, any note you've attached to a block name is displayed in the Choices list whenever you highlight that name. The second technique, creating a block name table, lets you see all the notes attached to block names.

Tip. If you write over existing data when you create a block name table, immediately press Alt-F5 to undo the table and restore the data.

Inserting a Block Name Table into the Spreadsheet

The /Edit, Names, Make Table command is especially helpful when you're using a lot of defined block names in a spreadsheet or for troubleshooting. This command places a table in your spreadsheet listing all the block names in alphabetical order, the cell coordinates associated with each, and in Quattro Pro 4.0, any notes attached to block names.

For example, to create a block name table for the block names in Figure 1.36, first preselect the upper-left cell where you want the table to begin, cell A9 for instance. (Make sure there are empty cells below and two columns to the right of the cell you choose so Quattro Pro doesn't write over existing data.)

When you select /Edit, Names, Make Table, Quattro Pro 4.0 creates the three-column table shown in A9..C15 of Figure 1.39 listing all the block names previously created in this spreadsheet. As this table shows, SALES is assigned to the block B2..D2. What's more, you can see the note attached to SALES, "Apr, May, and June." (In Quattro Pro 3.0, no block notes are included.)

Figure 1.39

Creating a block name table for the spreadsheet in Figure 1.36

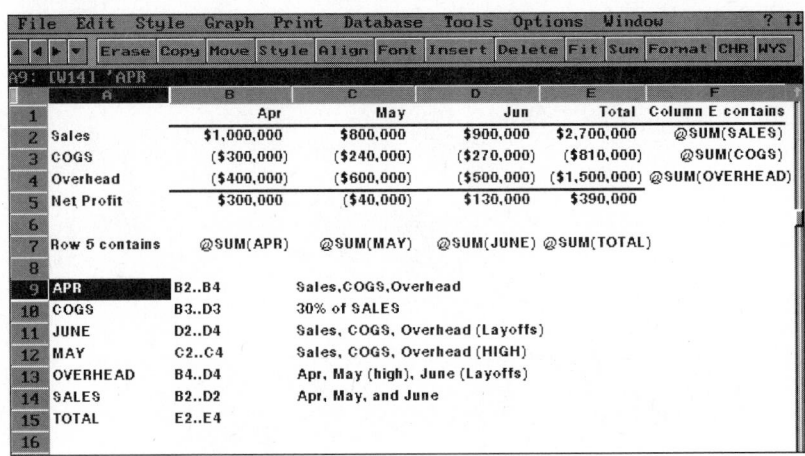

If you change or add block names and notes, you'll have to reuse /Edit, Names, Make Table; Quattro Pro doesn't update the table automatically.

Using Labels to Name Single-Cell Blocks

When you want to create a group of single-cell block names, consider using the /Edit, Names, Labels command to assign labels in adjacent cells. For instance, suppose you want to use the labels in column D of Figure 1.40 as block names for the corresponding cells in column E.

First, preselect the block of labels you want to use as block names, in this case D1..D8. Select /Edit, Names, Labels. In the menu shown in Figure 1.40, choose Right, Down, Left, or Up to tell Quattro Pro where the cells you want to name are in relation to the labels. Because the values in column E of Figure 1.40 are to the right of the labels in column D, the default, Right, is correct. When you press Enter, Quattro Pro assigns these labels as single-cell block names.

Tip. The /Edit, Names, Labels, Right command is particularly handy for naming macros (see Chapter 12).

Figure 1.40

Creating single-cell block names

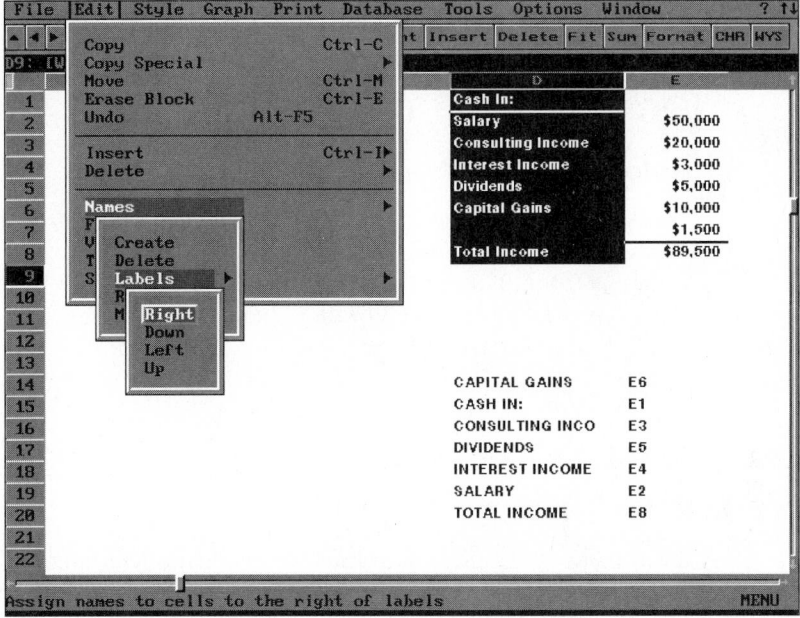

NOTE. *The cells you want to name must be next to the cells containing the labels. For example, if the values in column E of Figure 1.40 were in column F, and column E were blank, the labels in column D would be assigned as block names to the blank cells in column E.*

To see the named blocks Quattro Pro creates, /Edit, Names, Make Table is used in Figure 1.40 to create a block name table, beginning in cell D14. Now you can see that cell E6 is named Capital Gains, cell E2 is named Salary, and so on. Notice how Quattro Pro truncates any label to 15 characters when it's used as a block name, such as Consulting Inco assigned to E3. Although all labels are assigned as block names—even Cash In: is assigned to blank cell E1—Quattro Pro ignores any cells in the label block that are blank or contain numbers or formulas. That's why cell E7 isn't assigned a block name—cell D7 is blank.

Changing a Named Block

You can also use /Edit, Names, Create to change the block coordinates assigned to an existing block name. For example, imagine that you want to change the named block, SALES, which is assigned to B2..D2 in Figure 1.36, to refer to J3..J6. The easiest way is to preselect the new block coordinates, J3..J6. Then choose /Edit, Names, Create and select SALES from the list displayed. The block J3..J6 is now assigned to SALES. What's more, any formulas or functions that refer to SALES, such as @SUM(SALES) in cell E2 of Figure 1.36, now refer to J3..J6.

Deleting Block Names

Note. If you delete a block name by mistake, immediately press Undo (Alt-F5) to restore it.

To delete a defined block name, such as SALES in Figure 1.36, select /Edit, Names, Delete and then choose SALES. Quattro Pro automatically converts any formula using the deleted block name SALES to the cell addresses previously assigned to that block name. In Figure 1.36, for example, @SUM(SALES) in cell E2 changes back to the formula in Figure 1.34, @SUM(B2..D2). To remove all block names from a spreadsheet and start over, use /Edit, Names, Reset, Yes.

Searching and Replacing Data

By using the /Edit, Search & Replace command, you can quickly locate specific data in a spreadsheet, and if you want, replace it. You can search for and replace values, labels, or the occurrence of a text string—such as a cell reference, a function name, or a block name—within your formulas. The /Edit, Search & Replace command can be a real time saver when you want to make a substantial change to your spreadsheet logic.

Searching Formulas

The formulas in Figure 1.41 use block names created earlier in "Creating a Named Block." For example, you can see that cell E2 contains the formula @SUM(SALES), where SALES is a block name assigned to B2..D2. Using /Edit Search & Replace is the easiest way to check that a block name, such as SALES, is correctly used in your formulas. Here's how:

Note. /Edit, Search & Replace doesn't search hidden columns and rows unless you redisplay them first.

1. Move the cell selector to the upper-left cell of the block you want to search, in this case cell A1. (Otherwise, Quattro Pro will search the block you specify only from the cursor position onward.)

2. Select /Edit, Search & Replace. You'll see the menu shown in Figure 1.42.

3. Specify the Block you want to search as A1..F7. (If you don't, Quattro Pro for Windows will search the entire spreadsheet.)

Figure 1.41

Searching for a string in text and formulas

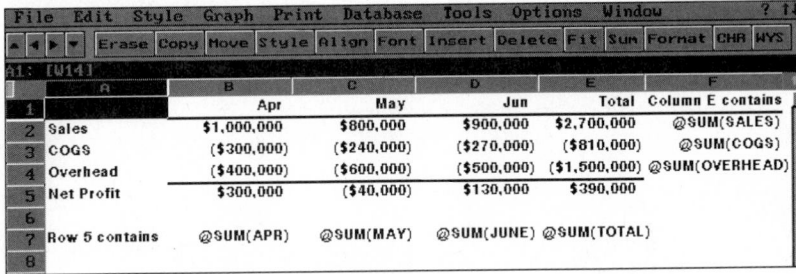

Figure 1.42

The Search & Replace menu

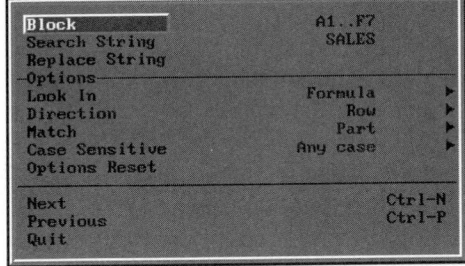

4. For the Search String, enter the string you want to find up to 512 characters. For this example, enter **SALES**.

5. Because, in this case, you don't care whether the search is case-sensitive, accept the default Case Sensitive setting, Any Case. (Choose Exact Case if you want to make the search case-sensitive.)

6. To search the contents of formulas, accept the Look In default setting, Formula. (As you'll see, a Formula setting also searches any cell that contains a label.)

7. Accept the Match default, Part. This setting tells Quattro Pro to consider it a match if the Search String occurs as part of a cell entry. (Whole tells Quattro Pro that a match occurs when the Search String exactly matches the *entire* entry in a cell.)

8. Accept the default Direction setting, Row. (To search column by column, choose Column.)

9. Select Next to begin the search.

Beginning in cell A1, Quattro Pro begins to search the cells in the search block containing formulas or labels for the Search String SALES. If no match is found, Quattro Pro beeps and displays the error message "not found." As you can see in Figure 1.43, however, Quattro Pro finds its first match in cell A2. Notice how the cell selector moves to this cell so you can see its contents in the input line, 'Sales.

Figure 1.43

The matches Quattro Pro finds during the search

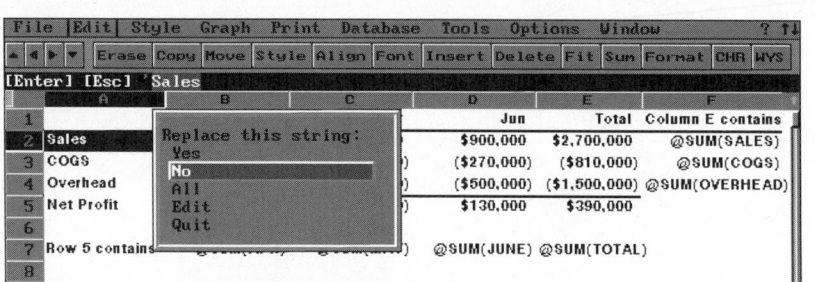

A

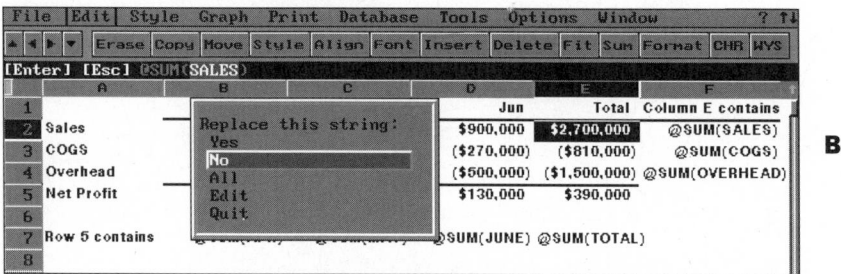

B

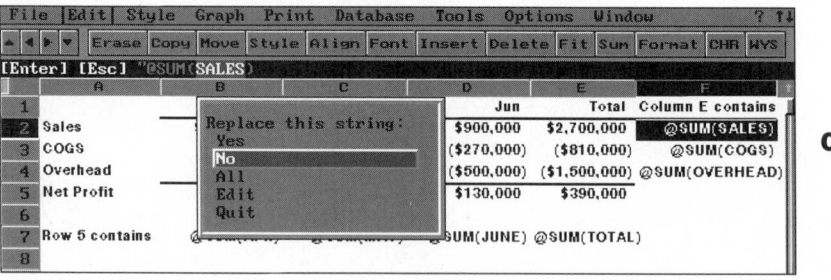

C

TIP. *When you're searching formulas for block names, which Quattro Pro always displays in uppercase letters, you can limit the search by specifying Case*

Sensitive Exact Case. Then the label 'Sales in cell A2 of Figure 1.43A wouldn't be found.

Because you are only searching for data, not replacing it, you'll want to choose from these three options in the menu displayed:

- **No** continues the search without replacing the contents of the cell.

- **Edit** displays the contents of the current cell in the input line. You can edit the contents of the cell and then press Enter to continue the search.

- **Quit** ends the search, leaving the cell selector in the current cell.

CAUTION! *If you select Yes during a search operation, Quattro Pro will delete the contents of the current cell because you haven't specified a Replace String.*

Tip. To search *backward* from the cursor, press Ctrl-P, the shortcut for /Edit, Search & Replace, Previous.

Select No, and Figure 1.43B shows that Quattro Pro finds another match to SALES in cell E2, which contains the formula @SUM(SALES). Choose No again to continue the search, and Quattro Pro finds the third match shown in Figure 1.43C, in the label "@SUM(SALES) in cell F2. When no other match is found, Quattro Pro returns the cell selector to its original location, cell A1.

Because Quattro Pro remembers your /Edit, Search & Replace settings until you close the file, just press Ctrl-N, the shortcut for /Edit, Search & Replace, Next, to perform the same search again. However, your settings are not saved with the file. If you want to clear these settings, choose Options Reset in the Search & Replace menu.

Searching for a Value

Things can get confusing when you try to use /Edit, Search & Replace to find a value. To see why, let's search for the value 300000 in column B of Figure 1.41. Before we begin, you'll need to know this information:

Cell	Contains	Displayed
B2	300000+700000	$1,000,000
B3	–300000	($300,000)
B4	–400000; assumes 300000 in cost cutting	($400,000)
B5	@SUM(APR)	$300,000

If you use the following Search String and Look In settings in the /Edit, Search & Replace command for the Block B1..B5, you'll get these results:

Search String	Look In	Found
300000	Value	No match
$300,000	Value	300000 in B3; $300,000 result in B5
$300,000	Formula	No match
300,000	Formula	300000 in B2; 300000 in B3; 300000 in B4 note

So what does this table say? Well, first you can make these conclusions about how the Look In settings evaluate values:

- **Value** evaluates cells containing only a value, such as B3, and cells where the result of a formula is a value, such as B5. It doesn't search notes, as in B4, because a note is a label, or formulas themselves, as in B2.

- **Formula** evaluates the cell *contents* for a value, whether the cell contains a value, as in B3, a note (label), as in B4, or a formula, as in B2. This setting does not, however, recognize a value resulting from a formula, as in B5.

What's more, this table shows how your Search String must include the *same* formatting in which the value you are searching for appears in. When you use a Search String of 300000 and Look In Value, Quattro Pro doesn't consider the 300000 in either cell B3 or B5 a match, because a Currency 0 places format makes them appear as $300,000. Use a Search String of $300,000, however, and Quattro Pro finds both these occurrences. Likewise, when you use the Search String $300,000 and Look In Formula, Quattro Pro doesn't find the occurrences in B2, B3, and B4 that it does when you use the Search String 300000.

Using a Condition to Limit the Search for a Value

You can further limit a search for a value by using Look In Condition and then specifying a special logical formula as your Search String. As discussed earlier in "Logical Formulas," a logical formula uses one of the logical operators listed in Table 1.9 to create a comparison test.

Note. When you specify a Look In condition, Quattro Pro replaces ? in the Search String with the cell it is currently evaluating in the Search Block. For example, ?>900000 might be converted to +A1>900000.

When you use a logical formula in /Edit, Search & Replace, it must take the form *?=Value* where = represents any logical operator such as >, and Value can be any value.

In Figure 1.44, for instance, the Search String ?>900000 and a Look In setting of Condition in /Edit, Search & Replace causes Quattro Pro to find all the cells in the Search Block A1..F7 of Figure 1.41 where the *resulting* value is greater than 900,000—cell B2, which contains $1,000,000, and cell E2, where the result of the formula @SUM(SALES) is $2,700,000.

Figure 1.44

Using a condition
as the Search String

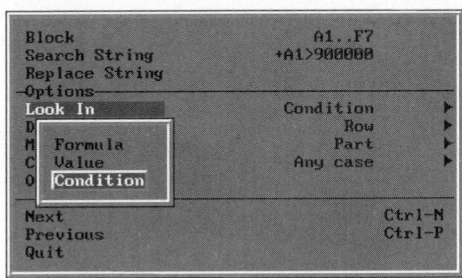

NOTE. *When you use a condition as the Search String, you can only perform a search operation—you can't perform a search and replace operation. That's why you won't see the menu shown in Figure 1.43. Instead, you have to press Ctrl-N to continue the search.*

Searching for a Label

When you want to search for a label or part of a label, you should use a Look In Value setting. A Look In Formula setting expands the search to include the text in formulas, such as the function name @SUM and the block name SALES in @SUM(SALES).

You can further limit a search for a label in two ways. First, use a Case Sensitive Exact Case setting to limit what Quattro Pro considers an exact match. Use the Search String Sales in Figure 1.43, for example, and only the label Sales in cell A2 is found; SALES in the label in cell F2 isn't.

A second way to limit a label search is to set Match to Whole. For the Search String Sales and a Look In setting of Value, Quattro Pro finds the label Sales in cell A2. But it won't find this string when Sales is only part of the entry in a cell. If you use Look In Formula, however, Quattro Pro includes the label prefix in its evaluation. In Figure 1.43, for instance, it would only consider the label in A2 a match when you use the Search String 'Sales.

Note. To see how Quattro Pro evaluates a text string that contains a value, see "Searching for a Value," earlier.

Replacing a String

Once you understand how the /Edit, Search & Replace command evaluates values, labels, and formulas in a search block, there's nothing difficult about replacing some or all of the occurrences of the Search String matches Quattro Pro finds. The only difference is that you specify a Replace String in the /Edit, Search & Replace menu.

When you perform a search and replace operation, all of the choices in the menu Quattro Pro displays (Figure 1.43) can be used. Here's what each option does:

- **Yes**   Replaces the Search String found with the Replace String, and then moves on to the next occurrence found.

- **No**   Continues the search without replacing the search string.

- **All**   Replaces the current occurrence and all remaining occurrences of the search string without prompting you further.

- **Edit**   Displays the contents of the current cell in the input line. The search string isn't replaced. You can edit the contents of the cell and then press Enter to continue the search.

- **Quit**   Cancels the search and replace operation and returns you to the spreadsheet. The cell selector comes to rest in the current cell.

Saving and Retrieving Files

When you enter information in a Quattro Pro spreadsheet, you are actually creating a spreadsheet *file*. Initially, however, that file and the information it contains is only temporary—that is, it exists only in your computer's RAM. If you turn your computer off or exit Quattro Pro, the spreadsheet file and the information it contains is lost.

To save the information in a spreadsheet file for future use, you must save the spreadsheet file itself to disk. Thereafter, you can safely turn off your computer or leave Quattro Pro, knowing that your information has been retained. You can then open that same spreadsheet file in a future Quattro Pro session to view or change the information contained in the file.

To save a new Quattro Pro spreadsheet file, use the /File, Save command. When you select this command Quattro Pro displays the "Enter save file name:" prompt box, as shown in Figure 1.45. Under the prompt, you'll see the path to the current directory followed by the file descriptor *.WQ1. Any spreadsheet files that have already been saved to the current directory are listed below. Type a new file name that is eight characters or less in length—for example, SALES_92. When you are ready, press Enter. Quattro Pro saves the current spreadsheet file to disk under the name you've specified, automatically appending a .WQ1 file name extension, as in SALES_92.WQ1. This extension is the default for Quattro Pro's spreadsheet file names.

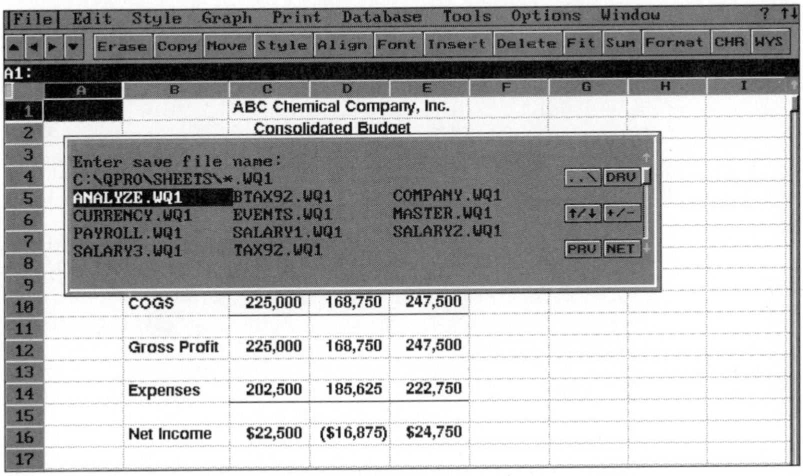

Figure 1.45
Using/File, Save to name your spreadsheet file and save it to disk

Once a spreadsheet file has been saved to disk, you can open that same file in a later Quattro Pro session using the /File, Retrieve command. For example, to open the SALES_92.WQ1 file discussed in the previous paragraph, select /File, Retrieve. Quattro Pro displays the "Enter name of file to retrieve:" prompt box, showing a list of files in the current directory. The first file in the list is highlighted. Use the arrow keys to move the highlight to the SALES_92.WQ1 file name, and press Enter to open the file. Alternatively, you can simply type **SALES_92** and press Enter. Either way, Quattro Pro opens the SALES_92.WQ1 file and displays it on the desktop. You can now view and edit the file. When you're done, use /File, Save to save your changes.

Note that the /File, Save and /File, Retrieve commands are only two of the commands Quattro Pro offers for managing your spreadsheet files. As you'll learn in Chapters 2 and 5, you can use the commands on the /File menu to open both new and existing spreadsheet files, and save them in different directories under different names. You'll also learn how you can open multiple spreadsheets on the Quattro Pro desktop at the same time.

Erasing the Entire Spreadsheet

Eventually, the time will come when you want to delete the spreadsheet in the current window. This may be when you've completed work on the current spreadsheet and saved it to disk, and you want to start a new spreadsheet with a new name. Or you may be working on a hopeless case and just want to start over again.

You can erase the spreadsheet in the current window and open a fresh, blank spreadsheet using the /File, Erase command. This command does not affect files on disk. It removes only the current spreadsheet and replaces it with a new one. If you've neglected to save your changes to the current spreadsheet, Quattro Pro gives you an opportunity to do so before it removes the current file from memory. You'll see a prompt box that says "Lose your changes?" along with a Yes/No choice (Figure 1.46). If you select No, Quattro Pro returns you to the spreadsheet and you can use /File, Save to save your changes. Select Yes, however, and the old spreadsheet is removed from memory and replaced with a new one.

Using the Undo Feature

Quattro Pro's Undo feature lets you reverse the effect of the last command. For example, suppose you've just used /Edit, Erase Block to delete a large block of cells. You then discover the block you specified was a little too large and you've deleted some important data. At this point, you can use Undo to reverse the effect of the /Edit, Erase command and restore the spreadsheet to the way it was. In this way, you can reclaim the data you've lost.

Enabling Undo

Initially, the Undo feature is disabled. Therefore, before you can use Undo, you must first enable it. Select the /Options, Other, Undo command, and you'll see another menu with the Enable and Disable options. Select Enable, and Quattro Pro activates the Undo feature. (To disable it, select Disable.) You can also save this setting for future sessions by selecting the Update command from the /Options menu.

When Undo is enabled, Quattro Pro keeps track of the state of your spreadsheet both before and after each command that can be reversed. (There are some commands Quattro Pro cannot undo.) It can thus reverse the effects of the most recent command. However, keeping track of your commands places an additional burden on Quattro Pro and may cause it to run noticeably slower. For this reason, the product ships with the Undo feature disabled.

Figure 1.46
The /File, Erase command's prompt to save your changes before erasing

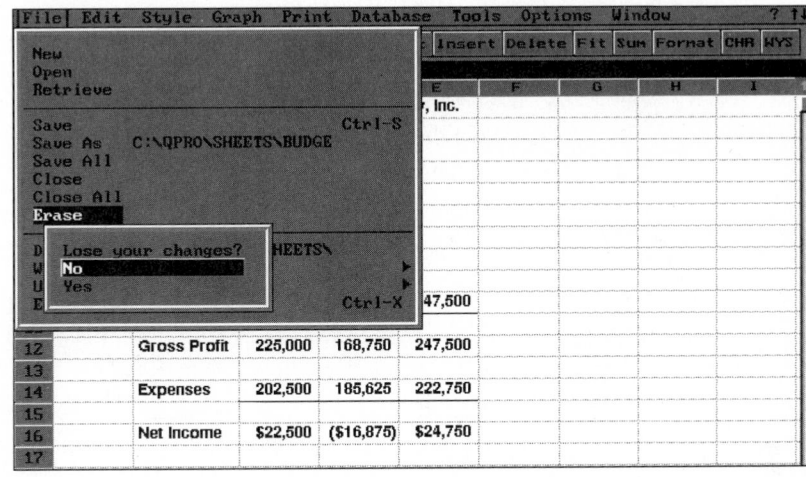

Using Undo to Reverse Commands

Tip. You can also use Undo to perform a little "what-if" analysis in the spreadsheet. Say you have a key cell in a model on which other cells depend. You can enter a value in that cell just to see what happens. If you don't like the results, select /Edit, Undo (Alt-F5) and try a new value.

Once you enable the Undo feature, you can use the /Edit, Undo command (or press Alt-F5) to reverse the effects of the previous command. However, Undo can *only* reverse the effects of the most recent command. Therefore, you must use /Edit, Undo *immediately* after the command you want to reverse. If you don't and you enter some other reversible command, you lose the opportunity to fix the damage.

As mentioned, there are some irreversible commands and operations. If you select /Edit, Undo after one of these commands, Quattro Pro cannot undo the most recent operation. Instead, it will undo the last command that it *can* undo, no matter how long ago you entered that command. The results of this can be unsettling, but fortunately, /Edit, Undo (Alt-F5) is also a toggle command. That is, if Undo reverses a command you decide that you don't want reversed after all, you can use /Edit, Undo again to redo what you just reversed.

The /Edit, Undo command is powerful; it reverses the following operations:

- Erasing spreadsheets in memory (/File, Erase)

- Retrieving files (/File, Retrieve)

- Deletions of block names (/Edit, Name, Delete)

- Deletions of named graphs (/Graph, Name, Reset)

■ Changes to the data in your spreadsheet, including new entries or entries you erased (/Edit, Erase Block)

Commands That Undo Cannot Reverse

Remember that some commands and operations cannot be reversed. These include:

■ Any operation that affects files on disk, such as /File, Save, or copying, moving, and deleting files with File Manager

■ Commands on the /Style or /Options menus that affect the formatting of the spreadsheet (fonts, label alignment, numeric format, line drawing, shading, column widths, row heights, and so on)

■ Settings for commands such as the Block setting for the /Database, Sort command and the Series setting for the /Graph command

■ /Print commands that send data to your printer or to a file on disk

NOTE. *You can also use the Transcript facility (described next) to undo changes to your spreadsheet. In fact, you'll find Transcript is somewhat more flexible than Undo. Transcript lets you rerun all the commands you've entered during the current work session, or just a selected portion of them. Consider using Transcript when the Undo feature is disabled or when you want to undo recent irreversible commands.*

The Transcript Facility

The Transcript facility keeps a running log of just about everything you do in Quattro Pro. It captures all of your keystrokes and commands and records them in a file on disk named QUATTRO.LOG. All of this takes place in the background. In fact, Borland has gone to great lengths to make the Transcript facility operation as transparent and unobtrusive as possible.

You can use Transcript to perform a number of important functions. First and foremost, you can use it to undo a mistake you've made. In fact, if the Undo feature discussed in the previous section is disabled (the default), you'll find the Transcript facility a lifesaver. You'll learn later how you can *play back* portions of the Transcript log file, thereby repeating commands and keystrokes you've previously entered. This allows you to recover lost data, should your system suffer a power outage. Finally, you can copy portions of the Transcript log file to your spreadsheet for use as a macro.

All your commands and keystrokes are captured and stored in the QUATTRO.LOG file in the form of macro commands. As you'll learn in

Chapter 12, Quattro Pro offers a full-fledged macro command language that lets you automate many of your routine Quattro Pro tasks (and some that are not so routine). Macro commands are simply instructions in the form of labels that tell Quattro Pro to select a given command, enter a given value or label in a cell, and so on.

On the surface, the macro command language may be intimidating to the novice. Many books about Quattro Pro place the discussion of the Transcript facility inconspicuously in the macros chapter, where you might never get the chance to find out about its uses. Here, on the other hand, you'll explore Transcript early in your Quattro Pro study. As you'll soon see, you don't have to be an expert macro programmer to make effective use of Transcript's power.

Viewing the Transcript Log File

To view the contents of the Transcript log file, select the /Tools, Macro, Transcript command. (You can also select this command by pressing Alt-F2 and typing **T**.) Quattro Pro opens the Transcript window, illustrated in Figure 1.47.

Figure 1.47
The Transcript window

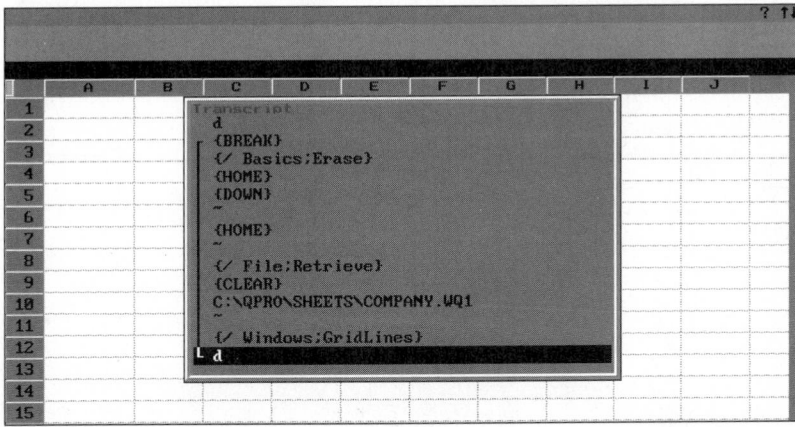

The Transcript window shows a sequential listing of the commands and keystrokes you've entered since you opened the current file. The last command you entered is highlighted. Often, you'll find that this list of commands exceeds the size of the Transcript window. You can scroll back through your previous commands by pressing the ↑ or PgUp key. To scroll back to where you started from, press ↓ or PgDn. In addition, the Home key takes you to the first command in the list, and the End key takes you to the last command.

The commands displayed in the Transcript window are referred to collectively as the *command history*. Later, under "Changing the Length of Your Command History," you'll learn how you can control the length of the command history that is displayed in the Transcript window.

As you view the Transcript window, you'll notice a thin vertical line to the left of some of the commands in the window. Look closely, and you'll see that each end of this vertical line has a small, connected horizontal line, thus forming a large bracket. The commands listed above this bracket have been written to the QUATTRO.LOG file on disk. The commands within the bracket have not—they exist only in your computer's memory. The beginning or top end of this vertical bracket marks a *checkpoint*. Quattro Pro creates this checkpoint each time you select the /File, Save, /File, Retrieve, or /File, Erase commands. Thus, each time you save a file or replace the contents of a window, a new checkpoint marks the start of a new bracket, and the commands prior to that checkpoint are saved to the QUATTRO.LOG file.

Transcript also comes with its own menu. You can open this menu by pressing the / (slash) key while the Transcript window is displayed. When you press this key, Quattro Pro opens a second window containing Transcript command options, shown in Figure 1.48. These commands perform the following functions:

- *Undo Last Command* rebuilds the current spreadsheet in which you are working, up to but not including the last command you entered.

Figure 1.48
The Transcript menu

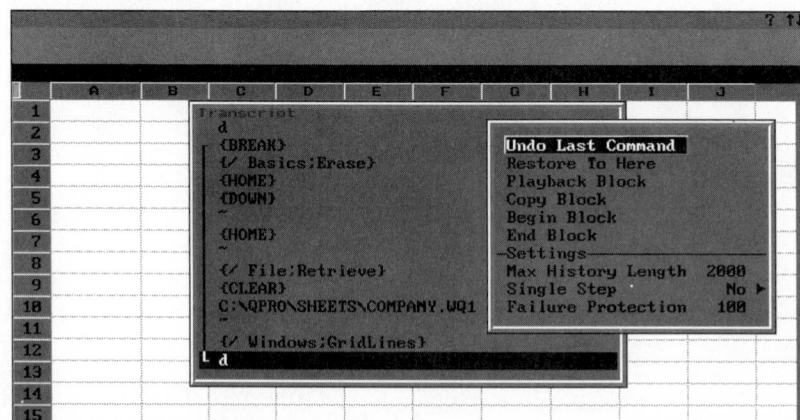

- *Restore To Here* plays back your commands from the last checkpoint (the point where you last used the /File, Save, Retrieve, or Erase command) up to the current command that is highlighted in the Transcript window. You can use this option to reclaim lost work.

- *Playback Block* lets you play back a block of commands. You define the block to play back by using the Begin Block and End Block command options.

- *Copy Block* copies a selected block of commands from the Transcript window to the current spreadsheet for printing or for use as a macro. You define the Block you want to copy by using the Begin Block and End Block command options.

- *Begin Block* defines the beginning of a block to play back or copy.

- *End Block* defines the end of a block to play back or copy.

- *Max History Length* lets you increase or decrease the number of characters stored in the QUATTRO.LOG file before Quattro Pro renames this file to QUATTRO.BAK and starts a new QUATTRO.LOG file.

- *Single Step* lets you choose the speed at which commands are played back.

- *Failure Protection* lets you specify the number of characters you can type before Quattro Pro saves your input to the QUATTRO.LOG file on disk.

NOTE. *As you'll learn in Chapter 12, Quattro Pro supports two styles of macro programming—keystroke-equivalent macros and menu-equivalent macros. Because menu-equivalent macros are compatible with custom menu trees, this form of macro is stored in the Transcript log by default. However, you can switch to capturing keystrokes and commands in the keystroke-equivalent format, by using the /Tools, Macro, Macro Recording command and selecting the Keystroke option. This command is discussed in detail in Chapter 12.*

Exiting Transcript

You can exit the Transcript facility at any time simply by pressing Esc. Keep this in mind as you read the sections that follow. When you press Esc, the Transcript window is removed from your screen and you are returned to the current spreadsheet.

Undoing Only the Last Command

Undo Last Command lets you rebuild a spreadsheet after a damaging command. It does this by playing back all commands, except the last one, from the last Transcript window checkpoint, which begins with the last /File, Retrieve, Save, or Erase command.

Imagine that the Undo feature has not yet been enabled with /Options, Other, Undo, Enable. Therefore, you cannot select /Edit, Undo (or Alt-F5) to reverse the effects of the last command. While working on a spreadsheet, you use the /Edit, Copy command to copy a large block of data from one area of the spreadsheet to another, accidentally overwriting a block of cells critical to your spreadsheet.

To reverse the damage you've done, select the /Tools, Macro, Transcript command (or press Alt-F2, T) *immediately*, before selecting any more commands. Quattro Pro displays the Transcript window. Press the / (slash) key to display the Transcript menu; then select the Undo Last Command option. Quattro Pro returns to the last checkpoint in the Transcript log file—the point at which you opened a spreadsheet window or erased its contents—and begins executing (playing back) all your commands and keystrokes from that point forward, leaving out the last command you entered and thereby rebuilding your spreadsheet.

While Quattro Pro is reexecuting your commands, the WAIT mode indicator is displayed in the status line. You can stop the playback process at any time by pressing Ctrl-Break. Quattro Pro will execute the last command it encountered before you pressed Ctrl-Break and then stop the playback. Whether you stop playback or let it run to completion, you are returned to the current spreadsheet.

CAUTION! *If you are working with multiple spreadsheets, Transcript may not be able to accurately rebuild the current spreadsheet. You'll get reliable playbacks only when you are working on one spreadsheet at a time.*

Playing Back Commands and Keystrokes

You can also play back selected keystrokes and commands in the Transcript log file. There are two ways to do this: You can play back the commands from the last checkpoint up to the command that is highlighted in the Transcript window; or you can select a block of commands you want to play back. You can also choose the speed at which playback occurs.

Playing Back Actions to a Specific Point

Transcript's Restore To Here option lets you play back all of your actions from the last checkpoint to the command currently highlighted in the Transcript window. You might use this option if you make a costly mistake, but you don't discover it until several commands later. At that point, neither the Undo feature nor Transcript's Undo Last Command option will do you any good.

To use the Restore To Here option, select /Tools, Macro, Transcript. The last command you entered appears highlighted in the Transcript window. Press ↑ to move the highlight to the last command or keystroke you want Quattro Pro to reexecute and select /Transcript, Restore To Here. Quattro Pro plays back your commands from the last checkpoint in the Transcript window up to the currently highlighted command. Essentially, it rebuilds your spreadsheet—from the last time you opened it or saved it up until the command you highlighted.

Playing Back Part of the Transcript Log File

You can also play back a selected portion of the Transcript log file by using the Playback Block option. You might use this option when you are creating a new spreadsheet and you want to enter most of the commands and keystrokes you've used in a previous spreadsheet.

To set up for Playback Block,

1. Select /Tools, Macro, Transcript (or press Alt-F2 and type **T**).

2. Highlight the *first* command or keystroke you want to execute.

3. Select /Begin Block from the Transcript menu. Quattro Pro places a small arrow next to the current command in the Transcript window.

4. Use the arrow keys to move to the *last* command in the block of commands you want to play back.

5. Select /End Block. Quattro Pro places small arrows next to all the command lines between the beginning and ending commands you've selected, as shown in Figure 1.49.

To initiate the playback process, select Playback Block. Quattro Pro plays back the commands that are marked in the Transcript window.

Choosing a Playback Speed

You can also choose the speed at which Transcript commands are played back when you select the Playback Block, Restore To Here, and Undo Last Command options. To do this, you use the Single Step option from the Transcript menu. When you select this option, Quattro Pro displays a submenu with three choices—No, Yes, and Timed. With the No option (the default), Quattro Pro plays back Transcript commands at full speed. Often, however, commands are executed so fast that you can't tell what is going on. If there is an error in the procedure, you may not be able to determine where that error lies. You can slow down the playback speed by selecting the Yes or Timed options from the Single Step menu.

Figure 1.49

Selecting a block of commands to play back from the Transcript window

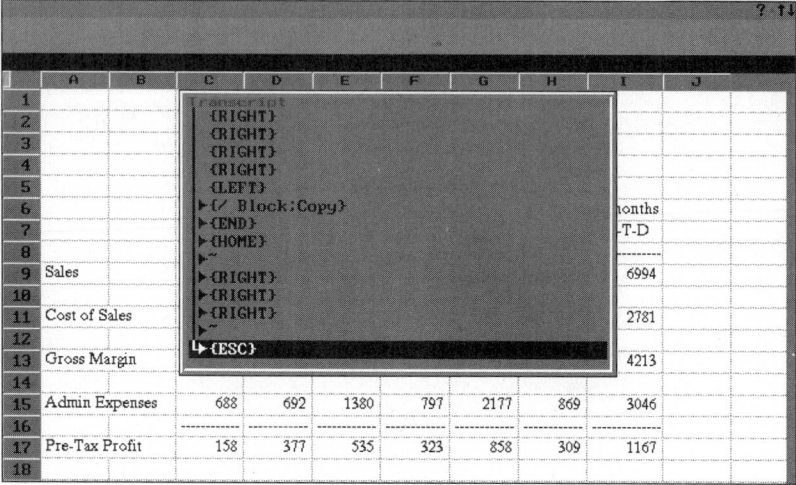

Choose Yes from the Single Step menu, and Quattro Pro will play back Transcript commands one command or keystroke at a time. In fact, to execute each command or keystroke, you must press a key. This option is useful when you want to search for an error in a command sequence. Or you can select Timed, and Quattro Pro will hesitate for a few seconds between executing each command. When you play back Transcript commands with either of these settings in force, Quattro Pro displays a DEBUG indicator in the status line at the bottom of your screen. To revert to full-speed playback, select the No option from the Single Step menu.

NOTE. *The effects of selecting Yes from the Single Step menu are similar to selecting the /Tools, Macro, Debugger command when you are debugging a macro stored in the current spreadsheet. See Chapter 12 for details.*

Copying Transcript Commands to Your Spreadsheet

As mentioned, the Transcript facility captures all of your commands and keystrokes and stores them as macro-command equivalents in the QUATTRO.LOG file. Therefore, you might think of the Transcript log contents as one long macro.

To copy a selection of commands from the Transcript window to the spreadsheet and thereby create a ready-made macro, you use the Copy Block option from the Transcript menu. The use of this option in creating ready-made macros is described in detail in Chapter 12; here is a summary.

Start by marking the block of commands you want to copy. Use the Begin Block and End Block options from the Transcript menu, as described earlier in "Playing Back Part of the Transcript Log File." Next, select the Copy Block command. Quattro Pro prompts you to name the block of commands. Type the name of your choice and press Enter. (You'll learn how this name is used in Chapter 12.) When prompted for the location in the spreadsheet where you want to copy the commands, move the cell pointer to an appropriate cell in the current spreadsheet and press Enter. Quattro Pro copies the block of commands into the spreadsheet, starting in the cell you specified. The commands are stored as a column of labels with one label or command line per cell.

Changing the Length of Your Command History

When the QUATTRO.LOG file reaches a certain size in characters, Quattro Pro renames the file QUATTRO.BAK and starts a new, empty QUATTRO-.LOG file. The default size setting for the Quattro Pro log file is 2,000 characters (2,000 bytes). Each time it reaches this threshold, QUATTRO.BAK is overwritten. Limiting the size of QUATTRO.LOG keeps it from occupying too much of your computer's memory that could potentially be used by your spreadsheets.

Nevertheless, Quattro Pro allows you to increase the size of the QUATTRO.LOG file up to 25,000 characters, using the Max History Length option on the Transcript menu. On the other end of the scale, you can disable the Transcript facility altogether, by entering 0 for this option.

Guarding Against System Failures

Quattro Pro adds your keystrokes to the QUATTRO.LOG file in 100-character segments. That way, if a power outage occurs, you'll only lose your last 100 keystrokes. When the power returns, you can open the Transcript window and use the Restore To Here option from the Transcript menu to rebuild your spreadsheet.

The act of periodically writing your keystrokes to the QUATTRO.LOG file can slow down Quattro Pro. If you find this becoming a problem, you can increase the number of keystrokes that are stored in memory before saving them to the QUATTRO.LOG file. To do this, select the Failure Protection option from the Transcript menu, and type a value greater than 100. The more keystrokes you specify, the less frequently Quattro Pro saves them to disk. If the power goes out, however, you may find that you can only rebuild part of your spreadsheet from the QUATTRO.LOG file.

Checking Available Memory

Whenever you work with large spreadsheets in Quattro Pro, it's wise to keep an eye on the amount of available memory in your computer. To check available memory, use the /Options, Hardware command. Quattro Pro shows you the settings for both conventional and expanded (EMS) memory, as shown in Figure 1.50. Chapter 15 gives you more information on how to control Quattro Pro's use of memory.

Figure 1.50

The /Options, Hardware command

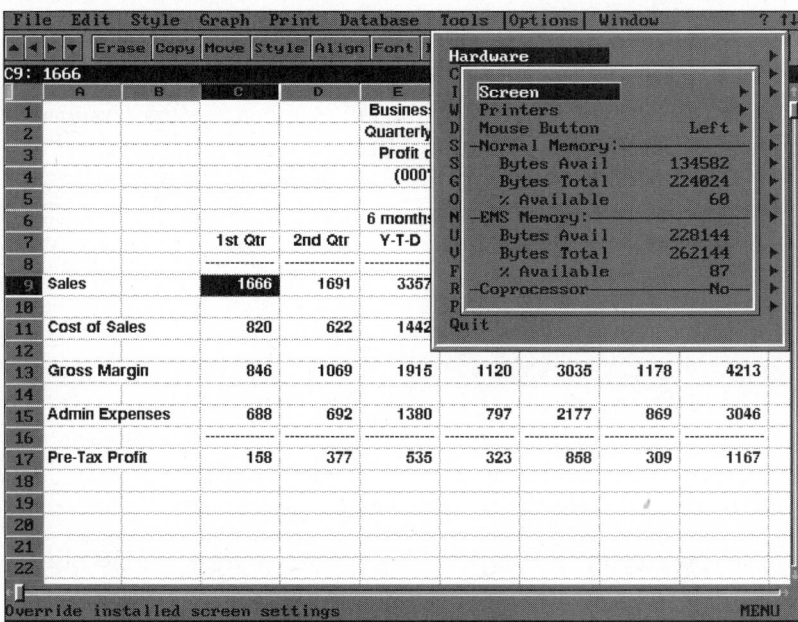

Inserting Columns and Rows

Many times you'll need to add new data in the middle of a previously created spreadsheet. Although you can move existing entries to another location (see Chapter 4), it's often easier to insert additional columns or rows.

Inserting Columns

Figure 1.51A contains the number of subscribers for three cable channels in October, November, and December in columns B, C, and D. Column E contains the total number of subscribers for these three months. Suppose you want to add the number of subscribers for July, August, and September in three columns to the left of column B. Here's the procedure to do this:

1. Place the cell selector in any cell of the column where you want to begin inserting the new columns. In this case, because you want to insert columns to the left of column B, place the cell selector in any cell in column B, cell B2 for instance.

2. Preselect the block that contains the number of columns you want to insert. Because you want to insert three columns, select block B2..D2, as shown in Figure 1.51A.

3. Select /Edit, Insert, Columns.

Figure 1.51

Inserting columns

Tip. Selecting `Insert` is equivalent to selecting /Edit, Insert.

As you can see in Figure 1.51B, Quattro Pro inserts three blank columns to the left of column B. Column B of Figure 1.51A is now column E, column C is now column F, column D is now column G, and so on. The inserted columns have the Quattro Pro default style attributes for alignment, numeric format, column width, and so on. To learn how to change these style attributes, see Chapter 3.

Inserting Rows

Inserting rows is similar to inserting columns. Figure 1.52A shows the same spreadsheet as Figure 1.51A. Suppose you want to insert two rows above row 2. To do this, place the cell selector in any cell of the row immediately below where you want to insert the new rows, cell B2 for example. Next, pre-select a block that contains the number of rows you want to insert. Because you want to insert two rows, select block B2..B3 as shown in Figure 1.52A and select /Edit, Insert, Rows.

As you can see in Figure 1.52B, Quattro Pro inserts two rows immediately above row 2. Row 2 of Figure 1.52A is now row 4, row 3 is now row 5, row 4 is now row 6, and so on.

The Effects of Inserting Columns or Rows

As you know, a block is a rectangular group of contiguous cells defined by the cell addresses of the diagonally opposite corners. Block A10..B11, for example, contains the cells A10, A11, B10, and B11. For more information on blocks, see "Working with Blocks," earlier in this chapter.

When you insert columns or rows in the middle of a block and that block is referenced in a formula, the block reference expands its cell addresses to include the additional columns or rows. By contrast, when you insert columns or rows at the beginning or the end of a block, the address doesn't expand. In both cases, Quattro Pro updates the block to reflect its new spreadsheet location due to the additional columns or rows.

To see how Quattro Pro updates block addresses, compare the three spreadsheets in Figure 1.52. In Figure 1.52A, Total October Subscribers are calculated in cell B5 using the formula @SUM(B2..B4). After you insert two rows above row 2, in Figure 1.52B the old row 2 becomes row 4, the old row 3 becomes row 5, and the old row 4 becomes row 6. So the formula in cell B7 is updated to @SUM(B4..B6) to reflect the new location of the referenced block address. However, the block address doesn't expand to include the inserted rows. If you enter a value in cell B2 or B3 of Figure 1.52B, this value won't affect Total October Subscribers calculated in cell B7.

On the other hand, a formula block address does expand when you insert columns or rows into the middle of the referenced block. Suppose you insert two rows above row 3 of Figure 1.52A. In this case, you've inserted rows in the middle of the referenced block of the formula @SUM(B2..B4) used to calculate Total October Subscribers. In cell B7 of Figure 1.52C, Quattro Pro expands the block reference so that the formula now reads @SUM(B2..B6). If you enter a value in cells B3 or B4 of Figure 1.52C, the value will be included in the calculation of Total October Subscribers.

When you insert columns or rows into a spreadsheet, you need to be aware of the following:

- You can't insert columns or rows in a globally protected spreadsheet (see Chapter 2).

Figure 1.52

Inserting rows

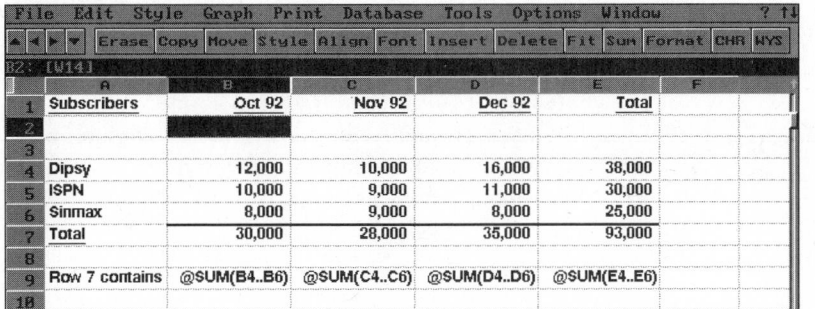

- In Quattro Pro 4.0, an inserted column or row has the default style attributes, including left label alignment, General numeric format, 12 point Swiss-SC font and (when inserting columns) a column width of 9. Quattro Pro 3.0 has the same default style attributes except the default font, which is Swiss 12 point (see Chapter 3).

- An inserted column or row may be included in the print block (see Chapter 6).

- When you are using a database in Quattro Pro, where each row is one record and each column is one field, inserting a row creates a blank record and inserting a column creates a blank field (see Chapter 10).

- Inserting columns and rows can adversely affect macros. For example, inserting a blank row in the middle of a macro will cause the macro to stop running when it reaches the blank row (see Chapter 12).

Deleting Columns and Rows

Tip. If Undo is enabled, you can reinsert the deleted columns or rows by selecting /Edit, Undo (see "Using the Undo Feature," earlier).

The procedure you use to delete columns and rows is similar to the one you use to insert them. Suppose, for example, you track monthly product sales in Figure 1.53A. Because of a product recall, you've had to make refunds on all sales of R3 Fuses. To delete row 4 from the spreadsheet, place the cell selector anywhere in that row, in cell B4 for example. Then select /Edit, Delete, Rows and when prompted for a block of rows to delete, press Enter. Quattro Pro deletes row 4 with all its data, as shown in Figure 1.53B. It moves all rows below row 4 up—row 5 of Figure 1.53A becomes row 4 of Figure 1.53B and row 6 becomes row 5.

TIP. *Selecting* `Delete` *is equivalent to selecting /Edit, Delete.*

The Effects of Deleting Columns or Rows

Quattro Pro automatically updates all formulas when you delete a column or row. If the deleted row or column contains a cell that defines a block referred to in a formula, the formula returns ERR.

To see this, compare the spreadsheets in Figure 1.53B and Figure 1.53C. Both are the results of deleting one row from Figure 1.53A, where Total January Sales are calculated in cell B6 using @SUM(B2..B5). Figure 1.53B is the result of deleting row 4 from Figure 1.53A, and the formula in cell B5 is correctly updated to @SUM(B2..B4). By contrast, Figure 1.53C is the result of deleting row 2. Here, the formula in cell B5 is converted to @SUM(ERR), which returns ERR. That's because the deleted row 2 contains cell B2, one of the cells that define the original formula reference in @SUM(B2..B5).

When you delete columns or rows, you should be aware of the following:

- You can't delete rows or columns in a globally protected spreadsheet (see Chapter 2).

- In Quattro Pro 4.0, if formula protection is enabled, you can't delete a column or row that contains a formula (see Chapter 4).

- Deleting a row that contains a macro line can affect how the macro runs (see Chapter 12).

Figure 1.53

Deleting rows

A

File	Edit	Style	Graph	Print	Database	Tools	Options	Window		? ↑↓

▲	◄	►	▼	Erase	Copy	Move	Style	Align	Font	Insert	Delete	Fit	Sum	Format	CHR	WYS

B4: (C0) [W8] 400

	A	B	C	D	E	F	G	H
1	Product	Jan	Feb	Mar	Cell D6 contains			
2	MT Grinders	$12,000	$15,000	$17,000				
3	F3C Distributors	$10,000	$9,000	$11,000				
4	R3 Fuses	$400	$500	$300				
5	7H Capacitors	$2,000	$1,000	$3,000				
6	Total	$24,400	$25,500	$31,300	@SUM(D2..D5)			
7								

B

File	Edit	Style	Graph	Print	Database	Tools	Options	Window		? ↑↓

▲	◄	►	▼	Erase	Copy	Move	Style	Align	Font	Insert	Delete	Fit	Sum	Format	CHR	WYS

B3: (C0) [W8] 10000

	A	B	C	D	E	F	G	H
1	Product	Jan	Feb	Mar	Cell D5 contains			
2	MT Grinders	$12,000	$15,000	$17,000				
3	F3C Distributors	$10,000	$9,000	$11,000				
4	7H Capacitors	$2,000	$1,000	$3,000				
5	Total	$24,000	$25,000	$31,000	@SUM(D2..D4)			
6								

C

File	Edit	Style	Graph	Print	Database	Tools	Options	Window		? ↑↓

▲	◄	►	▼	Erase	Copy	Move	Style	Align	Font	Insert	Delete	Fit	Sum	Format	CHR	WYS

B2: (C0) [W8] 10000

	A	B	C	D	E	F	G	H
1	Product	Jan	Feb	Mar	Cell D5 contains			
2	F3C Distributors	$10,000	$9,000	$11,000				
3	R3 Fuses	$400	$500	$300				
4	7H Capacitors	$2,000	$1,000	$3,000				
5	Total	ERR	ERR	ERR	@SUM(ERR)			
6								

Inserting and Deleting Blocks in Quattro Pro 4.0

Sometimes you may need additional space in just one section of a spreadsheet. Quattro Pro 4.0 allows you to insert blocks, instead of entire columns or rows, without changing the structure of the rest of the spreadsheet.

There are two types of blocks you can insert: column blocks and row blocks. The one you choose depends on whether you want columns or rows to shift as a block is inserted. Inserting a column block shifts affected columns to the right. Inserting a row block shifts affected rows down.

CAUTION. *After you insert or delete a block, you may need to check and update formula block addresses, block names, and macros. Because inserting and deleting blocks can cause structural changes in your spreadsheet, you may find it easier to insert an entire column or row and then move data as necessary.*

Inserting a Block

Suppose you track sales by region using the spreadsheet in Figure 1.54. For 1993 only, you want additional space to track sales semiannually instead of annually. Therefore, you need to insert a block immediately to the right of the current 1993 data in block B1..B5. Here's the procedure to insert a column block:

1. Place the cell selector in the cell where you want the inserted block to begin, in this case cell C1.

Figure 1.54

Inserting a column block

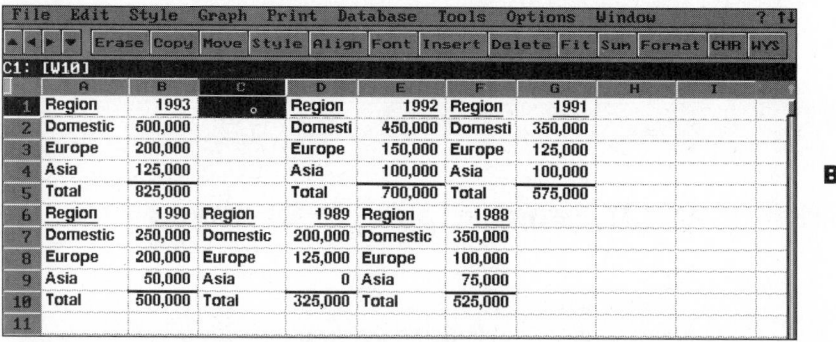

2. Preselect a block that covers the blank area you want to insert, in this case, C1..C5, as shown in Figure 1.54A.

3. Select /Edit, Insert, Column Block.

As you can see in Figure 1.54B, the data directly to the right of the inserted block moves right by the number of columns in the inserted block and all the formula references are adjusted accordingly. The data in all rows other than rows 1 through 5 isn't affected.

Inserting a row block is similar to inserting a column block. The only difference is that you select /Edit, Insert, Row Block, and the data in the rows directly below the inserted block shifts downward.

Deleting a Block

You may want to delete a block containing unneeded data without affecting entries in other cells. Deleting a block, however, may cause unexpected results in the spreadsheet (see "The Effects of Inserting and Deleting Blocks," next).

Figure 1.55A contains financial data for 12 months—July 92 through June 93. Suppose you don't need the data July 92 to Sept 92 and decide to delete block B1..D4 along with its data. To do this, first select the block, as shown in Figure 1.55A. When you choose /Edit, Delete, Column Block, you'll get the result in Figure 1.55B. Quattro Pro 4.0 deletes block B1..D4 and moves the data in rows 1 through 4 of columns E, F, and G to columns B, C, and D. The data in all other rows isn't affected.

If you use /Edit, Delete, Row Block to delete block B1..D4 of Figure 1.55A, you'll get the result in Figure 1.55C. This time the data in rows 5 through 8 of columns B, C, and D is moved to rows 1 through 4. The data in all other columns isn't affected. Of course, this produces a result you're unlikely to want in the current example, but it does illustrate the effect of the command.

The Effects of Inserting and Deleting Blocks

When you insert or delete a block, you should be aware of the following:

- You can't insert or delete a block in a globally protected spreadsheet.

- The cells in an inserted row or column block have the default style attributes, except for column width.

- Block addresses in formulas that reference any affected cells may give unexpected results.

- Inserting a block may cause previously assigned block names to refer to different blocks, so you may need to update block names after you insert a block.

- When you're using a database in Quattro Pro 4.0, inserting a block may corrupt the database.

Figure 1.55

Deleting a block

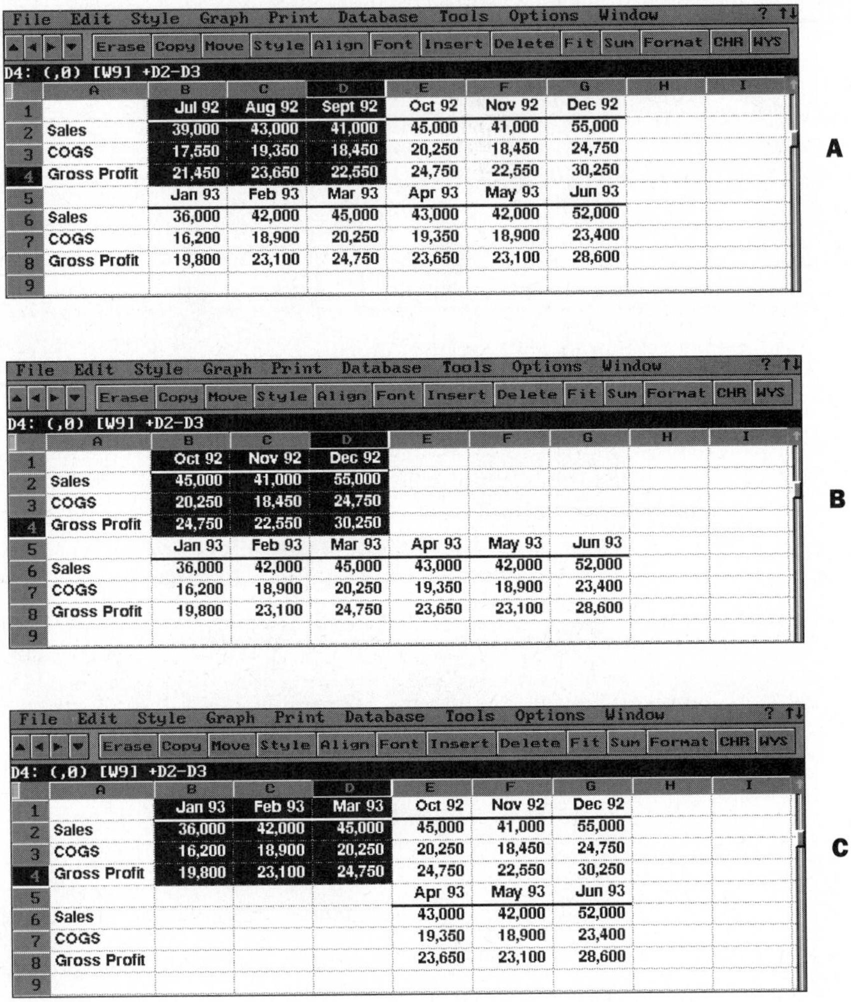

Recalculation

As you know, when you enter a formula that references other cells, Quattro Pro automatically updates the formula when you change the entries on which it relies. This automatic updating is known as *recalculation*.

In early spreadsheet programs, *foreground recalculation* caused the entire spreadsheet to be recalculated each time you changed a value in a cell. While recalculation took place, you couldn't use your computer. This wasn't a problem with small spreadsheets that contained relatively few formulas. But with large, formula-intensive spreadsheets, recalculation became a time-consuming process.

Like most modern spreadsheet programs, Quattro Pro reduces the amount of time it spends recalculating by using *minimal* and *background recalculation*. With minimal recalculation, when you add or edit a cell in a spreadsheet, only those cells that are affected by the change are recalculated. Also, recalculation occurs in the background while you continue to do your work. This means Quattro Pro uses the time between keystrokes to carry out its recalculation.

Quattro Pro's minimal recalculation happens automatically, and you cannot change it. You can, however, control when recalculation takes place and the order in which cells are evaluated during recalculation. You control these settings through the /Options, Recalculation command (Figure 1.56), as described in the following sections.

Controlling When Recalculation Takes Place

Quattro Pro provides three options for controlling when recalculation takes place: Automatic, Manual, and Background. You control these options through the /Options, Recalculation, Mode command.

- *Background* causes Quattro Pro to use the time between keystrokes to recalculate the spreadsheet. Recalculation takes place automatically on an ongoing basis, and your work is never interrupted (this is the default).

- *Automatic* recalculates the spreadsheet any time you change an entry in a cell. Therefore, your work may be interrupted as Quattro Pro pauses to recalculate the spreadsheet, especially if you are working on a large, formula-intensive model.

- *Manual* only recalculates the formula that you are currently adding or editing. Other formulas are not recalculated until you press Calc (F9).

Note. In Quattro Pro 4.0, `Calc` in the Edit SpeedBar is equivalent to F9.

In general, it is wise to leave Quattro Pro set for background recalculation, because this method offers the best combination of speed and accuracy. In fact, background recalculation is always preferable to automatic recalculation because you avoid the inevitable delay that the latter method imposes when you have a large spreadsheet and you change a value that is referenced by a formula. What's more, with background recalculation you need not be concerned about whether your spreadsheet is up to date, because Quattro Pro always finishes recalculating before saving, extracting, or printing the spreadsheet.

Although background recalculation works well for most spreadsheets, manual recalculation is appropriate in certain situations. For example, consider a large spreadsheet that takes a long time to recalculate, in which you want to change several values at once. In this case, setting Quattro Pro for manual recalculation makes sense, so that you can control precisely when recalculation takes place.

Figure 1.56

The /Options, Recalculation menu

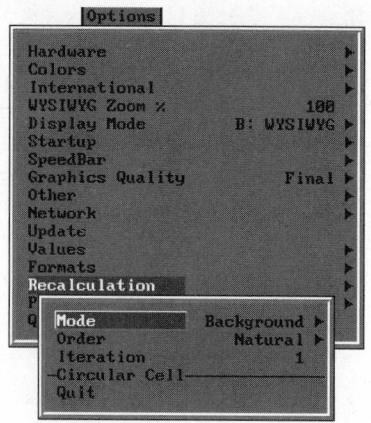

To illustrate how manual recalculation works, suppose you start with a fresh worksheet and enter **100** in cell B4, and **4** in cell C4. Next, move to cell D4 and enter the formula **+B4/C4**. Quattro Pro immediately displays the result, 25, in D4. Now switch from background to manual recalculation, using the /Options, Recalculation, Mode, Manual command. To see the effect of this change, move to cell B4 and enter **200** in that cell.

Now take a look at Figure 1.57. Notice that the CALC indicator appears in the status line, telling you that the spreadsheet needs recalculating. In addition, notice that the result of the formula in D4 remains at 25, though it should be 50. When you press Calc (F9), Quattro Pro instantly recalculates the formula and removes the CALC indicator.

Another good reason for using manual recalculation pertains to running Quattro Pro in WYSIWYG mode. You may have noticed that whenever you change the contents of a cell involved in a formula, Quattro Pro always repaints the entire screen in WYSIWYG mode. This results in a kind of ripple effect, especially on older EGA and VGA systems. If you switch to manual recalculation, however, Quattro Pro repaints only the line that contains the cell you are changing. Only when you press Calc (F9) to initiate recalculation does Quattro Pro update the entire screen.

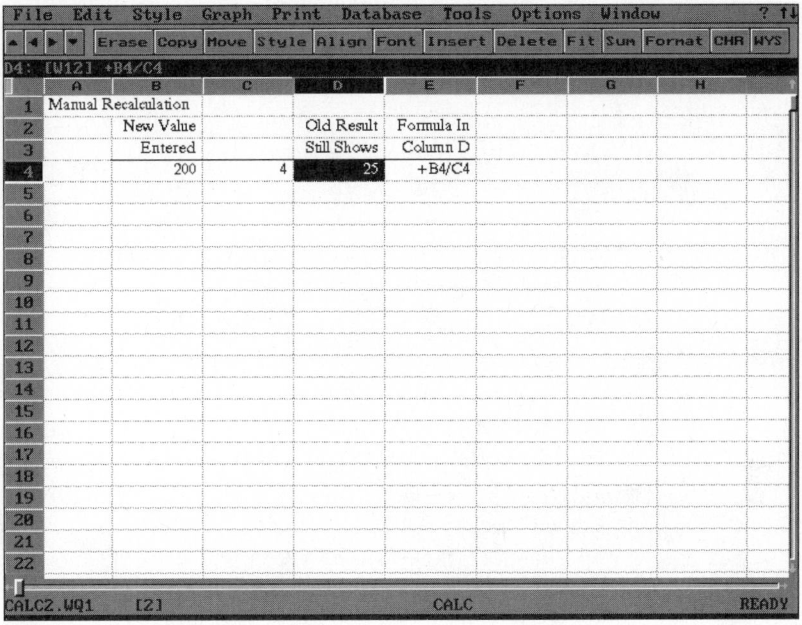

Figure 1.57

After setting a
spreadsheet for
manual recalculation

File	Edit	Style	Graph	Print	Database	Tools	Options	Window	? ↑↓

▲ ◄ ► ▼ | Erase | Copy | Move | Style | Align | Font | Insert | Delete | Fit | Sum | Format | CHR | WYS |

D4: [W12] +B4/C4

	A	B	C	D	E	F	G	H
1	Manual Recalculation							
2		New Value		Old Result	Formula In			
3		Entered		Still Shows	Column D			
4		200	4	25	+B4/C4			
5								
6								
7								
8								
9								
10								
11								
12								
13								
14								
15								
16								
17								
18								
19								
20								
21								
22								

CALC2.WQ1   [2]   CALC   READY

Changing the Order of Recalculation

Quattro Pro lets you choose between three orders of recalculation: Natural, Rowwise, and Columnwise. Natural order is the default way that Quattro Pro recalculates the spreadsheet. With natural order, Quattro Pro does not recalculate a formula until all the cells it references have been recalculated.

To see the benefit of natural recalculation, consider the spreadsheet in Figure 1.58, where cell C4 contains the formula +C3+C5, and cell C5, the formula +C3+C6. In this spreadsheet, Quattro Pro recalculates the formula in cell C5 first, even though it is not the first formula in the spreadsheet. Only then does the formula in C4, which depends on the formula in C5, get recalculated.

In the earliest spreadsheets—for example, Visicalc—natural recalculation was not available. These spreadsheets offered columnwise and rowwise recalculation order instead. In columnwise order, recalculation begins in cell A1 and works its way down column A, then column B, and so on. Rowwise recalculation is similar to columnwise, except that recalculation occurs row by row beginning in row 1. (In case you want to set Quattro Pro for columnwise or rowwise recalculation, use the /Options, Recalculation, Order, Column-wise and Row-wise commands.)

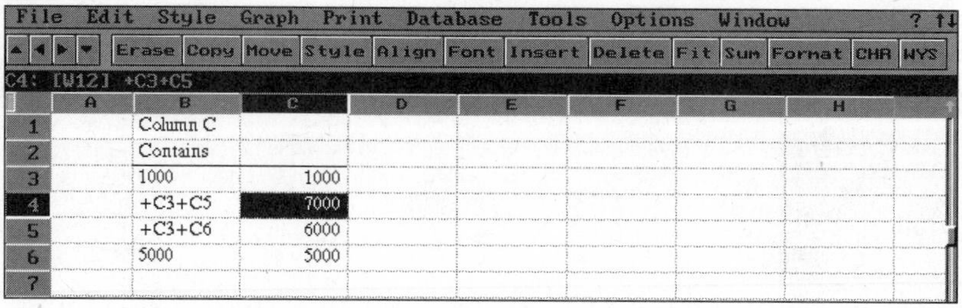

Figure 1.58

The advantage of
natural recalculation

In many spreadsheets, you get identical results regardless of the recalculation order you use. When a spreadsheet has a *forward reference*, however, columnwise and rowwise recalculation can give incorrect results. A forward reference occurs when a spreadsheet formula refers to another formula that occurs lower in the spreadsheet. For example, in Figure 1.58, the formula in C4 contains a forward reference to C5. If you use columnwise or rowwise recalculation with this spreadsheet, you won't get the proper results. Recalculate the spreadsheet, however, by pressing Calc (F9), and the results are properly updated.

Circular References

A *circular reference* occurs when you place a formula in a cell whose value depends on that same cell. A circular reference usually occurs by mistake, such as when you mistype a cell address. Occasionally, however, a circular reference is intentional.

The simplest form of circular reference is when a formula refers to itself. In Figure 1.59, for example, the formula in cell C3, +C3+C4, refers to itself. When you make these entries, Quattro Pro displays a CIRC indicator in the status line, telling you that the spreadsheet contains a circular reference.

Quattro Pro cannot resolve many circular references—the circular reference just discussed is one example. Others it can resolve, provided you increase the iteration count, as explained later in "Resolving Intentional Circular References."

Eliminating Accidental Circular References

To help you eliminate circular references that you've entered by mistake, Quattro Pro reveals the location of a cell involved in the circular reference when you select the /Options, Recalculation command. For example, in Figure 1.59, C3 appears to the right of the Circular Cell option.

Figure 1.59
Determining the
location of a cell
involved in a
circular reference

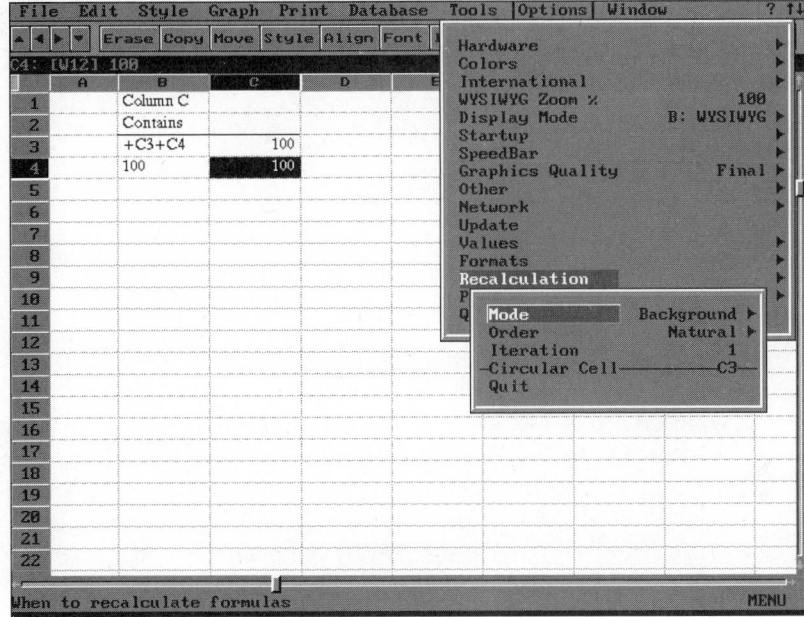

With some circular references, once Quattro Pro gives you a lead on the offending cell, you can easily eliminate the problem. Usually this involves changing a formula to reference another cell.

In Quattro Pro 3.0 and earlier releases, tracking down the cause of a circular reference was often a struggle, particularly when the spreadsheet contained many layers of dependencies. About all you could do was check each reference in the circular reference chain. Sometimes printing the cell formulas (see Chapter 6) helped.

Quattro Pro 4.0, however, finally provides a solution to the circular reference hunt: the /Tools, Audit command. See Chapter 11 for more details.

Resolving Intentional Circular References

Occasionally circular references are intentional, and you'll want Quattro Pro to resolve them as best it can. To resolve a circular reference, you must recalculate the spreadsheet more than once. The easiest way to do this is to use the /Options, Recalculation, Iteration command and specify the number of passes you want Quattro Pro to make before it completes recalculation. Figure 1.60, for example, shows such a situation.

Figure 1.60

The results of an intentional circular reference

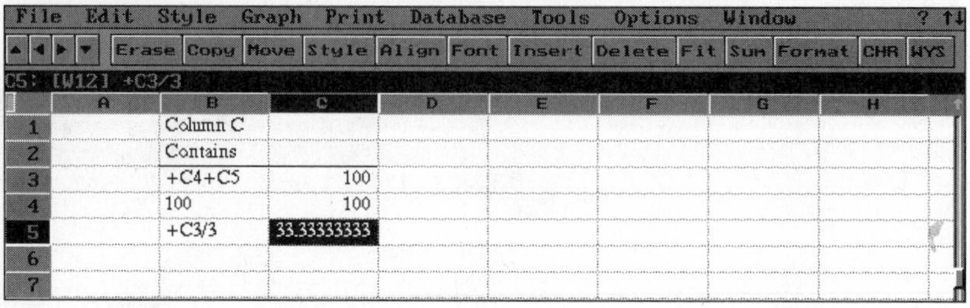

For Quattro Pro to resolve the circular reference you have created, you must increase the number of passes it makes when it recalculates the spreadsheet. To do this select the /Options, Recalculation, Iteration command and specify from 1 to 255 iterations (the default is 1). For the current example, enter **13**. Press Calc (F9) to have Quattro Pro recalculate the spreadsheet.

The following table shows how the formulas in the spreadsheet change as Quattro Pro performs its recalculation. Notice that with each pass, Quattro Pro comes closer to resolving the circular reference. Still, even by the thirteenth pass, it has not yet converged on the final values—150 for cell C3, and 50 for cell C5. You must press Calc (F9) again to have it recalculate the spreadsheet an additional thirteen times and finally reach the correct values.

Iteration Number	C3	C4	C5
1	100	100	33.33333
2	133.3333	100	44.44444
3	144.4444	100	48.14815
4	148.1481	100	49.38272
5	149.3827	100	49.79424
6	149.7942	100	49.93141
7	49.9314	100	49.97714
8	149.9771	100	49.99238
9	149.9924	100	49.99746
10	149.9975	100	49.99915
11	149.9992	100	49.99972

Iteration Number	C3	C4	C5
12	149.9997	100	49.99991
13	149.9999	100	49.99997

Accessing DOS

It's easy to access DOS without having to exit Quattro Pro. To do so, select the /File, Utilities, DOS Shell command. Quattro Pro then displays the prompt

```
Enter DOS Command, Press Enter for full DOS Shell
```

To execute your DOS command and return immediately to Quattro Pro, simply type the command, for example, **FORMAT A:**, and press Enter. When the command is completed, you are returned to the spreadsheet in Ready mode.

You can also exit to a full DOS session and return to Quattro Pro at your leisure, by simply pressing Enter in response to the above DOS Shell prompt. You'll then see a screen similar to Figure 1.61.

Figure 1.61

After using /File, Utilities, DOS Shell to exit temporarily

```
Type Exit to return to Quattro

Microsoft(R) MS-DOS(R) Version 5.00
         (C)Copyright Microsoft Corp 1981-1991.

C:\QPRO>
```

After exiting to DOS, you can use any number of DOS commands, such as COPY, CD, and FORMAT. You can also use other application programs, provided you have sufficient memory. To return from DOS to Quattro Pro, type **exit** and press Enter at the DOS prompt.

When you issue the /File, Utilities, DOS Shell command, Quattro Pro actually loads a second copy of COMMAND.COM (the DOS command interpreter) and then executes it. When you type **exit** to return to Quattro Pro or when the DOS command you provide is completed, Quattro Pro discards the second copy of COMMAND.COM and frees the memory for use by your worksheets. In order for Quattro Pro to load the second copy of COMMAND.COM, there must be sufficient memory available. If there is not, Quattro Pro will issue the error message "Not enough memory for that operation."

CAUTION! *Do not load any memory-resident utilities or TSRs while at the DOS level. If you do, you probably will not be able to return to Quattro Pro.*

Quitting Quattro Pro

To quit Quattro Pro and return to DOS, select /File, Exit or press Ctrl-X. If Quattro Pro senses that you haven't made any changes to the current spreadsheet, it immediately quits and returns you to DOS. On the other hand, if it determines that you've not yet saved changes to your work, it displays the confirmation menu in Figure 1.62. Here's an explanation of the options:

- *No* returns you to the spreadsheet so that you can save your work.

- *Yes* exits Quattro Pro without saving your work. Everything in your spreadsheet that is unsaved will be lost.

- *Save & Exit* saves the spreadsheet with its current name, and then exits Quattro Pro.

Figure 1.62
The /File, Exit
confirmation menu

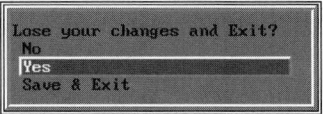

C H A P T E R

2

Managing
the Desktop

QUATTRO PRO'S PRIMARY DISPLAY AREA OR WORK SURFACE IS referred to as the desktop. The desktop is used to display your spreadsheets as you view and edit them; each of your spreadsheet files is displayed in a separate window. These windows overlay the Quattro Pro desktop. Unlike some spreadsheet software, however, Quattro Pro is not confined to displaying only a single spreadsheet window. Instead, you can have multiple spreadsheets open on the desktop, each in its own window. These windows can be resized, moved, tiled (displayed side by side), and so on, allowing you to work on several projects at the same time as well as to visually compare the spreadsheets.

Quattro Pro also lets you link your spreadsheets together—that is, you can "borrow" live data from one spreadsheet for use in another. When the data in the source spreadsheet changes, the spreadsheet containing the link to that data is automatically updated for the change. This linking feature lets you divide your work into smaller, more natural segments. For example, rather than shoehorning a table of values, a database, and your macros all into a single large spreadsheet file, you can divide them into smaller spreadsheet files and link them together as needed. That way, you don't have to navigate a massive spreadsheet to find the data you're looking for. Furthermore, Quattro Pro lets you link to files on disk. This lets you create large models that exceed the limits of the physical memory in your machine.

In addition to allowing you to open multiple spreadsheet files and link them together, Quattro Pro lets you split a spreadsheet window into two separate *panes*, each one focused on a different area of the spreadsheet. That way, you can simultaneously view and edit two widely distanced portions of the same spreadsheet.

This chapter shows you how to go about managing multiple spreadsheet files on the Quattro Pro desktop. As you'll soon see, there are various techniques for organizing and displaying multiple spreadsheet windows. You'll also learn how to group related spreadsheet files together, and save and retrieve them as a single unit. You'll see how to link two or more spreadsheets together, so you can reference data on another spreadsheet either in memory or on disk, and use it in the current spreadsheet. Finally, you'll learn how to split a spreadsheet window.

Note that when it comes to managing multiple spreadsheet windows, there are some minor functionality differences between Quattro Pro's WYSIWYG and Character display modes. This chapter will, of course, point out those differences where they occur. As a result, you'll notice that the discussion at times shifts back and forth between WYSIWYG mode and Character mode. Don't be confused or annoyed by this—you'll soon discover there are distinct advantages to be gained by using Quattro Pro in both of its available modes.

Working with Multiple Windows

As you know, Quattro Pro automatically creates and displays a fresh, blank spreadsheet window when you start the program—the so-called *startup spreadsheet*. You can open additional spreadsheet windows on the Quattro Pro desktop whenever you want to. In fact, provided you have sufficient memory, you can have as many as 32 spreadsheet windows open on the Quattro Pro desktop at any one time. Each new window you open can contain either a new, blank spreadsheet or an existing spreadsheet from disk. You can also easily replace one spreadsheet with another, and close one or more spreadsheet windows when they are no longer needed. All of these operations are performed by using the /File menu shown in Figure 2.1.

Figure 2.1
The /File menu

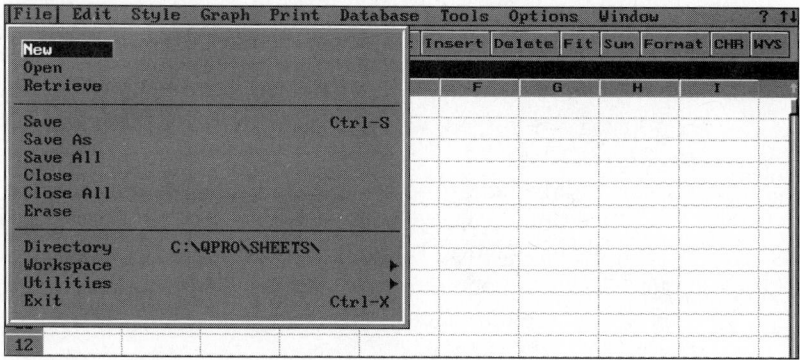

NOTE. *You can also open Quattro Pro's File Manager in its own window, or even multiple copies of File Manager, each in its own window. However, each copy of File Manager that you open counts toward the 32-window maximum allowed. The File Manager (see Chapter 5) lets you perform routine file-management chores (like copying and deleting files) without leaving Quattro Pro.*

Creating a New Spreadsheet

Suppose you are working on a spreadsheet—for example, a budget summary—and you develop a need for some supporting data. You can, of course, move to an empty area of the current spreadsheet, build the data there, and then reference it by formula in the budget summary. Alternatively, you can create an entirely new spreadsheet file, devoted just to the supporting data. Once that spreadsheet exists, you can link it to the current budget summary spreadsheet. (See "Linking Spreadsheet Files" later for details on how to link one spreadsheet file with another.)

Note. For additional information on using the /File, New command, see Chapter 5.

To create a new, blank spreadsheet file, use the /File, New command. When you select this command, Quattro Pro overlays the current spreadsheet window (if one is open on the desktop) with a new, blank spreadsheet window. That new window then becomes the *active* window (the cell selector shifts to it), and you can begin entering data in the new spreadsheet. It also means that the commands in Quattro Pro's menu bar now apply to the new spreadsheet. Any spreadsheet files you may already have open remain open, but they are shifted to the background, temporarily out of view. (You can move to one of these background windows at any time. See "How Quattro Pro Handles Multiple Windows" and "Moving Between Windows" later for details on what happens to background windows and how you can move to them.)

When you create a new spreadsheet file, Quattro Pro automatically assigns it a default file name and displays that name at the far left of the status line at the bottom of the screen. This default name takes the form SHEET#.WQ1, where # is a sequential integer. For example, as you've probably noticed, when you start Quattro Pro, it automatically offers you a new, blank spreadsheet named SHEET1.WQ1. In contrast, if you use /File, New again to create another new spreadsheet, Quattro Pro opens that spreadsheet in its own window and names it SHEET2.WQ1. The third new spreadsheet file is named SHEET3.WQ1, and so on. You can, of course, change this name to a more descriptive title when you later save the file to disk with the /File, Save command, explained later in the chapter.

Opening an Existing File

The /File, Open command lets you open an existing spreadsheet file from disk and display it in its own window. Any spreadsheet windows you already have open are not affected. They are simply shifted to the background, and the new window becomes the active window. /File, Open is convenient when you want to visually compare one spreadsheet with another or when you want to establish a link between two spreadsheets.

When you select the /File, Open command, Quattro Pro displays a *file dialog box* that prompts you to "Enter name of file to open:", as shown in Figure 2.2. At the top of the file list in this box, Quattro Pro displays the path to the current directory, followed by the file name extension *.W??. All the file names in the current directory with an extension that begins with *w* are displayed in the box, in alphabetical order by file name. The first name in the list is highlighted.

From the file dialog box, there are several ways to select a file to open. For example, imagine you want to open the file CASH.WQ1 that appears in the file dialog box in Figure 2.2. To do this, you can use the arrow keys to highlight the CASH.WQ1 file and press Enter to open it. Or you can click your mouse on the scroll bar located on the right-hand side of the box, to scroll the list of file names up or down. When CASH.WQ1 is displayed, click on it with your mouse. Finally, you can simply type the name of the file you want to open. As you begin to type, the file dialog box is replaced by a simple prompt box. This box shows the path to the current directory followed by what you've typed thus far, and two mouse buttons labeled Enter and Esc. When you finish typing the name of the file, you can press the Enter key on your keyboard or click on the Enter mouse button.

Figure 2.2

A file dialog box, with the prompt for a file name

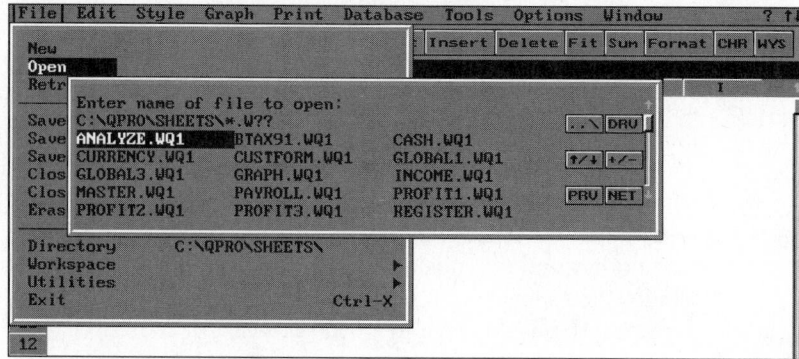

Once you select a spreadsheet file to open, Quattro Pro opens that spreadsheet in its own window, which overlays any windows that are already open on the desktop. The new window is now the active window, ready to accept your data entry and the commands you enter from the menu bar. The file name of the new active spreadsheet appears in the status line, as illustrated in Figure 2.3 for the CASH.WQ1 file.

The /File, Open command can be used to open any file located in any directory on your hard disk. You can also use it to open files located in shared directories on a network server. Chapter 5 gives you an in-depth description of how to use /File, Open to open files in different directories. For information on using Quattro Pro on a network, see Chapter 14.

Shortcuts in Quattro Pro 4.0

As you can see in Figure 2.2, the /File, Open dialog box in Quattro Pro 4.0 has six buttons that you can use to find the file you're looking for. Table 2.1 describes what each of these buttons does. (If you're using the keyboard, press / and then use one of the arrow keys to select a button.) All of these buttons except ⬜ are toggles. For example, press ▢DRU once to see all drives; press it again to remove the drive list.

Figure 2.3

The CASH.WQ1 file open on the desktop

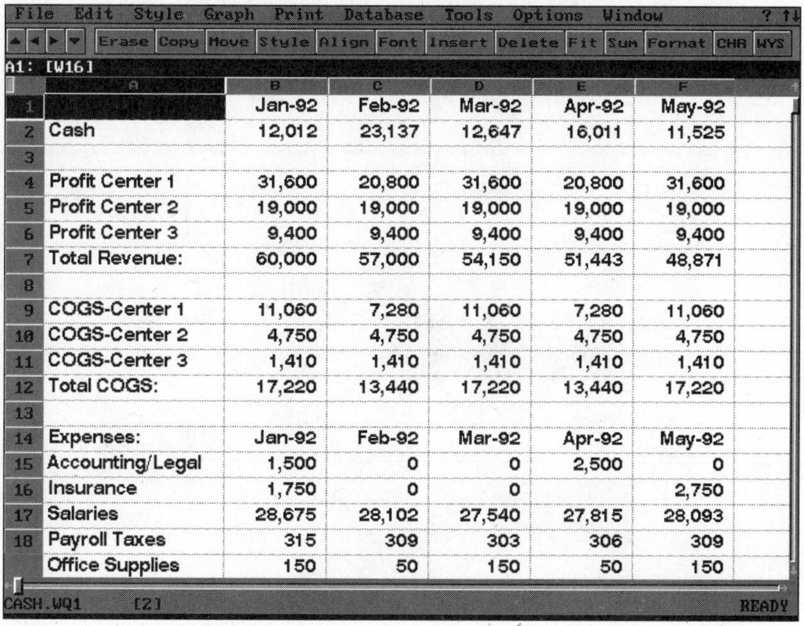

File Edit Style Graph Print Database Tools Options Window					? ↑↓
▲ ◀ ▶ ▼ Erase Copy Move Style Align Font Insert Delete Fit Sum Format CHR WYS					
A1: [W16]					

	A	B	C	D	E	F
1		Jan-92	Feb-92	Mar-92	Apr-92	May-92
2	Cash	12,012	23,137	12,647	16,011	11,525
3						
4	Profit Center 1	31,600	20,800	31,600	20,800	31,600
5	Profit Center 2	19,000	19,000	19,000	19,000	19,000
6	Profit Center 3	9,400	9,400	9,400	9,400	9,400
7	Total Revenue:	60,000	57,000	54,150	51,443	48,871
8						
9	COGS-Center 1	11,060	7,280	11,060	7,280	11,060
10	COGS-Center 2	4,750	4,750	4,750	4,750	4,750
11	COGS-Center 3	1,410	1,410	1,410	1,410	1,410
12	Total COGS:	17,220	13,440	17,220	13,440	17,220
13						
14	Expenses:	Jan-92	Feb-92	Mar-92	Apr-92	May-92
15	Accounting/Legal	1,500	0	0	2,500	0
16	Insurance	1,750	0	0		2,750
17	Salaries	28,675	28,102	27,540	27,815	28,093
18	Payroll Taxes	315	309	303	306	309
	Office Supplies	150	50	150	50	150

CASH.WQ1   [2]   READY

Table 2.1   **The /File, Open Buttons in Quattro Pro 4.0**

Button	What It Does
`..◣`	Lists files in the parent directory
`↑/↓`	Expands the File Open dialog box
`PRV`	Lists the current directory and the last eight files opened in Quattro Pro 4.0
`DRV`	Lists all available drives on your computer
`+/−`	Shows the date, time, and size of files in the current directory
`NET`	Lets you access files on a network drive

Because `..◣` lists files in the parent directory, it's a convenient way to open a file in a different directory without changing what Quattro Pro recognizes as the current directory (see Chapter 5). By contrast, `DRV` lets you access both local and network drives; select one to see the directory structure on a different drive.

Note. Pressing F3 (Choices) also expands the /File, Open dialog box; pressing F3 again shrinks it.

For each of the files currently listed in Figure 2.4, ⊞ displays the size as well as the date and time the file was created or last modified. When you're viewing a lot of information, you can maximize what you see by using ⊞ to increase the size of the /File,Open dialog box to the size in Figure 2.4. (In Character mode, ⊞ expands the dialog box to fill the entire screen.)

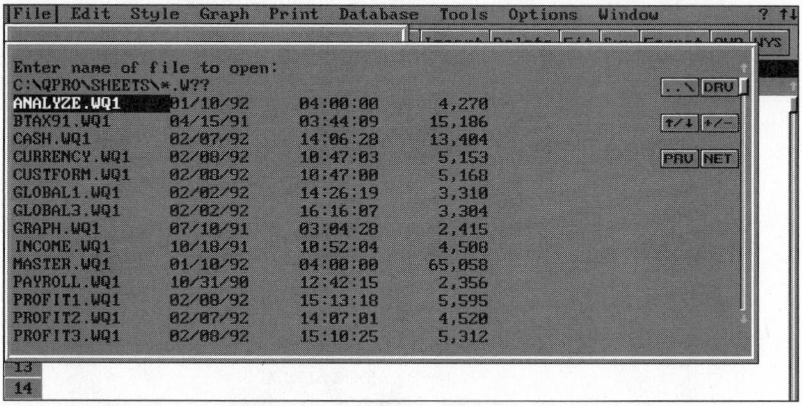

Figure 2.4

Using ⊞ and ⊞ to view additional information in an expanded /File Open dialog box

```
|File| Edit  Style  Graph  Print  Database  Tools  Options  Window      ? ↑↓
                                     |Insert  Delete  Fit  Sum  Format  CHR|WYS
 Enter name of file to open:
 C:\QPRO\SHEETS\*.WQ??                                           |..\|DRV|
 ANALYZE.WQ1       01/10/92      04:00:00      4,270
 BTAX91.WQ1        04/15/91      03:44:09     15,186            |↑↓|⊞|
 CASH.WQ1          02/07/92      14:06:28     13,404
 CURRENCY.WQ1      02/08/92      10:47:03      5,153            |PRV|NET|
 CUSTFORM.WQ1      02/08/92      10:47:00      5,168
 GLOBAL1.WQ1       02/02/92      14:26:19      3,310
 GLOBAL3.WQ1       02/02/92      16:16:07      3,304
 GRAPH.WQ1         07/10/91      03:04:20      2,415
 INCOME.WQ1        10/18/91      10:52:04      4,508
 MASTER.WQ1        01/10/92      04:00:00     65,058
 PAYROLL.WQ1       10/31/90      12:42:15      2,356
 PROFIT1.WQ1       02/08/92      15:13:18      5,595
 PROFIT2.WQ1       02/07/92      14:07:01      4,520
 PROFIT3.WQ1       02/08/92      15:10:25      5,312
 13
 14
```

If you frequently work with the same set of files, you'll probably find ▣PRV▣ to be one of the more useful enhancements to the /File, Open dialog box. As you can see in Figure 2.5, ▣PRV▣ lets you choose from a list that includes both the current directory and the path and name of the eight files you've most recently opened.

Figure 2.5

Using ▣PRV▣

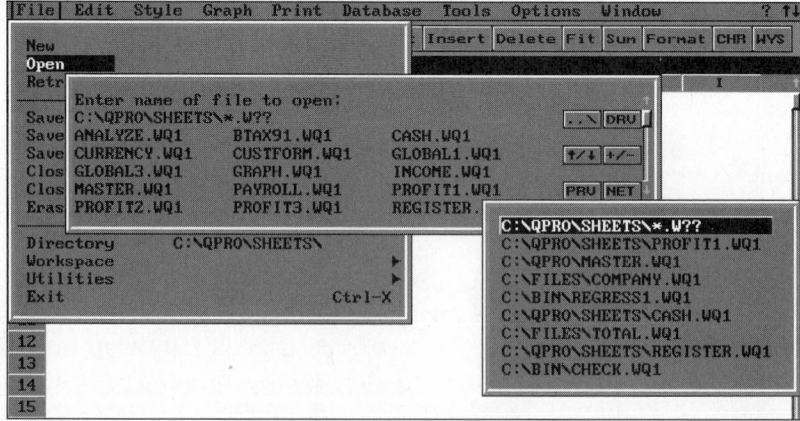

NOTE. PRU *lists only those files you've previously opened using the /File, Open command. It doesn't list any supporting files you may have opened with /File, Open's Load Supporting command (see "Loading a Spreadsheet with Links," later).*

NET shows your network drive mappings—the letters assigned to each logical drive. You must create these drive mappings in advance in order for them to be displayed. For more information on running Quattro Pro 4.0 on a network, see Chapter 14.

How Quattro Pro Handles Multiple Windows

Note. You can also stack or tile the windows on the Quattro Pro desktop so that you can see portions of each window (see "Tiling and Stacking Windows" later).

As explained, when you use /File, New or /File, Open to open a new or existing spreadsheet file, Quattro Pro displays that file in its own window, which then becomes the currently active window and overlays the Quattro Pro desktop. Any windows already open are shifted to the background, but remain open on the desktop, just as you left them. In fact, you can move to a background spreadsheet window whenever you want to (see the later section "Moving Between Windows"). Think of these background spreadsheet windows as being *stacked* in memory behind the currently active spreadsheet window, much like the pages in a book, as illustrated in Figure 2.6. The order of the stack is determined by the order in which you opened the spreadsheet files.

Figure 2.6

Multiple spreadsheet windows stacked in memory

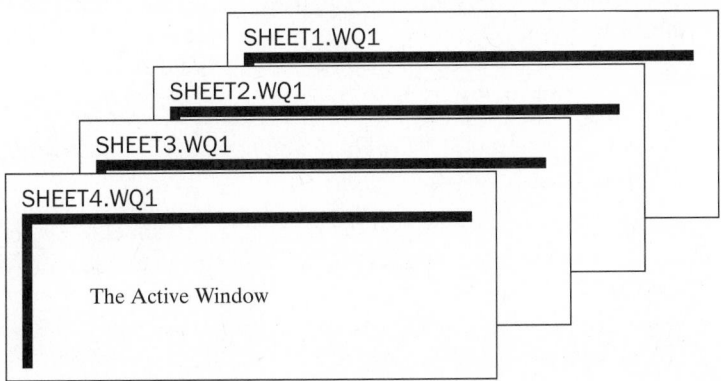

SHEET1.WQ1
SHEET2.WQ1
SHEET3.WQ1
SHEET4.WQ1

The Active Window

Each time you open a new window, Quattro Pro assigns a number to that window. As you might imagine, the first window opened (usually the startup spreadsheet) is assigned the number 1. The second window opened is number 2, the third window number 3, and so on. The spreadsheet number is displayed in square brackets [ ] just to the right of the file name in the status line. Take another look at the CASH.WQ1 file shown in Figure 2.3, and you'll see the number 2 in square brackets indicating that this file is the second file open on the desktop. Later, under "Moving Between Windows," you'll learn how to use these numbers to jump quickly to a specific window.

Replacing One Spreadsheet with Another

Note. For additional details on the /File, Retrieve command, see Chapter 5.

You don't have to open a separate spreadsheet window when you want to open an existing spreadsheet file on disk. Instead, you can simply *replace* the spreadsheet file in the current window with the spreadsheet of your choice. To do this, you use the /File, Retrieve command.

In preparation for replacing one spreadsheet file with another, begin by activating the window whose spreadsheet file you want to replace. You can do this by simply moving to the window. (See the next section for details on how to move between open windows.) When you're ready, select /File, Retrieve, and Quattro Pro displays a file dialog box similar to the one you saw earlier for the /File, Open command.

At the top of the file dialog box for /File, Retrieve, Quattro Pro displays the prompt "Enter name of file to retrieve:". Beneath this, the path to the current directory is displayed, followed by the file descriptor *.W??. As with /File, Open, you'll see all file names in the current directory that have an extension beginning with *w*. To increase the size of this dialog box, too, you can use the Choices key (F3). Also as before, you can select a file to retrieve by highlighting its name and pressing Enter, clicking on its name with your mouse, or typing its name and pressing Enter. The file in the current window is then replaced by the file you retrieved from disk.

TIP. *In Quattro Pro 4.0, the File Retrieve dialog box includes the same six shortcut buttons as the /File, Open dialog box. See "Shortcuts in Quattro Pro 4.0," earlier.*

When you try to replace the current spreadsheet file with another, Quattro Pro first checks the current file to see if you've made any changes to that file since you opened it. If Quattro Pro detects any unsaved changes, it gives you a chance to save those changes before replacing the file with the one you've asked to be retrieved. You'll see a "Lose your changes?" prompt box with the options No and Yes. If you select No, the /File, Retrieve command is cancelled and you are returned to the active spreadsheet, where you can use /File, Save to save your changes. On the other hand, if you select Yes, Quattro Pro proceeds to replace the current file with the file from disk. Any changes you made to the previous current file are lost.

You can also retrieve a specific file when you start Quattro Pro. The file you specify will replace the startup spreadsheet. One way to do this is to specify a file with the startup command you enter at the DOS prompt. Type **Q** followed by a space and the name of the file you want to retrieve, for example,

```
Q C:\ACCTG\BUDGET.WQ1
```

Alternatively, you can use the /Options, Startup, Autoload File command to specify a spreadsheet file that will always be retrieved automatically when you start Quattro Pro.

Loading Multiple Spreadsheet Files: An Example

You can use the /File, Retrieve and /File, Open commands in combination to set up your Quattro Pro work session. Imagine you are working on a cash-flow spreadsheet for a small company. Let's again use CASH.WQ1 as the name of your file. This spreadsheet is supported by three subsidiary spreadsheet files, named PROFIT1.WQ1, PROFIT2.WQ1, and PROFIT3.WQ1, which contain estimates of the income to be generated by the three major profit centers for your company over the upcoming year.

To set up your work session, you'll need to get all four spreadsheet files into memory. Here is one approach you might take.

1. Start Quattro Pro.

2. Select the /File, Retrieve command, and specify CASH.WQ1 as the file to retrieve. Quattro Pro replaces the startup spreadsheet with the CASH.WQ1 file.

3. Select the /File, Open command, and specify the PROFIT1.WQ1 file. Quattro Pro opens the PROFIT1.WQ1 file in its own window, which overlays the CASH.WQ1 file.

4. Use the /File, Open command twice more to open PROFIT2.WQ1 and PROFIT3.WQ1, each in its own window.

At this point, your work session is set up, and you can move among these four open windows, viewing and editing the spreadsheets. The next section will show you how to do just that.

NOTE. *You can also group related spreadsheets together as a single workspace. Using the /File, Workspace, Save command, you create and name a text file with a .WSP extension that lists the names of the windows currently open on the desktop. Then, by using /File, Workspace, Restore and selecting this .WSP file, you can open this same group of related files (workspace) in a single operation. See "Saving and Restoring the Workspace" later in the chapter.*

Moving Between Windows

Although you can have multiple windows open on the Quattro Pro desktop, only one of those windows can be the *active* window. You choose the active window by simply *moving* to it—that is, by moving the cell selector into that spreadsheet. This lets you enter and edit data in the active spreadsheet, and apply commands from Quattro Pro's menu bar.

There are several techniques for moving among the open windows on the desktop. One common way is with the /Window, Pick command. (There are two shortcuts for this command, Shift-F5 and Alt-0.) When you select /Window, Pick, Quattro Pro displays the Window Pick list of window names currently open on the desktop, as shown in Figure 2.7. In this example four windows are open on the desktop. Notice that the number assigned to each window appears next to its name. To move to a window, simply pick the window by highlighting its name and pressing Enter, or clicking on its name with your mouse. Quattro Pro moves the window you've selected to the foreground, and it becomes the active window. The rest of the open windows are shifted to the background.

Figure 2.7
The Window Pick list

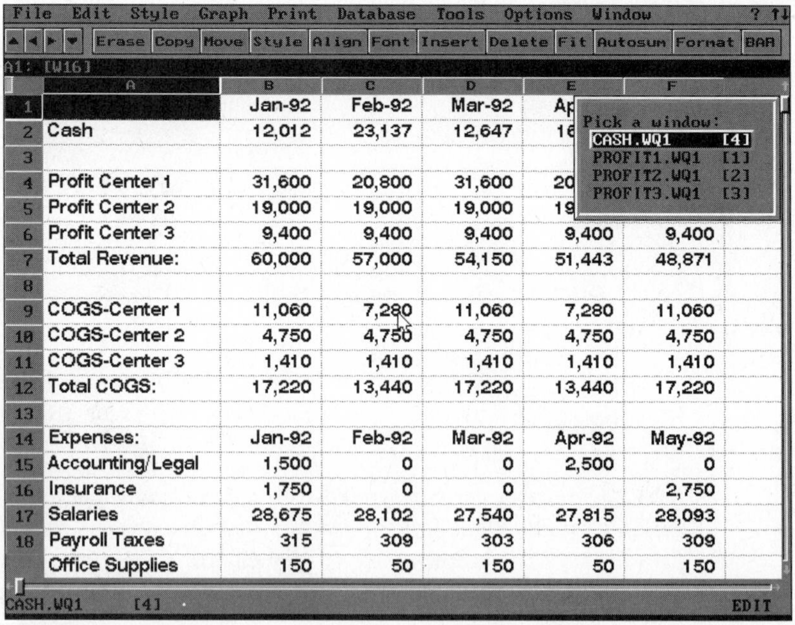

	A	B	C	D	E	F
1		Jan-92	Feb-92	Mar-92	Apr	
2	Cash	12,012	23,137	12,647	16	
3						
4	Profit Center 1	31,600	20,800	31,600	20	
5	Profit Center 2	19,000	19,000	19,000	19	
6	Profit Center 3	9,400	9,400	9,400	9,400	9,400
7	Total Revenue:	60,000	57,000	54,150	51,443	48,871
8						
9	COGS-Center 1	11,060	7,280	11,060	7,280	11,060
10	COGS-Center 2	4,750	4,750	4,750	4,750	4,750
11	COGS-Center 3	1,410	1,410	1,410	1,410	1,410
12	Total COGS:	17,220	13,440	17,220	13,440	17,220
13						
14	Expenses:	Jan-92	Feb-92	Mar-92	Apr-92	May-92
15	Accounting/Legal	1,500	0	0	2,500	0
16	Insurance	1,750	0	0		2,750
17	Salaries	28,675	28,102	27,540	27,815	28,093
18	Payroll Taxes	315	309	303	306	309
	Office Supplies	150	50	150	50	150

Pick a window:
CASH.WQ1 [4]
PROFIT1.WQ1 [1]
PROFIT2.WQ1 [2]
PROFIT3.WQ1 [3]

Once you know the window number assigned to a window, you can quickly jump to any window by holding down the Alt key and typing the appropriate number. For example, to jump to the open window number [4], press Alt-4. Quattro Pro activates that window and shifts your other open windows to the background.

Another convenient way to move between windows is to use the Next Window key sequence, Shift-F6. When you press Shift-F6 in an open window, Quattro Pro jumps to the next open window in the numerical sequence. In fact, if you continue to press Shift-F6, Quattro Pro will cycle through all of the open windows on the desktop. When you get to the last window in memory, Quattro Pro returns to the first window.

Another way to move among your open spreadsheet windows is by using the GoTo key (F5). This key lets you jump directly to a particular cell address or block name in an open spreadsheet file. When you press GoTo (F5), Quattro Pro prompts you for an address to "go to." Type the name of an open spreadsheet, enclosed in square braces, followed by a cell address or block name. Then press Enter to jump to that location. For example, imagine you want to go directly to cell B14 in the PROFIT.WQ1 file. To do this, press GoTo (F5), type **[PROFIT1]B14**, and press Enter.

The GoTo key (F5) is helpful when you want to take a quick glance at a spreadsheet and then return to your original location. First press GoTo (F5). When Quattro Pro prompts you for a cell address, rather than typing a cell address or block name, simply move to the location you want to have a look at. For example, press Alt-0 to display the Window Pick list and select a window to jump to. When you get to the location, take note of the data you need to see, and then press Esc to return to your original location.

Closing Windows

Each window that you open on the desktop requires additional memory. What's more, the more windows you open, the more crowded and disorderly the desktop can become. To cut down on memory usage and minimize possible confusion, remember to close windows that you no longer need, thus removing them from the desktop. You can close one specific window at a time, or you can close all the windows on the desktop.

Closing a Single Window

To close a specific window, you must activate that window. Once it is active, you can close it in one of two ways: Select the /File, Close command; or click your mouse on the *close box*, the small box in the upper-left corner of the spreadsheet, at the intersection of the column and row borders.

When you use either of these file closing methods, Quattro Pro immediately attempts to close the active window and remove it from the desktop. However, if the spreadsheet in the window contains unsaved changes, you are given a chance to save those changes. Quattro Pro displays a prompt box that says "Lose your changes?" along with a Yes/No choice. If you select No, the close operation is cancelled and you are returned to the current spreadsheet window, where you can use /File, Save to save your changes. Or, if you select Yes, Quattro Pro closes the window without saving your changes.

When you close a window, Quattro Pro removes it from the desktop, revealing the next background window in the stack. If no other windows are open, the desktop itself is revealed, as shown in Figure 2.8. In addition, only a single command, /File, appears in the menu bar. When you open this menu, an abbreviated /File menu is displayed, containing the following commands:

- *New* creates a new spreadsheet file.

- *Open* lets you open an existing file from disk.

- *Workspace* lets you open the files in a workspace you've previously saved.

- *Utilities* lets you shell out to DOS or open the File Manager.

- *Exit* leaves Quattro Pro and returns you to the DOS prompt.

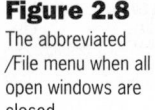

Figure 2.8

The abbreviated /File menu when all open windows are closed

Closing All Open Windows

Occasionally, you may want to close all the windows on the desktop and start with a clean slate—for example, to begin a new project that does not rely on any of the spreadsheets you currently have open. To close all open windows, select the /File, Close All command. Quattro Pro will then close all the windows on the desktop, one by one.

During the close operation, if Quattro Pro comes across a spreadsheet that is new or detects that you have made changes since you last saved a file, you are given a chance to save your changes. You'll see a prompt box that says "Lose your changes and close window?" followed by three options— No, Yes, and Save and Close. Select No, and the close operation is aborted. Select Yes, and Quattro Pro closes all open files without saving your changes. Choose Save and Close, and Quattro Pro saves each file, on a file-by-file basis, prior to closing it. If the file already exists on disk, you'll be prompted with the Cancel, Replace, Backup menu, just as though you were using /File, Save or /File, Save As for each individual file.

Tiling and Stacking Windows

When you have multiple windows open on the desktop, you are constantly faced with the challenge of keeping track of what they all contain. To help you in this task, Quattro Pro allows you to stack and tile your open windows.

Tiling Windows

When you *tile* windows, Quattro Pro arranges all of your open windows into a side-by-side configuration much like the tiles on a floor. Figure 2.9 shows an example of four tiled windows. When you tile windows, the currently active window is displayed at the upper-left corner of the desktop. To tile all of your open windows, you use the /Window, Tile command.

To move among tiled windows, you use the /Window, Pick command, or one of its equivalents, Shift-F5 or Alt-0. If you know the number of the window you want, hold down the Alt key and type that window number. You can also use Next Window (Shift-F6) to move sequentially from one window to the next. Or, if you are using a mouse, you can click anywhere on a window to activate it. As you might expect, when you move to a spreadsheet window, that window becomes the active window and contains the cell selector. Also, the commands in the menu bar will apply to that window.

Figure 2.10 shows tiling configurations for up to seven open windows. Notice that only when you tile an even number of open windows does Quattro Pro allocate an equal amount of display space to each window.

Figure 2.9

Using the /Window,
Tile command to
create a tiled
display of windows

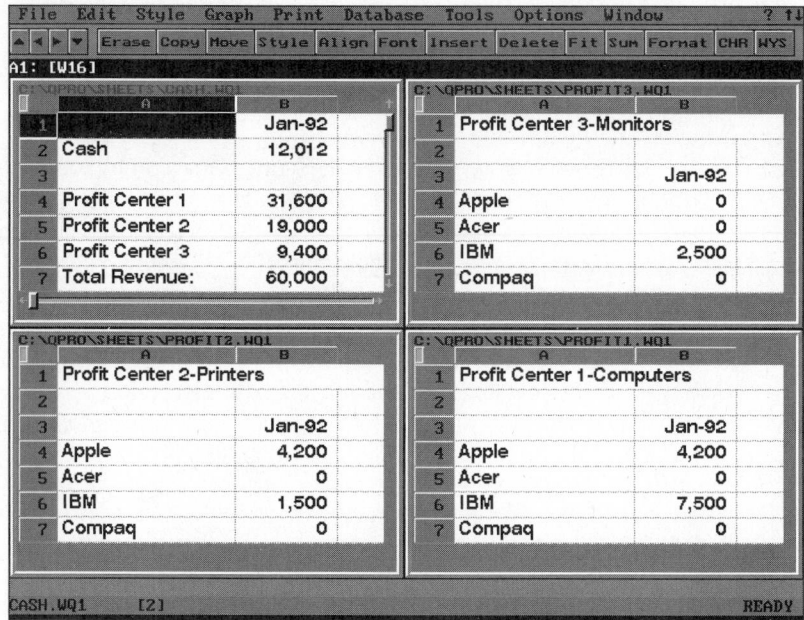

Figure 2.10

Tiling
configurations for
up to seven open
windows

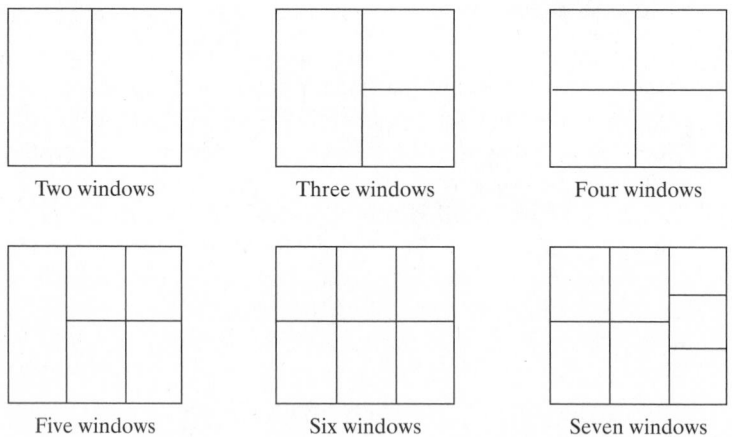

Two windows

Three windows

Four windows

Five windows

Six windows

Seven windows

Stacking Windows

You can also *stack* the windows that are open on the desktop, making them appear in a cascading stack, one behind the other. The top portion of each window is exposed to show both the name of the window and its number. The currently active window appears at the front of the stack. Stacked windows are allowed in Character mode only. To stack the windows on the desktop, use the /Window, Stack command. Figure 2.11 shows an example of stacked windows.

Figure 2.11

Stacked windows that are currently open on the desktop (in Character mode only)

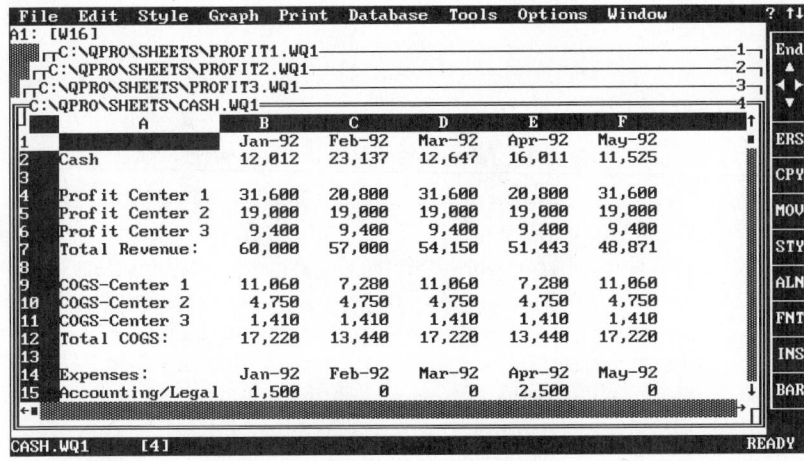

NOTE. *Unfortunately, you can stack windows only in Character mode. (If you select /Window, Stack while in WYSIWYG mode, Quattro Pro beeps at you.) If you are presently running in WYSIWYG mode, you can switch to Character mode by selecting /Options, Display Mode and choosing A: 80X25. Alternatively, you can click on the CHR button in the mouse palette in Quattro Pro 3.0., and in the SpeedBar in Quattro Pro 4.0.*

Note. To unstack windows, press Zoom (Alt-F6) to zoom one of the windows to full size. See "Zooming a Window" later in this chapter for details.

Notice that when Quattro Pro is operating in Character mode and the active window is less than full size, it has a double border around it. By contrast, inactive windows that are less than full size have only a single border. The name and number of each window appears at the top of the window, making the window easier to identify.

To move among stacked windows, just use the same techniques you use for tiled windows. For example, you can select the /Window, Pick command or press Shift-F5 or Alt-0 to display the Window Pick list, and then select the window you want. Quattro Pro moves it to the front of the stack, making it the active window. You can also hold down Alt and type the window number to have Quattro Pro activate that window at the front of the stack. To move sequentially from one window to the next, use Next Window (Shift-F6). Finally, if you are using a mouse, you can click on any exposed portion of a window to activate it.

Resizing and Moving Windows

Although you can't move or change the size of a window in WYSIWYG mode, you certainly can in Character mode. In fact, you may find yourself occasionally switching to Character mode just so you can take advantage of the useful resize feature. You can move and resize windows using either the keyboard or the mouse, and both methods are discussed in the sections that follow.

Resizing and Moving Windows with the Keyboard

To change the size of a window or move it to another area of the desktop, you must be in Character mode. Once you are in Character mode, activate the window you want to move or resize, and then select the /Window, Move/-Size command (or press Ctrl-R). Quattro Pro displays a box labeled MOVE in the upper-left corner of the current spreadsheet. For example, suppose that you have the stacked windows in Figure 2.11, and you want to resize and move the top one. Figure 2.12 shows how your screen appears after you activate the top window and select /Window, Move/Size.

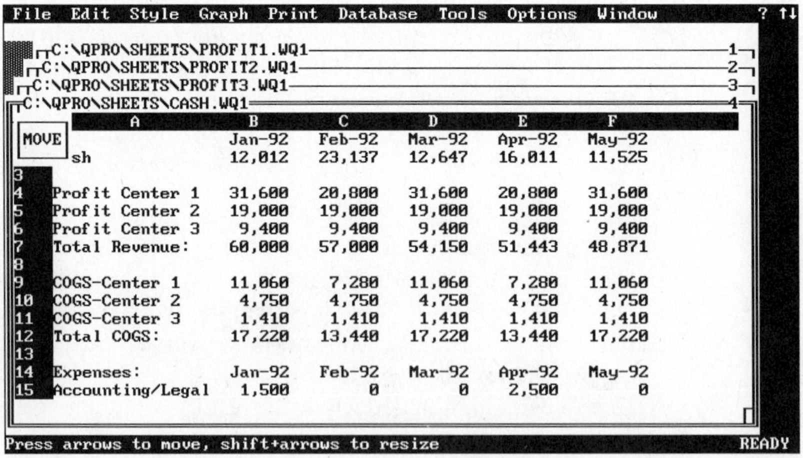

Figure 2.12

The MOVE box that appears when you select the /Window, Move/Size command

```
   File   Edit   Style   Graph   Print   Database   Tools   Options   Window        ? ↑↓

   ┌C:\QPRO\SHEETS\PROFIT1.WQ1───────────────────────────────────────1┐
   │┌C:\QPRO\SHEETS\PROFIT2.WQ1──────────────────────────────────────2┐
   ││┌C:\QPRO\SHEETS\PROFIT3.WQ1─────────────────────────────────────3┐
   │││┌C:\QPRO\SHEETS\CASH.WQ1═══════════════════════════════════════4
   ││││        A         B         C         D         E         F
   │││┌MOVE┐                Jan-92    Feb-92    Mar-92    Apr-92    May-92
   ││││    └sh            12,012    23,137    12,647    16,011    11,525
   │││3
   │││4  Profit Center 1  31,600    20,800    31,600    20,800    31,600
   │││5  Profit Center 2  19,000    19,000    19,000    19,000    19,000
   │││6  Profit Center 3   9,400     9,400     9,400     9,400     9,400
   │││7  Total Revenue:   60,000    57,000    54,150    51,443    48,871
   │││8
   │││9  COGS-Center 1    11,060     7,280    11,060     7,280    11,060
   │││10 COGS-Center 2     4,750     4,750     4,750     4,750     4,750
   │││11 COGS-Center 3     1,410     1,410     1,410     1,410     1,410
   │││12 Total COGS:      17,220    13,440    17,220    13,440    17,220
   │││13
   │││14 Expenses:        Jan-92    Feb-92    Mar-92    Apr-92    May-92
   │││15 Accounting/Legal  1,500         0         0     2,500         0
   │││                                                                   ┘

   Press arrows to move, shift+arrows to resize                    READY
```

You can't move a full-size window—after all, there's no place for it to go. So for the example in Figure 2.12, you'll need to change the size of the window before you can move it. To do this, hold down the Shift key and press the ← key several times on the numeric keypad. Notice that the window contents seem to disappear, leaving only the MOVE box. The right-hand border of the window moves toward the center of the screen, and the window appears smaller. Release the Shift key and press Enter. The contents of the window reappear and the window takes on the new smaller size. You can use this same procedure with the Shift and → keys to move the right border back to where it was. In like fashion, you can use the /Window, Move/Size command with the Shift-↑ or Shift-↓ key sequences to move the bottom border of a window up or down, thereby decreasing or increasing the size of a window.

Now that you have reduced the size of the current spreadsheet window to occupy less than the entire screen, you can practice moving the window around the desktop. Select the /Window, Move/Size command again, and you'll see the familiar MOVE box in the upper-left corner of the current spreadsheet. To move the window to the right, press → several times; each time you press this key, the window moves to the right. To complete the move, press Enter. You can use the /Window, Move/Size command with any of the arrow keys to move a window to the left, right, up, or down.

Before moving on, take a moment to look at the windows that have been resized in Figure 2.13. Because the window containing the file E:\QPRO\SHEETS\CASH.WQ1 has a double border around it, you can tell that it is the active window; the inactive windows that have been resized have only a single border.

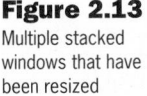

Figure 2.13
Multiple stacked windows that have been resized

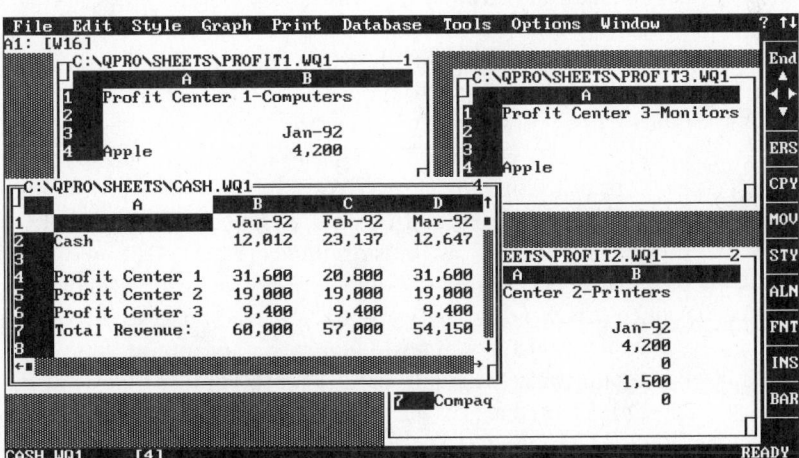

Moving and Resizing Windows with the Mouse

Moving and resizing windows with the mouse is easier and more intuitive than using the keyboard. For example, to resize the current window (CASH.WQ1), click your mouse on the resize box located at the lower-right corner of the window, where the scroll bar arrows converge (take a look at Figure 2.13 to get a fix on this). Continue to hold your mouse button down, and drag diagonally upward and to the left. As you drag, you'll notice a box labeled SIZE in the upper-left corner of the window you are dragging. Also, the bottom and right borders of the window contract dynamically with the movement of your mouse pointer. When you've got the window sized the way you want it, release your mouse button. Quattro Pro resizes the window to meet your new specifications.

Moving a window with the mouse is just as easy. To do this, click the mouse button anywhere on the top border of a resized window, and hold it down. Then you can drag that window in any direction. As you drag, a MOVE box appears in the upper-left corner of the window, and the window itself follows the movement of your mouse pointer. When you've got the window where you want it, release the mouse button, and Quattro Pro moves the window to the new location.

Zooming a Window

If you've reduced the size of a window (in Character mode only) or tiled the windows you have open, you can choose a specific window and *zoom* it to full size. This lets you get a closer look at just that window, without any visual interference from other windows you may have open on the desktop. As with other window manipulation features, your choice of WYSIWYG or Character mode will affect how the zoom feature is used.

To zoom a window to full size (in either Character or WYSIWYG mode), first activate the window, and then select the /Window, Zoom command (or press Alt-F6). The window expands to full size, completely covering your other open windows. You can then move around in the zoomed window, entering and editing data. In Character mode only, you can also return a zoomed window to its original size and position on the desktop. To do this, just select /Window, Zoom (or press Alt-F6) a second time. Quattro Pro reduces the window to its original size and restores it to its original position.

You can also zoom a window with your mouse. Simply click on one of the zoom icons (the small ↑ and ↓ on the mouse palette at the right of your screen). If you click on the ↑ icon, Quattro Pro zooms the current window to full size. Click on the ↓ icon (Character mode only), and Quattro Pro zooms the current window down to its original size and restores it to its original position on the desktop.

If you are running in Character mode, you can also use /Window, Zoom to zoom a full-size window down to a smaller size. For example, imagine the current spreadsheet is displayed as a full-size window. To zoom this window to a smaller size, select /Window, Zoom (or press Alt-F6), or click your mouse on the small ↓ icon on the mouse palette. Quattro Pro zooms the current window down to about half size, as shown in Figure 2.14. Notice that a portion of the full-size spreadsheet located directly behind the current half-size one is revealed. You might use this feature when you want to take a quick look at the spreadsheet located directly behind the current one. When you've seen what you need to see, you can zoom the current spreadsheet to full size again.

Figure 2.14
Zooming a window
to half size

```
 File  Edit  Style  Graph  Print  Database  Tools  Options  Window         ? ↑↓
A1: [W16]
        A           B        C        D        E        F        G      End
1  Profit Center 1-Computers                                              ▲
2                                                                         ◀ ▶
3           Jan-92   Feb-92   Mar-92   Apr-92   May-92   Jun-92           ▼
4  Apple     4,200        0    4,200        0    4,200        0
5  Acer          0    6,200        0    6,200        0    6,200      ERS
6  IBM       7,500        0    7,500        0    7,500        0
7  Compaq        0    4,800        0    4,800        0    4,800      CPY
 ┌─C:\QPRO\SHEETS\CASH.WQ1═══════════════════════════════2┐          MOV
        A           B        C        D        E        F    ↑
1                                                                         STY
2  Cash      12,012   23,137   12,647   16,011   11,525
3                                                                         ALN
4  Profit Center 1  31,600   20,800   31,600   20,800   31,600
5  Profit Center 2  19,000   19,000   19,000   19,000   19,000           FNT
6  Profit Center 3   9,400    9,400    9,400    9,400    9,400
7  Total Revenue:   60,000   57,000   54,150   51,443   48,871           INS
8
9  COGS-Center 1    11,060    7,280   11,060    7,280   11,060           BAR
10 COGS-Center 2     4,750    4,750    4,750    4,750    4,750    ↓
CASH.WQ1    [2]                                               READY
```

Scaling in WYSIWYG Mode

Note. The /Options, WYSIWYG Zoom % command affects only the on-screen display. It does not change the printed output.

In WYSIWYG mode, you can also zoom in on a portion of the contents of a window. To do this, you use the /Options, WYSIWYG Zoom % command. This command lets you scale (proportionally increase or decrease) the displayed size of the contents of your spreadsheet. When you increase the size of displayed contents, fewer columns and rows of the spreadsheet are displayed. Conversely, when you decrease the size of the contents, more columns and rows of data are displayed within the current window.

Suppose you are working with the spreadsheet in Figure 2.15, in WYSIWYG mode. To zoom in on this spreadsheet, select /Options, WYSIWYG Zoom %. Quattro Pro displays a prompt box asking you to specify the decrease or increase percentage desired for the spreadsheet, from 25% to

200% (100% is the default display size). For example, if you want the text in the current spreadsheet to be displayed at 1½ times (150%) its current size, type **150**, and press Enter. When Quattro Pro zooms in on the spreadsheet, all displayed spreadsheet contents appear at 1½ times original size, as shown in Figure 2.16. Notice that fewer rows and columns are now displayed to accommodate the larger text. Conversely, if you want the displayed spreadsheet to appear at half its normal size, you can use a zoom value of 50%. Although your spreadsheet may be hard to read at this scale, you'll be able to see about twice as many columns and rows of data in the same window.

Figure 2.15

A sample spreadsheet in the default display size

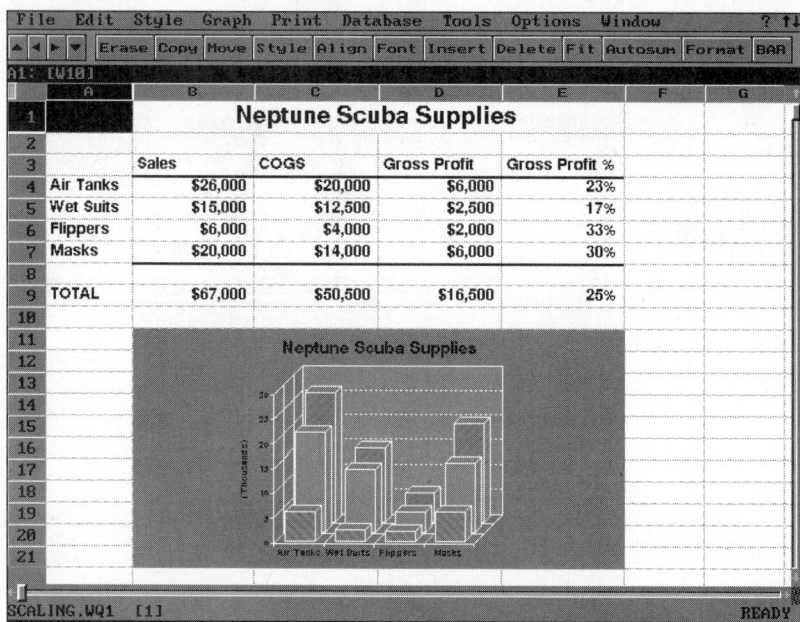

Saving All Open Files

In Chapter 1, you learned how to save your spreadsheet files one at a time by using the /File, Save command. However, if you have many files open on the desktop, using /File, Save to save each of these individual files one by one can become tedious. Another option is to save all your open files at once, using the /File, Save All command.

When you choose /File, Save All, Quattro Pro starts with the currently active spreadsheet and processes each of your open files one by one. If Quattro Pro encounters a new file that you have not yet saved to disk, that file is saved under its default SHEET#.WQ1 name in the current directory. For a file already saved on disk that you have changed since you opened it, Quattro Pro displays a Cancel, Replace, Backup menu for that file. The options on this menu for the /File, Save All command have the following effects:

- *Cancel* ends the /File, Save All operation without saving the current file.

- *Replace* replaces the file on disk with the file from memory, and moves on to the next open file.

- *Backup* renames the file on disk with same name but with a .BAK extension, saves the file from memory to disk, and moves on to the next open file.

Figure 2.16

The spreadsheet from Figure 2.15 zoomed to 150% of the default display size

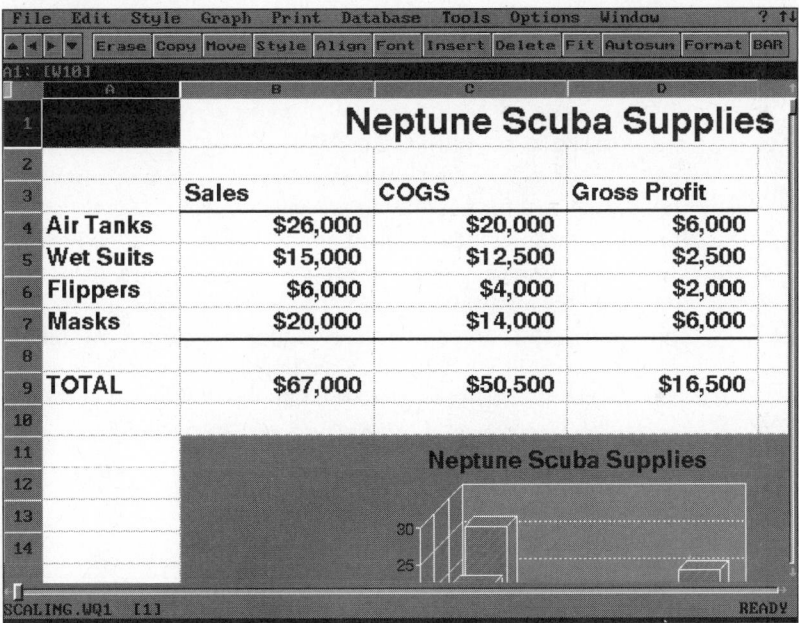

If you are running Quattro Pro in Character mode, the /File, Save All command saves not only the spreadsheet file itself, but also the position and size of its window on the desktop. That way, the next time you open the file, its window is restored to the same location it previously occupied and in the same size.

/File, Save All provides a quick and convenient way for you to save all your open files with a single command. However, in order to restore that same set of files to the Quattro Pro desktop for a future session, you must use the /File, Retrieve and/or /File, Open commands to open each of the files individually. There is a better way to do this: by grouping the currently open files under a workspace name and opening all of them on the desktop in a single operation, as described next.

Saving and Restoring the Workspace

The current configuration of open windows—their positions, sizes, and the files they contain—is called the *workspace*. Quattro Pro lets you assign a name to the current workspace configuration and save that information to disk in the form of an ASCII file with a .WSP extension. You can then restore the same set of files to the desktop in a future session by simply opening the appropriate .WSP file. To create and restore .WSP files, you use the /File, Workspace command. Before you use /File, Workspace to create a workspace file, it is important to be sure you have your open windows sized and positioned the way you want them. For example, if you want the current set of windows to be restored to the desktop in a tiled configuration, use the /Window, Tile command first. When you are satisfied with the appearance of the workspace, select the /File, Workspace command. Quattro Pro then displays two options, Save and Restore. Choose Save, and you'll see a prompt box asking you for a name under which to save the workspace. This prompt box also contains the names of any workspace files previously created in the current directory. Type a name of up to eight characters (the .WSP extension is added for you automatically), and press Enter. Quattro Pro creates a workspace file in the current directory under the name you specified.

As mentioned, when you save the workspace, Quattro Pro creates an ASCII text file including only the names of files currently open on the desktop and the positions of their windows. The actual files themselves are *not* saved. You must do this as a separate operation using an appropriate save command. For example, you might use the /File, Save All command described in the previous section to save all your open files at once.

To restore a particular set of files to the desktop at a later time, use the /File, Workspace, Restore command. Quattro Pro displays a prompt box showing a list of .WSP files, where you can highlight the name of the .WSP file you want. Press Enter, and Quattro Pro loads the files associated with that workspace. The windows for those files are sized and positioned as they were when you originally created the workspace file.

To give you an idea of what a .WSP workspace file looks like, Figure 2.17 shows a workspace file called CASH.WSP that has been opened in the Windows Notepad editor. (The Windows Notepad editor is used to read and write ordinary flat ASCII text files.) Notice that the file begins with the word Workspace, followed by the name of each file included in the workspace. Displayed with each file name is information indicating the position and size of the window when the workspace was saved.

Figure 2.17

A sample
workspace .WSP
file, listed in the
Windows Notepad
editor

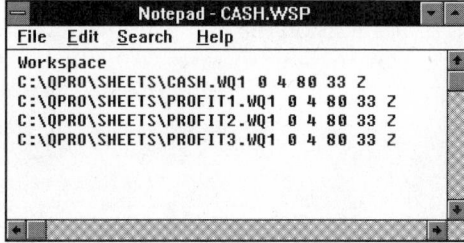

```
┌────────────────────────────────────────────┐
│ ─        Notepad - CASH.WSP            ▼ ▲  │
│ File  Edit  Search   Help                   │
├────────────────────────────────────────────┤
│ Workspace                                 ▲ │
│ C:\QPRO\SHEETS\CASH.WQ1 0 4 80 33 Z         │
│ C:\QPRO\SHEETS\PROFIT1.WQ1 0 4 80 33 Z      │
│ C:\QPRO\SHEETS\PROFIT2.WQ1 0 4 80 33 Z      │
│ C:\QPRO\SHEETS\PROFIT3.WQ1 0 4 80 33 Z      │
│                                             │
│                                           ▼ │
│ ◄ ▓▓▓▓▓▓▓▓▓▓▓▓▓▓▓▓▓▓▓▓▓▓▓▓▓▓▓▓▓▓▓▓▓▓▓▓▓ ►   │
└────────────────────────────────────────────┘
```

Splitting Windows

You have learned that a spreadsheet window is simply a rectangular area of your screen through which you view a much larger work surface. In fact, even a full-sized spreadsheet window shows you only a fraction of the available cells. When you work with a large spreadsheet, you may find yourself losing valuable time by continually moving back and forth between key areas of the spreadsheet. To cut down on this jumping around, Quattro Pro lets you split a spreadsheet window into two *panes*. You can then focus one pane in one area of the spreadsheet while the other pane is focused on a completely different area. What's more, you can easily jump from one pane to the other, letting you conveniently view, edit, and compare two widely distanced areas of the same spreadsheet.

To split a window, you use the /Window, Options command. The sections that follow show you how to split a window vertically into two side-by-side panes or horizontally into two panes, top and bottom. You'll also learn how to clear split windows and return to a single-pane display.

Splitting a Window Vertically

To split a window into two vertical (side-by-side) panes, begin by moving the cell selector to the column where you want the split to occur. For example, imagine you are working with the cash-flow spreadsheet in Figure 2.18, which shows twelve months of activity for a small company. Only the first six months (January through June) are displayed. However, you need to compare the various balances at the beginning and end of the year. To do this, you could split the spreadsheet vertically at column D and move the end-of-the-year column closer to the January column.

You begin by moving the cell selector to column D. Then select the /Window, Options command. From the submenu of Window options that appears, choose Vertical. Quattro Pro splits the current spreadsheet vertically at the location of the cell selector, as shown in Figure 2.19. Notice that a second set of row numbers now appears to mark the split. Notice, too, that the cell selector remains on the first window in column C.

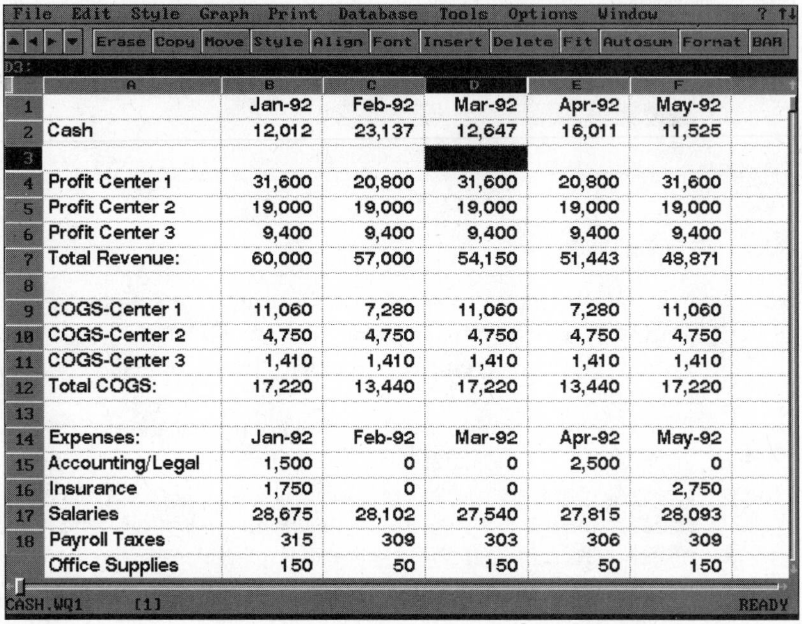

Figure 2.18

A sample cash-flow spreadsheet

File Edit Style Graph Print Database Tools Options Window		? ↑↓
▲ ◄ ► ▼ Erase Copy Move Style Align Font Insert Delete Fit Autosum Format BAR		

D3:						
	A	B	C	D	E	F
1		Jan-92	Feb-92	Mar-92	Apr-92	May-92
2	Cash	12,012	23,137	12,647	16,011	11,525
3						
4	Profit Center 1	31,600	20,800	31,600	20,800	31,600
5	Profit Center 2	19,000	19,000	19,000	19,000	19,000
6	Profit Center 3	9,400	9,400	9,400	9,400	9,400
7	Total Revenue:	60,000	57,000	54,150	51,443	48,871
8						
9	COGS-Center 1	11,060	7,280	11,060	7,280	11,060
10	COGS-Center 2	4,750	4,750	4,750	4,750	4,750
11	COGS-Center 3	1,410	1,410	1,410	1,410	1,410
12	Total COGS:	17,220	13,440	17,220	13,440	17,220
13						
14	Expenses:	Jan-92	Feb-92	Mar-92	Apr-92	May-92
15	Accounting/Legal	1,500	0	0	2,500	0
16	Insurance	1,750	0	0		2,750
17	Salaries	28,675	28,102	27,540	27,815	28,093
18	Payroll Taxes	315	309	303	306	309
	Office Supplies	150	50	150	50	150

CASH.WQ1 [1]	READY

To focus on and edit the information in a specific pane, you must move the cell selector to that pane. To move the cell selector back and forth between vertical or horizontal window panes, use the Pane key (F6). If you are using a mouse, you can simply click your mouse pointer on any cell in either pane to move the cell selector.

For example, in Figure 2.19, you'll need to press Pane to move the cell selector from the left pane to the right pane. Once this is done, you can use the cell selector movement keys or the mouse scroll bars to move around the spreadsheet. Continuing with our cash-flow example in Figure 2.19, you'll want to press the → key ten times to scroll the right-hand pane to the right, and display the year-end balances that you need for your comparison to the left pane. Your screen will appear as shown in Figure 2.20.

You'll notice when you move the cell selector up and down within one vertical window pane that Quattro Pro always keeps the same rows in view in both panes. This is, of course, for your convenience. There may be times, however, when you want to unsynchronize window pane scrolling so that different rows can be displayed in each vertical pane. Later, under "Unsynchronizing Window Pane Scrolling," we'll show you how to do just that.

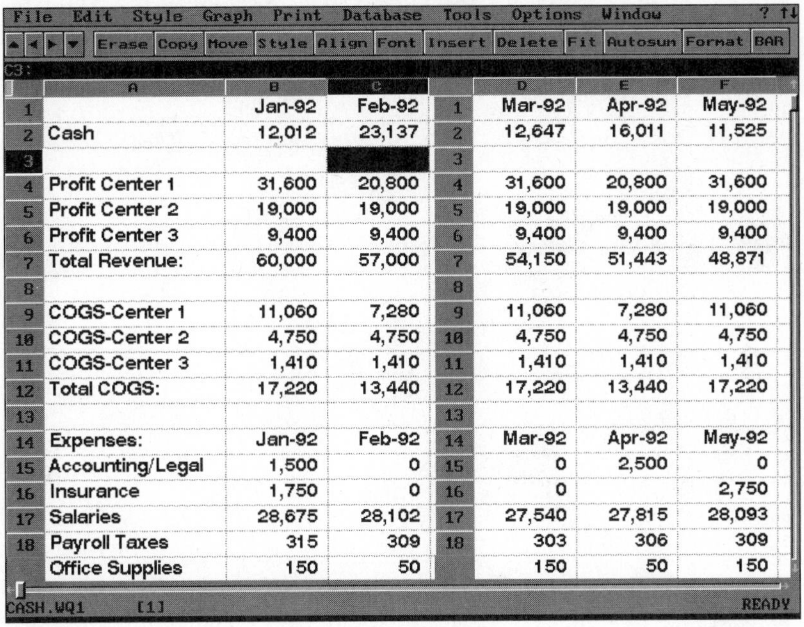

Figure 2.19

Splitting a spreadsheet window into two vertical panes

File	Edit	Style	Graph	Print	Database	Tools	Options	Window		? ↑↓

▲ ◄ ► ▼	Erase	Copy	Move	Style	Align	Font	Insert	Delete	Fit	Autosum	Format	BAR

C3:

	A	B	C		D	E	F
1		Jan-92	Feb-92	1	Mar-92	Apr-92	May-92
2	Cash	12,012	23,137	2	12,647	16,011	11,525
3				3			
4	Profit Center 1	31,600	20,800	4	31,600	20,800	31,600
5	Profit Center 2	19,000	19,000	5	19,000	19,000	19,000
6	Profit Center 3	9,400	9,400	6	9,400	9,400	9,400
7	Total Revenue:	60,000	57,000	7	54,150	51,443	48,871
8				8			
9	COGS-Center 1	11,060	7,280	9	11,060	7,280	11,060
10	COGS-Center 2	4,750	4,750	10	4,750	4,750	4,750
11	COGS-Center 3	1,410	1,410	11	1,410	1,410	1,410
12	Total COGS:	17,220	13,440	12	17,220	13,440	17,220
13				13			
14	Expenses:	Jan-92	Feb-92	14	Mar-92	Apr-92	May-92
15	Accounting/Legal	1,500	0	15	0	2,500	0
16	Insurance	1,750	0	16	0		2,750
17	Salaries	28,675	28,102	17	27,540	27,815	28,093
18	Payroll Taxes	315	309	18	303	306	309
	Office Supplies	150	50		150	50	150

CASH.WQ1   [1]   READY

Splitting a Window Horizontally

You can also split the current spreadsheet window horizontally, creating a view with top and bottom window panes. To do this, position the cell selector in the row where you want the split to occur. When you are ready, select /Window, Options and choose Horizontal. Quattro Pro splits the window horizontally at the current row and displays a second set of column letters to mark the split.

You can move between horizontal window panes using the same techniques as for vertical panes. Just press Pane (F6) on the keyboard to move between the panes, or simply click your mouse pointer on any cell in either pane to move the cell selector there.

Just like vertical panes, you can focus your horizontal panes on different areas of the spreadsheet. Press Pane (F6) (or use the mouse) to move the cell selector to the appropriate pane, and then use the cell selector movement keys or the mouse scroll bars to move to the area of the spreadsheet you want to view.

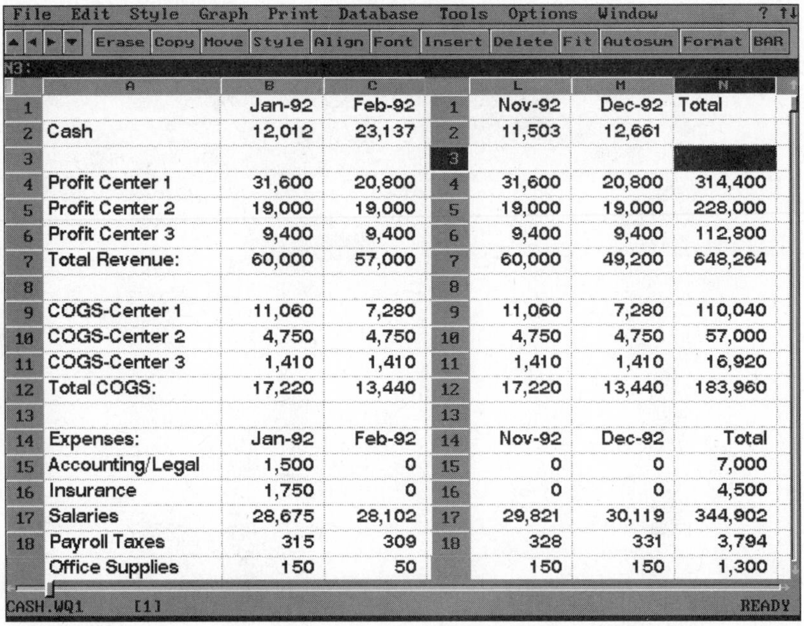

Figure 2.20

Splitting a window
so you can
simultaneously view
and edit two distant
portions of a
spreadsheet

You'll notice as you scroll around within a horizontal window pane that Quattro Pro always displays the same columns in both panes—just as it does for rows in a vertically split window. As with vertical splits, you can un-synchronize the scrolling of horizontal window panes by using the /Window, Options, Unsync command discussed next.

Unsynchronizing Window Pane Scrolling

When you need to, Quattro Pro lets you unsynchronize the scrolling of both horizontal and vertical panes. Normally, when you split the current spread-sheet window vertically or horizontally, Quattro Pro always keeps the same rows or columns in view for both panes. You'll find this default setting to be helpful in most situations. Occasionally, however, you may want to change this.

To unsynchronize window pane scrolling, use the /Window, Options, Unsync command. When you select this command, your window panes become independent of each other. That is, as you move the cell selector within one window pane, the other pane remains static on your screen.

Consider the current spreadsheet, split into two vertical panes, with the cell selector located in the right-hand pane, as shown in Figure 2.20. Normally, when you press ↓ to move beyond the bottom edge of one pane, Quattro Pro scrolls both window panes so that the same rows are displayed in each pane. However, with the /Window, Options, Unsync command in force, panes are no longer synchronized. You can move the cell selector in the right-hand pane up and down in the current window, and Quattro Pro will scroll the view in the right-hand pane to show the appropriate set of rows. The rows displayed in the left-hand pane, however, remain unchanged, as shown in Figure 2.21.

Figure 2.21
Unsynchronizing the scrolling of split window panes

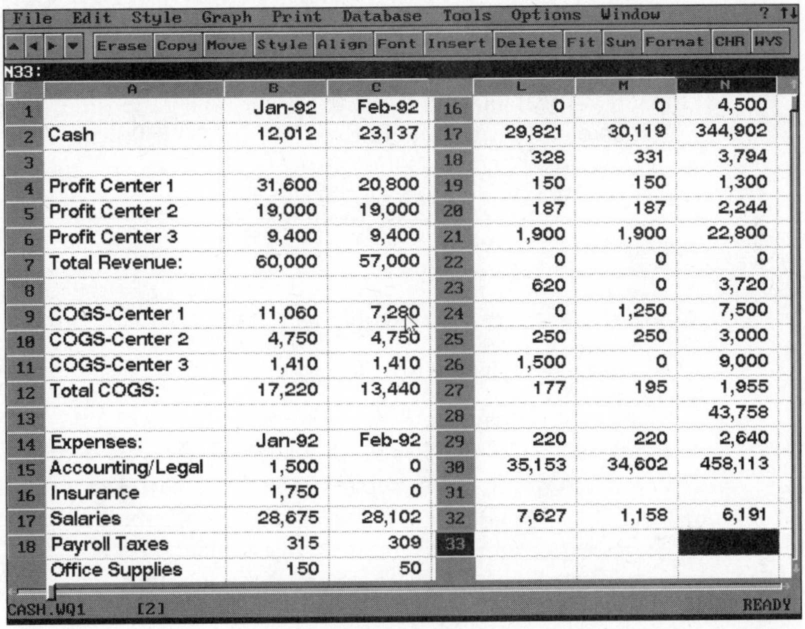

	A	B	C		L	M	N
1		Jan-92	Feb-92	16	0	0	4,500
2	Cash	12,012	23,137	17	29,821	30,119	344,902
3				18	328	331	3,794
4	Profit Center 1	31,600	20,800	19	150	150	1,300
5	Profit Center 2	19,000	19,000	20	187	187	2,244
6	Profit Center 3	9,400	9,400	21	1,900	1,900	22,800
7	Total Revenue:	60,000	57,000	22	0	0	0
8				23	620	0	3,720
9	COGS-Center 1	11,060	7,280	24	0	1,250	7,500
10	COGS-Center 2	4,750	4,750	25	250	250	3,000
11	COGS-Center 3	1,410	1,410	26	1,500	0	9,000
12	Total COGS:	17,220	13,440	27	177	195	1,955
13				28			43,758
14	Expenses:	Jan-92	Feb-92	29	220	220	2,640
15	Accounting/Legal	1,500	0	30	35,153	34,602	458,113
16	Insurance	1,750	0	31			
17	Salaries	28,675	28,102	32	7,627	1,158	6,191
18	Payroll Taxes	315	309	33			
	Office Supplies	150	50				

To return to synchronized scrolling, select /Window, Options and choose Sync. If you have vertical panes displayed, and matching rows are not displayed in both panes, Quattro Pro will update the pane that does not contain the cell selector to match the one that does. The same adjustment is made to synchronize the columns of a window that is split horizontally.

Clearing Split Window Settings

You can clear the current horizontal or vertical split window settings by using the /Window, Options, Clear command. When you select this command, Quattro Pro clears any horizontal or vertical window panes and returns the current spreadsheet to a single-pane display.

You must clear the current split window settings before establishing new ones. Suppose you have the current spreadsheet split into two vertical panes. You then decide that two horizontal panes would be more appropriate. If you enter /Window, Options, Horizontal at this point, Quattro Pro will refuse the command. You must first use /Window, Options, Clear to clear the current vertical split window setting. Then you can select /Window, Options, Horizontal.

Changing the Display Format in a Window Pane

When you split a spreadsheet window, not all of the display format changes you make in one pane will affect the other. In general, format changes in the left vertical pane or in the top horizontal pane will override the changes you make in the right and bottom panes. The following formatting settings are affected:

- Locked titles (/Window, Options, Locked Titles)

- Column widths (/Style, Column Width)

- Hidden and displayed columns (/Style, Hide Column, Hide and Expose)

- Default display format (/Options, Formats)

When you change one of these format settings in the right or bottom window pane, Quattro Pro seems to respond to your bidding. However, when you return to a single-pane display, Quattro Pro formats the entire spreadsheet to match the settings that currently exist in the left or top pane. The exceptions are any format changes you make with either the /Style, Numeric Format or /Style, Font command in the right or bottom pane; these will be retained when you return to a single-pane display.

Locking Titles

Perhaps one of the most useful features in Quattro Pro is its ability to let you lock column and row titles. Most spreadsheets that you build will have titles (dates or labels) in the top cell of each column, which identify the contents of each column. In addition, along the left edge of your spreadsheet, you'll probably want to have titles that identify the contents of significant rows of data. All these titles allow you, or someone else, to quickly determine what the numbers in your spreadsheet mean.

Unfortunately, when you scroll past the right or bottom edges of the current spreadsheet window, some or all of your titles will drop out of view, making it hard to determine what you're seeing in the continuing rows and columns of the spreadsheet. However, with the /Window, Options, Locked

Titles command, Quattro Pro lets you designate specific columns and rows of data that will always remain in view along the top and left edges of your spreadsheet. That way, you can move around the spreadsheet freely, without losing track of your column and row titles.

When you select /Window, Options, Locked Titles, Quattro Pro displays a menu with these four options:

- *Horizontal* lets you specify that all rows above the location of the cell selector will remain in view across the top edge of your spreadsheet.

- *Vertical* lets you specify that all the columns to the left of the location of the cell selector will remain in view along the left edge of your spreadsheet.

- *Both* lets you specify that all rows above the cell selector *and* columns to the left of the cell selector will remain in view at all times.

- *Clear* lets you clear the Locked Titles setting for the current spreadsheet.

Consider the cash-flow spreadsheet in Figure 2.22. As you can see, this spreadsheet includes labels in column A to identify the contents of each row, and dates at the top of each column to identify months. Below the month labels, the on-hand cash balance at the end of each month is shown in row 2.

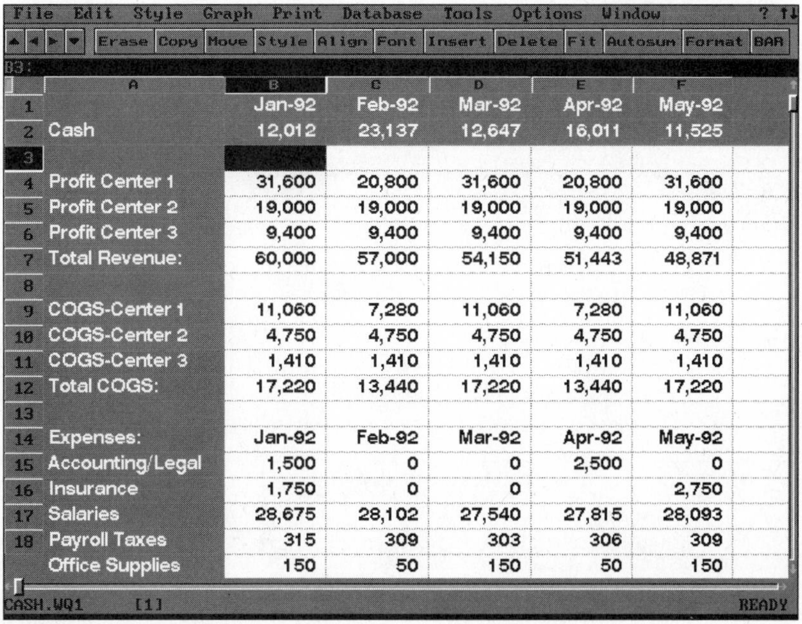

Figure 2.22

Using /Window, Options, Locked Titles to keep column and row titles in view

	A	B	C	D	E	F
1		Jan-92	Feb-92	Mar-92	Apr-92	May-92
2	Cash	12,012	23,137	12,647	16,011	11,525
3						
4	Profit Center 1	31,600	20,800	31,600	20,800	31,600
5	Profit Center 2	19,000	19,000	19,000	19,000	19,000
6	Profit Center 3	9,400	9,400	9,400	9,400	9,400
7	Total Revenue:	60,000	57,000	54,150	51,443	48,871
8						
9	COGS-Center 1	11,060	7,280	11,060	7,280	11,060
10	COGS-Center 2	4,750	4,750	4,750	4,750	4,750
11	COGS-Center 3	1,410	1,410	1,410	1,410	1,410
12	Total COGS:	17,220	13,440	17,220	13,440	17,220
13						
14	Expenses:	Jan-92	Feb-92	Mar-92	Apr-92	May-92
15	Accounting/Legal	1,500	0	0	2,500	0
16	Insurance	1,750	0	0		2,750
17	Salaries	28,675	28,102	27,540	27,815	28,093
18	Payroll Taxes	315	309	303	306	309
	Office Supplies	150	50	150	50	150

For the spreadsheet in Figure 2.22, the titles in column A and/or rows 1 and 2 need to be constantly visible. That way, no matter where you move within the spreadsheet, the meaning and effect of the numbers in the spreadsheet cells will remain clear. For example, Figure 2.23 shows column and row titles that are locked and thus remain visible when the cell selector is moved to a remote area of the spreadsheet.

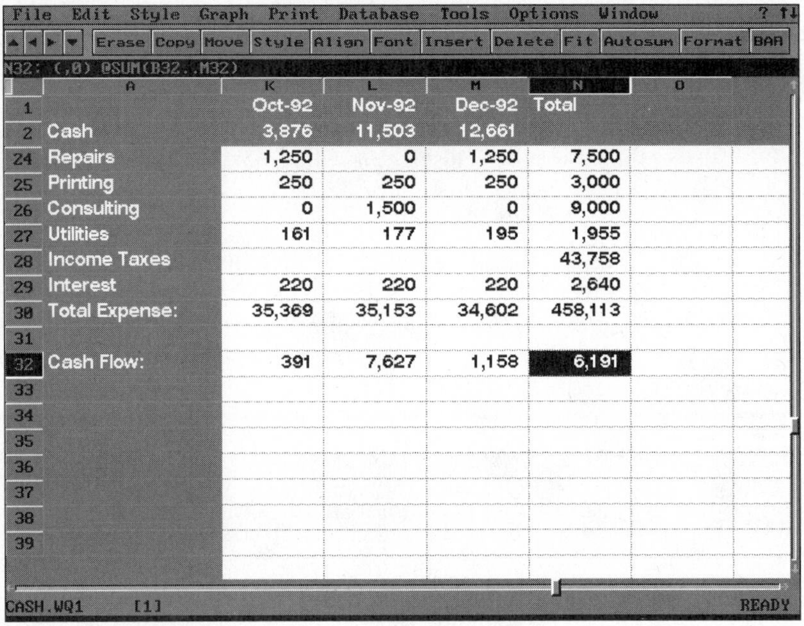

Figure 2.23

Locked column and row titles that remain in view

| File | Edit | Style | Graph | Print | Database | Tools | Options | Window | ? ↑↓ |

| Erase | Copy | Move | Style | Align | Font | Insert | Delete | Fit | Autosum | Format | BAR |

N32: (,0) @SUM(B32..M32)

	A	K	L	M	N	O
1		Oct-92	Nov-92	Dec-92	Total	
2	Cash	3,876	11,503	12,661		
24	Repairs	1,250	0	1,250	7,500	
25	Printing	250	250	250	3,000	
26	Consulting	0	1,500	0	9,000	
27	Utilities	161	177	195	1,955	
28	Income Taxes				43,758	
29	Interest	220	220	220	2,640	
30	Total Expense:	35,369	35,153	34,602	458,113	
31						
32	Cash Flow:	391	7,627	1,158	6,191	
33						
34						
35						
36						
37						
38						
39						

CASH.WQ1 [1]   READY

The /Window, Options, Locked Titles command relies on the location of the cell selector to determine which columns and rows of data to "freeze" along the top and left edges of your screen. To lock the titles in rows 1 and 2 and in column A of Figure 2.22, you'll begin by positioning the cell selector in cell B3. Then select the /Window, Options, Locked Titles command to display the menu of options.

■ If you select Horizontal, Quattro Pro will lock the titles in the rows that are above the location of the cell selector (cell B3). That way, rows 1 and 2 will always be displayed across the top of the current spreadsheet window.

■ If you select Vertical, Quattro Pro will freeze all columns to the left of the cell selector, in this case column A.

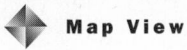

- Finally, if you select Both, Quattro Pro will freeze all rows above the location of the cell selector, as well as columns to the left of it. Thus the titles in rows 1 and 2 along the top edge of the spreadsheet window, and the titles in column A along the left edge, will remain visible.

The Both option is the obvious choice in this particular case.

Quattro Pro identifies columns and rows containing locked titles by displaying their entries in a different color. For example, Figure 2.22 shows an example of how locked titles appear in WYSIWYG mode. Notice that a gray shadow overlays the cells in locked columns and rows, and that the cell entries appear in white. In Character mode, the cells in locked columns and rows appear in light blue on a color screen.

Normally, Quattro Pro will not let you move the cell selector to cells within the locked title area. (If you try this, Quattro Pro will beep.) However, suppose you need to edit cells within a locked title area, and you don't want to have to clear the locked title setting (/Window, Options, Locked Titles, Clear). To do this, you must use the GoTo key (F5) to jump to the appropriate cell. Notice when the cell selector arrives within the locked title area that all of your column and row titles are displayed twice. Don't let this distract you. Simply edit the desired cells in the usual way. When you're done, you'll have to clear the double-title display by moving the cell selector beyond the edge of the spreadsheet window and then back again. You can do this for horizontal titles by pressing PgDn followed by PgUp. For vertical titles, press Tab followed by Shift-Tab. Finally, for both vertical and horizontal titles, press End-Home followed by Home.

TIP. *In Quattro Pro 4.0, the arrow buttons in the SpeedBar also move the cell selector beyond the edge of the window and back again.*

Map View

Quattro Pro's Map view lets you a get a bird's-eye view of a portion of your spreadsheet or an overall view of the structure and organization of the whole spreadsheet. In Map view, all columns in the spreadsheet are reduced to the width of one character. In addition, special symbols are used to represent the type of data (number, label, formula, and so on) in each cell. You can also use Map view to identify errant entries—for example, a stray label prefix in a cell that is supposed to be blank. Figure 2.24 shows a Map view of the spreadsheet pictured earlier in Figure 2.22.

To enable Map view, select the /Window, Options, Map View command. Quattro Pro displays a Yes/No menu. Select Yes, and you'll enter Map view.

The data in each cell of the current spreadsheet is identified by one of the following symbols:

Symbol	Meaning
l	Label
n	Number
+	Formula
-	Link formula
c	Circular reference cell
g	Inserted graph

To turn Map view off and restore the spreadsheet to its normal display mode, select /Window, Options, Map View, No.

Figure 2.24

An example of Map view

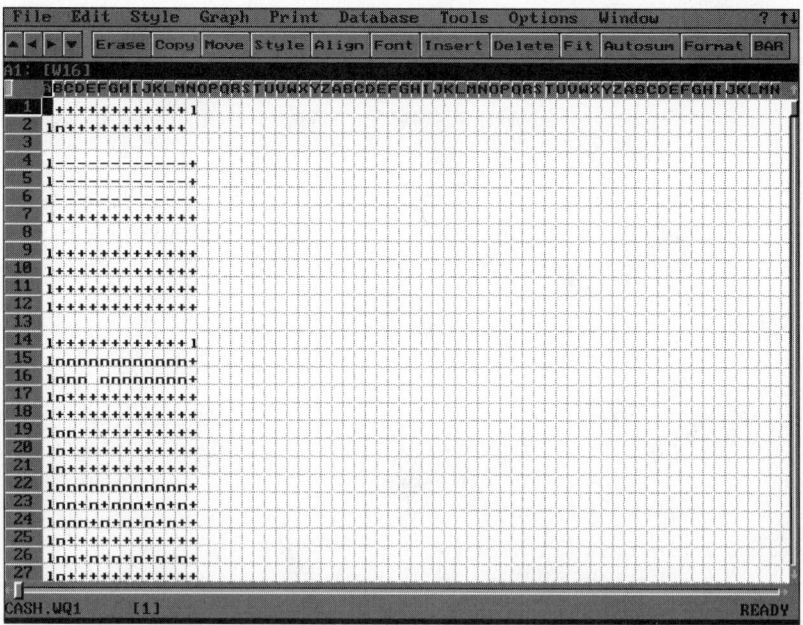

Linking Spreadsheet Files

Quattro Pro lets you link one spreadsheet with another through the use of *link formulas*. In essence, link formulas let you use data in the current spreadsheet from other spreadsheets located either in memory or on disk. What's more, the link is dynamic—when you change the block that is in the linked (supporting) spreadsheet, the link formula in the current spreadsheet is automatically updated for the change.

Linking your spreadsheets can have multiple advantages. For example, rather than building large, difficult-to-navigate spreadsheets, you can divide your work into smaller, more manageable segments. When each segment of the model is complete, you can build a summary spreadsheet composed of link formulas that summarize the results. Not only does this approach simplify your work, it also lets you divide a project among several people. In addition, because you can link spreadsheet files located on disk, you can create models that exceed the limits of your PC's RAM.

Creating Link Formulas

You can place a link formula that refers to another spreadsheet in any cell in the current spreadsheet. The spreadsheet containing the link formula is often called the *primary* spreadsheet, and the spreadsheet to which that link refers is often called the *supporting* spreadsheet. Of course, a supporting spreadsheet can serve as a primary spreadsheet when it contains a link formula to another spreadsheet.

Link formulas are the same as regular formulas except that they contain a reference to data in a cell or block of another spreadsheet, located either in memory or on disk. Link formulas take the following form:

```
+[filename]block
```

where + is any operator or @function that begins a formula; *filename* is a reference to a supporting Quattro Pro spreadsheet file, enclosed in brackets, as in [PAYABLE.WQ1]; and *block* is a reference to a cell, block, or block name in *filename*, for example A1, A1..A10, or TOTAL. If the supporting spreadsheet is located outside the current directory, you must precede *filename* with the appropriate path. Here is an example of a link formula.

```
+[C:\ACCTG\PAYABLE.WQ1]A10
```

Perhaps the best way to understand how link formulas actually work is through an example. Figure 2.25 shows two spreadsheet windows displayed side by side. The primary spreadsheet on the left (CASH.WQ1) contains a link formula that refers to the supporting spreadsheet on the right (PROFIT1.WQ1). The link formula itself resides in cell B4 of CASH.WQ1 and reads as follows:

```
+[PROFIT1]B14
```

This formula begins with a + (plus) operator, causing Quattro Pro to treat the entry as a formula. Next is the reference to the supporting PROFIT1.WQ1 file. Notice that the name of the file is enclosed in square brackets, followed immediately by a reference to a cell (B14) in that file. As you can see in Figure 2.25, this formula returns 31,600 in cell B4 of the CASH.WQ1 file, which is the same as the contents of B14 in the PROFIT1.WQ1 file.

Figure 2.25

Two linked spreadsheets

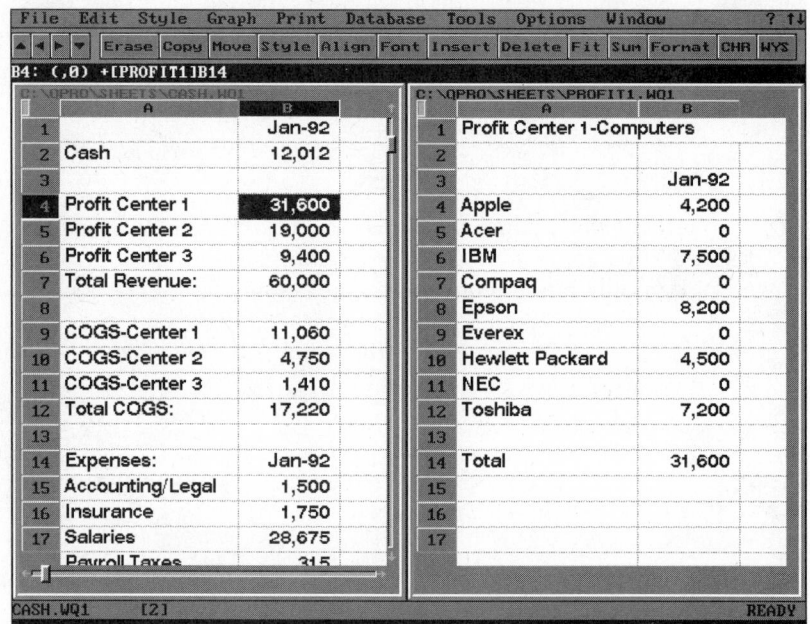

Similar formulas appear in cells B5 and B6 of CASH.WQ1 to reference two additional supporting spreadsheet files, PROFIT2.WQ1 and PROFIT3.WQ1. (Figure 2.26 shows the CASH.WQ1 file open on the desktop along with all three of its supporting spreadsheets.) In this way, you can use a single primary spreadsheet to summarize the data in multiple supporting spreadsheets in a meaningful way.

You can also reference a block name in another spreadsheet file. In fact, you should attempt to do this whenever you can. That way, if the referenced data in the supporting spreadsheet is moved, the link formula in the primary

Tip. You can also use link formulas in the criteria table for the /Database, Query command, to query an external database that has been created by a program other than Quattro Pro, like Paradox, dBASE, or Reflex. See "Querying an External Database" in Chapter 10.

spreadsheet will remain valid. For example, suppose you used /Edit, Name, Create to assign the name JAN_1 to cell B14 of the PROFIT1.WQ1 file, shown on the right side of Figure 2.25. With this block name in place, you can use the following formula in cell B4 of CASH.WQ1:

```
+[PROFIT1]JAN_1
```

In Quattro Pro, link formulas are not confined to single-cell references. In fact, you can use a link reference in just about any formula or macro. For example, the link formula in cell B4 of the CASH.WQ1 file in Figure 2.25 could just as easily read:

```
@SUM([PROFIT1]B4..B12)
```

You can also combine multiple *linking expressions* to build a formula. For example, suppose there are two block names, JAN_1 and TOTAL, in the PROFIT1.WQ1 spreadsheet. The JAN_1 block contains the total January sales, and the TOTAL block contains the total sales for the entire year. You can use these two block names to determine the percentage of total sales that January sales represents, by using the following formula:

```
+[PROFIT1]JAN_1/[PROFIT1]TOTAL_YR
```

Figure 2.26

The CASH.WQ1 spreadsheet, with its three supporting spreadsheets, PROFIT1.WQ1, PROFIT2.WQ1, PROFIT3.WQ1

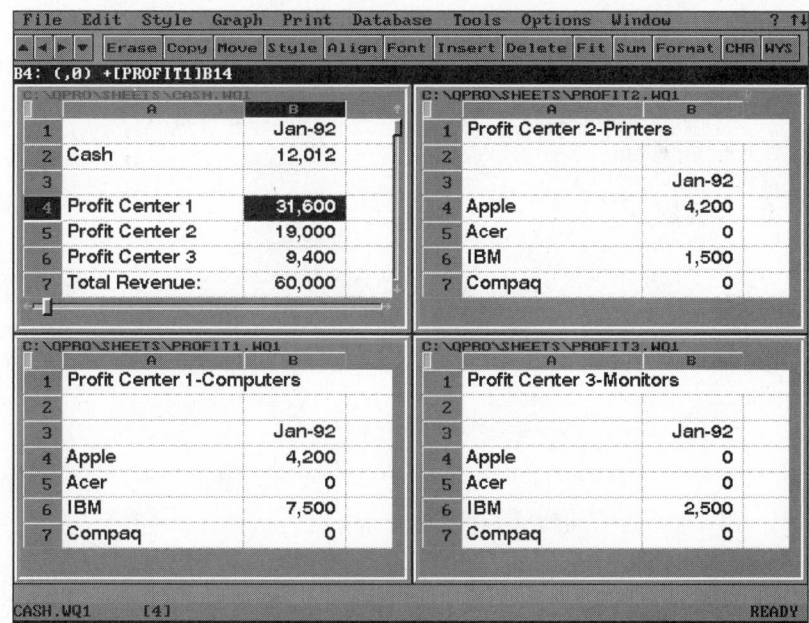

Entering Link Formulas

You can enter link formulas into the spreadsheet by either typing them in or pointing to them. Chapter 1 explains Quattro Pro's Point mode, which allows you to highlight and select cell blocks by pointing to them. This technique can be used to build formulas, including link formulas. In fact, you'll find that pointing to individual cells or blocks will improve both speed and accuracy as you build your link formulas.

To give you an idea of how easy it is to build a link formula by pointing, here is the procedure for building the link formula +[PROFIT1]B14 in cell B4 of CASH.WQ1, which contains a link to PROFIT1.WQ1. These same files are shown again in Figure 2.27.

Figure 2.27

A link formula in the making

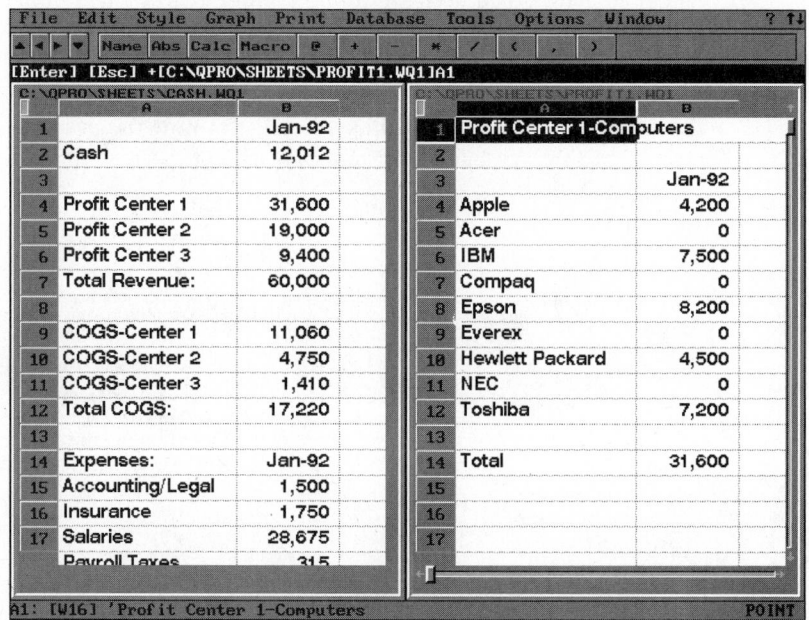

1. Make the CASH.WQ1 file active.

2. Move the cell selector to cell B4.

3. Press the + (plus) key. Quattro Pro enters Value mode.

4. Move the cell selector to cell B14 of the PROFIT1.WQ1 file.

You can perform step 4 in several ways. If the PROFIT1.WQ1 file is the next window in memory, you can press the Next Window key (Shift-F6).

Quattro Pro enters Point mode and moves the cell selector to the last active cell in the next spreadsheet in memory. If you take a moment to look at the edit line in Figure 2.27, you'll see it now shows the + symbol followed by the full path and name of the current file, and a reference to that cell. Instead of the Shift-F6 method, you can press Alt followed by the window number to jump directly to a window. Finally, if you are using a mouse, and the PROFIT1.WQ1 window is visible, you can simply click on the window.

5. Once the cell selector is located in the PROFIT1.WQ1 spreadsheet, move it to cell B14. Quattro Pro updates the information in the edit line accordingly.

6. Press Enter to complete the formula. Quattro Pro returns you to cell B4 of the CASH.WQ1 file and places the formula you've just built in that cell.

After these actions, Quattro Pro displays the same value in cell B4 of CASH.WQ1 as it does in cell B14 of PROFIT1.WQ1.

The link formed between these two spreadsheets is dynamic. If you make a change to the PROFIT1.WQ1 spreadsheet that affects cell B14, the link formula in cell B4 of the CASH.WQ1 file will be updated automatically—provided, of course, that both files are open on the desktop. If CASH.WQ1 isn't open when you change the PROFIT1.WQ1 spreadsheet, Quattro Pro will update the CASH.WQ1 file the next time you open it. See the later section "Loading a Spreadsheet with Links" for details on how Quattro Pro goes about doing this.

The above procedure showed you how to use Point mode to build a link formula with a single reference. However, you can also use Point mode to build formulas with multiple link references. For example, rather than pressing Enter in step 6 to complete the link formula, you can type another operator—for example, + (plus). Quattro Pro then returns you to the cell in which you are building the formula, in this case, B4 of CASH.WQ1. At this point, the edit line contains +[PROFIT1]B14+. You can now point to an address in yet another open spreadsheet file, and Quattro Pro will append that reference to the end of the formula. When you press Enter to complete the formula, Quattro Pro uses both references in calculating the formula's result.

Linking to Files on Disk

You have read that you can also link to supporting spreadsheet files that are located on disk. In this case, you need not have both the primary and supporting spreadsheets open on the desktop. For example, imagine you are working with the same two files, CASH.WQ1 and PROFIT.WQ1. Only the CASH.WQ1 spreadsheet is open on the desktop. To create the link to cell

B14 of PROFIT1.WQ1, move the cell selector to cell B4 of CASH.WQ1, type **+[PROFIT1.WQ1]B14**, and press Enter. Quattro Pro returns the appropriate value from the PROFIT.WQ1 file, even if it isn't open on the desktop.

If the file to which you are linking is not located in the current directory, make sure you include in your link formula the full path and name of the supporting file. For example, if PROFIT1.WQ1 is located in C:\QPRO\SHEETS, you would use the following formula:

```
+[C:\QPRO\SHEETS\PROFIT1.WQ1]B14
```

The ability to link to closed files on disk lets you build a large model that might otherwise exceed the limits of your PC's RAM. That is, instead of building one large spreadsheet, you can build several smaller supporting ones and link them together by using a primary consolidation spreadsheet. Because Quattro Pro does not load any of the supporting spreadsheets into memory, but merely reads linked data from them, the consolidation spreadsheet uses far less RAM.

Using Wildcards in Link Formulas

Quattro Pro also lets you use special *wildcard* symbols in your link formulas to link to other files that are currently open on the desktop. You can use this feature to create three-dimensional link formulas.

If you are familiar with DOS, you know that the standard wildcard symbols are * (asterisk) and ? (question mark). These symbols serve as substitutes for letters in file names that are used in commands (COPY *.WQ1 A:), directory searches (DIR *.*), and so on. The * symbol represents any group of letters, and the ? symbol represents any single letter. Quattro Pro lets you use these symbols in link formulas to represent the names of files that are open on the desktop.

For example, imagine you want to create a link formula in the current spreadsheet that sums the contents of the block B4..B12 in all other open spreadsheet files. To do this, you might use the following formula:

```
@SUM([*]B4..B12)
```

In this case the * wildcard is used as the *file name* argument to represent any combination of letters that may be included in a file name. You can also add letters to this wildcard pattern to limit the files that are referenced by the formula, for example,

```
@SUM([P*]B4..B12)
```

This formula limits the @SUM function to only those open spreadsheets whose file names begin with the letter *P*.

The ? wildcard lets you be even more specific. Imagine you want to sum the range B4..B12 in all open files with file names that begin with the letter *P* and are no more than seven characters long (not including the extension). To do this, you would use the following formula:

```
@SUM([P??????]B4..B12)
```

Using Indirect References in Link Formulas

You can save yourself time and effort by using *indirect references* in your link formulas. Suppose you have a block of data in another spreadsheet to which you often refer. Rather than including a reference to that block in each of your link formulas, you can create, in one cell of the current spreadsheet, a single link formula that references the appropriate block. Then, whenever you need the data, you can simply refer to that cell. For example, imagine you frequently use this reference:

```
@AVG([C:\QPRO\SHEETS\SALES.WQ1]B14..H14)
```

Rather than typing this lengthy reference each time you need it, you can enter it once in any cell in the current spreadsheet. Then use the /Edit, Name, Create command to assign a block name to that cell—for example, S_AVG. From then on, you can simply reference the S_AVG block name in your link formula to get the data you need.

Creating a Link Library

You can use the indirect reference technique just described to create a special spreadsheet as a *link library*, containing only link formulas referring to other files that you use frequently. Once the library spreadsheet is built, you can then use /Edit, Name, Create to assign a memorable block name to each of its cells that contain a link formula. With this file always open on the desktop, you can use simple link formulas in the current spreadsheet to reference library formulas. This technique helps cut down on the time you spend building link formulas.

Let's say you frequently refer to various blocks in the SALES_92.WQ1, COGS_92.WQ1, and EXP_92.WQ1 files. Rather than having to constantly reference each of these files individually, you can put all the appropriate link formulas into a single spreadsheet file, say LIB_92.WQ1. Assign easy-to-remember block names to each cell containing a link formula, like SALES_AVG, SALES_ANNUAL, or VARIANCE. That way, you only have one file to worry about, instead of three. In addition, instead of having to enter lengthy link formulas in the current spreadsheet, such as

```
@SUM([C:\QPRO\ACCTG\SALES_92]B14..B12)
```

you can get by with the simpler formula

```
+[LIB_92]SALES_AVG
```

Loading a Spreadsheet with Links

Quattro Pro does not update a primary spreadsheet file on disk when you make a change to one of its supporting spreadsheets. Instead, when you load a primary spreadsheet that contains link formulas, Quattro Pro prompts you to update the link formulas it contains. This lets you keep the formulas in the primary spreadsheet always up-to-date.

To remind you to "refresh" your spreadsheet's link formulas, Quattro Pro displays the menu box shown in Figure 2.28 when you use either the /File, Retrieve or /File, Open command to open the file on disk. This menu box contains the following three options:

- *Load Supporting* opens the file on disk to which the link formulas in the current (primary) file refer. If a supporting spreadsheet also contains links, those supporting spreadsheets will be opened, as well. That way, the primary spreadsheet and all its supporting spreadsheets will be present in memory. Bear in mind that if you have many links in a large spreadsheet, this process can take quite a while. It can also eat up available memory in a hurry.

- *Update Refs* updates the link formulas' references to supporting spreadsheet files on disk. The supporting spreadsheets themselves remain closed on disk. This option takes less time and requires less memory. If you decide later that you want to load a supporting spreadsheet, you can always do so using the /Tools, Update Links, Open command discussed later under "Opening Linked Files."

- *None* replaces link formulas in the current file with the value NA (not available). This replacement is only temporary, and your link formulas are not affected. Use this option when you want to quickly open a big spreadsheet and edit data that is not related to the link formulas in the file. If you later change your mind and want to update the links in the current file, you can do so by using the /Tools, Update Links, Refresh command discussed later under "Updating Link Formulas."

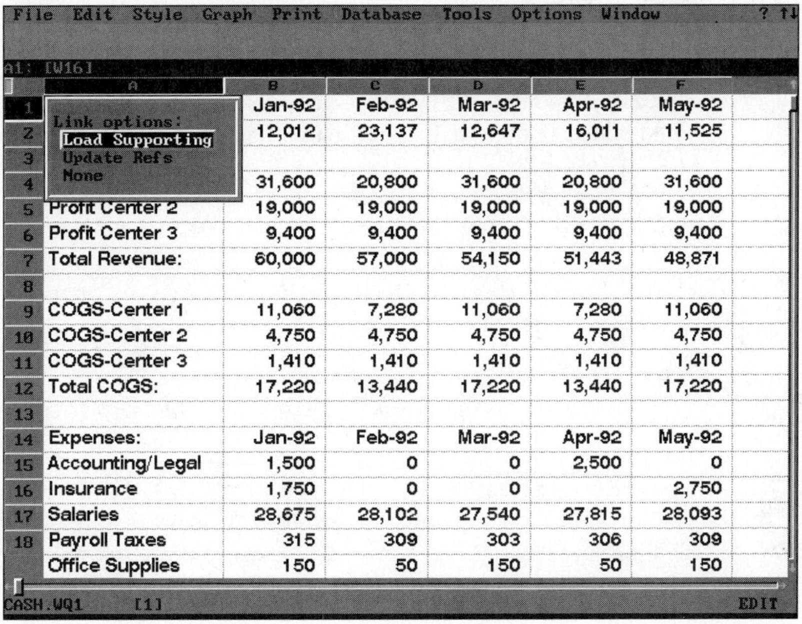

Figure 2.28
The prompt to update links that appears if you use /File, Open or Retrieve

```
 File  Edit  Style  Graph  Print  Database  Tools  Options  Window        ? ↑↓
A1: [W16]
            A              B        C        D        E        F
 1                      Jan-92   Feb-92   Mar-92   Apr-92   May-92
 2   Link options:     12,012   23,137   12,647   16,011   11,525
     Load Supporting
 3   Update Refs
 4   None              31,600   20,800   31,600   20,800   31,600
 5   Profit Center 2   19,000   19,000   19,000   19,000   19,000
 6   Profit Center 3    9,400    9,400    9,400    9,400    9,400
 7   Total Revenue:    60,000   57,000   54,150   51,443   48,871
 8
 9   COGS-Center 1     11,060    7,280   11,060    7,280   11,060
10   COGS-Center 2      4,750    4,750    4,750    4,750    4,750
11   COGS-Center 3      1,410    1,410    1,410    1,410    1,410
12   Total COGS:       17,220   13,440   17,220   13,440   17,220
13
14   Expenses:         Jan-92   Feb-92   Mar-92   Apr-92   May-92
15   Accounting/Legal   1,500        0        0    2,500        0
16   Insurance          1,750        0        0             2,750
17   Salaries          28,675   28,102   27,540   27,815   28,093
18   Payroll Taxes        315      309      303      306      309
     Office Supplies      150       50      150       50      150
CASH.WQ1    [1]                                              EDIT
```

Potential Problems with Linked Spreadsheets

You can run into problems with linked spreadsheets if you create circular links. For example, suppose you are working with three spreadsheets, SHEET1.WQ1, SHEET2.WQ1, and SHEET3.WQ1. SHEET1.WQ1 contains a link formula that refers to SHEET2.WQ1, and SHEET2.WQ1 contains a link formula that refers to SHEET3.WQ1. To complete the circle, SHEET3.WQ1 contains a link formula that refers to SHEET1.WQ1. Thus a network of circular links has been created, as shown in Figure 2.29.

Figure 2.29
A network of circular links in three spreadsheet

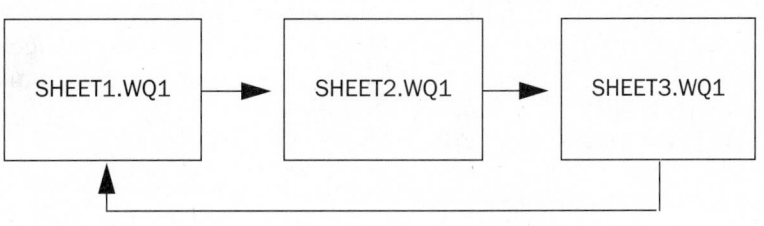

While all of these spreadsheets are open on the desktop, no problems occur. However, if only SHEET1.WQ1 is open, its link formulas may not be returning accurate results. As you can see in Figure 2.29, SHEET1 gets its data from SHEET2, SHEET2 in turn relies on SHEET3, and finally SHEET3 relies on SHEET1. If SHEET1 is the only spreadsheet open, however, and you make a change to it that will affect SHEET3, that change will not be passed on to SHEET3 because it is not open on the desktop. In addition, SHEET2 won't be current because it relies on SHEET3. Moving up the chain, SHEET1 won't be current because it relies on SHEET2, and so on. Obviously, you should avoid creating a network of circular link formulas, but if you must use this technique, make sure *all* the affected files are open on the desktop when you make changes to any of the files involved in the circle.

NOTE. *Although the new /Tools, Audit command can help you chase circular references within a spreadsheet, it won't help you trace circular references between spreadsheets.*

Occasionally, Quattro Pro may not be able to find the supporting spreadsheets referenced in your link formulas. This often happens when the supporting spreadsheet file is not in the current directory and you forget to precede its file name (in the formula) with the appropriate path. Quattro Pro helps you by displaying NA in the cell when you press Enter to complete the link formula, informing you that it cannot find the file you've referenced. All formulas whose values depend on that cell will, of course, return NA as well. If, at a later time, you use the /File, Directory command to make the appropriate directory current, Quattro Pro will thus gain access to the needed file. You can then select the /Tools, Update Links, Refresh command to make the formula return a valid result (see "Updating Link Formulas" later in this chapter).

Managing Link Formulas

To help you manage your link formulas, Quattro Pro offers the /Tools, Update Links command. When you select this command, Quattro Pro displays a menu with four options: Open, Refresh, Change, and Delete. You can use these options to open files linked to the current file, update the links in the current file, change the formula references in the current file to reference another supporting spreadsheet, and delete links in the current file that refer to a specific supporting spreadsheet.

Opening Linked Files

The /Tools, Update Links, Open command lets you open one or more of the supporting spreadsheets that are linked to the current file. For example, suppose you have used the /File, Open command to open a spreadsheet containing link formulas and you have selected the Update Refs option. Thus, the link formulas in the spreadsheet have been updated, but the supporting spreadsheets remain closed on disk. To open one or more of these supporting spreadsheets, select /Tools, Update Links, Open. Quattro Pro shows you a list of the spreadsheets linked to the current spreadsheet. Choose the name of the supporting spreadsheets you want to open by highlighting each name one at a time and pressing the Select key sequence (Shift-F7). Each file you select in this way appears with a check mark next to its name. To unselect a file, press Select (Shift-F7) a second time. To select all the names in the list, use the Select All key sequence (Alt-F7). To complete the command, press Enter, and Quattro Pro opens all the files you've selected on the desktop.

Updating Link Formulas

The /Tools, Update Links, Refresh command lets you update the link formulas in the current spreadsheet file. However, the supporting spreadsheet files remain closed on disk. You might want to use this option in a network environment where multiple users have access to Quattro Pro data files in shared directories and a file you are linked to may be changed without your knowledge.

When you select /Tools, Update Links, Refresh, Quattro Pro displays a list of supporting spreadsheets that are linked to the current spreadsheet. Choose the supporting spreadsheets whose links you want to update, as described in the previous section. When you've chosen the names you want, press Enter, and Quattro Pro updates all the link formulas in the current file that refer to the files you've selected.

Changing Links to Reference a New File

The /Tools, Update Links, Change command lets you switch the link formula references in the current primary file from one supporting spreadsheet to another. You can use this command to evaluate the link formulas in the primary spreadsheet under different supporting scenarios. This feature is also useful when you've renamed a supporting spreadsheet.

CAUTION! *Be aware that when the links are changed to reference the new file, they will reference the same blocks as they did in the old file. Therefore, the new supporting spreadsheet must have the same structure as the old one. Otherwise, the affected link formulas will evaluate to ERR.*

When you select the /Tools, Update Links, Change command, Quattro Pro displays a list of supporting spreadsheets that are linked to the current spreadsheet. Highlight the name of the supporting spreadsheet you no longer want to reference in the link formulas, and press Enter. Quattro Pro displays a prompt box asking you for the name of the new file you want the links to reference. Type the name of the new file and press Enter. Quattro Pro changes the affected links in the current primary file from the old supporting file to the new one. The affected link formulas are updated accordingly.

Deleting Links

Use the /Tools, Update Links, Delete command to delete the links to a specific supporting spreadsheet in the primary file. When you select this command, Quattro Pro displays a list of supporting spreadsheets linked to the current file. Select the name of each supporting file you want to unlink from the current file, using the techniques described in "Opening Linked Files." When you've chosen the name(s) you want, press Enter, and Quattro Pro unlinks all the supporting files you've selected from the current file.

When you delete links, be aware that all the affected link formulas remain in the primary file. What's more, they now evaluate to ERR. You'll have to go through the spreadsheet and manually edit these formulas to return a valid result.

NOTE. *For additional information about copying and moving link formulas, both within the current file and between files, see Chapter 4.*

Linking to Lotus 1-2-3 Files

It is possible to create a link formula in a Quattro Pro spreadsheet that references a block (range) in a Lotus 1-2-3 file. That file can either be open on the Quattro Pro desktop or closed on disk. In fact, there are no special considerations for linking to 1-2-3 files, other than to make sure you use the extension in your file reference. For example, here is a formula that references a 1-2-3 file:

```
+[C:\LOTUS\ACCT23\ACCTPAB.WK3]B4
```

As long as you include the .WK3 extension with the referenced file name, you can link to a 1-2-3 Release 3 file whenever you want.

NOTE. *In Quattro Pro 4.0, you can link to both .WK1 and .WK3 files. In Quattro Pro 3.0, you're limited to .WK1 files (Lotus 1-2-3 Release 2.2).*

If you are familiar with 1-2-3 Releases 2.2 or 3, you know that they, too, support file-linking formulas. In fact, the syntax used by 1-2-3 is somewhat similar to that of Quattro Pro. Here are examples of linking formulas in all three applications:

- **Quattro Pro**: [SALES_92]B12

- **1-2-3 Release 2.2**: +<<SALES_92.WK1>>B12

- **1-2-3 Release 3.x**: +<<SALES_92.WK3>>B12

You'll notice that the primary difference here is the brackets used to enclose the file reference. Quattro Pro uses square brackets, and 1-2-3 requires double-arrow brackets.

In Quattro Pro 3.0, when you load a 1-2-3 file that contains formula links, the double-arrow brackets in those formulas are replaced by square brackets. That way, the formula links continue to return valid results under Quattro Pro. Then you can use the /File, Save As command and specify a .WQ1 extension to save the file in Quattro Pro's file format. However, if you try to use /File, Save to save a .WK1 file in Quattro Pro, you'll see a warning prompt with three menu options: No, Yes, and Use 2.2 Syntax. These menu options have the following effects:

- *No* cancels the save operation. Quattro Pro displays a warning message that the file has been deleted from disk. At this point you are on dangerous ground, because the only copy that exists of that file is in your computer's RAM. So if you wish to use this 1-2-3 file again, you *must* save it to disk. Select the /File, Save As command, specify a .WQ1 extension for the file, and press Enter.

- *Yes* saves the file to disk but converts all link formulas to their current values. The original link references are lost.

- *Use 2.2 Syntax* saves the current file in 1-2-3 Release 2.2 file format, using the appropriate 1-2-3 file-linking syntax.

Quattro Pro 4.0 handles 1-2-3 Release 2.2 files with link formulas in much the same way as Quattro Pro 3.0. However, Quattro Pro 4.0 also lets you open and save 1-2-3 Release 3.x and 1-2-3 for Windows .WK3 files that contain link formulas. These files are handled a little differently.

When you open a 1-2-3 Release 3.x file that contains link formulas, Quattro Pro displays

```
Formula contains hot links
```

in the cell containing the formula. The formula continues, however, to return valid results, and you can build other formulas in the file that refer to that formula. If you save the file with a .WK3 extension (meaning it will be saved in Release 3 format), Quattro Pro 4.0 will not save the link formulas in a format that 1-2-3 can use. Instead, it will replace the formulas with zeros.

Protecting Areas of the Spreadsheet

Now that you've learned so many facts about using Quattro Pro's spreadsheet windows and files, let's take a look at a new subject: protecting your data.

If the spreadsheet you are preparing is to be used by others, you may want to *protect* it. By protecting a spreadsheet, you can shield certain cell blocks to prevent users (even yourself!) from accidentally changing their contents. You can also eliminate the risk of damaging the spreadsheet with the /Edit, Erase Block command, where a single mistake might accidentally destroy hours of work.

When you start a new spreadsheet, every cell in it is unprotected; global spreadsheet protection is not active. This means that you can change the contents of cells without any thought as to whether cells are protected or not. Only when you activate global spreadsheet protection—using the /Options, Protection, Enable command—are cells actually shielded from harm. With protection enabled, you can move around the spreadsheet in the usual fashion, but you cannot enter new data or edit existing data in any cells. If you want to be able to change the contents of a spreadsheet's cells, you must selectively unprotect them using the /Style, Protection, Unprotect command.

Turning Protection On and Off

Because Quattro Pro's spreadsheet protection feature is a little puzzling at first, you may find it easier to understand in an example. Imagine that you have created a spreadsheet that will be used by others, and you want to protect certain cells from any edits, deletions, or overwrites. To start with, you select /Options, Protection, Enable to turn on global protection for the *entire* spreadsheet. At this point, all the cells in the spreadsheet are protected. Look at the input line as you move the cell selector around the spreadsheet, and you'll notice that every cell address is followed by the letters PR (for protected), like this:

```
D21: PR 2436
```

Of course, it's not practical to have every cell in the spreadsheet protected. Therefore, you use the /Style, Protection, Unprotect command to unprotect the cells you want users to be able to edit. When you select this command, Quattro Pro prompts you for the block of cells you want to unprotect and shows the current cell address after the prompt. Once you select a block and press Enter, Quattro Pro shows U in place of PR in the input line for each cell or block of cells you unprotect.

If you want to disable global protection entirely so you can change the contents of any spreadsheet cell, just turn off global protection with the /Options, Protection, Disable command. Then, after you've finished editing the spreadsheet, you can turn global protection on again with /Options, Protection, Enable.

The foregoing example assumes that you turn on global protection at the start, but you don't have to do it this way. You may prefer instead to selectively unprotect and protect cells, and then turn on global protection. The most common protection method of all, however, is to jump back and forth—turning global protection on and off, protecting and unprotecting cells as needed—until you get your spreadsheet just the way you want it.

NOTE. *Normally Quattro Pro displays unprotected cells in cyan on a color screen. In WYSIWYG mode, the command to change the display color of unprotected cells is /Options, Colors, Spreadsheet, WYSIWYG Colors, Unprotected. In Character mode, the command is /Options, Colors, Spreadsheet, Unprotected.*

The Effects of Protection

Note. If you want to restrict cell selector movement to unprotected cells only, use the /Database, Restrict Input command. See Chapter 10.

Of course, the most significant effect of enabling global spreadsheet protection is that you cannot modify the contents of protected cells. Here are some side effects that are not so apparent:

- You cannot use /Edit, Erase Block or the Del key to delete the contents of protected cells.

- You cannot use /Edit, Move or /Edit, Copy to move or copy data to a protected cell. You can, however, move or copy the contents of a protected cell to an unprotected cell.

- You cannot use /Edit, Insert, Rows or Columns, or /Edit, Delete, Rows or Columns to insert/delete columns and rows when global protection is enabled.

CAUTION! *Even when you enable global spreadsheet protection, users can still use the /File, Erase command to erase the contents of the spreadsheet from memory. Likewise, the /File, Close command can be used to erase a protected file from memory and close its window. Quattro Pro has no way to guard against the use of these commands.*

Protecting Formulas in Quattro Pro 4.0

If you've ever created a spreadsheet for clients or for use by others, you'll be interested in a new feature in Quattro Pro 4.0: /Options, Protection, Formulas. Because you can now password-protect only the formulas and functions in a spreadsheet, this command makes it easy to protect your logic while still allowing limited user access.

To turn on the protection, simply select /Options, Protection, Formulas, Protect, as shown in Figure 2.30. This accesses a prompt box where you must type in a password consisting of 1 to 15 letters, numbers, and/or nonalphabetic characters. (Remember, passwords are case-sensitive.) Press Enter, and then reenter the password for verification purposes. Press Enter a second time; when you return to the spreadsheet, all the formulas and functions in the spreadsheet are protected.

Figure 2.30

Protecting formulas

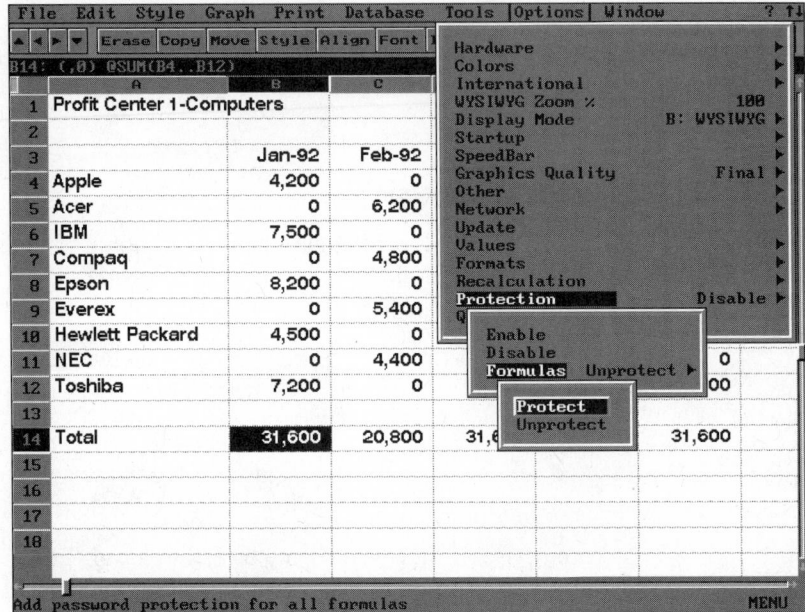

NOTE. *A password is saved with the spreadsheet file. If you don't save the file after protecting formulas, they won't be protected the next time the file is opened.*

If you need to edit any protected formula, you have to unprotect all of them by using /Options, Protection, Formulas, Unprotect and entering the password. To turn on the protection again, reuse /Options, Protection, Formulas, Protect. At this point, if you so choose, you can use a new password; the first one is history.

3

Changing the
Appearance of Data

A S YOU BECOME SKILLED IN BUILDING SPREADSHEETS, YOU'LL DISCOVER that there are several elements to spreadsheet design. The initial challenge is to develop a layout that is relevant to your data. The more subtle component of spreadsheet design, however, is the art of presentation. Your comprehensive data, intricate formulas, and perceptive analyses will go unnoticed if the final product appears cluttered and difficult to read.

In this chapter, you will learn how to *format* spreadsheets, adding the finishing touches that make them more inviting to read. When you *format* a spreadsheet, you arrange the layout of your data. For example, you can use Quattro Pro's impressive collection of formatting commands to realign the data in blocks of cells, change the format of values (such as adding commas, dollar signs, or percent symbols), adjust the width of columns, and hide blocks or columns of cells. You can also use Quattro Pro's presentation-quality format commands to add impact to your final draft by including lines and boxes around cells, bulleted lists with any of the seven bullet symbols, shading, and up to eight different typestyles (fonts).

Formatting techniques in Quattro Pro are discussed in three sections in this chapter: changing how labels and numbers appear, manipulating columns, and adding presentation-quality effects.

Global Formats Versus Block Formats

Quattro Pro allows you to assign global formats and block formats to a spreadsheet. *Global formats* affect the entire spreadsheet; *block formats* affect smaller areas of the spreadsheet, such as single cells or groups of cells. Every format option in Quattro Pro, except line drawing and shading, can be set globally as the default for the entire spreadsheet using the /Options, Formats and /Options, International commands, and locally for specific blocks using the /Style command.

Global Formats

During installation, Quattro Pro preassigns certain settings that affect the appearance of data. These settings become the *default formats* for each new spreadsheet. Many of these settings are accessible through the /Options, Formats menu shown in Figure 3.1. Because these default settings affect every cell in a new spreadsheet, they are known as *global* formats.

As you can see, Quattro Pro's global default settings include a nine-character column width, left label alignment, the General numeric format, and displayed zeros. The Font 1 typestyle, accessed through the /Style command, is the default font displayed in the spreadsheet in WYSIWYG mode and for printing to a printer in graphics mode.

Figure 3.1
The /Options,
Formats menu

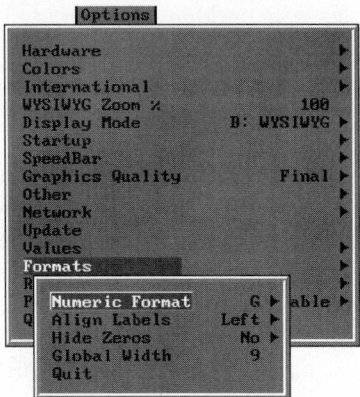

You can change the global formats for each spreadsheet with the /Options, Formats command. When you alter a global setting, it becomes the new default for the current spreadsheet. Any data that you enter uses this new global setting, except for the blocks you have previously formatted with the /Style command (see "Block Formats," just below).

The exception is /Global, Formats, Hide Zeros, which controls the display of zeros in a spreadsheet. The default setting is No, which means zeros are displayed. If you choose to set /Global, Formats, Hide Zeros to Yes, Quattro Pro does not save this setting when you save a spreadsheet. So you must choose this setting each time you retrieve a file.

When you change global format settings with the /Options, Formats command, they affect only the *current* spreadsheet. The /Options, Update command does not store them as the defaults for other spreadsheets. For all *new* spreadsheets, Quattro Pro always uses the defaults shown in Figure 3.1.

Certain global settings—currency symbol and placement, punctuation symbols, as well as international date and time formats—are accessed through the /Options, International command (Chapter 15). These global default settings can be saved for all future sessions by using the /Options, Update command.

TIP. *In Quattro Pro 4.0, /Options, Formats, Numeric Format and Align Labels are also controlled by the numeric format and alignment settings of the named style NORMAL. See "Creating Named Styles in Quattro Pro 4.0" at the end of this chapter.*

Block Formats

You can assign a different format to small areas of a spreadsheet using the /Style command, illustrated in Figure 3.2. A block format set with one of the /Style options *overrides* any /Options, Formats global default settings. So use block formats to assign a variety of other format settings in addition to your global default settings.

Figure 3.2
The /Style menu

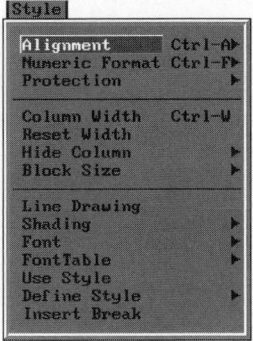

Memory Usage Considerations

Quattro Pro requires little or no extra RAM to store Global settings assigned with the /Options, Formats command. On the other hand, because numeric, alignment, and font formats set with the /Style command use up available RAM, you'll want to exercise some caution when formatting large blocks. Table 3.1 shows the approximate RAM required to format a cell with some of the /Style commands.

Table 3.1   **Memory (RAM) Usage of Some /Style Commands**

Command	Minimum RAM per Cell
/Style, Alignment	2 bytes
/Style, Numeric Format	4 bytes
/Style, Font (Fonts 2–8)	2 bytes

Since Quattro Pro's memory management scheme allocates RAM differently depending on the size and shape of a block of data, the amount of RAM required to store cell formats may differ from one spreadsheet to another. For example, say you want to format columns A through D of a spreadsheet with /Style, Numeric Format, Currency 2. Because you aren't sure how many rows you'll be using, you indicate the block A1..D8192, just for good measure. If you check available RAM (using the /Options, Hardware command) before and after specifying this /Style setting, you'll notice that it takes approximately 131,000 bytes of RAM to format this large, mostly blank area.

Clearly, haphazard use of the /Style command can significantly reduce the amount of available RAM. You should therefore use the global format commands to set formats that apply to the majority of a spreadsheet, saving the /Style command for smaller areas of data. This strategy allows you to conserve your computer's RAM for your data, formulas, and graphics.

Formatting Data

Once you've entered data and formulas into a new spreadsheet, you will want to make adjustments to create a more readable layout. Columns may need widening to space data better; descriptive labels at the top of columns may be out of sync with the values below them, and values may not line up on the decimal point. In Quattro Pro, a few simple changes can turn a rough layout into a crisp and easy-to-read format.

NOTE. *When you format data, Quattro Pro only changes the way data is displayed. If you place the cell selector on a formatted cell and examine the data in the input line, you'll notice that it is stored just as you entered it.*

Adjusting Data Alignment

For values and labels in a spreadsheet, Quattro Pro's /Options, Formats default settings (Figure 3.1) include the general numeric format, which aligns *values* at the *right* edge of a cell (see "Changing the Appearance of Numbers" later in this chapter), and the Align Labels, Left setting, which aligns *labels* at the *left* edge of a cell.

Specifying Label Alignment for a Cell

To specify a label alignment for a specific cell, include one of the following *label prefix* characters at the beginning of the label:

Label Prefix	Effect
^	Centers a label
"	Right-aligns a label
,	Left-aligns a label

These label prefixes override *both* the /Style, Alignment and /Options, Formats, Align Labels settings. (See "Entering Data in Cells" in Chapter 1.)

Aligning a Block of Data

The /Style, Alignment command aligns the contents (labels and values) of each cell in a block, to the left, right, or center of the cell. Use this command to align blocks of data to a nondefault format. You can also use /Style, Alignment to realign blocks of data to the global default setting.

The /Style, Alignment command aligns labels and values, including those returned by formulas, as follows:

/Style, Alignment Option	Effect
Left	Aligns data at the left edge of a cell
Right	Aligns data at the right edge of a cell
Center	Aligns data in the center of a cell
General	Aligns data using the current global default settings

If these have not been changed, values are right-aligned and labels left-aligned by default. (See "Setting the Global Label Alignment" later in this chapter.)

TIP. *In Quattro Pro 4.0,* `Align` *in the SpeedBar is a shortcut for /Style, Alignment.*

Consider the Regional Sales data in Figure 3.3, which has been aligned using the following /Style, Alignment options:

Column	/Style, Alignment option
A	General
C	Left
E	Center
G	Right

You can see immediately that, for this particular set of data, the right-aligned column G is easiest to read. When selecting an alignment option for labels and values, you'll want to choose the one most appropriate for the type of data you are presenting.

Figure 3.3

Examples of various Alignment settings

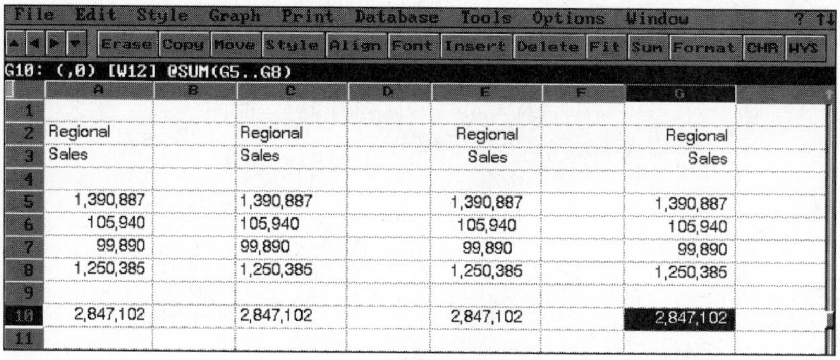

Now take a look at the quarterly sales information for the Action Video store, shown in Figure 3.4, which is entered without changing Quattro Pro's global default settings. The store organizes its video tapes by category and assigns a shelf location to each. Notice that the shelf location entries in column C almost look like they're in two different columns. The label entries New and Beta align to the left edge of the cell, and the shelf numbers, entered as values, align to the right. Furthermore, although the descriptive labels at the top of columns D, E, F, and G align to the left, the sales figures entered in rows 5 through 11 line up to the right. As you look at the spreadsheet, it's hard to tell which column heads apply to the data below them.

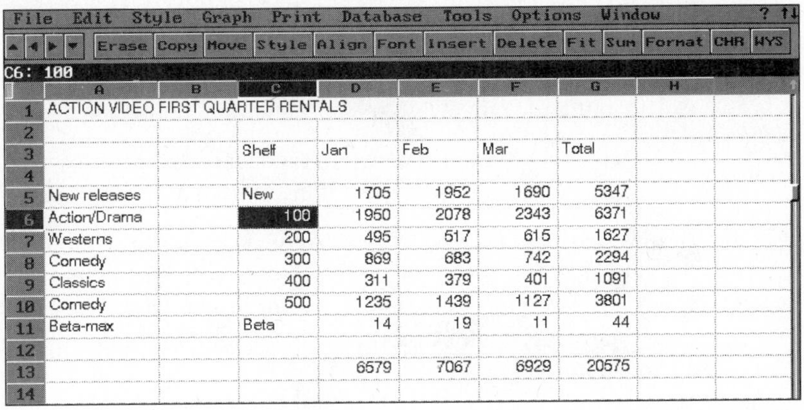

Figure 3.4
Data using the global default left-alignment

File	Edit	Style	Graph	Print	Database	Tools	Options	Window		? ↑↓

| ▲ ◄ ► ▼ | Erase | Copy | Move | Style | Align | Font | Insert | Delete | Fit | Sum | Format | CHR | WYS |

C6: 100

	A	B	C	D	E	F	G	H
1	ACTION VIDEO FIRST QUARTER RENTALS							
2								
3			Shelf	Jan	Feb	Mar	Total	
4								
5	New releases		New	1705	1952	1690	5347	
6	Action/Drama		100	1950	2078	2343	6371	
7	Westerns		200	495	517	615	1627	
8	Comedy		300	869	683	742	2294	
9	Classics		400	311	379	401	1091	
10	Comedy		500	1235	1439	1127	3801	
11	Beta-max		Beta	14	19	11	44	
12								
13				6579	7067	6929	20575	
14								

Here's how to correct this awkward alignment, using the /Style, Alignment command or the Align button:

- The shelf locations in column C will be easier to read if all the entries are aligned to the left, under the shelf label. To do this, assign a Left alignment to C6..C11 by using /Style, Alignment, Left.

- Next you'll want to change the alignment so the month names appear directly above the sales figures by assigning a Right alignment to D3..G3.

The result of these simple alignment changes, shown in Figure 3.5, is a spreadsheet that is crisp and easy to read.

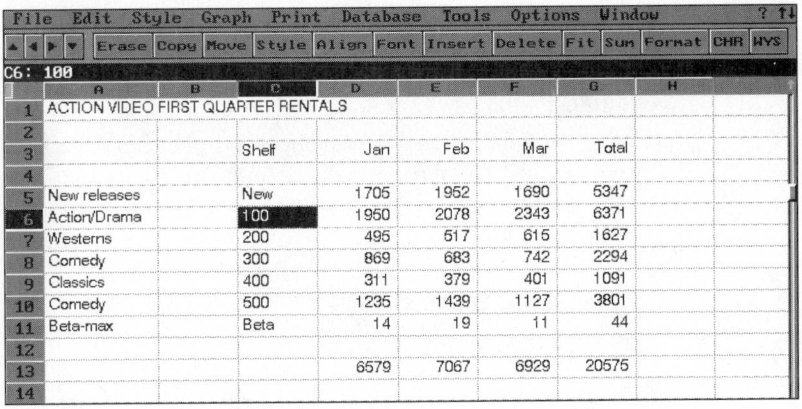

Figure 3.5
The spreadsheet from Figure 3.4 after using /Style, Alignment

File	Edit	Style	Graph	Print	Database	Tools	Options	Window		? ↑↓

| ▲ ◄ ► ▼ | Erase | Copy | Move | Style | Align | Font | Insert | Delete | Fit | Sum | Format | CHR | WYS |

C6: 100

	A	B	C	D	E	F	G	H
1	ACTION VIDEO FIRST QUARTER RENTALS							
2								
3			Shelf	Jan	Feb	Mar	Total	
4								
5	New releases		New	1705	1952	1690	5347	
6	Action/Drama		100	1950	2078	2343	6371	
7	Westerns		200	495	517	615	1627	
8	Comedy		300	869	683	742	2294	
9	Classics		400	311	379	401	1091	
10	Comedy		500	1235	1439	1127	3801	
11	Beta-max		Beta	14	19	11	44	
12								
13				6579	7067	6929	20575	
14								

Keep in mind the following when you use the /Style, Alignment command:

- Ctrl-A is the shortcut key for /Style, Alignment.

- The /Style, Alignment command is stronger than the /Options, Formats command, and always overrides default spreadsheet settings.

- Any row or column you insert in a spreadsheet uses the /Options, Formats default settings, even if inserted in a block previously formatted.

- When label entries appear out of sync with the numeric data below them, it's easier to align the *labels* to conform to the *value* alignment, rather than try to realign the values to match the labels. As illustrated in Figure 3.3, center or left alignment sometimes makes values more difficult to read or analyze.

- When you enter data in a cell that has been formatted with /Style, Alignment, only a value or date entry reflects the /Style, Alignment setting. A new label entry aligns according to the global setting in the /Options, Formats, Align Labels command.

- When you use the /Edit, Copy or Move commands, these commands also copy or move any /Style, Alignment settings assigned to the block.

- Block or global alignment settings may not appear to affect labels or values that are the same width or wider than a cell. Increase the column width, and the alignment settings will become apparent. (See "Working with Columns" later in this chapter.)

Setting the Global Label Alignment

Tip. The /Style, Alignment, General command resets labels to the global /Options, Formats, Align Labels setting currently in effect.

You can have Quattro Pro center- or right-align labels as you enter them; just change the global default Left label alignment using /Options, Formats, Align Labels. This command allows you to preset the label alignment for the entire spreadsheet, so you don't have to change the alignment of a block of labels after you've entered them. /Options, Formats, Align Labels has no effect on existing labels in a spreadsheet; it only affects new labels as they are entered, aligning them to the new default setting.

For example, suppose you want to type some descriptive labels at the top of each column in a spreadsheet, and you'd like each one to right-align as you enter it. Select /Options, Formats, Align Labels, Right; as you enter the labels, each one will align to the right edge of the cell. When you are done, reset the global alignment to the original setting using /Options, Formats, Align Labels, Left. Existing labels are unchanged, but any future label entries will use the default Left alignment.

TIP. *In Quattro Pro 4.0, the /Options, Formats, Align Labels default is also controlled by the alignment setting in the named style NORMAL (accessed through /Style, Define Style, Create). That is, if you change the NORMAL Alignment setting to Center, then /Options, Formats, Align Labels automatically changes to reflect this. Likewise, change the /Options, Formats, Align Labels setting to Right, and the NORMAL alignment changes to this setting. See "Creating Named Styles in Quattro Pro 4.0," later.*

Changing the Appearance of Numbers

When you enter values into a spreadsheet, they are seldom displayed the way you envisioned them. Values may appear somewhat erratic, for example, because numbers with decimals don't line up with whole numbers, and large numbers are hard to read without comma separators between the hundreds and thousands. What's worse, a number that is too large for a cell may end up looking something like 1.2E+08, which makes many new users shut off their computer and abstain from any further spreadsheet activities.

The manner in which Quattro Pro displays values is known as *numeric format*. The default numeric format, General, typically displays values in a somewhat disorganized fashion. However, Quattro Pro offers a variety of other numeric formats, shown in Table 3.2. For example, you can set uniform decimal places, add commas between hundreds and thousands, and add currency symbols. You can also display percent symbols, choose among various date and time formats for date values, and even hide cell contents. All eleven formats are discussed in detail in this section.

Table 3.2 **Numeric Format Options**

Format	Description	Example
Fixed	Displays values with a specified number of decimal places from 0 to 15. Displays leading zeros.	12.00 0.7759 –1500
Scientific	Displays values in an exponential format called scientific notation. Only one integer is displayed, with 0 to 15 decimal places.	1.5E+08 2.22E+14 3.23E–05
Currency	Displays values with a leading currency symbol, commas separating thousands, and negative numbers in parentheses.	$2,150.00 (15.75) ¥190

Table 3.2 **(Continued)**

Format	Description	Example
,(Comma)	Separates thousands with commas. Negative values appear in parentheses. 0 to 15 decimal places.	7,500 (14.95) 150,750.00
General	Displays values as entered. Leading or trailing zeros are not displayed. If values are too long for the cell, they are rounded if fractional, or displayed in scientific notation.	14.759 –35 1500000
+/–	Creates a horizontal bar graph by converting a value to a corresponding number of + or – symbols, depending on the sign. Zero values are represented with a . character.	+++++++++++ ——————— .
Percent	Multiplies values by 100, with 0 to 15 decimal places. Adds a trailing percent symbol.	75% 12.50% –.03%
Date	Offers five different formats for date values, and four formats for time values.	Nov-90, 15-Jan-91 12:01:35PM, 08:56
Text	Displays the underlying formula instead of its results.	+A4*B6 @SUM(B15..H15)
Hidden	Hides the contents of a cell. Cell entries are still visible on the input line when the cell is selected.	
Reset	Returns the cell to the global numeric format. Cells formatted with the Hidden format redisplay their contents.	

Quattro Pro's numeric formats, listed in Figure 3.6, affect only the way values are displayed, not the way they are stored. For example, if you enter the value .0115 in a cell and format it as Percent 2 (Percent format using two decimal places), it will be displayed as 1.15%. However, when the cell pointer is in that cell, the input line shows the value is still stored in its original form, .0115.

How the Font and Numeric Format Affect the Size of Values Displayed

Both the font and the numeric format you choose affect the size of values that are displayed within a given column width. Changing from a streamlined numeric format, such as General, to another format, such as Currency, decreases the size of the values displayed in a given column width. That's because extra characters such as $, and . usually take up one column-width space each. For large numbers, sometimes a proportionally spaced font requires less space. For example, the proportional Swiss font requires a column width of 13 to display $2,000,000.00 although the fixed-width Monospace and Courier fonts need a column width of 14.

Figure 3.6

The /Options, Formats, Numeric Format menu

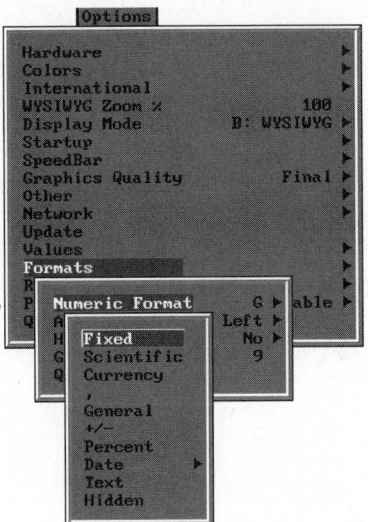

NOTE. *In Quattro Pro, each column-width character represents one 10-cpi fixed-width character; the default column width of 9 represents nine 10-cpi characters. This means that, especially for a proportionally spaced font, this character-based unit of measurement doesn't indicate the number of characters that will fit. See "Fonts" for further discussion.*

Setting a Global Numeric Format

You can use the /Options, Formats, Numeric Format command to specify a new default numeric format for an entire spreadsheet. Suppose, for example, that you want all values to be displayed using the Fixed 2 format (Fixed format with two decimal places). To do this,

1. Select /Options, Formats, Numeric Formats. Quattro Pro displays the pull-down menu shown in Figure 3.6, which lists all the numeric format options.

2. Select Fixed and press Enter.

3. You'll be prompted to "Enter number of decimal places [0..15]: 2." Just press Enter to confirm the default of two decimal places.

4. Select Quit twice to return to the spreadsheet.

Now all existing values in the spreadsheet are displayed with two decimal places, with the exception of any you have previously formatted with /Style, Numeric Format. Any new values you enter will also use this default Fixed 2 format.

The /Options, Formats, Numeric Format setting only controls the default format for the current spreadsheet. Selecting /Options, Update won't change the global numeric format for future sessions.

TIP. *In Quattro Pro 4.0, the /Options, Formats, Numeric Format default is also controlled by the numeric format setting in the named style NORMAL (accessed through /Style, Define Style, Create). That is, if you change the NORMAL Numeric Format setting to Currency 0 places or even to a custom numeric format, the /Options, Formats, Numeric Format setting automatically changes to reflect this. Likewise, change the /Options, Formats, Numeric Format setting to Percent 2 places, and the NORMAL numeric format changes to this setting. See "Using Custom User-Defined Numeric Formats in Quattro Pro 4.0," later.*

Setting the Numeric Format for Specific Blocks

Tip. In Quattro Pro 4.0, `Format` in the SpeedBar is a shortcut for /Style, Numeric Format.

Although your default numeric format may be working perfectly for most values in your spreadsheet, you may need percent symbols or currency signs to clarify the meaning of some values. In Quattro Pro, you can format a specific block using any of the /Style, Numeric Format options shown in Figure 3.7. (Note that except for the Reset option, these are identical to the global numeric format options shown in Figure 3.6.)

Say, for example, that you are setting up your checkbook register in Quattro Pro. Since you're entering financial information, you'll want to preset this spreadsheet to display the values in financial format: dollar signs, comma separators, and decimal places. To do this, you use the /Options, Formats, Numeric Format, Currency 2 command.

As you enter your first check, however, the flaw in your scheme becomes glaringly apparent: The data looks great—except for the check numbers! Because you entered these check numbers as values, they are displayed in Figure 3.8 with the global default Currency 2 format. Naturally, they bear no resemblance to check numbers and make your check register difficult to understand.

Figure 3.7

The /Style,
Numeric Format
menu

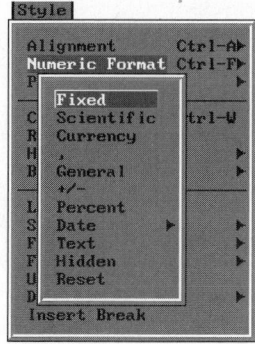

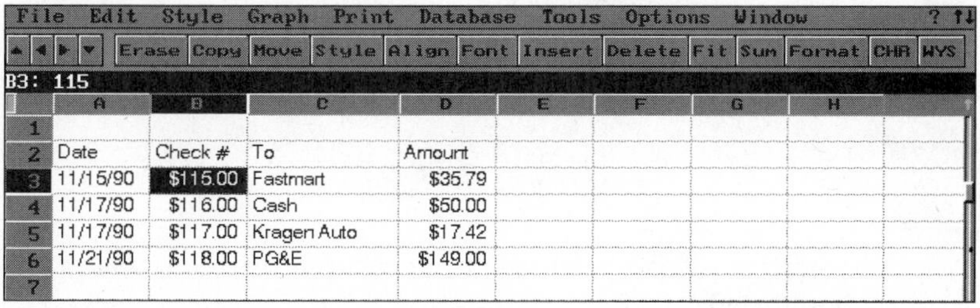

Figure 3.8

A global numeric
format
inappropriate for
column B

File	Edit	Style	Graph	Print	Database	Tools	Options	Window		? ↑↓

▲ ◀ ▶ ▼	Erase	Copy	Move	Style	Align	Font	Insert	Delete	Fit	Sum	Format	CHR	WYS

B3: 115

	A	B	C	D	E	F	G	H	
1									
2	Date	Check #	To	Amount					
3	11/15/90	$115.00	Fastmart	$35.79					
4	11/17/90	$116.00	Cash	$50.00					
5	11/17/90	$117.00	Kragen Auto	$17.42					
6	11/21/90	$118.00	PG&E	$149.00					
7									

To correct the problem in column B, you need to override the global setting with a more appropriate format. So preselect B3..B6, and then use
/Style, Numeric Format or the Format button. Assigning a General format
correctly displays each check number without dollar signs and decimal places.

Once you use /Style, Numeric Format to assign a block's numeric format,
this block will be unaffected if you select a new global default format for the
spreadsheet. In other words, the /Style, Numeric Format command is stronger than the /Options, Formats, Numeric Format command, and always overrides the default spreadsheet setting.

You can tell at a glance if a specific cell has been assigned a non-global
format. Place the cell selector on the cell and examine the input line. If you
see an indicator in parentheses, such as (F0), the cell has been formatted
with /Style, Numeric Format. Table 3.3 lists some examples of formats and
their indicators. (You'll learn about the numeric format options in the next
section.)

Note. To reset a
numeric format to
the global numeric
format, use the
/Style, Numeric
Format, Reset
command.

Table 3.3   **Numeric Format Indicators in the Input Line**

Format Option	Format Indicator
Fixed 0	(F0)
Scientific 0	(S0)
Currency 2	(C2)
, 2	(,2)
General	(G)
+/−	(+)
Percent 3	(P3)
Date 1	(D1)
Date Time 1	(D6)
Text	(T)
Hidden	(H)

Here are a few things to keep in mind when you are using /Style, Numeric Format:

- Ctrl-F is the shortcut keystroke for /Style, Numeric Format.

- If you insert a row or column within a block formatted with /Style, Numeric Format, the cells in the new row or column will use the spreadsheet's global numeric format.

- When you create a large spreadsheet and are concerned with memory limitations, use /Options, Formats, Numeric Format to change the numeric format for the entire spreadsheet. This technique uses little or no RAM, but the /Style, Numeric Format command does. Save the /Style commands for changing the formats in small areas of the spreadsheet. (See "Memory Usage Considerations" at the beginning of this chapter.)

- The /Edit, Copy and Move commands also copy or move the numeric format assigned to each cell in a block.

Numeric Format Options

As you explore Quattro Pro's 11 numeric format options, remember that each of them can be assigned globally for the entire spreadsheet using /Options, Formats, Numeric Format, or for a smaller area of the spreadsheet using /Style, Numeric Format or the Format button.

Five of Quattro Pro's numeric formats allow you to vary the number of decimal places displayed after the decimal point: Fixed, Scientific, Currency, ,(Comma), and Percent. If you enter a value that has more decimal places than you selected during formatting, Quattro Pro rounds the displayed value.

Imagine, for example, that you select Fixed 2 as the global numeric format. If you enter the value 10.375 in a cell, it is displayed as 10.38. When you look at the input line, however, you see that this value is stored as 10.375; only the appearance of this value has changed. Furthermore, any formulas that reference this value use the stored value, 10.375.

Rounding has interesting consequences. To see this, suppose you use /Options, Formats, Numeric Formats and select Fixed 0 as the global numeric format. Then you enter the following values in column A of a spreadsheet, starting in row 1, and observe how Quattro Pro displays them:

Tip. To prevent the appearance of an incorrect total, use the @ROUND function to round stored values to match their assigned format. See Chapter 7 for more about the @ROUND function.

Cell	Value Entered	Resulting Display
A1	100.51	101
A2	45.75	46
A3	375.01	375
A5	@SUM(A1..A3)	521

Tip. In Quattro Pro 4.0, you can access predefined numeric formats or even create your own. See "Using Custom User-Defined Numeric Formats in Quattro Pro 4.0," later.

If you enter the formula in cell A5 as shown, the actual result, 521.27, is rounded to 0 decimals and displayed as the integer 521. However, use a calculator to add the values as they are displayed in the spreadsheet, and the result is 522. Although the spreadsheet appears to be inaccurate, the difference occurs because Quattro Pro is adding the stored values, whereas the calculator is adding the rounded values as they're displayed in the spreadsheet.

General

The General format is Quattro Pro's default numeric format that is set during installation. This is the most unadorned (and seemingly inconsistent) of the format types. It displays values as you enter them, with these exceptions:

- Trailing decimals are eliminated. If you enter 10.00, it is displayed as 10; 1.750 is displayed as 1.75.

- Values less than 1 are displayed with a leading 0. For example, the value .15 is displayed as 0.15.

- Decimal values that are too large for a cell's column width are rounded when displayed. For example, the value π is stored as 3.1415926535898, but is displayed as 3.1415926 in a cell with a width of 9.

- Integers that are too wide for the current cell are displayed in scientific notation. For example, if you enter 150000000 in a cell with the default column width of 9, this value is displayed as 1.5E+08. When this happens, increase the column width using /Style, Column Width to display the number.

- Integers larger than 14 digits are stored in scientific notation. If you edit the value, it is still displayed in scientific notation in the input line. Once this has happened, widening the column has no effect on the value; it remains stored and displayed in scientific notation. Values stored in this format are not affected when used in calculations, however. See the section on Scientific format for more information.

The foregoing exceptions cause the General format to display values in a seemingly disorganized fashion, so you'll probably use this format less than others. However, General is an effective choice when you are entering integers—symbols or codes, such as account numbers, check numbers, or part numbers.

,(Comma)

Note. The ,(Comma) format is identical to the Currency format except it does not display a currency symbol.

The ,(Comma) format, appropriately named, uses commas to separate hundreds from thousands, thousands from millions, and so on. Parentheses surround negative numbers, and you can display 0 to 15 decimal places. Although this format is known as the "Financial" format, it can be used in any application to make large numbers easier to read.

A combination of the ,(Comma) and Currency formats is often used in financial statements, as shown in Figure 3.9. In this example, the default format is set to ,(Comma) 0 using /Options, Formats, Numeric Format. Then the first account in the balance sheet—the Sales amounts in row 3—and the Net Income/Loss result in row 20 are formatted with /Style, Numeric Format Currency 0. The result is a better presentation of the balance sheet.

Remember that the additional characters displayed with the ,(Comma) format (commas, parentheses, and decimal places) may demand a wider column width. If Quattro Pro displays a row of asterisks for a value, you need to widen the column.

Figure 3.9

An example of the ,(Comma) format, used with the Currency format

File Edit Style Graph Print Database Tools Options Window						? ↑↓	
▲ ◄ ► ▼ Erase Copy Move Style Align Font Insert Delete Fit Sum Format CHR WYS							
G16: [W9] @SUM(B16..F16)							

	A	B	C	D	E	F	G	H
		NW	SW	MW	SE	NE	TOTAL	
1								
2	INCOME							
3	Sales	$150,000	$175,000	$145,000	$135,000	$170,000	$775,000	
4	Returns	(9,000)	(5,600)	(3,500)	(8,000)	(7,500)	(33,600)	
5								
6	GROSS REVENUE	141,000	169,400	141,500	127,000	162,500	741,400	
7								
8	EXPENSES							
9	Commission	1,500	1,750	1,450	1,350	1,700	7,750	
10	Freight	1,200	1,400	1,160	1,080	1,360	6,200	
11	Interest	1,350	1,575	1,305	1,215	1,530	6,975	
12	Legal	1,500	1,500	1,500	1,500	1,500	7,500	
13	Materials	49,500	57,750	47,850	44,550	56,100	255,750	
14	Transport.	1,800	2,100	1,740	1,620	2,040	9,300	
15	Utilities	750	875	725	675	850	3,875	
16	Wages	22,500	26,250	21,750	20,250	25,500	116,250	
17								
18	TOTAL EXPENSES	80,100	93,200	77,480	72,240	90,580	413,600	
19								
20	NET INCOME/LOSS	$60,900	$76,200	$64,020	$54,760	$71,920	$327,800	
21								
22								

FORMATS.WQ1   [2]   READY

Currency

You can use the Currency format to dress up values with leading dollar signs (or other currency symbols) and commas. Negative numbers are surrounded with parentheses; you can display 0 to 15 decimal places. Figure 3.10 shows several examples of how the Currency format can affect the display of values.

Figure 3.10

Examples of the Currency format

File Edit Style Graph Print Database Tools Options Window					? ↑↓	
▲ ◄ ► ▼ Erase Copy Move Style Align Font Insert Delete Fit Sum Format CHR WYS						
G7: (C2) [W14] 1111000						

	A	B	C	D	E	F	G	H
1							AFTER COLUMN	
2	FORMAT		STORED		DISPLAYED		WIDENED	
3	OPTION		VALUE		VALUE		TO 14	INDICATOR
4								
5	Currency 0		1979.99		$1,980		$1,980	(C0)
6	Currency 1		175.56		$175.6		$175.6	(C1)
7	Currency 2		1111000		*********		$1,111,000.00	(C2)
8	Currency 2		-2700		*********		($2,700.00)	(C2)
9								

The Currency format often creates a column width problem, as you can see in Figure 3.10. When the value 1111000 is entered in cell C7, the default column width of 9 accommodates this value in the global General format with ease. When the Currency 2 format is assigned to the same value in cell E7, however, six characters are added to the display—a dollar sign, two commas, a decimal point, and two decimal places. Because this formatted value is too wide for the column, Quattro Pro displays a row of asterisks instead. In column G, the /Style, Column Width command (Ctrl-W) has been used to widen it to 14 characters, just to display the formatted value in G7. (See "Working with Columns" later in this chapter for more information on adjusting column widths.)

Unfortunately, the Currency format (especially Currency 2 places) is one of the most misused of the format options, cluttering the display with dollar signs and unneeded decimal places. What's more, the extra spaces needed by the dollar signs and commas usually require wider columns, reducing the amount of data you can display on the screen or printed page.

A typical example of formatting an entire spreadsheet using the more practical Currency 0 format is shown in Figure 3.11. Compare this to Figure 3.9, which is the same spreadsheet with only the top and bottom rows formatted in Currency 0, and the rest in the ,(Comma) 0 format. You be the judge about which one is easier to read. As you can see, the Currency format is most effective when used in small doses. Setting the decimal places to 0 streamlines the display even more. It's best to use the Currency format to draw the reader's eye to the important data in a spreadsheet, such as the Sales and Net Income Loss values in Figure 3.9.

Keep in mind the following when you use the Currency format:

- The type of currency symbol and its placement before or after a value is determined by the /Options, International, Currency setting. See Chapter 15 for more information.

- If you want blank spaces between the currency symbol and a value, use the /Options, International, Currency command. To place two spaces between the currency symbol and each value, for instance, specify the Currency setting as a $ (dollar sign) followed by two spaces, and Prefix. When you enter the value 100 in a cell formatted for Currency 0 places, this value will be displayed as $ 100.

Fixed

Quattro Pro's Fixed format is an all-purpose format that creates a uniform display of values lined up on the decimal point. You can use this format to display 0 to 15 decimal places, leading zeros for decimal values, and minus signs (–) preceding negative numbers. Because the Fixed format uses no extra characters, such as commas or dollar signs, you can fit more data on a screen or printed page. Figure 3.12 demonstrates four examples of how the Fixed format affects values.

Figure 3.11
A spreadsheet using the global format Currency 0

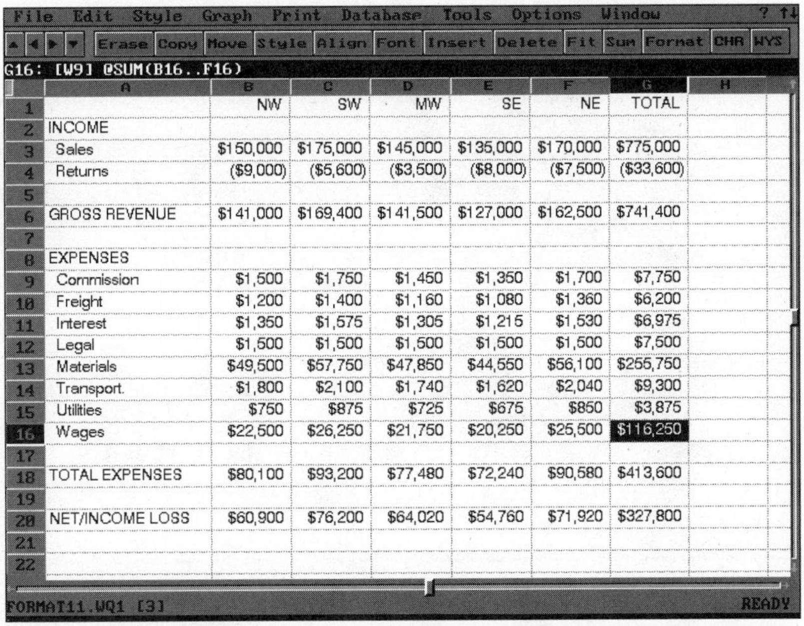

	A	B	C	D	E	F	G	H
1		NW	SW	MW	SE	NE	TOTAL	
2	INCOME							
3	Sales	$150,000	$175,000	$145,000	$135,000	$170,000	$775,000	
4	Returns	($9,000)	($5,600)	($3,500)	($8,000)	($7,500)	($33,600)	
5								
6	GROSS REVENUE	$141,000	$169,400	$141,500	$127,000	$162,500	$741,400	
7								
8	EXPENSES							
9	Commission	$1,500	$1,750	$1,450	$1,350	$1,700	$7,750	
10	Freight	$1,200	$1,400	$1,160	$1,080	$1,360	$6,200	
11	Interest	$1,350	$1,575	$1,305	$1,215	$1,530	$6,975	
12	Legal	$1,500	$1,500	$1,500	$1,500	$1,500	$7,500	
13	Materials	$49,500	$57,750	$47,850	$44,550	$56,100	$255,750	
14	Transport.	$1,800	$2,100	$1,740	$1,620	$2,040	$9,300	
15	Utilities	$750	$875	$725	$675	$850	$3,875	
16	Wages	$22,500	$26,250	$21,750	$20,250	$25,500	$116,250	
17								
18	TOTAL EXPENSES	$80,100	$93,200	$77,480	$72,240	$90,580	$413,600	
19								
20	NET/INCOME LOSS	$60,900	$76,200	$64,020	$54,760	$71,920	$327,800	
21								
22								

Figure 3.12
Effect of the Fixed format on values

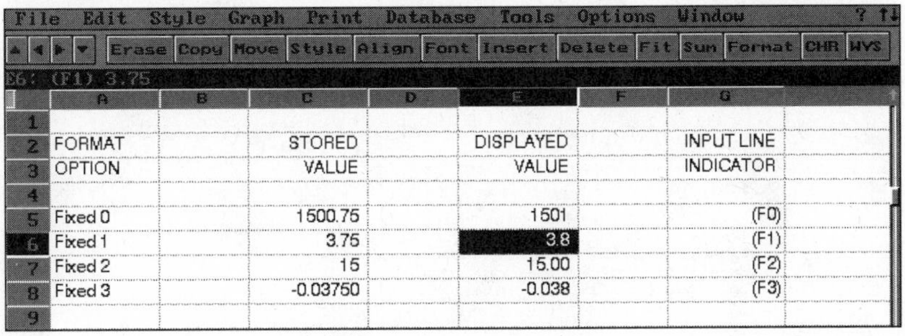

	A	B	C	D	E	F	G
1							
2	FORMAT		STORED		DISPLAYED		INPUT LINE
3	OPTION		VALUE		VALUE		INDICATOR
4							
5	Fixed 0		1500.75		1501		(F0)
6	Fixed 1		3.75		3.8		(F1)
7	Fixed 2		15		15.00		(F2)
8	Fixed 3		-0.03750		-0.038		(F3)
9							

As you can see, values in the Fixed format are displayed using the number of decimal places you specify. For example, the input line shows that 3.75 is stored in cell E6. The Fixed 1 format, however, displays this value as 3.8. The input line also displays (F1), indicating the cell has been formatted with the Fixed 1 option.

Suppose you have created the spreadsheet in Figure 3.13 using Quattro Pro's default global General numeric format. The Unit Prices in column E and the Total Prices in column F look disorganized and are hard to read. Figure 3.14 shows the same spreadsheet after assigning a Fixed 2 places format in columns E and F. Because the prices are now aligned on the decimal point, they are neat and easy to understand.

Figure 3.13

A spreadsheet using the default General format

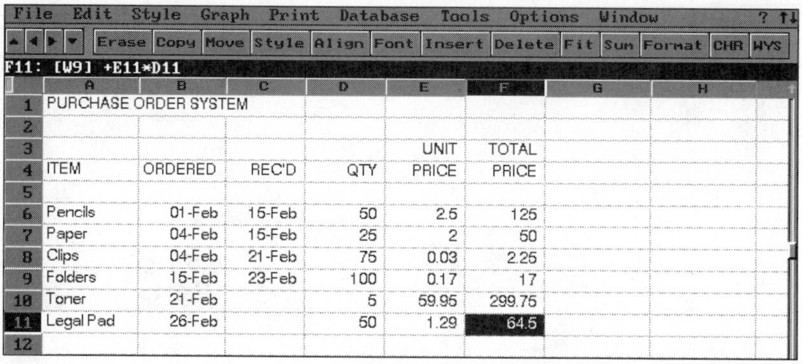

Figure 3.14

The spreadsheet from Figure 3.13 using Fixed 2 format in columns E and F

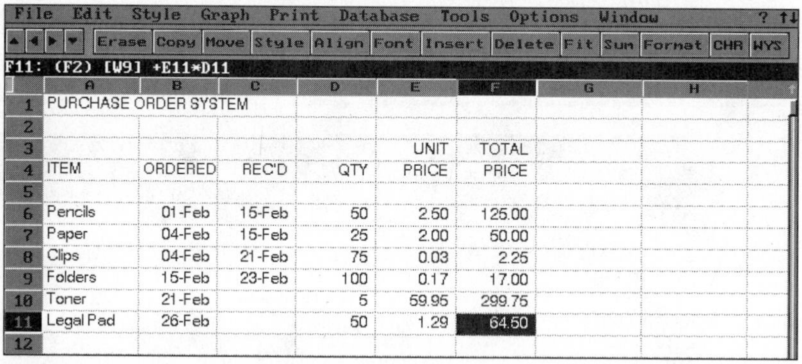

Percent

In Percent format, values are multiplied by 100 and then displayed with comma separators and a trailing % (percent) symbol. Negative values are preceded by a minus sign. You can specify 0 to 15 decimal places; however, values that have more decimal places than your format setting are rounded when displayed. For example, if you assigned a Percent 2 places format, .10375 is displayed as 10.38%.

Note. Since the
Percent format
multiplies a value
by 100, make sure
you enter values
correctly, or you
may get some
unexpected results.
For example, to
display 1.5%, enter
.015; to display
150%, enter 1.5.

This next table shows how values are displayed when formatted with the
Percent format.

Format Setting	Stored Value	Displayed Value
Percent 0 [P0]	.1075	11%
Percent 1 [P1]	.08325	8.3%
Percent 2 [P2]	–.000545	–0.05%
Percent 3 [P3]	.12625	12.625%

Dates and Times

As you learned in Chapter 1, Quattro Pro for Windows represents a date as
a date-value, and a time as a time-value. You can assign a date-value any of
the five date formats shown in Figure 3.15, and a time-value any of the four
time formats shown. In fact, to successfully enter a date using Ctrl-D, you
must enter it in the International D4 or D5 date format; you must enter a
time using the International D8 or D9 format.

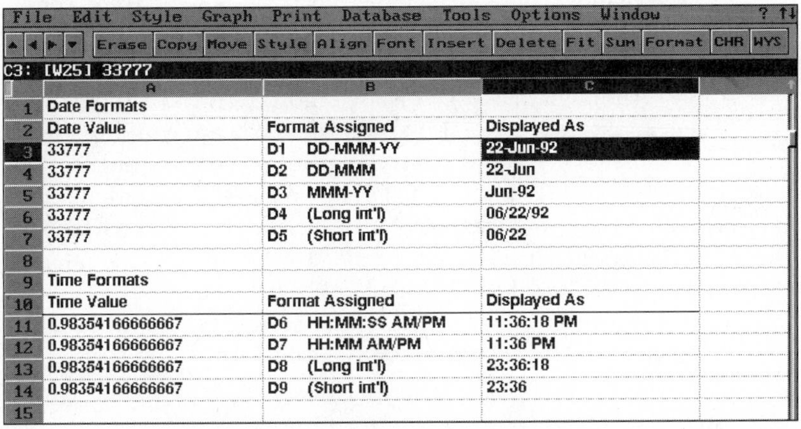

Figure 3.15

Date and time
formats

| File | Edit | Style | Graph | Print | Database | Tools | Options | Window | ? ↑↓ |

| ▲ ◄ ► ▼ | Erase | Copy | Move | Style | Align | Font | Insert | Delete | Fit | Sum | Format | CHR | WYS |

C3: [W25] 33777

	A	B	C
1	Date Formats		
2	Date Value	Format Assigned	Displayed As
3	33777	D1 DD-MMM-YY	22-Jun-92
4	33777	D2 DD-MMM	22-Jun
5	33777	D3 MMM-YY	Jun-92
6	33777	D4 (Long int'l)	06/22/92
7	33777	D5 (Short int'l)	06/22
8			
9	Time Formats		
10	Time Value	Format Assigned	Displayed As
11	0.98354166666667	D6 HH:MM:SS AM/PM	11:36:18 PM
12	0.98354166666667	D7 HH:MM AM/PM	11:36 PM
13	0.98354166666667	D8 (Long int'l)	23:36:18
14	0.98354166666667	D9 (Short int'l)	23:36
15			

In Figure 3.15, for instance, you can see that the date June 22, 1992, represented by the date-value 33777, is displayed as 22-Jun-92 in the D1 format,
22-Jun in the D2 format, and 06/22/92 in the D4 format. The D3 format disregards the day component of the date-value and returns Jun-92; the D5 format disregards the year component and returns 06/22.

Similarly, the time 11:36:18 PM, represented by the time-value 0.9835416667, is displayed as 11:36:18 PM in the D6 format and in the D8 military time format as 23:36:18. The D7 and D9 time formats disregard the seconds component of the time-value and return 11:36 PM and 23:36, respectively.

You can use the /Options, International command to change the default Long and Short int'l date and time formats. You can also use this command to specify a new date separator, which is / (slash) by default, as well as a new time separator, which is : (colon) by default. See Chapter 15.

TIP. *In Quattro Pro 4.0, the new user-defined numeric formats allow you to customize your date and time formats virtually any way you wish. For example, you can add the day of the week a date represents or display the date and time a combined date- and time-value represent. See "Using Custom User-Defined Numeric Formats in Quattro Pro 4.0," later.*

Scientific

You can use the Scientific format to display values in scientific, or exponential notation. This format displays a value using its *base* and *exponent:* The base is a single-digit value with up to 15 decimal places, and the exponent indicates the power of ten to which the base is raised. The value 1000, for example, looks like 1E+03 when displayed in Scientific 0 format. The 1 represents the base number, and the 03 represents the exponent, or power of 10 to which the base is raised (in other words, 1*10*10*10). To interpret this notation, you simply multiply the base value (1), by 10 three (the exponent) times.

Although this format is used most frequently for scientific and engineering applications, it is also useful when you are working with numbers that are so large or so small that they require very wide columns. In fact, you've probably already discovered that Quattro Pro's default numeric format, General, automatically converts a value to Scientific format whenever it is too long for the current cell. Take the number 100000000, for example. In ,(Comma) 0 format and the default Swiss SC 12-point font, it is displayed as 100,000,000 and requires a column width setting of 12. In Scientific format, Quattro Pro displays the same value as 1E+08, which only requires a column width of 6.

Text

You will want to use the Text format to display an actual formula rather than the result returned by that formula. A formula formatted as Text still calculates, and can be referenced by other cells, even though you cannot see the results of the formula.

For instance, suppose you have entered the value 100 in cell F10, and the value 200 in cell F11. You then add the contents of the two cells by entering the formula **@SUM(F10..F11)** in F13. Normally, the result (300) is displayed in cell F13. If you assign a Text format to F13, the 300 disappears and the formula @SUM(F10..F11) is displayed in place of this value. Your formula is still working, however. If you reference cell F13 in another formula, it will use the value 300.

The Text format is useful when the actual formula needs to be visible. The What-If table in Figure 3.16, for example, is easier to interpret when the formula in cell B7 is visible, showing how the values in the table were derived. You may also find the Text format helpful in debugging a formula that isn't working properly.

Figure 3.16

The formula in B7 is formatted as text

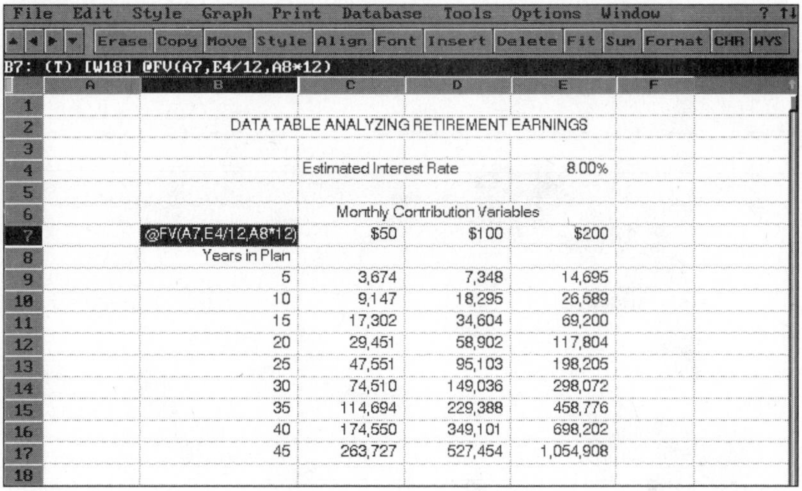

File	Edit	Style	Graph	Print	Database	Tools	Options	Window	? ↑↓
▲ ◄ ► ▼	Erase	Copy	Move	Style	Align	Font	Insert	Delete	Fit	Sum	Format	CHR	WYS

B7: (T) [W18] @FV(A7,E4/12,A8*12)

	A	B	C	D	E	F
1						
2			DATA TABLE ANALYZING RETIREMENT EARNINGS			
3						
4			Estimated Interest Rate		8.00%	
5						
6			Monthly Contribution Variables			
7		@FV(A7,E4/12,A8*12)	$50	$100	$200	
8		Years in Plan				
9		5	3,674	7,348	14,695	
10		10	9,147	18,295	26,589	
11		15	17,302	34,604	69,200	
12		20	29,451	58,902	117,804	
13		25	47,551	95,103	198,205	
14		30	74,510	149,036	298,072	
15		35	114,694	229,388	458,776	
16		40	174,550	349,101	698,202	
17		45	263,727	527,454	1,054,908	
18						

NOTE. *Since the Text display is limited to the cell width, longer formulas may get truncated.*

Keep the following in mind when using the Text format:

- To redisplay the results of a formula, assign any format except Text.

- If you format value entries with the Text option, they are displayed in the General numeric format.

- If you want to display a long formula for debugging or teaching purposes, you can convert it to a label by using the ' (apostrophe) label prefix at the beginning of the formula. With the formula displayed as text, you can study it, copy it without losing the cell references, print it, or show it to someone else. (Remember to convert it back to a formula—delete the ' label prefix—when you are done, or it won't calculate.)

Hidden

The Hidden format, as its name indicates, makes the contents of a cell invisible, although the data is still stored in the cell and can be used in calculations. Place the cell selector on a cell formatted as Hidden, and you can see that Quattro Pro still stores the cell contents.

Suppose you are preparing to print and distribute the employee roster shown in Figure 3.17. However, the home phone numbers listed in column D are confidential, and the personnel department requests that they be omitted from the printed roster. It's easy to conceal this information by preselecting the block D3..D24, and then using /Style, Numeric Format or the Format button to assign a Hidden format. As you can see in Figure 3.18, the home phone numbers are no longer displayed. To redisplay this hidden information, just select any format other than Hidden.

Figure 3.17

An employee roster

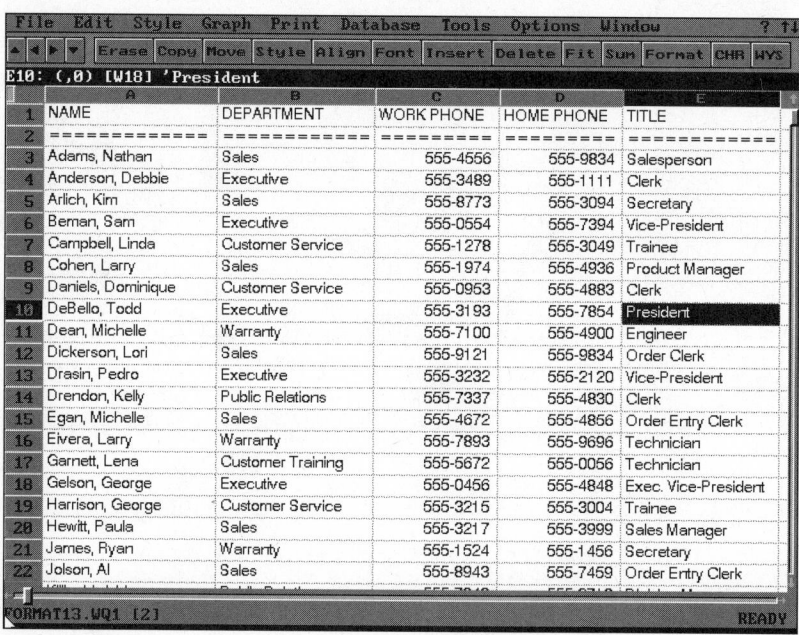

TIP. *Sometimes hiding the data in a block of cells arouses more curiosity than it's worth. In the example in Figure 3.18, for instance, the remaining column heading, HOME PHONE, calls attention to the missing data. Another alternative is to hide the entire column. (See "Working with Columns" later.) Be aware, however, that neither of these two methods hides information from a knowledgeable Quattro Pro user.*

Figure 3.18

The employee roster after hiding the contents of column D

| File | Edit | Style | Graph | Print | Database | Tools | Options | Window | ? ↑↓ |

| ▲ ◄ ► ▼ | Erase | Copy | Move | Style | Align | Font | Insert | Delete | Fit | Sum | Format | CHR | WYS |

D3: (H) [W14] "555-9834

	A	B	C	D	E
1	NAME	DEPARTMENT	WORK PHONE	HOME PHONE	TITLE
2	=========	=========	=========	=========	=========
3	Adams, Nathan	Sales	555-4556		Salesperson
4	Anderson, Debbie	Executive	555-3489		Clerk
5	Arlich, Kim	Sales	555-8773		Secretary
6	Beman, Sam	Executive	555-0554		Vice-President
7	Campbell, Linda	Customer Service	555-1278		Trainee
8	Cohen, Larry	Sales	555-1974		Product Manager
9	Daniels, Dominique	Customer Service	555-0953		Clerk
10	DeBello, Todd	Executive	555-3193		President
11	Dean, Michelle	Warranty	555-7100		Engineer
12	Dickerson, Lori	Sales	555-9121		Order Clerk
13	Drasin, Pedro	Executive	555-3232		Vice-President
14	Drendon, Kelly	Public Relations	555-7337		Clerk
15	Egan, Michelle	Sales	555-4672		Order Entry Clerk
16	Eivera, Larry	Warranty	555-7893		Technician
17	Garnett, Lena	Customer Training	555-5672		Technician
18	Gelson, George	Executive	555-0456		Exec. Vice-President
19	Harrison, George	Customer Service	555-3215		Trainee
20	Hewitt, Paula	Sales	555-3217		Sales Manager
21	James, Ryan	Warranty	555-1524		Secretary
22	Jolson, Al	Sales	555-8943		Order Entry Clerk

FORMAT14.WQ1 [2]   READY

+/– (Horizontal Bar Graph)

The +/– format creates a horizontal bar graph using + or – symbols to represent a formatted value. For example, the value 10 formatted with +/– is displayed as ++++++++++; –3 as – – –; and values that fall between –1 and 1 are displayed as a . (decimal). Values that include decimals, such as 3.75, are truncated rather than rounded to a higher or lower integer. For example, 3.99 is displayed as +++. If these symbols are longer than the column width, Quattro Pro displays a row of asterisks, reminding you to widen the column.

NOTE. *Due to screen width limitations, you can only display values between –72 and 72 in +/– format. To compensate for this, enter large values using consistent increments of hundreds, thousands, or millions. The value 25,000,000, for example, can be entered as 25; the value 12,000,000 can be entered as 12.*

Reset

The Reset format option resets a block's numeric format to the spreadsheet's numeric format, the /Options, Formats, Numeric Format setting. You can also use Reset to undo a numeric format that you've assigned to a block or to redisplay cell entries hidden using the Hidden format.

Using Custom User-Defined Numeric Formats in Quattro Pro 4.0

Although the /Style, Numeric Format command enables you to create many different numeric format permutations, it doesn't allow you to save the ones you frequently use. What's more, if the numeric format options don't meet your needs, you're out of luck. In Quattro Pro 4.0, these deficiencies have finally been addressed through user-defined numeric formats. Not only can you access predefined named styles for commonly used numeric formats, but you can create your own custom numeric formats that can be significantly better than Quattro Pro's. Figure 3.19 shows just a few examples of the formats you can create.

Figure 3.19

Creating custom numeric formats

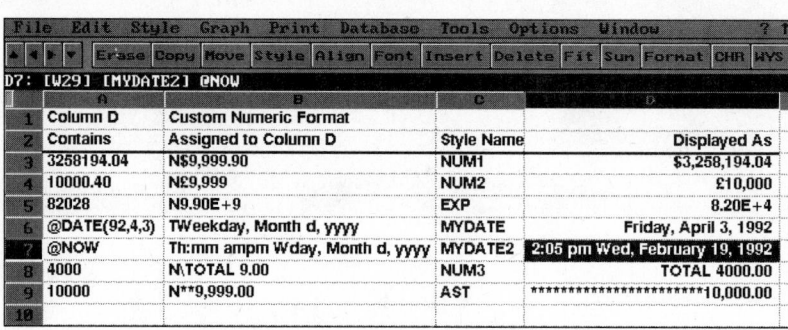

Using Predefined Custom Numeric Formats

You can use the /Style, Use Style command to assign these five predefined, commonly used numeric formats:

Style	Assigns
CURRENCY	Currency 2 places
COMMA	, (Comma) 2 places
DATE	Date with full name of month (for example, April 3, 1992)
FIXED	Fixed 2 places
PERCENT	Percent 2 places

For example, choose COMMA in the dialog box shown in Figure 3.20 to assign a ,(Comma) 2 places format to the block B6..E12. If you look at the input line, you can see that Quattro Pro assigns a [COMMA] named style to each cell in this block.

Figure 3.20
Using a predefined named numeric format

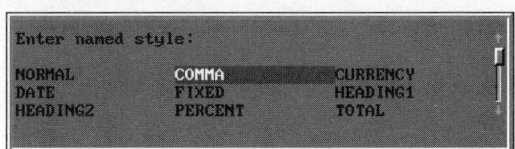

TIP. *As you'll see in the next section, Quattro Pro 4.0 builds these predefined styles as user-defined numeric formats. This means that you can assign another format you frequently use to one of these names. For example, if you're always using a ,(Comma) 0 places format, consider changing the COMMA predefined style to this. In fact, the NORMAL named style, discussed in "Creating Named Styles in Quattro Pro 4.0," controls the default numeric format Quattro Pro uses.*

Creating Custom User-Defined Numeric Formats

You create a custom numeric format by putting together *format codes* like building blocks. The collection of format codes is then assigned a name. The only difficult thing about this process is understanding the format codes and unraveling the somewhat obscure intricacies of putting them together.

In Figure 3.21, for instance, Style, Define Style, Create Name is first chosen to create the BASIC named style. Then Numeric Format, User Defined is used to create the custom numeric format code N9.9 shown in the dialog box. Here, the format code "N" says that you're creating a format for a value. The first "9" describes the format of the integer portion, while the second "9" describes the format of the decimal portion. When the /Style, Use Style command is used to assign BASIC to cell C5 of Figure 3.22, for example, the value 3500.290 is displayed in this numeric format as 3500.3.

NOTE. *Once you're in the dialog box labeled "Enter custom numeric format," shown in Figure 3.21, the named style remains in effect even if you abort the operation.*

Figure 3.21

Creating a custom
numeric format

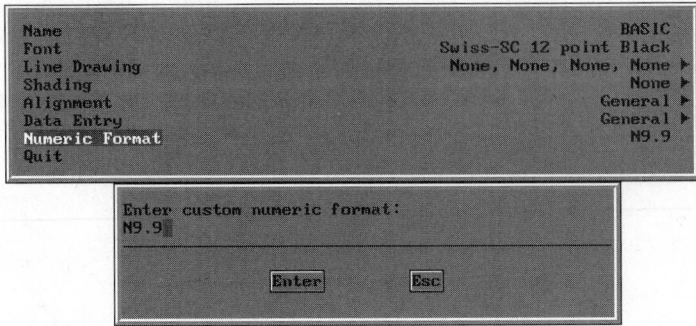

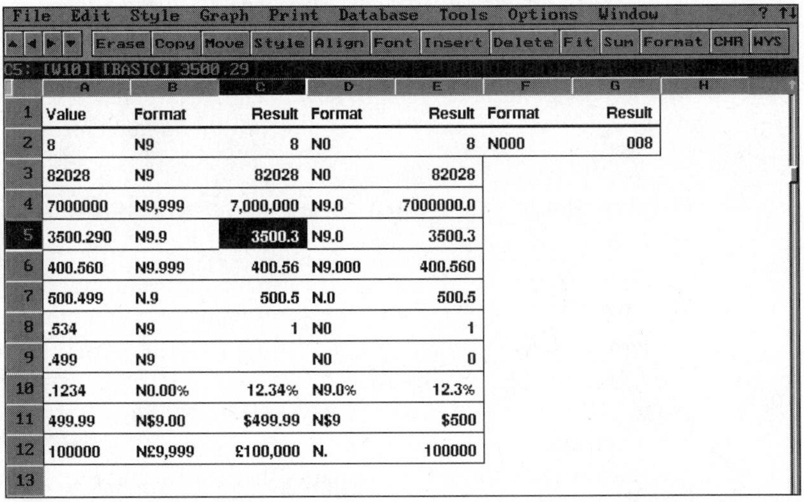

Figure 3.22

User-defined
numeric formats in
action

	A	B	C	D	E	F	G	H
1	Value	Format	Result	Format	Result	Format	Result	
2	8	N9	8	N0	8	N000	008	
3	82028	N9	82028	N0	82028			
4	7000000	N9,999	7,000,000	N9.0	7000000.0			
5	3500.290	N9.9	3500.3	N9.0	3500.3			
6	400.560	N9.999	400.56	N9.000	400.560			
7	500.499	N.9	500.5	N.0	500.5			
8	.534	N9	1	N0	1			
9	.499	N9		N0	0			
10	.1234	N0.00%	12.34%	N9.0%	12.3%			
11	499.99	N$9.00	$499.99	N$9	$500			
12	100000	N£9,999	£100,000	N.	100000			
13								

Number Formats

A number format, made up of a combination of format codes, displays a number exactly the way you want it. First, a number format always begins with "N". This tells Quattro Pro that the codes that follow represent a format for numbers. After the "N", a . (period) is used to separate the integer from the decimal portion. The integer portion and the decimal portion are represented by either 9 or 0, depending on how you want the number to appear.

To see the difference 9 and 0 produce, let's dissect how the number formats in Figure 3.22 display the values shown in column A. First off, you only need to enter *one* 9 or 0 to display the *entire* integer portion. That's why the N9 and N0 formats in rows 2 and 3 both display 8 as 8, and 82028 as 82028.

There are two instances when you'll want to include additional 0 or 9 format codes in the integer portion: to add leading zeros and to include a comma as the thousands separator. Additional 0 format codes at the beginning of the integer portion adds leading zeros. For example, the N000 format displays 8 as 008. To include a comma as the thousands separator, you only have to include one , (comma) code. For example, you can see in Figure 3.22 that N9,999 in row 4 returns 7,000,000. (If you enter an abbreviated version of this format code—for example 9,9—Quattro Pro automatically converts it to 9,999.)

NOTE. *The /Options, International command, discussed in Chapter 15, controls the thousands and decimal separators. If you've changed this setting, Quattro Pro automatically converts the , or . format code you enter to match this setting.*

Tip. Actually, you don't even have to include an integer portion in the format code as long as you include a decimal portion. For example, both N9.0 and N.0 display 50,000.69 as 50000.7.

When you're defining the decimal portion of a number format, however, the number of 9's and 0's does affect the number of decimal places displayed. That is, the number of 9's or 0's defines the number of decimal places to which a value is rounded. Otherwise, there's only one difference: 0 displays a trailing 0 while 9 doesn't. For example, both the N9.9 and N9.0 formats in row 5 round the value 3500.290 to 3500.3. Although the N9.999 format in row 6 truncates the trailing 0 in 400.560 to 400.56, N9.000 includes it and returns 400.560.

To handle decimal values, you must include a decimal portion in the format code. Otherwise, you'll get some odd results. For example, both N.9 and N.0 in row 7 display .499 as .5. Although N9 and N0 in row 8 both round .534 to 1 and N0 rounds .499 down to 0 in row 9, N9 returns a null string (nothing).

There's one more number format code, %, which acts just like the Percent numeric format. This code multiplies a value by 100 and adds a trailing % symbol. For example, N0.00% in row 10 displays .1234 as 12.34%.

If you're wondering how to include a currency sign in a numeric format, just enter it. For example, N$9.00 in row 11 displays 499.99 as $499.99; N$9 displays $500.

TIP. *You can include special characters to enhance a numeric format. For example, to add the English pound sign, keep Alt depressed, and then enter its extended character code, 156, from the numeric keypad. You can see the result in row 12 of Figure 3.22.*

Scientific Notation
In a number format, using E+ or E– followed by either 0 or 9 tells Quattro Pro to display that number in scientific notation. E– or e– adds a minus sign (–) to negative exponents. E+ or e+ also adds a plus sign (+) to positive exponents.

To create a code for scientific notation, here's the format you have to follow:

```
N(Base format)(E or e)(+ or -)(Exponent format)
```

In the code N9.90E+9 in Figure 3.19, for example, everything preceding the E—9.90—is the number format of the base. Everything after the + is the exponent format. This code displays 82090 as 8.21E+4; the base 8.21 is rounded because the base format specifies two places. On the other hand, N9.99E–00 would display 82090 as 8.21E4.

TIP. *By including a zero in the exponent, you can tell when a value is raised to the 0 power. For example, N9E+0 displays 2 as 2E+0. N9E+9 would make it appear as 2E+.*

Dates and Times

A custom date or time format always begins with "T", and then includes one or a combination of the codes in Table 3.4. For example, the code TWeekday, Month d, yyyy represents the date entered as @DATE(92,4,3) in row 6 of Figure 3.19 as Friday, April 3, 1992. As you can see, Quattro Pro automatically determines the correct day of the week for any date-value you enter.

In Quattro Pro 4.0, you can format a cell containing a combined date/time-value to show *both* the date and time. In row 7 of Figure 3.19, for instance, the format code

```
TH:mm ampm Wday, Month d, yyyy
```

displays the combined date/time-value @NOW returns as 2:05 pm Wed, February 19, 1992.

Table 3.4   **Date and Time Format Codes**

Format Code	Displays
d or D	Day of the month as a one- or two-digit number. The day 8 appears as 8, the day 12 as 12.
dd or DD	Day of the month as a two-digit number. The day 8 appears as 08, the day 12 as 12.
wday, Wday, or WDAY	Day of the week as a 3-character abbreviation. The capitalization of the code indicates the capitalization of the result—wday produces fri, for instance.
weekday, Weekday, or WEEKDAY	Day of the week. The capitalization of the code indicates the capitalization of the result—weekday produces monday, for instance.

Table 3.4   **(Continued)**

Format Code	Displays
m or mo	Month as a one or two digit number; m represents minutes as a one- or two-digit number if preceded by h, H, hh, or HH.
mm or MMo	Month as a two-digit number; mm represents minutes as a two-digit number if preceded by h, H, hh, or HH.
mon, Mon, or MON	Month as a three-character abbreviation. The capitalization of the code indicates the capitalization of the result—mon produces jan, for instance.
month, Month, or MONTH	Name of the month. The capitalization of the code indicates the capitalization of the result—month produces january, for instance.
yy or YY	Year as a two-digit number 00 to 99.
yyyy or YYYY	Year as a four-digit number.
h or H	Hour as a one- or two-digit number in a 24-hour format unless followed by ampm or AMPM.
hh or HH	Hour as a two-digit number in 24-hour format unless followed by ampm or AMPM.
Mi	Minutes as a one- or two-digit number.
MMi	Minutes as a two-digit number.
s or S	Seconds as a one- or two-digit number.
ss or SS	Seconds as a two-digit number.
ampm or AMPM	Abbreviations *am* for morning and *pm* for afternoon.

Special Numeric Format Codes

Quattro Pro provides three additional codes that you can use anywhere in any custom number, date, or time format:

Code	Displays
\	All characters, including blank spaces, after \ that aren't format codes. For example, the value 4000 in the N\TOTAL 9.00 format is displayed in cell D8 of Figure 3.19 as TOTAL 4000.00.

Code	Displays
" "	Characters enclosed within the quotation marks. For example, the value 911 in the N9 "Help Me!" format appears as 911 Help Me!.
*	The characters following * in any remaining blank space in the cell, provided they aren't format codes. For instance, the value 10000 in the N*+9,999.00 format might appear as ++++++10,000.00.

Working with Columns

By now you may have discovered that Quattro Pro's default column width setting at 9 is often inappropriate for the labels and values you enter into a spreadsheet. Labels are truncated if they overlap into adjacent nonempty cells, and values are displayed as a row of asterisks or in scientific notation if they are too large for a cell. Quattro Pro makes it easy to adjust column widths, however, by offering a variety of options for widening or narrowing a single column, a block of columns, or all the columns in a spreadsheet at once. You can even hide entire columns to make the contents invisible.

Because fonts are displayed in WYSIWYG mode, you can visually evaluate your column width needs on the screen. So it has become much easier to adjust column width settings to accommodate any fonts you have specified.

If you work in Character mode or do not use an EGA or VGA monitor, you will still encounter the same problems with column width settings and fonts that you may have experienced in earlier Quattro Pro releases. This occurs because the font you see on the screen, Monospace 12 point, does not change when you assign one of Quattro Pro's fonts to a spreadsheet block (see "Fonts," later). Therefore, on the screen, column width settings will appear adequate; only when you print will the problem of truncated text resulting from inadequate column width settings become apparent. You can avoid this problem by using Quattro Pro's Screen Preview feature discussed in Chapter 6.

Setting the Column Width for a Single Column

Use the /Style, Column Width command to widen or narrow a single column. For instance, suppose you have entered the spreadsheet data in Figure 3.23. All columns use the /Options, Format, Global Width setting of 9. Notice that this causes the labels in column A to overflow into column B. To widen column A, follow the procedure below.

Tip. You can also use /Style, Block Size, Auto Width (discussed later) to automatically size a column width to accommodate the longest width.

1. Position the cell selector anywhere in column A; let's use cell A4. Then select /Style, Column Width or press Ctrl-W. Quattro Pro displays

   `Alter the width of the current column [1..254]:`

   followed by the current cell width, 9.

2. Press the → key until the label in cell A4 is fully displayed (or fully encompassed by the cell selector) and Quattro Pro displays 16 in the input line. Or you can just enter the value **16**. (To decrease a column width, use the ← key.) Press Enter to confirm.

In Figure 3.24, you can see how the width of column A has changed to reflect the new 16-character setting. When you place the cell selector in any cell in this column, the input line displays the column width setting in brackets: [W16].

Figure 3.23

An inadequate column width setting

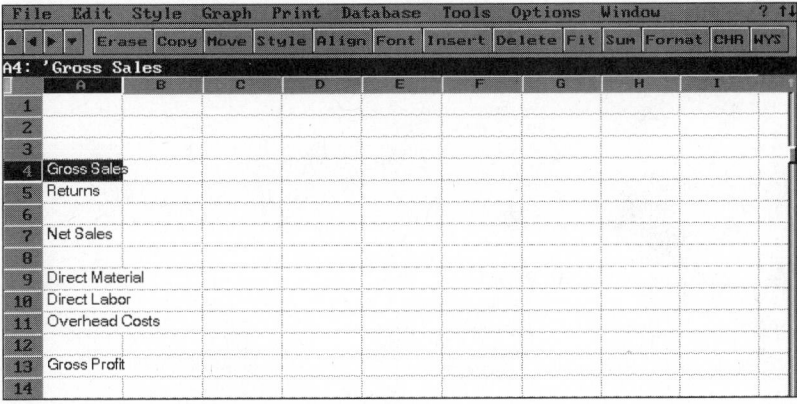

Setting the Global Column Width

Sometimes you will want to change the global column width setting of 9 that Quattro Pro automatically uses in every spreadsheet. For example, consider Figure 3.25, which contains financial data in columns B through E. The global column width setting of 9 is too small to properly display the data—labels are truncated and some values are displayed as asterisks. To remedy this, set all column widths in this spreadsheet to 12, except column A. Select /Options, Formats, Global Width. Specify the new column width, **12**, and press Enter. Select Quit twice to return to the spreadsheet. In Figure 3.26, all columns in the spreadsheet except A are now set to the new width of 12. However, because it is a global width setting, no format indicator is included in the input line.

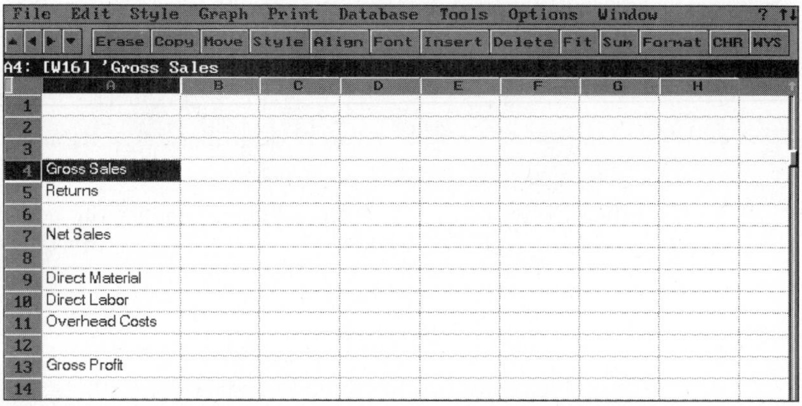

Figure 3.24

Using /Style, Column Width to change the width of one column

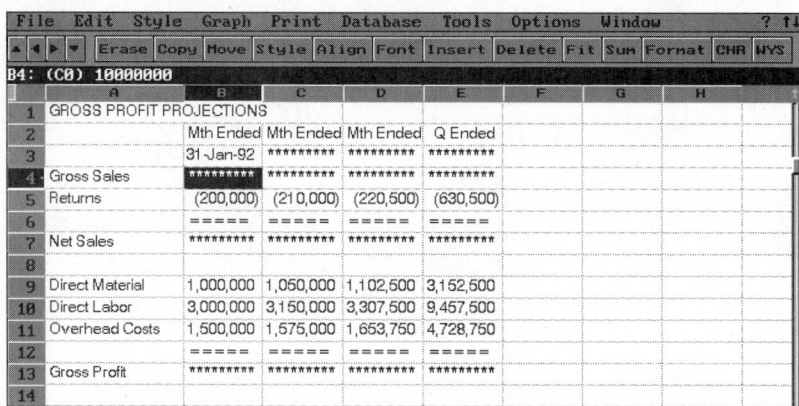

Figure 3.25

An inadequate global column width

The /Options, Formats, Global Width command does not affect column width settings that have been previously set with /Style, Column Width, Block Size, or Hide Column. These commands are stronger than /Options, Formats, Global Width. You can use /Style, Reset Width, and /Style, Block Size, Reset Width, however, to override /Style, Column Width, Block Size, and Hide Column settings and reset a column width to the /Options, Formats, Global Width setting.

Figure 3.26
Changing the global column width setting

File Edit Style Graph Print Database Tools Options Window ? ↑↓

```
▲ ◀ ▶ ▼  Erase Copy Move Style Align Font Insert Delete Fit Sum Format CHR WYS
B4: (C0) 10000000
```

	A	B	C	D	E	F
1	GROSS PROFIT PROJECTIONS					
2		Mth Ended	Mth Ended	Mth Ended	Q Ended	
3		31-Jan-92	29-Feb-92	31-Mar-92	31-Mar-92	
4	Sales	$10,000,000	$10,500,000	$11,025,000	$31,525,000	
5	Returns	(200,000)	(210,000)	(220,500)	(630,500)	
6		========	========	========	========	
7	Net Sales	$9,800,000	$10,290,000	$10,804,500	$30,894,500	
8						
9	Direct Material	1,000,000	1,050,000	1,102,500	3,152,500	
10	Direct Labor	3,000,000	3,150,000	3,307,500	9,457,500	
11	Overhead Costs	1,500,000	1,575,000	1,653,750	4,728,750	
12		========	========	========	========	
13	Gross Profit	$4,300,000	$4,515,000	$4,740,750	$13,555,750	
14						

TIP. *You can easily tell if a column width has been changed from the global setting. Place the cell selector on one cell in the column and look at the input line. An indicator showing the current column width enclosed in brackets, such as [W16], informs you that the column width setting was set with one of the /Style commands.*

Setting the Column Width for a Block of Columns

Tip. You can preselect a block of adjacent columns before you choose /Style, Block Size.

You can simultaneously change the width of contiguous columns with the /Style, Block Size command (Style, Block Widths in earlier releases) using these options:

Option	Effect
Set Width	Changes all the columns in a block to the same width
Auto Width	Adjusts the width of each column in a block to that of the longest entry in each column
Reset Width	Resets the width for all the columns in a block to the global default width (set with /Options, Formats)

Note. For a discussion of the /Style, Block Size, Height command, see "Working with Row Heights" later in this chapter.

Specifying the Same Width for a Block of Columns

You can change the width of a group of adjacent columns with /Style, Block Size, Set Width. For instance, suppose in Figure 3.25 you want to keep the global width setting at 9; however, you still need to change the column width settings in columns B through E to 12. Here's how to do this.

1. Position the cell selector anywhere in column B, for example, B3, and select /Style, Block Size, Set Width.

2. In response to the prompt, specify at least one cell in each column. In this case, specify the block **B3..E3** and press Enter.

3. Indicate the new width by entering **12** or by using the → and ← keys to adjust the column width. Press Enter, and all the columns in this block (B, C, D, and E) now use this new width.

You can see the results in Figure 3.27. The cells in columns B through E display [W12] in the input line, but the global column setting of 9 is still in effect for all other columns (except A).

Figure 3.27
Using /Style, Block Size, Set Width to alter the width of columns B through E

	File	Edit	Style	Graph	Print	Database	Tools	Options	Window		? ↑↓

| ▲ | ◄ | ► | ▼ | Erase | Copy | Move | Style | Align | Font | Insert | Delete | Fit | Sum | Format | CHR | WYS |

B4: (C0) [W12] 10000000

	A	B	C	D	E	F	G
1	GROSS PROFIT PROJECTIONS						
2		Mth Ended	Mth Ended	Mth Ended	Q Ended		
3		31-Jan-92	29-Feb-92	31-Mar-92	31-Mar-92		
4	Gross Sales	$10,000,000	$10,500,000	$11,025,000	$31,525,000		
5	Returns	(200,000)	(210,000)	(220,500)	(630,500)		
6		========	========	========	========		
7	Net Sales	$9,800,000	$10,290,000	$10,804,500	$30,894,500		
8							
9	Direct Material	1,000,000	1,050,000	1,102,500	3,152,500		
10	Direct Labor	3,000,000	3,150,000	3,307,500	9,457,500		
11	Overhead Costs	1,500,000	1,575,000	1,653,750	4,728,750		
12		========	========	========	========		
13	Gross Profit	$4,300,000	$4,515,000	$4,740,750	$13,555,750		
14							

Automatically Setting Column Widths to the Longest Entry

The /Style, Block Size, Auto Width command quickly becomes a favorite for most users. Because it automatically adjusts the width of each column in a block to the longest entry in each column, you can use it to efficiently set column widths in your spreadsheet.

Tip. In Quattro Pro 4.0, Fit in the SpeedBar is a shortcut for /Style, Block Size, Auto Width.

Setting individual column widths can be painstaking and tedious. You want each column wide enough to display data fully, but you also want to conserve space by using narrower column widths wherever possible, in order to fit more on your screen or reports. /Style, Block Size, Auto Width or the Fit button lets you enter data without concern for the column width, and later adjust column widths for the whole block at once. You can even specify how many blank spaces you want between each column.

The example in Figure 3.28 is Exotic Tours, Ltd's tour bookings spreadsheet for the month of August. All the data is entered using the default column width of 9, rendering it almost impossible to read because the data is obscured by this global column width setting. The long labels—client names and tour descriptions in columns C and D—seem truncated because the columns are too narrow. Conversely, the account numbers and trip codes in columns B and E look a little lost because the columns are too wide. It's obvious that each column needs to be adjusted individually in order to best display this information. Rather than doing this one column at a time, however, you can let Quattro Pro do the work for you.

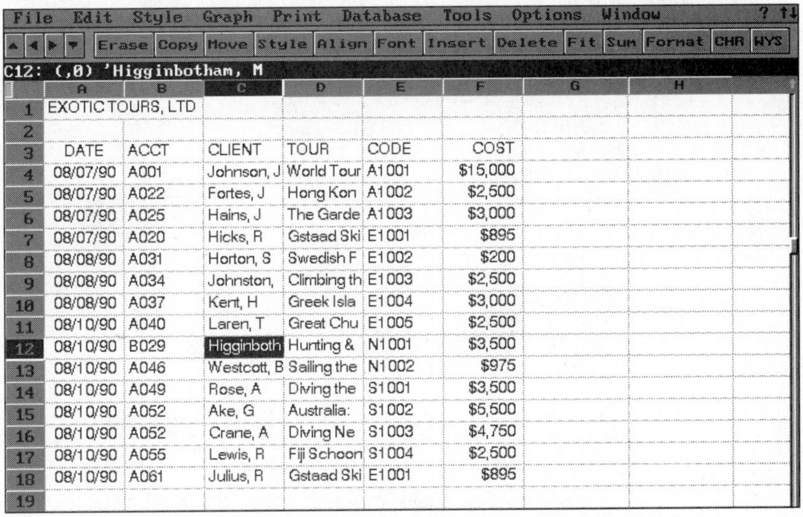

Figure 3.28

A poorly arranged spreadsheet using the default column width of 9

Here's how to improve Exotic Tours' spreadsheet.

1. Position the cell selector on the first column in the block you want to modify, such as A3, and select /Style, Block Size, Auto Width.

2. You will be prompted to "Enter extra space between columns [0-40]:1". Accept the default of 1 by pressing Enter.

3. In response to the prompt for the block address, indicate **A3..F3**, and press Enter.

As shown in Figure 3.29, Quattro Pro makes each column in this block wide enough to display its longest entry, plus one extra space. Thus, the width of column A is 10; columns B and E are 7; column F is 9; and column C is 14 characters wide to display the longest name, Higginbotham, M, in cell C12. Likewise, column D is now 23 characters wide to fully display all tour names with one extra space. Notice that for the current cell, C12, Quattro Pro displays the column width format indicator [W14] in the input line.

Figure 3.29

The Exotic Tours spreadsheet after using the Auto Width option

File	Edit	Style	Graph	Print	Database	Tools	Options	Window		? ↑↓

| ▲ | ◄ | ► | ▼ | Erase | Copy | Move | Style | Align | Font | Insert | Delete | Fit | Sum | Format | CHR | HYS |

C12: (,0) [W14] 'Higginbotham, M

	A	B	C	D	E	F	G
1	EXOTIC TOURS, LTD						
2							
3	DATE	ACCT	CLIENT	TOUR	CODE	COST	
4	08/07/90	A001	Johnson, J	World Tour by Baloon	A1001	$15,000	
5	08/07/90	A022	Fortes, J	Hong Kong Buying Trip	A1002	$2,500	
6	08/07/90	A025	Hains, J	The Gardens of Japan	A1003	$3,000	
7	08/07/90	A020	Hicks, R	Gstaad Ski Week	E1001	$895	
8	08/08/90	A031	Horton, S	Swedish Folk Dance Tour	E1002	$200	
9	08/08/90	A034	Johnston, K	Climbing the Alps	E1003	$2,500	
10	08/08/90	A037	Kent, H	Greek Island Art Seminar	E1004	$3,000	
11	08/10/90	A040	Laren, T	Great Churches of Italy	E1005	$2,500	
12	08/10/90	B029	Higginbotham, M	Hunting & Fishing Alaska	N1001	$3,500	
13	08/10/90	A046	Westcott, B	Sailing the NW Passage	N1002	$975	
14	08/10/90	A049	Rose, A	Diving the Barrier Reef	S1001	$3,500	
15	08/10/90	A052	Ake, G	Australia: The Outback	S1002	$5,500	
16	08/10/90	A052	Crane, A	Diving New Zealand	S1003	$4,750	
17	08/10/90	A055	Lewis, R	Fiji Schooner Cruise	S1004	$2,500	
18	08/10/90	A061	Julius, R	Gstaad Ski Week	E1001	$895	
19							

Here are some things to keep in mind when you use /Style, Block Size, Auto Width or the Width button:

- Any blank columns get reset to the default /Options, Formats, Global Width setting.

- Any cells within a column using a Hidden numeric format are treated as blank cells, and are therefore not evaluated by this command. Therefore, the column width is set to accommodate unhidden entries; otherwise, it is reset to the global column width setting.

- The column width of any hidden columns are correctly adjusted.

- The Auto Width option does not accurately assess the column width required to display values formatted with the +/– horizontal bar graph format. For example, suppose the value 10 is in +/– format, and is displayed as ++++++++++. The Auto Width option sets the column width incorrectly, because it analyzes the two digits in the stored value, 10, rather than the ten + characters in the formatted display. The result is a row of asterisks.

Resetting the Column Width

Any column width setting you specify using the /Style command is stronger than the global column width setting. Thus, the /Options, Formats, Global Width command is ineffective in resetting any column widths previously set with the /Style command. However, Quattro Pro provides two commands that accomplish this task. Use /Style, Reset Width to reset one column. Or use /Style, Block Size, Reset Width, first offered in version 3.0, to reset a block of columns.

For example, let's return to Figure 3.27. All the columns in this spreadsheet use the global column width setting of 9, except column A, assigned a width of 14, and columns B through E, assigned a width of 12. Suppose you now decide to change all the column widths in the spreadsheet to 15, using /Options, Formats, Global Width. The widths of columns A through E, however, are unaffected, because you set the width of these columns using the /Style command, which overrides the global default setting.

You can, nevertheless, return columns A through E to the new global default setting. Place the cell selector anywhere in column A, such as A3, select /Style, Block Size, Reset Width, and specify A3..E3. Quattro Pro resets all column widths in this block to the global default setting of 15.

Hiding Columns

You can hide and redisplay entire columns in a spreadsheet with the /Style, Hide Column, Hide and Expose commands. The Hide option hides the *entire* column, including the column letter at the top, and makes it appear as though it doesn't exist. When you hide a column, all columns to the right move to the left. However, these columns retain their original column letters.

Consider the mail-order inventory spreadsheet shown in Figure 3.30.

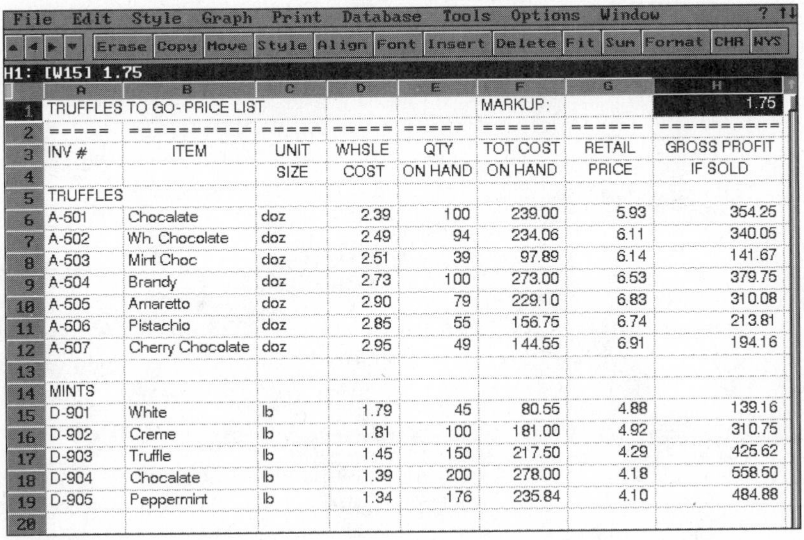

Figure 3.30

An inventory spreadsheet with all columns displayed

File	Edit	Style	Graph	Print	Database	Tools	Options	Window	? ↑↓

▲ ◄ ► ▼	Erase	Copy	Move	Style	Align	Font	Insert	Delete	Fit	Sum	Format	CHR	WYS

H1: [W15] 1.75

	A	B	C	D	E	F	G	H
1	TRUFFLES TO GO- PRICE LIST					MARKUP:		1.75
2	=====	==========	=====	=====	=====	======	======	==========
3	INV #	ITEM	UNIT	WHSLE	QTY	TOT COST	RETAIL	GROSS PROFIT
4			SIZE	COST	ON HAND	ON HAND	PRICE	IF SOLD
5	TRUFFLES							
6	A-501	Chocalate	doz	2.39	100	239.00	5.93	354.25
7	A-502	Wh. Chocolate	doz	2.49	94	234.06	6.11	340.05
8	A-503	Mint Choc	doz	2.51	39	97.89	6.14	141.67
9	A-504	Brandy	doz	2.73	100	273.00	6.53	379.75
10	A-505	Amaretto	doz	2.90	79	229.10	6.83	310.08
11	A-506	Pistachio	doz	2.85	55	156.75	6.74	213.81
12	A-507	Cherry Chocolate	doz	2.95	49	144.55	6.91	194.16
13								
14	MINTS							
15	D-901	White	lb	1.79	45	80.55	4.88	139.16
16	D-902	Creme	lb	1.81	100	181.00	4.92	310.75
17	D-903	Truffle	lb	1.45	150	217.50	4.29	425.62
18	D-904	Chocalate	lb	1.39	200	278.00	4.18	558.50
19	D-905	Peppermint	lb	1.34	176	235.84	4.10	484.88
20								

This spreadsheet tracks the inventory on hand, cost of inventory, and potential gross profit were everything sold. The markup, or margin, factor is displayed in cell H1, and is referenced by formulas in columns G and H to calculate the retail price of each item, as well as the gross profit.

This inventory spreadsheet actually serves a dual purpose, however. If you hide the columns that contain information applicable for internal accounting purposes only, you can turn it into a price list. For example, the quantity of product on hand, wholesale price, total cost of inventory, and the markup factor are confidential. To hide columns D, E, F, and H from view:

1. Place the cell selector anywhere in column D, such as cell D6, and select /Style, Hide Column, Hide. In response to the prompt, "Hide columns from view:", specify **D6..F6**, and press Enter. As shown in Figure 3.31, columns D, E, and F disappear, and column G appears adjacent to column C.

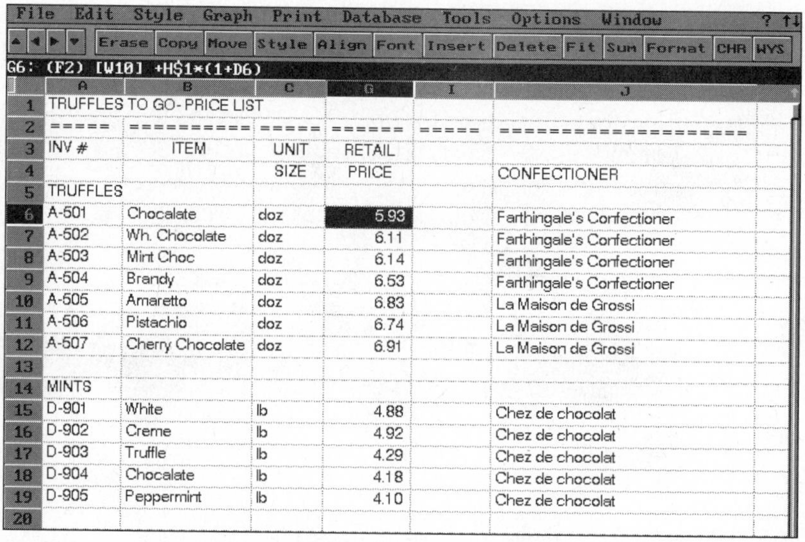

Figure 3.31
The spreadsheet shown in Figure 3.30 after using /Style, Hide Column

2. Move the cell selector to any cell in column H, such as cell H6, and again invoke /Style, Hide Column, Hide. Specify any cell in column H, such as H6, press Enter, and Quattro Pro hides column H, moving column I next to column G.

This inventory list has now become the price list shown in Figure 3.31, which can be printed and mailed to customers. As you can see, Quattro Pro conceals columns D, E, F, and H; this makes room for column J, which lists the source confectioner for each inventory item. The proprietary markup information in cells F1 and H1 is no longer displayed, because these columns are now hidden. The result is a spreadsheet that is simple and to the point, rather than cluttered with irrelevant (or confidential) information. What's more, since you've reduced the size of the block, you can use a larger font to print the price list and still fit it on a standard 8 1/2-by-11-inch page. (See "Spreadsheet Publishing," next.)

Only the data in columns, D, E, F, and H are hidden from view. This information is still stored in the spreadsheet, and any formulas that reference this data return the same results.

To expose all the hidden columns in Figure 3.31, select /Style, Hide Column, Expose. As shown in Figure 3.32, Quattro Pro temporarily displays hidden columns D, E, F, and H with an * (asterisk) next to their column letters. Specify the block **D1..H1** (you can include columns that aren't hidden), and press Enter. The columns you hid now reappear on screen, data intact. Asterisks no longer appear next to the column letters. The spreadsheet once more looks like Figure 3.30.

Figure 3.32
Redisplaying hidden columns

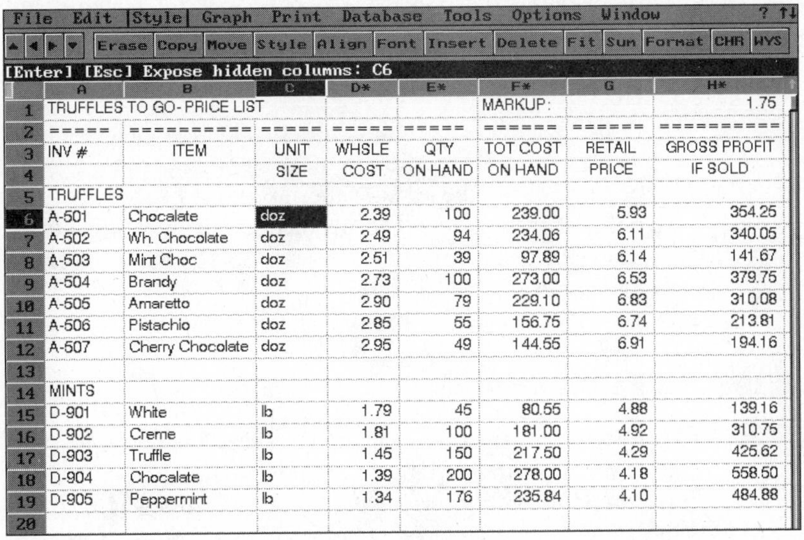
File Edit Style Graph Print Database Tools Options Window ? ↑↓
Erase Copy Move Style Align Font Insert Delete Fit Sum Format CHR WYS
[Enter] [Esc] Expose hidden columns: C6

	A	B	C	D*	E*	F*	G	H*
1	TRUFFLES TO GO- PRICE LIST					MARKUP:		1.75
2	=====	==========	=====	=====	=====	======	======	==========
3	INV #	ITEM	UNIT	WHSLE	QTY	TOT COST	RETAIL	GROSS PROFIT
4			SIZE	COST	ON HAND	ON HAND	PRICE	IF SOLD
5	TRUFFLES							
6	A-501	Chocalate	doz	2.39	100	239.00	5.93	354.25
7	A-502	Wh. Chocolate	doz	2.49	94	234.06	6.11	340.05
8	A-503	Mint Choc	doz	2.51	39	97.89	6.14	141.67
9	A-504	Brandy	doz	2.73	100	273.00	6.53	379.75
10	A-505	Amaretto	doz	2.90	79	229.10	6.83	310.08
11	A-506	Pistachio	doz	2.85	55	156.75	6.74	213.81
12	A-507	Cherry Chocolate	doz	2.95	49	144.55	6.91	194.16
13								
14	MINTS							
15	D-901	White	lb	1.79	45	80.55	4.88	139.16
16	D-902	Creme	lb	1.81	100	181.00	4.92	310.75
17	D-903	Truffle	lb	1.45	150	217.50	4.29	425.62
18	D-904	Chocalate	lb	1.39	200	278.00	4.18	558.50
19	D-905	Peppermint	lb	1.34	176	235.84	4.10	484.88
20								

Here are some things to keep in mind when using /Style, Hide Columns, Hide and Expose:

- *All* hidden columns are temporarily displayed when you create a new formula and enter Point mode, allowing you to point to data in the hidden columns. Additionally, other commands that require a block address also cause Quattro Pro to temporarily redisplay hidden columns (such as /Edit, Copy and /Style, Numeric Format), marking them with an * (asterisk).

■ When you are working in a split window and you hide a column in the current window, the column won't be hidden in the second window. Also bear in mind that any changes made to this column in either the bottom or right pane are *not* retained when you close the window. To retain any changes to values or format settings in the hidden column, you *must* make these changes in the top or left window pane. (See Chapter 2.)

■ /Style, Hide Column, Hide can be an important tool in creating concise reports from complex spreadsheets. Spreadsheet users are forever trying to squeeze reports onto letter-size pages, yet trying to keep them informative and easy to read. By hiding columns of data that may be extraneous to a report and using Quattro Pro's array of small fonts, you can reduce many reports to fit a standard page.

■ Hiding columns does *not* protect information from being viewed by other Quattro Pro users. A sharp eye can pick up the missing column letter in the horizontal border of the spreadsheet. To further camouflage a hidden column, turn off the spreadsheet borders with /Window, Options, Row & Col Borders, Hide; this removes the column letter display entirely. Remember, though, that commands such as /Edit, Copy and Move cause information in hidden columns to be displayed. So another person editing the spreadsheet will most likely view hidden data at some point. You can, however, protect data from being altered using the /Options, Protection command (see "Protecting Areas of the Spreadsheet" in Chapter 2).

Spreadsheet Publishing

Traditionally, spreadsheets have been used for recordkeeping, financial analysis, graphing data, and myriad other functions. Many users feel that they can "do it all" with a spreadsheet. The one area where spreadsheets have characteristically fallen short, however, is in presentation—or printed reports.

You'll want to take advantage of Quattro Pro's spreadsheet publishing /Style commands to give your printed data the zip it needs. For example, you can emphasize blocks of data by outlining or shading them, create shadow boxes and thick black rules, and use Quattro Pro's impressive assortment of typefaces (fonts) to print a report. You can even produce sharp-looking bulleted lists by selecting one of the seven bullet symbols available in version 2.0 and later releases.

Hardware Considerations

Note. Some IBM PC XTs and compatibles may not have a built-in graphics card.

To use Quattro Pro's spreadsheet-enhancement /Style commands effectively, you need

- An EGA or VGA monitor, so you can view fonts and special effects using WYSIWYG mode.

- A printer that supports a graphics mode. (Many of today's dot-matrix and laser printers do.) See Chapter 6, Chapter 15, and your printer manual for more information.

Even if you don't have an EGA or VGA monitor, you can still preview special effects if your computer includes a graphics card. See "Previewing a Document" in Chapter 6 for more information.

Fonts

One of Quattro Pro's most powerful features is its fonts capability. You can assign fonts included in Quattro Pro during installation or even create your own custom fonts. WYSIWYG mode, first offered in Quattro Pro version 3.0, makes it considerably easier to use fonts because you can actually view fonts on screen.

For many of you, Quattro Pro may be the first time you have easy access to fonts in a spreadsheet. For this reason, the first part of this section covers font basics—typefaces, point sizes, attributes, soft versus printer-specific fonts, and proportionally spaced versus fixed-width fonts. The remainder of this section is devoted to using fonts in Quattro Pro.

Typeface

A *typeface* is the design, or style of a printed character. Most typefaces are either *serif* or *sans serif* styles. (A serif is a small hook that embellishes the ends of each stroke and corner of a character.) The Dutch typeface illustrated in Figure 3.33 is an example of a serif typeface. The Swiss typeface, which lacks serifs, is an example of a sans serif typeface.

Both Quattro Pro versions 3.0 and 4.0 offer the 11 basic typefaces shown in Figure 3.33. They range from the elegant Roman Light and the spare Monospace, to the heavy, ornate Old English. Quattro Pro also supports some printer-specific fonts, depending on the printer you specified during installation. (See "Default Font Library" later in this section.)

Tip. Two additional typefaces are offered in the ProView Power Pak included with version 3.0. See Chapter 9 for more details.

Scalable (SC) Typefaces in Quattro Pro 4.0

The original Bitstream fonts found in Quattro Pro 3.0 are *raster fonts*. With raster fonts, each character in a typeface is represented by a bitmap, and all the bitmaps for a given typeface are stored in an .FON file. (That's why you have one .FON file in your Quattro Pro 3.0 FONTS directory for every typeface and type size.) When you call for a typeface or type size for which Quattro Pro doesn't currently have an .FON file, it must synthesize the file on the fly. When this happens, you see the message "Now building font."

Figure 3.33
Quattro Pro's
typeface selection

In a new twist, Quattro Pro 4.0 also offers scalable *outline fonts* (designated as -SC within menus), but only for the Dutch, Swiss, and Courier typefaces. Outline fonts are smaller and more flexible than the older raster fonts because with outline font technology, the outline of a character is placed on the screen and the remaining area within the outline is then filled in; bitmaps are rasterized (built) as needed from a single outline (.SPO) font file, at least when displaying fonts on the screen. If you were to compare the FONTS directories of Quattro Pro 3.0 and 4.0, though, you'd notice that there are an equal number of font files. The only difference is that with Quattro Pro 4.0, these font files are used for printing, not for displaying fonts on the screen as they are in Quattro Pro 3.0.

Fixed-Width Versus Proportionally Spaced Fonts

Font typefaces are categorized as either *fixed-width* or *proportionally spaced*. A fixed-width typeface allots the same amount of space to each character. Compare the five *i*'s and five *m*'s in Figure 3.34, for example. Because the fixed-width Monospace typeface has been used, these labels are the same length. It is for this reason that fixed-width fonts are easy to work with. You can use the character width of a fixed-width font, designated as *cpi* (characters per inch) or *pitch*, to calculate the number of characters that will fit across a row on a particular page size. A fixed-width font of 10 cpi, for instance, will fit 75 characters on 7 1/2 inches.

Figure 3.34
Fixed-width versus
proportionally
spaced fonts

File Edit Style Graph Print Database Tools Options Window					? ↑↓

```
File  Edit  Style  Graph  Print  Database  Tools  Options  Window        ? ↑↓
▲ ◄ ► ▼  Erase Copy Move Style Align Font Insert Delete Fit Sum Format CHR WYS
A20: [W35]
                         A              B        C      D      E      F
  1
  2  Monospace                11111
  3  (Fixed width font)       mmmmm
  4
  5  Swiss                    iiiii
  6  (Proportionally spaced font) mmmmm
  7
```

Note. For a discussion of printing fonts, see Chapter 6.

A proportionally spaced typeface, on the other hand, uses different amounts of space for each character—the character *i*, for instance, uses less space than the character *m*. In Figure 3.34, you can see the difference in length of the five *i*'s and five *m*'s in the Swiss typeface. Although a proportionally spaced typeface results in a "tighter fit," it's difficult to determine the number of characters that will fit on a printed page.

If you use a dot-matrix printer, this proportional width adjustment is not what you are accustomed to. Dot-matrix printers can only print characters of a limited height with their built-in character sets, so they measure character size in pitch or cpi. Quattro Pro, however, can print in the more complex graphics mode, so you'll be astonished at the report quality you can produce using a dot-matrix printer. Most 24-pin, dot-matrix printers can produce near-laser-quality fonts and graphics for data with Quattro Pro.

Point Size

Note. Working with different point sizes in a spreadsheet affects the row height. See "Working with Row Heights" later in this section.

The size of a printed character is measured vertically in points. A *point* is approximately $1/72$ of an inch high, and all typefaces are measured in increments of one point. For example, the point size of all eleven typestyles in Figure 3.28 is 18. You can translate this into a more familiar measurement by expressing it this way: $18/72$, or $1/4$ of an inch. This means that the *maximum* height of each character is approximately $1/4$-inch high.

Quattro Pro provides 13 different point sizes ranging from 6 to 72. You can use any of these point sizes with all of the typefaces listed in Figure 3.33. Regardless of the point size, the width-to-height ratio of each character is maintained. You can see this in Figure 3.35, which shows the Bitstream Swiss typeface in six different point sizes, ranging from the tiny 6 point to the formidable 72 point.

Attributes

Quattro Pro offers three different type styles or *attributes*—Bold, Italic, and Underline—that you can assign to a typeface. You can also use a combination of these attributes. Not all type styles, however, work with all typefaces. The Roman typeface, for instance, is the only Hershey font that can be italicized. For a discussion of Hershey fonts, see "Soft Versus Printer-Specific Fonts," next.

Figure 3.35
Some of the point sizes available for each typeface

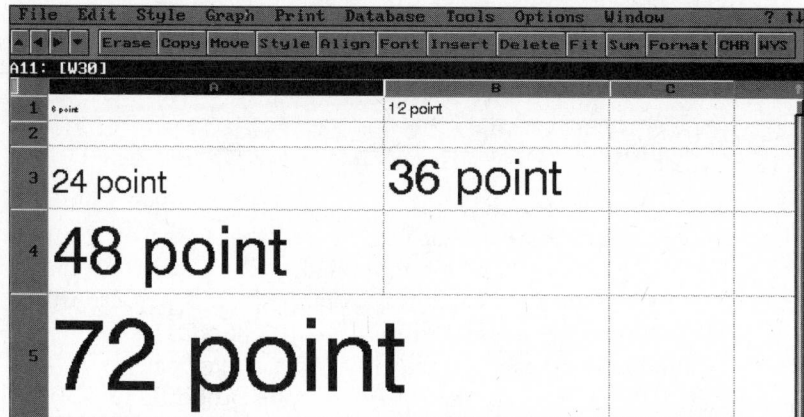

In general, the style attributes only work with the following typefaces:

Attribute	Typeface Affected
Bold	Swiss and Dutch
Italic	Roman, Dutch, Swiss, and Courier
Underline	All typefaces

Soft Versus Printer-Specific Fonts

Quattro Pro supports both *soft fonts* and *printer-specific fonts*. Soft fonts, which can be printed on most graphics printers, are combinations of typeface, point size, and attributes that are provided by Quattro Pro. They are created with software instructions from Quattro Pro telling the printer how to form each character as it is being printed. Although a printer can print a specific Quattro Pro font, it may not be able to print the same font with other software, such as a word processor or database program unless those programs also have soft font capability.

Two types of soft fonts, Hershey and Bitstream, are included with Quattro Pro. *Hershey fonts* are basic type fonts that can be instantly output to the screen or most graphic printers. These fonts are the Roman, Sans Serif, Script, Monospace, Old English, and Eurostyle typefaces.

Bitstream fonts, on the other hand, are sent to the printer in a "bitmap" format that produces a higher-quality character resolution, especially at the larger point sizes. Because of this special format, each combination of typeface, point size, and style requires that a *bitmap font file* be built before the font can be displayed or printed.

Note. Quattro Pro requires, on average, approximately 125k of available RAM to build a new font file. If your hard disk is full and Quattro Pro cannot save the font file, it switches to draft mode and replaces a Bitstream font with the closest Hershey font.

You have the option of building bitmap font files for the Bitstream fonts when you install Quattro Pro, or later as needed. If you choose not to build the font files at installation, Quattro Pro builds them as needed during your Quattro Pro sessions.

Printer-specific fonts—internal character sets built into a printer—are unique to your printer model. A dot-matrix printer, for instance, may have several internal fonts such as Pica, Elite, and Compressed. PostScript printers have a more exotic list of internal typefaces, such as Palatino, Times, and Zapf Dingbats. Printer-specific fonts can be used with almost any program and often can be selected from a menu on the front panel of the printer.

Quattro Pro supports printer-specific fonts for the LaserJet and PostScript families of printers. See "Default Font Library" next for more details.

Default Font Library

During installation, Quattro Pro 4.0 automatically includes the eight fonts shown in Figure 3.36 as the *default font library*. All of these fonts are scalable fonts. (See "Scalable (SC) Typefaces in Quattro Pro 4.0," earlier.) Quattro Pro 3.0 has the same default font library except that the fonts are Bitstream fonts. For example, Font 1 is Bitstream 12 point Swiss.

When you retrieve a spreadsheet file created in an earlier release, the default library is updated only in certain circumstances. For instance, imagine that you created a file in Quattro Pro 3.0 and you open it in Quattro Pro 4.0. If this file used version 3.0's default font library, then the library is updated. Font 1, for example, is converted from Bitstream Swiss 12 point to SC Swiss 12 point. But if you previously changed the font library in any way, then the font library isn't updated and it uses Bitstream rather than SC (scalable) fonts.

If you specify an HP LaserJet or PostScript printer during installation, Quattro Pro also attaches printer-specific fonts to your font library. For instance, when you specify an HP LaserJet III printer, just some of the printer-specific fonts included are shown in Figure 3.37. (To choose one of these fonts, see "Customizing the Font Library" later in this section.)

You can change the fonts in your font library for one spreadsheet or for all future sessions. See "Customizing the Font Library."

Figure 3.36

Quattro Pro 4.0's default font library

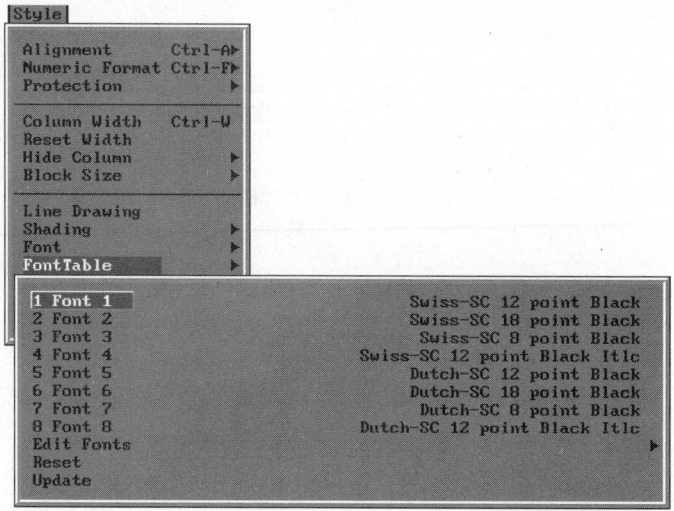

Figure 3.37

Some of the HP LaserJet III fonts automatically added to the font library

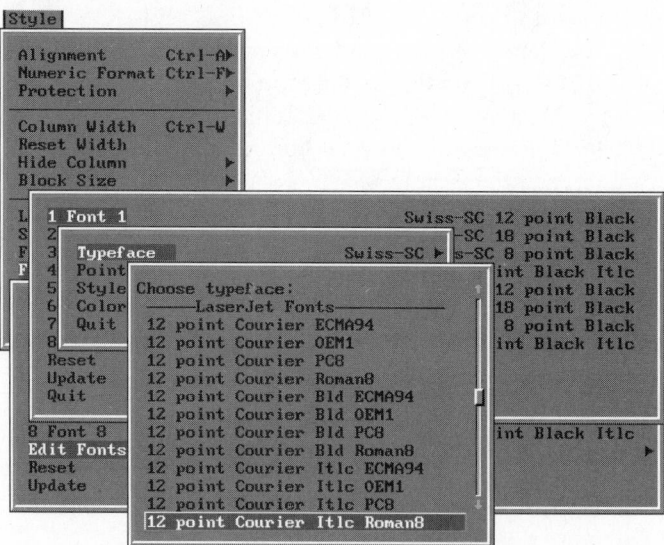

The Default Spreadsheet Font

By default, Quattro Pro always assigns Font 1 to the data in a spreadsheet. During installation, SC Swiss 12 point Black is assigned to Font 1 (see Figure 3.36). In version 3.0, Font 1 is Bitstream Swiss 12 point Black.

Note. Any headers or footers you assign using the /Print command *always* use Font 1. See Chapter 6.

TIP. *In Quattro Pro 4.0, the /Style, Font Table, 1 Font 1 setting is also controlled by the Font Setting of the named style NORMAL (accessed through /Style, Define Style, Create). That is, if you change the NORMAL Font setting, this becomes the new default font and is reflected as the /Style, Font Table 1 Font 1 setting. Likewise, change the /Style, FontTable, 1 Font 1 setting, and the NORMAL font changes to this setting. See "Creating Named Styles in Quattro Pro 4.0," later.*

When you work in WYSIWYG mode, Quattro Pro displays your spreadsheet data using Font 1—you can see this in Figure 3.38. When you work in Character mode, however, or if you are not using an EGA or VGA monitor, all spreadsheet data is displayed using a 12-point Monospace font. Then the only way to see Font 1 (or any other fonts you assign) on the screen is by using Quattro Pro's Screen Preview feature discussed in Chapter 6.

Figure 3.38

A spreadsheet using default Font 1

| File | Edit | Style | Graph | Print | Database | Tools | Options | Window | ? ↑↓ |

| ▲ ◄ ► ▼ | Erase | Copy | Move | Style | Align | Font | Insert | Delete | Fit | Sum | Format | CHR | WYS |

B4: (C0) 10000000

	A	B	C	D	E	F
1	GROSS PROFIT PROJECTIONS					
2		Mth Ended	Mth Ended	Mth Ended	Q Ended	
3		31-Jan-92	29-Feb-92	31-Mar-92	31-Mar-92	
4	Gross Sales	$10,000,000	$10,500,000	$11,025,000	$31,525,000	
5	Returns	(200,000)	(210,000)	(220,500)	(630,500)	
6		========	========	========	========	
7	Net Sales	$9,800,000	$10,290,000	$10,804,500	$30,894,500	
8						
9	Direct Material	1,000,000	1,050,000	1,102,500	3,152,500	
10	Direct Labor	3,000,000	3,150,000	3,307,500	9,457,500	
11	Overhead Costs	1,500,000	1,575,000	1,653,750	4,728,750	
12		========	========	========	========	
13	Gross Profit	$4,300,000	$4,515,000	$4,740,750	$13,555,750	
14						

Assigning Existing Fonts

In Quattro Pro, you can use up to eight different fonts in one spreadsheet. When you use different fonts, it's best to

- Decide first on the font setting you want to use for the majority of the spreadsheet, and make that the default setting (Font 1).

- Assign other fonts to small blocks in the spreadsheet, as needed.

For example, suppose you have previously entered the data shown in Figure 3.38. Since you have not assigned any specific fonts, this data is displayed (in WYSIWYG mode) using Font 1, or SC Swiss 12 point. You have assigned a global column width setting of 12, and to column A only, a column width of 14. Let's say you now want to use different fonts to differentiate the spreadsheet title, column and row headings, and data. Here's how to do this:

Note. In Quattro Pro 3.0, you use the /Style, Font command.

1. Select /Style, Font Table to access the font menu shown in Figure 3.36. Assign Swiss 18 point Black to the title by selecting 2 Font 2 and then specifying the single-cell block A1..A1. When you press Enter, Quattro Pro 4.0 returns you to the spreadsheet, where the label in cell A1 now uses this font.

2. Assign Swiss 12 point Black Italic to the column and row headings by selecting /Style, Font Table, 4 Font 4, and then specifying the block B2..E3. When you press Enter, Quattro Pro 3.0 returns you to the spreadsheet, so select /Style, Font Table again and assign this font to the block A4..A13.

You can see the results in Figure 3.39. Because you can view the assigned fonts in WYSIWYG mode, you can see that Quattro Pro automatically adjusts the height of row 1 to accommodate the 18-point title in cell A1. (See "Working with Row Heights" later in this section.) However, column width settings are not automatically adjusted. Although this is not a problem here, you will see in the next section the difficulties it can cause.

Figure 3.39
Assigning existing fonts to a spreadsheet

File	Edit	Style	Graph	Print	Database	Tools	Options	Window	? ↑↓
▲ ◄ ► ▼	Erase	Copy	Move	Style	Align	Font	Insert	Delete	Fit	Sum	Format	CHR	WYS

B4: (C0) 10000000

	A	B	C	D	E	F
1	GROSS PROFIT PROJECTIONS					
2		Mth Ended	Mth Ended	Mth Ended	Q Ended	
3		31-Jan-92	29-Feb-92	31-Mar-92	31-Mar-92	
4	Gross Sales	$10,000,000	$10,500,000	$11,025,000	$31,525,000	
5	Returns	(200,000)	(210,000)	(220,500)	(630,500)	
6		========	========	========	========	
7	Net Sales	$9,800,000	$10,290,000	$10,804,500	$30,894,500	
8						
9	Direct Material	1,000,000	1,050,000	1,102,500	3,152,500	
10	Direct Labor	3,000,000	3,150,000	3,307,500	9,457,500	
11	Overhead Costs	1,500,000	1,575,000	1,653,750	4,728,750	
12		========	========	========	========	
13	Gross Profit	$4,300,000	$4,515,000	$4,740,750	$13,555,750	
14						

Customizing the Font Library

Sometimes you will prefer to use fonts not currently available in your font library. You can customize the font library using the /Style, Font Table, Edit Fonts command and assigning a different typeface, point size, style (attribute), and/or color to one or all of the eight font choices in the Font menu. Then you can assign these fonts to areas of a spreadsheet.

Note. In Quattro Pro 3.0, select /Style, Font.

For instance, you might prefer a sans serif 12-point font for most spreadsheet data in Figure 3.39. To specify this font as Font 1,

1. Select /Style, Font Table to view the Font menu in Figure 3.36. Choose Edit Fonts, and then 1 Font 1 (or type **1**). Quattro Pro displays the frontmost menu in Figure 3.40, which lists the current Font 1, SC Swiss 12 point Black.

Figure 3.40

The /Style, Font Table, Edit Fonts, Font 1 menu

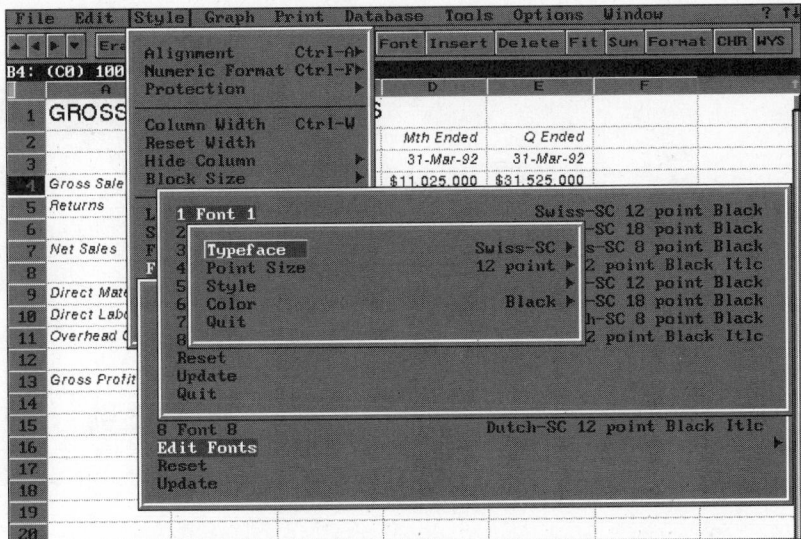

2. Choose Typeface to access the typefaces shown in Figure 3.41. (If you specified a PostScript or LaserJet printer during installation, this menu will also include printer-specific fonts.) Select Sans Serif, and Quattro Pro returns you to the Font 1 menu, which now displays a Sans Serif typeface.

NOTE. *When you select one of the LaserJet or PostScript typefaces Quattro Pro attaches to a font library during installation, such as 12 point Courier Bld OEM1, you cannot change the point size and style.*

3. Since the other settings (12 point and Black) are already specified, you needn't make any other changes. Select Quit twice to return to the Font Table menu, where Sans Serif 12 point Black is now displayed as Font 1.

Note. Although Quattro Pro lets you choose any of the Style attributes for any typeface, not all of them work. See "Attributes" earlier in this section.

The block A4..E13 now uses this new Font 1. Additionally, any new data entered in this spreadsheet will use this font. Some of the values in the block are represented by asterisks, indicating that the column width settings are too small for this font. We'll adjust column widths and other settings after we have finished assigning fonts in this spreadsheet.

Figure 3.41

Changing the Font 1 typeface

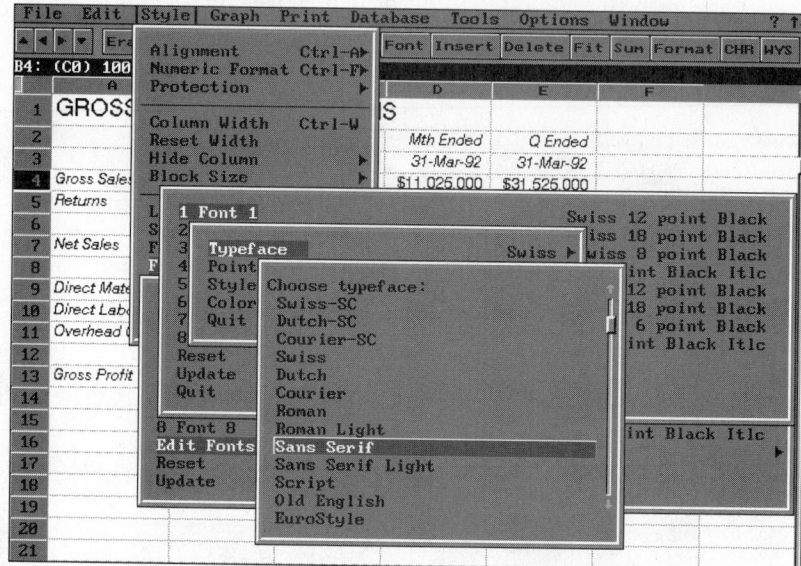

Any changes you make to the font library are saved with the current spreadsheet. To make these settings the font library for all future sessions, select /Style, Font Table, Update. To reset the font library to the default settings, select /Style, Font Table, Reset. (In Quattro Pro 3.0, use /Style, Font, Update and Reset.)

Although you'll want to change the font library for fonts you often use, Quattro Pro 4.0 offers you a more flexible alternative when you want to assign a font not currently in the font library.

Assigning New Fonts

One of the frustrating limitations in Quattro Pro 3.0 is that you can only assign 8 fonts to a spreadsheet—the number of fonts in the font library. In Quattro Pro 4.0, however, you can assign a virtually unlimited number of fonts by using the /Style, Font command.

Tip. If you preselect a block, Font in Quattro Pro 4.0's SpeedBar accesses the /Style, Font dialog box.

For example, here's how to add other fonts for the labels and headings in Figure 3.39 without changing the font library:

1. Assign a Sans Serif 14 point Black font to emphasize the Net Sales and Gross Profit values. First, preselect B7..E7, and then select /Style, Font. You'll see the backmost menu shown in Figure 3.42, which displays the font currently assigned to the upper-left cell in this block or the default spreadsheet font. Choose Typeface, and then select Sans Serif from the list. Choose Point Size, and you'll see the frontmost menu in Figure 3.42. From the 13 available point sizes (6 to 72), choose 14 point. When you select Quit, Quattro Pro returns you to the spreadsheet, where B7..E7 is now assigned this font. Repeat this procedure for the block B13..E13.

Figure 3.42

Changing the point size

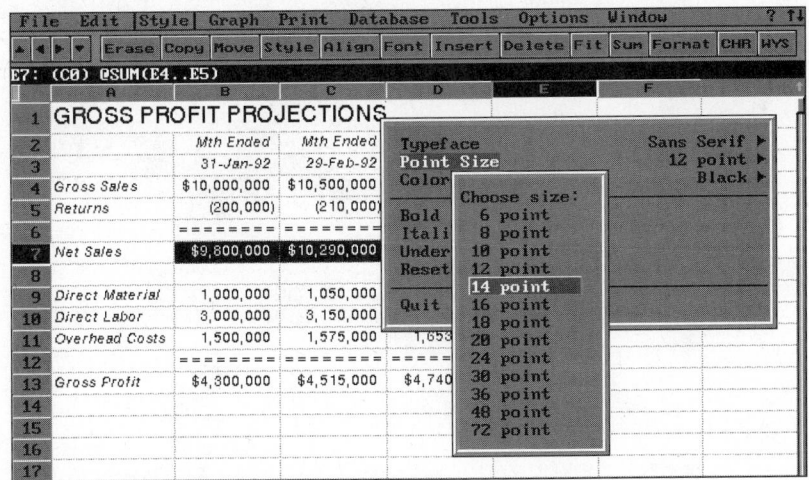

NOTE. *Quattro Pro 3.0 users: To perform step 1 above, first use the /Style, Font, Edit Fonts command to assign Sans Serif 14 point Black as part of the font library. Let's say you assign it to 3 Font 3. You can then use the /Style, Font command to assign 3 Font 3 to B7..E7 and to B13..E13, just as you would any other existing font. Repeat this technique to complete steps 2 and 3, below.*

2. Assign an SC Swiss 20 point Black Italic font to the Net Sales spreadsheet title in cell A1. First, preselect A1, and then select /Style, Font or the Font button. You'll again see a menu with the default font, SC Swiss 12 point Black. Choose Point Size and specify 20 point. Next, select Italic to turn this style attribute on, just as you see in Figure 3.43. (You can choose one or more of these styles; Reset turns off all style attributes.) Choose Quit to return to the spreadsheet where this font will be assigned to A1.

3. Use the /Style, Font command to assign an SC Swiss 10 point Black Bold font to the column and row headings in the block A4..A5 and A9..A11. Likewise, assign an SC Swiss 14 point Black Bold font to emphasize the labels "Net Sales" in A7 and "Gross Profit" in A13.

You can see the results in Figure 3.44. The widths of columns B through E are too small to accommodate the new fonts. Column A, on the other hand, is a little too large. To overcome this problem, you can either adjust the column width settings (see "Fonts and Column Widths" next), or assign other fonts to the data.

Figure 3.43

Assigning a style attribute

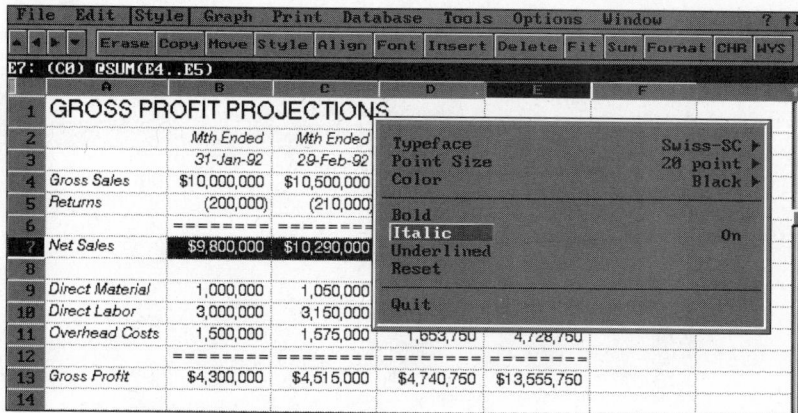

Figure 3.44

Using large fonts sometimes requires column width adjustments

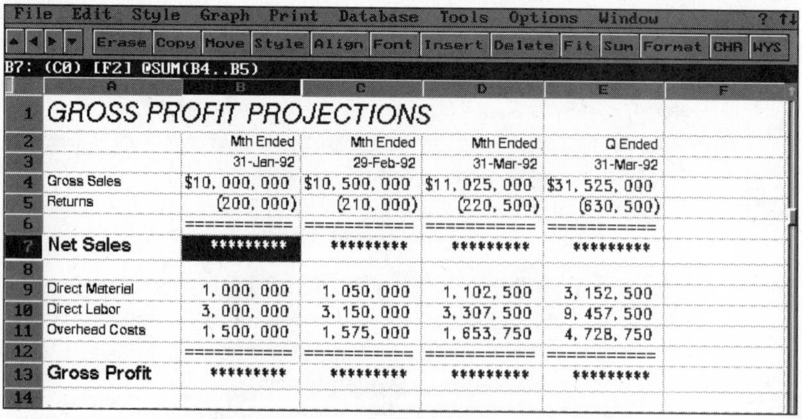

When you assign new fonts to a spreadsheet, you will often find that you need to make other presentation-style changes. These types of changes are made to Figure 3.44 in "Fonts and Column Widths" next.

You can display spreadsheet data in color (and print it in color if you are blessed with a color printer) by assigning a font color. In Quattro Pro 4.0, you can access a menu with 16 different color choices through /Style, Font, Color, or when you change a library font through the /Style, Font Table, Edit Fonts command. In Quattro Pro 3.0, you access this same menu through /Style, Font, Edit Fonts.

Fonts and Column Widths

When you use fonts in Quattro Pro, remember these two important principles:

- Larger fonts require larger column widths. If you switch to a large font in one cell, it can affect the width of the entire column.

- For the same point size, one typeface may require a different column width than another typeface.

Note. If you work in Character mode (not WYSIWYG), you may encounter problems with column width settings and fonts. See "Working with Columns" earlier in this chapter.

For example, examine the title GROSS PROFIT PROJECTIONS at the top of Figure 3.44, which uses a 20-point font. In this case, the large point size does not affect the width of column A, because cells B1, C1, and D1 are empty and handle the overflow. Consider, however, that if you had to size column A to fit this title, it would take up the space of four columns. In general, you'll want to use large fonts only in limited instances.

Furthermore, take another look at Figure 3.44: the font assigned to Font 2, Sans Serif 14 point Black, causes some of the data to be displayed as asterisks. Compare this to Figure 3.38 and to Figure 3.39. All three spreadsheets use a column width of 12 for columns B through E, but in Figure 3.44 this doesn't work. Therefore, to display the data in Figure 3.44, columns B through E must have a column width of 15, as shown in Figure 3.45. Whenever you encounter this problem, either adjust the column width or try changing the typeface.

In contrast, the fonts assigned to the labels in column A (except for the title in cell A1) reduce the displayed length of these labels. To reflect this, the column A width has been decreased from 14 in Figure 3.44 to 12 in Figure 3.45.

NOTE. *Quattro Pro's character-based column width setting assumes a fixed-width, 10-cpi font. So when you use proportionally spaced fonts, such as SC Swiss, the correct character-based column width setting may not correspond to the actual number of characters in the column.*

Finally, after you make the appropriate column width adjustments, you may find that some additional changes will enhance presentation even further.

The /Style, Alignment, Center command, for instance, has been used for block B2..E3 in Figure 3.45 to center the column headings. Additionally, the \= labels in Figure 3.44 look odd because of the Bold style assigned to the majority of the spreadsheet. In Figure 3.45 these labels have been changed to \- for a cleaner effect.

Figure 3.45

Adjusted column widths accommodate larger assigned fonts

File	Edit	Style	Graph	Print	Database	Tools	Options	Window	? ↑↓

| ▲ | ◄ | ► | ▼ | Erase | Copy | Move | Style | Align | Font | Insert | Delete | Fit | Sum | Format | CHR | WYS |

B7: (C0) [W15] [F2] @SUM(B4..B5)

	A	B	C	D	E
1	GROSS PROFIT PROJECTIONS				
2		Mth Ended	Mth Ended	Mth Ended	Q Ended
3		31-Jan-92	29-Feb-92	31-Mar-92	31-Mar-92
4	Gross Sales	$10,000,000	$10,500,000	$11,025,000	$31,525,000
5	Returns	(200,000)	(210,000)	(220,500)	(630,500)
6		-----------	-----------	-----------	-----------
7	**Net Sales**	$9,800,000	$10,290,000	$10,804,500	$30,894,500
8					
9	Direct Material	1,000,000	1,050,000	1,102,500	3,152,500
10	Direct Labor	3,000,000	3,150,000	3,307,500	9,457,500
11	Overhead Costs	1,500,000	1,575,000	1,653,750	4,728,750
12		-----------	-----------	-----------	-----------
13	**Gross Profit**	$4,300,000	$4,515,000	$4,740,750	$13,555,750
14					

CAUTION! *Column width settings that appear adequate on the screen may not be sufficient when you print. See Chapter 6 for details.*

Working with Row Heights

You'll find /Style, Block Size, Height, first introduced in version 3.0, extremely helpful when you work with fonts in a spreadsheet. When you assign fonts to a spreadsheet, Quattro Pro follows these rules for row height:

Note. Even in Character mode, Quattro Pro automatically adjusts the row height to accommodate the largest font in each row—but you can't see it on the screen. So you must use Screen Preview, discussed in Chapter 6, to view the effect of fonts on a spreadsheet.

■ The default row height is 15, which accommodates the default Font 1, a 12-point font (see "The Default Spreadsheet Font" earlier).

■ If you change the point size of Font 1, the height of *all* spreadsheet rows changes to accommodate the height of the new point size.

■ The height of a row is adjusted to accommodate the *largest* font in that row (see Figure 3.46). If you later assign an even larger font to the row, Quattro Pro once again adjusts the row height to accommodate the largest font. If you later assign a smaller font to that row or delete the largest font in the row, Quattro Pro does not adjust the row height; it retains the setting that accommodated the larger font.

Figure 3.46

Quattro Pro's row
height adjustments

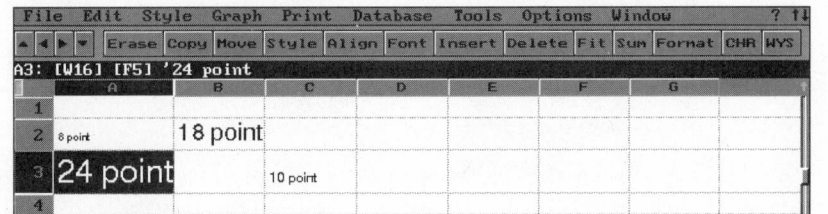

A

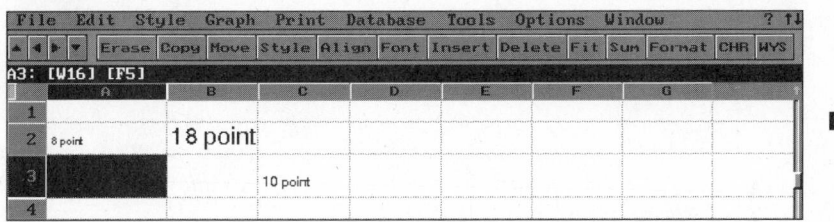

B

You can see this in Figure 3.46. Notice in Figure 3.46A that cell A3 is assigned a 24-point font. If you press Del and erase the contents of A3, you can see in Figure 3.46B that Quattro Pro does not adjust the row height. Instead, you must do so using /Style, Block Size, Height. In the menu shown in Figure 3.47, choose Reset Row Height and specify any cell in row 3.

Figure 3.47

The /Style, Block
Size, Height menu

```
 File   Edit  |Style| Graph   Print   Database   Tools   Options   Window        ? ↑↓
 ▲ ◄ ► ▼   Er:  Alignment      Ctrl-A►   Font  Insert  Delete  Fit  Sum  Format  CHR  WYS
A3: [W16] [F    Numeric Format Ctrl-F►      D        E        F        G
               Protection             ►
  1
  2  8 point    Column Width    Ctrl-U
               Reset Width
  3            Hide Column            ►
               Block Size            ►
  4         L   Set Width
  5         S   Reset Width          ►
  6         F   Auto Width           ►
  7         F   Height        ►       ►
  8         U
  9         Def i    Set Row Height
 10         Inse   Reset Row Height
 11
```

Quattro Pro automatically adjusts the height of all cells in row 3 back to the default height determined by Font 1. However, if any cell in the row contains a font *larger* than the point size of Font 1, Quattro Pro adjusts the height to accommodate this font.

The /Style, Block Size, Height command includes another option, Set Row Height. Use this to

- Decrease the height of a row that contains a large font. The text using this large font will then be truncated on the screen. This setting does not affect your printed output, however (see Chapter 6).

- Change the height of a row for other presentation effects. For instance, you may want to decrease a row height when you create the shadow in a shadow box.

CAUTION! *When you assign large fonts close together in a spreadsheet, Quattro Pro does not always adjust the row heights correctly when you print, even though the row heights may appear adequate on your screen. This seems to happen when the largest font in a row is not in the first column of the printed output. So make sure you use Screen Preview, discussed in Chapter 6, to preview a document before you print. And use the /Style, Block Size, Height command to overcome this problem.*

Shading Blocks of Data

Quattro Pro offers two shading options, Grey and Black, that you can employ to emphasize areas of a spreadsheet and to create dramatic effects such as thick black rules or shadow boxes. Figure 3.48 shows some of the special effects you can achieve with the /Style, Shading command and a printer that supports graphics mode.

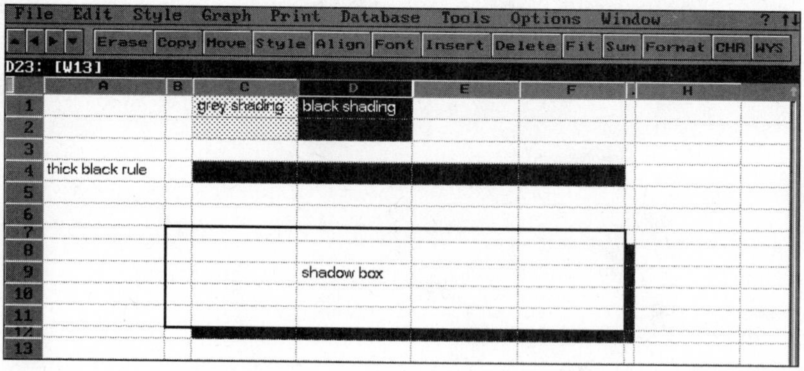

Figure 3.48
Shading effects using /Style, Shading

Note. To print shaded cells, see "Printing Special Effects" in Chapter 6.

As you can see, the Grey option creates a soft grey backdrop for data; Black shading produces a more dramatic "reverse-highlight" effect—the background in black and data in gray. Quattro Pro shades only the part of the block that does *not* contain data. Text and labels are also displayed in their normal mode. So use these shading effects to call attention to important data, create easy-to-follow forms, and produce reports that look professionally done.

Here is the procedure to create a thick black rule like the one in Figure 3.48.

1. Position the cell selector in the upper-left corner of the block you want to shade, in this case, C4.

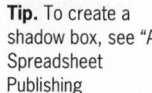

Tip. To create a shadow box, see "A Spreadsheet Publishing Example" later in this chapter.

2. Select /Style, Shading, and Quattro Pro offers you the three selections in Figure 3.49. Select Black.

3. In response to the prompt for the block to shade, specify **C4..F4**, and press Enter.

Figure 3.49
The /Style, Shade menu

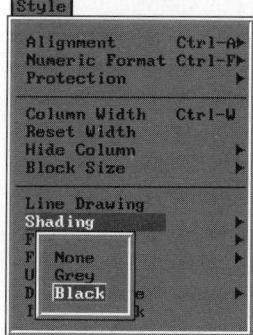

Keep in mind the following when using /Style, Shading:

- When you work in Character mode, or use a black-and-white monitor, shading on the screen and when printed may differ. For instance, when you use gray shading in a cell that contains data, the shading looks black on the screen, but is gray when you print.

- Shaded cells can be copied or moved just like other cells. When you use the /Edit, Copy and Move commands, a /Style, Shade setting is also copied or moved right along with the data.

- When you use /Edit, Erase, only the data is removed; any shading is left intact. Use /Style, Shading, None to remove shading from a cell or block.

- Cells that have both shading and line drawing settings may appear to have a gap between the shading and lines, making them look out of kilter on the screen. When you print, however, the shading and line drawing effects are in perfect alignment.

- You can control the intensity of gray shading when you print on an HP LaserJet printer, with the /Options, Hardware, Printers, Fonts, Cartridge Fonts, Shading Level command discussed in Chapter 15.

- Use /Options, Colors, Spreadsheet, Shading (see Chapter 15) to change the color of shading displayed on the screen.

Drawing Lines and Boxes

In the past, spreadsheet users have gone to great lengths to create grid effects around their data in an attempt to make the printed data easier to read. This involved inserting lots of extra rows and columns, using = or | characters. Quattro Pro's /Style, Line Drawing command gives you the capability to draw "real" boxes and lines around data, without having to add any extra rows or columns. You can select single, double, or thick lines to create border, grid, or underline effects that accentuate your data.

Adding Lines and Boxes

You can easily create boxes and lines in your spreadsheet. (Take a look ahead at Figure 3.52.) You can do this before or after you enter data in the spreadsheet. Just use the following procedure:

1. Create the double lines along the bottom of cells A1 through F1. Place the cell selector in A1 and select /Style, Line Drawing. In response to the prompt, indicate the block **A1..F1**, and press Enter.

2. From the Placement menu shown in Figure 3.50, select Bottom from the following list of options. (Quit returns you to the spreadsheet.)

Line Drawing Option	Lines Drawn
All	Box around each cell in the block, creating a grid effect
Outside	Box around the outside edge of the block, creating a border

Line Drawing Option	Lines Drawn
Top	Horizontal line above the top row of cells in the block
Bottom	Horizontal line below the last row of cells in the block
Left	Vertical line along the left edge of the block
Right	Vertical line along the right edge of the block
Inside	Vertical and horizontal lines between all cells in the block, creating a grid effect with no border
Horizontal	Horizontal line between each row in the block
Vertical	Vertical line between each column in the block

Figure 3.50

The /Style, Line Drawing, Placement menu

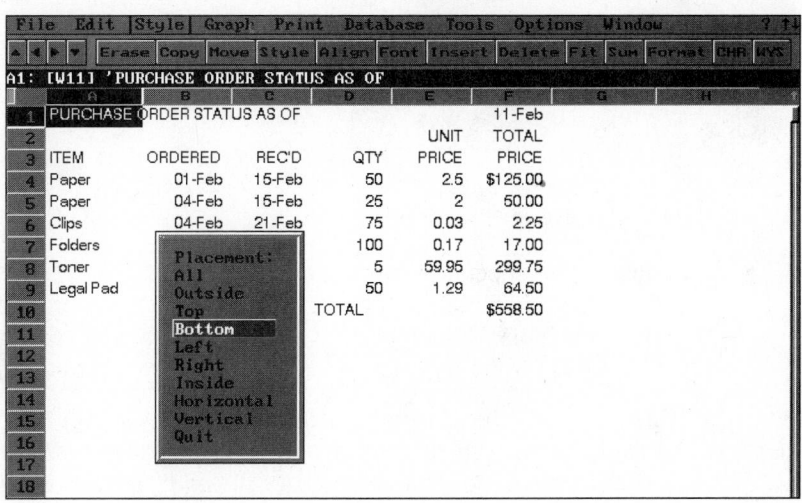

3. From the Line Types menu shown in Figure 3.51, select Double from this list of options:

Line Type Option	Effect
None	Removes lines previously drawn
Single	Draws a single line
Double	Draws double lines
Thick	Draws a single, heavy line

Figure 3.51

The /Style, Line Drawing, Line Types menu

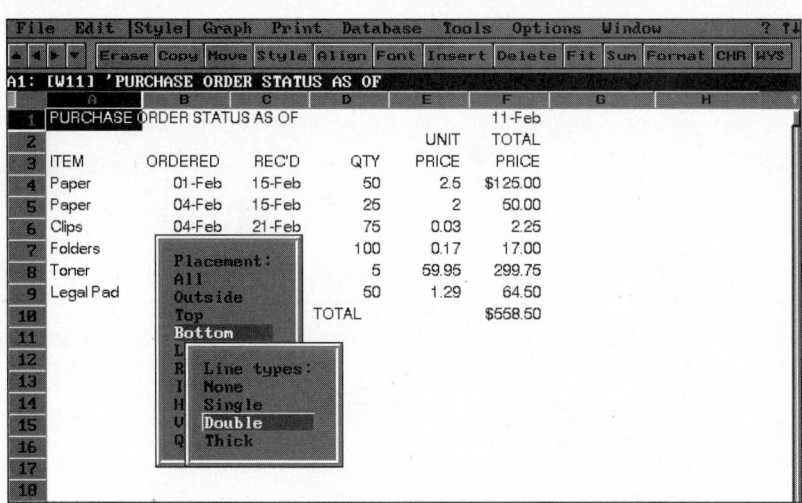

A double line appears across the bottom of the block A1..F1. Quattro Pro returns you to the Placement menu. From here, you can draw additional lines in the same block, or press Esc to back up one step and continue to define other blocks for line drawing, or select Quit to return to the spreadsheet.

4. Now specify lines around the block A4..F9 (see Figure 3.52). Press Esc, and Quattro Pro displays "Enter block to draw lines:". Press Esc again to unanchor the cell selector, specify **A4..F9**, then press Enter. Select Outside from the Placement menu, and then Thick from the Line Type menu. Quattro Pro draws a thick line around the *outside* of this block.

5. Next draw single vertical lines between the columns in the same block, A4..F9. Since this block is still selected, and you are now located in the Placement menu, just choose Vertical and then Single from the Line Type menu.

6. Draw thick lines around cell F10. Since you are located in the Placement menu, press Esc twice to return to the block definition prompt, and unanchor the cell selector. Specify **F10** as the block, Outside Placement, and Thick Line Type. Quattro Pro draws a box around cell F10.

7. Select Quit to return to the spreadsheet.

Your spreadsheet now looks like Figure 3.52. Double lines are displayed along the bottom of the title block, A1..F1; thick lines outline the block A4..F9 and thin lines delineate each column in this block; and cell F10 is encased in a box.

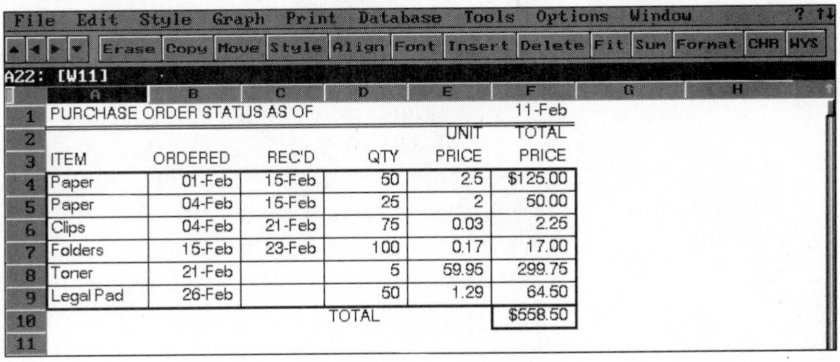

	A	B	C	D	E	F
1	PURCHASE ORDER STATUS AS OF					11-Feb
2					UNIT	TOTAL
3	ITEM	ORDERED	REC'D	QTY	PRICE	PRICE
4	Paper	01-Feb	15-Feb	50	2.5	$125.00
5	Paper	04-Feb	15-Feb	25	2	50.00
6	Clips	04-Feb	21-Feb	75	0.03	2.25
7	Folders	15-Feb	23-Feb	100	0.17	17.00
8	Toner	21-Feb		5	59.95	299.75
9	Legal Pad	26-Feb		50	1.29	64.50
10				TOTAL		$558.50
11						

Figure 3.52 A spreadsheet with lines and boxes

The /Style, Line Drawing command does not affect the data inside the lines. You can still enter or edit the data within these cells, and reference it with formulas. You can even draw lines in an empty spreadsheet, creating a data entry form for future use.

In WYSIWYG mode, line drawing will look almost the same in the displayed spreadsheet and the printed one. (Be sure to read "Printing Special Effects" in Chapter 6.) If you don't use an EGA or VGA monitor, however, or if you are working in Character mode, line drawing may appear to take up more space on screen. Some rows and columns will look larger than others, for example, and thick lines will be unsightly. When you print, however, or use Screen Preview (see Chapter 6), you will see that line drawing does not actually consume additional space.

Quattro Pro does not assign line drawing to the same cells that you originally specified. In Figure 3.52, for instance, you created the thick box around cell F10 by using the /Style, Line Drawing command and specifying cell F10. When you did this, Quattro Pro assigned the top line and left line of the box to cell F10. But it assigned the bottom line to cell F11, and the right line to cell G10. This has important implications when you move or copy cells (see Chapter 4) that contain line drawing, and when you print (see Chapter 6).

NOTE. *You may notice that the /Style, Line Drawing command seems a little "sticky" if you attempt to leave the menu with the Esc key rather than selecting the Quit option. Esc backs you up only one step, allowing you to define another block and select a placement option for it. You have to press Esc twice more to return to the spreadsheet. So use Quit to leave this command, rather than Esc.*

Removing Lines and Boxes

Note. The /Edit, Erase Block command (see Chapter 4) does not erase line drawing.

You can remove all or some of the lines from a block as easily as you assign them. For example, suppose you use the command /Style, Line Drawing, All, Single to draw lines around every cell in the block A1..D4. After viewing the results, you decide that the spreadsheet is a little cluttered. You decide to remove *only* the horizontal lines between the rows to improve the effect of the lines. To do this, select /Style, Line Drawing, indicate the same block (A1..D4) and then choose Horizontal placement. Then select None from the Line Type menu, and Quit to return to the spreadsheet. Quattro Pro removes only the horizontal lines within this block, leaving intact the vertical lines between columns and the border around the outside; the result is a cleaner look.

Creating Bulleted Lists

You can create stylish bulleted lists in a spreadsheet using any of the seven special bullet characters provided by Quattro Pro. In version 3.0, bullets are usually displayed in a spreadsheet in WYSIWYG mode. Figure 3.53 shows the entries you must make to create the seven bullets.

NOTE. *When you create a bullet that includes a checkmark and the checkmark overflows into the cell above, you have to erase the contents of both cells to eradicate the checkmark.*

To create a bullet, enter the appropriate bullet code where you want the bullet to appear. If you precede a label entry with a bullet code, for example, Quattro Pro prints a bullet preceding the label. You can even embed a bullet code in the middle or end of a label.

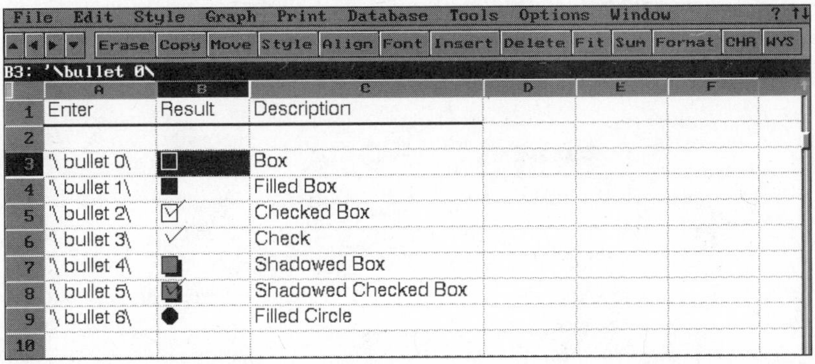

Figure 3.53

Quattro Pro's bullet codes and resulting bullets

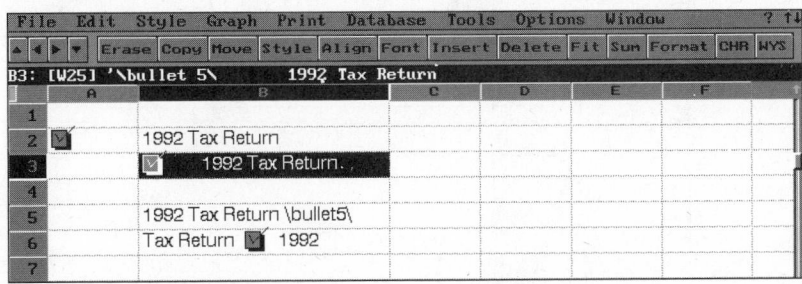

	File Edit Style Graph Print Database Tools Options Window	? ↑↓
	▲ ◀ ▶ ▼ Erase Copy Move Style Align Font Insert Delete Fit Sum Format CHR WYS	

B3: '\bullet 0\

	A	B	C	D	E	F
1	Enter	Result	Description			
2						
3	\ bullet 0\	☐	Box			
4	\ bullet 1\	■	Filled Box			
5	\ bullet 2\	☑	Checked Box			
6	\ bullet 3\	✓	Check			
7	\ bullet 4\	◪	Shadowed Box			
8	\ bullet 5\	☑	Shadowed Checked Box			
9	\ bullet 6\	●	Filled Circle			
10						

Suppose you want to create a shadowed checked box (bullet 5) preceding the label 1992 Tax Return. You can use either of two methods (demonstrated in Figure 3.54):

- In cell A2, separate from the label, enter **'\bullet 5**, and press Enter. (When a bullet code is the first thing entered in a cell, a label prefix must precede the bullet code.) In cell B2, enter the label **'1992 Tax Return** and press Enter.

- In the *same* cell as the label (B3) type **'\bullet 5**. Press the spacebar seven times to add seven blank spaces, type **1992 Tax Return**, and press Enter.

Figure 3.54

Different ways of entering bullet codes

	File Edit Style Graph Print Database Tools Options Window	? ↑↓
	▲ ◀ ▶ ▼ Erase Copy Move Style Align Font Insert Delete Fit Sum Format CHR WYS	

B3: [W25] '\bullet 5\   1992 Tax Return

	A	B	C	D	E	F
1						
2	☑	1992 Tax Return				
3		☑ 1992 Tax Return.				
4						
5		1992 Tax Return \bullet5\				
6		Tax Return ☑ 1992				
7						

Tip. Bullet characters can also be included in graphs (see Chapter 9).

You can also add a bullet after a label or even embed a bullet in the middle of a label. When you do, a label prefix before the bullet code is not needed. In Figure 3.54, the label in cell B5, 1992 Tax Return \bullet 5\, creates a bullet at the end of the label. In cell B6 the bullet is embedded in the middle of the label Tax Return \bullet 5\ 1992. Notice that an embedded bullet is displayed, while a bullet at the end of a label is not.

Before you print a spreadsheet that contains bullets, be sure to read "Printing Special Effects" in Chapter 6.

A Spreadsheet Publishing Example

Now that you have explored Quattro Pro's spreadsheet formatting capabilities, you are ready to combine the array of /Style commands to create a presentation-quality report that will grab the attention of anyone who sees it.

The example in Figure 3.55 depicts an invoice that incorporates most of the formats presented in this chapter. Column width settings, various numeric formats, shading, line drawing, and different fonts are used to create a form that appears professionally typeset.

Figure 3.55

A spreadsheet
publishing example

Rancho de Luna
Invoice

ACCOUNT: Beaucoup Bouquets	DATE		03/02/92

Bulb Type	Price	Qty	Total
Wedgewood	$10.95	25	$35.95
King Alfred	$14.75	25	$39.75
Yellow Flag	$5.95	30	$35.95
Cristata, white	$7.50	50	$57.50
Acapulco	$15.95	25	$40.95
Spectacular Sun	$16.95	30	$46.95
		Sub-Total	$514.10
		Sales Tax	$33.42
		Total	$547.52

To reproduce this invoice, you will

- Enter data

- Set numeric formats, column widths, and alignment

- Draw invoice lines

- Create the shadow box and line shading

- Assign fonts

Entering the Data

To replicate the invoice form in Figure 3.55, you'll need to enter labels and formulas in a spreadsheet. Just use the following procedure. (Your spreadsheet will eventually look like Figure 3.56.)

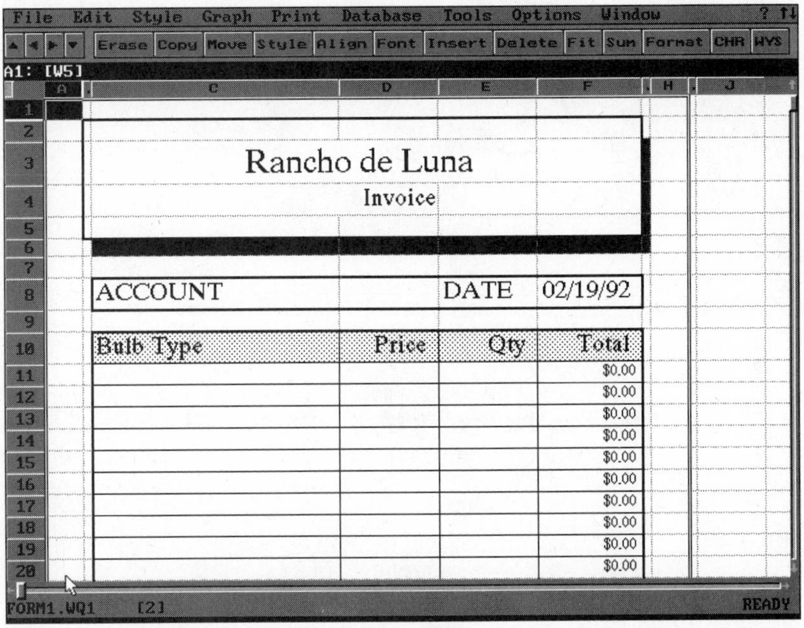

Figure 3.56

The finished invoice form

1. In cell C3, press the spacebar 20 times, type **Rancho de Luna**, and press Enter. The 20 blank spaces preceding the label will make it appear centered when you print the invoice form.

2. In cell C4, press the spacebar 43 times, type **Invoice**, and press Enter. When you print, these 43 blank spaces will make this line appear centered.

(Later you will assign this label a smaller font than the one used for the company name.)

3. In the cells listed, enter the following labels:

Cell	Label Entry	Cell	Label Entry
C8	ACCOUNT:	F10	Total
E8	DATE	E24	Sub-Total
C10	Bulb Type	E25	Sales Tax
D10	Price	E26	Total
E10	Qty		

4. In cell F11, enter the formula **+D11+E11** to calculate the extended price of each line item. Copy this formula to the block F12..F23.

5. In the cells listed, enter these formulas:

Cell	Formula
F24	@SUM(F11..F23)
F25	+F24*.065
F26	+F24+F25
F8	@NOW

Setting the Numeric Formats, Column Widths, and Alignment

Now that you have entered the data, you need to use the /Options and /Style commands to format this information.

1. Use /Options, Formats, Numeric Format, Currency 2 to set the global numeric format to Currency 2 places.

2. Use /Style, Numeric Format or the Format button to assign a Date 4 format in cell F8 and a Fixed 0 format for the block E11..E23.

3. To right-align the labels in block D10..F10, use /Style, Alignment or the Align button and choose Right.

4. Set the column widths using /Style, Column Width (Ctrl-W) as follows:

Column	Column Width
A, H	5
B, G	1
C	33
D, E	13
F	14

Although some of these column widths may not make sense at this point, they are necessary to complete the shadow box created later.

Drawing Invoice Lines

Now let's draw lines and boxes around the blocks listed below using the /Style, Line Drawing command:

Block	/Style, Line Drawing Options
A1..H28	Outside, Double
B2..F5	Outside, Thick
C8..F8	Outside, Thick
C10..F23	All, Single
E24..F26	All, Thick

After you are done, select Quit from the Placement menu to return to the spreadsheet.

Creating the Shadow Box and Shading

You can create the shadow box at the top of Figure 3.55 using a combination of black shading, column widths, and small font sizes. Notice how the shadow box seems to leap off the paper because of the black shadow that appears behind it. To create this effect, you need to use narrow columns and rows. You have already set the widths of columns B and G to 1, so all you need to do now is adjust row heights and assign the shading. At the same time, you can assign gray shading to row 10.

1. To decrease the height of row 6, select /Style, Block Size, Height, Set Row Height. Indicate any cell in row 6, such as **C6**, and press Enter. Then specify a row height of **11** and press Enter.

2. Now you need to assign Black shading to row 6 and to column G at the right of the box. To make the shadow appear behind, below, and to the right of the box, don't shade the entire width of row 6 or height of column G. Leave a corner off each. Select /Style, Shading, Black and specify row **C6..G6**. Select /Style, Shading, Black again and specify row **G3..G5**. Finally, use /Style, Shading, Grey to shade the block **C10..F10**.

You cannot fully see the three-dimensional effect of the shadow box on screen. So use the Screen Preview feature (Chapter 6) to view special effects before you print.

Assigning Fonts
Use the /Style, Font Table command to assign these fonts:

/Style, Font Command	Assigned to
Dutch 24 point	C3
Dutch 18 point	C4, C8..F8, C10..F10
Dutch 12 point	C11..F26

When you finish, the spreadsheet looks similar to the one in Figure 3.56.

NOTE. *In Quattro Pro 3.0, you'll first have to assign Dutch 24 point as part of the font library using /Style, Font, Edit Fonts. Then use /Style, Font to assign these fonts in the spreadsheet.*

Save this file to create a master invoice form that can be used for all of Rancho de Luna's customers. You can then save this spreadsheet under another file name and enter the billing information for a specific account—Beaucoup Bouquets, for instance. When you print this spreadsheet (read "Printing Special Effects" in Chapter 6 first!), the result will be the professional-looking invoice shown in Figure 3.55.

Creating Named Styles in Quattro Pro 4.0

You can create a named style in Quattro Pro 4.0 and then assign it to cells in the spreadsheet. Or you can use a predefined named style. A *named style* can consist of any combination of /Style settings—font, line drawing, shading, numeric format, and label alignment. You can even limit data entry to only dates or only labels. In effect, a named style lets you easily copy /Style settings as if you were using the new /Edit, Copy Special, Format option.

Although Quattro Pro 4.0 lets you create up to 120 named styles in a spreadsheet, there's still one drawback. You can only create a named style that reflects /Style settings for one cell. You can't create a named style that automatically formats a block of cells as a single entity.

Assigning Predefined Named Styles

Tip. `Style` takes you directly to the named styles list.

Quattro Pro 4.0 comes with predefined named styles, accessed through the /Style, Use Style command. You can see them in Figure 3.57. Five of these— COMMA, CURRENCY, DATE, FIXED, and PERCENT—assign commonly used numeric formats. See "Using Custom User-Defined Numeric Formats in Quattro Pro 4.0," earlier.

Figure 3.57
Predefined named styles in Quattro Pro 4.0

	A	B	C	D	E	F
1	Annual $ales Projection - 1993					
2						
3	Pacific Region	First Qtr	Second Qtr	Third Qtr	Fourth Qtr	Total 1993
4	California	540,000	570,000	600,000	650,000	2,360,000
5	Oregon	220,000	235,000	250,000	280,000	985,000
6	Washington	280,000	300,000	325,000	360,000	1,265,000
7	Region Total	$1,040,000	$1,105,000	$1,175,000	$1,290,000	$4,610,000
8						
9	Mountain Region	First Qtr	Second Qtr	Third Qtr	Fourth Qtr	Total 1993
10	Arizona	105,000	110,000	120,000	130,000	465,000
11	Colorado	190,000	200,000	215,000	230,000	835,000
12	Idaho	70,000	75,000	80,000	85,000	310,000
13	Montana					210,000
14	Nevada					370,000
15	New Mexico					320,000
16	Utah					540,000
17	Wyoming					190,000
18	Region Total					240,000
19						
20	Total Sales	1,760,000	1,880,000	2,015,000	2,195,000	7,850,000
21						
22						

File Edit |Style| Graph Print Database Tools Options Window ? ↑↓

▲ ◀ ▶ ▼ Erase Copy Move Style Align Font Insert Delete Fit Sum Format CHR WYS

B7: (C0) [W13] @SUM(B4..B6)

Enter named style:

NORMAL	COMMA	CURRENCY
DATE	FIXED	HEADING1
HEADING2	PERCENT	TOTAL

CUSTSTY1.WQ1 [2]   NAMES

Here are what some of the other predefined named styles do:

Style	Assigns
HEADING1	SC Swiss 18 point bold font
HEADING2	SC Swiss 12 point bold font
TOTAL	Double line at top of cell

If you want, you can change the settings assigned to a predefined named style. See "Changing Style Settings Assigned to a Name," later.

Using NORMAL to Change the Global Default Settings

The NORMAL named style contains the /Options, Formats global default settings automatically assigned to each spreadsheet—a General numeric format, left label alignment, and an SC Swiss 12 point Black font.

If you change one of the NORMAL settings—Alignment to Center, perhaps—/Options, Formats, Align Labels automatically changes to reflect this. Likewise, change the /Options, Formats, Align Labels setting to Right, and the NORMAL Alignment changes to this setting.

The NORMAL settings, however, only apply to the current spreadsheet. That is, if you change the NORMAL settings, save Quattro Pro's predefined named styles, and then retrieve them in another spreadsheet, Quattro Pro doesn't transfer these changes to the new spreadsheet. (See "Creating a Library of Named Styles," later.)

Creating Named Styles

You can create a named style in either of two ways.

- Assign new /Style settings to a name.

- Assign existing /Style settings in a cell to a name.

In fact, sometimes it's easiest to begin with a cell that already has most of the /Style settings you want.

For example, cell B7 in Figure 3.57 is assigned a Currency 0 places numeric format, a single top line, gray shading, and a bolded Swiss 12 point font. To name these /Style settings, preselect B7, and then select Style, Define Style, Create. In the prompt box displayed, enter a style name such as **TOTAL1**.

NOTE. *If you specify label alignment in a named style, it only applies to existing data. Any new data entered in a cell after the named style has been assigned won't take on the label alignment.*

Next, you'll see the TOTAL1 dialog box shown in Figure 3.58, which lists the /Style settings currently assigned to cell B7. If these are the settings you want, selecting Quit will save them as TOTAL1 and return you to the spreadsheet. If you want to assign different /Style settings, you can do so through the options shown. For example, selecting Font moves you to the /Style, Font dialog box; choosing Line Drawing accesses the options that apply to a single cell in the first /Style, Line Drawing menu. The Data Entry option, the equivalent of the /Database, Data Entry command (see Chapter 10), allows you to limit data entry to only labels or only dates. The default, General, allows any type of data entry.

Figure 3.58

Creating a named custom style

Once you create the named style TOTAL1, you can assign it to one cell or a block of cells in the spreadsheet. For example, to assign it to A20..F20 of Figure 3.57, preselect this block, select /Style, Use Style or the Style button, and then choose TOTAL1 from the list of names. Figure 3.59 shows how Quattro Pro assigns the TOTAL1 style to each cell in this block. TOTAL1 has also been assigned in A18..F18.

In most instances, Quattro Pro 4.0 treats a named style just like any other /Style setting. In other words, a named style is moved when you use /Edit, Move and copied when you use /Edit, Copy. The exception occurs when you delete or change settings in a cell defined by a named style.

To see how this works, imagine that you've created and assigned a named style called SPECIAL, which includes line drawing and a font. Even if you change the font or line drawing in a cell assigned SPECIAL, the cell is still assigned SPECIAL. In other words, the settings of a named style don't override other /Style settings you apply. The exception is if you try to assign a different font. To do so, Quattro Pro makes you first remove the named style.

To delete a named style from a cell, use /Style, Define Style, Erase. /Edit, Erase Block won't work. Use /Style, Define Style, Remove to delete the named style SPECIAL from the named style list and from any cells assigned SPECIAL.

Changing Style Settings Assigned to a Name

If you've created a named style using existing /Style settings in a cell, changing the /Style settings in that cell won't affect the named style. Change the font in cell B7 of Figure 3.59, for instance, and the new font won't automatically be assigned to TOTAL1. Instead, use /Style, Define Style, Create and change the font assigned to TOTAL1. Then each cell assigned TOTAL1 is updated to reflect this change.

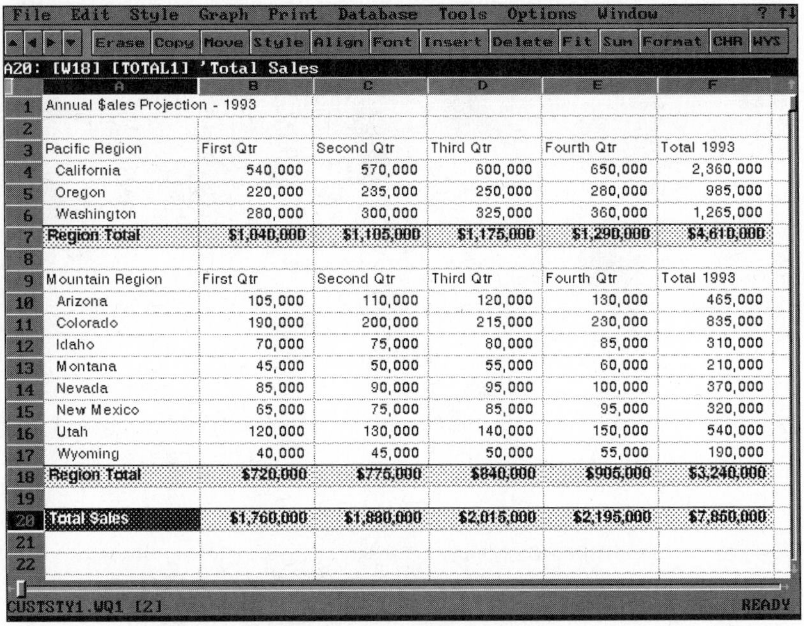

	A	B	C	D	E	F
1	Annual $ales Projection - 1993					
2						
3	Pacific Region	First Qtr	Second Qtr	Third Qtr	Fourth Qtr	Total 1993
4	California	540,000	570,000	600,000	650,000	2,360,000
5	Oregon	220,000	235,000	250,000	280,000	985,000
6	Washington	280,000	300,000	325,000	360,000	1,265,000
7	Region Total	$1,040,000	$1,105,000	$1,175,000	$1,290,000	$4,610,000
8						
9	Mountain Region	First Qtr	Second Qtr	Third Qtr	Fourth Qtr	Total 1993
10	Arizona	105,000	110,000	120,000	130,000	465,000
11	Colorado	190,000	200,000	215,000	230,000	835,000
12	Idaho	70,000	75,000	80,000	85,000	310,000
13	Montana	45,000	50,000	55,000	60,000	210,000
14	Nevada	85,000	90,000	95,000	100,000	370,000
15	New Mexico	65,000	75,000	85,000	95,000	320,000
16	Utah	120,000	130,000	140,000	150,000	540,000
17	Wyoming	40,000	45,000	50,000	55,000	190,000
18	Region Total	$720,000	$775,000	$840,000	$905,000	$3,240,000
19						
20	Total Sales	$1,760,000	$1,880,000	$2,015,000	$2,195,000	$7,850,000
21						
22						

Figure 3.59 Assigning a named custom style to a block

Creating a Library of Named Styles

Once you create named styles in a spreadsheet, you can save them in a separate file which can be accessed in other spreadsheets. In effect, Quattro Pro allows you to create a library of easily accessible named styles.

For example, to save all the named styles in the spreadsheet in Figure 3.59, choose /Style, Define Style, File, Save, and then specify a name, such as NEW. Quattro Pro automatically adds a .STY extension to the file name and saves it in the QPRO directory. (Quattro Pro's predefined named styles are already incorporated in the QUATTRO.STY file.)

To retrieve this set of named files in a different spreadsheet, use /Style, Define Style, File, Retrieve. (Because each spreadsheet is limited to 120 named styles, Quattro Pro stops importing when the number of styles currently in the spreadsheet and those retrieved exceed 120.) When you save this spreadsheet file, the imported named styles are saved with it.

NOTE. *You can't transfer changes you make to the NORMAL named style to other spreadsheets. That is, if you make changes to NORMAL and save the named styles to QUATTRO.STY, the NORMAL changes aren't transferred when you retrieve this group of named styles in another spreadsheet.*

4

Manipulating Data

ONE OF THE MOST IMPORTANT FEATURES OF ANY SPREADSHEET program is the capability it gives you to efficiently manipulate data. For this reason, Quattro Pro includes the menu of /Edit commands, shown in Figure 4.1.

The /Edit, Fill command, for instance, fills a block with values. You can use this command as a shortcut to enter equally spaced, sequential values in a spreadsheet, including dates and times. The most basic types of data manipulation, however, are erasing, moving, and copying data. Quattro Pro's /Edit, Erase Block, Move, and Copy commands provide a number of different methods you can use to erase unneeded information, and move or copy data from one location to another—even to another open file. If you've upgraded to Quattro Pro 4.0, you'll find a new command, /Edit, Copy Special, which lets you copy only cell contents or only style settings.

Note. Chapter 1 covers /Edit, Name, /Edit Undo, /Edit, Search & Replace, and /Edit, Insert or Delete

Figure 4.1
The /Edit menu

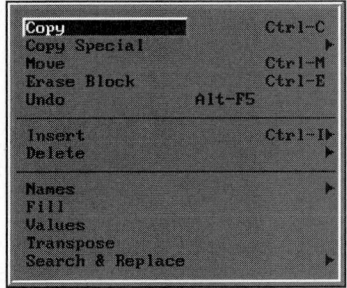

Quattro Pro also includes two special copy commands. /Edit, Values is useful in scenario generation and in large files when you need to decrease memory consumption. You can use it to copy the current values and labels returned by formulas, rather than the underlying formulas themselves. /Edit, Transpose, on the other hand, both copies and transposes data. This command is handy when you need to "flip" the orientation of values and labels—from columns to rows, or rows to columns.

Filling a Block with Values

Quattro Pro provides you with an easy way to fill a spreadsheet block with equally spaced, sequential values. The /Edit, Fill command is helpful whenever you need to enter sequential invoice numbers, check numbers, serial numbers, dates, times, or even percentages.

Entering Evenly Spaced Values

Note. If you specify a multicolumn destination block, Quattro Pro fills each cell in the first column, then each cell in the second column, and so on.

Suppose you want to enter the integers 1 through 12 in column A of a spreadsheet, beginning in cell A3, to represent each payment made during the first year of a 30-year mortgage. Do this using the following procedure:

1. Position the cell selector in the upper-left cell of the *fill block* (the block you want to fill with integers), cell A3. Then select /Edit, Fill. In response to "Destination for cells:", specify the fill block **A3..A14** and press Enter.

2. Specify a *start value* (the first value you want to appear in the fill block). The default is 0, so type **1** and press Enter.

You can enter a start, step, or stop value as a number, a function, or even a formula that references information in the spreadsheet. Quattro Pro, however, converts any formula you use in the /Edit, Fill command to its resulting value. Therefore, you must reenter a formula used in /Edit, Fill, if a value the formula references in the spreadsheet changes.

1. Specify a *step value* (the increment between each value in the fill block). The default is 1, so press Enter.

2. Specify a *stop value* (the highest value in the fill block). The default is 8191, so type **12** and press Enter.

TIP. *When you are filling a block with ascending values, use a very high stop value such as 999999. Because Quattro Pro automatically stops entering values when the fill block is full, a high stop value is easier to use than a calculated stop value. Similarly, use a very low stop value , such as –999999, when you are filling a block with descending values.*

Tip. If you inadvertently write over existing spreadsheet information, immediately use /Edit, Undo (Alt-F5) to cancel the completed /Edit, Fill command.

As soon as you press Enter after entering the stop value, Quattro Pro begins filling the block A3..A14. It first enters the start value, 1, in the first cell, A3. It then adds the step value, 1, to this value and arrives at the next value 2, which is entered in cell A4. This process continues until *either* the fill block is filled or the stop value is reached.

You can see the results in Figure 4.2. Quattro Pro has filled the block A3..A14 with equally spaced values from 1 to 12, writing over any existing information in the process.

You can also use /Edit, Fill to enter sequential values in descending order. To fill a block with descending values, specify the *highest* value as the start value, a *negative* step value, and a stop value considerably *lower* than the start value. For instance, in Figure 4.2, /Edit, Fill has been used with the fill block B3..B14, a start value of 360, a step value of –1, and a stop value of 0. These settings create the Remaining Payments (for a 30-year mortgage) shown in column B.

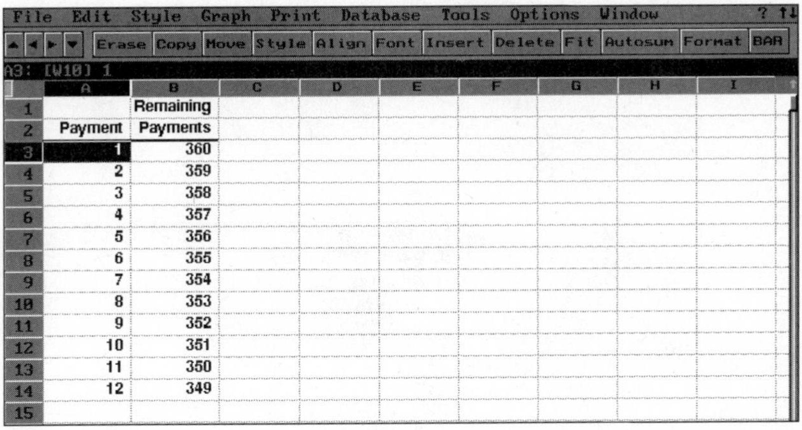

Figure 4.2

Using /Edit, Fill to
fill one block with
ascending integers
and another block
with descending
integers

File	Edit	Style	Graph	Print	Database	Tools	Options	Window		? ↑↓
▲ ◄ ► ▼	Erase	Copy	Move	Style	Align	Font	Insert	Delete	Fit	Autosum	Format	BAR

A3: [W10] 1

	A	B	C	D	E	F	G	H	I
1		Remaining							
2	Payment	Payments							
3	1	360							
4	2	359							
5	3	358							
6	4	357							
7	5	356							
8	6	355							
9	7	354							
10	8	353							
11	9	352							
12	10	351							
13	11	350							
14	12	349							
15									

Here are some tips for using the /Edit, Fill command.

■ Quattro Pro remembers the latest /Edit, Fill settings. (It also saves the latest /Edit, Fill settings when you save a file.) To clear a fill block setting, press Esc when it is highlighted, and then specify a new block. To reenter a new start, step, or stop value, simply enter a new value or formula—Quattro Pro automatically erases the old setting.

■ If you realize before completing an /Edit, Fill command that you entered an incorrect fill block, start, step, or stop value, you can back up and change the value. For example, if you are about to specify the stop value and realize that you specified an incorrect start value, press Esc twice to return to the start value prompt. Specify the correct start value, press Enter, and then press Enter again to confirm the current step value and return to the stop value prompt.

Entering Evenly Spaced Dates or Times

Now suppose you want to create a column of dates in the block B1..I1, beginning with Jan-92. To do this, select /Edit, Fill, and specify the fill block **B1..I1**. Next, specify the start value as **@DATE(92,1,15)** (or press Ctrl-D and type **1/15/92**). Press Enter. Type a step value of **30** and the stop value **999999**. Using these parameters, Quattro Pro enters the date numbers shown in row 1 of Figure 4.3A. To format date *values*, as shown in Figure 4.3B, select /Style, Numeric Format, Date, 3 (MMM-YY) and specify the block **B1..I1**.

Figure 4.3

Using /Edit Fill to fill a block with equally spaced, sequential date numbers, and a second block with equally spaced, sequential time numbers

File	Edit	Style	Graph	Print	Database	Tools	Options	Window	? ↑↓

| ▲ ◄ ► ▼ | Erase | Copy | Move | Style | Align | Font | Insert | Delete | Fit | Autosum | Format | BAR |

B1: 33618

	A	B	C	D	E	F	G	H	I
1	Date	33618	33648	33678	33708	33738	33768	33798	33828
2	Time	0.333333	0.375	0.416667	0.458333	0.5	0.541667	0.583333	0.625
3									

A

File	Edit	Style	Graph	Print	Database	Tools	Options	Window	? ↑↓

| ▲ ◄ ► ▼ | Erase | Copy | Move | Style | Align | Font | Insert | Delete | Fit | Sum | Format | CHR | HYS |

B1: (D3) 33618

	A	B	C	D	E	F	G	H	I
1	Date	Jan-92	Feb-92	Mar-92	Apr-92	May-92	Jun-92	Jul-92	Aug-92
2	Time	08:00 AM	09:00 AM	10:00 AM	11:00 AM	12:00 PM	01:00 PM	02:00 PM	03:00 PM
3									

B

Note. When you enter a start, step, or stop value as a date or time, Quattro Pro automatically converts it to a date or time number. For additional discussion of dates and times, see "Date and Time Functions" in Chapter 7.

TIP. *You can use /Edit, Fill to create a very large block of sequential date headings before the same month is repeated in two consecutive cells. Simply use a start value in the middle of the first month, like January 15 in the current example, and a step value of 30.7. Then format the resulting date numbers using the MMM-YY date format.*

You can also use /Edit, Fill to enter evenly spaced, sequential times in a block. For example, suppose you want to fill a block with increasing sequential times, beginning at 8:00 AM and increasing by one hour thereafter. In the /Edit, Fill command, specify the fill block **B2..I2**. Specify the start value **@TIME(08,00,00)** (or press Ctrl-D and type **8:00**). Finally, specify the step value **@TIME(01,00,00)** (or press Ctrl-D and type **1:00**), and the stop value **999999**. When you press Enter, Quattro Pro fills in the time values shown in row 2 of Figure 4.3A. You can then use /Style, Numeric Format, Date, Time, 2 (HH:MM AM/PM) in this block to display the time numbers as the sequential hours shown in Figure 4.3B.

Erasing Data

Once you enter information in Quattro Pro, you will invariably need to remove some of it. Quattro Pro gives you a variety of methods to erase data in one cell or a block of cells.

Erasing Data in a Single Cell

Suppose you want to delete the data in a single cell, such as Dick's assets in cell C2 of Figure 4.4A. Simply position the cell selector in cell C2, and press

Del. As you can see in Figure 4.4B, Quattro Pro deletes the *contents* of C2. However, Quattro Pro does not erase the cell *format*. Compare the input lines in Figures 4.4A and 4.4B, and you will see that cell C2 is formatted for (C0), Currency 0 places, both before and after the erase operation. In general, all /Style formats except Alignment are maintained when you erase the contents of a cell.

Figure 4.4

Using Del to erase the contents of cell C2

File	Edit	Style	Graph	Print	Database	Tools	Options	Window		? ↑↓
▲ ◄ ► ▼	Erase	Copy	Move	Style	Align	Font	Insert	Delete	Fit	Autosum	Format	BAR

C2: (C0) [W10] 500000

	A	B	C	D	E	F	G	H	
1		Tom	Dick	Harry					**A**
2	Assets	$50,000	$500,000	$100,000					
3	Liabilities	$30,000	$750,000	$50,000					
4	Net Worth	$20,000	($250,000)	$50,000					
5									

File	Edit	Style	Graph	Print	Database	Tools	Options	Window		? ↑↓
▲ ◄ ► ▼	Erase	Copy	Move	Style	Align	Font	Insert	Delete	Fit	Autosum	Format	BAR

C2: (C0) [W10]

	A	B	C	D	E	F	G	H	
1		Tom	Dick	Harry					**B**
2	Assets	$50,000		$100,000					
3	Liabilities	$30,000	$750,000	$50,000					
4	Net Worth	$20,000	($750,000)	$50,000					
5									

TIP. *To erase shading in a cell, select /Style, Shading, None. To erase line drawing in a cell, such as a bottom line, select /Style, Line Drawing, Bottom. Then select None. See Chapter 3 for complete information on /Style settings.*

Erasing Data in a Block of Cells

There are different methods you can use to erase the contents of a block of cells. You can

Tip. You can cancel /Edit, Erase Block during the command. Either press Esc repeatedly until you return to the main menu, or use Ctrl-Break.

- Select /Edit, Erase Block or its shortcut, Ctrl-E, and then specify the block to be erased

- Preselect the block; then select /Edit, Erase Block, or press Ctrl-E or Del

TIP. *In Quattro Pro 4.0,* Erase *is also a shortcut for /Edit, Erase Block.*

For instance, suppose you want to erase Tom, Dick, and Harry's liabilities in the block B3..D3 of Figure 4.5A. First, position the cell selector in the upper-left cell of this block, cell B3. Next, select /Edit, Erase Block, Ctrl-E, or the Erase button. After the prompt "Block to be modified:", Quattro Pro displays the current cell selector location as the block B3..B3. Specify the range B3..D3, as demonstrated in Figure 4.5A, and press Enter. As you can see in Figure 4.5B, Quattro Pro deletes the contents of the cells in this block, but not the cell formats.

Figure 4.5

Using /Edit, Erase Block to delete the contents of B3..D3

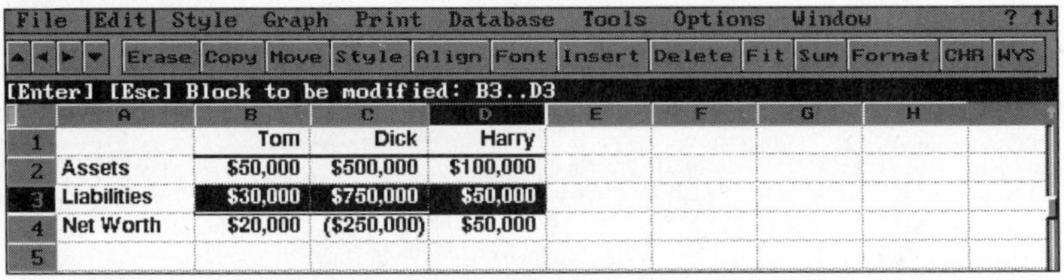

NOTE. *If you select /Edit, Erase, Ctrl-E, or the Erase button, and then realize the cell pointer is positioned in the wrong cell, press Esc to unanchor the cell selector. Then move the cell selector to the correct cell. If you are erasing a block, type a . (period) to anchor the cell selector in the upper-left cell, and then highlight the block.*

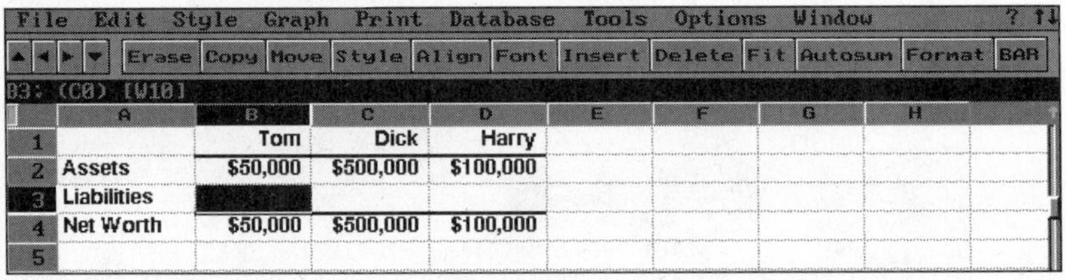

In the current example, you can also preselect the block B3..D3—before invoking the erase operation. Quattro Pro then automatically erases the contents of these cells when you select /Edit, Erase Block, Ctrl-E, Del, or the Erase button. Bear in mind, however, that although preselecting a block is the most efficient method of erasing information, you cannot abort the erase operation midstream when you use this method.

Hidden columns are temporarily redisplayed *only* when you select /Edit, Erase Block, Ctrl-E, or the Erase button *without* preselecting a block. When you preselect a block, information in hidden areas is not redisplayed. For example, suppose you use /Style, Hide Column, Hide to hide column C from view. Columns B and D will then appear as adjacent columns. Imagine you now preselect B3..D3, and select Del, Ctrl-E, /Edit, Erase Block, or the Erase button. Because Quattro Pro erases the data in the preselected block without asking for confirmation, you will also erase the contents of the hidden cell C3.

Likewise, suppose you use /Style, Numeric Format, Hidden to hide the information in cell D3 from view. Cell D3 thus appears to be blank. If you erase the block A3..E3 using *any* method, the hidden information will not be temporarily redisplayed and is also erased. To avoid this, you may want to protect hidden information so that it cannot be inadvertently erased (see Chapter 2).

Keep in mind the following when you are erasing the contents of a cell or a block of cells:

- If you accidentally erase the wrong information, immediately use /Edit, Undo (Alt-F5) to restore the data. See Chapter 1.

- If you erase the contents of a cell that is referenced by a string formula, you change the results of that formula. Because Quattro Pro assigns a value of 0 to a blank cell, a string formula referencing a blank cell returns ERR. See Chapter 1 for a discussion of string formulas.

- You cannot erase information in protected cells unless you first use the /Style, Protection command to unprotect these cells.

- To remove an entire row or column from a spreadsheet, including the cell contents, use /Edit, Delete as discussed in Chapter 1.

- To delete the contents of an entire spreadsheet, use /File, Erase (Chapter 5). This command removes the entire file from memory, but does not affect the original file on disk.

- To return a cell's format settings to the global settings without erasing the cell's contents, use /Style, Reset Width and /Style, Numeric Format, Reset (see Chapter 3).

Moving Data

Note. To move a line drawing, you specify the source block differently than you might expect. See "Copying a Single Cell" later in this chapter.

Moving information in Quattro Pro is a straightforward process. The /Edit, Move command lets you move data from one cell or a block of cells to another location in a spreadsheet. You can even move data between two open files.

When you use /Edit, Move, the following occurs:

- The data in the *source* block is moved to a new *destination* location, including format, protection status, and other settings such as shading.

- Any preexisting information in the destination location is overwritten.

- The cells in the source block are cleared and returned to the global default settings.

- Cell references throughout the spreadsheet are automatically adjusted to reflect the new location of the moved data. The exceptions to this rule are discussed in "When Cell References Are Not Automatically Adjusted," later in this section.

Moving Data Within a File

The easiest way to see how the /Edit, Move command works is through an example. Suppose you create the spreadsheet in Figure 4.6. You decide to move the January shoes sales information from block B1..B7 to the block C1..C7. Use the following procedure:

1. Position the cell selector in the upper-left cell of the block you want to move, in this case, B1.

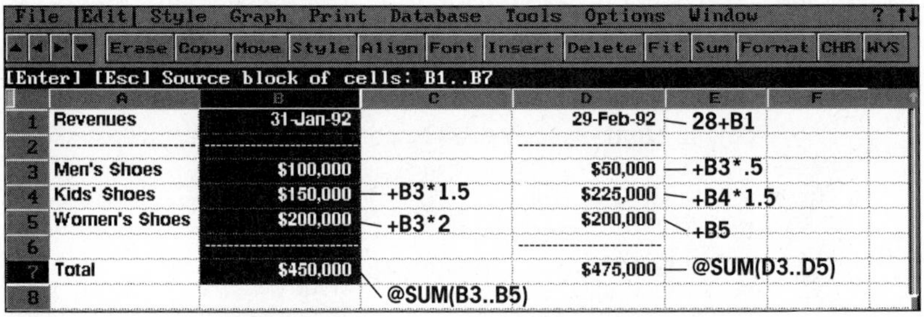

Figure 4.6

Selecting block B1..B7 to be moved to a new location

File	Edit	Style	Graph	Print	Database	Tools	Options	Window	? ↑↓

| ▲ | ◄ | ▶ | ▼ | Erase | Copy | Move | Style | Align | Font | Insert | Delete | Fit | Sum | Format | CHR | WYS |

[Enter] [Esc] Source block of cells: B1..B7

	A	B	C	D	E	F
1	Revenues	31-Jan-92		29-Feb-92	— 28+B1	
2	--------	--------		--------		
3	Men's Shoes	$100,000		$50,000	— +B3*.5	
4	Kids' Shoes	$150,000	— +B3*1.5	$225,000	— +B4*1.5	
5	Women's Shoes	$200,000	⌐ +B3*2	$200,000	⌐ +B5	
6		--------		--------		
7	Total	$450,000		$475,000	— @SUM(D3..D5)	
8			⌐ @SUM(B3..B5)			

Tip. You can cancel an /Edit, Move command in midstream by either pressing Esc repeatedly until you return to the main menu or by using Ctrl-Break.

2. Select /Edit, Move or its shortcut, Ctrl-M. Quattro Pro displays "Source block of cells:" followed by the current selection in the form of a block address, B1..B1.

TIP. ▶ *In Quattro Pro 4.0,* Move *is also a shortcut for /Edit, Move.*

3. Specify the source block **B1..B7**, as illustrated in Figure 4.6, and press Enter. Quattro Pro now displays the prompt "Destination for cells:" followed by the first cell in the current selection, B1.

4. Specify the destination as a single cell address, **C1**, and press Enter. Quattro Pro uses this cell as the upper-left corner of the destination block and moves the information from the source block—maintaining its size and shape—into the destination. The cell selector returns to B1, its location before you selected /Edit, Move.

CAUTION! *Be sure the destination area is blank, because Quattro Pro uses the destination cell as the "starting point" of the move operation and then moves in the entire source block. If you do inadvertently write over existing information in the destination, immediately use /Edit, Undo (Alt-F5) to cancel the completed move.*

Figure 4.7 shows the result. As you can see, the information originally located in B1..B7 has moved to the new location C1..C7. The original location, B1..B7, is now empty, and its cells have reverted to the global default settings.

Figure 4.7

The moved block in its new location, C1..C7

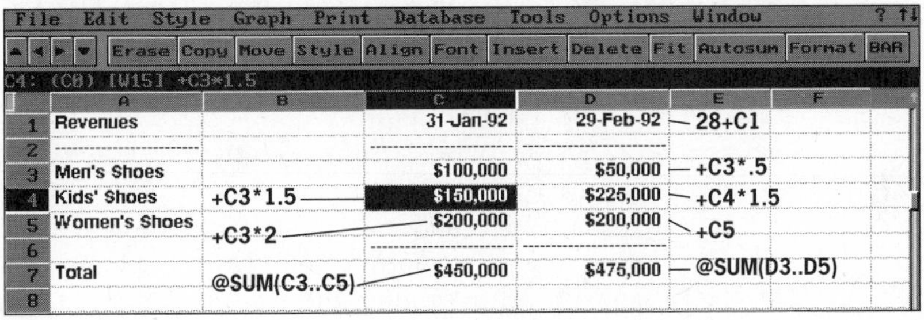

| File | Edit | Style | Graph | Print | Database | Tools | Options | Window | ? ↑↓ |

| ▲ ◀ ▶ ▼ | Erase | Copy | Move | Style | Align | Font | Insert | Delete | Fit | Autosum | Format | BAR |

C4: (C0) [W15] +C3*1.5

	A	B	C	D	E	F
1	Revenues		31-Jan-92	29-Feb-92	— 28+C1	
2	---------		-----------	-----------	-----------	
3	Men's Shoes		$100,000	$50,000	— +C3*.5	
4	Kids' Shoes	+C3*1.5 —	$150,000	$225,000	— +C4*1.5	
5	Women's Shoes	+C3*2	— $200,000	$200,000	— +C5	
6			-----------	-----------		
7	Total	@SUM(C3..C5)	— $450,000	$475,000	— @SUM(D3..D5)	
8						

NOTE. *If you select /Edit, Move, Ctrl-M, or the Move button, and then realize the cell pointer is positioned in the wrong cell, press Esc to unanchor the cell selector. Then move the cell selector to the correct cell. If you are moving a block, type a . (period) to anchor the cell selector in the upper-left cell, and then highlight the block.*

You can preselect a source block before you begin a move operation. For instance, suppose in the shoe sales example you preselect the source block B1..B7. When you select /Edit, Move, Ctrl-M, or the Move button, Quattro Pro automatically assumes this selection is the source block and only prompts you for the destination cell.

In addition, you can manipulate the /Edit, Move command so that the cell selector ends up in the destination location rather than the source block. For further details see "Using Alternative Copy Methods," later in this chapter.

Tip. Use /Edit, Insert, Rows or Columns (see Chapter 3) to insert a column or row.

You may want to protect information that has been hidden using /Style, Numeric Format, Hidden; otherwise, you run the risk of overwriting it when you move data. Protected information can be moved as a source block, but it cannot be overwritten in a destination. Hidden columns, on the other hand, are redisplayed and marked by an * (asterisk) during a move.

Cell Reference Adjustments

When you move formulas, Quattro Pro automatically adjusts any cell references

- Outside the moved block that refer to moved cells

- Inside the moved block that refer to other cells within this block

Note. When you move a cell or block of cells, Quattro Pro even adjusts any absolute or mixed cell references that are affected. For a discussion of absolute, relative, and mixed addressing, see "Copying Formulas," later in this chapter.

For instance, Figures 4.6 and 4.7 show the contents of the cells in columns B, C, and D before and after using /Edit, Move. Notice in Figure 4.6 that the formulas in cells B4 and B5 reference the value in cell B3. After block B1..B7 is moved to column C in Figure 4.7, however, Quattro Pro adjusts the formulas in C4 and C5 to refer to C3, which is the new location of the information previously in B3. Likewise, the formula @SUM(B3..B5) in cell B7 of Figure 4.6 is converted to @SUM(C3..C5) in cell C7 of Figure 4.7. Quattro Pro automatically adjusts the cell references *within* the moved block that refer to other moved cells.

Similarly, Quattro Pro automatically adjusts cell references *outside* a moved block that refer to the moved cells. Notice in Figure 4.6 that D1 contains the formula 28+B1 to produce the date 28-Feb-91. Furthermore, the February revenue values in D3, D4, and D5 are all derived from formulas that reference values in column B, such as the formula +B3*.5 in D3. After block B1..B7 is moved to column C in Figure 4.7, however, the formulas in column D still produce the same February revenue values. Quattro Pro has adjusted the cell references in D1, D3, D4, and D5 to correspond to the new location of the moved cells. Thus, cell D1 now contains the formula 28+C1.

Notice also that the formula in D7, @SUM(D3..D5), is the same in both Figures 4.6 and 4.7. Because this formula does not contain any references to cells in the moved block, it is unaffected by the move operation.

When Cell References Are Not Automatically Adjusted

There are two situations when moving data can cause problems in your spreadsheet. These occur when

- You move data and in the process write over information that is referenced by a formula in another cell

- You move the upper-left or lower-right cell that defines a block used in a formula

Writing over a Cell Reference

Suppose you enter the information shown in the spreadsheet in Figure 4.8A. Cell A1 contains the value 20, and B2 contains the value 40. Cell C1 contains the formula +B1 (look at the input line), which produces the value 40. If you move the contents of A1 to B1, you'll write over the contents of B1 in the process and get the results shown in Figure 4.8B. As you can see, cell C1 displays ERR, even though cell B1 now contains the value 20. In fact, C1 does *not* reference the new information in B1 and no longer contains the formula +B1. Instead, it now contains +ERR.

Figure 4.8
The error that results when you move the contents of A1 to B1, when C1 contains the formula +B1

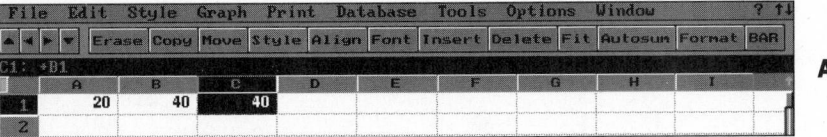

This problem also occurs when you move the contents of one cell to another cell that defines a block—either the upper-left or lower-right cell—in a formula. For instance, suppose you enter ticket sales in a spreadsheet as shown in Figure 4.9. You have received two different January ice hockey ticket sales figures: 15,000, which you enter in cell C2, and 20,000, which you enter in cell B2. When you receive confirmation that 20,000 is the correct number of ice hockey tickets sold in January, you move this value to C2, overwriting the 15,000 value in the process. The results are shown in Figure 4.10. Because C2 is used to define the block in the formula @SUM(C2..C4) in C5, and in the formula @SUM(C2..E2) in F2, these cells now contain the formula @SUM(ERR). Because you wrote over the existing information in C2 when you performed the move operation, Quattro Pro replaces the block reference in these formulas with ERR. However, the formula @SUM(F2..F4) in F5 is still intact and only produces ERR because the formula in cell F2 returns ERR.

In both of these examples, you moved a *value* and overwrote another value. In this instance, it is better to copy the value to the new location (see "Copying Data" in this chapter). Then you can erase the value in the original location. The advantage to this method is that it does not wreak havoc with existing formulas. If you are moving a formula, no "best" method exists—especially if the moved formula contains relative references.

Figure 4.9

A spreadsheet that includes @SUM formulas

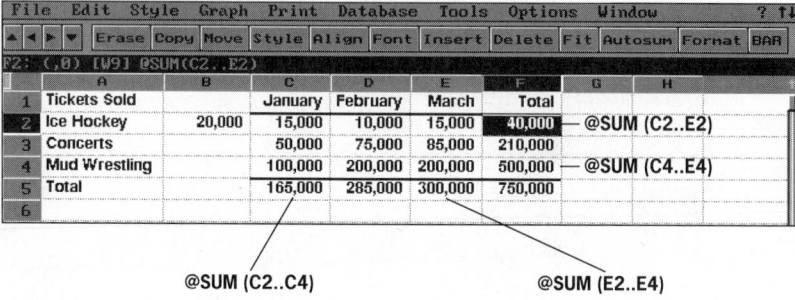

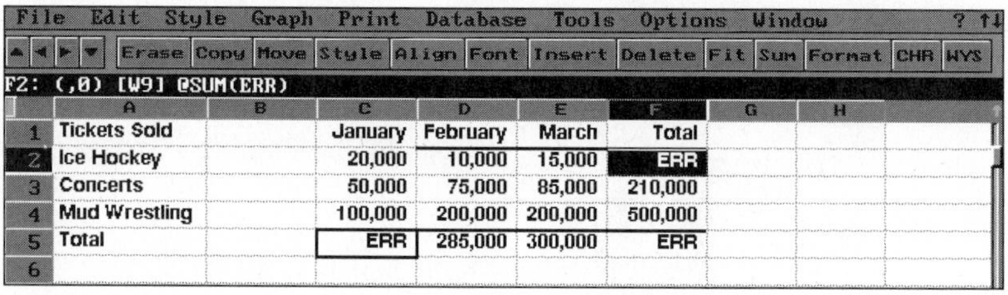

@SUM (C2..C4)   @SUM (E2..E4)

Figure 4.10

Figure 4.9's spreadsheet after moving data into a cell that defines a block referenced by formulas

	A	B	C	D	E	F	G	H
			January	February	March	Total		
1	Tickets Sold							
2	Ice Hockey		20,000	10,000	15,000	ERR		
3	Concerts		50,000	75,000	85,000	210,000		
4	Mud Wrestling		100,000	200,000	200,000	500,000		
5	Total		ERR	285,000	300,000	ERR		
6								

Moving a Cell That Defines a Block

When you move information into or out of *cells that are part of a block referenced in a formula,* the results you get vary depending upon the location of the cells within the block. Move a cell that is in the middle of a block, and any formulas referencing that cell are unaffected. However, move a cell that *defines* a referenced block—either the upper-left or lower-right cell—and the size of the block is changed to reflect this new location. Side effects can occur; the formula may return an incorrect result, and a circular reference may be created in the spreadsheet.

For instance, let's return to the spreadsheet in Figure 4.9. Total ticket sales are summed down each month column, and summed by event across each row. Thus, cell D5 contains the formula @SUM(D2..D4), and cell F3 contains the formula @SUM(C3..E3). Figure 4.11 shows the results of moving the contents of cell D3, 75,000, to cell G3. Notice that the formulas in D5 and F3 are unaffected, because cell D3 is in the *middle* of the block each formula references. However, because D3 is now blank, the *results* produced by these formulas do change. The formula in D5 now returns 210,000 tickets sold in February, and the formula in F3 calculates 135,000 total concert tickets sold.

Figure 4.11

Results of moving a
cell from the
middle of a
referenced block

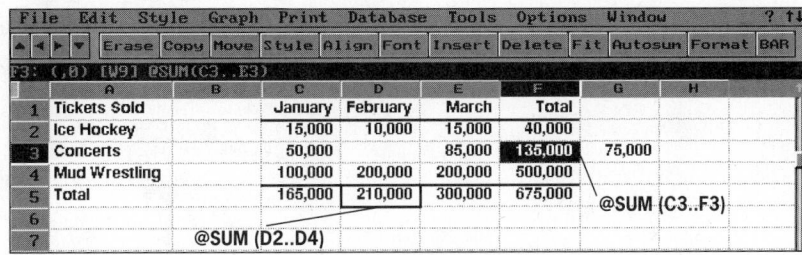

On the other hand, you get substantially different results when you move a cell that *defines* a block used in a formula. For example, suppose you move the contents of cell E2 in Figure 4.9, 15,000, to cell G2. Notice that the formula @SUM(E2..E4) in E5 uses E2 as the upper-left corner of its block reference. Also, the formula @SUM(C2..E2) in F2 uses E2 as the lower-right corner of its block reference. Look at the result in Figure 4.12. Cell F2 now contains the formula @SUM(C2..G2), which calculates the value 80,000. Quattro Pro has adjusted the original block reference in this formula, C2..E2, to correspond to the new location of the corner cells, C2..G2. Like-wise, cell E5 now contains the formula @SUM(G2..E4) and returns the value 1,090,000. In addition, these two adjusted formulas now create circular references in this spreadsheet.

NOTE. *A named block is also affected in the same manner when you move the contents of a cell that defines it.*

Moving Data to Another File

Note. Chapter 2 tells you how to open multiple files on the desktop.

You can also move data between two open files. The procedure is very similar to moving information within a file. Suppose you have two files, MONTH.WQ1 and TOTAL.WQ1, open on the desktop, as shown in Figure 4.13. You decide to move the total cash values in the block E1..E6 of MONTH.WQ1 to column A of TOTAL.WQ1.

With both files open, locate the cell selector in the upper-left cell of the block you want to move, cell E1 in file MONTH.WQ1. Select /Edit, Move, Ctrl-M, or the Move button. Specify the source block **E1..E6**. Now specify the destination, cell A1 in TOTAL.WQ1, as **[C:\FILES\TOTAL.WQ1]A1**. Notice that in Figure 4.13, because you are pointing to this destination, Quattro Pro automatically includes the destination file name (and path if the file is not located in the current directory) enclosed in brackets.

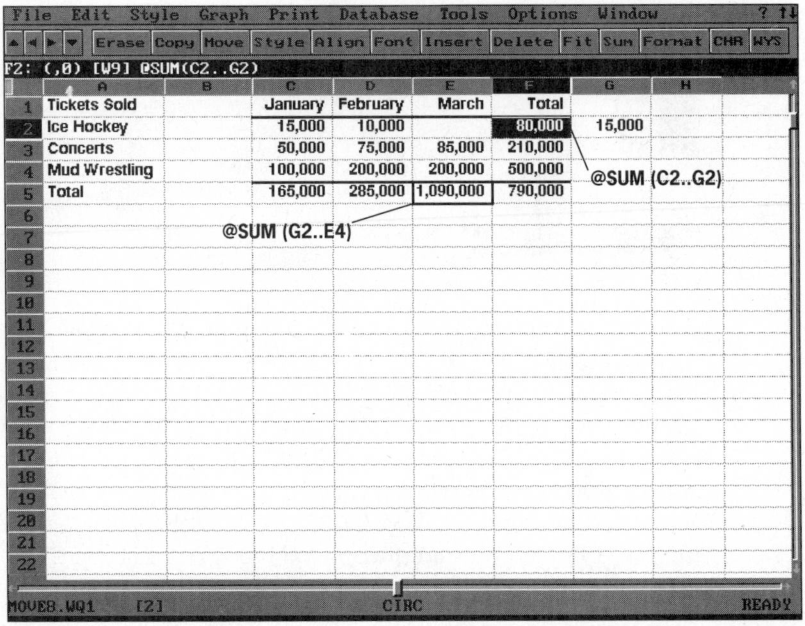

Figure 4.12
Results of moving a cell that defines the upper-left or lower-right corner of a referenced block

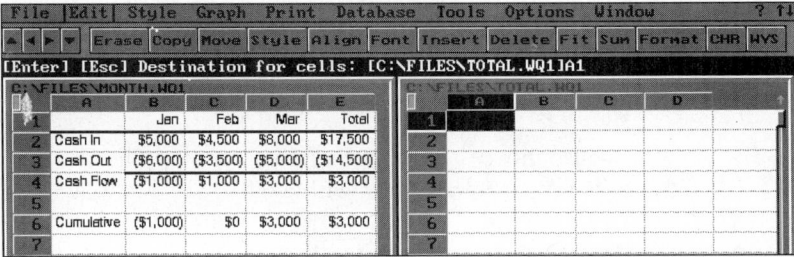

```
 File   Edit   Style   Graph   Print   Database   Tools   Options   Window        ? ↑↓
 ▲ ◄ ► ▼  Erase Copy Move Style Align Font Insert Delete Fit Sum Format CHR WYS
 F2: (,0) [W9] @SUM(C2..G2)
        A              B        C        D        E        F        G        H
  1  Tickets Sold            January February  March    Total
  2  Ice Hockey               15,000   10,000            80,000   15,000
  3  Concerts                 50,000   75,000   85,000  210,000
  4  Mud Wrestling           100,000  200,000  200,000  500,000    @SUM (C2..G2)
  5  Total                   165,000  285,000 1,090,000 790,000
  6
  7                          @SUM (G2..E4)
  8
  9
 10
 11
 12
 13
 14
 15
 16
 17
 18
 19
 20
 21
 22
 MOVEB.WQ1    [2]                        CIRC                          READY
```

Figure 4.13
Moving information between open files

```
 File   Edit   Style   Graph   Print   Database   Tools   Options   Window        ? ↑↓
 ▲ ◄ ► ▼  Erase Copy Move Style Align Font Insert Delete Fit Sum Format CHR WYS
 [Enter] [Esc] Destination for cells: [C:\FILES\TOTAL.WQ1]A1
 C:\FILES\MONTH.WQ1                      C:\FILES\TOTAL.WQ1
      A         B        C        D        E            A     B     C     D
  1            Jan      Feb      Mar     Total      1
  2  Cash In  $5,000   $4,500   $8,000  $17,500     2
  3  Cash Out ($6,000) ($3,500) ($5,000)($14,500)   3
  4  Cash Flow($1,000)  $1,000   $3,000   $3,000     4
  5                                                  5
  6  Cumulative($1,000)    $0    $3,000   $3,000     6
  7                                                  7
```

Tip. If you are using the keyboard, press Shift-F6 to move the cell selector between open files.

You can see the results of this move operation in Figure 4.14. The data originally located in the block E1..E6 of MONTH.WQ1 is now located in TOTAL.WQ1, beginning in cell A1. The original location, E1..E6 in MONTH.WQ1, is now empty, and its cells have reverted to the global default settings.

Figure 4.14
Moving data to
another file to
create linked files

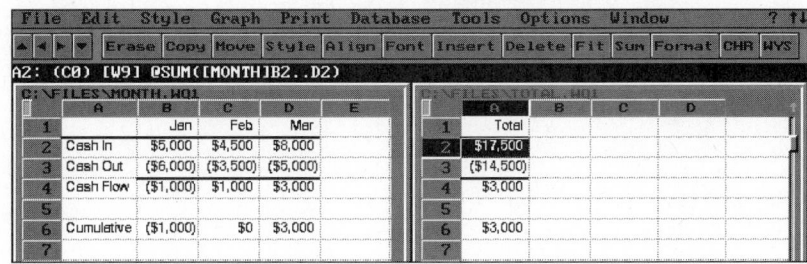

When you move information *between* files, cell references are affected in the same way as though you moved information *within* a file. In the current example, the moved cells that contain formulas are affected as follows:

Before /Edit, Move:		After /Edit, Move:	
Cell in MONTH.WQ1	**Contents**	**Cell in TOTAL.WQ1**	**Contents**
E2	@SUM(B2..D2)	A2	@SUM ([MONTH]B2..D2)
E3	@SUM(B3..D3)	A3	@SUM ([MONTH]B3..D3)
E4	@SUM(E2..E3)	A4	@SUM(A2..A3)
E6	+D6	A6	+[MONTH]D6

This table shows you that cell E4 in MONTH.WQ1 originally contained the formula @SUM(E2..E3), which sums total cash inflows and outflows and returns the total net cash flow. However, because cells E2, E3, and E4 were *all* moved to TOTAL.WQ1, Quattro Pro adjusted the E4 formula to @SUM(A2..A3), which references the new locations of the moved cells. Therefore, this formula produces the same value, $3,000, before and after the move operation.

In contrast, the formulas moved to cells A2, A3, and A6 of TOTAL.WQ1 (from cells E2, E3, and E6 of MONTH.WQ1) *link* the two files. Because cell E6 in MONTH.WQ1 originally contained the formula +D6, after the move this formula *still* references D6—cell A6 in TOTAL.WQ1 now contains the formula +[MONTH]D6. Therefore, if the information in D6 of MONTH.WQ1 changes, the value in A6 of TOTAL.WQ1 will reflect this change. Likewise, cell E2 in TOTAL.WQ1 originally contained the formula @SUM(B2..D2), summing monthly cash inflows. A similar formula in cell E3, @SUM(B3..D3), sums monthly cash outflows. When these formulas are moved to TOTAL.WQ1, they still reference the same cells in MONTH.WQ1, and thus link the two files. (See Chapter 2 for further details about linking files.)

Copying Data

You will find the /Edit, Copy command one of the most powerful and efficient commands in Quattro Pro. You can use it to copy data from one cell to a block of cells, from a block of data to another block, or even from one file to another open file. The real power of /Edit, Copy is fully used, however, when you copy formulas. In this capacity, /Edit, Copy is a tremendous time-saving tool.

Because /Edit, Copy is so versatile, it can be used in many different ways. With this versatility, however, comes complexity. Therefore, this powerful command is presented to you here in two parts: To begin with, you'll learn the mechanics of copying, such as how to copy a block of data. In Quattro Pro 4.0, you'll also learn how to use the new /Edit, Copy Special command to copy either cell contents or style settings. Then you'll see how to copy formulas, and will examine the effects of relative, mixed, and absolute cell addressing.

The Mechanics of Copying

When you use /Edit, Copy, the following occurs:

- The data in the *source* block is copied to a *destination* location, including formatting, protection status, and other settings, such as shading.

- Any existing information in the destination is overwritten.

- The cells in the source block are unaffected.

/Edit, Copy produces different results depending on the type of source and destination blocks you specify.

Tip. You can cancel an /Edit, Copy command midstream by pressing Esc repeatedly until you return to the main menu or by using Ctrl-Break.

Copying a Single Cell

The easiest type of copying in Quattro Pro is copying the contents of a single cell. You can copy the contents of one cell to another cell or to a block of cells.

For example, consider Figure 4.15A. You can copy the value in cell A2 to cell C2 by using this procedure:

1. Position the cell selector in cell A2.

Figure 4.15

Using /Edit, Copy to copy a single cell to another cell and to a block of cells

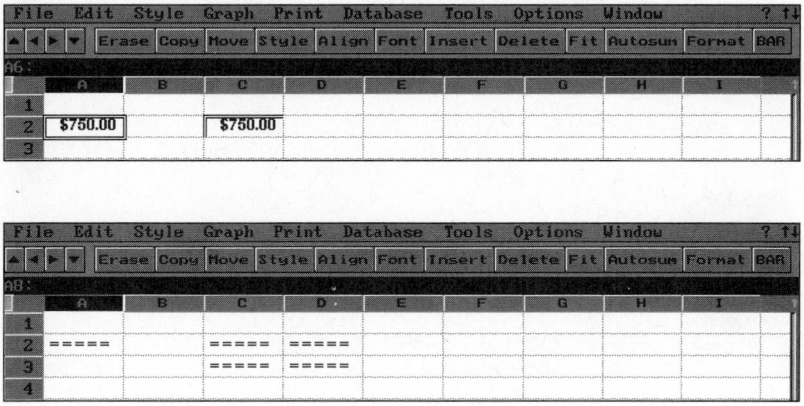

2. Select /Edit, Copy or use its shortcut, Ctrl-C. Quattro Pro displays "Source block of cells:" followed by the current selection in the form of a block, A2..A2. Press Enter.

TIP. *In Quattro Pro 4.0,* [Copy] *is also a shortcut for /Edit, Copy.*

3. In response to the prompt for a destination location, specify **C2** and press Enter. Quattro Pro returns the cell selector to its location before you selected /Edit, Copy—in this case, A2.

The results of your copy operation are shown in Figure 4.15A. As you can see, Quattro Pro has copied the contents of cell A2 to cell C2, as well as the numeric format (C2), Currency 2 places. The contents of cell A2, however, are unaffected.

Figure 4.15A also demonstrates a Quattro Pro quirk that appears when you copy (or move) line drawing. Notice in Figure 4.15A that the /Style, Line Drawing command has been used to create a double line box around cell A2. When you copy the contents of A2 to C2, Quattro Pro copies only the top and left segments of the line drawing. To get Quattro Pro to copy the entire box, you must specify A2..B3 as the source block in the /Edit, Copy command. This is because Quattro Pro assigns the right segment of the box to B2 and the bottom segment to A3.

Now let's look at what happens when you copy the contents of one cell to a multicell block. Imagine that you enter \= in cell A2 of Figure 4.15B, which produces the broken double line shown in this cell. To copy this label to the block C2..D3, position the cell selector in A2, and select /Edit, Copy or press Ctrl-C. Specify **A2** as the source block, and **C2..D3** as the destination block.

As you can see in Figure 4.15B, Quattro Pro copies the label in cell A2, \=, to each cell in the block C2..D3.

TIP. *After you select /Edit, Copy, Ctrl-C, or the Copy button, if you realize the cell pointer is positioned in the wrong cell, press Esc to unanchor the cell selector. Then move the cell selector to the correct cell. If you are copying a block, type a . (period) to anchor the cell selector in the upper-left cell, and then highlight the block.*

Copying a Multicolumn, Multirow Block

In many cases, you will need to copy a multicolumn, multirow block to another location in a spreadsheet. Let's look at an example of this technique. Imagine you own a startup company and want to project its personnel requirements for 1992. To do this, you create the spreadsheet in Figure 4.16 and enter the number of employees needed during the first two months. You then realize that the January and February levels will be maintained through March and April.

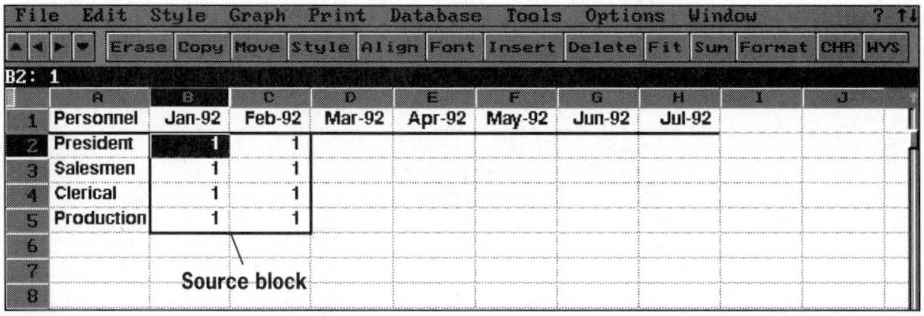

Figure 4.16

Copying the multicolumn, multirow block B2..C5

To copy the January-February block of data, position the cell selector in the upper-left cell of the block, cell B2. Select /Edit, Copy or press Ctrl-C. Specify the source block as **B2..C5** and the destination as the single cell **D2**. (Be sure the area below and to the right of the destination cell is blank, because any existing information will be written over by the copied data.) After the copy operation is completed, Quattro Pro returns the cell selector to its location before you selected /Edit, Copy, in this case, B2.

Figure 4.17 illustrates how Quattro Pro uses the destination cell D2 as the upper-left corner of the destination block. It then copies the information in the source block, B2..C5, mirroring its size and shape, to the block D2..E5. It also copies all /Style settings, except the column width, to the new location. The information in the source block B2..C5 is unchanged.

Figure 4.17
The personnel
spreadsheet after
using /Edit, Copy

File	Edit	Style	Graph	Print	Database	Tools	Options	Window		? ↑↓
▲ ◀ ▶ ▼	Erase	Copy	Move	Style	Align	Font	Insert	Delete	Fit	Autosum Format BAR

	A	B	C	D	E	F	G	H	I	J
1	Personnel	Jan-92	Feb-92	Mar-92	Apr-92	May-92	Jun-92	Jul-92		
2	President	1	1	1	1					
3	Salesmen	1	1	1	1					
4	Clerical	1	1	1	1					
5	Production	1	1	1	1					
6										
7		Source block								
8										

Tip. If, during an
/Edit, Copy
command, you
inadvertently write
over existing
information in the
destination location,
immediately use
/Edit, Undo (Alt-F5)
to cancel the
completed copy
operation.

When you copy a multicolumn, multirow block, Quattro Pro will only copy the source block *once*, even if you specify a multicell destination block. In the current example, if you specify the destination block D2..G2, or even D2..E100, Quattro Pro copies the block B2..B5 *once*—to the block D2..E5.

NOTE. *When you use /Edit, Copy, or one of its shortcuts, hidden columns are redisplayed and marked by an * (asterisk), but information hidden using /Style, Numeric Format, Hidden is not. You may want to protect hidden information (which can be copied, but not overwritten in a destination); otherwise, you run the risk of overwriting it.*

Using Alternative Copy Methods

Quattro Pro offers you two alternative copying techniques you can use with the /Edit, Copy command. You can

- Preselect a source block

- Copy "in reverse," so that the cell selector ends up in the destination location

For instance, suppose you preselect the block B2..C5 in the current example (Figure 4.16). When you invoke /Edit, Copy, Ctrl-C, or the Copy button, Quattro Pro automatically assumes your selection is the source block and only prompts you for the destination cell.

Quattro Pro also lets you copy "in reverse." As you know, after a completed copy operation, Quattro Pro always returns the cell selector to its original position before you used /Edit, Copy. Therefore, if you position the cell selector in the source block *before* you select /Edit, Copy, Quattro Pro returns you to the source block after the command. In the current example, Figure 4.16, you can do so by following this procedure:

1. Position the cell selector in the upper-left corner of the destination block, cell D2.

2. Select /Edit, Copy, Ctrl-C, or the Copy button. As usual, Quattro Pro assumes that the current selection, D2, is the source block. To delete this block address from the input line, press Esc.

3. Move the cell selector to the upper-left cell of the source block, cell B2. Then specify the block B2..C5 and press Enter. Quattro Pro moves the cell selector back to its *original* location, D2, and displays this cell as the destination in the input line. Press Enter.

The result is the spreadsheet shown in Figure 4.17, *except* that the cell selector will be located in cell D2 of the destination block after the completed /Edit, Copy command.

Copying a Single Column or Row

Copying a single column or row is different from other multicell copy operations because you can create *multiple* copies of the single column or row in the destination block.

For example, let's return to the personnel spreadsheet example. Suppose you now enter the May personnel requirements in column F of Figure 4.18, and you know these levels will be adequate in June and July as well. Therefore, you want to copy column F to columns G and H. To do this, position the cell selector in cell F2, select /Edit, Copy, Ctrl-C, or the Copy button, and specify the source block as **F2..F5**. Then specify the destination block, **G2..H2**.

Figure 4.18
Copying a single column to two other columns

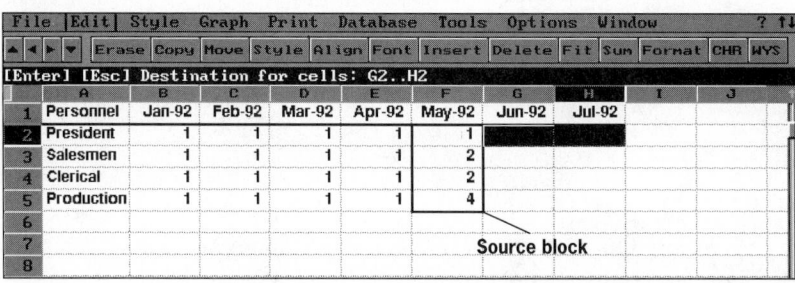

Tip. You can use /Edit, Transpose to copy labels or values in a column and transpose them to a row, and vice versa. See "Transposing Data" in this chapter.

You can see the results in Figure 4.19. As in other copy operations, Quattro Pro uses cell G2 as the upper-left corner of the destination block and copies the information from the source block, F2..F5, to the block G2..G5. The column shape of the source block is retained. In addition, using cell H2, which you also specified in the destination block, Quattro Pro also replicates the contents of the source block in the block H2..H5.

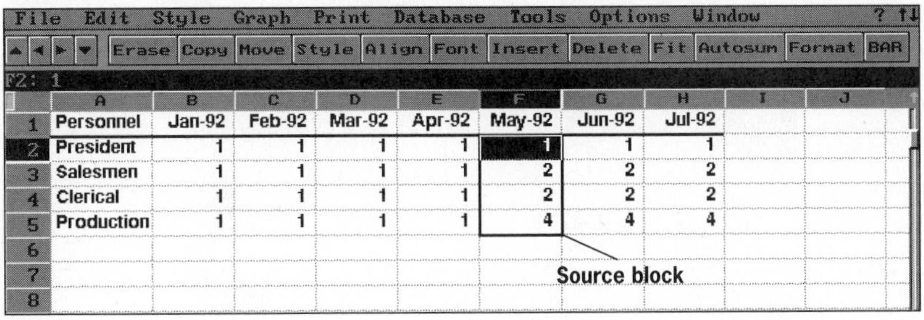

Figure 4.19

The results of copying a single column to a multicell destination

When you specify a single-row source block with the /Edit, Copy command, Quattro Pro evaluates it in the same way as a single-column source block. Thus, if you copy a single row, such as A5..H5 in Figure 4.19, to a multicell destination block, such as A6..A8, Quattro Pro copies the information three times: to row 6 beginning in cell A6, to row 7 beginning in cell A7, and to row 8 beginning in cell A8.

Copying Repetitively

There is an easy way to copy data repetitively in a spreadsheet. This is especially helpful when you want to copy headings that you use repetitively in a spreadsheet. For instance, suppose you create the column and row headings in the block A1..H4 in Figure 4.20. You want to copy this block down the length of the spreadsheet three times. You will then use these headings to create profit data for four different years.

To copy this information repetitively in one /Edit, Copy operation, you must specify

- A source block that encompasses the data you want to copy *and* the entire area to which you want the data copied

- A single cell destination *within* the source block

In the current example, you want the four-row block A1..H4 to be repeated four times, so the correct source block is A1..H16. You want to copy the headings beginning in cell A5, so this is the destination cell to use. You can see the results of this /Edit, Copy command in Figure 4.21. By using this technique, you tell Quattro Pro to repeat the labels in the block A1..H4 four additional times within the source block A1..H16. (Actually, the data is also copied to A1..A4, the source block, overwriting the existing information.)

Figure 4.20

Copying repetitively by specifying the source block A1..H16 in the /Edit, Copy command

Figure 4.21

The results of the copy operation in Figure 4.20

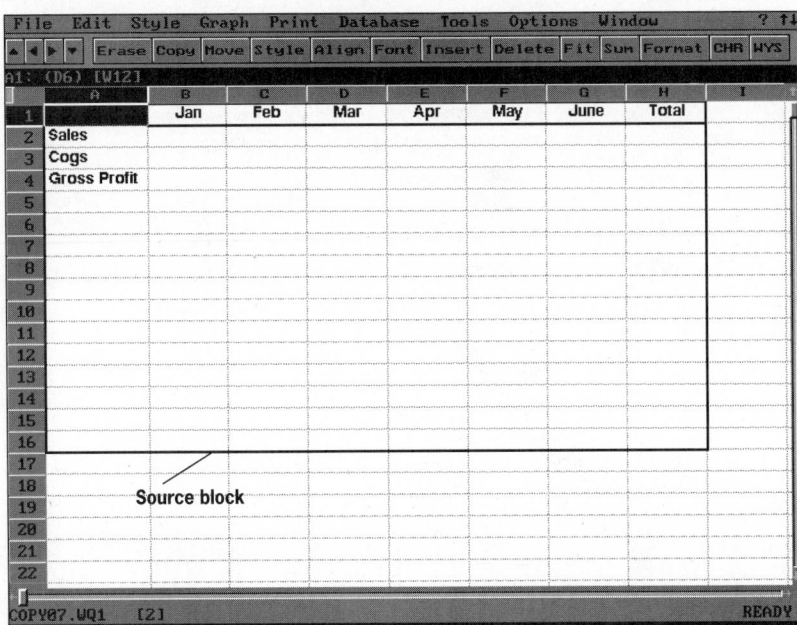

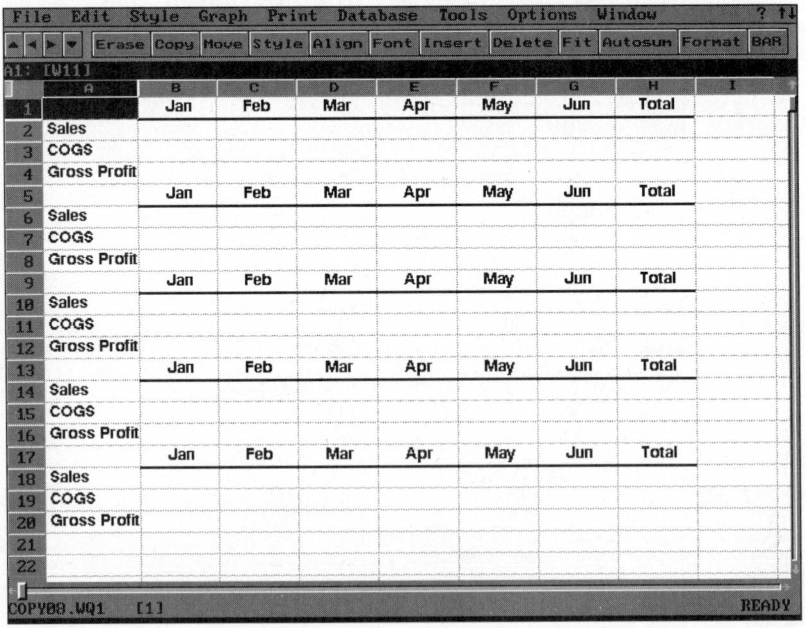

Copying Data Between Two Open Files

Note. Chapter 2 tells how to open multiple files on the desktop.

The procedure used for copying data *between* files is very similar to that for copying information *within* a file. For example, suppose you are an electrical distributor with locations in numerous cities, including Topeka. Topeka has sent you a spreadsheet, TOPEKA.WQ1, listing sales by product line during the first two months of the year. You want to copy this data, which is in the block A1..C6, to the same block in a corporate file called COMPANY.WQ1.

With both files TOPEKA.WQ1 and COMPANY.WQ1 open on the desktop, as shown in Figure 4.22, locate the cell selector in the upper-left cell of the block you want to copy—cell A1 in TOPEKA.WQ1. Select /Edit, Copy, Ctrl-C, or the Copy button, and specify the source block **A1..C6**. Specify the destination (cell A1 in COMPANY.WQ1) as

```
[C:\FILES\COMPANY.WQ1]A1.
```

If you point to this destination as shown in Figure 4.22, Quattro Pro automatically supplies the path and file name, enclosed in brackets.

Figure 4.22

Copying information between two open files

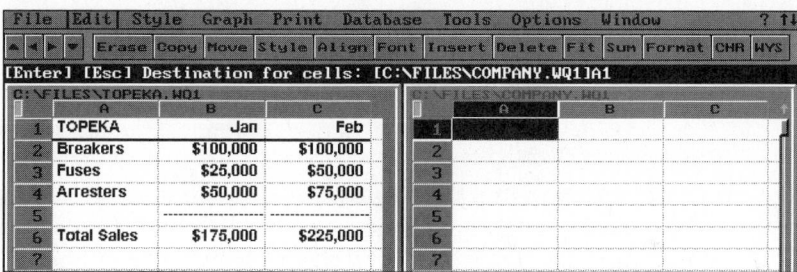

Tip. From the keyboard, you can press Shift-F6 to move the cell selector between open files.

As you can see in Figure 4.23, Quattro Pro leaves intact the information in the source block, A1..C6 in TOPEKA.WQ1, and copies this data (as well as all /Style settings except the column width), to the same block in COMPANY.WQ1. Quattro Pro then returns the cell selector to its location before you selected /Edit, Copy—in this case, cell A1 in TOPEKA.WQ1.

CAUTION! *Copying a block that contains formulas to another file can be tricky and may produce unexpected results, unless these formulas use absolute addressing or are copied to the same location in the destination file. See the section "Copying Formulas" for details.*

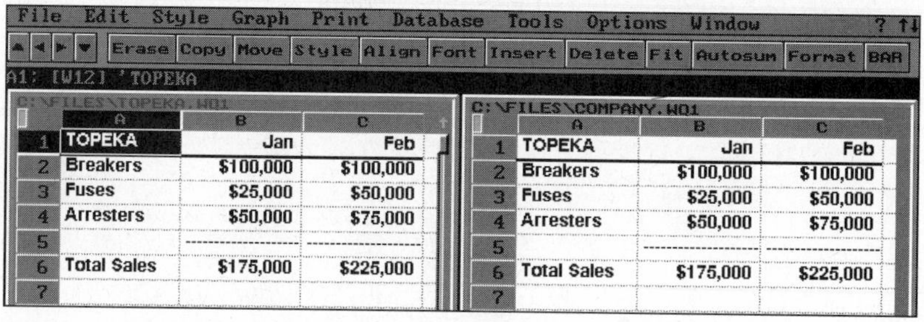

Figure 4.23
The results of
copying data
between two open
files

Copying Only Cell Contents or /Style Settings

Quattro Pro 4.0 includes a new command, /Edit, Copy Special, that performs
two functions. It can copy just the cell contents, leaving any /Style settings or
attributes—numeric format, line drawing, font, shading, and so on—in the
destination intact. Or it can copy just /Style settings, leaving any data in the
destination intact.

In Figure 4.24A, for example, the block F1..I3 is assigned a Dutch 12-
Point Bold font, different numeric formats, alignments, and line drawing.
Let's use the /Edit, Copy Special command and examine the results you get
by copying the block F1..I3 to a destination beginning in cell F5.

Copying Only Cell Contents

If you use /Edit, Copy Special and choose Contents from the menu shown in
Figure 4.24A, you'll get the results in Figure 4.24B. Although the contents of
F1..I3 are copied to F5..I7, the /Style settings—font, numeric format, and line
drawing—previously assigned to the destination are unaffected and still intact. If no /Style settings have been assigned to the destination, the copied
data takes on the global default settings for the spreadsheet.

Copying Only Style Attributes

If you use /Edit, Copy Special and choose Format, you'll get the results in
Figure 4.24C. Here the bold font, numeric formats, and line drawings assigned to F1..I3 are copied to F9..I11, although the centered label alignment
is not. (To learn why the bottom line drawing of cell H3 isn't copied, see
"Copying a Single Cell," earlier.) The existing data in the F9..I11 destination
is unaffected.

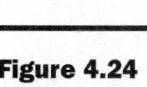

Figure 4.24
Copying only style attributes or only cell contents

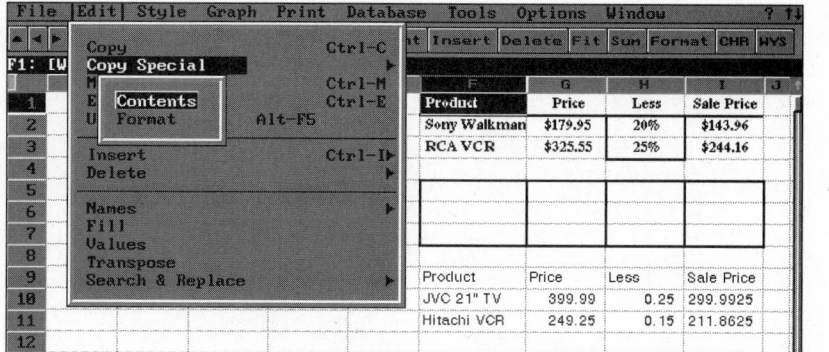

Copying Formulas

Only when you copy formulas do you really use the /Edit, Copy command's full power and time-saving capability. To correctly use /Edit, Copy in this capacity and maintain accuracy in your spreadsheet, however, you must have a sound understanding of how Quattro Pro copies formulas.

When a formula contains cell references, such as +C10, and you copy the formula to another location in the spreadsheet, Quattro Pro automatically adjusts each cell reference to correspond to the formula's new location. However, each of the following types of cell reference is adjusted differently:

- Relative

- Absolute

- Mixed

Using Relative References

You may not be aware of it, but by default you create a *relative reference* each time you enter a formula. For example, the formula +B10 contains a relative reference to cell B10; the formula @SUM(A1..A3) uses three relative references: A1, A2, and A3.

When you copy a formula that contains a relative reference, Quattro Pro automatically adjusts the reference *relative to* the formula's new location in the spreadsheet. Let's look at an example of this principle. Imagine that you own a hotdog stand, and you have created the spreadsheet in Figure 4.25A listing the sales for each product during your highest grossing months. Cell B5 contains the formula @SUM(B2..B4), summing the July sales of hotdogs, ice cream, and soda. You want to use a similar formula to sum the sales in August and September. You could take the "longhand" approach and create another formula in cell C5, and yet another in cell C6. Instead, you can use a much more efficient method and copy the formula in B5 to cells C5 and D5. You can do this by copying the formula in B5 to the destination C5..D5.

Take a look at the results of this copy operation in Figure 4.25B. Examine the formula in the input line, and you'll see that C5 now contains the formula @SUM(C2..C4). Quattro Pro has automatically adjusted the formula's cell references *relative to* this new location. Because cell C5 is one column to the right of cell B5 (the source location of the formula), Quattro Pro adjusted the *column* component of the relative cell references by one column. Likewise, because cell D5 is two columns to the right of cell B5, Quattro Pro has adjusted the column component of the relative references by two so that D5 contains the formula @SUM(D2..D4).

Figure 4.25

Copying the formula in B5, which contains relative references, to C5 and D5

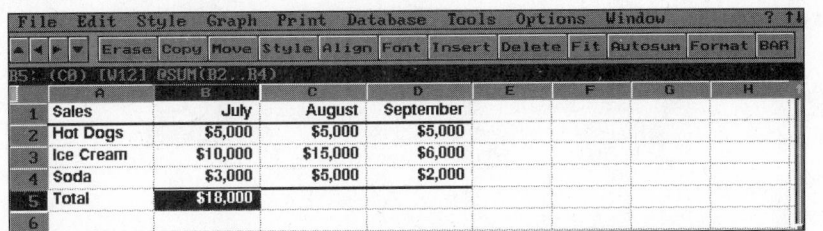

Now suppose that you want to calculate the total for each product, and you enter the formula @SUM(B2..D2) in cell E2 of Figure 4.26A. You then use /Edit, Copy to copy this formula to the block E3..E4. Notice in Figure 4.26B that Quattro Pro has automatically adjusted the relative references to correspond to the formula's new location. Cell E3 now contains the formula @SUM(B3..D3) because this cell is located one row down from the source cell, E2. Likewise, because cell E4 is two rows down from cell E2, E4 now contains the formula @SUM(B4..D4).

As you can see from these examples, relative referencing makes it easy to copy a formula from one location in a spreadsheet to another. However, if you copy relative references indiscriminately, you can create large-scale errors in your spreadsheet.

Avoiding Problems with Relative References

Relative references, although extremely useful, are sometimes inappropriate. Most commonly an incorrect use of relative references occurs when you copy a formula to a cell in a different column and row.

For example, imagine that you are expanding your enterprise, Mighty Munchies. You already are selling muffins, generating monthly revenues of $1,000. Bagels and doughnuts, on the other hand, are new, so you only expect sales of $100 for each of these products during the first month you offer them, January. You create the spreadsheet in Figure 4.27A using these estimates.

Figure 4.26

Copying the formula in E2, which contains relative references, to E3 and E4

A

E2: (C0) @SUM(B2..D2)

	A	B	C	D	E
1	Sales	July	August	September	Total
2	Hot Dogs	$5,000	$5,000	$5,000	$15,000
3	Ice Cream	$10,000	$15,000	$6,000	
4	Soda	$3,000	$5,000	$2,000	
5	Total	$18,000	$25,000	$13,000	
6					

B

E4: (C0) @SUM(B4..D4)

	A	B	C	D	E	
1	Sales	July	August	September	Total	
2	Hot Dogs	$5,000	$5,000	$5,000	$15,000	@SUM(B2..D2)
3	Ice Cream	$10,000	$15,000	$6,000	$31,000	@SUM(B3..D3)
4	Soda	$3,000	$5,000	$2,000	$10,000	@SUM(B4..D4)
5	Total	$18,000	$25,000	$13,000		
6						

Figure 4.27

Incorrect use of relative references

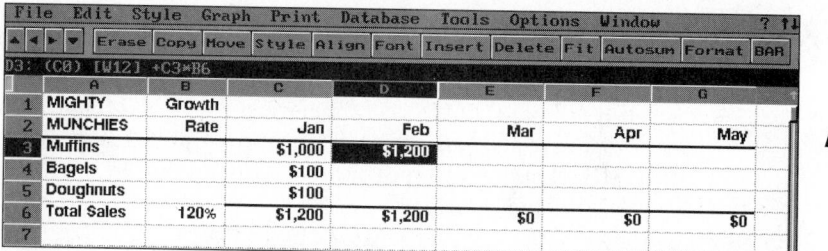

A

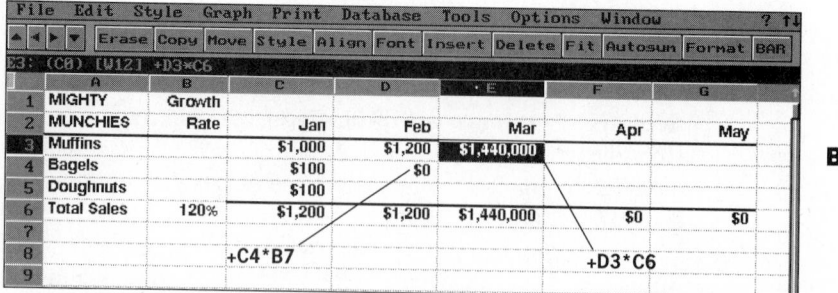

B

By opening a retail location, however, you expect total revenues to grow 20% per month. Therefore, in cell D3, you calculate projected February muffin sales as $1,200 using the formula +C3*B6. This formula uses the preceding month's (January) muffin sales value of $1,000 from cell C3 and multiplies it by the 120% growth rate from cell B6.

If you copy this formula to other cells, however, you won't get correct formulas. Look at what happens when you copy it to cell E3 to calculate March muffin sales; you get the formula +D3*C6, or $1,440,000, as illustrated in Figure 4.27B. The reference to February muffin sales, +D3, is correct, but the copied formula incorrectly references cell C6, January total sales, not the 120% growth rate in cell B6. Likewise, when you copy the formula in cell D3 to cell D4 to calculate February bagel sales, you get the incorrect formula +C4*B7, which returns $0. The cell reference +C4 correctly references January bagel sales, but the copied formula incorrectly references the blank cell B7, instead of the growth rate in cell B6.

In both cases—when you copy across a row and when you copy down a column—the copied formulas do not reference cell B6, the monthly growth rate. Thus the use of the relative reference B6 is inappropriate in this instance. However, by using an *absolute reference*, described next, you can copy the formula in D3 anywhere in the spreadsheet and still maintain the reference to cell B6.

Using Absolute References

An *absolute reference* is the opposite of a relative reference. As you know, a relative cell reference changes to reflect the spreadsheet location to which it is copied. An absolute reference, on the other hand, remains unchanged no matter where you copy it.

Tip. You can also use ABS (F4) or the Abs button in the Edit SpeedBar to create an absolute reference. See "Using ABS (F4)."

You create an absolute reference by placing a dollar sign ($) in front of both the column component and row component of a cell address. $A$1 is an absolute reference. Additionally, if SALES is a defined block name, $SALES is an absolute reference. (For more about using an absolute address with block names, see "Using ABS (F4)," later in this chapter.)

Returning to the Mighty Munchies example, suppose you now calculate projected February muffin sales in cell D3 with the formula +C3*$B$6, as shown in Figure 4.28A. This formula still references the preceding month's (January) muffin sales, using the relative reference C3. However, it now uses the absolute address, $B$6, to reference the 120% monthly growth rate. This time, when you copy the formula by specifying cell D3 as the source cell and D3..G5 as the destination block, the absolute cell address $B$6 is maintained throughout the destination block. You can see this by examining the input line in Figure 4.28B. Notice that cell G5 contains the formula +F5*$B$6. So May doughnut sales are correctly calculated as the April doughnut sales ($173 in cell F5) multiplied by the 120% growth rate in cell B6, for a result of $207.

Figure 4.28

Copying the formula in D3, which uses an absolute reference, to B6

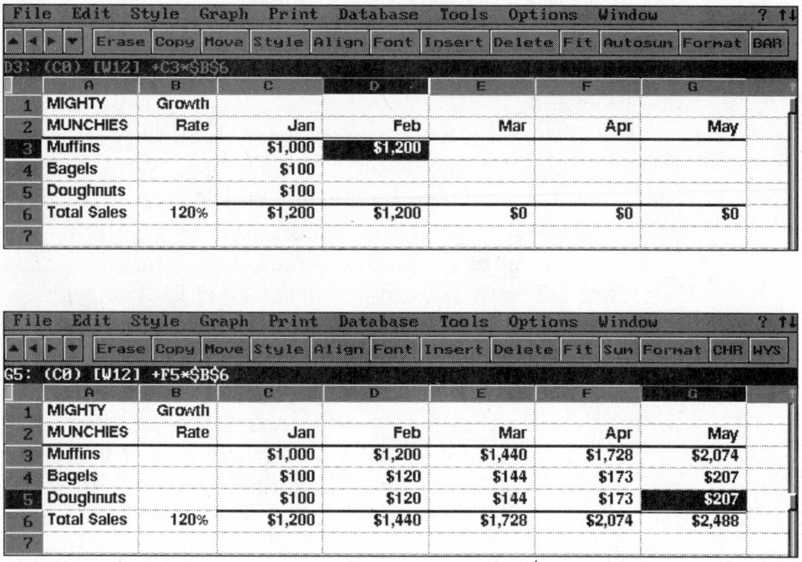

A

| File | Edit | Style | Graph | Print | Database | Tools | Options | Window | | ? ↑↓ |

Erase Copy Move Style Align Font Insert Delete Fit Autosum Format BAR

D3: (C0) [W12] +C3*$B$6

	A	B	C	D	E	F	G
1	MIGHTY	Growth					
2	MUNCHIES	Rate	Jan	Feb	Mar	Apr	May
3	Muffins		$1,000	$1,200			
4	Bagels		$100				
5	Doughnuts		$100				
6	Total Sales	120%	$1,200	$1,200	$0	$0	$0
7							

B

| File | Edit | Style | Graph | Print | Database | Tools | Options | Window | | ? ↑↓ |

Erase Copy Move Style Align Font Insert Delete Fit Sum Format CHR WYS

G5: (C0) [W12] +F5*$B$6

	A	B	C	D	E	F	G
1	MIGHTY	Growth					
2	MUNCHIES	Rate	Jan	Feb	Mar	Apr	May
3	Muffins		$1,000	$1,200	$1,440	$1,728	$2,074
4	Bagels		$100	$120	$144	$173	$207
5	Doughnuts		$100	$120	$144	$173	$207
6	Total Sales	120%	$1,200	$1,440	$1,728	$2,074	$2,488
7							

TIP. *When you create a formula in the upper-left cell of a block and then want to copy that formula to the other cells in the block, you can specify this source cell as part of the destination block. For instance, in the Mighty Munchies example, the formula in cell D3 is copied to the block D3..G5. During the copy operation, Quattro Pro simply overwrites the formula in the source cell, D3, with the same formula.*

Absolute references are also commonly used to create running totals using the @SUM function. A *running total* is a balance calculated at the end of each time period, equal to

accumulated balance for prior periods + current period balance

Running totals are often maintained for balance sheet items, like cash, retained earnings, and depreciation. In fact, monthly checkbook balances are running totals.

For instance, suppose you and another investor in Mighty Munchies together put up $20,000 in cash on December 31. Your retail location opens on January 1, and generates the monthly cash flow shown in Figure 4.29A. To create running cash totals, enter the formula **+$B$3+@SUM($C$4..C4)** in cell C6. As shown in the input line, this formula includes two absolute references—$B$3, referencing the $20,000 beginning cash balance, and $C$4 in the @SUM function, referencing the January cash flow ($1,000).

Figure 4.29
Using absolute
references in
running totals

A

| File | Edit | Style | Graph | Print | Database | Tools | Options | Window | ? ↑↓ |

▲ ◀ ▶ ▼ | Erase | Copy | Move | Style | Align | Font | Insert | Delete | Fit | Sum | Format | CHR | WYS

C6: (C0) +$B$3+@SUM($C$4..C4)

	A	B	C	D	E	F	G	H
1	MIGHTY							
2	MUNCHIES	01-Jan-92	Jan	Feb	Mar	Apr	May	
3	Beginning Cash	$20,000						
4	Net Cash Flow		($1,000)	($2,000)	($500)	$100	$500	
5								
6	Cash Balance		$19,000					
7								

B

| File | Edit | Style | Graph | Print | Database | Tools | Options | Window | ? ↑↓ |

▲ ◀ ▶ ▼ | Erase | Copy | Move | Style | Align | Font | Insert | Delete | Fit | Sum | Format | CHR | WYS

G6: (C0) +$B$3+@SUM($C$4..G4)

	A	B	C	D	E	F	G	H
1	MIGHTY							
2	MUNCHIES	01-Jan-93	Jan	Feb	Mar	Apr	May	
3	Beginning Cash	$20,000						
4	Net Cash Flow		($1,000)	($2,000)	($500)	$100	$500	
5								
6	Cash Balance		$19,000	$17,000	$16,500	$16,600	$17,100	
7								

If you copy this formula to the block D6..G6, you can see the results in Figure 4.29B. Notice that the input line displays the formula in cell G6, +$B$3+@SUM($C$4..G4), which returns the May cash balance of $17,100. Only the relative reference in the @SUM formula has changed. The absolute reference to the beginning balance in cell B3 remains fixed, as well as the absolute reference in the @SUM formula. Thus, the @SUM block expanded as you copied across row 6, while maintaining the initial reference to cell C4.

Using Mixed References

You can also create a *mixed reference*, which includes both relative and absolute components in the same cell address. For example, the mixed address formula +$A1 includes the absolute column component $A and the relative row component 1. The column component therefore remains fixed, regardless of where you copy this formula, but the row component can vary. If you copy the mixed address formula +A$1, on the other hand, the absolute row component (1) remains constant, but the relative column component can vary.

Mixed references are especially helpful when you need to copy a formula. To see this let's return to the startup of Mighty Munchies. Suppose you now decide to project total revenues, and then assign a proportion of these revenues to the three product lines: bagels, doughnuts, and muffins.

Tip. You can use the ABS (F4) key to create a mixed reference. See "Using ABS (F4)" for details.

First, you'll need to create a spreadsheet like that in Figure 4.30A and enter the formula **+C3*$B3** in cell D3. This formula calculates February sales of $1,200 as January sales (C3) multiplied by the 120% growth rate in B3. Notice the mixed address $B3. When you copy this formula across row 3 to the block E3..G3, the $B3 mixed address keeps the $B column component fixed. As you can see in Figure 4.30B, after the copy operation cell G3 contains the correct formula +F3*$B3. However, you don't need to freeze the row component, 3, because it does not change when you copy across the same row the source cell is located in.

Figure 4.30

Copying a mixed reference across a column

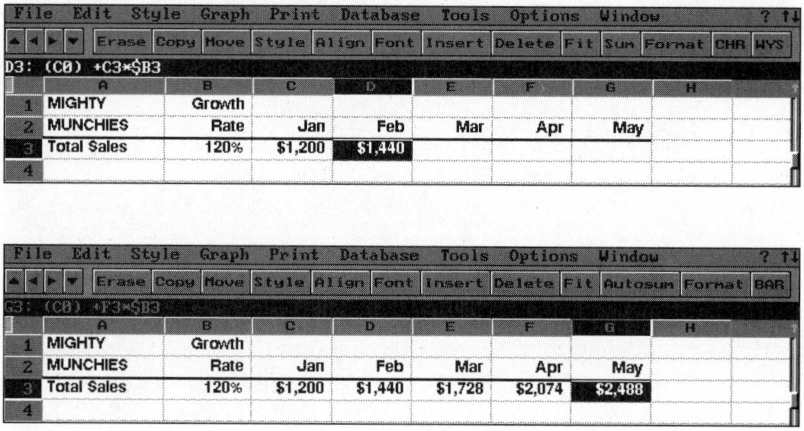

Figure 4.31A shows how to calculate the sales attributable to each product line. If muffins represent 60% of total sales, bagels 25%, and doughnuts 15%, the formula in cell C6, **+C$3*$B6**, calculates projected January muffin sales of $720. When you copy this formula to the block C6..G8, the references behave as follows:

■ C$3 allows the column component, C, to vary as you copy across a row. Therefore, if you copy the formula to column D, the column component then refers to column D. The row component, $3, remains fixed, so that all copied formulas in rows 6, 7, and 8 refer to a sales value in row 3.

■ $B6 allows the column component, $B, to remain fixed when it is copied across a row. The row component, however, can vary when the formula is copied to rows 7 and 8. Thus all copied formulas in row 6 refer to cell B6, formulas in row 7 refer to cell B7, and those in row 8 refer to cell B8.

Figure 4.31
Copying a mixed
reference to a block

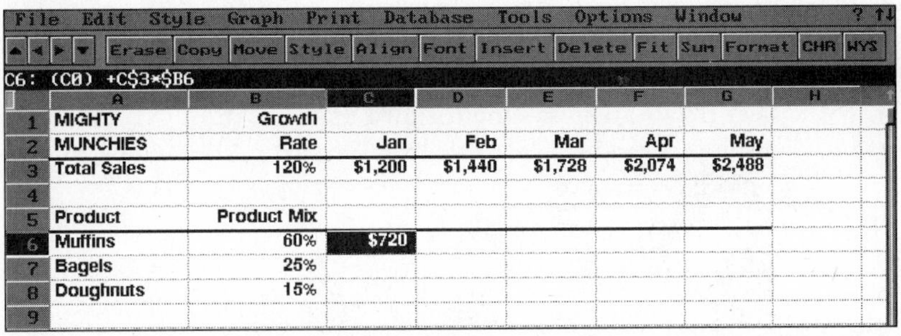

A table/screenshot showing a Quattro Pro spreadsheet (panel A):

File Edit Style Graph Print Database Tools Options Window   ? ↑↓
▲ ◀ ▶ ▼ Erase Copy Move Style Align Font Insert Delete Fit Sum Format CHR WYS

C6: (C0) +C$3*$B6

	A	B	C	D	E	F	G	H
1	MIGHTY	Growth						
2	MUNCHIES	Rate	Jan	Feb	Mar	Apr	May	
3	Total Sales	120%	$1,200	$1,440	$1,728	$2,074	$2,488	
4								
5	Product	Product Mix						
6	Muffins	60%	$720					
7	Bagels	25%						
8	Doughnuts	15%						
9								

A

Panel B:

File Edit Style Graph Print Database Tools Options Window   ? ↑↓
▲ ◀ ▶ ▼ Erase Copy Move Style Align Font Insert Delete Fit Sum Format CHR WYS

G8: (C0) +G$3*$B8

	A	B	C	D	E	F	G	H
1	MIGHTY	Growth						
2	MUNCHIES	Rate	Jan	Feb	Mar	Apr	May	
3	Total Sales	120%	$1,200	$1,440	$1,728	$2,074	$2,488	
4								
5	Product	Product Mix						
6	Muffins	60%	$720	$864	$1,037	$1,244	$1,493	
7	Bagels	25%	$300	$360	$432	$518	$622	
8	Doughnuts	15%	$180	$216	$259	$311	$373	
9								

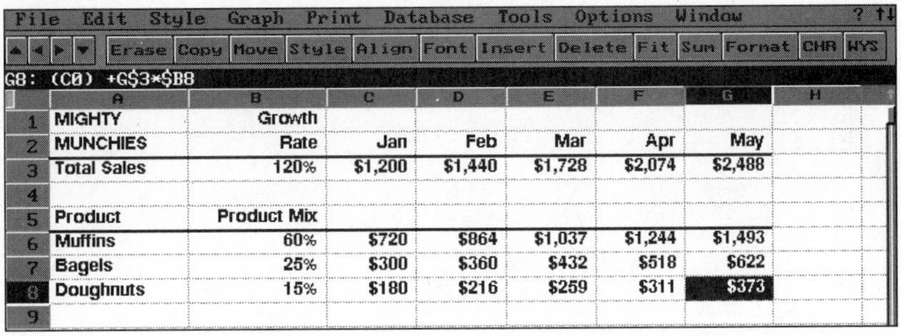

B

You can see these results in Figure 4.31B. Observe in the input line that cell G8 now contains the formula +G$3*$B8. Projected May doughnut sales of $373 is therefore calculated as the May total sales of $2,488 in cell G3, multiplied by the 15% doughnut percentage in cell B8.

Using ABS (F4)

Instead of typing a dollar sign ($) to create an absolute or mixed reference, you can use the ABS key (F4). The ABS key is easier because it saves keystrokes, and because you can use it in any of the following modes:

- Point mode, when pointing to a cell
- Value mode, when entering a formula
- Edit mode, when editing a formula

Tip. In Quattro Pro 4.0, [Abs] in the Edit SpeedBar is also a shortcut for ABS (F4).

Suppose you want to enter the formula +B1 as an absolute reference in cell A1. Type **+** in A1 and then point to B1. Quattro Pro enters Point mode and displays the formula +B1 in the input line. To convert this relative reference to an absolute reference, press ABS (F4) or the Abs button in the Edit

SpeedBar. Your formula is now displayed as +$B$1. Press Enter to accept this formula in cell A1.

On the other hand, suppose you want this formula to become a mixed reference. Press ABS (F4) or the Abs button twice while in Point mode, and Quattro Pro displays the formula as +B$1; press ABS three times, and it is displayed as +$B1. You can keep pressing ABS and cycle through the following cell references:

Press ABS (F4) or the Abs button	Formula	Cell Address	Column	Row
1 time	+$B$1	Absolute	Fixed	Fixed
2 times	+B$1	Mixed	Changes	Fixed
3 times	+$B1	Mixed	Fixed	Changes
4 times	+B1	Relative	Changes	Changes

You can also use ABS (F4) or the Abs button when you edit an existing formula. For example, suppose cell A1 already contains the formula +B1–B2, and you want to change the relative reference B1 to an absolute address. Press Edit (F2) to enter Edit mode, then Home to move to the beginning of your formula, and then press the → key once. Press ABS (F4), and Quattro Pro displays the formula as +$B$1–B2. Press Enter to accept this formula in A1.

Be aware that ABS has some limitations. When you use a block reference in a formula, ABS always converts both cell addresses to the same type of reference. For example, if you enter the formula **@SUM(B1..C3)** in A1 and press ABS once, Quattro Pro displays the formula @SUM($B$1..$C$3). Press ABS again, and it displays @SUM(B$1..C$3). Therefore, you have to manually insert or delete the appropriate $ if the cell references need to be different types of references.

ABS also has limited application when you use a block name in a formula. For instance, assign the name SALES to the block B1..C3, and enter the formula **@SUM(SALES)** in cell A1. Press ABS (F4) once, and Quattro Pro displays this formula as @SUM($SALES), which is equivalent to @SUM($B$1..$C$3). Therefore, if you need to use different types of cell addressing in a formula, do not use a block name.

Copying Link Formulas

As discussed in Chapter 2, you can create a formula that links two spreadsheet files. You get different results, however, when you copy a link formula that contains an absolute address and when you copy one that contains a relative address.

Consider Figure 4.32A. Here you have three files open on the desktop: DAY, MONTH, and YEAR. Cell A1 in the file DAY contains the value 5. As you can see in the input line, cell A1 of the file MONTH contains the link formula +[DAY]$A$1, which includes an absolute reference to cell A1 of DAY. Figure 4.32B shows what happens if you copy this link formula to cell A2 of YEAR. Quattro Pro copies the formula, +[DAY]$A$1, to cell A2 of YEAR, which also produces the value 5. Not only are the files DAY and MONTH linked, but the two files DAY and YEAR are also now linked.

Figure 4.32

Copying a link formula that contains an absolute address

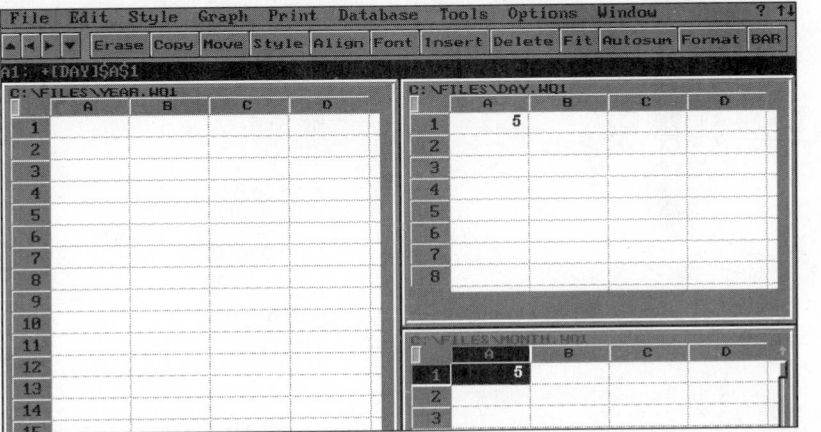

When you copy a link formula containing a relative address into another file, however, you get different results. For example, in Figure 4.33A, cell A1 of MONTH contains the link formula +[DAY]A1. Copy this link formula to cell A2 of YEAR, and you get the result +[DAY]A2, as shown in Figure 4.33B. Because [DAY]A2 is blank, this link formula produces the value 0 in [YEAR]A2. Thus, although the formula links the files DAY and YEAR, Quattro Pro adjusts the relative cell reference to correspond to the formula's new location in YEAR.

Figure 4.33

Copying a link formula that contains a relative address

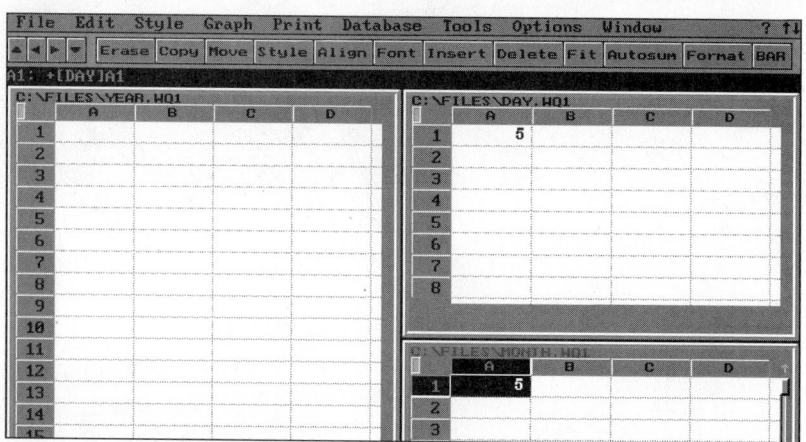

You get the same result when you copy a link formula containing a relative or absolute block name. Imagine, for instance, that you use /Edit, Names, Create to assign the absolute block name $SALES to cell A1 of DAY. Then you enter the formula +[DAY]$SALES in cell A1 of MONTH. When you copy this formula to cell A2 of YEAR, Quattro Pro maintains the absolute block name. On the other hand, suppose you use /Edit, Name, Create to assign the relative block name SALES to cell A1 of DAY, and then enter the formula +[DAY]SALES in cell A1 of MONTH. When you copy this formula to cell A2 of YEAR, Quattro Pro treats the relative block name SALES as the relative cell reference A1. The copied result in cell A2 of YEAR is the formula +[DAY]A2.

Converting and Copying Formulas as Values

In some instances, such as in scenario generation, you may want to copy the current values and labels returned by formulas, rather than the underlying formulas themselves, to another location in a spreadsheet. Or perhaps—to decrease memory consumption (in a large file, for example)—you want to convert unneeded formulas to the displayed values and labels in their current location. Quattro Pro's /Edit, Values command can be used in both of these situations.

Copying Values and Labels Returned by Formulas

Note. Using /Edit, Values is very similar to using /Edit, Copy. See "The Mechanics of Copying" earlier in this chapter.

Consider the model in Figure 4.34A, which projects financial data for a company. The current scenario assumption—that sales will grow by 10% each month—is used to project sales in February, March, and April. For instance, examine the input line in Figure 4.34A, and you see that February sales of $11,000 are calculated using the formula +C3*(1+$B3). This scenario also assumes that cost of goods sold (COGS) is 60% of sales; the $6,600 February COGS in cell D4, for example, is calculated as +D3*$B4. The quarter's totals in column F, however, are summations of the monthly totals.

Suppose you want to run a second scenario using different assumptions. However, you want to save the current results so you can compare the two scenarios. To accomplish this, you must first copy the *results* of the current scenario (block A1..F5) to a blank location in the spreadsheet. You can use this procedure:

1. (OPTIONAL) If Recalculation is set to manual, press Calc (F9) to update the values in the spreadsheet; otherwise, the values you copy may not be current.

Figure 4.34
Using /Edit, Values to copy the displayed values and labels in the block A1..F5 to another location

A

	A	B	C	D	E	F	G
1						Quarter Ended	
2		Assumptions	31-Jan-92	29-Feb-92	31-Mar-92	31-Mar-92	
3	SALES	10%	$10,000	$11,000	$12,100	$33,100	
4	COGS	60%	$6,000	$6,600	$7,260	$19,860	
5	GROSS PROFIT		$4,000	$4,400	$4,840	$13,240	
6							

D3: [W10] +C3*(1+$B3)

B

D9: [W10] 11000

	A	B	C	D	E	F	G
1						Quarter Ended	
2		Assumptions	31-Jan-92	29-Feb-92	31-Mar-92	31-Mar-92	
3	SALES	10%	$10,000	$11,000	$12,100	$33,100	
4	COGS	60%	$6,000	$6,600	$7,260	$19,860	
5	GROSS PROFIT		$4,000	$4,400	$4,840	$13,240	
6							
7						Quarter Ended	
8		Assumptions	31-Jan-92	29-Feb-92	31-Mar-92	31-Mar-92	
9	SALES	10%	$10,000	$11,000	$12,100	$33,100	
10	COGS	60%	$6,000	$6,600	$7,260	$19,860	
11	GROSS PROFIT		$4,000	$4,400	$4,840	$13,240	
12							

Tip. If you inadvertently write over existing information in the destination during an /Edit, Values command, immediately use /Edit, Undo (Alt-F5) to cancel the completed copy operation.

2. Position the cell selector in the upper-left cell of the block whose values and labels you want to copy (in this example, cell A1).

3. Select /Edit, Values. Quattro Pro displays "Source block of cells:" followed by the current selection in the form of a block, A1..A1. Specify the source block **A1..F5** and press Enter.

4. In response to "Destination for cells:", specify the single cell address **A7** and press Enter. Quattro Pro returns the cell selector to its location before you selected the /Edit, Values command—in this case, A1.

You can see the results in Figure 4.34B. Using the destination cell A7 as the upper-left corner of the destination block, Quattro Pro copies only the displayed values and labels, not the underlying formulas, in the source block A1..F5 to the block A7..F11 (writing over any existing information in the process). Cell D9 thus contains the value 11000, shown in the input line. The underlying formulas in the source block A1..F5 are unchanged.

Notice in Figure 4.34B that Quattro Pro did not copy the line drawing in the source block to the destination. /Edit, Values does, however, copy alignment, numeric format, font, and shading settings.

Since the formulas in A1..F5 are still intact, you can now change the assumptions and run a new scenario. For example, if you enter .05 (a 5% monthly sales growth assumption) in cell B3, you can see the results in Figure 4.35. Although the information in A1..F5 changes to reflect the new assumptions, the information in A7..F11 remains "frozen" because it only contains values and labels. You can now compare these two scenarios.

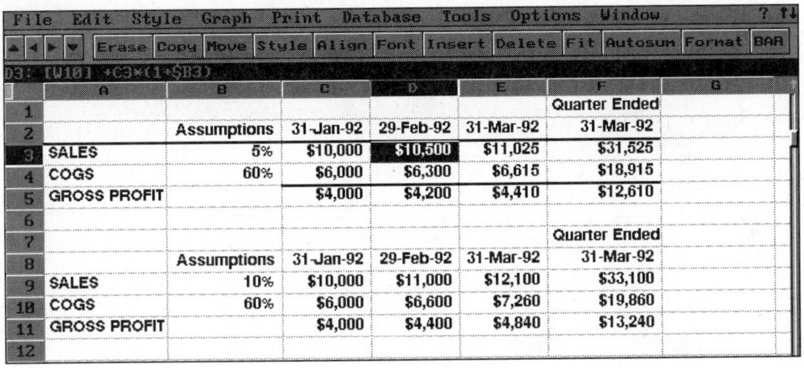

Figure 4.35

Comparing a second scenario with the Figure 4.33B scenario "frozen" in the block A7..F11

File	Edit	Style	Graph	Print	Database	Tools	Options	Window	? ↑↓

| ▲ ◄ ► ▼ | Erase | Copy | Move | Style | Align | Font | Insert | Delete | Fit | Autosum | Format | BAR |

D3: [W10] +C3*(1+$B3)

	A	B	C	D	E	F	G
1						Quarter Ended	
2		Assumptions	31-Jan-92	29-Feb-92	31-Mar-92	31-Mar-92	
3	SALES	5%	$10,000	$10,500	$11,025	$31,525	
4	COGS	60%	$6,000	$6,300	$6,615	$18,915	
5	GROSS PROFIT		$4,000	$4,200	$4,410	$12,610	
6							
7						Quarter Ended	
8		Assumptions	31-Jan-92	29-Feb-92	31-Mar-92	31-Mar-92	
9	SALES	10%	$10,000	$11,000	$12,100	$33,100	
10	COGS	60%	$6,000	$6,600	$7,260	$19,860	
11	GROSS PROFIT		$4,000	$4,400	$4,840	$13,240	
12							

NOTE. *Quattro Pro also offers two methods for copying the values and labels returned by formulas to another file. You can use /Edit, Values to copy them to another open file. (The mechanics of /Edit, Values and /Edit, Copy operations are very similar; see the earlier section "Copying Data Between Two Open Files.") Or you can use the /Tools, Xtract, Values command discussed in Chapter 5 to copy the displayed values and labels in an open file to a file on disk.*

Converting Formulas to Values and Labels in Their Current Location

You can also use the /Edit, Values command to convert underlying formulas to the values and labels *currently* returned by these formulas. This is useful when you need to decrease memory consumption of a large file, because literal values and labels use less memory than formulas.

For example, suppose you create the spreadsheet in Figure 4.36A. Only columns A and B contain labels and values; all other columns contain formulas. Even the label Month Ended in C1 is created by the formula +B1; similarly, the $10,000 February sales value in C3 is calculated as +B3. In the input line, the date 30-Apr-92 in cell E2 is the result of the formula +30+D2.

Figure 4.36
Using /Edit, Values to convert the underlying formulas in a block to the displayed values and labels

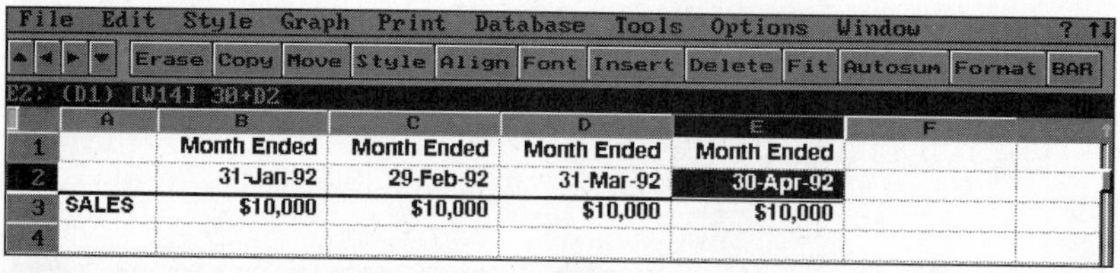

Here is how to convert the contents of all these cells to displayed labels and values: Select /Edit, Values, specify the source block **A1..E3**, and specify the *same* block as the destination (or just the upper-left cell of this block, cell A1). As illustrated in Figure 4.36B, the input line shows that cell E2 now contains the date value 33724.

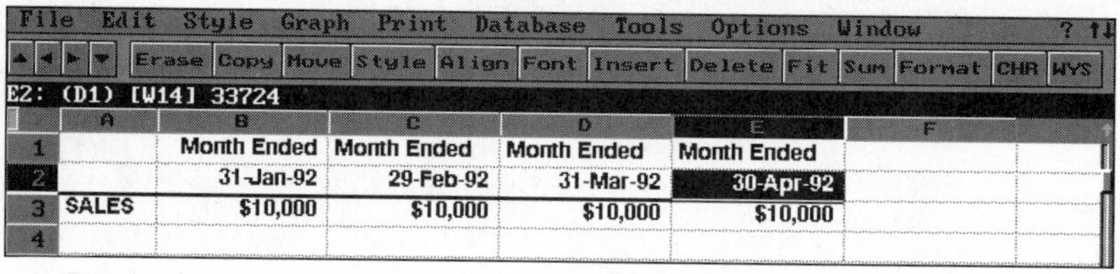

TIP. *To convert a single formula to its current value or label, move the cell selector to the cell containing this formula, press Edit (F2), Calc (F9), or the Calc button in the Edit SpeedBar, and then Enter.*

Transposing Data

Quattro Pro includes the /Edit, Transpose command, which you can use to *transpose*, or change, the orientation of data in a spreadsheet. This is a handy command when you need to "flip" the orientation of values and labels from columns to rows, or from rows to columns. Transposing data that contains formulas, however, is successful only in certain situations.

Transposing a Block of Values and Labels

The easiest way to see how the /Edit, Transpose command works is through an example. Suppose you create the spreadsheet in Figure 4.37A by entering dates in row 1 and sales values in row 2. You enter all the data as values, labels, or dates. For instance, you enter the formula **@DATE(92,2,29)** in C1, and the sales value **20000** in C2. After you enter this data, however, you realize that you should have entered it in columns. Instead of reentering all this data, you can use the /Edit, Transpose command to transpose these rows to columns, using a blank area of the spreadsheet. To do so, follow these steps:

1. Position the cell selector in the upper-left cell of the block you want to transpose, cell A1.

2. Select /Edit, Transpose. Quattro Pro displays "Source block of cells:" followed by the current selection in the form of a block, A1..A1. Specify the source block **A1..E2** and press Enter.

3. In response to "Destination for cells:", specify the single cell address, **A4**, and press Enter. Quattro Pro returns the cell selector to its location before you selected the /Edit, Transpose command (in this case, cell A1).

Figure 4.37

Transposing a block of values and labels

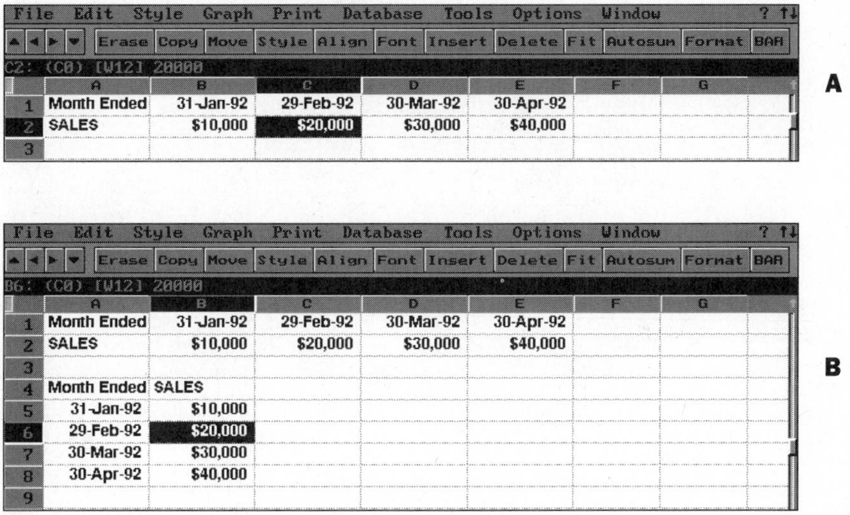

As you can see in Figure 4.37B, Quattro Pro uses cell A4 as the upper-left corner of the destination block. It copies *and transposes* the values and labels in the source block A1..E2 to the block A4..B8. The data in row 1 is transposed to column A; the data in row 2 is transposed to column B. Quattro Pro also copies all /Style settings except column width to this destination. The data in the source block A1..E2 is unaffected.

It is important to note that the size and shape of the transposed block, A4..B8, is quite different from that of the source block A1..E2. So be sure the area below and to the right of your specified destination cell is empty, because any existing information is overwritten by the transposed data. (If you do accidentally write over existing information in the destination when you use /Edit, Transpose, immediately use /Edit, Undo (Alt-F5) to reverse the effects of the completed command.)

CAUTION! *You cannot use /Edit, Transpose to transpose data in one location. That is, you cannot specify the same source and destination; nor can you specify a destination cell located within the source block. If you do, Quattro Pro "loses" some of the data during the transposition. Instead, first transpose the data to another location in the spreadsheet, and then use /Edit, Copy or Move to transfer it back to the source area. Remember, however, that unless it is square in shape, the shape of the transposed data will be different from that of the source block.*

You can also use /Edit, Transpose to copy and transpose data to a destination in another open file. Because the mechanics of /Edit, Transpose and /Edit, Copy are very similar, see "Copying Data Between Two Open Files," earlier, for details.

Transposing a Block of Formulas

Note. See "Copying Formulas" earlier in this chapter for a discussion of relative and absolute references.

Transposing a block of data that contains formulas requires special attention and forethought. To see this, let's return to our current example. This time, suppose you enter the data in the block C1..E2 as formulas that include relative references (Figure 4.38A). Thus, the date 29-Feb-92 in cell C1 is the result of the formula +B1+29, and the dates in D1 and E1 are calculated similarly. The $20,000 February sales value in cell C2 is calculated as +B2*2, as shown in the input line. This formula is then copied to cells D2 and E2.

If you now use /Edit, Transpose, specifying the source block A1..E2 and the destination cell A4, you get the results in Figure 4.38B. Here, Quattro Pro has incorrectly transposed this data because of the relative references. The $20,000 February sales value in cell C2 is calculated as +B2*2; in the transposed block it is calculated as +A6*2 in cell B6, which returns $67,326. You can see this formula in the input line.

You can avoid this problem and successfully transpose this data by using any of these methods:

■ Convert all relative addresses in the source block to absolute addresses, *before* you use /Edit, Transpose. Any formulas in the transposed (destination) block, however, still refer to the cells in the source block.

■ Use /Edit, Values first to copy the current values and labels returned by these formulas, not the underlying formulas themselves, to another location in a spreadsheet. Then you can use /Edit, Transpose to transpose these values and labels in yet another location.

Figure 4.38
Unsuccessfully
transposing a block
of formulas
containing relative
references

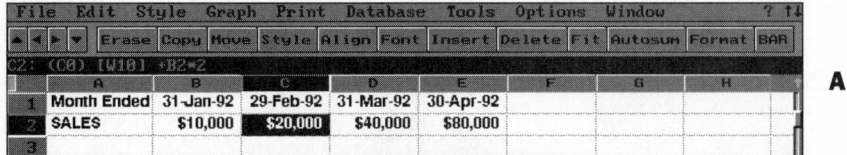

A

B

- Use /Edit, Move to separately move the contents of each cell to its new location. Although time-consuming, this is the only way, short of reentering the formulas, to ensure that cell addresses reference the correct data in the new location.

CHAPTER

5

File Management

TO GET THE MOST OUT OF QUATTRO PRO, YOU SHOULD KNOW ITS BASIC housekeeping functions, especially those that manage and manipulate files. You can access most of these using the /File command on Quattro Pro's main menu bar. Its pull-down menu is the gateway for you to create, open, replace, close, erase, and save spreadsheet files. It also enables you to work with directories and workspaces, to SQZ! (compress) files, and to gain access to the File Manager.

In addition to covering the /File command menu in detail, this chapter will also explore other aspects of managing files in Quattro Pro. For example, you'll learn how to save a spreadsheet file with a password, so that others cannot access it without knowing the password. You will also learn about various commands in the /Tools menu that let you import ASCII files into the spreadsheet, extract a portion of a spreadsheet to a file on disk, and combine several spreadsheet files into one.

If you've upgraded to Quattro Pro 4.0, you'll find two noteworthy enhancements. First, the File command dialog boxes now include shortcut buttons that make selecting files easier. Second, Quattro Pro 4.0 supports some new file formats, including 1-2-3 Release 3.x .WK3 files, Allways .ALL files, and Impress .FMT files. In addition, Quattro Pro 4.0 supports Harvard Graphics .CHT files.

File Basics

When you first bring up Quattro Pro, it displays a new, blank spreadsheet file named SHEET1.WQ1 that is displayed in its own window. Thus, immediately, Quattro Pro suggests a default file name for the new spreadsheet file. At this point, you can begin entering data into the new spreadsheet. However, the entries you make are only temporary—that is, they are stored in your computer's RAM. The moment you turn off your machine, the data you've entered will be lost.

To save a permanent record of your data for future use, you must assign a name to the spreadsheet file and save that file to disk. When saving the file, you can use the default file name suggested by Quattro Pro, or you can provide a more descriptive file name of your own. However, before you are ready to assign file names, you'll need a basic understanding of Quattro Pro's file-naming conventions.

Quattro Pro conforms to the same file-naming conventions as DOS. Therefore, like DOS files, Quattro Pro files begin with a name of up to eight characters in length, followed by a period, and an extension of up to three characters. File names may contain the characters A through Z, the numbers 0 through 9, and an underscore (_). In addition, you can include the following symbols:

~ ^ / ! @ # $ % & ( ) – { } '

File names may not contain spaces. Further, when you assign a file name, DOS will convert all letters in that name to uppercase. Moreover, Quattro Pro requires that all the spreadsheet files in a given directory have a unique name. If you try to save a file under a name that already exists, Quattro Pro will warn you of this and ask for a confirmation from you before overwriting the file on disk.

Note. You should avoid assigning your own file extensions to minimize the risk of mistakenly erasing or changing important system files.

Note that if you attempt to assign a file name that is longer than eight characters, DOS will truncate the file name to eight characters. This can cause problems if the first eight characters of two file names are the same. For example, INCOME-QUARTER1.WQ1 and INCOME-QUARTER2-.WQ1 would both be truncated to INCOME-QU.WQ1, and saving one would overwrite the other.

You can assign just about any file name you want to a spreadsheet file. However, you do not have to provide an extension. Quattro Pro does this for you. In fact, as you'll soon see, Quattro Pro uses the extensions it assigns to identify its own files. For example, Quattro Pro automatically assigns the default extension of .WQ1 to all its spreadsheet files. You can modify this default extension by using the /Options, Startup, File Extension command (discussed in Chapter 15).

Although you will seldom assign extensions to file names, having a good working knowledge of significant extensions used by Quattro Pro can help you to ascertain the origin or type of a file. Table 5.1 lists those file extensions used by Quattro Pro that you may encounter, including new ones supported in version 4.0.

In addition to those file extensions listed in Table 5.1, five other extensions are reserved for special DOS functions. You should avoid using them when naming your files. These extensions are .BAT, .BAS, .COM, .EXE, and .SYS.

As mentioned, when you start Quattro Pro, it creates a new spreadsheet file and displays that file in its own window. You can do several things with this "startup" spreadsheet. You can begin entering data and then save the spreadsheet to disk. You can retrieve an existing file from disk that replaces the startup spreadsheet and work on that file. Or, you can ignore the startup spreadsheet, leaving it in memory, and open an existing or new file in a separate window.

The sections that follow explore Quattro Pro's file-management options in detail. For example, you'll learn how to create a new spreadsheet and open existing ones. You'll also learn how to save spreadsheet files to disk.

Table 5.1 Commonly Used File Extensions in Quattro Pro 3.0 and 4.0

File Extension	Description
Quattro Pro 3.0 & 4.0	
.BAK	Quattro Pro backup file
.BGI	Graph/font printing file
.CA1	File used by INSTALL
.CA2	File used by INSTALL
.CA3	File used by INSTALL
.CHR	Hershey font file
.CLP	Clip art file
.DAT	Data file
.DEF	Default settings file
.FON	Bitmap font file
.HLP	Quattro Pro Help file
.ICO	Windows icon file
.INI	Windows install file
.LOG	Transcript log file
.MU	Quattro Pro Menu file
.PIF	Windows program information file
.PRN	Print file
.RSC	Resource file
.SFO	Bitstream outline font file
.SND	Sound file
.SOM	Network serial number file
.SOR	Sort order file
.TRN	File translator file
.VRM	Memory management file

Table 5.1	**(Continued)**	
	File Extension	**Description**
	.WKZ	Early Quattro version SQZ! file
	.WQ!	Quattro Pro SQZ! file
	.WQ1	Quattro Pro spreadsheet file
	.WSP	Workspace date file
	.ZIP	ZIP compressed file[*]
New in Quattro Pro 4.0		
	.FN2	Bitmap font file
	.HDX	Help index file
	.PAK	PAK compressed file
	.PCX	PCX splash file
	.QLL	Add-in @function library
	.RF	Resource file
	.STY	Named style file
	.SPO	Speedo outline font file
	.SPR	Speedo outline font file

*   Used by Quattro Pro 3.0 only

Creating New Files: /File, New

When you select the /File command, Quattro Pro displays the menu options shown in Figure 5.1.

To create a new spreadsheet file and open it in a separate window, you use the /File, New command. When you select this command, Quattro Pro immediately responds by overlaying the current window with a new window that contains a fresh spreadsheet file. That window then becomes the active window and the commands in Quattro Pro's menu bar now apply to that window.

When you create a new spreadsheet file, Quattro Pro assigns it both a window number and a file name that conforms to its default file-naming scheme. The file name assigned takes the form SHEET#.WQ1, where # corresponds to the number of new spreadsheet windows you have opened since you started the current Quattro Pro session. For example, if only one window (the startup spreadsheet, SHEET1) was open before you selected the /File, New command, the new window is assigned the number [2]. The default file name assigned to the spreadsheet in that window is SHEET2.WQ1. The next new file is assigned a window number of [3] and a file name of SHEET3.WQ1, and so on. Both the window number and the default file name appear in the status bar at the bottom of your screen. You can, of course, assign a more descriptive file name when you later save the file. See "Saving Files" later in this chapter for details on saving files.

Figure 5.1

The /File pull-down menu

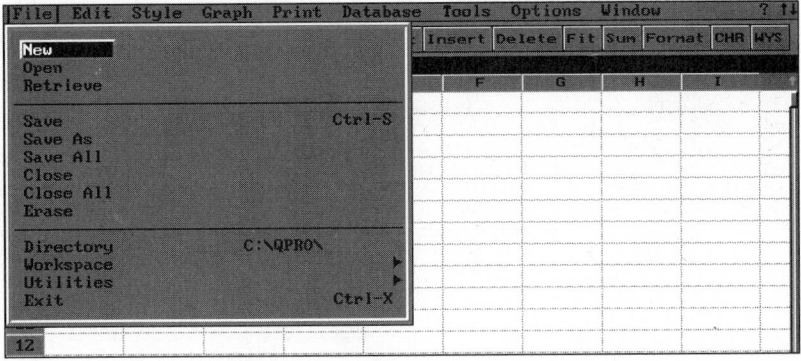

When you create a new spreadsheet file, the window in which it resides overlays other existing windows, hiding them from view. However, those windows are still there in the background and you can access them at any time. In fact, if you use the /Window, Tile command discussed in Chapter 2, you can see the exposed portions of each of your open spreadsheet windows. Figure 5.2 shows an example.

As mentioned, you can easily move to an open spreadsheet window at any time. The techniques and commands for moving between windows are discussed at length in Chapter 2, and they are briefly reviewed here:

- Use the /Window, Pick command, press Shift-F5 or Alt-0. Quattro Pro displays a list of names for your selection.

- Click on the exposed portion of a window with the mouse.

- Press the Alt key and the key corresponding to the window number. For example, to move to window number 3, press Alt-3.

- Press Next Window (Shift-F6) to cycle through open windows one at a time.

Figure 5.2

Multiple
spreadsheet
windows open on
the desktop

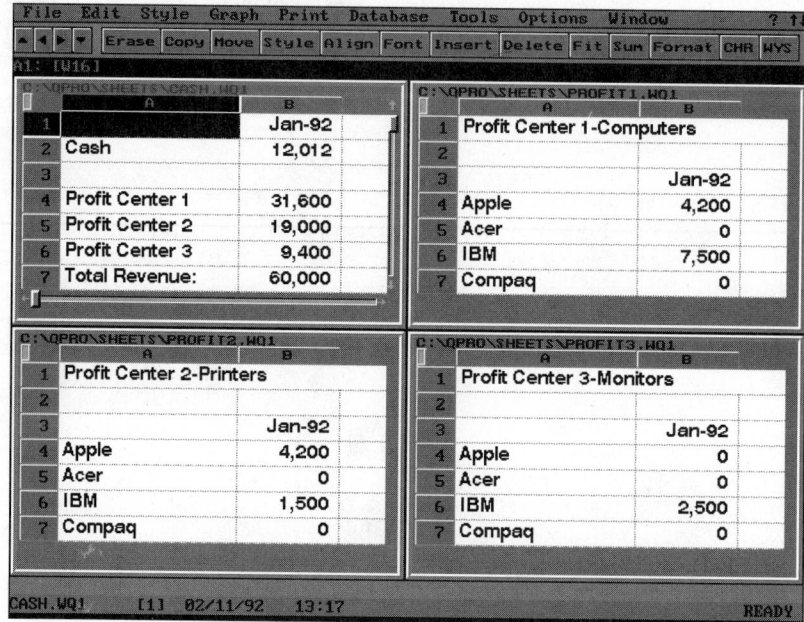

Opening Existing Files: /File, Open

To open an existing file from disk in a separate window, you use the /File, Open command. When you select this command, Quattro Pro displays a file dialog box like that in Figure 5.3. This box contains a listing of spreadsheet files in the current directory. Type the name of the file you want to open or use the arrow keys to highlight it in the list of files. Press Enter to confirm your selection. Quattro Pro opens the file you've selected in its own window. Normally, that window overlays the others on the desktop. However, if you resized or moved the window for that file before you last saved it, Quattro Pro restores its window to the desktop in the same size and position. That window then becomes the active window and the commands in Quattro Pro's menu bar now apply to it.

There are a number of techniques that you can use to enhance the functionality of the file list box shown in Figure 5.3. For example, you can expand the file dialog box to full screen size. You can also change the contents of the list box, or you can open a file from a directory other than the current directory. See "Techniques for Selecting Files" later for more details.

Figure 5.3

The file dialog box displayed when /File, Open is selected

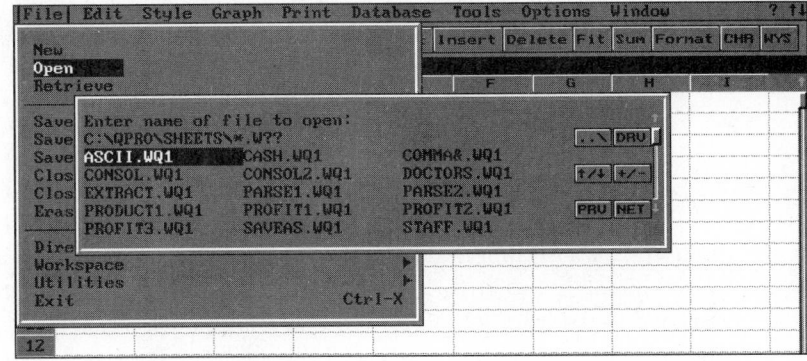

Retrieving Files: /File, Retrieve

To replace the spreadsheet file in the current window with another spreadsheet file from disk, you use the /File, Retrieve command. In contrast to /File, Open, which loads a specified spreadsheet file into its own window, /File, Retrieve closes the spreadsheet file in the current window and removes it from memory. That file is then replaced by a file you select.

The first thing Quattro Pro does when you enter the /File, Retrieve command is attempt to remove the spreadsheet file in the current window from memory. However, if Quattro Pro detects that you have changed the spreadsheet since you last saved it, you are given an opportunity to save your work. To do this, Quattro Pro displays a prompt box that asks "Lose your changes?" If you enter **N**, the /File, Retrieve command is aborted and you will be returned to the /File pull-down menu so that you can save the spreadsheet. (The default response is No, so pressing Enter will accomplish the same thing.) If you enter **Y** or you've made no changes to the file in memory, Quattro Pro displays a file dialog box similar to the one in Figure 5.3. However, this time the box contains the prompt "Enter name of file to retrieve" and a list of files in the current directory is displayed below it. At this point, you can either type the name of the file you want to retrieve or highlight it from the list box below. Press Enter to confirm your selection. Quattro Pro loads the file you've selected into the current window, replacing the file in that window.

Techniques for Selecting Files

Quattro Pro allows you to open an existing file from any directory you want. To do this, it provides a uniform system of dialog and prompt boxes to assist you in the selection of a file. This system is used for both the /File, Open and /File, Retrieve commands discussed above as well as for the /File, Save, /File, Save As, and /File, Save All commands covered later in this chapter.

For example, when you select the /File, Open command, Quattro Pro displays a file dialog box similar to the one shown in Figure 5.3. The first line of this box is a prompt that is specific to the command you are using. The second line of the list box shows the drive and path to the current directory followed by a wildcard filter, for example:

```
C:\QPRO\*.W??
```

This causes Quattro Pro to display in the dialog box all those files in the current directory (C:\QPRO) that have an extension that conforms to the *.W?? file descriptor. The asterisk and question mark in the file descriptor are wildcards. They let you control what groups of file names and extensions are displayed in the list. For example, *.W?? causes Quattro Pro to display all .WQ1 spreadsheet files, all .WSP workspace files, and possibly files that do not belong to Quattro Pro, for example, Lotus 1-2-3 Release 2.2 files (.WK1).

The * (asterisk) wildcard character in a file name or in an extension indicates that any character can occupy that position and all remaining positions in the file name or extension. For example, typing **B*.WQ1** at the prompt causes Quattro Pro to list all files in the current directory that begin with B and have an extension of .WQ1—for example, BUDPROJ.WQ1, B1.WQ1, and BILLS90.WQ1. Likewise, typing **XYZ.*** causes Quattro Pro to list all files named XYZ regardless of their extension—for example, XYZ.WQ1, XYZ.BAK, and XYZ.WSP.

The ? (question mark) wildcard character in a file name or extension indicates that any character can occupy that position. For example, typing **PR?.WQ1** lists all files that begin with PR and have a .WQ1 extension—for example, PRD.WQ1, PR1.WQ1, and PR.WQ1. As another example, typing **WOODS.W?1** lists all files named WOODS that have an extension that begins with W and ends with 1—for example, WOODS.WQ1 and WOODS.WK1.

Once the dialog box is displayed, you can use any one of several techniques to select a file to open, retrieve, or save. The sections that follow explain each of these techniques.

Selecting a File Name

To select a file from the files dialog box in Figure 5.3, you can use the arrow keys to move the highlight to the file name you want and then press Enter to select it. Alternatively, you can simply click on the name of a file with the mouse. Although either of these methods will get the job done, both Quattro Pro 3.0 and Quattro Pro 4.0 offer some keyboard and mouse alternatives that can make selecting a file much easier. These are summarized in Table 5.2 and discussed briefly in the following paragraphs.

In particular, the six buttons on the right side of the files dialog box can make selecting a file downright convenient in Quattro Pro 4.0. You can access these buttons by pressing the / (slash) key and then using the arrow keys to move between buttons, or you can simply click on a button with your mouse. For example, when you press the DRV button, Quattro Pro 4.0 shows you a list of both local and network drives. To see a list of files and directories on a particular drive, simply select it.

When you're viewing a lot of files, you can increase the size of the files dialog box, as shown in Figure 5.4, by pressing F3 (Choices), or in Quattro Pro 4.0, pressing the ↑/↓ button. (In Character mode, the ↑/↓ button expands the dialog box to fill the entire screen.) This button is a toggle; pressing it once expands the dialog box and pressing it again contracts it.

Figure 5.4

Expanding the files dialog box

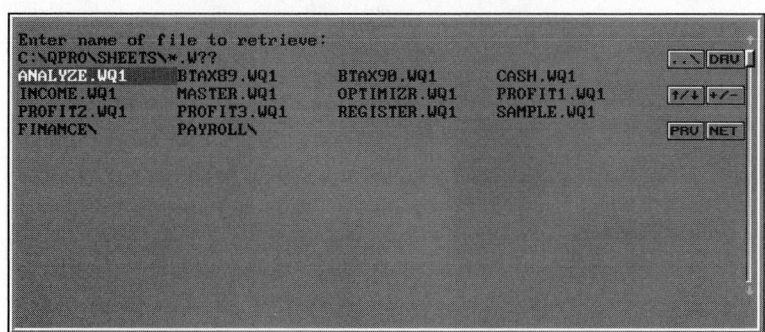

To get information about files before you select them, such as the file size, date and time created, or date last modified, press the + (plus) key or, in Quattro Pro 4.0, the +/− button. Quattro Pro will list your files in alphabetical order with a full set of details for each file. The +/− button in Quattro Pro

4.0 is a toggle; pressing it again reverts to the normal files-list display. In either version, pressing the – (minus) key reverts to a normal files display.

When you select the PRV button, Quattro Pro 4.0 displays a list like the one in Figure 5.5, showing the paths and names of the last eight files you've opened. If you use a particular set of files frequently, you'll find this new feature is a real time saver.

Table 5.2   **Special Keys in the File Dialog or Prompt Box**

Key	Quattro Pro 4.0 Button	Result in File Dialog Box	Result in Prompt Box
Esc		Removes file list, moves to prompt-line, and clears the wildcard file descriptor from prompt-line	Clears directory and path from prompt-line
Ctrl-Backspace		Removes file list, moves to prompt-line, and removes entire prompt-line entry	Clears entire prompt-line entry
Spacebar		Highlights next file in list	Adds space to prompt-line entry
Backspace	`..\`	Displays list of all files in the parent directory	Deletes character to left of cursor
F2		Prompts for "Search for" wildcard pattern; enter desired search characters	
F3	`↑/↓`	Acts as a toggle key to expand or shrink the file dialog box	
+	`+/–`	Displays file information for each file in the list	Adds + character to prompt-line entry
–	`+/–`	Returns file list to file names only format	Adds – character to the prompt-line entry
	`PRV`	Lists the default directory and the path and filename of the last eight files opened	
	`NET`	Shows the local and network drives	
	`DRV`	Lists all available drives on your computer system	

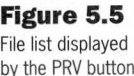

Figure 5.5

File list displayed
by the PRV button

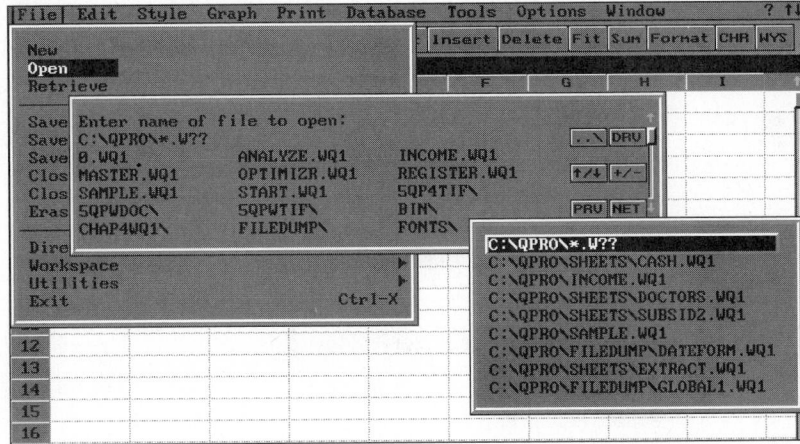

The NET button shows your network drive mappings. You can use this button to quickly access files stored on a network server. See Chapter 14 for more details on using this button.

Choosing a Different Directory

What if the file you want is not in the current directory? For example, suppose the current directory is C:\QPRO\SHEETS, and you select /File, Open. To move up one directory level and view the contents of the parent directory, press Backspace once, or in Quattro Pro 4.0, press the ..\ button. Quattro Pro shifts the second line in the files dialog box from C:\QPRO\SHEETS*.W?? to read C:\QPRO*.W??. Press Backspace or the ..\ button again, and you'll see the contents of the next parent directory—in this case, the root directory C:*.W??.

NOTE. *When you choose a file from a different directory, the current directory for Quattro Pro is not changed. The next time you open the files dialog box, Quattro Pro will again show you its current default working directory. See "Changing Directories" later for details on how to change this.*

Moving down one directory level to a subdirectory of the current directory is just as easy. In addition to showing you the files in the current directory, Quattro Pro also shows you all subdirectories of the current directory. These are marked with a \ (backslash) following the directory name. In Figure 5.4, for example, selecting PAYROLL\ displays all the files and subdirectories in the PAYROLL directory.

Searching a Dialog Box

As you create more files with Quattro Pro, the number of files in the file dialog box will grow, making it harder to scan the box and find the file you want. However, Quattro Pro offers a handy facility that lets you search a dialog box. To do this, enter a command (for example, /File, Open) that causes the file dialog box to be displayed, and then press Search (F2). Quattro Pro displays "Search for: *" at the bottom of the screen. Type the name of the file you want. As you type, Quattro Pro moves the highlight around the dialog box, locating that file whose name is closest to what you type. When the highlight is located on the file you want, press Enter to select it.

Typing the File Name

You can also type the name of the file you want to select. For example, when you select the /File, Open command, Quattro Pro displays a file dialog box. If you begin typing the name of a file, however, Quattro Pro clears the dialog box and displays the file prompt box shown in Figure 5.6. Once this box is displayed, you can finish typing the name of the file in the current directory and press Enter to open it.

Figure 5.6

The file prompt box

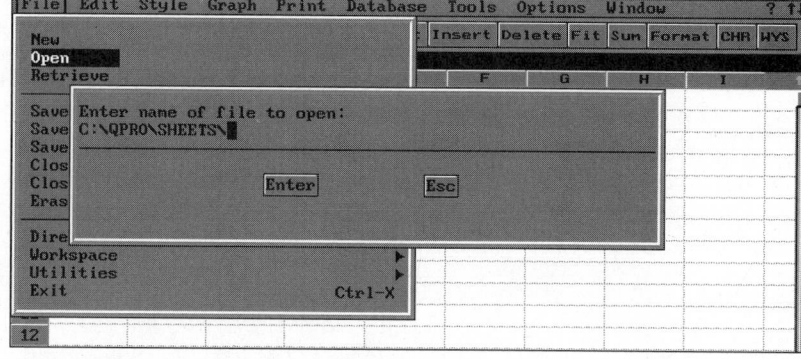

Note. With certain commands, such as /File, Save As, you must press Esc three times— the first time to remove the name of the existing file, the second time to remove the *.W?? file descriptor, and the third time to remove the path. You can then type a new path and press Enter.

You can also type the name of a file in a different directory. To do this, press Esc when the file dialog box is displayed. Quattro Pro displays the file prompt box. You can then press Backspace as needed to clear the current directory and type a new one, followed by an appropriate file name.

You can also press Esc twice—the first time to clear the wildcard file descriptor and again to clear the current path. (Pressing Ctrl-Backspace has the same effect.) You can then enter a new path, including the drive designation and an appropriate file name.

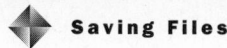

You can also type just the path in the file prompt box and let Quattro Pro help you to find the file. For example, suppose the current directory is C:\QPRO and you want to open a file in C:\ARCHIVE\TAX91. When you select the /File, Open command, Quattro Pro displays C:\QPRO*.W?? in the second line of the file dialog box. After pressing ESC twice to clear the file filter and path, you can then specify the new path by typing **C:\ARCHIVE\TAX91** and pressing Enter. (Don't forget the last backslash.) Quattro Pro automatically appends the *.W?? file filter to the end of the path as soon as you press Enter. It then displays the file dialog box showing the files in the directory you've chosen. You can then select the one you want.

Saving Files

This section discusses three commands for saving your spreadsheet files: /File, Save; /File, Save As; and /File, Save All. The /File, Save As command is used when you want to save a file for the first time or when you want to save an existing file under a new name. By contrast, the /File, Save command is used when you want to save an existing file under the same name. Finally, /File, Save All is used when you want to save all the currently open spreadsheets.

You can also save a file with a password. That way, if someone does not know the password, Quattro Pro will not allow them to open the file.

Saving a File for the First Time

To save a new file for the first time, you use the /File, Save As command. When you select this command, Quattro Pro displays the file dialog box shown in Figure 5.7. Below the prompt "Enter save file name:" is a list of files in the current directory. Type the name of the file you want to save. As soon as you begin typing, Quattro Pro clears the file dialog box and displays the file prompt box in Figure 5.8. Finish typing the name of the file (you don't have to provide the .WQ1 extension, since Quattro Pro does this for you automatically) and press Enter. Quattro Pro saves the file under the name you specified.

You can also save a new file in a directory other than the current directory. When Quattro Pro displays the file dialog box in Figure 5.7, press Esc twice, once to display the file prompt box in Figure 5.8 and again to clear the current path and directory. You can then type the new path and name for the file and press Enter.

Figure 5.7

The file dialog box for the /File, Save As command

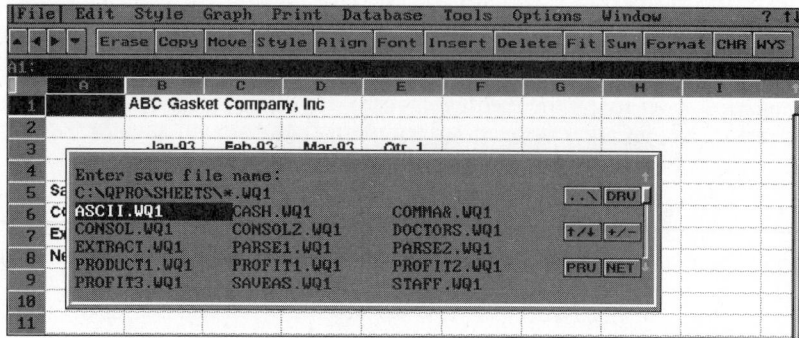

Figure 5.8

The file prompt box for the /File, Save As command

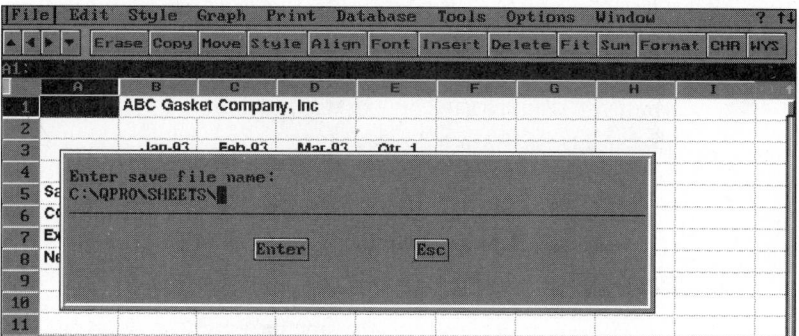

Saving an Existing File

To save an existing file under the same name, you use the /File, Save command. (The shortcut key for this command is Ctrl-S.) This command replaces a file on disk with the new, updated version of the file in memory. In addition, before you replace the file on disk, the /File, Save command gives you the option of creating a backup copy of that file before replacing it with the file from memory.

Unlike the /File, Save As command, Quattro Pro does not prompt you for a file name when you select /File, Save. It assumes you want to save the current file under its present name. Instead, Quattro Pro displays a "File already exists:" box that offers the following options:

- *Cancel*   Cancels the /File, Save command and returns you to the current spreadsheet

- *Replace*   Overwrites the existing spreadsheet file on disk with the newer version from memory

- *Backup*   Renames the original version with the same file name and a .BAK file extension, and then saves the current version of the file to disk with a .WQ1 extension

The Backup option allows you to save only one backup copy of each file in a given directory. However, you can easily save several versions of the same file in the same directory by saving each of them under different names. See the next section for details on how to do this.

Saving a File Under a New Name

To save an existing file under a new name or in a different directory, you use the /File, Save As command. When you select this command, Quattro Pro displays a file prompt box that contains the path and directory of the current file followed by its current name. To change the name or path, press Edit (F2), and then press Backspace to delete the characters to the left of the cursor. Alternatively, you can use the arrow keys to move the cursor to any point in the file name, press the Del key to delete only selected characters, type the new path and/or file name, and press Enter. Quattro Pro saves the current file under the name and in the directory you specified.

TIP. *In Quattro Pro 4.0, it's become easy to save the current open file in another directory using the /File, Save As command. Pressing Esc converts the file prompt box to the enhanced file dialog box. Once this box is displayed, you can use the techniques described in the previous sections to navigate to a new directory.*

Saving a File as a Template

Another useful application for /File, Save As is to create a custom spreadsheet *template* with the organization and layout for spreadsheets you use often. Templates enable you to save time by not having to repeatedly set up the same spreadsheet. In a sense you can recycle your work.

To create a template, simply build a spreadsheet with the structure, headings, settings, numeric formats, and macros you frequently use. Then, save it to disk with the /File, Save As command. The next time you want to use those settings, simply open the template file by using /File, Open or /File, Retrieve. Once the file is open, enter data as you normally would, taking full advantage of your previously established settings. When you're done, use the /File, Save As command to save the file under a different name.

Saving All Open Files

Note. When the Cancel/Replace/ Backup menu is displayed, selecting the Cancel option causes Quattro Pro to skip saving the file in the current window and move on to the next window. Pressing Esc has the same effect.

When you have more than one file open on the desktop, instead of saving them individually you may want to save them all at once. Quattro Pro's /File, Save All command lets you save all open files, starting with the current window. Quattro Pro then activates windows in the reverse of the order in which they were opened, from most recent to least recent. In each case, if a file already exists, Quattro Pro displays the Cancel/Replace/Backup menu, allowing you to overwrite or back up each file. If a file does not yet have a valid name, Quattro Pro displays the file prompt box and requests one.

Protecting Files with a Password

You can prevent unauthorized access to your Quattro Pro spreadsheet files by assigning passwords. When you protect a file with a password, the file cannot be retrieved unless the correct password is supplied.

CAUTION! *Once a file is saved with a password, it cannot be opened without the correct password. If you forget the password, the data in that spreadsheet is irretrievably lost. Therefore, you may want to make a note of the password you assign to a file.*

To assign a password to a file, you use the /File, Save As command. If you are saving the file for the first time, type a name for the file, press the spacebar once, type **P**, and press Enter. If you are saving an existing file, Quattro Pro displays the file prompt box shown when you select /File, Save As. This box already contains the path and name of the file, so simply press the spacebar once, type **P**, and press Enter. In either case, Quattro Pro displays the password prompt box shown in Figure 5.9.

Figure 5.9

The password prompt box

| File | Edit | Style | Graph | Print | Database | Tools | Options | Window | ? ↑↓ |

| Enter password: ■■■■■■■ | Verify password: ■■■■■■■ |

	ABC Gasket Company, Inc				
1	ABC Gasket Company, Inc				
2					
3		Jan-93	Feb-93	Mar-93	Qtr. 1
4					
5	Sales	$100,000	$120,000	$125,000	$345,000
6	COGS	$20,000	$24,000	$25,000	$69,000
7	Expenses	$6,000	$72,000	$153,000	$153,000
8	Net Profit	$74,000	$24,000	$25,000	$123,000
9					

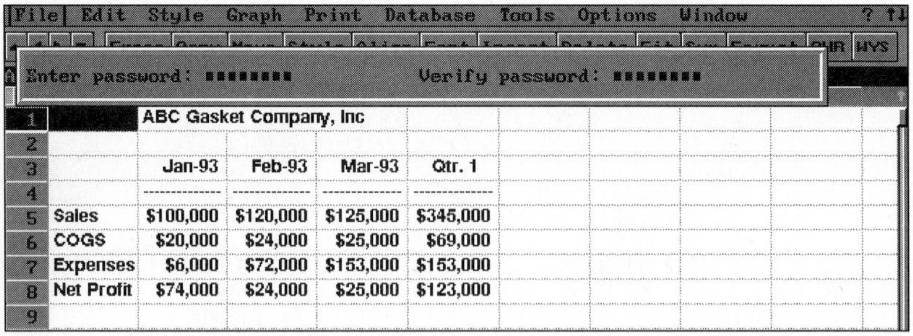

Type the password you want to assign to the file at the "Enter password:" prompt. You can enter up to 15 characters. Keep in mind that a password is case-sensitive. As you type, Quattro Pro displays square bullets in place of the characters. When you're done, press Enter. Quattro Pro displays a "Verify password:" prompt. Type the exact same password again and press Enter. If the password is verified, the spreadsheet will be saved with the password protection. If, for one reason or another, the password you entered for verification did not exactly match your original entry, Quattro Pro will beep and display a "Passwords do not match" error message. Press Esc or Enter and you will be sent back to the prompt screen, with the cursor at the end of the file name and in position for you to press the spacebar, type **P**, press Enter, and try again.

Once you have assigned a password to a file, Quattro Pro will prompt you for that password when you use /File, Open or /File, Retrieve to open the file. Simply type the password and press Enter to open the file.

Note. In Quattro Pro 4.0, you can password-protect the formulas in a spreadsheet. See Chapter 2.

You can also remove password protection or change the password for a file. To do this, begin by loading the file into memory by using the /File, Retrieve or /File, Open command and supplying the old password when requested to do so. Once the file is in memory, select the /File, Save As command. Quattro Pro displays the file prompt box containing the path and name for the file, followed by the designation "[Password Protected]." Press the Backspace key to remove the "[Password Protected]" message. If you want to supply a new password, press the spacebar, type **P**, and follow the steps outlined above. Otherwise, press Enter. Quattro Pro presents the Cancel/Replace/Backup menu. Select Replace. Quattro Pro replaces the file on disk with the updated file from memory.

Tips on Saving Files

An important nuance of both /File, Save and /File, Save As is that even though you saved the file to disk, that file still remains open on the desktop. Saving the file does *not* close the window; you can even continue to work on it after you have saved it. To close the file and remove it from the desktop, you can use the /File, Close command discussed in "Closing Files."

When you save a spreadsheet file, Quattro Pro saves the formatting, protection, recalculation, graphs, block names, and current directory settings. However, the /Options, Formats settings and the system defaults such as hardware and color display are not saved in the spreadsheet file. The next time you call up the saved spreadsheet, it will use the current default settings.

You can also organize your spreadsheet files into *workspaces*. Workspaces are essentially groups of related files. To create a workspace, you use the /File, Workspace, Save command. This command causes Quattro Pro to scan the files on the desktop and record their names in a file with a .WSP extension. Thus, by simply opening the .WSP workspace file, you can quickly restore the desktop to its former state. See "Saving and Retrieving Work-spaces" later in this chapter for details on how to save the current workspace.

Conserving Disk Space with SQZ! Plus

Quattro Pro's built-in SQZ! Plus file compression utility can help you con-serve storage space on your hard disk. This utility can be useful when you need to conserve space on your hard disk or when you need to archive large spreadsheets on a floppy disk.

To compress an existing Quattro Pro file, select the /File, Save As com-mand and replace the .WQ1 extension with a .WQ! extension. When you press Enter to save the file, Quattro Pro saves it in a compressed format. The next time you need the file, simply use the /File, Retrieve or /File, Open com-mand to load the compressed file into memory. Quattro Pro will automati-cally decompress the file and restore it to memory just as you saved it.

You also can use SQZ! Plus to save files from other software programs in compressed format. To do this, simply provide one of the following extensions:

- WKZ compresses files from earlier versions of Quattro.

- WK$ compresses Lotus 1-2-3 .WKS files (version 1A).

- WK! compresses Lotus 1-2-3 .WK1 files (version 2.01).

- WR$ compresses Symphony .WRK files (version 1.2).

- WR! compresses Symphony .WR1 files (version 2.0).

You can also configure SQZ! Plus by using the /File, Utilities, SQZ! com-mand. When you select this command, Quattro Pro displays a menu with the three options Remove Blanks, Storage of Values, and Version.

Remove Blanks lets you specify whether you want Quattro Pro to save blank cells when it compresses files. Normally blank preformatted cells are saved. However, you can save additional space on your hard disk or floppy disk by saving only filled cells. To do this, select the Remove Blanks option and then select Yes. However, be aware that blank preformatted cells will be permanently removed from your spreadsheet when you save. If saving the formatting for these cells is important to you, do not use this option.

Storage of Values determines how Quattro Pro stores spreadsheet values. Quattro Pro usually stores both formulas and their resulting values with up to 15 significant digits after the decimal, if required. However, when you se-lect this option, Quattro Pro displays a menu with three options: Exact, Ap-proximate, and Remove. *Exact* is the default and stores values and formulas with the usual 15 digits of precision. *Approximate* stores formulas and their values in half-precision, with up to seven significant digits after the decimal, requiring less disk space. *Remove* achieves the highest compression by removing values and storing only formulas. When you retrieve the spreadsheet after selecting Remove, Quattro Pro will automatically recalculate the formulas.

There is one special consideration to keep in mind when you use the Storage of Values option. You should save your spreadsheet with the Exact option rather than Remove if you plan to use those formulas in other Quattro Pro spreadsheets. For example, later in this chapter you'll learn about the /Tools, Combine command, which allows you to combine two or more spreadsheet files. You'll also learn about the /Tools, Xtract command, which allows you to extract a portion of a spreadsheet file to another file on disk. In either of these cases, if you remove values with SQZ! Plus, Quattro Pro will read in zero values (or NA) when it combines the spreadsheet into the current spreadsheet or when it extracts a portion of the spreadsheet to disk.

In most other cases, though, you can use the Remove option without penalty or fear of losing your formulas. In fact, you may be using unnecessary disk space if you don't use the Remove or Approximate setting.

The third SQZ! option, Version, lets you select whether you want to use the older version of SQZ! (the default) or the newer SQZ! Plus. You should use SQZ! Plus unless you plan to share files with someone else who uses version 1.x of the SQZ! add-in with Lotus 1-2-3 or Symphony. Note, however, that Quattro Pro's SQZ! Plus is compatible with SQZ! v.1.5 and SQZ! Plus for Lotus 1-2-3.

Translating to and from Other File Formats

Another powerful feature of Quattro Pro is its ability to automatically translate files from other programs when you retrieve them, and conversely, translate your Quattro Pro spreadsheet files to other file formats for use with other programs. You can use this feature to share data with Lotus 1-2-3, Symphony, and dBASE, among others.

Here are some points to consider as you translate files. You can also combine or extract files in other file formats (see /Tools, Combine and /Tools, Xtract below). In addition, you can compress files with the SQZ! utility and save them under one of the special SQZ! extensions shown in Table 5.3. You can also bring up Quattro Pro and Paradox at the same time and share data between them. (see Chapter 10).

Table 5.3 **File Extensions of Programs Directly Importable to Quattro Pro 3.0 and 4.0**

File Extension	File Source
Quattro Pro 3.0 & 4.0	
.DB	Paradox
.DB2	dBASE II (see note)
.DBF	dBASE III, III Plus, and IV
.DIF	Visicalc
.R2D	Reflex 2
.RXD	Reflex
.SLK	Multiplan
.WK!	SQZ! (Lotus 1-2-3 Release 2.01)
.WK$	SQZ! (Lotus 1-2-3 Release 1A)
.WK1	Lotus 1-2-3 Release 2.01
.WKE	Lotus 1-2-3 Educational Version
.WKP	Surpass
.WKQ	Quattro 1.x
.WKS	Lotus 1-2-3 Release 1A
.WKZ	SQZ! (Quattro, all versions)
.WQ!	SQZ! (Quattro Pro, all versions)
.WQ1	Quattro Pro
.WR!	SQZ! (Symphony Release 2.0)
.WR$	SQZ! (Symphony Release 1.2)
.WRK	Symphony Release 1.2
.WR1	Symphony Release 2.0
New in Quattro Pro 4.0	
.ALL	Allways files
.CHT	Harvard Graphics

Table 5.3	(Continued)	
File Extension	**File Source**	
.FM3	Impress files	
.FMT	Impress files	
.WK3	Lotus 1-2-3 Release 3.x	

NOTE. *dBASE II and dBASE III both use the .DBF file extension, but use different file formats. Therefore, when translating a Quattro Pro spreadsheet into dBASE II format, you must use the .DB2 extension to differentiate it from a dBASE III file. Then, prior to retrieving this file in dBASE II, change the extension to .DBF. Files in dBASE III, on the other hand, retain their .DBF extension.*

By merely editing file name extensions, you can translate files automatically as you save them without using a separate translate utility. Table 5.3 shows the types of files Quattro Pro can translate and their respective file name extensions.

To save a Quattro Pro file for use in another spreadsheet or database, use the /File, Save As command and edit the file name extension to the one in Table 5.3 that corresponds to the file format you're exporting to. For example, if you want to save a Quattro Pro spreadsheet file named PRODUCT1.WQ1 to a 1-2-3 Release 2.01 file (also readable by 1-2-3 Release 2.2), you would do the following:

1. Make PRODUCT1.WQ1 the active spreadsheet.

2. Select the /File, Save As command.

3. When Quattro Pro presents the file dialog box, press Edit (F2) and revise the file extension to read .WK1 so the file will be saved as PRODUCT1.WK1, and press Enter.

You can now load 1-2-3 Release 2.01 or 2.2 and retrieve the file named PRODUCT1.WK1.

CAUTION! *If you have added unique Quattro Pro features such as linking formulas or presentation-quality graphics, Quattro Pro will warn you that these features are not exportable. If you don't want to lose these features, you must save the spreadsheet again as a .WQ1 file.*

When you save a Quattro Pro spreadsheet file in Paradox, Reflex, or dBASE format, a translator box appears with three options:

- *View Structure* shows how Quattro Pro proposes to format the file. Quattro Pro draws the field names from the first row of the spreadsheet. If the first row contains numbers or labels with embedded spaces, Quattro Pro cannot create the field names in the usual way. In this case, it uses column letters to identify the fields (A, B, C). You can change any field name, type, or size by highlighting the field in the list and pressing Enter. You can then edit the settings as you like. To remove a field from the structure, highlight it and press Del.

- *Write* carries out the translation.

- *Quit* returns you to the spreadsheet.

Suppose you want to save a Quattro Pro file named PRODUCT1.WQ1 as a dBASE III PLUS file. You would use the following procedure:

1. Make PRODUCT1.WQ1 the active spreadsheet.

2. Select the /File, Save As command.

3. When Quattro Pro prompts you for the file name, press Edit (F2) and revise the name to read PRODUCT1.DBF, and press Enter. Quattro Pro displays the list box with the View Structure, Write, and Quit options.

At this point you could choose to see the structure by selecting View Structure. Quattro Pro displays the field names and their type and width, as shown in Figure 5.10.

You could also choose to modify the structure by highlighting an item in the list and pressing Enter. You can then edit the field name, type, and/or width using the options that Quattro Pro presents. Press Esc after you've completed your modifications.

4. Select Write from the list box. Quattro Pro carries out the translation and returns you to the spreadsheet.

You can now load dBASE III PLUS and use the file PRODUCT1.DBF.

Lotus 1-2-3 Release 3.x Files

Quattro Pro version 4.0 supports Lotus 1-2-3 Release 3.x files. Simply specify a .WK3 file extension when you open, retrieve, or save a spreadsheet. If the file has no Release 3.x–specific features—for example, multiple worksheets—Quattro Pro will simply open the file and convert it to its own format. When you go to save the file, Quattro Pro will save in the .WK3 format that is usable by 1-2-3 Release 3.x.

Figure 5.10

Viewing the
database structure
with View Structure

| File | Edit | Style | Graph | Print | Database | Tools | Options | Window | ? ↑↓ |

| ◄ | ◀ | ▶ | ▼ | Erase | Copy | Move | Style | Align | Font | Insert | Delete | Fit | Sum | Format | CHR | WYS |

A1: 'Invoice

	A	B	C	D	E	F	G
1	Invoice	Payee	Amount				
2	132	PG&E	51.90				
3	133	MAS Custom Printing	2965.36				
4	134	Outdoor			dBase – File Save:		
5	135	Atchiso			View Structure	▶	
6	136	TOCK E		Field name	Type	Width	Decimals
7	137	C.T.W. 1		INVOICE	Numeric	9	0
8	138	Cummir		PAYEE	Text	23	
9	139	Valley Resource Center	428.52	AMOUNT	Numeric	9	2
10	140	San Benito Bank	235.16				
11	141	Outdoor World	616.72				
12	142	Express Personnel	465.25				
13	143	Whitings Foods	32.52				
14	144	Dell Williams	579.10				
15	145	PacMed Paramedics	500.45				
16	146	Baikie and Alcantara	100.44				
17	147	Soquel Spirits	35.78				
18	148	Ocean Chevrolet	125.52				
19							

Problems may arise, however, when you attempt to open a file that has Release 3.x–specific features. A list of these problems follows:

- *Multiple worksheets*   If you attempt to open a file that contains multiple worksheets, Quattro Pro opens each of them in its own spreadsheet window. Each is assigned the same name and a special extension. For example, if you open the file EXPENSES.WK3 that contains three worksheets, the files EXPENSES.W0A, EXPENSES.W0B, and EXPENSES.W0C are created. Using this method, Quattro Pro allows you to open a file that contains up to 32 worksheets. If the file contains more than 32 worksheets, you must split up the file beforehand by using 1-2-3.

- *3-D cell references*   When you load a file that contains three-dimensional cell references, Quattro Pro converts the references to its own linking format. For example, the formula +B:D20+C:H1 becomes

  ```
  +[EXPENSES.W0B]D20+[EXPENSES.W0C]H1
  ```

- *Long labels*   A label longer than 256 characters is truncated.

- *Formulas*   External file references and formulas longer than 256 characters are converted to their literal values and followed by a label that reads either "external reference not allowed" or "formula too long."

- *@functions*   @functions not supported by Quattro Pro are converted to labels.

- *Graphs*   Any Release 3.x graph feature not directly supported by Quattro Pro is lost.

- *Macros*   Cell references in macros are not updated. Therefore, your macros may not run correctly.

- *Formula notes*   All 1-2-3 formula annotation is lost.

- *Values*   A value larger than 10E+308 is converted to ERR; a value smaller than 10E-308 is converted to 0.

- *Formatting*   The formatting of blank cells is ignored.

Allways .ALL Files

Quattro Pro 4.0 provides support for Lotus 1-2-3 Release 2.01 and 2.2 spreadsheets formatted with Allways. If you are familiar with this product, you know that special formatting is provided by separate .ALL files. When you load a .WK1 file, Quattro Pro looks for an .ALL file with the same name. If one is found, a prompt is displayed asking you if you also want to load the .ALL file along with the .WK1 file. If you answer Yes, Quattro Pro loads the .WK1 file and automatically applies the Allways formatting.

Quattro Pro doesn't support .AFS, .ALS, or .ENC files, which contain custom font sets and formats. You'll need to create a separate .WK1 file and .ALL file for each format before attempting to load the files into Quattro Pro.

Although Quattro Pro supports most Allways options, it doesn't support all of them. For example, the following options are not supported:

- *Inserted graphs*   Because graphs are stored in separate .PIC files, Quattro Pro cannot support this feature.

- *Labels*   Labels with left-side spillover, usually found in centered labels, are not supported.

- *Screen colors*   Custom screen colors.

- *Worksheet options*   Worksheet options for page breaks, column page breaks, and display zoom.

- *Layout options*   Layout options for page size, bottom borders, and grid on printing.

- *Print options*   Print options for printer type, orientation, print settings, and port bin.

Impress .FMT Files

Quattro Pro version 4.0 also supports Lotus 1-2-3 files that use either the WYSIWYG or Impress add-in. If you load a .WK1, .WKS, or .WK3 file, Quattro Pro checks for a corresponding .FMT or .FM3 file and asks if you also want to load the WYSIWYG/Impress file. If you select Yes, Quattro Pro automatically applies the formatting. If a corresponding .ALL file is found along with the .FMT file, the .ALL file is ignored.

As with Allways, Quattro Pro supports many WYSIWYG/Impress settings, but not all of them. Here are the ones that Quattro Pro doesn't import:

- *Graphs*   Inserted graphs based on external files and blank graphs

- *Labels*   Labels that spill over to the left

- *Formatting*   Formatting embedded in text

- *Worksheet options*   Worksheet options for column page breaks and column width

- *Display options*   Display options for colors, mode, font directory, rows, and zoom

- *Format options*   Format options for line shadow and colors (except text color)

- *Print settings*   Print settings for page size, borders on bottom, grid on printing, frame, settings, and print configuration

Harvard Graphics

You can import or export a Harvard Graphics file with Quattro Pro 4.0 by simply specifying the .CHT file extension. There are some limitations you should be aware of, however, due primarily to inherent differences between these two applications.

When you save a Quattro Pro file in Harvard Graphics (.CHT) format, keep the following in mind:

- Harvard Graphics deals only with graphs. Therefore, non-graph data, such as formatting, formulas, and macros, will not be exported.

- Harvard Graphics does not support multiple graphs. Therefore, graphs other than the current graph will not be exported, nor will named graphs.

Quattro Pro lets you load Harvard Graphics (.CHT) version 2.x graph files. When the files are loaded, Quattro Pro converts them to its own format. During this conversion process, the following problems may crop up.

- *Graph types*   Quattro Pro will convert the graph to its closest graph type. In some cases, there is not a corresponding graph type. When this happens, the incoming file is empty. Organization charts, combinations of graph types, and multiple pie graphs are not converted. (Only the first in a series of multiple pie graphs is imported.)

- *Options*   Fill patterns and graph options will be converted to the closest matching Quattro Pro option.

- *Data series*   Data series are converted to spreadsheet values.

- The Annotator doesn't work with .CHT files.

Closing Files

Tip. You can also close the current spreadsheet by clicking the mouse on the close block (in the upper-left corner of the window).

To close the currently active file and its window, select /File, Close. If you haven't made any changes or additions to your spreadsheet since it was last saved, Quattro Pro will immediately close the window. If you've entered data after the last time you saved it, Quattro Pro displays the prompt box "Lose your changes?" with No and Yes options.

If you select No, the /File, Close command is aborted and you will be returned to the spreadsheet so that you can save your data with /File, Save or /File, Save As. When the file has been saved, use /File, Close again. If you select Yes, Quattro Pro will close the window and any changes you've made will be lost.

When you close the last open spreadsheet, you get a blank screen with the File command as your sole command option. To activate the command, type / followed by Enter. Quattro Pro displays a shortened /File menu, from which you can create a new file, open an existing file or workspace, or exit.

If you want to close all of the currently open files and windows at once, use the /File, Close All command. This command closes your windows one by one after prompting you whether you want to lose your changes. Quattro Pro starts with the active window and proceeds to close windows from last opened to first.

Clearing a Window: /File, Erase

The /File, Erase command is used to erase all data from the current spreadsheet without opening another window. This is perhaps Quattro Pro's most perplexing command, because it does not refer to erasing the file from disk. Rather, it refers to eliminating the file from RAM. The result of using this command is a totally blank, unformatted spreadsheet. Quattro Pro assigns the spreadsheet the generic name SHEET#.WQ1, where # is an integer that

Quattro Pro automatically assigns (see "Creating New Files: /File, New" earlier for more on this).

In a way, /File, Erase works just like the /File, Close command, except that it does not close the window. Like /File, Close, if you have not saved the spreadsheet since last modifying it, Quattro Pro displays the prompt "Lose your changes?" with No and Yes options. Select No to return to the spreadsheet and save your changes before removing the file from memory. Select Yes to eliminate the file from memory and lose your changes in the process.

NOTE. *To delete a file from disk, you have two options. You can exit temporarily to DOS using the /File, Utilities, DOS Shell command, and then use the DOS DEL command. Or, you can delete a file from within Quattro Pro by using the File Manager's /Edit, Erase command (see "Managing Files").*

Changing Directories

Note. See "Techniques for Selecting Files" earlier in this chapter for details on how you can change the current directory for a /File command.

When you select a /File command and Quattro Pro displays a list of file names in a dialog box, it draws those names from the *default* or *current directory*. If you want to choose a file in another directory, you can change to that directory in three ways, depending on the degree of permanence you want. The first way is to specify a different directory and when you select a /File command, Quattro Pro prompts you for a file name; this method only affects the outcome of work done with the one command.

There are two other ways, however. You can use the /File, Directory command to change the default directory for the duration of the current session. You also can use the /Options, Startup Directory command to change the directory for all future sessions. This section describes both of these methods.

Changing the Default Directory for the Current Session

Suppose you want to change the default directory so that every time you use a /File command, Quattro Pro lists the files in the new directory. You can change the default directory for the duration of the current session with the /File, Directory command.

For example, if the current directory is C:\QPRO and you want to change this setting for the rest of the current session to C:\ARCHIVE\TAX91, select the /File, Directory command, type **C:\ARCHIVE\TAX91**, and press Enter. From that point on, when you select a /File command, Quattro Pro will list the files in C:\ARCHIVE\TAX91.

Changing the Default Directory Permanently

When you load Quattro Pro for the first time, it automatically uses the directory that contains your Quattro Pro program files as the default directory, typically C:\QPRO. To change this setting to another directory on a permanent basis, you use the /Options, Startup, Directory command. After selecting this command, press Esc to erase the current setting, type the new setting, and press Enter. To make this change permanent, select the Update option from the /Options menu. Remember that any time you use Update, all your /Options menu settings (above the Values option) are recorded at their current values.

For example, suppose you want to permanently change the default directory setting from C:\QPRO to C:\ARCHIVE\TAX91. Select the /Options, Startup, Directory command, press Esc, type **C:\ARCHIVE\TAX91**, and press Enter. Quattro Pro checks to see whether you've entered a valid directory. If you have, the /Options, Startup menu reappears. Select Quit to return to the /Options menu, and then choose Update. If you have entered an invalid directory, Quattro Pro cancels the command.

When you change the default directory using the /Options, Startup Directory command, Quattro Pro also changes the /File Directory setting to match. If you use the /File, Directory command to temporarily change the default directory, however, the setting you provide will take precedence over the /Options, Startup, Directory setting during the current session.

Saving and Retrieving Workspaces

Tip. You can load a workspace from the command line when you start Quattro Pro. For example, if the workspace file is named SALES.WSP, type **Q SALES** at the DOS prompt.

If you've arranged your windows in a special way on the screen, and you don't want to have to manually re-create that same arrangement the next time you load Quattro Pro, you can save the arrangement as a workspace and restore it again later. A workspace includes the position and size of your open windows as well as a record of the files that reside within the windows.

To save a workspace, use the /File, Workspace, Save command. When Quattro Pro prompts you for a file name, type a name without an extension; Quattro Pro automatically assigns a .WSP extension to workspace files.

To retrieve a workspace, use /File, Workspace, Restore. When Quattro Pro displays a list box containing workspace files, highlight a file in the list and press Enter. When you retrieve a workspace, Quattro Pro always uses the latest versions of the files that are involved in that workspace. Therefore, if you save a workspace and then later change a file involved in it, don't be surprised by the contents of the file the next time you retrieve the workspace.

File Manager

The File Manager is a semi-independent module of Quattro Pro that allows you to manage files. You can use it to perform many of your routine file management chores (as well as some that are not so routine) without having to leave Quattro Pro. For example, you can use File Manager to copy, move, sort, rename, and delete files. You can also perform numerous other operations, including searching your hard disk for a specific file, printing files, and even selecting a specific spreadsheet file to be opened in a Quattro Pro window.

To start File Manager, select the /File, Utilities, File Manager command from Quattro Pro's main menu bar. When you select this command, the File Manager window appears on your screen as shown in Figure 5.11. Notice that File Manager's window is laid over the currently active spreadsheet window. In addition, some of the menu options in Quattro Pro's main menu bar have changed and now apply to File Manager. As you'll soon see, some of the commands on this menu duplicate those accessible from Quattro Pro's main menu bar for spreadsheet windows, while others are unique to File Manager.

Figure 5.11
The File Manager window

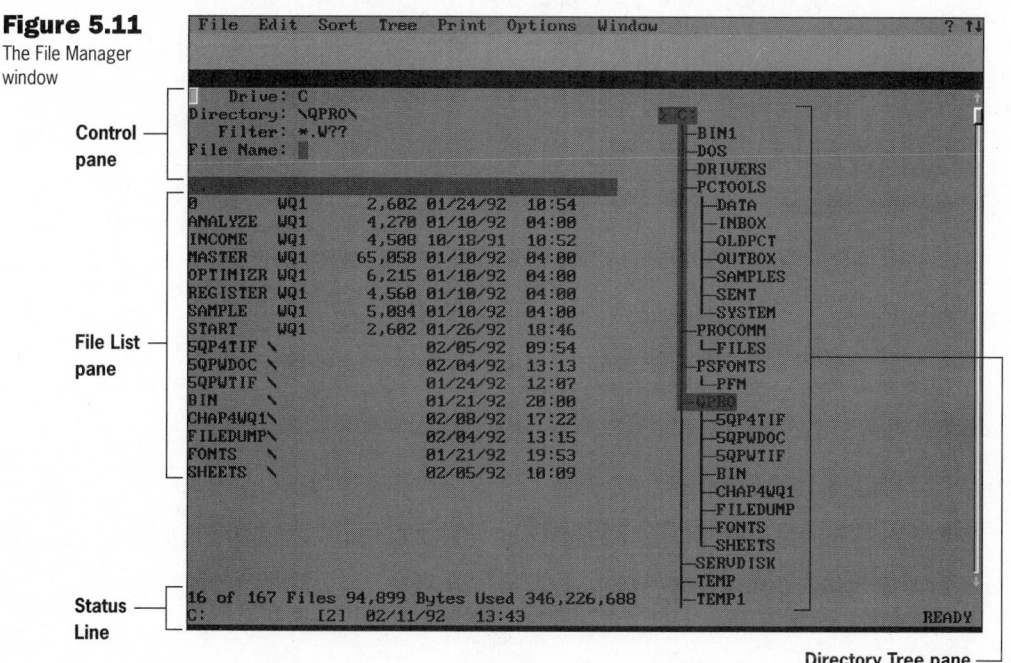

Control pane

File List pane

Status Line

Directory Tree pane

The sections that follow take you on a tour of File Manager and its screens, and show you how to use them. This is followed by specific discussions of those commands that are unique to File Manager. These commands are not duplications of commands covered earlier in this chapter with regard to managing files in spreadsheet windows.

Managing the File Manager Window

When File Manager is activated, it occupies its own window, as shown in Figure 5.11. This window is subject to the same activation, closing, moving, sizing, zooming, tiling, and stacking commands used on spreadsheet windows. The window occupied by File Manager also counts toward the 32-window maximum capacity of Quattro Pro.

As you begin to learn more about the powerful features that File Manager has to offer, you may decide to leave a copy of it open on your desktop (provided, of course, that you can afford the memory required). That way, it's always there whenever you need it. You can easily switch to another window by using the techniques and commands you learned about in Chapter 2. For example, you can use the /Window, Pick command to select another window, or you can click the mouse on the exposed portion of any window to move to that window.

You also can have several File Manager windows open at the same time. In fact, each time you select the /File, Utilities, File Manager command during a session, Quattro Pro will open another File Manager window. If several File Manager windows are open and you want to look at all of them, select the /Window, Stack command to display the titles of all open spreadsheet windows and File Manager windows. Alternatively, you can select Ctrl-T (or /Window, Tile) for a tiled display of the open windows. Choose the window you want by using the /Window, Pick command or by clicking on a specific window with the mouse.

You can close the File Manager window by using /File, Close from File Manager's menu. This command was discussed earlier in this chapter in the context of closing spreadsheet windows. It performs the same function here and works in exactly the same way. It is but one of the many commands that are duplicated on both the standard spreadsheet menu and the File Manager menu. Nevertheless, when you close the File Manager, Quattro Pro removes its window from the desktop and displays the next active window in its place. If that window happens to be a spreadsheet window, the File Manager menu is replaced by the standard spreadsheet menu.

The File Manager Screen

As you can see in Figure 5.11, File Manager's window is different from a standard spreadsheet window. You'll notice there are no row and column designators. Furthermore, the window name information on the status line at the bottom of the screen consists only of the drive designation and a colon; there is nothing to identify the current directory. Instead, this information appears on the second line at the top of the File Manager window. Moreover, additional information about the current directory appears on the left side of the top border. You'll learn more about how this directory information is used in this section.

In other ways, though, the File Manager window is similar to a spreadsheet window. For example, it has a menu bar running across the top of the screen. Further, along the bottom of the File Manager window is the status line.

However, the similarities stop there. The remainder of the File Manager screen consists of two sections—the Control pane and the File List pane—plus, at your option, a third section—the Directory Tree pane. The Directory Tree pane appears only when you select the /Tree, Open command from File Manager's menu bar. Each of these panes is outlined in Figure 5.11. In general, the panes in the File Manager window perform the following functions:

- *Control pane*   Controls the files listed in the File List pane

- *File List pane*   Displays files for your selection

- *Directory Tree pane*   Displays directories on the current drive for your selection, and, to some degree, works in conjunction with the Control pane to control the list of files displayed in the File List pane

You'll notice in Figure 5.11 that the File Manager window occupies the entire screen. This is the default in WYSIWYG mode. However, in Character mode, you can have the File Manager occupy only about half of your screen, as shown in Figure 5.12. To contract (or expand) the File Manager window, press Alt-F6 or use the /Window, Zoom command. Alternatively, you can click the mouse on the small up arrow at the upper-right corner of the desktop. When the File Manager window is not expanded, its layout appears as shown in Figure 5.12. Notice that its organization is changed slightly—that is, the Directory Tree pane is now displayed on the bottom of the File Manager window.

NOTE. *Once you expand or contract the File Manager window, Quattro Pro remembers this setting.*

Figure 5.12

The File Manager window displayed at half-screen size in Character mode

Control pane

File List pane

Directory Tree pane

Status Line

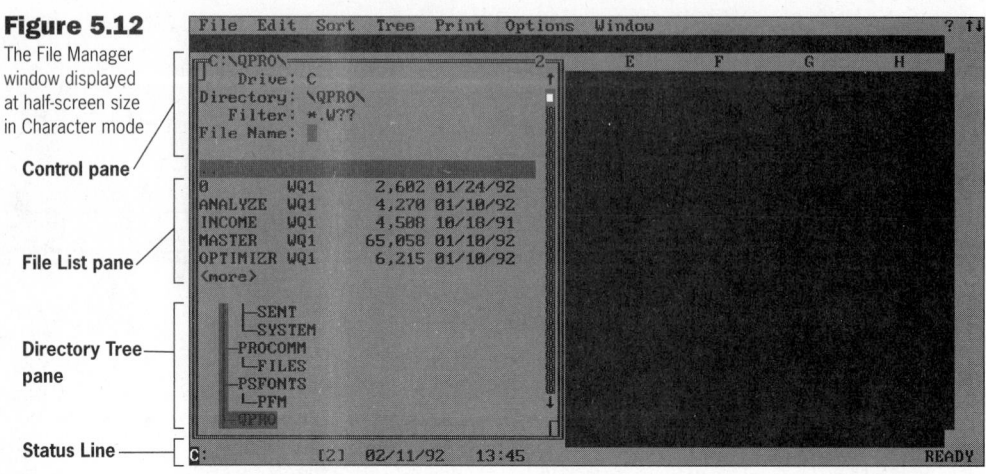

Moving Around the File Manager Screen

Each of the File Manager panes has a set of special-purpose keys and key combinations that take on functions unique to that pane. However, there are several key combinations that operate throughout File Manager, regardless of which pane is active. Most of them are oriented toward moving around the File Manager screen. These keys are described in Table 5.4.

Table 5.4 **Keys Used in All Panes of File Manager**

Key	Name	Function
Shift-F5	Pick window	Displays a listing of open windows. Highlight the name of the window you want and press Enter to activate it. Equivalent to /Window, Pick.
F6 or Tab	Pane	Jumps to the next pane in the File Manager window. Pressing this key repeatedly cycles you through all File Manager panes.
Alt-F6	Zoom window	Toggles the open window between zoomed (full screen) and nonzoomed. Performs the same function as the /Window, Zoom command. Works in Character mode only.
Alt-N	Jump	Jumps to window number N.[*]

* The window number appears at the right side of the top edge of each frame or the center of the status line.

You can move from pane to pane by pressing F6 or the Tab key. If the Directory Tree pane is in use, the sequence of movement is: Control pane, File List pane, Directory Tree pane, Control pane, and so on. If the Directory Tree pane is not in use (closed), the F6 and Tab keys act as a toggle to jump between the Control and File List panes.

The most common "pane-jumping" move is to the File Name line in the Control pane from either the File List or Directory Tree pane. Quattro Pro lets you do this with the Shift-Tab combination. The use of the File Name line is explained in detail in the next section.

The Control Pane

The Control pane comprises the first four lines of the File Manager window. The lines in this pane control the list of files displayed in the File List pane. These lines are permanently labeled as Drive, Directory, Filter, and File Name. Each label (and its accompanying text box) is a prompt for entering the parameters of the files that you want to appear in the File List pane.

To change the contents of any of the lines in the Control pane, simply use the ↑ and ↓ keys to move to the appropriate line and type a suitable entry. (The format and type of entry you can make for each of these lines is discussed in further detail below.) While making an entry, keep in mind that the Home key jumps the cursor to the first character position on the current line, and the End key jumps it to the last position. To complete an entry, press Enter or the ↑ or ↓ keys.

The entries you make in the Control pane have a direct impact on the other panes in the File Manager window. What's more, Quattro Pro does not wait for you to change all of the lines before updating the File List and Directory Tree panes. As soon as you change any Control pane line and accept the new entry, the other panes in the File Manager are immediately updated to reflect that change.

You can also change the contents of the lines in the Control pane by using the Directory Tree pane. For example, if you point to a directory name in the Directory Tree pane, the appropriate lines in the Control pane (and the File List pane) are automatically updated.

The Drive Prompt

The Drive prompt lets you designate the current drive for File Manager. It consists of a letter (with no colon) that identifies the current drive. To change the current drive, simply move to the Drive prompt and type the letter of the drive you want to make current.

The drive letter in the Drive prompt (plus a colon) also becomes the name of the current File Manager window. When you change the drive designation, you'll notice that the window name in the status line at the bottom of File Manager's window also changes. What's more, when you select the

/Window, Pick command to display a list of windows for your selection, the current drive letter plus a colon appears as a name for the File Manager window. Finally, the name at the top border of the File Manager window will consist of the current drive letter followed by the path that appears next to the Directory prompt in the Control pane.

Changing the current drive has an immediate effect on the other components of the File Manager window. As soon as you make a change and accept it, File Manager generates a new File List pane (and Directory Tree display, if the Directory Tree pane is open) to reflect the new drive setting.

The Directory Prompt

Note. When the File Manager is activated, the default directory is the directory that contains the Quattro Pro program files, and not the current data directory, as you might expect.

The directory named here determines the directory whose files are displayed in the File List pane. You can use normal text editing techniques to change or delete all or any part of the path in the Directory line. When you've entered the directory name, press Enter, ↑, or ↓ to complete the entry. File Manager immediately generates a new File List pane (and Directory Tree display, if open) to reflect the new directory parameter.

You can also specify a different directory for File Manager by using the File List pane or the Directory Tree pane. See "The File List Pane" and "The Directory Tree Pane" for details.

Filter Prompt

The Filter prompt allows you to enter a standard DOS wildcard pattern (using the * and ? symbols) to describe the files you want displayed in the File List pane. You can use this entry to filter out unwanted files so that only those files that are of immediate interest to you are displayed.

The default wildcard pattern for the Filter prompt is *.W??. This causes all files in the current directory (designated by the Directory prompt) whose extension begins with W to appear in the File List pane. You can, of course, change this filter to display a different group of files. For example, you might change it to *.* to list all the files in the current directory.

You can also specify multiple wildcard patterns at the Filter prompt. Each should be separated by a comma. These commas are interpreted by Quattro Pro as "and." For example, if you specify a filter like

```
*.WQ?,*.WK?
```

both Quattro Pro files (.WQ1) and Lotus 1-2-3 files (.WKS or .WK1) will be displayed in the File List pane.

In addition, Quattro Pro lets you specify a negative filter, which is a wildcard pattern that will exclude those file names that meet its criteria. A

negative filter is indicated by enclosing it within square brackets, such as [*.WK?]. Thus, a filter prompt of

```
Filter: *.W??,[*.WR!],[*.WK!]
```

will list all files whose extensions start with W, but will exclude any SQZ'd files of Lotus 1-2-3 (*.WK!) or Symphony (*.WR!).

To reinstate the default *.W?? wildcard pattern when the cursor is anywhere on the Filter line, press Esc followed by Enter.

The File Name Prompt

When File Manager is first activated, the cursor is positioned on the File Name prompt line. This prompt allows you to specify the name of a spreadsheet file that you want to open. When you specify a file name and press Enter to accept it, Quattro Pro opens that file on the desktop in its own window. That window then becomes the active window. The File Manager window remains open, but it is shifted to an inactive position in the background.

You can specify a file name at the File Name prompt in one of several ways. If you know the name of the file, simply type it and press Enter to open it. If Quattro Pro cannot find a file under that name in the current directory, it creates a new file under that name and opens it in its own window.

You also can search for files on your hard disk by using GoTo (F5). For example, suppose you know the name of a file but you can't remember where it is located. To find it, type its name at the File Name prompt and press GoTo (F5). Quattro Pro searches the hard disk until it finds the file, and then updates the current entries in the Control pane (as well as the File List and Directory Tree panes) accordingly. Once the file is found, press Enter to open it. If Quattro Pro cannot find the file, it issues an error message.

Or suppose you almost know the correct file name. In this case, enter it as best you can using wildcards (? or *) for the part of the file name that escapes you. Quattro Pro will search your entire hard disk until it finds the first occurrence of a file name that meets the criteria you entered. If this is not the file you are seeking, press F5 again; and Quattro Pro will look for the next acceptable occurrence. If the desired file appears several times in various directories or if there are several files in various directories that satisfy the wildcard pattern, repeatedly pressing GoTo (F5) will eventually display all the appropriate files.

CAUTION! *Once all directories have been searched, File Manager will cycle through the disk again, redisplaying directories and files that you have already reviewed. There is no indication given that you are being cycled through previously displayed items.*

Control Pane Keys

Table 5.5 shows a list of keys you'll find useful when working in the Control pane. Most of these have been discussed previously. However, they are summarized here.

Table 5.5　　**Special Keys Used in the Control Pane**

Key	Name	Function
Esc	Escape	Deletes the entire line entry where the cursor is located. If the cursor is moved elsewhere without making an entry to the line, the original entry will be restored.
Del	Delete	Deletes the character at the cursor.
F2	Rename	Shortcut key for /Edit, Rename. Brings up the Rename prompt box. See "Renaming a File" for details.
F5	GoTo	Starts a disk-wide search for the first file it can find that matches the name, or the name and wildcards, entered at the File Name prompt. The directory path of the file, if found, will appear in the Directory prompt. Press F5 again for the next matching occurrence.
Enter	Enter	If the cursor is on the File Name line, it will open the file highlighted on the File List or, if a directory is highlighted, will move to that directory.
Home	Home	Jumps the cursor to the first position of whichever line of the Control pane the cursor is on.
End	End	Jumps the cursor to the last position of whichever line of the Control pane the cursor is on.

The File List Pane

The File List pane provides a means for you to select files and then apply actions to them. For example, you might select a spreadsheet file and then open it on the desktop. Or you might select a file and then copy, move, erase, or rename it. Selecting files and applying actions to them is covered later under "Managing Files." This section explains how to manage the File List pane itself. For example, you'll learn how to change the appearance of the file list, sort the files it contains, and use the file list to change the current directory for File Manager.

The File List pane can list up to 15 lines of file names on screen that meet the parameters noted in the Control pane. If there are more files in a directory than will fit in the File List pane, Quattro Pro displays *<more>* at the bottom of the list.

Changing the Display of the File List Pane

When you open File Manager, the File List pane appears as shown previously in Figure 5.11. As mentioned, the contents of this list are determined by current entries in the Control pane. The list is organized into four columns of information about each file, including its name, the size of the file expressed in bytes, the date of creation, and the time of creation. This view of the File List pane is referred to as a *full view*.

You can change the display of the File List pane so that only file names are listed without the size, date, and time of creation information. An example of this configuration, referred to as a *wide view*, appears in Figure 5.13.

Figure 5.13
A wide view of the File List pane

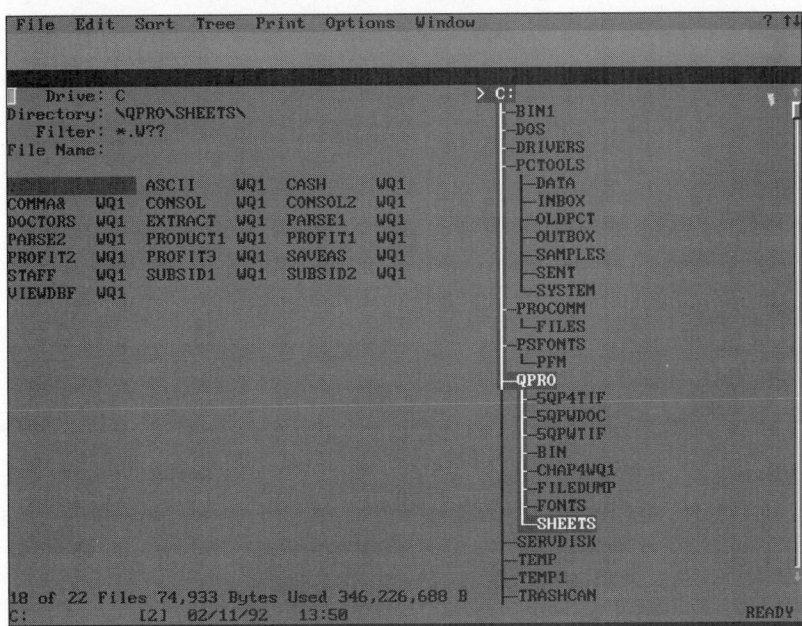

Note. Both the number of lines and the number of columns displayed in the File List pane depend on whether or not the Directory Tree is active and, if so, how large a portion of the screen is set aside for its use. See "The Directory Tree Pane" later in this section for details on how to increase or decrease the size of the Directory Tree pane.

To change the display of the File List pane, you use the /Options, File, List command. When you select this command, Quattro Pro presents an option box with two selections, Wide View and Full View. Select Wide View to display the File List pane as shown in Figure 5.13.

Sorting the File List

Normally, the File List pane is composed of a listing of the files displayed in multiple columns, sorted alphabetically in ascending order by file name. However, you can sort the list of files in the File List pane in a variety of ways. To do this, select the /Sort command from File Manager's menu. When you select this command, Quattro Pro displays a pull-down menu with different sort options. All of these options sort the file list in ascending order. They start with the lowest, smallest, or oldest files and proceed to the highest, largest, or newest. The following choices are available:

- *Name* sorts the files alphabetically.

- *Timestamp* sorts the files into chronological order by the date and time they were last saved.

- *Extension* sorts the files alphabetically by extension, and then by file name.

- *Size* sorts the directory by file size.

- *DOS Order* sorts the directory in the same fashion as DOS directories, usually in the order of initial file origination.

When you choose a sort order, all of the subdirectories on the tree also will be sorted in that order. The sort order you select remains in effect until you change it or end the current Quattro Pro session. To make it permanent, select the /Options, Update command from File Manager's menu. That way, the new sort order will become the default setting for Quattro Pro.

Using the File List Pane to Change the Directory

You can use the File List pane to change the current directory for File Manager. To do this, you must move to the File List pane (press Tab or F6 until the highlight comes to rest on the File List pane). Once there, you can switch to either a parent directory or a subdirectory of the current directory.

If you want to go to the parent directory, select the first entry in the file list, which is marked by two periods (..)—the DOS designation for "parent directory"—and press Enter. The Directory prompt in the Control pane is immediately updated to display the name of the parent directory. What's more, the entire File Manager window is also updated to reflect your selection. However, if you are in the root directory and thus no parent directory exists, the cursor will simply highlight the first entry in the file list.

If you want to switch to a subdirectory, press End and the cursor will highlight the final entry in the File List pane. (Subdirectories appear at the end of the file list and are recognizable by having no extensions and a backslash (\) in the position that normally separates the file name from its extension.) Use the arrow keys to highlight the desired subdirectory, and then press Enter. The Control pane Directory prompt will change to show the name and path of the directory you've selected and the entire File Manager window will be updated to reflect this change.

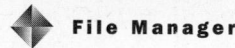

File List Pane Keys

Table 5.6 lists some special keys that you'll find useful when you are working in the File List pane. Many of these keys allow you both to select files in the File List pane and to apply actions to them. In addition, some of these keys allow you to move around quickly within the File List pane.

Table 5.6   **File List Pane Keys**

Key	Name	Function
F2	Rename	Lets you rename the currently selected file in the file list. This key is equivalent to the /Edit, Rename command. See "Renaming Files" later for more information.
Shift-F7 or +	Select	Selects a file in the file list (shortcut for the /Edit, Select File command). Once a file has been selected, you can apply an action to that file. See "Managing Files" later for descriptions of actions you can apply to selected files.
Alt-F7	All Select	Selects all the files in the file list for an action (shortcut for the /Edit, All Select command). If one or more files are already selected, they will be unselected.
Shift-F8	Move	Moves the files into the paste buffer, thereby removing them from the file list. See "Moving Files" later for details on how this works.
Del	Delete	Deletes the currently highlighted or selected files. Exercise care when using this key.
F9	Calc	Reads the current directory and updates the file list (shortcut for the /File, Read Dir command). This key is useful on a network where other users may create files without your knowledge.
Shift-F9	Copy	Copies the highlighted or selected file(s) to the paste buffer, but they remain on the file list. Once the file is in the paste buffer, you can copy that file to another directory or disk. See "Copying Files" later for details.
Shift-F10	Paste	Inserts the file(s) currently on the paste buffer into the file list for the current directory, starting at the location of the cursor. See "Copying Files" and "Moving Files" later for details.
Esc	Escape	Cancels all current selections in the file list, activates the Control pane, and positions the cursor on the File Name prompt in that pane.

Table 5.6   **(Continued)**

Key	Name	Function
Enter	Enter	When a spreadsheet file is highlighted or selected, pressing Enter opens that file in a Quattro Pro window. If the highlight is on the first line of the file list (the "double dot"), pressing Enter moves to the parent directory. If the highlight is on a subdirectory name, it moves to that subdirectory.
Home	Home	Moves the highlight to the first line in the file list.
End	End	Moves the highlight to the last line in the file list.
PgUp	Page Up	Moves up one screenful in the file list.
PgDn	Page Down	Moves down one screenful in the file list.

The Directory Tree Pane

The Directory Tree lets you quickly change the current directory for File Manager. It presents a pictorial view of the directories on the current drive. You can select the directory you want by simply pointing to it. When you make a selection from the Directory Tree, the Control and File List panes are automatically updated to reflect your selection. However, the Directory Tree is only displayed at the user's option. If you want to use the Directory Tree, you must first open it.

Opening the Directory Tree

To open the Directory Tree pane, select the /Tree, Open command from File Manager's menu bar. When you open the Directory Tree, Quattro Pro displays it in one of two places, depending upon the size of the File Manager window. If the size of the window is less than full-screen size (unzoomed), the Directory Tree is displayed at the bottom of the File Manager window. The File List pane is appropriately shortened to make room for it. If the File Manager window has been zoomed to full-screen size, the Directory Tree is displayed on the right side of the File Manager window and the File List pane is not affected. An example of a zoomed File Manager window with the Directory Tree displayed appears in Figure 5.11, shown previously in this chapter.

Once you open the Directory Tree, that setting becomes the default for future Quattro Pro sessions. However, you can easily revert to the default setting of a closed Directory Tree by selecting the /Tree, Close command. Quattro Pro closes the Directory Tree and expands the File List pane to take up the space formerly occupied by the Directory Tree.

Changing the Directory

To change the current directory for File Manager, all you need to do is move to the Directory Tree and select the directory you want. To move to the Directory Tree, press Tab or F6 until the highlight rests on the Directory Tree. You'll notice immediately that the current directory in the Directory Tree is identified by a highlight that traces the path to that directory. At this point, you can easily change the current directory by using the keyboard or the mouse.

With the keyboard, simply use the arrow keys to move up and down the Directory Tree. As you move to each directory, Quattro Pro updates the File List and Control panes to reflect your selection. However, using the arrow keys to change directories can become slow and awkward if the change entails moving to a distant subdirectory. This is because Quattro Pro must read your hard disk to display each directory as you go.

The mouse, on the other hand, is a more efficient tool for changing directories. Just click on the directory you want and it's done. You don't even have to make the Directory Tree pane active to use this technique. Just point and click. If the desired directory is off screen, point and drag to scroll the tree.

As mentioned, the directory shown in the Control pane determines the directory whose files are displayed in the File List pane. However, this also determines which part of the directory tree is shown on the screen; Quattro Pro ensures that the Directory prompt line and the Directory Tree pane match each other.

Changing the Size of the Directory Tree

You can also change the size of the Directory Tree to occupy more or less of the File Manager window. To do this, you use the /Tree, Resize command. When you select this command, Quattro Pro displays the prompt box shown in Figure 5.14. This prompt lets you specify the approximate percentage of the File Manager window that you want the Directory Tree to occupy. Type a number between 10 and 100 to specify the percentage you want. (Obviously, the higher the number the more space the Directory Tree will occupy.) When you press Enter to confirm your entry, Quattro Pro adjusts the size of the Directory Tree accordingly. Quattro Pro reduces the display space allocated to the File List pane if more room is needed for the Directory Tree.

When you change the size of the Directory Tree, that setting becomes the default for future Quattro Pro sessions until you change it. Experiment with this setting to determine what works best for you.

Figure 5.14

The prompt box for resizing the Directory Tree

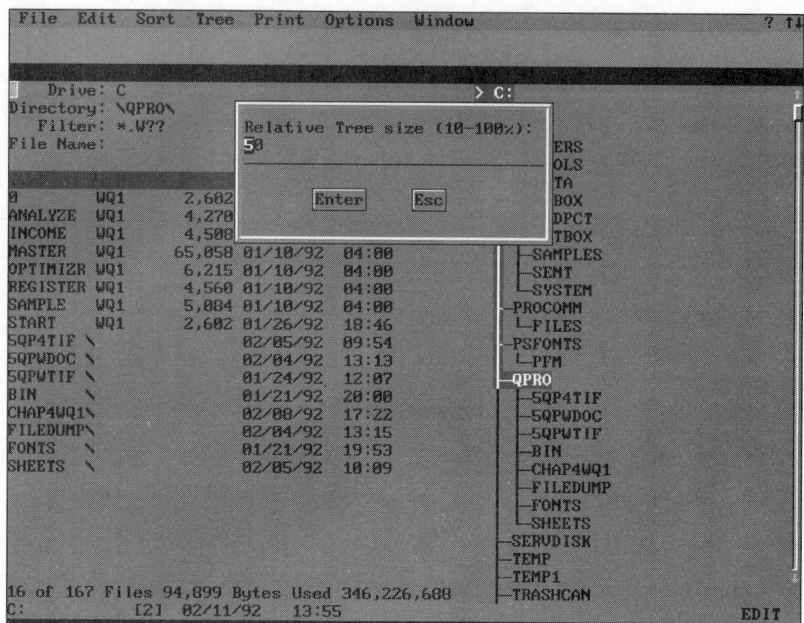

Managing Files

You can use File Manager to perform many of your routine file management chores without having to leave Quattro Pro. For example, you can select, open, copy, move, erase, and rename files simply by selecting the appropriate command from the File Manager menu. Most of the activity for these tasks centers around the File List pane. As you may recall, this pane provides a means for you to select specific files and then apply actions to them.

Selecting Files

Before you can perform an action on a file, you must select that file from the File List pane. To do this, move to the File List pane to activate it, and then select the file or files you want.

To select a single file, use the arrow keys to move to it (or click the mouse on the file name) and then select the /Edit, Select command from File Manager's menu. Alternatively, you can press Shift-F7 or the + (plus) key to select the file. Quattro Pro marks the file as having been selected. To select more than one file, simply repeat this action for each file you want. If you change your mind about a file, you can easily unselect it by selecting /Edit, Select again or by pressing Shift-F7 or + a second time.

Note. All marked files can also be unselected by pressing Esc when the File List or the Tree Pane is active. The cursor then jumps to the first character position of the File Name line of the Control pane.

You can also select all the files at once in the File List pane. To do this, choose the /Edit, All Select command from File Manager's menu. Alternatively you can press Alt-F7. If any files have been previously selected, Quattro Pro unselects them.

To limit the files in the File List pane for the /Edit, All Select command, you can use the Filter prompt in the Control pane. As you may recall, the Filter prompt lets you define a wildcard pattern that describes a select group of files for display in the File List pane.

If you have used /Edit, All Select and then realize that you want to further limit the file listing by changing the Filter prompt, go ahead and do so. However, if you change the filter to add files to the listing, the added file names will not be marked as selected. To mark the entire list, you will have to use the /Edit, All Select command again (or press Alt-F7) to unselect the first batch, and then once more select all the files in the list.

Opening Spreadsheet Files

You can open a spreadsheet file from the File List pane in several ways. The easiest way to open a single file is to simply move the highlight to the file you want and press Enter. Quattro Pro opens the file you've selected in its own window. Alternatively, you can highlight the name of a file and use the /Edit, Select Command (or press Shift-F7 or +) to select it, and then press Enter to open it. In fact, you can use this technique to open several files at once. To do this, first select all the files you want to open, and then press Enter. Quattro Pro displays a prompt box asking you if you want the marked documents opened. If you press Enter or Y, Quattro Pro will open each of them in separate windows. If you press N, you will be returned to the file list.

You can also use the mouse to select and open files in the File List pane. To do this, simply double-click on the name of the file you want to open. Quattro Pro opens that file in its own window. To open more than one file, click once on each file to select it, and then double-click on any selected file name. Quattro Pro opens each of the files you've selected, each in its own window.

Copying Files

To copy a file, you can use the /Edit, Copy command or press Shift-F9. This command does the same thing as the DOS COPY command—that is, it places a copy of a file in a different directory using the same file name. However, Quattro Pro accomplishes this in a slightly different fashion than DOS does.

Unlike DOS, copying files with Quattro Pro is a two-step operation. First, select the source file(s) you want to copy. If just one file is to be copied, highlight the file name in the file list. If two or more files are to be copied, select and mark them as described earlier. Then, use the /Edit, Copy command or press Shift-F9. Quattro Pro places a copy of the selected file(s) into a paste buffer, where they will remain until you recall them. Now, change to the directory where you want the copy of the file(s) to reside and recall the contents of the paste buffer by entering the /Edit, Paste command or by pressing Shift-F10. The contents of the paste buffer will be emptied into the current File List pane and their file names will be placed into the proper sort order in the listing.

You can also copy a file and give it a different name. To do this, you use the /Edit, Duplicate command. Its use is simplicity itself. First highlight the name of the file in the File List pane, and then select /Edit, Duplicate. Type the new file name at the prompt (you can enter a different path if you want to have the file stored in a different directory); then press Enter. Quattro Pro copies the file under the new name.

Moving Files

You can also use the File Manager to move a file from its present directory to another directory. Similar to copying a file, moving a file is a two-step operation. To move one or more files, begin by selecting them from the File List pane. Then select the /Edit, Move command or press Shift-F8. Quattro Pro places the marked files on the paste buffer, removing them from the file list. To complete the move, switch to the target directory and use the /Edit, Paste command or press Shift-F10. Quattro Pro empties the paste buffer into the directory you've selected and displays the files in the File List pane for the directory.

Erasing Files

Note. If you deleted all the files in a directory, you can also delete the directory itself from within Quattro Pro. Select the name of the directory in the File List pane and then choose the /Edit, Erase command. After you respond to the confirmation prompt, Quattro Pro will delete the directory.

You can also erase one or more files from disk. To erase a single file, move the highlight in the File List pane to the name of the file you want to erase (or click on it with your mouse). When you're ready, select the /Edit, Erase command or press Del. Quattro Pro displays a Yes/No prompt box asking you to confirm the deletion. Select Yes to delete the file.

To erase more than one file, use the /Edit, Select or Shift-F7 key to select each of the files you want to delete from the File List pane. After you make your selections, select the /Edit, Erase command or press Del. Quattro Pro displays a Yes/No prompt asking you to confirm the deletion. Choose Yes to delete the files you've selected.

Renaming Files

To rename a file, highlight the name of the file in the File List pane and select the /Edit, Rename command or press F2. Type the new name at the prompt. If you want to move the file to a new directory as well, include the desired path as part of the new file name. When you're ready, press Enter. Quattro Pro renames the file you've selected.

Managing Directories

File Manager has two unique commands on its /File menu that let you reread the current directory and create a new subdirectory of the current directory. These commands are /File, Read Dir and /File, Make Dir, respectively. (The rest of the commands on the /File menu duplicate their namesakes on the regular Quattro Pro spreadsheet menu and are covered earlier in this chapter.) In addition, through the /Options, Directory command, you can select a default directory that will be used by File Manager each time you open its window.

Reading a Directory

You can reread the current directory by using the /File, Read Dir command or by pressing F9. This tells Quattro Pro to reread the specified directory and update the File List pane accordingly. This command is useful when you are connected to a local area network (LAN) where another user might have added or deleted files since the last time the directory was read.

Creating a Directory

To create a new directory, you use the /File, Make Dir command. This command enables you to simulate the DOS MKDIR or MD (make directory) command from within Quattro Pro, without having to leave the program or use the DOS Shell command.

To create a new directory, move to the directory under which you wish to create the new one. To do this, use the Directory prompt in the Control pane, or select the appropriate directory from the Directory Tree pane, if it is open. Then select the /File, Make Dir command. You will see the Create a New Directory box shown in Figure 5.15, with the cursor in the first character position.

Although the Create a New Directory box doesn't show it, it assumes that whatever directory name you are going to enter will be a subdirectory to the one shown on the Directory line of the Control pane. If this is the case, enter the subdirectory name and press Enter. However, if this is not the case, you can enter the full path and name, starting with a backslash and the root directory's name and working down the entire path, concluding the entry with the name of the directory you wish to create. The name you choose must comply with the standard DOS rules that govern directory names. The Create a New Directory box will accept a path and name of up to 62 characters.

If you try to create a directory whose name does not conform to the DOS rules or if you try to create a subdirectory under a nonexistent directory (either by intent or because of bad spelling), File Manager will beep and display an error message. When this happens, press Esc and the File

Manager screen will return with the cursor positioned where it was before
you entered the /File, Make Dir command.

Choosing a Default Directory for File Manager

You can also choose a default directory that File Manager will automatically
use when you open its window. To do this, you use the /Options, Startup Directory command from File Manager's menu. When you select this command,
Quattro Pro displays a submenu with two options, Previous and Current.
Select Previous to have the current directory displayed the next time you start
File Manager. (This option is the default.) Select Current to have File Manager
use the directory you were in when you started Quattro Pro.

Figure 5.15

The Create a New
Directory box

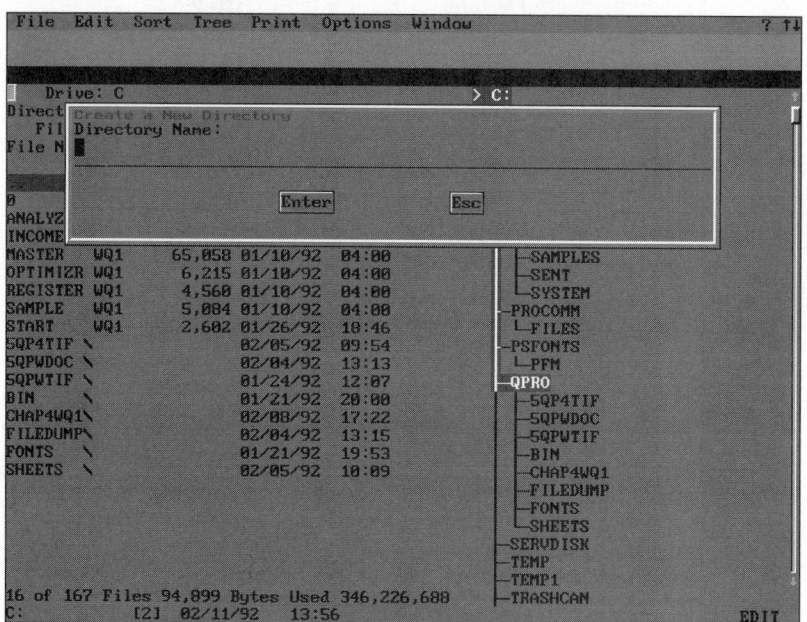

Printing from File Manager

File Manager also offers a modified /Print menu that lets you print information from the File List and Directory Tree panes. Actually, the File Manager
/Print menu is very similar to the one covered in Chapter 6. The exception to
this is the File Manager's Block option. When you select Block, Quattro Pro
displays a submenu with the following options.

■ *Files* prints the contents of the File List pane for the current directory. The printout includes those files not shown because of screen-length limitations. The list is printed one file per line and includes the file size and timestamp data.

■ *Tree* prints the contents of the Directory Tree pane. This includes any portion not presently displayed on your screen.

■ *Both* prints the file listing, followed by the Directory Tree. Figure 5.16 shows a sample printout using the Both option.

Combining Files: /Tools, Combine

To combine all or part of the contents of a spreadsheet file on disk with the current spreadsheet, you use the /Tools, Combine command. This command was originally designed to allow you to transfer data between files. However, Quattro Pro's file-linking capabilities discussed in Chapter 2 reduce the need for this command. In fact, in most cases where flexibility, memory use, and live interactive spreadsheet communication are high-priority considerations, using link formulas is preferable to using the /Tools, Combine command.

You will find the /Tools, Combine command preferable for files in which formula links are not appropriate, but still require periodic sharing of data between spreadsheets. You will probably find this command most useful when you need to combine large amounts of data. In this case, using the /Tools, Combine command is preferable to setting up multiple link formulas.

You will also prefer /Tools, Combine in specific situations where continuous updating is not required. Other common applications include consolidating monthly spreadsheets into a single annual spreadsheet or combining subsidiary spreadsheets into a single consolidated spreadsheet.

You should be aware that there are drawbacks with /Tools, Combine. Most notably, you must re-execute this command whenever the information you combine is changed. In addition, you must know the exact cell coordinates for both the block source and destination; otherwise the operation will be completed incorrectly.

The /Tools, Combine command offers the following three options:

■ *Copy* copies the specified block of data in a spreadsheet file on disk to the current spreadsheet.

■ *Add* adds numeric data in a spreadsheet file on disk to numbers or blank cells in the current file.

■ *Subtract* subtracts numeric data in a spreadsheet file on disk from numbers or blank cells in the current file.

Figure 5.16

The printout generated when you choose File Manager's /Print, Block, Both command

```
C:\QPRO\SHEETS\
*.W??

ASCII     WQ1     3,457 02/06/92 09:36
CASH      WQ1    13,195 02/98/91 04:38
COMMA&    WQ1     3,549 02/06/92 10:06
CONSOL    WQ1     3,249 02/05/92 18:45
CONSOL2   WQ1     3,255 02/05/92 18:49
DOCTORS   WQ1     2,812 02/05/92 20:16
EXTRACT   WQ1     3,018 02/05/92 19:11
PARSE1    WQ1     3,448 02/06/92 10:32
PARSE2    WQ1     4,094 02/06/92 11:17
PRODUCT1  WQ1     3,547 02/05/92 17:37
PROFIT1   WQ1     5,365 02/08/91 04:38
PROFIT2   WQ1     4,326 02/08/91 04:38
PROFIT3   WQ1     5,118 02/08/91 04:38
SAVEAS    WQ1     3,073 02/05/92 11:53
STAFF     WQ1     3,337 02/05/92 20:17
SUBSID1   WQ1     3,256 02/05/92 18:36
SUBSID2   WQ1     3,257 02/05/92 18:49
VIEWDBF   WQ1     3,549 02/06/92 09:17
18 of 22 Files 74,905 Bytes Used 346,406,912 Bytes Free


> C:
  +-Bin1
  |
  +-DOS
  |
  +-DRIVERS
  |
  +-QPRO
  |  +-5QP4TI
  |  |
  |  +-5QPWDOC
  |  |
  |  +-5QPWTIF
  |  |
  |  +-BIN
  |  |
  |  +-CHAP4WQ1
  |  |
  |  +-FILEDUMP
  |  |
  |  +-FONTS
  |  |
  |  +-SHEETS
  +-SERVDISK
  |
  +-TEMP
  |
  +-TEMP1
  |
  +-TRASHCAN
  |
  +-WINDOWS
```

Quattro Pro always assumes that you want to combine information in the current file starting at the location of the cell pointer and begins the combining process at that location. Therefore, it is very important that you correctly position the cell pointer where you want to begin combining data before issuing the command.

It is also important to note that the /Tools, Combine command does not copy from an active source spreadsheet but copies the data from a source file on disk. For this reason, you don't have to have the source file open to perform a /Tools, Combine operation.

It is also useful to keep in mind that, should an error occur, Alt-F5 (Undo) can undo a multitude of sins, including a mistake in combining data. However, Alt-F5 *must* be the first keystroke you press after you have completed a /Tools, Combine operation.

The Copy Option

You can use the /Tools, Combine, Copy command to copy spreadsheet data on disk to the current spreadsheet. You can think of this command as an /Edit, Copy operation between files, except that the cell block destination is implied by the current location of the cell pointer. When you select the Copy option, Quattro Pro then copies the contents, format, and display settings (such as shading and line drawing) from the source file or block into the current spreadsheet. This command copies all forms of data including values, labels, and formulas.

You can use the /Tools, Combine, Copy command to copy an entire file or a specific block of data from the source file. If you specify the entire file, Quattro Pro only copies the cells containing data, since blank cells have no data to copy. For example, if a source file only contains data in the cells A1..G1, and you elect to copy the entire file, only the data in A1..G1 from the source file will be combined with the currently active file.

The /Tools, Combine, Copy command copies formulas just as they are in the source spreadsheet. So, if any formulas reference cells outside of the block being copied, they will most likely be inaccurate in their new location in the destination spreadsheet.

Before you begin a /Tools, Combine copying operation, it's important that you note the position of the cell selector in the currently active spreadsheet (the destination file). Obviously you want to make sure that you are copying the appropriate data to the appropriate spots. In addition, be aware of the size of the incoming block from the source file. With the Copy option, once the combining operation begins, Quattro Pro will overwrite all cells in the path of the incoming data.

The example that follows will take you through a sample /Tools, Combine, Copy session. In this example, you'll combine a portion of a subsidiary income statement with a consolidated master income statement. Both of the files involved are shown in Figure 5.17. The master statement (the destination file) is CONSOL.WQ1 (the left side of the figure), and the source data is located in the block B5..B21 of SUBSID1.WQ1 (the right side of the figure). Both files are shown as being open in memory for your convenience. However, as mentioned, when the combining operation occurs, Quattro Pro will copy information from the SUBSID1.WQ1 file on disk, not the file in memory.

Tip. To copy the values returned by formulas to another file, rather than the formulas themselves, use the /Tools, Extract Values command.

Figure 5.17

Two files prepared for the /Tools, Combine, Copy command

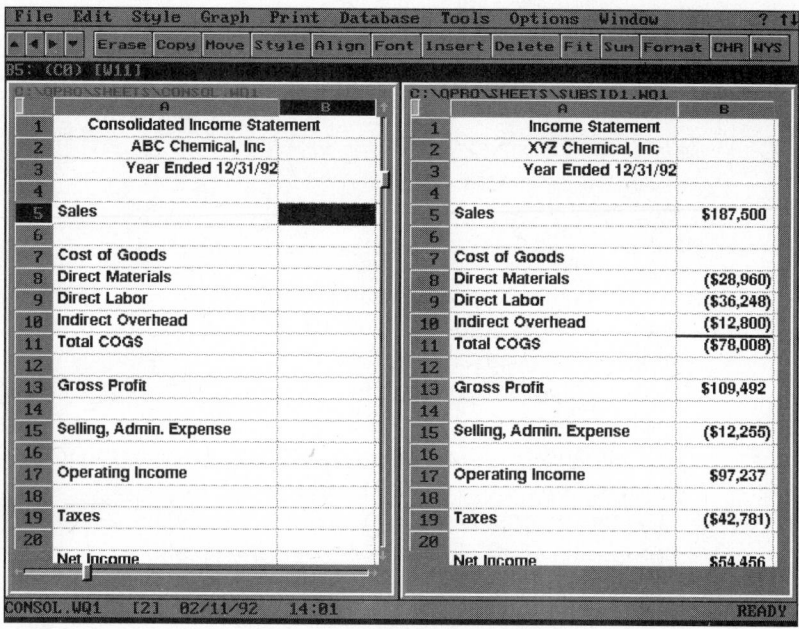

To prepare for this example, open the CONSOL.WQ1 file in memory and make sure its window is active. Then perform the following steps:

1. Locate the cell pointer in the upper-left cell of the block where you want the incoming information to be combined, in this case cell B5 of CONSOL.WQ1.

2. Select /Tools, Combine, Copy.

3. Since you want to copy only a portion of the file SUBSID1.WQ1, next select Block. In response to Quattro Pro's prompt "Enter block name or coordinates:", specify the source block **B5..B21** and press Enter. Quattro Pro displays a file list box prompting you for a file to combine. If you want to specify a file in another directory, you can press Esc twice to eliminate the current directory and drive displayed by Quattro Pro; then enter the drive and directory you want, ending the entry with a back-slash (\), and press Enter. Quattro Pro automatically displays the appropriate file list.

4. In response to the prompt "Enter name of file to combine", specify **SUBSID1.WQ1** and press Enter. Quattro Pro writes the block B5..B21

from the source file to the block B5..B21 in the destination file. Your
screen should look like Figure 5.18.

Figure 5.18

Using /Tools,
Combine, Copy to
combine data from
two spreadsheet
files

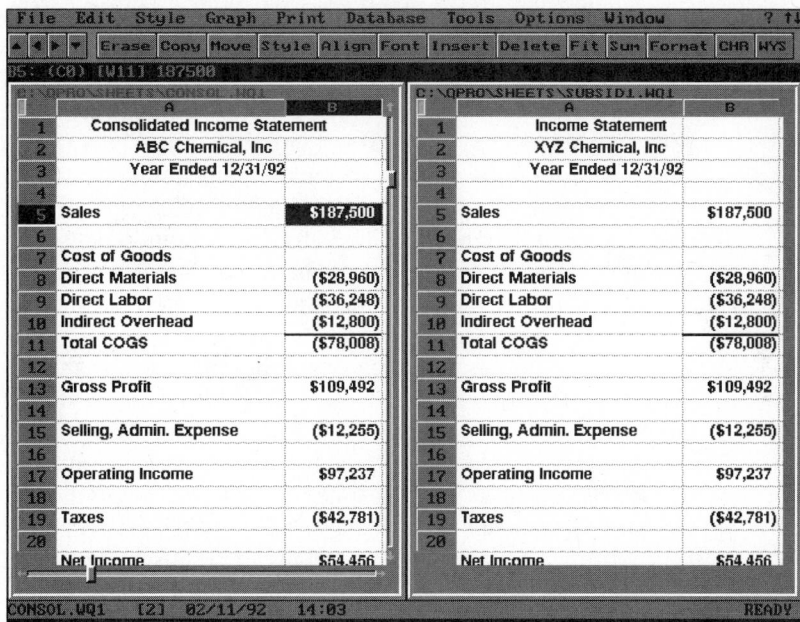

In the above example, Quattro Pro copied the information from SUBSID1-
.WQ1 to CONSOL.WQ1. However, the source block in SUBSID1.WQ1 was
unaffected by this copy operation. Also, remember, even though the source file
SUBSID1.WQ1 is displayed in Figure 5.17, Quattro Pro actually copied the information from the SUBSID1.WQ1 file on disk.

The Add Option

You can use /Tools, Combine, Add to add numeric values in a file on disk to
corresponding values or blank cells in the current spreadsheet. When you use
this command, Quattro Pro first converts any incoming formulas to their displayed values. It also interprets labels and blank cells in the source file as 0; it
does not include this information in the combine operation, nor does it include ERR or NA values. In short, the /Tools, Combine, Add command only
imports values, which can be either literal numbers or the results of formulas.

With /Tools, Combine, Add, you have the option of adding data from either an entire file or a block. If you elect to add the contents of an entire file,

Quattro Pro adds all the cells that contain values in the source spreadsheet to existing values below or to the right of the cell pointer in the destination spreadsheet. It does not add those labels and formulas it cannot convert to values in the source spreadsheet file. The /Tools, Combine, Add command replaces the existing value entries in the current (destination) spreadsheet with new values, representing the combined sum of the original and incoming values.

If a cell in the active (destination) file is blank, it will take on the value of the corresponding (source) cell in the file on disk. However, if a cell in the active file contains a label or formula, the incoming value that corresponds to that cell is ignored. The formula remains unchanged, thus producing an incorrect consolidation value. Therefore you should *not* use /Tools, Combine, Add if cells in the active or destination file contain formulas or labels.

To add or subtract combined values properly, you must take necessary precautions to ensure that values are combined precisely. To consolidate values correctly, you must make certain the spreadsheets share a common layout and that you specify blocks correctly during the /Tools, Combine, Add command. The cell pointer cannot be even one cell off when you combine the files, or your combined value totals will be inaccurate and meaningless.

Before you use /Tools, Combine, Add, make sure the most recent version of your source file has been saved to disk. This actually serves two purposes: It provides a way of checking your results, and it serves as a "safety net" from which to retrieve original data should the Add operation go awry. If you do make a mistake, remember to press Alt-F5 (Undo) immediately thereafter to undo the error.

Suppose that you want to add the values from the spreadsheet of a second subsidiary (SUBSID2.WQ1) to the consolidated income statement file, CONSOL.WQ1 (Figure 5.19). To do this, you would locate the cell pointer in CONSOL.WQ1 at the beginning of the cell block where you want the consolidation to occur, in this case cell B5.

Next, you would select /Tools, Combine, Add Block and specify the block, B5..B21. When Quattro Pro prompts you for a source file, you would specify **SUBSID2.WQ1**. As you can see in Figure 5.19, the values are added to those already there from the previous /Tools, Combine, Copy operation. You have now created a consolidated income statement for the company.

The Subtract Option

The /Tools, Combine, Subtract command works identically to the /Tools, Combine, Add command with one exception: It subtracts numbers and the current results of numeric formulas in the spreadsheet file on disk (the source) from corresponding cells in the current (destination) spreadsheet. Like the Add option, the Subtract option does not subtract values from

Note. When you use the Subtract option with date and time numbers, you may lose your formatting. However, the resulting date or time value will be valid.

corresponding cells in the source file when cells in the current destination file contain formulas or labels. The incoming values are simply ignored. Further, if a cell in the destination file is blank, the incoming value is subtracted from zero.

Figure 5.19
Using /Tools, Combine Add to add data from two spreadsheet files

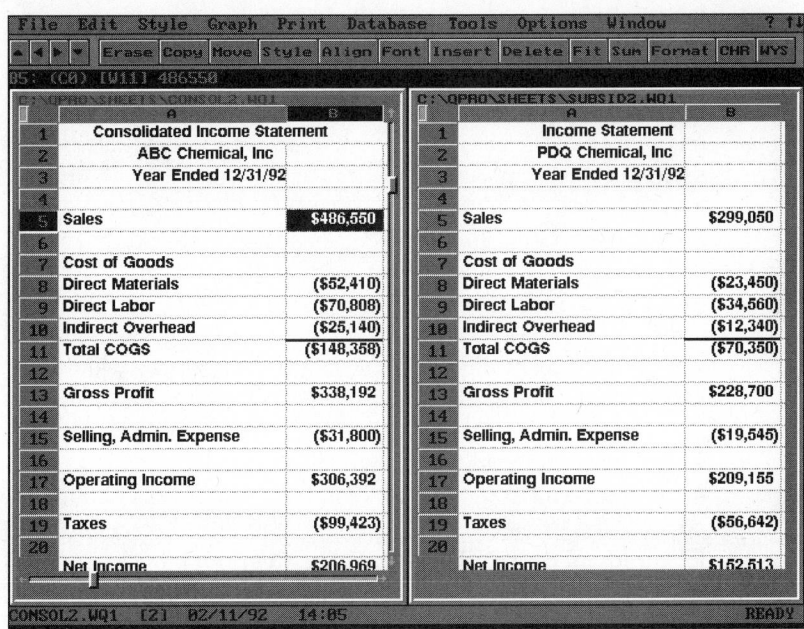

As is the case with all /Tools, Combine options, make sure you carefully position the cell selector in the upper-left corner of where you want the combining (subtraction) process to begin. And make certain you designate the data block from the source file precisely. Otherwise, your results will be inaccurate, and you may overwrite existing data. If you should overwrite data, press Alt-F5 immediately to undo the damage.

You can use the /Tools, Combine, Subtract command to subtract values from statements. For example, you might want to analyze what the corporate statements would look like without the contributions of a certain subsidiary or without certain accounts. Or, you may need to remove the accounts of a certain business segment to correct errors and then reconsolidate the account with /Tools, Combine, Add.

Extracting Data to Disk: /Tools, Xtract

You can use Quattro Pro's /Tools, Xtract command to copy a specified cell block in a spreadsheet and save it to a file on disk. All data from a specified block in the current spreadsheet, including block names, named graphs, and defaults, is copied to the file on disk. The original source data, however, is left intact.

In Quattro Pro versions prior to 3.0, the /Tools, Extract command was used for breaking down very large spreadsheets into several smaller, and more manageable, spreadsheet files. You would then use /Tools, Combine to recombine all or parts of the files. However, with Quattro Pro's file-linking capabilities (discussed in Chapter 2), files can be made interactive, which makes /Tools, Xtract more or less outmoded. However, it remains useful because of its compatibility with other spreadsheet products, and for use in macros.

/Tools, Xtract also remains a viable tool for other reasons. For example, you may want to extract a certain part of a spreadsheet and work on it independently of its original spreadsheet ties to explore what-if scenarios. By using it to copy a portion of a spreadsheet that you don't use often, it could also serve as a memory-saving device. You might also use this command when you want to share data with other users, but you don't want to give them access to your formulas. You can even use the command to extract a portion of a spreadsheet to a file and password protect it (see "Protecting Files with a Password" for details on this).

The /Tools, Xtract command offers two options, Formulas and Values. The Formulas option copies your spreadsheet exactly (including underlying formulas) to the file on disk. The Values option extracts only values that are either literal numbers or the results of formulas.

When you extract data to a file on disk, the data begins in the upper-left cell, cell A1, of the destination file. Therefore, when you use /Tools, Xtract Formulas, make sure you include any cell blocks that the formulas reference or you may get some unpredictable results in the new file. Further, if you extract a formula that refers to a named cell block, make sure you extract the named cell block as well. Otherwise, the formula will evaluate to ERR in the new file. In addition, if you extract formulas that refer to other files, you should make sure these formulas contain absolute references to those files. Otherwise, you may get unexpected results when the formulas arrive in the new file.

Perhaps the best way to illustrate the /Tools, Xtract command is through an example. Suppose you are the controller of an outpatient surgery clinic, and you have developed the surgical staffing labor estimate shown in Figure 5.20. You need to extract the data for the physician staffing component to

Tip. If you want to extract only values, formulas, and labels from a spreadsheet block, you might find it easier to open a new file using the /File, New command. Then, copy the values to the new file by using /Edit, Copy.

justify your rate structure to a local health insurance company. You could use the following procedure:

1. Open the file that contains your staffing estimates. An example file (STAFF.WQ1) appears in Figure 5.20.

2. Position the cell pointer in the upper-left cell of the intended source data block (cell A4 in STAFF.WQ1) and select /Tools, Xtract.

Figure 5.20

A sample staffing spreadsheet

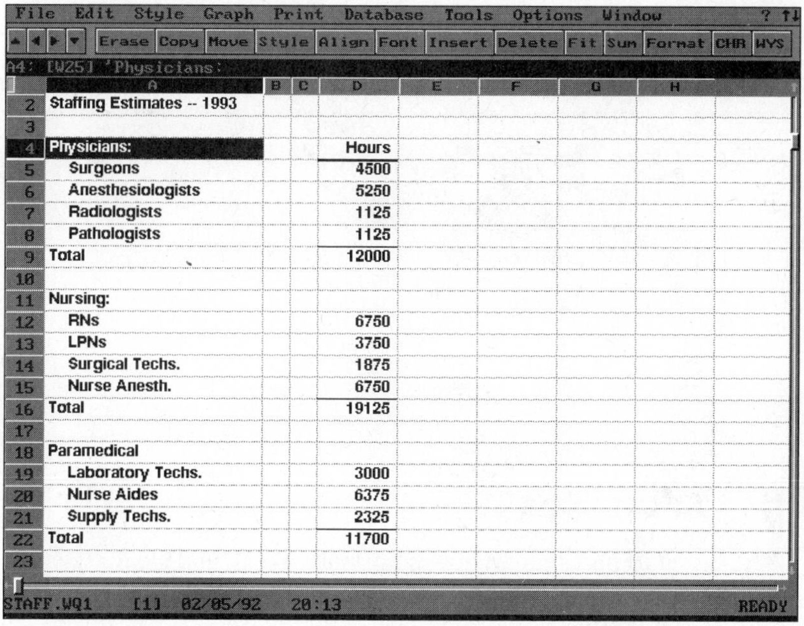

File Edit Style Graph Print Database Tools Options Window	? ↑↓

| ▲ ◀ ▶ ▼ | Erase | Copy | Move | Style | Align | Font | Insert | Delete | Fit | Sum | Format | CHR | WYS |

A4: [W25] 'Physicians:

	A	B	C	D	E	F	G	H
2	Staffing Estimates -- 1993							
3								
4	Physicians:			Hours				
5	Surgeons			4500				
6	Anesthesiologists			5250				
7	Radiologists			1125				
8	Pathologists			1125				
9	Total			12000				
10								
11	Nursing:							
12	RNs			6750				
13	LPNs			3750				
14	Surgical Techs.			1875				
15	Nurse Anesth.			6750				
16	Total			19125				
17								
18	Paramedical							
19	Laboratory Techs.			3000				
20	Nurse Aides			6375				
21	Supply Techs.			2325				
22	Total			11700				
23								

STAFF.WQ1 [1] 02/05/92 20:13 READY

3. In response to the prompt "Formulas or Values", select Formulas to save the block exactly as it is to disk, including all labels, values, and formulas. (You would choose Values instead of Formulas if you wanted Quattro Pro to save labels and values, but have formulas displayed as their current values.) Quattro Pro prompts you for a file name with the prompt "Enter File Name" and displays the file names in the current directory.

4. Type the file name **DOCTORS**. Quattro Pro prompts you for a block to extract.

5. Select the block of data you want to extract, in this case A4..D9, and press Enter to execute the command. Quattro Pro creates the file DOC-TORS.WQ1 and extracts the specified block to that file.

Once you have extracted the cell block to the file DOCTORS.WQ1, you can then retrieve that file using the /File, Retrieve command as shown in Figure 5.21. You can see that DOCTORS.WQ1 contains all labels, values, and their underlying formulas. For example, in cell D6 of DOCTORS.WQ1, you can see that the input line displays the formula @SUM(D2..D5). Notice that the formula has been adjusted to reflect its new position in the spreadsheet. As you can see in Figure 5.20, this same formula in cell D9 originally read @SUM(D5..D8).

Figure 5.21

Data extracted to disk

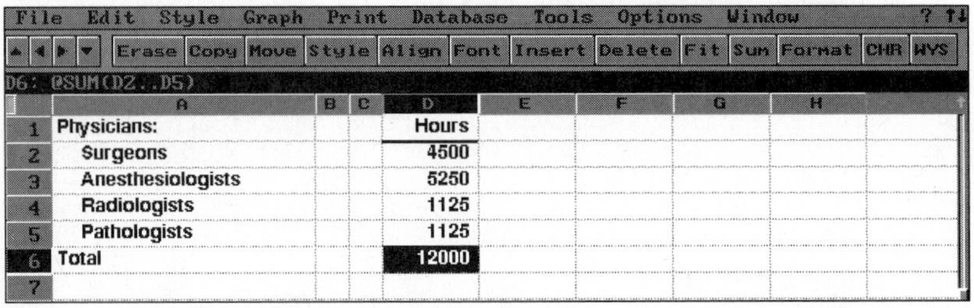

Importing ASCII Files

ASCII files contain only unformatted text, and for that reason are sometimes called *flat text files*. An example of an ASCII file is a mailing list you create in WordPerfect and save in ASCII format, rather than WordPerfect's native format. Another example is the .PRN files you create when printing to a text file in Quattro Pro.

Quattro Pro's /Tools, Import command lets you load three different kinds of ASCII files into the current spreadsheet—standard text files, comma-and-quote delimited files, and comma-only delimited files. A standard ASCII text file can contain lines that are a maximum of 254 characters in length, each line ending in a carriage-return or line-feed character. Figure 5.22 shows an example of such a file.

A *comma-and-quote delimited text file* has each field separated (delimited) by commas with string data enclosed in quotes. Figure 5.23 shows an example of a comma-and-quote delimited text file. Many database programs are capable of producing comma-and-quote delimited files, which you can then import into Quattro Pro.

Figure 5.22

A standard ASCII
text file

```
Invoice# Payee                    Amount
     132 PG&E                      51.90
     133 MAS Custom Printing     2965.36
     134 Outdoor Visions          515.16
     135 Atchison and Anderson    181.16
     136 TOCK Enterprises          51.15
     137 C.T.W. Tire Warehouse    400.00
     138 Cumming-Henderson, Inc.   56.62
     139 Valley Resource Center   428.52
     140 San Benito Bank          235.16
     141 Outdoor World            616.72
     142 Express Personnel        465.25
     143 Whitings Foods            32.52
     144 Dell Williams            579.10
     145 PacMed Paramedics        500.45
     146 Baikie and Alcantara     100.44
     147 Soquel Spirits            35.78
     148 Ocean Chevrolet          125.52
```

Figure 5.23

A comma-and-quote
delimited text file

```
"Invoice#","Payee","Amount"
132,"PG&E",51.90
133,"MAS Custom Printing",2965.36
134,"Outdoor Visions",515.16
135,"Atchison and Anderson",181.16
136,"TOCK Enterprises",51.15
137,"C.T.W. Tire Warehouse",400.00
138,"Cumming-Henderson, Inc.",56.62
139,"Valley Resource Center",428.52
140,"San Benito Bank",235.16
141,"Outdoor World",616.72
142,"Express Personnel",465.25
143,"Whitings Foods",32.52
144,"Dell Williams",579.10
145,"PacMed Paramedics",500.45
146,"Baikie and Alcantara",100.44
147,"Soquel Spirits",35.78
148,"Ocean Chevrolet",125.52
```

In a *commas-only delimited text file*, all the fields are separated by commas, regardless of whether they are strings or values. Figure 5.24 shows an example. It's rare to find such a file, but you may encounter one in your travels.

When you select the /Tools, Import command, Quattro Pro presents three menu options: ASCII Text File, Comma & "" Delimited File, and Only Commas. The option you choose depends on the type of ASCII file you have.

Figure 5.24
A commas-only
delimited text file

```
Invoice#,Payee,Amount
132,PG&E,51.90
133,MAS Custom Printing,2965.36
134,Outdoor Visions,515.16
135,Atchison and Anderson,181.16
136,TOCK Enterprises,51.15
137,C.T.W. Tire Warehouse,400.00
138,Cumming-Henderson,56.62
139,Valley Resource Center,428.52
140,San Benito Bank,235.16
141,Outdoor World,616.72
142,Express Personnel,465.25
143,Whitings Foods,32.52
144,Dell Williams,579.10
145,PacMed Paramedics,500.45
146,Baikie and Alcantara,100.44
147,Soquel Spirits,35.78
148,Ocean Chevrolet,125.52
```

The ASCII Text File Option

The /Tools, Import, ASCII Text File command lets you import a standard ASCII text file into the spreadsheet, beginning at the current cell selector location. Quattro Pro imports each line of the text file as a long label. The labels are entered in a single column, one cell after the next. If the ASCII file contains a blank line, Quattro Pro creates a blank label (') for it.

For example, suppose you have the text file in Figure 5.22 and you want to import it into the current spreadsheet beginning at cell A1. Start by moving the cell selector to cell A1 and choose the /Tools, Import, ASCII Text File command. When Quattro Pro presents a list of file names, select the file name in the list and press Enter. (Quattro Pro assumes that ASCII files have a .PRN extension, so you may need to change the *.PRN filter to *.TXT, for example, to see a list of your text files.) Figure 5.25 shows how your spreadsheet would appear. Notice that the entry in cell A1 is a long label, meaning that it spills over into the cells to the right. The same is true for all the entries in column A.

After loading an ASCII file into the spreadsheet, if you want to separate the strings and numbers into separate cells, use the /Tools, Parse command (see "Breaking Up Long Labels: /Tools, Parse").

Tip. You can use blank spaces in place of commas in a comma-and-quote delimited file; Quattro Pro will treat it just as though you had used commas.

The Comma & "" Delimited File Option

The /Tools, Import, Comma & "" Delimited File command lets you import files that are comma-and-quote delimited. Quattro Pro places each delimited data item in a separate cell, beginning at the current cell selector location.

Figure 5.25

Results of
importing a file with
the /Tools, Import
ASCII Text File
command

	A	B	C	D	E	F	G	H	I
File	Edit	Style	Graph	Print	Database	Tools	Options	Window	? ↑↓

Erase Copy Move Style Align Font Insert Delete Fit Sum Format CHR WYS

A1: 'Invoice #Payee   Amount

	A	B	C	D	E	F	G	H	I
1	Invoice #Payee		Amount						
2	132 PG&E		51.90						
3	133 MAS Custom Printing		2965.36						
4	134 Outdoor Visions		515.16						
5	135 Atchison and Anderson		181.16						
6	136 TOCK Enterprises		51.15						
7	137 C.T.W. Tire Warehouse		400.00						
8	138 Cumming-Henderson, Inc.		56.62						
9	139 Valley Resource Center		428.52						
10	140 San Benito Bank		235.16						
11	141 Outdoor World		616.72						
12	142 Express Personnel		465.25						
13	143 Whitings Foods		32.52						
14	144 Dell Williams		579.10						
15	145 PacMed Paramedics		500.45						
16	146 Baikie and Alcantara		100.44						
17	147 Soquel Spirits		35.78						
18	148 Ocean Chevrolet		125.52						
19									

For example, suppose you want to import the comma-and-quote delimited file in Figure 5.23 into the current spreadsheet. You would move the cell
selector to cell A1, select the /Tools, Import, Comma & "" Delimited File
command, and then specify the name of the file and press Enter. You would
get the results in Figure 5.26. Notice that each delimited data item occupies
its own separate cell. In addition, each string becomes a label and each number becomes a value.

The Only Commas Option

The /Tools, Import, Only Commas command lets you import files whose
fields are separated only by commas. Each data item is placed in a separate
cell, starting at the current cell selector location. For example, suppose you
use the /File, Import, Only Commas command with the file shown in Figure
5.24. You get the same results as shown in Figure 5.26.

Breaking Up Long Labels: /Tools, Parse

You can parse a block of long labels into individual cells using the /Tools,
Parse command. In spreadsheet parlance, *parsing* means "breaking up" a
long label so that individual numbers and words within the label are separated into their own cells. You can then use the numbers and labels just as
you would any other Quattro Pro data.

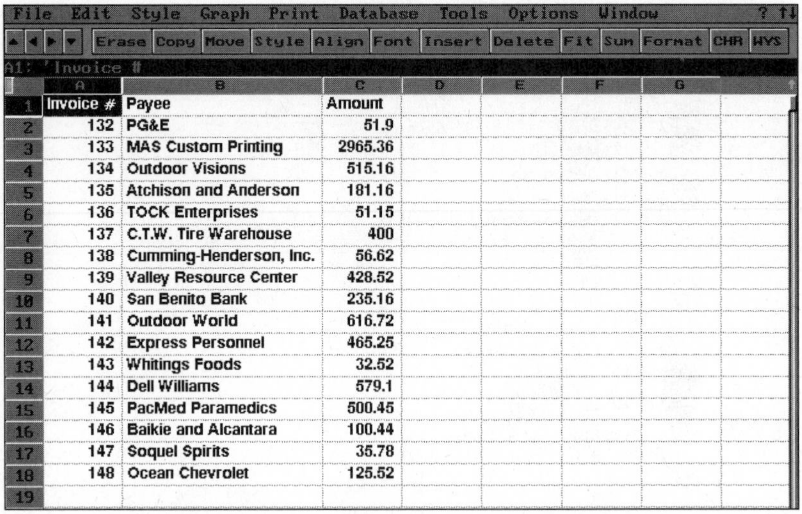

Figure 5.26

Results of importing a file with the /Tools, Import, Comma & " " Delimited File command

	A	B	C	D	E	F	G
1	Invoice #	Payee	Amount				
2	132	PG&E	51.9				
3	133	MAS Custom Printing	2965.36				
4	134	Outdoor Visions	515.16				
5	135	Atchison and Anderson	181.16				
6	136	TOCK Enterprises	51.15				
7	137	C.T.W. Tire Warehouse	400				
8	138	Cumming-Henderson, Inc.	56.62				
9	139	Valley Resource Center	428.52				
10	140	San Benito Bank	235.16				
11	141	Outdoor World	616.72				
12	142	Express Personnel	465.25				
13	143	Whitings Foods	32.52				
14	144	Dell Williams	579.1				
15	145	PacMed Paramedics	500.45				
16	146	Baikie and Alcantara	100.44				
17	147	Soquel Spirits	35.78				
18	148	Ocean Chevrolet	125.52				
19							

You will most commonly use /Tools, Parse after you have imported an ASCII file using the /Tools, Import, ASCII Text File command. For example, Figure 5.27 shows the long labels that are produced when you import an ASCII text file into the spreadsheet. The labels come from an ASCII file of stock quotations, very similar to the kind of file you might trap with a communications program while working on CompuServe. As you can see, the labels are all long labels beginning in column A and spilling over into columns to the right. Suppose you want to parse this stock data so that you can perform some calculations with it.

Here are the steps for parsing long labels into individual cells using the /Tools, Parse command:

1. Insert a format line into the spreadsheet with the /Tools, Parse, Create command. A *format line* is a special nonprinting label that tells Quattro Pro how to break up the labels that follow into individual cells.

2. If necessary, edit the format line using the /Tools, Parse, Edit command.

3. Specify an input column using /Tools, Parse, Input. This is the column that contains the format line and long labels.

4. Specify an output block using /Tools, Parse, Output. This is the block that is to contain the parsed data.

5. Launch the parsing operation with /Tools, Parse, Go.

The sections that follow describe these steps in detail.

Figure 5.27

Labels in the spreadsheet prior to using /Tools, Parse

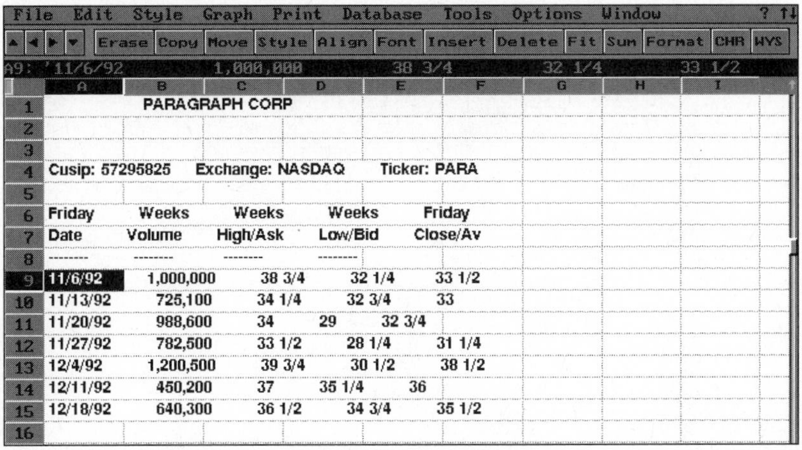

File Edit Style Graph Print Database Tools Options Window						? ↑↓
▲ ◄ ► ▼	Erase Copy Move Style Align Font Insert Delete Fit Sum Format CHR WYS					

A9: '11/6/92   1,000,000   38 3/4   32 1/4   33 1/2

	A	B	C	D	E	F	G	H	I
1		PARAGRAPH CORP							
2									
3									
4	Cusip: 57295825		Exchange: NASDAQ		Ticker: PARA				
5									
6	Friday	Weeks	Weeks	Weeks	Friday				
7	Date	Volume	High/Ask	Low/Bid	Close/Av				
8	--------	--------	--------	--------	--------				
9	11/6/92	1,000,000	38 3/4	32 1/4	33 1/2				
10	11/13/92	725,100	34 1/4	32 3/4	33				
11	11/20/92	988,600	34	29	32 3/4				
12	11/27/92	782,500	33 1/2	28 1/4	31 1/4				
13	12/4/92	1,200,500	39 3/4	30 1/2	38 1/2				
14	12/11/92	450,200	37	35 1/4	36				
15	12/18/92	640,300	36 1/2	34 3/4	35 1/2				
16									

Creating a Format Line

The format line is the heart of a parsing operation. It is a graphic representation of the way you want Quattro Pro to break up the labels that follow.

To insert a format line into the spreadsheet, you use the /Tools, Parse, Create command. Before using this command, however, you should always move the cell selector to the first cell that contains the data you want to parse. Quattro Pro will pattern the format line from the label in that cell. For example, in Figure 5.27, because cell A9 contains the first label you want to parse, you should place the cell selector in that cell. (Although you could parse the labels above A9, they are not as useful as the labels that contain numeric data.)

Figure 5.28 shows the results of inserting a format line with the /Tools, Parse, Create command. Notice that when Quattro Pro inserted the format line in the spreadsheet, it inserted a row, causing all the data below row 9 to shift down by one row. All the labels below the format line will be parsed. The labels above the format line (in the block A1..A8) will remain untouched.

The format line begins with a split vertical bar (¦), which prevents Quattro Pro from printing the format line when you print your spreadsheet. Following the bar are a series of special symbols that tell Quattro Pro how to break up the labels below. Table 5.7 shows a list of the available format-line characters.

When Quattro Pro inserts a format line into the spreadsheet, it takes its "best guess" as to what symbols to include in that line. It bases its guess on the label that resided in the cell when you entered the /Tools, Parse, Create command.

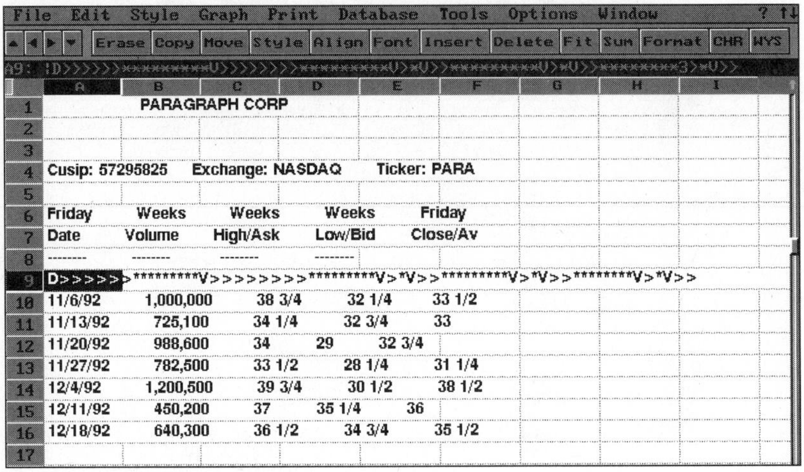

Figure 5.28

A format line
inserted with
/Tools, Parse,
Create

Table 5.7   Format-Line Symbols

Symbol	Description
D	Marks the first character in a date that will be translated into a serial number.
L	Marks the first character in a label.
S	Tells Quattro Pro to skip (delete) the character in this position (you can only insert this character when you are editing a format line).
T	Marks the first character in a time that will be translated into a serial number.
V	Marks the first character in a value.
>	Continues an entry.
*	Indicates a blank space that can be filled in by longer entries beneath the first.

The symbols that Quattro Pro uses in a format line correspond to four different data types: date (D), label (L), time (T), and value (V). When Quattro Pro encounters one of these data types, it uses continuation characters (>) for as long as the entry lasts. In addition, when Quattro Pro sees a blank space, it automatically uses the format-line symbol for a space (*). For example, the format line in Figure 5.28 contains only two types of data: date (D) and value (V). As another example, suppose you had the label "Sales after

11/19/90 were $1,200,000", which contains three data types. Here is how Quattro Pro would create the format line:

```
L>>>>*L>>>>*D>>>>>>>*L>>>*V>>>>>>>>>
Sales after 11/19/90 were $1,200,000
```

If you want to exclude a portion of a label from being parsed, you can use the skip symbol (S). Quattro Pro does not use this symbol when it creates a format line. However, you can insert this symbol when you edit a format line.

Editing the Format Line

More often than not, you will have to edit a format line to fine-tune how Quattro Pro interprets the data below. For example, the format line in Figure 5.28 has problems with the stock quotation values. Wherever there is a fraction (for example, 38 $^3/_4$), Quattro Pro mistakenly assumes that you want to parse the label into two separate values. Because you want each share price treated as a single value, you need to modify the three occurrences of V>*V>> to read V>>>>. This will cause Quattro Pro to treat a share price such as 38 $^3/_4$ as the single value 38.75.

To edit a format line, position the cell selector on the cell containing the line (for example, on cell A9 in Figure 5.28) and use /Tools, Parse, Edit. When you select this command, Quattro Pro displays a FRMT indicator and changes to overstrike (OVR) mode. You can then edit the format line in the spreadsheet by typing the characters shown in Table 5.7. You can also use ←, →, Home, and End to move around in the format line. Figure 5.29 shows how your screen looks while editing the format line.

One thing to remember about a format line is that it is like any other label, except that it has the unusual distinction of beginning with a split vertical bar (¦). As such, you can build your own format line simply by starting it with ¦ and then typing the characters you want. In addition, you can copy a format to another area of the spreadsheet and reuse it.

Parsing the Data

To parse the labels into individual cells, you must specify an input block that includes the format line and an output block to parse the data to. As the final step, you must select Go from the /Tools, Parse menu.

To specify an input block, select the Input option from the /Tools, Parse menu, highlight a range, and press Enter. For example, in Figure 5.29 the block you want to parse is A9..A16. This block includes the format line as well as the labels you want to parse.

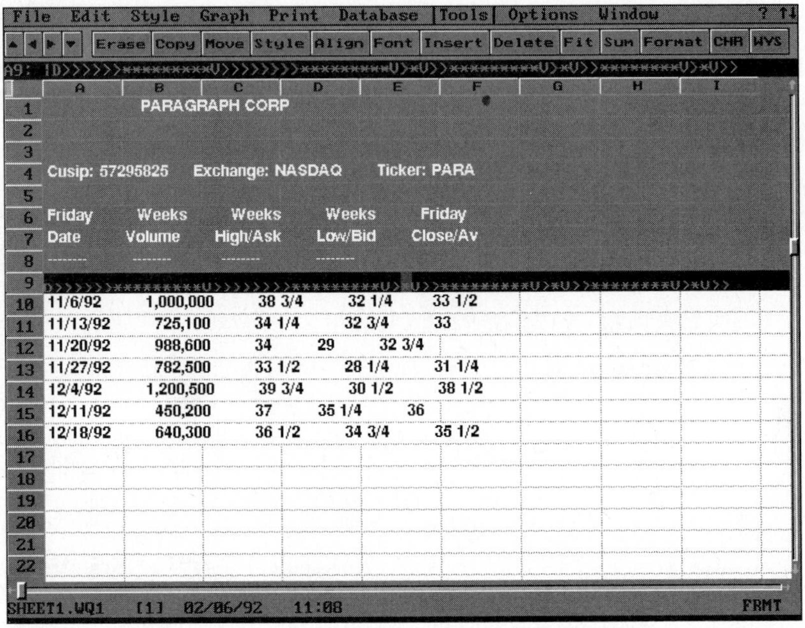

Figure 5.29

Editing the format
line with /Tools,
Parse, Edit

The output block defines the location where you want Quattro Pro to write the parsed data. To specify an output block, you use the Output option in the /Tools, Parse menu. When you select this command, Quattro Pro prompts you for the output range. Move the cell selector to the upper-left corner of the block you want (for example, cell A18 in Figure 5.29), and press Enter.

To carry out the parsing operation, select Go from the /Tools, Parse menu. In the current example, Quattro Pro parses the labels in the range A9..A16 and copies them to the cells in A18..E24. Figure 5.30 shows the results. You can now use the parsed data as you would any other spreadsheet data.

You shouldn't be concerned if the results you are shooting for don't happen the first time. It usually takes several tries to get long labels parsed the way you want them. If you are not pleased with the results of your first attempt, use /Tools, Parse, Edit to modify your format line; then use /Tools, Parse, Go to repeat the parse again.

Figure 5.30
The results of
parsing long labels

| File | Edit | Style | Graph | Print | Database | Tools | Options | Window | ? ↑↓ |

| ▲ ◀ ▶ ▼ | Erase | Copy | Move | Style | Align | Font | Insert | Delete | Fit | Sum | Format | CHR | WYS |

A18: 33914

	A	B	C	D	E	F	G	H	I
6	Friday	Weeks	Weeks	Weeks	Friday				
7	Date	Volume	High/Ask	Low/Bid	Close/Av				
8	--------	--------	--------	--------					
9	D>>>>>>>********V>>>>>>>>********V>>>>>********V>>>>>********V>>>>>								
10	11/6/92	1,000,000	38 3/4	32 1/4	33 1/2				
11	11/13/92	725,100	34 1/4	32 3/4	33				
12	11/20/92	988,600	34	29	32 3/4				
13	11/27/92	782,500	33 1/2	28 1/4	31 1/4				
14	12/4/92	1,200,500	39 3/4	30 1/2	38 1/2				
15	12/11/92	450,200	37	35 1/4	36				
16	12/18/92	640,300	36 1/2	34 3/4	35 1/2				
17									
18	33914	1000000	38.75	32.25	33.5				
19	33921	725100	34.25	32.75	33				
20	33928	988600	34	29	32.75				
21	33935	782500	33.5	28.25	31.25				
22	33942	1200500	39.75	30.5	38.5				
23	33949	450200	37	35.25	36				
24	33956	640300	36.5	34.75	35.5				
25									
26									
27									

SHEET1.WQ1   [1] 02/06/92   11:16   READY

Autoloading Spreadsheets

You can have Quattro Pro automatically load a specific file when you start
the program. To set up this autoloading spreadsheet, simply create the file
you want to have autoloaded and then save it under the name QUATTRO-
.WQ1. Make sure you use this exact name. Also make sure that you save the
file in the default directory that Quattro Pro uses on startup. (As you may recall, you can specify a startup directory for Quattro Pro by using the /Op-
tions, Startup, Directory command and then selecting the Update option
from the /Options menu.) The next time you start Quattro Pro, it will automatically search the current default directory for the QUATTRO.WQ1 file,
and, if it exists, will automatically load it in place of the startup spreadsheet.

Autoloading spreadsheets can be used in a number of ways. For example, if you have a particular spreadsheet that you use at the beginning of
each Quattro Pro session, you can set it up as an autoloading spreadsheet.
This file might contain data or it might contain a series of settings that you
use frequently in Quattro Pro. On the other hand, you might want to use an
autoloading spreadsheet to ensure the execution of an autoloading macro.

As you'll learn in Chapter 12, you can create a macro and give it a name of /0. That macro will be automatically executed when you open the file that contains it. By putting this autoexecuting macro in an autoloading spreadsheet, you can literally take control over Quattro Pro. That is, when you start Quattro Pro, it comes up under the control of your macro.

If you would prefer to have a file other than QUATTRO.WQ1 automatically loaded on startup, you can use the /Options, Startup, Autoload File command to change the default autoload file name. When you select this command, Quattro presents a prompt box showing the current autoload file name. Use the Backspace key or press Esc to delete this entry and type a new one of your own. Press Enter to complete the command. From that point forward, Quattro Pro will use the file you specified as its autoloading file.

TIP. *You can also autoload a particular spreadsheet file on Quattro Pro startup without using the /Options, Startup, Autoload command. However, you must do so from the DOS prompt. To do this, type* **Q**, *leave a space, and type the name of the file you want to open (you do not need to supply the extension). For example, if you want to load MYFILE.WQ1, enter* **q myfile**. *When you're ready, press Enter to start Quattro Pro. When Quattro Pro comes up, it automatically loads the file you specified, overriding the current autoload file setting.*

6

Printing Spreadsheets

FOR MOST QUATTRO PRO USERS, CREATING A PRINTED OR "HARD" COPY of the information in a spreadsheet is a virtual necessity. You can use Quattro Pro's /Print command to define, format, preview, and print information in a spreadsheet, a graph, or even a spreadsheet and a graph together.

Quattro Pro's /Print command is a flexible tool that you can tailor to your own requirements. For example, you can easily create a printed document using Quattro Pro's default /Print settings. As you become more sophisticated, you can utilize the /Print command's full range of custom capabilities, such as downloading fonts or previewing a page before you print.

Quattro Pro's /Print command also offers you different print *destinations* that handle virtually all of your printing needs. In version 3.0, you will usually print spreadsheet data to a graphics printer, so that presentation-quality effects such as fonts, lines, and shading are printed in the highest quality. By using Quattro Pro's Screen Preview as your print destination, you can see how information will appear in a document before you actually print it. You can even print to a file and then use the output with another software package, or direct it to the printer later.

In addition, Quattro Pro 4.0 includes a feature that lets you quickly process multiple print jobs. Print jobs are "spooled" to disk, and printing takes place in the background while you keep on working. To manage your spooled output—cancel print jobs or put them on hold—a new application called Print Manager is also provided.

In this chapter you will learn to use Quattro Pro's /Print command to print

- Spreadsheet data using Quattro Pro's default /Print settings

- Large spreadsheets and custom reports using settings that you specify, such as margins, page length, headings (borders), footers, and headers

- Sideways (landscape) pages, even across continuous-feed paper

- Spreadsheet data that has been reduced or enlarged to fit within a particular page size or on the smallest number of pages

- Fonts and special effects, such as lines, block shading, and bullets

- A "screen dump"—everything currently displayed on the computer screen

- Cell contents (as opposed to the information displayed in the spreadsheet)

As you can see, this chapter emphasizes printing information in a spreadsheet. See Chapter 8 for a discussion of how to print graphs, including how to print a graph and a spreadsheet together.

WYSIWYG Mode and Print Destinations

WYSIWYG mode has major implications for printing. Consider for a moment the advantage WYSIWYG mode offers you: the ability to see fonts and special effects on the screen. Both Quattro Pro version 3.0 and version 4.0 can do this because they are displayed on your EGA or VGA monitor in *graphics* mode.

Note. For further discussion, see "Fonts Used in Draft Mode" and "Fonts Used in Graphics Mode" later in this chapter.

Now examine the /Print, Destination menu in Figure 6.1. Quattro Pro divides these print destinations into Draft Mode Printing and Final Quality Printing. The implications are as follows:

- If you print to a *final quality* destination, Quattro Pro uses graphics mode. Thus, what you see on the screen in WYSIWYG mode and what your printer produces will essentially be the same.

- If you print to a *draft mode* destination, the quality of the printed output is usually inferior to that of the spreadsheet data in WYSIWYG mode.

Figure 6.1

The /Print, Destination menu

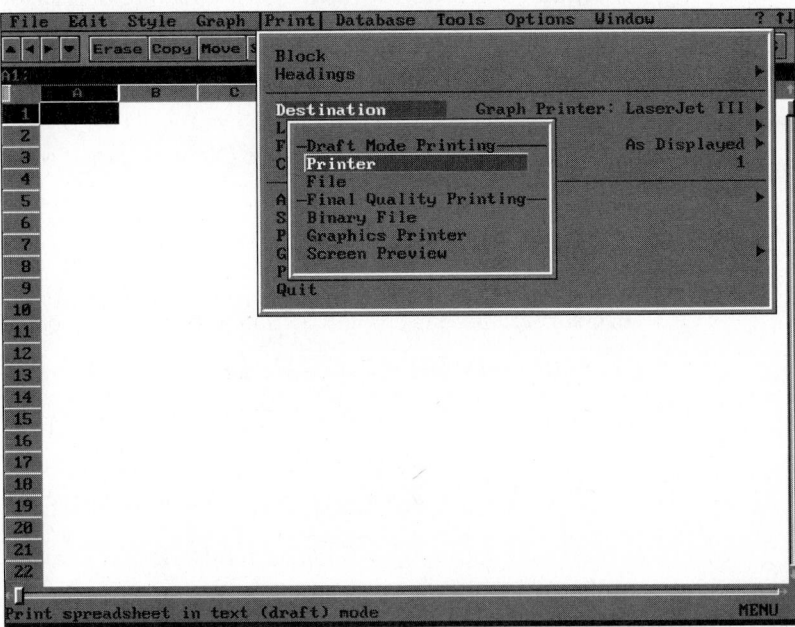

To fully understand why this occurs, let's examine and compare how Quattro Pro prints to a printer in draft mode and in final quality (graphics) mode.

Note. See Chapter
15 for details on
how to change the
printer selection
you specified
during installation.

Printing to a Printer in Draft Mode

Quattro Pro makes it easy to print a single-page document in draft mode.
For example, suppose you want to print the information in Figure 6.2. (Notice that this data is displayed in WYSIWYG mode.) Assuming that the
printer is on line, follow this procedure:

1. Select the /Print command. Quattro Pro displays a /Print menu like that
   in Figure 6.3.

Figure 6.2

Spreadsheet data
to be printed

	A	B	C	D	E	F
	Date	House Expense	Description	Amount		
2	========	=================	============	========		
3	03-Oct-89	Fed Ex to Realtor	Realtor	$12.00		
4	28-Oct-89	House Inspection	House Inspection	$225.00		
5	07-Nov-90	Coast Commercial Bank	Closing Costs	$1,780.05		
6	09-Nov-89	Farmers Exchange	Miscellaneous	$11.66		
7	03-Dec-89	Sears	Varnish	$37.31		
8	08-Dec-89	Orchard Supply	Miscellaneous	$10.97		
9	09-Dec-89	Orchard Supply	Varnish	$53.71		
10	12-Dec-89	Vapor Cleaners	Drapes	$22.50		
11	15-Dec-89	Orchard Supply	Stripper	$38.25		
12	16-Dec-89	KMart	Paint Supplies	$9.84		
13	16-Dec-89	Sears	Varnish Remover	$19.89		
14	17-Dec-89	Ace Hardware	Varnish Remover	$14.73		
15	21-Dec-89	Orchard Supply	Varnish	$53.95		
16	22-Dec-89	King's Paint	Varnish	$18.62		
17	22-Dec-89	King's Paint	Floor Supplies	$18.62		
18		Total to Date		$2,327.10		
19						
20						
21						
22						

PRINT1.WQ1   [1]   READY

2. Select Block, and in response to "The block of the spreadsheet to
   print:", specify **A1..E19** and press Enter. (You must include cells E18
   and D19 to print the bottom and right lines of the line drawing.)

3. Set Quattro Pro's line/page counter to correlate to the print head's position at the top of a page. Select Adjust Printer, and specify Align from
   the Adjust Printer menu shown in Figure 6.4. Quattro Pro returns to the
   /Print menu.

4. Specify draft mode printing by choosing Destination and then Printer
   (the default). Quattro Pro returns you to the Destination menu, where
   the draft printer is displayed. In this example, Quattro Pro displays

"Printer: LaserJet III" as in Figure 6.3 because this is the default printer. Obviously, Quattro Pro will display whatever printer you have specified as the default.

Figure 6.3

The /Print menu

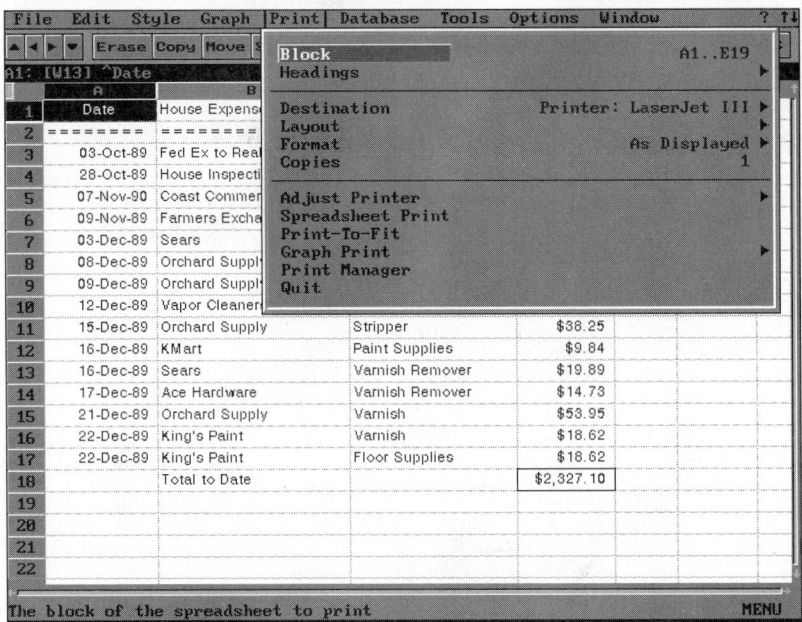

5. Select Spreadsheet Print to print this block. The READY indicator reappears after Quattro Pro completes sending data to the printer buffer.

6. Choose Adjust Printer, Form Feed to eject this printed page and position the print head at the top of a new page. Quattro Pro returns you to the /Print menu.

7. Select Quit to complete the /Print command and return to the spreadsheet.

NOTE. *In this instance, you used the default /Print, Layout settings to format the printed document. (See "Default /Print, Layout Settings" later.) You also used the /Print, Adjust Printer command to control the paper in the printer. (See "Controlling the Paper in the Printer.")*

Quattro Pro prints the information in the block A1..E19 on one page, as shown in Figure 6.5. If you compare Figures 6.2 and 6.5, you will see that the

Tip. You can abort a print operation that is in process by pressing Ctrl-Break. This command stops Quattro Pro from sending information to the printer buffer; however, printing may continue until any information already in the buffer is printed.

spreadsheet data in WYSIWYG mode is superior in quality to the document printed in draft mode. The reasons why are discussed next.

Figure 6.4

The /Print, Adjust Printer menu

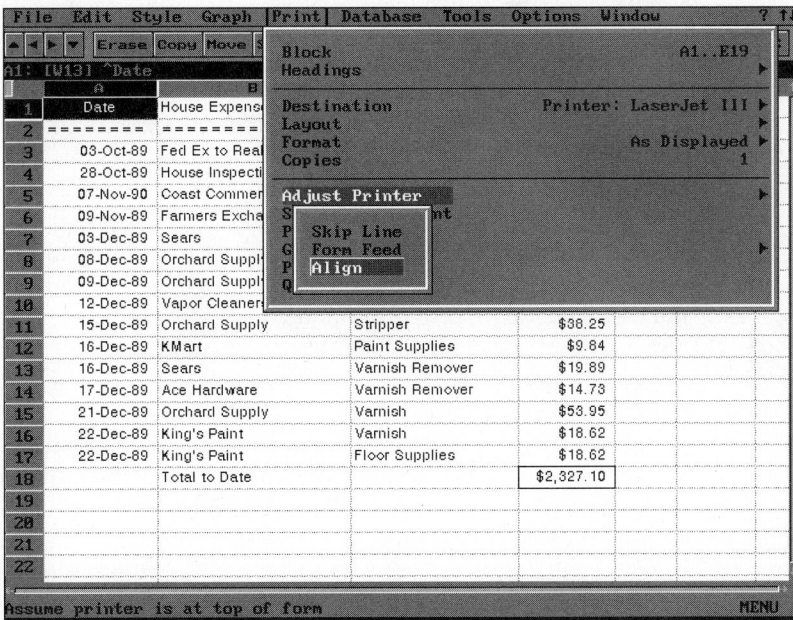

Figure 6.5

The data from Figure 6.2 printed in draft mode

```
Date       House Expense        Description      Amount
=========  ===================  ===============  ============
03-Oct-89  Fed Ex to Realtor    Realtor              $12.00
28-Oct-89  House Inspection     House Inspection    $225.00
07-Nov-90  Coast Commercial Bank  Closing Costs   $1,780.05
09-Nov-89  Farmers Exchange     Miscellaneous        $11.66
03-Dec-89  Sears                Varnish              $37.31
08-Dec-89  Orchard Supply       Miscellaneous        $10.97
09-Dec-89  Orchard Supply       Varnish              $53.71
12-Dec-89  Vapor Cleaners       Drapes               $22.50
15-Dec-89  Orchard Supply       Stripper             $38.25
16-Dec-89  KMart                Paint Supplies        $9.84
16-Dec-89  Sears                Varnish Remover      $19.89
17-Dec-89  Ace Hardware         Varnish Remover      $14.73
21-Dec-89  Orchard Supply       Varnish              $53.95
22-Dec-89  King's Paint         Varnish              $18.62
22-Dec-89  King's Paint         Floor Supplies       $18.62
                                                 +----------+
           Total to Date                         |$2,327.10 |
                                                 +----------+
```

The Differences Between the WYSIWYG Display and a Document Printed in Draft Mode

When Quattro Pro prints spreadsheet data in draft mode, it passes ASCII characters to the printer. The printer then reproduces the characters in its own resident font. This causes two major differences between how a spreadsheet appears in WYSIWYG mode and how it appears when printed in draft mode.

The first difference is that a draft-quality document is printed using the printer's resident font, regardless of the fonts used in the spreadsheet. Remember, if you have not assigned any fonts to a spreadsheet, data is displayed in WYSIWYG mode using Font 1; even in this instance, the font you see on the screen in WYSIWYG may differ from the printed font. So *even if* you assign fonts to a spreadsheet and you can see them in WYSIWYG mode, when you print in draft mode these fonts are not printed. (For further discussion, see "Printing Fonts" later.) Since the data in Figure 6.2 is printed to an HP LaserJet III printer, the document in Figure 6.5 uses the Courier 12-point printer-resident font.

Second, the print quality of special effects such as block shading, bullets, and line drawing is substantially degraded. You can see this in the draft-quality document in Figure 6.5; the line around cell D18 is printed using plus signs, vertical bars, and dashes. In some instances, special effects may not be printed at all. See "Printing Special Effects" later in this chapter.

In some ways then, Quattro Pro has outdistanced many printers. If your printer only supports draft (text) mode, it may not print Quattro Pro's fonts, or it may limit the print quality of special effects.

Printing to a Printer in Graphics Mode

Note. To print sideways in graphics or draft mode, see "Printing Sideways" later.

To print Quattro Pro's fonts, or final-quality special effects, such as line drawing, block shading, and bullets, that you can see in WYSIWYG mode, you must print in graphics mode. For example, you would follow these steps to print the information in Figure 6.2 in graphics mode:

1. Select /Print, Block, specify **A1..E19**, and press Enter. (You must include cells E18 and D19 to print the bottom and right lines of the line drawing.) Quattro Pro returns you to the /Print menu.

2. Specify graphics mode printing by choosing Destination and then Graphics Printer. Quattro Pro returns you to the /Print menu, and now displays the destination as "Graphics Printer: LaserJet III."

3. Set Quattro Pro's line/page counter to correlate to the print head's position at the top of a page. Select Adjust Printer, and then Align. Quattro Pro returns you to the /Print menu.

Note. It is not necessary to use Adjust Printer, Form Feed when you print in graphics mode. For details, see "Controlling the Paper in the Printer" later.

4. Select Spreadsheet Print to print this block. If you print to an HP Laser-Jet or compatible printer, you will see the message "Downloading char #" while Quattro Pro downloads the fonts in the print block to the printer. The READY indicator reappears after Quattro Pro finishes sending data to the printer buffer.

TIP. *If an "I/O error" warning is displayed on the status line during printing, and a confirmation menu appears in the spreadsheet, you most likely have a printer problem. The printer may be out of paper, not turned on, not on line, or not hooked to the correct port. Choose Abort to discontinue the print operation, or correct the situation, and select Continue.*

5. Select Quit to complete the /Print command and return to the spreadsheet.

Note that in this instance, you used the default /Print, Layout settings to format the printed document. See "Default /Print, Layout Settings" later to learn about these settings. You also used the /Print, Adjust Printer command to control the paper in the printer. See "Controlling the Paper in the Printer" later for more details.

Once again, Quattro Pro prints the information in the block A1..E19 on one page, as shown in Figure 6.6. However, notice that the printed document is of higher quality than that in Figure 6.5. This is because

- The data is printed using Quattro Pro's Font 1, Swiss-SC 12 point, rather than a printer-resident font. (Obviously, if you assign other fonts to a print block, these will be printed.)

- The line drawing around cell D18 is printed using graphic characters rather than printer characters. (Graphic characters are discussed in the next section.)

In fact, the printed data in Figure 6.6 has more similarities to the spreadsheet data displayed in WYSIWYG mode in Figure 6.2. The reasons why are discussed next.

How Quattro Pro Prints in Graphics Mode

When you print to a printer in graphics mode (using /Print, Destination, Graphics Printer), Quattro Pro builds a graphic image of each page—essentially a bit pattern composed of tiny dots—and then passes this image to the printer. The printer then reproduces this image on paper. Thus, printing in graphics mode results in a higher-resolution document than printing in draft mode.

Figure 6.6

Printing the data from Figure 6.2 in graphics mode

Date	House Expense	Description	Amount
========	===============	=============	======
03-Oct-89	Fed Ex to Realtor	Realtor	$12.00
28-Oct-89	House Inspection	House Inspection	$225.00
07-Nov-90	Coast Commercial Bank	Closing Costs	$1,780.05
09-Nov-89	Farmers Exchange	Miscellaneous	$11.66
03-Dec-89	Sears	Varnish	$37.31
08-Dec-89	Orchard Supply	Miscellaneous	$10.97
09-Dec-89	Orchard Supply	Varnish	$53.71
12-Dec-89	Vapor Cleaners	Drapes	$22.50
15-Dec-89	Orchard Supply	Stripper	$38.25
16-Dec-89	KMart	Paint Supplies	$9.84
16-Dec-89	Sears	Varnish Remover	$19.89
17-Dec-89	Ace Hardware	Varnish Remover	$14.73
21-Dec-89	Orchard Supply	Varnish	$53.95
22-Dec-89	King's Paint	Varnish	$18.62
22-Dec-89	King's Paint	Floor Supplies	$18.62
	Total to Date		$2,327.10

To see this, compare the line drawing in Figure 6.6, which is printed in graphics mode using an HP LaserJet III printer, and the line drawing in Figure 6.5, which is printed using the same printer, but in draft mode.

When Quattro Pro builds a graphic image of a page, it doesn't actually store the entire page of graphics in memory. After all, a 300-dpi (dots per inch) laser printer using 8½-by-11-inch paper would require over a megabyte of data to define one page. Instead, Quattro Pro's printer drivers use a technique called *banding*, which divides a page into smaller rectangles called *bands*. The bands are passed to the printer one at a time until the entire page is realized on the printer. By using banding, Quattro Pro is able to draw complex images without consuming large portions of valuable RAM.

Likewise, this is why Quattro Pro can print any of the numerous fonts you can assign using the /Style command. It sends a "picture" of each page to the printer, rather than passing the ASCII characters as it does in draft mode printing.

Tip. Version 2.0 and later releases include improved printing performance for HP LaserJet printers. Quattro Pro now prints faster and can download up to eight Bitstream fonts directly to the printer (not to the printer buffer). See Chapter 15.

This print method is also why WYSIWYG mode on your screen and printing in graphics mode are alike; remember, in WYSIWYG mode, Quattro Pro "prints" to the screen in graphics mode. Typically, you'll find the only major difference to be the inferior quality of some fonts displayed in WYSIWYG mode compared with the printed quality in graphics mode. This difference is due to the quality of your monitor. The higher the resolution of the screen you use, the closer the quality of the display in WYSIWYG mode to the printed output in graphics mode. In fact, WYSIWYG mode on a high-quality monitor may display data even better than data printed on a low-quality graphics printer.

Some of Quattro Pro's "spreadsheet publishing" features, however, are still limited by many graphics printers. For example, many colors that

Quattro Pro can display on the screen—such as a color background or different colors for negative and positive numbers—can only be printed by color printers.

Final Versus Draft Graphics Quality

You will get different results when you print in graphics mode, depending on the /Options, Graphics Quality setting. To take full advantage of the print quality available in graphics mode, /Options, Graphics Quality must be set to Final (the default). If /Options, Graphics Quality is set to Draft, then Bitstream fonts, for instance, are approximated by Hershey fonts.

Controlling the Paper in the Printer

Tip. To print page numbers in a document, see "Numbering Pages" later in this chapter.

As shown in both of the previous exercises, you can and should use the /Print command to control the paper in your printer. Quattro Pro controls the printer paper using its internal line and page counters. The *line counter* automatically tracks Quattro Pro's position on a printed page by counting the number of lines printed; when the number of printed and blank lines equals the /Print command's page length setting (see "Default /Print, Layout Settings" later), Quattro Pro advances to a new page, resets its internal line counter to 0, and starts counting again.

If you advance the paper either manually or using a printer's form or line feed button, this internal line counter does not record the advance. Quattro Pro then incorrectly assesses the print head's actual position and will print future pages incorrectly.

Quattro Pro's internal *page counter* tracks the page being printed during each print session. Each time the internal line counter is reset to 0, Quattro Pro adds 1 to the page counter. (See "How Quattro Pro Divides a Print Block into Pages" for further discussion.)

The /Print, Adjust Printer command provides three selections—Align, Skip Line, and Form Feed (see Figure 6.4)—which you can use to control the paper in a printer. Each of these selections is affected by the type of printing that is taking place—draft or graphics mode.

Align

The Align selection correlates the print head's position to a line-counter reading of 0. Quattro Pro then assumes the print head is at the top of a new page. It simultaneously sets the page counter to 1. You should use Align

- At the beginning of a Quattro Pro print session, to initially correlate the internal line counter to the print head's position at the top of a blank page.

- During a print session, to reset the page counter to 1.

- Whenever you have moved the printer paper without using Quattro Pro—either manually, or using the printer's form or line feed command—to reset the line counter to 0.

For example, in both "Printing to a Printer in Draft Mode" and "Printing to a Printer in Graphics Mode" earlier, Align was selected before Spreadsheet Print to ensure that Quattro Pro's internal line counter was set to 0 and its page counter to 1.

At the start of a print session, Quattro Pro's internal line counter automatically corresponds to the top of the printer paper in laser printers. However, if you use continuous-feed paper in a printer, you must first *manually* align the top of the first page with the print head. Then specify /Print, Adjust Printer, Align before you print for the first time. Otherwise, Quattro Pro's line counter will not correspond correctly to the page positioning, and Quattro Pro will break pages incorrectly.

Skip Line

The Skip Line selection moves the print head one line. Use this selection when you print multiple blocks on the same page (in draft mode only) and want Quattro Pro to insert blank lines between each block. You must select Skip Line for each blank line you want to include. To insert three blank lines on a page, for instance, select Skip Line three times.

Remember, Quattro Pro prints in graphics mode by creating a "picture" of each page. This means you can't print two separate print blocks on one page in graphics mode, rendering the Skip Line selection irrelevant.

Form Feed

Note. If you select Adjust Printer, Form Feed or Skip Line after you have printed a spreadsheet to a file in draft mode, Quattro Pro automatically adds one or more blank lines to the end of the file.

When you print in draft mode, the Form Feed selection advances the print head to the top of the next page. Quattro Pro's internal line counter evaluates how many lines have been printed on the current page, and then advances the paper by the number of lines required to reach the top of the next page. Quattro Pro then resets its internal line counter and updates its page counter. Use this Form Feed selection after you have completed a print operation *in draft mode* to eject the last printed page and to position the print head at the top of a new page.

That is why in "Printing to a Printer in Draft Mode" you selected Adjust Printer, Form Feed—to move the print head to the beginning of a new page after printing was completed. In this example, Quattro Pro uses a 66-line default page length, determines the number of remaining lines on the page, and moves the print head that number of lines. This locates the print head on the first line of a new page, resets Quattro Pro's internal line counter to 0, and adds 1 to the page counter to set it to 2.

When you print in graphics mode, however, Quattro Pro takes a "picture" of the entire last page (even though data may only fill part of it), automatically resets the internal counter to 0, and updates the internal page counter by adding 1. So it is not necessary for you to use Form Feed after Quattro Pro finishes printing in graphics mode.

Default /Print, Layout Settings

When you use the /Print command, Quattro Pro 4.0 automatically employs the default settings shown in Figure 6.7. You can view these settings by selecting /Print, Layout. To view a similar menu in version 3.0, select /Print, Layout, Values. These settings determine the overall way information is displayed, the amount of data printed on each page, and the amount of space between the printed data and the edge of a page.

Figure 6.7

/Print, Layout default settings

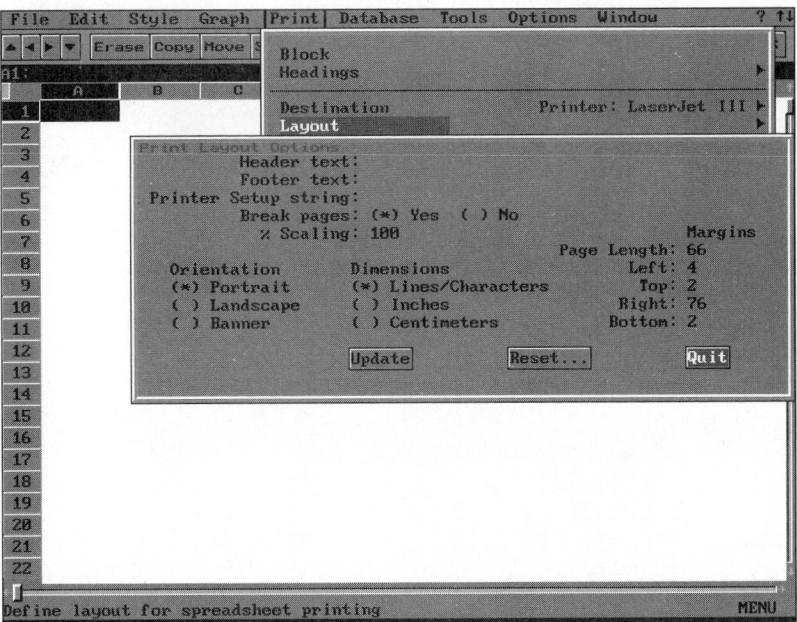

Three default /Print settings control the overall way a printed document is displayed:

- Destination, Printer prints a block to a text printer in draft form. To print what you see in WYSIWYG mode, you must change the Destination setting to Graphics Printer.

- Format, As Displayed prints the information displayed in a block. (Later you'll learn how to print the contents of each cell in a print block.)

Tip. To print in landscape orientation (sideways) in draft mode, see "Using Setup Strings" later in this chapter.

- Layout, Orientation, Portrait prints data vertically on a page. Actually, this setting is ignored when you print in draft mode; only when you print in graphics mode does the Layout, Orientation setting have any bearing on a printed document.

NOTE. *The /Print, Layout Options dialog box in Figure 6.7 is new for Quattro Pro 4.0. From this dialog box you can control most of Quattro Pro's page layout settings. Quattro Pro 3.0, on the other hand, uses a different approach. When you select /Print, Layout in this version, a menu of page layout options is presented; you can then choose the one you want. To see the current page layout settings, select /Print, Layout, Values. Quattro Pro will present a dialog box showing the current page layout settings. This dialog box is for information only; you cannot modify its contents.*

Default Page Layout

All the other default settings control the amount of data and blank space on a printed page. Figure 6.8 shows the default page layout these settings create.

The Dimensions default setting, Lines/Characters, specifies the page length and margin settings in terms of characters. Remember, the /Print command's default is a draft mode printer destination. So the character-based page length and margin settings assume a 12-point, 6-lines-per-inch, 10-cpi resident printer font.

Tip. When you print Quattro Pro fonts, it is much easier to specify margin settings in inches using /Print, Dimensions, Inches. See "Changing Margins" later for further details.

To change margin and page length settings to accommodate different paper sizes and orientations in draft mode, see "Changing Margins" later in this chapter. Changing these settings to accommodate fonts is a different matter. See "Effect of Proportionally Spaced Fonts on Margin Settings" and "Effect of Fonts on the Page Length Setting."

Default Left and Right Margins

As you can see in Figure 6.7, Quattro Pro uses a 4-character 10-cpi left margin and a 76-character right margin by default. A 4-character left margin is equivalent to $4/10$ or 0.4 inch. The 76-character right margin setting corresponds to a portrait orientation on an $8^{1}/_{2}$-by-11-inch page. So this margin setting creates an 0.4 inch right margin.

CAUTION! *Many LaserJet printers with Canon engines cannot print on the half-inch border of a page. Thus, even when you use these default margins, the actual top, bottom, left, and right margins will be 0.5 inch.*

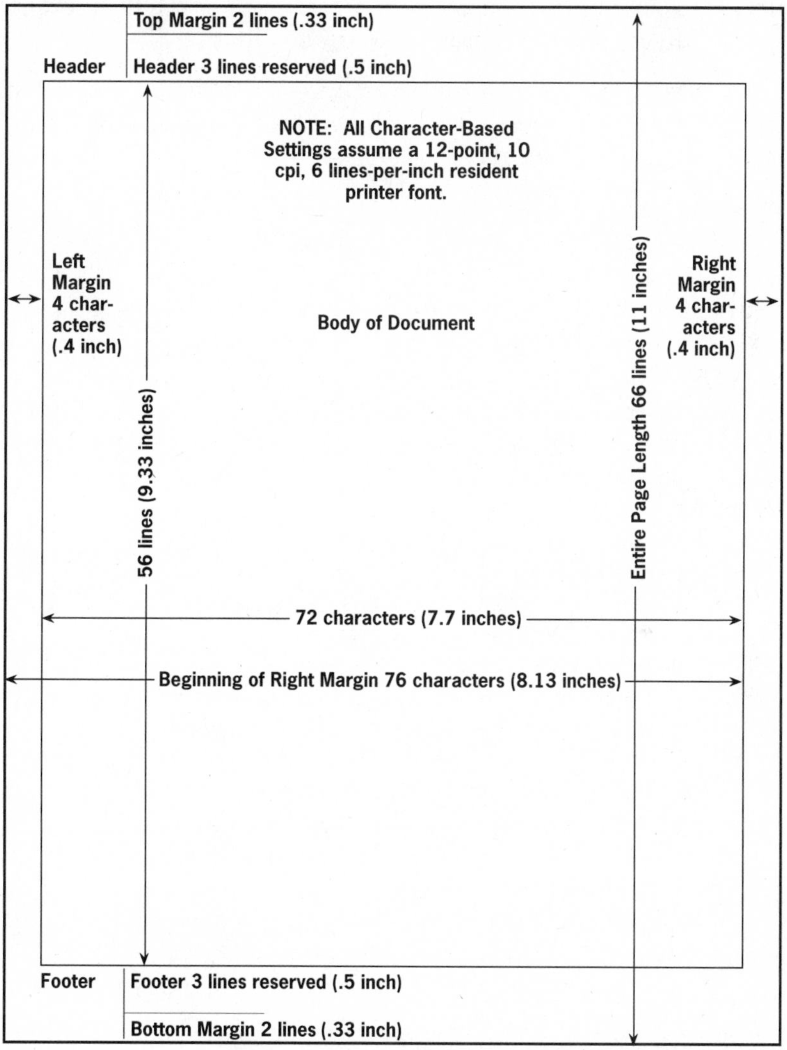

Figure 6.8

Default page layout scheme

Top Margin 2 lines (.33 inch)

Header | Header 3 lines reserved (.5 inch)

NOTE: All Character-Based Settings assume a 12-point, 10 cpi, 6 lines-per-inch resident printer font.

Left Margin 4 characters (.4 inch)

Body of Document

56 lines (9.33 inches)

Entire Page Length 66 lines (11 inches)

Right Margin 4 characters (.4 inch)

72 characters (7.7 inches)

Beginning of Right Margin 76 characters (8.13 inches)

Footer | Footer 3 lines reserved (.5 inch)

Bottom Margin 2 lines (.33 inch)

Maximum Data Printed per Line

A standard Quattro Pro printed page can include seventy-two 12-point, 10-cpi characters per line (76 right margin minus 4 left margin). However, Quattro Pro never divides the information within a column between two pages. So a standard Quattro Pro printed page can include any number of columns as long as the combined width is equal to or less than seventy-two 12-point, 10-cpi characters (using a fixed-width font).

TIP. *If labels in the rightmost column of a print block are partially printed, then the labels are too long for the column and have spilled into the next column. The right margin setting is not the culprit. Either increase the column width or increase the print block by one column.*

Default Top and Bottom Margins

Quattro Pro automatically includes 2-line top and bottom margins on each page. So for a 12-point, 6-lines-per-inch font, this translates into a 0.333 inch ($2/6$) margin at the top of each page and at the bottom of each page.

However, as you can see in Figure 6.8, there are actually five blank lines at the top and bottom of each page, because Quattro Pro also automatically reserves an additional three lines at the top of the page for a header, and another three lines at the bottom of each page for a footer. (See "Adding Headers and Footers" later.) Therefore, when a header and footer are *not* included, the blank space from the top of the paper to the first line of spreadsheet data is 0.83 inch ($5/6$); the blank space from the last line of spreadsheet data to the bottom of a page is also 0.83 inch.

Default Page Length

Quattro Pro assumes a default page length of 66 lines, equivalent to 11 inches (11 times 6 lines per inch). The Layout, Break Pages, Yes setting automatically breaks each page using this default page length setting, 66 lines.

Maximum Lines of Data Printed on a Page

Since the default page length is 66, and ten lines are reserved for a header, a footer, and top and bottom margins, a standard Quattro Pro printed page can include 56 (66 minus 10) lines of 12-point, 6-lines-per-inch spreadsheet data. Therefore, by default the maximum amount of printed space allotted to print block data on an 11-inch page is 9.33 inches ($56/6$).

Printing a Multipage Document

You will find that Quattro Pro's default /Print settings usually work best when you print a single-page, $8\frac{1}{2}$-by-11-inch document in draft mode. When you print a multipage document, you will usually encounter additional formatting requirements that you can best handle by customizing your /Print settings.

For example, suppose you want to print the checking account and budget information in the block A1..P80 shown in Figure 6.9. (This data is used throughout the rest of this chapter.) This block consists of 80 lines and 16 columns. The width of column B ("Check") is 8 characters, column C ("Paid To") is 16 characters, column N ("Misc House Ex") is 10 characters, and all other columns are 9 characters wide. The height of row 3 is 1. (See "Adding Headings" later for the reason.) Since this spreadsheet data is displayed in WYSIWYG mode, you can see that all the data uses Font 1, Swiss-SC 12 point.

Let's print this block in graphics mode so that the fonts and line drawings in the printed document are similar to what you see in WYSIWYG mode. For all other /Print settings, let's use the defaults (Figure 6.7) and then examine the printed document these settings create. These steps assume the printer is on line.

1. Select /Print, Block and indicate **A1..P80**. Quattro Pro returns you to the /Print menu.

2. Select Destination and then Graphics Printer to specify graphics mode printing. Quattro Pro returns you to the /Print menu.

3. Choose Adjust Printer, Align to correlate Quattro Pro's line/page counter to the print head's position at the top of a page. Quattro Pro returns you to the /Print menu.

4. Choose Spreadsheet Print. If you are printing to an HP LaserJet or compatible printer, you will see the message "Downloading char #" while Quattro Pro downloads the fonts in the print block to the printer. The READY indicator reappears after Quattro Pro completes the print operation.

5. Select Quit to return to the spreadsheet.

Quattro Pro prints the information in the block A1..P80 on four pages, as shown in Figure 6.10.

Note. To include page numbers in a printed document, see "Numbering Pages" later in this chapter.

How Quattro Pro Divides a Print Block into Pages

Quattro Pro evaluates the length of the print block in Figure 6.9 in relation to the default page length, top margin, and bottom margin settings shown in Figure 6.7. Whenever Quattro Pro evaluates a print block larger than one page, such as A1..P80, it divides the printout into several pages. In this case,

Figure 6.9

A multipage block to print

Date	Check	Paid To	Amount	Deposit	Balance	Mortgage	House Utilities	Phone	Food	Health Expense	Other Ins	Car Expense	Misc House Exp	Other	Misc
		Balance			$423										
		Deposit		$4,000	$4,423										
Mar-91	850	Mortgage	($1,500)		$2,923	$1,500									
Mar-91	851	Cash	($100)		$2,823										$100
Mar-91	852	Shell	($75)		$2,748							$75			
Mar-91	853	Electric	($120)		$2,628		$120								
Mar-91	854	Sewer/Water	($65)		$2,563		$65								
Mar-91	855	Baby Sitter	($50)		$2,513										$50
Mar-91	856	Safeway	($175)		$2,338				$175						
Mar-91	857	Phone	($85)		$2,253			$85							
Mar-91	858	Health Ins	($175)		$2,078					$175					
Mar-91	859	Cash	($50)		$2,028										$50
Mar-91	860	Firestone	($200)		$1,828							$200			
Mar-91	861	Cleaners	($20)		$1,808										$20
Mar-91	862	Am Ex	($150)		$1,658									$150	
Mar-91	863	Nob Hill	($40)		$1,618				$40						
Mar-91	864	Car Ins	($450)		$1,168						$450				
Mar-91		Deposit		$2,000	$3,168										
Mar-91	865	VOID	$0		$3,168										
Mar-91	866	Mastercard	($250)		$2,918									$250	
Mar-91	867	House Ins	($800)		$2,118						$800				
Mar-91	868	Cash	($100)		$2,018										$100
Mar-91	869	Safeway	($60)		$1,958				$60						
Mar-91	870	Fishing Trip	($150)		$1,808										$150
Mar-91	871	Alumni Fund	($50)		$1,758									$50	
Mar-91	872	Bookstore	($25)		$1,733										$25
Mar-91	873	Cleaners	($25)		$1,708										$25
Mar-91	874	Paint Store	($100)		$1,608								$100		
Mar-91	875	Cash	($200)		$1,408										$200
Mar-91	876	TWA	($150)		$1,258									$150	
Mar-91	877	Nob Hill	($75)		$1,183				$75						
Mar-91	878	Ace Hardware	($40)		$1,143							$40			
Mar-91	879	Roter Rooter	($70)		$1,073							$70			
Mar-91	880	Magazine Subs	($35)		$1,038										$35
Mar-91	881	Cleaners	($15)		$1,023										$15
Mar-91	882	Lawn Service	($80)		$943								$80		
Mar-91	883	Dog Food	($40)		$903										$40
Mar-91	884	Dentist	($150)		$753					$150					
Mar-91	885	Cash	($75)		$678										$75
Mar-91	886	Safeway	($100)		$578				$100						
Mar-91		Service Charge	($10)		$568										$10
Mar-91		Total For March	($5,855)	$6,000	$568	$1,500	$185	$85	$450	$325	$1,250	$275	$290	$600	$895
Apr-91	887	Baby Sitter	($25)		$543										$25
Apr-91		Deposit		$4,000	$4,543										
Apr-91	888	Mortgage	($1,500)		$3,043	$1,500									
Apr-91	889	YMCA	($75)		$2,968										$75
Apr-91	890	Phone	($120)		$2,848			$120							
Apr-91	891	Electric	($95)		$2,753		$95								
Apr-91	892	Cable	($44)		$2,709		$44								
Apr-91	893	Cash	($100)		$2,609										$100
Apr-91	894	Safeway	($150)		$2,459				$150						
Apr-91	895	Cleaners	($30)		$2,429										$30
Apr-91	896	RE Taxes	($1,100)		$1,329								$1,100		
Apr-91	897	IRS	($250)		$1,079									$250	
Apr-91	898	State of Calif	($75)		$1,004									$75	
Apr-91	899	Health Ins	($175)		$829					$175					
Apr-91	900	Am Ex	($50)		$779									$50	
Apr-91	901	VOID	$0		$779										
Apr-91	902	Mastercard	($125)		$654									$125	
Apr-91	903	VOID	$0		$654										
Apr-91		Deposit		$1,500	$2,154										
Apr-91	904	Cash	($100)		$2,054										$100
Apr-91	905	To Savings	($1,000)		$1,054									$1,000	
Apr-91	906	Baby Sitter	($35)		$1,019										$35
Apr-91	907	Cleaners	($15)		$1,004										$15
Apr-91	908	Lawn Service	($80)		$924								$80		
Apr-91	909	Plumber	($200)		$724								$200		
Apr-91	910	Cash	($75)		$649										$75
Apr-91	911	Nob Hill	($125)		$524				$125						
Apr-91	912	Midas Muffler	($250)		$274							$250			
Apr-91	913	Cleaners	($20)		$254										$20
Apr-91		Deposit		$500	$754										
Apr-91	914	WS Journal	($120)		$634										$120
Apr-91	915	Local Paper	($22)		$612										$22
Apr-91		Service Charge	($10)		$602										$10
Apr-91		Total For April	($5,966)	$6,000	$602	$1,500	$139	$120	$275	$175	$0	$250	$1,380	$1,500	$627

- Beginning at the upper-left corner of the block, Quattro Pro assigns the first 43 lines to page 1.

- Because there are only 37 remaining lines in this block, Quattro Pro prints rows 44 through 80 on the second page.

Remember, Quattro Pro's default page length setting, 66 (approximately 9.3 inches), is for a 12-point, 6-lines-per-inch resident printer font. Thus, for default Font 1, the proportionally spaced Swiss-SC 12 point, Quattro Pro can fit only 42 lines within the same space allotted to spreadsheet data. (Actually, it's 43 lines, but row 3 has a height of 1.) See "Changing Page Lengths" later for further discussion.

Figure 6.10
Printed multipage block

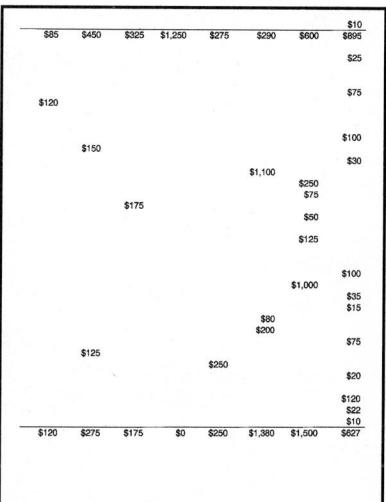

Date	Check	Paid To	Amount	Deposit	Balance	Mortgage	House Utilities
		Balance			$423		
		Deposit		$4,000	$4,423		
Mar-91	850	Mortgage	($1,500)		$2,923	$1,500	
Mar-91	851	Cash	($100)		$2,823		
Mar-91	852	Shell	($75)		$2,748		
Mar-91	853	Electric	($120)		$2,628		$120
Mar-91	854	Sewer/Water	($65)		$2,563		$65
Mar-91	855	Baby Sitter	($50)		$2,513		
Mar-91	856	Safeway	($175)		$2,338		
Mar-91	857	Phone	($85)		$2,253		
Mar-91	858	Health Ins	($175)		$2,078		
Mar-91	859	Cash	($50)		$2,028		
Mar-91	860	Firestone	($200)		$1,828		
Mar-91	861	Cleaners	($20)		$1,808		
Mar-91	862	Am Ex	($150)		$1,658		
Mar-91	863	Nob Hill	($40)		$1,618		
Mar-91	864	Car Ins	($450)		$1,168		
Mar-91		Deposit		$2,000	$3,166		
Mar-91	865	VOID	$0		$3,166		
Mar-91	866	Mastercard	($250)		$2,916		
Mar-91	867	House Ins	($800)		$2,116		
Mar-91	868	Cash	($100)		$2,016		
Mar-91	869	Safeway	($60)		$1,956		
Mar-91	870	Fishing Trip	($150)		$1,806		
Mar-91	871	Alumni Fund	($50)		$1,756		
Mar-91	872	Bookstore	($25)		$1,733		
Mar-91	873	Cleaners	($25)		$1,708		
Mar-91	874	Paint Store	($100)		$1,608		
Mar-91	875	Cash	($200)		$1,408		
Mar-91	876	TWA	($150)		$1,258		
Mar-91	877	Nob Hill	($75)		$1,183		
Mar-91	878	Ace Hardware	($40)		$1,143		
Mar-91	879	Roter Rooter	($70)		$1,073		
Mar-91	880	Magazine Subs	($35)		$1,038		
Mar-91	881	Cleaners	($15)		$1,023		
Mar-91	882	Lawn Service	($80)		$943		
Mar-91	883	Dog Food	($40)		$903		
Mar-91	884	Dentist	($150)		$753		
Mar-91	885	Cash	($75)		$678		
Mar-91	886	Safeway	($100)		$578		

Date	Check	Paid To	Amount	Deposit	Balance	Mortgage	House Utilities
Mar-91		Service Charge	($10)		$568		
Mar-91		Total For March	($5,855)	$6,000		$1,500	$185
Apr-91	887	Baby Sitter	($25)		$543		
Apr-91		Deposit		$4,000	$4,543		
Apr-91	888	Mortgage	($1,500)		$3,043	$1,500	
Apr-91	889	YMCA	($75)		$2,968		
Apr-91	890	Phone	($120)		$2,848		
Apr-91	891	Electric	($95)		$2,753		$95
Apr-91	892	Cable	($44)		$2,709		$44
Apr-91	893	Cash	($100)		$2,609		
Apr-91	894	Safeway	($150)		$2,459		
Apr-91	895	Cleaners	($30)		$2,429		
Apr-91	896	RE Taxes	($1,100)		$1,329		
Apr-91	897	IRS	($250)		$1,079		
Apr-91	898	State of Calif	($75)		$1,004		
Apr-91	899	Health Ins	($175)		$829		
Apr-91	900	Am Ex	($50)		$779		
Apr-91	901	VOID	$0		$779		
Apr-91	902	Mastercard	($125)		$654		
Apr-91	903	VOID	$0		$654		
Apr-91		Deposit		$1,500	$2,154		
Apr-91	904	Cash	($100)		$2,054		
Apr-91	905	To Savings	($1,000)		$1,054		
Apr-91	906	Baby Sitter	($35)		$1,019		
Apr-91	907	Cleaners	($15)		$1,004		
Apr-91	908	Lawn Service	($80)		$924		
Apr-91	909	Plumber	($200)		$724		
Apr-91	910	Cash	($75)		$649		
Apr-91	911	Nob Hill	($125)		$524		
Apr-91	912	Midas Muffler	($250)		$274		
Apr-91	913	Cleaners	($20)		$254		
Apr-91		Deposit		$500	$754		
Apr-91	914	WS Journal	($120)		$634		
Apr-91	915	Local Paper	($22)		$612		
Apr-91		Service Charge	($10)		$602		
Apr-91		Total For April	($5,966)	$6,000		$1,500	$139

Quattro Pro also evaluates the width of the print block using the default right and left margins in Figure 6.7. Because columns are not divided between pages, only columns A through H fit on one page (8, plus 6 times 9, plus 16, or 78 *proportionally spaced* characters). Therefore,

- On the first page, Quattro Pro prints the leftmost columns, A through H, or the block A1..H43.

- On the second page, Quattro Pro prints the block A44..H80 using the same column calculations.

- Because columns I through P (7 times 9 plus 10, or 73 *proportionally spaced* characters) cannot fit on the first two pages, two more pages are printed—page 3 containing the block I1..P43, and page 4 containing the block I44..P80.

Remember, Quattro Pro's character-based margin settings are for a 12-point, 10-cpi, fixed-width font. Thus, for default Font 1 (proportionally spaced Swiss-SC 12 point), Quattro Pro can fit more characters per line. See "Changing Margins" later for further discussion.

Unfortunately, the default /Print format does not display the printed information in Figure 6.10 in a highly readable manner. For example, this information would be presented better if

- All of the March information through row 45 were printed on pages 1 and 3, and the April information were printed in a similar manner on pages 2 and 4.

- Page 3 contained all the March budget information, beginning in column G, while Page 4 contained the April budget data.

- Pages 3 and 4 included the dates, check numbers, and descriptive labels in columns A, B, and C, so you could easily determine what the budget value in a row represented.

- Pages 2 and 3 included the column labels in rows 1 and 2, so you could easily determine what each column of information represented.

This information would be even more readable if it were printed on fewer pages. One alternative would be to print this information sideways (landscape) on two pages, with March information on the first page and April information on the second. Then columns A through P would be printed on each page. Or you could try using one of Quattro Pro's /Print commands—Print to Fit or Layout, Percent Scaling—if you wanted to fit all of the information on one page.

Fortunately, you can manipulate the /Print command to create these presentation-quality documents. Before you do so, however, you should become familiar with Quattro Pro's Screen Preview option. This feature comes in very handy when you are in the process of designing a custom document.

NOTE. *In WYSIWYG mode, Quattro Pro 4.0 can display the current print block and your page breaks by using dotted gray lines. This allows you to see what data is included in the print block and how your pages will break when printed. (This feature is not available in Quattro Pro version 3.0.) For this feature to be active, a printer must be selected, either when you install Quattro Pro 4.0, or later with the /Options, Hardware, Printers command. In addition, /Print, Destination must be set to either Graphics Printer, Screen Preview, or Binary File. Finally, you must select /Window, Options, Print Block and select Display. To turn off this feature, select /Window, Options, Print Block, and then select Hide.*

Previewing a Document

Note. If you cannot display WYSIWYG mode, Screen Preview is the only method of checking fonts and column widths in Quattro Pro. See "Printing Fonts" for further details.

Quattro Pro's Screen Preview option allows you to preview a printed document on the screen. Using this option can save you considerable time, paper, and headaches by enabling you to locate and solve problems before you actually print. So use Screen Preview to check the overall appearance of a printer document as well as individual entries. You can examine fonts, margins, headers, footers, page breaks, headings—anything that affects a printout.

Screen Preview prints to the screen in graphics mode and thus displays fonts accurately. Be aware, however, that even if you view the correct fonts during Screen Preview, they are not printed unless you also print to a printer in *graphics mode.* Be sure to read "Printing Fonts" later in this chapter if you are using fonts in a print block.

If you are printing in draft mode to an HP LaserJet or PostScript printer, you can use Screen Preview to view the document using one of the printer's fonts. If you specify an HP LaserJet or PostScript printer during installation, Quattro Pro includes the appropriate printer-specific fonts in your font library. You can then use the /Style command (see Chapter 3) to assign a printer-specific font to Font 1, such as 12 point Courier Bold for an HP Laser-Jet Series III. Now when you use Screen Preview, Quattro Pro displays the document using this font.

Accessing Screen Preview

You should use Screen Preview after you specify all your /Print settings but before you print. Returning to the example in Figures 6.9 and 6.10, if you had used Screen Preview first, you would have discovered the deficiencies in the finished document before you actually printed it. Once you specify the print block in Figure 6.9,

Note. Unlike earlier
releases, Screen
Preview in versions
3.0 and 4.0 turns
the displayed pages
sideways when you
view a document
with a landscape
(sideways)
orientation.

1. Select /Print, Destination, and then choose Screen Preview. Quattro Pro returns you to the /Print menu, where the destination is displayed as "Screen Preview: LaserJet III."

2. Select Spreadsheet Print.

Quattro Pro now builds a preview of the document using the /Print settings. Sometimes it takes a while, especially if Quattro Pro has to build fonts used in the document; then you will see messages such as "Now building fonts." displayed on the screen. Finally, Quattro Pro displays the Screen Preview in Figure 6.11, which includes the menu options listed in Table 6.1.

Figure 6.11

Quattro Pro's
Screen Preview

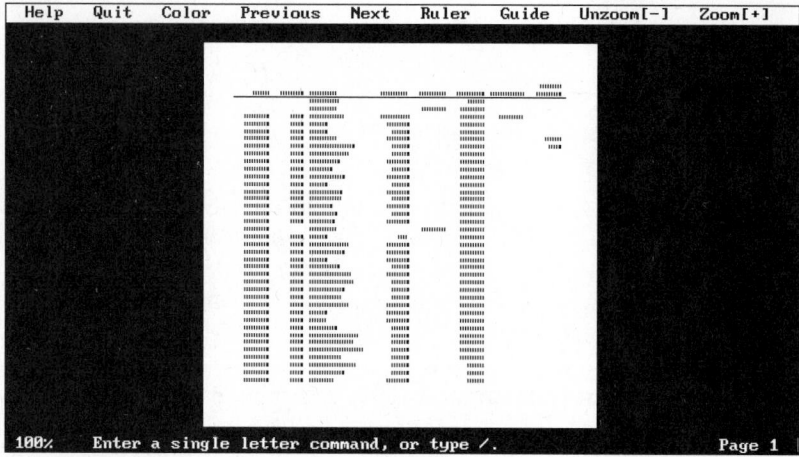

Quattro Pro initially displays the first page in the document using its 100% mode. As you can see in Figure 6.11, this initial display mode makes the text appear like gibberish. Only in Zoom mode can you identify and evaluate the lines in a document.

Working in Zoom Mode

To enter Zoom mode, select Zoom or press +. Quattro Pro now displays the magnified Screen Preview in Figure 6.12. Since this is 200% Zoom mode, only a portion of the page is displayed—in this case, the top of page 1. The 200% Zoom level is helpful to check column widths, margin settings, and the overall appearance of a printed document.

As you can see in Figure 6.12, by default Quattro Pro includes a *guide*—the miniature page display in the upper-right corner—which tells you what portion of a page you are currently viewing. You can use many of the Screen Preview commands in Table 6.1, and the keys listed in Table 6.2, to move this guide and examine different segments of the document.

Table 6.1   **Screen Preview Commands**

Screen Preview Command[*]	Function
Help (F1)	Displays the Screen Preview help menu. Press Esc to return to Screen Preview.
Quit (Esc)	Leaves Screen Preview and returns you to the /Print menu.
Color	Changes the screen display. Screen Preview is initially displayed in the current screen display mode, such as color screen, black-on-white display. Select Color once to change to black on white, twice for white on black, three times to return to the first display mode, color. If a color printer is your default, selecting Color three times changes Screen Preview to a color screen and color data display. A monochrome monitor displays only white on black and black on white.
Ruler	Overlays a 1-inch grid on the displayed page. Select Ruler again to remove this grid.
Previous (PgUp)	Displays the previous page. This is not a toggle, so at the first page you must use Next repeatedly to move to the last page.
Next (PgDn)	Displays the next page. This is not a toggle, so at the last page you must use Previous repeatedly to return to the first page.
Guide	Turns the guide display on or off. In Zoom mode, a miniature page display is created in the upper-right corner, along with a guide. The guide position indicates the portion of the page currently displayed. Changing the position of the guide—using one of the keys shown in Table 6.2—changes the portion of the current or new page displayed in Zoom mode. Pressing Del also removes the guide during Zoom mode; pressing Insert redisplays it.
Unzoom (–)	Decreases the 200% or 400% Zoom mode by one level.
Zoom (+)	Assuming the initial Screen Preview mode is 100%, Zoom enlarges a page to 200% and 400% of this size. Use 200% to check the overall appearance of the document, 400% to check individual entries.

*   You can use these commands at any time during Screen Preview. If you are using the keyboard during Zoom mode, select one of these commands by typing the first letter of a command *without* preceding it by a slash (/), such as **Q** to quit Screen Preview. Or use the alternative methods displayed in parentheses.

You can select Previous or Next from the menu to display different pages in the document. Quattro Pro then automatically displays the portion of the new page within the guide. In the current example, if you press either PgDn or N (for Next), Quattro Pro will display page 2 of the document in this 200% Zoom mode.

You cannot use Next to flip through a document continuously. Once you get to the last page, you must select Previous (P or PgUp) repeatedly to return to earlier pages; Next does not return you to the first page.

Figure 6.12
200% Zoom mode

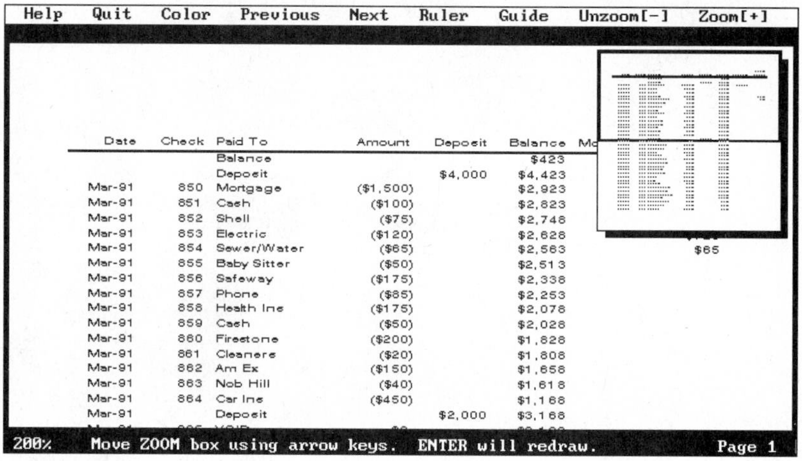

Table 6.2   **Keys That Control Zoom Display**

Key	Moves Guide to
PgDn	Same position on the next page
PgUp	Same position on the previous page
↑ or ↓	One guide increment up or down from current guide position
→ or ←	One guide increment right or left from current guide position
Home	The top of the current page in 200% Zoom; the upper-left corner of the current page in 400% Zoom
End	The bottom of the current page in 200% Zoom; the bottom-left corner of the current page in 400% Zoom

You can also view a different portion of the current page by using one of the keys shown in Table 6.2. For example, you can press End to move the guide to the bottom of the current page. However, when you use one of these keys and the guide is active, Quattro Pro does not automatically display the selected portion of the page. Only after you press Enter does Quattro Pro preview the portion of the page now located within the guide. (This does not apply to PgDn and PgUp, which are equivalents for Next and Previous.)

If you select Zoom or press + a second time, Quattro Pro displays the 400% Zoom mode, as shown in Figure 6.13. As you can see, 400% Zoom mode displays only a small portion of a page. Use this level to check font sizes, spelling, and anything relating to individual entries.

At any point in Screen Preview, you can press Esc to return to the /Print menu. Your foray in Screen Preview may indicate that you need to make changes to spreadsheet data or /Print settings. After you make these changes, you can follow these steps to return to Screen Preview:

1. From the /Print menu, select Adjust Printer, Align to reset Quattro Pro's internal page counter to 1. (See "Controlling the Paper in the Printer" earlier.) Otherwise, Quattro Pro numbers the pages incorrectly in Screen Preview.

Figure 6.13
400% Zoom mode

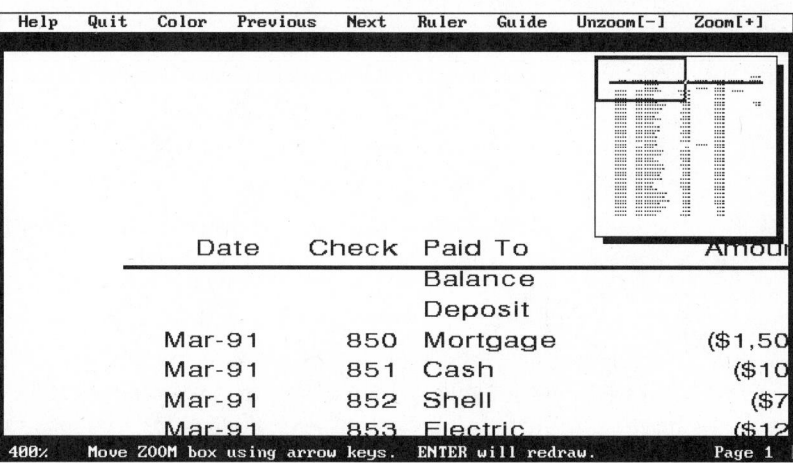

2. Select Spreadsheet Print from the /Print menu. Quattro Pro remembers your previous destination, and thus prints to Screen Preview. You can now check the effect of any changes you have made. When you are satisfied with how the printed document will look,

3. Press Esc to return to the /Print menu.

4. Select Destination and choose another graphics mode (final quality) print destination, such as Graphics Printer. Quattro Pro returns you to the /Print menu.

5. Choose Adjust Printer, Align to reset Quattro Pro's internal line and page counters.

6. Select Spreadsheet Print, and Quattro Pro prints the document previously displayed in Screen Preview.

Customizing a Document

You can use the /Print command to create custom, presentation-quality documents by

- Adding column and/or row headings on each page

- Changing the document page length, and/or specifying different page lengths for individual pages

- Adding headers and/or footers on each page

- Using custom margin settings

- Hiding portions of data from being printed

- Adding setup strings

- Printing sideways (landscape orientation), even across continuous-feed paper

- Reducing (or enlarging) the size of printed text to fit within a specified page size or within the smallest number of pages

- Including special effects, such as bullets, line drawing, and block shading

For instance, let's return to the printout in Figure 6.10. You can use the /Print settings in Table 6.3 to improve the appearance of this output and create the document in Figure 6.14. By changing the font, column widths, and page lengths, and adding headers, footers, and column and row headings, you can create a document that includes March checking data on page 1, April checking data on page 2, March budget data on page 3, and April budget data on page 4. This section will show you how to specify the /Print settings used in this document.

Figure 6.14

A custom-printed
document

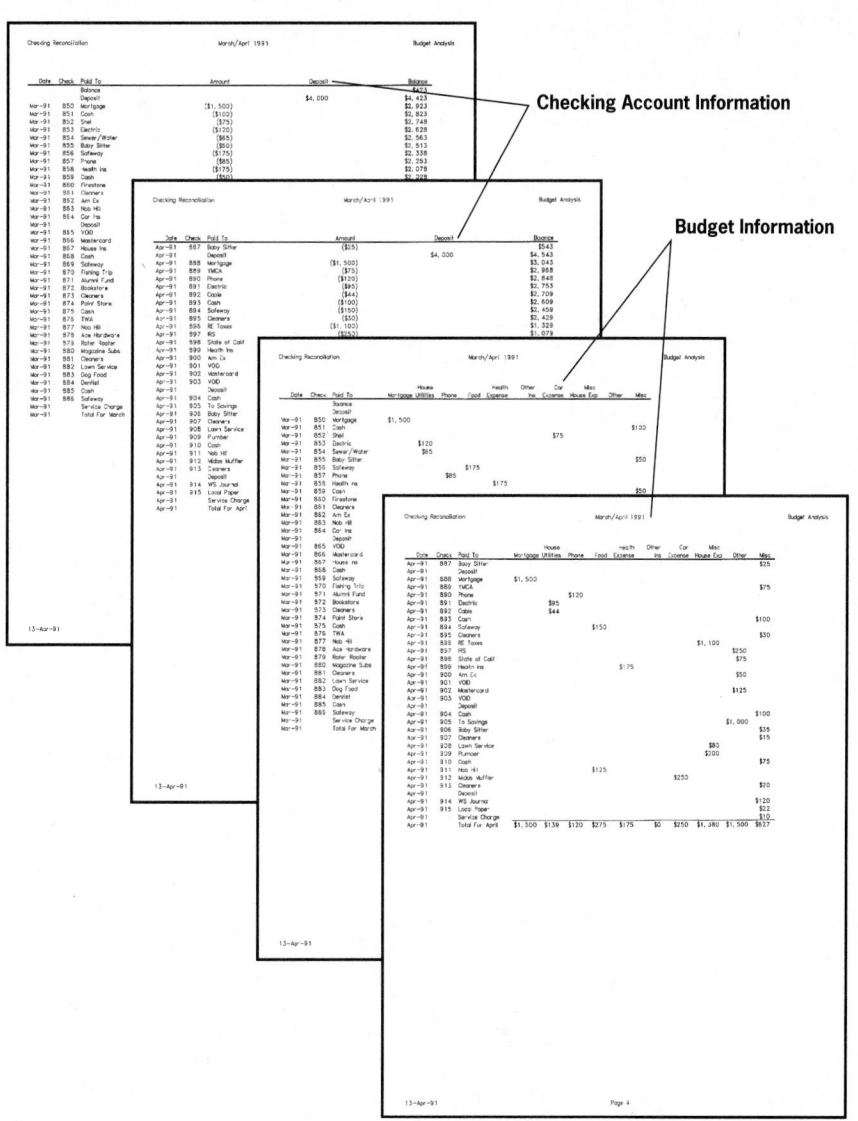

Checking Account Information

Budget Information

One of the nice features of Quattro Pro's /Print command is that you can
present the same spreadsheet data in different ways by changing the printed
appearance of a document. For instance, using the same information in Figure 6.9, you can also create a totally different-looking document by hiding
some of the data before you print, or by using different fonts. Or you can

Table 6.3   /Print Settings Used for Figure 6.14

Command	Setting
/Print, Block	D4..P80
/Print, Headings	
Left Heading	A1..C1
Top Heading	C1..C3
/Print, Layout, Margins	
Top	.33
Bottom	.33
Left	.40
Right	7.6
Page Length	11.0
/Print, Layout	
Dimensions	Inches
Orientation	Portrait
Header text	Checking Reconciliation|March/April 1991|Budget Analysis
Footer text	@|Page #
/Print, Destination	Graphics Printer
|:: (manual hard page break)	D46
/Style, Font Table, Edit Fonts	
1 Font 1	Sans Serif 8 point
/Style, Column Width	
6	Columns B, H, I, J, P
7	Columns A, G, K, L, M, O
8	Column N
12	Column C
22	Columns D, E, F

print the data sideways (landscape) on two pages. You can even print this data on one page by reducing the printed size of the text until it fits. (You'll see examples of these different print methods in this section.) In fact, you will find that Quattro Pro's /Print command offers you the flexibility to print spreadsheet data almost any way you choose.

You will find that fonts affect virtually every aspect of printing. For this reason, a recap of fonts is presented next, before any other /Print options are discussed.

Printing Fonts

Note. To specify and edit fonts, see Chapter 3.

One of the most powerful features in Quattro Pro is its font library. You can use Quattro Pro's fonts to create professional-looking documents equal to those created using stand-alone publishing software.

Quattro Pro uses different fonts depending on the destination and default printer you specify. Fonts affect virtually every aspect of a printed document, even if you haven't specified any fonts in a spreadsheet. In WYSIWYG mode, "what you see is what you get" is *not* necessarily true when you print.

Fonts Used in Draft Mode

When you print in draft mode, Quattro Pro uses the resident printer font. For example, the printed document you saw in Figure 6.5 uses a 12-point Courier font because it is printed using the default /Print, Destination, Printer setting (a draft mode destination), and a LaserJet III as the default printer. Even if you assign fonts to a spreadsheet and you can see them in WYSIWYG mode, when you print to a draft mode destination, these fonts are not printed.

Note. To print fonts assigned to a spreadsheet, you must print in graphics mode.

Be aware that in draft mode, there is a difference between what you see in Screen Preview and in the printed document. Remember, when you use Screen Preview, Quattro Pro prints to the screen in graphics mode, and thus displays a document using Quattro Pro's Font 1 (and any other assigned fonts), not the resident printer font. Therefore, Screen Preview may not accurately depict the default printer font used when you print in draft mode. For the exceptions—HP LaserJet and PostScript fonts—see "Previewing a Document" earlier.

An additional problem with column width settings can occur when the point size of the resident printer font differs from Font 1 (or any other assigned fonts). Remember, Quattro Pro's column widths are always sized for a 12-point 10-cpi font, and the default font, Font 1, is a 12-point font (so a column width of 20 accommodates twenty 10-cpi characters). If your printer's resident font is a different point size, column width settings that appear fine on the screen may cause truncated characters when printed. Likewise, margin and page length settings specified in the /Print command also assume a 12-point 10-cpi font, and may need to be adjusted to accommodate a different printer font. Therefore, when you print in draft mode you should specify a Font 1 point size equal to the point size of your resident printer font. Then you can use Screen Preview to determine the correct column width settings for the printed document. See "Changing Page Lengths" and "Changing Margins" later for further details.

Fonts Used in Graphics Mode

Tip. To increase the amount of data on each printed page, you can also use two /Print commands—Print to Fit and Layout, Percent Scaling. Both are discussed in this chapter.

When you print in graphics mode, by default Quattro Pro prints the document using Font 1, Swiss-SC 12 point Black. Likewise, to print fonts assigned to a spreadsheet, you *must* print in graphics mode. (See "Printing to a Printer in Graphics Mode" earlier.)

For instance, by printing in graphics mode, you can print the font specified in Table 6.3, and create the document in Figure 6.14. As you can see, Font 1 is specified as Sans Serif 8 point, which by default is assigned to the spreadsheet data. This 8-point font is used to fit more columns and lines on each page.

When you use Quattro Pro's fonts in a printed document, they can affect the printed lines per page, column width settings, margin settings, and even headers and footers. Only the implications for column width are discussed here; the effects of fonts on the other /Print settings are discussed in the respective sections.

In Quattro Pro 3.0, if you do not choose to build fonts during installation, Quattro Pro will build fonts as needed to print or preview a document. This font building can be time-consuming and can use considerable disk space. (Each font file uses on average approximately 125k and then resides permanently on disk.) Instead, you can choose a Hershey typeface that doesn't need any font building, rather than a Bitstream font, by selecting /Options, Graphics Quality, Draft before you print. The trade-off, however, is that Hershey fonts are not as aesthetically pleasing as Bitstream fonts, and can be slower than previously constructed Bitstream fonts. This problem can be avoided in Quattro Pro 4.0 by using scalable (SC) fonts.

Effect of Quattro Pro Fonts on Column-Width Settings

One of the most important features in Quattro Pro in respect to printing is the ability in WYSIWYG mode to view fonts on the screen. This enables you to evaluate and change column-width settings to accommodate fonts you assign in a spreadsheet. For example, the spreadsheet data in Figure 6.9 by default uses Font 1, Swiss-SC 12 point. This font is printed in Figure 6.10 (though the type size was reduced for reproduction in this book). To create

the document in Figure 6.14, however, the spreadsheet data is assigned Sans Serif 8 point and the following changes are made to the column widths:

Column	Figure 6.10 Width	Figure 6.14 Width
B	8	6
A, G, K, L, M, O	9	7
H, I, J, P	9	6
C	16	12
D, E, F	9	22
N	10	8

The column widths of D, E, and F are expanded so that only the March checking data is printed on page 1 and the April checking data on page 2. The other column widths are decreased (made possible by the smaller 8-point font) so that all of the March budget data fits on page 3, and the April budget data on page 4.

In versions 3.0 and 4.0, evaluating column widths is much easier than in previous releases because you can view fonts in WYSIWYG mode. If you work in Character mode (or use an earlier version), however, Quattro Pro does not display any of its fonts on the screen (see Chapter 3). This can cause substantial mistakes in a printed document; column-width settings that appear fine on the screen may cause truncated characters when spreadsheet data is printed in graphics mode. (Remember, Quattro Pro's character-based column width settings assume a 12-point, 10-cpi font.) So to check column-width settings in relation to any fonts you have specified, be sure to use Screen Preview before you print.

Using Printer-Specific Fonts When Printing in Graphics Mode

In some instances, you can print spreadsheet data in graphics mode using printer-specific fonts. If you specified a PostScript or LaserJet Series II (or later) printer during installation, Quattro Pro includes printer-specific fonts in your font library. You can then use the /Style command to specify these printer fonts. See Chapter 3 for further details.

In addition, you can use the /Options, Hardware, Printers, Fonts, Cartridge Fonts command to specify a cartridge you are using with a LaserJet Series II or later printer. Quattro Pro then adds these additional printer-specific fonts to your font library.

Adding Headings

In many cases, descriptive labels are used across the top and down the left side of a spreadsheet, as in Figure 6.9. In this example, row 1 contains labels describing the entries in each column, and row 2 contains labels as well as a line drawing that offsets these descriptive labels from the body of the data. Additionally, column A contains the date, column B the check number, and column C a description of the expense in each row.

When you use Quattro Pro's default /Print settings to print a large spreadsheet, many times these descriptive *headings* are not printed on most of the pages. This occurs, for instance, when the information from Figure 6.9 is printed in Figure 6.10—pages 2 and 4 do not contain the column headings in rows 1 and 2, while pages 3 and 4 do not contain the row headings in columns A, B, and C.

You can use the /Print, Headings command to include row headings, column headings, or both on every printed page. For example, here's how to create headings when you print the data in Figure 6.9:

Caution! You must specify a print block that excludes the Heading blocks; otherwise Quattro Pro prints this information twice on some pages.

1. Select /Print, Headings. Quattro Pro displays a menu like that in Figure 6.15. Choose Left Heading, and in response to "Row headings to print on the left of each page:", specify **A1..C1**. (You only need to specify one cell in each column, not the entire block A1..C80.) Press Enter. Quattro Pro returns you to the /Print menu.

2. Select Top Heading, and in response to "Column headings to print on the top of each page:", specify **C1..C3**. (You only need to specify one cell in each row, not the entire block A1..P3.) Press Enter. Quattro Pro returns you to the /Print menu.

NOTE. *Unless you also include row 3 in the Top Heading block, the line drawing in row 2 is not printed on pages 2 and 4. Remember, any bottom line drawing is assigned to the cell below the one to which it was originally assigned. (See Chapter 3 for further discussion.) That is why row 3 was assigned a height of 1 and included in the heading block.*

3. Choose Block and indicate **D4..P80**, which *excludes* the Heading blocks, and press Enter.

How Headings Affect the Amount of Data Printed on Each Page

Tip. Remember to use Screen Preview to examine a document with headings before printing.

Because Quattro Pro includes headings in the spreadsheet data that it prints on each page, it may divide printed pages differently. For example, the left heading adds three columns (A, B, and C) to pages 2 and 4. Therefore, if you print the data in Figure 6.9, instead of printing four pages as in Figure 6.10, Quattro Pro will not be able to fit all of the columns on four pages, and will add two more pages—5 and 6. In Figure 6.14, this problem is overcome by decreasing the point size of the printed font. Since the data in Figure 6.10 uses Font 1 (Swiss-SC 12 point by default), the /Style command is used to specify a Sans Serif 8-point font.

Figure 6.15

The /Print, Headings menu

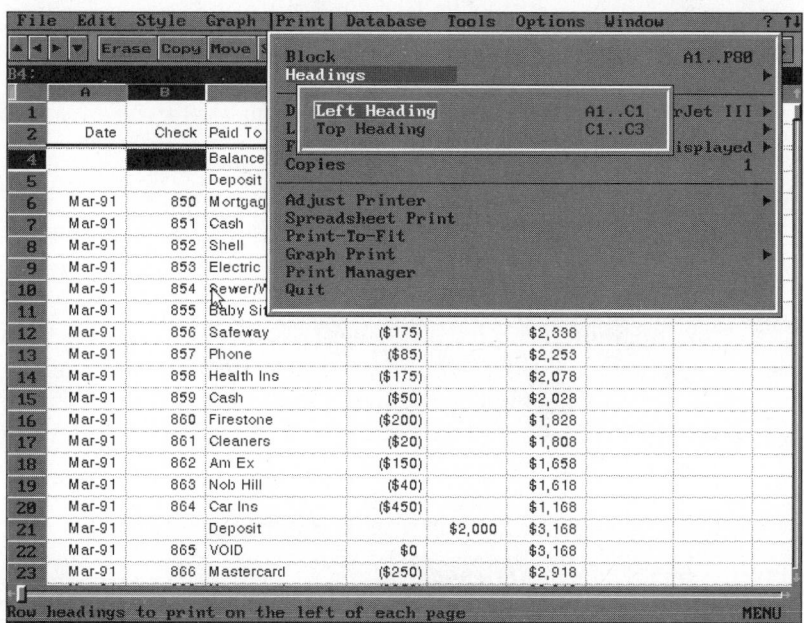

Row headings, on the other hand, affect the lines of spreadsheet data printed on a page. For instance, if you specify a two-row top heading without changing the font, Quattro Pro will print fewer lines of spreadsheet data per page after the first page. In Figure 6.14, however, the smaller 8-point font allows Quattro Pro to print *more* lines per page than in Figure 6.10. (See "Changing Page Lengths" for the reason.)

If you print the Figure 6.9 data using the /Print, Layout default settings and a graphics mode destination, you will get the printed output in Figure 6.14, which includes these additional headings:

Note. Obviously, more lines could be printed on Page 2; a hard page break (see "Changing Page Lengths" later) is used to separate the March and April data on different pages.

■ On page 2, the row (top) heading A1..I3

■ On page 3, the column (left) heading A1..C49 (notice that the smaller font allows six additional rows to be printed compared with Figure 6.10)

■ On page 4, the row (top) heading I1..P3 and the column (left) heading A50..C80

Quattro Pro prints only those headings that correspond to the /Print Block data printed on a particular page.

Changing Layout Dimensions

You can use /Print, Layout, Dimensions to change the unit of measurement Quattro Pro uses for the /Print, Layout, Margin settings. By default, the Dimensions setting is Characters/Lines, which you can change to either Inches or Centimeters. Quattro Pro then automatically converts the /Print, Layout, Margins settings to this unit of measure. However, the Dimensions setting does not affect any settings in the spreadsheet, such as the character unit of measurement Quattro Pro uses for column widths.

Tip. To save a Dimensions, Inches setting as the default for all future Quattro Pro sessions, select /Printer, Layout, Update.

You should use a Dimensions, Inches setting when you print Quattro Pro fonts. The reasons are discussed in "Changing Page Lengths" and "Changing Margins" later.

For instance, you can change the Dimensions setting to specify the margins and page length settings in inches rather than in characters. The Print Layout Options dialog box in Figure 6.7 shows Quattro Pro's default margins and page length settings expressed in characters, while the same dialog box in Figure 6.16 displays these settings converted to inches.

Figure 6.16
Using /Print, Layout, Dimensions to convert margin settings to inches

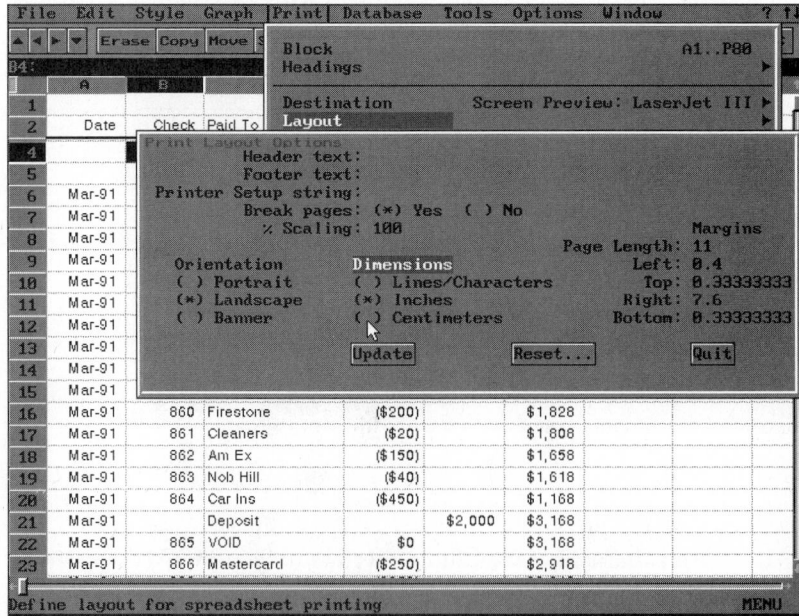

Changing Page Lengths

By default, Quattro Pro breaks printed pages every 66 lines, or every 56 lines of spreadsheet data. This default /Print, Layout, Margins, Page Length setting assumes

- A portrait (vertical) orientation on 8½-by-11-inch paper
- Printing in draft mode using the resident printer font
- A 12-point, fixed-pitch font that can fit six lines per inch

Thus, the standard page length setting is 66 lines, or 11 inches.

In many instances, however, you will want to use a different page length for an entire document or even different page lengths for certain pages in a document. For instance, a 60-line page length setting may be appropriate for all pages except one, which should use a 35-line setting. For this reason, Quattro Pro recognizes both soft and hard page breaks.

Soft Page Breaks

A *soft page break* is created by the /Print, Layout, Margins, Page Length setting. This setting determines where Quattro Pro breaks a block of data into pages. So for a large print block, Quattro Pro prints on the first page the number of lines specified by the Page Length setting (66 by default), breaks the page, resets its internal line counter to 1, updates its page counter to 2, prints the number of lines specified by the Page Length setting on the second page, and so on. (For further details, see "How Quattro Pro Divides a Print Block into Pages.")

To change the page length setting, select /Print, Layout, Margins, Page Length, and specify a setting between 0 and 100 (lines).

Although Quattro Pro accepts any page length setting between 1 and 100 lines, you must specify a minimum page length equal to 1 line of data plus top and bottom margins plus 6 lines (the header and footer allocation). If the top and bottom margins are both set to 2 lines, for example, the minimum page length setting is 11 lines. If you specify too small a number, when you try to print, Quattro Pro displays the error message "No room for text. Please change margins."

The /Print, Layout, Margins, Page Length setting works in tandem with the /Print, Layout, Break Pages setting. When you use /Print, Layout, Break Pages, Yes (the default), Quattro Pro creates soft page breaks using the page length setting specified.

These factors affect the page length setting:

- The information you want to print on each page
- The paper size

Note. The /Print, Layout, Margins, Page Length setting also controls Quattro Pro's internal line/page counter and the /Print, Adjust Printer, Align command. See "Controlling the Paper in the Printer" earlier for details.

- The printer you use

- The font(s) specified in the print block

For instance, the paper size you use directly impacts the correct page length setting. You may need to print on a form smaller than the standard page size. Or you may want to print on legal-size 8½-by-14-inch paper. You may even want to print sideways on standard or legal-size paper, so that the page length is 8½ inches.

CAUTION! *Some printers have a switch that controls the page length. Unless you adjust this switch to correspond to Quattro Pro's Page Length setting, you may get page breaks in unexpected places.*

For example, to print the document in Figure 6.14 using an HP LaserJet III printer, the /Print, Layout, Margins, Page Length setting is maintained at 11 inches. (Notice in Table 6.3 that Dimensions is set to Inches.) Quattro Pro then creates soft page breaks every 11 inches unless it encounters a hard page break. A page length setting in inches was used because the character/-line unit of measurement is confusing when you print Quattro Pro fonts.

Effect of Fonts on the Page Length Setting

Remember, the default page length of 66 accommodates a 12-point, 6-lines-per-inch resident printer font, which translates into 11 inches. When you print in graphics mode, however, this page length setting remains at 66 regardless of the point size of Font 1 or of other fonts in the print block.

Therefore, the page length setting *in number of lines* always represents a 12-point, 6-lines-per-inch font, regardless of the fonts being printed. If you change the page length to 44, it represents the amount of space taken up by 44 lines of that same font.

To see this, let's examine Table 6.4. To derive the values in this table, the same data was printed using different point sizes. In all instances, the page length setting remained at the default, 66, and the default top and bottom margins remained at 2. In each case, Quattro Pro printed the number of lines that can fit in approximately 8.75 inches. Likewise, it maintained a consistent 1-inch blank space at the top of the page and a 1.25-inch space at the bottom of the page; this space includes Quattro Pro's allocation for headers and footers. (See "Changing Margins" and "Adding Headers and Footers" later for further discussion.) The conclusion you can draw is that Quattro Pro maintains the page length setting in inches, not in character-based lines.

As Table 6.4 shows, when you work with fonts, you are better off using /Print, Layout, Dimensions, Inches to convert the page length and other margin settings to inches. You can then specify a new Page Length setting in inches. Quattro Pro responds by printing as many lines as can fit in this chosen page length.

Table 6.4   **Approximate Printed Lines per Inch for Different Point Sizes***

Point Size	Printed Lines in 8.75"	Calculated Lines Per Inch
6 point	80	9.14
8 point	63	7.20
10 point	51	5.83
12 point	42	4.80
14 point	36	4.11
16 point	32	3.66
18 point	29	3.31
20 point	26	2.97
24 point	21	2.40
30 point	17	1.94
36 point	14	1.60
48 point	11	1.26
72 point	6	0.69

* For Bitstream Swiss-SL printed on an HP LaserJet III, 300-by-300 dpi resolution.

Effect of Fonts on the Number of Printed Lines per Page

In a printed document, the number of lines per page will vary depending on the size of the font. You can see this in Table 6.4. For instance, when a 10-point Swiss-SC font is specified, Quattro Pro prints 51 lines of spreadsheet data on each page. For a 16-point Swiss-SC font, only 32 lines per page are printed. In both cases, the 51 lines of 10-point data and the 32 lines of 14-point data take up approximately 8.75 inches.

You can use Table 6.4 to estimate the number of lines of spreadsheet data that will be printed on a given page. For instance, when you print sideways (landscape orientation) on an 8 ½-by-11-inch page using Swiss-SC 10 point, approximately 36 lines will fit on each page. To arrive at this value, take the page length (8.5), subtract the space at the top and bottom (2.25), and multiply the result by the number of lines per inch from Table 6.4 (5.83).

Note. Because of the variations in lines per inch between typefaces and point sizes, be sure to use Screen Preview to preview a document before you print.

Be aware that the values in Table 6.4 are only approximate values, so they may vary depending on the typeface you use and the printer resolution. For example, if you specify a 150-by-150-dpi resolution for an HP LaserJet printer, fewer lines per inch will be printed than if you specify a 300-by-300-dpi resolution.

Hard Page Breaks

Tip. When you don't want to insert an unneeded row in an adjacent print block, or into a macro (see Chapter 12), insert a hard page break manually.

You can use hard page breaks to override the current soft page break (the Page Length setting). A *hard page break* separates the information above it into one page, and that below it into another page. When Quattro Pro encounters a hard page break in a print block, it immediately ends that page, moves the print head to the top of the next page, and resets its internal line and page counters.

Quattro Pro does not print any information that resides in the same row as a hard page break. Therefore, Quattro Pro allows you to create a hard page break in two ways to cover different situations. You can

- Manually enter a hard page break symbol, |::, in a spreadsheet, without inserting a blank line.

- Use the /Style, Insert Break command to insert a blank line containing a hard page break.

In either case, Quattro Pro does not include this symbol and the row in which it resides in the printed document.

For instance, to create the document in Figure 6.14, a hard page break is needed in row 46. Since this row is already blank (see Figure 6.9), a hard page break symbol, |:: (a split vertical bar followed by two colons), is entered manually in cell D46.

Quattro Pro applies this hard page break for the entire print block. Thus, both page 1 and page 3 end at row 46 in Figure 6.14 so that the March and April information is printed on separate pages. In addition, row 46 is not printed.

If you specify two separate print blocks, Quattro Pro will only evaluate the hard page break for the block in which it is located. Imagine, for example, that you specify the settings in Table 6.3 (except the /Print, Block). These settings include a manual hard page break in cell D46. If you print the block D4..H80 (the March and April checking data), the hard page break in row 46 will be used. However, if you print the block I4..P80 (the March and April budget data), only the soft page break specified by the /Print, Layout, Margins, Page Length setting will be used.

CAUTION! *Remember to place a hard page break in a leftmost cell in a print block, not in the leftmost cell in the spreadsheet. For instance, if you place the hard page break in cell A46 of Figure 6.9 and use the settings in Table 6.3,*

Quattro Pro will treat this page break symbol as a label, since it is located in the Left Heading block, not in the print block.

If you want to use the /Style, Insert Break command in Figure 6.9,

1. Position the cell selector in cell D46, the leftmost cell directly below the block containing the March information.

2. Select /Style, Insert Break.

As shown in Figure 6.17, Quattro Pro automatically inserts a row above this line and inserts a hard page break in cell D46. The old row 46 becomes row 47. Quattro Pro also adjusts the /Print, Block to D4..P81 to include this new line.

Figure 6.17

Using /Style, Insert Break to insert a hard page break in a print block

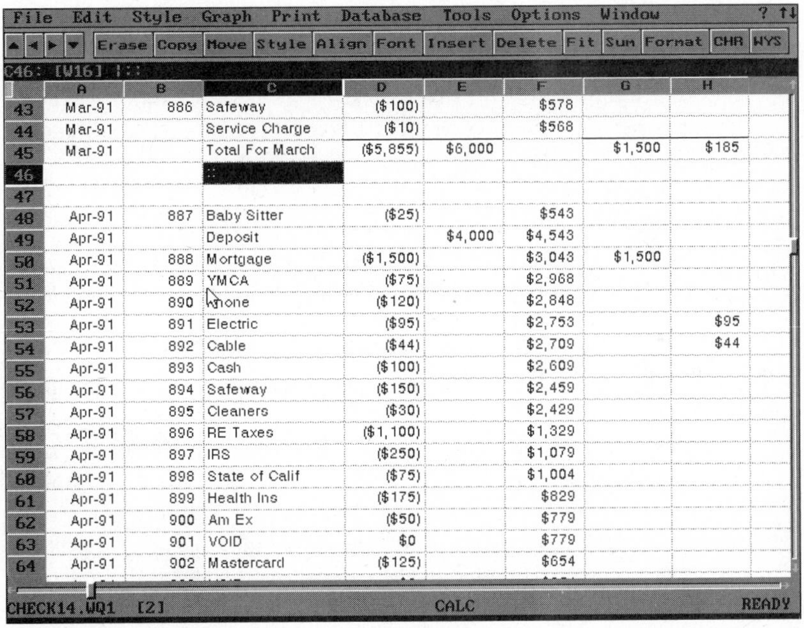

	A	B	C	D	E	F	G	H
43	Mar-91	886	Safeway	($100)		$578		
44	Mar-91		Service Charge	($10)		$568		
45	Mar-91		Total For March	($5,855)	$6,000		$1,500	$185
46			::					
47								
48	Apr-91	887	Baby Sitter	($25)		$543		
49	Apr-91		Deposit		$4,000	$4,543		
50	Apr-91	888	Mortgage	($1,500)		$3,043	$1,500	
51	Apr-91	889	YMCA	($75)		$2,968		
52	Apr-91	890	Phone	($120)		$2,848		
53	Apr-91	891	Electric	($95)		$2,753		$95
54	Apr-91	892	Cable	($44)		$2,709		$44
55	Apr-91	893	Cash	($100)		$2,609		
56	Apr-91	894	Safeway	($150)		$2,459		
57	Apr-91	895	Cleaners	($30)		$2,429		
58	Apr-91	896	RE Taxes	($1,100)		$1,329		
59	Apr-91	897	IRS	($250)		$1,079		
60	Apr-91	898	State of Calif	($75)		$1,004		
61	Apr-91	899	Health Ins	($175)		$829		
62	Apr-91	900	Am Ex	($50)		$779		
63	Apr-91	901	VOID	$0		$779		
64	Apr-91	902	Mastercard	($125)		$654		

File Edit Style Graph Print Database Tools Options Window ? ↑↓
Erase Copy Move Style Align Font Insert Delete Fit Sum Format CHR WYS
C46: [W16] : : :

CHECK14.WQ1 [2]   CALC   READY

TIP. *To delete both the blank row and the hard page break included in a print block, use /Edit, Delete Rows. To delete only the hard page break and not the row it resides in, move the cell selector to the cell containing the hard page break and press Del.*

No Page Breaks

Note. You cannot specify No as the Break Pages default.

In some instances you will not want page breaks to occur in a document, such as when you print continuous-feed mailing labels, or when you print to a file and will use that file with another software package. (See "Printing to a File" later.) In these instances, you should specify /Print, Layout, Break Pages, No. Quattro Pro then ignores the Page Length setting and does not create soft page breaks. If your laser printer cannot print on the half-inch edge of the paper, you still will get half-inch blank spaces at the top and bottom of each page.

The /Print, Layout, Break Pages command also controls headers, footers, and headings in a document. (Headers and footers are discussed later in this chapter.) If you select the No option, Quattro Pro does not include any headers or footers. However, it does print a Top Heading once at the top of the block.

Changing Margins

Tip. Use /Print, Layout, Update to save Margins settings as the default.

By default, Quattro Pro uses the settings shown in Figure 6.7, which create approximately 0.4 inch left and right margins, and 0.33 inch top and bottom margins. These settings assume that you are printing in draft mode using a portrait (vertical) orientation on an 8½-by-11-inch page and a 12-point fixed-width font one-tenth of an inch wide (10 cpi) and one-sixth inch high. You can see this default page-layout scheme in Figure 6.8.

You will want to change these margin settings when you use a different font or page size, or when you want to fit more or less information on a printed page. For instance, when you print sideways on 8½-by-11-inch paper using a printer-specific compressed font (16.67 cpi), a right margin of 176 works well.

For example, to change the left margin to 5 characters, select /Print, Layout, Margins, Left. Because Dimensions is set to the default, Lines/Characters, simply type **5** and press Enter. You can now change other margin settings, or press Quit twice to return to the /Print menu. The margin range that Quattro Pro accepts for each of the Dimensions settings is displayed in Table 6.5.

Table 6.5   Acceptable /Print, Layout, Margins Settings

Selection	Default Character	Allowed Range (Characters)	Allowed Range (Inches)	Allowed Range (Centimeters)
Page Length	66	1–100	0–24	0–60
Left	76	0–254	0–24	0–60

Table 6.5   (Continued)

Selection	Default Character	Allowed Range (Characters)	Allowed Range (Inches)	Allowed Range (Centimeters)
Top	2	0–32	0–24	0–60
Right	4	0–511	0–24	0–60
Bottom	2	0–32	0–24	0–60

The /Print command accepts unrealistic character-based and inches margin settings. However, Quattro Pro warns you if these settings do not allow text to be printed. For instance, suppose by mistake you specify a left margin larger than the right margin setting. Or suppose the top and bottom margin settings plus seven lines (one for data, six for header and footer) exceed the page length setting. When you try to print, Quattro Pro will display the error message "No room for text. Please change margins."

Quattro Pro does not warn you if you specify margins that are too large for a printed page. Imagine, for instance, that you specify a character-based right margin of 120 when you are printing vertically on an 8½-by-11-inch page. Or suppose you specify a right margin of 10.5 inches. (The correct right margin is 76 or 7.6 inches for most 12-point, 10-cpi fonts.) Quattro Pro will print the document accordingly; however, only those characters that can fit on this page are printed, and no right margin is displayed. Furthermore, the unprinted information is not printed on an additional page since Quattro Pro thinks that it has printed the entire block. Luckily, Quattro Pro's Screen Preview feature is especially helpful in determining and checking margin settings before you print.

TIP. *If you do not use headers and footers in a document, you can increase the number of lines of spreadsheet data printed on a page and still retain top and bottom margins. When a header and a footer are not specified and you print in draft mode, approximately 1 inch of blank space occurs at the top of a page, and 1.25 inches at the bottom. If you set both the top and bottom margins to 0, each printed page still includes 3-line top and bottom margins, which Quattro Pro reserves for headers and footers. If you print in draft mode, this creates approximately half-inch margins. Furthermore, you can now add four lines of data to a printed page when using a 12-point, 6-lines-per-inch font. If you print in graphics mode, the top and bottom margins will be equal to three times the height of Font 1.*

Effect of Fixed-Width Fonts on Margin Settings

If your printer has a fixed-pitch font and you print in draft mode, you can use the font's *cpi* (characters per inch) value to determine the correct margin settings. To do so, you multiply the desired margin in inches by the font's cpi value to obtain the margin in characters. Suppose, for example, the resident printer font is 12 point, 10 cpi. Then to calculate a 0.5-inch left margin setting you multiply 10 (the cpi value) by 0.5 (the margin in inches), resulting in a 5-character left margin setting. Conversely, a 4-character margin setting results in a 0.4-inch margin ($^4/_{10}$).

Effect of Proportionally Spaced Fonts on Margin Settings

Note. See "Effect of Fonts on the Page Length Setting" earlier for a discussion of the amount of spreadsheet data printed on each page.

Calculating correct margin settings for a font can get tricky when you use Quattro Pro's proportionally spaced fonts. To see this, imagine that you print a block using Quattro Pro's default /Print settings, which include a left margin of 4 characters and top and bottom margins of 2. You get the following results for Swiss-SL font:

On Printed Page

Point Size	Left Margin	Top Margin	Bottom Margin
8 point	10/16 inch	10/16 inch	11/16 inch
12 point	11/16 inch	9/16 inch	10/16 inch
16 point	11/16 inch	10/16 inch	9/16 inch

Now compare these actual printed margins to those you would get if you printed in draft mode with the default 12-point, 10-cpi, 6-lines-per-inch resident printer font. A right margin of 4 is equal to $^4/_{10}$ or 0.4 inch. A top margin of 2 lines is equal to $^2/_6$ or 0.33 inch; likewise, the bottom margin is 0.33 inch. Thus, when you print fonts in graphics mode, character-based margin settings are generally not reliable.

Even if you do use /Print, Layout, Dimensions, Inches to convert these default margin settings to inches, Quattro Pro still leaves the same space shown in this table at the left, top, and bottom of each printed page. Nevertheless, it is still worthwhile using a Dimensions, Inches setting because you are working with an understandable unit of measurement. So the general rule when printing Quattro Pro fonts is to use /Print, Layout, Dimensions, Inches to specify margins in inches rather than in characters.

Furthermore, when you print a large font, Quattro Pro may not be able to print the amount of characters on a page specified by the right margin setting. Likewise, if you specify a small font, a character-based right margin setting may limit the number of characters you can actually print on a page. For this reason alone, it is best to use a Dimensions, Inches setting.

Adding Headers and Footers

A *header* is a single line of text, up to 251 characters, that Quattro Pro prints at the top of every page in a print block. Likewise, a *footer* is a single line of text, up to 251 characters, that is printed at the bottom of every page. In Quattro Pro, you can use headers and footers to

- Include descriptive titles or information

- Date printed material

- Number pages

On every printed page, Quattro Pro always reserves three lines for a header—two blank and one for the header itself—even if you do not specify one. If you do print a header, Quattro Pro prints the header line first, and then two blank lines. Likewise, Quattro Pro also reserves three lines for a footer; however, it prints the two blank lines first, and then the footer line. The blank lines serve to separate the header and/or footer from the body of your document. You can see this default page layout in Figure 6.8.

The number of characters Quattro Pro actually prints in a particular header or footer is determined by the left and right margin settings, as well as

- In draft mode, the typeface and point size of the resident printer font.

- In graphics mode, the typeface and point size of Font 1. (Headers and footers are always printed using Font 1.)

Note. You cannot enter a header or footer as a formula (e.g., +C3) that references spreadsheet data.

The first header or footer character is offset from the left edge of the page by the left margin setting. Furthermore, Quattro Pro only prints the portion of a header or footer that can fit between the right and left margin settings; it does not wrap a header or footer.

For example, suppose you want to add the header *Checking Reconciliation* to each printed page in Figure 6.10. Select /Print, Layout, Header text, type **Checking Reconciliation**, and press Enter.

Now when you print, Quattro Pro includes the header at the top of each printed page, as shown in Figure 6.18. As you can see, this header is aligned with the left margin.

CAUTION! *When you print in draft mode, you must select /Print, Adjust Printer, Form Feed after Quattro Pro is finished printing. Otherwise, a footer is not included on the last printed page.*

Figure 6.18

A left-aligned header in Screen Preview

Help	Quit	Color	Previous	Next	Ruler	Guide	Unzoom[-]	Zoom[+]

Checking Reconciliation

Date	Check	Paid To	Amount	Deposit	Balance	Mortgage	House Utilities
		Balance			$423		
		Deposit		$4,000	$4,423		
Mar-91	850	Mortgage	($1,500)		$2,923	$1,500	
Mar-91	851	Cash	($100)		$2,823		
Mar-91	852	Shell	($75)		$2,748		
Mar-91	853	Electric	($120)		$2,628		$120
Mar-91	854	Sewer/Water	($65)		$2,563		$65
Mar-91	855	Baby Sitter	($50)		$2,513		
Mar-91	856	Safeway	($175)		$2,338		
Mar-91	857	Phone	($85)		$2,253		
Mar-91	858	Health Ins	($175)		$2,078		
Mar-91	859	Cash	($50)		$2,028		
Mar-91	860	Firestone	($200)		$1,828		
Mar-91	861	Cleaners	($20)		$1,808		
Mar-91	862	Am Ex	($150)		$1,658		
Mar-91	863	Nob Hill	($40)		$1,618		
Mar-91	864	Car Ins	($450)		$1,168		
Mar-91		Deposit		$2,000	$3,168		

200%   Change position on page using arrow keys.   Page 1

To clear a header, select /Print, Layout, Header, press Esc, and then press Enter. You can also use /Print, Layout, Reset, All (the only Reset command that affects headers and footers) to clear both the header and footer settings.

Changing the Alignment of Headers and Footers

Quattro Pro automatically left-aligns headers and footers with the left margin. However, you can change this alignment by including the split vertical-bar character (|) in a header or footer.

For example, you can enter **Checking Reconciliation** in the /Print, Layout, Header command in the following ways and achieve vastly different results:

Tip. You can further indent a header or footer by including blank spaces. For instance, if you begin a header with three blank spaces, such as _ _ _Checking Reconciliation, then the header is offset from the left margin by three spaces.

Header Entry	**Printed Header**
Checking Reconciliation	Left-aligned with left margin setting
|Checking Reconciliation	Centered between left and right margin settings
||Checking Reconciliation	Right-aligned with right margin setting

You can also use split vertical bars within a header or footer to align certain portions of the text. For example, to create the header in Figure 6.14, use the Header setting

Checking Reconciliation|March/April 1991|Budget Analysis

As you can see, Quattro Pro prints this header by left-aligning Checking Reconciliation, centering March/April 1991, and right-aligning Budget Analysis.

Dating Printouts

When you print multiple versions of a spreadsheet, many times you want to know which is the latest version. One way to automatically keep track of the latest version is to put the date in a header or footer.

In Quattro Pro, you can include the special symbol @ in a header or footer. When you print, Quattro Pro then substitutes the current date for this symbol. This date is always printed using the DD-MMM-YY format, regardless of the date format currently specified in the spreadsheet.

For instance, suppose you use /Print, Layout, Footer and enter ‖@. When you print, Quattro Pro will print a right-aligned footer on each page showing today's date, such as 19-Feb-93.

Numbering Pages

Quattro Pro automatically numbers the printed pages in a document when you include the special symbol # in a header or footer. When you print, the appropriate page number is substituted for this symbol.

For example, to create the footer in Figure 6.14, use /Print, Layout, Footer and specify **@‖Page #**. When you print the block D4..P80, Quattro Pro left-aligns the current date at the bottom of each printed page. However, Quattro Pro centers the footer portion *Page 1* on the first page, *Page 2* on the second page, and so on.

When you include page numbers in a header or footer, Quattro Pro assigns the numbers by the order in which it prints pages. Quattro Pro's page ordering system, however, may not always create the page order you desire. In Figure 6.14, the March data is printed on the first and third printed pages, page 1 containing the checking data (D4..H45), and page 3 containing the budget data (I4..P45). (Since cell D46 contains a hard page break, row 46 is not printed.) Likewise, Quattro Pro prints the April information on pages 2 and 4. (See "How Quattro Pro Divides a Print Block into Pages" earlier.)

For better presentation, however, you may want the March information printed on pages 1 and 2, and the April information on pages 3 and 4. To overcome this problem,

1. Print the March data by specifying the block **D4..P46**.

2. Print the April data by specifying the block **D47..P80**, but do not use Adjust Printer, Align before you select Spreadsheet Print (otherwise, Quattro Pro resets its internal page counter).

Quattro Pro will print the March checking data on page 1, the March budget data on page 2, the April checking data on page 3, and the April budget data on page 4.

Quattro Pro's page numbering method is also the cause of many incorrectly numbered printouts. Notice when you print the second block, D47..P80, Quattro Pro assigns sequential page numbers 3 and 4. It does not reset the page numbers. Likewise, if you print block D4..P46 again without first selecting Adjust Printer, Align, then Quattro Pro will assign page numbers 5 and 6 to these pages. Whenever you print blocks sequentially Quattro Pro does not automatically reset its internal page counter. To reset the page numbers, you must select the /Print, Adjust Printer, Align command before you print each block. This internal page counter is also reset when you close the file or quit Quattro Pro.

NOTE. *Quattro Pro does not reset its internal page counter when you quit the /Print command and return to the spreadsheet.*

Effect of Fonts on Headers and Footers

When you print in draft mode, headers and footers, like the rest of the document, are printed using the resident printer font. When you print in graphics mode, however, headers and footers are always printed using Font 1. For instance, the headers and footers in Figure 6.14 use the Sans Serif 8 point assigned to Font 1.

Obviously, you can print headers and footers in one font and spreadsheet data in another font. (Take a peek at Figure 6.22.) For example, you can

Note. To change the fonts in your font library, and to assign fonts to data in a spreadsheet, see Chapter 3.

- Assign the font you want for headers and footers to Font 1.

- Assign another font to the spreadsheet data.

Font 1 also controls (look at Figure 6.8) the height of the top and bottom margin lines as well as the height of the two blank header lines and the two blank footer lines. So the larger the point size of Font 1, the larger the blank space at the top and bottom of each page. Therefore, keep the point size of Font 1 and the font assigned to spreadsheet data relatively close. Or better yet, use a Dimensions, Inches setting and specify margins in inches. So the moral, once again, is to use a Dimensions, Inches setting when you print Quattro Pro fonts.

Hiding Information During Printing

You can easily *hide* portions of a print block from being printed. This is an efficient method of creating a presentation-quality document without affecting the placement of spreadsheet data. You can hide columns and/or rows from view, or you can hide only the information itself.

For example, when a spreadsheet appears cluttered with too much information, you can hide information from being printed without hiding the cell in which it resides. Use the /Style, Numeric Format, Hidden command (see Chapter 3), and any cells you specify now appear blank.

Hiding Columns

You can use Quattro Pro's /Style, Hide Column, Hide command to hide columns from view. Quattro Pro then moves together the remaining displayed columns to create an uninterrupted spreadsheet (see Chapter 3).

For example, suppose in Figure 6.9 you only want to print the budget data related to house expenses—columns G, H, L, and N—and the explanatory information in columns A, B, and C. You can use the settings in Table 6.3, with the following addition. Use /Style, Hide Column, Hide to hide columns D through F, I through K, M, and O through P. (You'll have to use this command four times to hide nonadjacent columns.) When you print, you will end up with a two-page document showing only the nonhidden columns A through C, G, H, L, and N. You can see a portion of page 1 in Figure 6.19.

To redisplay hidden information, use /Style, Hide Column, Expose.

Figure 6.19

Keeping some columns from being printed

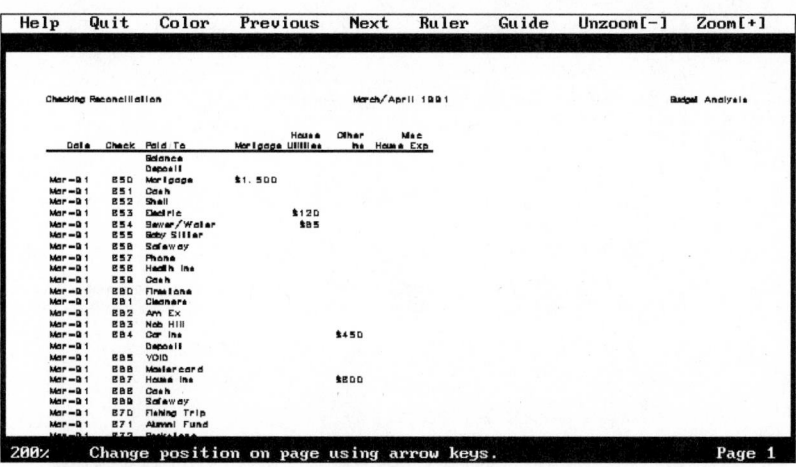

Hiding Rows

You can also hide rows from being printed. For instance, suppose in Figure 6.19 you want to exclude rows 4 and 5 (balance and deposit data) from being printed. To do so,

Tip. Assigning a row height of 1 also hides a row.

1. Because column D, the first column in the print block, is hidden, first use /Style, Hide Column, Expose to redisplay column D.

2. Enter ⁞⁞ (two split vertical-bar characters) in cell D4, the leftmost cell in row 4 in the print block. This cell must contain only these characters, nothing else. Likewise, enter ⁞⁞ in cell D5.

3. Use /Style, Hide Column, Hide to rehide column D.

Now when you print, rows 4 and 5 are not printed. Instead, row 6 is printed immediately after row 3, as if these two rows were adjacent in the spreadsheet. You can see this in Figure 6.20.

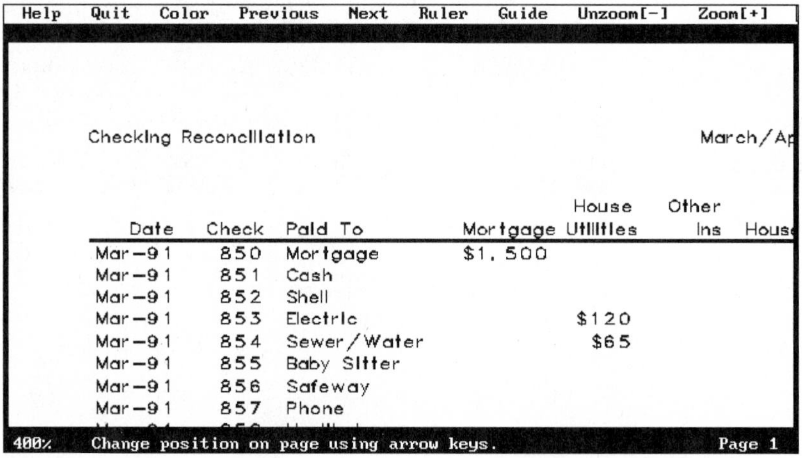

Figure 6.20
Keeping some rows from being printed

Help	Quit	Color	Previous	Next	Ruler	Guide	Unzoom[-]	Zoom[+]

Checking Reconciliation   March/Ap

	Date	Check	Paid To	Mortgage	House Utilities	Other Ins	House
	Mar-91	850	Mortgage	$1,500			
	Mar-91	851	Cash				
	Mar-91	852	Shell				
	Mar-91	853	Electric		$120		
	Mar-91	854	Sewer/Water		$65		
	Mar-91	855	Baby Sitter				
	Mar-91	856	Safeway				
	Mar-91	857	Phone				

400%   Change position on page using arrow keys.   Page 1

Using Setup Strings

A *setup string* is a character sequence, specific to a printer, that activates or deactivates special print features. In the past, setup strings were used with Quattro to print different fonts and type styles, compressed or expanded pitch, or sideways (landscape) orientation.

Quattro Pro, however, makes setup strings obsolete in many cases. Using the /Style, Font command to access Quattro Pro's font capabilities is a much better method of assigning fonts (see Chapter 3). Likewise, you can use the /Print command to print sideways (see "Printing Sideways" ahead) and to specify the number of printed copies.

A setup string still has a limited role in printing. For instance, you can use a setup string to

- Specify the paper tray used

- Change the number of printed lines per inch for a printer-specific font

- Control different settings, such as sideways (landscape) printing, for a portion of a print block

Be aware, however, that Quattro Pro lets you send setup strings to the printer when you print in draft mode (/Print, Destination, Printer). If you try to send a setup string to a graphics printer (/Print, Destination, Graphics Printer), in some cases Quattro Pro will simply ignore it. In other cases, the printer may hang.

Creating a Setup String

Each type of printer uses its own control codes to represent different print features or *attributes*. You can find these control codes in your printer manual. The control code sequence that tells an Epson printer to print eight lines per inch, for instance, is [Esc]0. To convey this information in Quattro Pro, you must convert this control sequence to a setup string using ASCII codes. (Most printer manuals include an ASCII conversion table in an appendix.)

A setup string begins with a *delimiter* (backslash), followed by a three-digit ASCII code in decimal notation. Each delimiter and ASCII code represents a portion of a control sequence. For instance, the control sequence [Esc]0 is represented by the setup string \027\048. (Esc is converted to the ASCII decimal equivalent \027, and 0 is converted to \048.) Notice that no blank spaces are included in a setup string because the remaining portion after a blank space is not evaluated.

However, when a portion of a control sequence is a number, letter, or other character on the keyboard (ASCII equivalents between 032 and 127), you can use the character instead of the ASCII code. For example, since the number 0 is represented by the ASCII code 048, you can use \0270 in place of \027\048. In addition, when you use an ASCII code to represent a letter, number, or other keyboard character, you must precede it with a backslash (\). When you use the character itself, however, the backslash is not necessary.

CAUTION! *Be very careful that you use the exact control code shown in your printer manual. For instance, the number 0 is equivalent to ASCII code 048, uppercase O is ASCII code 079, while lowercase o is ASCII code 111. Each code represents a different control sequence in a setup string.*

You can also specify multiple print attributes in one setup string. For example, the setup string \027\038\108\056\068 tells an HP LaserJet printer to print eight lines per inch, while the setup string \027\038\108\051\072 tells it to print on manually fed envelopes. You can collapse and combine these setup strings into

```
\027\038\108\056\068\038\108\051\072
```

Within a single control sequence, the order of the characters is important. When you combine multiple sequences, however, you may be able to change their order. See your printer manual.

Since & (038), lowercase l (108), 8 (056), uppercase D (068), 3 (051), and uppercase H (072) are represented by ASCII codes between 032 and 127, you can use the alphanumeric representations if you wish. Thus, this setup string could also be represented as \027&l8D&l3H. You will want to use alphanumeric characters whenever possible, since a setup string is limited to 39 characters in the /Print command.

TIP. *The uppercase letters A through Z are represented by the ASCII codes 065 through 090. Moreover, Ctrl-A is equivalent to ASCII code 001, Ctrl-B to 002, and so on. Therefore, if a print attribute is represented by Ctrl with an uppercase letter, subtract 64 from the ASCII code number for the uppercase letter to derive the proper code number.*

Once you create a setup string, you can specify it for an entire print block, or you can embed it in a spreadsheet so that it affects only a portion of the print block. The upcoming sections explain these techniques.

Specifying a Setup String for a Print Block

You can use the /Print, Layout, Setup String command to specify a setup string of up to 39 characters. Quattro Pro then sends this setup string to the printer each time you print a block in the spreadsheet in draft mode. For example, suppose you want to print eight lines per inch using an HP LaserJet printer. Select /Print, Layout, Setup String, and in response to "Specify printer code to be sent to the printer:", type **\027E\027&l8D** and press Enter.

Quattro Pro saves the /Print, Layout, Setup String setting when you save the current file. You can also use /Print, Layout, Update to specify this setup string as the default for all future Quattro Pro sessions.

Deleting and Turning Off a Setup String

You can delete a setup string using either of the following methods:

- Select /Print, Layout, Setup String, press Esc, and press Enter. Quattro Pro clears the setup string setting.

■ Select /Print, Layout, Reset, Layout. Quattro Pro returns the setup string setting to the current default, along with other Layout settings. (There is no default setup string unless you have previously used /Print, Layout, Update to specify one.)

Once you have used a setup string to "turn on" a print attribute, the printer uses this attribute until you turn the printer off or you send a new setup string that reverses the effect of the previous string. Thus, if you delete a setup string, be sure to turn the printer off and then on again to clear the old control sequences the printer is using. Or send the printer its "reset" setup string.

A "reset" or "initialize printer" setup string resets a printer to its default settings. For instance, the setup string \027E resets HP LaserJet printers. Your printer manual should include a reset control sequence.

Creating Embedded Setup Strings

Note. Embedded setup strings do not work when you print in graphics mode.

When you print in draft mode, you can use an *embedded setup string*, inserted in a row in the spreadsheet, to specify print attributes for only a portion of a print block. When the printer encounters an embedded setup string, it uses those print attributes until you specify otherwise. To cancel an embedded setup string, you must include a second embedded setup string. This string might specify new print attributes or cancel all existing attributes.

You *must* enter an embedded setup string in the leftmost column of a print block; otherwise, it is not recognized by the printer. Furthermore, a setup string should be entered in a blank row, since information in this row is not printed. Since an embedded setup string is entered in a cell, it can be up to 254 characters long, the maximum length of a cell entry in Quattro Pro.

For instance, suppose you are using an HP LaserJet III printer to print the data in Figure 6.21 in a vertical (portrait) orientation. Since you will be printing in draft mode, the LaserJet font 12 point Courier Roman8 has been assigned to Font 1. This font setting allows you to view in WYSIWYG mode the HP LaserJet printer-specific font that will appear when you print the document in draft mode.

You decide to print the block A1..H10 sideways. Although you could specify two separate print blocks and orientation settings, you decide to use embedded setup strings and still specify one print block. Here's how to do this:

1. Enter an embedded setup string in an empty row above the block A2..H10. Since row 1 is blank, move the cell selector to cell A1, the leftmost cell directly above this block. (If this row is not blank, use /Edit, Insert Rows to insert a blank row first.) Enter ||\027&11O (two split vertical-bar characters followed by a setup string specifying landscape orientation).

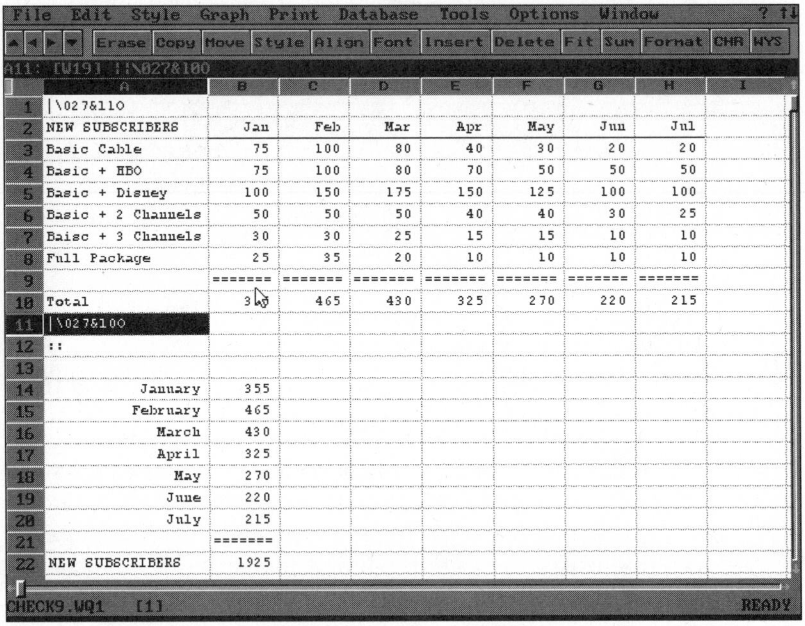

Figure 6.21

Adding embedded strings to spreadsheet data

File	Edit	Style	Graph	Print	Database	Tools	Options	Window	? ↑↓

| ▲ ◄ ► ▼ | Erase | Copy | Move | Style | Align | Font | Insert | Delete | Fit | Sum | Format | CHR | WYS |

A11: [U19] |:\027&10O

	A	B	C	D	E	F	G	H	I
1	|:\027&11O								
2	NEW SUBSCRIBERS	Jan	Feb	Mar	Apr	May	Jun	Jul	
3	Basic Cable	75	100	80	40	30	20	20	
4	Basic + HBO	75	100	80	70	50	50	50	
5	Basic + Disney	100	150	175	150	125	100	100	
6	Basic + 2 Channels	50	50	50	40	40	30	25	
7	Baisc + 3 Channels	30	30	25	15	15	10	10	
8	Full Package	25	35	20	10	10	10	10	
9		=======	=======	=======	=======	=======	=======	=======	
10	Total	3▵	465	430	325	270	220	215	
11	|:\027&10O								
12	::								
13									
14	January	355							
15	February	465							
16	March	430							
17	April	325							
18	May	270							
19	June	220							
20	July	215							
21		=======							
22	NEW SUBSCRIBERS	1925							

CHECK9.WQ1 [1]   READY

2. Turn off this setup string for the rest of the spreadsheet by entering another embedded setup string in an empty row directly below this block. Since row 11 is blank, move the cell selector to cell A11, the leftmost cell directly below this block. Enter |:\027&10O (two split vertical-bar characters followed by a setup string specifying portrait orientation).

3. Enter a hard page break to end this page and begin a new page. Since row 12 is blank, move the cell selector to the leftmost cell in this row, cell A12. Then type |:: (one split vertical-bar character followed by two colons), and press Enter. (If this row is not blank, use /Style, Insert Break to simultaneously insert a blank row and a hard page break in that row.)

You can see these setup strings and the hard page break in Figure 6.21. When you print the block A1..H22 in draft mode, Quattro Pro will print the portion A2..H10 sideways (landscape orientation) as the first page, and then the block A13..H22 as the second page using a vertical (portrait) orientation. Quattro Pro does not print rows 1, 11, and 12, which contain the embedded setup strings and hard page break. However, for the printer to recognize these printer instructions, these rows *must* be included in the print block.

Printing Sideways

Note. The /Print, Layout, Orientation setting is saved when you save a file.

By default, Quattro Pro prints a block in vertical or *portrait* orientation, such as the data from Figure 6.9 printed in Figure 6.10. Many times you will want to print spreadsheet data sideways on a page—that is, using a *landscape* orientation. The advantage to printing in landscape is that you can include more columns on each printed page than when you use a portrait (vertical) orientation.

You can use these different methods to print in landscape:

■ Use /Print, Layout, Orientation, Landscape and print in graphics mode. You can also use this method to print a printer-resident landscape font.

■ Use /Print, Layout, Orientation, Banner to print in graphics mode across continuous-feed paper (*banner printing*).

■ Use a setup string to print sideways in draft mode.

The upcoming sections describe each of these techniques.

Printing Sideways in Graphics Mode

Note. When you use Screen Preview to view a document printed in landscape, the page is displayed sideways.

If you specify /Print, Layout, Orientation, Landscape, then Quattro Pro only prints sideways in graphics mode. For example, using a LaserJet III printer you can print the information from Figure 6.9 sideways on an $8\frac{1}{2}$-by-11-inch page by using the settings in Table 6.6. The results can be seen in Figure 6.22.

By adjusting the font size down from 12 to 10 point, reducing the column widths to reflect this smaller font, and printing in landscape, you can fit all of the March data on one page and all of the April data on a second page.

TIP. *If you are printing sideways (landscape) and not all of the columns in the print block appear on the page, check the right margin setting. It may still be set for a portrait orientation.*

Whenever you print sideways, you should also adjust the right margin and the page length accordingly. These settings depend on the paper and fonts used. For instance, when you print sideways on $8\frac{1}{2}$-by-11-inch paper, the page width is now 11 inches while the length is 8.5 inches. Therefore, a right margin setting of 10.5 inches and a page length setting of 8.5 inches are appropriate.

Printing Sideways in Graphics Mode Using Printer-Specific Fonts

Tip. You can also use a landscape font included in a LaserJet Series II (or later) cartridge. See "Printing Fonts" earlier for details.

If you specified a PostScript or LaserJet Series II (or later) printer during installation, Quattro Pro includes printer-specific fonts in your font library. Some of these are landscape fonts. You can use the /Style, Font command to specify these printer fonts.

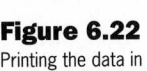

Figure 6.22

Printing the data in Figure 6.9 sideways (landscape)

Page 1

Checking Reconciliation — March/April 1991 — Budget Analysis

Date	Check	Paid To	Amount	Deposit	Balance	Mortgage	House Utilities	Phone	Food	Health Expense	Other Ins	Car Expense	Misc House Exp	Other	Misc
		Balance			$423										
		Deposit		$4,000	$4,423										
Mar-91	850	Mortgage	($1,500)		$2,923	$1,500									
Mar-91	851	Cash	($100)		$2,823										$100
Mar-91	852	Shell	($75)		$2,748							$75			
Mar-91	853	Electric	($120)		$2,628		$120								
Mar-91	854	Sewer/Water	($65)		$2,563		$65								
Mar-91	855	Baby Sitter	($50)		$2,513										$50
Mar-91	856	Safeway	($175)		$2,338				$175						
Mar-91	857	Phone	($85)		$2,253			$85							
Mar-91	858	Health Ins	($175)		$2,078					$175					
Mar-91	859	Cash	($50)		$2,028										$50
Mar-91	860	Firestone	($200)		$1,828							$200			
Mar-91	861	Cleaners	($20)		$1,808										$20
Mar-91	862	Am Ex	($150)		$1,658									$150	
Mar-91	863	Nob Hill	($40)		$1,618				$40						
Mar-91	864	Car Ins	($450)		$1,168						$450				
Mar-91		Deposit		$2,000	$3,168										
Mar-91	865	VOID	$0		$3,168										
Mar-91	866	Mastercard	($250)		$2,918									$250	
Mar-91	867	House Ins	($800)		$2,118						$800				
Mar-91	868	Cash	($100)		$2,018										$100
Mar-91	869	Safeway	($60)		$1,958				$60						
Mar-91	870	Fishing Trip	($150)		$1,808										$150
Mar-91	871	Alumni Fund	($50)		$1,758									$50	
Mar-91	872	Bookstore	($25)		$1,733										$25
Mar-91	873	Cleaners	($25)		$1,708										$25
Mar-91	874	Paint Store	($100)		$1,608								$100		
Mar-91	875	Cash	($200)		$1,408										$200
Mar-91	876	TWA	($150)		$1,258									$150	
Mar-91	877	Nob Hill	($75)		$1,183				$75						
Mar-91	878	Ace Hardware	($40)		$1,143								$40		
Mar-91	879	Rotor Rooter	($70)		$1,073								$70		
Mar-91	880	Magazine Subs	($35)		$1,038										$35
Mar-91	881	Cleaners	($15)		$1,023										$15
Mar-91	882	Lawn Service	($80)		$943								$80		
Mar-91	883	Dog Food	($40)		$903										$40
Mar-91	884	Dentist	($150)		$753					$150					
Mar-91	885	Cash	($75)		$678										$75
Mar-91	886	Safeway	($100)		$578				$100						
Mar-91		Service Charge	($10)		$568										$10
Mar-91		Total For March	($5,855)	$6,000		$1,500	$185	$85	$450	$325	$1,250	$275	$290	$600	$895

13-Apr-91

Page 2

Checking Reconciliation — March/April 1991 — Budget Analysis

Date	Check	Paid To	Amount	Deposit	Balance	Mortgage	House Utilities	Phone	Food	Health Expense	Other Ins	Car Expense	Misc House Exp	Other	Misc
Apr-91	887	Baby Sitter	($25)		$543										$25
Apr-91		Deposit		$4,000	$4,543										
Apr-91	888	Mortgage	($1,500)		$3,043	$1,500									
Apr-91	889	YMCA	($75)		$2,968										$75
Apr-91	890	Phone	($120)		$2,848			$120							
Apr-91	891	Electric	($95)		$2,753		$95								
Apr-91	892	Cable	($44)		$2,709		$44								
Apr-91	893	Cash	($100)		$2,609										$100
Apr-91	894	Safeway	($150)		$2,459				$150						
Apr-91	895	Cleaners	($30)		$2,429										$30
Apr-91	896	RE Taxes	($1,100)		$1,329								$1,100		
Apr-91	897	IRS	($250)		$1,079									$250	
Apr-91	898	State of Calif	($75)		$1,004									$75	
Apr-91	899	Health Ins	($175)		$829					$175					
Apr-91	900	Am Ex	($50)		$779									$50	
Apr-91	901	VOID	$0		$779										
Apr-91	902	Mastercard	($125)		$654									$125	
Apr-91	903	VOID	$0		$654										
Apr-91		Deposit		$1,500	$2,154										
Apr-91	904	Cash	($100)		$2,054										$100
Apr-91	905	To Savings	($1,000)		$1,054									$1,000	
Apr-91	906	Baby Sitter	($35)		$1,019										$35
Apr-91	907	Cleaners	($15)		$1,004										$15
Apr-91	908	Lawn Service	($80)		$924								$80		
Apr-91	909	Plumber	($200)		$724								$200		
Apr-91	910	Cash	($75)		$649										$75
Apr-91	911	Nob Hill	($125)		$524				$125						
Apr-91	912	Midas Muffler	($250)		$274							$250			
Apr-91	913	Cleaners	($20)		$254										$20
Apr-91		Deposit		$500	$754										
Apr-91	914	WS Journal	($120)		$634										$120
Apr-91	915	Local Paper	($22)		$612										$22
Apr-91		Service Charge	($10)		$602										$10
Apr-91		Total For April	($5,966)	$6,000		$1,500	$139	$120	$275	$175	$0	$250	$1,380	$1,500	$627

13-Apr-91

Table 6.6   /Print Settings Used for Figure 6.22

Command	Setting
/Print, Block	A4..P80
/Print, Headings, Top Heading	C1..C3
/Print, Layout, Margins	
Top	.33
Bottom	.33
Left	.50
Right	10.5
Page Length	8.5
/Print, Layout	
Dimensions	Inches
Orientation	Landscape
Header text	Checking Reconciliation¦March/April 1991¦ Budget Analysis
Footer text	@¦Page #
/Print, Destination	Graphics Printer
¦:: (Manual Hard Page Break)	D46
/Style, FontTable, Edit Fonts,	
1 Font 1	Swiss-SC 10 point Bold
2 Font 2	Swiss-SC 10 point
/Style, FontTable, 2 Font 2	D4..P80
/Options, Formats, Global Width	9
/Style, Column Width	
Column B	7
Column A	8
Column N	11
Column C	15

For example, if a LaserJet III printer is the default printer and you select /Style, FontTable, Edit Fonts, 1 Font 1, Typeface, Quattro Pro includes the printer-specific fonts in Figure 6.23. If you choose 12 point Courier Bld ECMA94, for instance, Quattro Pro then assigns this font to Font 1. In addition, Orientation must be set to Landscape. When you print in graphics mode to the HP LaserJet III printer, Quattro Pro will print in landscape orientation using this printer font.

Figure 6.23

Some of the HP LaserJet III landscape fonts attached to the font library

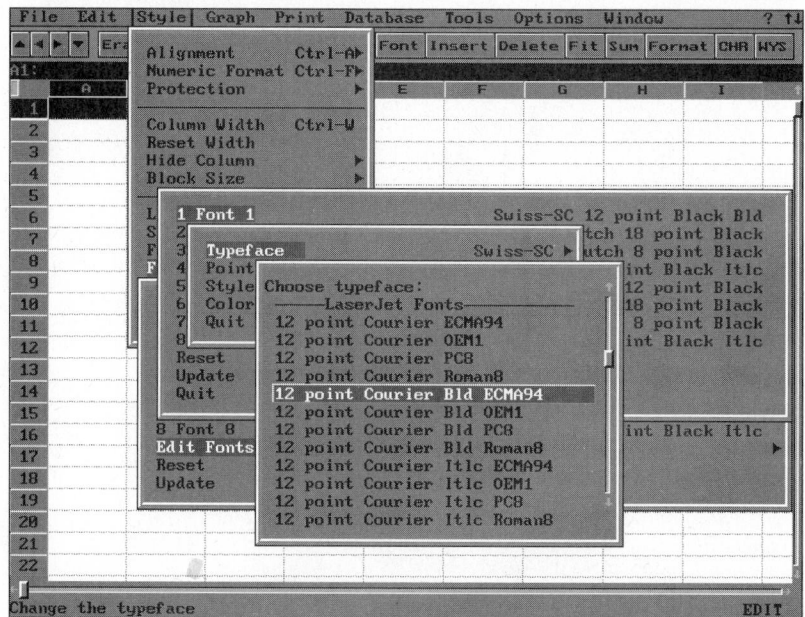

Banner Printing

Starting with version 3.0, Quattro Pro includes a new command, /Print, Layout, Orientation, Banner, which allows you to perform *banner printing*. In banner printing, the output is printed lengthwise across continuous-feed paper. Banner printing only works on dot-matrix printers with graphics capabilities; it does not work on laser or daisy-wheel printers. In addition, banner printing only works when you use Destination, Graphics Printer; otherwise, Quattro Pro ignores the Orientation, Banner setting.

CAUTION! *You cannot use Screen Preview to view a document with a banner orientation.*

For example, suppose you want to print the data in Figure 6.14 (from Figure 6.9) across continuous-feed paper. To do so, use the settings in Table 6.3, *except* use /Print, Layout, Orientation, Banner. In addition,

- The default printer, set with /Options, Hardware, Printers (see Chapter 15), must be a dot-matrix printer using continuous-feed paper.

- For the default printer, the Single Sheet setting must be No to indicate continuous-feed paper.

Note. When Quattro Pro prints using a banner orientation, it ignores the right margin setting.

Banner printing is *left-facing*—the printed data begins at the top-left corner of the page and continues across page perforations. So when you print this data, Quattro Pro prints it on four continuous-feed sheets. All of the March data is printed sideways across two continuous-feed pages. Remember, there is a hard page break in line 46. Likewise, the April data is printed across another two continuous-feed pages.

In addition, headers and footers are treated as if you were printing on one wide sheet. So on the first two-sheet page—the March data—the header *Checking Reconciliation|March/April 1991|Budget Analysis* is printed as follows:

Note. If you use headings when you print in a banner orientation, they only appear on the topmost and leftmost pages.

- *Checking Reconciliation* is aligned with the left margin on the first sheet.

- *March/April 1991* is centered near the page perforation.

- *Budget Analysis* is aligned with the right margin on the second sheet.

This header is also printed on the second two-sheet "page"—the April data. The footer @| Page # is printed twice in a similar manner.

Printing Sideways in Draft Mode Using a Setup String

Another way to print sideways using a resident printer font is to use the /Print, Layout, Setup String command. For instance, imagine you are using an HP LaserJet III printer and want to print a document using the LaserJet's default 12-point Courier font. Before you print,

1. Choose /Print, Layout, Setup String and enter **\027&l1O**. (To create setup strings, see "Using Setup Strings" earlier.)

2. Adjust the Layout, Margins settings to conform to a landscape orientation. In this instance, a 10.5-inch right margin and an 8.5-inch page length are appropriate.

3. Specify a draft mode destination. Otherwise, the Setup String setting is ignored.

Tip. To print only a portion of a print block sideways, use embedded setup strings (see "Using Setup String").

4. Turn the printer off and on again to clear the old control sequence the printer is using, or add the printer's reset control sequence to the beginning of the setup string.

You cannot preview this printed output, because Quattro Pro always prints to Screen Preview in graphics mode.

When you print, the HP LaserJet printer reads this setup string and prints sideways; the Layout, Orientation setting is irrelevant in draft mode. Furthermore, the block is printed using the LaserJet's default 12-point Courier font and 6 lines per vertical inch.

However, suppose you want to fit even more data on the page. If you use the setup string

```
\Ø27&11Ø\Ø27(s16.66H\Ø27&18D
```

you can print the same block sideways using an 8.5-point printer font in compressed print (16.66 characters per horizontal inch), with reduced line spacing of 8 lines per vertical inch. Because you previously specified margin settings in inches, you do not need to change them. So stick with the 10.5-inch right margin and 8.5-inch page length setting.

Proportional Printing

Note. In Quattro Pro 3.0, the % Scaling option appears as Percent Scaling in the /Print, Layout menu.

Quattro Pro version 3.0 offers you two new /Print commands—Print To Fit and Layout, % Scaling—which make printing large spreadsheets considerably easier. As you become comfortable with these commands, you will find yourself using them more and more.

So far in this chapter, we have printed the data in Figure 6.9 in graphics mode using Quattro Pro's default /Print, Layout settings. This resulted in the four-page document in Figure 6.10. Then custom features like headings, headers, and footers were added to create the four-page document in Figure 6.14. However, the font had to be reduced from 12 point to 8 point and the column widths had to be adjusted. Otherwise, the document would have been printed on six pages. Likewise, to create Figure 6.22, the font had to be reduced to 10 point and the column widths adjusted to create this two-page document printed in landscape orientation.

Instead of making these font and column-width adjustments, you can use either Print To Fit or % Scaling to automatically fit data on one page or on the smallest number of pages possible. You can even use the % Scaling option to enlarge the size of a printed block.

Scaling to Fit

The /Print, Layout, % Scaling command proportionally reduces or enlarges the print block by the scaling percentage you specify. The default is 100%.

So think of this command as being similar to a photocopier that reduces or enlarges. The difference, however, is that the margins are not reduced or enlarged.

The easiest way to see how the /Print, Layout, % Scaling option works is through an example. Let's return once again to the data in Figure 6.9. This data uses Quattro Pro's default Font 1, Swiss-SC 12 point. Let's use most of Quattro Pro's default /Print, Layout settings, add the header and footer in Table 6.3, and examine the results that different % Scaling settings produce. To do this,

1. Select /Print, Block and specify **A1..P80**. Quattro Pro returns you to the /Print menu.

2. Choose Layout, % Scaling. Quattro Pro displays the default, 100 (percent). You can enter any number between 1 and 1000. For this example, type **75** and press Enter. Quattro Pro returns you to the Layout menu. Select Quit to return to the /Print menu.

3. Choose Destination and select a final quality destination, such as Graphics Printer or Screen Preview. Quattro Pro returns you to the /Print menu.

4. Select Adjust Printer, Align. When Quattro Pro returns to the /Print menu, choose Spreadsheet Print.

Tip. Rather than use the trial-and-error process to create a one-page document with % Scaling, use the /Print, Print To Fit command discussed next.

Before it prints, Quattro Pro reduces the size of the print block by 25%. However, the default margins (see Figure 6.8) are not changed. The result is that this data is still printed on four pages. However, the columns through *Other Ins* (column L) and the lines through *896 RE taxes* (row 57) all fit on the first page. The other three pages contain the "overflow" that does not fit on the first page.

If you use /Print, Layout, % Scaling, specify **60**, and then print this block, Quattro Pro reduces the print block by 40%. The printed data fits on two pages—all of the columns A through P fit on one page—but a second page is needed to print the last eight lines (rows 72 through 80).

Tip. To reduce the margins, change the Margins settings.

Trial and error demonstrates that to print the data on one page, you must specify a % Scaling setting of **51** (%). You can see the printed result in Figure 6.24. Notice that the margins are unaffected by the scaling.

On the other hand, if you use an Orientation, Landscape setting (remember to change the Margins settings!), you must use a % Scaling setting of 40 (%) before the print block fits on one page. You can see the result in Figure 6.25. Notice that to fit all the lines on a page length of 8.5 inches, the columns only take up approximately half of the page; the end result is not as aesthetically pleasing. In addition, this small scaling level results in small, hard-to-read print.

Figure 6.24

Printing the data from Figure 6.9 using a 51% setting for % Scaling

Checking Reconciliation   March/April 1991   Budget Analysis

Date	Check	Paid To	Amount	Deposit	Balance	Mortgage	House Utilities	Phone	Food	Health Expense	Other Ins	Car Expense	Misc House Exp	Other	Misc
		Balance			$423										
		Deposit		$4,000	$4,423										
Mar-91	850	Mortgage	($1,500)		$2,923	$1,500									
Mar-91	851	Cash	($100)		$2,823										$100
Mar-91	852	Shell	($75)		$2,748							$75			
Mar-91	853	Electric	($120)		$2,628		$120								
Mar-91	854	Sewer/Water	($65)		$2,563		$65								
Mar-91	855	Baby Sitter	($50)		$2,513										$50
Mar-91	856	Safeway	($175)		$2,338				$175						
Mar-91	857	Phone	($85)		$2,253			$85							
Mar-91	858	Health Ins	($175)		$2,078					$175					
Mar-91	859	Cash	($50)		$2,028										$50
Mar-91	860	Firestone	($200)		$1,828							$200			
Mar-91	861	Cleaners	($20)		$1,808										$20
Mar-91	862	Am Ex	($150)		$1,658									$150	
Mar-91	863	Nob Hill	($40)		$1,618				$40						
Mar-91	864	Car Ins	($450)		$1,168						$450				
Mar-91		Deposit		$2,000	$3,168										
Mar-91	865	VOID	$0		$3,168										
Mar-91	866	Mastercard	($250)		$2,918									$250	
Mar-91	867	House Ins	($800)		$2,118						$800				
Mar-91	868	Cash	($100)		$2,018										$100
Mar-91	869	Safeway	($60)		$1,958				$60						
Mar-91	870	Fishing Trip	($150)		$1,808									$150	
Mar-91	871	Alumni Fund	($50)		$1,758									$50	
Mar-91	872	Bookstore	($25)		$1,733										$25
Mar-91	873	Cleaners	($25)		$1,708										$25
Mar-91	874	Paint Store	($100)		$1,608								$100		
Mar-91	875	Cash	($200)		$1,408										$200
Mar-91	876	TWA	($150)		$1,258										$150
Mar-91	877	Nob Hill	($75)		$1,183				$75						
Mar-91	878	Ace Hardware	($40)		$1,143								$40		
Mar-91	879	Roter Rooter	($70)		$1,073								$70		
Mar-91	880	Magazine Subs	($35)		$1,038										$35
Mar-91	881	Cleaners	($15)		$1,023										$15
Mar-91	882	Lawn Service	($80)		$943								$80		
Mar-91	883	Dog Food	($40)		$903										$40
Mar-91	884	Dentist	($150)		$753					$150					
Mar-91	885	Cash	($75)		$678										$75
Mar-91	886	Safeway	($100)		$578				$100						
Mar-91		Service Charge	($10)		$568										$10
Mar-91		Total For March	($5,855)	$6,000		$1,500	$185	$85	$450	$325	$1,250	$275	$290	$600	$895
Apr-91	887	Baby Sitter	($25)		$543										$25
Apr-91		Deposit		$4,000	$4,543										
Apr-91	888	Mortgage	($1,500)		$3,043	$1,500									
Apr-91	889	YMCA	($75)		$2,968										$75
Apr-91	890	Phone	($120)		$2,848			$120							
Apr-91	891	Electric	($95)		$2,753		$95								
Apr-91	892	Cable	($44)		$2,709		$44								
Apr-91	893	Cash	($100)		$2,609										$100
Apr-91	894	Safeway	($150)		$2,459				$150						
Apr-91	895	Cleaners	($30)		$2,429										$30
Apr-91	896	RE Taxes	($1,100)		$1,329								$1,100		
Apr-91	897	IRS	($250)		$1,079									$250	
Apr-91	898	State of Calif	($75)		$1,004									$75	
Apr-91	899	Health Ins	($175)		$829					$175					
Apr-91	900	Am Ex	($50)		$779									$50	
Apr-91	901	VOID	$0		$779										
Apr-91	902	Mastercard	($125)		$654									$125	
Apr-91	903	VOID	$0		$654										
Apr-91		Deposit		$1,500	$2,154										
Apr-91	904	Cash	($100)		$2,054										$100
Apr-91	905	To Savings	($1,000)		$1,054									$1,000	
Apr-91	906	Baby Sitter	($35)		$1,019										$35
Apr-91	907	Cleaners	($15)		$1,004										$15
Apr-91	908	Lawn Service	($80)		$924								$80		
Apr-91	909	Plumber	($200)		$724								$200		
Apr-91	910	Cash	($75)		$649										$75
Apr-91	911	Nob Hill	($125)		$524				$125						
Apr-91	912	Midas Muffler	($250)		$274							$250			
Apr-91	913	Cleaners	($20)		$254										$20
Apr-91		Deposit		$500	$754										
Apr-91	914	WS Journal	($120)		$634										$120
Apr-91	915	Local Paper	($22)		$612										$22
Apr-91		Service Charge	($10)		$602										$10
Apr-91		Total For April	($5,966)	$6,000		$1,500	$139	$120	$275	$175	$0	$250	$1,380	$1,500	$627

When you use the % Scaling option, Quattro Pro limits the size of the printed output. Regardless of the scaling setting you use, the minimum size of each reduced character is 1 point, and the maximum size of each enlarged character is 72 points. However, on a more practical level, the minimum and maximum character size depend more on the printer resolution. For a 300-by-300-dpi printer resolution, for instance, Quattro Pro can use a smaller point size than for a 150-by-150-dpi resolution.

Figure 6.25

Printing the data from Figure 6.9 using a 40% setting for Scaling and a landscape orientation

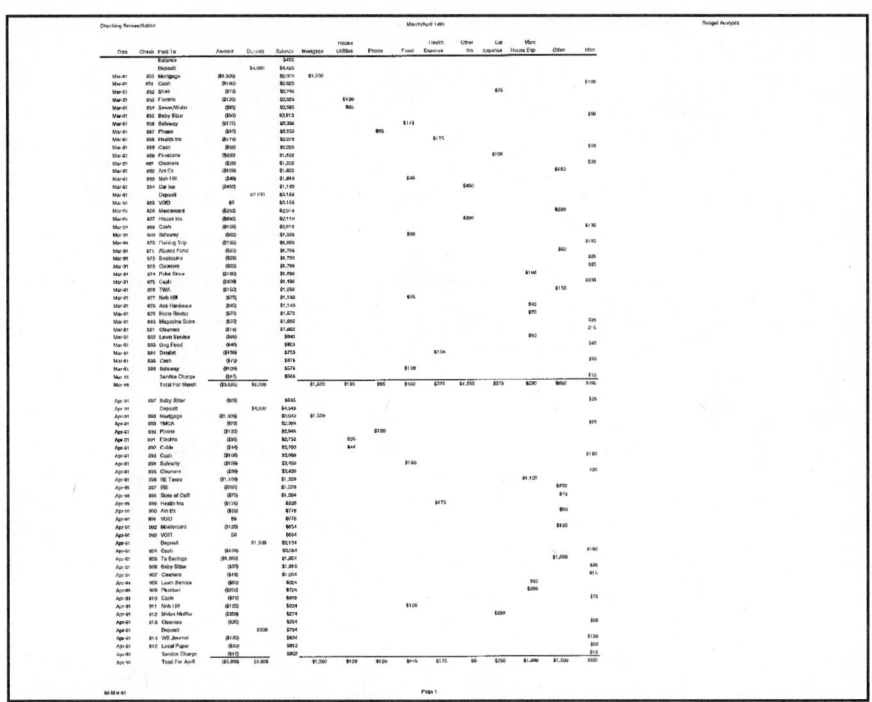

As you can see by these examples, % Scaling is a trial-and-error process. However, it is considerably easier than fooling with fonts and column widths. Keep in mind the following when you use /Print, Layout, % Scaling:

- You must print in graphics mode. % Scaling does not work in draft mode.

- Quattro Pro also scales headers and footers.

- When you use the /Print, Print-To-Fit command (see next section), the % Scaling setting is ignored.

Printing to Fit

One of the main disadvantages of the /Print, Layout, % Scaling command is that you have to use trial and error to determine the precise percent scaling needed to fit a multipage document on one page. To get around this problem, Quattro Pro offers the /Print, Print-To-Fit command. With this command, Quattro Pro automatically shrinks printed data to fit on one page by reducing it proportionally. Note that if the printed output normally fits on one page, the /Print, Print-To-Fit command has no effect.

Let's return once again to the data in Figure 6.9 to see the results that the /Print, Print-To-Fit command produces. Recall that this data uses Quattro Pro's default Font 1, Swiss-SC 12 point. Using the default /Print, Layout settings, perform the following:

1. Select /Print, Block and specify **A1..P80**. Quattro Pro returns you to the /Print menu.

2. Choose Destination and select a final quality destination, such as Graphics Printer or Screen Preview. Quattro Pro returns you to the /Print menu.

3. Select Adjust Printer, Align.

4. When Quattro Pro returns to the /Print menu, choose Print-To-Fit.

Quattro Pro prints all the data on one page, as shown in Figure 6.24. (Recall that these were the same results produced by using the /Print, Layout, % Scaling command and specifying a scaling setting of 51%.) Likewise, if you perform the same steps outlined above but with the orientation set to landscape (/Print, Layout, Orientation, Landscape), you get the results shown in Figure 6.25.

Keep in mind the following when you use the /Print, Print-To-Fit command:

■ You must print in graphics mode. Print-To-Fit does not work in draft mode.

■ Print-To-Fit ignores the Layout, % Scaling setting.

■ Like the Layout, % Scaling option, the Print-To-Fit option does not affect the margins; they remain constant.

■ The minimum character size is 1 point. However, on a more practical level, the minimum character size is a function of the printer resolution. With a 300-by-300-dpi printer, for example, Quattro Pro can use a smaller font than with a 150-by-150-dpi resolution. This limitation may not allow Quattro Pro to fit the data on one page; the data is then printed on as few pages as possible.

Printing Special Effects

Note. See Chapter 3 to learn how to create special effects.

Quattro Pro's /Style command allows you to enhance a spreadsheet with professional-looking special effects such as line drawing, shadow boxes, and cell shading. You can also include seven types of bullets in a document. Suppose,

for example, you create the spreadsheet in Figure 6.26, which includes different types of line drawing, rules, cell shading, and bullets. Figure 6.27 is the result you get when you print in graphics mode to an HP LaserJet III printer.

Figure 6.26

A spreadsheet of
special effects

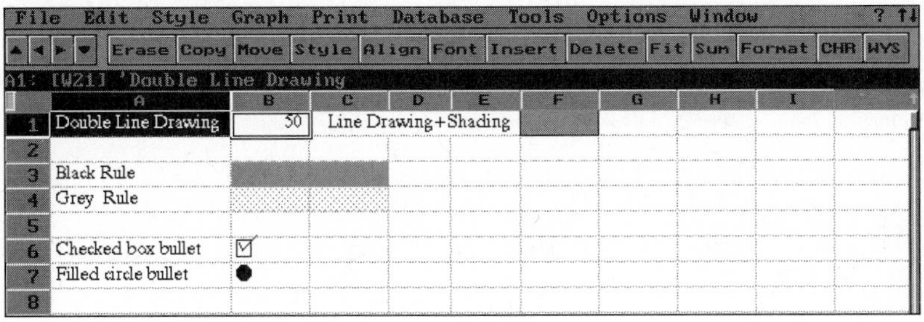

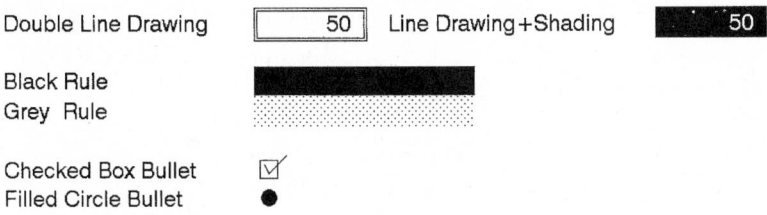

Figure 6.27

Line drawing, rules,
cell shading, and
two types of bullets
printed in graphics
mode

| Double Line Drawing | 50 | Line Drawing+Shading | 50 |

Black Rule

Grey Rule

Checked Box Bullet ☑

Filled Circle Bullet ●

You can view many of these special effects when you work in WYSI-
WYG (graphics) mode. To print high-quality special effects, you *must* print
in graphics mode and set /Options, Graphics Quality to Final. (See "Printing
to a Printer in Graphics Mode" earlier.)

If you print in draft mode to a printer, some special effects, such as block
shading, do not appear. Likewise, bullets are printed as labels, rather than as
graphic symbols.

On the other hand, the print quality of other special effects suffers
greatly when you print in draft mode to your text printer. For instance, in
draft mode the quality of line drawing may appear inconsistent on a printed
page, because Quattro Pro prints horizontal lines using dashes (--) and vertical lines using split vertical-bar characters (¦). You can see how line drawing
appears in Figure 6.5 when you print in draft mode to an HP LaserJet
printer. However, if you print a spreadsheet block to a printer in graphics
mode, line drawing is printed in presentation quality as shown in Figure 6.6.

Tip. You can control the printed shading level used by an HP LaserJet. This shading level will affect any block shading you have assigned in a spreadsheet, but not the shading of bullets. (See /Options, Hardware, Printers, Fonts, Cartridge Fonts, Shading Level discussed in Chapter 15.)

Keep in mind the following when you print special effects:

■ Screen Preview is temperamental when it comes to displaying special effects, and does not always reflect the quality of the actual printed output. For example, gray shading sometimes appears as light dots, other times as black dots on an olive background. Double lines are sometimes squished together, while block shading does not always appear to cover the entire area. However, these deficiencies do not appear when you print in graphics mode.

■ When you print a line drawing, make sure that you include each cell surrounding the lines in the print block; otherwise, only part of the line drawing is printed. For instance, to print the line drawing around cell D18 in Figure 6.2 (in the beginning of this chapter), cells D19 and E18 must be included in the print block.

■ In Character mode, a bullet code (not the bullet itself) is displayed in the spreadsheet. When you print in graphics mode or use Screen Preview, however, the bullet will be printed.

Printing Cell Contents

By default, Quattro Pro prints the displayed information in a print block. However, you can use the /Print, Format, Cell-Formulas command to print the contents of each cell. You will find this setting useful when you want to create documentation for a large spreadsheet model, or to debug formulas.

For instance, suppose you want to analyze the logic that creates the information in Figure 6.28.

1. Select /Print, Block and specify **A1..D3**. Quattro Pro returns you to the /Print menu.

2. Choose Format, and select Cell-Formulas from the menu shown in Figure 6.29. Quattro Pro returns you to the /Print menu.

3. Select Spreadsheet Print.

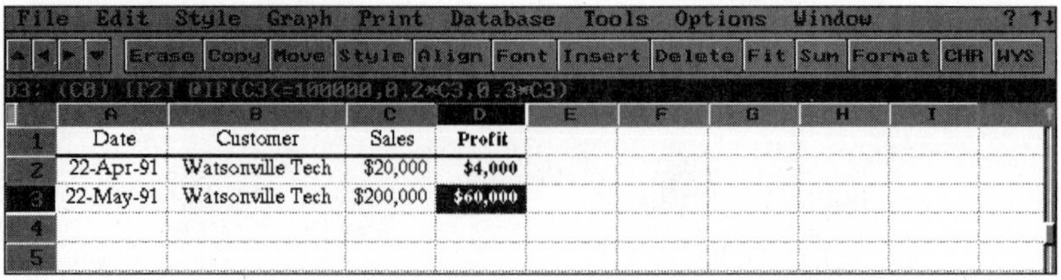

Figure 6.28

Information printed using /Print, Format, As Displayed

File	Edit	Style	Graph	Print	Database	Tools	Options	Window	? ↑↓

| ▲ | ◄ | ▼ | Erase | Copy | Move | Style | Align | Font | Insert | Delete | Fit | Sum | Format | CHR | WYS |

D3: (C0) [F2] @IF(C3<=100000,0.2*C3,0.3*C3)

	A	B	C	D	E	F	G	H	I
1	Date	Customer	Sales	Profit					
2	22-Apr-91	Watsonville Tech	$20,000	$4,000					
3	22-May-91	Watsonville Tech	$200,000	$60,000					
4									
5									

Figure 6.29
The /Print, Format menu

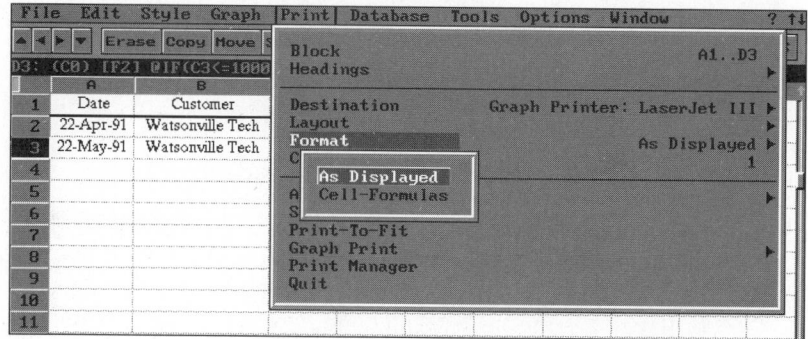

Quattro Pro prints the cell contents as shown in Figure 6.30. Notice that the contents are printed by rows—cells A1, B1, C1, and D1 first, then the cell contents in row 2, and so on. Additionally, all format settings, such as hard page breaks, footers, margins, and headings, are ignored in this print format. Likewise, Quattro Pro does not print anything for a blank cell in the Cell-Formulas format.

Figure 6.30
Using /Print, Format Cell-Formulas

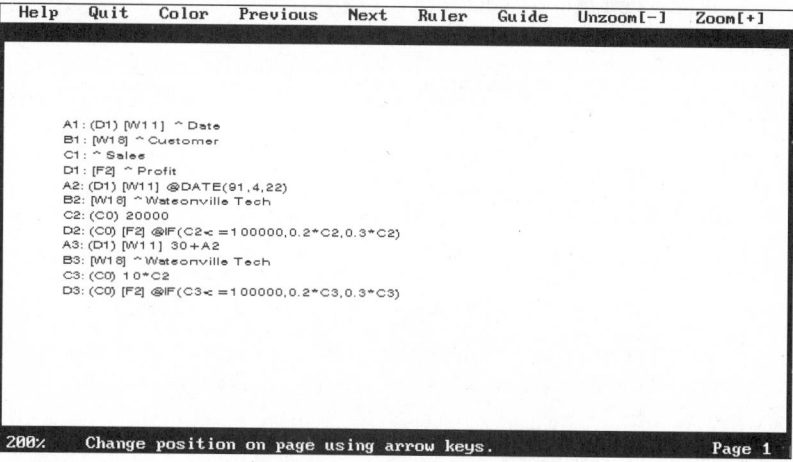

Note. The Format, As Displayed setting is always the default; it cannot be changed. In fact, the Format, As Displayed setting is not even saved when you save a file.

When you print the cell contents, Quattro Pro includes the following for each cell:

■ Cell address

- Numeric format, if different from the global numeric format

- Font, if not Font 1 by default

- Column width, if different from the global width

- Content as it appears on the input line

- Any comment you have added to the cell content

As you can see in Figure 6.30, (C0) and [F2] indicate that cell D2 uses a nondefault Currency 0 format, and Font 2, all set with the /Style command. On the other hand, [W18] ^ indicates that cell B1 is assigned a column width of 18 and a centered label alignment; otherwise, it uses default settings. Notice that line drawing is not indicated either in the block to which it was originally assigned—A1..D1—or in the block to which Quattro Pro attaches the bottom line drawing—A2..D2.

Note. The Cell-Formulas format takes considerable printing time for medium to large spreadsheets.

Specifying the Number of Copies to Be Printed

Starting with version 3.0, Quattro Pro includes a new command, /Print, Copies, which you can use to specify the number of printed copies of a document. The default is 1.

Suppose, for example, you want to print two copies of Figure 6.14. Before you print, select /Print, Copies and specify 2. When you print—remember to select Adjust Printer, Align first—Quattro Pro prints the first copy of Figure 6.14, numbering the pages 1 through 4 (since the footer includes the special symbol #). It then automatically resets its internal line and page counters, and prints the second copy of Figure 6.14, numbering the pages 1 through 4.

After Quattro Pro finishes printing, the /Print, Copies setting always returns to 1.

Resetting and Updating /Print Settings

The /Print, Layout, Update command can be used to change the Destination, and the Layout, Margins, Setup String, Dimensions, and Orientation default settings.

On the other hand, use /Print, Layout, Reset to return /Print settings to their defaults. As you can see in Figure 6.31, the /Print, Layout, Reset command offers four options, which you can use as follows:

- *All* resets the Page Length, Margins, Setup String, Dimensions, Orientation, and Destination to the latest default settings. The Block, Headings, Header, and Footer settings are cleared. The Format, % Scaling, and Page Break settings are returned to Quattro Pro's default settings.

Figure 6.31
The /Print, Layout,
Reset menu

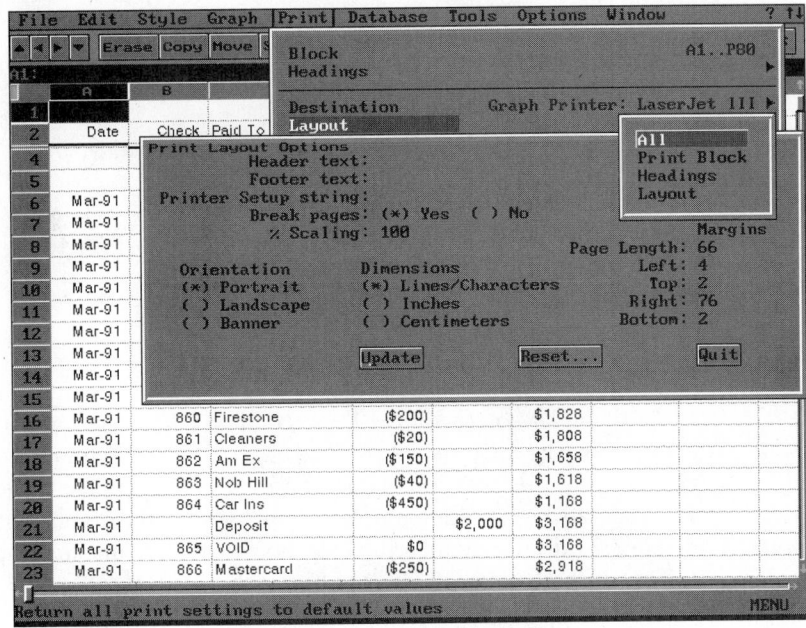

- *Print Block* clears the current Block setting.

- *Headings* clears the current Left and Top Headings settings.

- *Layout* resets only the Page Length, Margins, and Setup String settings to the current defaults. It does not affect the Layout, Header, Footer, Orientation, Break Pages, Percent Scaling, or Dimensions settings.

Printing a Screen Dump: Shift-PrtSc or PrtSc

Note. You cannot print a screen dump of a graph.

A screen dump is the easiest form of printing in Quattro Pro. Although a screen dump only produces an unformatted "snapshot" of a computer screen, it is a quick and easy print method that can be useful in many situations.

For example, suppose you want to print the information in Figure 6.32, which is displayed on your computer screen. You *must* be working in Character mode; otherwise, the screen dump will consist of uninterpretable graphic symbols. Assuming that the printer is on line, press Shift-PrtSc. (You can also press just PrtSc if you have a 101-key extended keyboard.)

Figure 6.32

Spreadsheet data
displayed in
Character mode

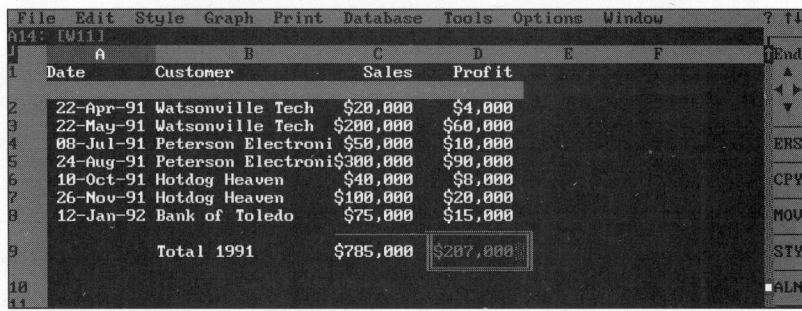

Quattro Pro does not control a screen dump. Rather, pressing Shift-PrtSc triggers a routine in the PC's ROM (read-only memory), which prints everything currently displayed. As you can see in Figure 6.33, the result is certainly not presentation quality. Your spreadsheet data as well as Quattro Pro's spreadsheet border, mode indicators, and control panel contents are all printed. Additionally, line drawing is printed using unusual characters, and the block shading in cell D9 is not printed.

Figure 6.33

Results of Shift-
PrtSc

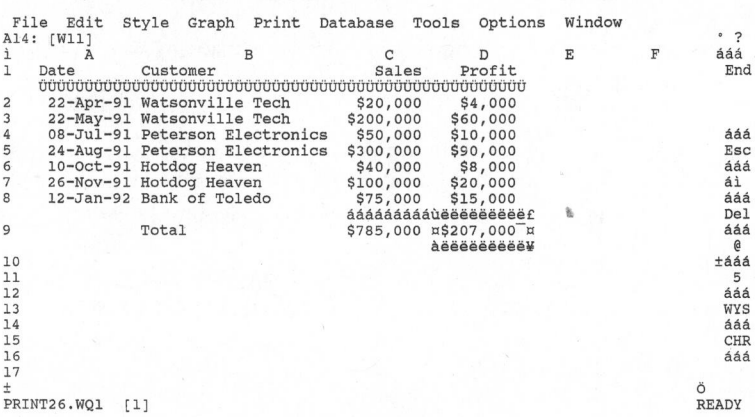

Keep in mind the following when you print a screen dump:

- The printer must be connected to the first parallel port, LPT1. If it is hooked to a serial port, you must first exit to DOS and reassign the port to LPT1 using the MODE command in DOS. (For more information, see your DOS manual.)

- Since Quattro Pro does not control a screen dump, its internal line/page counter is not activated by this print method. Thus, before you print anything else, you must correlate the print head and Quattro Pro's internal line/page counter. If you are using a laser printer, simply turn the printer off and on before you print again. If you are using continuous-feed paper, you must manually position the print head at the top of a new page, and then use the /Print, Adjust Printer, Align command so that the print head and Quattro Pro's internal line/page counter correspond. (See "Controlling the Paper in the Printer" earlier for more information.)

Printing in the Background

Quattro Pro 4.0 ships with the Borland Print Spooler (BPS). When the BPS is active, your print jobs are directed to a queue—a temporary holding area on your computer's hard disk. They are then released to your printer in the order in which they were sent. The primary advantage to using the BPS is that Quattro Pro can usually print to your hard disk much faster that it can to your printer (especially if you're printing in graphics mode). The upshot is that you spend less time waiting for Quattro Pro to finish printing. Because less time is required to print, control of the spreadsheet is returned to you that much quicker. In the meantime, the BPS continues printing from the queue in the background while you continue to work in Quattro Pro.

The BPS is not "hardwired" into Quattro Pro's executable code and cannot be called from a menu. Instead, it comes as a separate program, BPS.COM. You must run this program from the DOS prompt before you start Quattro Pro. To do this, make your C:\QPRO directory current—for example, type **CD\QPRO**—and type the following two commands at the DOS prompt, pressing Enter after each one:

```
BPS
Q
```

The BPS will be loaded and Quattro Pro will start. Any print jobs you initiate will be spooled to disk and released to the default printer for Quattro Pro in the order in which they were sent. To accomplish this, the BPS creates temporary files with an .SPL extension in your Quattro Pro program directory, usually C:\QPRO. The first print job is assigned the name QPPRN1.SPL, the second QPPRN2.SPL, and so on. When a print job is complete, its .SPL file is removed from your hard disk.

The BPS is a memory-resident program. This means it remains in memory after you leave Quattro Pro. To avoid conflicts with your other programs, it's always a good idea to clear the BPS from memory after you quit

Quattro Pro. You can do this by entering the BPS command at the DOS prompt with the U (unload) switch; for example:

```
BPS U
```

If you turn off your machine or unload the BPS while a print job is underway, the print job will not be cancelled, but only suspended temporarily. The part of the print job that was not sent to the printer before the BPS was unloaded will continue to print the next time the BPS is loaded into memory. You can avoid this, however, by simply deleting the .SPL files in your Quattro Pro program directory.

TIP. *Place the BPS command lines in a DOS .BAT (batch) file, thereby automating the process of loading and unloading the BPS. You can create a .BAT file by using any text editor capable of reading and writing ASCII text. You can also use the DOS COPYCON command to create a .BAT file. Whichever method you choose, you'll want to include the following command lines:*

```
BPS
Q
BPS U
```

These command lines will run BPS.COM and then start Quattro Pro (Q.EXE). When you leave Quattro Pro, the BPS U command line will unload the BPS from memory.

In addition to the U (Unload) switch, there are two other command-line switches for the BPS that you should know about:

- *BPS Sn*   Specifies the rate at which data is released to your printer. The *n* argument must be a number between 0 and 9, with 0 being the slowest and 9 being the fastest. The default setting is 3, which should be adequate for most printing configurations.

- *BPS Cn*   Specifies the handshake method (asynchronous communication protocol) used to communicate with the printer. You'll only need to use this setting when your printer is connected to a COM (serial) port. The *n* argument must be a number between 0 and 3 as follows:

  0=none

  1=Xon/Xoff

  2=DTR, then CTS/DTR (the default)

  3=CTS only

You'll have to check your printer's manual to determine which setting is appropriate.

CAUTION! *If you're running Quattro Pro on a network, the BPS may cause a conflict with the network print spooler. When this happens, your machine will lock up. To avoid this, load the BPS before you load the network shell. If you continue to have difficulty, don't load the BPS. Instead, use the network print spooler.*

If you are running Quattro Pro 4.0 on a network, you can use the /Options, Network, Queue Monitor command to monitor the status of your BPS print jobs as they are sent to the network print queue. Quattro Pro will display the status of your print jobs in relation to others in the network print queue—for example, 1jobs|3ahead|Actv—in the Status line at the bottom of your screen. See Chapter 14 for more details on this.

Using Print Manager

If you've got the Borland Print Spooler (BPS) loaded when you start Quattro Pro, you can use the Print Manager feature, new in Quattro Pro 4.0, to monitor and control the print jobs stored in the BPS queue. For example, you can cancel a print job or suspend it temporarily and then release it to the printer later.

To activate the Print Manager, select /Print, Print Manager. Quattro Pro opens a window similar to the one in Figure 6.34, showing the status of the print jobs in the queue.

The content of the Print Manager window is determined by your current printer connection. If the default printer for Quattro Pro is directed to a network print queue, Print Manager will show you the contents of that queue. If the printer is connected to a local port and the BPS has been loaded, Print Manager will show you the status of the BPS queue, similar to Figure 6.34. If the BPS has not been loaded, Print Manager will display the message "No queue selected" when its window first appears.

Print Manager's Window

The information displayed in Print Manager's window identifies the position of each print job in the BPS queue and its present status. The following information is available:

- *Seq*   The order of print jobs in the queue.

- *File Name*   The file name assigned to the print job by Quattro Pro—for example, QPPRN1.SPL, QPPRN2.SPL, and so on.

Figure 6.34

Print Manager's window

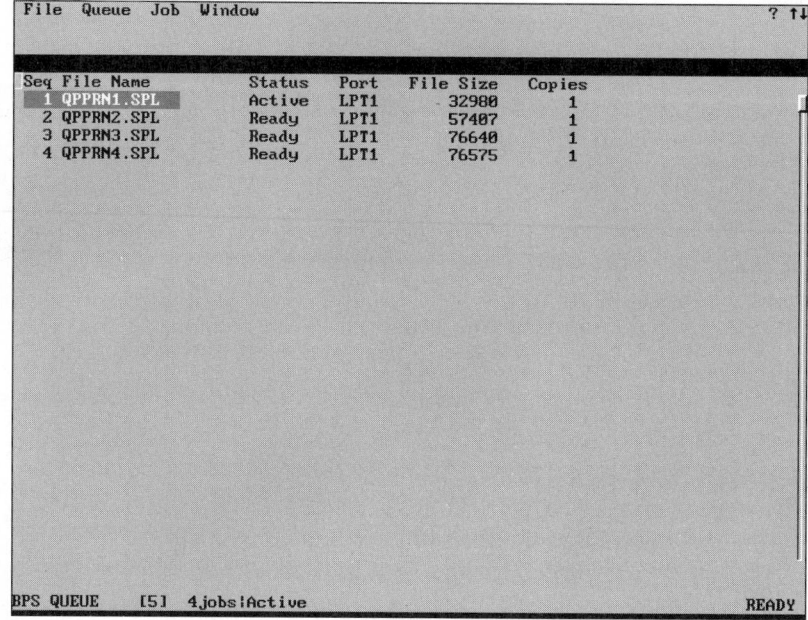

- *Status*   The current status of the print job. There are three designations here: Active, Ready, or Held. Active means the print job is printing, Ready means it is waiting in the queue, and Held means that it has been temporarily suspended.

- *Port*   The port to which the print job is being sent. This is determined by the /Options, Hardware, Printers, 1st (or 2nd) Printer, Device setting that was in effect when you initiated the print job.

- *File size*   The file size of the print job expressed in bytes.

- *Copies*   The number of copies that will be printed. This is determined by the /Print, Copies setting that was in effect when you initiated the print job.

To keep you abreast of the status of your print jobs, the Print Manager window is periodically updated. The interval at which these updates occur is determined by the current /Options, Network, Refresh Interval setting.

Using Print Manager's Menus

Print Manager's menus are relatively straightforward. You open the menu by pressing the / (slash) key and then selecting an option. The following menus are available:

- *File* Contains two options, Close and Close All. The Close option closes Print Manager's window. Close All closes all open windows.

- *Queue* Contains two options, Background and Network. As mentioned, Print Manager lets you view the status of either the local BPS queue or a network print queue to which you have access. As you might imagine, the Background option shows you the contents of the local BPS queue. The Network option, on the other hand, lets you specify the name of the network queue to monitor. See Chapter 14 for more details on using this option.

- *Job* Contains three options—Delete, Hold, and Release—that let you manage print jobs in a print queue.

- *Window* Contains five options, Zoom, Tile, Stack, Move/Size, and Pick. These options match those available on the standard Window menu that is available when a spreadsheet window is displayed. You'll find them discussed in Chapter 2.

Controlling Print Jobs

In addition to showing you the print jobs in the BPS queue, Print Manager also lets you suspend print jobs and resume them, or cancel them altogether. For example, suppose you have the four print jobs shown in Figure 6.34 currently in the BPS queue. You want to put the first one on hold temporarily and delete the last three. To do this, select the first print job (even though it is currently printing) and select /Job, Hold. Quattro Pro changes the Status for the print job from Active to Held, indicating that it is temporarily suspended. To delete the last three jobs, select the appropriate job line and then select /Job, Delete, Yes. When you are ready to resume the first job again, select it and then select /Job, Release.

Printing to a File

As you can see in Figure 6.35, Quattro Pro provides two file destinations: File under Draft Mode Printing, and Binary File under Final Quality Printing. Here are a few applications of these Destination settings.

■ Creating an ASCII text file or binary file, and then using DOS to direct the file to a printer. This is helpful when a printer is not currently connected to your PC, and you will print later on another PC.

■ Creating an ASCII text file that can be used in another software package, such as a word processor or a database program.

■ Creating a binary graphics file that can then be converted and used in another graphics program (see Chapter 8).

Figure 6.35

The /Printer, Destination, File or Binary File menu

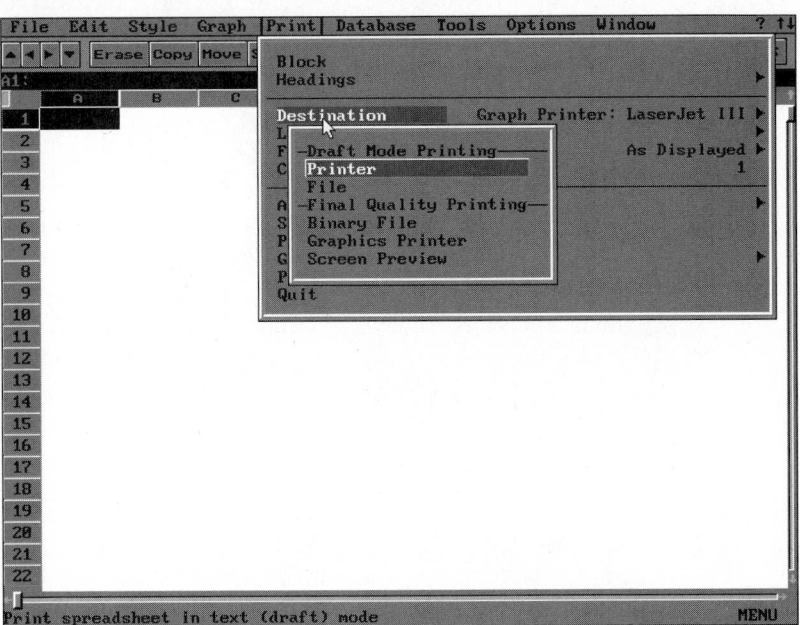

If you choose Destination, File, then Quattro Pro prints to a "flat" ASCII text file. This file is flat in the sense that it does not include any of the special codes needed to produce fonts, shading, and line drawing. On the other hand, if you select Destination, Binary File, then Quattro Pro prints to a file in graphics mode using bit patterns. Therefore, any presentation-quality settings, such as fonts and special effects, that exist in the print block are printed to this file. Although the resulting text and binary files are quite different, creating these files is very similar.

Printing a File from DOS

Imagine that you are currently working on the file LISA.WQ1. You want to print this file to a LaserJet printer, but the printer is not currently connected to your PC. Instead, you direct the output to a file, such as LISA.PRN, and print the contents of the file later using DOS. The procedures for printing to an ASCII text file or to a binary file are nearly identical, as follows:

1. Select /Print, Destination, File or Binary File, and Quattro Pro displays the menu in Figure 6.35. In response to "Enter print file name:", type **LISA** and press Enter. By default, Quattro Pro includes a .PRN extension. (If you want another extension, be sure to include it in the file name.) Quattro Pro returns to the /Print menu, and now displays "File" or "Binary File" as the destination.

NOTE. *If you have previously created any .PRN files in the current directory, Quattro Pro will display these file names. For instance, suppose LISA.PRN already exists. If you select this file from the list, Quattro Pro will display a Cancel/Replace/Backup/Append menu. Select Replace to overwrite the existing file, or Append to add the current print block to the end of an existing file.*

2. Select Adjust Printer, Align.

3. Select Spreadsheet Print. Quattro Pro writes the data to the file name you specified, in this instance LISA.PRN.

4. Choose Adjust Printer, Form Feed.

5. Select Quit to close the text file and return to the spreadsheet.

Quattro Pro does not close the text file until you quit the /Print menu, choose a new destination, or specify another text file. Otherwise, Quattro Pro continues to append data to the open text file.

If you have created an ASCII text file, you can now view it on the screen. Exit to DOS and enter **TYPE LISA.PRN** to scroll the contents of this file across the screen. Press Ctrl-S at any time to stop the scrolling, and Enter to resume.

You can use DOS to print both ASCII text or binary files. Suppose your printer is hooked to LPT1. To print the text file, use **COPY LISA.PRN LPT1**. If LISA.PRN is a binary file, use **COPY LISA.PRN /B LPT1**. DOS now sends the file contents to the printer connected to LPT1.

When you use the COPY command in DOS to copy a binary file to a printer, you must make sure to use the /B switch. This switch directs DOS to use the file length setting in the file header. (You can see this setting when you use the DIR command.) Without this switch, DOS will stop copying when it encounters a Ctrl-Z character (1A in hexadecimal). In an ASCII text file, a Ctrl-Z character normally occurs at the end of the file; but in a binary file, a Ctrl-Z may occur almost anywhere, depending on the graphic image you are printing.

Creating a Text File to Be Used with Another Software Package

If you want to create a text file that will be used in another software package, you should remove any formatting that might interfere with this software package before you create the file. So be sure to

- Set the top, bottom, and left margins to 0, and the right margin to 254.

- Prevent Quattro Pro from using soft page breaks, headers, footers, and setup strings. Therefore, specify /Print, Layout, Page Breaks, No; and clear any setup string, header, and footer settings.

Now you can create the text file. Select /Print, Destination, File and specify the file name, such as **LISA.PRN**. If this is already an existing .PRN file, select Replace to overwrite the existing file, or Append to add the print block to the end of an existing file. Choose Spreadsheet Print, and Quattro Pro writes the data to the file name you specified, LISA.PRN. Finally, choose Quit to close the text file and return to the spreadsheet; otherwise, Quattro Pro continues to append data to the open file.

CHAPTER

7

Functions

AFUNCTION IS A BUILT-IN TOOL OR FORMULA THAT ALLOWS YOU TO perform a specialized, sometimes complex task quickly and easily. For instance, mathematical and statistical functions perform numeric calculations such as summing numbers, calculating an average, or computing a standard deviation. Other functions execute trigonometric, date and time, financial, and depreciation calculations; perform logical analysis; retrieve information from tables; and manipulate strings. Some functions perform specialized tasks, such as returning information about the operating system, the current session, or the location of the cell pointer.

Note. Database functions are discussed in Chapter 10.

This chapter is geared to help you use functions as a time-saving tool, regardless of your level of expertise. If you're trying to use functions for the first time, this chapter will teach you the basics. But if you're an experienced user, consider this chapter a convenient, in-depth function reference. Because functions cover such a wide range of disciplines—accounting, statistics, engineering, and finance, just to name a few—this chapter also provides you with a refresher course on the underlying mathematical computations a function performs.

If you're upgrading from Quattro Pro 3.0 or an earlier version, the big news in Quattro Pro 4.0 is that you can now create your own functions to perform specialized tasks, store them in a function library, and then use them as needed. Two new functions, @ISAPP and @ISAAF, allow you to test for the presence of add-ins.

NOTE. *Because Quattro Pro has many functions unavailable in 1-2-3, your spreadsheet logic may be corrupted if you import a Quattro Pro file into Lotus 1-2-3. However, you shouldn't have any problems with your functions when you import a 1-2-3 file into Quattro Pro.*

Function Basics

Most functions must be entered in a cell in this form:

```
@FUNCTION(Argument1,Argument2,........,Argumentn)
```

The @ symbol tells Quattro Pro that you're entering a function, not a label. You can enter the function name in any combination of upper- and lower-case characters. The maximum length of a function is 254 characters, the maximum length of a cell entry in Quattro Pro. If you include spaces between the function name and the first parenthesis, between the arguments, or between the last argument and the last parenthesis, Quattro Pro automatically deletes them for you.

You can also enter a function by pointing-and-shooting. First, select ⌹ from the SpeedBar or press Alt+F3 (Functions). You'll see the @Function Index, shown in Figure 7.1, which lists all functions alphabetically. Scroll down this list and choose the one you want by clicking on it or highlighting it, and then press Enter. For example, if you choose AVG, then @AVG(will be displayed in the input line along with its left parenthesis. If you choose a function that doesn't use an argument (such as @RAND), however, you'll have to delete the beginning parenthesis.

Figure 7.1
The @Function Index

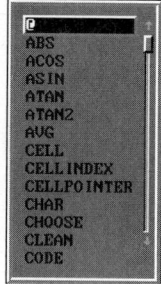

Function Arguments

Arguments, enclosed in parentheses, are the parameters on which a function acts. You specify arguments while entering a function; Quattro Pro won't let you preselect an argument, such as a block.

Some functions require no arguments, such as @PI and @ERR. Others act on one argument, like @SUM(B6..E7). Many functions, however, use multiple arguments, as in @IF(A1>0,A1+B1,B1). Multiple arguments are separated by a comma, the default *argument separator,* which you can change to a semicolon or a period using the /Options, International, Punctuation command (see Chapter 15).

When a function requires multiple arguments, you must enter them in the order specified. Otherwise, you'll get ERR or incorrect results. In the @DATE(*Yr,Mo,Day*) function, for example, the first argument must be the year, the second, the month, and the third, the day.

Some functions include one or more optional arguments, designated by < >. For example @PVAL(*Rate,Nper,Pmt,<FV>,<Type>*) has two arguments you don't have to include, *FV* and *Type.*

Functions use different types of arguments. Many functions act on a *value* argument—a number, a numeric formula or function that returns a value, or a cell or block address or name (even in another open file) that contains values or formulas that return values. For example, all these functions use valid arguments: @ABS(-14.6), @SQRT(6*E19), @AVG(A1..C1), and @SUM(RATES), where RATES is a defined block name.

NOTE. *You create file linking when you use a function argument that references a location in another Quattro Pro file. If you're working in the active file WON.WQ1, for instance, the average value returned by @AVG([LOST]A1..E20) is automatically updated whenever the data in A1..E20 of LOST.WQ1 changes. File linking is discussed in Chapter 3.*

Other functions act on a *string* argument—a *literal string* or label enclosed in double quotes, a formula or function that returns a string, or a cell or block address or name (even in another open file) that contains strings or formulas that return strings. The arguments in @REPLACE(A1,0,@LENGTH(A1),"Delta Queen"), for instance, are the cell address A1, the start-point at character Ø, the function @LENGTH(A1), and the literal string "Delta Queen". (Don't forget the double quotes!) When you include a function, such as @LENGTH, as an argument of another function, it's called *nesting*.

In some cases, a function acts on both a value and a string argument. For example, @LEFT("United States",6) returns the first 6 characters of the literal string "United States".

Some functions use other types of arguments. An @IF function compares two items using a *condition argument*—a logical test that includes a logical operator such as = or <=. For example, @IF(B5<200,C7,"Error") uses the conditional argument B5<200 to compare the contents of cell B5 with the value 200. On the other hand, some special functions like @CELL-POINTER("address") act on an *attribute argument* to return information about an attribute of a cell, such as the cell address.

TIP. *You can attach a note to the end of a function by preceding the note with a ; (semi-colon), as in @SUM(B5..B7); May to June. Notes are discussed in Chapter 1.*

Help with Functions

When you're working with functions in Quattro Pro, here's how to access online help. Press F1 (Help), choose Functions, and then select @Function Index. You can then choose the function for which you want help from the alphabetized list displayed in Figure 7.1. Select SUM, for instance, and you'll see the help screen shown in Figure 7.2. To see examples of @SUM, choose Examples.

General Mathematical Functions

A general mathematical function either calculates or manipulates a value, and returns a value result. Table 7.1 includes Quattro Pro's general mathematical functions, which are the same as in previous releases.

Figure 7.2

Getting help for the @SUM function

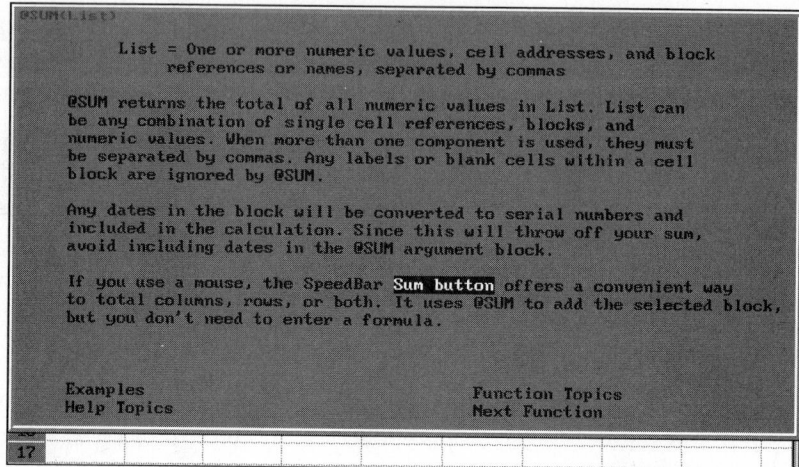

@SUM(list)

List = One or more numeric values, cell addresses, and block references or names, separated by commas

@SUM returns the total of all numeric values in List. List can be any combination of single cell references, blocks, and numeric values. When more than one component is used, they must be separated by commas. Any labels or blank cells within a cell block are ignored by @SUM.

Any dates in the block will be converted to serial numbers and included in the calculation. Since this will throw off your sum, avoid including dates in the @SUM argument block.

If you use a mouse, the SpeedBar Sum button offers a convenient way to total columns, rows, or both. It uses @SUM to add the selected block, but you don't need to enter a formula.

Examples   Function Topics
Help Topics   Next Function

17

Table 7.1   General Mathematical Functions

Function	Returns
@ABS	Absolute, or positive value of a number
@SQRT	Square root of a number
@ROUND	Number rounded to the specified precision
@INT	Integer part of a number
@MOD	Modulus (remainder) of a division operation
@RAND	Random number

Absolute Value: @ABS

@ABS determines the absolute or positive value of a number. The form of this function is

    @ABS(x)

where x must evaluate to a value. Use @ABS(x) to force a value to be positive; use −@ABS(x) to force a negative value. For example, @ABS(−1.5) returns 1.5, but −@ABS(1.5) returns −1.5. You can calculate the square root of a negative number using −@SQRT(@ABS(x)).

Calculating the Square Root: @SQRT

@SQRT calculates the square root of any nonnegative value. The form of this function is

    @SQRT(x)

where x must result in 0 or a positive number. For example, @SQRT(16) returns 4. But @SQRT returns ERR when x is negative. To calculate the square root of a negative value, you must use –@SQRT(@ABS(x)). For example, –@SQRT(ABS(–16)) returns –4; @SQRT(–16) returns ERR.

@SQRT(x) is the same as x^0.5—raising x to the $\frac{1}{2}$ power. For example, the result of either @SQRT(16) or 16^0.5 is 4.

NOTE. *The* ^ *operator raises a value to the power you specify. For instance, 5^3 cubes the value 5 and returns 125. Conversely, 125^(1/3) returns the cube root of 125, which is 5. But because of Quattro Pro's order of precedence, 125^1/3 is evaluated as (125^1)/3 or 41.67. (See Chapter 1.)*

Rounding a Value: @ROUND

@ROUND rounds a value to the number of decimal places, or *precision*, you specify. The form of this function is

    @ROUND(x , Num)

where x and *Num* must both evaluate to numbers. X is the value to be rounded. *Num* is the number of digits (up to 15) to the left or the right of the decimal point where rounding should occur. A digit between 0 and 4 is rounded down; a digit between 5 and 9 is rounded up.

Specify a positive *Num* to round to the right of the decimal point. For example, @ROUND(912.64,1) returns 912.6. Specify a negative *Num* to round to the left of the decimal point—@ROUND(917.64,–1) returns 920.

A formula that references a cell containing the @ROUND function uses the rounded value. For example, suppose your company has determined that three employees sharing a printer is considered 100% capacity. A new printer is purchased whenever an existing printer is being used at 150% capacity. Column B in Figure 7.3 shows the number of printers needed for different employee levels. In cell B5, for example, +A5/3 calculates that 1.667 printers are needed for five employees. Following your company's printer policy, @ROUND(B5,0) in cell C5 correctly returns that 2 printers are needed. You can see in cell D5 how this rounded value is used in the formula +C5*1000 to compute that a $2,000 investment in printers is needed.

Figure 7.3
Using @ROUND
and @INT

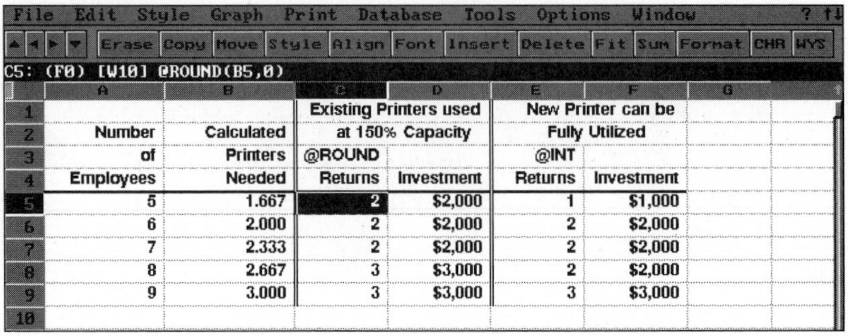

File Edit Style Graph Print Database Tools Options Window						? ↑↓
◢ ◀ ▶ ▼ Erase Copy Move Style Align Font Insert Delete Fit Sum Format CHR WYS						

C5: (F0) [W10] @ROUND(B5,0)

	A	B	C	D	E	F	G
1			Existing Printers used		New Printer can be		
2	Number	Calculated	at 150% Capacity		Fully Utilized		
3	of	Printers	@ROUND		@INT		
4	Employees	Needed	Returns	Investment	Returns	Investment	
5	5	1.667	2	$2,000	1	$1,000	
6	6	2.000	2	$2,000	2	$2,000	
7	7	2.333	2	$2,000	2	$2,000	
8	8	2.667	3	$3,000	2	$2,000	
9	9	3.000	3	$3,000	3	$3,000	
10							

Returning an Integer: @INT

@INT returns the integer portion of a value without rounding the value. The form of this function is

    @INT(x)

where x must result in a value. For example, @INT(574.7) drops the decimal portion without rounding and returns 574.

A formula that references a cell containing @INT uses the integer returned. To see how @INT works, let's build on the previous example in Figure 7.3. Now imagine that although the corporate policy is still that three employees should share a printer (100% capacity), a new printer is purchased only when it will immediately be fully utilized—that is, when there are three employees to share it. You can use @INT to model this printer policy. At five employees, for example, @INT(B5) in cell E5 truncates the decimal portion of 1.667 and returns 1. The formula +E5*1000 in cell F5 then uses this truncated value to compute that only a $1,000 investment in printers is needed.

Returning the Remainder: @MOD

@MOD determines the remainder, or *modulus*, of a division operation. For example, 7 divided by 3 is 2, with 1, the modulus, remaining. The form of this function is

    @MOD(Numerator,Denominator)

where the *Numerator* is the value you want to divide, and the *Denominator* is the value you divide the *Numerator* by. @MOD returns ERR when the *Denominator* is 0.

The sign of the *Numerator* controls the sign of the result. For example, @MOD(7,3) returns 1, while @MOD(–7,3) returns –1. What's more, when the *Numerator* is smaller than the *Denominator*, @MOD returns the *Numerator*—@MOD(3,7), for example, returns 3.

Tip. You can use @MOD to calculate the day of the week a particular date falls on. See "Date Functions," later.

Figure 7.4 shows how @MOD can be used to calculate the number of leftover units when 5 units are shipped to a box. On Monday, when 12 units are available for shipping, @MOD(B4,B6) in cell B7 calculates 2 leftover units. Here, the 12 units on hand in B4 is the *Numerator*, while the 5 units per box in B5 is the *Denominator*. Notice that the 2 remaining units @MOD returns become Tuesday's beginning inventory.

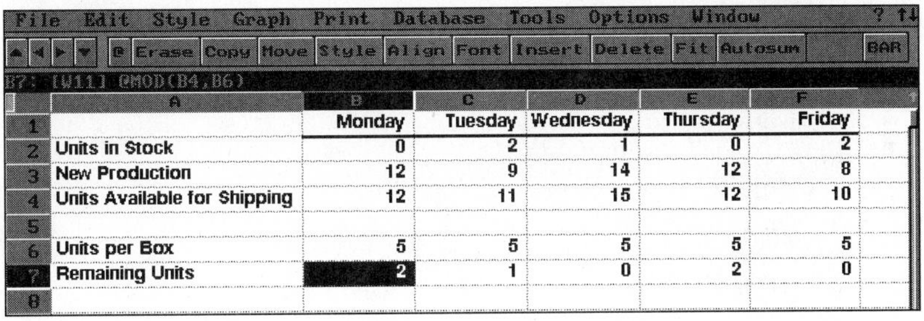

Figure 7.4
Using @MOD

File Edit Style Graph Print Database Tools Options Window	? ↑↓

| ▲ ◄ ► ▼ | ℗ Erase | Copy | Move | Style | Align | Font | Insert | Delete | Fit | Autosum | | BAR |

B7: [W11] @MOD(B4,B6)

	A	B	C	D	E	F	
1		Monday	Tuesday	Wednesday	Thursday	Friday	
2	Units in Stock	0	2	1	0	2	
3	New Production	12	9	14	12	8	
4	Units Available for Shipping	12	11	15	12	10	
5							
6	Units per Box	5	5	5	5	5	
7	Remaining Units	2	1	0	2	0	
8							

Generating Random Values: @RAND

@RAND, which doesn't use an argument, generates a random number between 0 and 1, up to 15 decimal places. To generate a table of random values, you'll need to enter @RAND in each cell of the table.

@RAND generates a new number whenever the spreadsheet is automatically or manually recalculated. To save a current random number as a literal value, use /Edit, Values.

Use @RAND to generate

- Invoice numbers, check numbers, and so on in a test of internal controls (a test that verifies the accuracy of internal accounting procedures).

- Serial numbers to test quality control procedures.

- Integers below a certain value. For example, @INT(@RAND∗100) returns random numbers below 100; @ROUND(@RAND∗1000000,0) creates a random value between 0 and 1 million rounded to zero places.

Trigonometric and Logarithmic Functions

Quattro Pro's trigonometric and logarithmic functions are summarized in Table 7.2. They are used mainly in engineering and scientific applications. Three functions, new to Quatro Pro 4.0, calculate hyperbolic relationships.

Table 7.2 **Trigonometric and Logarithmic Functions**

Function	Returns
@PI	Value of π, 3.141592653589794
@RADIANS	Conversion of an angle β from degrees to radians
@DEGREES	Conversion of an angle β from radians to degrees
@SIN	Sine of an angle β
@COS	Cosine of an angle β
@TAN	Tangent of an angle β
@ASIN	Arcsine of the sine of an angle β
@ACOS	Arccosine of the cosine of an angle β
@ATAN	Arctangent of the tangent of an angle β
@SAMPLE.SINH	Hyperbolic sine
@SAMPLE.COSH	Hyperbolic cosine
@SAMPLE.TANH	Hyperbolic tangent
@ATAN2	Arctangent of x and y
@EXP	Value of e raised to the power x
@LN	Natural logarithm of x in base e
@LOG	Base 10 logarithm of x

Calculating Pi: @PI

@PI is equal to 3.141592653589794 or π, the ratio of a circle's circumference to its diameter. As you can see in Figure 7.5, the 360 degrees of a circle equal 2π radians. The circumference of a circle is @PI*d, where d is the diameter. The area of the circle is @PI*r^2, where r is the radius.

Figure 7.5

The relationship between π (pi) and a circle

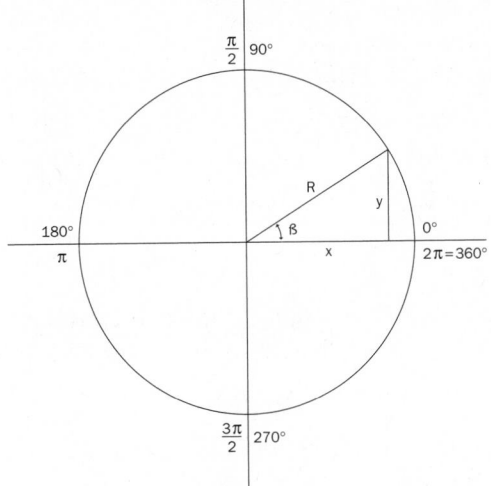

@PI doesn't require an argument—simply enter @PI into a cell. The resulting value is always expressed to 15 significant digits. This means that using @PI will maintain accuracy in your calculations, regardless of the numeric format.

Converting Between Degrees and Radians: @DEGREES and @RADIANS

Most of the trigonometric functions in Quattro Pro require arguments expressed in radians. You're probably much more familiar, however, with the concept of degrees. For example, π radians equals 180 degrees. You can see the relationship between degrees and radians in Figure 7.5.

When you're working with a value expressed in degrees, you'll first need to convert it to radians using

```
@RADIANS(x)
```

where x must be expressed in degrees. In effect, @RADIANS multiplies x by $\pi/180$. For example, a right angle (90 degrees) is converted using @RADIANS(90) to 1.5708 radians; @RADIANS(–45) returns .7854 radians.

Because Quattro Pro's inverse trigonometric functions return values in radians, you'll most likely want to convert their results into degrees using

```
@DEGREES(x)
```

where x must be expressed in radians. In effect, this function multiplies x by $180/\pi$. For example, @DEGREES(π/2) returns 90 degrees.

Other Trigonometric Conversions: @SIN, @COS, and @TAN

@SIN, @COS, and @TAN compute the sine, cosine, and tangent of an angle. The forms of these functions are

```
@SIN(angle ß in radians)
@COS(angle ß in radians)
@TAN(angle ß in radians)
```

where angle β must be expressed in radians. If you're working with an angle expressed in degrees, first convert it to radians—use @SIN(@RADIANS(β)), for example.

Table 7.3 summarizes these trigonometric functions for the triangle in Figure 7.5, as well as other trigonometric relationships such as the secant, cosecant, and cotangent.

Table 7.3   **Trigonometric Functions**

Trig Function	Mathematical Formula	Function
Sine	y/r	@SIN(β)
Cosine	x/r	@COS(β)
Tangent	y/x	@TAN(β)
Cotangent	$x/y = 1/\text{Tangent } \beta$	1/@TAN(β)
Secant	$r/x = 1/\text{Cosine } \beta$	1/@COS(β)
Cosecant	$r/y = 1/\text{Sine } \beta$	1/@SIN(β)

In Figure 7.5, for instance, suppose that angle β is 40 degrees and x is 10 feet. Because the tangent of β is y/x, you can calculate y using @TAN. Because β is in degrees, use @TAN(@RADIANS(40)) to return 0.83910. So Tan(β) = 0.83910 = $y/10$; therefore y is 8.391 feet.

Inverse Trigonometric Functions: @ASIN, @ACOS, @ATAN, and @ATAN2

@ASIN, @ACOS, @ATAN, and @ATAN2 are the inverse functions of @SIN, @COS, and @TAN. These inverse functions return the angle in radians whose sine, cosine, or tangent is specified in the argument. Table 7.4 shows the forms of these functions, the range of minimum and maximum arguments, and the range of results returned.

Table 7.4   **Inverse Trigonometric Functions**

Trig Function	Quattro Pro Function	Argument		Result	
		Min.	Max.	Min.	Max.
Arcsine ß	@ASIN(sine ß)	−1	1	−π/2	π/2
Arccosine ß	@ACOS(cosine ß)	−1	1	0	π
Arctangent ß	@ATAN(tangent ß)	none	none	−π/2	π/2
Arctangent ß	@ATAN2(x,y)	none*	none*	−π	π

---

* @ATAN2(x,0) returns 0; @ATAN(0,0) returns ERR.

All the inverse trigonometric functions return a result in radians. In Figure 7.5, for example, suppose y is 20 and R (the radius) is 40. Sin $ß$ then is 20/40, or 0.5. The arcsine can be calculated as @ASIN(0.5), or 0.5236. Then use @DEGREES(0.5236) to convert this value to 30 degrees. Or simply use @DEGREES(@ASIN(20/40)) to complete this calculation in one step.

@ATAN2(x,y) computes the arctangent of x and y coordinates (see Figure 7.5). Here's an example: Imagine that you want to determine the angle of trajectory for a field-goal kicker to kick a football through the goalpost. The defensive line, 15 yards (45 feet) away, can jump 12 feet high to block the ball. To clear the defense, what is the minimum angle the kicker should use? Using Figure 7.5, x is 45 and y is 12. Using @DEGREES(@ATAN2(45,12)) returns 14.9 degrees. At a minimum then, the kicker should kick the ball at a 15-degree angle.

Hyperbolic Trigonometric Functions: @SINH, @COSH, and @TANH

Note. To learn how to load an add-in function, see "Add-In Functions" at the end of this chapter.

Hyperbolic functions are usually used to solve physical problems, such as the tension on a cable suspended between two points. To return the hyperbolic sine, cosine, and tangent, use one of the new Quattro Pro 4.0 add-in functions

```
@SAMPLE.SINH(x)
@SAMPLE.COSH(x)
@SAMPLE.TANH(x)
```

Instead of describing a circular relationship, the non-periodic hyperbolic functions are described through the identity $\cosh^2 x - \sinh^2 x = 1$ and these relationships:

Hyperbolic Function	Mathematical Formula	Function
Sinh	$1/2(e^x - e^{-x})$	@SAMPLE.SINH(x)
Cosh	$1/2(e^x + e^{-x})$	@SAMPLE.COSH(x)
Tanh	Sinh$x$/Cosh$x$	@SAMPLE.TANH(x)
Coth	Cosh x/Sinh x = 1/Tanh x	1/@SAMPLE.TANH(x)*
Sech	1/Cosh$x$	1/@SAMPLE.COSH(x)
Cosh	1/Sinh$x$	1/@SAMPLE.SINH(x)*

* When x=0, function returns ERR.

Because the hyperbolic cosine is an even function ($\cosh(-x) = \cosh x$), its curve is symmetric about the y-axis. Since the hyperbolic sine is an odd function ($\sinh(-x) = -\sinh x$), its curve is symmetric about the origin. As you may recall, at the origin when x equals 0, cosh$x$ is 1 and sinh$x$ is 0, so the hyperbolic functions all have the same values as the corresponding trigonometric functions.

Logarithmic Functions: @EXP, @LN, and @LOG

Quattro Pro has three closely related logarithmic functions: @EXP, @LN, and @LOG. @EXP calculates the value of e^x, the constant value e raised to the power of x. The form of this function is

    @EXP(x)

where x must return a number between 709 and –703. For example, @EXP(1) returns 2.7182818. @EXP(@LN(10)) returns 10 because the natural logarithm, @LN, is the inverse of @EXP. If x is greater than 709, Quattro Pro can't display or store the results, and @EXP returns ERR. When x is less than –703, @EXP returns 0.

@LN, the inverse of @EXP, calculates the natural logarithm of a value x in base e. Mathematically, $e^y = x$, where $\ln(x) = y$. The form of this function is

    @LN(x)

where x must be a positive value. For example, @LN(10) returns 2.3025, @LN(0.0001) returns –9.2103, but @LN(0) and @LN(–0.0001) return ERR. @LN(@EXP(10)) returns 10 because the natural logarithm is the inverse of the constant value e.

@LOG solves for the base 10 logarithm of a value x. Mathematically, $10^y = x$, where $\log(x) = y$. The form of this function is

```
@LOG (x)
```

where x must evaluate to a positive value. For example, @LOG(7) returns 0.8451, @LOG(0.07) returns –1.1549, but @LOG(0) returns ERR. Because this function uses base 10, @LOG(100) returns 2.

Statistical Functions

Quattro Pro includes ten statistical functions listed in Table 7.5. @AVG and @SUM are among the most commonly used functions.

Table 7.5 **Statistical Functions**

Function	Returns
@SUM	Total of a list of values
@SUMPRODUCT	Total of the products of congruent blocks of values
@COUNT	Number of nonblank cells in a list
@AVG	Mean of a list of values
@MIN	Minimum value in a list of values
@MAX	Maximum value in a list of values
@VAR	Population variance of a list of values
@STD	Population standard deviation of a list of values
@VARS	Sample variance of a list of values
@STDS	Sample standard deviation of a list of values

Adding Values: @SUM

@SUM, which adds a list of values, is the most widely used Quattro Pro function. The form of this function is

    @SUM(*List*)

where *List* is composed of one or more values or groups of values, each separated by a comma. For example, the *List* in @SUM(7,A9,B1..B4) contains three items representing six values: 7, and the values in A9, B1, B2, B3, and B4. Normally, you'll use a block as *List*, as in @SUM(A1..A10).

In the spreadsheet named TOTAL1 in Figure 7.6, for example, @SUM(A4..A8) in cell A9 returns 600. Entering @SUM(A4,A5,A6,A7,A8) or +A4+A5+A6+A7+A8 would give the same result. @SUM([TOTAL2]A1..D1) in cell A1 returns 170. Notice that you must include the file name TOTAL2 when you reference a block in another file.

Figure 7.6

Adding values using @SUM

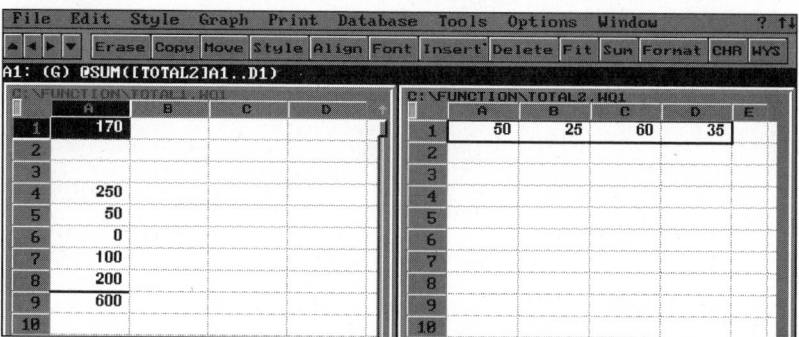

TIP. *In Quattro Pro 4.0,* Sum *is a shortcut for @SUM. In Figure 7.6, for instance, pressing* Sum, *selecting the block A4..A8, and then specifying) also produces @SUM(A4..A8).*

Adding Products: @SUMPRODUCT

@SUMPRODUCT, a specialized statistical function, multiplies the values in corresponding cells of two blocks and adds the products. The form of this function is

    @SUMPRODUCT(*List1*,*List2*)

where *List1* and *List2* must consist of equal-sized, multiple-cell, parallel blocks, each separated by a comma. @SUMPRODUCT returns ERR when the *List1* and *List2* blocks are unequal in size, not parallel, or different in shape.

Figure 7.7, for example, contains the number of Iguana cars sold and the average unit price in four different sales regions. To calculate total sales, you could enter +B3*C3 in cell D3, copy this formula to cells D4, D5, and D6, and then enter @SUM(D3..D6) in cell D7. By using @SUMPRODUCT(B3..B6,C3..C6) in cell E7 instead, you can get the same result in one step. In this case, each block is one column wide, so @SUMPRODUCT multiplies across rows—it first multiplies +B3*C3, +B4*C4, +B5*C5, and +B6*C6, then adds the results to return $1,614,000,000.

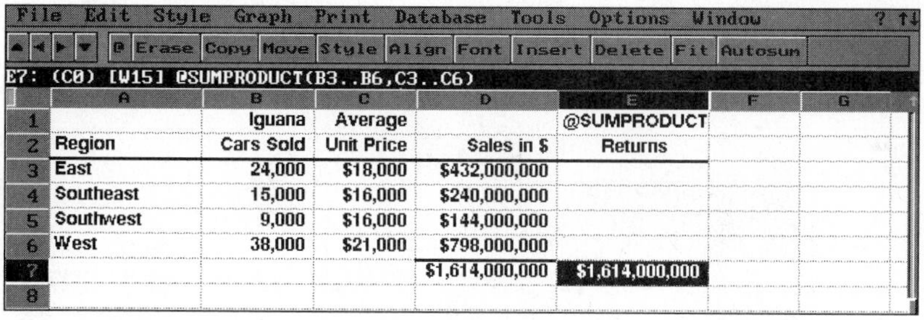

Figure 7.7
Using
@SUMPRODUCT
with single column
blocks

File	Edit	Style	Graph	Print	Database	Tools	Options	Window	? ↑↓

| ▲ | ◀ | ▶ | ▼ | P | Erase | Copy | Move | Style | Align | Font | Insert | Delete | Fit | Autosum |

E7: (C0) [W15] @SUMPRODUCT(B3..B6,C3..C6)

	A	B	C	D	E	F	G
1		Iguana	Average		@SUMPRODUCT		
2	Region	Cars Sold	Unit Price	Sales in $	Returns		
3	East	24,000	$18,000	$432,000,000			
4	Southeast	15,000	$16,000	$240,000,000			
5	Southwest	9,000	$16,000	$144,000,000			
6	West	38,000	$21,000	$798,000,000			
7				$1,614,000,000	$1,614,000,000		
8							

When your blocks are more than one column wide, however, @SUMPRODUCT performs its calculations differently. You can see how this works in Figure 7.8, which contains the same information as Figure 7.7—units sold and average unit price—but for two products, Iguanas and Newts. To calculate the total combined sales, @SUMPRODUCT(B3..C6,D3..E6) in cell G7 first multiplies each cell in the first column (column B) of the first block by the corresponding cell in the first column (column D) of the second block. That is, it calculates +B3*D3, +B4*D4, +B5+D5, and +B6*D6. This process is then repeated for the second column of each block, columns C and E, through the formulas +C3*E3, +C4*E4, +C5*E5, and +C6*E6. Finally, the results are summed to return $4,092,000,000.

Finding the Number of Values in a Cell Block: @COUNT

Tip. To count the number of values within frequency intervals, use the /Tools, Frequency command discussed in Chapter 11.

@COUNT counts the number of nonblank cells in a specified block. The form of this function is

    @COUNT(*List*)

where *List* consists of one or more values or groups of values, each separated by a comma. Normally, *List* is a block.

Figure 7.8

Using @SUMPRODUCT with multiple-column blocks

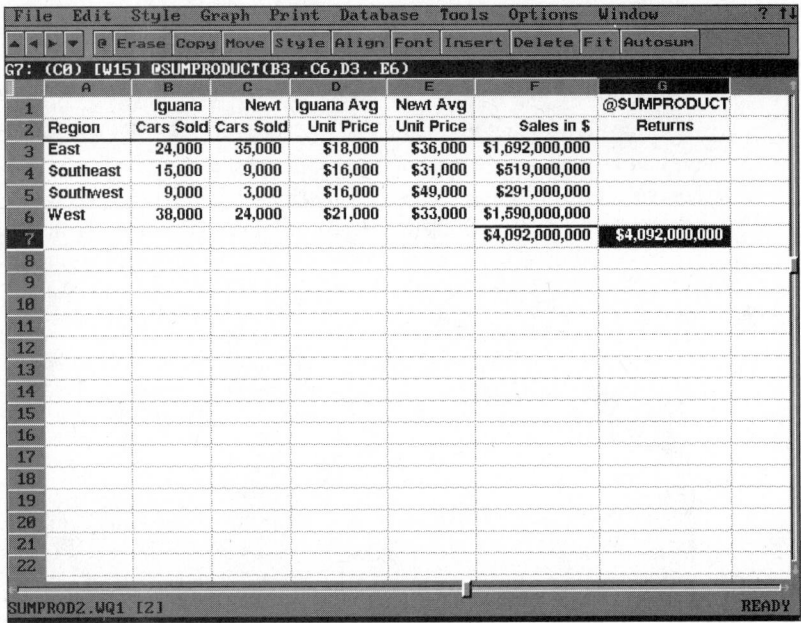

		Iguana	Newt	Iguana Avg	Newt Avg		@SUMPRODUCT
1	Region	Cars Sold	Cars Sold	Unit Price	Unit Price	Sales in $	Returns
3	East	24,000	35,000	$18,000	$36,000	$1,692,000,000	
4	Southeast	15,000	9,000	$16,000	$31,000	$519,000,000	
5	Southwest	9,000	3,000	$16,000	$49,000	$291,000,000	
6	West	38,000	24,000	$21,000	$33,000	$1,590,000,000	
7						$4,092,000,000	$4,092,000,000

Understanding @COUNT will help you better use the more frequently applied @AVG function. @COUNT counts, or assigns a value of 1 to, each cell in *List* that contains a value (including the special values ERR and NA) a formula, a label, or a label prefix. You can see examples of @COUNT in row 9 of Figure 7.9. For instance, @COUNT(B3..B6) in cell B9 counts all 4 values in the block B3..B6.

Figure 7.9

Using @COUNT and @AVG

	A	B	C	D	E	F	G
1		List	List	List	List	List	
2		B3..B6	C3..C6	D3..D7	E3..E6	F3,F4,F5,F6	
3		15	15	15	15	15	
4		5	5	5	5	5	
5		0	Text	0			
6		20	20	20	20	20	
7				Text			
8	@SUM Returns	40	40	40	40	40	
9	@COUNT Returns	4	4	5	3	4	
10	@AVG Returns	10	10	8	13.33	10	
11	@SUM/@COUNT Returns	10	10	8	13.33	10	

Problems with @COUNT

Sometimes you'll get incorrect results with @COUNT because of the way it counts blank cells. Consider Figure 7.9, for example. The problem occurs when a blank cell is a single item in *List*, such as the blank cell F5 included in @COUNT(F3,F4,F5,F6), which returns 4. Quattro Pro evaluates this as @COUNT(F3)+@COUNT(F4)+@COUNT(F5)+@COUNT(F6), or 1+1+1+1. But when a blank cell is part of a block in *List*, as in @COUNT(E3..E6) in cell item E9, blank cell E5 isn't counted and the correct result, 3, is returned. Obviously then, it's usually a good idea to avoid using a single cell item in *List*.

When you're trying to count the number of values in a block, you should also keep in mind that you'll get an incorrect result when a label or a blank cell containing spaces is inadvertently included in *List*. In fact, that's why @COUNT(C3..C6) in cell C9 returns a count of 4—it counts the label in cell C5 of Figure 7.9.

Finding the Average: @AVG

Tip. Use @MAX and @MIN, described later, to calculate the average after excluding the largest and smallest values.

@AVG determines the average, or *arithmetic mean*, of a set of values by adding all the values and dividing the result by the number of values. The form of this function is

```
@AVG(List)
```

where *List* consists of one or more values or groups of values, each separated by a comma. Normally, you'll use a block—in Figure 7.9, for example, @AVG(B3..B6) in cell B10 returns 10.

Problems with @AVG

The @AVG function has many of the same problems as @COUNT. To understand why, you'll need to think of @AVG(*List*) as equal to @SUM(*List*)/@COUNT(*List*). In fact, by comparing rows 10 and 11 in Figure 7.9, you'll see that @AVG returns the same values as @SUM/@COUNT.

The @AVG function returns an incorrect result when *List* includes

■ A cell containing a label, a label prefix, or blank spaces

■ A blank cell included in *List* by itself, not as part of a block

In cell D10 of Figure 7.9, for example, @AVG(D3..D7) returns an incorrect average, 8, because the label in D7 is included in the calculation. Although this label is evaluated as 0 in the numerator, the @SUM function, it's also counted in the denominator, the @COUNT function.

What's more, @AVG returns an incorrect result when a blank cell, like cell F5, is included by itself in *List*. This problem occurs in cell F10 because Quattro

Pro evaluates @AVG(F3,F4,F5,F6) as @SUM(F3,F4,F5,F6)/(1+1+1+1) or 10. See "Problems with @COUNT" earlier, for a full explanation.

Returning Maximum and Minimum Values: @MAX and @MIN

@MAX returns the highest value in a set of values; @MIN returns the lowest value. The forms of these functions are

```
@MAX(List)
@MIN(List)
```

where *List* consists of one or more values or groups of values, each separated by a comma. Usually, *List* is a block. About the only problem you'll run into happens when *List* includes a blank cell or a label, which Quattro Pro evaluates as 0.

Figure 7.10 shows a typical example of how you use @MAX and @MIN. For example, @MAX(B3..B5) in cell B7 correctly returns the maximum damage losses for the first quarter, $20,000. Likewise, @MIN(B3..B5) in cell B8 correctly returns the minimum damage loss, $5,000. Notice in both cases that blank cell B4 is ignored. By contrast, @MIN(C3..C5) in cell C11 incorrectly returns a minimum damage loss in the second quarter because it evaluates the label "Unavailable" in cell C4, as 0.

Figure 7.10
Using @MAX and @MIN

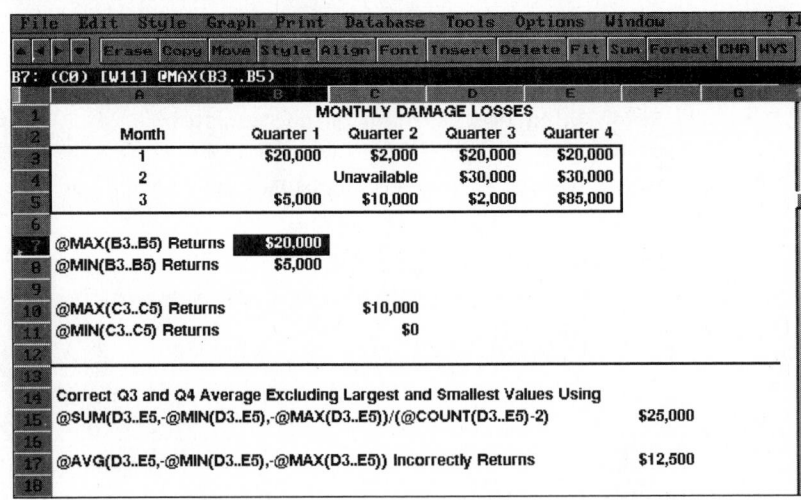

Using @MAX and @MIN to Calculate the Average after Excluding the Largest and Smallest Values

@MAX and @MIN can be used to help calculate the average after throwing out the largest and smallest values. In Figure 7.10, for instance, you can calculate the average monthly loss for the last two quarters using this formula:

```
@SUM(D3..E5,-@MIN(D3..E5),-@MAX(D3..E5))/(@COUNT(D3..E5)-2)
```

Notice that the largest and smallest values are excluded in the @SUM function (the numerator) through the @MAX and @MIN functions. These values are also excluded in the denominator by subtracting 2 from the result of the @COUNT function. Quattro Pro evaluates this formula as $100,000/4 and returns $25,000.

If you try to use the @AVG function shown in Figure 7.10, @AVG-(D3..E5,-@MAX(D3..E5),-@MIN(D3..E5)) returns the incorrect average of $12,500 in cell F17. That's because the total (excluding the largest and smallest values) is divided by 8 items (6 values in D3..E5, the largest value, and the smallest value) instead of 4.

Advanced Statistical Functions: @VAR, @STD, @VARS, and @STDS

You can use Quattro Pro's advanced statistical functions to evaluate a population or a sample of a population. A population consists of all the values in a particular group—the income of each person in the United States, for example. Typically, however, it's practical and economical to analyze only a sample of the population. As you may already know, a sample must include 30 or more *random* selections to statistically profile a population.

The *mean*, or average, is perhaps the most common statistic used to analyze a population or a sample of that population. In Quattro Pro, you use @AVG to calculate the population mean and the sample mean.

Two other statistical calculations evaluate the reliability of the (mean) average by determining whether values are widely dispersed or closely clustered around the mean. The *variance* indicates the total variation of all values from the mean. The *standard deviation* measures the degree of dispersion to which all values deviate from the mean. When you calculate these statistics for a population, you use @VAR and @STD; for a population sample, use @VARS and @STDS.

Population Statistics: @VAR and @STD

The *population variance*, which measures the variation of all values from the mean, is mathematically equivalent to

$$\text{Population Variance} = \frac{\Sigma (i - \text{avg})^2}{N} = \frac{\Sigma (i - @\text{AVG}\,(List))^2}{@\text{COUNT}\,(List)}$$

where i is one value in the population and N is the total number of values in the population. The population variance, then, is mathematically calculated by subtracting each value from the mean, squaring each result, adding the squared values, and dividing the total by N, the number of values in the population.

The variance demonstrates the reliability of the average. For example, the *lower* the variance, the less individual values vary from the mean. A variance of 0 indicates that all values are the same—that is, each value equals the mean.

Actually, the *standard deviation*, equal to

$$\text{Population Standard Deviation} = \sqrt{\text{Population Variance}}$$

is more commonly used than the variance because it's easier to understand. A low standard deviation indicates that individual values are closely clustered around the mean. In a normally distributed population, about 68% of the values are within plus or minus one standard deviation of the mean, 95% are within plus or minus two standard deviations, and 99% are within plus or minus three standard deviations.

The forms of Quattro Pro's population variance and standard deviations functions are

@VAR(*List*)
@STD(*List*)

Tip. To determine if your *List* is normally distributed, use the /Tools, Frequency command discussed in Chapter 11.

where *List*, although usually a block, can consist of one or more values or groups of values, each separated by a comma.

NOTE. *@VAR and @STD have the same problems as @AVG and @COUNT. Therefore, don't include in your* List *any cells containing labels, label prefixes, or blank cells. (See "Problems with @COUNT," earlier in this chapter.)*

In Figure 7.11, for example, suppose that the block A2..E7 contains the incomes of all 30 members of a club—an entire population. @AVG(A2..E7) in cell G3 returns that the mean income of this population is $40,400. Because @STD(A2..E7) in cell G4 returns 14,865, 68% of this population have incomes between $25,535 (Avg – 1Std Dev) and $55,265 (Avg + 1Std Dev). In cell G5, @VAR(A2..E7) calculates the population variance as 220,973,333, which is simply the square of the standard deviation or $(14,865)^2$.

Sample Statistics: @VARS and @STDS

The *sample variance*, which calculates the variation of all values in a sample from the sample mean, is mathematically equivalent to

$$\text{Sample Variance} = \frac{\Sigma (j - \text{avg})^2}{n-1} = \text{Population Variance} \times \frac{n}{n-1}$$

where *j* is one value in the sample and *n* is the total number of values in the sample. The term *n/(n–1)*, or the *degrees of freedom*, modifies the population variance to account for sampling errors. Because *n/(n–1)* is always greater than 1, this term means that the sample variance is always greater than the population variance.

Figure 7.11
Using @VAR, @STD, @VARS, and @STDS

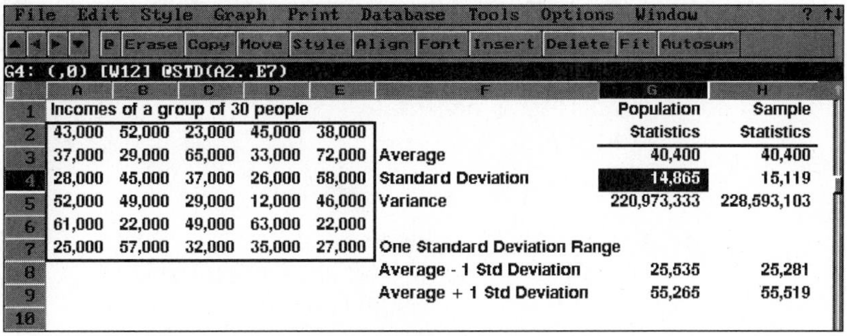

	A	B	C	D	E	F	G	H
1	Incomes of a group of 30 people						Population	Sample
2	43,000	52,000	23,000	45,000	38,000		Statistics	Statistics
3	37,000	29,000	65,000	33,000	72,000	Average	40,400	40,400
4	28,000	45,000	37,000	26,000	58,000	Standard Deviation	14,865	15,119
5	52,000	49,000	29,000	12,000	46,000	Variance	220,973,333	228,593,103
6	61,000	22,000	49,000	63,000	22,000			
7	25,000	57,000	32,000	35,000	27,000	One Standard Deviation Range		
8						Average - 1 Std Deviation	25,535	25,281
9						Average + 1 Std Deviation	55,265	55,519
10								

The sample standard deviation, equal to

$$\text{Sample Standard Deviation} = \sqrt{\text{Sample Variance}}$$

measures how much the sample values vary from the sample mean.

The forms of Quattro Pro's functions are

```
@VARS(List)
@STDS(List)
```

where *List*, although usually a block, can consist of one or more values or groups of values, each separated by a comma.

NOTE. *@VARS and @STDS also return incorrect results when* List *includes any cells containing labels, label prefixes, or blank cells containing spaces. (See "Problems with @COUNT," earlier in this chapter.)*

If you now assume that the 30 values in A2..E7 of Figure 7.11 represent a sample of incomes, then @AVG(A2..E7) in cell H3 calculates the sample mean, 40,400. Although this is the same as the population average, the sample standard deviation indicates that this sample mean is less reliable. Because @STDS(A2..E7) in cell H4 returns a sample standard deviation of 15,119, the sample indicates that 68% of the incomes in the *population* are between \$25,281 (Avg – 1Std Dev) and \$55,519 (Avg + 1Std Dev). In cell H5, @VARS(A2..E7) computes the sample variance of 228,593,103—the square of the sample standard deviation or $(15,119)^2$.

Date and Time Functions

Date and time functions are among the most useful functions Quattro Pro offers. Simply put, they calculate dates and times. In fact, because Quattro Pro calculates dates and times as numeric values, you can manipulate them just as you would any other number in a spreadsheet.

You can use date and time functions to return a specific date or time, to compute the number of days between two dates, or to measure the time elapsed between two times. This allows you to calculate interest, create loan amortization and production schedules, age accounts receivables and payables, and manage time-sensitive projects.

Date Functions

Table 7.6 shows the date functions available in Quattro Pro. Two new functions, @SAMPLE.ADD_MONTHS and @SAMPLE.LAST_DAY. will help you create a series of dates falling on the last day of each month.

Table 7.6 **Date Functions**

Function	Returns
@DATE	Date-value of a date
@DATEVALUE	Date-value of a date string
@SAMPLE.ADD_MONTHS	A series of date-values falling on the last day of each month
@DAY	Day of the month of a date-value
@MONTH	Number of the month of a date-value
@YEAR	Year of a date-value
@SAMPLE.LAST_DAY	Date-value of the last day of a month
@TODAY	Date-value of the current date

Date Function Basics

Note. Formatting dates is discussed in Chapter 3.

To represent dates, Quattro Pro uses a serial numbering system. Each day is identified by an integer called a *date-value*. Date-value 0 is assigned to December 30, 1899, date-value 1 is assigned to Dec 31, 1899, and so on. The highest date-value Quattro Pro recognizes is 73050, representing December 31, 2099.

Because a date function returns a date-value, to make it recognizable you must format it using /Style, Numeric Format or the Format button in Quattro Pro 4.0, and choose Date. Quattro Pro continues to store it as a date-value, however, so you can use it in calculations.

Entering a Date into the Spreadsheet: @DATE

@DATE converts a date to its corresponding date-value (see "Date Function Basics," earlier), which can then be used in calculations. The form of this function is

`@DATE (Yr,Mo,Day)`

where the *Yr*, *Mo*, and *Day* arguments must be within these limits:

Argument	Minimum	Maximum
Yr	0 (year 1900)	199 (year 2099)
Mo	1 (January)	12 (December)
Day	1	last day of a particular month

Here are some examples using @DATE:

Date	@DATE Function	Date-Value Result	Displayed in the D1 Format as
Jan 1, 1900	@DATE(0,1,1)	2	01-Jan-00
Jul 17, 1994	@DATE(94,7,17)	34532	17-Jul-94
Feb 29, 2004	@DATE(104,2,29)	38046	29-Feb-2004
The number of days between July 4 and Christmas in 2010	@DATE(110,12,25) –@DATE(110,7,4)	174	

@DATE uses only the integer portion of an argument, and truncates the rest. For example, @DATE(93,6.7,20) evaluates the 6.7 *Mo* as 6.

@DATE has a built-in error checking feature. It won't accept dates that don't exist—for example, @DATE(95,11,31) returns ERR because there are only 30 days in November. @DATE(93,2,29) also returns ERR because 1993 isn't a leap year.

TIP. *In Quattro Pro, it's actually easier to enter dates using Ctrl-D rather than @DATE (see Chapter 1). For example, if you press Ctrl-D, and enter* **17-Jul-94**, *Quattro Pro displays the date 17-July-94 in the D1 DD-MMM-YY format, but stores it as the date-value 34532. However, you can't use this method to enter a formula containing a date. Try to enter* **17-Jul-94+30**, *for instance, and you'll get an error message. (Using Ctrl-D to enter dates is discussed in Chapter 1.) The easiest way to fill a block with sequential, evenly spaced dates is to use the /Edit, Fill command discussed in Chapter 4.*

Using @SAMPLE.ADD_MONTHS to Fill a Block with End of the Month Dates

To create sequential dates on the last day of each month, you can use the new add-in function

```
@SAMPLE.ADD_MONTHS(DateNumber,Months)
```

where *DateNumber* represents the date-value of the first date, and *Months* is a positive integer representing the number of months you want to step each date. Although you can use a negative *Months* integer, the results aren't always consistent.

To see how to do this, let's create the sequential monthly payment dates in column B of the loan amortization table in Figure 7.12. Payments are made on the last day of each month; the first payment is due on January 31, 1992.

Figure 7.12 Using @SAMPLE.-ADD_MONTHS to create dates at the end of each month

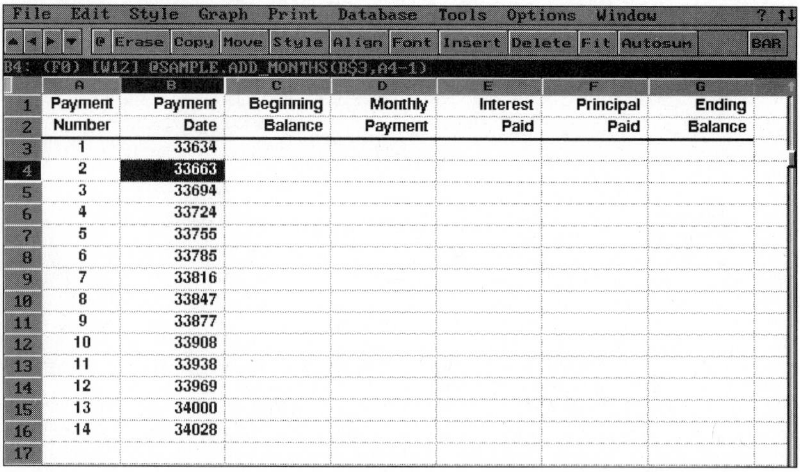

	A	B	C	D	E	F	G
1	Payment	Payment	Beginning	Monthly	Interest	Principal	Ending
2	Number	Date	Balance	Payment	Paid	Paid	Balance
3	1	33634					
4	2	33663					
5	3	33694					
6	4	33724					
7	5	33755					
8	6	33785					
9	7	33816					
10	8	33847					
11	9	33877					
12	10	33908					
13	11	33938					
14	12	33969					
15	13	34000					
16	14	34028					
17							

Note. To load an add-in function, see "Add-in Functions" at the end of this chapter.

Enter the first payment date, January 31, 1992, as @DATE(92,1,31) in cell B3 (or use Ctrl-D). In the next cell, B4, enter @SAMPLE.ADD_MONTHS-(B$3,A4–1). This function uses the date in B3 as the *DateNumber* and a *Months* of 1 to increase each date by 1 month; the result is the date-value for 29-Feb-92, 33663.

When you copy this function to B5..B16, the mixed reference freezes the B$3 address. The correct number of months are added to the date-value 33634 (31-Jan-92) in each cell. In cell B5, this function adds 2 months and returns the date-value 33694 for 31-Mar-92; in cell B6, it adds 3 months and returns the date-value 33724 for 30-Apr-1992. You can see these date-values formatted in Figure 7.13.

It's also easy to create sequential payment dates by quarter or year. For example, @SAMPLE.ADD_MONTHS(B$3,3) in Figure 7.12 would add 3 months to the date-value in B3 and return the date-value 33724 representing 30-Apr-92. @SAMPLE.ADD_MONTHS(B$3,6) adds 6 months and would return the date-value 33816, or 31-Jul-92.

Using Dates in Calculations

Note. @IPAYMT assigns 365.25/12 or 30.4375 days of interest to each month.

Because @DATE returns a numeric date-value, this function can be used to add and subtract dates. In fact, because many banks calculate mortgage interest daily, using the actual number of days in each month is the only way to recreate their loan amortization table. For example, suppose the payment dates in column B of Figure 7.13, created earlier, represent the first fourteen payment dates in a $100,000, 12% fixed rate, 20-year mortgage. The beginning balance in column C is the previous month's ending balance in column G. The $1,101 monthly payment in column D is calculated as @PMT(100000,.12/12,20*12). (See "Fixed Payment per Period to Repay a Loan: @PMT and @PAYMT," later in this chapter.)

In column E, the interest each month is calculated using the number of days in that month through the formula

Days Between Payments ∗ Principal Balance ∗ Daily Interest Rate

In cell E4, for example, the $950 February interest is computed using (B4–B3)∗C4∗0.12/366. (366 days are used because 1992 is a leap year.) Here, B4–B3 returns 29 days, or the number of days between 31-Jan-92 and 29-Feb-92. The exception is the January interest of $1,016, which is computed using (B3–@DATE(91,12,31)∗C3∗0.12/366). Because interest begins accruing on 1-Jan-92, this formula creates 31 days of interest. In 1993, the daily interest in this formula is adjusted to 0.12/365 because 1993 isn't a leap year.

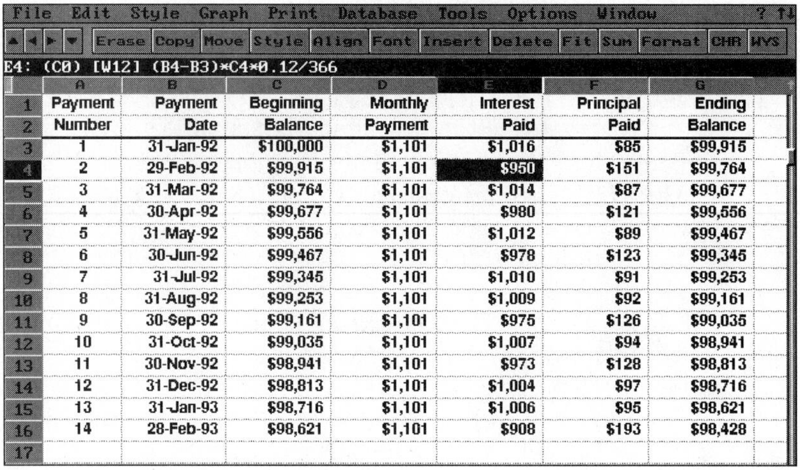

Figure 7.13
Using @DATE to
create a loan
amortization
schedule

```
File  Edit  Style  Graph  Print  Database  Tools  Options  Window        ? ↑↓
▲ ◄ ► ▼   Erase Copy Move Style Align Font Insert Delete Fit Sum Format CHR WYS
E4: (C0) [W12] (B4-B3)*C4*0.12/366
```

	A	B	C	D	E	F	G
1	Payment	Payment	Beginning	Monthly	Interest	Principal	Ending
2	Number	Date	Balance	Payment	Paid	Paid	Balance
3	1	31-Jan-92	$100,000	$1,101	$1,016	$85	$99,915
4	2	29-Feb-92	$99,915	$1,101	$950	$151	$99,764
5	3	31-Mar-92	$99,764	$1,101	$1,014	$87	$99,677
6	4	30-Apr-92	$99,677	$1,101	$980	$121	$99,556
7	5	31-May-92	$99,556	$1,101	$1,012	$89	$99,467
8	6	30-Jun-92	$99,467	$1,101	$978	$123	$99,345
9	7	31-Jul-92	$99,345	$1,101	$1,010	$91	$99,253
10	8	31-Aug-92	$99,253	$1,101	$1,009	$92	$99,161
11	9	30-Sep-92	$99,161	$1,101	$975	$126	$99,035
12	10	31-Oct-92	$99,035	$1,101	$1,007	$94	$98,941
13	11	30-Nov-92	$98,941	$1,101	$973	$128	$98,813
14	12	31-Dec-92	$98,813	$1,101	$1,004	$97	$98,716
15	13	31-Jan-93	$98,716	$1,101	$1,006	$95	$98,621
16	14	28-Feb-93	$98,621	$1,101	$908	$193	$98,428
17							

In column F, the principal paid is simply the payment in column D less the interest in column E. The ending balance in column G is the beginning balance in column C less the principal paid in column F.

Determining the Day of the Week

To determine what day of the week a particular date falls on, you use substantially different techniques in Quattro Pro 3.0 and 4.0. In Quattro Pro 4.0, all you have to do is create a user-defined date format that includes the day of the week. See Chapter 3.

In Quattro Pro 3.0, you can determine what day of the week a particular date falls on with

```
@CHOOSE(@MOD(@DATE(Yr,Mo,Day),7),"Saturday","Sunday","Monday","Tuesday",
"Wednesday","Thursday","Friday")
```

Saturday is always the first item in the @CHOOSE *List*, which has an offset of 0, because December 30, 1899 (date value 0) fell on a Saturday. (@CHOOSE is discussed in "String Functions" later in this chapter.)

For instance, to determine what day of the week July 17, 1994 falls on, use @DATE(94,7,17) in this formula. @MOD divides the 34532 date-value by 7 and returns the modulus 1. @CHOOSE then uses 1 as its *Offset* argument to retrieve the second item in *List*, Sunday.

Returning the Day, Month, and Year: @DAY, @MONTH, and @YEAR

@DAY, @MONTH, and @YEAR return the day, month, and year of a specified date-value. The forms of these functions are

```
@DAY(DateValue)
@MONTH(DateValue)
@YEAR(DateValue)
```

where *DateValue* must result in a date-value between 0 and 73050, corresponding to dates between Dec. 30, 1899 and Dec. 31, 2099. The results of these functions correspond to the arguments in the @DATE function. For example, @DATE(94,7,17) returns 34532. @DAY(34532) returns 17, @MONTH(34532) returns 7, and @YEAR(34532) returns 94.

TIP. *In Quattro Pro 4.0, you can create a user-defined date format that displays the year in a four-digit display, such as 1993; see Chapter 3. In Quattro Pro 3.0, you have to use @YEAR(*DateValue*)+1900. For instance, @YEAR(34001)+1900 returns 93+1900, or 1993.*

Returning the Name of a Month

To determine the name of the month a particular date falls on, you use substantially different techniques in Quattro Pro 3.0 and 4.0. In Quattro Pro 4.0, all you have to do is create a user-defined date format that includes the name of the month—see Chapter 3.

In Quattro Pro 3.0, you must use

```
@CHOOSE(@MONTH(DateValue)-1,"January","February","March","April","May","June",
"July","August","September","October","November","December")
```

where the first item, January, has an offset value of 0, the second item, February, has an offset value of 1, and so on. But because @MONTH returns 1 through 12, @MONTH–1 is used to get the correct result; for example, when @MONTH returns 1, @MONTH–1 equals 0, which returns January. For @MONTH(36526), representing January 1, 2000, this formula returns January. (@CHOOSE is discussed in "String Functions" later in this chapter.)

Calculating the Years, Months, and Days Between Two Dates

Figure 7.14 shows how you can use @YEAR, @MONTH, and @DAY to return the years, months, and days between two dates: July 20, 1969, or date-value 25404 in cell C3, and January 1, 2000, or date-value 36526 in cell C4. The difference of 11122 in cell C5 is used in @YEAR(C5) to return 30 years, in @MONTH(C5)–1 to return 5 months, and in @DAY(C5) to return 13 days. Therefore, on January 1, 2000, it will be 30 years, 5 months, and 13 days since Neil Armstrong set foot on the moon.

Figure 7.14
Using @YEAR,
@MONTH, and
@DAY

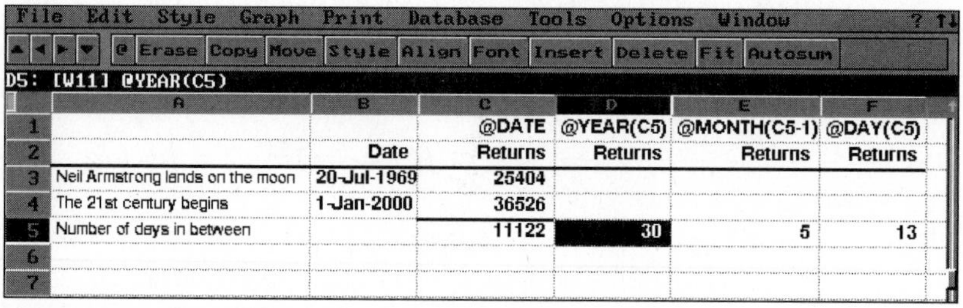

| File | Edit | Style | Graph | Print | Database | Tools | Options | Window | ? ↑↓ |

▲ ◀ ▶ ▼ @ Erase Copy Move Style Align Font Insert Delete Fit Autosum

D5: [W11] @YEAR(C5)

	A	B	C	D	E	F
1			@DATE	@YEAR(C5)	@MONTH(C5-1)	@DAY(C5)
2		Date	Returns	Returns	Returns	Returns
3	Neil Armstrong lands on the moon	20-Jul-1969	25404			
4	The 21st century begins	1-Jan-2000	36526			
5	Number of days in between		11122	30	5	13
6						
7						

Returning the Last Day of a Particular Month

The new add-in function

```
@SAMPLE.LAST_DAY(DateNumber)
```

Note. To learn how to load an add-in function, see "Add-In Functions" at the end of this chapter.

returns the date-value for the last day of a particular month. For example, try using the date-value for April 4, 1993, as *DateNumber*, as in @SAMPLE.LAST_DAY(@DATE(93,4,4)). You'll get the date-value 34089, representing April 30, 1993. Use the date-value for February 2, 1992, in @SAMPLE.LAST_DAY(@DATE(92,2,2)), and the result is the date-value 33663, or February 29, 1992.

Returning the Date-Value of a String: @DATEVALUE

@DATEVALUE returns the date-value that corresponds to a date string. This function is commonly used to convert dates entered as labels to date-values, which can then be used in calculations. Another application is to convert dates imported from another file, such as a ValueLine or a word processing document. The form of this function is

```
@DATEVALUE(DateString)
```

where *DateString* must be a date label from Dec 30, 1899, to Dec 31, 2099, in one of Quattro Pro's five date formats (see Chapter 3). If you enter *DateString* as a literal string, remember to enclose it in double quotes. @DATEVALUE returns ERR if *DateString* isn't in a supported format or if the date doesn't exist. (See "Date Function Basics," earlier.)

For example, @DATEVALUE returns the following date-values for each of the five Quattro Pro date formats:

Numeric Format	@DATEVALUE Function	@DATEVALUE Returns
D1. DD-MM-YY	@DATEVALUE ("26-Jun-98")	35972

Numeric Format	@DATEVALUE Function	@DATEVALUE Returns
D2. DD-MMM	@DATEVALUE ("26-Jun")	33781
D3. MMM-YY	@DATEVALUE ("Jun-98")	35947
D4. (Long Intl.)	@DATEVALUE ("06/26/98")	35972
D5. (Short Intl.)	@DATEVALUE ("06/26")	33781

As you can see, @DATEVALUE returns the date-value 35972 for the D1 and D4 date formats. The D2 and D5 formats don't evaluate the year, so @DATEVALUE gets the current year from your computer's system clock and returns 33781 (June 26, 1992). Since the D3 format doesn't evaluate the day, @DATEVALUE returns the date-value for the first day of the month, 35947 (June 1, 1998).

Entering the Current Date into the Spreadsheet: @TODAY

The @TODAY function, which requires no arguments, returns the current date from your computer's system clock as a date-value. It's often used to date-stamp a spreadsheet or in date calculations. Enter @TODAY in a cell on July 17, 1994, for example, to return the date-value 34532. Then format that cell to display 17-Jul-94.

The result @TODAY returns is updated each time you open the file or the spreadsheet is recalculated. To save the date that @TODAY currently returns, use /Edit, Values.

Figure 7.15 shows how you can use @TODAY to flag all past due accounts receivable every time the file is opened. Here, column C contains the invoice date entered using @DATE, and column D contains the due date calculated by adding 30 to the date-value of the invoice date. Each cell in column E contains a formula similar to the one in cell E2, @IF(D2>=@TODAY,"Current",@TODAY-D2).

Here's how to translate this formula: If the date-value of the due date in cell D2 equals or exceeds today's date-value generated by @TODAY, the account isn't past due and "Current" is returned. Otherwise, the number of days past due is calculated as the date-value of the due date less today's date-value. If today is February 1, 1992, for example, the formula in cell E2 returns "Current" because the due date in cell D2 is greater than today's date. In cell E3, however, this formula calculates that Wagner's Cafe's payment is 15 days overdue.

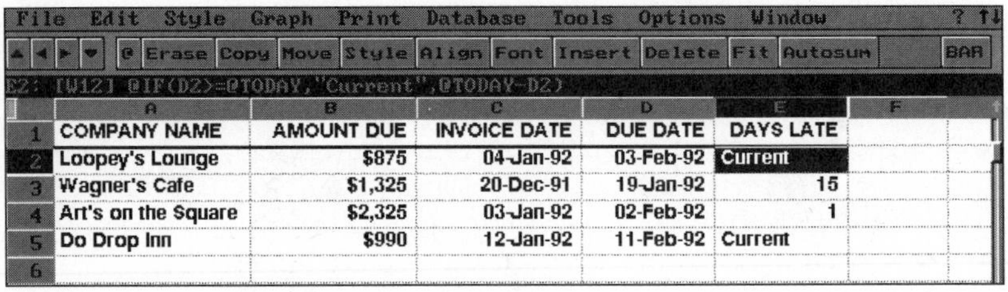

Figure 7.15
Using @TODAY to
age accounts
receivables

Time Functions

Table 7.7 shows the six time functions available in Quattro Pro, all available in previous releases.

Table 7.7   **Time Functions**

Function	Returns
@TIME	Time-value of a time
@TIMEVALUE	Time-value of a time string
@SECOND	Seconds from a time-value
@MINUTE	Minutes from a time-value
@HOUR	Hours from a time-value

Time Function Basics

Quattro Pro represents a time as a *time-value*—a decimal value between 0 and 1, where a 24-hour period, from midnight to midnight, is equal to the value 1. In effect, a time-value measures the time lapsed since midnight. Here's how Quattro Pro evaluates units of time:

Unit	Time-Value
1 day	1.0
1 hour	1.0/24 hours per day = 0.041667
1 minute	1.0/1440 minutes per day = 0.0006944
1 second	1.0/86,400 seconds per day = 0.000011574

For example, 0.041667 times 6 equals 0.25, which represents 6 hours after midnight or 6 a.m.

Because Quattro Pro's time-values are cyclical, starting over every midnight, a particular time-value represents the same time on each day; for instance, 0.25 represents 6 a.m. today *and* 6 a.m. the next day.

To recognize a time-value, you'll need to format it using /Style, Numeric Format (or the Format button in Quattro Pro 4.0), Date, Time. (See Chapter 3.) But because Quattro Pro stores a formatted time as a time-value, you can still use it in time calculations.

Entering Times: @TIME

@TIME converts a time into its corresponding time-value. The form of this function is

    @TIME (Hr,Min,Sec)

where *Hr*, *Min*, and *Sec* must be within these limits:

Argument	Minimum	Maximum
Hr	0	23
Min	0	59
Sec	0	59

The @TIME function uses the 24-hour military clock. For example, 3 p.m. is represented by an *Hr* of 15. @TIME returns ERR, however, when any argument is outside these ranges—when *Hr* is 24, for example. Here are some examples of time-values returned using @TIME:

Time	Enter	Time-Value Result	Displayed in the D8 Format as
12:30:00 A.M.	@TIME(0,30,0)	0.020833	00:30:00
12:30:01 P.M.	@TIME(12,30,1)	0.520845	12:30:01
3:00:59 P.M.	@TIME(15,00,59)	0.625683	15:00:59

TIP. *It's easier to enter a time by pressing Ctrl-D and then entering the time in one of Quattro Pro's four time formats (see Chapter 1). Although the time is displayed in the time format you use, it's still stored as a time-value, so you can use it in calculations. You'll get an error message, however, if you try to use this method to enter a formula containing a time—for example, 11:30:59+6.*

Using @TIME to Add and Subtract Times

You have to use @TIME in time calculations or you'll get incorrect results. In Figure 7.16, @TIME is used to create a use schedule for Room 101. For example, for a two-hour meeting beginning at 9 p.m., +D1+@TIME(2,0,0) in cell D2 returns that the room will be in use until the time-value 0.9583333, or 11:00 p.m. You can't use +D1+2—Quattro Pro will return the value 2.875, which means nothing.

Figure 7.16

Using @TIME to add and subtract times

	A	B	C	D	E	F	G	H
	File Edit Style Graph Print Database Tools Options Window						? ↑↓	
	▲ ◀ ▶ ▼ Erase Copy Move Style Align Font Insert Delete Fit Sum Format CHR WYS							
	D2: [W10] +D1+@TIME(2,0,0)							
1	Room 101	Formula	08:00 PM	09:00 PM	10:00 PM	11:00 PM	12:00 PM	
2	2-hour	+D1+@TIME(2,0,0)		0.9583333				
3	Meeting			11:00 PM				
4	4-hour	+F1+@TIME(4,0,0)				1.125		
5	Meeting					03:00 AM		
6	23-hour	+D1-@TIME(23,0,0)		-0.083333				
7	Marathon			10:00 PM				
8								
9								

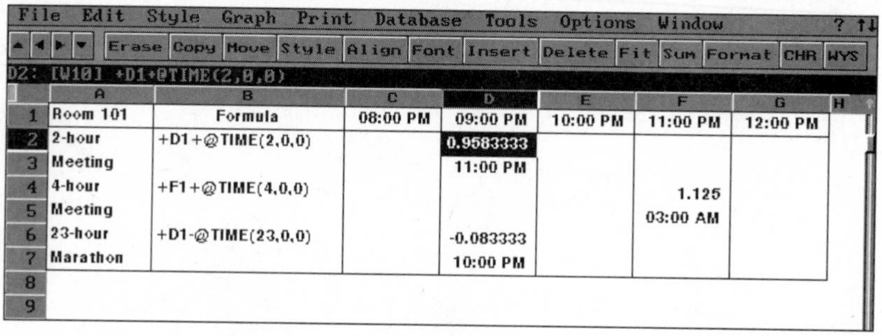

If a late-night 4-hour meeting starts at 11:00 p.m., +F1+@TIME(4,0,0) returns the time-value 1.125 in cell F4. Since time-values start over every midnight, this time-value actually means that the room will be in use until 3:00 a.m. the next day. Likewise, if the room was vacated at 9:00 p.m. after a 23-hour marathon negotiating session, +D1–@TIME(23,0,0) returns the time-value –0.083333 in cell D6. This means that the room has been in use since 10:00 p.m. the previous day.

TIP. *Use the /Edit, Fill command, discussed in Chapter 4, to create a block of sequential time-values that increase or decrease by hours, minutes, or seconds.*

Returning the Hour, Minute, and Second: @HOUR, @MINUTE, and @SECOND

@HOUR, @MINUTE, and @SECOND return the hours, minutes, and seconds of a time-value. The forms of these functions are

```
@HOUR(TimeValue)
@MINUTE(TimeValue)
@SECOND(TimeValue)
```

where *TimeValue* must result in a time-value between 0 and 0.999999. The results of these functions correspond to the arguments in the @TIME function. For example, @TIME(9,33,3) returns .397951; @HOUR(.397951) returns 9 hours, @MINUTE(.397951) returns 33 minutes, and @SECOND(.397951) returns 3 seconds.The results are arithmetic values, not time-values.

In Quattro Pro 4.0, you can create a user-defined time format that returns a time-value in standard time, 3 p.m. for instance, instead of the corresponding military time format, 15. (See Chapter 3.) In Quattro Pro 3.0, you have to use @MOD with @HOUR. For example, @HOUR(.625) returns 15, representing 15:00, but @MOD(@HOUR(.625),12) returns 3, representing 3 p.m.

Returning the Time-Value of a String: @TIMEVALUE

@TIMEVALUE returns the time-value that corresponds to a time string. It's often used to convert times entered or imported as labels. The form of this function is

```
@TIMEVALUE(TimeString)
```

where *TimeString* must be a time label from 00:00:01 to 23:59:59 in one of Quattro Pro's four time formats. If you enter *TimeString* as a literal string, remember to enclose it in double quotes. @TIMEVALUE returns ERR if *TimeString* isn't in one of the four time formats or if any part of the label is outside the @TIME argument limits. (See "Entering Times: @TIME," earlier.)

Here's how @TIMEVALUE evaluates each of Quattro Pro's four time formats:

Time Format	@TIMEVALUE Function	Time-Value Result
D6. HH:MM:SS am/pm	@TIMEVALUE("03:30:45 pm")	0.646354
D7. HH:MM am/pm	@TIMEVALUE("03:30 pm")	0.625
D8. (Long Intl.)	@TIMEVALUE("15:30:45")	0.646354
D9. (Short Intl.)	@TIMEVALUE("15:30")	0.625

As you can see, when *TimeString* is in the D6 and D8 formats, @TIMEVALUE returns 0.646354, the time-value representing 3:30:45 p.m. But since the D7 and D9 formats don't evaluate the seconds, Quattro Pro assumes 0 seconds, and returns the time-value 0.625 for 3:30:00 p.m.

Combining Dates and Times

When you combine date- and time-values in a single value, Quattro Pro evaluates the integer portion as a date-value and the decimal portion as a time-value. (See "Date Function Basics," and "Time Function Basics," earlier.) For example, @DATE(94,7,4)+@TIME(12,1,30) returns 34519.50104, corresponding to July 4, 1994 at 12:01:30 p.m.

In Quattro Pro 3.0, you can only format a cell to display either the date or the time. In Quattro Pro 4.0, however, you can create a user-defined format that displays both; see Chapter 3.

Calculating with Date and Time Combinations

Suppose you plan to drive from San Francisco to New York, beginning on June 1, 1992 at 6 a.m., or @DATE(92,6,1)+@TIME(6,0,0). If you believe the trip will take 8 days and 4 hours, your travel time is 8+@TIME(4,0,0). Here, the 8 represents 8 days in date/time units. You can calculate your estimated time of arrival, then, as

```
@DATE(92,6,1)+@TIME(6,0,0)+(8+@TIME(4,0,0))
```

This formula returns 33764.41667, so assign a D1 date format to display the arrival date, 09-Jun-92; assign a D6 time format to display the arrival time, 10:00 a.m., Eastern time (7:00 a.m. Pacific time). In Quattro Pro 4.0, you can create a combined date/time format that displays 09-Jun-92 10:00 a.m.

Entering the Current Date and Time: @NOW

@NOW, which requires no arguments, checks the current date and time on your computer's system clock, and returns a combined date-and-time-value. Consider using this function to time-stamp a spreadsheet.

Note. @TODAY returns only the current date.

Enter @NOW into a cell at 3:15 p.m. on January 30, 1993, for example, to return 33999.635416667. Assign a date format to display 30-Jan-93 or a time format to display 3:15:00 PM, or in Quattro Pro 4.0, create a user-defined format that displays both. The value @NOW returns is automatically recalculated each time you open the file or the spreadsheet is recalculated. To save the date and time currently returned by @NOW, use /Edit, Values, discussed in Chapter 4.

Logic and Error-Trapping Functions

Quattro Pro's logic and error-trapping functions are decision-making tools that let you evaluate and test conditions in a spreadsheet, macro, or database. Table 7.8 shows these functions, including @ISAPP and @ISAAF, new in version 4.0.

Table 7.8   **Logic and Error-Trapping Functions**

Function	Returns
@IF	True result if the conditional test is true, false result otherwise
@TRUE	Value 1
@FALSE	Value 0
@ERR	Value ERR
@NA	Value NA
@ISERR	Value 1 for the value ERR, 0 otherwise
@ISNA	Value 1 for the value NA, 0 otherwise
@ISSTRING	Value 1 for a string, 0 otherwise
@ISNUMBER	Value 1 for a value or blank cell, 0 otherwise
@ISAPP	Value 1 for a currently loaded add-in, 0 otherwise
@ISAAF	Value 1 for a function defined in a loaded add-in, 0 otherwise

Conditional Tests: @IF

One of the most versatile functions in Quattro Pro, @IF, lets you perform decision-making tests in almost any situation which has at least two possible outcomes. The form of this function is

```
@IF(Condition,TrueExpression,FalseExpression)
```

where *Condition* is the test you want to analyze. If *Condition* is true, @IF returns the *TrueExpression*; if *Condition* is false, @IF returns the *FalseExpression*.

The *Condition* Argument

The *Condition* argument defines the *conditional test* that compares two items to each other using a *logical operator* like < or =. Table 7.9 shows Quattro Pro's simple logical operators. If the Condition created by a logical operator is true, Quattro Pro returns the true value 1; if the Condition is false, it returns the false value 0.

For example, the *Condition* 95>12.5 returns 1 (true) because 95 is greater than 12.5. The *Condition* B5="SUNDAY" is true and returns 1 when cell B5 contains the label SUNDAY, and 0 (false) otherwise. A *Condition* can also include a formula or a function, such as (+A1+A2)/2<100 or

@AVG([SALES]A1..F25)>=1000. (Remember, when you reference cells in another file, include the file name.)

Table 7.9	**Simple Logical Operators**	
	Operator	**Operation**
	=	Equal to
	<>	Not equal to
	>	Greater than
	>=	Greater than or equal to
	<	Less than
	<=	Less than or equal to

The *TrueExpression* and *FalseExpression* Arguments

When the *Condition* argument in an @IF function is true (value 1), Quattro Pro returns *TrueExpression*; when the *Condition* is false (value 0), *FalseExpression* is returned. The *TrueExpression* and *FalseExpression* arguments can be a value, a string, a formula, or another condition. In fact, you can even use another @IF function as *TrueExpression* or *FalseExpression*, which is called *nesting*. (See "Nesting @IF Functions," later in this section).

For example, @IF(B5>=35,"MILD","COLD") compares the contents in cell B5 to 35. When the value in cell B5 is greater than or equal to 35, the *Condition* is true and returns the *TrueExpression* MILD. Otherwise, the *Condition* is false and returns the *FalseExpression* COLD.

NOTE. *If you enter a literal string in @IF, remember to enclose it in double quotes, just like "MILD" and "COLD" above.*

Evaluating Values with @IF

Note. Quattro Pro assigns a 0 value to a blank cell.

Suppose that a video store has a clearance sale. If you buy up to 5 cassettes, you pay $10 each; buy 6 or more, and you pay $8 each. The @IF function is used in Figure 7.17 to model this price structure. In cell B6, for example, the *Condition* in @IF(A6>5,+A6*8,+A6*10) evaluates that the 6 cassettes in cell A6 are greater than 5, and returns the *TrueExpression* +A6*8, or $48. By contrast, @IF(A7>5,+A7*8,+A7*10) in cell B7 evaluates that the value in A7, 5, is not greater than 5 and returns the *FalseExpression* +A7*10, or $50.

Figure 7.17
Evaluating values
with @IF

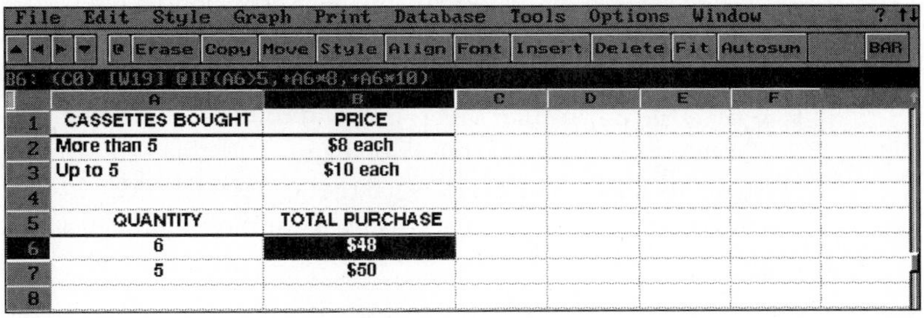

File Edit Style Graph Print Database Tools Options Window	? ↑↓
▲ ◄ ► ▼	@ Erase Copy Move Style Align Font Insert Delete Fit Autosum	BAR

B6: (C0) [W19] @IF(A6>5,+A6*8,+A6*10)

	A	B	C	D	E	F
1	CASSETTES BOUGHT	PRICE				
2	More than 5	$8 each				
3	Up to 5	$10 each				
4						
5	QUANTITY	TOTAL PURCHASE				
6	6	$48				
7	5	$50				
8						

Evaluating Strings with @IF

When you use a string in a *Condition* argument, capitalization differences
and label alignment (designated by label prefixes) won't affect your results.
But because Quattro Pro evaluates two strings with spelling differences and
spacing differences (including extra leading or trailing spaces) as unequal,
these differences will affect your results.

Note. The mixed
references freeze
the row references
in C1 and C2 and
the column
references in A5
and B5 when the
formula is copied
to C5..F11.

Figure 7.18 shows a spreadsheet that uses strings in the @IF function to
keep a running inventory of parts for a bicycle shop. For example, cell C5
contains @IF($A5=C$1,$B5*C$2,""). Because @IF evaluates the proper
case string "Frame" in cell A5 as equal to the uppercase string "FRAME" in
cell C1, it uses the *TrueExpression*, $B5*C$2, and returns 12*50 or 600. But
because "Whels" in cell A9 is spelled differently than "WHEELS" in cell
E1, @IF($A9=E$1,$B9*E$2,"") in cell E9 returns the *FalseExpression*, a
null string. A null string is also returned in cell C10 because the right-aligned
label " Frame" in cell A10 includes trailing spaces.

Figure 7.18
Evaluating strings
with @IF

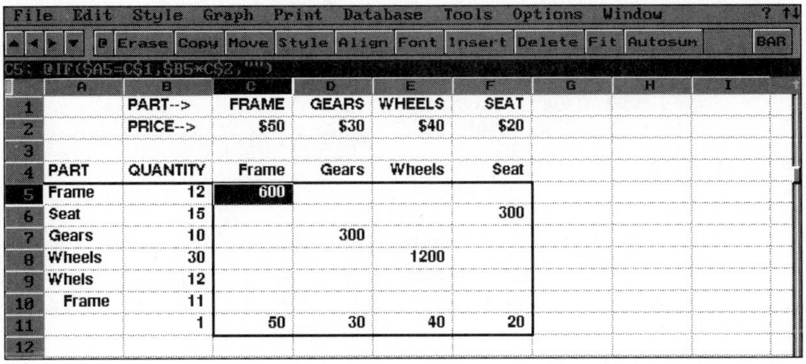 File Edit Style Graph Print Database Tools Options Window	? ↑↓
▲ ◄ ► ▼	@ Erase Copy Move Style Align Font Insert Delete Fit Autosum	BAR

C5: @IF($A5=C$1,$B5*C$2,"")

	A	B	C	D	E	F	G	H	I
1		PART-->	FRAME	GEARS	WHEELS	SEAT			
2		PRICE-->	$50	$30	$40	$20			
3									
4	PART	QUANTITY	Frame	Gears	Wheels	Seat			
5	Frame	12	600						
6	Seat	15				300			
7	Gears	10		300					
8	Wheels	30			1200				
9	Whels	12							
10	Frame	11							
11		1	50	30	40	20			
12									

Figure 7.18 shows a common problem that can occur when you use @IF to evaluate strings. Quattro Pro evaluates a string and a blank cell as both equal to the value 0; this is why each @IF function in row 11 evaluates blank cell A11 as equal to the labels in row 1. For example, @IF($A11=C$1,$B11*C$1,"") uses the *True Expression* $B11*C$1 and returns 1*50 or 50.

When you're evaluating two strings and want to differentiate between capitalization, use the @EXACT function as the @IF *Condition*. For an example, see "Testing Two Strings for Equality: @EXACT" later in this chapter.

Concatenating Strings and Blank Cells with @IF

@IF is the only way you can *concatenate*, or join, a string and a blank cell in Quattro Pro. In Figure 7.19, for example, the first, middle, and last names are being concatenated; when a person doesn't have a middle name, the cell in column B, such as B3, is left blank.

Figure 7.19

Concatenating strings with @IF

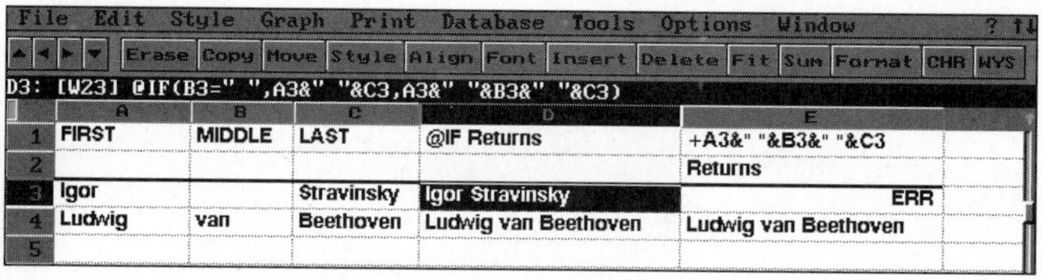

In cell D3, @IF(B3=" ",+A3&" "&C3,+A3&" "&B3&" "&C3) evaluates whether cell B3 is blank. Because it is, @IF uses the *TrueExpression*, which uses the *concatenation operator* & to join only the first and last names in cells A3 and C3. The result is "Igor Stravinsky". Notice that the *TrueExpression* adds a space between the concatenated names. By contrast, you can see what happens in cell E3 when you use the formula +A3&" "&B3&" "&C3: blank cell B3 causes this formula to return ERR.

Because cell B4 contains a string, the *Condition* in

```
@IF(B4="  ",+A4&"  "&C4,+A4&"  "&B4&"  "&C4)
```

and the *FalseExpression* joins the first, middle, and last names to return Ludwig van Beethoven. Notice that this *FalseExpression* concatenation formula adds a space between the first and middle name, and between the middle and last name.

Compound Logical Operators: #AND#, #NOT#, and #OR#

You can use the complex logical operators #AND#, #NOT#, and #OR# shown in Table 7.10 to create a *multicondition test*—a test for more than one condition in a single @IF function. For instance, the #AND# operator in @IF(A1>2#AND#A2>5000,"TAKE VACATION","WORK OVERTIME") tests two conditions. Only when both A1>2 *and* A2>5,000 are true is the *TrueExpression* TAKE VACATION returned. If one of these conditions is false, @IF returns the *FalseExpression* WORK OVERTIME.

The #OR# operator returns the *TrueExpression* if any one of the conditions is true. In @IF(A1>2#OR#A2>5000,"TAKE VACATION","WORK OVERTIME"), the *TrueExpression* TAKE VACATION is returned whenever either A1>2 *or* A2>5000 *or* both are true. Only when both of the conditions are false does @IF return the *FalseExpression* WORK OVERTIME.

Table 7.10 **Compound Logical Operators**

Operator	Operation	Example
#AND#	And	A1>2#AND#A2>5000
#OR#	Or	A1>2#OR#A2>5000
#NOT#	Not	#NOT#A2>5000

The #NOT# operator is different because it negates a conditional test by forcing @IF to analyze the *opposite* of the condition. For example,

```
@IF(#NOT#A2>5000,"TAKE VACATION","WORK OVERTIME")
```

returns the *TrueExpression* TAKE VACATION when A2<=5000, and the *FalseExpression* WORK OVERTIME when A2>5000.

Note. Because #NOT# has a higher order of precedence than the #AND# and #OR# (see Chapter 1), it's evaluated first regardless of its location in an *@IF Condition*.

Using Parentheses to Change the Order of Precedence

By default, Quattro Pro evaluates complex logical operators from left to right. For example, in

```
@IF(A1>2#AND#A2>5000#OR#A3>40,"TAKE VACATION","WORK OVERTIME")
```

here's how @IF evaluates the *Condition*: First, it evaluates whether A1>2 *and* A2>5000 are true. If both conditions are true, only then does it evaluate whether A3>40.

You can, however, use parentheses to control the *order of precedence*—the order in which Quattro Pro evaluates each condition in a multicondition test. For example, in

```
@IF(A1>2#AND#(A2>5000#OR#A3>40),"TAKE VACATION","WORK OVERTIME")
```

the *Condition* is evaluated differently. Here, the parentheses force (A2>5000#OR#A3>40) to be evaluated first. Therefore, if either A2>5000 or A3>40 is true, only then is A1>2 evaluated.

Nesting @IF Functions

When you need to test multiple conditions, you can create a logical hierarchy by *nesting* @IF functions—including another @IF as the *TrueExpression* and/or the *FalseExpression*. Nesting allows you to perform complex decision making while using a formula that remains relatively easy to understand and debug. When you're nesting @IF functions, however, keep in mind that you're limited to 254 characters total, the maximum length of a cell entry in Quattro Pro.

Figure 7.20 shows how nesting @IF functions can help you create logic that evaluates more than two solutions. Here, a stock recommendation is based on three minimum financial indicators: sales of $20,000,000, net profit of 8%, and a growth rate of 10%. A company earning at least 8% of sales is given a HOLD recommendation. One earning at least 8% and either generating $20,000,000 in sales or experiencing a 10% growth rate is rated a BUY. A company not generating at least 8% in profits is rated a SELL, regardless of its other financial ratios. In cell B6, all of these conditions are incorporated into the formula

```
@IF(B2>=0.08,@IF(B3>=20000000#OR#B4>=0.10,"BUY","HOLD"),"SELL")
```

Figure 7.20
Nesting @IF functions

File Edit Style Graph Print Database Tools Options Window   ? ↑↓
▲ ◀ ▶ ▼ @ Erase Copy Move Style Align Font Insert Delete Fit Autosum   BAR
B6: @IF(B2>=0.08,@IF(B3>=20000000#OR#B4>=0.1,"BUY","HOLD"),"SELL")

	A	B	C	D	E
1		Centron Corp	Genome Corp	Altos Airline	
2	Profit on Sales	7%	10%	9%	
3	Sales	$25,000,000	$50,000,000	$18,000,000	
4	Sales Growth Rate	11%	6%	9%	
5					
6	@IF Returns	SELL	BUY	HOLD	
7					

Here's how the first @IF function is evaluated:

B2>=0.08 Condition	Result
True	Evaluates *TrueExpression* @IF(B3>=20000000#OR#B4>=0.10, "BUY","HOLD")
False	Returns *FalseExpression* SELL

Since Centron Corp. generated only 7% profits in cell B2, which is less than the required 8%, the *Condition* in the first @IF is false, and the *FalseExpression* SELL is returned. Because Genome Corp. in column C generated a 10% profit, however, the *Condition* in the first @IF is true, and the second @IF function is evaluated in this way:

C3>=20000000 Condition	C4>=0.10 Condition	Result
True	True or False	Returns *TrueExpression* BUY
True or False	True	Returns *TrueExpression* BUY
False	False	Returns *FalseExpression* HOLD

When *either* sales are at least $20,000,000 *or* the growth rate is at least 10%, the second @IF function returns its *TrueExpression* BUY. For example, although Genome Corp.'s sales of $50,000,000 easily exceed the minimum $20,000,000 sales level, this company is only experiencing a 6% growth rate, which is lower than the 10% target. Because it meets just one of the conditions, the second @IF returns a BUY recommendation for this stock.

By contrast, Altos Airline in column D generated a 9% profit so the second @IF function is also evaluated. But neither its $18,000,000 sales nor its 9% growth rate meet the $20,000,000 sales or 10% growth rate conditions in the second @IF. In this case, Quattro Pro evaluates the *Condition* of the second @IF function as false, and returns the *FalseExpression* recommendation, HOLD.

True and False Values: @TRUE and @FALSE

@TRUE returns the true value 1; @FALSE returns the false value 0. Neither require an argument. Typically, @TRUE and @FALSE are used in macros, as the *TrueExpression* and *FalseExpression* arguments in @CHOOSE or in @IF. For instance, @IF(D4>10,@TRUE,@FALSE) returns 1 when cell D4 contains a value greater than 10 and 0 when it doesn't.

Flagging Errors: @ERR

@ERR returns the special value ERR, not the label ERR. Because it doesn't require an argument, simply enter @ERR in a cell.

Consider using @ERR in an @IF function to create error-trapping logic that flags errors. For example, imagine that cell E20 contains the number of employees, which can't be negative. The function @IF(E20>=0,+E20,@ERR) returns the number of employees when cell E20 contains 0 or a positive value, and ERR otherwise—that is, when it's a negative value.

Note. The functions @COUNT, @DCOUNT, @ISERR, @ISNA, @ISNUMBER, @ISSTRING, @CELL, @CELLINDEX, and @CELLPOINTER don't return ERR if they reference a cell containing the value ERR.

@ERR can produce a ripple effect in your spreadsheet. Because the value ERR has the highest precedence of all values (see Chapter 1), a cell that references a cell containing ERR returns ERR. To understand this, imagine that cell F14 contains @ERR, which returns ERR. If cell F15 contains +F14, it returns ERR. If cell F16 indirectly references cell F14 through the formula +F15, it also returns ERR. When this happens, use @ISERR to stop the ripple effect. (See "Blocking the Ripple Effect of ERR or NA," later in this section.)

Flagging an Unknown Value: @NA

@NA, which doesn't require an argument, returns the special value NA (not available), not the label NA. Use it as a placeholder for incomplete spreadsheet data or to determine which formulas in a spreadsheet reference a particular cell.

A formula that directly or indirectly references a cell containing @NA returns NA, unless ERR overrides it. For instance, if cell F14 contains @NA, which returns NA, and cell F15 contains +F14, the formula returns NA. But if cell F16 contains ERR, +F15+F16 returns ERR, not NA, because ERR has a higher order of precedence.

Checking for ERR and NA: @ISERR and @ISNA

@ISERR tests for the special value ERR (error). @ISNA tests for the special value NA (not available). The forms of these functions are

```
@ISERR(x)
@ISNA(x)
```

where x, normally a cell reference, can be a formula, value, string, or condition. @ISERR returns 1 (true) when x evaluates to the special value ERR, and 0 otherwise. @ISNA returns 1 when x evaluates to the special value NA, and 0 otherwise. Typically, you'll use these functions either to divide by 0 or to stop the ripple effect of ERR or NA.

Using @ISERR to Divide by Zero

Many times, ERR results from a division by 0. If cell B6 is blank or contains 0, for example, +5/B6 in cell A1 returns ERR. Instead, use @IF(@ISERR(+5/B6),0,+5/B6) which returns 0 when B6 is blank or contains 0, and the results of +5/B6 otherwise.

Blocking the Ripple Effect of ERR or NA

@ISERR prevents ERR from rippling through your spreadsheet. Likewise, @ISNA stops the ripple effect of NA. To see how this works, imagine that cell A1 evaluates to ERR. Therefore, in cell B1 the formula +A1 also returns ERR, as does +B1 in cell C1. By contrast, if cell B1 contains the formula @IF(ISERR(A1),0,A1), it returns 0 when A1 contains ERR, and the contents of cell A1 otherwise. What's more, the formula +B1 in cell C1 no longer returns ERR, but 0 instead.

Testing for Strings or Values: @ISSTRING and @ISNUMBER

@ISSTRING and @ISNUMBER test for a string, a value, or a blank cell. The forms of these functions are

```
@ISSTRING(x)
@ISNUMBER(x)
```

where x, though normally a cell reference, can be a value, string, or condition. Here's how these functions work:

x Evaluates to a	@ISSTRING Returns	@ISNUMBER Returns
Label, label prefix, or blank cell with spaces	1	0
Value, including special values ERR and NA	0	1
Blank cell	0	1

Note. Macros are discussed in Chapters 12 and 13.

@ISSTRING and @ISNUMBER are often used in interactive macros to test for improper data entry in a cell. The TEST_CELL macro in Figure 7.21, for example, uses {IF @ISNUMBER(ZIP)}{BRANCH ERROR} in cell B13 to make sure that the zip code was entered as a label in the cell named ZIP, B6.

If ZIP is blank or contains a value, @ISNUMBER evaluates to 1, which makes the {IF} statement true. This causes the macro to branch to the ERROR routine, beginning in cell B16, and display the error message

"Enter zip code as a LABEL". If the zip code is entered in B6 as a label, however, @ISNUMBER returns 0, the macro continues to the {BRANCH ADD} line in cell B14, and the ADD routine adds the record in B1..B6 to the database. (See also "Returning Cell Attributes: @CELL, @CELLINDEX, @CELLPOINTER" later in this chapter.)

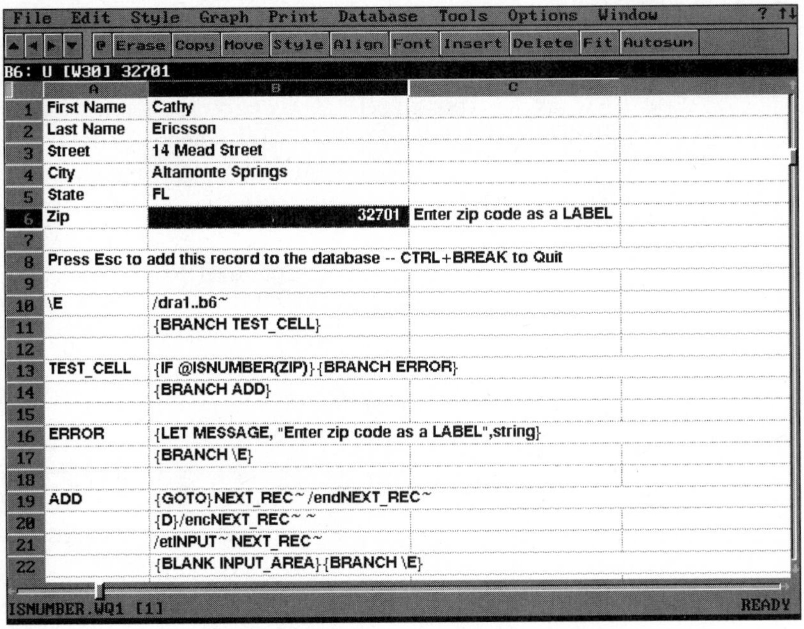

Figure 7.21
Using @ISNUMBER in a macro to test data entry

Checking for Add-ins: @ISAPP and @ISAAF

Two new functions in Quattro Pro 4.0, @ISAPP and @ISAAF, test for currently loaded add-ins. The forms of these functions are

```
@ISAPP(Addin)
@ISAAF(Addin.Function)
```

If you enter *Addin* or *Addin.Function* as a literal string, remember to enclose it in double quotes.

@ISAPP tests whether a particular add-in library is currently loaded. If *Addin* is a module loaded in memory, @ISAPP returns 1; otherwise it returns 0. @ISAAF tests whether a particular @function is defined in a currently loaded add-in library. For example, if the add-in library Custom.QLL is currently loaded, @ISAAF("Custom.Budget") returns 1 if the add-in function Budget is defined in the Custom library, and 0 if it isn't.

Lookup Functions

You can use Quattro Pro's lookup functions, listed in Table 7.11, to "look up" or retrieve a string or value from a list or a table. All of these functions were offered in previous releases.

Table 7.11 **Lookup Functions**

Function	Retrieves
@CHOOSE	Item from a list
@INDEX	Item from an index table
@VLOOKUP	Item from a vertical lookup table
@HLOOKUP	Item from a horizontal lookup table

Choosing an Item from a List: @CHOOSE

@CHOOSE retrieves an item, such as a string or value, from a list. The form of this function is

```
@CHOOSE(Number,List)
```

Note. If a cell address in *List* references a blank cell, @CHOOSE will return 0 when it's selected.

List is the set of items you want to select from. It can contain values, formulas, literal strings enclosed in double quotes, and single cell addresses, each separated by a comma. The entire *List* can't exceed 254 characters. Because a block can't be an item in *List*—@CHOOSE returns ERR—use @CHOOSE only when *List* consists of a few items. (For a large group of items, use one of the other lookup functions discussed later.)

The integer portion of the *Number* argument determines the item @CHOOSE selects from *List*. The first item in *List* has an offset value of 0; the last item has an offset value of $n-1$, where n is the number of items in *List*. If *Number* is negative or greater than $n-1$, @CHOOSE returns ERR.

Figure 7.22 shows how you can incorporate a price structure in @CHOOSE to calculate the price of different-sized hotel banquets. Here, cells C4, C5, and C6 contain the price per person for different group sizes, which are used as *List* in @CHOOSE.

Figure 7.22

Incorporating a pricing structure into @CHOOSE

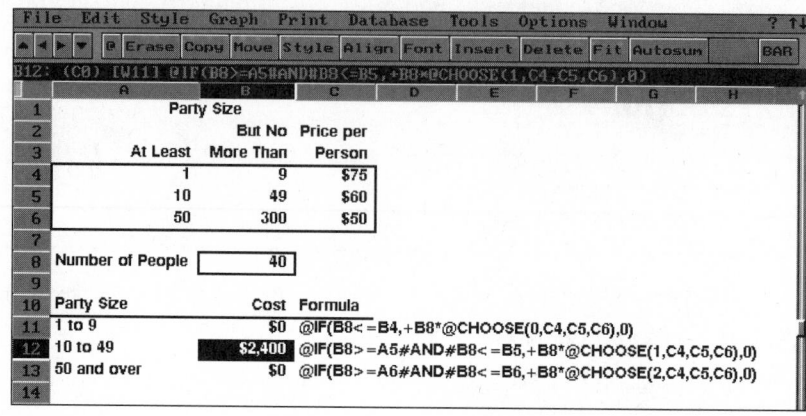

To calculate the actual price for a specific party, 40 in cell B8 for instance, three different @IF functions use @CHOOSE as the *TrueExpression*. In cell B12 for example, the *Condition* B8>=A5#AND#B8<=B5 in

```
@IF(B8>=A5#AND#B8<=B5,+B8*@CHOOSE(1,C4,C5,C6),0)
```

compares the party size in B8, 40, with the 10 to 49 party size limits in A5 and B5. Because it's true that 40 is within this range, @IF uses the *TrueExpression* +B8*@CHOOSE(1,C4,C5,C6) and calculates the price of the party. In @CHOOSE, the *Number* offset of 1 retrieves the second item in *List*, $60 per person in cell C5. The cost of dinner is calculated then, as the 40 people in cell B8 times $60 per person, or $2,400.

This @IF function is designed to return the *FalseExpression* 0 when the party size in B8 falls outside of the *Condition* range 10 to 49. Depending on the size of the party, the *Condition* argument in one of the other @IF functions is then true, and the price is calculated by the @CHOOSE function in its *TrueExpression*.

Retrieving an Item from an Index Table: @INDEX

The @INDEX function retrieves an item from an *index table*, which is any continuous block containing values and/or strings. You'll find an index table an efficient way to categorize and retrieve nonlinear data—for example, taxes or accelerated depreciation.

The form of this function is

```
@INDEX (Block,Column,Row)
```

where *Block* is the block address or name of the index table. @INDEX returns 0 if it selects a blank cell in the *Block* index table.

You tell @INDEX which item to select through *offset coordinates*. In an index table, each cell has two unique offset coordinates, *Column* and *Row*. The leftmost column in an index table has a *Column* offset value of 0; the rightmost column *c* has a *Column* offset of *c*–1. The top row has a *Row* offset of 0; the last row *r* has a *Row* offset of *r*–1. Therefore, the upper-left cell in an index table is represented by a *Column* offset of 0 and a *Row* offset of 0. The lower-right cell has a *Column* offset of *c*–1, and a *Row* offset of *r*–1. Obviously, a *Column* offset of *c* or greater, or a *Row* offset of *r* or greater, specifies a cell outside the index table, and @INDEX returns ERR.

The index table B4..E8 in Figure 7.23 contains a nonlinear sales commission schedule. Columns B and C contain the rates for Region 1 during the first two quarters, columns D and E the rates for Region 2.

Figure 7.23
Using @INDEX with an index table

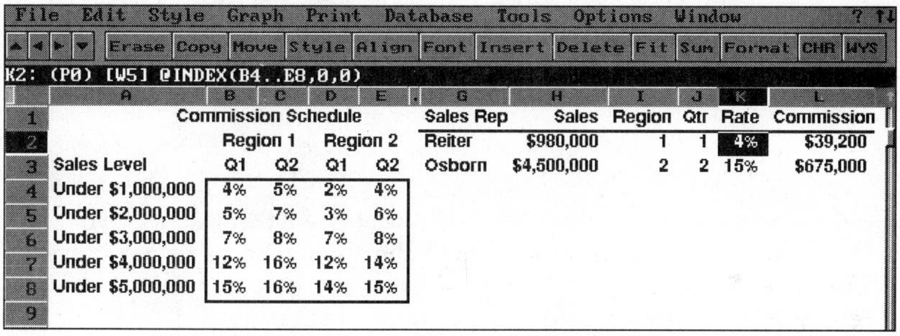

	A	B	C	D	E	G	H	I	J	K	L
1		Commission Schedule				Sales Rep	Sales	Region	Qtr	Rate	Commission
2		Region 1		Region 2		Reiter	$980,000	1	1	4%	$39,200
3	Sales Level	Q1	Q2	Q1	Q2	Osborn	$4,500,000	2	2	15%	$675,000
4	Under $1,000,000	4%	5%	2%	4%						
5	Under $2,000,000	5%	7%	3%	6%						
6	Under $3,000,000	7%	8%	7%	8%						
7	Under $4,000,000	12%	16%	12%	14%						
8	Under $5,000,000	15%	16%	14%	15%						
9											

In cell K2, Reiter's commission rate is retrieved by @INDEX(B4..E8,0,0). To return a commission rate for Region 1, Quarter 1, a *Column* offset of 0 says to look in the first column of the table, column B. Because Reiter generated sales less than $1,000,000, the *Row* offset of 0 tells Quattro Pro to look in the first row of the table, row 4. So @INDEX retrieves the 4% commission rate in cell B4—the upper-left cell of the table.

Because Osborn is from Region 2, and his commission is for sales in Quarter 2, @INDEX(B4..E8,3,3) uses a *Column* offset of 3 to return data from the fourth (last) column in the index table. Since he generated less than $5,000,000 in sales, a *Row* offset of 4 says to fetch an item from the fifth (last) row in the table. As you can see in cell K3, @INDEX retrieves 15% from column 4, row 5, or cell E8.

Retrieving an Item from a Vertical Lookup Table: @VLOOKUP

The @VLOOKUP function retrieves an item from a *vertical lookup table*, a two-dimensional block with at least two columns and two rows and no blank columns. The leftmost column, called the *index column*, must contain only values or only strings. If @VLOOKUP finds the value or string you're searching for in the index column, it returns an item from the same row in the lookup table, but from the column you specify.

The form of this function is

```
@VLOOKUP(x,Block,Column)
```

where *x* is the value or string you're looking for in the index column, and *Block* is the block address or block name of the vertical lookup table.

Column represents an offset value that tells @VLOOKUP which column to retrieve data from. Because the index column has an offset value of 0, specify a *Column* offset between 1 and *c*–1, where *c* is the number of columns in the lookup table. If you use an offset value of *c* or greater, @VLOOKUP returns ERR since you've specified a column outside of the lookup table.

If the index column contains values, a *Column* offset of 0 retrieves the value in the index column specified by *x*. But if the index column contains strings, a *Column* offset of 0 rather unexpectedly returns an offset value representing the row location of the string *x* in the index column.

Using @VLOOKUP with Values

Figure 7.24 shows how you can use @VLOOKUP with values. This spreadsheet contains a vertical lookup table in A4..C7, which is used to calculate the federal tax withheld in 1992 when an employee receives a paycheck every two weeks, known as biweekly income. The *Block* A4..C7 is a valid vertical lookup table because the leftmost column—the index column—contains

- Values in ascending order

- No duplicate values

- No blank cells

- The lowest income level, $0, for which the lowest values in columns B and C apply

- *Critical values*, the values at which the values in columns B and C change

- The lowest income value, $1,944, for which the highest values in columns B and C apply

Figure 7.24

Using @VLOOKUP
with values

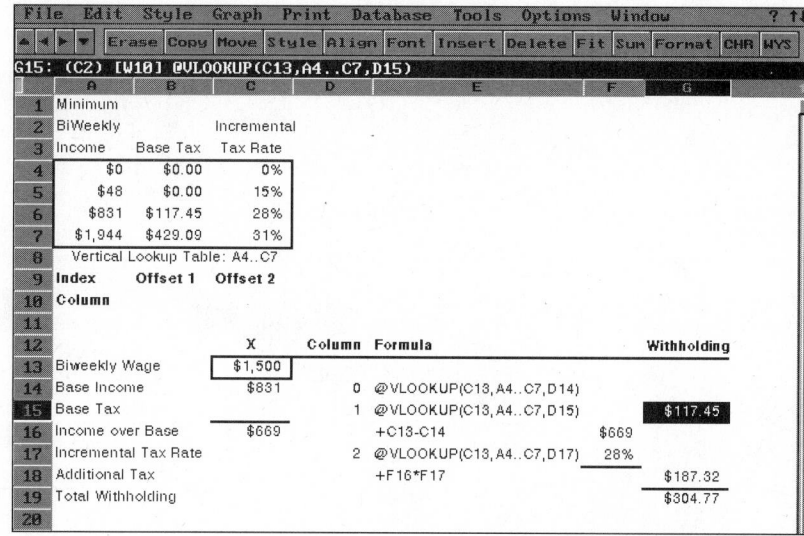

When you use values in the index column, @VLOOKUP moves down the index column and stops searching the first time it finds a value equal to but not greater than *x*. That's why it's so important that the index column values be unique and in ascending order.

For the $1,500 *x* wage in cell C13, the Base Tax is returned in cell G15 by @VLOOKUP(C13,A4..C7,D15). @VLOOKUP searches the index column for a value closest to but not greater than *x*, and finds $831 in cell A6. The *Column* offset of 1 in cell D15 then tells @VLOOKUP to return the corresponding value in column 2 of the table, or the base tax of $117.45 from cell B6.

To calculate the additional tax due, we've used @VLOOKUP two different ways. In a slightly unconventional approach, @VLOOKUP(C13,A4..C7,D14) in cell C14 uses a *Column* offset of 0 to return the Base Income value, $831—the value @VLOOKUP uses in the index column for the $1,500 wage. This makes it easy to calculate the $669 Income over Base in cell C16. Then @VLOOKUP-(C13,A4..C7,D17) in cell F17 uses a *Column* offset of 2 to return the Incremental Tax Rate of 28% from cell C6. The Income over Base is multiplied by this Incremental Tax Rate to return the Additional Tax of $187.32 in cell G18. This is then added to the $117.45 Base Tax to compute a Total Withholding of $304.77.

Using @VLOOKUP with Strings

Although you can use strings in the index column of a vertical lookup table, @VLOOKUP will only "find" one when the *x* string is an exact match. @VLOOKUP only considers two strings to be an exact match when they have the same spelling, capitalization, spacing between words, and leading and trailing spaces.

In Figure 7.25, the vertical lookup table in A3..C8 uses state names in index column A to return a corresponding abbreviation and nickname. In cell G3, for example, @VLOOKUP(E3,A3..C8,F3) finds an exact match for the *x* string New Jersey in cell A4 of the index column. It then uses the *Column* offset of 2 to move to the third column, column C, and returns the nickname "The Garden State" from cell C4.

Figure 7.25

Using @VLOOKUP with strings

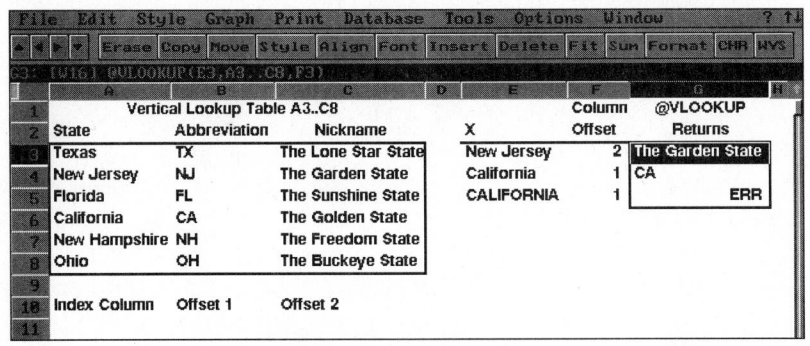

Likewise, @VLOOKUP(E4,A3..C8,F4) in cell G4 finds an exact match for the *x* string California in cell A6 of the index column, and then uses the *Column* offset of 1 to return the abbreviation "CA" from cell B6. In cell G5, however, @VLOOKUP(E5,A3..C8,F5) returns ERR because it doesn't find an exact match in the index row for the uppercase *x* string CALIFORNIA.

Retrieving an Item from a Horizontal Lookup Table: @HLOOKUP

@HLOOKUP works the same as @VLOOKUP except that it retrieves an item from a horizontal lookup table. A *horizontal lookup table* must be composed of at least two rows and two columns without any empty rows. @HLOOKUP, however, compares *x* against the contents of the *index row*—the uppermost row of the table. In the index row, @HLOOKUP works from left to right, beginning in the leftmost cell. When it finds the first value closest to but not greater than *x*, or the first string that matches *x*, @HLOOKUP retrieves an item from that column, but in the row you specify.

The form of this function is

`@HLOOKUP(x,Block,Row)`

where *x* is the value or string you're looking for in the index row, and *Block* is the block address or block name of the horizontal lookup table.

The *Row* offset tells @HLOOKUP which row in the horizontal lookup table to retrieve data from. Because the index row has an offset value of 0, specify a *Row* offset between 1 and *r*–1, where *r* is the number of rows in the lookup table. If you use a negative *Row*, or one greater than *r*, then @HLOOKUP returns ERR since you've specified a row outside of the lookup table. If the index row contains values, a *Row* offset of 0 retrieves the value in the index row specified by *x*. But if the index row contains strings, a *Row* offset of 0 returns an offset value representing the column location of the string *x* in the index row.

Using @HLOOKUP with Values and Strings

The horizontal lookup table B2..E10 in Figure 7.26 is designed to return the used car price for the models in the index row, row 2. In cell J6, for example, @HLOOKUP(H6,B2..E10,I6) begins in the leftmost cell of the index row, cell B2. Moving right, it compares *x*, the string "4-door" in cell H6, to each cell in this row. When it encounters an exact match in cell C2, @HLOOKUP uses the *Row* offset of 3 to move down column C and retrieve a value in the fourth row of the table, $7,000 in cell C5, which is the price for a used 1986 4-door.

Figure 7.26
Using @HLOOKUP with strings and values

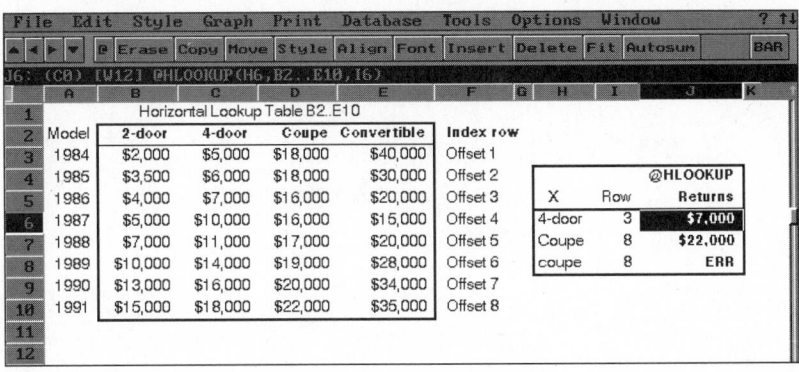

Likewise, @HLOOKUP(H7,B2..E10,I7) in cell J7 finds an exact match for *x*, Coupe, in cell D2 of the index row. It then uses the *Row* offset of 8 to move down column D to the 9th or last row, cell D10. The result is $22,000, the price for a used 1991 Coupe. By contrast, because of the capitalization differences, @HLOOKUP in cell J8 doesn't find an exact match in the index row for *x*, coupe, and returns ERR instead.

String Functions

The functions listed in Table 7.12 manipulate strings. Typically, you'll use these functions to:

- Concatenate (join) strings, or strings and values
- Edit strings and labels
- Convert strings to values, and values to strings
- Test for strings and values

Table 7.12   **Quattro Pro's String Functions**

Function	Operation
Information	**Returns**
@LENGTH	Number of characters in a string
@FIND	Starting position of a substring in a string
Text Editing	**Performs**
@LOWER	Converts all characters to lowercase
@UPPER	Converts all characters to uppercase
@PROPER	Converts first character in every word to uppercase, all other characters to lowercase
@TRIM	Removes extra blank spaces
@CLEAN	Removes all non-ASCII characters
@LEFT	Returns specified number of characters starting from left end of string
@RIGHT	Returns specified number of characters starting from right end of string
@MID	Returns specified number of characters, beginning at a start point
@REPLACE	Replaces specified number of characters in string with another string, or adds new string at beginning or end of string
@REPEAT	Repeats string a specified number of times
Conversion	**Converts**
@STRING	A value to a string
@VALUE	A string to a value

Table 7.12	(Continued)
Function	**Operation**
Testing	**Tests**
@EXACT	Two strings for equality
@N	First cell in block for a value
@S	First cell in block for a string
Character	**Converts**
@CHAR	IBM PC Character Set code to its character
@CODE	Character to its IBM PC Character Set code
Hexadecimal	**Converts**
@NUMTOHEX	Base 10 value to its base 16 string
@HEXTONUM	Hexadecimal string to its base 10 value

String Information Functions

@LENGTH and @FIND provide information about a string. Usually, you'll nest one of these functions in @LEFT, @RIGHT, @MID, or @REPLACE when you're editing a string. @LENGTH and @FIND are also used in macros to return information about strings.

Determining the Length of a String: @LENGTH

Because @LENGTH returns the number of characters in a string, including blank spaces, it's usually used to calculate the length of a string or a substring when you're working with the text editing functions shown in Table 7.12. @LENGTH is also commonly used in a macro to check that entries requiring a specific length, such as Social Security numbers and zip codes, are entered correctly.

The form of this function is

```
@LENGTH(String)
```

If you use a literal *String*, remember to enclose it in double quotes. In cell C3 of Figure 7.27, for example, @LENGTH(A3) returns that the string "San Jose" is 8 characters long. But because @LENGTH(A4) in cell C4 returns 9, the identical-looking string in cell A4 must have 1 trailing space.

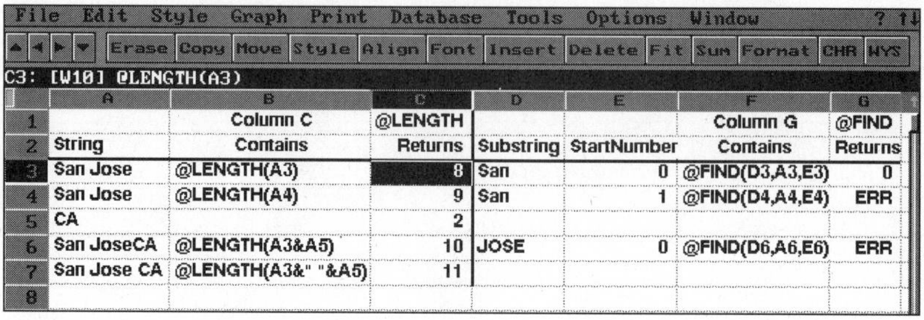

Figure 7.27
Using @LENGTH
and @FIND

| File | Edit | Style | Graph | Print | Database | Tools | Options | Window | ? ↑↓ |

| ▲ ◄ ▼ | Erase | Copy | Move | Style | Align | Font | Insert | Delete | Fit | Sum | Format | CHR | WYS |

C3: [W10] @LENGTH(A3)

	A	B	C	D	E	F	G
1		Column C	@LENGTH			Column G	@FIND
2	String	Contains	Returns	Substring	StartNumber	Contains	Returns
3	San Jose	@LENGTH(A3)	8	San	0	@FIND(D3,A3,E3)	0
4	San Jose	@LENGTH(A4)	9	San	1	@FIND(D4,A4,E4)	ERR
5	CA		2				
6	San JoseCA	@LENGTH(A3&A5)	10	JOSE	0	@FIND(D6,A6,E6)	ERR
7	San Jose CA	@LENGTH(A3&" "&A5)	11				
8							

Note. @LENGTH
returns ERR if your
argument
references a blank
cell or a cell
containing a value.

When two strings are concatenated, @LENGTH returns the length of the new string. In cell C6, for instance, @LENGTH(A3&A5) returns the information that the new string "San JoseCA" is 10 characters long. In cell C7, however, @LENGTH(+A3&" "&A5) returns a length of 11 because the formula +A3&" "&A5 adds a space between the concatenated strings.

Locating a Substring within a String: @FIND

@FIND returns the position of the first occurrence of a substring in a string after the starting point you specify. @FIND is frequently used to search a macro for a character sequence, such as keystrokes or macro commands. @FIND can also be a good way to return the *StartNumber* or *Number* arguments in @MID, @LEFT, @RIGHT, and @REPLACE. (See "Text Editing Functions," later in this chapter).

The form of this function is

`@FIND(Substring,String,StartNumber)`

where *Substring* is what you're searching for in *String*. For @FIND to find the *Substring*, it must exactly match the spelling, spacing, capitalization, and accent marks of what you're looking for in *String*. If no match is found, @FIND returns ERR.

The *StartNumber* specifies the place within *String* that @FIND begins searching. Because *StartNumber* uses an offset of 0, the leftmost character in *String* has a *StartNumber* of 0; the last character has a *StartNumber* of $n-1$, where n is the length of *String*. If *StartNumber* is negative or greater than $n-1$, @FIND returns ERR.

In cell G3 of Figure 7.27, for example, @FIND(D3,A3,E3) detects an exact match for the *Substring* "San" beginning at character 1 in *String*, and returns an offset value of 0. By contrast, @FIND(D4,A4,E4) in cell G4 doesn't find a match and returns ERR because the *StartNumber* of 1 says to start searching for "San" at character 2 of *String*. @FIND(D6,A6,E6) in cell

G6 returns ERR for a different reason—there isn't a match for the *SubString* "JOSE" because of its capitalization.

Text Editing Functions

The ten text editing functions listed in Table 7.12 can help you edit text. All of these functions were available in previous Quattro Pro releases.

Case Conversion of Strings: @UPPER, @LOWER, and @PROPER

@UPPER, @LOWER, and @PROPER convert the case, or capitalization, of a string. When you're performing a case-sensitive sort, these functions are often used beforehand to convert labels in a database to the same case. They're also used to make labels in a spreadsheet consistent. The forms of these functions are

    @UPPER(*String*)
    @LOWER(*String*)
    @PROPER(*String*)

@UPPER converts all characters in *String* to uppercase. @LOWER converts everything to lowercase. @PROPER capitalizes the first letter in *String* and the first letter after a blank space or a nonalphabetic character, such as . (period), 4, and #.

Figure 7.28 shows the effect @UPPER, @LOWER, and @PROPER have on the *String* "Depreciation Method—MACRS" in cell A2. In cell C2, for example, @UPPER(A2) capitalizes all letters. By contrast, @LOWER(A2) in cell C3 converts all letters to lowercase. In cell C4, @PROPER(A2) capitalizes the first letter in every word because each is preceded either by a blank space or by the nonalphabetic hyphen character (-) and converts all other letters to lowercase.

Figure 7.28
Using @UPPER, @LOWER, and @PROPER

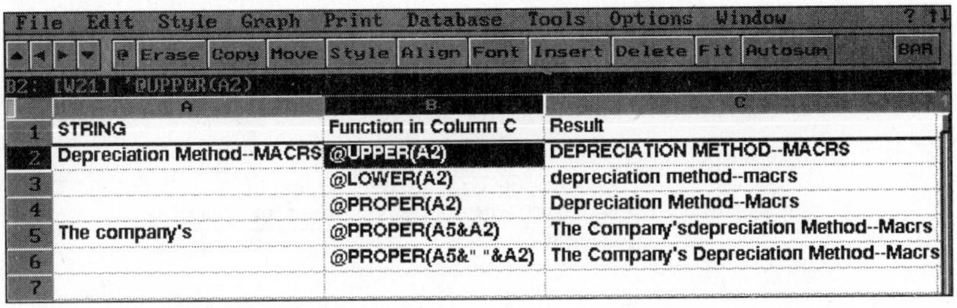

When you concatenate strings, @PROPER returns different results depending on the spacing between the concatenated strings. In cell C5, for example,

@PROPER(A5&A2) doesn't capitalize the first letter "d" in the A5 string because it's joined to the string in A2 without a space. In cell C6, however, the "D" is capitalized because the concatenation formula @PROPER(A5&" "&A2) adds a space before the second string.

Trimming Unnecessary Spaces: @TRIM

@TRIM removes (trims) all unneeded spaces from a string. Here are some ways to use it:

- In a macro, to create consistent spacing in each data entry.

- Before you sort a database, to create consistent spacing. (Blank spaces can affect how data is sorted.)

- To remove extra spaces when concatenating strings.

- To edit labels in a spreadsheet.

    The form of this function is

    @TRIM(*String*)

@TRIM removes all leading spaces from the beginning of *String*, all trailing spaces from the end of *String*, and any additional blank spaces after a blank space. However, it always leaves one blank space between concatenated strings.

Figure 7.29 illustrates how @TRIM works. In column C, @LENGTH says that the *String* in cell B2 is 45 characters long, but the same string in cell B3 is 60 characters long—it includes 5 leading spaces, 5 trailing spaces, and 5 unnecessary spaces between "of" and "8%". Now you can evaluate how @TRIM(B3) works in cell B4. Because @LENGTH in column C shows that the string @TRIM returns is 45 characters, you know that @TRIM removed all leading and trailing spaces, and all spaces except one between words.

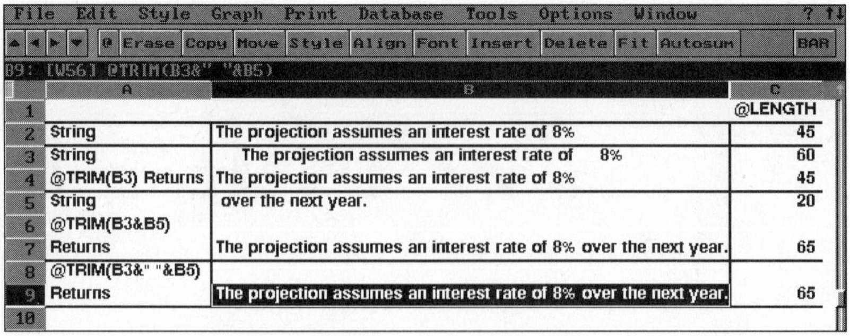

Figure 7.29
Using @TRIM

	A	B	C
			@LENGTH
1			
2	String	The projection assumes an interest rate of 8%	45
3	String	The projection assumes an interest rate of 8%	60
4	@TRIM(B3) Returns	The projection assumes an interest rate of 8%	45
5	String	over the next year.	20
6	@TRIM(B3&B5)		
7	Returns	The projection assumes an interest rate of 8% over the next year.	65
8	@TRIM(B3&" "&B5)		
9	Returns	The projection assumes an interest rate of 8% over the next year.	65
10			

When *String* is the result of two concatenated strings, @TRIM always leaves one space between them. In cells B7 and B9, for example, @TRIM (+B3&B5) and @TRIM(+B3&" "&B5) both leave a space between the concatenated strings and return a string 65 characters long.

Removing All Non-Printable ASCII Characters: @CLEAN

@CLEAN removes all non-printable ASCII characters (0 to 31) from a string. The form of this function is

`@CLEAN(String)`

When you import data files, such as database or word processing files, you can use @CLEAN to delete characters that Quattro Pro can't evaluate. You can also use @CLEAN to remove non-printable ASCII characters from files imported from services like CompuServe or Dow Jones News/Retrieval.

Extracting Strings: @LEFT, @RIGHT, and @MID

@LEFT, @RIGHT, and @MID extract a portion of a string while leaving the string intact. You can use these functions to make labels consistent (for example, to convert both *Revenues* and *Revenue* to *Rev*); to copy only a portion of a label to a cell; or to employ only a portion of a label in a macro or database. The forms of these functions are

`@LEFT(String,Number)`
`@RIGHT(String,Number)`
`@MID(String,StartNumber,Number)`

Beginning from the left of *String*, @LEFT extracts the *Number* of characters you specify. @RIGHT begins from the right of *String* when it extracts the *Number* of characters.

@MID, however, starts extracting characters at the *StartNumber* position. Because the leftmost character has an offset value of 0, *StartNumber* must be between 0 and $n-1$, where n is the length of *String*. If *StartNumber* is negative, @MID returns ERR; if *StartNumber* is greater than $n-1$, @MID returns a null string (""").

Assuming n is the length of *String*, a *Number* from 1 to n tells Quattro Pro the length of the substring to extract. If *Number* is negative, you'll get ERR; when *Number* is 0, you'll get a null string (""). When *Number* is n or greater, @LEFT and @RIGHT return the entire string; @MID returns all characters after *StartNumber*.

Figure 7.30 shows how these functions affect the 16-character *String* "Year Ending 1992". @LEFT starts from the left, and @RIGHT starts from the right. Here's the different results they return for the same *Number* argument:

String	**Number**	**Characters @LEFT Returns**	**Characters @RIGHT Returns**
Year Ending 1992	1	Leftmost "Y"	Rightmost "2"
Year Ending 1992	4	4 leftmost "Year"	4 rightmost "1992"
Year Ending 1992	17	Entire 16-character string "Year Ending string 1992"	Entire 16-character string "Year Ending string 1992"

Figure 7.30
Using @LEFT, @RIGHT, and @MID

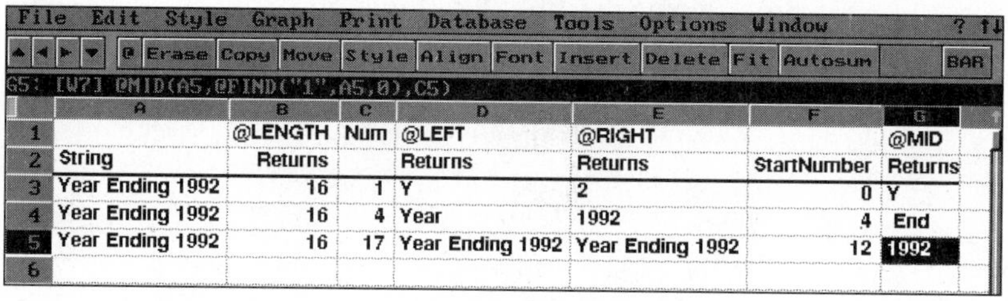

	A	B	C	D	E	F	G
1		@LENGTH	Num	@LEFT	@RIGHT		@MID
2	String	Returns		Returns	Returns	StartNumber	Returns
3	Year Ending 1992	16	1	Y	2	0	Y
4	Year Ending 1992	16	4	Year	1992	4	End
5	Year Ending 1992	16	17	Year Ending 1992	Year Ending 1992	12	1992
6							

@MID begins at the *StartNumber*, counting from the left end of *String*. When *StartNumber* is 0, as in @MID(A3,F3,C3) in cell G3, @MID produces the same result as @LEFT. The *Number* argument of 1 extracts the leftmost character "Y", which has an offset value 0. In cell G4, the *StartNumber* 4 tells @MID(A4,F4,C4) to start extracting at the fifth character, the first blank space. The *Number* argument of 4 then returns the 4 characters " End".

TIP. *When you want to start extracting at a unique character in* String, *consider using @FIND(*Substring,String,StartNumber*) as the @MID* StartNumber *argument. Because the 1 in "Year Ending 1992" is unique, for example, @MID(A5,@FIND("1",A5,0),C5) in cell G5 of Figure 7.30 begins extracting at the "1". Even if a character isn't unique, you can still use @FIND as the* StartNumber *by incorporating a unique character into your logic. @MID(A5,@FIND("g",A5,0)+1,C5), for instance, would begin extracting at the second blank space because @FIND("g",A5,0)+1 represents the second blank space as 1 character after the unique "g".*

Replacing or Adding a String: @REPLACE

You can use @REPLACE to replace all or part of a string with another string or to add another string to the beginning or end of a string. The form of this function is

@REPLACE(*String*, *StartNumber*, *Number*, *NewString*)

Use the *StartNumber* to say where, from the left, you want the *New-String* to begin replacing *String*. The leftmost character in *String* has an offset value or *StartNumber* of 0; the last character an offset of *n*–1 when the *String* is *n* characters long.

Beginning at the *Start Number*, the *Number* argument represents the number of characters, including blank spaces, that you want to replace in *String*. Naturally then, *Number* can be between 0 and *n*.

Depending on the *StartNumber* and *Number* arguments you use, @REPLACE accomplishes the following:

StartNumber	Number	@REPLACE
0	0	Adds *NewString* in front of *String*
	1 to *n*–1	Beginning from the left, replaces the length of *String* equal to *Number* with *NewString*
	n or greater	Replaces entire *String* with *NewString*
1 to *n*–1	1 to *n*–1	Beginning at *StartNumber*, replaces the length of *String* equal to *Number* with *NewString*
n or greater	Any positive number	Adds *NewString* to the end of *String*

Figure 7.31 shows how @REPLACE works. Column A contains the *String* "Coca Cola". In column B, @LENGTH returns the number of characters in this string. As explained in column G, Column F contains the results returned by @REPLACE using the *StartNumber* arguments in Column C, the *Number* arguments in Column D, and the *NewString* arguments in Column E.

Adding a New String at the Beginning or End of an Existing String
By using @REPLACE to add a *NewString* at the beginning or the end of *String*, you produce the same result as concatenating two strings. In

cell F3, for example, @REPLACE(A3,C3,D3,E3) uses a *StartNumber* of 0 and *Number* of 0 to add the *NewString* to the beginning of *String*; the result is "Diet Coca Cola".

Figure 7.31
Using @REPLACE

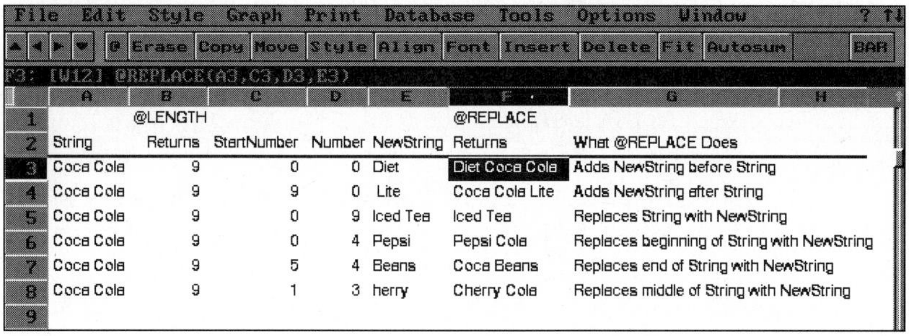

| File | Edit | Style | Graph | Print | Database | Tools | Options | Window | ? ↑↓ |

| ▲ ◀ ▶ ▼ | @ | Erase | Copy | Move | Style | Align | Font | Insert | Delete | Fit | Autosum | | BAR |

F3: [W12] @REPLACE(A3,C3,D3,E3)

	A	B	C	D	E	F	G	H
1		@LENGTH				@REPLACE		
2	String	Returns	StartNumber	Number	NewString	Returns	What @REPLACE Does	
3	Coca Cola	9	0	0	Diet	Diet Coca Cola	Adds NewString before String	
4	Coca Cola	9	9	0	Lite	Coca Cola Lite	Adds NewString after String	
5	Coca Cola	9	0	9	Iced Tea	Iced Tea	Replaces String with NewString	
6	Coca Cola	9	0	4	Pepsi	Pepsi Cola	Replaces beginning of String with NewString	
7	Coca Cola	9	5	4	Beans	Coca Beans	Replaces end of String with NewString	
8	Coca Cola	9	1	3	herry	Cherry Cola	Replaces middle of String with NewString	
9								

Tip. Use @LENGTH(*String*) as your *StartNumber* when you're adding *NewString* to the end of *String*.

In cell F4, the *Start Number* of 9 (equal to the length of the string) and a *Number* of 0 tells @REPLACE to add the *NewString* at the end of *String* to produce "Coca Cola Lite".

Replacing a String with a New String By using a *StartNumber* of 0 and a *Number* of 9, the length of the string, @REPLACE in cell F5 replaces all the characters in *String* with the *NewString* "Iced Tea". (Remember that using @LENGTH as your *Number* argument will automatically calculate the length of *String* for you.)

Replacing Part of a String with a New String The way you use @REPLACE to replace the beginning or end of a string is quite straightforward. In cell F6, for example, @REPLACE uses a *StartNumber* of 0 to begin replacing at the beginning of *String*. The *Number* argument of 4 says to replace the first four characters "Coca"; the result is "Pepsi Cola".

In cell F7, @REPLACE uses the *Number* argument of 4 to substitute the last four characters of the *String* "Cola" with the *NewString* "Beans" to return "Coca Beans". Here, the easiest way to specify the *StartNumber* offset of 5 is to use @LENGTH(*String*)–*Number*, or 9–4. This forces @REPLACE to begin replacing at the second "C", which has an offset of 5.

TIP. *Because you want to replace all characters before the unique blank space, using @FIND(" ",A6,0) as the* Number *argument would return an offset of 4 and produce the same result.*

The hardest situation is to replace characters in the middle of a *String*. To change "Coca Cola" to "Cherry Cola" as in cell F8, @REPLACE needs a

StartNumber of 1, the offset value of the first "o", and a *Number* of 3 to re-place the first occurrence of "ola". Sometimes, you can use @FIND to help you determine the *StartNumber* and *Number* arguments.

Repeating a Text String: @REPEAT

@REPEAT, naturally, repeats a string or character pattern as many times as specified. The form of this function is

```
@REPEAT(String,Number)
```

Number is the number of times you want *String* repeated. *String* can include any displayable character, including all foreign-language, special mathematical, and graphics symbols in the IBM PC Character Set.

Figure 7.32 shows how @REPEAT works for the *String* arguments in column A and the *Number* arguments in column B. In cell C3, for instance, @REPEAT(A3,B3) repeats the five-character *String* "Sales" 2 times to create a ten-character label. In cell C4, @REPEAT(A4,B4) repeats the *String* "9%" 4 times.

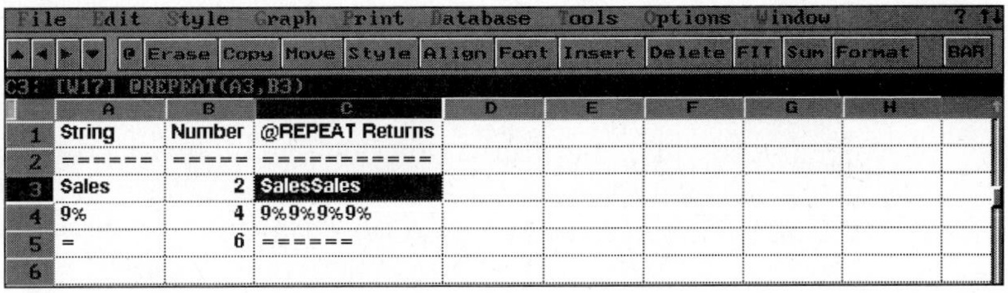

Figure 7.32
Using @REPEAT

Figure 7.32 also shows how @REPEAT differs from the repeating label prefix \ (backslash). In cell C5, @REPEAT(A5,B5) repeats the *String* "=" six times; the column width has nothing to do with the length of the label displayed. But \= in cell C2 fills the entire width of column C with the label "=".

TIP. *To repeat a special character, use @CHAR in* String. *For example,* @REPEAT(@CHAR(227),5) *repeats the special character π five times. To access special characters, see "Converting an IBM PC Character Set Code Number to Its Character: @CHAR," later. You may have to change your typeface, however, to view the result. Some typefaces, such as Swiss and Dutch, substitute ? (question mark) in place of a special character.*

String Conversion Functions

Quattro Pro includes two string conversion functions offered in previous releases. @STRING converts a value to a string. @VALUE does the opposite—it converts a numeric string to a value.

Converting a Value to a String: @STRING

Because @STRING converts a value to a string, it's often used in databases to convert data entered as values, such as a zip code, to a string. It's also sometimes used to create headings or labels in spreadsheets. More importantly, @STRING is the only way to concatenate, or join, a value and a string into one string.

The form of this function is

```
@STRING(x,DecPlaces)
```

where *x* is the value you want to convert to a label. Quattro Pro ignores any formatting included in *x*, such as a comma or a dollar sign. If *x* refers to a blank cell or a label, @STRING returns a string for the value 0, using the *DecPlaces* specified.

DecPlaces is the number of decimal places between 0 and 15 that you want the label to appear with. If *DecPlaces* is negative or greater than 15, @STRING returns ERR.

@STRING first rounds the value *x* to the *DecPlaces* specified, just like @ROUND, but returns this value as a label. Figure 7.33 shows how @STRING works for *x* in column A and *DecPlaces* in column B. In cell C2, @STRING(A2,B2) converts the value 47 to a string, adds 3 places and returns the *label* 47.000. In cell C3, @STRING(A3,B3) rounds the value $2,500.50 to 0 places, drops the formatting, and returns the label 2501. In cell C4, however, @STRING(A4,B4) returns 0 because cell A4 contains the left-aligned label 1997.

Concatenating a Value and a Label

@STRING is the only way you can concatenate a value and a label together to produce a label. In cell D2 of Figure 7.34, the concatenation formula +A2&" "&B2&" "&@STRING(C2,0) returns the label "Soquel CA 95073". The portion +A2" "&B2 joins the labels in A2 and B2 and adds a blank space in between. The segment B2&" "&@STRING(C2,0) rounds the value 95073 in C2 to 0 places, converts it to a label, and then adds it along with a blank space after the B2 string.

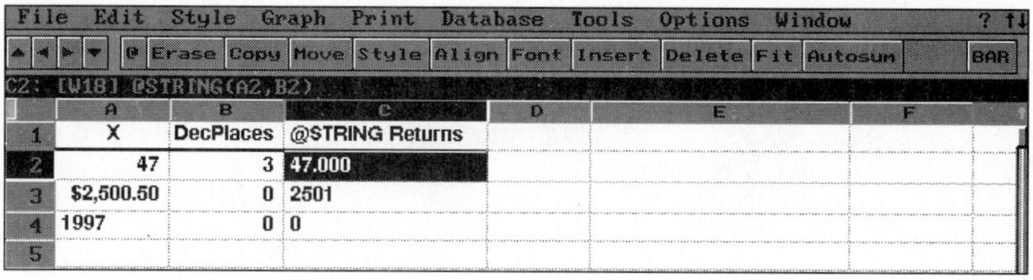

Figure 7.33
Using @STRING

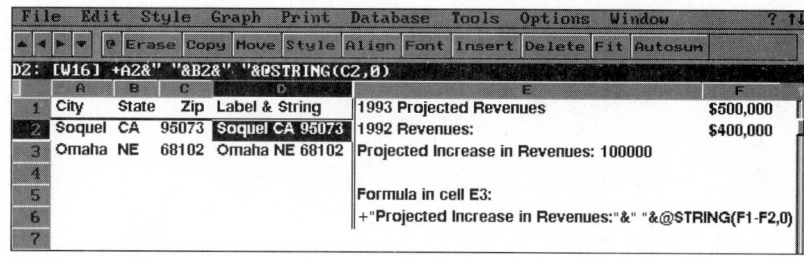

Figure 7.34
Using @STRING to
concatenate a
value and a string

You can also use @STRING in a concatenation formula to create a dynamic label that changes each time the included value changes. The concatenation formula in cell E3,

```
+"Projected Increase in Revenues:&"  "&@STRING(F1-F2,0)
```

uses the $500,000 1993 Projected Revenues in F1 and the $400,000 1992 Revenues in F2 to produce the label "Projected Increase in Revenues: 100000". But if the 1993 Revenues in F1 changes to $1,000,000, this label will change to read "Projected Increase in Revenues: 600000".

Converting Strings to Values: @VALUE

@VALUE converts a string into a numeric value that you can use in calculations. Typically, @VALUE is used to convert data imported as text from external sources, such as CompuServe or Dow Jones News/Retrieval. The form of this function is

```
@VALUE(String)
```

where *String* must evaluate to a *numeric string*—a value expressed as a string. For example, @VALUE can convert the number 2.2, the mixed number 9 7/8, a number in scientific notation, such as 2.56E5, or a number in one of Quattro

Pro's standard numeric formats, as in \$23.45 or 23.45%. @VALUE disregards any leading or trailing spaces.

@VALUE can't convert a numeric string that includes nonnumeric characters (as in "45lbs") or that contains formatting separated from the number (as in "7.5 %"). What's more, @VALUE can't convert a numeric string that contains a function, such as @AVG(B1..C1) or a formula like 2*5. The exception is the division operator /.

For example, @VALUE returns the following for different numeric strings:

Tip. Use /Tools, Parse, discussed in Chapter 5, to convert a block of numeric strings to values.

String	Result	What @VALUE Does
@VALUE("57 1/4")	57.25	Converts fraction to decimal
@VALUE(" 150")	150	Ignores three leading spaces
@VALUE("7.65% ")	0.0765	Drops % sign and percent format
@VALUE("75 % ")	ERR	Can't convert because % sign is separated from number
@VALUE(@AVG(B1..C1))	ERR	Can't convert a function
@VALUE("2*5")	ERR	Can't convert most formulas
@VALUE("10/2")	5	Can convert a formula containing a division operator

Test Functions: @EXACT, @N, and @S

Three string functions, @EXACT, @N, and @S, test spreadsheet entries. Normally, they're used in database applications. @EXACT, however, can also be used with or instead of @IF to test strings.

Note. For more information on conditional tests, see "Logic and Error-Trapping Functions," earlier in this chapter.

Testing Two Strings for Equality: @EXACT
@EXACT performs a conditional test by comparing two strings for equality. In fact, @EXACT provides a more stringent test than @IF. That's why @EXACT is often used to test database entries.

The form of this function is

@EXACT(*String1,String2*)

where *String1* and *String2* must both evaluate to a string. For @EXACT to consider *String1* and *String2* equal and return 1 (true), they must have the same spelling, capitalization, accent marks, punctuation, and blank spaces; however, differences in label prefixes are ignored. Otherwise, @EXACT returns 0 (false). @EXACT returns ERR when either *String1* or *String2* evaluates to a value or a blank cell.

Figure 7.35 shows how @EXACT in column C provides a more stringent test than @IF in column D for the strings in columns A and B. In row 2, @EXACT and @IF both evaluate the strings in A2 and B2 as equal and return 1 (true). They both evaluate the *String2* misspelling in row 3 and incorrect spacing in row 4 the same way and return 0 (false). But in row 5, @EXACT evaluates the capitalization differences and returns 0 (false), while @IF(A5=B5,1,0) ignores the difference and returns 1 (true).

Figure 7.35
Comparing @EXACT and @IF

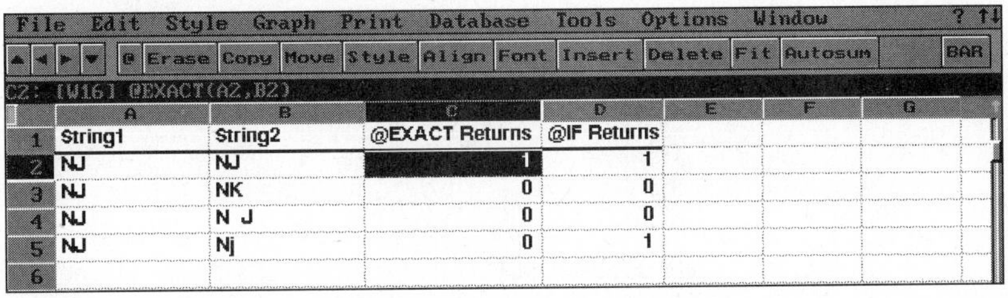

	A	B	C	D	E	F	G
1	String1	String2	@EXACT Returns	@IF Returns			
2	NJ	NJ	1	1			
3	NJ	NK	0	0			
4	NJ	N J	0	0			
5	NJ	Nj	0	1			
6							

When you need to differentiate between a null string (""), a blank cell, or a cell containing only spaces, use @IF rather than @EXACT. If F14 is a blank cell, for instance, and F15 is either a blank cell, a cell containing a null string, or only spaces, @IF(F14,F15) considers the cell contents equal and returns 1; @EXACT(F14,F15) returns ERR.

Testing a Block for Values and Strings: @N and @S

@N and @S test whether the first cell in a block contains a value or a string. The forms of these functions are

```
@N(Block)
@S(Block)
```

where *Block* can be a block address or name, even in another open file. If *Block* is a single cell address, Quattro Pro converts it to a block address.

@N tests whether the upper-left cell of *Block* contains a value; @S tests that cell for a string. Here are the results these functions return:

Upper-Left Cell in Block Contains	@N Returns	@S Returns
Value or formula returning a value	Value in cell	Null string ("")
String or formula returning a string	0	String in cell
Blank cell	0	Null string ("")

NOTE. *The logical functions @ISNUMBER and @ISSTRING also test a cell for a value or a string, but return the logical true and false values 1 and 0. See "Logic and Error-Trapping Functions," earlier in this chapter.*

During data entry, both @N and @S are commonly used to test for the correct type of data entry. For example,

```
{IF @S(ZIP)=""}{BRANCH ERROR}
```

ensures that the zip code is entered as a label in the cell named ZIP. If it's entered as a value, @S(ZIP) returns a null string "", which causes the macro to branch to the ERROR subroutine, where an error message like "Enter zip code as a LABEL" is displayed.

Character Functions

When you type a character in Quattro Pro, it's stored using the IBM PC Character Set. This character set is made up of 256 characters, each assigned a code number from 0 to 255. Code numbers 0 to 127 represent the standard ASCII Character set; of these, codes 32 to 127 represent characters that you can type on your keyboard. Code numbers outside of this range represent special characters, such as fractions, accent marks, mathematical symbols, and screen-graphics characters. In Quattro Pro, you can use @CHAR to access these characters and @CODE to find out the code number a character represents.

Converting an IBM PC Character Set Code Number to Its Character: @CHAR

@CHAR uses an IBM PC Character Set code number to return the equivalent on-screen character. The form of the function is

```
@CHAR(Code)
```

where *Code* must be a value representing an IBM Character Set code number between 0 and 255. Otherwise, @CHAR returns ERR. For example, @CHAR(70) returns "F"; @CHAR(227) returns π; @CHAR(270) returns ERR. Any decimal portion of *Code* is truncated—for instance, @CHAR(70.8) also returns "F".

NOTE. *Some of Quattro Pro's typefaces, such as Swiss and Dutch, display a special character as a ? (question mark). If this happens to you, try another typeface like Sans Serif or Roman.*

If you're printing in graphics mode, you'll be able to print special characters like π because Quattro Pro essentially takes a "picture" of the block to be printed. If your printer can't handle graphics mode, the special characters you can print may be severely limited. Screen-graphics characters, however, are always non-printable irrespective of the printer.

Determining the IBM Character Set Code Number of a Character: @CODE

@CODE produces the opposite of @CHAR because it uses a character to return the corresponding IBM PC Character Set code number. The form of the function is

```
@CODE(String)
```

where *String* must evaluate to a *label*, even if the character is a number. Otherwise, @CODE returns ERR. For instance, @CODE("7") returns the IBM Character set code number 55. If cell B1 contains the string "Arachnid", @CODE(B1) only evaluates the first letter of *String* and returns 65, the code number for the character A.

Hexadecimal Functions

When you need to convert a base 10 number to its *hexadecimal* or base 16 equivalent, or vice versa, use one of the hexadecimal functions, @NUMTOHEX or @HEXTONUM.

As you may already know, 16 is represented by 10 in base 16, 32 as 20, 256 by 100, and so on. The base 10 values 0 through 9 are the same in base 16, but 10 through 15 are represented by the letters *A* through *F.* In base 16, for example, *D* represents the base 10 value 13; *2D* represents 45, or 2∗16+13.

Converting from Decimal to Hexadecimal Numbers: @NUMTOHEX

@NUMTOHEX converts the integer portion of a base 10 number to a *label* representing its hexadecimal (base 16) equivalent. The form of this function is

```
@NUMTOHEX(x)
```

where *x* must evaluate to a numeric value; otherwise, @NUMTOHEX returns 0. For example @NUMTOHEX(24) returns '18, a string representing the base 16 equivalent of the base 10 number 24. Both @NUMTOHEX(127) and @NUMTOHEX(127.6) return '7F; the 7 represents 7 units of 16, and the F represents the 15 units remaining.

Converting from Hexadecimal to Decimal Values: @HEXTONUM

@HEXTONUM converts a *label* representing a hexadecimal (base 16) number to its base 10 equivalent. The form of the function is

```
@HEXTONUM(String)
```

where *String* must evaluate to a hexadecimal numeric label; otherwise @HEXTONUM returns ERR. For example, @HEXTONUM("B") returns the base 10 value 11. If cell D2 contains the hexadecimal numeric string '2A, @HEXTONUM(D2) returns 42. @HEXTONUM("100J") produces ERR, however, because J isn't used in the hexadecimal system.

Financial Functions

Quattro Pro's financial functions let you analyze opportunities based on the time value of money. Because of the interest you can earn, cash in hand today is worth more than cash received in the future. Financial analysis then, determines the present value by *discounting* future cash flows at an interest rate that compensates you for the risk of the investment.

When you use a financial function, it's crucial that your assumptions match the underlying assumptions built in by Quattro Pro; otherwise, the result returned may not be for the problem you're analyzing. Because these underlying assumptions are so important, they've been listed in the upcoming sections for each financial function.

As you become familiar with Quattro Pro's financial functions, or if you've used them before, you'll find Table 7.13 a convenient reference guide. This table lists what each financial function does, the arguments it acts on, and the all-important underlying assumptions it makes.

Table 7.13   Quattro Pro's Financial Functions

Quattro Pro Function	Calculates	Cash Flow Argument	Interest or Discount Rate	Payment Occurs in Period
@PV(Pmt,Rate,Nper)	Present value of an annuity	One annuity payment entered as Pmt	Per period of annuity	Ending

Table 7.13   (Continued)

@PVAL(*Rate,Nper,–Pmt, <–FV>,<Type>*)	Present value of an annuity or an annuity due, with or without a terminal value	One annuity or annuity due payment, entered as a negative *Pmt*; terminal value entered as a negative *FV*	Per period of annuity or annuity due	*Type* of 0 for ending, 1 for beginning
@PMT(*PV,Rate,Nper*)	Fixed payment per period	Loan amount entered as *PV*	Per period of payment	Ending
@PAYMT(*Rate,Nper, –PV,<FV>,<Type>*)	Annuity or annuity due payment, with or without a balloon payment	Loan amount entered as a negative *PV*; balloon payment entered as *FV*	Per period of annuity or annuity due	*Type* of 0 for ending, 1 for beginning
@IPAYMT(*Rate,Per,Nper, –PV,<FV>,<Type>*)	Component of fixed payment allocated to interest	Loan amount entered as a negative *PV*; balloon payment entered as *FV*	Per period of annuity or annuity due	*Type* of 0 for ending, 1 for beginning
@PPAYMT(*Rate,Per,Nper, –PV,<FV>,<Type>*)	Component of fixed payment allocated to principal	Loan balance entered as a negative *PV*; balloon payment entered as *FV*	Per period of annuity or annuity due	*Type* of 0 for ending, 1 for beginning
@FV(*Pmt,Rate,Nper*)	Future value of an annuity	One annuity payment entered as *Pmt*	Per period of annuity	Ending
@FVAL(*Rate,Nper,–Pmt, <–PV>,<Type>*)	Future value of an annuity or an annuity due, with or without an initial investment	One annuity or annuity due payment, entered as a negative *Pmt*; initial investment entered as a negative *PV*	Per period of annuity or annuity due	*Type* of 0 for ending, 1 for beginning
@NPV(*Rate,Block,<Type>*)	Net present value	*Block* of positive cash inflows and negative cash outflows	Per period between cash flows	*Type* of 0 for ending, 1 for beginning
@IRR(*Guess,Block*)	Internal rate of return	*Block* of positive cash inflows and negative cash outflows	Rate calculated for one period	Ending or beginning
@RATE(*FV,PV,Nper*)	Implied interest rate for an initial investment to reach a future value	Initial investment entered as *PV*; future value at the end of all compounding periods entered as *FV*	Rate calculated for one period	Ending
@IRATE(*Nper,Pmt,–PV,FV, <Type>*)	Implied interest rate for an initial investment generating annuity or annuity due payments	One annuity or annuity due payment entered as *Pmt*; initial investment entered as a negative *PV*; value at the end of all compounding periods entered as *FV*	Rate calculated for one period	*Type* of 0 for ending, 1 for beginning
@CTERM(*Rate,FV,PV*)	Number of periods for an initial investment to reach a future value	Future value entered as *FV*; initial investment entered as *PV*	Per period of compounding periods	Ending
@TERM(*Pmt,Rate,FV*)	Number of fixed payments to reach a future value	One payment entered as *Pmt*; future value entered as *FV*	Per period of compounding periods	Ending
@NPER(*Rate,–Pmt,–PV,FV, <Type>*)	Number of annuity payments or annuity due payments to reach a future value, with or without an initial investment	One annuity or annuity due payment entered as a negative *Pmt*; initial investment entered as a negative *PV*; future value entered as *FV*	Per period of annuity or annuity due	*Type* of 0 for ending, 1 for beginning

- *Pmt* = one of the equal payments

- *Rate* = interest rate per period in percent or decimal form

- *Nper* = number of payments

- *Per* = specific payment period

  Relevant assumptions:

- All interest payments are reinvested at interest or discount *Rate* until end of investment period.

- Interest *Rate* remains constant over investment periods.

- All periods must be equal.

- Interest *Rate* determines time period between cash flows.

- *Nper* is the largest interval that makes intervals between cash flows equal.

How the Rate Argument Determines the Time Period Between Cash Flows

Because discounting cash flows to their present value is the underlying basis of financial analysis, all of Quattro Pro's financial functions either use or solve for an interest or discount rate. Although you may not know it, the interest rate you use determines an implicit variable—the equal time period between cash flows.

In financial analysis, all time periods between cash flows must be the same. For instance, if payments occur every six months, then six months is the equal period between cash flows. If one payment occurs in three months and the next nine months later, the period between cash flows is three months—there just isn't a cash flow in periods 2 and 3.

Note. In Quattro Pro's financial functions, the *Rate* can't be less than –1.0; you'll get an incorrect result or ERR.

In a financial function, you use a *Rate* argument for one time period to tell Quattro Pro the time period between cash flows. If all cash flows occur yearly, then you use a yearly rate. But if cash flows occur every three months, then you must use a quarterly rate (yearly/4). If the annual rate is 12%, for instance, you'd use a *Rate* of .03.

Because the interest rate and time period between cash flows are so closely related, it's a good idea to clarify the underlying assumptions for both:

- The *Rate* corresponds to one time period, and all time periods are equal.

- The *Rate* is constant over the life of the investment.

- Any cash received is immediately reinvested at the *Rate* until the end of the investment.

- Interest is compounded at the *Rate* at the end of each time period.

How to Specify When Cash Flows Occur in a Time Period

Because future cash flows are discounted back to the present, *when* a cash flow occurs affects its value today. In the earliest versions of Quattro Pro, all the financial functions implicitly assumed that cash flows occurred at the end of each time period. These functions, still included in Quattro Pro today, were designed for compatibility with Lotus 1-2-3.

Beginning in Quattro Pro 1.0, however, Borland introduced additional financial functions that include an optional *<Type>* argument. If you don't use this argument, or if you specify a *Type* of 0, Quattro Pro assumes that cash flows occur at the end of each period. By using a *Type* of 1, you can specify that all cash flows occur at the beginning of each period. If you switch between Quattro Pro and 1-2-3, however, including a *Type* argument makes your Quattro Pro function incompatible with 1-2-3.

Present Value of an Annuity and Annuity Due: @PV and @PVAL

The *present value* (PV) is the value today of a future stream of equal cash flows discounted at some fixed interest rate. Mathematically, it's expressed as

$$\text{PV} = \text{Payment Per Period} * \frac{1 - (1 + \text{Interest Rate})^{-n}}{\text{Interest Rate}}$$

where *n* represents the number of equal payments made. The PV equation assumes:

- Equal payments occur at equally spaced time periods.

- All payments (cash received) are immediately reinvested at the interest rate until the end of the investment.

- The interest rate remains constant over the investment period.

    Quattro Pro has two functions that calculate the present value:

    `@PV(Pmt,Rate,Nper)`
    `@PVAL(Rate,Nper,-Pmt,<-FV>,<Type>)`

where *Pmt* is the value of one of the equally spaced payments. If you're using @PV, enter a payment made as a positive number. If you're using @PVAL, a payment made is entered as a negative value because it's an outflow. (Otherwise, you'll get a negative PV.) *Nper* is the number of equal payments, and *Rate* is the interest rate for one time period entered in decimal or percentage form. If payments occur each month, for instance, use a monthly *Rate*.

By default, @PV and @PVAL both assume that payments occur at the end of each period. To specify that payments occur at the beginning of each period, use an optional *Type* argument of 1 in @PVAL.

Note. To calculate the PV of a stream of unequal cash flows, see "Net Present Value: @NPV," later.

The optional @PVAL *FV* argument allows you to specify a *terminal value* that occurs on the last day of the investment, such as a large cash balloon payment or repayment of an initial investment. Remember to enter it using the same sign as the *Pmt* argument. If you want to include a *Type* argument when there isn't a terminal value, use an *FV* of 0.

To see the different results @PVAL can return, let's evaluate the three annuity opportunities shown in Figure 7.36, which all require the same initial investment. Regardless of the investment you choose, it's assumed that you can reinvest the payments received and earn 7% a year.

Figure 7.36
Calculating the PV of an annuity, an annuity with a terminal value, and an annuity due

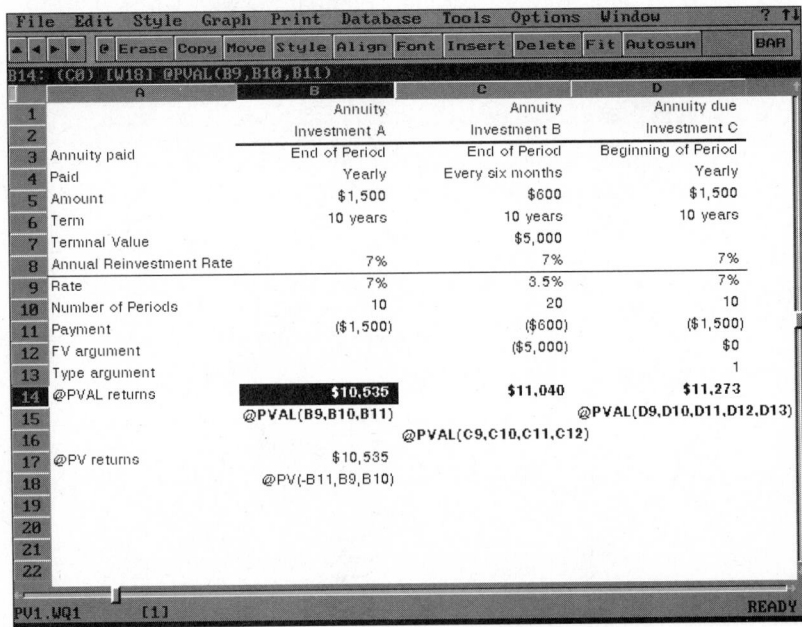

Calculating the PV of an Annuity

Column B of Figure 7.36 contains Annuity A, which pays $1,500 at the end of each year for 10 years. In cell B14, @PVAL(B9,B10,B11) uses a 7% yearly

Rate, a –$1,500 yearly *Pmt*, and 10 yearly *Nper* periods to return a PV for this investment of $10,535. By making the payment positive, you can see in cell B17 how @PV(–B11,B10,B9) produces the same result.

Calculating the PV of an Annuity with a Terminal Value

Column C of Figure 7.36 contains Annuity B, which pays $600 at the end of every six months for 10 years and then a final balloon payment of $5,000. This time a six-month *Rate* of 3.5%, a semiannual *Pmt* of –$600, an *Nper* of 20 six-month periods, and an *FV* of –$5,000 in @PVAL(C9,C10,C11,C12) returns a PV of $11,040. So far then, Annuity B is the better investment because its PV exceeds the PV of Annuity A.

Calculating the PV of an Annuity Due

Column D of Figure 7.36 contains Annuity C, an annuity due that pays $1,500 at the beginning of every year for 10 years. This time, you need to use a yearly *Rate* of 7%, a yearly *Pmt* of –$1,500, an *NPer* of 10 yearly periods, and an *FV* argument of 0 so you can include an ending period *Type* argument of 1. Then @PVAL(D9,D10,D11,D12,D13) in cell D14 calculates a PV of $11,273, the highest PV of all three investment alternatives.

Fixed Payment per Period to Repay a Loan: @PMT and @PAYMT

The fixed payment to pay off a fixed-rate loan (principal) in a specified number of payments is mathematically expressed as

$$\text{Payment Per Period} = \text{Principal} * \frac{\text{Interest Rate}}{1 - (1 + \text{Interest Rate})^{-n}}$$

where *n* is the number of equal payments made. This equation assumes

- Equal payments occur at equally spaced time periods until the principal is repaid.

- The payment amount applied to interest and principal varies for each period.

- The interest rate remains constant over the repayment period.

  Quattro Pro has two functions that calculate a fixed payment:

  ```
  @PMT(PV,Rate,Nper)
  @PAYMT(Rate,Nper,-PV,<FV>,<Type>)
  ```

Here, *PV* is the principal or current loan balance. If you're using @PMT, enter the principal as a positive number. But if you're using @PAYMT, the principal is entered as a negative value because it's an outflow. (Otherwise, you'll get a negative payment.) *Nper* is the number of equal payments, and *Rate* is the fixed interest rate for one time period entered in decimal or percentage form. If payments occur each month, for instance, use a monthly *Rate*.

By default, @PMT and @PAYMT both assume that payments occur at the end of each period. If payments occur at the beginning of each period, use an optional *Type* argument of 1 in @PAYMT.

The optional @PAYMT *FV* argument allows you to specify an outstanding principal balance, such as a balloon payment, remaining on the day of the last fixed payment. Remember to enter it using the opposite sign as the *PV* argument. To include a *Type* argument of 1 when there isn't an outstanding ending balance, use an *FV* of 0.

To see how @PAYMT works, let's calculate the monthly payments for a 9% fixed-rate, 20-year, $200,000 mortgage shown in Figure 7.37 using the terms offered by three different banks. All assume a 0.09/12 or 0.75% monthly rate, 240 monthly payments, and a $200,000 principal balance. Therefore, each formula uses 240 monthly *Nper* periods, a fixed 0.75% monthly *Rate*, and a –$200,000 *PV* principal balance in @PAYMT.

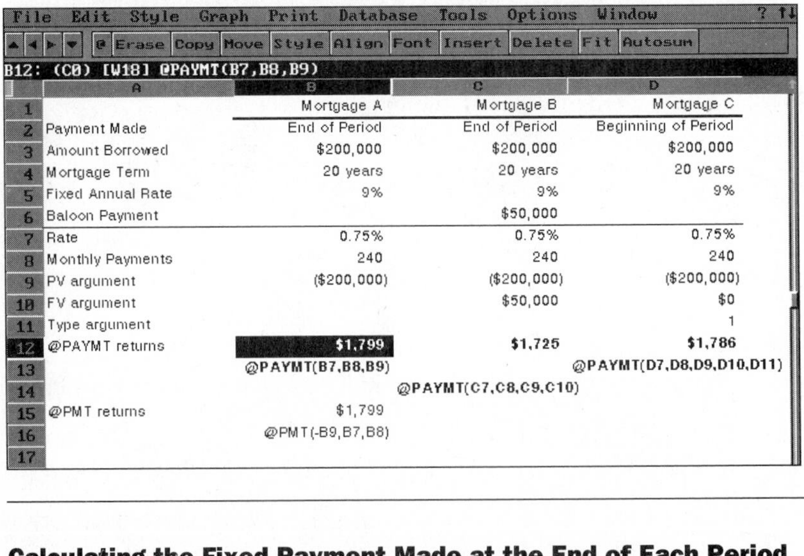

Figure 7.37
Calculating the fixed payment to retire different loans

	Mortgage A	Mortgage B	Mortgage C
Payment Made	End of Period	End of Period	Beginning of Period
Amount Borrowed	$200,000	$200,000	$200,000
Mortgage Term	20 years	20 years	20 years
Fixed Annual Rate	9%	9%	9%
Baloon Payment		$50,000	
Rate	0.75%	0.75%	0.75%
Monthly Payments	240	240	240
PV argument	($200,000)	($200,000)	($200,000)
FV argument		$50,000	$0
Type argument			1
@PAYMT returns	$1,799	$1,725	$1,786
	@PAYMT(B7,B8,B9)		@PAYMT(D7,D8,D9,D10,D11)
		@PAYMT(C7,C8,C9,C10)	
@PMT returns	$1,799		
	@PMT(-B9,B7,B8)		

B12: (C0) [W18] @PAYMT(B7,B8,B9)

Calculating the Fixed Payment Made at the End of Each Period

Because Mortgage A is paid at the end of each month, @PAYMT(B7,B8,B9) in cell B12 calculates that you'd have to pay $1,799 per month to repay this mortgage in 20 years. By making the principal positive, you can see in cell B15 how @PMT(–B9,B7,B8) produces the same result.

Calculating the Fixed Payment Made at the End of Each Period with a Balloon Payment

Although Mortgage B is also paid at the end of each month, it has a balloon payment of $50,000 at the end of the mortgage. That's why @PAYMT(C7,-C8,C9,C10) in cell C12 uses an *FV* of $50,000 and returns $1,725, a lower payment than Mortgage A.

Calculating the Fixed Payment Made at the Beginning of Each Period

Mortgage C, however, is paid at the beginning of every month. Therefore, an *FV* argument of 0 is included in @PAYMT(D7,D8,D9,D10,D11) so that an ending period *Type* of 1 can be specified. As you can see, the monthly payment of $1,786 in cell D12 is lower than Mortgage A because all payments have essentially been moved up one month.

Allocating a Fixed Payment to Interest and Principal Each Period: @IPAYMT and @PPAYMT

As you know, in a fixed-rate mortgage a different amount of interest and principal is allocated each month. Quattro Pro includes two functions that automatically calculate the allocation each period:

```
@IPAYMT(Rate,Per,Nper,-PV,<FV>,<Type>)
@PPAYMT(Rate,Per,Nper,-PV,<FV>,<Type>)
```

Nper is the number of equal payments made over the life of the loan. *Rate* is the fixed interest rate for one time period entered in decimal or percentage form; for monthly payments, use a monthly *Rate*. *PV* is the current loan balance entered as a negative value. (Otherwise, you'll get negative interest and principal amounts.) The optional *FV* argument, entered in the opposite sign as the *PV*, represents an outstanding principal balance, such as a balloon payment on the day of the last fixed payment.

The *Per* argument tells Quattro Pro the specific payment being made. In a 20-year mortgage for instance, the first payment has a *Per* of 1; the last payment has a *Per* of 240.

By default, payments occur at the end of each period, so use an optional *Type* of 1 for payments made at the beginning of each period. If there isn't an outstanding loan balance at the end of the mortgage, use an *FV* of 0 so you can include a *Type* argument.

The loan amortization schedule in Figure 7.38 shows how @IPAYMT and @PPAYMT work for a $200,000, 9% fixed, 20-year mortgage. (Earlier, in Figure 7.37, the @PAYMT function was used to calculate the fixed payment per month, $1,799 in column C.) In column D, the @IPAYMT function calculates the interest paid each month; in column E, the @PPAYMT function

Note. The mixed addressing in @PAYMT, @IPAYMT, and @PPAYMT keeps the references to the monthly rate, number of monthly payments, and the principal fixed when these formulas are copied down a column.

computes the principal paid each month. The ending balance in column F is the beginning balance in column B less the principal paid.

Figure 7.38
Using @IPAYMT and
@PPAYMT to create
a loan amortization
schedule

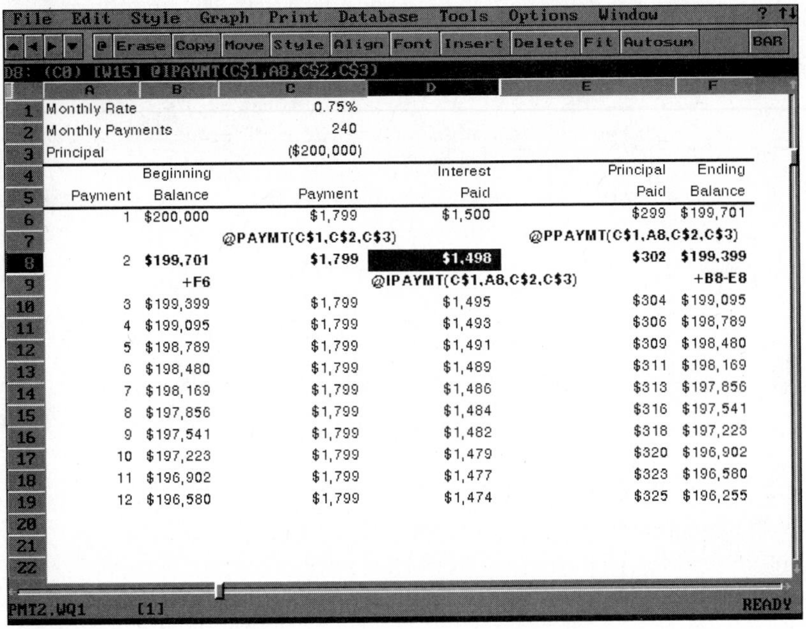

File	Edit	Style	Graph	Print	Database	Tools	Options	Window		? ↑↓

▲ ◀ ▶ ▼ @ Erase Copy Move Style Align Font Insert Delete Fit Autosum   BAR

D8: (C0) [W15] @IPAYMT(C$1,A8,C$2,C$3)

	A	B	C	D	E	F
1	Monthly Rate		0.75%			
2	Monthly Payments		240			
3	Principal		($200,000)			
4		Beginning		Interest	Principal	Ending
5	Payment	Balance	Payment	Paid	Paid	Balance
6	1	$200,000	$1,799	$1,500	$299	$199,701
7			@PAYMT(C$1,C$2,C$3)		@PPAYMT(C$1,A8,C$2,C$3)	
8	2	$199,701	$1,799	$1,498	$302	$199,399
9		+F6		@IPAYMT(C$1,A8,C$2,C$3)		+B8-E8
10	3	$199,399	$1,799	$1,495	$304	$199,095
11	4	$199,095	$1,799	$1,493	$306	$198,789
12	5	$198,789	$1,799	$1,491	$309	$198,480
13	6	$198,480	$1,799	$1,489	$311	$198,169
14	7	$198,169	$1,799	$1,486	$313	$197,856
15	8	$197,856	$1,799	$1,484	$316	$197,541
16	9	$197,541	$1,799	$1,482	$318	$197,223
17	10	$197,223	$1,799	$1,479	$320	$196,902
18	11	$196,902	$1,799	$1,477	$323	$196,580
19	12	$196,580	$1,799	$1,474	$325	$196,255
20						
21						
22						

PMT2.WQ1   [1]   READY

For the second payment in row 8, for instance, @IPAYMT(C$1,A8,C$2,C$3) uses *Payment* number 2 in cell A8 and calculates that $1,498 of the $1,799 fixed payment is eaten up by interest. How does @IPAYMT do this? Well, first you must know that Quattro Pro treats these functions this way:

```
@IPAYMT + @PPAYMT = @PAYMT
```

Therefore, the @IPAYMT function first figures out the fixed-payment amount for the mortgage, $1,799 in this case. Then, based on the payment specified by the *Per* argument, @IPAYMT figures out what the beginning balance should be. For example, because the second payment is being calculated here, @IPAYMT first computes the $199,701 loan balance in cell B8. You can think of @IPAYMT as keeping a "running balance" of where it stands in the loan schedule.

To actually calculate the interest each period, @IPAYMT assumes that there are 365.25 days in a year assigned evenly over 12 months. If payments occur monthly, the interest each month is computed for 365.25/12 days. The interest is then computed as

Beginning Balance ∗ (Annual Interest Rate ∗ 365.25/12 Days)

Try out this formula in Figure 7.38, and you'll get the same result @IPAYMT returns. For example, $199,701∗.09∗365.25/12 returns $1,498, just like @IPAYMT returns in cell D8.

Note. To compute interest based on the actual number of days in a month, see "Using Dates in Calculations," earlier.

It'll help to think of the @PPAYMT function as calculating @PAYMT–@IPAYMT. That is, @PPAYMT first figures out the fixed-payment amount for the mortgage, $1,799, that @PAYMT would return. Then it calculates the interest amount @IPAYMT would return for the *Per* payment specified. The difference between the fixed payment and the interest paid is the amount applied to principal—$302 in cell E8, for instance. In fact, if you examine the interest and principal amount that @IPAYMT and @PPAYMT return in Figure 7.38, you'll see that each month the combined total equals the fixed payment of $1,799.

Future Value of an Annuity and Annuity Due: @FV and @FVAL

The *future value* (FV) is the value on the last day of the investment period of a stream of equal cash flows invested at some fixed interest rate. Mathematically, it's expressed as

$$FV = Payment \ Per \ Period \ * \frac{(1 + Interest \ Rate)^{-n} - 1}{Interest \ Rate}$$

where *n* represents the number of equal payments made. The FV equation assumes

- Equal payments occur at equally spaced time periods.

- All payments received (interest) are immediately reinvested at the interest rate until the end of the investment.

- The interest rate remains constant over the investment period.

- The FV is calculated on the date of the last payment.

    Quattro Pro has two functions that calculate the future value:

    ```
    @FV(Pmt,Rate,Nper)
    @FVAL(Rate,Nper,-Pmt,<-PV>,<Type>)
    ```

where *Pmt* is the value of one of the equally spaced payments. If you're using @FV, enter a payment made as a positive number. If you're using

@FVAL, a payment made is entered as a negative value because it's an outflow. Otherwise, you'll get a negative FV. *Nper* is the number of equal payments, and *Rate* is the interest rate for one time period entered in decimal or percentage form. If payments occur semiannually, for instance, use a semiannual (year/2) *Rate*.

By default, @FV and @FVAL both assume that payments occur at the end of each period. To specify that payments occur at the beginning of each period, use an optional *Type* argument of 1 in @FVAL. The optional @FVAL *PV* argument allows you to specify a initial investment, entered as a negative outflow, occurring on day 1 of the investment period. If you want to include only a *Type* argument, use a *PV* of 0.

Figure 7.39 shows the results @FVAL returns for the three different investment strategies being evaluated. All three guarantee an 8% return and require the same total investment of $60,000, spread over 20 years. Naturally, the objective is to choose the one which generates the highest future value at the end of 20 years.

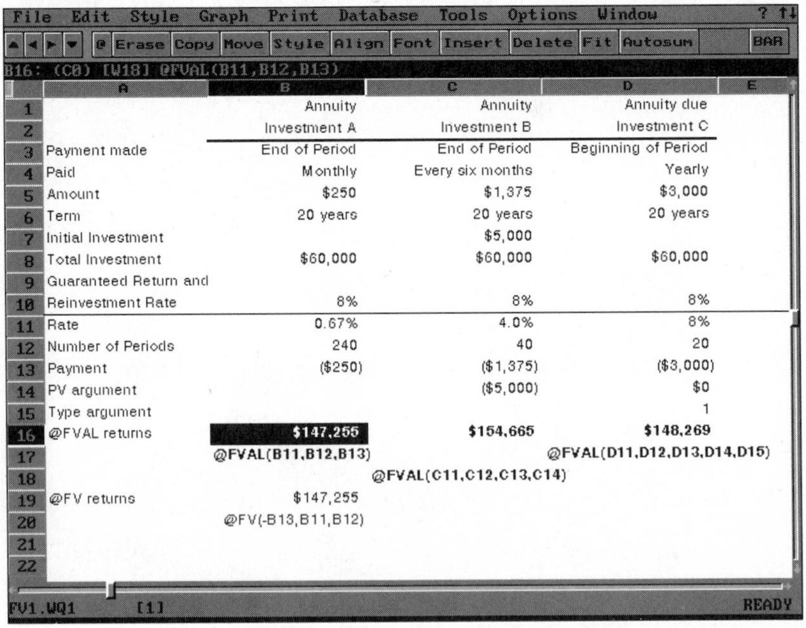

	A	B	C	D
1		Annuity	Annuity	Annuity due
2		Investment A	Investment B	Investment C
3	Payment made	End of Period	End of Period	Beginning of Period
4	Paid	Monthly	Every six months	Yearly
5	Amount	$250	$1,375	$3,000
6	Term	20 years	20 years	20 years
7	Initial Investment		$5,000	
8	Total Investment	$60,000	$60,000	$60,000
9	Guaranteed Return and			
10	Reinvestment Rate	8%	8%	8%
11	Rate	0.67%	4.0%	8%
12	Number of Periods	240	40	20
13	Payment	($250)	($1,375)	($3,000)
14	PV argument		($5,000)	$0
15	Type argument			1
16	@FVAL returns	**$147,255**	**$154,665**	**$148,269**
17		**@FVAL(B11,B12,B13)**		**@FVAL(D11,D12,D13,D14,D15)**
18			**@FVAL(C11,C12,C13,C14)**	
19	@FV returns	$147,255		
20		@FV(-B13,B11,B12)		
21				
22				

Figure 7.39 Calculating the FV of an annuity, an annuity with an up-front investment, and an annuity due

Calculating the FV of an Annuity

Investment A in column B of Figure 7.39 requires you to invest $250 at the end of every month for 20 years. In cell B16, @FVAL(B11,B12,B13) uses an 0.08/12 or 0.67% monthly *Rate*, a –$250 monthly *Pmt*, and 240 monthly *NPer* periods to return an FV of $147,255. By making the payment positive, you can see in cell B19 how @FV(–B13,B11,B12) produces the same result.

Calculating the FV of an Annuity with an Initial Investment

In column C, Investment B requires an up front investment of $5,000, and $1,375 at the end of every six months for 20 years. Here, a six-month *Rate* of 4%, a semiannual *Pmt* of –$1,375, an *Nper* of 40 six-month periods, and a *PV* of –$5,000 in @FVAL(C11,C12,C13,C14) return an FV of $154,665. The large up-front payment on day 1 generates a larger FV than Investment A, so Investment B is the current front-runner.

Calculating the FV of an Annuity Due

Investment C is an annuity due that requires a $3,000 investment at the beginning of every year for 20 years. Therefore, a yearly *Rate* of 8%, a yearly *Pmt* of –$3,000, and an *Nper* of 20 yearly periods are used. A *PV* of 0 is also added so that an ending period *Type* of 1 can be specified. In cell D16, @FVAL(D11,D12,D13,D14,D15) returns an FV of $148,269. Therefore, although the timing of these payments at the beginning of each year generates a larger FV than Investment A, Investment B with a large up-front investment is still the best choice.

Net Present Value: @NPV

Net present value (NPV) is the present value of a stream of future cash flows. The NPV is calculated by discounting the cash flow stream at some rate in the mathematical equation

$$NPV = \Sigma \frac{\text{Cash Inflows} - \text{Cash Outflows}}{(1 + \text{Discount Rate})^n} - \text{Initial Investment}$$

where *n* represents the number of equal time periods over which the cash flows occur. The *discount rate* at which these cash flows are discounted represents the return you require, given the risk of the investment. Notice that an initial investment on day 1 is included in the equation. The NPV equation assumes

- Equal time periods between cash flows.

- All cash inflows (cash received) are immediately reinvested at the discount rate until the end of the investment.

■ The discount rate remains constant over the investment period.

Quattro Pro's function that calculates the Net Present Value takes the form

`@NPV(Rate,Block,<Type>)`

where *Rate* is the discount rate in decimal or percentage form for one time period. For example, if cash flows occur each month, use a monthly *Rate*.

The *Block* represents the stream of unequal cash flows, positive cash inflows, and negative cash outflows (investments). Each cell represents one time period. If cash flows in or out every year for five years, for example, you need a five-cell *Block*, even if no cash flow occurs in one of the years. How you enter your cash flows, however, depends on whether they occur at the beginning or end of each time period.

Calculating the NPV for Cash Flows at the End of Each Period

By default, when no *Type* argument is included, @NPV assumes that all cash flows occur at the *end* of each period. Using this assumption, each cell in *Block* represents the cash flow at the end of a period. For example, the first cell represents the first cash flow at the end of period 1 (*not* the initial investment), the second cell represents the first cash flow at the end of period 2, and so on. Enter cash inflows as positive and cash outflows (investments) as negative. *Don't* include any initial investment in the cash flow stream.

Figure 7.40, for example, shows how the cash flow stream for a potential investment is entered. Here, the investment occurs in two stages: a $1,000,000 initial investment on day 1, December 31, 1992, and another $300,000 infusion on December 31, 1993. In return, this investment produces four payouts of $500,000 every six months, beginning June 30, 1994, and ending with a payout of $1,000,000 on December 31, 1996. Because of the riskiness of this venture, a 25% annualized discount rate is considered appropriate.

As you can see, the cash flow *Block* C6..J6 excludes the initial investment. Because cash flows occur at least every six months, each cell represents the *last* day of a six-month time period, even when no cash flow occurs. For example, cell C6 represents June 30, 1992, even though no cash flow occurs during the prior six months. Because each cell in the cash flow *Block* represents a six-month time period, a six-month discount rate of 12.5% is used in cell B8.

In cell B9, @NPV(B8,C6..J6) returns 1,340,120. The NPV of this investment, however, is calculated in cell B11 as the result of @NPV less the initial investment, or 340,120.

Figure 7.40

Calculating the NPV of an investment when the cash flows occur at the end of time periods

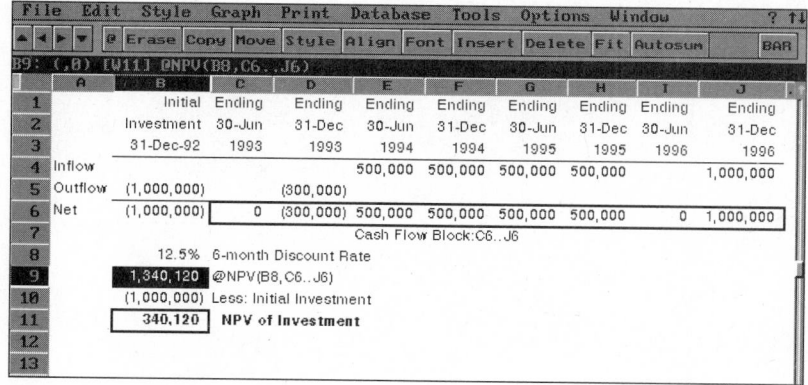

Evaluating the NPV Result

Because the @NPV discount rate represents the rate that compensates you for the risk of the particular investment being analyzed, an NPV of 0 indicates that you'd be no better off if you made the investment. A negative NPV says that you shouldn't make the investment because the return doesn't compensate you for the risk.

In theory, any investment that generates a positive NPV should be made. For example, because the NPV of 340,120 in Figure 7.40 is positive, this investment should be made. In the real world of scarce funds, however, a project with a positive NPV is usually evaluated against other positive NPV projects.

Calculating the NPV for Cash Flows at the Beginning of Each Period

The @NPV function can handle cash flows that occur at the beginning of each period, including the initial investment. To see how this works, let's assume that all cash flows in Figure 7.40 now occur at the beginning of each six-month period. That is, each cell in the cash flow *Block* now represents the first day of a six-month period.

In Figure 7.41, the $1,000,000 initial investment on day 1 now occurs on January 1, 1993, and is included in the cash flow *Block*; the second investment is made on July 1, 1993; the four $500,000 payouts still occur every six months, but beginning on January 1, 1994; the $1,000,000 final payout is scheduled for July 1, 1996.

In cell B11, @NPV(B8,C6..J6,1) returns the NPV of this investment, 507,635. The *Type* argument of 1 tells Quattro Pro to assume that the cash flows in *Block* occur at the beginning of each period. Because the NPV is positive, this investment should be made. This NPV is larger than the one in Figure 7.40 because essentially all payments have moved up one period.

Figure 7.41

Calculating the NPV of an investment when the cash flows occur at the beginning of time periods

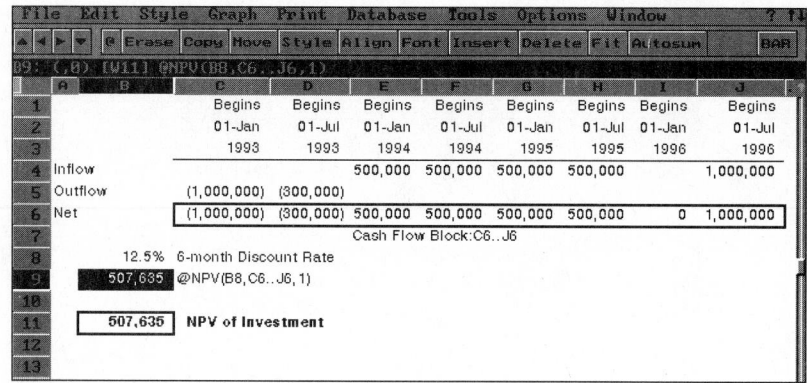

Internal Rate of Return: @IRR

The *internal rate of return* (IRR) for an investment is the discount rate that makes the NPV mathematical equation equal to 0. In other words, IRR is the rate that makes the present value of cash flows equal to the present value of cash outflows (investments). Mathematically, it's expressed as

$$0 = NPV = \Sigma \frac{\text{Cash Inflows} - \text{Cash Outflows}}{(1 + IRR)^n} - \text{Initial Investment}$$

where *n* represents the number of time periods over which the cash flow occurs. Because this equation is the NPV equation, it assumes

- Equal time periods between cash flows.

- All cash inflows (cash received) are immediately reinvested at the IRR rate until the end of the investment.

- The IRR rate remains constant over the investment period.

Before the advent of spreadsheets like Quattro Pro, you calculated an IRR by trial and error—entering IRR guesses into the NPV mathematical equation to find the IRR that made NPV equal to 0. Fortunately, you can get Quattro Pro to perform this iterative process for you by using

```
@IRR(Guess,Block)
```

where *Block* represents the stream of negative cash outflows and positive inflows. Because the time period between cash flows must be equal, the first cell represents the first day of the investment, when the initial investment occurs. All other cells represent the ending day of equally spaced time periods. Remember to include a cell for each period, even if no cash flow occurs.

The *Guess*, in decimal or percentage form, is what @IRR begins with to calculate the actual IRR. In most instances, you should use a *Guess* between 0 and 1 or 0% to 100%. Quattro Pro uses this *Guess* and tries, in 20 or fewer iterations, to calculate the actual IRR. If an answer is returned, it represents the IRR for one time period, so you may want to convert it to an annual IRR.

TIP. For a normal *cash flow stream, with one or more periods of cash outflows (investments) followed by periods of cash inflows (returns), you don't need to estimate your IRR. Simply enter @NA as the Guess argument.*

Calculating the IRR for an Investment

Let's calculate the IRR for the investment in Figure 7.40, where the cash flows occur at the end of six-month periods. Figure 7.42 shows how you must first change the cash flow *Block* to accommodate the @IRR function. Here, the initial investment is included as the first cell in the cash flow *Block* B6..J6; each cell thereafter represents the last day of a six-month period. In cell B9, @IRR(B8,B6..J9) starts with the 30% *Guess* in cell B8 and returns an actual IRR of 18.34%. But because the cash flow *Block* uses a six-month time period, this value is multiplied by 2 to return the annualized IRR of 9.17% in cell B11.

Figure 7.42
Computing the IRR for a normal cash flow

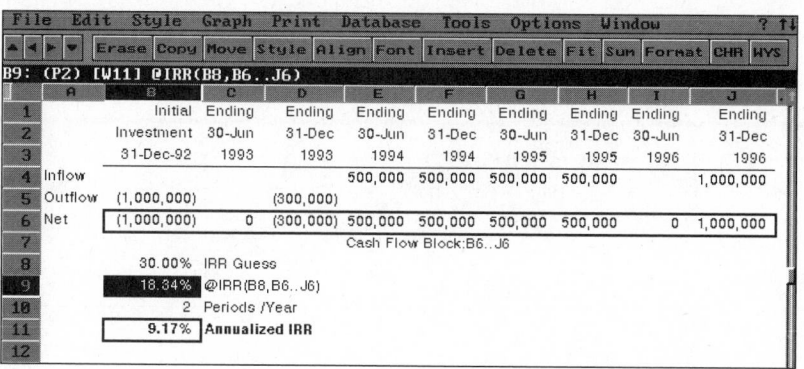

Evaluating the IRR Result

The IRR result, the rate of return for an investment, is usually compared to a *hurdle rate*—a minimum return taking into account the risk of the investment being analyzed. For example, imagine that your firm requires a 7% annualized rate of return for an investment like the one in Figure 7.42. Because its 9.17% annualized IRR exceeds the hurdle rate, this investment should be approved. In a world of scarce funds, though, a project whose IRR exceeds the hurdle rate is usually ranked against other projects.

When @IRR Returns ERR or Incorrect Values

Although @IRR can handle a normal cash flow stream, with one or more periods of cash outflows (investments), followed by periods of cash inflows (returns), it has problems handling certain situations. For example, @IRR returns ERR when your *Guess* is so far from the actual IRR that it can't converge on an IRR value within 20 iterations.

@IRR returns either ERR or an incorrect IRR when cash flow is *nonnormal*; that is, it includes one or more of the following:

■ An initial investment of 0.

■ An investment (outflow) near the end of the investment period, which causes the sign of the cash flow to change more than once.

■ A relatively large outflow near the end of the investment period.

■ An IRR less than 0% or greater than 100%.

Note. If you use @NA as your *Guess*, @IRR will return ERR instead of multiple returns.

For example, Figure 7.43 shows a situation when @IRR returns one of two IRR values, depending on the *Guess*. Here, the sign changes more than once because three investments are required, $500,000 on day 1, $800,000, and an additional $200,000 near the end of the investment. What's more, the actual IRR is obviously negative because the return (cash inflows) and the total investment, most of which occurs early, are about equal. Depending on the *Guess* in row 6, @IRR returns either –20.4% or 8.1% in row 7.

Figure 7.43
A situation when
@IRR returns
different IRR values

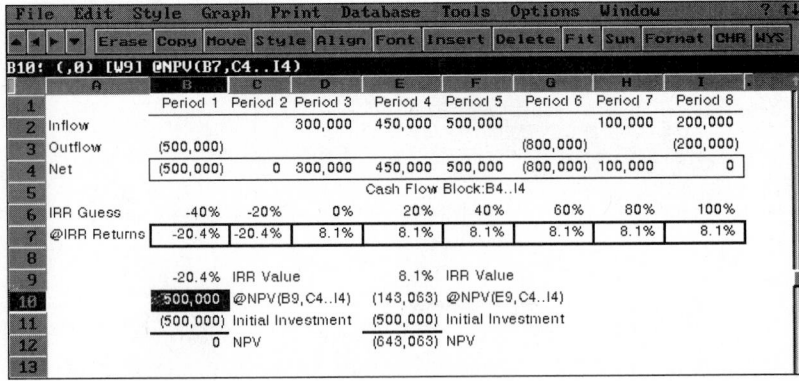

Note. Sometimes, the NPV for the correct IRR will be close to 0 due to rounding.

By trying these IRR values in the @NPV function, you can confirm which is the correct IRR. In cell B10, for example, @NPV(B9,C4..I4) returns 500,000 for a *Rate* of –20.4%. (Remember, in @NPV, the initial investment isn't included in *Block*.) When the initial investment is subtracted from this value, the end result is a 0 NPV. So –20.4% is the actual IRR for this cash flow. When you use the 8.1% IRR value, you can see that its NPV isn't 0.

NOTE. *In rare instances, a cash flow may be nonnormal to the extent that there are two IRR values—one positive and one negative. In this case, both have an NPV of 0.*

Implied Interest Rate: @RATE and @IRATE

Many times you'll need to calculate the implied compound rate earned on zero-coupon bonds, compound rates of returns on an equity investment, such as a stock, or even the implied compound growth rate for a financial indicator like sales or net profit. When you need to calculate the implied rate returned by an initial investment, you can calculate it using either @RATE or @IRATE.

To calculate the implied compound rate for an initial investment that generates a stream of fixed payments, however, you must use @IRATE. For example, you might want to figure out the return of a dividend-paying bond or the implied compound rate that your state is using when it spreads a lottery jackpot over 20 years.

Calculating the Implied Interest Rate for an Initial Investment

The compounded, implied fixed rate earned by an initial investment over the investment period is mathematically expressed as

$$\text{Compound Interest Rate} = (\text{FV/PV})^{1/n} - 1$$

where *n* represents the total number of equal payments. This equation assumes

- All payments (cash received) are immediately reinvested at the interest rate until the end of the investment.

- The interest rate remains constant over the investment period.

- Interest is compounded at the end of each time period.

When you're working with a single investment, two functions calculate the implied rate:

```
@RATE(FV,PV,Nper)
@IRATE(Nper,Pmt,-PV,FV,<Type>)
```

PV is the initial investment value, entered as positive in @RATE, but as a negative outflow in @IRATE. (Otherwise, you'll get a negative rate.) *FV* is the value achieved or received at the end of all compounding periods, entered as positive in both @RATE and @IRATE. Because only a single investment is being evaluated, set *Pmt* in @IRATE to 0.

Nper is the number of equal periods over which interest is compounded. If interest is compounded quarterly, for instance, use the annual rate divided by 4. By default, @RATE and @IRATE both assume that interest is compounded at the end of each period. If compounding happens at the beginning of each period, use @IRATE and specify an optional *Type* argument of 1.

Column A of Figure 7.44, for example, shows how you can use @IRATE to compute the implied interest on a zero-coupon bond. A *zero-coupon bond* is sold at a deep discount, such as 50% of its face value, and then redeemed at the full face value at a later date. Because no interest is paid, the return is the implied rate of interest.

Figure 7.44

Using @IRATE to calculate the implied interest rate of different investments

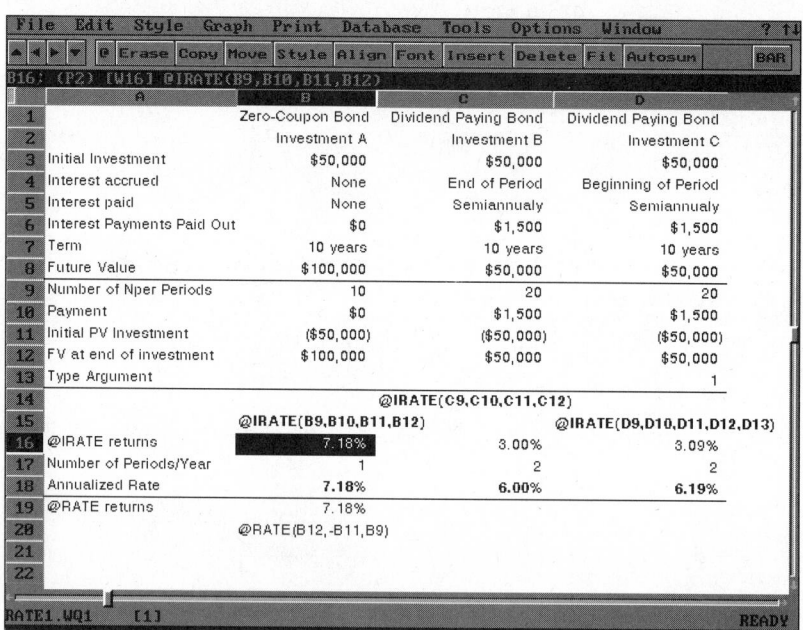

For example, the implied return of a $100,000, 10-year, zero-coupon bond purchased for $50,000 is calculated by @IRATE(B9,B10,B11,B12) in cell B16. This function uses 10 *Nper* yearly periods, a $0 *Pmt* because no interest is paid, an initial –$50,000 *PV* investment, and a $100,000 *FV* redemption value to return a 7.18% rate of return. The *Nper* periods are years, so it's already an annualized rate.

Calculating the Implied Interest Rate for an Initial Investment Generating Annuity Payments

To calculate the implied rate of an investment which pays dividends or interest, you must use @IRATE(*Nper,Pmt,–PV,FV,<Type>*). *Pmt* is the amount of interest or dividends paid each *Nper* period, entered as positive because it's an inflow to you. If interest or dividends are paid at the end of each *Nper* period, you don't need the optional *Type* argument; @IRATE already assumes this.

Column C of Figure 7.44 uses @IRATE to calculate the implied rate of return for a $50,000, 10-year bond paying a $1,500 dividend every six months. Because this bond is purchased at face value, a –$50,000 *PV* initial investment and a $50,000 *FV* redemption value are used. Adding 20 six-month *Nper* periods and a $1,500 semiannual dividend *Pmt*, @IRATE(C9,-C10,C11,C12) in cell C16 returns a 3.00% semiannual rate of return; the annualized rate is 6.00%.

Calculating the Implied Interest Rate for an Initial Investment Generating Annuity Due Payments

If you assume the bond in column C of Figure 7.44 pays interest at the beginning of every period, in column D the function @IRATE(D9,D10,D11,D12,D13) adds a *Type* argument of 1 and returns a slightly higher semiannual rate, 3.09%, in cell D16. In cell D18, this rate is annualized to 6.19%.

Term of an Initial Investment: @CTERM

The *term*, or number of periods it takes for an initial investment to reach a future value at a fixed interest rate, can be mathematically expressed as

$$\text{Term of a Single Investment} = \frac{\text{Ln (Future Value / Investment)}}{\text{Ln (1 + Interest Rate)}}$$

where Ln is the natural logarithm. This equation assumes:

- The investment occurs on day 1 of the investment period.

- The interest rate remains constant over the investment period.

- All payments received (interest) are immediately reinvested at the interest rate until the end of the investment.

- Interest is compounded at the end of each time period.

In Quattro Pro, you use this function to calculate the term of an initial investment:

@CTERM(*Rate*,*FV*,*PV*)

where *PV* is the investment made on day 1, although it's entered as a positive value. *Rate* is the fixed interest rate for one time period entered in decimal or percentage form. If payments occur semiannually, for instance, use the annual rate divided by 2. *FV* is the investment objective, also entered as positive.

@CTERM returns a term representing the number of compounding periods it takes to grow the *PV* into the *FV*. Because this term is in the same time period used in the *Rate* argument, you may want to convert it to an annualized rate.

In Figure 7.45, @CTERM is used to determine the time it takes two different investment schemes to turn a $20,000 *PV* investment into a $50,000 *FV*. Because Investment A pays a 10% annual rate compounded monthly, @CTERM(B7,B8,B9) in cell B11 uses a monthly *Rate* of 0.10/12 or 0.83%. Although the calculated term is 110.41 months, for comparison purposes it's converted in cell B13 to 9.2 years.

Note.
@NPER(*Rate*,0, –*PV*,*FV*) is also equivalent to @CTERM.

Figure 7.45
Using @CTERM to evaluate lump sum investments

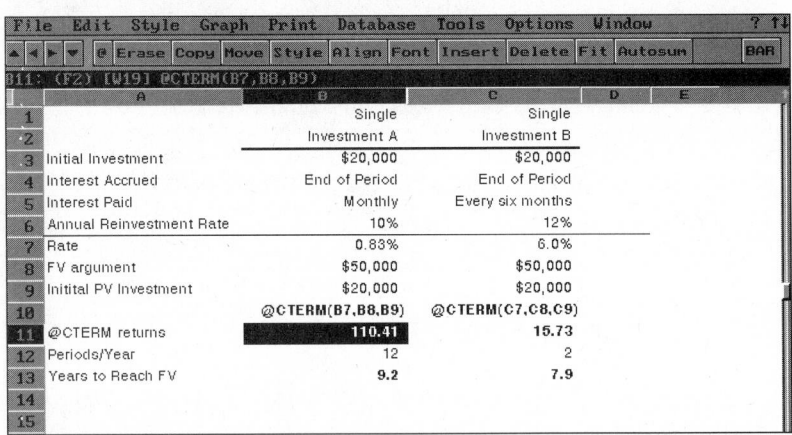

Investment B, on the other hand, pays a 12% annual return, compounded semiannually. Therefore, @CTERM(C7,C8,C9) in cell C11 uses a 6% semiannual *Rate* to calculate that it takes 15.73 six-month periods for Investment B to reach $50,000. Because this term is equivalent to 7.86 years in cell C13, Investment B is the obvious choice.

Number of Fixed Payments to Reach a Future Value: @TERM and @NPER

The term, or number of periods it takes for equal payments invested at a fixed rate to reach a future value, such as a retirement goal, can be mathematically expressed as

$$\text{Term} = \frac{\text{Ln}\,[\,1 + (\text{FV} * \text{Interest Rate})\,/\,\text{Payment}\,]}{\text{Ln}\,(1 + \text{Interest Rate})}$$

where Ln is the natural logarithm. This equation assumes

- Equal payments occur at the end of equally spaced time periods.

- The interest rate remains constant over the investment period.

- All payments received (interest) are immediately reinvested at the interest rate until the end of the investment. Interest is compounded at the end of each time period.

    In Quattro Pro, you can calculate the term using

    ```
    @TERM(Pmt,Rate,FV)
    @NPER(Rate,-Pmt,-PV,FV,<Type>)
    ```

where the *Pmt* is the value of one payment, entered as a positive value in @TERM, but as a negative value in @NPER because it's a cash outflow. *Rate* is the interest rate for one time period entered in decimal or percentage form. If payments are made each month, for instance, use a monthly *Rate*. *FV* is the desired investment objective, entered as positive in both functions.

   In @NPER, *PV* allows you to specify an initial investment; if there isn't one, use $0. Because it's a cash outflow, remember to enter it as a negative value.

   By default, @TERM and @NPER both assume that you make payments at the end of each period. If payments are made at the beginning of each period, use an optional *Type* argument of 1 in @NPER.

   @TERM and @NPER calculate the number of compounding periods that it takes to reach the *FV*. Because this term is in the same units as the *Rate*, you may want to annualize it.

   Figure 7.46 shows how you can use @NPER to calculate the time it takes to amass $200,000 when you put aside $2,000 every month. If you assume a 10% annualized return, all three scenarios use a fixed 0.83% monthly *Rate*, a –$2,000 monthly *Pmt*, and a $200,000 *FV* goal in @NPER.

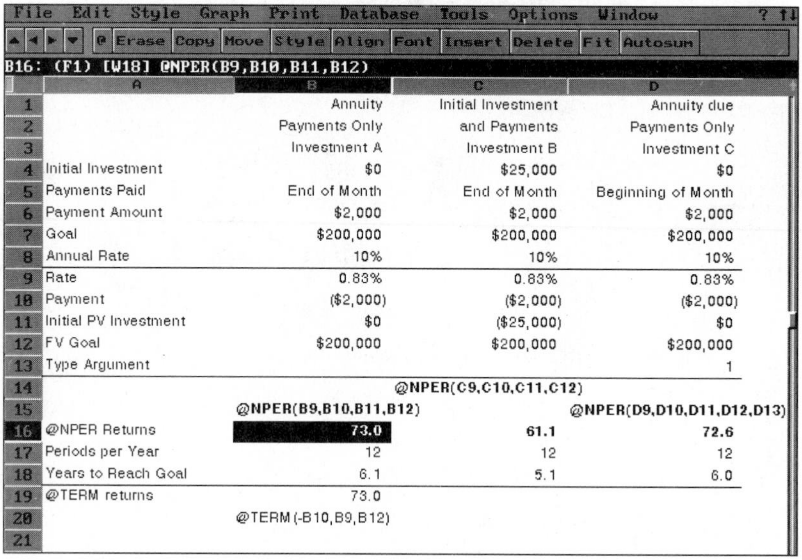

Figure 7.46
Using @NPER to evaluate how long it takes to reach an FV

	File Edit Style Graph Print Database Tools Options Window		? ↑↓
	▲ ◄ ► ▼ @ Erase Copy Move Style Align Font Insert Delete Fit Autosum		
	B16: (F1) [W18] @NPER(B9,B10,B11,B12)		

	A	B	C	D
1		Annuity	Initial Investment	Annuity due
2		Payments Only	and Payments	Payments Only
3		Investment A	Investment B	Investment C
4	Initial Investment	$0	$25,000	$0
5	Payments Paid	End of Month	End of Month	Beginning of Month
6	Payment Amount	$2,000	$2,000	$2,000
7	Goal	$200,000	$200,000	$200,000
8	Annual Rate	10%	10%	10%
9	Rate	0.83%	0.83%	0.83%
10	Payment	($2,000)	($2,000)	($2,000)
11	Initial PV Investment	$0	($25,000)	$0
12	FV Goal	$200,000	$200,000	$200,000
13	Type Argument			1
14			@NPER(C9,C10,C11,C12)	
15		@NPER(B9,B10,B11,B12)		@NPER(D9,D10,D11,D12,D13)
16	@NPER Returns	73.0	61.1	72.6
17	Periods per Year	12	12	12
18	Years to Reach Goal	6.1	5.1	6.0
19	@TERM returns	73.0		
20		@TERM(-B10,B9,B12)		
21				

Calculating the Term for Fixed Annuity Payments Only

In Investment A, an initial investment of $0 *PV* is used because the only investment is the $2,000 paid at the end of each month. @NPER(B9,B10,B11,B12) in cell B16 returns that it'll take 73 months, or 6.1 years, to amass $200,000. By converting the monthly payment to a positive value, @TERM(−B10,B9,B12) returns the same result.

Calculating the Term for an Initial Investment and Fixed Annuity Payments

If you add an initial −$25,000 *PV* investment to the monthly payments, @NPER(C9,C10,C11,C12) in cell C16 returns that it'll take Investment B 61.1 months or 5.1 years to reach $200,000. Because of the relatively short investment time span, this large initial investment only decreases the term by 1 year.

Calculating the Term for Fixed Annuity Due Payments Only

If the $2,000 payment is made at beginning of every month, and no initial investment is made, @NPER(D9,D10,D11,D12,D13) uses an ending period *Type* of 1 and a *PV* of 0. As you can see, it will take 72.6 months or 6 years to reach $200,000.

Depreciation Functions

Quattro Pro's depreciation functions, listed in Table 7.14, use three commonly accepted methods for calculating depreciation: straight-line, sum-of-the-years'-digits, and double-declining-balance.

Table 7.14   **Depreciation Functions**

Function	Method Used to Calculate Depreciation
@SLN	Straight-line
@SYD	Sum-of-the-years'-digits
@DDB	Double-declining-balance

NOTE. When *you're using Quattro Pro's depreciation functions, you must use realistic values. Otherwise, you can end up with incorrect results or ERR. For example, an asset's salvage value, very logically, must be less than the asset's cost; both must also be positive values.*

The Partial-Year Convention

Often, depreciation methods use a *partial-year convention*—especially tax depreciation methods. The most common, a *half-year convention*, assumes that all new assets are placed in service on July 1. Only one-half of a full year's depreciation is expensed in the first year. This means that an asset is depreciated over one more year than its life classification because it takes an additional year to expense the remaining one-half year of depreciation. For example, a 7-year asset is depreciated over 8 years.

Straight-Line Depreciation: @SLN

Straight-line allocates the same expense over each depreciation period. The depreciation each period is calculated as

$$\text{Depreciation per Period} = \frac{(\text{Cost-Salvage Value})}{(\text{Periods of Useful Life})}$$

The form of Quattro Pro's function is

```
@SLN(Cost,Salvage,Life)
```

where *Cost* represents the total cost—purchase price, freight-in, and installation. *Life* is the total number of equal periods over which the asset is depreciated. Using a half-year convention, *Life* is the number of six-month periods. *Salvage* is the estimated value at the end of the asset's useful life. @SLN calculates the depreciation for one *Life* period.

Using @SLN with the Half-Year Convention

Figure 7.47 shows how to use @SLN to calculate straight-line depreciation for a $100,000 asset placed in service during 1993. It has a life of 5 years and an estimated $10,000 salvage value at the end of this time period.

Figure 7.47

Using @SLN to calculate straight-line depreciation with a half-year convention

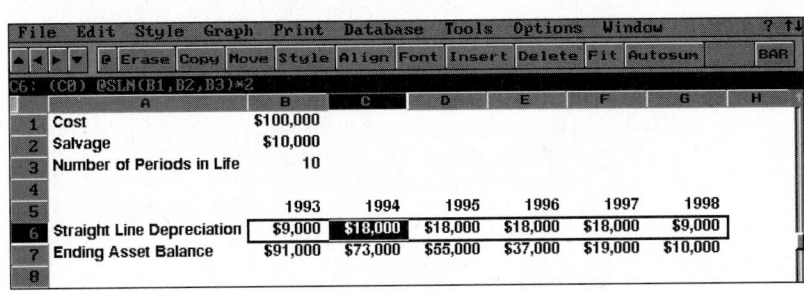

Under the half year convention, you use a *Life* of 10 six-month periods. The asset, however, is depreciated over 6 years. For example, because only half of a year's depreciation is expensed in the first year, 1993, and the last year, 1998, @SLN(B1,B2,B3) returns a $9,000 expense. In the other 4 years, a full year's depreciation expense of $18,000 is returned by @SLN(B1,B2,B3)*2. Notice how the fully depreciated asset value in G7 equals the $10,000 salvage value.

Sum-of-the-Years'-Digits Depreciation: @SYD

Sum-of-the-years'-digits (SYD) is an accelerated method that allocates the largest depreciation expense during the earlier years. The depreciation in each period is calculated by

$$\text{SYD per Period} = (\text{Cost} - \text{Salvage Value}) * \frac{(n-p+1)}{(n \times (n+1)/2)}$$

where *n* is the number of periods of useful life and *p* is the period depreciation is being calculated for. In this equation, the depreciation *rate* per period is represented by the remaining life, or $(n-p+1)$, divided by the sum of the years of life, or $(n*(n+1)/2)$. In the first year of depreciation of a three-year asset, the numerator evaluates to 3–1+1 or 3, and the denominator to 3*(4/2) or 6—the sum-of-the-years'-digits 1+2+3. This means that ³⁄₆ or one-half of the total depreciation is expensed in the first year.

The form of Quattro Pro's function is

`@SYD(Cost,Salvage,Life,Period)`

where *Cost* represents the total cost—purchase price, freight-in, and installation. *Life* is the total number of equal periods over which the asset is depreciated. *Salvage* is the estimated asset value at the end of its useful life. @SYD calculates the expense for the depreciation *Period* specified. If *Period* is 4, for instance, @SYD calculates the depreciation in period 4.

Figure 7.48 shows how @SYD calculates depreciation for the same asset as before with a $100,000 *Cost* and a $10,000 *Salvage* value. Here though, it's being depreciated over 5 years, so *Life* is 5. The only argument that varies is the *Period* in row 6. For example, @SYD(B1,B2,B3,1) in cell B7 uses a *Period* of 1 and returns a $30,000 depreciation expense for period 1; in cell E7, @SYD(B1,B2,B3,4) returns a $12,000 depreciation expense for period 4. In cell F8, you can see that the fully depreciated asset equals the $10,000 salvage value.

Figure 7.48
Using @SYD to calculate sum-of-the-years'-digits depreciation

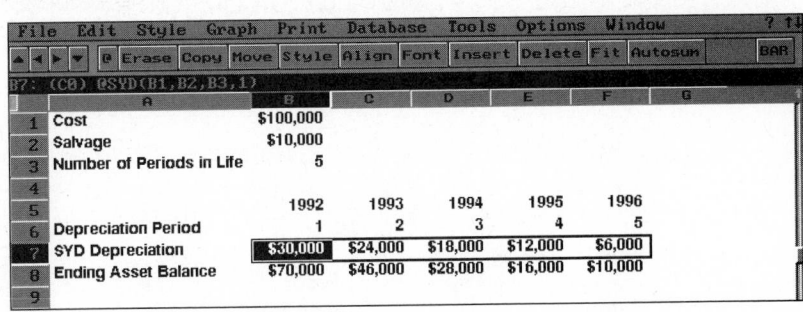

Double-Declining Balance: @DDB

Double-declining balance depreciation, or 200% DDB, is another accelerated depreciation method. The 200% DDB depreciation per period is represented by

$$DDB \; per \; Period \; = \; (2/n) * Remaining \; Book \; Value$$

where *n* is the number of periods of useful life and the *Remaining Book Value* equals the original cost less the depreciation to date.

The depreciation rate (2/*n*) remains constant; it's the remaining book value that decreases each period. For instance, each year 40% (2/5) of the remaining book value of a 5-year asset is depreciated. Because DDB never fully depreciates an asset, a "plug" value is always used in the last year to write off the remaining depreciable amount not expensed.

The form of this function is

@DDB(*Cost,Salvage,Life,Period*)

where *Cost* represents the total cost—purchase price, freight-in, and installation. *Life* is the total number of equal periods over which the asset is depreciated. Using a half-year convention, *Life* is the number of six-month periods. *Salvage* is the estimated disposal value at the end of its useful life. @DDB calculates the expense for the depreciation *Period* specified. If *Period* is 6, for instance, @DDB calculates the depreciation in period 6.

Using @DDB with the Half-Year Convention

Figure 7.49 shows how a $100,000, 5-year asset with a $12,000 salvage value is depreciated using double-declining balance depreciation and a half-year convention. In each of the depreciation periods, a *Cost* of $100,000 in cell B1, a *Salvage* of $12,000 in cell B2, and a *Life* of 10 six-month periods in cell B3 is used. Only the *Period* changes in @DDB. Here's how the depreciation is calculated for each year:

Year	Depreciation Periods	Formula Used
1992	1	@DDB(B1,B2,B3,1)
1993	2 and 3	@DDB(B1,B2,B3,2) + @DDB(B1,B2,B3,3)
1994	4 and 5	@DDB(B1,B2,B3,4) + @DDB(B1,B2,B3,5)
1995	6 and 7	@DDB(B1,B2,B3,6) + @DDB(B1,B2,B3,7)
1996	8 and 9	@DDB(B1,B2,B3,8) + @DDB(B1,B2,B3,9)
1997	10	@DDB(B1,B2,B3,10)

Notice that Quattro Pro correctly calculates the "plug" value of $1,422 in the last period—cell G6.

Figure 7.49
Using @DDB to calculate double-declining balance depreciation with a half-year convention

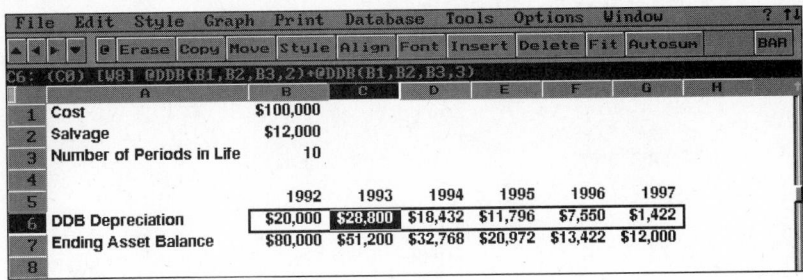

CAUTION! *Often, for small asset values, or for a $0 salvage value, or a salvage value in the neighborhood of 12% or less, Quattro Pro calculates the "plug" value incorrectly. So when you use @DDB, make sure you check the total depreciation expensed against the amount that should be expensed. In fact, don't be surprised if you get some really odd results when you fall below these limits.*

How @DDB Differs from Tax Depreciation

You should take considerable care if you decide to use @DDB to calculate tax depreciation. The first reason is that @DDB won't calculate the most advantageous tax depreciation for you. At the time this book was written, current tax laws allowed you to switch to a *modified* form of straight-line depreciation in the first tax year in which it yielded a larger expense than declining balance depreciation. The modified straight-line depreciation is based on the remaining book value, *not* the total asset value. (See a tax publication for details.)

Second, for most asset classes, tax depreciation assumes a $0 salvage value. Because of the problems @DDB has when you use a $0 salvage value, you'll have a difficult time using it to create an accurate depreciation table.

Special Functions

Quattro Pro's special functions, listed in Table 7.15, return information about your spreadsheet or about the current work session.

Table 7.15   **Special Functions**

Function	Returns
@COLS	Number of columns in a block
@ROWS	Number of rows in a block
@@	Contents of a cell referenced through another cell
@CELL	Attribute of the first cell in a block
@CELLINDEX	Attribute of a specified cell in a block
@CELLPOINTER	Attribute of the current cell
@CURVALUE	Result of most recent use of commands
@MEMAVAIL	Memory currently available
@MEMEMSAVAIL	Expanded memory currently available
@VERSION	Version of Quattro Pro in use
@FILEEXISTS	1 if specified file exists, 0 otherwise

Number of Columns and Rows in a Block: @COLS and @ROWS

The @COLS and @ROWS functions return the number of columns and rows in a block. The forms of these functions are

```
@COLS(Block)
@ROWS(Block)
```

where *Block* is the address or name of a block. For example, @COLS(A1..D5) returns 4 columns; @ROWS(A1..D5) returns 5 rows.

Normally, you'll use these functions to find the number of rows or columns in a named block. They're also used in a macro when the number of rows or columns in a block affects how the macro runs. For example, if each row in a database contains a record, you could use @ROWS to determine the number of records.

Note. Macros are discussed in Chapters 12 and 13.

Indirect Cell Referencing: @@

@@ retrieves the contents of a cell by indirectly referencing it through another cell. The form of this function is

    @@(Cell)

where *Cell* must be the address or name of one cell, entered as a string. For example, if cell F14 contains 100 and cell F15 contains +F14, then @@("F15") returns 100, the contents of cell F14 indirectly referenced through the label "F15". If *Cell* is the address or name of a block, @@ returns ERR.

You can create powerful conditional formulas by using the @@ function as the *Condition* in @IF. For example, imagine that cell D5 contains @IF(C1="","C2","C3"), and cell D6 contains @@(D5). If C1 is blank, the *Condition* is true, and @IF returns the *TrueExpression* label "C2" in cell D5. @@(D5) then uses this string and returns the contents of cell C2. But if cell C1 isn't blank, @IF returns the *FalseExpression* label "C3", and @@(D5) returns the contents of cell C3.

Returning Cell Attributes: @CELL, @CELLINDEX, and @CELLPOINTER

The @CELL, @CELLINDEX, and @CELLPOINTER functions return information about an attribute of a cell. Usually, you'll use these functions in macros to check the attributes of a cell before a certain type of entry is allowed.

NOTE. *The results obtained by @CELL, @CELLINDEX, and @CELL-POINTER aren't updated when the spreadsheet is automatically recalculated. You'll have to update the results yourself by pressing F9 (Calc).*

Returning Attribute Information for the Upper-Left Cell in a Block

To return information about the attribute of the upper-left cell of a block, use

    @CELL(Attribute,Block)

where *Attribute* is one of the attributes listed in Table 7.16 entered as a string. Remember to enclose an *Attribute* in double quotes if you enter it directly into @CELL. *Block* is the address or name of a block.

In column B of Figure 7.50, @CELL returns information for A1, the upper-left cell of the *Block* A1..E2. For the *Attribute* "prefix", @CELL returns the centered label prefix ^ because cell A1 contains a centered label; for the *Attribute* "address", it returns the absolute address $A$1. @CELL returns 1 when *Attribute* is "col" or "row" because A1 is in the first column and first row of the spreadsheet.

Table 7.16   **Cell Attributes Used in @CELL, @CELLINDEX, and @CELLPOINTER**

Attribute	@CELL, @CELLINDEX, and @CELLPOINTER Return
"address"	Cell address as an absolute address, as in $B$5
"col"	Column number of a cell between 1 and 256 corresponding to columns A through IV
"contents"	Cell contents
"format"	Numeric format of a cell: C0 to C15 for Currency, ,0 to ,15 for Comma, E0 to E15 for Exponential, F0 to F15 for Fixed, G for General or a user-defined format, H for Hidden, P0 to P15 for Percent, S0 to S15 for Scientific, T for formulas displayed as Text, D1 to D5 for Date, D6 to D9 for Time, + for +/– format
"prefix"	Label prefix in a cell: ' for left-aligned, ^ for centered, " for right-aligned, \ for repeating
"protect"	Protection status of a cell: 1 for protected, 0 for unprotected
"row"	Row number of a cell, 1 to 8,192
"rwidth"	Number of columns in *Block*
"type"	Type of data in a cell: b for blank, v for a number or formula, l for a label
"width"	Column width of a cell, 1 to 254

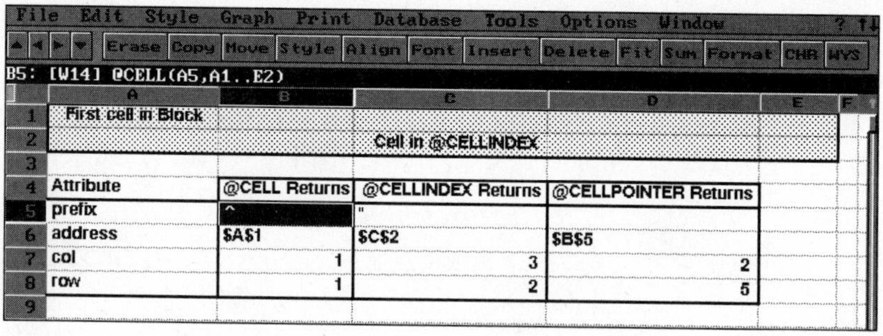

Figure 7.50
Using @CELL, @CELLINDEX, and @CELLPOINTER to return information about the attributes of different cells

Returning Attribute Information for Any Cell in a Block

To return information about the attribute of any cell of a block, use

@CELLINDEX(*Attribute,Block,Column,Row*)

where *Attribute* is one of the attributes listed in Table 7.16 entered as a string. Remember to enclose an *Attribute* in double quotes if you enter it directly into @CELLINDEX. *Block* is the address or name of a block.

You use the *Column* and *Row* arguments to specify the cell you want to examine in *Block*. The leftmost column in *Block* has an *Column* offset value of 0; the rightmost column *c* has an *Column* offset of *c*–1. The top row in *Block* has a *Row* offset of 0; the last row *r* has a *Row* offset of *r*–1. Therefore, the upper-left cell in *Block* is represented by a *Column* offset of 0 and a *Row* offset of 0. The lower-right cell has a *Column* offset of *c*–1 and a *Row* offset of *r*–1. Obviously, values outside of these ranges specify a cell outside of the *Block*, and @CELLINDEX returns ERR.

In Figure 7.50, for instance, @CELLINDEX uses the *Block* A1..E2, a *Column* offset of 2 and a *Row* offset of 1 to examine the cell in the third column, second row of A1..E2, or cell C2. For the *Attribute* "prefix", it returns the right label prefix " because cell C2 contains a right-aligned label. For the *Attribute* "address", @CELLINDEX returns the absolute address $C$2. And since C2 is in the third column and second row of the spreadsheet, @CELLINDEX returns 3 for "col" and 2 for "row".

Returning Attribute Information for the Current Cell Pointer Location

To return information about the attribute of the current cellpointer location, use

@CELLPOINTER(*Attribute*)

where *Attribute* is one of the attributes listed in Table 7.16 entered as a string. Remember to enclose *Attribute* in double quotes if you enter it directly into @CELLPOINTER.

Column D of Figure 7.50 shows how @CELLPOINTER works for the *Attribute* arguments in column A. Because the cell selector is currently located in cell B5, @CELLPOINTER returns information about this cell. @CELLPOINTER returns a null string for the *Attribute* "prefix", so you know that cell B5 hasn't been assigned a nonglobal label format. For the *Attribute* "address", @CELLPOINTER returns the absolute address $B$5. Because B5 is in the second column and fifth row of the spreadsheet, @CELLPOINTER returns 2 for "col" and 5 for "row".

Returning What a Command Acted On: @CURVALUE

For a particular command, @CURVALUE returns the most recent item—block, file name, printer, and so on—that was acted on. Typically, you'll use @CURVALUE in a macro when you want to base the next action on a previous command setting. The form of this function is

@CURVALUE(*GeneralAction*,*SpecificAction*)

GeneralAction describes a general menu command category. *SpecificAction* is a specific menu command selection. Enter each as a literal string enclosed in double quotes. *GeneralAction* and *SpecificAction* must evaluate to a valid menu-equivalent command listed in Chapter 3 of Quattro Pro's *@Functions and Macros* handbook.

For example, if the last file saved was COSTS.WQ1 in the C:\QPRO directory, @CURVALUE("file","save") returns C:\QPRO\COSTS.WQ1. If the last block specified in /Print, Block was A1..E10, @CURVALUE("print","block") returns A1..E10.

Returning Information About the Operating System: @MEMAVAIL, @MEMEMSAVAIL, and @VERSION

Quattro Pro includes three commands that provide information about the current session:

Function	Returns
@VERSION	The version of Quattro Pro currently in use.
@MEMAVAIL	The number of bytes of conventional memory currently available for Quattro Pro to use.
@MEMEMSAVAIL	The number of bytes of expanded (EMS) memory available. (If your system doesn't have expanded memory, it returns NA.)

Testing for a File Name: @FILEEXISTS

To test for the existence of a file, use

@FILEEXISTS(*FileName*)

where *FileName* represents a file name, including the file extension, entered as a literal string enclosed in double quotes—@FILEEXISTS("SALES1.WQ1"), for instance. To search for a file in a directory other than the default directory, include the full path name in *FileName*. @FILEEXISTS performs a logical test and returns the true value 1 if the file name exists, and 0 otherwise.

Add-in Functions

Note. Quattro Pro also includes two new functions @ISAPP and @ISAAF that test for a particular library and function. See "Checking for Add-Ins: @ISAPP and @ISAAF," earlier.

Quattro Pro 4.0 allows you to use customized add-in functions, including some provided with the program, to perform specialized tasks. Add-in functions are written in a lower level language like C. They are then stored in a file called a *library* which has a .QLL extension.

To access an add-in function, you first use the /Tools, Library, Load command to load the library that holds the function. For example, in the dialog box shown in Figure 7.51, select the SAMPLE.QLL library to load add-in functions Quattro Pro has provided. Once a library is loaded, it remains attached to Quattro Pro for all future sessions. (To detach it, use the /Tools, Library, Unload command.)

Figure 7.51

Loading an add-in function library

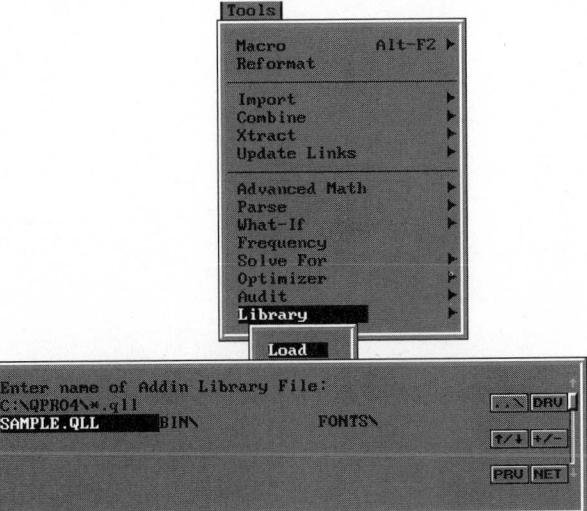

Once a library is loaded, you can use the add-in functions it contains, just like you would any other function. For example, Table 7.17 contains the functions from the @SAMPLE.QLL library. These functions are discussed in "Hyperbolic Trigonometric Functions: @SINH, @COSH, @TANH," "Returning the Last Day of a Particular Month," and "Using @SAMPLE.ADD_MONTHS to Fill a Block with End of Month Dates" earlier in this chapter.

Table 7.17   SAMPLE.QLL Add-in Functions

Add-in Function	Returns
@SAMPLE.SINH(x)	Hyperbolic sine of x
@SAMPLE.COSH(x)	Hyperbolic cosine of x
@SAMPLE.TANH(x)	Hyperbolic tangent of x
@SAMPLE.ADD_MONTHS	Date-value of a date obtained by adding specified number of months to a given date
@SAMPLE.LAST_DAY	For a date, the last day of a month

CHAPTER

8

Creating Graphs

A GRAPHIC REPRESENTATION OF DATA CAN SAY A LOT MORE THAN words and numbers in a spreadsheet, by visually illustrating relationships, and highlighting differences and similarities. Best of all, a graph often reveals trends and patterns that are not immediately apparent in an examination of raw data. In fact, graphs can give you a whole new perspective on your data. For instance, compare the data in Figure 8.1 to the 3-D graph in Figure 8.2. As you can see, the graph reveals more than the spreadsheet and dramatically illustrates the overwhelming U.S. dependence on petroleum during the time period shown.

Figure 8.1

Spreadsheet data used to make a graph

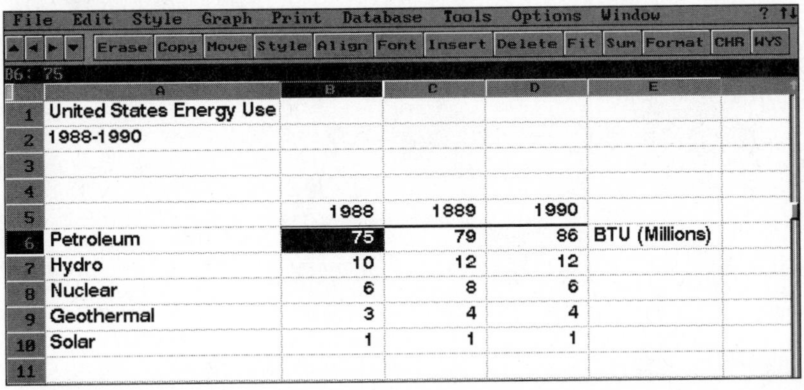

Quattro Pro gives you powerful yet flexible graphics capability. For instance, it provides eleven types of 2-D graphs (ten in Quattro Pro 3.0) and four types of 3-D graphs. To create a graph style all your own, you can combine line and bar graphs. You can even print spreadsheet data and a graph together.

In Quattro Pro, you use the /Graph command to customize graphs almost any way you like. For example, you can add descriptive text like titles, labels, and legends. The /Graph, Annotate command offers you even more presentation-quality finishing touches, such as arrows, lines, buttons, and notes (see Chapter 9).

Hardware Considerations

Naturally, for you to display graphs on your screen, your computer must have a graphics card. Most present-day PC-compatible computers include some kind of graphics board. Quattro Pro supports most of them, displaying your graphs using the highest-resolution graphics mode that your machine can produce. (See Chapter 15 for further discussion.)

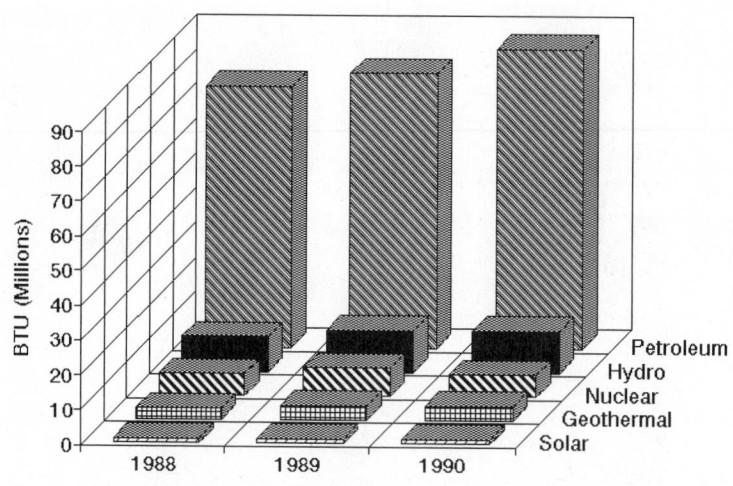

Figure 8.2
A 3-D bar graph
based on Figure 8.1

United States Energy Use
1988 - 1990

Tip. You can also use /Graph, Insert to simultaneously review spreadsheet data and a graph.

If you have two monitors connected to your PC, you can view a graph on one monitor and the spreadsheet data on the other. This way, you can view the resulting changes in a graph as you change the data in the spreadsheet. To set this up, you use the /Options, Hardware, Screen command discussed in Chapter 15.

Even if your computer can't display graphs on the screen, you can still create graphs and print them on a printer that supports graphics mode. Some of Quattro Pro's custom graph features, such as its color capability, may not be supported by your printer.

Graph Basics

Before you can create a graph, you need to familiarize yourself with Quattro Pro's graph terminology. The different components that together make up a presentation-quality graph are illustrated in Figure 8.3.

The *first* and *second titles* at the top of this bar graph are used to succinctly explain the graph information. Figure 8.3 is a graph comparing 1992 automobiles that were rated the best in fuel efficiency.

The values you want to graph are categorized into *data series*. For example, the graph in Figure 8.3 is created by separating spreadsheet data into two data series. The *1st data series* represents the city mileage for all vehicles, and the *2nd data series* includes the highway mileage for the same vehicles. (This is explained in the *legend*, which is the key to each data series.) The number of data series that you use depends on the amount of information you want to graph and the type of graph you want to create.

Figure 8.3

The parts of a graph and the data used to create it

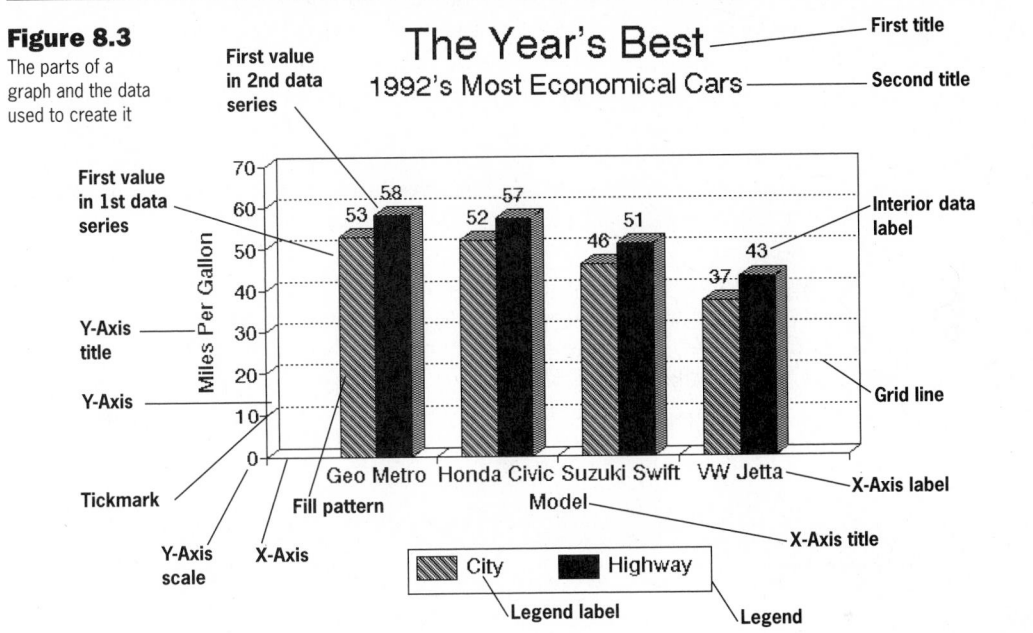

When you create a two-dimensional (2-D) graph, Quattro Pro displays a border composed of an x-axis and a y-axis (except for pie, text, and column graphs). The *y-axis* displays a numeric scale representing the range of values in the graph (0 through 70 in Figure 8.3). Quattro Pro automatically creates this *y-axis scale* using equally-spaced intervals so that all data series values are represented. The *y-axis labels* designate these intervals, and also correspond to the *tickmarks* displayed on the y-axis. Quattro Pro automatically creates the y-axis labels, but you can change them when you customize your graph. The *y-axis title* (Miles Per Gallon in Figure 8.3) conveys the y-axis unit of measurement.

Additional features in this graph allow easier interpretation of the *y-values*. Quattro Pro automatically includes a horizontal *grid* corresponding to the y-axis tickmarks. *Data labels* have been added to display the y-value each bar represents.

In most Quattro Pro graphs, the *x-axis* is used to convey descriptive information about each item in a data series. It is not a numeric scale. In Figure 8.3, the 1st and 2nd data series each include a value for Geo Metro, Honda Civic, Suzuki Swift, and VW Jetta, and these descriptive categories are used as the *x-axis labels*. The *x-axis title*, "Model," further describes these categories.

Only in an XY graph does the *x-axis* represent a sliding numeric scale. Quattro Pro then automatically creates equally spaced x-axis labels covering all x-values in your data. For example, each tickmark may represent an equally spaced time period, such as days, expense values, number of employees, or whatever progressive values you are graphing on the x-axis.

As you can see, a big part of creating a graph is enhancing it. Only the two data series in Figure 8.3 actually represent the data being graphed. Many of the other graph components—titles, axis labels, axis titles, legends, data labels, and grids—enhance the graphed data.

Creating a Graph: A Simple Example

In Quattro Pro, graphing data is much easier than you might expect. It takes only a few steps to create a basic graph, and only a few more steps to customize it. To clearly see this, let's go step by step through the creation of a basic line graph, which we'll then customize. In the process, you will get a taste of just a few of Quattro Pro's graphics capabilities.

Suppose you have entered the spreadsheet information in Figure 8.4, which presents the resale price of used vehicles as a percentage of original list price. Although it is clear in the spreadsheet that resale value decreases with vehicle age, little else is obvious. Look carefully at this data, and you can also see that cars lose their value much more rapidly than trucks. However, this trend would be more easily apparent if it were visually displayed in a graph.

Figure 8.4
The spreadsheet data used in the line graphs in Figure 8.6 and 8.7

File	Edit	Style	Graph	Print	Database	Tools	Options	Window		? ↑↓

| ▲ ◄ ► ▼ | Erase | Copy | Move | Style | Align | Font | Insert | Delete | Fit | Sum | Format | CHR | WYS |

B5: [W11] 100

	A	B	C	D	E	F
1	Value of Used Vehicles					
2						
3	Age in Years	Percentage of List Price				
4		Trucks	Cars			
5	0	100	100			
6	1	84	78			
7	2	74	64			
8	3	67	54			
9	4	61	46			
10	5	58	41			
11	6	54	37			
12	7	51	33			
13	8	49	30			
14	9	47	27			
15	10	46	25			
16						

Tip. Use the Fast Graph command to create and view a "bare bones" graph of spreadsheet data. See "Creating a Fast Graph" later in this chapter.

Before you create this graph, you must first plan its layout. To begin with, you need to determine the type of graph you should use. In this example, you want to examine a trend—resale price versus vehicle age—and see if this pattern holds up. Therefore, a *line graph* is ideally suited, because it will dramatically display any deviations in the spreadsheet data from the linear trend.

The next step is to classify the spreadsheet data into different data series. In a line graph, Quattro Pro graphs each data series as a separate line and identifies each value in a data series with a *marker*. In this case, you'll want to graph the Trucks data from column B as one line, and the Cars data from column C as another line. So you will specify each column of data as a separate data series; the line graph will then contain two separate lines of values (markers), each representing one data series. Furthermore, you can use the column A values as the x-axis labels.

Next, you need to develop label text that succinctly explains this graphed information. For instance, for the title at the top of the graph you use the text "Value of Used Vehicles" in cell A1 of the spreadsheet. You can also develop a second graph title, "Cars Versus Trucks." You'll want to identify the y-axis values using "Percentage of List Price" in cell B3, and the x-axis values using the label "Age in Years" in cell A3. Legends are also needed to identify each graphed line—for the 1st data series, use "Trucks" from cell B4, and for the 2nd data series, use "Cars" from cell C4. (Take a look ahead at Figure 8.7 to see how all this will look.)

After you determine the components of the graph, you can use Quattro Pro's /Graph command to create it. For the data in Figure 8.4, you can use the following procedure to do this:

Note. If you do not select a graph type, Quattro Pro will automatically create a stacked bar graph.

1. Select the /Graph command, and Quattro Pro displays the /Graph menu in Figure 8.5. Now specify a line graph by choosing Graph Type, then Line. Quattro Pro returns to the /Graph menu.

Figure 8.5

The /Graph menu

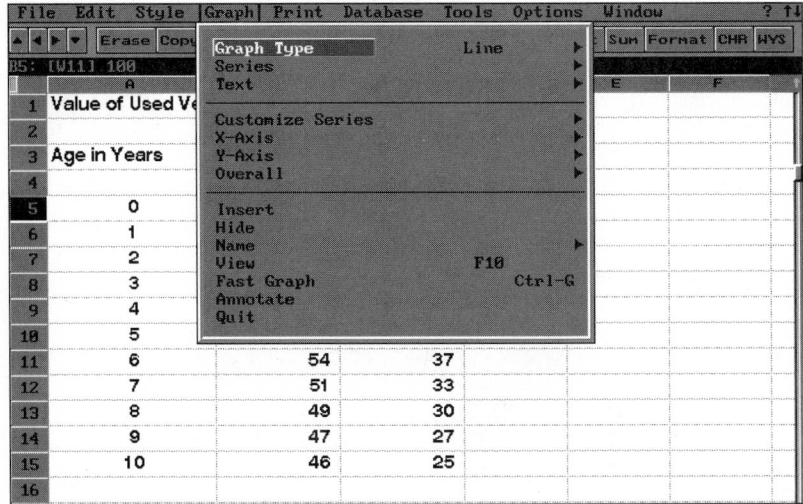

2. Specify the two data series. First, choose Series from the /Graph menu, and then select 1st Series. In response to the prompt, specify the Trucks block **B5..B15** from Figure 8.4 and press Enter. Next, select 2nd Series. Specify the Cars block **C5..C15** and press Enter. Select Quit to return to the /Graph menu.

3. View the graph so far by pressing F10 (Graph). Quattro Pro displays the unadorned graph shown in Figure 8.6. Notice that Quattro Pro has automatically defined the y-axis labels, even though you haven't specified any. Press any key to return to the /Graph menu.

4. Define the x-axis labels. Choose Series from the /Graph menu, and then X-Axis Series. Specify the block **A5..A15** containing the values 0 through 10. Press Enter, and then select Quit (or press Esc) to return to the /Graph menu.

Figure 8.6

A line graph with 1st and 2nd Series defined

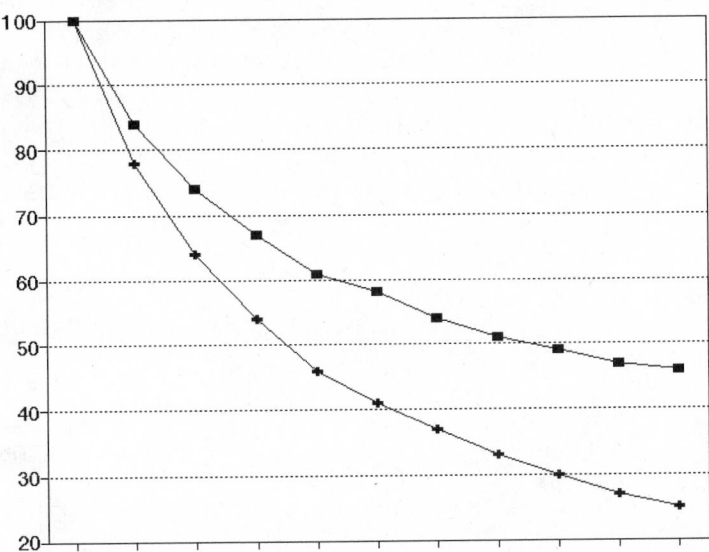

At this point, your graph is beginning to take shape, but it needs text to further identify the graphed data.

5. Next add the graph titles. Choose Text from the /Graph menu. Then select 1st Line, enter **\A1** (a backslash followed by the cell address), and press Enter. Note that you can specify a graph label as a cell address. The label "Value of Used Vehicles" in cell A1 then appears as the first title line in the graph. Now choose 2nd Line, and type **Cars Versus Trucks**. Press Enter, and Quattro Pro returns to the Text menu.

6. Add the x-axis and y-axis titles. Select X-Title from the Text menu. Enter **\A3**, and press Enter. Next, select Y-Title, type **\B3**, and press Enter. Quattro Pro returns to the Text menu.

7. Create a legend. Choose Legends from the Text menu, and then select 1st Series to define the legend for the first column of the data. Type **\B4**, and press Enter. When the Legends menu reappears, select 2nd Series, type **\C4**, and press Enter. Finally, position the legend at the right side of the graph by selecting Position from the Legends menu, then Right. (Otherwise, Quattro Pro places the legend in the default position below the graph.) Select Quit twice to return to the /Graph menu.

8. Press F10 (Graph) to view the graph again. As you can see in Figure 8.7, your line graph now includes text that defines the graphed data. Press

any key to return to the /Graph menu, and then Quit to return to the spreadsheet.

The line graph you have created now displays the data effectively, with identifying labels that define the information for a reader. You can stop at this point, or you can add some custom features to make this graph even more effective, as described in the next section. (If you decide not to continue and customize this graph, be sure to save it, as discussed in "Saving a Graph" below.)

Figure 8.7
The line graph after defining Series and Text settings

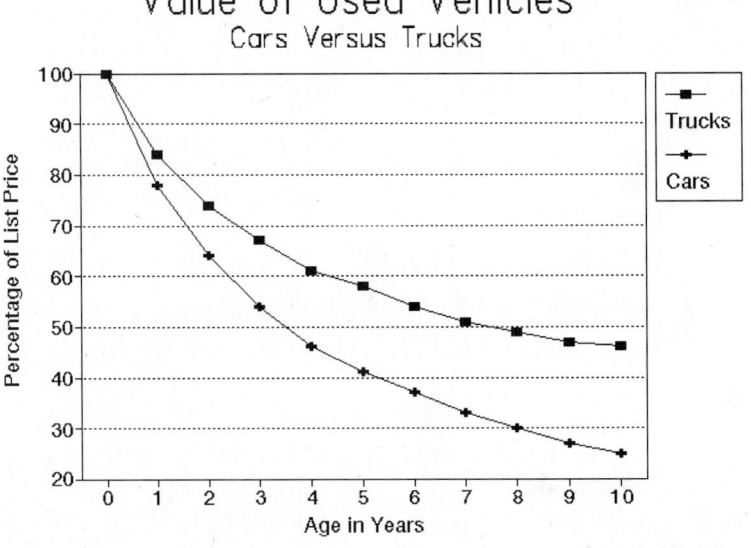

Viewing a Graph

Once you have used the /Graph, Series command to specify just one data series, you can view a graph using any of the following methods:

■ Select /Graph, View.

■ Press F10 (Graph) from anywhere within the /Graph menu, or even when you are in the spreadsheet.

■ Use Quattro Pro's Screen Preview feature (see "Printing a Graph" at the end of this chapter).

By far the most versatile of these methods is the Graph key (F10). Since Quattro Pro remembers the latest /Graph settings, you can be in any /Graph menu or even in the spreadsheet when you press F10. Thus you can change spreadsheet data, or change a /Graph setting, and immediately see its effect on a graph.

Saving a Graph

When you save a spreadsheet, Quattro Pro automatically saves the latest graph. However, you will often use the same spreadsheet information to create more than one graph. In this case, you must name each graph in order to save all of them within the same spreadsheet file. Quattro Pro includes an option that automatically saves changes to a named graph. For more information, see "Naming Graphs" later in this chapter.

Specifying Data to Be Graphed

The heart of any graph is the data it displays. In Quattro Pro, you use the /Graph, Series command to specify your data series—the spreadsheet information you want graphed. When you select this command, Quattro Pro displays the menu shown in Figure 8.8.

Figure 8.8

The /Graph, Series menu

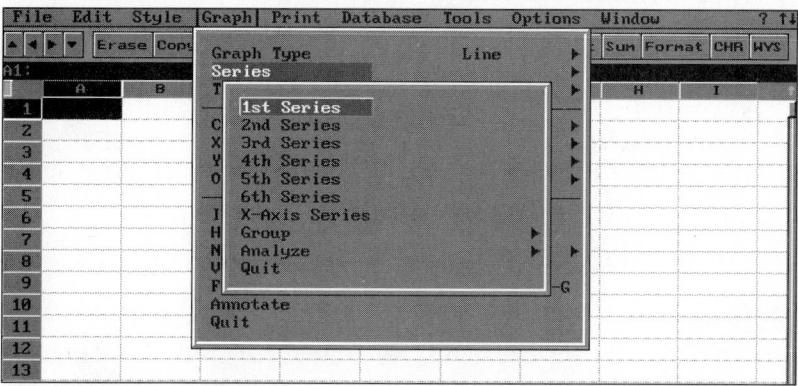

You can plot up to six different series on one graph. (Some graph types limit the number of series you can specify; these limitations are discussed in "Choosing a Graph Type" in the next section.) Quattro Pro automatically assigns each series a unique fill pattern, color, or marker symbol, depending on the graph type. You will see how to change these default characteristics in "Customizing a Graph" later in the chapter.

The way Quattro Pro graphs data is determined by the way information is categorized in *series blocks*, and by the type of graph you select. For instance, in Step 3 of the first exercise in this chapter, Quattro Pro graphed two lines in the line graph because you specified the data in two different series blocks. However, if you specify all the data in one series block, Quattro Pro will graph one line representing both the Cars and Trucks data points. Thus, the way you specify data series is a major factor in creating an effective graph. The appropriate use of series blocks is discussed for each graph type in "Choosing a Graph Type."

Keep in mind the following when you specify /Graph, Series blocks:

- The easiest way to enter information for a particular series block is to place it in one column or one row of the spreadsheet. Quattro Pro will, however, accept a multicolumn, multirow block for the 1st through 6th series.

- Quattro Pro evaluates all entries in a series block as *values*. A label is evaluated as the value 0 and is graphed accordingly. Quattro Pro evaluates a blank cell as missing data, and does not include the data point in the graph.

- *To specify a new series block setting*, just use the /Graph, Series command again. Since Quattro Pro remembers the last series block setting you specified, select /Graph, Series, choose the series you want to redefine, and press Esc to clear the old setting. Then specify the new block and press Enter.

- *To remove a selected series from a graph* without affecting other series, use the /Graph, Customize Series command and choose the Reset option. For example, suppose you have previously specified five series blocks, and you want to remove the 4th Series setting. Select Reset, 4th Series, and Quattro Pro eliminates the 4th Series setting from both the Reset and Series menus.

- You can *temporarily suppress a series* from being graphed, without deleting its series setting. For instance, to suppress the 2nd Series block for a line graph in Quattro Pro 4.0, use /Graph, Customize Series, turn on the Series 2 option, and choose Neither from the Format options. (In Quattro Pro 3.0, use /Graph, Customize Series, Markers & Lines, Formats, 2nd Series, Neither.) When you press F10 (Graph), Quattro Pro will graph all other defined series blocks except for the 2nd Series.

■ You can use Quattro Pro's *file linking* capability to access series blocks from different files. One method is to create linking references in cells of the active spreadsheet, and then include those cells in your /Graph, Series settings. You can also specify series settings as information from another open file, and even from an unopened file on disk. When you use this method, specify a series block using the appropriate directory, file name, and block address. (For more information about linking files, see Chapter 2.)

Grouping Data Series

Tip. To assign data series and x-axis labels in one block, use the Fast Graph command as discussed later in this chapter.

You can use the /Graph, Series, Group command to quickly define multiple data series blocks. When you use this command, all spreadsheet information you want to graph must be entered in adjacent columns or rows, one series to a column or row. You cannot, however, use /Graph, Series, Group for an XY graph.

For instance, in Figure 8.4, the data is entered in adjacent columns. To specify all these series at once, you can use /Graph, Series, Group, Columns. You'll be prompted to "Enter block for column series:"; specify the block **B5..C15** and press Enter. Quattro Pro returns to the Series menu, in which it automatically assigns the leftmost column in the block, B5..B15, as the 1st Series block, and the next column, C5..C15, as the 2nd Series block. If you now press F10, Quattro Pro displays the same graph that you originally created by specifying separate data series blocks (Figure 8.7).

Specifying X-Axis Labels

As you know, most Quattro Pro graphs include an x-axis along the bottom. In many cases, you will want to include *x-axis labels* to better describe the data in the graph. For instance, the 3-D bar graph in Figure 8.2 uses the x-axis labels 1988, 1989, and 1990 to differentiate its information. The 2-D bar graph in Figure 8.3 includes x-axis labels describing the type of car model being compared, such as Geo Metro and Honda Civic.

In Quattro Pro, you use the /Graph, Series, X-Axis Series command to specify x-axis labels. Beginning with the first label in the block you specify, Quattro Pro then creates x-axis labels from left to right in the graph. Even if the X-Axis Series block contains values, they are evaluated as labels along the x-axis (*except* in XY graphs, as discussed in a later section).

When Quattro Pro cannot fit all of the labels along the x-axis, the rightmost labels in the block are not displayed. You can overcome this problem, and the related problem of cramped labels, in three ways: by carefully selecting the type of graph you use, by adjusting Quattro Pro's placement of tickmarks on the x-axis, or by using a smaller font. You'll see how to use these customization techniques in "Customizing a Graph" later in this chapter.

Choosing a Graph Type

Note. The Graph Type, Text selection is used with Quattro Pro's Annotator discussed in Chapter 9.

By default, Quattro Pro creates a stacked bar graph. However, you can use /Graph, Graph Type to choose from 12 different graph selections: Line, Bar, XY, Stacked Bar, Pie, Area, Rotated Bar, Column, High-Low, Text (see note), Bubble, and 3-D Graphs. (Bubble graphs are new to Quattro Pro 4.0.)

Many of these graph types are similar. For instance, a pie chart and column graph are almost identical. Likewise, stacked bar and rotated bar graphs are both variations of a bar graph. Line, XY, Area, and High-Low graphs are all closely related. Quattro Pro also offers four types of 3-D graphs—Bar, Ribbon, Step, and Area.

You can also combine graph types in a single graph. For instance, you might create a graph that portrays one series of data as a bar graph and another series as a line graph. (See "Mixed Graphs" later in this chapter.)

If your monitor can display graphics (WYSIWYG mode), you will find the Graph Type menu (Figure 8.9) to be of significant help in selecting a graph type. This menu gives you a visual sample of each type of graph.

Once you have created a graph, you may want to experiment a little to see which graph type best displays the information. You can switch to a different type at any time by simply making another Graph Type selection. Press F10 (Graph), and Quattro Pro displays your data using the new graph type. (In some instances, you may first need to respecify some /Graph settings.)

2-D Graphs with a Three-Dimensional Effect

Unless you specify otherwise, Quattro Pro displays all 2-D bar graphs, pie charts, and column charts with a three-dimensional effect. However, sometimes this 3-D effect can get in the way of an effective graph. In Quattro Pro 4.0, set /Graph, Overall, Add Depth to No to remove the three-dimensional effect, as has been done for many of the graphs in this section. (In Quattro Pro 3.0, use /Graph, Overall, Three-D, No.) To reinstate the 3-D effect, change this setting to Yes.

Do not confuse 2-D graphs, which display a three-dimensional effect, with Quattro Pro's 3-D graphs, discussed later in this chapter.

Figure 8.9

The Graph Type and 3-D Graphs menus displayed in WYSIWYG mode. (In Quattro Pro 4.0, the Bubble sample is hidden from view when you select 3-D graphs.)

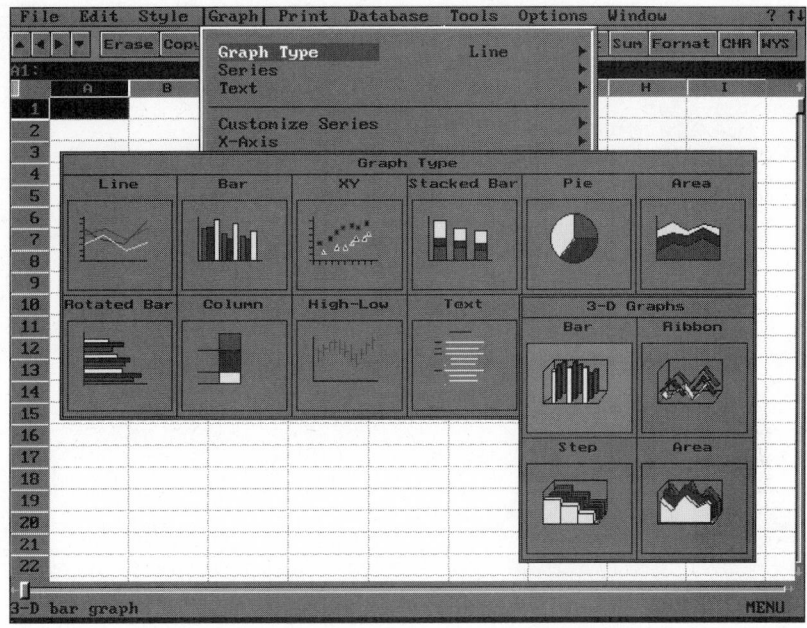

Pie Chart

Tip. To display information as sections of a column, use a column graph.

A *pie chart* displays each value as a portion of a pie, or circle. The best time to use a pie chart is when you want to illustrate the percentage each value contributes to the total. For example, you might use a pie chart to show the market share percentage each competitor currently holds in an industry, or to illustrate the portion of your take-home pay each of your expenses represents.

Suppose you want to graph your total 1992 expenditures, with each expense shown as a percentage. You can use the information in Figure 8.10 and the /Graph settings in Table 8.1 to create the pie chart in Figure 8.11. When you press F10 (Graph), Quattro Pro automatically calculates the total value of the pie, and then places the appropriate percentage next to each slice

As you can see, the pie chart in Figure 8.11 represents each expense as a percentage of the total expenditures, clearly portraying the predominance of rent (37.5%) and entertainment (22.5%) expenses, as well as the relatively small insurance expense (5.6%). Quattro Pro automatically includes the shading patterns shown in Figure 8.11 to differentiate each slice of the pie.

Figure 8.10

Data graphed in pie chart (Figure 8.11) and column graph (Figure 8.12)

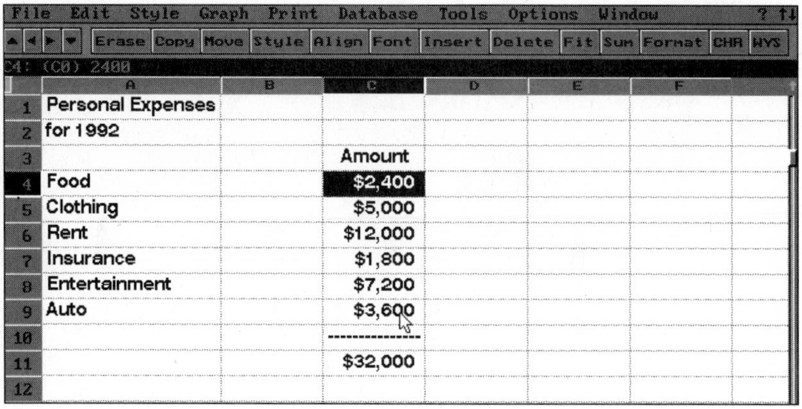

File	Edit	Style	Graph	Print	Database	Tools	Options	Window	? ↑↓

| ▲ | ◄ | ► | ▼ | Erase | Copy | Move | Style | Align | Font | Insert | Delete | Fit | Sum | Format | CHR | WYS |

C4: (C0) 2400

	A	B	C	D	E	F
1	Personal Expenses					
2	for 1992					
3			Amount			
4	Food		$2,400			
5	Clothing		$5,000			
6	Rent		$12,000			
7	Insurance		$1,800			
8	Entertainment		$7,200			
9	Auto		$3,600			
10			-------------			
11			$32,000			
12						

Figure 8.11

A pie chart of the data from Figure 8.12

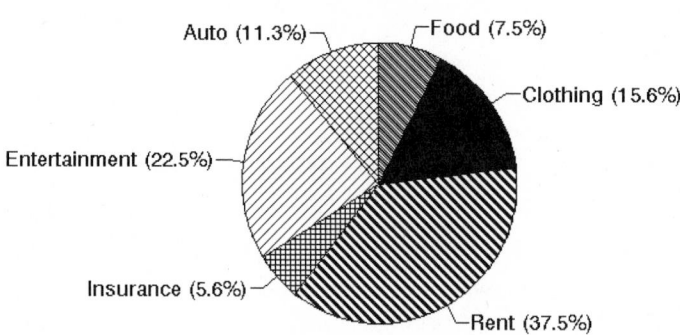

Personal Expenses
for 1992

When you create a pie chart, you must specify the graphed values in one series block (the 1st Series). Otherwise, Quattro Pro can't create the pie chart and displays the error message "Series undefined." You must enter your values in one column, row, or a continuous block. Remember, too, that Quattro Pro cannot graph negative numbers in a pie chart—instead, it graphs the absolute (positive) value of that negative number.

Table 8.1	/Graph Settings Used with Figure 8.10 to Create Graphs in Figures 8.11 and 8.12	
/Graph Commands	**Settings**	
Graph Type	Pie or Column	
Series		
1st Series	C4..C9	
X-Axis Series	A4..A9	
Text		
1st Line	\A1	
2nd Line	\A2	
Overall, Add Depth (or Three-D)	No	

Quattro Pro creates a pie chart beginning at the 12 o'clock position. It then arranges successive slices clockwise. In Figure 8.11, the first value in the 1st Series block, $2,400 in cell C4, is the first pie slice, Food. Then the second value, $5,000 in cell C5, is the Clothing slice, and so on. To change the graphed order of the slices, you must change the order of the data in the spreadsheet.

An effective pie chart displays each slice and label clearly. Here are some other guidelines to remember when you are organizing the data for your pie charts.

- Place a relatively small value between larger values—do not group small values together.

- Do not plot too many values in one pie; instead, combine several smaller values together into a "group" value if possible.

- Specify a relatively large value as the first or last entry in the series block.

Tip. To "hide" the labels in a pie chart without deleting the X-Axis Series block, select /Graph, Customize Series, Label Format, None. (In Quattro Pro 3.0, use /Graph, Customize Series, Pies, Label Format, None.)

If the data labels in your graph are not clearly displayed, try reordering the data in the series block. You can also reduce the font point size used for the labels (see "Customizing a Graph" later in this chapter). Sometimes using the /Graph, Overall, Add Depth (or Three-D), No setting—to eliminate the 3-D effect—also helps.

Should you wish to display the value of each slice, rather than the percentage, you can use /Graph, Customize Series to do this. You can also explode, color, or change the shading of the slices. See "Customizing Pie and Column Charts" later in this chapter for more details.

Column Graph

A *column graph* depicts values as parts of a whole by stacking the components on top of one another in a vertical column. In all other respects, a column graph and a pie chart are the same. Choosing between the two is mostly a matter of personal style. However, a column chart is better able to accommodate longer data labels than a pie chart.

To graph the expenses from Figure 8.10 as a column graph, use the /Graph settings shown in Table 8.1. Quattro Pro will create the column chart shown in Figure 8.12. Quattro Pro automatically includes the percentage for each segment, as well as the differentiating shading patterns shown in the figure.

Figure 8.12
A column graph of
the data in Figure
8.10

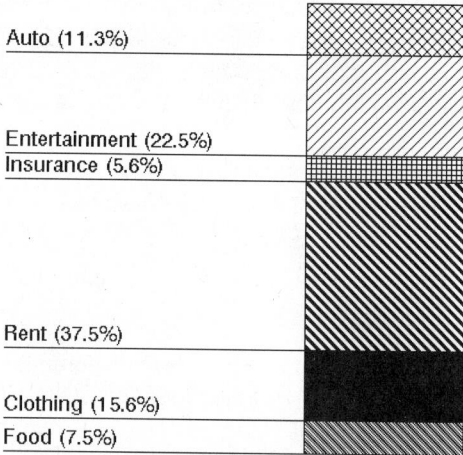

As in a pie chart, only the 1st Series block in a column graph is graphed. So when you enter your data in the spreadsheet, you should place it in one column, row, or continuous block. Furthermore, Quattro Pro always creates a column graph using the absolute (positive) values in the 1st Series block.

As you can see in Figure 8.12, Quattro Pro creates a column graph beginning at the *bottom* segment. In the current example, the first value in the 1st Series block, $2,400 in cell C4, is graphed as the bottommost expense, Food.

Tip. Use the
Annotator
discussed in
Chapter 9 to call
attention to a
particular segment
of a column graph.

The program then works its way *down* the series block but *up* the graphed column. For this reason, the series block seems to be plotted upside down. To change the graphed order of these values, you must change the order of the data in the spreadsheet.

Like a pie chart, a column graph may also suffer from the problem of cramped data labels. If you graph many values, or if some values are significantly smaller than others, the labels identifying the individual segments get clumped together. For instance, the Insurance (5.6%) label in Figure 8.12 appears "squeezed in," because insurance expense is significantly smaller than the other expenses. To avoid this, make sure you place a relatively small value between larger values, to allow sufficient room for each label. Additionally, you can try a smaller font for the data labels (see "Customizing a Graph"). Using the /Graph, Overall, Add Depth (or Three-D in version 3.0), No setting to eliminate the three-dimensional effect also helps.

As with pie charts, when you create a column chart, you can use /Graph, Customize Series, Pies to display the value for each segment rather than a percentage, and to color or change the shading of each segment (see "Customizing Pie and Column Charts" later in this chapter).

Bar

A *bar graph* displays each positive data point in a series as an individual vertical bar rising from the x-axis. Negative values are displayed as vertical bars below the x-axis. The height of each bar represents that value plotted against the y-axis.

Though typically used to compare values at a specific point in time, you can also use a bar graph to compare values at different points in time. For instance, you can create a bar graph that effectively contrasts the sales generated by three different salespeople in two different years.

Tip. The width of each bar depends on the number of values in the graph. The more values graphed, the smaller the width of each bar. However, you can use /Graph, Customize Series, Bar width to change the bar width. See "Customizing the Series Display" later.

Suppose your city is experiencing a drought. Water rationing is about to be instituted. You want to portray, in graphic form, the typical water usage for various two-person households over the four low-rainfall months (Figure 8.13). Using the /Graph settings in Table 8.2, you can create the bar graph in Figure 8.14.

In Figure 8.14, Quattro Pro clusters three bars around the May tick-mark—the first bar is the first value in the 1st Series block (7), followed by a second bar representing the first value in the 2nd Series block (also 7), and a third bar for the first value in the 3rd Series block (18). It then repeats this process for all values, or *data points*, in the assigned Series blocks. The height of each bar represents the y-value. The result is a bar graph that effectively displays the widely varying water consumption for these different households.

Figure 8.13

Water consumption
of three households

| File | Edit | Style | Graph | Print | Database | Tools | Options | Window | ? ↑↓ |

| ▲ ◀ ▶ ▼ | Erase | Copy | Move | Style | Align | Font | Insert | Delete | Fit | Sum | Format | CHR | WYS |

B11: [W12] @SUM(B6..B10)

	A	B	C	D	E	F	G
1	Water Usage						
2	2-Person Households						
3							
4	Months	Desert Lawn	Grass Lawn	Pool			
5	========	========	========	========			
6	May	7	7	18	Cubic Feet		
7	June	8	9	13			
8	July	9	13	13			
9	August	9	16	17			
10		--------	--------	--------			
11	Total	33	45	61			
12							

Figure 8.14

A bar graph of the
data from Figure
8.13

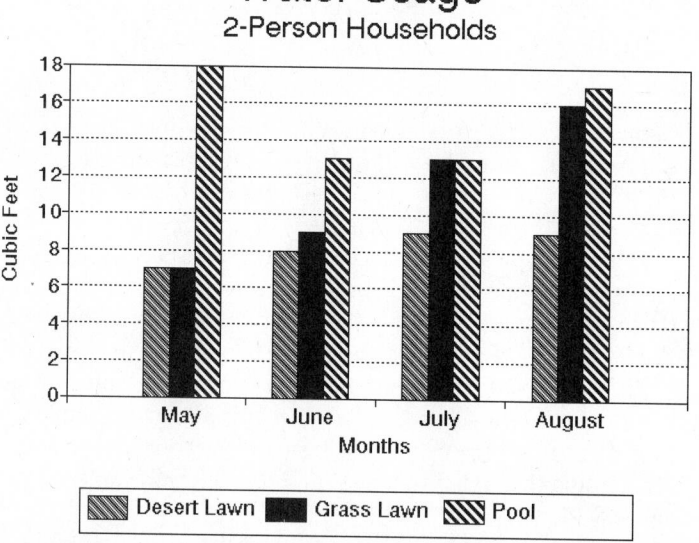

In a bar graph, Quattro Pro evaluates a blank cell, a cell containing 0, and a cell containing a label all in different ways. Imagine, for instance, that the May value in cell C6 (the Grass Lawn household) is 0. Quattro Pro will graph this 0 value by leaving a blank space between the 1st Series and 3rd Series bars. If cell C6 contains a label or is blank, however, Quattro Pro will ignore this cell and plot the 1st Series and 3rd Series bars adjacent to each other.

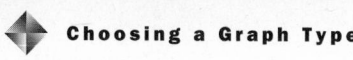

Table 8.2 **/Graph Settings Used with Figure 8.13 to Create Graphs in Figures 8.14 and 8.15**

/Graph Commands	Settings
Graph Type	Bar or Stacked Bar
Series	
1st Series	B6..B9
2nd Series	C6..C9
3rd Series	D6..D9
X-Axis Series	A6..A9
Text	
1st Line	\A1
2nd Line	\A2
X-Title	\A4
Y-Title	\E6
Text, Legends	
1st Series	\B4
2nd Series	\C4
3rd Series	\D4
Overall, Add Depth (or Three-D)	No

Quattro Pro uses the default fill patterns shown in Figure 8.14 to differentiate each data series in a bar graph, but does not automatically include a legend to explain what each fill pattern represents. The /Graph settings to create this legend are included in Table 8.2.

As you become familiar with the program's graphing capabilities, you will want to customize your bar graphs. You can add data labels that display the value of each bar, for instance, or you can change the default fill patterns. Be sure to read "Customizing a Graph" later in this chapter.

Stacked Bar

A *stacked bar* graph is Quattro Pro's default graph type. Like a bar graph, a stacked bar graph uses bars to indicate values, except that values from each series are stacked in every bar. The first stacked bar is composed of all the first values from each Series block, the second stacked bar represents the second values from each Series block, and so forth. Thus each bar emphasizes the contribution each part makes to the total; a bar graph also contrasts the total values represented by each bar.

For instance, if you use the /Graph settings in Table 8.2, Quattro Pro uses the information from Figure 8.13 to create the stacked bar graph in Figure 8.15. In this example, the first data point in the 1st Series (Desert Lawn) block, 7, is graphed first at the bottom of the May bar. Then the first value in the 2nd Series block, also 7, is stacked on top of this segment. Finally, the first value in the 3rd Series block, 18, is added on top. The combined height of this stacked bar indicates the sum of the total of these values, or 32. Quattro Pro then repeats this process for all data points in the assigned series blocks.

Figure 8.15
A stacked bar graph of information from Figure 8.13

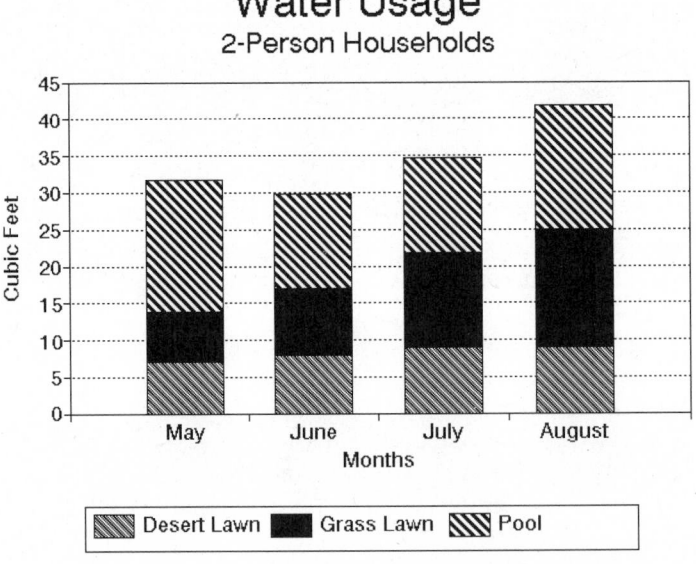

A stacked bar graph does not emphasize the difference between each data point. Rather, it emphasizes the difference between the combined totals—for example, the difference between May's total water consumption and June's total water consumption.

In Figure 8.15, you see the same default fill patterns that were shown in Figure 8.14. As usual, you can change these fill patterns and add other enhancements to a stacked bar graph. For example, by specifying the /Graph, Text, Legends settings in Table 8.2, you can add a legend to the graph, explaining what each fill pattern represents. You can also use the /Graph command to add data labels that display the total value of each bar. See "Customizing a Graph" in this chapter.

Rotated Bar

A *rotated bar graph* is a hybrid graph that is similar to a regular bar graph, except for the following:

■ It reverses the positions of the x- and y-axes. Each data point is represented by a bar, but the bars extend horizontally from the y-axis—positive values to the right, and negative values to the left.

■ The first data point in a series block is plotted at the bottom of a rotated bar graph; the last data point is plotted at the top.

Tip. Use the /Style, Alignment command to create consistent y-axis labels. For instance, /Style, Alignment, Right is used for the block A5..A17 so that the y-axis labels are all right-aligned in the rotated bar graph in Figure 8.17.

Like a bar graph, you can use a rotated bar graph to compare and contrast values—the choice between the two is a matter of presentation style. The rotated bar graph does allow for longer x-axis labels. Consider the data in Figure 8.16—the energy requirements of different means of transportation. Because the labels in column A are too long to fit along the x-axis at the bottom of a bar graph, a rotated bar graph is a better choice. The /Graph settings in Table 8.3 result in the rotated bar graph in Figure 8.17.

When you create a rotated bar graph, specifying axis settings can get a little confusing, since Quattro Pro actually *rotates* the x- and y-axes. Notice in Table 8.3 that the x-axis title (KCAL/KM per Person) is specified using Text Y-Title. Similarly, custom settings for the x-axis are specified using the /Graph, Y-Axis command. (These custom settings overcome the cramped x-axis labels that would occur if you used the /Graph default settings.) Likewise, you use the Series, X-Axis Series block, A5..A17, to create the y-axis labels.

As mentioned, Quattro Pro does not graph the data in a rotated bar graph like that of a bar graph. As you can see in Figure 8.17, the first data point from the 1st Series block is plotted at the bottom of the graph—820 in cell B5. The final 1st Series value is plotted at the top of the graph—8.4 in cell B17. Be sure to enter your spreadsheet data to reflect this graphing sequence.

Figure 8.16

Data used for the
rotated bar graph
in Figure 8.17

	File	Edit	Style	Graph	Print	Database	Tools	Options	Window		? ↑↓

▲ ◄ ► ▼	Erase	Copy	Move	Style	Align	Font	Insert	Delete	Fit	Sum	Format	CHR	WYS

B5: 820

	A	B	C	D	E
1	Energy Cost of Movement				
2	by Various Means				
3					
4		KCAL/KM per Person			
5	Auto and 1 rider @ 30 mph	820			
6	Auto and 1 rider @ 60 mph	539			
7	Swimmer @ 1.5 mph	269.6			
8	Horse and 1 rider @ 10 mph	245.4			
9	Auto and 5 riders @ 30 mph	183			
10	Commuter Train @ 30 mph	112			
11	Moped and 1 rider @ 20 mph	88.3			
12	Runner @ 10 mph	68.3			
13	Walker @ 4 mph	55.3			
14	Bicyclist @ 15 mph	24.4			
15	Auto and 5 riders @ 60 mph	20.5			
16	Bicyclist @ 10 mph	15.6			
17	Bicyclist @ 4 mph	8.4			
18					

Figure 8.17

A rotated bar graph
of the data from
Figure 8.16

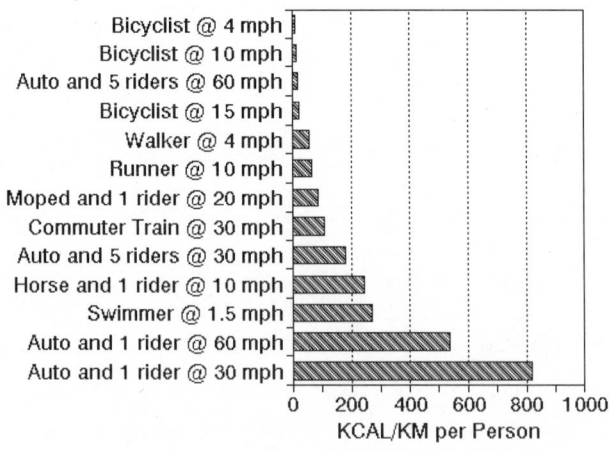

Table 8.3 **/Graph Settings Used with Figure 8.16 to Create Rotated Bar Graph in Figure 8.17**

/Graph Commands	Settings
Graph Type	Rotated Bar
Series	
1st Series	B5..B17
X-Axis Series	A5..A17
Text	
1st Line	\A1
2nd Line	\A2
Y-Title	\B4
Y-Axis	
Scale	Manual
High	1000
Increment	100
No. of Minor Ticks	1
Overall, Add Depth (or Three-D)	No

In many cases you will want to use the /Database, Sort command when you create a rotated bar graph, to improve its readability. For instance, imagine you initially enter the Figure 8.16 spreadsheet data in the block A5..B17 in any order. Then you can use /Database, Sort, specifying the Sort block A5..B17, and the 1st Key block B5..B17. To organize the data as it is shown in Figure 8.16, with largest values on the bottom and smallest values at the top, choose a descending sort order. Because the largest value is now the first data point in this block, it is plotted at the bottom of the rotated bar graph in Figure 8.17. Conversely, to graph the smallest values at the bottom of the graph, you would use an ascending sort order. (/Database, Sort is explained in Chapter 10.)

Like other types of bar graphs, you can add many enhancements to your rotated bar graphs. The rotated bar graph in Figure 8.17, for example, includes a custom y-axis. See "Customizing a Graph" in this chapter.

Line

A *line graph* is commonly used to plot and compare data over time. When you create a line graph, Quattro Pro plots each value in a series block, and then connects these points with a line. Each series block is graphed as a separate line, and each data point along the line is represented by a marker. This graph type emphasizes the patterns in data, and is useful when you are trying to spot trends.

Suppose you want to graph your monthly electric and gas expenses (Figure 8.18). To graph these expenses separately, as well as the combined expense, you need to create a line graph that contains three different lines. The /Graph settings in Table 8.4 create the line graph shown in Figure 8.19.

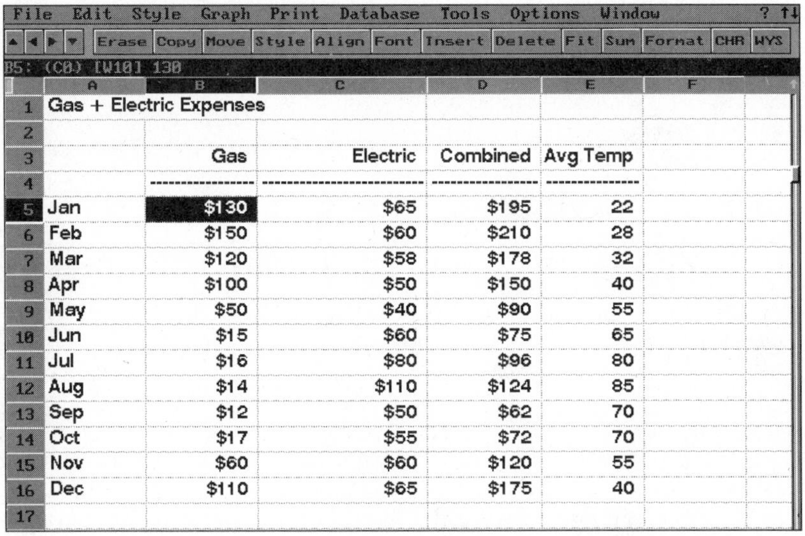

	A	B	C	D	E	F
1	Gas + Electric Expenses					
2						
3		Gas	Electric	Combined	Avg Temp	
4		----------	----------	----------	----------	
5	Jan	$130	$65	$195	22	
6	Feb	$150	$60	$210	28	
7	Mar	$120	$58	$178	32	
8	Apr	$100	$50	$150	40	
9	May	$50	$40	$90	55	
10	Jun	$15	$60	$75	65	
11	Jul	$16	$80	$96	80	
12	Aug	$14	$110	$124	85	
13	Sep	$12	$50	$62	70	
14	Oct	$17	$55	$72	70	
15	Nov	$60	$60	$120	55	
16	Dec	$110	$65	$175	40	
17						

Figure 8.18 Data used in graphs in Figures 8.19, 8.20, 8.21, and 8.22

Here Quattro Pro graphs each series block as a separate line. By default, Quattro Pro uses the same line style, but different marker styles, for all data series. In Figure 8.19, however, we have used custom Line Styles settings to more clearly differentiate each expense. Additionally, the /Graph, Text, Legends command has been used to add a legend explaining what each line represents. See "Customizing a Graph" later in this chapter for additional features you can add to a line graph.

Figure 8.19

A line graph of the data from Figure 8.18, using three series blocks

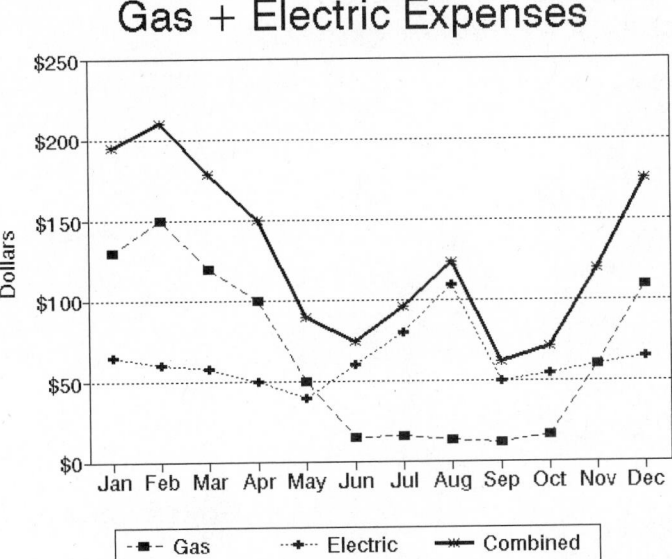

Area

An *area graph*, like a line graph, uses lines to represent values, but the data series are stacked on top of one another, similar to a stacked bar graph. An area graph is a good method of showing the extent to which each component contributes to the whole over time. Additionally, an area graph is superior to a stacked bar graph when you want to emphasize a connection between time periods.

Let's look again at the data in Figure 8.18. An area graph is a good way to display the total combined utility expense as a function of both gas and electric expenses, as shown in Figure 8.20. The /Graph settings in Table 8.4 were used to create this area graph.

Quattro Pro first plots the 1st Series block, gas expense in cells B5..B16, along the bottom of this area graph. It then stacks the area for the 2nd Series block, electric expense in cells C5..C16, on top of the 1st Series area. At each x-axis tickmark, the combined areas represent the sum of the corresponding values for each series. Quattro Pro automatically fills in the area beneath each line using a different fill pattern. Thus, the area filled with a particular pattern represents the contribution of a particular data series to the total. The /Graph, Text, Legends command is used to create a legend defining these fill patterns.

Tip. In most instances, an area graph does not effectively portray negative numbers.

Table 8.4 **/Graph Settings Used with Figure 8.18 to Create Line Graph in Figure 8.19 and Area Graph in Figure 8.20**

/Graph Commands	Settings	Settings
Graph Type	Line	Area
Series		
1st Series	B5..B16	B5..B16
2nd Series	C5..C16	C5..C16
3rd Series	D5..D16	
X-Axis Series	A5..A16	A5..A16
Text		
1st Line	\A1	\A1
Y-Title	Dollars	Dollars
Text, Legends		
1st Series	\B3	\B3
2nd Series	\C3	\C3
3rd Series	\D3	
Y-Axis		
Format of Ticks	Currency 0	Currency 0
Customize Series, Line Style (Customize Series, Markers & Lines, Line Styles in version 3.0)		
1st Series	Center-line	
2nd Series	Dotted	
3rd Series	Heavy Solid	

To see how to change default fill patterns and the legend placement, or add other enhancements to an area graph, read "Customizing a Graph" in this chapter.

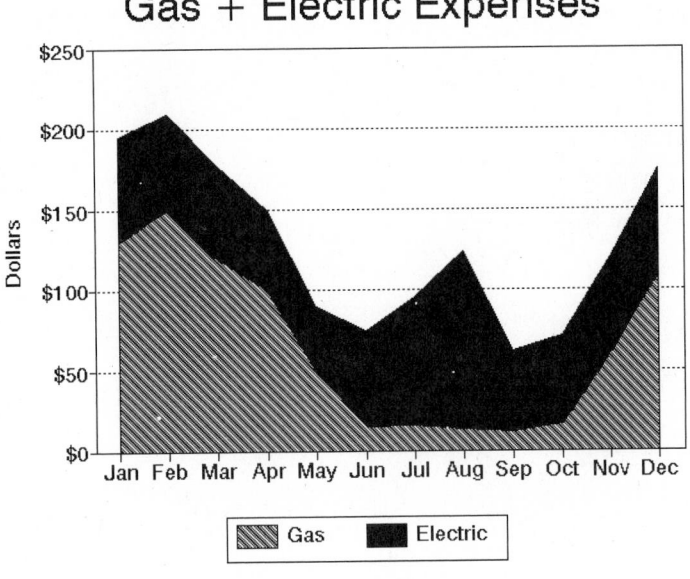

Figure 8.20
An area graph of the data from Figure 8.18, using two series blocks

XY

An *XY graph* looks like a line graph, but is actually quite different. An XY graph plots both x- and y-values for each data point. You can use this graph type to plot sales versus marketing expenses, for example, or interest rates over time.

When you specify an XY graph, Quattro Pro assumes that the /Graph, Series, X-Axis Series block contains x-values. It evaluates all the other series you specify, such as the 1st Series block, as containing corresponding y-values.

If you specify more than one series in an XY graph, such as 1st Series, 2nd Series blocks, the same x-values are used for both of these series. Quattro Pro then graphs two lines; one line represents the 1st Series y-values and the X-Axis Series x-values, and a second line represents the 2nd Series y-values and the same X-Axis Series x-values.

Let's return to the information in Figure 8.18. Suppose you want to plot the combined utility expense versus average monthly temperature. With a new set of /Graph settings (Table 8.5), you can create the XY graph shown in Figure 8.21. (We'll improve on its appearance later.)

Notice in the /Graph settings in Table 8.5 that the X-Axis Series block, E5..E16, represents the average temperature corresponding to each value in the 1st Series block. Therefore, in Figure 8.21, Quattro Pro plots the first value as the x-value 22 (cell E5), and the y-value 195 (cell D5). The Text, X-Title setting, \E3, is used to define the x-values as "Avg Temp."

Note. Many of Quattro Pro's shortcut methods do not work when you create an XY graph. You can only use /Graph, Series, Group to assign the y-value data series, and you must specify the X-Axis Series separately. Also, you cannot create an XY Fast Graph.

Figure 8.21

An XY graph of the data from Figure 8.18

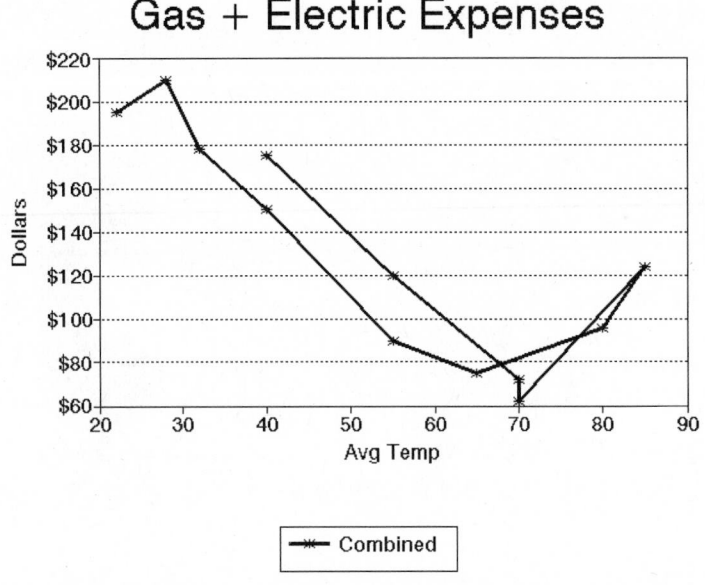

As you can see in Figure 8.21, the plotted line is not straight. This is because Quattro Pro plots the first value using the first data points in the 1st and X-Axis Series blocks, then the second value using the second data points, and so on. Thus the line "backtracks"—after the x-value 85 in cell E12, all x-values still to be plotted are less than this value. Therefore, the line doubles back on itself when these remaining values are plotted.

When backtracking occurs in an XY graph, you can create a straighter line using one of the following techniques.

- Use the /Database, Sort command. For example, use it on the Sort block D5..E16 in Figure 8.18. Specify the 1st Key as the average temperature block E5..E16, and an ascending sort order; specify the 2nd Key as the combined expense block D5..D16, and an ascending sort order. Then when you graph this data, Quattro Pro will graph the data points sequentially by ascending average temperature (x-values).

- Use the /Tools, Advanced Math, Regression command to perform a linear regression on this data. Then graph the calculated regression line. See Chapter 11 for more details.

Table 8.5 **/Graph Settings Used with Figure 8.18 to Create XY Graphs in Figures 8.21 and 8.22**

/Graph Commands	Settings
Graph Type	XY
Series	
1st Series	D5..D16
X-Axis Series	E5..E16
Text	
1st Line	\A1
Y-Title	Dollars
X-Title	\E3
Text, Legends	
1st Series	\D3
Y-Axis	
Format of Ticks	Currency 0
Customize Series, Line Style (Customize Series, Markers & Lines, Line Styles in version 3.0)	
1st Series	Heavy Solid

- In Quattro Pro 4.0, use the new /Graph, Series, Analyze, Linear Fit command to have Quattro Pro automatically perform linear regression and generate a line that best fits the data. See "Analytical Graphing in Quattro Pro 4.0," later.

The first method, using the /Database, Sort command, has been employed to create the XY graph shown in Figure 8.22. This improved graph conveys much more effectively the strong relationship between total utility expense and extreme high or low average monthly temperatures.

Both of the XY graphs in Figures 8.21 and 8.22 use custom settings to better set off and explain the data. A Line Style setting of Heavy Solid is used to create a thick line, and a Legend is included to explain what this line represents. (See "Customizing a Graph" later in this chapter.)

Figure 8.22

An XY graph of Figure 8.18 with X-Series values entered in ascending order

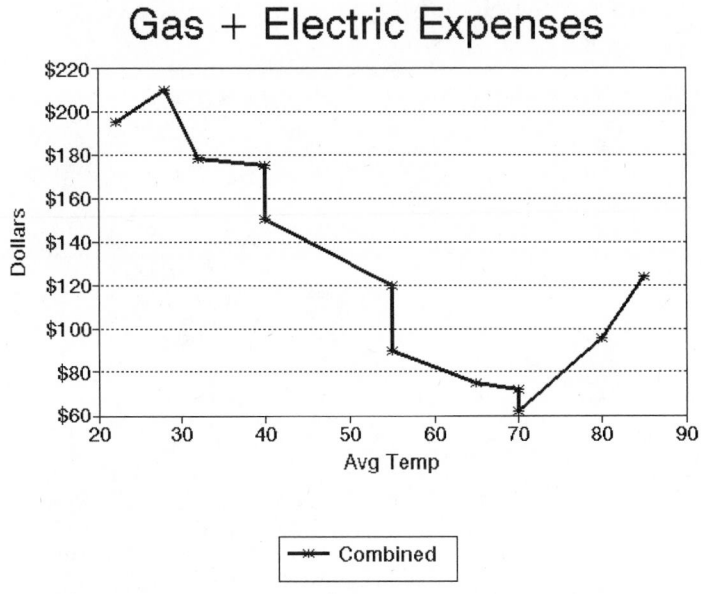

You can use the XY graph type to create a *scatter diagram* of data points. For instance, to change the current example to a scatter diagram, use the /Graph settings from Table 8.5, and then select Customize Series, Formats, 1st Series, Symbols. When you view the graph, Quattro Pro will plot only the data points, without a line connecting them.

Bubble

A *bubble graph*, new to Quattro Pro version 4.0, is a variation of the XY graph. It lets you use bubbles of various sizes to add another level of comparison to an XY graph. For example, Figure 8.23 shows the data from a survey of cold remedies. A typical XY graph of the data might compare the Effectiveness series (B5..B9) versus the Stomach Upset series (C5..C9). By adding a third series, Votes (D5..D9), you can portray the number of survey respondents that voted for a particular cold remedy, as shown in Figure 8.24. Table 8.6 shows the settings used to produce the graph.

As with an XY graph, Quattro Pro uses the X-Axis Series block for the x-values and the 1st Series block for the y-values. What is different about a bubble graph is that the 2nd Series block is used for determining the size of the bubbles.

Notice also that the bubble graph has several custom settings to enhance its appearance. For example, interior data labels have been added to help identify the bubbles, and the fill patterns have been adjusted to make the data labels more readable. See "Customizing a Bubble Graph" later for other ways to adjust the appearance of a bubble graph.

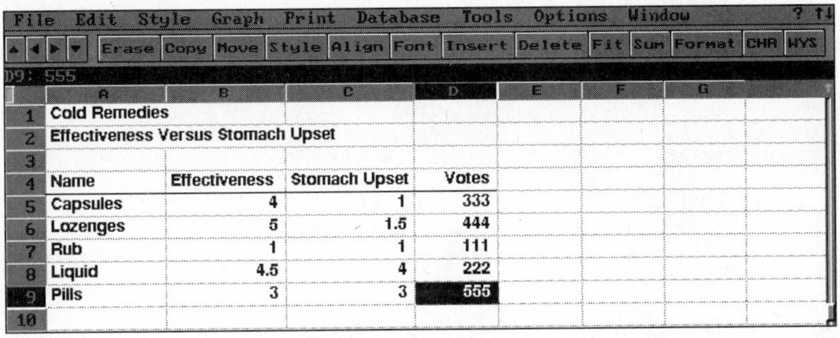

Figure 8.23

Bubble graph data used to create the graph in Figure 8.24

File	Edit	Style	Graph	Print	Database	Tools	Options	Window		? ↑↓

▲	◀	▶	▼	Erase	Copy	Move	Style	Align	Font	Insert	Delete	Fit	Sum	Format	CHR	WYS

D9: 555

	A	B	C	D	E	F	G	
1	Cold Remedies							
2	Effectiveness Versus Stomach Upset							
3								
4	Name	Effectiveness	Stomach Upset	Votes				
5	Capsules	4	1	333				
6	Lozenges	5	1.5	444				
7	Rub	1	1	111				
8	Liquid	4.5	4	222				
9	Pills	3	3	555				
10								

Figure 8.24

The data from Figure 8.23 graphed using the settings in Table 8.6

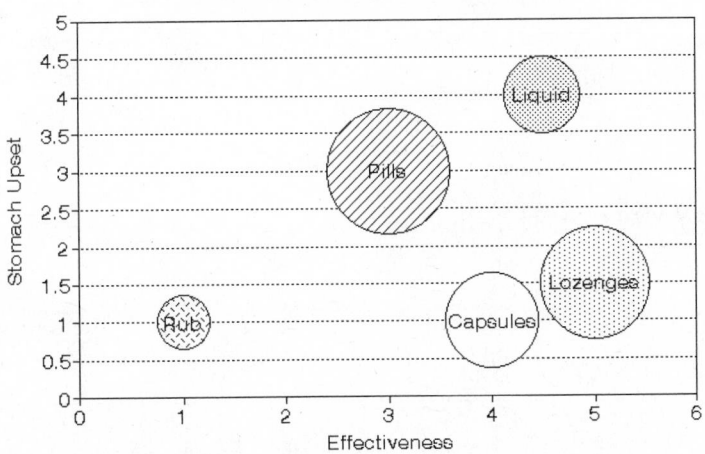

High-Low

A *high-low* graph, also called an *open-close* graph, is primarily used to track daily stock market prices; however, it can also be used in other applications.

For example, you can create a high-low graph that tracks daily high, low, and average temperatures. Or you can use this graph type to plot experimental data showing the high, low, and median values for each trial experiment.

Table 8.6 **/Graph Settings Used with Figure 8.23 to Create Bubble Graph in Figure 8.24**

/Graph Commands	Settings
Graph Type	Bubble
Series	
1st Series	C5..C9
2nd Series	D5..D9
X-Axis Series	B5..B9
Text	
1st Line	\A1
2nd Line	\A2
X-Title	\B4
Y-Title	\C4
Customize Series	
Interior Label Block	A5..A9 (with Center alignment)
Bubble 1, Fill Pattern	Empty
Bubble 2, Fill Pattern	Light Dots
Bubble 3, Fill Pattern	Stitch
Bubble 4, Fill Pattern	Heavy Dots
Bubble 5, Fill Pattern	Lt ///

Suppose you want to track the daily stock price of Takeover Ltd. during the month of January 1992, when takeover rumors are rife. Figure 8.25 shows a portion of the high, low, open, and close stock values during this time period. If you use the /Graph settings in Table 8.7, you can create the high-low graph shown in Figure 8.26.

Figure 8.25

Stock price
information for
Takeover Ltd.

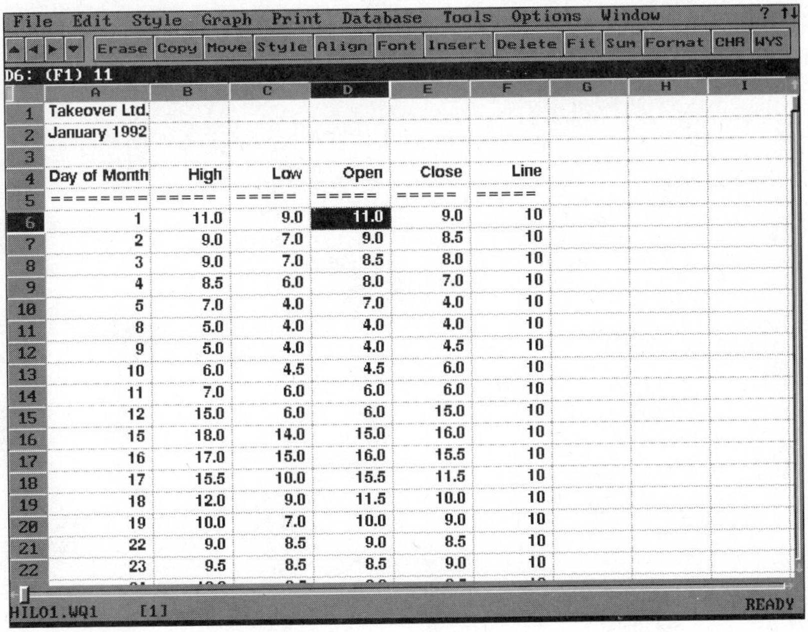

```
 File   Edit   Style   Graph   Print   Database   Tools   Options   Window        ? ↑↓
 ▲ ◄ ► ▼  Erase Copy Move Style Align Font Insert Delete Fit Sum Format CHR WYS
D6: (F1) 11
        A            B        C        D        E        F        G        H        I
 1  Takeover Ltd.
 2  January 1992
 3
 4  Day of Month    High     Low     Open     Close    Line
 5  ========    =====   =====   =====   =====   =====
 6           1     11.0     9.0     11.0     9.0      10
 7           2      9.0     7.0      9.0     8.5      10
 8           3      9.0     7.0      8.5     8.0      10
 9           4      8.5     6.0      8.0     7.0      10
10           5      7.0     4.0      7.0     4.0      10
11           8      5.0     4.0      4.0     4.0      10
12           9      5.0     4.0      4.0     4.5      10
13          10      6.0     4.5      4.5     6.0      10
14          11      7.0     6.0      6.0     6.0      10
15          12     15.0     6.0      6.0    15.0      10
16          15     18.0    14.0     15.0    16.0      10
17          16     17.0    15.0     16.0    15.5      10
18          17     15.5    10.0     15.5    11.5      10
19          18     12.0     9.0     11.5    10.0      10
20          19     10.0     7.0     10.0     9.0      10
21          22      9.0     8.5      9.0     8.5      10
22          23      9.5     8.5      8.5     9.0      10
                    ...     ...      ...     ...      ...
HIL01.WQ1    [1]                                                    READY
```

Figure 8.26

A high-low graph of
the data from
Figure 8.25

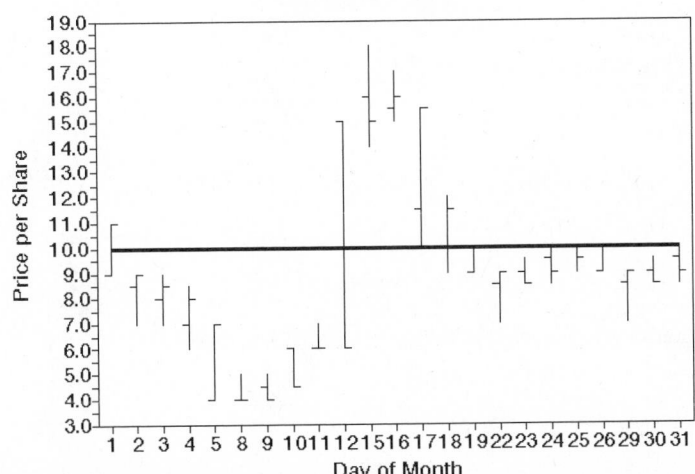

Table 8.7 **/Graph Settings Used with Figure 8.25 to Create High-Low Graph in Figure 8.26**

/Graph Commands	Settings
Graph Type	High-Low
Series	
1st Series	B6..B28
2nd Series	C6..C28
3rd Series	D6..D28
4th Series	E6..E28
5th Series	F6..F28
X-Axis Series	A6..A28
Text	
1st Line	\A1
2nd Line	\A2
Y-Title	Price Per Share
X-Title	\A4
Y-Axis	
Scale	Manual
Low	3
High	19
Increment	.5
Format of Ticks	Fixed 1
No. of Minor Ticks	1
Customize Series, Markers & Lines, Line Styles, 5th Series*	Heavy Solid
Formats, 5th Series*	Lines
Overall, Grid	Clear

* These are the settings for Quattro Pro 3.0. To change the format of the line in Quattro Pro 4.0, you must temporarily switch the graph type to line and then use Customize Series to modify the settings for Series 5.

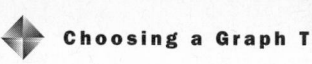
In this high-low graph, Quattro Pro portrays each set of corresponding values in the 1st and 2nd Series blocks as a vertical line. It uses the first data points in the 1st and 2nd Series blocks (11 in cell B6 and 9 in cell C6) to create a vertical line between 9.0 and 11.0.

The 3rd and 4th series blocks are normally used to represent open and close prices, as in our example. Quattro Pro represents values in the 3rd and 4th Series blocks as tickmarks extending from the corresponding vertical line. As you can see in Figure 8.26, the first opening stock price value in the 3rd Series block, 11 in cell D6, is depicted as a right tickmark on the first vertical line; the first closing value stock price in the 4th Series block, 9 in cell E6, is a left tickmark.

Tip. Before you create a high-low graph, make sure you turn off Quattro Pro's default horizontal grid lines by specifying /Graph, Overall, Grid, Clear. Otherwise it can be very difficult to see the tickmarks.

If you include a 5th Series block, Quattro Pro uses the values in this block to plot a line on the high-low graph. Likewise, if you include a 6th Series block, Quattro Pro adds a second line. So, you might use one of these series when you want to emphasize a trend in a high-low graph. For instance, in Figure 8.26, the variability of Takeover Ltd.'s stock price from $10 per share is emphasized by using a 5th Series block, F6..F28, that creates a horizontal line through the value 10.

As usual, you can add custom features to a high-low graph. For instance, the /Graph, Y-Axis settings in Table 8.7 are used to customize the y-axis of this graph. Be sure to read "Customizing a Graph" later in this chapter.

3-D Graphs

Note. 3-D graphs are more complex than regular graphs and therefore take considerable time to print.

Quattro Pro includes four types of *3-D graphs*: Bar, Ribbon, Step, and Area. A 3-D graph plots the positive and negative values in data series on a three-dimensional grid (x-, y-, and z-axes)—one series in front of another along the z-axis. Thus a 3-D graph, correctly designed, can dramatically emphasize the differences in data, as illustrated in the 3-D bar graph in Figure 8.2.

Do not confuse 3-D graphs with regular 2-D graphs that are displayed with the three-dimensional effect turned on (with /Graph, Overall, Three-D, Yes). If you turn this option off, 3-D graphs are still plotted on a three-dimensional grid, but the series appear flat (two-dimensional) rather than thick (three-dimensional). For instance, 3-D ribbon graphs just look like regular line graphs.

3-D Bar

A *3-D bar* graph is similar to a 2-D bar graph, except that the graph is plotted on a three-dimensional grid. The bars of each series are graphed in front of one another along the z-axis.

A 3-D bar graph is most effective when there is a distinct and progressive difference between each series—that is, series with the largest values appear in the back of the graph, progressing to series with the smallest values in the front of the graph. If the bars in the front of the graph are larger than bars in the other series, they may hide them from view.

Suppose you want to graph the Sales, Gross Profit, and Net Income data shown in Figure 8.27. You can use the /Graph settings in Table 8.8 to create the 3-D bar graph for Acme Financial Corp. in Figure 8.28.

Figure 8.27

Three-year financial data for Acme Financial Corp.

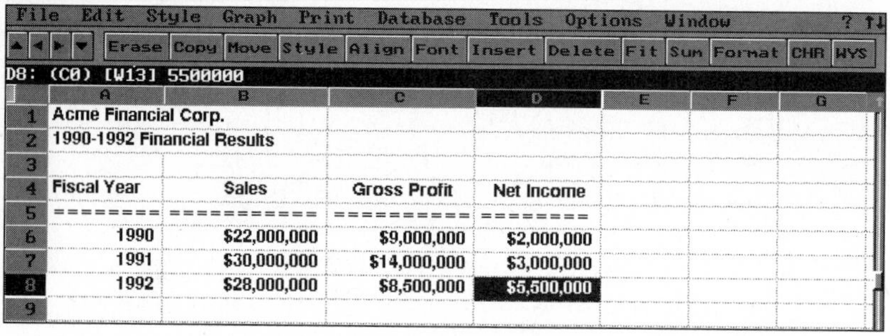

Notice in Figure 8.28 how Quattro Pro graphs the 1st Series block first, at the back of the graph. That is why this graph was designed so that the 1st Series block includes the largest values to be graphed—the Sales values in B6..B8. The 2nd Series block, containing the Gross Profit information in C6..C8, is plotted next. Finally comes the Net Income values from the 3rd Series block, D6..D8. *Remember*, if the values in the frontmost series (in this case the 3rd Series) are higher than the values in the other series, these bars may obscure the bars graphed behind them.

Quattro Pro automatically uses a different fill pattern to distinguish each series. When you use the Text, Legends settings in Table 8.8, however, Quattro Pro does not create a legend defining these fill patterns. Instead, it produces labels along the right side of the z-axis, as shown in Figure 8.28. You cannot change the placement of these legends.

3-D Step

A *3-D step* graph is similar to a 3-D bar graph, except that each series is plotted as a continuous block rather than discrete bars. You can see this effect in Figure 8.29. When you compare this 3-D step graph with the 3-D bar graph in Figure 8.28, you can see that the 3-D step graph illustrates the data variations more dramatically. Be careful, however—in some cases a step graph makes it harder to see the series in the back of the graph.

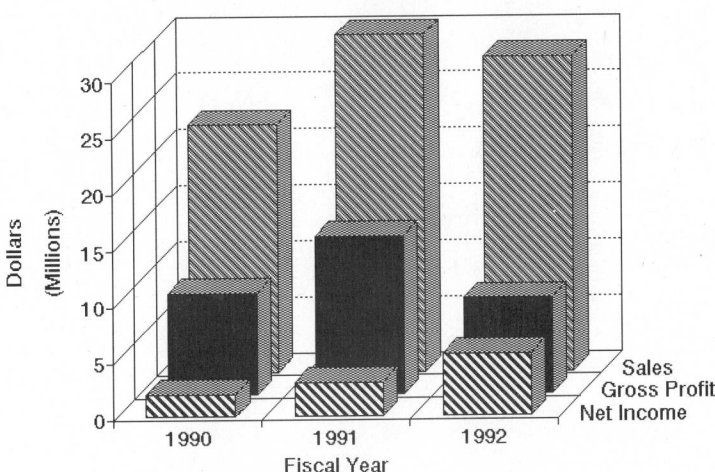

Acme Financial Corp.
1990-1992 Financial Results

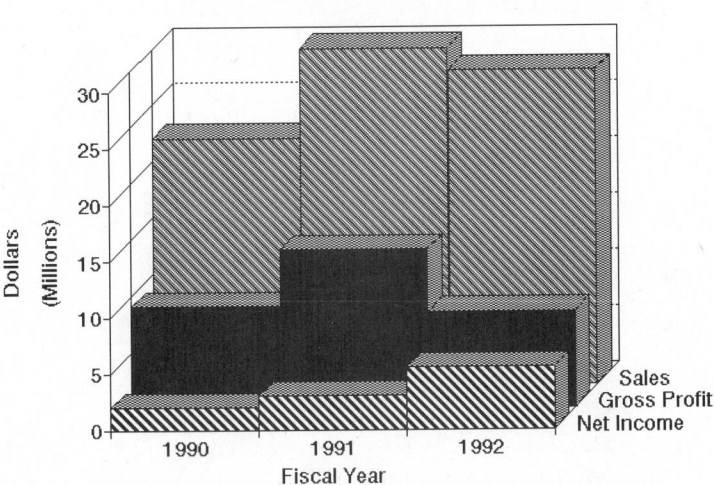

Acme Financial Corp.
1990-1992 Financial Results

Table 8.8 **/Graph Settings Used with Figure 8.27 to Create 3-D Graphs in Figures 8.28, 8.29, 8.30, and 8.31**

/Graph Commands	Settings
Graph Type, 3-D Graphs	Bar, Ribbon, Step, or Area
Series	
1st Series	B6..B8
2nd Series	C6..C8
3rd Series	D6..D8
X-Axis Series	A6..A8
Text	
1st Line	\A1
2nd Line	\A2
X-Title	\A4
Y-Title	Dollars
Text, Legends	
1st Series	\B4
2nd Series	\C4
3rd Series	\D4
Overall, Add Depth (or Three-D in version 3.0)	Yes

You can use the same /Graph settings in Table 8.8 to create the 3-D step graph in Figure 8.29. As in the 3-D bar graph, Quattro Pro graphs a 3-D step graph by first plotting the 1st Series block (Sales) at the back of the graph, then the 2nd Series block (Gross Profit), and finally the Net Income values from the 3rd Series block at the front of the graph.

3-D Area

Unlike a 2-D area graph, a *3-D area* graph does not stack the data series, but rather plots each series separately. For instance, for the information in Figure 8.27, you can use the /Graph settings in Table 8.8 to create the 3-D area graph shown in Figure 8.30. Of all the 3-D graphs created using the information in Figure 8.27, this 3-D area graph best conveys the upward Net Income trend.

Figure 8.30
A 3-D area graph of
the data in Figure
8.27

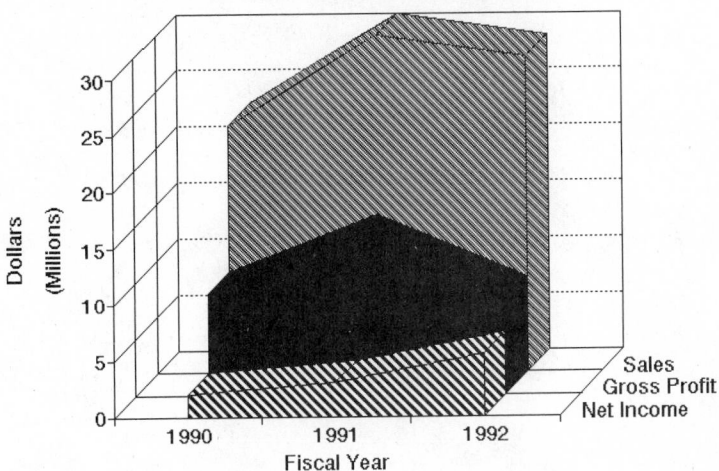

Once again, Quattro Pro first plots the 1st Series block (Sales) at the back of the 3-D area graph, then the 2nd Series block (Gross Profit), and finally the Net Income values in the 3rd Series block at the front of this 3-D area graph. Notice that the series are not stacked, but are graphed separately.

3-D Ribbon

A *3-D ribbon* graph portrays each series as a line, stretched into a flat ribbon. You can see a 3-D ribbon graph in Figure 8.31, created using the information in Figure 8.27 and the /Graph settings in Table 8.8. For portraying this particular data, this style of 3-D graph is probably the least effective.

When you first examine Figure 8.31, you can see the 1st Series block (Sales) is the topmost ribbon, the Gross Profit values included in the 2nd Series block are represented by the middle ribbon, and the bottom ribbon is the 3rd Series block, Net Income. Thus, a typical legend that defines the fill patterns would be very helpful in a 3-D ribbon graph. However, when you specify a legend in a 3-D graph, Quattro Pro only adds labels along the right side of the z-axis.

Figure 8.31

A 3-D ribbon graph of the data in Figure 8.27

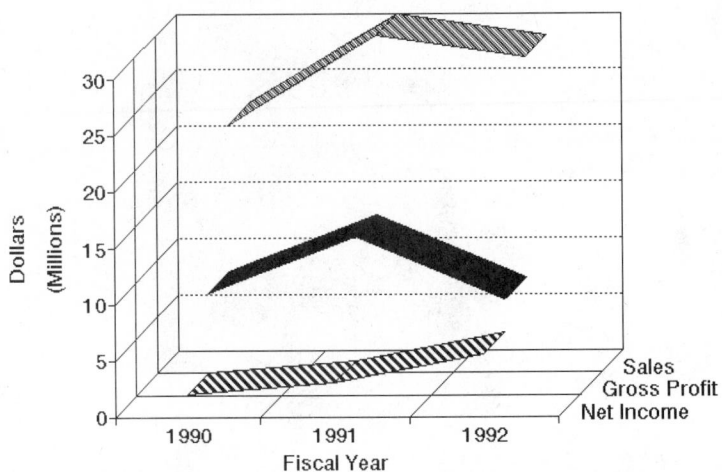

Mixed Graphs

In Quattro Pro you can combine line and bar graphs into a single graph. Mixing graph types is helpful when you need to compare related information, such as net income and stock prices.

For example, let's return to Acme Financial Corp., whose 1990–1992 net income and year-ending stock price values are shown in Figure 8.32. Now suppose you want to graph these values together in one graph. You can use the /Graph settings in Table 8.9 to create the mixed line and bar graph shown in Figure 8.33.

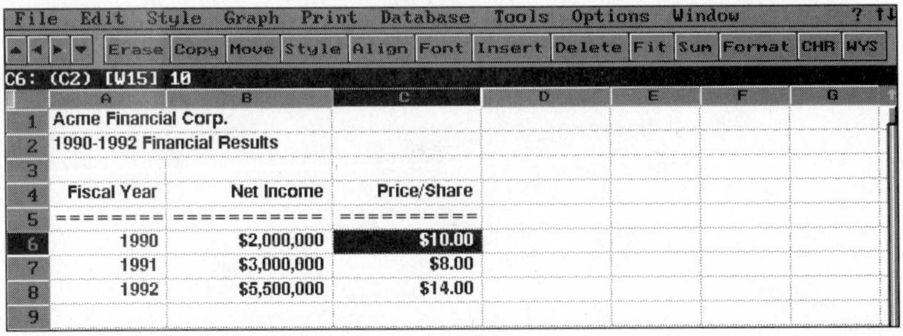

Figure 8.32

Data for Acme Financial Corp.

| File | Edit | Style | Graph | Print | Database | Tools | Options | Window | ? ↑↓ |

| ▲ ◀ ▶ ▼ | Erase | Copy | Move | Style | Align | Font | Insert | Delete | Fit | Sum | Format | CHR | WYS |

C6: (C2) [W15] 10

	A	B	C	D	E	F	G
1	Acme Financial Corp.						
2	1990-1992 Financial Results						
3							
4	Fiscal Year	Net Income	Price/Share				
5	========	=========	=========				
6	1990	$2,000,000	$10.00				
7	1991	$3,000,000	$8.00				
8	1992	$5,500,000	$14.00				
9							

Figure 8.33
A mixed line/bar graph created with the data from Figure 8.32

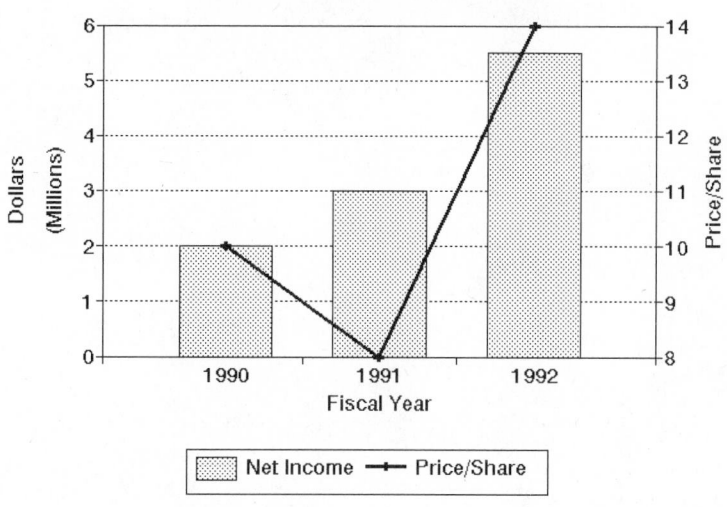

Acme Financial Corp.
1990-1992 Financial Results
Dollars (Millions)
0
1
2
3
4
5
6
Price/Share
8
9
10
11
12
13
14
1990
1991
1992
Fiscal Year
Net Income
Price/Share

Note. If you select Default from the Override Type menu, Quattro Pro uses the current Graph Type setting.

You want to graph the 1st Series values (Net Income) as bars, so specify Graph Type, Bar. This setting becomes the default graph type for this mixed graph. Since you also want to plot the 2nd Series block (Price per Share) as a line, use Customize Series, Override Type, 2nd Series. When Quattro Pro displays the menu of override options, select Line.

The mixed bar and line graph in Figure 8.33 shows you two additional uses of Quattro Pro's custom graph capabilities. First, to prevent the line from being obscured by the bars' fill patterns, the Customize Series settings in Table 8.9 are used to specify a dotted fill pattern for the bars, and a heavy solid line style.

Additionally, the Customize Series, Series 2, Y-Axis, Secondary selection (Customize Series, Y-Axis, 2nd Series, Secondary Y-Axis in Quattro Pro 3.0) creates a second y-axis on the right side of the graph for the share prices. You will want to add a second y-axis whenever you create a mixed graph of values that vary widely in magnitude. For instance, in Figure 8.33, the share price ranges from 8 to 14, while the net income values are in the millions. A Text, Secondary Y-Axis setting is also used to label this second y-axis as Price per Share. (For further discussion of adding a second y-axis, see the next two sections on customizing graphs.)

Table 8.9   **Graph Settings Used with Figure 8.32 to Create Mixed Line/Bar Graph in Figure 8.33**

/Graph Commands	Settings
Graph Type	Bar
Series	
1st Series	B6..B8
2nd Series	C6..C8
X-Axis Series	A6..A8
Text	
1st Line	\A1
2nd Line	\A2
Y-Title	Dollars
Secondary Y-Axis	\C4
X-Title	\A4
Text, Legends	
1st Series	\B4
2nd Series	\C4
Overall	
Add Depth (Three-D in Quattro Pro 3.0)	No
Customize Series	
Series 2, Override Type (Override Type, 2nd Series in Quattro Pro 3.0)	Line
Series 2, Y-Axis (Y-Axis, 2nd Series in Quattro Pro 3.0)	Line
Markers & Lines, Line Styles, 2nd Series[*]	Heavy Solid
Series 1, Fill Pattern (Fill Pattern, 1st Series in Quattro Pro 3.0)	L - Heavy Dots

[*] This is the setting for Quattro Pro 3.0. To change the format of the line in Quattro Pro 4.0, you must temporarily switch the Line Style graph type to line and then use Customize Series to modify the settings for Series 2.

Customizing a Graph in Quattro Pro 4.0

Quattro Pro 4.0's new dialog boxes make it much easier to customize a graph than in previous versions. For example, Figure 8.34 shows the new /Graph, Customize Series dialog box for bar graphs. (The settings that appear in the dialog box vary with the graph type.) This one dialog box alone replaces what took four layers of menus in Quattro Pro 3.0. Dialog boxes also make it much easier to see your settings once you've made them.

Figure 8.34

The /Graph, Customize Series dialog box for bar graphs

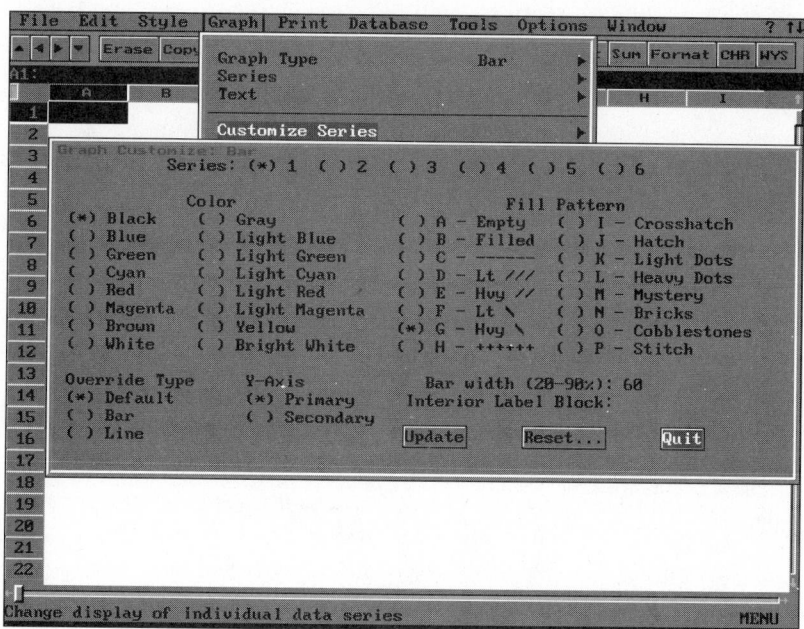

Besides /Graph, Customize Series, here are the three other /Graph commands that display dialog boxes in Quattro Pro 4.0:

/Graph, X-Axis

/Graph, Y-Axis

/Graph, Overall

Customizing a Bubble Graph

Quattro Pro 4.0's bubble graph offers the following new ways for customizing data series:

- The /Graph, Customize Series command lets you set the color and fill pattern for bubbles in the same way you would set them for the slices in a pie graph (see "Customizing the Series Display" later).

Note. If more than nine bubbles appear in a bubble graph, Quattro Pro starts repeating the color and fill pattern. For example, the color and fill pattern for the tenth bubble is the same as for the first, the eleventh is the same as for the second, and so on.

- By choosing /Graph, Customize Series, Max Bubble Size, you can specify that the radius of the largest bubble be a certain percentage of the x-axis (from 1 to 25 percent). For example, if you were to select a setting of 20 percent, the radius of the largest bubble would be 20 percent of the size of the x-axis. (The default setting is 10 percent.)

- Almost every bubble graph can benefit from having interior data labels that appear in front of or adjacent to the bubbles. Each data label usually identifies the corresponding bubble, making it easier to interpret the graph. To set interior data labels for a bubble graph, use /Graph, Customize Series, Interior Label Block and choose a range that contains the labels that are to be applied. The label in the first cell is used for the first bubble, the label in the second cell for the second bubble, and so on. Figure 8.24 shows an example.

Customizing a Graph in Quattro Pro 3.0

One of the best features of Quattro Pro is the custom graphing capabilities it offers you. When you create a graph, you can use the /Graph command to

- *Customize text.* You can add graph titles, x- and y-axis titles, and legends. To enhance this text, you can also access Quattro Pro's powerful font capability.

- *Change the graphed appearance of series blocks.* You can change the default fill patterns and colors used in area graphs and all types of bar graphs. You can change the width of bars and the line and marker styles, add interior data labels, and customize pie and column charts.   .

- *Customize axes.* You can rescale the x- and y-axes to your own specifications, and even add a secondary y-axis.

- *Tailor the overall graph.* You can include or remove grid lines, add boxes around text or a legend, control the three-dimensional effect of pie, column, and bar graphs, change the background color of a graph, and choose between a color or black-and-white display of your graph.

■ *Add enhancements to the graph.* Using /Graph Annotate (discussed in Chapter 9), you can move text around, and add arrows, buttons, lines, and callouts.

All of the customization features (except those offered by the Annotator) are discussed in the following sections.

NOTE. *The settings that appear in Quattro Pro 4.0's dialog boxes are nearly identical to those in Quattro Pro 3.0's menus. Therefore, in the sections that follow, whenever a Quattro Pro 3.0 menu command appears, you should easily be able to find its corresponding setting in a Quattro Pro 4.0 dialog box.*

Updating and Resetting Default Settings

If you find yourself using certain /Graph commands often, consider using /Graph, Customize Series, to save these settings for all future sessions. The Update option saves the current settings for the following /Graph commands as the new defaults:

/Graph, Graph Type

/Graph, Text, Font

/Graph, Text, Legends, Position

/Graph, Customize Series (except Interior Labels)

/Graph, X-Axis

/Graph, Y-Axis

/Graph, Overall

Be careful: Quattro Pro *does not* ask for confirmation when you invoke /Graph, Customize Series, Update. Therefore, before you select this command, be certain that you do in fact want to use the current settings for the commands listed above as defaults.

When you select /Graph, Customize Series, Reset, Graph, Quattro Pro clears all the /Graph, Series settings and all the /Graph, Text settings (*except* for those listed above). All other /Graph settings are returned to the *current* default settings.

You can also use Reset to clear one or all /Graph, Series blocks without affecting the other /Graph settings. For more details, see "Specifying Data to Be Graphed" earlier in the chapter.

Note. In Quattro Pro 4.0, Update and Reset are available as buttons in the /Graph, Customize Series dialog box.

Adding Text

The /Graph, Text command lets you add titles, labels for x-, y- and secondary y-axes, and even a legend. You can also specify Text Font settings to customize the typeface, size, typestyle, and text color of graph text.

Suppose you are analyzing the Peterson Manufacturing income data in Figure 8.35, and you use the following /Graph settings:

/Graph Commands	Settings
Graph Type	Area
Series	
1st Series	B6..B9
2nd Series	C6..C9
X-Axis Series	A6..A9

Figure 8.35

Data for Peterson Manufacturing

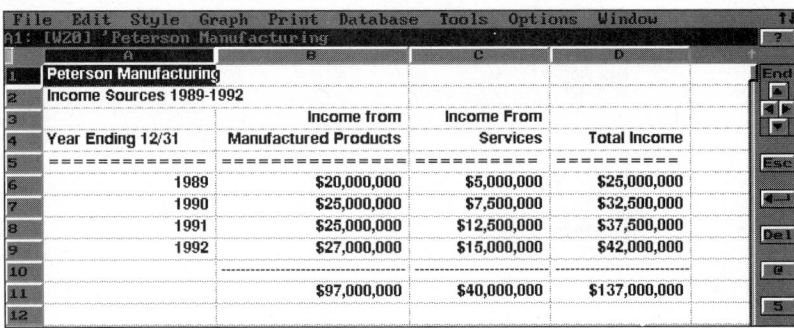

As you can see in Figure 8.36, the resulting area graph is rather austere, and does not convey what this graphed information represents. In the following sections, you'll see how to use the /Graph, Text command to add explanatory information to this graph.

Titles

You can use the following Graph Text settings to add descriptive labels to the graph in Figure 8.36:

■ The 1st Line setting, \A1, creates a main title at the top of the graph, "Peterson Manufacturing."

Figure 8.36

An area graph of data from Figure 8.35, using two series blocks

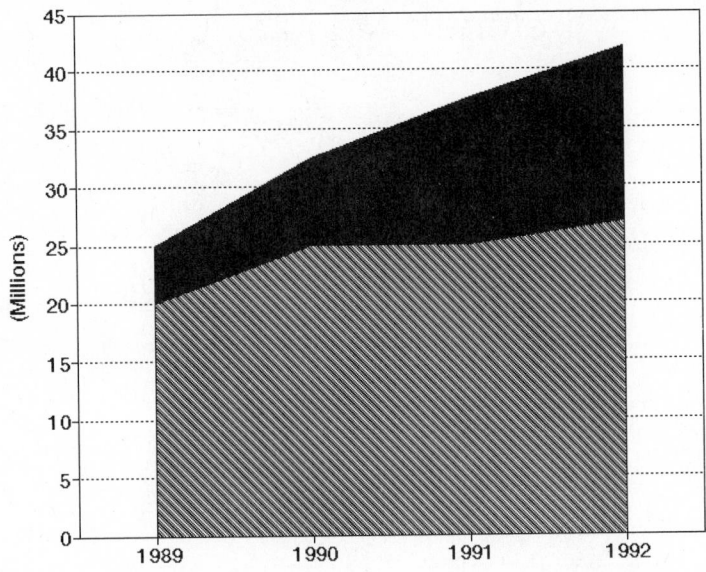

- The 2nd Line setting, \A2, creates a subtitle below the main title, "Income Sources 1989–1992."

- The X-Axis Title setting, \A4, adds explanatory text along the bottom of the graph, "Year Ending 12/31."

- The Y-Axis Title setting, Income, adds this explanatory text along the left side of the graph.

Now look at the area graph in Figure 8.37, which includes graph titles and x-axis and y-axis descriptive labels. Notice that the "(Millions)" label along the y-axis has not been specified in a /Graph, Text setting. Quattro Pro automatically divides each value in both series blocks by 1,000,000, and then indicates this scaling multiplier, (Millions), next to the y-axis. (See "Customizing the Y-Axis" later in this chapter for a further discussion of this scaling multiplier.)

When you specify a Text setting, you can enter either a label, or a cell address—preceded by a backslash (\)—that references a label in the spreadsheet. For instance, the 1st Line setting in our example, \A1, references the label Peterson Manufacturing in cell A1. Be aware, however, that if you move this text, say to cell A20, or insert or delete rows or columns in the spreadsheet, a cell address setting is not automatically adjusted to reflect the new position of the label.

Figure 8.37
The Peterson Manufacturing area graph with added graph titles, and x- and y-axis labels

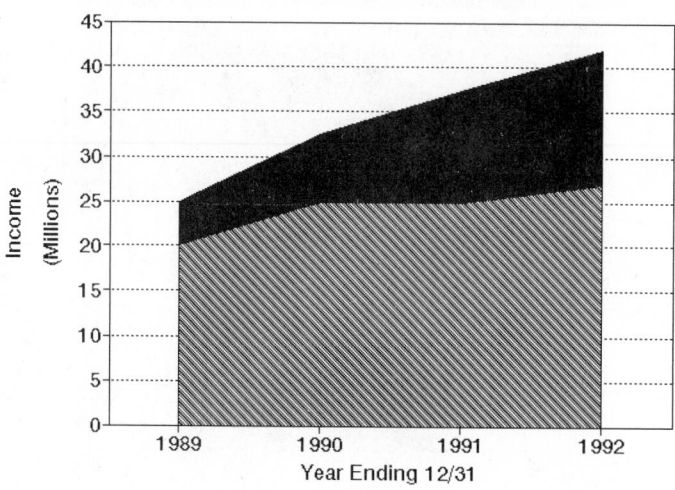

Peterson Manufacturing
Income Sources 1989-1992

Keep in mind the following when you are adding text to a graph:

Note. You'll find Quattro Pro 4.0's Outlines option in the /Graph, Overall dialog box.

- In a rotated bar graph, you must use Text, X-Axis Title to specify the y-axis title, and Text, Y-Axis Title to add an x-axis title.

- You can specify a Text setting that is a string formula, and thereby combine labels already in a spreadsheet. See "String Functions" in Chapter 7.

- You can use the /Graph, Overall, Outlines command to add boxes around your text. See "Customizing the Overall Graph" later in this chapter.

- To clear one Text setting, such as the 1st Line setting, simply select the /Graph, Text, 1st Line option, press Esc, and then Enter.

- Quattro Pro clears all Text settings when you choose /Graph, Customize Series, Reset, Graph. See "Updating and Resetting Default Settings" at the beginning of this section.

Legend
Even though descriptive labels have been added to the Peterson Manufacturing graph in Figure 8.37, these labels do not explain what each graphed series represents. A legend or key is needed to do this. A legend tells you what

each of the fill patterns, colors, line styles, and/or markers represent in the graph.

To add a legend to the graph in Figure 8.37, choose /Graph, Text, Legends. Quattro Pro displays the Legends menu in Figure 8.38. Specify the 1st Series setting, \B4, and the 2nd Series setting, \C4. As you can see in Figure 8.39, Quattro Pro creates a legend with two keys at the bottom of the graph. This legend ties the Heavy Filled (\\\\) fill pattern to Manufactured Products, and the Filled fill pattern to Services.

Figure 8.38

The /Graph, Text, Legends menu

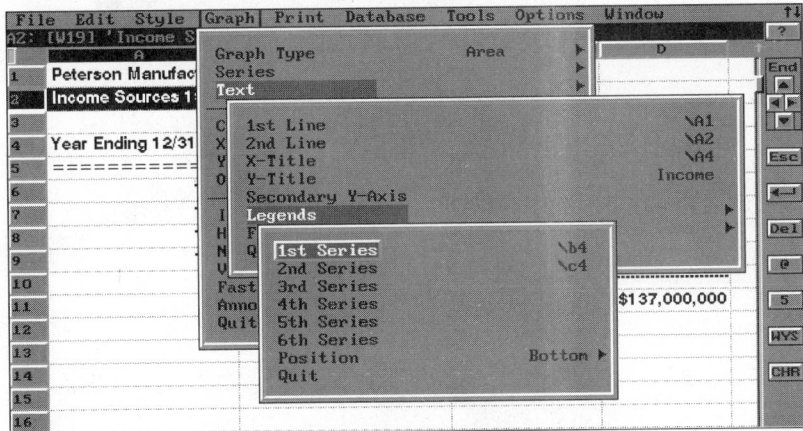

The default position for a legend is below the graph. However, you can use Legends, Position, Right to place it at the right of the graph. Quattro Pro will automatically resize the graph to accommodate this placement, as in Figure 8.40. One advantage of drawing the legend on the right is that this placement can usually accommodate longer legend labels.

Keep in mind the following when you are adding a legend:

Note. You can specify a Legends setting as a label, or as a cell address—preceded by a backslash (\ )—that references a label in the spreadsheet. Be aware, however, that if you move the label text or insert/delete rows or columns in the spreadsheet, Quattro Pro does not automatically adjust the cell address setting.

■ Quattro Pro only produces a legend label for each series block graphed. Thus, if you specify Legends settings for the 1st through 3rd Series, but then graph just the 1st and 2nd Series, Quattro Pro only displays legend keys for the first two series.

■ Quattro Pro automatically includes a box around a legend, but you can use /Graph, Overall, Outlines to change this. For example, you can eliminate the box altogether, or choose a double-line box. (See "Graph, Title, and Legend Outlines" later in this chapter.)

Figure 8.39

The Peterson Manufacturing graph with an added legend

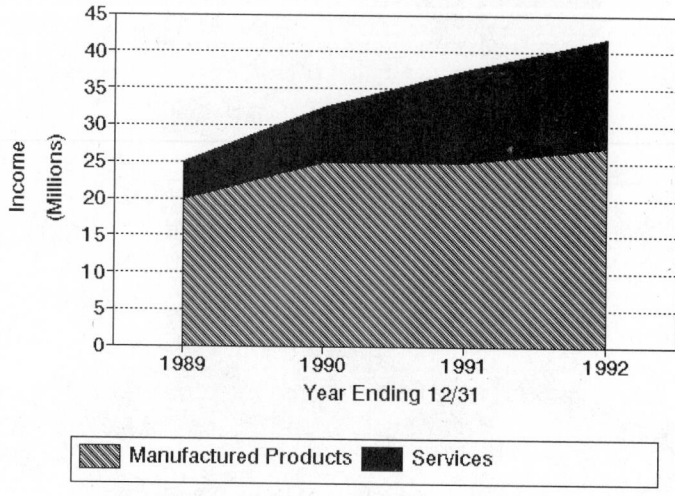

Figure 8.40

The graph with a right-positioned legend

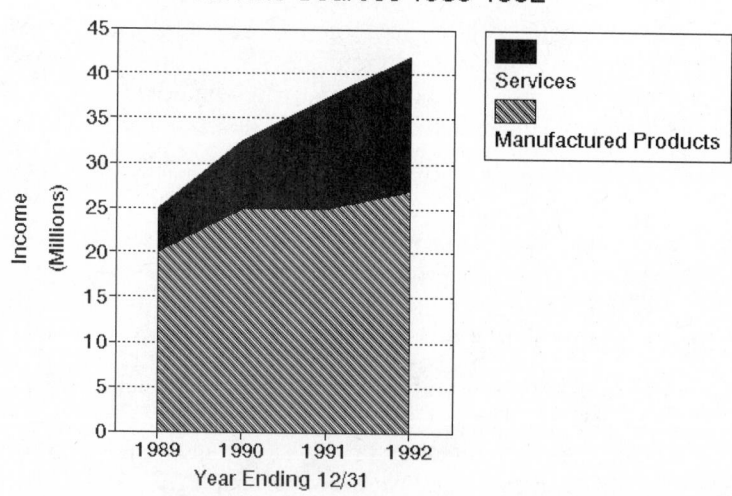

■ To suppress a legend from being displayed in a graph, without affecting the Legends settings, use /Graph, Text, Legends, Position, None.

■ If you designate a legend for a 3-D graph, Quattro Pro places the descriptive text at the bottom right of the 3-D graph along the z-axis, as illustrated in Figure 8.28.

■ To clear one Legends setting, simply select /Graph, Text, Legends, choose the series name, press Esc, and then press Enter. Quattro Pro also clears all the Legends settings when you select the Reset, Graph option.

Changing Fonts

Quattro Pro's substantial font capability is accessed through the /Graph, Text, Font command. You can use this command to choose various custom fonts for, and customize the typestyle of graph titles, axis titles, and legends, as well as data and tickmark labels. The Font menu is shown in Figure 8.41.

Figure 8.41
The /Graph, Text, Font menu

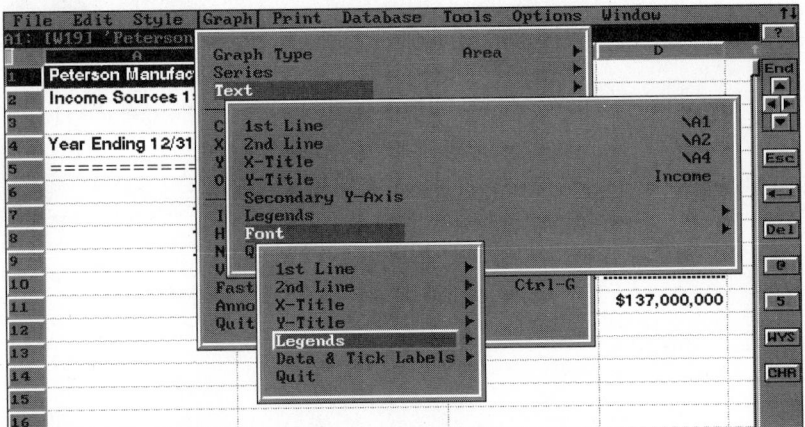

Quattro Pro's default font settings are listed in Table 8.10. You will want to change the fonts used in a graph if the text overwhelms the graph, if the x-axis labels run together, or when you want to emphasize certain text.

Consider, for instance, the Peterson Manufacturing graph in Figure 8.40. Suppose you want to change the Legends font to 14-point Roman Italic.

Note. For a full discussion of the fonts Quattro Pro offers, as well as selecting and editing fonts, see Chapter 3.

1. Select /Graph, Text, Font, Legends. Quattro Pro displays a menu like that in Figure 8.42.

2. Select Typeface, and from the Typeface menu, choose Roman. Quattro Pro returns to the Font, Legends menu.

Table 8.10   **Default Graph Font Settings**

/Graph, Text, Font	Typeface	Point Size	Color
1st Line	Bitstream Swiss	36	Blue
2nd Line	Bitstream Swiss	24	Blue
X-Title	Bitstream Swiss	18	Blue
Y-Title	Bitstream Swiss	18	Blue
Legends	Bitstream Swiss	18	Blue
Data & Tick Labels	Bitstream Swiss	18	Blue

Figure 8.42

The /Graph, Text, Font, Legends menu

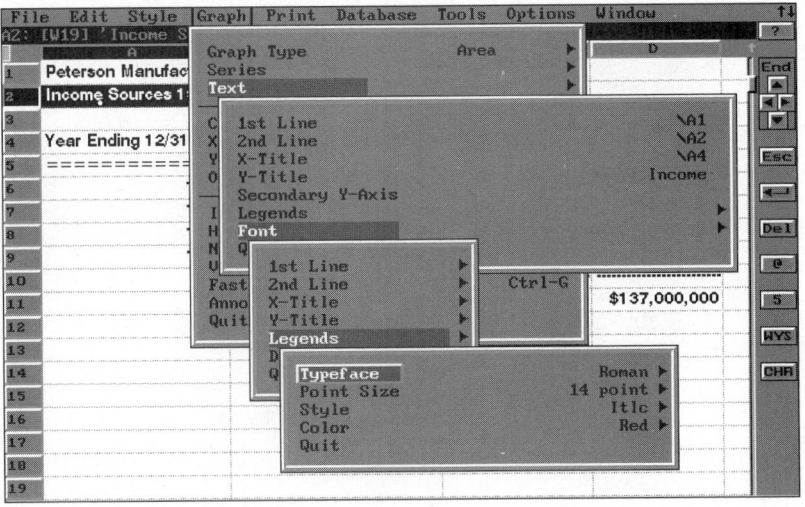

3. Select Point Size, and choose 14 point from the available selections (6 to 72). Quattro Pro returns to the Font, Legends menu.

4. Select Style from the menu in Figure 8.42, and then Italic. Quattro Pro then displays that Italic is turned On. (To turn it off, either select Italic again, or choose Reset, which clears all Style selections in this menu.) Select Quit to return to the Font, Legends menu.

If you have a color printer, you can change the color in which the text is printed. For example, suppose you want to change the legend text to red.

Note. You can also display a font using bold, italic, underlined, drop shadow, or a combination of these typestyles.

Select Color on the Font, Legends menu, and Quattro Pro displays a menu listing 16 different color selections. (If you are working in WYSIWYG mode, the Color menu actually displays the 16 different colors.) Choose Red, and Quattro Pro returns to the Font, Legends menu, where you'll see this new font, Roman 14-point Italic Red, as illustrated in Figure 8.42. (To see this legend color when you display the graph, you must first select /Graph, Overall, Color/B&W, Color.)

NOTE. *To display text colors in Quattro Pro 4.0, select Use Colors, Yes in the /Graph, Overall dialog box.*

After making these font changes, press F10 (Graph), and Quattro Pro displays the graph in Figure 8.43. Notice how the smaller legend font de-emphasizes the legend, and allows a larger version of the area graph to be displayed.

Figure 8.43
Using a smaller font for the legend

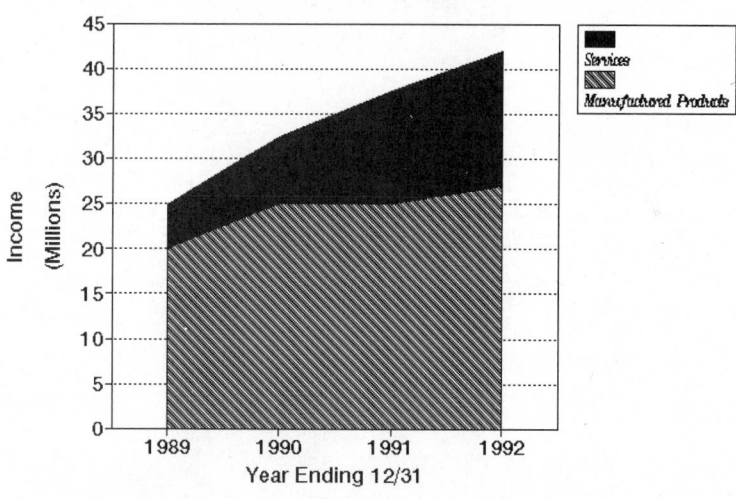

Note. When you select a new point size for data and tickmark labels in Quattro Pro 4.0, all markers and symbols are automatically scaled to match.

Be aware of the following when you specify text fonts in a graph:

- In a 3-D graph, to change the default legend font, you must use the Font, Data & Tick Labels selection rather than the Font, Legends selection. Furthermore, Quattro Pro does not display the legend in a 3-D graph using the new drop shadow typestyle, even if you select this option.

- To more easily view text assigned smaller fonts, use Quattro Pro's Screen Preview Zoom mode, discussed in "Previewing a Graph" later in this chapter.

- You can also use the Annotator (Chapter 9) to change the size of text.

- To save Text, Font settings as the new defaults, use /Graph, Customize Series, Update discussed earlier in this chapter.

The Drop Shadow Typestyle   Quattro Pro offers you an additional typestyle, drop shadow. For example, to create the 1st Line title illustrated in Figure 8.43, select /Graph, Text, Font, 1st Line Style, and then choose Drop Shadow. Quattro Pro will indicate that the Drop Shadow Style is On. (To remove the drop shadow typestyle select Drop Shadow again.) Remember to select Quit to return to the Style menu.

When you use a drop shadow typestyle, the *text* color is determined by the /Graph, Text, Font command. In Figure 8.43, for example, the Text, Font, 1st Line Color setting is Blue, so Quattro Pro displays the 1st Line title text in blue.

Note. In Quattro Pro 4.0, use the Drop Shadow colors button in the /Graph, Overall dialog box to set text shadow colors.

To control the color of the text *shadow*, you select /Graph, Overall, Drop Shadow, Color, to get the menu in Figure 8.44. Notice that this menu includes two columns of color names. The first column lists the color choices you are offered in the /Graph, Text, Font command. The second column lists the corresponding *default* shadow color Quattro Pro uses for each text color. Therefore, because the 1st Line text in Figure 8.43 is set to Blue, Quattro Pro automatically uses a Light Blue shadow.

Figure 8.44
The default settings for /Graph, Overall, Drop Shadow Color

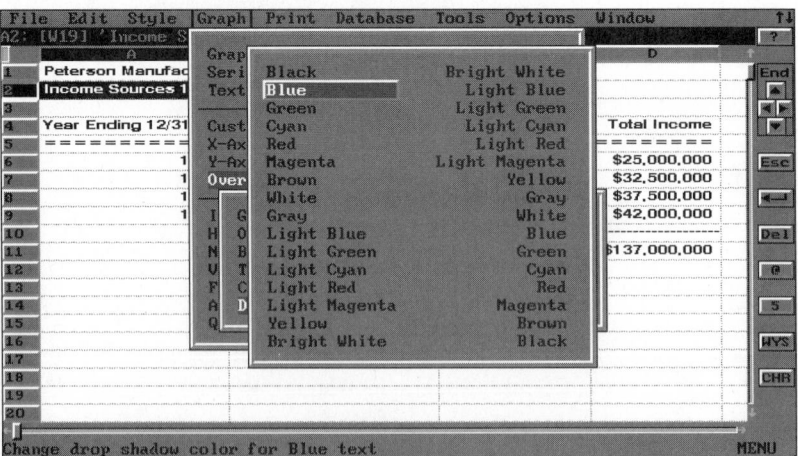

You can change the shadow color Quattro Pro uses. To change the corresponding shadow color for a Blue text color, for example, select Blue in the left column of the Drop Shadow color menu. You'll see a pictorial menu (if you are in WYSIWYG mode) of 16 color selections. Make a selection, such as Yellow, and Quattro Pro displays this shadow color to the right of the corresponding text color.

Customizing the Series Display

The /Graph, Customize Series command lets you improve the appearance of the data in a graph. You can use this command to

- Change the fill patterns and colors used for area graphs and all types of bar graphs

- Adjust the width of bars

- Choose the line and marker styles, as well as whether each line is represented by a line and markers, a line, or just markers

- Add interior data labels

- Enhance pie and column charts

NOTE. *There is a substantial difference in the way Quattro Pro 4.0 responds to the /Graph, Customize Series command. Instead of seeing individual menus and submenus, you'll see a dialog box that is tailored to the graph type you've selected. Additionally, you won't find a display of fill patterns like the one in Figure 8.48.*

Fill Patterns

Quattro Pro automatically fills in the bars in all types of bar graphs, and the area underneath the lines of area graphs, with *fill patterns*. These fill patterns are used to differentiate the information represented by each series block. The contrast between Quattro Pro's default fill patterns is distinct, but you can choose other fill patterns that contrast more subtly.

For example, suppose you want to graph the high and low temperature values in Figure 8.45. The /Graph settings in Table 8.11 will create the bar graph in Figure 8.46, which uses Quattro Pro 3.0's default fill patterns. (You'll see slightly different fill patterns in Quattro Pro 4.0.)

You can easily change the fill patterns for each series to those in Figure 8.49.

1. Select /Graph, Customize Series, Fill Patterns, and Quattro Pro 3.0 displays a menu like that in Figure 8.47.

Figure 8.45

Temperature data for some metropolitan areas

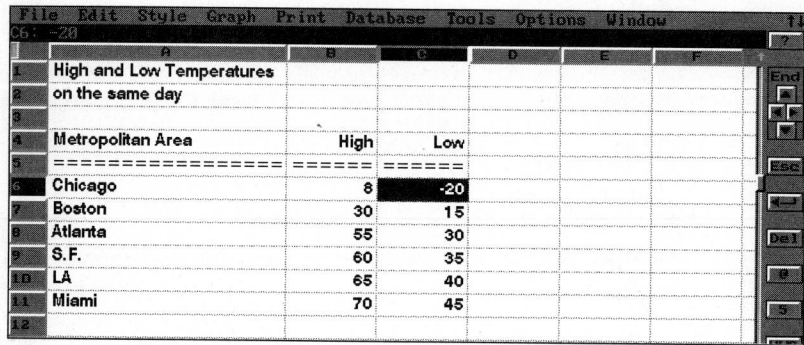

2. To change the 1st Series fill pattern, choose 1st Series, and Quattro Pro 3.0 displays a list of available patterns. If you are working in WYSIWYG mode, Quattro Pro displays the pictorial gallery of fill patterns shown in Figure 8.48. Choose K - Light Dots, and press Enter. Quattro Pro returns to the Fill Patterns menu.

Figure 8.46

A bar graph using Quattro Pro 3.0's default fill patterns and bar width

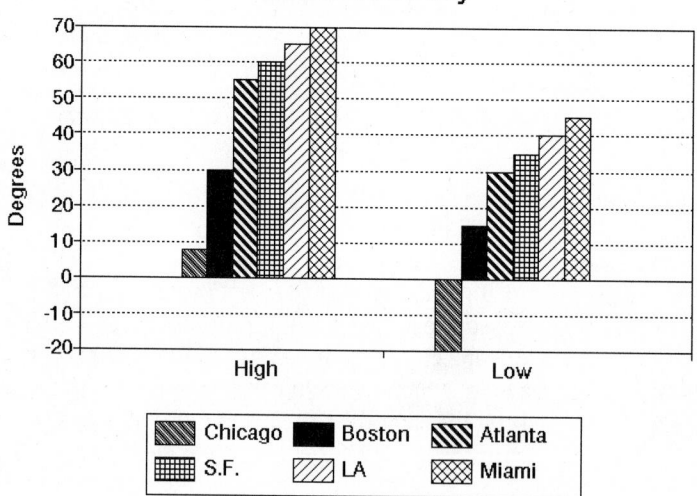

Table 8.11 **/Graph Settings Used in Figure 8.45 to Create Bar Graph in Figure 8.46**

/Graph Commands	Settings
Graph Type	Bar
Series	
1st Series	B6..C6
2nd Series	B7..C7
3rd Series	B8..C8
4th Series	B9..C9
5th Series	B10..C10
6th Series	B11..C11
X-Axis Series	B4..C4
Text	
1st Line	\A1
2nd Line	\A2
Y-Title	Degrees
Text, Legends	
1st Series	\A6
2nd Series	\A7
3rd Series	\A8
4th Series	\A9
5th Series	\A10
6th Series	\A11

3. Repeat this selection process to establish the following Fill Patterns settings:

1st Series—K - Light Dots

2nd Series—D - Light \\\

3rd Series—B - Filled

4th Series—J - Hatch

5th Series—P - Stitch

6th Series—L - Heavy Dots

When you press F10 (Graph), a bar graph like that in Figure 8.49 is displayed. As you can see, the new fill patterns display the information more subtly than the default fill patterns in Figure 8.46.

Figure 8.47

The /Graph, Customize Series, Fill Patterns menu listing Quattro Pro 3.0's default fill patterns

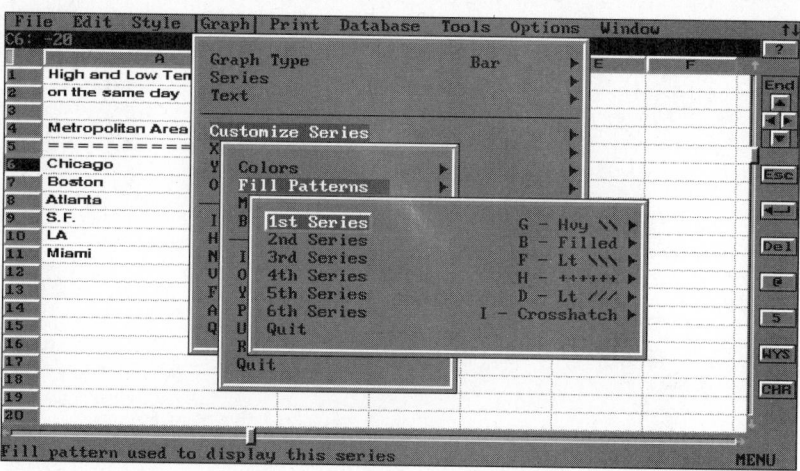

Keep in mind the following when you specify fill patterns:

■ Use /Graph, Customize Series, Pies, Patterns to change the fill patterns used in a pie or column chart. This process is explained later in this chapter.

■ To save a new set of fill pattern settings as the defaults for all future sessions, use /Graph, Customize Series, Update as explained earlier in this section.

Figure 8.48
Quattro Pro 3.0's
Fill Patterns menu
displayed in
graphics mode

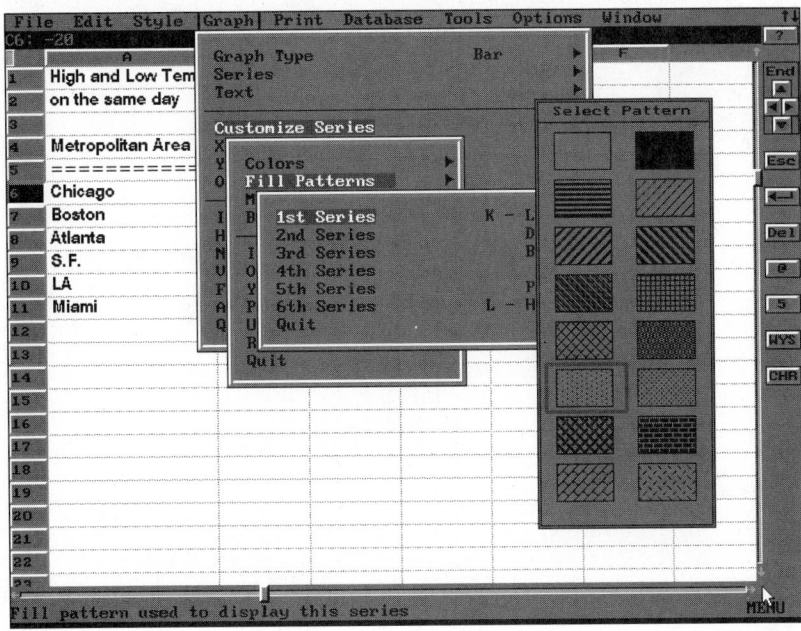

NOTE. *In Quattro Pro 4.0, both the fill pattern settings and the Update button are found in the /Graph, Customize Series dialog box.*

Adjusting Bar Thickness

When Quattro Pro draws any type of bar graph, it divides the available space along the x-axis, into *drawable* space and blank space. By default, Quattro Pro allots 60% of the available space as drawable space for the bars. The other 40% is left blank, resulting in a fairly wide space between each group of bars, between the y-axis and the leftmost bar, and between the rightmost bar and the right edge of the graph. Therefore, the more values graphed, the less space Quattro Pro allots to each bar. In fact, if you plot too many values, the bars get toothpick-thin.

Tip. Reduce the Bar Width setting if your data doesn't fit in a graph.

Take the bar graph in Figure 8.46, for example, which uses Quattro Pro's default drawable area of 60%. You can increase this drawable area percent, and thus the width of each bar, to those shown in Figure 8.49. Select /Graph, Customize Series, Bar Width, and when Quattro Pro prompts you for a percentage between 20 and 90, type **90** and press Enter. Now 90% of the drawable space is devoted to the bars.

To make this Bar Width setting the new default, you can use /Graph, Customize Series, Update, as explained in "Updating and Resetting Default Settings."

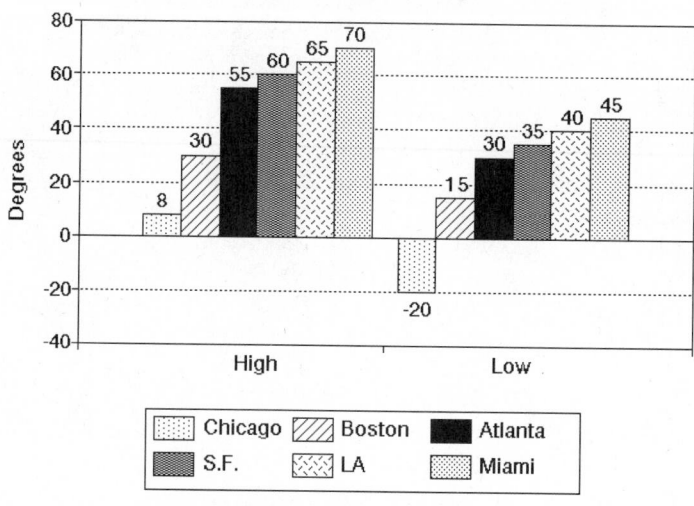

Figure 8.49
The bar graph from
Figure 8.46, with
custom fill
patterns, interior
data labels, and a
90% bar width

Interior Data Labels

Sometimes a graph does not distinctly convey the values graphed. When this
happens, *data labels* help. A data label, either text or a value, labels a specific
data point. Data labels are particularly useful for Quattro Pro 4.0's new bubble graphs. See "Customizing a Bubble Graph," earlier. You can use data labels in all graph types except pie, column, and 2-D area graphs.

Note. In Quattro
Pro 4.0, specify
data labels using
Interior Label Block
in the /Graph,
Customize Series
dialog box.

For instance, take another look at the graph in Figure 8.46. It does not
convey the actual temperature represented by each bar. You can use /Graph,
Customize Series, Interior Labels to specify a data label for each bar. In
Quattro Pro, you can specify data labels as spreadsheet information. So, in
our example, the 1st through 6th Interior Labels blocks are the same as the
1st through 6th /Graph, Series blocks shown in Table 8.11. You will often
find this is the case.

You can specify the data labels by using this procedure:

1. Select /Graph, Customize Series, Interior Labels. Quattro Pro displays
the menu shown in Figure 8.50.

2. Select 1st Series, and specify the spreadsheet block B6..C6. Quattro Pro
now displays the Placement menu shown in Figure 8.51.

3. From the Placement menu you can choose the label position that best
suits the graph. In this case, however, you are labeling a bar graph, so

Quattro Pro automatically places data labels above their bars, regardless of the position you specify.

4. Repeat the process, using the Interior Labels settings in Table 8.11, for the 2nd through 6th series.

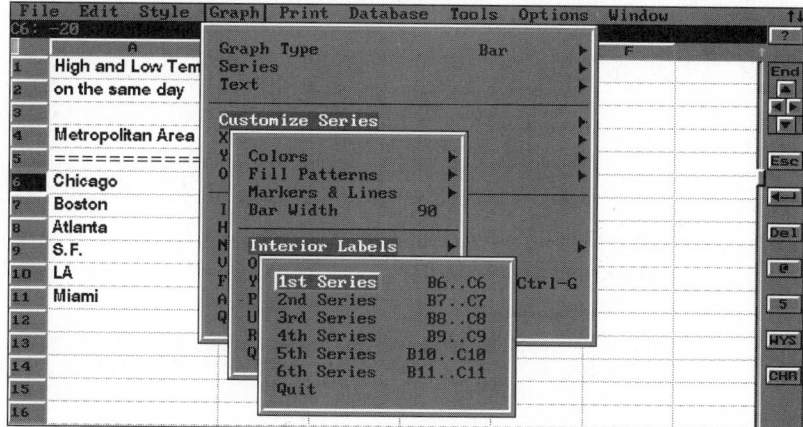

Figure 8.50

The /Graph, Customize Series, Interior Labels menu with the settings used in Figure 8.51

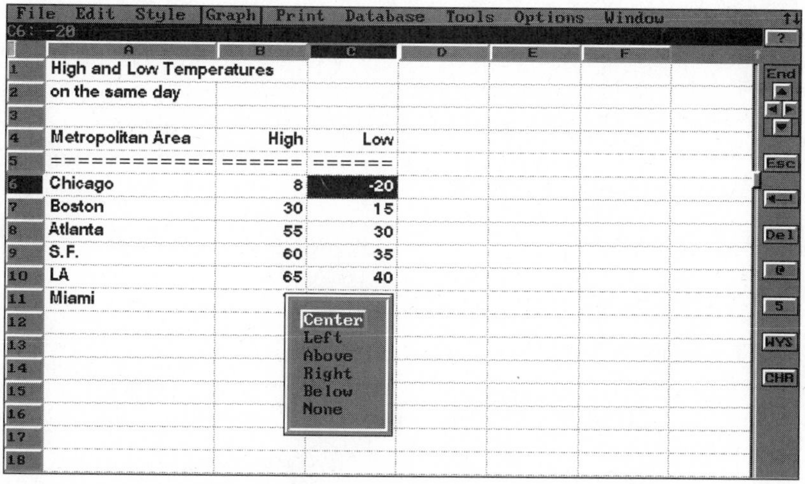

Figure 8.51

The Interior Labels, Placement menu

5. Press F10 (Graph), and Quattro Pro adds the data labels shown in Figure 8.49.

Keep in mind the following when you are creating custom interior data labels:

- If you wish, you can label only some of the values in a series block. See "Customizing the Y-Axis" later in the chapter for an example.

- You can also temporarily suppress the interior data labels in a graph without deleting the Interior Labels settings. To do this, for each Interior Labels series block, specify None in the Placement menu.

Interior Labels in Bar Graphs   In a bar graph, Quattro Pro always places an interior data label immediately *above* its bar, regardless of the data label position you specify. In a rotated bar, Quattro Pro always places an interior data label at the *end* of the bar. Avoid using interior data labels in a stacked bar graph, because Quattro Pro places them *above each segment* of the bar. Thus, the data label for the bottom segment appears inside the second segment, and so on. In addition, if a stacked bar includes a relatively small segment, its data label can run together with the next segment's data label.

In a bar graph, Quattro Pro sometimes places an interior data label a little off center, to the left. Unfortunately, you cannot use the Annotator to move these labels. Furthermore, you can't use /Style, Alignment to realign them in the spreadsheet, because Quattro Pro only uses the text of the label (not the alignment character) in an interior data label. What you can do is use the following trick:

- First, copy the information you want to use for interior data labels as values and labels to another part of the spreadsheet. (If this information contains formulas, use /Edit, Values to copy the results of formulas to this new block.)

- Next, edit each label in the new location, adding three or four spaces before the text in each cell. (If you copied values, convert them to labels by adding an apostrophe in front of each value.) This skews the text to the right.

- Now specify these cells as the appropriate /Graph, Customize Series, Interior Data Labels settings.

Interior Labels in 3-D Graphs   You can change the interior data label placement in 3-D area and ribbon graphs. Interior data labels are always placed above data points in 3-D bar and step graphs, however. Thus, the data labels for the frontmost series appear within the body of the next series, and so on. Not only does this placement cause confusion, but the data labels can be obscured by the fill patterns.

Colors

By default, Quattro Pro assigns the colors in Figure 8.52 to each data series. If you have a color screen, you can display these colors by first selecting /Graph, Overall, Colors/B&W, Colors. When you press F10 (Graph), Quattro Pro displays your graph using the default colors.

Figure 8.52

The /Graph, Customize Series, Colors menu, listing Quattro Pro's default color assignments

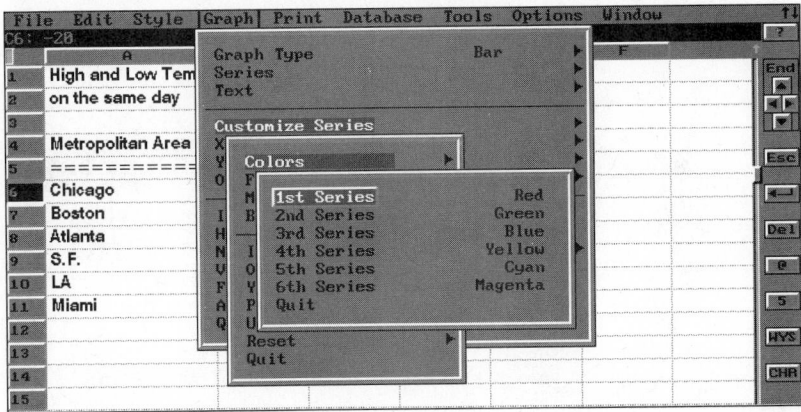

Note. You can display colors in Quattro Pro 4.0 by selecting Use Colors, Yes in the /Graph, Overall dialog box. To change the color assigned to a series, use the /Graph, Customize Series dialog box.

You can easily change the color assigned to a series. For example, to assign another color to the 1st Series, select /Graph, Customize Series, Colors. Quattro Pro displays the menu in Figure 8.52. Select 1st Series, and a list of the 16 available colors is displayed. (If you are working in WYSIWYG mode, Quattro Pro displays the actual colors.) Choose Light Blue, press Enter, and Quattro Pro displays this selection in the Colors menu.

Keep in mind the following when specifying colors for a graph:

- You can create a graph that displays colors without fill patterns. Use /Graph, Customize Series, Fill Patterns and specify B - Filled for each data series. Quattro Pro will display each data series using its Colors setting and no fill pattern.

- If your computer includes a color graphics card, but you have a black-and-white monitor, only some of the available color selections are translated to shades of black and white; others are indistinguishable. You'll need to try other colors until you find ones that are more easily discerned.

- Use /Graph, Customize Series, Update to save the current Colors settings as new defaults.

Marker and Line Symbols

When you create a line or XY graph, Quattro Pro automatically uses a solid line for each data series, but uses different markers on each line to differentiate the data series. For instance, suppose you graph the data in Figure 8.53 using the /Graph settings in Table 8.12. Quattro Pro creates the line graph in Figure 8.54 using its default line styles and markers, as explained in the legend at the bottom of the graph.

If you want, you can change the line styles and markers assigned to each data series and remove the markers, lines, or both for any of the data series.

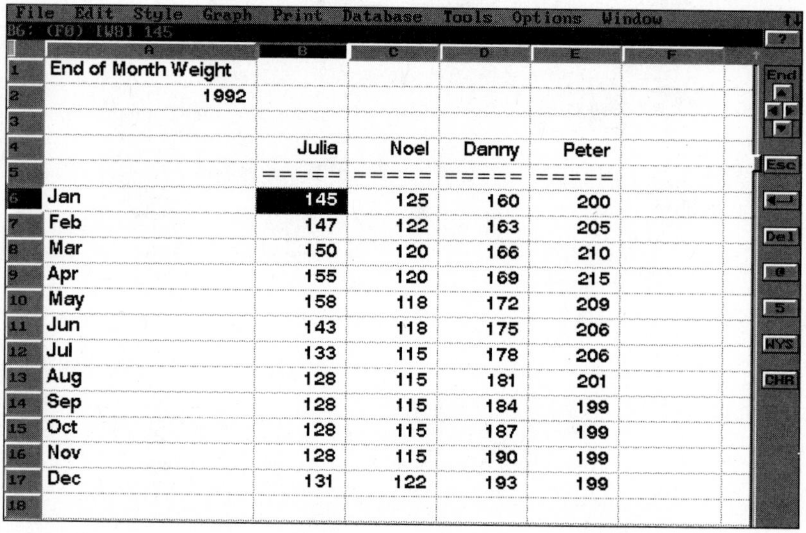

Figure 8.53

Spreadsheet data used in Figures 8.54, 8.58, and 8.60

File Edit Style Graph Print Database Tools Options Window						
B6: (F0) [W8] 145						
	A	B	C	D	E	F
1	End of Month Weight					
2	1992					
3						
4		Julia	Noel	Danny	Peter	
5		=====	=====	=====	=====	
6	Jan	145	125	160	200	
7	Feb	147	122	163	205	
8	Mar	150	120	166	210	
9	Apr	155	120	169	215	
10	May	158	118	172	209	
11	Jun	143	118	175	206	
12	Jul	133	115	178	206	
13	Aug	128	115	181	201	
14	Sep	128	115	184	199	
15	Oct	128	115	187	199	
16	Nov	128	115	190	199	
17	Dec	131	122	193	199	
18						

Note. In Quattro Pro 4.0, line styles are set in the /Graph, Customize Series dialog box.

For example, let's represent each data series graphed in Figure 8.53, using lines but no markers. Of course you'll want to assign different line styles to differentiate each series. Here's how:

1. Select /Graph, Customize Series, Markers & Lines. Quattro Pro displays the Markers & Lines menu shown in Figure 8.55.

2. Select Formats, and Quattro Pro displays a Formats menu in which each series is assigned the default setting Both (markers and lines).

Table 8.12 **/Graph Settings Used with Figure 8.53 to Create Line Graph in Figure 8.54**

/Graph Commands	Settings
Graph Type	Line
Series	
1st Series	B6..B17
2nd Series	C6..C17
3rd Series	D6..D17
4th Series	E6..E17
X-Axis Series	A6..A17
Text	
1st Line	\A1
2nd Line	\A2
Y-Title	Pounds
Text, Legends	
1st Series	\B4
2nd Series	\C4
3rd Series	\D4
4th Series	\E4

3. Choose 1st Series, and you'll see the menu shown in Figure 8.56. Here, select Lines, and Quattro Pro returns to the Formats menu, where your Lines selection is now displayed.

4. Repeat this process for the 2nd, 3rd, and 4th Series blocks, choosing Lines each time.

5. Select Quit to return to the Markers & Lines menu.

Next, let's change the line styles to differentiate the four series blocks.

6. Choose Line Styles to view the Line Styles menu, where each series is currently assigned the Solid default setting.

Figure 8.54

A line graph of the data in Figure 8.53, using default Line Styles and Markers settings

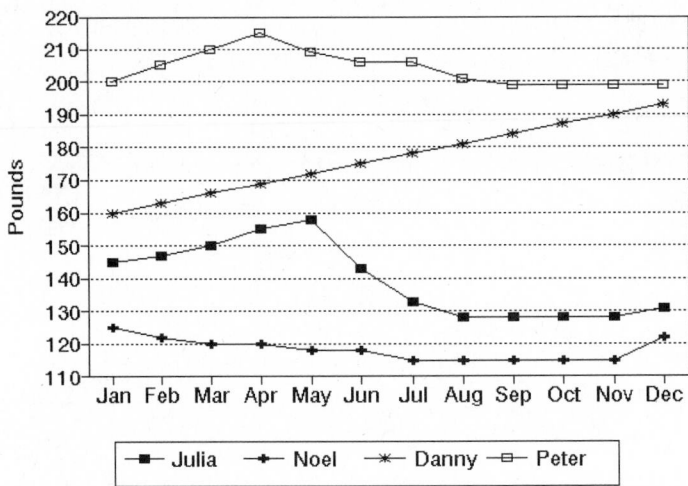

Figure 8.55

The /Graph, Customize Series, Markers & Lines, Series menu

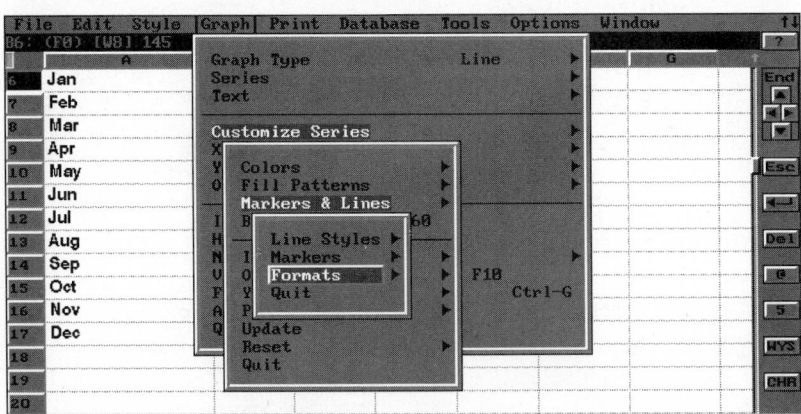

7. Select 1st Series, and Quattro Pro displays a menu of available line styles. If you are working in WYSIWYG mode to change your screen mode, you'll see the pictorial menu shown in Figure 8.57.

8. Choose Heavy Solid, and Quattro Pro returns to the Line Styles menu, where this selection is now displayed.

Figure 8.56

The /Graph, Customize Series, Markers & Lines, Formats, 1st Series menu

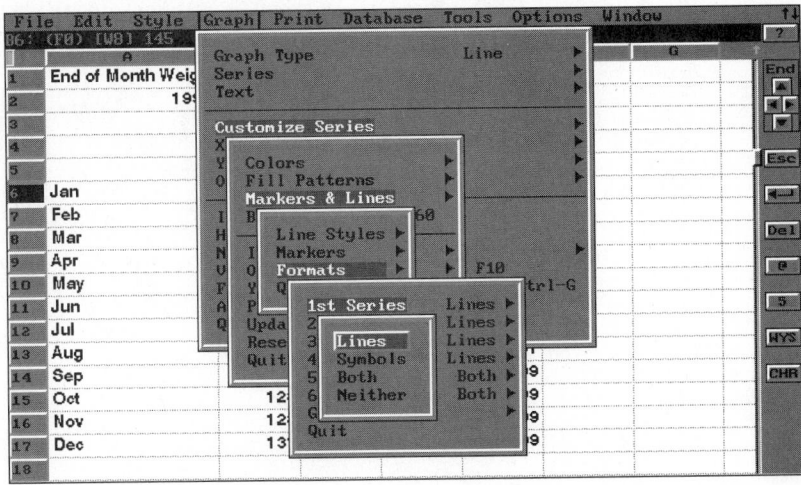

9. Repeat this process to select all the following Line Styles settings:

/Graph, Customize Series, Markers & Lines	Setting
Line Styles, 1st Series	Heavy Solid
Line Styles, 2nd Series	Heavy Dotted
Line Styles, 3rd Series	Heavy Centered
Line Styles, 4th Series	Heavy Dashed

Now when you press F10 (Graph), Quattro Pro displays the line graph in Figure 8.58. Notice that each data series is now represented by a different line style, and that the use of Heavy line styles makes the lines more apparent in the graph. Additionally, the legend automatically changes to reflect the new line style.

Next we'll change our line graph to portray the data using various markers, and no lines. Use the following procedure.

1. Select /Graph, Customize Series, Markers & Lines, Formats, and specify Symbols for the 1st through 4th Series. Select Quit to return to the Markers & Lines menu.

Figure 8.57

The Line Styles selections in WYSIWYG mode

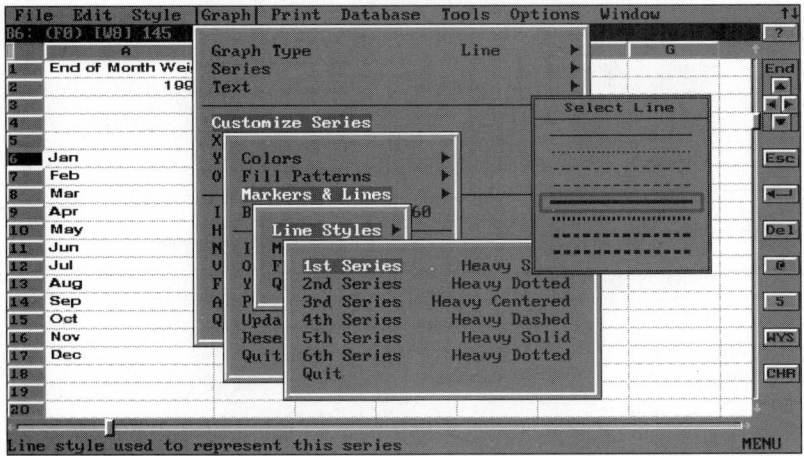

Figure 8.58

The improved graph, with custom line styles and no markers

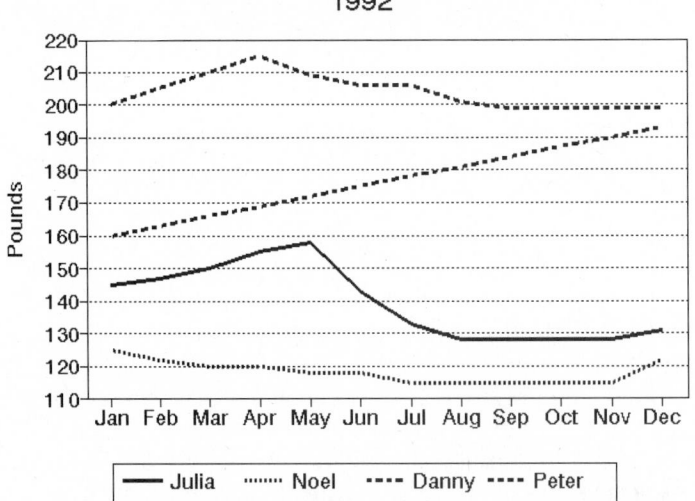

2. Select Markers to view the Markers menu. Here, select 1st Series. If you are working in WYSIWYG mode, the pictorial menu of marker styles in Figure 8.59 is displayed. Choose the Filled Triangle marker, and Quattro Pro returns to the Markers menu, where this selection is now displayed.

Figure 8.59
The Markers selection in WYSIWYG mode

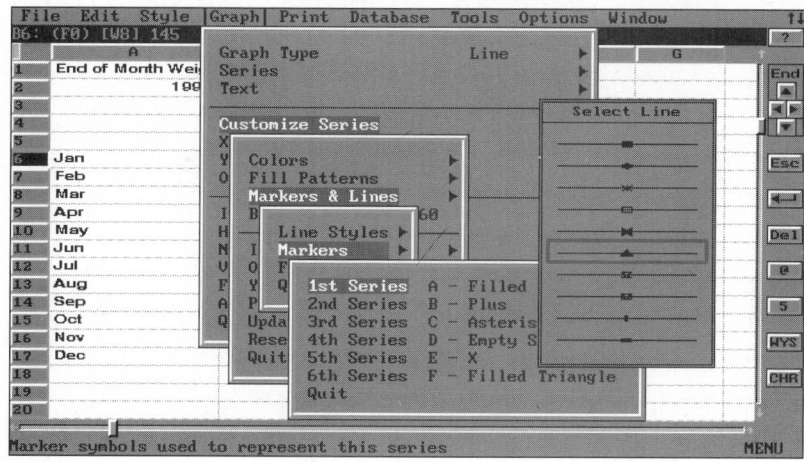

Note. You can change the Markers settings in Quattro Pro 4.0's /Graph, Custom Series dialog box.

3. Repeat this process to specify all these Markers selections:

/Graph, Customize Series, Markers & Lines	Setting
Markers, 1st Series	F - Filled Triangle
Markers, 2nd Series	G - Hourglass
Markers, 3rd Series	H - Square with X
Markers, 4th Series	C - Asterisk

Press F10 (Graph) to see your graph with its new marker settings (Figure 8.60). Notice that the data points in each series are represented by markers of different styles. Once again, Quattro Pro automatically adjusts the legend to display the appropriate marker next to each legend label.

When you change Markers & Lines settings, be aware of the following:

■ You can temporarily suppress a data series from being graphed—without deleting its /Graph, Series setting. For instance, to suppress the 2nd Series block, use /Graph, Customize Series, Markers & Lines, Formats,

2nd Series, Neither. Quattro Pro will graph all the defined series blocks except the 2nd Series.

Figure 8.60
The graph with customized markers and no lines

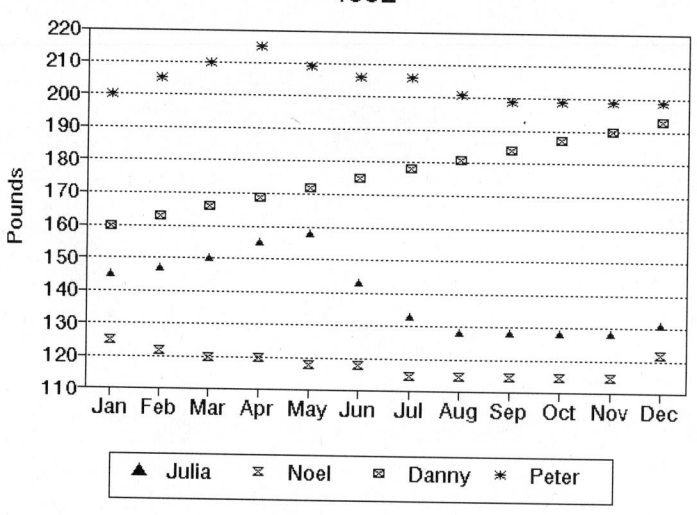

End of Month Weight
1992

- When you use markers in a line graph, it is usually best to use a Solid line style for all data series; otherwise, the graph appears cluttered.

- You can use the Formats, Symbols setting to create a scatter diagram of data points, as explained earlier for XY graphs.

- You can save the current Markers & Lines settings as new defaults, using /Graph, Customize Series, Update.

Customizing the Y-Axis and X-Axis

Note. All of these items are available in Quattro Pro 4.0's /Graph, X-Axis and /Graph, Y-Axis dialog boxes. To add a second Y-Axis, choose the 2nd Y-Axis button.

All graphs except pie and column charts include an x-axis and a y-axis. The graphed values are plotted along the y-axis, which Quattro Pro automatically scales to include the highest and lowest values. When you want to customize the y-axis, you can do it in the following ways:

- Change the *scale*. You can specify the smallest and largest values, the *increment* that controls when values are displayed, as well as the number of minor tickmarks between each displayed value.

- Change the way values are displayed, such as their numeric format, or the type of scale display.

- Use a logarithmic scale.

- Add a second y-axis, which you can also customize.

Remember that the x-axis is not usually a numeric scale. Rather, it conveys descriptive information about the data graphed. So, you usually don't customize the x-axis in the same way as the y-axis. An important customization option, however, is that you can display x-axis labels in two tiers. This is an effective way to handle a graph that includes many or long x-axis labels, as demonstrated later in this chapter in "Customizing the X-Axis."

The x-axis in an XY graph, however, does represent a sliding numeric scale, and in this graph Quattro Pro plots values against both the x- and y-axes. So Quattro Pro provides you most of the same customization options for the x-axis. One exception is that you cannot add a second x-axis.

Customizing the Y-Axis

Suppose you are the lucky owner of Hotdog Heaven, Inc. As shown in Figure 8.61, you started the firm in 1982 with one store. By 1992, your company owns and operates 100 locations that generate $20,000,000 in gross revenues. To graph this impressive sales growth, you can use the /Graph settings in Table 8.13 to create the line graph in Figure 8.62.

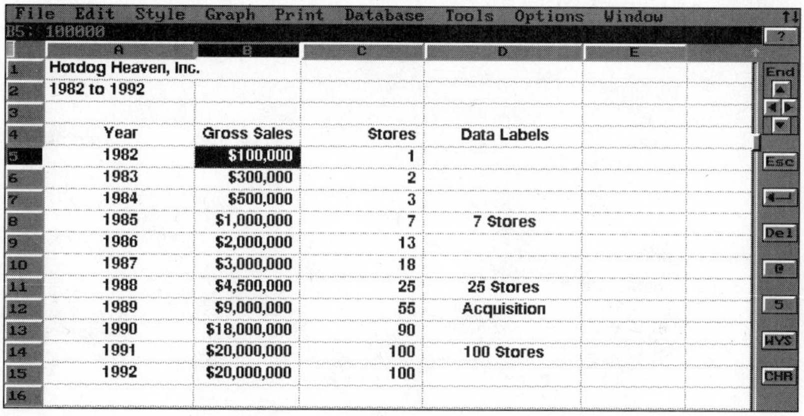

Figure 8.61

Hotdog Heaven's data, used to create the graphs in Figures 8.62, 8.65, 8.66, and 8.69

	A	B	C	D	E
1	Hotdog Heaven, Inc.				
2	1982 to 1992				
3					
4	Year	Gross Sales	Stores	Data Labels	
5	1982	$100,000	1		
6	1983	$300,000	2		
7	1984	$500,000	3		
8	1985	$1,000,000	7	7 Stores	
9	1986	$2,000,000	13		
10	1987	$3,000,000	18		
11	1988	$4,500,000	25	25 Stores	
12	1989	$9,000,000	55	Acquisition	
13	1990	$18,000,000	90		
14	1991	$20,000,000	100	100 Stores	
15	1992	$20,000,000	100		
16					

File Edit Style Graph Print Database Tools Options Window
B5: 100000
End Esc Del @ 5 HYS CHR

Table 8.13 **Graph Settings Used with Figure 8.61 to Create Line Graphs in Figures 8.62, 8.65, 8.66, and 8.69**

/Graph Commands	Figure 8.62 Settings	Figure 8.65 Settings	Figure 8.66 Settings	Figure 8.69 Settings
Graph Type	Line	Line	Line	Line
Series				
1st Series	B5..B15	B5..B15	B5..B15	B5..B15
2nd Series				C5..C15
X-Axis Series	A5..A15	A5..A15	A5..A15	A5..A15
Text				
1st Line	\A1	\A1	\A1	\A1
2nd Line	\A2	\A2	\A2	·\A2
X-Title	\A4	\A4	\A4	\A4
Y-Title	\B4	\B4	\B4	\B4
Secondary Y-Axis				\C4
Text, Legends				
1st Series				\B4
2nd Series				\C4
Y-Axis				
Scale		Manual	Automatic	Manual
Low		0		0
High		22000000		22000000
Increment		1000000		1000000
Format of Ticks		Currency 0	Comma 0	Currency 0
No. of Minor Ticks		1		1
Display Scaling		Yes		Yes
Mode		Normal	Log	Normal

Table 8.13 **(Continued)**

/Graph Commands	Figure 8.62 Settings	Figure 8.65 Settings	Figure 8.66 Settings	Figure 8.69 Settings
2nd Y-Axis				
Scale			Automatic	
Format of Ticks			General	
Customize Series, Interior Labels				
1st Series Block		D5..D15	D5..D15	
1st Series Position		Above	Above	
Customize Series, Markers & Lines,				
Line Styles				
1st Series			Heavy Solid	
2nd Series			Heavy Dashed	
Customize Series, Markers & Lines,				
Formats				
1st Series			Lines	
2nd Series			Lines	
Customize Series, Y-Axis				
1st Series			Primary Y-Axis	
2nd Series			Secondary Y-Axis	
X-Axis				
Alternative Ticks		Yes	Yes	
Overall, Grid		Clear	Clear	

Figure 8.62

The data from Figure 8.61 graphed using Table 8.13's settings for Figure 8.62, and the default /Graph, Y-Axis and X-Axis settings

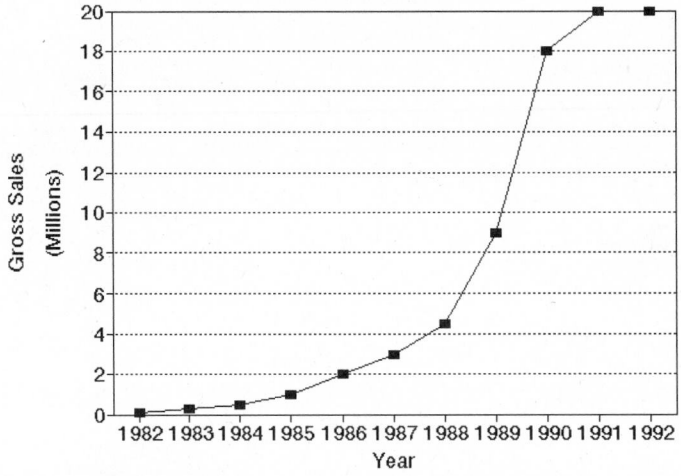

Note. When you graph extremely large values, Quattro Pro will display a scaling multiplier label of "(Times 10E9)", not "Billions".

Quattro Pro automatically adjusts a y-axis scale to accommodate all of the graphed values. In Figure 8.62, it creates the y-axis scale from 0 to 20 million, labeling these low and high values as well as each 2 million increment between these values.

Notice in Figure 8.62 that Quattro Pro automatically divides each y-axis value by 1,000,000, and then uses (Millions) as the identifying label, or *scaling multiplier.* Quattro Pro creates this type of y-axis scale when the values in a graph are in the thousands or greater, and so many 0's would create a cluttered y-axis. You can control this scaling display; select /Graph, Y-Axis, Display Scaling, No to turn it off, or Yes to restore it.

In many instances, you will want to specify your own Y-Axis settings. Customizing the y-axis in Figure 8.62, for example, will create a better-looking graph. In addition, to include the data labels shown in Figure 8.61, you must add space at the top of the graph by increasing the upper value displayed on the y-axis. You can use the following procedure to customize the y-axis and to add these data labels:

1. Select /Graph, Y-Axis. You'll see the Y-Axis menu in Figure 8.63, which lists Quattro Pro's default Y-Axis settings.

2. Choose Scale to see a menu with two options: Automatic and Manual. Select Manual so that Quattro Pro uses the other Y-Axis settings you will specify. The Y-Axis menu reappears.

3. Select Low to specify the smallest value in the y-axis scale. In response to the "Enter Y-Axis Minimum:" prompt, type **0** and press Enter. The Y-Axis menu returns.

4. Choose High to specify the highest value in the y-axis scale. Remember, you need to include extra space at the top of the graph to leave room for the last data label. Therefore, in response to the prompt for the Y-Axis Maximum, type **22000000** and press Enter. The Y-Axis menu returns.

5. Select Increment. This option lets you tell Quattro Pro when to display a tickmark labeled with the corresponding value. You'll be prompted to enter "The values by which to increment numbers labeling the axis." Enter **1000000**, and press Enter.

6. Choose Format of Ticks to specify the numeric format for the y-axis values. A menu is displayed listing the numeric formats. Select Currency, and Quattro Pro displays the Places screen shown in Figure 8.64. Type **0** places, and press Enter. The Y-Axis menu reappears.

7. Select No. of Minor Ticks. You want the y-axis to include tickmarks every $1 million; however, only every other tickmark needs to be labeled. Therefore, in response to the prompt "Number of minor ticks between each labeled tick (0 to 240):", type **1** and press Enter. When the Y-Axis menu returns, select Quit to return to the /Graph menu.

Figure 8.63
The /Graph, Y-Axis menu, with default settings

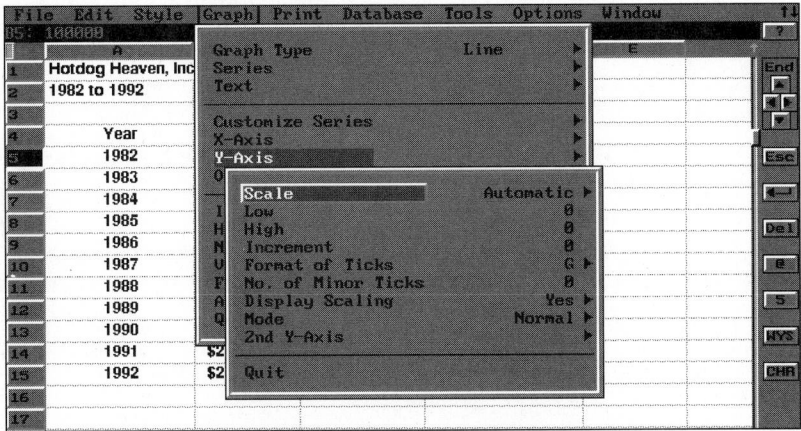

8. Choose Customize Series, Interior Labels, 1st Series and specify **D5..D15**. When Quattro Pro displays the Placement menu, select Above.

Figure 8.64

The /Graph, Y-Axis, Format of Ticks, Currency Places screen

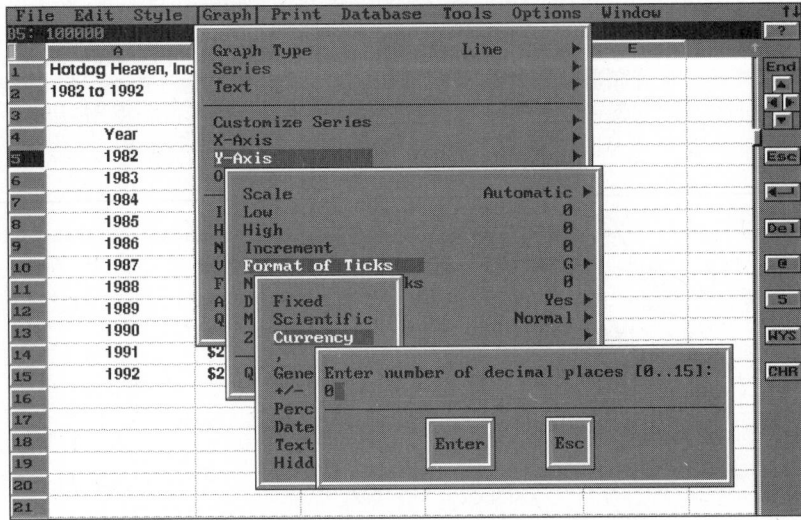

Now when you press F10 (Graph), Quattro Pro creates the graph in Figure 8.65. As you can see, the y-axis scale includes values from $0 to $22 million, which allows room for the data label 100 Stores at the top of the graph. It labels every other tickmark—$2 (Million), $4 (Million), and so on—and includes one minor tickmark between each labeled tickmark. Finally, each value on the y-axis scale is preceded by a $, reflecting your Currency Format selection.

Using a Logarithmic Scale

Note. You cannot use a logarithmic scale when the graphed data includes 0 or negative values.

In Quattro Pro, you can also create a graph that uses a *logarithmic*, or *log scale*. In a log scale, each value displayed along the y-axis represents ten times the previous value. You will want to use a log scale when a graph includes values that vary wildly in magnitude. Additionally, logarithmic scaling is often used to graph values that increase or decrease geometrically, such as population growth.

The values in Figure 8.61 are good candidates for a log scale, because the Gross Sales values range from $100,000 all the way to $20 million. To create the graph in Figure 8.66,

- Select /Graph, Y-Axis, Mode, and Quattro Pro displays two mode choices: Normal and Log. Choose Log, and Quattro Pro returns to the Y-Axis menu.

Figure 8.65

The Hotdog Heaven graph using the /Graph settings from Table 8.13, including custom Y-Axis settings

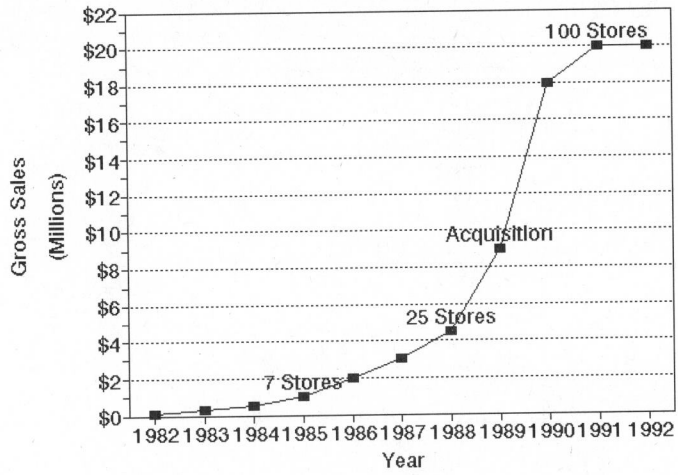

Hotdog Heaven, Inc.
1982 to 1992

- Because you have chosen Log mode, you should also specify Scale, Automatic; Quattro Pro takes it from there.

- The only other Y-Axis setting you need to specify is Format of Ticks. Choose , (Comma) and 0 places. (If you use a Currency 0 format, Quattro Pro displays the highest y-axis value, $100,000,000, as asterisks.)

When you press F10 (Graph), Quattro Pro displays the graph with a logarithmic y-axis in Figure 8.66 (this graph also uses the other /Graph settings in Table 8.13).

Notice that four y-axis values are displayed, each increasing by a factor of ten. As you can see, a logarithmic scale often makes a nonlinear relationship (like that in Figure 8.62) appear linear.

Customizing the X-Axis

Because you are creating a line graph in the Hotdog Heaven example, the x-axis conveys descriptive information about the graphed data. The /Graph, Series, X-Axis Series setting (A5..A15 in Figure 8.61) is used to specify the x-axis labels. Beginning with the first label in this block, 1982 in cell A5, Quattro Pro creates x-axis labels from left to right as shown in Figure 8.65.

When you use a logarithmic y-axis scale, however, Quattro Pro resizes the graph and decreases the length of the x-axis. You can see this by comparing Figures 8.65 and 8.66. This often happens when you change the range of values graphed, or change the y-axis scale, or use a different graph type. A common result can be cramped x-axis labels. (You may encounter a similar problem when Quattro Pro cannot fit all of the labels along the x-axis.) This problem has been solved in Figure 8.66 by adjusting the placement of tickmarks on the x-axis.

Figure 8.66
A graph of the data from Figure 8.61, using the /Graph settings from Table 8.13, with a logarithmic y-axis and alternative x-axis tickmarks

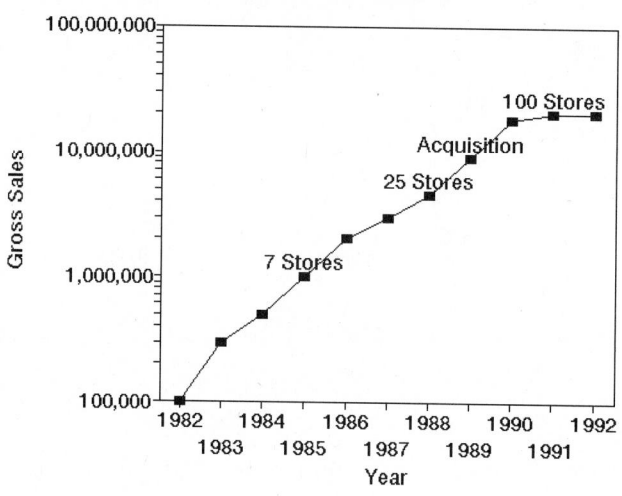

Note. You can also use a smaller font to solve many x-axis label problems. See "Changing Fonts" earlier in this chapter.

As you can see in Table 8.13, the settings for Figure 8.66 include /Graph, X-Axis, Alternative Ticks, Yes. When you set this option to Yes, Quattro Pro displays the x-axis labels in two tiers, which you can see in Figure 8.66.

When the x-axis conveys descriptive information, the only X-Axis selections that work (besides Alternative Ticks) are No. of Minor Ticks and Format of Ticks. For instance, specify No. of Minor Ticks 1, and Quattro Pro will only label every other tickmark, such as 1982, 1984, 1986, and so on, in the Hotdog Heaven graph. Keep this in mind as another option when x-axis labels are not effectively displayed. Additionally, Format of Ticks lets you change the numeric format of spreadsheet values that are used as x-axis labels. (Format of Ticks does *not* affect labels.)

In an XY graph, you can use the /Graph, X-Axis command to customize the x-axis in the same manner as /Graph, Y-Axis to customize the y-axis. See the earlier section, "Customizing the Y-Axis," for details.

Adding a Second Y-Axis

In some instances, a single y-axis does not accurately portray the graphed data. Look again at Figure 8.61; suppose you want to include both the Gross Sales and the number of stores in the same graph. The number of stores varies from 1 to 100, and the Gross Sales revenue varies from $100,000 to $20,000,000. If you use one y-axis you won't be able to differentiate the number of Stores values.

To overcome just such a problem, Quattro Pro lets you add a second y-axis to a line, bar, XY, or mixed graph. This second y-axis is displayed on the right side of the graph, and employs a scale based on the values in the series blocks that use this second y-axis.

For instance, you can use Table 8.13's /Graph settings for Figure 8.69 to create a graph of the data from Figure 8.61, using two y-axes. Select /Graph, Y-Axis, 2nd Y-Axis, and you see the menu in Figure 8.67. Notice how similar this menu is to the Y-Axis menu. In this case, however, there is no need to specify custom settings; you can use the default settings shown in this menu.

Figure 8.67

The /Graph, Y-Axis, 2nd Y-Axis menu with the default settings

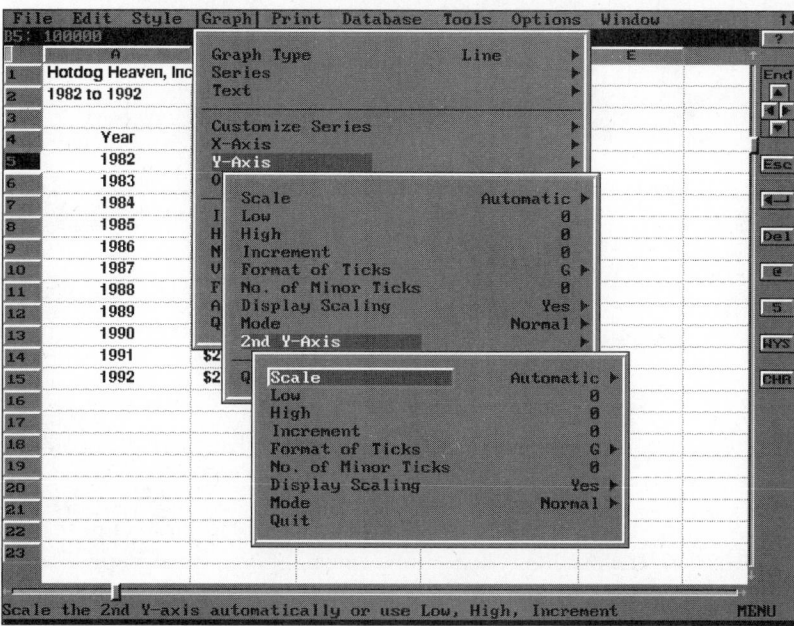

To specify which series blocks are graphed against each y-axis, select /Graph, Customize Series, Y-Axis. The default assignment for each series

block is the Primary Y-Axis. So select 2nd Series, and Quattro Pro displays the menu in Figure 8.68. Here, choose Secondary Y-Axis. Based on these settings, Quattro Pro plots the 1st Series block, B5..B15 containing the sales values, using the primary y-axis. On the same graph, it plots the 2nd Series block, C5..C15 containing the number of stores, using the secondary y-axis. Because you opted for the 2nd Y-Axis default settings, Quattro Pro scales the second y-axis using the values in the 2nd Series block. You can see the resulting graph in Figure 8.69.

Figure 8.68

Using /Graph, Customize Series, Y-Axis to specify the data series graphed against the primary and secondary y-axes

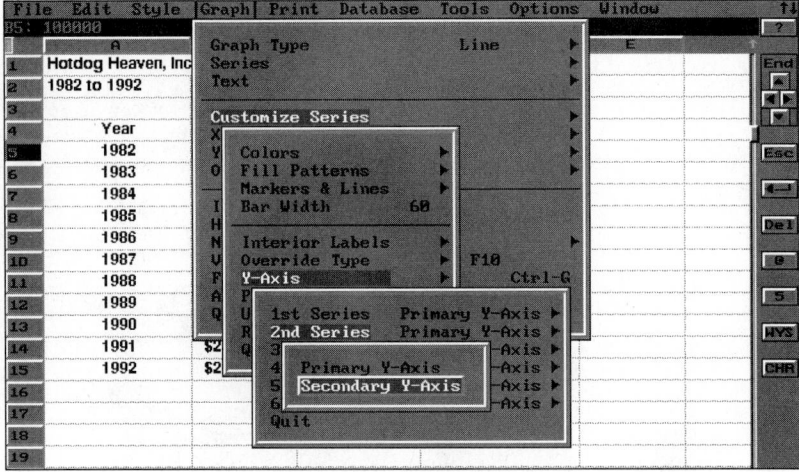

Keep in mind the following when you define a second y-axis:

■ Use /Graph, Text, Secondary Y-Axis to designate a title for this axis.

■ If you add a second y-axis to a stacked bar, rotated bar, or area graph, Quattro Pro only includes the primary y-axis, and *only* the series graphed against the primary y-axis. Neither the secondary y-axis nor the series graphed against this axis is displayed.

■ If you include a second y-axis in a 3-D graph, Quattro Pro only graphs the primary y-axis; however, it ignores the /Graph, Customize Series, Y-Axis settings and graphs all data series against this primary y-axis, including those assigned to the secondary y-axis.

Figure 8.69
A graph of the data from Figure 8.61, using the /Graph settings in Table 8.13, with two y-axes

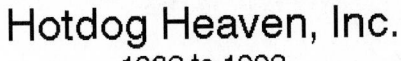
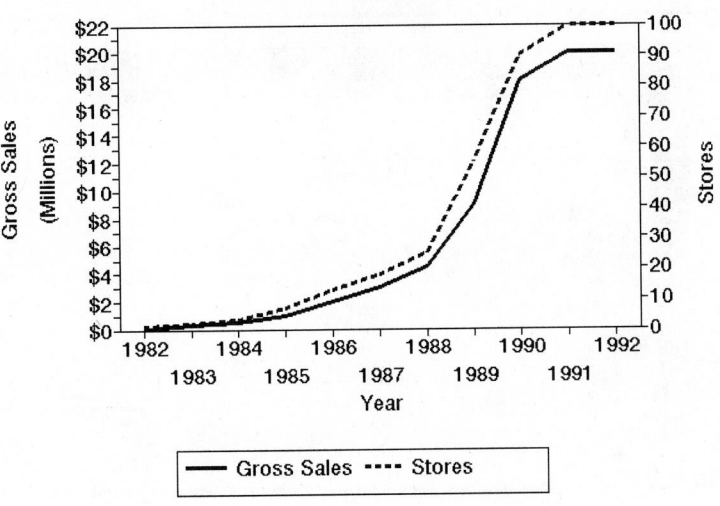

Customizing Pie and Column Charts

The /Graph, Customize Series, Pies command lets you customize pie and column charts by

- Changing the label format (the type of value included in the labels describing each pie wedge or column segment)

- Changing the fill patterns and colors

- Deleting the tickmark connecting each pie slice or column segment to its identifying label

- Emphasizing (exploding) one or more wedges of a pie chart

Tip. You can also use /Graph, Series, 2nd Series to assign fill patterns and colors, and to explode wedges of a pie chart. See the end of this section.

NOTE. *In Quattro Pro 4.0, the commands for customizing pie and column charts are in the /Graph, Customize Series dialog box.*

For instance, suppose your company, Kleinmann Electronics, achieves the 1992 financial information shown in Figure 8.70. You can use the /Graph settings in Table 8.14 to represent this data as the pie chart in Figure 8.71. This pie chart uses Quattro Pro's default pie chart settings: a percentage label format, default fill patterns, tickmarks, and no exploded wedges.

However, you can use the same financial data and the /Graph command to create the pie chart in Figure 8.72. The relevant /Graph, Customize Series, Pies settings are discussed in the subsequent paragraphs.

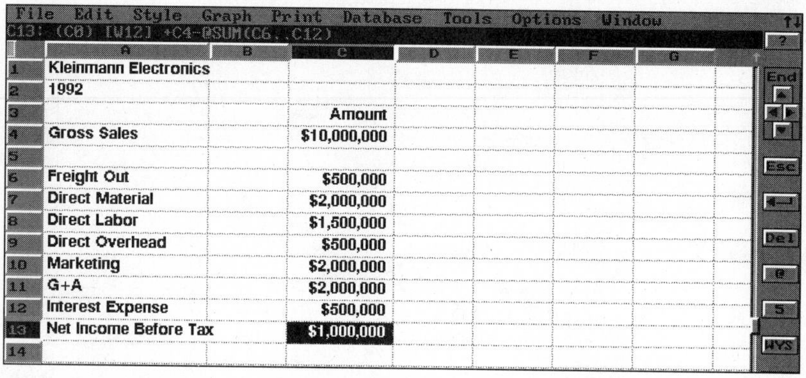

Figure 8.70
The spreadsheet data used to create the pie charts in Figures 8.71 and 8.72

	A	B	C	D	E	F	G
	File Edit Style Graph Print Database Tools Options Window						
	C13: (C0) [W12] +C4-@SUM(C6..C12)						
1	Kleinmann Electronics						
2	1992						
3			Amount				
4	Gross Sales		$10,000,000				
5							
6	Freight Out		$500,000				
7	Direct Material		$2,000,000				
8	Direct Labor		$1,500,000				
9	Direct Overhead		$500,000				
10	Marketing		$2,000,000				
11	G+A		$2,000,000				
12	Interest Expense		$500,000				
13	Net Income Before Tax		$1,000,000				
14							

Figure 8.71
The "default" pie chart of the data from Figure 8.70

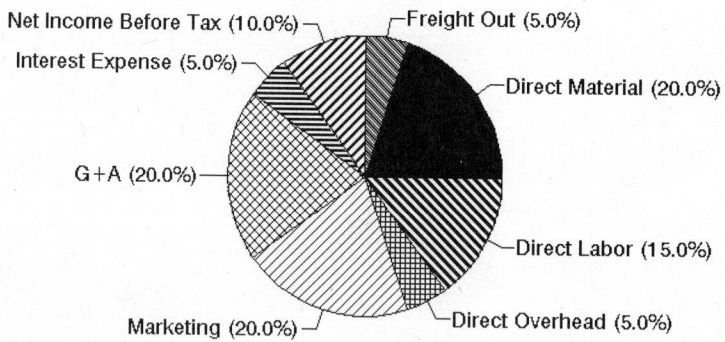

Kleinmann Electronics
1992

Net Income Before Tax (10.0%)
Freight Out (5.0%)
Interest Expense (5.0%)
Direct Material (20.0%)
G+A (20.0%)
Direct Labor (15.0%)
Marketing (20.0%)
Direct Overhead (5.0%)

Note. Use /Graph, Customize Series, Update to save your customized Pies settings as defaults.

Label Format

By default, Quattro Pro labels each slice in a pie chart with the percentage that slice represents of the total pie, as illustrated in Figure 8.71. If you have included a /Graph, Series, X-Axis Series block, the appropriate percentage is placed directly after each label. Likewise, Quattro Pro automatically includes this percentage for each segment in a column graph.

Table 8.14 **Graph Settings Used with Figure 8.70 to Create Pie Chart in Figure 8.71**

/Graph Commands	Settings
Graph Type	Pie
Series	
1st Series	C6..C13
X-Axis Series	A6..A13
Text	
1st Line	\A1
2nd Line	\A2

Figure 8.72

The customized pie chart of the data from Figure 8.70

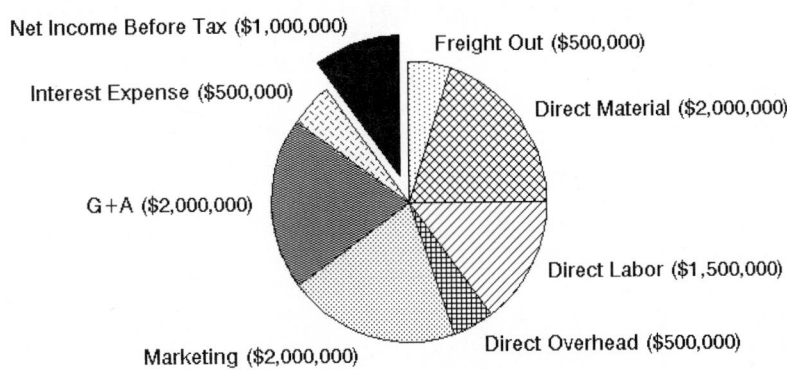

Kleinmann Electronics
1992

Net Income Before Tax ($1,000,000)
Freight Out ($500,000)
Interest Expense ($500,000)
Direct Material ($2,000,000)
G+A ($2,000,000)
Direct Labor ($1,500,000)
Marketing ($2,000,000)
Direct Overhead ($500,000)

Instead, you can display the value of each slice or segment, and even precede it with a $ sign if you wish. For example, here's how to include the dollar values shown in Figure 8.72.

1. Select /Graph, Customize Series, Pies. Quattro Pro displays the Pies menu in Figure 8.73, with the default Label Format, %.

2. Choose Label Format, and you see the menu in Figure 8.74. Select $, and Quattro Pro now displays this format in the Pies menu.

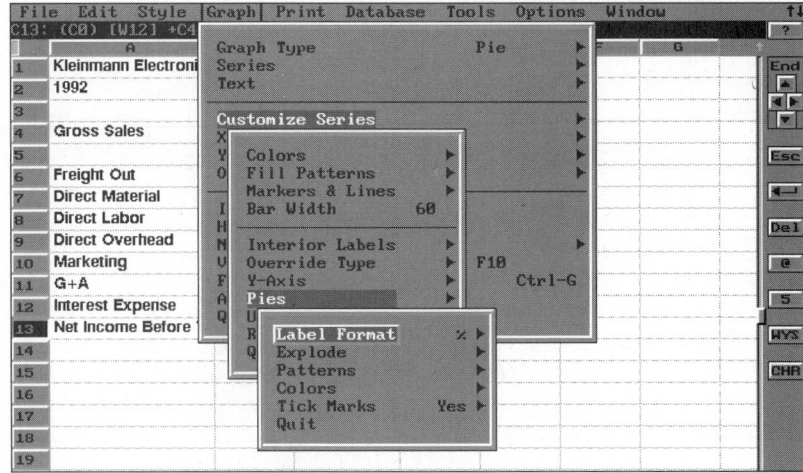

Figure 8.73
The /Graph, Customize Series, Pies menu

Keep in mind the following when you are working with Pie labels:

- To suppress the labels from a pie or column chart without deleting the /Graph, Series, X-Axis Series block, select /Graph, Customize Series, Pies, Label Format, None.

- Value and $ label formats usually result in longer labels than the % format.

Tickmarks

Note. Remember, the first value in the data series is assigned to the first slice at the 12 o'clock position, the second value is represented by the second slice, and so on, in a clockwise direction.

Quattro Pro automatically draws a tickmark from each slice of a pie to its corresponding label (see Figure 8.71). Similarly, Quattro Pro draws a tick-mark from each segment of a column graph to its corresponding label. A tickmark helps to associate a label to the appropriate pie wedge or column segment. However, many times these relationships are obvious, and the tick-marks only make the graph look cluttered.

For example, in Figure 8.71 it is obvious which label belongs to each pie wedge. To remove the tickmarks select /Graph, Customize Series, Pies to see the menu in Figure 8.73. Choose Tick Marks, and then select No to remove all tickmarks. Quattro Pro returns to the Pies menu. Now when you press F10 (Graph), Quattro Pro creates a pie chart without tickmarks, like that in Figure 8.72.

Figure 8.74

The list of formats for pie labels

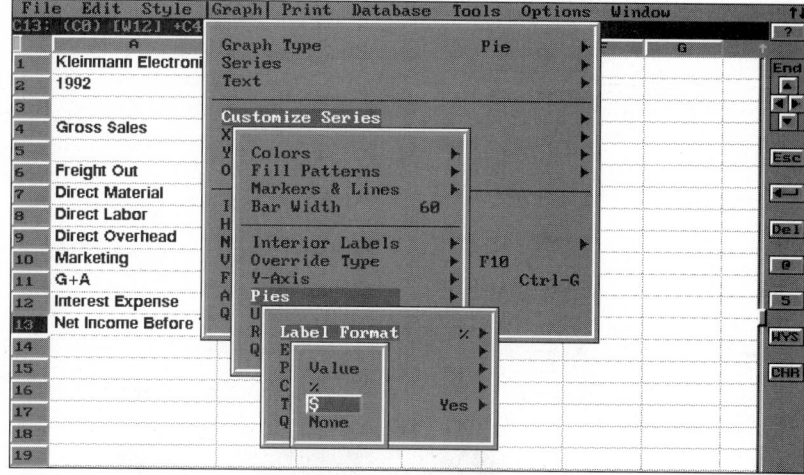

Fill Patterns

Quattro Pro automatically uses the fill patterns, shown in Figure 8.71, in a pie or column chart to differentiate each wedge or segment. As you can see, the contrast between the default fill patterns is distinct; you may prefer to use different fill patterns.

For example, do the following to assign the fill patterns in Figure 8.72:

Note. If a pie or column chart has more than nine slices, Quattro Pro repeats the assigned patterns, so the tenth slice will appear in the same pattern as the first slice.

1. To change the fill pattern of the first slice, select /Graph, Customize Series, Pies, Patterns. Quattro Pro displays the Patterns menu in Figure 8.75, with nine different slice selections.

2. Choose 1st Slice, and Quattro Pro displays a list of available patterns. If you are working in WYSIWYG mode, you'll see the pictorial menu in Figure 8.75. Choose K - Light Dots, and press Enter. Quattro Pro returns to the Patterns menu.

3. Repeat this process to complete the following Patterns settings:

/Graph, Customize Series, Pies, Patterns	Setting
1st Slice	K - Light Dots
2nd Slice	I - Crosshatch
3rd Slice	D - Light \\\

/Graph, Customize Series, Pies, Patterns	Setting
4th Slice	H - ++++++
5th Slice	L - Heavy Dots
6th Slice	J - Hatch
7th Slice	P - Stitch
8th Slice	B - Filled

Figure 8.75
The /Graph, Customize Series, Pies, Patterns choices

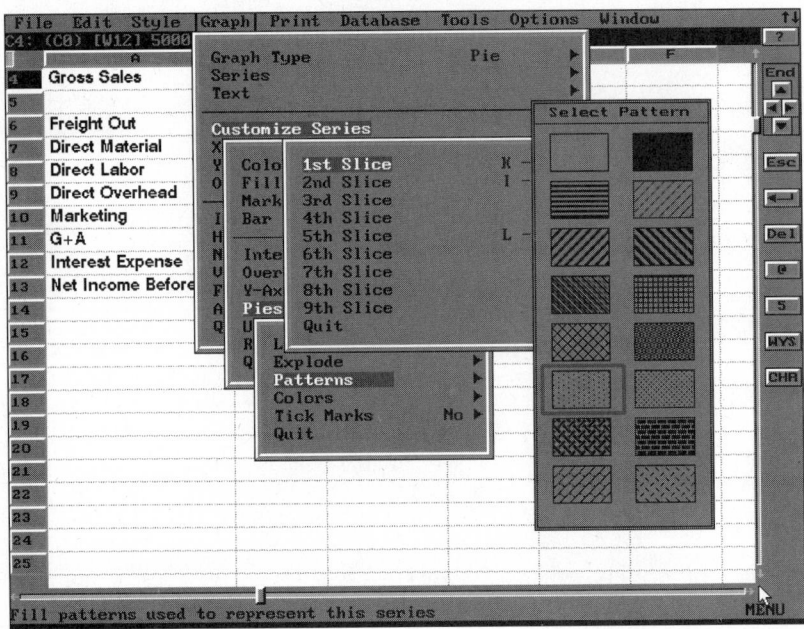

Note. If a pie or column chart has more than nine values, Quattro Pro repeats the assigned colors, so the tenth pie slice will appear in the same color as the first slice.

The result is a pie chart like Figure 8.72. As you can see, the new fill patterns portray the information more subtly than the default patterns in Figure 8.71.

Colors

Quattro Pro assigns a different color to each slice of a pie chart and to each segment of a column chart. (If you have a color monitor, you can display these colors by first selecting /Graph, Overall, Colors/B&W, Color.)

The /Graph, Customize Series, Pies, Colors command lets you change these colors to your liking. For example, to assign Light Blue to the first slice (value) in Figure 8.71, choose 1st Slice, and Quattro Pro displays the list of colors shown in Figure 8.76. (If you are working in WYSIWYG mode, Quattro Pro displays the actual colors.) For this example, choose Light Blue, and then press Enter. Your selection is reflected in the Colors menu. When you view this graph, Quattro Pro displays the first slice in Light Blue and with the assigned fill pattern.

Figure 8.76

The /Graph, Customize Series, Pies, Colors choices

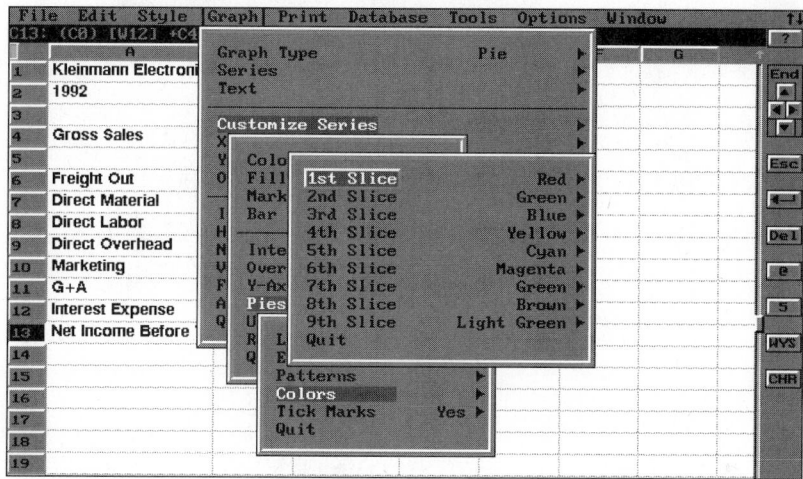

TIP. *You can create a pie or column chart that uses colors and no fill patterns. Use /Graph, Customize Series, Pies, Patterns and specify B - Filled for each slice. Quattro Pro represents each slice using its Colors setting but with no fill pattern.*

Exploding Pieces of a Pie

In a pie chart, you can emphasize one or more slices by *exploding* them, or pulling them away from the center of the pie. (You cannot explode segments of a column chart.)

For instance, in Figure 8.71, the Net Income Before Tax value, $500,000, is the most important value portrayed in the pie chart. Here's how to emphasize this slice.

1. Select /Graph, Customize Series, Pies, Explode. Quattro Pro displays the menu in Figure 8.77.

Figure 8.77
The /Graph,
Customize Series,
Pies, Explode menu

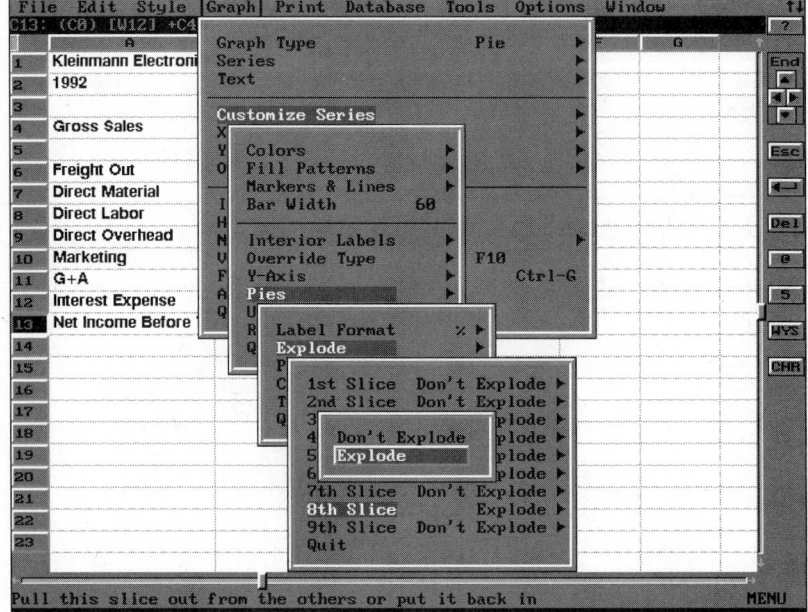

2. Select 8th Slice. Remember—Quattro Pro graphs a pie chart by placing the first slice at the 12 o'clock position, and then proceeding clockwise. Since Net Income is the eighth value in the 1st Series block, it is represented by the 8th Slice.

3. From the frontmost menu in Figure 8.77, choose Explode to pull this slice away from the pie. You can see the result in Figure 8.72.

Using a 2nd Series to Enhance Pie and Column Charts

As you know, when Quattro Pro creates a pie chart, it only graphs the values in the 1st Series block. However, you can specify a 2nd Series block to explode, color, and fill the slices of a pie chart. You can also use this method to assign colors and fill patterns to segments of a column chart.

When you graph a pie or column chart, Quattro Pro evaluates the data in the 2nd Series block in a special way. The value 0 represents the first color and pattern specified in the Pies, Colors and Pies, Patterns menus. The value 1 represents the second color and pattern; the value 2 represents the third color and fill pattern; and so on. The value 100 tells Quattro Pro to explode a slice.

The easiest way to see this is through an example. Let's return to Kleinmann Electronics' 1992 financial data. A second data series is specified with

/Graph, Series, 2nd Series as D6..D13 in Figure 8.78. In this second data series, Quattro Pro evaluates the value 7 in cell D7 and assigns the eighth fill pattern and color to the second slice. The eighth value, 107 in cell D13, assigns the eighth fill pattern to the eighth slice, and also explodes this slice. You can see the results in Figure 8.79, which also uses the other custom Pies, Patterns settings assigned earlier.

Figure 8.78

Using a 2nd Series to explode and assign patterns and colors to sections of a pie chart

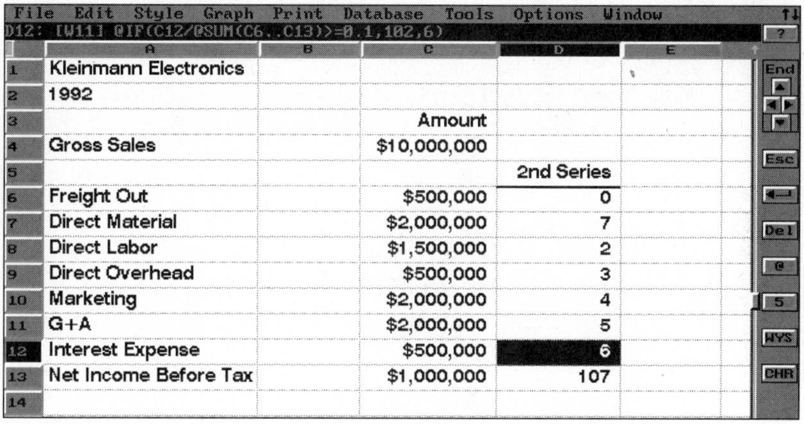

File Edit Style Graph Print Database Tools Options Window				
D12: [W11] @IF(C12/@SUM(C6..C13)>=0.1,102,6)				

	A	B	C	D	E
1	Kleinmann Electronics				
2	1992				
3			Amount		
4	Gross Sales		$10,000,000		
5				2nd Series	
6	Freight Out		$500,000	0	
7	Direct Material		$2,000,000	7	
8	Direct Labor		$1,500,000	2	
9	Direct Overhead		$500,000	3	
10	Marketing		$2,000,000	4	
11	G+A		$2,000,000	5	
12	Interest Expense		$500,000	6	
13	Net Income Before Tax		$1,000,000	107	
14					

Figure 8.79

A pie chart using the 2nd Series block from Figure 8.78

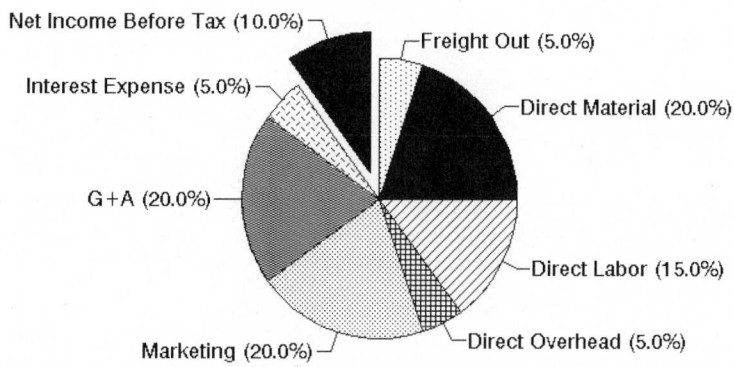

Kleinmann Electronics
1992

Net Income Before Tax (10.0%) — Freight Out (5.0%) — Direct Material (20.0%) — Interest Expense (5.0%) — G+A (20.0%) — Direct Labor (15.0%) — Marketing (20.0%) — Direct Overhead (5.0%)

You can also control the appearance of a slice by using a formula. For instance, look at the input line in Figure 8.78. Cell D12 contains the formula

```
@IF(C12/@SUM(C6..C13)>=.1,102,6)
```

Since the value in C12, $500,000, is less than 10% of the total value, this formula returns the value 6. Therefore, this slice is graphed using the seventh pattern and color. However, if the value in C12 were equal to or greater than $1 million, this formula would return the value 102, and the slice would be exploded and graphed using the third fill pattern and color.

Customizing the Overall Graph

The /Graph, Overall command lets you customize certain features of the entire graph. When you select this command, Quattro Pro offers you the following choices:

Note. In Quattro Pro 4.0, to change the settings that affect the entire graph regardless of the graph type, use the /Graph, Overall dialog box.

- *Grid* lets you control the type of grid displayed, the graph background color within the x- and y-axes, the color and line style of the grid lines, and the color of most other lines in the graph.

- *Outlines* lets you remove or add boxes around the graph titles, the legend, and even the entire graph.

- *Background Color* controls the background color *outside* of the x- and y-axes.

- *Overall, Three-D* controls the three-dimensional effect in all types of bar graphs, in pie and column charts, and in 3-D graphs. The default is Yes, which enables the three-dimensional effect; No removes it.

- *Color/B&W* determines whether a graph is displayed on screen in color or black and white.

- *Drop Shadow Color* controls the shadow color for the drop shadow typestyle. See "Changing Fonts" earlier in this chapter.

Grid Settings

Let's return to Hotdog Heaven, Inc. Imagine that you use the data in Figure 8.80 to create the two-line graph in Figure 8.81. This graph uses the /Graph, Overall default settings, which create bright white, dotted grid lines extending horizontally from each *labeled* y-axis tickmark.

Figure 8.80
Hotdog Heaven data graphed in Figures 8.81, 8.83, and 8.84

File Edit Style Graph Print Database Tools Options Window

E5: [W15] +B5/C5

	A	B	C	D	E
1	Hotdog Heaven, Inc.				
2	1982 to 1992				
3					
4	Year	Gross Sales	Stores	Data Labels	Sales Per Store
5	1982	$100,000	1		$100,000
6	1983	$300,000	2		$150,000
7	1984	$500,000	3		$166,667
8	1985	$1,000,000	7	7 Stores	$142,857
9	1986	$2,000,000	13		$153,846
10	1987	$3,000,000	18		$166,667
11	1988	$4,500,000	25	25 Stores	$180,000
12	1989	$9,000,000	55	Acquisition	$163,636
13	1990	$18,000,000	90		$200,000
14	1991	$20,000,000	100	100 Stores	$200,000
15	1992	$20,000,000	100		$200,000
16					

Figure 8.81
A line graph of the data from Figure 8.80, using the /Graph, Overall default settings

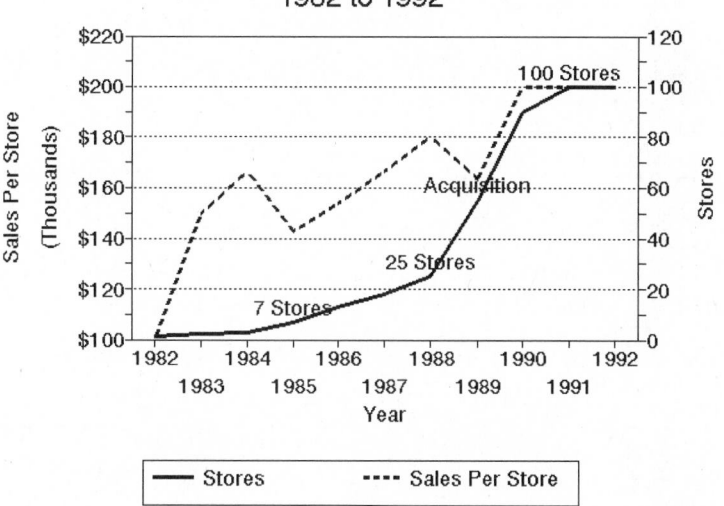

Looking at this graph, you see that it is clearly difficult to determine the value that corresponds to a particular year. You can improve the graph by including both horizontal and vertical grid lines, and by changing the grid line style, as follows:

1. Select /Graph, Overall, Grid, and you'll see the menu in Figure 8.82, which includes the default settings.

Figure 8.82

The /Graph, Overall Grid menu listing the default settings

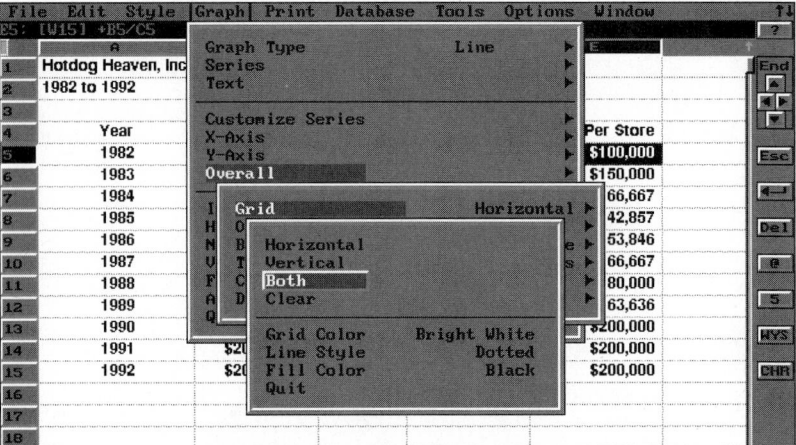

2. Select Both to create both horizontal and vertical grid lines.

3. Next choose Line Style from the Grid menu.

4. From the list of eight different line styles (a pictorial menu if you are in WYSIWYG mode), choose Solid.

5. Select Quit, and Quattro Pro returns to the Overall menu, which now displays your selections.

6. Press F10 (Graph) to view the graph in Figure 8.83.

Now that you have changed this graph, you can see that, in this instance, trends are more important than specific points. Furthermore, this grid style makes the graph look cluttered. A solution is to delete all grid lines to create a cleaner effect. To do this, select /Graph, Overall, Grid, Clear; this clears any previous Horizontal, Vertical, or Both selection. The result is a graph like that in Figure 8.84.

Figure 8.83
The graph from
Figure 8.81 after
using /Graph,
Overall, Both, and
Line Style, Solid

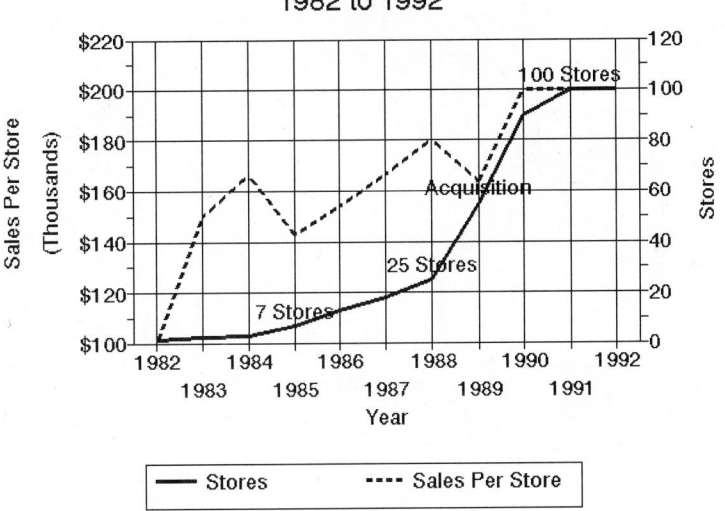

NOTE. *Typically, Quattro Pro creates a vertical grid line extending from each labeled x-axis tickmark. The exception, however, can be seen in Figure 8.83. When a graph includes two tiers of x-axis labels (specified by /Graph, X-Axis, Alternate Ticks, Yes), Quattro Pro includes a vertical grid line at each x-axis tickmark, even if the tickmark is not labeled.*

Graph, Title, and Legend Outlines

Quattro Pro automatically includes a single-line box around a legend, like that shown in Figure 8.81. However, you can use /Graph, Overall, Outlines to remove this box, and to add other types of boxes around the graph titles, the legend, and even the entire graph.

Here is how to create a sculpted box around the entire graph, as illustrated in Figure 8.84, as well as the shadow box around the legend and the rounded rectangle around the graph titles.

Note. To remove an outline setting— for example, the box around the legend in Figure 8.81—select /Graph, Overall, Outlines, Legend, None.

1. Select /Graph, Overall, Outlines, and Quattro Pro displays the menu in Figure 8.85, which includes the default settings.

2. Select Titles to see the menu in Figure 8.86.

3. Choose Rnd Rectangle, and Quattro Pro returns to the Outlines menu. Specify Legend, Shadow and then Graph, Sculpted.

Figure 8.84

The graph from
Figure 8.81,
without grid lines

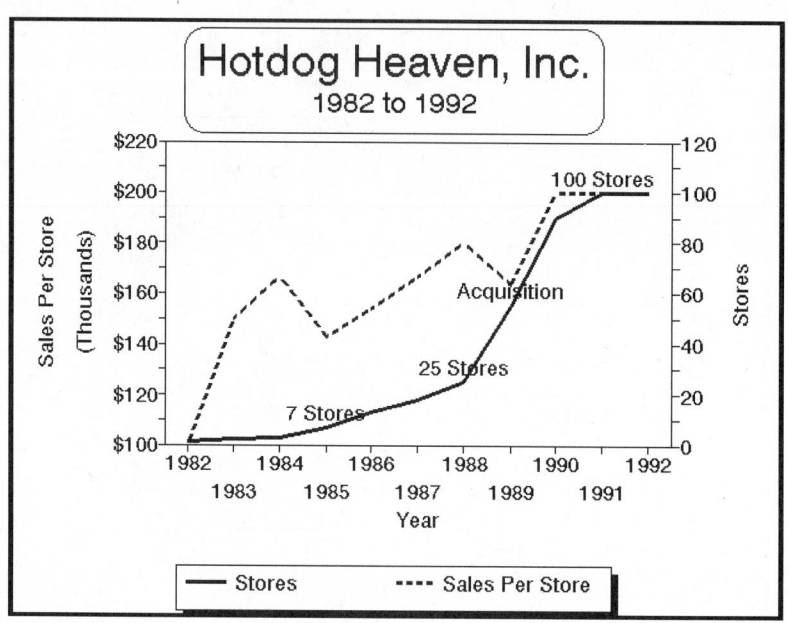

Figure 8.85

The /Graph,
Overall, Outlines
menu with the
default settings

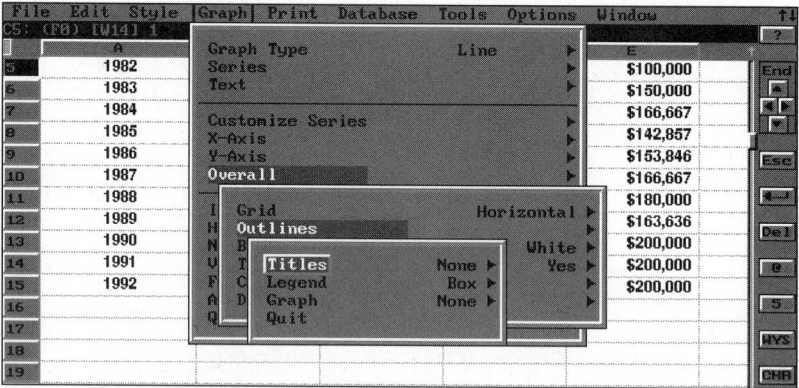

Figure 8.86

The /Graph, Overall, Outlines, Titles choices

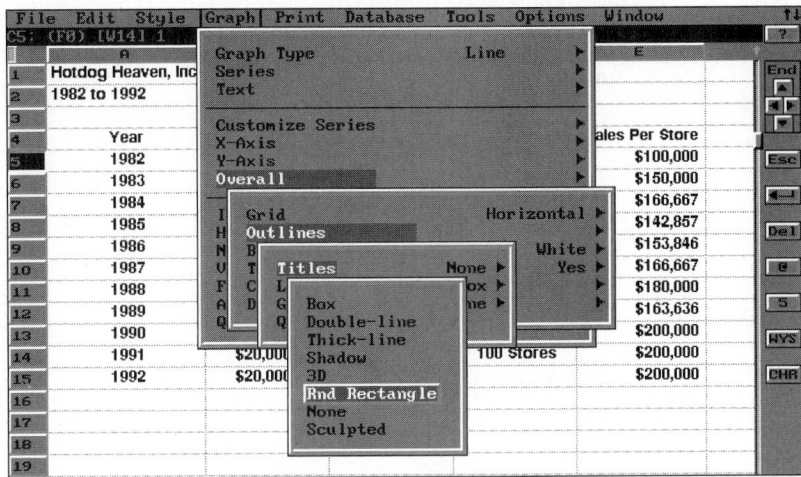

Graph Colors

The /Graph, Overall command also manages the screen display of colors, as well as many of the colors in a graph. The /Graph, Overall command has the following options:

- *Color/B&W* controls the color display of a graph on the screen. The Color selection displays a graph in color. The default is B&W.

- *Grid, Grid Color* controls the color of the grid lines, the x-axis and y-axis lines, and tickmarks, as well as any lines around graph titles, the graph, and the legend. Additionally, it controls the color of the lines defining a pie and each pie slice, the lines defining each area in an area graph, and those encasing each bar and bar segment in all types of bar and column graphs. The default is bright white.

- *Grid, Fill Color* determines the background color *within* the x- and y-axes of the graph. The default is gray.

- *Background Color* sets the background color *outside* the x- and y-axes— the area containing graph and axis titles and the legend. The default is black.

- *Drop Shadow Color* determines the shadow color of any text assigned a drop shadow typestyle.

For any of these options, you can choose from 16 different colors, which Quattro Pro displays in a pictorial menu if you are working in WYSIWYG mode.

The other colors in a graph are controlled as follows:

- /Graph, Text, Font governs the colors of the graph titles, x- and y-axis titles, legend text, y-axis scale, and x-axis labels. The exception is text assigned a drop shadow typestyle; the shadow color for this typestyle is controlled by /Graph, Overall, Drop Shadow, Color.

- /Graph, Customize Series, Colors controls the display color of each /Graph, Series block—regardless of whether the data is graphed as a line with or without markers, as any type of bar, or as part of an area graph. /Graph, Customize Series, Pies, Colors controls the colors of each slice in a pie chart, and each segment in a column graph. Remember, to display only the color, and not the fill pattern, select the B - Filled pattern for each slice or block.

Creating a Fast Graph

Quattro Pro includes Fast Graph, a convenient feature that you can use to create a graph without even entering the /Graph menu. Fast Graph is helpful when you want to get a general feel for how graph data will look.

When you create a Fast Graph, you specify only one block to be graphed, called the Fast Graph block. Quattro Pro will then create a different Fast Graph depending on the number of rows versus columns in the Fast Graph block and the cell contents (label versus value) in the first column and row of the Fast Graph block.

For example, consider the spreadsheet in Figure 8.87 that contains salary and savings data. Column A contains years entered as *labels*. Suppose the only /Graph setting you have specified is /Graph, Graph Type, Bar, and you want to get a rough idea of what this data will look like graphed. From the spreadsheet, press Ctrl-G to view a Fast Graph of your data. (You can also select /Graph, Fast Graph.) In response to the "Enter Fast Graph block:" prompt, specify the block **A1..C12** and press Enter.

Because the number of rows (12) in the block A1..C12 exceeds the number of columns (3), Quattro Pro creates the Fast Graph in Figure 8.88 using the following logic:

- It ignores the upper-left cell of the Fast Graph block, A1, because all other cells in the first column, A2..A12, are labels. (This would also happen if these cells contained values formatted as dates.) The cells A2..A12 are assigned to the X-Axis Series block.

Figure 8.87

The spreadsheet data used to create the Fast Graph in Figure 8.88

	File Edit Style Graph Print Database Tools Options Window							
	▲ ◄ ► ▼	Erase	Copy	Move	Style	Align	Font	Insert	Delete	Fit	Sum	Format	CHR	WYS

A1: 'Year

	A	B	C	D	E	F	G	H
1	Year	Gross Salary	Amount Saved					
2	1982	$17,000	$200					
3	83	$19,000	$600					
4	84	$22,000	$1,000					
5	85	$30,000	$1,500					
6	86	$35,000	$1,750					
7	87	$45,000	$1,000					
8	88	$25,000	($5,000)					
9	89	$60,000	$6,000					
10	90	$65,000	$6,500					
11	91	$70,000	$7,000					
12	92	$80,000	$8,000					
13								

Figure 8.88

The Fast Graph of data from Figure 8.87

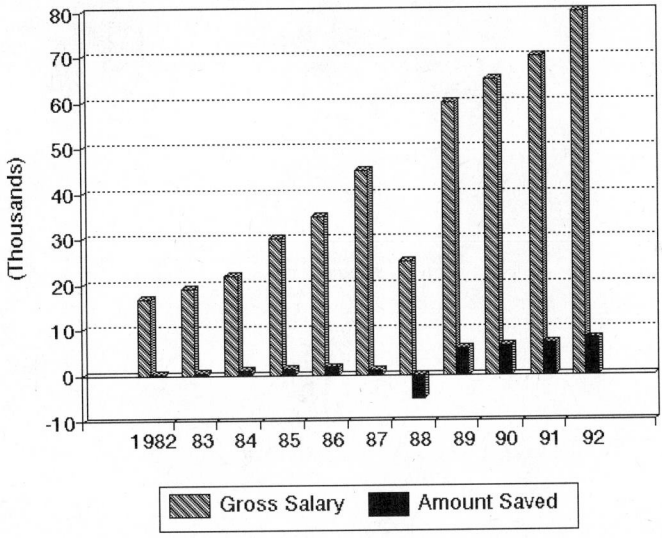

- The first cell in the second column, B1, is assigned as the /Graph, Text, Legends, 1st Series setting, and creates the first legend label, "Gross Salary." The remaining cells in this column, B2..B12, are assigned to the 1st Series block.

- The contents of the first cell in the third column, "Amount Saved" in C1, becomes the 2nd Series legend label. The remaining cells in column C, C2..C12, are assigned to the 2nd Series block.

■ Quattro Pro uses all other /Graph settings you have previously specified. In the current example, Bar is the current Graph Type; all other /Graph settings are defaults.

Quattro Pro also assigns these Fast Graph settings to the appropriate /Graph commands. For instance, when you next select /Graph, Series, Quattro Pro will display the menu in Figure 8.89, which includes the Fast Graph series blocks.

Figure 8.89

The /Graph, Series menu after creating the Fast Graph

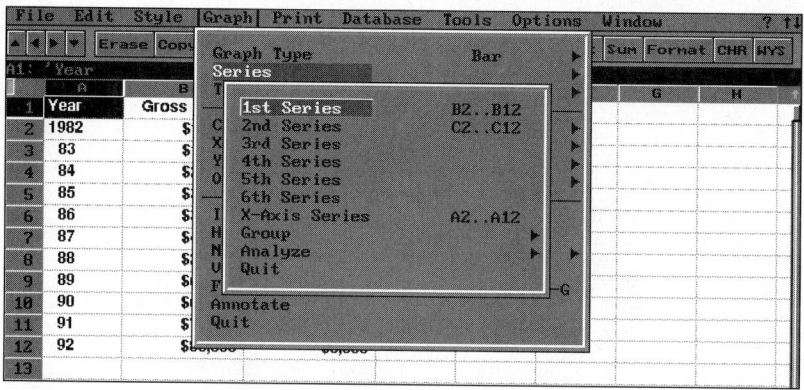

Quattro Pro uses other rules to create a Fast Graph, depending upon the contents of the Fast Graph block.

■ *If the entire Fast Graph block contains values*, Quattro Pro assigns all cells to series blocks, and creates a Fast Graph without x-axis labels and a legend. For instance, if you specify the Fast Graph block B2..C12 in Figure 8.87, Quattro Pro assigns cells B2..B12 to the 1st Series block and cells C2..C12 to the 2nd Series block. In this example, the Fast Graph produces the same results as /Graph, Series, Group.

■ *If the cells in the first column after the first cell contain values* (cells A2..A12 in Figure 8.87), Quattro Pro assigns all of these cells to the 1st Series block, and cell A1 becomes the 1st Series Legend setting. The first cell in the second column, B1, becomes the 2nd Series legend, and cells B2..B12 are assigned to the 2nd Series block. No X-Axis Series is assigned, regardless of the number of columns in the Fast Graph block.

■ If the number of rows in a Fast Graph block equals or exceeds the number of columns, Quattro Pro assigns /Graph, Series blocks by rows. *If the first row contains labels*, or values formatted as dates, these cells are assigned to the X-Axis Series block. The second row becomes the 1st Series block, the third row is the 2nd Series block, and so on. The data in the first column become legend labels. On the other hand, *if the first row contains values*, the entire first row is assigned to the 1st Series block, the second row to the 2nd Series block, and so on.

In addition, keep the following in mind when you create a Fast Graph:

- Make sure that cells in the Fast Graph block contain the correct contents, or you can get some unexpected results. If a cell assigned to a series block contains a label, for example, Quattro Pro assigns a value of 0 to this data point. A blank cell assigned to a series block, on the other hand, is ignored.

- You cannot create a Fast Graph for an XY graph. If you try, Quattro Pro displays the error message "Invalid X block."

Naming Graphs

Note. A graph name can be up to 15 characters long and follows exactly the same rules as for block names (Chapter 1).

In the previous section, you used the data in Figure 8.87 to create the Fast Graph bar graph in Figure 8.88. Suppose now that you want to save this graph, but you also want to create a line graph using the same data. You can solve this dilemma by *naming* the current bar graph.

Here is the procedure for assigning a graph name to the existing bar graph in Figure 8.88.

1. Select /Graph, Create, and you'll see the "Enter graph name:" prompt and a list of the existing named graphs in this spreadsheet file, like that in Figure 8.90.

2. Type the name you want to give this graph—for example, **BAR1**—and press Enter. Quattro Pro returns you to the /Graph menu.

When you save the spreadsheet, you save the named graph BAR1, any other named graphs created in this spreadsheet, and the current graph.

The major advantage of naming graphs is that you can save multiple graphs in one spreadsheet file. Otherwise, Quattro Pro only saves the current graph when it saves the file. Additionally, only named graphs can be copied to another spreadsheet file or included in a slide show.

Automatically Saving Graph Changes

Quattro Pro provides the command /Graph, Name, Autosave Edits. Set this to Yes, and you can *automatically* save the changes you make to a named graph.

Figure 8.90

The /Graph, Name, Create menu and prompt window

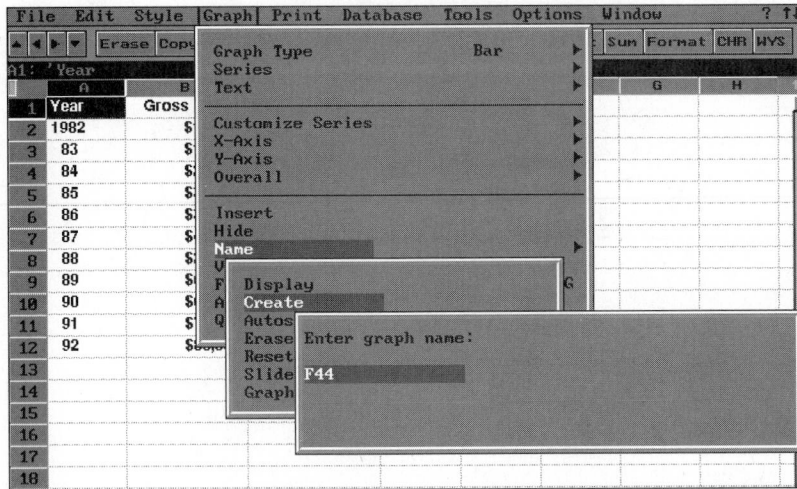

Normally, whenever you select /Graph, Name, Display and choose a named graph, the current graph settings are lost. If you enable /Graph, Name, Autosave Edits, however, any changes to /Graph settings and spreadsheet data are automatically saved under the current named graph when you select

- /Graph, Name, Autosave Edits, Erase, Slide, or Graph Copy

- /Graph, View (F10)

- /Print, Graph, Print Name

You will want to enable /Graph, Name, Autosave Edits as you first begin to create a graph. For example, now that you have saved the current graph as the named graph BAR1, you can create a line graph using the same data. You can also tell Quattro Pro to automatically save any /Graph settings and spreadsheet changes that will be made under a new graph name, such as LINE1. To do this, use the following procedure:

Note. Because Quattro Pro does not save the Autosave, Yes setting when you save a file, or when you use /Graph, Customize Series, Update, you must enable autosave each time you retrieve a file.

1. Set /Graph, Name, Autosave Edits to Yes to enable Quattro Pro's autosave capability. Quattro Pro returns you to the Name menu.

2. Choose Create from the Name menu. In response to the prompt, specify the new graph name **LINE1**. Quattro Pro returns you to the Name menu. Select Quit to return to the /Graph menu.

3. Select Graph Type from the /Graph menu, and then choose Line.

4. Press F10. Quattro Pro displays a line graph using the data in Figure 8.87 *and* automatically saves this graph as LINE1.

You can now continue to make changes to LINE1. Whenever you select one of the previously listed commands or press F10, Quattro Pro will automatically save the current /Graph settings under the graph name you specified.

Displaying a Named Graph

Now suppose that you want to redisplay the named graph, BAR1. Select /Graph, Name, Display, and you'll see a menu listing the existing named graphs in this spreadsheet file. Select BAR1, and the /Graph command now contains the BAR1 settings. Press F10 (Graph), and Quattro Pro will display the BAR1 graph (Figure 8.88).

Any changes you make to spreadsheet data after you create a named graph are automatically included the next time you display this graph. Imagine that you change the 1992 Amount Saved value in cell C12 of Figure 8.87 to $10,000. When you retrieve the named graph, BAR1, it will display this $10,000 value—not the original $8,000.

When you are displaying a named graph, keep in mind the following:

- You can only retrieve a named graph within the spreadsheet file in which it is created. You can, however, use /Graph, Name, Graph Copy to copy a named graph to another spreadsheet file. See "Copying a Named Graph to Another Spreadsheet," below, for details.

- When you display a named graph with /Graph, Name, Display, its settings become the current /Graph settings. Therefore, make sure you name the current graph before you retrieve a named graph.

- If the cell selector is positioned in the block where a named graph is inserted in the spreadsheet, this is the only graph you can display with /Graph, Name, Display. Thus, you can display a graph inserted in the spreadsheet by positioning the cell selector anywhere in the block it occupies, and pressing F10 (Graph). To display a different named graph, you must move the cell selector outside of this block, then reselect /Graph, Name, Display. See "Inserting a Graph into a Spreadsheet" later in this chapter.

Deleting Named Graphs

When you create a named graph, Quattro Pro saves it in the spreadsheet file; however, the size of a spreadsheet file grows with each named graph you create. Therefore, in a large spreadsheet where memory is a consideration, or to save disk space, you may need to delete unused named graphs.

Should you decide you no longer need the LINE1 named graph, for example, select /Graph, Name, Erase. When Quattro Pro displays the list of named graphs in the active spreadsheet, select LINE1 and press Enter. Quattro Pro returns to the /Graph menu.

You can use /Graph, Name, Reset, Yes to delete all named graphs in a spreadsheet. This command wipes out *all* of the named graphs in the active spreadsheet.

Copying a Named Graph to Another Spreadsheet

You can use the /Graph, Name, Graph Copy to copy a named graph from the active spreadsheet to another open spreadsheet. This command is especially helpful when you create complicated custom /Graph settings in one spreadsheet and want to use them in another file, but you don't want to specify them as the /Graph default settings.

For instance, suppose the named graph, BAR1, is located in the file SAVE. You have created a similar file for the years 1993 and on, and you want to copy BAR1 to this new file, called SAVEMORE. Here's how to do it:

Tip. When you copy a graph to another file, the target (destination) file need not be open. In response to "Point to target spreadsheet:", enter [*filename*]*anycell*. (If the target file is in a different directory, remember to include the path in this destination.)

1. Open both files, SAVE and SAVEMORE, and use /Window, Tile to display them side by side. Position the cell selector in the source spreadsheet, SAVE.

2. Select /Graph, Name, Graph Copy. Quattro Pro displays a menu listing the existing named graphs in this spreadsheet file and prompts you for the named graph. Select BAR1 and press Enter.

3. You'll see a prompt in the input line, "Point to target spreadsheet:". Move the cell selector to any cell in the target file SAVEMORE, and press Enter.

Quattro Pro copies the named graph BAR1 to the file SAVEMORE, returns the cell selector to the source file SAVE, and redisplays the /Graph menu. To see BAR1 in the target file, move the cell selector to SAVEMORE. Make BAR1 the current graph by selecting /Graph, Name, Display. Specify **BAR1** and press Enter. Press F10 to view this graph.

The named graph, BAR1, in the target file not only uses the same /Graph settings, but it also still references the spreadsheet information of the *source* file, SAVE. Thus, when you copy a named graph to another file, you *link* the source and target files. (Chapter 2 discusses linking files.) The exception is when you copy a named text graph—the copied graph remains independent of the source file. (Text graphs are discussed in Chapter 9.)

CAUTION! *If the target file already contains a named graph of the same name, Quattro Pro writes the incoming named graph over the existing one, without asking for confirmation.*

Analytical Graphing in Quattro Pro 4.0

Quattro Pro 4.0 offers several *analytical graphing* commands. They are analytical in the sense that they perform calculations on your spreadsheet data before graphing it. Here are the four types of analytical graphing offered:

- *Aggregation*   Combines multiple data points into a single graph point by calculating a sum, average, standard deviation, minimum value, or maximum value.

- *Moving average*   Smooths a graph's contour by plotting the average of a series of data points. You can have Quattro Pro give equal weight to all the data points, or more weight to recent data points.

- *Linear fit*   Performs simple linear regression on a series of data points and plots the resulting line.

- *Exponential fit*   Generates an exponential curve to fit a series of data points.

NOTE. *One of the problems with Quattro Pro's analytical graphing is that it is a "black box": You don't always know what calculations are being performed on your data before the results are graphed. For example, when Quattro Pro gives more emphasis to recent data points in a weighted moving average, it doesn't tell you how much extra weight is being given to those points. Likewise, when it plots a line using simple linear regression, you're given no measure of how well the line fits the data. If it's important to know these measures (and it usually is), you're better off performing your own calculations in the spreadsheet and using conventional /Graph commands to graph the results.*

Aggregation

Aggregation is handy when you have multiple data points, like daily sales, and you want to graph them in an aggregate form—for example, showing only weekly sales averages. Suppose you have the spreadsheet in Figure 8.91, for example, which contains 3 months of daily memorabilia sales. When you graph this data using a standard line graph, the large number of data points may give more detail than you actually need (Figure 8.92). By graphing the data in aggregate, though, you can get a better overall feel for trends in the data.

Figure 8.91

Daily sales data

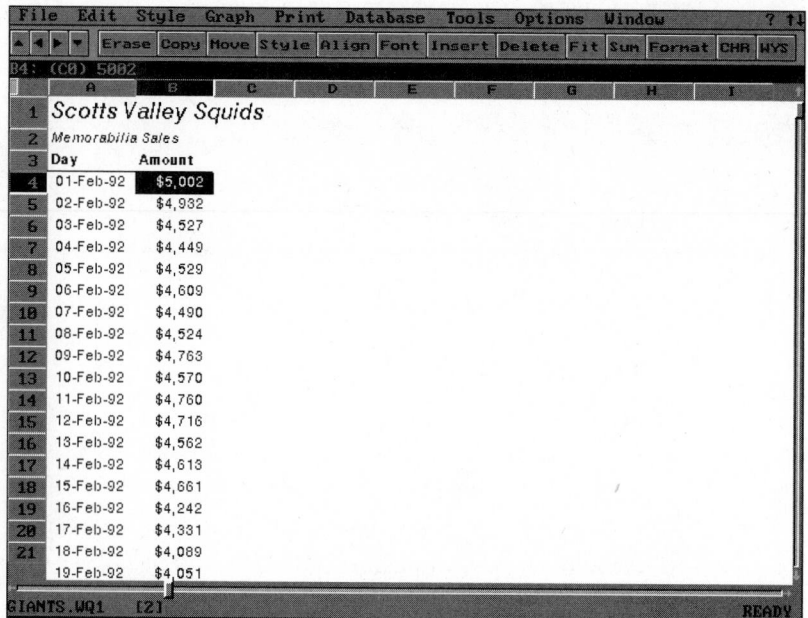

Figure 8.92

A standard line graph of the data in Figure 8.91

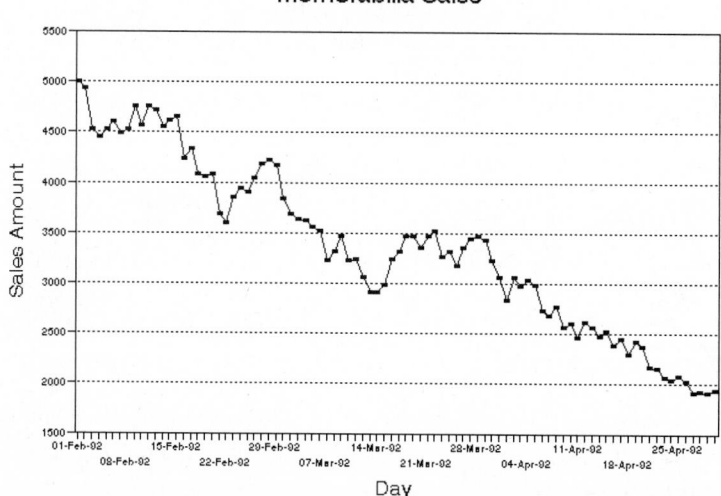

Table 8.15 shows the /Graph settings for creating the standard line graph in Figure 8.92. With these settings in place, you can easily change the display of the line from daily sales to weekly sales averages. Begin by selecting /Graph, Series, Analyze, 1st Series, Aggregation (Figure 8.93).

Table 8.15 **Standard /Graph Settings Used with Figure 8.91 to Create Line Graph in Figure 8.92**

/Graph Commands	Settings
Graph Type Series	Line
1st Series	B4..B93
X-Axis Series	A4..A93
Text	
1st Line	\A1
2nd Line	\A2
X-Title	Day
Y-Title	Sales Amount
X-Axis	
No. of Minor Ticks	6
Alternative Ticks	Yes

Here's an explanation of the various aggregation settings you'll encounter and how to set them for the current example:

- *Series Period*   Indicates what time period the data items in the series represent. The choices are Days (the default), Weeks, Months, Quarters, and Years. Table 8.16 shows the assumptions that Quattro Pro makes for the number of days in each period. In the current example, the original data represents daily sales, so you would accept the default setting, Days.

- *Aggregation Period*   This setting indicates how many data points to combine in each graph point. Weeks (the default) combines 7 data points, Months combines 30, Quarters combines 90, and Years combines 360. By choosing Arbitrary, you can specify your own aggregation period. For example, setting Arbitrary to 5 combines five data points into a single graph point (provided Series Period is set to Days). In the current example, because you want to show weekly averages, you'd accept the default of Weeks.

Figure 8.93

The Aggregation settings in Quattro Pro 4.0

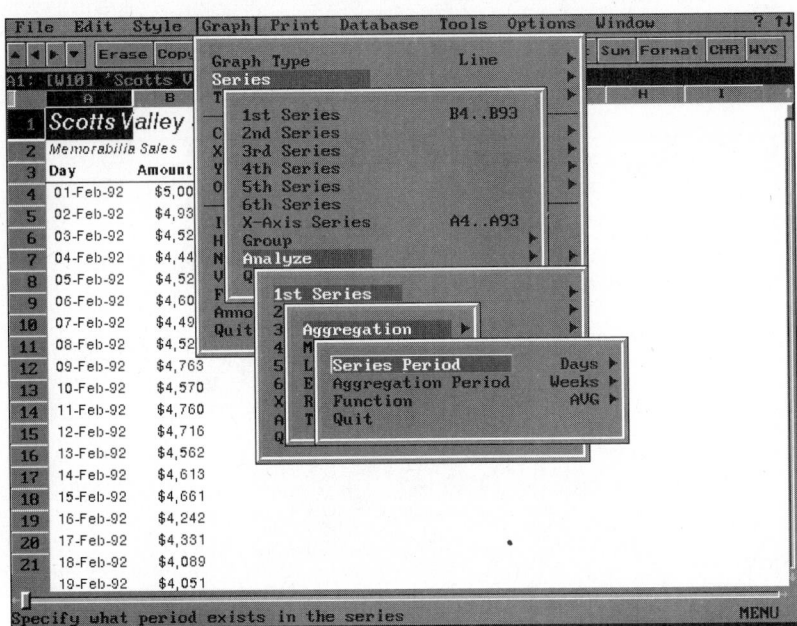

Table 8.16   **Quattro Pro's Time Period Assumptions for Aggregation**

Period	Is Equal to			
Week	7 days			
Month	30 days	4 weeks		
Quarter	90 days	12 weeks	3 months	
Year	360 days	51 weeks	12 months	4 quarters

■ *Function*   Controls the @function that Quattro Pro uses to recast the data. The choices are SUM, AVG, STD, STDS, MIN, and MAX. (See Chapter 7 for an explanation of these functions.) In the current example, because you want to graph weekly averages, you'd choose AVG.

Figure 8.94 shows the result of these aggregation settings.

Occasionally you may want to view a data series in two different aggregate forms. For example, besides seeing weekly sales averages, you may also want to see cumulative sales per week. To add a second view of the data to a graph, use /Graph, Series to assign the same block to the 2nd Series. You can then use /Graph, Series, Analyze, 2nd Series, Aggregation and specify options to control the method of display for that series. You can view up to six different series in this way.

Figure 8.94

The data in Figure 8.91 graphed using aggregation

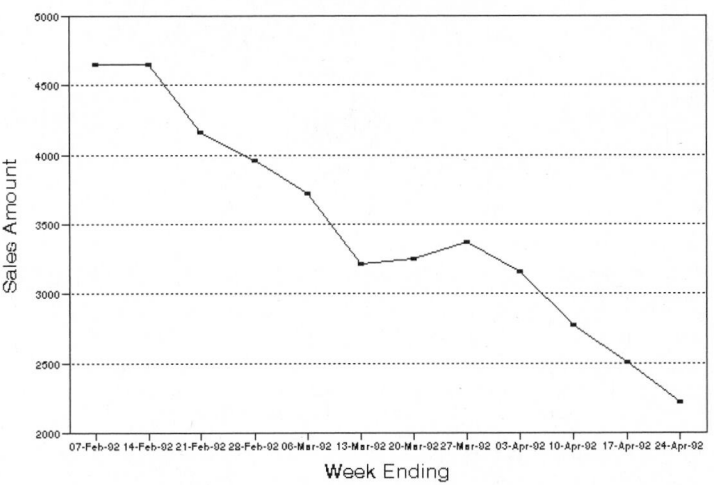

Moving Average

A moving average smooths the contour of a graph by averaging data points. Starting with the first point in a series, Quattro Pro calculates the average for a specified number of previous data points. The number of points it averages is known as the *period*. As Quattro Pro moves from one point to the next, it maintains the fixed period by dropping the oldest data point and replacing it with the current one. It then recalculates the average for the new set of points.

To control the period, use the /Graph, Series, Analyze, 1st Series through 6th Series, Moving Average, Period command and choose a setting from 1 to 1000. For example, to smooth the contour of the line graph in Figure 8.92, you could select a Period setting of 7 (for 7 days). Figure 8.95 illustrates the difference between daily sales and a 7-day moving average of the same sales. To produce this graph, you use the settings in Table 8.15 along with these additional settings:

/Graph Commands	Settings
Series	
2nd Series	B4..B93
Text, Legends	
1st Series	Daily sales
2nd Series	\F2 (where cell F2 contains the label "7-day moving average")
Customize Series	
Series:2, Format	Lines
Series, Analyze, 2nd Series, Moving Average	
Period	7
Weighted	No

Normally, Quattro Pro gives equal weight to each point in a moving average. If you prefer to give more weight to recent data points, you can select Yes for the Moving Average, Weighted option.

TIP. *You can see the values that Quattro Pro has calculated for a given data series by placing them in the spreadsheet. See "Generating a Table of Graphed Values," later.*

Linear Fit

Another form of analytical graphing uses simple linear regression to generate a line that best fits a data series. The command to draw such a line is /Graph, Series, Analyze, 1st Series through 6th Series, Linear Fit. If you use this command with the data in Figure 8.91, for example, you'll see the graph in Figure 8.96. Table 8.17 shows all the settings that were used to produce the graph.

Figure 8.95

Comparing daily sales to a 7-day moving average

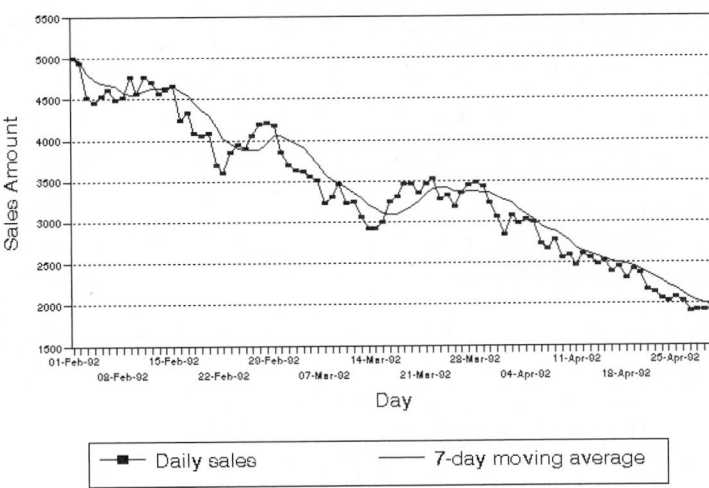

Figure 8.96

Linear Fit draws a regression line

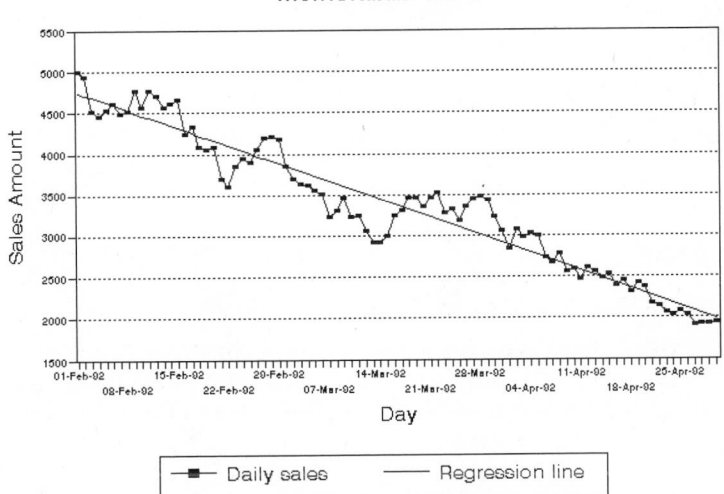

Table 8.17   /Graph Settings Used with Figure 8.91 to Create Linear Fit Graph in Figure 8.96

/Graph Commands	Settings
Graph Type	Line
Series	
1st Series	B4..B93
2nd Series	B4..B93
X-Axis Series	A4..A93
Text	
1st Line	\A1
2nd Line	\A2
X-Title	Day
Y-Title	Sales Amount
Legends, 1st Series	Daily sales
Legends, 2nd Series	Regression line
X-Axis	
No. of Minor Ticks	6
Alternative Ticks	Yes
Customize Series	
Series: 2, Format	Lines
Series, Analyze, 2nd Series	Linear Fit

As mentioned, one of the problems with the Linear Fit option is that you can't tell how well the line actually fits the data points. In fact, Quattro Pro generates a line even when the data has no general trend. If you want to determine the validity of the line, you should use the /Tools, Advanced Math, Regression command and check the value of R^2. See Chapter 11 for more on this topic.

Exponential Fit

If the data you're graphing increases or decreases exponentially, you can use the Exponential Fit option to fit an exponential curve to the data. For example Figure 8.97 shows some promising sales data for Tucson Tile and the results of using the Exponential Fit option to produce a graph. Table 8.18 shows the settings that were used to produce the graph.

Figure 8.97

Using Exponential Fit to draw an exponential curve

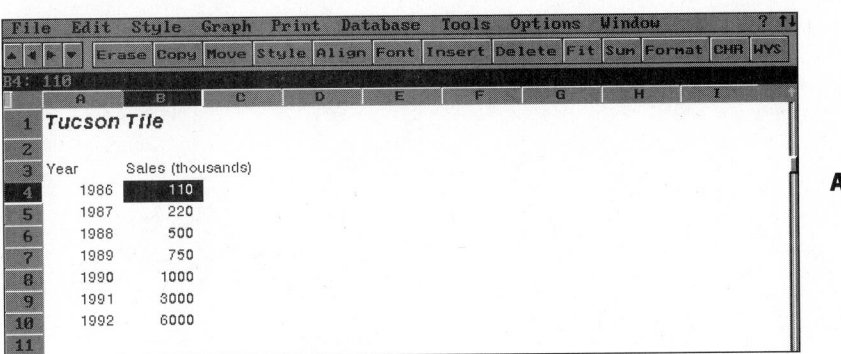

A

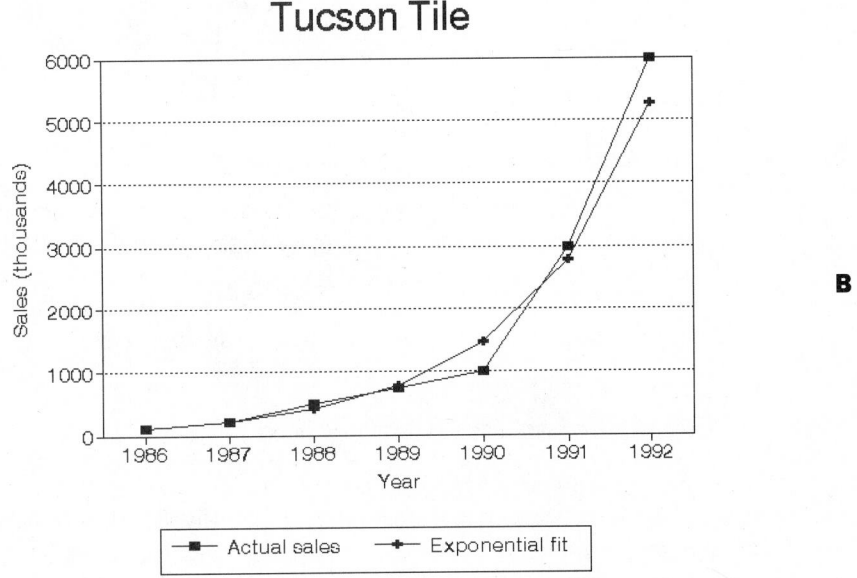

B

Table 8.18   **/Graph Settings Used to Create Exponential Fit Graph in Figure 8.97**

/Graph Commands	Settings
Graph Type	Line
Series	
1st Series	B4..B10
2nd Series	B4..B10
X-Axis Series	A4..A10
Text	
1st Line	\A1
X-Title	\A3
Y-Title	\B3
Legends, 1st Series	Actual sales
Legends, 2nd Series	Exponential fit
Customize Series	
Series: 2, Format	Lines
Series, Analyze, 2nd Series	Exponential Fit

Generating a Table of Graphed Values

If you're wondering what values Quattro Pro is using for an analytical graph, you can use the /Graph, Series, Analyze, 1st Series through 6th Series, Table command to place a table of them in the spreadsheet and examine them. By selecting a destination block of one cell, you can have Quattro Pro place the data starting in that cell and working its way downward as needed.

Zooming and Panning in Quattro Pro 4.0

In earlier versions of Quattro Pro, the only way you could get a better view of the important details in a crowded, data-intensive graph was to create another graph representing a portion of the original. Quattro Pro 4.0's new zoom and pan feature solves this problem. Zoom lets you enlarge a portion of a graph to view the data in greater detail. Once you've used graph zoom, you can then pan right or left to view other segments of the graph at the same level of detail. You can even return to the spreadsheet and print a segment exactly as displayed.

Zoom and pan are only available when viewing a graph, and they only work with a mouse. To activate zoom and pan, press the left and right mouse buttons at the same time. If you're viewing the graph in Figure 8.92, for example, you'll see the view shown in Figure 8.98A with the zoom and pan palette at the top. Figure 8.98B shows the view after zooming in three steps. By repeatedly selecting the pan control buttons, you can view the entire graph one segment at a time. Table 8.19 summarizes how the palette buttons work.

The position bar gives you a rough idea of both the zoom level and the pan position in the graph. Each time you select ++ or −−, the position bar shrinks or grows to approximate the portion of the graph displayed. Pan left or right, and the position bar moves to indicate your position in the graph.

You can click either the left or right mouse button anywhere on the screen to clear the zoom and pan palette and leave the graph displayed. Clicking either mouse button again after clearing the zoom and pan palette clears the graph display and returns you to the spreadsheet.

Creating a Slide Show

Quattro Pro's *slide show* capability provides you with a powerful vehicle for displaying your graphs. With sound effects, substantially improved visual effects, and a bevy of other new features, Quatro Pro holds its own with many stand-alone desktop presentation programs.

Slide Show Basics

Tip. You can use the Annotator (see Chapter 9) to create a text graph for a title slide.

A simple slide show automatically displays a series of named graphs, each for a specified number of seconds. You use the /Graph, Name, Slide command to create a slide show.

Suppose you want to create a slide show of four named graphs, TITLE, PAST, CURRENT, and FUTURE. You must first prepare a two-column block in a spreadsheet; the first column (A) contains the names of the graphs you want to display, and the second column (B) lists the number of seconds you want each graph to be displayed. To create this slide show, you would enter the following data, as shown in columns A and B of Figure 8.99:

Cell	Named Graph	Cell	Duration
A3	TITLE	B3	60
A4	PAST	B4	120
A5	CURRENT	B5	90
A6	FUTURE	B6	0

Figure 8.98

Using the zoom and pan palette to zoom in on Figure 8.92

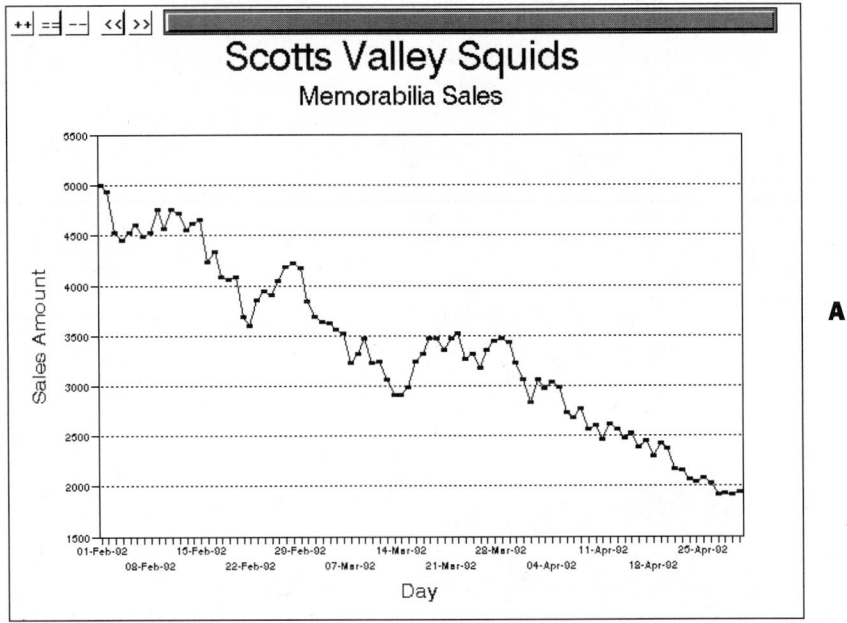

A

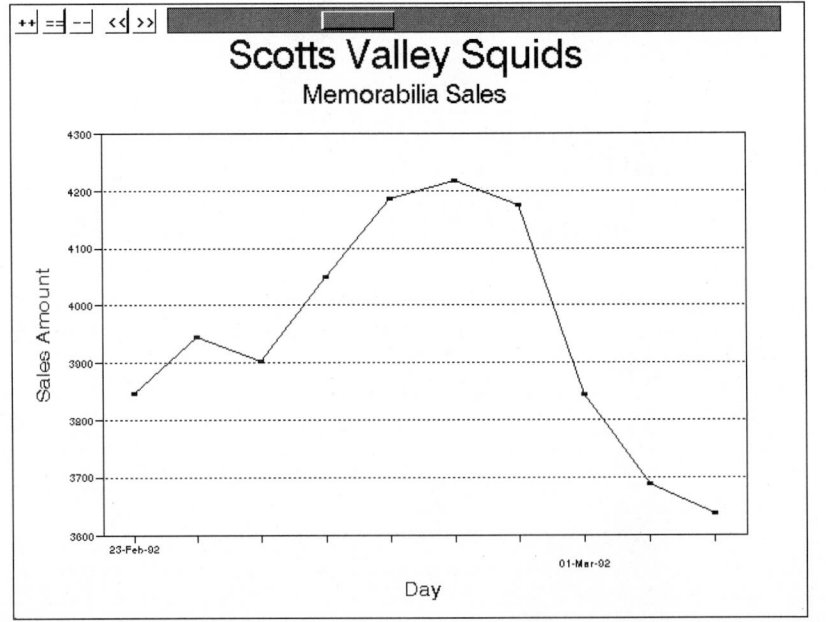

B

Figure 8.99

Data used in a slide show

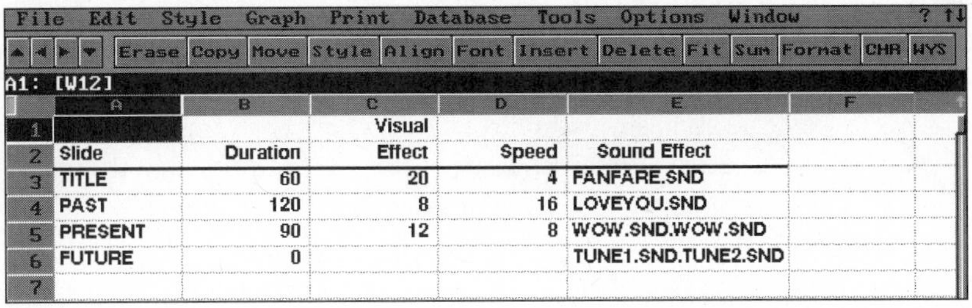

| File | Edit | Style | Graph | Print | Database | Tools | Options | Window | ? ↑↓ |

| ▲ | ◀ | ▶ | ▼ | Erase | Copy | Move | Style | Align | Font | Insert | Delete | Fit | Sum | Format | CHR | WYS |

A1: [W12]

	A	B	C	D	E	F
1			Visual			
2	Slide	Duration	Effect	Speed	Sound Effect	
3	TITLE	60	20	4	FANFARE.SND	
4	PAST	120	8	16	LOVEYOU.SND	
5	PRESENT	90	12	8	WOW.SND.WOW.SND	
6	FUTURE	0			TUNE1.SND.TUNE2.SND	
7						

To run this slide show as defined so far, choose /Graph, Name, Slide. In response to the prompt for the block of graph names, specify **A3..B6** and press Enter. Quattro Pro instantly starts the slide show. In this case, it displays the TITLE graph for 60 seconds, the PAST slide for 120 seconds, and then the CURRENT slide for 90 seconds. Finally, since cell B6 contains 0, the FUTURE graph is displayed indefinitely until you press any key.

NOTE. *If you leave a cell blank in the second column (B), Quattro Pro evaluates it as zero and displays the corresponding named graph indefinitely until you press any key.*

Table 8.19   **Zoom and Pan Buttons**

Button	Action
++	Zooms in on (enlarges) the center portion of a graph in steps to view less of the graph in greater detail. After the first zoom step, the left data point remains fixed; subsequent steps enlarge the graph portion in reference to this point.
−−	Zooms out in steps to view more of the graph after using ++ to zoom in.
==	Returns to full graph view after zooming in.
<<	Pans left after zooming in to display the graph segment to the left at the same level of detail.
>>	Pans right after zooming in to display the graph segment to the right.

When the slide show has run its course (when you press any key in the current example), Quattro Pro returns you to the /Graph menu. Select Quit to return to the spreadsheet.

Tip. Another way to start a slide show is to create a simple macro that invokes the /Graph, Name, Slide command. You can even assign that macro to a graph button, and launch it by clicking on the button. See Chapter 12 for more information about these topics.

While a slide show is running in Quattro Pro, you can review a previous slide. Press the Backspace key or click the right mouse button at any time during the show to reverse the sequence of slides. Quattro Pro works its way consecutively backward through the previous slides until you press any other key; the slide show then resumes a forward sequence.

Quattro Pro 2.0 and later versions include slide show features not available in earlier releases. You can

- Copy slides (named graphs) from one spreadsheet to another spreadsheet. See "Copying a Named Graph to Another Spreadsheet."

- Create large slide shows by storing slides in expanded memory. For details about expanded memory, see Chapter 15.

- Create a user-driven slide show by including graph buttons in your slides. Graph buttons let you control the progression of slides by clicking on the screen, rather than depending on a timed display. You can even create graph buttons that branch into different slide sequences. See Chapter 9 for more details.

In this section, you created a simple slide show that displayed each slide for a specified period of time. In Quattro Pro 3.0, however, you can use additional visual effects to add drama to your slide shows.

Adding Visual Effects

During a simple slide show, Quattro Pro progresses between slides by removing the current slide from view and then drawing the next slide on the screen. This works well as long as slides are simple, but when they are complex, the redrawing process can be time consuming and distracting to the audience.

To ease the transition between slides, Quattro Pro 3.0 offers 24 visual transition effects, listed in Table 8.20, that you can incorporate in your slide shows. These visual effects can also add real flair to any slide show.

Look at the Visual Effect column in Table 8.20, and you can see that visual effects are categorized into Fades, Horizontal wipes (single- and double-edged), Vertical wipes (single- and double-edged), Spirals, and Dissolves. The best way to see how each of these visual effects works is by trying them out. You will probably agree that the barn door and iris visual effects (7 through 12) are the most dramatic.

You can also control the speed of visual effects. For instance, you can specify a speed from 0 to 16, where 0 is the fastest speed and 16 is the slowest speed.

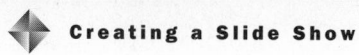

Table 8.20   **Slide Show Visual Effect Settings**

Visual Effect	Value	*Speed Range
Instantaneous cut	1	0
Switch to black, then display new image when drawn. Speed setting is the number of 1/70 of a second that screen remains black before new slide appears. For instance, a setting of 3 makes the screen black for 3/70 seconds.	2	Not a speed range. Enter any value ≥ 0.
Wipe right	3	0-16
Wipe left	4	0-16
Wipe bottom	5	0-16
Wipe top	6	0-16
Barn door close (right/left to center)	7	0-16
Barn door open (center to right/left)	8	0-16
Barn door top/bottom to center	9	0-16
Barn door center to top/bottom	10	0-16
Iris close	11	0-16
Iris open	12	0-16
Scroll up	13	0-16
Scroll down	14	0-16
Vertical stripes right	15	0-16
Stripes right and then left	16	0-16
Spiral in	17	0-16
Dissolve, 2x1 rectangles	18	0
Dissolve, 2x2 rectangles	19	0
Dissolve, 4x4 squares	20	0-2
Dissolve, 8x8 squares	21	0-4
Dissolve, 16x16 squares	22	0-8
Dissolve, 32x32 squares	23	0-16
Dissolve, 64x64 squares	24	0-32

*   0 is the fastest speed in the range

Imagine, for example, that you want to add some visual transition effects to the slide show. Quattro Pro reserves the third column (C) in a slide show block for visual effects, and the fourth column (D) for the speed of the visual effect. Suppose you enter this additional information in the spreadsheet shown in Figure 8.99:

Cell	Visual Effect	Cell	Duration
C3	20	D3	4
C4	8	D4	16
C5	12	D5	8
C6		D6	

Note. If you enter 0 or leave a blank in the visual effect (third) column, no visual effect occurs during a slide transition.

To overlay the next slide, enter a visual effect value as a negative number. If you use the visual effect –19, for instance, the next slide is added on top of the existing slide using a slow dissolve.

To create and run this enhanced slide show, specify the block **A3..D6** in the /Graph, Name, Slide command. Quattro Pro now runs the slide show, incorporating the following visual effects:

■ Between slide 1, TITLE, and slide 2, PAST, you'll see a dissolve transition (20), 4x4 squares, in the slowest speed (4 in cell D5 is the slowest speed for this transition).

■ Between slide 2, PAST, and slide 3, CURRENT, you'll see a barn door open transition (8), starting in the center and expanding both left and right in the slowest speed (16 in cell D4 is the slowest speed for this transition).

■ Between slide 3, CURRENT, and slide 4, FUTURE, you'll see an iris open transition (12) in a medium speed (8 in cell D5 is in the middle of the range 0 to 16).

Notice that no transition is needed for the last slide, FUTURE, in cell A6.

Transition visual effects require extra video memory. For this reason, Quattro Pro evaluates a slide show block before it begins the slide show. If a visual effect column (a third column) is included in this block, these visual effects are automatically displayed using 640x350 EGA resolution, even if your computer includes a VGA graphics adapter. Quattro Pro automatically returns to your default graphics resolution after the slide show ends.

If you use visual effects in graph buttons when Quattro Pro is set for VGA resolution, it does not automatically change the screen to an EGA resolution. Therefore, you should manually change to a 640x350 EGA resolution

(using /Options, Hardware, Screen Resolution) before beginning a slide show. Otherwise, Quattro Pro will ignore any visual effect when you choose a graph button that includes one. See Chapter 9 for information about graph buttons.

Adding Sound Effects

Note. If you've installed a Sound Blaster (or compatible) sound card and appropriate driver, Quattro Pro 4.0 automatically detects its presence and uses the card for slide show sound effects.

You can also add sound effects—digitized sound files on disk with an .SND file name extension—to your Quattro Pro slide shows. When you install version 3.0, it automatically adds three .SND files to your Quattro Pro directory. Other .SND files are also available in the ProView Power Pack. You will find that many of the .SND file names indicate the sound effect they produce, for instance, KABOOM.SND.

Imagine, for example, that you want to add sound effects for the slide show in Figure 8.99. Quattro Pro reserves the fifth column (E) in a slide show block for sound effects. So you might add the following values to your slide show block:

Cell	Sound Effect
E3	FANFARE.SND
E4	LOVEYOU.SND
E5	WOW.SND, WOW.SND
E6	TUNE1.SND,TUNE2.SND

This time, specify the block **A3..E6** in the /Graph, Name, Slide command. Quattro Pro runs the slide show in Figure 8.99, and produces the following sound effects:

- As soon as the TITLE slide is displayed, FANFARE.SND begins to play.

- After the dissolve transition to the PAST slide is completed, you hear "I love you."

- After the barn door open transition to the CURRENT slide is completed, WOW.SND plays twice.

- After the iris open transition to the FUTURE slide is completed, TUNE1.SND plays, immediately followed by TUNE2.SND.

Make sure that you coordinate the timed display of a slide (column B) with the duration of a sound effect. Quattro Pro continues to play a sound effect until it is completed, even if the next slide is displayed.

CAUTION! *In some instances sound effects may be distorted or may fail to play. This may occur, for example, when you are running Quattro Pro within Microsoft Windows, in which case you can simply run it stand-alone (see Chapter 15). If your computer is logged on to a network, or RAM-resident (TSR) programs are running, you can try removing unnecessary TSRs and device drivers from your CONFIG.SYS and AUTOEXEC.BAT files—but do so with great caution.*

Inserting a Graph into a Spreadsheet

One of the best features of the /Graph command is its ability to insert graphs directly into a spreadsheet. An inserted graph is "live"; that is, changes in the spreadsheet data and /Graph settings instantly affect the graph.

For instance, suppose you use the /Graph command to graph the competitive analysis in Figure 8.100. As you make adjustments to this data, you want to simultaneously view their effects on the graph. You can accomplish this by inserting the current graph in the spreadsheet. To do so,

1. Make sure you are working in WYSIWYG mode. Otherwise, the inserted graph will appear as a highlighted empty block on the screen.

Figure 8.100

Competitive analysis used to create the inserted graph in Figure 8.101

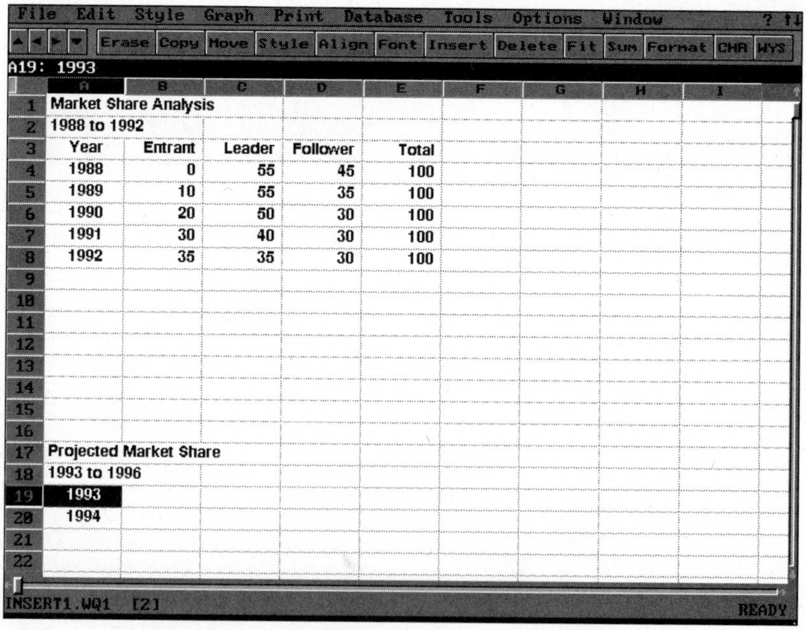

Note. The largest inserted graph Quattro Pro accepts in a spreadsheet is 12 columns by 32 rows, regardless of the column width used. Remember, however, if you print an inserted graph, that you are further limited to a maximum printed size of 8 by 10 inches.

2. To insert this graph in the spreadsheet, choose /Graph, Insert. Quattro Pro lists all the named graphs in this spreadsheet, as well as a <Current Graph> selection that reprints the current /Graph settings. In response to the "Enter graph name:" prompt, select <Current Graph> and press Enter.

3. Quattro Pro returns you to the spreadsheet, and prompts you for the spreadsheet block in which to insert the graph. Specify **A9..F19** and press Enter.

4. Quattro Pro inserts this graph in the spreadsheet, and returns to the /Graph menu. Select Quit to return to the spreadsheet.

In Figure 8.101, you can see how Quattro Pro includes a scaled version of the current graph to fit the spreadsheet block you specify. In fact, even if you specify a one-cell block, Quattro Pro will display a miniature version of the graph. In our example, the size of the block A9..F19 displays the graph so that the titles and labels can be read.

Figure 8.101

The current graph inserted in the Figure 8.100 spreadsheet

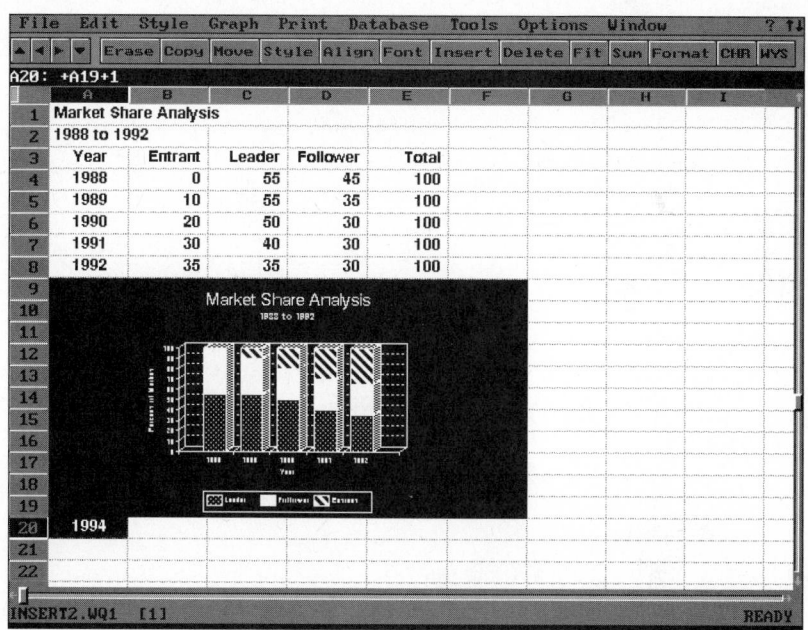

You can now print this spreadsheet, including the inserted graph. (See "Printing a Graph" at the end of this chapter.) Or you can change the spreadsheet data and simultaneously view the effect on this graph. You can even change the /Graph settings, such as Graph Type, and view the revised graph in the spreadsheet.

It is important to understand that an inserted graph is essentially a screen location—it does not affect the spreadsheet cells beneath it. You can see this by comparing Figures 8.100 and 8.101. In Figure 8.101, the cell selector is located in A20, which contains the formula 1+A19 displayed in the input line. Even though this formula references a cell covered by the inserted graph, it still returns the value 1994. Furthermore, once you remove this inserted graph, any information in these cells is once again displayed.

To remove this inserted graph, choose /Graph Hide. In response to the "Enter graph name:" prompt, select <Current Graph>. Quattro Pro removes this graph from the spreadsheet, which reverts back to Figure 8.100. /Graph Hide has no effect on the /Graph command settings, however. If you press F10 (Graph), you can view the current graph once again.

Note that if you insert a named graph in a spreadsheet that is *not* the current graph, the location of the cell selector will affect the current /Graph settings. For example, suppose you insert the named graph INSERT1. If the cell selector is located anywhere within the block occupied by INSERT1 (the input line displays INSERT1), in effect this graph temporarily becomes the "current" graph. You can press F10 (Graph) to view a full-screen version of INSERT1; you can also use the /Graph command to change its /Graph settings. However, once you move the cell selector outside the INSERT1 block, the /Graph settings revert to those of the true current graph. If you press F10 (Graph), the current graph is displayed.

Printing a Graph

Printing a graph is much like printing a spreadsheet. All of the commands you need are accessed through the /Print command. (For a thorough discussion of printing, see Chapter 6.)

For instance, suppose you want to print a graph of the information in Figure 8.101. (This figure shows you a scaled version of the graph you will print.) Here's how to print this graph using Quattro Pro's /Print, Graph Print default settings.

1. Select /Options, Graphics Quality, which controls the quality of a printed graph. The default setting is Draft, so select Final.

2. Press F10 (Graph) to ensure that the graph you want to print is the current graph. Press Esc to return to the spreadsheet.

3. Select /Print, Adjust Printer, Align. This command adjusts Quattro Pro's internal line counter to the print head's position at the top of a page. The /Print menu reappears.

4. Select Graph Print, and Quattro Pro displays the Graph Print menu in Figure 8.102. Select Destination, and then Graph Printer. The Graph Print menu reappears, and now displays Graph Printer as the Destination.

Figure 8.102

The /Print, Graph Print menu

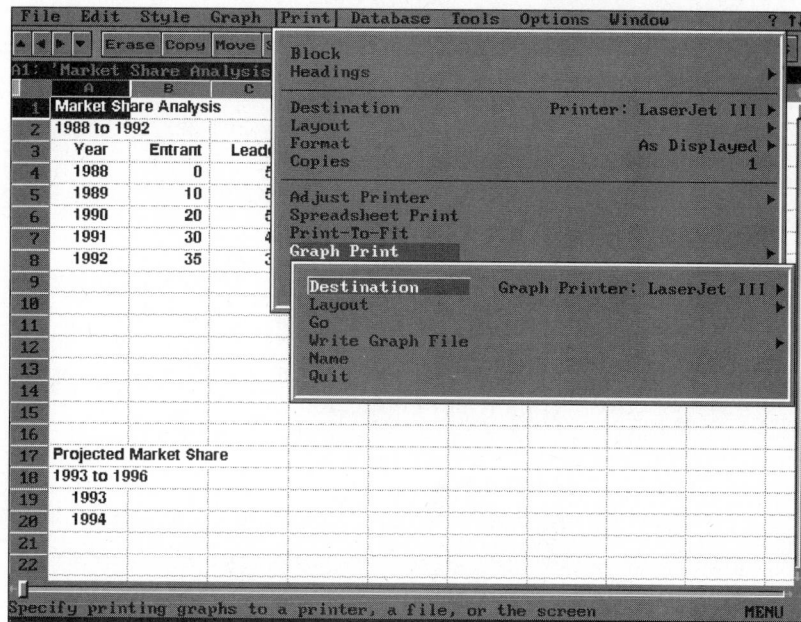

5. Select Go to print this graph. When Quattro Pro finishes printing, it returns to the Graph Print menu. Select Quit to return to the /Print menu.

6. Select Quit to complete the /Print command and return to the spreadsheet.

Quattro Pro prints this graph using the current /Graph settings, and the /Print, Graph Print, Layout default settings (explained just below in "Changing the Layout of a Printed Graph"). You'll see the printed graph in "Previewing a Graph" later in this section.

You can also use the /Print command to retrieve and then print a named graph. For instance, suppose you have previously created a graph and used /Graph, Name, Create to name it LINE1. So, be sure to name the current graph before you use the /Print command to access another named graph. To print LINE1, select /Print, Graph Print, Name, and Quattro Pro displays the named graphs in this spreadsheet. Choose LINE1 and press Enter. Quattro

Pro will now use this graph in the /Print command. Additionally, when you return to the spreadsheet, LINE1 will be the current graph.

Keep in mind the following when you print a graph in Quattro Pro:

- A graph takes considerably longer to print than a spreadsheet. See "Printing a Document in Graphics Mode" in Chapter 6 for details.

- By default, Quattro Pro prints a graph to the default printer. Use /Options, Hardware, Printers, Default Printer to change the default printer.

- If a graph includes Bitstream fonts (the default), and you did not choose to build them during installation, Quattro Pro builds fonts as needed to print, and displays a "Now building font..." message. See Chapter 6 for a further discussion of how Quattro Pro prints fonts.

- If, during printing, an "I/O error" warning appears in the status line and a confirmation menu appears in the spreadsheet, you probably have a printer problem. The printer may not be turned on or may be off line, out of paper, or incapable of printing in graphics mode. Choose Abort to discontinue the print operation. Or, correct the problem and then select Continue.

- To abort a print operation in process, press Ctrl-Break. Remember then to clear the printer buffer before you print anything else.

Changing the Layout of a Printed Graph

Note. Some laser printers cannot print on the top half-inch and bottom half-inch of a page. So if you specify a Top Edge setting less than one-half inch, your laser printer may not be able to carry out this instruction.

The default Graph Print, Layout settings work in many situations, like the previous example. However, you can change the Layout settings, discussed below, to customize a printed graph.

- *Dimensions* determines the unit of measurement used by the other Layout settings. The default is Inches, but you can also specify Centimeters.

- *Left Edge* designates the left margin—the amount of blank space the graph is offset from the left edge of the page. The default is 0 inches.

- *Top Edge* indicates the top margin—the amount of blank space the graph is offset from the top edge of the page. The default is 0 inches.

- *4:3 Aspect* controls the width-to-height ratio of a printed graph. Quattro Pro, by default, maintains a default 4:3 ratio (4 inches of width for every 3 inches of height) when it prints a graph. This is the typical aspect ratio of most screens, so by default the graph is printed as it appears on the screen. Select No to override this aspect ratio, and then use Height and Width to specify your own dimensions.

- *Height* is the height of the printed graph. This setting also indirectly controls the bottom margin. You can specify any height from 1 to 10 inches.

- *Width* is the width of the printed graph. You can specify any width from 1 to 8 inches. The Width setting indirectly sets the right margin.

NOTE. *If 4:3 Aspect is set to No, Quattro Pro prints the graph using the Height and Width settings. However, if 4:3 Aspect is set to Yes, the printed result may not follow the exact Height and Width settings if they do not conform to this 4:3 ratio. For example, if you set Width to 6 and Height to 3, Quattro Pro prints a graph 4 inches wide and 3 inches high.*

- *Orientation* controls the page orientation. The default, Portrait, prints a graph vertically on a page. Choose Landscape to print a graph sideways (horizontally) on a page; however, remember to adjust the Width and Height settings accordingly.

- *Reset* sets the Graph Print, Layout settings to the current defaults.

- *Update* saves the current Graph Print, Layout settings as the new defaults, to which you are returned whenever you select Reset.

You can use the 4:3 Aspect setting to print a graph on an entire page. For instance, to print the stacked bar graph in Figure 8.101 vertically on a page, specify Orientation, Portrait and 4:3 Aspect, No. (Keep the default Height and Width settings of 0.) The result is a graph almost as large as the page, with elongated stacked bars. However, if you print this graph sideways, using Orientation, Landscape and 4:3 Aspect, No, you get a graph with wide stacked bars and an elongated x-axis.

You can use /Print, Graph Print, Layout to create a graph different in appearance from that produced by the Layout default settings. Before you print the graph, however, you will want to preview the effect of these Layout settings. The section just below tells you how to preview a graph.

Previewing a Graph

Quattro Pro's Screen Preview feature (see Chapter 6) allows you to preview a printed graph on screen before you actually print it. Since Quattro Pro prints to Screen Preview in graphics mode, the graph appears as though you printed it to your default graphics printer.

For instance, to preview the graph in Figure 8.101, choose /Print, Graph Print, Destination, Screen Preview, as shown in Figure 8.103. Then select Go from the Graph Print menu. Quattro Pro displays the Screen Preview in Figure 8.104, using the Orientation and Layout settings you selected, as well as the /Graph settings—including any specified fonts. Press Esc at any time to return to the Graph Print menu.

Note. If you did not choose to install Bitstream fonts during installation, Quattro Pro builds them as needed. Thus, when you print to Screen Preview, you may see the message "Now building fonts."

Figure 8.103

The /Print, Graph Print, Destination, Screen Preview menu

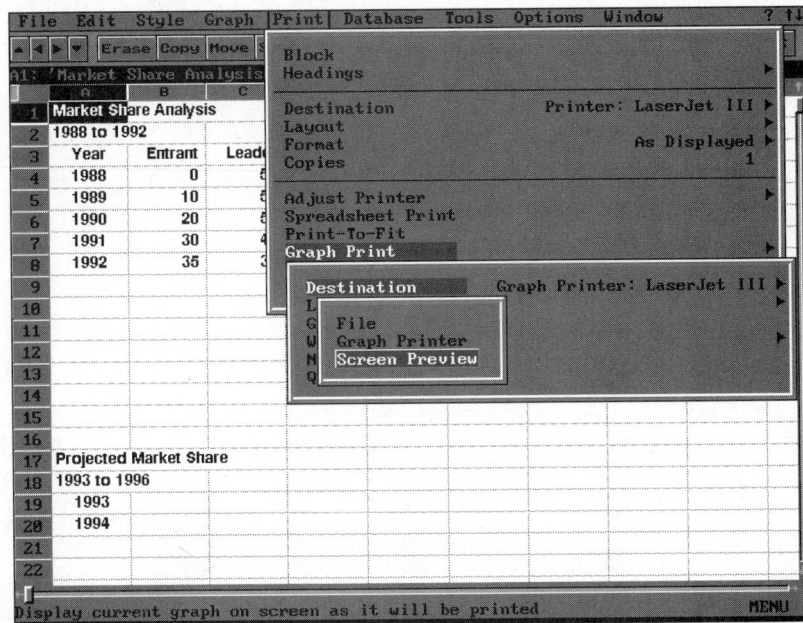

Quattro Pro initially displays the graph using the 100% Screen Preview mode shown in Figure 8.104. You can use this mode to check the overall appearance of the printed graph. In addition, Screen Preview includes 200% and 400% zoom levels that you can use to examine small portions of the document. So use Zoom mode to check margins, the aspect ratio, fonts, spelling, and so on. See "Previewing a Document" in Chapter 6 for a complete discussion of Screen Preview.

Printing to a File

You can save a graph for future printing by "printing" it to a file. When you print to a file, the graph is sent as though directed to the default graphics printer. (For a complete discussion, see "Printing to a File" in Chapter 6.)

Suppose you want to print the current graph to a file named COMP.

1. Select /Print, Graph Print, Destination. From the Destination menu (Figure 8.103), select File.

Figure 8.104
Previewing a graph
using Screen
Preview

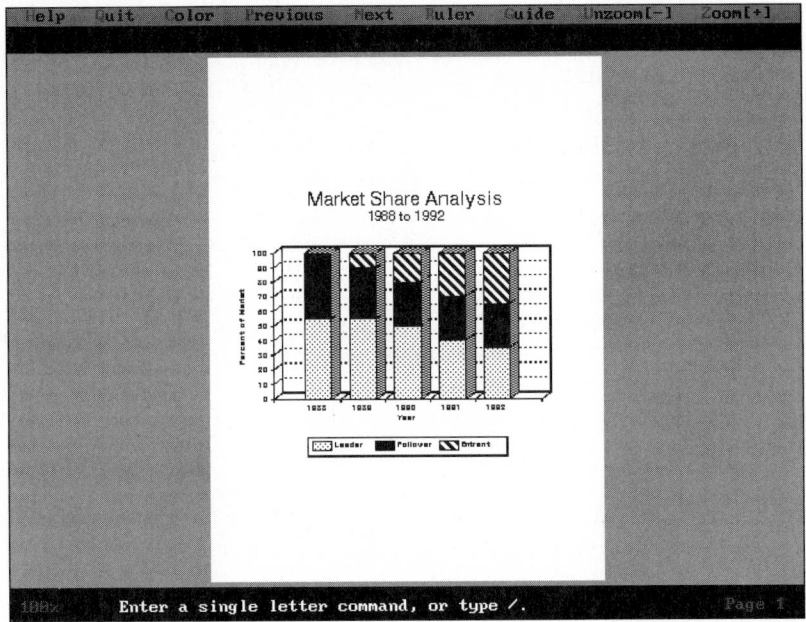

2. In response to the prompt for the file name, type **COMP** and press Enter. Quattro Pro returns to the Graph Print menu, and displays "Binary File" as the Destination.

3. Choose Go, and Quattro Pro prints this graph to the disk file COMP.PRN.

4. Select Quit to leave the /Print command. Otherwise, Quattro Pro does not close the file. However, since the file is not automatically closed, you can save as many graphs in the same file as you like.

You can now use the DOS COPY command

```
COPY COMP.PRN /B LPT1
```

to print the binary graph file COMP.PRN. DOS will send the file contents to the printer connected to LPT1.

The /B (Binary) switch in the COPY command directs DOS to use the file length setting in the file header, which you can see when you use the DIR command. In the file itself, the end-of-file character is Ctrl-Z. However, a Ctrl-Z character (1A in hexadecimal) can occur almost anywhere in a graph. By using the /B switch, you tell DOS not to evaluate any Ctrl-Z character it encounters until it reaches the file length.

Printing to Other Graphics File Formats

In Quattro Pro, you can save a graph in different graphics file formats. This is especially helpful when you want to use a Quattro Pro graph with another program. When you select /Print, Graph Print, Write Graph File, Quattro Pro displays the Graph File menu, listing four file formats: EPS, Slide EPS, PIC, and PCX.

When you choose one of these selections, Quattro Pro prompts you for a file name. You do not need to designate a file name extension; Quattro Pro automatically provides one based on the file format you choose.

CAUTION! *Once a graph is in a foreign file format, it can only be brought back into Quattro Pro using /Graph Annotate. (The exception is the PCX format, which cannot be brought back into Quattro Pro at all.) Therefore, make sure you save a copy of the graph in Quattro Pro before you write it to another file format.*

EPS and Slide EPS File Formats

The EPS file format creates an encapsulated PostScript file with an .EPS extension. This file format is compatible with many word processing and desktop publishing programs.

If the graph includes Bitstream fonts, the closest PostScript font is substituted in its place. You can take full advantage of the many PostScript fonts, however, by specifying a PostScript printer as the current printer.

The Slide EPS file format also creates an encapsulated PostScript file. Once you've created a file with the Slide EPS command, you can send it to a slide service that creates 35-mm slides from encapsulated PostScript files.

If you are creating slides, the Slide EPS format is by far the best choice. The quality of a slide using a PCX format is only as good as your screen resolution, whereas the quality of an EPS file is as good as your output device. Therefore, there is almost no limit to the quality of the picture you can produce from an EPS file.

PIC File Format

The PIC file format stores a graph in a file format compatible with Lotus 1-2-3. This file can then be used with PrintGraph in 1-2-3 Release 2.2 and earlier versions. This format creates a file with a .PIC extension.

PCX File Format

The PCX format creates a file that is compatible with several commercial paint programs, such as PC Paintbrush. Once a graph is in PCX format, it cannot be recalled into Quattro Pro.

Many slide services can create 35-mm slides from a PCX file. However, the quality of a PCX file is only as good as the screen resolution. If you have a monochrome graphics card, for example, the quality of the PCX file may be very poor indeed. Unless you have a very high quality graphics screen, use the Slide EPS format instead.

9

Using the Graph Annotator

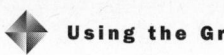

WITH MANY SPREADSHEET PROGRAMS, ANNOTATING GRAPHS IS limited to adding lines, arrows, and boxed text to an otherwise finished graph. If this is all you expect from Quattro Pro, however, then you aren't setting your sights high enough. Quattro Pro's Graph Annotator is a powerful built-in tool that lets you do far more than add simple annotations to existing graphs. Here are some examples of what you can do.

- Create freehand images with the same kinds of design tools that you usually find only in paint programs. You can draw lines, arrows, rectangles, ellipses, and polygons in a variety of colors and sizes.

- Create text graphs, such as flow charts, organizational charts, and bulleted lists.

- Add buttons to a graph so that you can select different slide sequences during a slide show. A graph button can even invoke a macro to drive a nonsequential slide show.

- Import clip art in CGM (Computer Graphics Metafile) format or Quattro Pro's Clipboard format.

- Copy, move, or resize existing design elements. You can also copy or move these elements from one graph to another, even when the graphs reside in different files.

Whether you perform these operations on an existing graph or start from a blank screen is entirely up to you. The end result is a finished graph that can be incorporated into a slide show or sent to a graphics printer or graph file. Figure 9.1 shows two examples of the kinds of graphs you can create with the Annotator.

When it comes to annotating an existing graph (one you have created with the /Graph commands), the Annotator offers some unique capabilities. You can, for example,

- Link a design element (boxed text, for example) to a particular data point in a data series, so that if the graphed value moves in the graph, the design element moves with it.

- Resize and move graph titles, legends, or even the graph itself. You can also change other graph features, such as text fonts, grid color, and background colors.

Figure 9.1

Examples of
annotated graphs

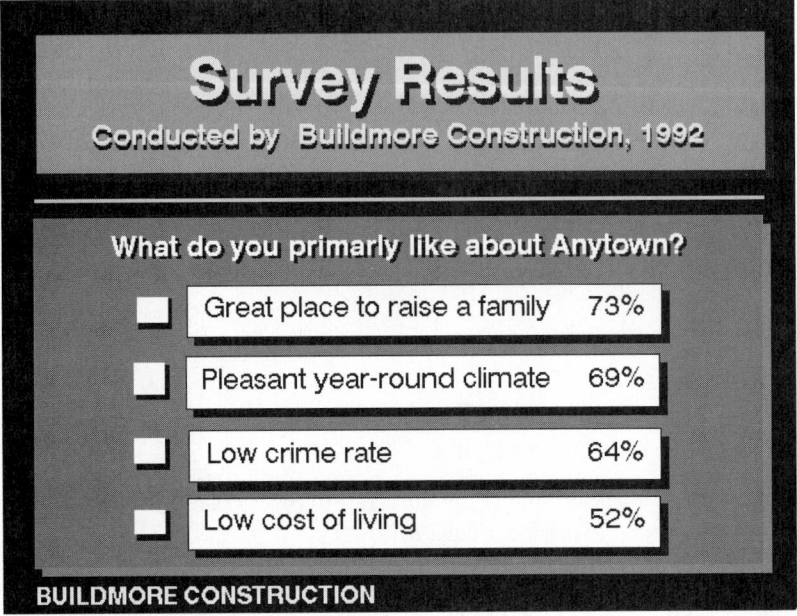

The Canadian Mounted Police

Annotator Basics

As you can see in Figure 9.2, the Graph Annotator screen looks considerably different from the screens you see in the rest of Quattro Pro. Actually, it resembles the screen of a stand-alone graphics editor—which is a good indication of the Annotator's function.

Figure 9.2

The Graph
Annotator screen
with a sample graph

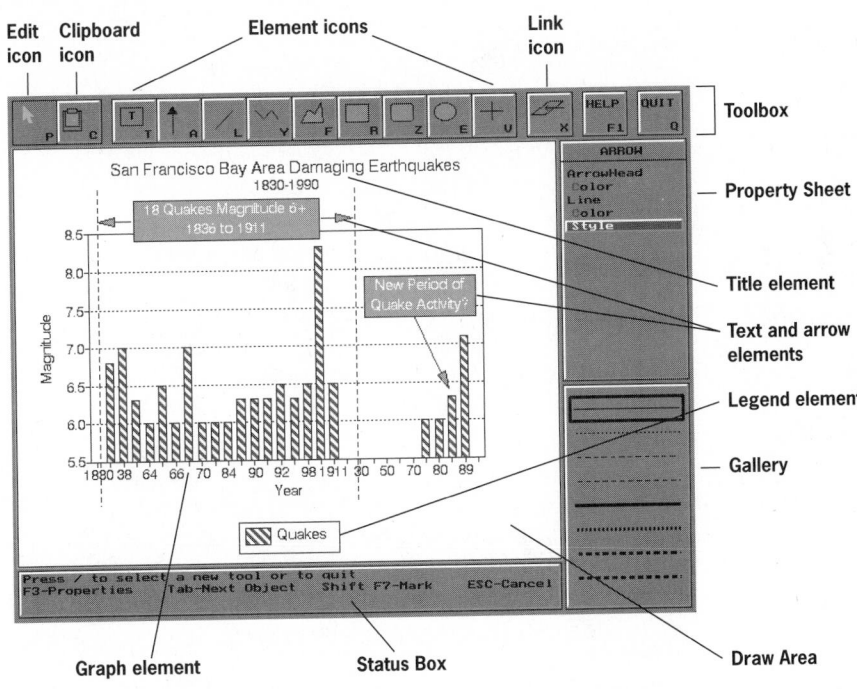

Edit icon   Clipboard icon   Element icons   Link icon

Toolbox — Property Sheet — Title element — Text and arrow elements — Legend element — Gallery

Graph element   Status Box   Draw Area

When you work with an existing graph in the Annotator, as shown in Figure 9.2, the Draw Area contains the graph. Everything within this *Draw Area*—the graph, text, lines, and shapes—are called *elements*. (In contrast, when you create a text graph, the Draw Area is blank.)

The top of the Annotator screen includes the Toolbox, a collection of multipurpose tools. The function of each tool is depicted by an icon, accompanied by a letter at the lower-right corner. The letter represents the keystroke that activates the tool (when you precede it with a / (slash)). You can use

■ *Edit (P)* to copy, move, delete, and resize elements.

Note. To annotate an existing graph that is current, select /Graph, Annotate, or press Graph (F10) to display the graph and then type /. To access the Annotator through a text graph, select /Graph, Graph Type, Text, and choose Annotate from the /Graph menu.

- *Clipboard (C)* to reposition, delete, and cut and paste elements within or between graphs.

- The nine element icons—*Text (T), Arrow (A), Line (L), Polyline (Y), Polygon (F), Rectangle (R), Rounded Rectangle (Z), Ellipse (E), and Vertical/Horizontal Line (V)*—to create design elements.

- *Link (X)* to connect one or more elements to a particular data point in a graph. When this point changes, the elements move with it.

- *Help (F1)* to enter Quattro Pro's on-line help system.

- *Quit (Q)* to leave the Annotator. This is the only way to exit the Annotator; Esc does not work.

In the Graph Annotator, there are two types of elements: *design elements* and *graph elements*. You use the nine element tools to create the design elements—text, lines, arrows, and shapes. For instance, in Figure 9.2, text boxes, dotted lines, and arrows are design elements that have been added to the graph.

Furthermore, each design element has certain *properties* that control its appearance. When you select an element icon, Quattro Pro displays its properties in the Property Sheet, on the right side of the Graph Annotator screen. For instance, in Figure 9.2 the Arrow element is currently selected, and the Property Sheet is displaying three properties: Arrowhead Color, Line Color, and Line Style. Because Line Style is selected, Quattro Pro displays a Gallery of eight different line styles you can choose from in the bottom right corner of the Annotator.

On the other hand, *graph elements* are created using the /Graph command. The three graph elements are the

- *Graph*, which includes the axes and the data series

- *Legend*, which usually appears below or to the right of the graph

- *Title*, which includes both the first and second title lines at the top of a graph

You can use the Annotator to move, resize, or delete these graph elements, as well as to change their attributes, which Quattro Pro lists in the Property Sheet. For instance, in Figure 9.2, we used the Graph Annotator to separately move and resize the legend, title, and even the graph. In addition, smaller fonts were assigned to the graph titles.

Quattro Pro uses a Status Box at the bottom of the Annotator screen to convey helpful information. In our example, Style in the Arrow Property Sheet is currently selected so the Status Box lists your available options if you are using the keyboard.

Mouse Versus Keyboard

When working with the Graph Annotator, you have the option of using the mouse, the keyboard, or both. For most tasks you will find the mouse easiest to use; in fact, the Annotator screen and its icon menu are designed with the mouse in mind. Furthermore, a mouse is by far the preferred tool for creating lines and shapes, and resizing or moving elements, because of the speed it offers and the freedom of movement it allows. Over all, this chapter emphasizes mouse techniques.

For a few operations, however, using the keyboard is best. For example, the keyboard's arrow keys work well for moving an element a precise distance or direction. Moreover, the keyboard and the mouse together provide shortcuts for other Annotator operations. You can select multiple elements at once, for instance, by holding down the Shift key as you click on elements with the mouse.

Table 9.1 defines the Annotator keys, and Table 9.2 lists the function keys that you can use in the Annotator.

Changing the Annotator Background Color

When you create a text graph, Quattro Pro displays the Draw Area in a non-descript grey color. To change this color to white, follow these steps:

1. Click anywhere on the Draw Area, or select the Edit (P) tool. Quattro Pro displays a Background menu (this menu is shown in Figure 9.28).

2. Click on Color in the Background menu, and you'll see a Gallery of 16 color choices in the lower-right corner. Choose white, the very last color box. Quattro Pro will now display a white Draw Area.

You can also change other features of the Draw Area. For instance, you can add a visible grid, discussed later in "Aligning Elements."

Design Elements

Note. Quattro Pro assigns properties, which you can change, to each design element. See "Assigning Design Element Properties" later in this chapter.

You can create and manipulate three different types of design elements—lines (including arrows), shapes, and text. Once you create a design element, you can move, copy, resize, or delete it. The easiest way to understand design elements is to work with them in a text graph. You can also use them when annotating an existing graph, however. To create a text graph, select /Graph, Graph Type, Text, and select Annotate from the /Graph menu. Quattro Pro enters the Annotator and displays a blank screen.

Table 9.1   **Annotator Keys**

Key	Function
Tab	Selects the next element.
Shift-Tab	Selects the previous element.
Shift	To select a group of elements, hold down Shift as you click on each element one at a time.
	After selecting the polygon or polyline elements, to draw a curve press Shift as you drag the mouse.
	When used in combination with the arrow keys, Home, End, PgUp, or PgDn, moves the selected element in large steps.
Del	Deletes the currently selected element or group of elements.
. (period)	Lets you resize an element or group of elements, using the keyboard. After selecting an element, press . (period), and Quattro Pro displays a rectangular outline with one handle in the lower-right corner of the element. You can then use the arrow keys to resize the element. Pressing . also moves the handle from one corner to the next, in a clockwise direction.
Home, End, PgUp, PgDn	Move the corners of a selected element diagonally. After selecting a design element tool and typing a period, use these keys to draw the element.
Arrow keys	Move or resize a selected element. After selecting a design element tool and typing a period, use these keys to draw the element.
Ctrl-Enter	When entering or editing a text element, starts a new line.
Backspace	When entering or editing a text element, deletes the character to the left of the cursor.
/ (slash)	Activates the Toolbox.
Esc	Cancels the current drawing operation. When a tool is active, cancels the current command selection.
Enter	Accepts the current drawing operation.
Alt	Pressing Alt and dragging the mouse selects a group of elements and automatically enters Proportional Resizing mode. Releasing the mouse button causes handles to appear, which you can drag to resize all the elements in the group at once.

Table 9.2	**Graph Annotator Function Keys**

Key	Function
F2	Enters Edit mode after a text element is selected.
F3	Activates the Property Sheet.
F7	After you select a group of elements, activates Proportional Resizing mode, where size and spacing between elements are adjusted at the same time.
Shift-F7	Lets you select a group of elements with the keyboard. Retains the current element, so that Tab or Shift-Tab will add an additional element to the group.
F10	Redraws the Draw Area. Lets you refresh the screen to eliminate partially drawn elements when the moving and resizing of elements obscures other elements.

Creating a Design Element

Tip. Use the visible grid and Snap-to features to easily create design elements. See "Aligning Elements" later in this chapter.

When working in the Annotator, you use the nine element tools to create design elements. Because of their similarity, design elements are grouped into three categories: lines and arrows, shapes, and text.

The Annotator includes four tools that create different types of lines and arrows, and four tools that create shapes, described as follows:

- *Vertical/Horizontal Line (V)* draws a horizontal or vertical line.

- *Line (L)* creates a straight line at any angle.

- *Arrow (A)* draws a line with an arrowhead at one end, or only an arrowhead.

Tip. When creating a design element, you can press Esc at any time to abort the creation process.

- *Polyline (Y)* creates a line that is anchored at more than two points.

- *Rectangle (R)* draws a rectangle of any dimensions, including a square.

- *Rounded Rectangle (Z)* creates a rectangle with rounded corners.

- *Ellipse (E)* draws an elliptical figure, including a circle.

- *Polygon (F)* draws a multisided figure of any shape.

Vertical and Horizontal Lines

You can use the Vertical/Horizontal Line (V) tool to draw straight horizontal and vertical lines using the beginning and ending points you specify. Here is the procedure for creating a vertical line.

Note. Quattro Pro's default style for line elements is a solid blue line. To change this property (as well as the color of an arrowhead), see "Line and Arrow Properties" later in this chapter.

1. Select the Vertical/Horizontal Line (V) tool.

2. Position the mouse where you want the line to begin.

TIP. *You do not have to be exact when you use the Vertical/Horizontal Line tool. If your beginning and ending points suggest more of a vertical line, Quattro Pro creates a vertical line. On the other hand, if the beginning and ending points approximate a horizontal line, you'll get a horizontal line.*

3. Click to anchor the line's beginning point, and drag the mouse in a vertical direction. Quattro Pro draws a vertical line as you go, as shown in Figure 9.3. You can also use the same method to create the other horizontal and vertical lines shown.

Figure 9.3
Drawing a vertical line

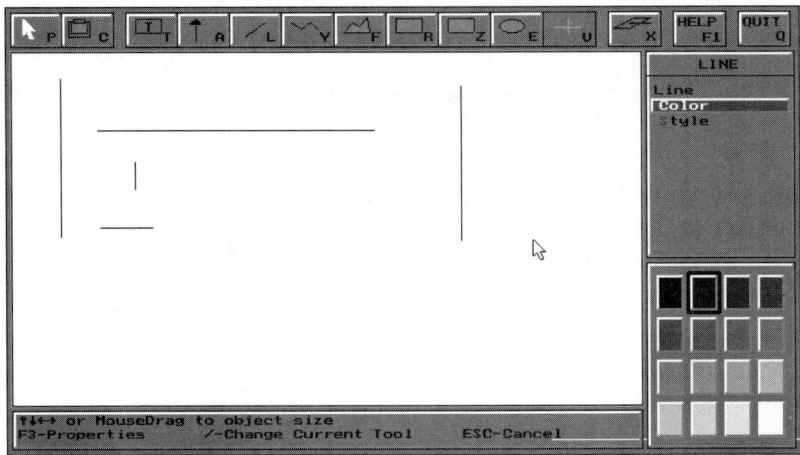

4. Release the mouse button to complete the line.

Other Lines

The Line (L) tool, as its name implies, creates all types of lines—horizontal, vertical, and diagonal. For example, to create any of the lines in Figure 9.4, select the Line (L) tool. Position the mouse where you want the line to begin, click to anchor this point, then drag the mouse in the direction you want Quattro Pro to draw the line. (The smoother the displayed line, the straighter the finished line.) When you're satisfied with the length, straightness, and position of the line, release the mouse button to complete the line.

Tip. To draw a straight horizontal or vertical line, use the Vertical/ Horizontal Line (V) tool.

Figure 9.4

Using the Line (L)
tool to draw lines

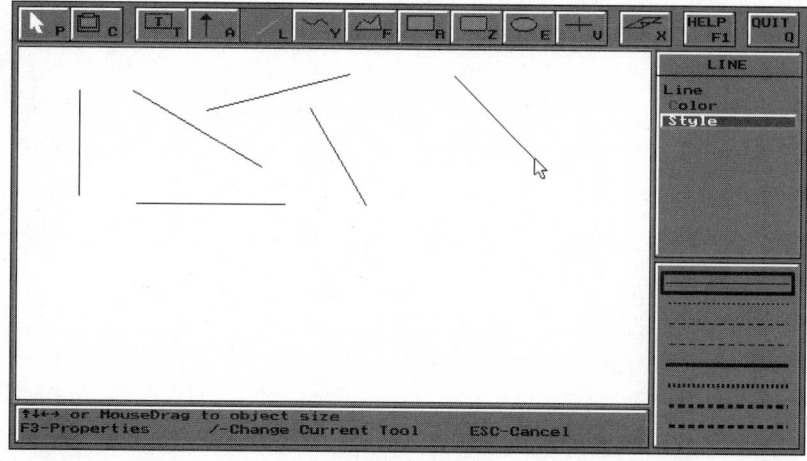

Arrows

Drawing an arrow is much like drawing a line. Just select the Arrow (A) tool, position the mouse where you want the arrow to begin, and click to anchor this point. As you drag the mouse, a line like the one at the right of the screen in Figure 9.5 is drawn as you go. To create a smooth-looking line, adjust the pointer position so the drawn line is smooth, not jagged. To complete the arrow, release the mouse button, and Quattro Pro creates an arrowhead at the ending point of the line. Figure 9.5 shows other arrows drawn with the Arrow (A) tool.

To draw just an arrowhead, use the Arrow (A) tool and draw a very small line. You can see some examples in Figure 9.5.

Polylines

A *polyline* is composed of line segments. These line segments can go in different directions, and can even cross each other.

Creating a polyline differs from drawing other line types. Here's the easiest way.

1. Select the Polyline (Y) tool.

2. Position the mouse pointer at the starting point in the polyline and click to anchor this point. To create the first segment, drag the mouse pointer (a line is drawn as you go), and release the mouse button to end this segment.

Figure 9.5

Using the Arrow (A) tool

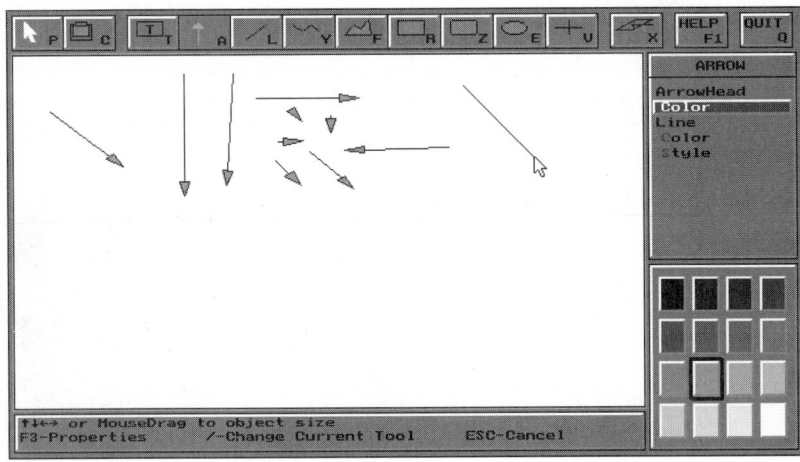

3. To create the next line segment, move the mouse pointer (don't drag it) and click at the end point of this new segment. Quattro Pro draws a line between the starting point and this new point. Continue this process, moving the pointer to the end point of each successive line segment, and then clicking. Each time you click, Quattro Pro draws a line between the last end point and the new end point. You can see this by comparing Figures 9.6 and 9.7.

Figure 9.6

Using the Polyline (P) tool

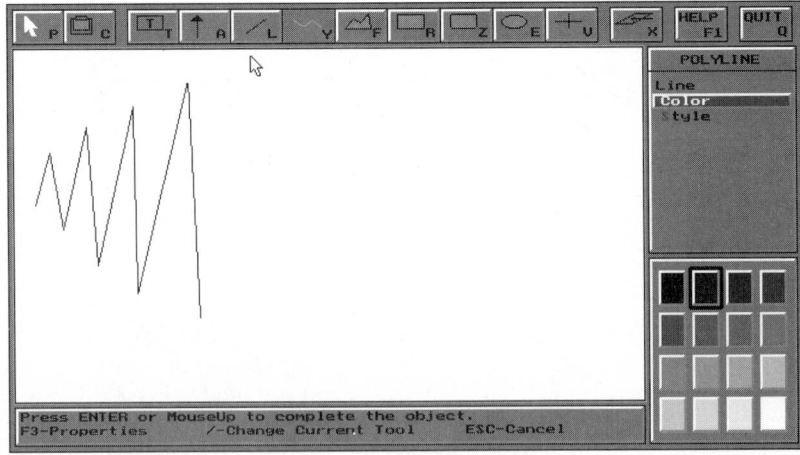

Figure 9.7
After adding more
lines to the polyline
in Figure 9.6

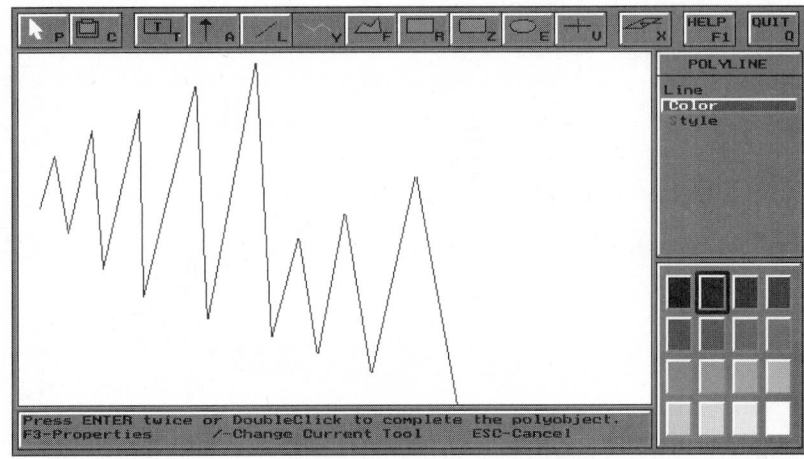

4. To end the polyline, click twice, or press Enter, or select another tool.

You can also create a polyline by dragging the mouse to the end of a line segment, clicking to establish the end point, dragging the mouse to draw the second line segment, clicking to establish this end point, and so on. Click twice to end the polyline.

Rectangles, Rounded Rectangles, and Ellipses

To create a rectangle, rounded rectangle, or ellipse, you use the same procedure as for lines and arrows. The only difference is the tool you use. For example, to create a rounded rectangle,

1. Select the Rounded Rectangle (Z) tool.

2. Position the mouse pointer at the upper-left corner where you want to begin, and click to anchor this corner.

3. Drag the mouse to the diagonally opposite corner. As you can see in Figure 9.8, Quattro Pro creates an outline of a rectangle as you go.

4. Release the mouse button. Quattro Pro creates a filled rectangle with rounded corners like the one shown in the upper-left corner of the Draw Area in Figure 9.8.

Tip. To create an irregular ellipse, see "Resizing Elements" later in this chapter.

Quattro Pro automatically creates a solid rounded rectangle. Since the interior and border are both blue, it is difficult to distinguish between the two. If you look in the menu at the right of Figure 9.8, however, you will see that you can change the properties of a rounded rectangle. (Ellipses and regular

Figure 9.8

Using the shape tools to draw rounded rectangles, rectangles, and ellipses

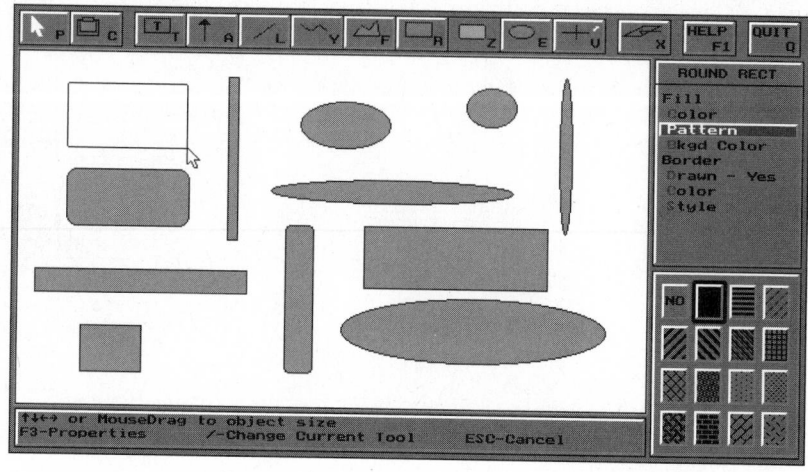

rectangles have the same properties.) See "Assigning Design Element Properties" later in the chapter.

You can also use the foregoing procedure to create the ellipses and circles shown in Figure 9.8. Even when you draw an ellipse, using the Ellipse (E) tool, Quattro Pro creates an outline of a rectangle; however, the end result is a filled ellipse using the height and width dimensions of the outline displayed.

Polygons

Creating a polygon differs from creating other shape elements. For polygons, you use a technique similar to that for creating a polyline.

Tip. To draw symmetrical polygons, use the Annotator's visible grid option (see "Aligning Elements" later). You can then draw from grid point to grid point.

1. Select the Polygon (F) tool.

2. Position the mouse pointer at the first point in the polygon and click to anchor this point. Create the first side by dragging the mouse pointer, and release the mouse button to complete this side.

3. To create the second side, *move* the mouse pointer (don't drag it) and click at the end point of this side. Quattro Pro draws a line between these two points. Continue this process to add as many sides as you wish, *except* the last side. To create the shape in Figure 9.9, for example, you need to repeat this step seven times.

4. To create the last side and close the polygon, locate the pointer as shown in Figure 9.9. Click twice, or press Enter twice, or select another tool.

Figure 9.9
Drawing the sides
of a polygon

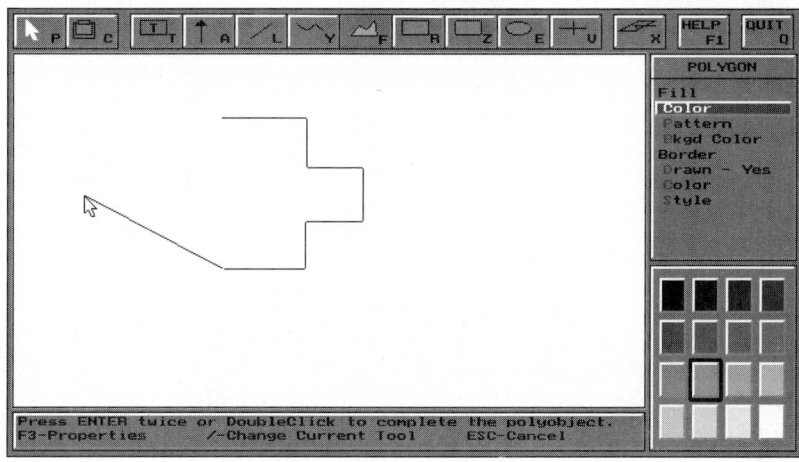

As you can see in Figure 9.10, Quattro Pro automatically connects the first and last points of the polygon, and fills in the shape. Like other shape elements, a polygon by default has a blue interior and border, which makes it hard to distinguish them. To change polygon properties, see "Assigning Design Element Properties" later in the chapter.

Figure 9.10
A completed
polygon

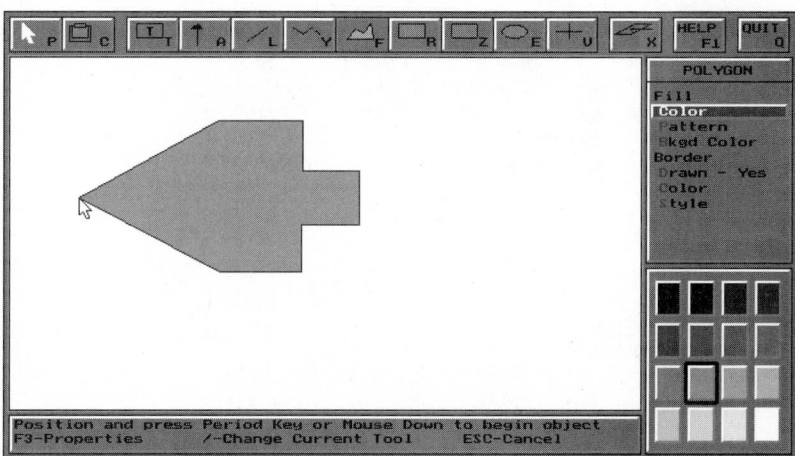

You can also create a polygon by dragging the mouse to the end of a side, releasing the mouse button to establish the end point, then dragging the mouse to draw the second side, releasing the mouse button to establish this end point, and so on. Click twice at the end of the last side.

Text Elements

You can add text to a graph with the Text (T) tool. Entering text in the Annotator is similar to entering text in a spreadsheet cell, except that you can wrap text to a new line.

To create a text element, follow these steps:

Tip. The easiest way to enter text in the Draw Area is to start typing. Quattro Pro will automatically activate the Text tool and display your text at the location of the mouse pointer.

1. Position the pointer where you want text to begin.

2. Select the Text (T) tool. A small text box appears along with the text cursor, which appears as a vertical line. Move the mouse pointer out of the way, so you can see what you are typing.

3. Type the text you want to enter. For instance, to create the text shown in Figure 9.11, press the spacebar three times, type **Strain Rate**, and press the spacebar three more times. Press Ctrl-Enter to end this line and begin a new line of text. The element will look like the text box on the left in Figure 9.11. Press the spacebar three times; then type **.076 in/yr.** (At any time, you can use the arrow keys and Backspace key to edit text you have previously typed.)

Figure 9.11
Creating a text element

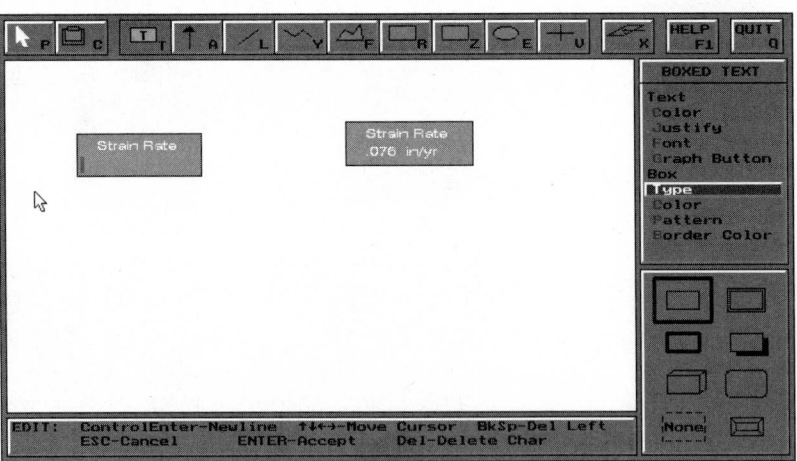

4. When you have the text the way you want it, press Enter to complete the text box. The completed element looks like the text box on the right in Figure 9.11.

5. To leave the Text tool, select another tool; otherwise, if you click the mouse or press Enter, Quattro Pro will create another text box.

Quattro Pro automatically left-justifies text and encloses it in a box with a single-line border. Usually the box is only large enough to fit the text; that is why you entered three spaces before and three spaces after the first line of text—to create a larger text box. (Later you'll learn how to change the size of the box; see "Resizing Elements.")

You can change the text alignment, the box style (or remove the box), the font, and other properties of text boxes. See "Assigning Design Element Properties" later in this chapter. To edit the contents of an existing text box, see "Editing a Text Element."

Note. If you select the Text (T) tool before you position the pointer, a text box is created at the current position. To overcome this problem, press Esc, move the pointer to the proper location, and then click.

Selecting Elements

Once you've created design elements, you may want to move, copy, resize, or delete them. You can perform these actions on a single element or a group of elements. Before you can do so, however, you must select the elements you want to manipulate.

Selecting a Single Element

Selecting a single element is easy. For example, here are the steps to select the ellipse portion of the sun in Figure 9.12 using the mouse.

1. Select the Edit (P) tool.

2. Move the pointer to any part of the element you want to select (the ellipse). Click, and Quattro Pro adds the *handles* (small rectangles) you see in Figure 9.12.

Note. To unselect one element or group of elements, press Esc, or select another element (or group), or select another tool.

To select an element using the keyboard, press Tab. If the Edit (P) tool is not active, Quattro Pro automatically makes it active and places handles around the most recently created element. Press Tab repeatedly to cycle through all the available elements. To get to a previously selected item, press Shift-Tab.

Tip. Using Tab is particularly helpful for selecting hidden elements.

Selecting a Group of Elements

It is also a simple matter to select a group of elements. Here is how to select all the elements that make up the sun in Figure 9.13 using the mouse.

1. Select the Edit (P) tool.

Figure 9.12

Selecting a single element

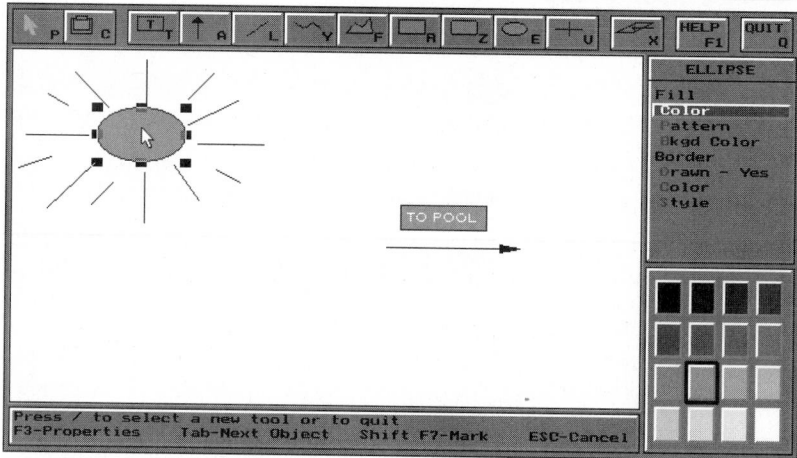

Figure 9.13

Selecting a group of elements

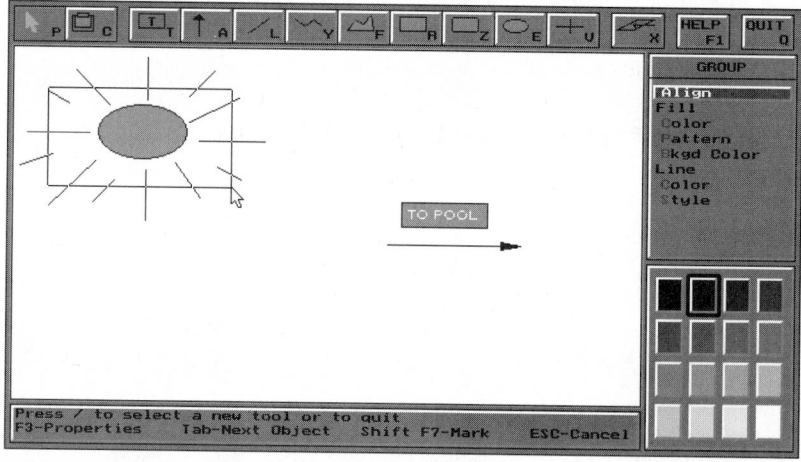

2. Move the mouse pointer to the upper-left corner of the group of elements you want to select (the sun). Click to anchor this point, and then drag the mouse pointer to the lower-left corner of the group of elements. You only have to select a portion of each element. Quattro Pro displays the rectangular outline shown in Figure 9.13.

CAUTION! *When you use the Edit (P) tool to select a group, take care to encompass at least a portion of each element in the group. Otherwise, Quattro Pro will not place handles around all the elements.*

3. Release the mouse button. All elements within the area are selected. As you can see in Figure 9.14, Quattro Pro adds handles to each element selected.

Figure 9.14
Handles indicating
the group of
elements selected

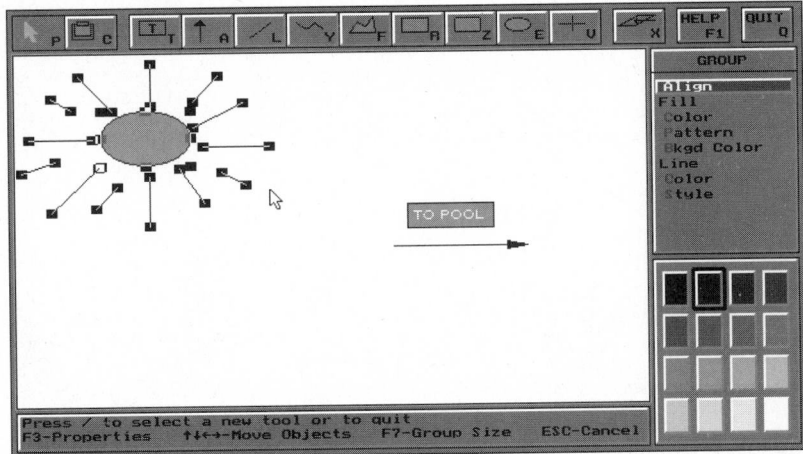

To select a group of elements with the keyboard,

1. Press Tab until handles appear around the first item in the group.

2. Press Shift-F7 to select that element.

3. Press Tab or Shift-Tab to add an additional element to the group.

4. Repeat steps 2 and 3 as many times as necessary until all the items in the group are selected.

Bringing Elements to the Top

Sometimes you will create design elements that partially or completely obscure smaller ones. When you do so, Quattro Pro "stacks" elements one on top of another in the Draw Area; the most recently created element appears on top, and the previously created elements lie beneath. So even if you cannot see them, some elements may be behind others.

For example, take a look at the arrow and the text box containing TO POOL that appear in Figure 9.14. In Figure 9.15, a larger rectangle and a vertical line have been added to create the effect of a pool-side sign. Because these elements were created last, they obscure the arrow and text box beneath.

Figure 9.15
Stacked elements

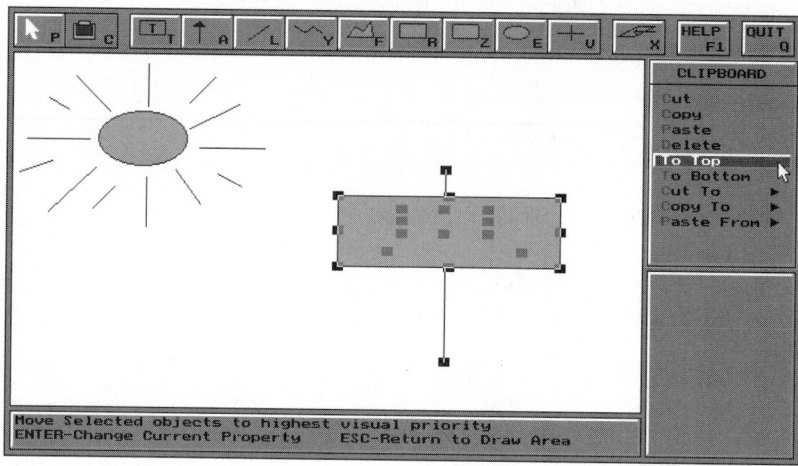

You can use the Clipboard (C) tool to reshuffle or bring hidden elements to the top of the stack. To see this, let's use the Clipboard in Figure 9.15.

1. Use the Edit (P) tool to select all the elements in the pool-side sign group. Notice in Figure 9.15 that Quattro Pro attaches handles to all the elements in the group—even to the arrow and text elements you cannot see.

2. Select the Clipboard (C) tool, and you'll see the Clipboard menu.

3. Choose the To Top option. The Status Box explains that the To Top option moves selected objects to the highest visual priority.

Now look at the result in Figure 9.16. The previously created elements—the text box and the arrow—have been moved to the top so they can now be seen.

Note that the To Bottom option in the Clipboard menu performs the reverse operation of the To Top option. Select To Bottom, and the group of elements returns to the stacking arrangement in Figure 9.15.

Figure 9.16
Reshuffling stacked
elements

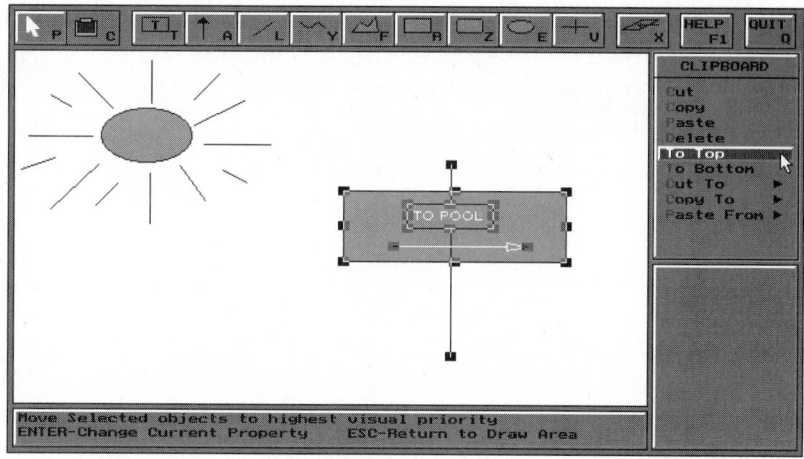

Moving Elements

You can use the Annotator to move a single element or a group of elements anywhere in the Draw Area. By moving elements you can completely reorganize your graph.

NOTE. *To move one element or a group of elements to another graph, you must use the Clipboard. See "Copying and Moving with the Clipboard" at the end of this section.*

Moving a Single Element

The easiest move operation in the Annotator is moving a single element at a time. Suppose, for instance, you want to move the ellipse shown in Figure 9.17.

Tip. The visible grid option lets you place an element in a precise location. See "Aligning Elements" for details.

1. Use the Edit (P) tool to select the ellipse. The ellipse will now have handles.

2. Position the mouse pointer within the center of the ellipse. *Make sure the pointer is not located on one of the handles.* Click, and then drag the mouse pointer to the new location for the element. Quattro Pro represents the ellipse by the empty rectangle shown in Figure 9.17. The ellipse in its current location is not affected.

3. Release the mouse button. As shown in Figure 9.18, Quattro Pro moves the ellipse to the new location indicated by the empty rectangle. Because the ellipse is still selected, handles are displayed. Press Esc to unselect it.

Figure 9.17
Moving an ellipse

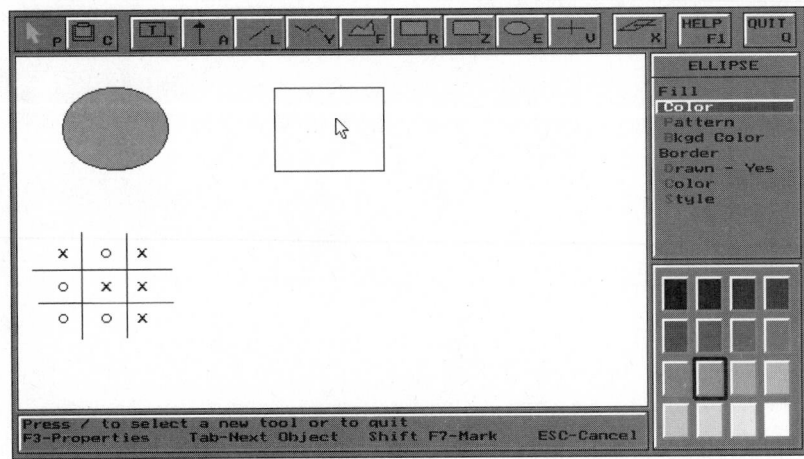

Figure 9.18
After moving an ellipse

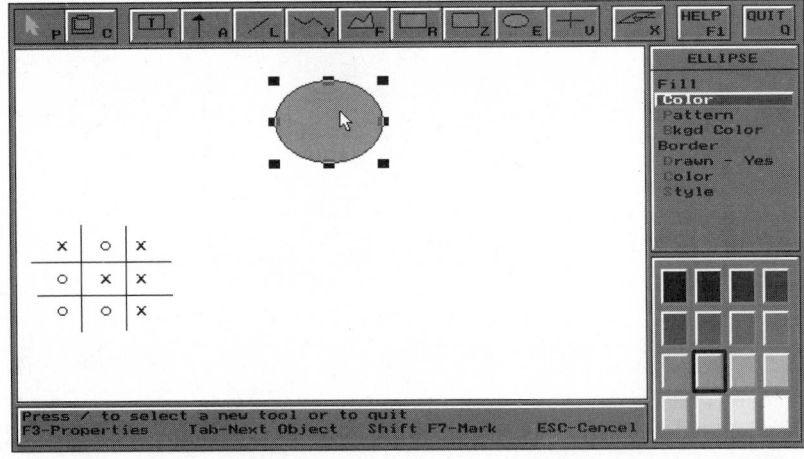

When you move a group of elements, Quattro Pro maintains the same spatial relationship between the elements when it moves them in the new location.

Moving a Group of Elements

The procedure to move a group of elements is nearly identical to that of moving a single element. For instance, suppose you want to move the tic-tac-toe board shown at the left in Figure 9.19. This is composed of vertical and horizontal lines, as well as boxless text (see "Text Properties" later). To do so,

1. Use the Edit (P) tool to select the group of elements (the tic-tac-toe board), all of which will have handles.

Figure 9.19
Moving a group of elements

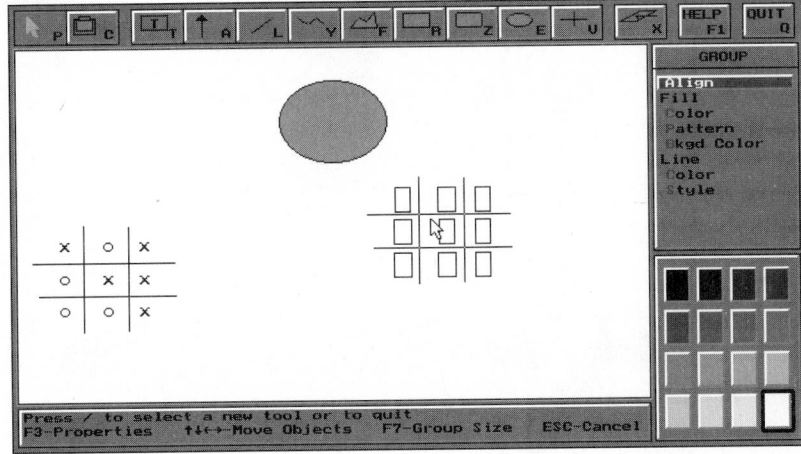

2. Position the mouse pointer within the center of the group, *and make sure the pointer is not located on one of the handles.* Click, and then drag the mouse pointer to the new location. As you can see at the right in Figure 9.19, Quattro Pro represents the group in the new location using lines and boxes.

3. Release the mouse button, and Quattro Pro moves the group to the new location (Figure 9.20). Since all of the elements are still selected, the handles are still displayed. Press Esc to unselect them.

Copying and Moving with the Clipboard

Tip. Because Quattro Pro never deletes the QUATTRO.CLP file, any elements it holds will be available for pasting the next time you load Quattro Pro.

The Annotator, like many graphics editors, lets you use the Clipboard to cut and paste design elements. Quattro Pro's Clipboard is a special file—QUATTRO.CLP on the Quattro Pro program directory (usually, C:\QPRO)—that holds the design elements last cut or copied. After cutting (moving) or copying an element to the Clipboard, you can then paste the element from the Clipboard to as many places as you want in the Draw Area.

You can even use the Clipboard to share design elements between graphs, even when those graphs reside in different files. You can also access the clip art files that come with Quattro Pro. See the later sections "Copying and Moving Design Elements to Another Graph" and "Importing Quattro Pro Clip Art."

Figure 9.20

After moving a group of elements

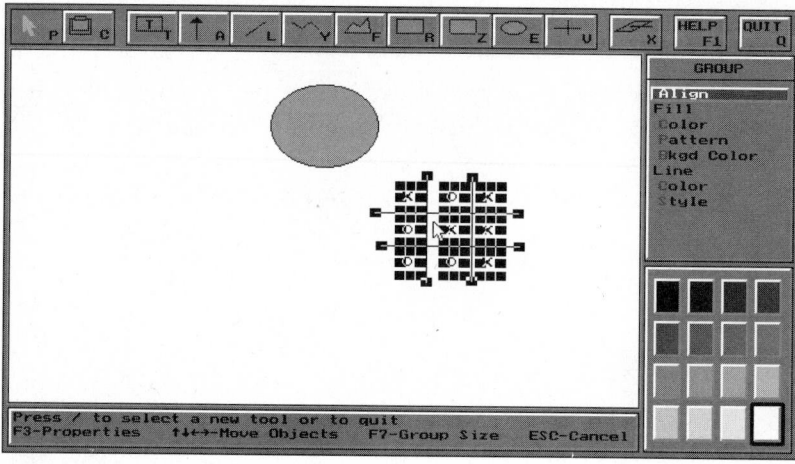

Copying Elements

Suppose you have created the text graph in Figure 9.21, and you want to copy the bouncing ball (the ellipse) to another location in the Draw Area. Follow these steps:

1. Use the Edit (P) tool to select the ellipse.

2. Select the Clipboard (C) tool, and you'll see the Clipboard menu in Figure 9.21.

3. Choose the Copy option from the Clipboard menu. Quattro Pro copies the ellipse to the Clipboard. The ellipse in the current graph is unaffected.

4. Choose the Paste option from the Clipboard menu. Quattro Pro pastes the ellipse from the Clipboard to the Draw Area in the same place from which you copied it; that is, the copied ellipse overlays the original ellipse. Handles are displayed around the pasted ellipse.

5. Now you can move the copied (pasted) element to a new location. Make sure the mouse pointer is located in the middle of the ellipse. Click, drag the mouse to the new location, and then release the mouse button. You can see the moved copy in Figure 9.22.

6. Because the copied ellipse is still selected, press Esc to unselect it.

Note. After copying to the Clipboard, you can perform any operation in the Draw Area, or even leave the Annotator and Quattro Pro. The elements in the Clipboard remain intact as long as you do not cut or copy other elements to the Clipboard.

Because you copied the ellipse, the Clipboard still contains it, and will continue to do so until you copy or cut (move) another element to the Clipboard. Therefore, if you want to add a third ellipse to Figure 9.22, just repeat the preceding steps 4 through 6.

Figure 9.21
Using the Clipboard to copy an element

Note. After cutting to the Clipboard, you can perform any operation in the Draw Area, or even leave the Annotator and Quattro Pro. The elements in the Clipboard remain intact as long as you do not cut or copy other elements to the Clipboard.

Cutting and Pasting Elements

Rather than copy the data to the Clipboard in the previous example (Figure 9.22), you can cut (move) it instead. To do so, you use the Edit (P) tool to select the ellipse, select the Clipboard (C) tool, and then choose the Cut option. Quattro Pro will move the ellipse from the graph to the Clipboard. Then choose the Paste option from the Clipboard menu. Keep in mind, however, when you paste the ellipse to the same graph, that Quattro Pro will paste it in the same place that you cut it from. For this reason, you will typically use the Clipboard's Cut and Paste options only when you move elements between graphs.

Figure 9.22
After copying and
moving the ellipse

Resizing Elements

You can increase or decrease the size of any element or group of elements
you create. However, the best way to resize a single element differs from the
best method to resize a group of elements.

Resizing a Single Element

Suppose you want to resize the rectangle in Figure 9.23.

1. Use the Edit (P) tool to select the element you want to resize—in this example, the rectangle. Quattro Pro adds handles to all of the movable
   parts of the element.

2. Position the mouse pointer on the handle you want to move. For example, to move the right side of the rectangle, position the mouse on the
   middle handle on the right side. To move both the bottom and right side
   at once, as in the current example, position the mouse on the handle in
   the lower-right corner.

3. Click on this handle and then drag the mouse. Only the bottom and right
   portions of the rectangle move; the upper-right corner remains fixed.

Quattro Pro displays an outline conforming to the new dimensions of the element, which you can see in Figure 9.23.

4. Release the mouse button, and Quattro Pro resizes the rectangle using these new dimensions. (You can see the result in Figure 9.24.)

Figure 9.23

Resizing an element

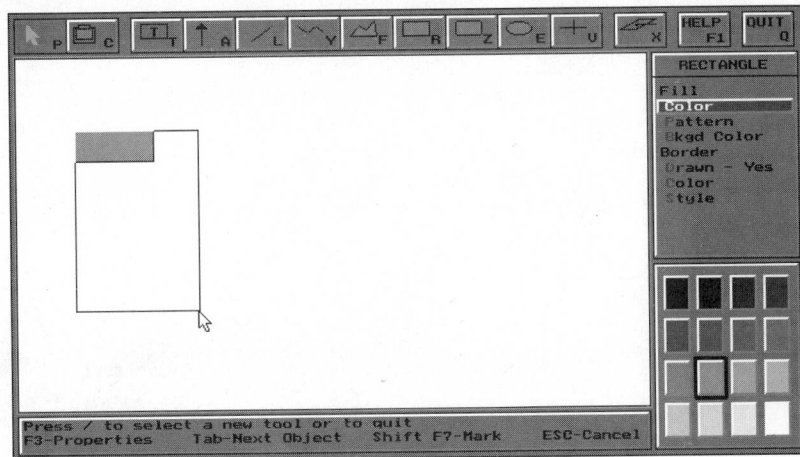

NOTE. *When you shrink the size of a boxed text element, Quattro Pro won't let you shrink the box any smaller than the minimum size required to contain the text. To shrink a text box further, you must first decrease the text font by changing the text element's font property (see "Changing Properties" later). On the other hand, if you increase the font size used in a text box, Quattro Pro automatically adjusts the size of the text box.*

Resizing a Group of Elements

You can also resize a group of elements simultaneously. However, you may get unexpected results if you use the same method as for resizing a single element. To see this, look at Figure 9.24. The Clipboard's Copy and Paste commands have been used to create two identical rectangles (see "Copying and Moving with the Clipboard" earlier.) The Edit (P) tool has been used to select both of them. When you do so, Quattro Pro displays handles around each rectangle.

In Figure 9.24, the lower-right corner handle of the rightmost rectangle is being dragged. Notice that the separate outlines Quattro Pro displays for each rectangle have increased by the same amount. So if you increase the right rectangle by one inch, the left rectangle also increases by one inch. However, look again at the outlines in Figure 9.24. Notice that the relative relationship (space) between the rectangles is *not* maintained. To maintain this proportionality, you must use a different technique, discussed next.

Figure 9.24

Resizing a group of elements without retaining proportionality

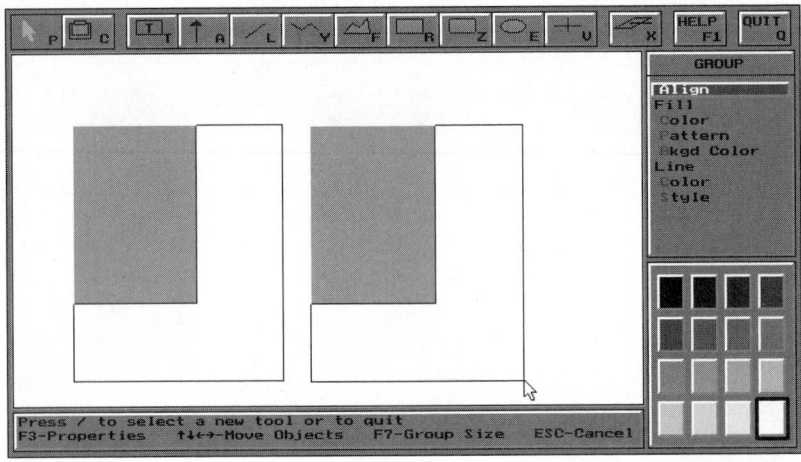

Resizing Elements Proportionately

When resizing a group of elements, you will probably want to maintain the relationship between these elements by adjusting their sizes proportionately. The easiest way to do this is to put Quattro Pro in Proportional Resize mode. Using this mode, you can resize a group of elements in the same way you would a single element, but have Quattro Pro automatically adjust their sizes proportionately.

For example, to proportionately expand the two rectangles in Figure 9.25 as a group, follow these steps:

1. Select the elements to be resized and enter Proportional Resize mode. First, use the Edit (P) tool to encompass the elements (the two rectangles in the current example). A set of handles appear around each item in the selected group. Next, press F7. Now a set of handles (like those in Figure 9.26) appear around the entire group—the elements are not individually selected.

NOTE. *Another method you can use is to keep the Alt key pressed while you select a group of elements. When you release the mouse button, Quattro Pro automatically enters Proportional Resize mode.*

Figure 9.25
Proportionately
resizing a group of
elements

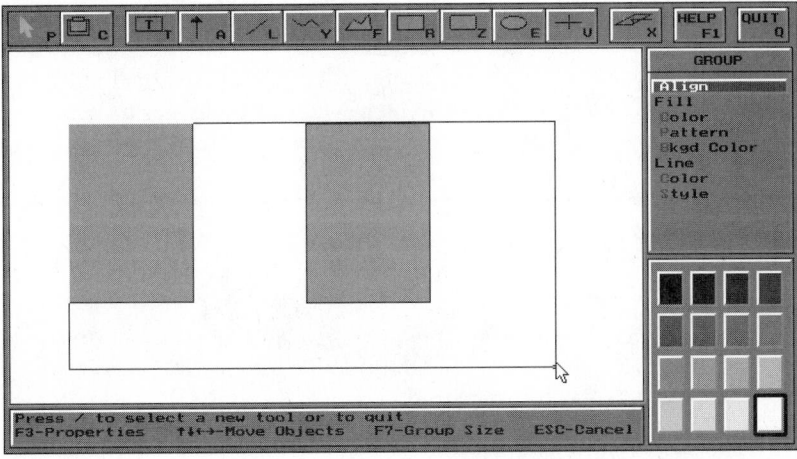

Figure 9.26
The results of
proportionately
resizing Figure 9.25

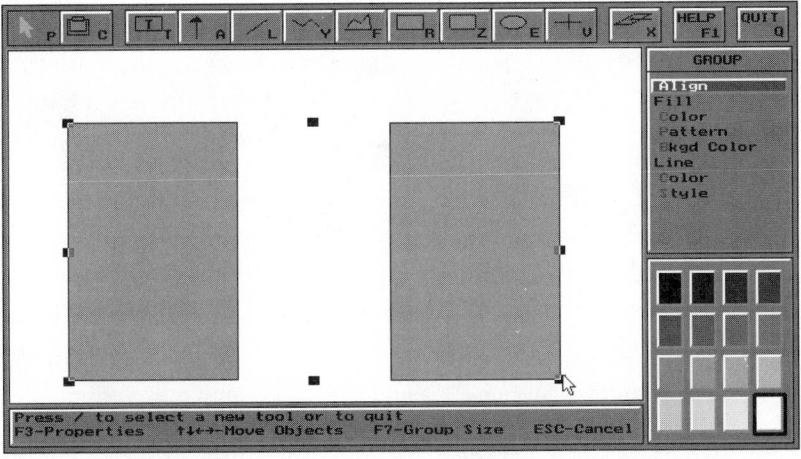

2. To proportionately expand all the elements in the group, click on the
bottom-right corner handle. Then drag this handle toward the lower-
right corner of the Draw Area. The rectangular outline in Figure 9.25
represents the new size of the element group. Release the mouse button,
and each rectangle increases proportionately to fit within this outline.
You can see the result in Figure 9.26. The group is still selected; press
Esc to unselect it.

Aligning Elements

The Annotator offers several commands for simultaneously aligning elements within a group. To access these commands, you must first select a group of elements. For example, the Property Sheet in Figure 9.27 shows the Group commands that appear when you select as a group (using F7) the large white rectangle and the text box labeled Original Position.

Figure 9.27
Result of the Group
Align options

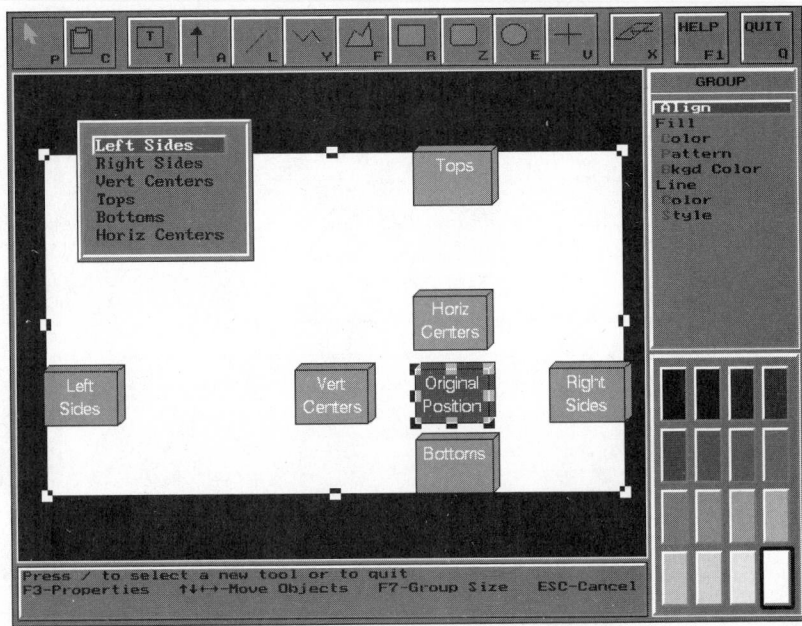

After selecting a group, you can simultaneously align the elements within it by choosing Align from the Group menu. Figure 9.27 illustrates the menu that appears listing the Alignment choices. For example, choose Left Sides to arrange all the elements of the group so that they align with the leftmost edge of the leftmost object—in this case, the left edge of the white rectangle.

Figure 9.27 shows the effect on the Original Position box if you select each of the different Group Align options. For example, choose Tops, and all the elements of the group align with the top edge of the topmost object—in this case the top edge of the white rectangle. Or choose Vert Centers, and all the group elements align so that their vertical centers correspond.

Aligning Elements Using the Placement Grid

Although you cannot normally see it, Quattro Pro has an invisible grid for locating elements in the Draw Area. There are two primary uses for this grid:

- By making the grid visible, you can use it to manually align elements.

Tip. You can also use the grid to create symmetrical shapes.

- By turning on the Snap-to feature of the grid, you can have Quattro Pro align design elements with the nearest grid line. Thus the grid lines act like magnets—when you move an element and release the mouse button, the element "snaps to" the nearest line in the grid.

Let's look at an example. Suppose you want to align the bottoms of the largest triangle and the rectangle in Figure 9.28.

Figure 9.28
Using the Annotator's visible grid and Snap-to features

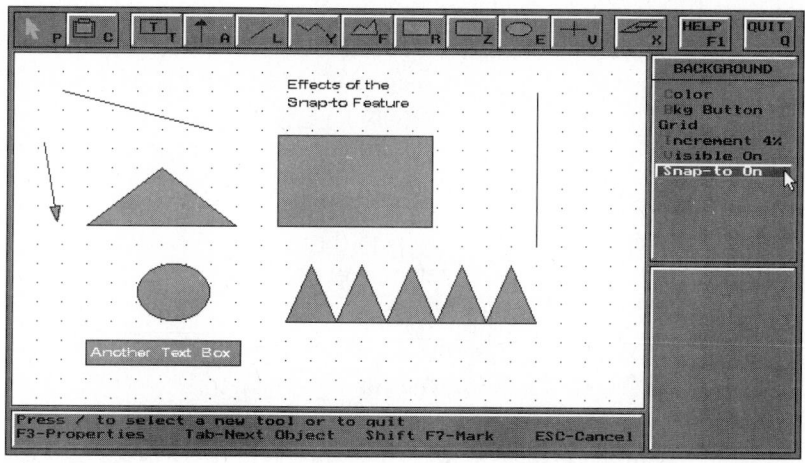

1. To access the grid features, click on the Draw Area. Figure 9.28 shows the Background menu that is displayed.

2. To make the grid visible, select Grid Visible from the Background menu. Quattro Pro now displays that Visible is On. The dots in Figure 9.28 represent the grid. (Because Visible is a toggle, you can turn the grid off by selecting this option again.)

3. To turn on the Snap-to feature, select Grid Snap-to from the Background menu. Quattro now displays that Snap-to is On. (Like Visible, this option is also a toggle.) Each element automatically "snaps to" the nearest horizontal and vertical grid lines.

When you create, move, or resize an element when the Snap-to feature is enabled, your dragging motion won't be as smooth as usual—Quattro Pro "jumps" to each grid line along the way. When you finish the operations, the element automatically aligns with the nearest vertical and horizontal grid lines.

If you like, you can use the Increment option to control the spacing of the dots in the grid. You can set this option from 1 to 25, which represents the ratio of the distance between the dots to the total width or height of the Draw Area. The default of 4, for example, means that dots appear at 4% increments; therefore, a grid of 25×25 dots will appear across the screen (100/4). A setting of 1, on the other hand, means a grid of 100x100 (100/1).

Deleting Elements

To delete a design element (or a group of elements), simply select it, and then press Del. Quattro Pro removes the element(s) from the Draw Area.

You can also delete a design element without preselecting it, by locating the mouse pointer on the item you want to delete and pressing Del. This approach is particularly helpful when you have just completed drawing a design element and you decide you don't like it. Rather than shifting to Edit (P) mode, selecting the item, and deleting it, all you have to do is press Del. You can then continue on with the current drawing tool.

To clear the Annotator of all its contents, use the /Graph, Customize Series, Reset, Graph command.

Editing a Text Element

Tip. If your text includes a bullet code, pressing F2 (Edit) makes the displayed bullet appear as its code, which you can then edit. When you press Enter, the bullet code will again be displayed as a bullet.

You can edit the text in a text element in much the same way that you edit text in a spreadsheet. For example, suppose you have previously created a text box. To edit this text, first use the Edit (P) tool to select the element. You'll see the familiar selection handles around its outer edges.

To edit the text, follow these guidelines:

- There are two ways to remove the existing text. You can just begin typing, and the old text is overwritten. Or press F2 (Edit) to bring up an edit cursor at the end of the entry. Then use the arrow keys to reposition the cursor. Pressing Del deletes characters to the right; pressing Backspace deletes characters to the left.

- To enter new text, press F2 (Edit), position the cursor where you want the text to start, and start typing.

- To consolidate two lines of text into one, press F2 (Edit), move the cursor to the beginning of the second line, and press Backspace.

- To align lines of text, see "Text Properties" later.

When you finish making changes, either press Enter or choose another tool.

Assigning Design Element Properties

Each design element has properties that define how it is displayed in the Annotator. For example, when you create an arrow element, you can specify the arrowhead color, the line color, and the line style. However, as you will see, design element properties are interrelated. The arrow line style, for instance, can affect the border style of shape properties. For this reason, the properties assigned to each type of element—line and arrow, shape, and text—are covered first in this section. Next, the relationships between properties are discussed followed by the mechanics of assigning properties to one or a group of elements.

Line and Arrow Properties

Take another look at Figure 9.3, and you'll see the Property Sheet for line elements (lines, polylines or horizontal/vertical lines). This Property Sheet contains two selections.

- *Line Color* changes the color of the line. The default is blue, but choosing this option lets you select from a Gallery of 16 colors (see Figure 9.3).

- *Line Style* changes the style of the line. Besides the default solid-line style, Quattro Pro offers seven other styles in a Gallery, shown in Figure 9.4.

When you create an arrow element, Quattro Pro displays a slightly different Property Sheet (Figure 9.5), which contains this additional selection:

- *Arrowhead Color* changes the color of the arrowhead. The default is blue, but choosing this option lets you select from a Gallery of 16 colors.

Note that if you specify a fill pattern for a group, any arrowheads in the group automatically use this fill pattern (see "Assigning Properties to a Group of Elements" later). You cannot stop this from happening. Fill patterns are discussed in the next section.

Shape Properties

All shape elements (polygon, rectangle, rounded rectangle, or ellipse) use the same Property Sheet, illustrated in Figure 9.8. Thus, all shape elements share a common set of properties.

Note. If you use a CGA monitor, you will see 8 color options.

- *Fill Color* changes the color used to fill in the shape. The default is blue, but choosing this option lets you select from a Gallery of 16 colors (Figure 9.9). This color selection also controls the color of any fill pattern.

- *Fill Pattern* controls the fill pattern used within the shapes. The default is solid, but this option offers you a Gallery of 16 fill patterns (Figure 9.8). Chose the NO option to display an empty shape outline with no interior color or fill pattern.

- *Fill Bkgd (Background) Color* changes the color behind the fill pattern. The default here is the default screen background color, grey. Select this option to choose from a Gallery of 16 colors.

- *Border Drawn* is a toggle that controls whether a shape's outline uses a color different from the fill color setting, and a border style other than a solid-line style. Because the default is Yes (as in Figure 9.8), Quattro Pro displays the shape's outline using the default border color setting, dark blue. If you select border drawn so No is displayed, the shape's outline is automatically a solid-line style in the same color as the current Fill Color Setting.

- *Border Color* specifies the color of the shape's outline. When Border Drawn is set to Yes, the default is dark blue. Select this option to choose from a Gallery of 16 colors. Don't choose a border color that matches the overall background color; otherwise, the shape border will be hard to distinguish.

- *Border Style* controls the line style of a shape's outline. When Border Drawn is set to Yes, you can change the default solid-line style to any of the seven other styles displayed in the Gallery (the same as in Figure 9.4).

Text Properties

When you select the Text (T) icon from the Toolbox, the Property Sheet (see Figure 9.11) lists the following properties:

- *Text Color* changes the text color. The default is bright white, but you can choose from a Gallery of 16 colors (Figure 9.3). You can only choose one color per text element.

- *Text Justify* aligns (justifies) multiple lines of text. Choose one of the three pictorial selections in the Gallery to left-align (the default), center, or right-align text.

- *Text Font* controls the typeface, point size, and style of the text font. The default for a design element text box is Bitstream Swiss 18 point. Choose this option, and Quattro Pro displays a menu with Typeface,

Point Size, and Style options (see Chapter 8 for further discussion of these font options).

- *Box Type* changes the text box type from the default, single line, to one of the seven other pictorial styles you can choose from the Gallery shown in Figure 9.11—double line, thick line, drop shadow, 3-D, rounded rectangle, None, or sculpted. None creates a boxless text element.

- *Box Color* controls the color within a text box in two ways. If a solid fill pattern is selected (the default,) this setting controls the background color of the text box. Although the default is blue, you can choose from a Gallery of 16 colors. However, if another fill pattern is chosen, this setting only determines the color of the fill pattern within a text box.

- *Box Pattern* controls the fill pattern used within the text box. The default is solid, but you'll get a Gallery of 16 fill patterns (the same as in Figure 9.9). Choose NO to display a text box with no interior color or fill pattern. When a pattern is displayed, the background color of a text box is determined by the shape's Fill Bkgd Color setting.

- *Box Border Color* controls the color of the text box border. The default is blue, and you can choose from a Gallery of 16 colors. This option also controls the shadow color of a drop shadow box type.

Property Relationships

Although each of the different groups of design elements—line and arrows, shapes, and text—have different Property Sheets, many of their properties are interrelated. You can see these relationships in Table 9.3.

Thus, the latest Line Color, Border Color, or Box Border Color selection you make determines the following for all future elements:

- Line color of line and arrow elements

- Border color of all shape elements

- Box border color for all text elements

Likewise, the latest Arrowhead Color, Fill Color, or Box Color you choose determines the color of arrowheads, the fill color of shapes, and the fill pattern color of shapes and text boxes. Your choice also controls the background color of shapes and text boxes if a solid fill pattern is selected. You can see how this works as you read the next sections.

Table 9.3   **Property Relationships**

Line and Arrow Properties		Shape Properties		Text Properties
Line color	=	Border color	=	Box border color
Arrowhead color	=	Fill color	=	Box color
Line style	=	Border style		
		Fill pattern	=	Box pattern
		Bkgd color	=	Bkgd color within box when fill pattern is other than solid or empty*

* Not a Property Sheet selection

Assigning Properties During Element Creation

One way to specify properties of a design element is to do so while you are creating the element. For example, here's how to choose the border style and fill pattern of a rectangle you are about to create.

1. Select the element you want to create—for this example, the Rectangle (R) icon. Quattro Pro displays the Rectangle Property Sheet shown in Figure 9.29.

Figure 9.29
Assigning properties during element creation

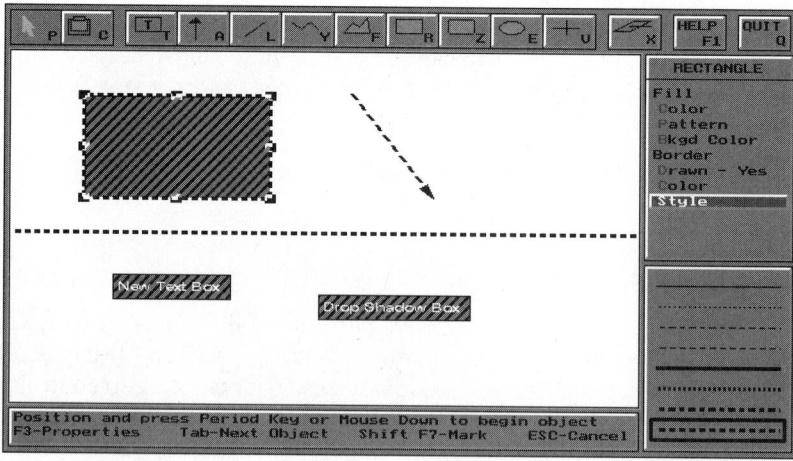

2. Choose Style by clicking on this option. Quattro Pro displays the Gallery of eight line styles. The default, thin solid line, is currently chosen. Click on the last style, heavy dotted. Make sure Border Drawn is set to Yes; otherwise, no border will be included.

NOTE. *If you are using the keyboard, press F3 to access the Property Sheet. Then use the arrow keys to select the property, such as Style, and press Enter. Quattro Pro transfers the cursor to the Gallery, where you can use the arrow keys to select the line style you want. Press Enter, and Quattro Pro returns you to the Property Sheet. You can select another property, or press Esc to return to the Draw Area.*

3. Click on Pattern in the Property Sheet. In the Gallery, choose the fifth pattern, Heavy ////.

4. Now create your rectangle using these properties, by moving the mouse pointer to the Draw Area. Click to begin the rectangle, drag the mouse to the diagonally opposite corner, then release the mouse button. Quattro Pro creates the rectangle in Figure 9.29, using a heavy-dotted line style and a heavy //// fill pattern.

Notice that the default background color in Figure 9.29 is grey. So the solid-blue fill color you see by default is really the default fill pattern.

The Border Style and Fill Pattern properties, until changed, will affect new elements. For instance, if you draw the arrow, ellipse, and horizontal line in Figure 9.29, you will see that all now use a heavy-dotted line style. However, notice that this border style does not affect the outline of new text boxes. Likewise, the heavy //// fill pattern is now used within the ellipse and text boxes (see "Property Relationships" earlier).

Assigning Properties To an Existing Element

When you want to change the properties of an existing element, use the Edit (P) tool to select the element. Suppose you select an existing rounded rectangle; you'll see the Rounded Rectangle Property Sheet at the right of the screen. Now you can change any of the shape properties listed on this sheet. For instance, you might select Fill Color, and then the apricot color from the Gallery displayed. Quattro Pro automatically updates the selected rounded rectangle to reflect your choice because the Property Sheet remains active. You can continue to change other shape properties, because the property sheet remains active until you unselect the element by pressing Esc or select another tool.

When you change the properties of an existing element, only the selected element is affected. However, your property selections will automatically affect any new elements you create. Since the rounded rectangle fill color was changed, any new solid-color shape elements will automatically use an apricot fill color. In addition, any new arrows will have an apricot arrowhead color, and any solid-background text elements will display an apricot box color (see "Property Relationships" earlier). Moreover, if you specify a fill pattern other than solid or empty, any new shape and text elements will use apricot as the fill pattern color.

Assigning Properties to a Group of Elements

When you assign properties to a group of elements, you can easily see the relationships between properties. To see this, let's return to Figure 9.29, which contains numerous design elements. We'll change the Line Style and Fill Pattern settings and examine the results.

1. Use the Edit (P) tool to select this group of elements. Quattro Pro displays the Group Property Sheet shown in Figure 9.30, and adds handles around each element selected.

Figure 9.30

Assigning properties to a group of elements

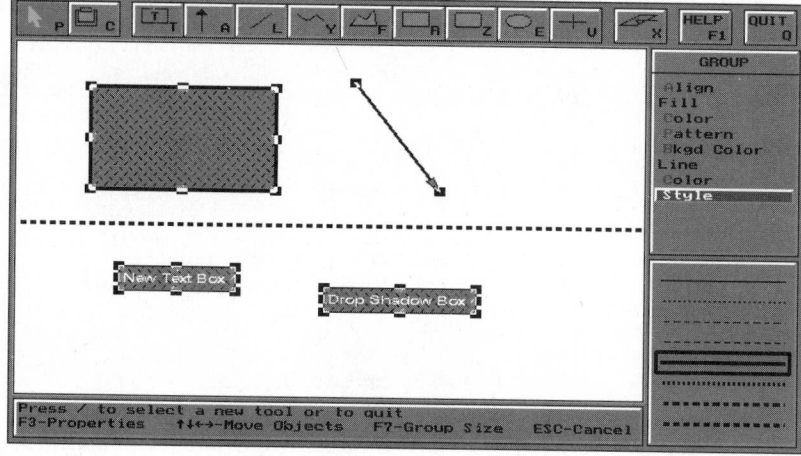

2. Select Line Style. Then choose the fifth style, thick solid, in the Gallery in Figure 9.30. Because design element properties are interrelated, you can see in Figure 9.30 that your selection affects the line and arrow line styles, and the border styles of shapes. It does not, however, affect the text box border style.

3. Select Fill Pattern, and choose the last fill pattern style (stitch) from the Gallery (see Figure 9.8). You can see in Figure 9.30 how this selection changes the fill pattern of the shapes and text boxes. Look closely, and you'll notice Quattro Pro even adds a fill pattern to the arrowhead. (This

only happens when a fill pattern is assigned to a group that contains arrows.) The grey background color is a default setting, and is controlled by the Fill Bkgd Color. The blue fill pattern is determined by the Fill Color setting (which is the shape color you see when the Fill Pattern is solid).

4. When you are finished making changes, press Esc to unselect the element group, or select another tool. Otherwise, the Group Property Sheet remains active.

Creating a Text Graph

Although Quattro Pro provides text graphs, the term "text graph" is really a misnomer. In reality, a text graph is merely a blank screen to which you add text using the Annotator. (Of course, you can also add arrows, rectangles, ellipses, and all the other graphic design elements available in the Annotator.) Some of the most common examples of text graphs are organization charts, flow charts, and bulleted lists, but text graphs can also contain graph buttons that can be used to drive a slide show. This section shows you how to create a simple text graph. You'll also learn how to create graph buttons and how to use them to drive a slide show.

Accessing the Annotator for a Text Graph

When you first start Quattro Pro, the default graph type is Stacked Bar. (You can verify this by selecting the /Graph command and reading the setting to the right of the Graph Type option.) If you immediately activate the Annotator, however, the graph type shifts to Text, and Quattro Pro displays a blank Draw Area to which you can add text and any other design element.

Of course, if a graph is already active when you switch to the Annotator, Quattro Pro displays that graph in place of the blank screen. In this case, if you want to create a text graph starting with a blank screen, you'll need to select the /Graph, Graph Type, Text command prior to activating the Annotator. (To save the current graph settings before you create a new text graph, use /Graph, Name, Create to assign a name to them. See Chapter 8 for more on naming graphs.)

An Example Text Graph

In its simplest form, a text graph is nothing more than a collection of text boxes. For example, Figure 9.31 shows a simple text graph that is a partial organization chart for ABCDEF Corporation. Each rectangle in the chart is a text box that was created with the Text (T) tool.

Figure 9.31

A sample text graph

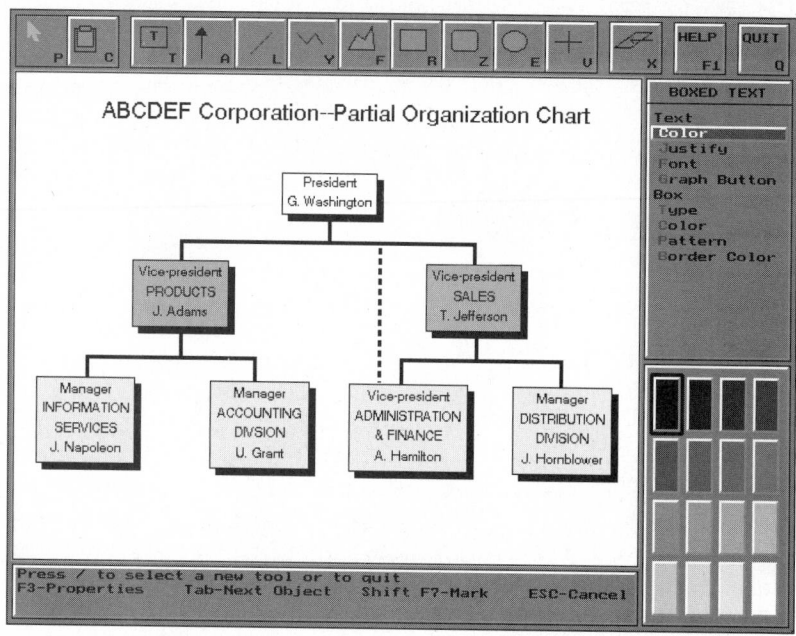

Here are the steps to create the first text element at the top of the chart.

1. Start with a clean spreadsheet and select /Graph, Annotate to enter the Annotator. Quattro Pro displays a blank Draw Area.

2. Select the Text (T) tool. Click on the area of the screen where you want the first entry in the organization chart to begin. Quattro Pro displays a small blue box with a cursor in it.

3. To change the color of the box to white, click on Box Color in the Property Sheet, and then on the white color tile in the Gallery.

4. To change the color of the text to black, click on Text Color, and then on the black color tile in the Gallery.

5. To have the text appear centered in the box, click on Text Justify, and then on the box in the Gallery that represents center-justified text.

6. To have the box appear shaded, click on Box Type, and choose the shaded box in the Gallery.

7. Type the text as you see it in the top box of Figure 9.31. Be sure to press Ctrl-Enter at the end of the first line; this causes the text to wrap to a new line. When you are finished, press Enter.

To create each of the remaining text boxes in the chart, simply click on the appropriate area of the screen. Then use the Property Sheet to change any properties you need to, such as Box Color. Only then type the entry. Whenever you want the text to wrap to a new line, press Ctrl-Enter.

After you've created all the text boxes, use the Vertical/Horizontal Lines (V) tool to create the connecting lines that you see in the chart. See the earlier section "Creating a Design Element" if you need specific instructions.

Here are some things to keep in mind as you create text graphs:

- To change the properties of an element after you have created it, see "Assigning Design Element Properties."

- Because it is nearly impossible to get the positioning of text boxes right the first time, you will probably need to move them. See "Moving Elements" earlier in the chapter. Or use Quattro Pro's visible grid for easier placement. See "Aligning Elements" earlier.

- If you've made a mistake in a text box and want to edit its contents, simply select the box and press Edit (F2). Quattro Pro shifts to Edit mode and places the cursor at the end of the text entry. See "Editing a Text Element."

Using Graph Buttons with a Slide Show

A graph button starts out as a simple text box. You then assign either a graph or a macro to the button. If you assign a graph, choosing the button instantly displays the graph; you can then press Enter or another key to make the graph disappear and return to the spreadsheet. By assigning a macro to the graph button, however, you can launch a slide show from the button. Depending on the sophistication of your macro, you can even create branching presentations that a user can view at his or her own pace.

Assigning a Graph to a Graph Button

Before you can create a graph button, you must first make and name the graph that you want to assign to the button, as described in detail in Chapter 8. The next step is to create a separate text graph that contains the graph button. For example, suppose you have a graph named 3DBAR. You then use the Annotator to create the text graph in Figure 9.31, which contains three 3-D text boxes. To assign the graph 3DBAR to the first text box, perform the following steps from the Annotator:

1. Use the Edit (P) tool to select the Marketing Data text box.

2. Choose the Text, Graph Button option from the Boxed Text menu. Quattro Pro displays a list of graph names in this spreadsheet file.

3. Type (or point to) the name **3DBAR**, and press Enter.

Now that you've created one graph button, you can easily create two others for the remaining two text boxes. Follow the steps outlined above, substituting different graph names for each text box.

When you have the graph buttons the way you want them, the final step is to leave the Annotator and use the /Graph, Name, Create command to save the text graph. When you select this command, Quattro Pro prompts you for a graph name. Type **SLIDE_MENU** (or another suitable name) and press Enter. (Naming a graph is always a good idea, but it is especially important if you plan to use the graph from within a macro, as you will in the next section.)

Now you can use one of the graph buttons you've just created. Display the Winter Sales Meeting graph (Figure 9.32) full screen, and click on the Marketing Data button. (You can also press the first letter of the text within the button, for example, *M* for Marketing Data.) Quattro Pro immediately displays the associated 3DBAR graph.

One thing you quickly discover after assigning a named graph to a graph button is that Quattro Pro sends you back to the spreadsheet (or to the /Graph menu) when you press a key to leave the named graph. If you want to return to the text graph that contains the graph buttons, so you can continue the slide show, you'll have to create a simple macro that tells Quattro Pro to do so. The next section shows you how, as well as how to attach the slide show macro to a graph button.

Note. Graph buttons are not active in the Annotator. They are active, however, when you press F10 to view the graph, or during a slide show.

Assigning a Macro to a Graph Button

As mentioned, besides attaching a named graph to a graph button, you can also assign a macro to a graph button. The function of the macro might be to launch a simple slide show or, in the case of a more sophisticated macro, to control the order and timing of slides.

Consider the \G macro, illustrated in Figure 9.33, which launches the slide show listed in column A. To understand how this macro works, recall from Chapter 8 that you can create the most fundamental type of slide show by placing a list of graph names in one column of the spreadsheet. You then use the /Graph, Name, Slide command, specify the block containing the graph names, and press Enter. Quattro Pro will display one graph after another, moving from one graph to the next when you press a key. When all the graphs have been shown, Quattro Pro returns you to the spreadsheet in Ready mode.

Note. You can also add sophisticated visual and sound effects to your slide shows. See Chapter 8 for details.

Figure 9.32
A text graph with
graph buttons

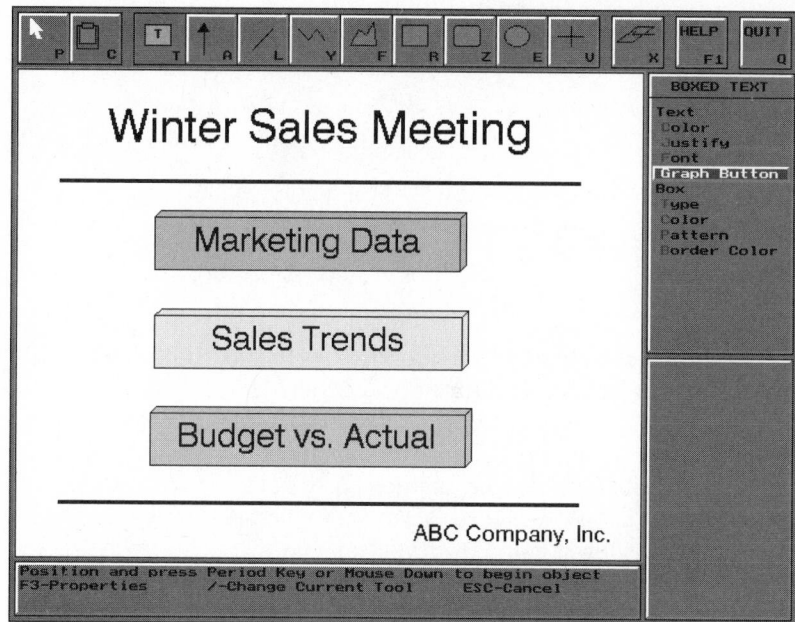

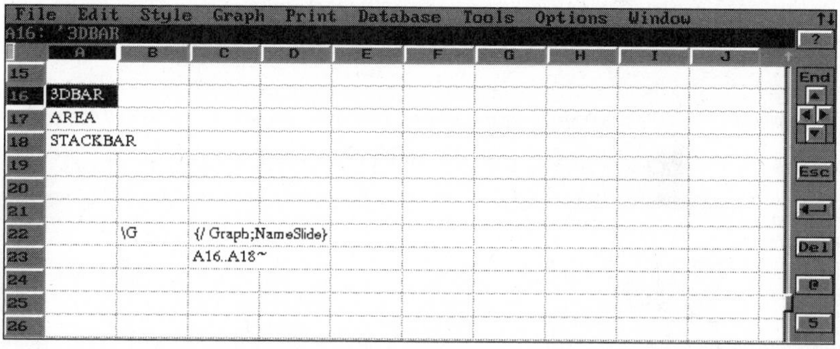

Figure 9.33
A macro to start a
slide show

In this example macro, the {/ Graph;NameSlide} command is the menu-equivalent command for /Graph, Name, Slide. In addition, the command A16..A18~ specifies the block A16..A18 as the location for the graph names, where ~ (tilde) is the equivalent of the Enter key. (See Chapter 12 for more on creating macros and interpreting macro commands.)

Here is the procedure for attaching the \G macro to the Marketing Data text box in Figure 9.32.

1. Activate the Annotator using /Graph, Annotate, and select the Marketing Data text box.

2. Choose the Text Graph Button option from the Boxed Text menu.

3. When Quattro Pro asks for a graph name, type the name of the macro, enclosed in braces—for this example, **{\G}**—and press Enter.

4. Use the Quit (Q) tool to leave the Annotator. Then save the graph with /Graph, Name, Create.

To test the new graph button, press F10 to display the Winter Sales Meeting text graph full screen, and select the Marketing Data graph button in the usual way. Quattro Pro automatically runs the macro and starts the slide show. When the slide show is completed, Quattro Pro returns you to the spreadsheet in Ready mode.

If you'd rather return to the text graph than to the spreadsheet when the slide show is completed, you can modify the macro as shown in Figure 9.34. In this macro, the commands

```
{/ Graph;NameUse}
SLIDE_MENU~
```

issue the /Graph, Name, Use command and then specify SLIDE_MENU (the name you assigned to the text graph in the previous example) as the next graph to display. You can then choose another graph button to execute another slide show.

Figure 9.34

A macro to start the slide show and then return to the text graph

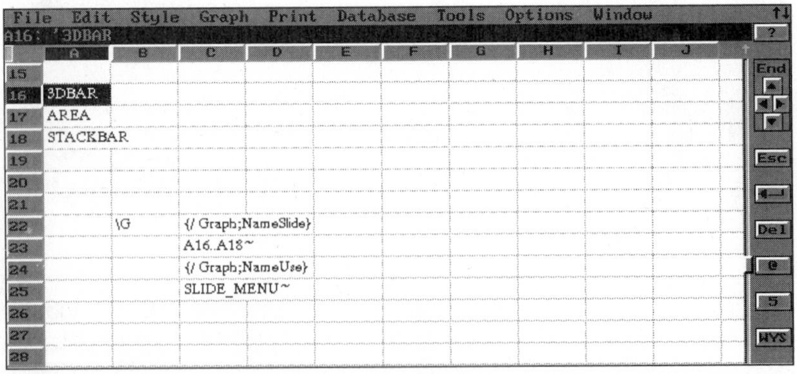

Using the Background Default Button

When you're running a Quattro Pro slide show that includes graph buttons, it's not unusual for a mouse click to miss a graph button and send your slide show skidding to a halt. To get around this problem, Quattro Pro lets you establish a *background default button*. By creating such a button, you can have your slide show display a certain graph or execute a specified macro whenever your mouse click misses its mark and you accidentally select the background.

Here are the steps for setting the background default button:

1. Select /Graph, Annotate to activate the Annotator.

2. Select the graph background by clicking on the Draw Area or by choosing the Edit (P) tool.

3. Choose the Bkg Button command from the Background Property Sheet. Quattro Pro requests a graph file name.

4. Enter the name of the graph file or macro you want to assign to the background. (If you specify a macro name, be sure to enclose it in curly braces.)

5. Use the Quit (Q) tool to leave the Annotator. Then save the text graph with /Graph, Name, Create.

6. Repeat this procedure for each slide in your slide show.

To see the effect of your new setting, press F10 to display the text graph full screen and click on the background. Quattro Pro automatically displays the graph or runs the macro you have specified. By using this feature in each slide, you can guarantee that a stray mouse click won't prematurely end your slide show.

Saving and Retrieving Clipboard Files

As you know, you can use the Annotator's Clipboard (C) tool to cut, copy, and paste graphic design elements. Two reasons for using these commands are that they let you manage elements in the current graph file and share elements between graph files.

Another advantage of the Clipboard commands is that they let you save and retrieve Clipboard (.CLP) files. Clipboard files provide a convenient way to store elements that you want to use again. What's more, Quattro Pro includes a library of Clipboard files that you can use as clip art.

Copying and Moving Elements to Another Graph

Note. To copy and move elements within the same graph, see "Copying and Moving with the Clipboard" earlier.

You can use two methods to copy design elements to another graph. The first method, using the Clipboard's Copy, Cut, and Paste commands, allows you to move or copy elements to the Clipboard, and then use the Paste command to paste the data from the Clipboard to another graph in the same file, or even in another file. The second method, using the Clipboard's Copy To, Cut To, and Paste To commands, allows you to create .CLP files. You can then retrieve these files at a later date, regardless of the data currently in the Clipboard.

Using the Clipboard

The Clipboard's Copy and Cut commands let you move or copy design elements to the Clipboard. You can then use the Paste command to paste the data from the Clipboard to another graph within the same file, or a graph in another file.

For example, suppose that you've created a particularly attractive polygon and ellipse that you would like to use in a new graph in the same file. The current graph is not named. Here's how to do this.

1. Use the Edit (P) tool to select the polygon and ellipse.

2. Select the Clipboard (C) tool, and choose the Copy command from the Clipboard menu (see Figure 9.21). Quattro Pro copies this group of elements to the Clipboard. (To move these elements, select Cut To. Quattro Pro then cuts this group to the Clipboard.)

3. Press Esc twice to unselect the ellipse. Select the Quit (Q) tool to leave the Annotator and return to the /Graph menu.

Tip. You can also use the /Graph, Name, Autosave Edits command to name a graph and automatically save any changes to it. See Chapter 8 for more details.

4. Name the current graph. Select Name from the /Graph menu and then Create. Type in the name you want, for example, **SHAPES1**. Press Enter, and Quattro Pro returns you to the /Graph menu.

5. Clear the current /Graph settings by selecting Customize Series from the /Graph menu, and then Reset, Graph. Select Quit to return to the /Graph menu, and choose Graph Type, Text to specify a Text graph. When you are once more at the /Graph menu, choose Annotate. You are returned to the Annotator with a blank Draw Area.

6. Select the Clipboard (C) tool, and choose Paste from the Clipboard menu. Quattro Pro copies the polygon and ellipse to the Draw Area, in the same position as in the original graph. The space between these elements is maintained. Handles are displayed, indicating that both these elements are currently selected as a group. Press Esc twice to leave the Clipboard menu and unselect them.

Remember, because Quattro Pro never deletes the QUATTRO.CLP file, (Clipboard), its contents will be available for pasting the next time you load Quattro Pro; these elements remain in the Clipboard until you cut or copy another element to it. To store elements for future use without tying up the Clipboard, you need to create Clipboard (.CLP) files, as explained next.

Creating .CLP Files

You can also use other Clipboard commands to copy or move design elements into a .CLP file. Clipboard (.CLP) files are a convenient means of storing elements that you want to reuse. To copy a design element, use the Copy To command; to move a design element, use the Cut To command. Both commands place the element in a .CLP file. Then, later you can use the Paste From command to place the contents of a .CLP file into an active graph.

For example, suppose you're not sure when you will use the polygon and ellipse you have previously created. The solution is to save these elements to one or more .CLP files. (You can save both elements to one .CLP file, maintaining the relationship between them, or you can save the polygon to one .CLP file and the ellipse to another.) Here's how to do this.

1. Use the Edit (P) tool to select the polygon.

2. Select the Clipboard (C) tool, and then the Copy To command from the Clipboard menu. (To move the polygon, select Cut To.) Quattro Pro displays a menu of existing .CLP files (by default in the QPRO directory), and prompts you for a file name.

3. Type the new file name (for instance, **POLY1**) and press Enter. Quattro Pro saves this file to disk, automatically adding a .CLP file name extension. You are returned to the Clipboard menu; press Esc.

4. Repeat steps 1 through 3 to copy the ellipse to a .CLP file, with a name such as CIRCLE1.

These two .CLP files are now saved on disk, and you can retrieve them whenever you want using the Paste From command, regardless of the data currently residing in the Clipboard. For example, suppose you have a new graph in the Annotator. To add the ellipse from CIRCLE1.CLP to this new graph:

1. Select the Clipboard (C) tool, and choose Paste From on the Clipboard menu. Quattro Pro displays a list of existing .CLP files (by default in the QPRO directory), and prompts you for a file name.

2. Choose CIRCLE1, and Quattro Pro copies the ellipse in this .CLP file to your current graph. Handles around the ellipse show that it is currently selected. Press Esc twice to leave the Clipboard menu and unselect the ellipse.

The CIRCLE1.CLP file is unaffected, so you can paste its contents again whenever needed.

As you save design elements to .CLP files, be aware that the .CLP format is Borland's own proprietary format, used exclusively for saving the Annotator's clipboard data. If you want to save a graph in a format that can be used by another graphics program, select the /Print, Graph Print, Write Graph File command (see Chapter 8). You can use this command to create EPS (encapsulated PostScript), PIC (Lotus picture), slide EPS, HPGL (Hewlett-Packard plotter), or PCX (PC Paintbrush) files.

Importing Quattro Pro Clip Art

Quattro Pro comes with over 40 professional clip art images, each in a separate .CLP file on the Quattro Pro program directory. You can import these images into the Annotator to create professional-looking graphs. Suppose, for example, that you want to import the clip art file USMAP.CLP that comes with Quattro Pro. To import this .CLP file into the current graph displayed in the Annotator, follow these steps:

1. Select the Clipboard (C) tool.

2. Choose the Paste From option on the Clipboard menu. Quattro Pro prompts you for a file name.

3. Specify the .CLP file you want to import—in this case, **USMAP.CLP**—and press Enter.

Quattro Pro copies the contents of the file to the Draw Area, as shown in Figure 9.35.

CAUTION! *Unlike Quattro Pro's other file-related commands, when using the Paste From command, you must make sure to include a file name extension. If you omit the extension, Quattro Pro will tell you that it cannot find the file.*

After pasting a clip art image into the current graph, you can move, resize, or change the properties of elements within the image just as you would other design elements. For example, Figure 9.36 shows a modified version of the United States map from Figure 9.35.

Importing CGM Files

You can also use the Clipboard's Paste From command to import files in CGM (Computer Graphics Metafile) format, an ANSI-standard graphics file format that is used by a number of graphics programs and clip art libraries. In fact, the ProView Power Pack (included with Quattro Pro) is a library of

over 100 color images that you can import into the Annotator. (See the following section, "About the ProView Power Pack.")

Figure 9.35
The USMAP .CLP file imported into the Annotator with the Clipboard Paste From command

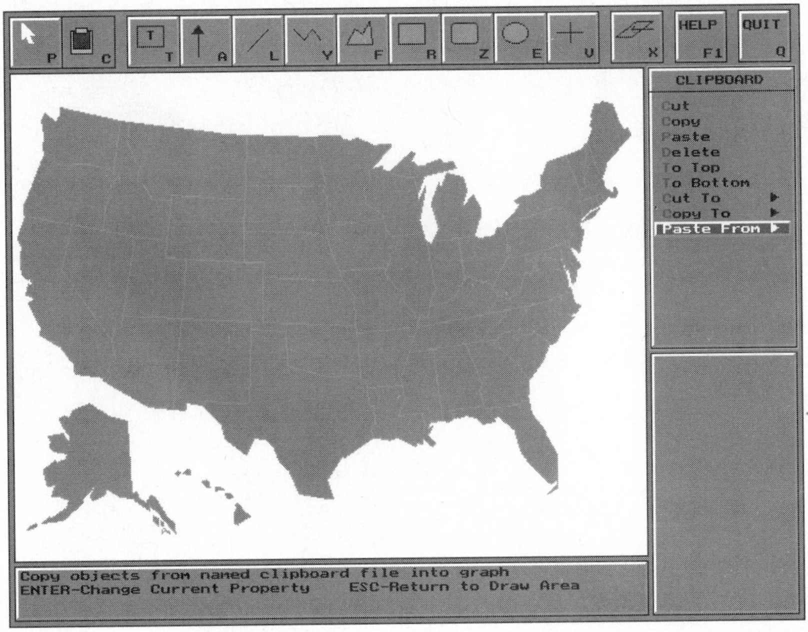

Note. Although Quattro Pro is capable of importing CGM files, it cannot export them. If you want to export a graph object, you must first store it to a .CLP file; use Copy To from the Clipboard menu.

The steps for importing CGM files are the same as for importing .CLP files. For example, suppose you've installed the ProView Power Pack, and you want to import one of its clip-art files, **USSLANT.CGM**. To import this file into the current graph displayed in the Annotator, select the Clipboard (C) tool. Then choose Paste From on the Clipboard (C) menu. When Quattro Pro prompts you for a file name, type USSLANT.CGM and press Enter. (You can also select it from the list of file names displayed.) Figure 9.37 shows the imported image. Of course, once you've imported a CGM file, you can modify its elements just as you would any other design element.

About the ProView Power Pack

You can use the ProView Power Pack included with Quattro Pro when you create slide shows. This pack is especially designed for creating presentations with Quattro Pro, and includes

■ A library of macros for creating, duplicating, and printing graphs.

Figure 9.36

The modified map from Figure 9.35

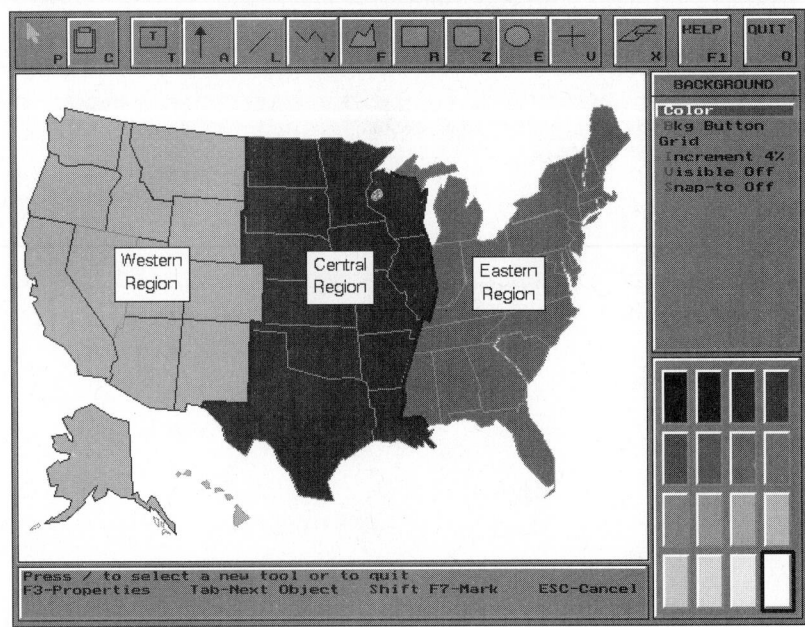

Figure 9.37

The USSLANT .CGM file imported into Annotator from the ProView Power Pack

- Two additional Bitstream typefaces, Script and Slate Bold.

- A collection of sound-effect files for adding drama to your slide shows.

- Over 100 professional clip art images from Marketing Graphics Incorporated (MGI).

- Some sample spreadsheet and template files. These files contain graph and text chart templates, as well as some nice examples of presentations you can create with Quattro Pro.

Keep in mind that the ProView Power Pack does not add any additional features to Quattro Pro. It merely contains some useful graphics elements, example files, and macros that augment the features Quattro Pro already provides.

Graph Elements

The Annotator recognizes three graph elements: the graph, the graph titles, and the legend. Graph elements differ from design elements in three ways. First, graph elements are created using the /Graph command, not the Annotator. Second, the way in which graph elements are manipulated—copied, moved, deleted, and resized—makes them different from design elements. Finally, you cannot select graph elements as a group, and then change the group properties.

Only these differences are fully discussed in this section. Otherwise, graph elements are the same as design elements as described throughout this chapter.

Selecting Graph Elements

Selecting a graph element is actually easier than selecting a design element. For example, to select the graph titles, simply choose the Edit (P) tool, and click anywhere on the graph titles. Quattro Pro will display the familiar handles around the titles (look ahead to Figure 9.40). Notice, however, that both graph titles are one element—you cannot select them separately.

When you use Edit (P) to select the graph, Quattro Pro displays handles only around the graph itself (see Figure 9.38, later). However, even though the x- and y-axis titles don't appear to be included, they are. This is discussed further in "Moving and Copying Graph Elements" below.

Remember: don't bother to select graph elements as a group, because the selections in the Group Property Sheet don't work for graph elements.

Moving and Copying Graph Elements

When you work with graph elements in the Annotator, Quattro Pro imposes some limits on moving and copying graph elements. You cannot move or copy graph elements using the Clipboard; Quattro Pro will issue an error message. Thus you cannot use the Clipboard to copy graph elements at all. Nor can you use the Annotator to move graph elements to another graph or to a .CLP file.

TIP. *You can, however, use the Clipboard to paste clip art into a graph. See the earlier sections, "Importing Quattro Pro Clip Art" and "Importing CGM Files."*

To move a graph element in the Annotator, you must select it using the Edit (P) tool, move the mouse pointer to the middle of the graph element, and then drag it to the new location. You will see how this works in "Modifying an Existing Graph: An Example" later, where the graph, graph titles, and the legend are all moved.

When you move a graph, Quattro Pro simultaneously moves the x- and y-axis titles, even though they don't appear to be selected. In addition, Quattro Pro maintains the space between the y-axis and its title, and between the x-axis and its title. This is also true for a secondary y-axis and its title, if included. When you move a graph to the left, and the y-axis title seems to disappear, it's still there—it's just not displayed on the Annotator screen. Move the graph to the right, and it will reappear.

Resizing Graph Elements

The only graph element you can resize in the usual manner is the graph itself. Later in "Modifying an Existing Graph: An Example" you'll see how a graph is resized by selecting it with the Edit (P) tool, and dragging one of the handles Quattro Pro displays.

You cannot, however, resize either graph titles or the legend using this technique. (Actually, Quattro Pro lets you do it, but the result is no different from what you started with.) Instead, you must resize the font used for graph titles or the legend, as described in "Properties of Graph Elements" later in the chapter.

Deleting Graph Elements

When you delete graph elements (by using the Edit (P) tool to select the element and then pressing Del, just like design elements), Quattro Pro follows these rules:

- If you delete the graph titles, the /Graph, Text, 1st Line and 2nd Line settings are automatically cleared.

- If you delete the graph legend, the /Graph, Text, Legends, Position setting is automatically changed to None; Quattro Pro does not clear the other Legends setting /Graph, Text.

- You cannot use the Annotator to delete the graph. Instead, use /Graph, Customize Series, Reset, Graph.

Properties of Graph Elements

Like design elements, graph elements also have properties you can change in the Annotator. Graph element properties, however, differ from design element properties in three respects. The first difference is obvious: Since graph elements are created using the /Graph command, you can only use the Annotator to change the properties of existing graph elements. Second, you cannot select graph elements as a group, and then change the group properties. Instead, you must change the properties of each graph element separately (the one exception, Box Color, is discussed below). And finally, the text font properties of graph elements do not include a Custom Drop Shadow Style selection.

Graph Properties

When you select the graph itself, the Property Sheet (see Figure 9.38 in the next section) lists the graph properties you can change. For instance:

- *Reset Scale* restores the size and orientation of the graph. Quattro Pro, however, does not always restore the graph precisely in relation to the other graph elements. For instance, after being reset, the graph may overlap the legend or titles. So you may have to reposition these other graph elements.

  Many of the options on the Property Sheet for graph properties control the colors used in the background of the graph. In all cases, you can choose from a Gallery of 16 colors like the one in Figure 9.38. (If you use a CGA monitor, you will see 8 color options.)

Note. Grid Color controls the same settings as Box Color in the Legends and Graph Titles Property Sheets. Thus the latest setting for any of these properties determines the color displayed.

- *Grid Color* governs the color of the graph grid lines, tickmarks, and the y- and x-axis lines, as well as the box outline and drop shadow color of any type of graph element. Additionally, it controls the color of the lines defining a pie and each pie slice, defining each area in an area graph, and encasing each bar and bar segment in all types of bar and column graphs. For a particular graph, the default is the /Graph, Overall, Grid, Grid Color setting.

- *Chart Color* controls the background color within the x- and y-axes. The default is the /Graph, Overall, Grid, Fill Color setting.

■ *Background* governs the background color outside of the x- and y-axes—the color behind the axis titles and graph titles. It also controls the background color behind interior data labels, and behind graphed data—bars, pies, and areas—that use fill patterns. The default is the /Graph, Overall, Background Color setting.

Three other options control the typeface, point size, and style of different labels.

Note. To change the color of the x-axis title, the y-axis title, and the interior data labels, you must use the /Graph, Text, Font command.

■ *Text Label Font* controls interior data labels, the x-axis labels, and the y-axis labels. The default is the /Graph, Text, Font, Data & Tick Labels setting.

■ *Text X Title Font* governs the x-axis title; *Text Y Title Font* controls the y-axis title. The defaults are the /Graph, Text, Font, X Title and Y Title settings. When you choose any of these options, Quattro Pro displays a menu with Typeface, Point Size, and Style options (see Chapter 8 for further discussion of these font options).

When you change any of these settings, Quattro Pro automatically adjusts the appropriate /Graph settings to conform to your selections. For instance, if you select green for the Background option, Quattro Pro changes the /Graph, Overall, Background Color setting to Green.

Graph Titles Properties

When you select the graph titles, the Property Sheet (see Figure 9.40, below) lists the following options you can change:

■ *Text Color* controls the color of both the 1st Line and 2nd Line graph titles. When the graph titles use different colors, the default is the /Graph, Text, Font, 1st Line, Color setting. You can choose from a Gallery of 16 colors shown in Figure 9.40. To assign different colors for each title line, you must use the /Graph, Text, Font command.

■ *Text Line 1 Font* changes the typeface, point size, and style of the first graph title; *Text Line 2 Font* changes these settings for the second graph title. The defaults are the /Graph, Text, Font, 1st Line and 2nd Line settings. Quattro Pro displays a menu with Typeface, Point Size, and Style options (see Chapter 8).

■ *Box Type* governs the graph titles box style. The default is the /Graph, Overall, Outlines, Titles setting. Choose from a Gallery (like the one shown later in Figure 9.39) of eight options.

■ *Box Color* controls the same settings as *Grid Color* in the Graph Property Sheet, and *Box Color* in the Legends Property Sheet. So the latest setting for any of these properties determines the color displayed.

When you change any of these settings, Quattro Pro automatically adjusts the appropriate /Graph settings to conform to your selections.

Legend Properties

Note. For a complete discussion of Legend properties, see Chapter 8.

The Annotator also displays a Property Sheet (see Figure 9.39) when you select the third graph element—the legend. Choose from these options:

■ *Text Color* controls the text color in the legend. The default is the /Graph, Text, Font, Legends, Color setting. (For 3-D graphs, the default is the /Graph, Text, Font, Data & Tick Labels, Color setting. See Chapter 8.) You can choose from a Gallery of 16 colors like the one shown in Figure 9.40.

■ *Text Font* changes the typeface, point size, and style of the legend text. The defaults are the /Graph, Text, Font, Legends settings. When you choose this property, Quattro Pro displays a menu with Typeface, Point Size, and Style options (see Chapter 8).

■ *Box Color* controls the same settings as *Grid Color* in the Graph Property Sheet, and *Box Color* in the Graph Titles Property Sheet. So the latest setting for any of these properties determines the color displayed.

■ *Box Type* governs the legend box style. The default is the /Graph, Overall, Outlines, Legend setting. Choose from a Gallery (like the one in Figure 9.39) of eight options.

Quattro Pro automatically adjusts the appropriate /Graph settings to reflect your selections.

Modifying an Existing Graph: An Example

By changing existing graph elements and adding new design elements to a finished graph, you can really make the graph come alive. Quattro Pro's Annotator makes it easier than ever to experiment with your graphs, and determine just the right combination of detail, focus, and appearance for the message you want to convey. Take for example, the graph in Figure 9.38. Although this graph is technically complete, it looks like a thousand other graphs you've seen and promptly ignored.

Figure 9.38

An unembellished graph in the Annotator

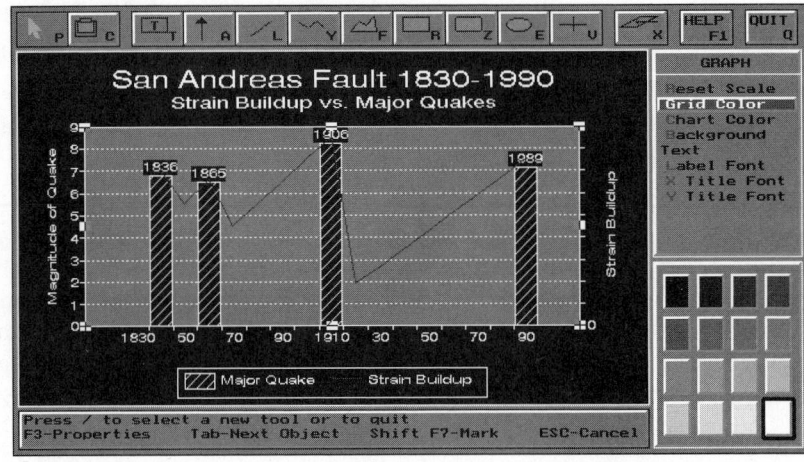

For a graph to be effective and memorable, it must be balanced, yet striking, and focus the reader's attention on a point that begs to be made. Compare the annotated graph in Figure 9.39 with the unadorned one in Figure 9.38 to see the difference the Annotator can make. Adding properly-sized elements helps to provide proper emphasis; element placement and color contrast can be equally effective methods of drawing a reader's attention.

Accessing the Annotator

You can display an existing graph that is current in the /Graph command using either of two methods:

- Press F10 to view the graph. Then press / (slash).

- Select /Graph, Annotate.

Changing Graph Elements

Figure 9.39 shows the San Andreas Fault 1830-1990 graph (Figure 9.38) after graph elements have been customized using the Annotator. To achieve such improvement, you need to make changes to the graph elements by following the procedure below.

1. Resize the graph titles' fonts. While you are doing this, also change the styles of these titles for emphasis. To select the graph titles, click first on the Edit (P) tool and then anywhere on the titles; handles will

be displayed. Click on Text Line 1 in the Titles Property Sheet (see Figure 9.40). By default, the first graph title uses 36 point, and the second graph title uses 24 point. So from the menu displayed, select Point Size, and choose 18 point. Then select Style from the menu, and specify Drop Shadow. Select Quit twice to return to the Titles Property Sheet. Use the same procedure again to change Text Line 2 to a 14 point font and a Bold style.

Figure 9.39

The Figure 9.38 graph after changing graph elements

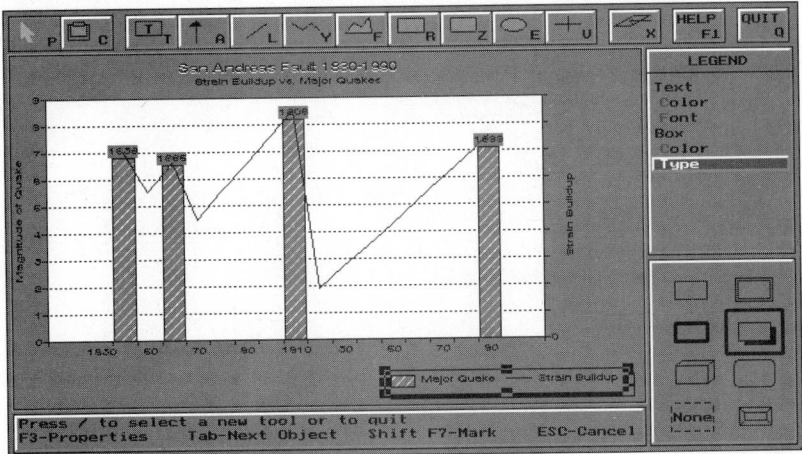

2. Reduce the other fonts in the graph, except the legend, to 14 point (the default for all other graph fonts is 18 point). To select the graph, click first on the Edit (P) tool and then anywhere within the x- and y-axes; handles will be displayed around the graph. Select Label Font in the Graph Property Sheet (see Figure 9.38). This setting affects the x-axis labels, the y-axis labels, and interior data labels. From the menu displayed, select Point Size, and choose 14 point. Select Quit to return to the Property Sheet. Use this same method to reduce the Y Title Font to 14 point.

3. Now that you have reduced the fonts of the labels and graph titles, and since the graph is still selected, you can resize and move this graph. First, position the mouse pointer on the handle in the upper-left corner, and drag it a little toward the upper-right corner of the Annotator. When you're satisfied with the change, release the mouse button. (Don't worry if the graph covers the graph titles a little—you'll move them later.) Next, move the graph to the left by positioning the mouse pointer in the center of the graph, and dragging it to the left. Release the mouse button. (If

you can't see the y-axis title, you've moved the graph too far to the left.) Later you'll add some text on the right side.

Figure 9.40

The Figure 9.39 graph after adding design elements

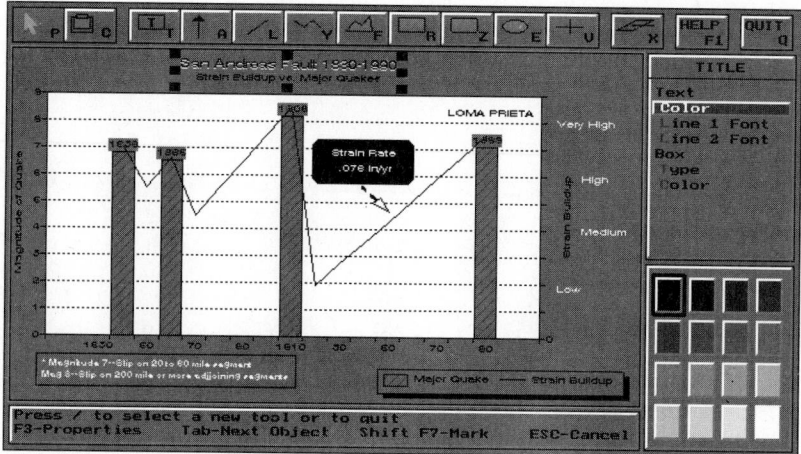

4. Change the color of the backgrounds for emphasis. The graph element is still selected, so click on Chart Color in the Graph Property Sheet, and then White in the Gallery. This changes the color within the x- and y-axes to white. Repeat this process to specify a grey Graph Background; this controls the background outside of the axes.

5. Center the graph titles over the graph. Use the Edit (P) tool to select them. Then position the mouse pointer in the center, and drag it to the left so that the middle handles line up with the middle of the bar labeled 1906. Release the mouse button.

6. Reduce the Legend to 14 point (to conform to the other labels), and change the box style. Then move the legend to the right corner to create space for a text box you'll add later. To select the legend, click first on the Edit (P) tool and then anywhere within the legend; handles will be displayed. Select Text Font in the Legend Property Sheet (see Figure 9.39). Using the menu displayed, choose Point Size and 14 point. Select Quit to return to the Property Sheet. Select Box Type in the Property Sheet, and the pictorial shadow box in the Gallery is displayed. Since the legend is still selected, move it to the lower-right corner by positioning the mouse pointer in the center and dragging it to the right. Release the mouse button.

Adding Design Elements

You can also add interest and give more emphasis to certain areas of your graph by adding some of the design elements you've learned about in this chapter. For instance, Figure 9.40 shows the design elements described below.

Tip. Don't be concerned when small point-size fonts are hard to distinguish in the Annotator. When you view the graph in the spreadsheet by pressing F10, it becomes easier to see these fonts. Or use Screen Preview (see Chapter 8) to view small fonts before you print.

The text box labeled Strain Rate .076 in/yr emphasizes the most recent data. This element uses these Text Property Sheet settings: Font Point Size 14, white Text Color, center Justify, rounded rectangle Box Type, black Box Color and Box Border Color, and a solid Pattern. An arrow logically connects this text box to the graphed line indicating strain buildup. Its properties are a white Arrowhead Color, black Line Color, and a heavy dotted Line Style.

The boxless text element labeled Loma Prieta is used to identify a particular data point. Its Text Property Sheet settings are Font Point Size 14, black Text Color, and no Box Type.

The text element in the lower-left corner of the graph provides additional magnitude information useful to the reader. Its Text Property Sheet settings are Font Point Size 12, black Text Color, and Border Box Color, and no Box Pattern.

Boxless text elements—Low, for example—are added along the second y-axis to convey non-numeric levels of magnitude. Their Text Property Sheet settings are Font Point Size 12, white Text Color, and no Box Type. The Group Align Left Sides command is used once to left-align Moderate and High, and again to left-align Low and Very High.

Notice that different point sizes, colors, and box styles are assigned to these text elements to emphasize and deemphasize data. Conversely, use uniform point sizes, colors, and box styles to assign an equal weight to explanatory text.

Linking an Element to a Graphed Data Point

One way to keep a design element paired with a specific data point in a graph is to *link* the two together. Then, when the graphed data changes, or you change /Graph settings, the two will move together. So linking a design element to a data point can be a real timesaver.

When Quattro Pro links an element to a specific data point, the element will follow the data point wherever it moves in the graph, even if the data series containing the point is moved. The link is retained even if you change the graph type.

You can also link multiple elements to the same data point. For example, it is not uncommon to create a text box and an arrow that correspond to a particular data point, as demonstrated in Figure 9.41. In this example, a text box and arrow emphasize a dramatic rise in projected company sales attributable to a Pentagon purchase order for aircraft in June of 1992.

Figure 9.41

Linking design elements to a data point

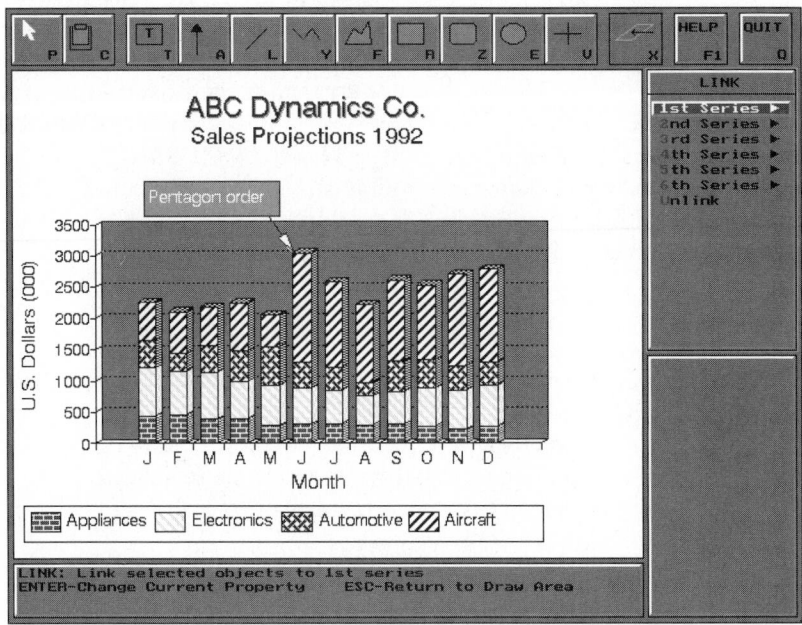

Here's how to link these text and arrow elements to the June order.

1. Use the Edit (P) tool to select the Pentagon text box and arrow elements as a group.

2. Select the Link (X) tool. Quattro Pro displays the Link Property Sheet shown in Figure 9.41.

3. In the Link Property Sheet, click on the data series that contains the value you want to link. In our example, Aircraft sales were previously assigned as the /Graph, Series, 4th Series block (look at the Legend), so click on 4th Series. Quattro Pro now displays a link index menu.

4. In response to the prompt Quattro Pro displays, enter the link index. This identifies the relative position of the value you want to link in the data series you have specified. Since the June Aircraft value is the sixth value in the 4th Series block, type **6** and press Enter.

5. Press Esc twice to leave the Property Sheet and unselect these elements.

NOTE. *If you select a data series from the Property Sheet or specify a link index value that has not been assigned a value, Quattro Pro will display the error message "Cannot link to an undefined series or point."*

From this point on, Quattro Pro links the text box and arrow elements with the sixth value in the 4th Series block. In Figure 9.41, this value is 1.75 million; the total for June is 3 million. However, if you change this value in the spreadsheet, say to 2.2 million, both the text box and arrow follow the new graphed value. You can see this in Figure 9.42. Compare Figures 9.41 and 9.42, and you'll see that Quattro Pro maintains the relationship (space) between the elements and the graphed value.

Figure 9.42
Changing the value
of the linked data
point

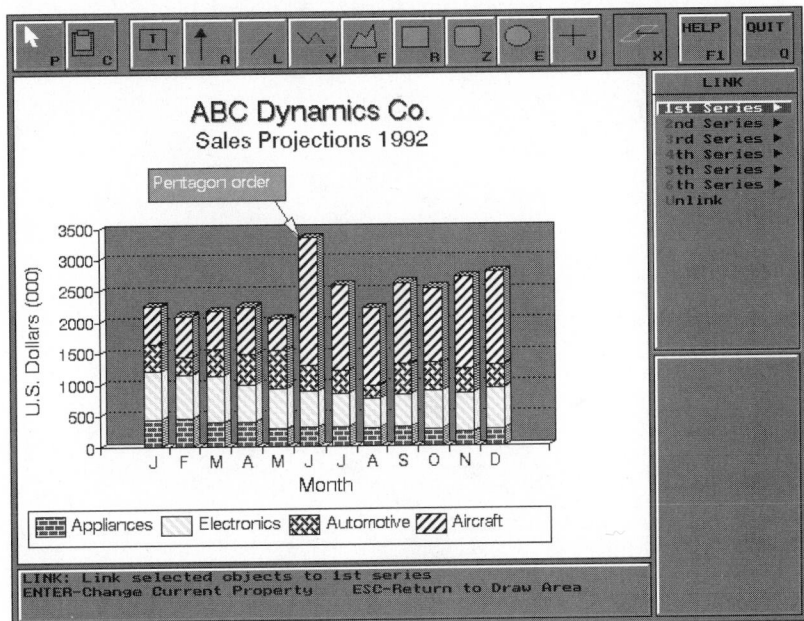

On the other hand, suppose the Pentagon intends to cancel this order. The linked text box and arrow elements will follow the smaller data point graphed, even if the graphed value is negative. Quattro Pro can do this because it "memorizes" each linked element and a point in the center of the graphed data point's image.

You also use the Link Property Sheet to unlink design elements from a data point. Use the Edit (P) tool to select the linked design elements you want to unlink, choose the Link (X) tool, and click on Unlink in the Property Sheet. Quattro Pro unlinks the selected elements from any previously assigned data points.

Should you delete a linked value from the spreadsheet, however, Quattro Pro does not graph either the data point or any design elements linked to this value. The design elements are not lost, though. If you later reenter a value in this cell, Quattro Pro will redisplay the linked elements when it graphs this data point. Likewise, if you reassign the data series block that contains the linked value to another /Graph, Series setting, Quattro Pro retains the link, and thus the linked design elements. However, if you clear the series block setting containing the linked value (using /Graph, Customize Series, Reset), and then reassign this series block, you will irretrievably lose the linked design elements.

10

Database
Management

Why Use a Database?

Building a Database

Sorting the Database

Querying the Database

Querying an
External Database

Using Quattro Pro's
Paradox Access Feature

Using the Database
@Functions

Creating a Custom
Data-Entry Form

THE COLUMN AND ROW ARRANGEMENT OF THE QUATTRO PRO SPREAD-sheet lends itself quite nicely to the task of database creation and management. Once you create the database, you can use the commands on the /Database menu to sort the information in the database in a certain order. You can also *query* the database (search it) to find information that meets specific criteria you define.

To assist you in analyzing the information stored in a database, Quattro Pro offers the database @functions. These special functions let you perform statistical analysis on the contents of a database. For example, you can get a quick count of all records that meet a specific condition. This chapter shows not only what database @functions are available, but also how you can use them to analyze the information in a database.

Quattro Pro also lets you query information contained in an *external* database. An external database is simply a database that has been created by another software program such as Paradox, dBASE, or Reflex. The results of the query are displayed in your Quattro Pro spreadsheet. In addition, through its Paradox Access feature, Quattro Pro lets you directly access information in database tables you've created with Paradox 3.5 (or later). This unique feature lets you run Quattro Pro and Paradox simultaneously and switch back and forth between them. At any time, you can load the results of your most recent Paradox query into your Quattro Pro spreadsheet. You can then use Quattro Pro's analytical, formatting, and graphing tools to work with that data.

Why Use a Database?

A database provides a structured environment for the storage and retrieval of related data. You'll find databases all around you, if you know where to look. A classic example of a database is your local telephone directory. Each *record* (listing) in this database contains four *fields* (items) of information: first name, last name, address, and telephone number. The records in this database are sorted by last name, so you can quickly *query* (search) the database to find the information you need—that is, someone's telephone number. In this way, databases provide an organized means of storing related information for easy and efficient access.

Building a Database

Figure 10.1 shows an example of a Quattro Pro database stored in a spreadsheet named EMPDATA.WQ1. You might use this database, or one like it, to store information about the employees in your company. In the sections that follow, you'll learn how to build the database in Figure 10.1 as well as how to sort it and query it. From here on, the database in Figure 10.1 will be referred to as simply the "employee database."

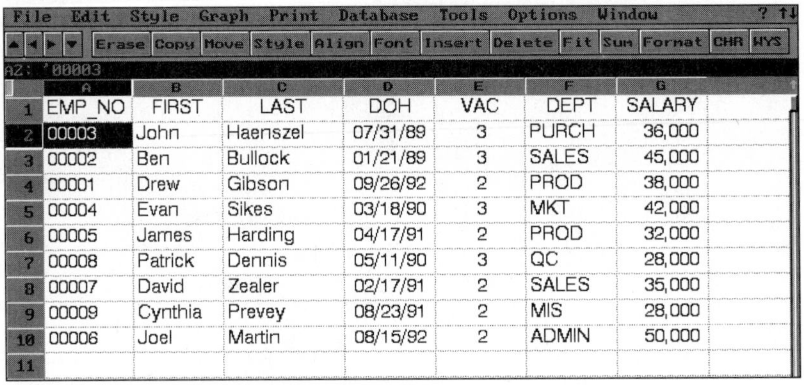

Figure 10.1

A sample database

	A	B	C	D	E	F	G
	EMP_NO	FIRST	LAST	DOH	VAC	DEPT	SALARY
2	00003	John	Haenszel	07/31/89	3	PURCH	36,000
3	00002	Ben	Bullock	01/21/89	3	SALES	45,000
4	00001	Drew	Gibson	09/26/92	2	PROD	38,000
5	00004	Evan	Sikes	03/18/90	3	MKT	42,000
6	00005	James	Harding	04/17/91	2	PROD	32,000
7	00008	Patrick	Dennis	05/11/90	3	QC	28,000
8	00007	David	Zealer	02/17/91	2	SALES	35,000
9	00009	Cynthia	Prevey	08/23/91	2	MIS	28,000
10	00006	Joel	Martin	08/15/92	2	ADMIN	50,000
11							

File   Edit   Style   Graph   Print   Database   Tools   Options   Window   ? ↑↓
▲ ◄ ► ▼ Erase Copy Move Style Align Font Insert Delete Fit Sum Format CHR WYS
A2: '00003

Database Structure

The information in a database is no different from any other information you enter in your Quattro Pro spreadsheet. The only difference lies in how you organize the information.

In Quattro Pro, a database is any collection of related information organized into columns and rows. The information in each row is called a *record*. A record contains all of the pertinent information about a particular item in the database. The first record in the database in Figure 10.1 resides in row 2. It describes employee number 00003, named John Haenszel, hired on 7/31/89, currently entitled to three weeks of vacation, working in the Purchasing department, and earning $36,000 per year. As you can see, the database contains the records for nine employees.

Each column in a database contains a *field* of information for each record. For example, the first field in the database in Figure 10.1 resides in column A and it contains employee numbers (entered as labels). The second and third fields, in columns B and C, respectively, contain the first and last names of each employee. The fourth field, column D, contains the date each employee was hired, and so on.

Notice that each field contains the same type of information—that is, all labels, all numbers, or all date values. As you'll see later under "Sorting the Database" and "Querying the Database," this uniformity of data type among the fields is critical to managing the database. See "Entering the Data" later for tips on how you can control the data type of the information that is entered into fields in a database.

At the top of each field (or column) in a database are the *field names*. You'll notice these appear in row 1 of Figure 10.1. The first field name (in cell A1) is EMP_NO, the second field name (cell B1) is FIRST, and so on. As you'll see later under "Querying the Database," Quattro Pro uses these field names to search for information (records) in a database table. For the search operation to be successful, you must observe a few important formatting rules. First of all, each field name in a database table must be unique. If two fields have the same name, Quattro Pro will use the first field name it encounters when searching the database and you may not get the results you expect. Another important formatting rule is that there cannot be any blank rows between the row of field names and the first record in the database. Finally, you must enter the field names at the top of the database as labels or as formulas that evaluate to labels. You cannot use literal values or formulas that evaluate to values.

The capitalization, font, and alignment of your field names are not important. For example, you can enter your field names in uppercase, as shown in Figure 10.1, or as a combination of uppercase and lowercase letters. (Nobody will care.) Further, you can use the /Style, Alignment command to specify any alignment setting you desire (left, right, or center) and you can use the /Style, Font command to specify the font of your choice.

On a more personal note, though, you should try to keep your field names short (15 characters or fewer) and descriptive. If you do this, you'll find that the field names are easier to remember when you later query the database. You'll also find you can use them to assign block names to the cells in the first row of the database. Later, under "Querying the Database," you'll learn how block names assigned to the first row of cells in a database can be useful in searching for records.

Database Size Limitations

The size of a Quattro Pro database is limited by two factors: the size of a Quattro Pro spreadsheet, and the amount of memory in your machine. The latter is usually the determining factor. Technically, a Quattro Pro database can contain 8191 records (the number of rows in a Quattro Pro spreadsheet minus one row for field names) with 256 fields in each record (the number of available columns). Realistically, though, the number of records that will fit in a Quattro Pro database is determined by the amount of memory required to store the spreadsheet containing that database.

Quattro Pro must keep your entire spreadsheet in memory while you are viewing and editing it. Unlike conventional database packages, Quattro Pro cannot "swap" or store part of the database file on disk and read it back into memory when it's needed. Therefore, your entire spreadsheet, and thus your database, remains in memory all the time. Of course, if you have an expanded-memory card available, Quattro Pro will take advantage of that card, often allowing you to build larger spreadsheets, and therefore, larger databases. (See Chapter 15 for discussion of how Quattro Pro uses expanded memory.)

Nevertheless, if you intend to build a relatively large database (3000 records or more), you're probably better off going with a conventional database software package—for example, Quattro's Pro "sister" product, Paradox. These packages let you build databases of virtually any size, depending on the amount of disk space you have available. Obviously, your learning curve and startup costs will be higher, but you'll thank yourself in the long run.

Location and Field Contents

You can locate a Quattro Pro database anywhere in your spreadsheet. Although Figure 10.1 shows the first row of field names starting in cell A1, you could just as easily start the first cell of the database in cell AU100.

The fields in a database can contain just about anything—values (including date and time values), labels, formulas (including link formulas), and so on. You can also leave fields (cells) in a record blank, if you so desire. However, if you decide to use a formula in a database field, you must follow two simple rules. First, if the formula refers to a cell block located outside the database, use an absolute reference. This will prevent Quattro Pro from changing the cell references in your formulas when you later sort the database. Otherwise, the cell references in your formulas will be updated to reflect their new positions in the spreadsheet and may return the wrong results.

Second, if the formula in a database field refers to cell blocks located within a database, make sure it refers to data in the same record. That way, when you later sort the database, the referenced data and the formula will travel together. When your formulas are updated for their new locations, they will continue to reference the appropriate blocks and return valid results.

Be wary of assigning block names to specific fields of information in a database record. When you later sort the database, that record may be moved to another location in the database, but your block name will remain behind. Therefore, any formulas referring to that block name may be referencing the wrong data.

Entering the Data

To build a database, start by entering the row of field names at the top of the database. For example, if you want to build the database shown earlier in Figure 10.1, move the cell pointer to cell A1 and enter the row of field names (labels), one field name per cell, as you see them in the figure. (The database in Figure 10.1 will be used in most of the examples throughout this chapter. Therefore, you may want to create this database, or one that is substantially similar.)

Once you enter your field names at the top of the database, you are ready to begin entering the contents of your records. To do this, move the cell selector to the first cell of the first row below your field names (cell A2) and begin typing in your data. Enter each field item, working from left to right, one item per cell, as you see them in Figure 10.1. For example, the first record in Figure 10.1 contains the following entries:

A2	'00003
B2	John
C2	Haenszel
D2	@DATE(89,31,7)
E2	3
F2	PURCH
G2	36000

When you finish entering the data for the first record, move on to the second one, and so on. Make sure that each field in each record contains the same type of data. For example, make sure that all of your employee numbers are entered as labels and that they are placed in column A.

As you begin entering the data in each of your records, you'll notice that your spreadsheet does not look at all like Figure 10.1. For example, column D contains date values rather than actual dates, the vacation numbers in column E are not centered, and the salary numbers in column G appear in general format rather than the more readable , (Comma) format in Figure 10.1. You can fix these problems with a little formatting. For example, you can use the /Style, Numeric Format, Date 4 command to format the date values in column D in Date 4 format. You can also use the /Style, Alignment, Center command to center the values in column E, and you can use the /Style, Numeric Format, , (Comma), 0 command to format the values in column G in Comma format with zero places after the decimal.

You can insert a new record into the middle of a database simply by using the /Edit, Insert, Rows command to insert a new row into the middle of a spreadsheet. You can then enter the information for the new record. Conversely, you can add a field to a database by using the /Edit, Insert, Columns command to insert a new column into the spreadsheet; you can then add a field name at the top of the database and enter the new field contents for each record.

CAUTION! *Inserting new rows and columns into the spreadsheet to add records or fields to a database may cause havoc elsewhere in your spreadsheet. For example, you might insert a row into the middle of a macro, causing it to run improperly. Conversely, inserting a new column may inadvertently expand a print block, causing a blank column to appear in your printout. Therefore, instead of inserting a row in the spreadsheet to add a database record, you may want to add the record to the end of the database and sort it into position later by using the /Database, Sort command. See "Sorting the Database" later for details on this command. Rather than inserting a column to add a field to the database, you may want to copy all the records in the database to an output block that includes a blank column. See "Querying the Database" later for details on how to copy the records in the database to an output block.*

Controlling Data Entry

Quattro Pro also offers a special command, /Database, Data Entry, that can assist you in entering the field information in a database. This command lets you format the fields (columns) within a database to only accept a certain type of entry. You can use this command to help you control the data type of entries made in specific fields within a database, as well as to speed up the data-entry process itself. When you select the /Database, Data Entry command, Quattro Pro displays a submenu with the following options:

- *General* Allows data of any type including values, labels, dates, times, or formulas that evaluate to any of these. This is the default setting.

- *Labels Only* Restricts data entry to labels only. If you enter a value, Quattro Pro will format it as a label, preceding it with a label prefix.

- *Dates Only* Restricts data entry to dates in one of Quattro Pro's acceptable date or time formats. (See Chapter 3 for more on Quattro Pro's acceptable date and time formats.) Simply type the entry in the date format you want—for example, **11/1/92**. Quattro Pro records the appropriate date value in the current cell and formats it accordingly. In this case, the cell would be formatted as Date 4. If you attempt to enter anything other than a date, Quattro Pro beeps and enters Edit mode.

You should use the /Database, Data Entry command for each column whose entries you want to control. To do this, begin by moving the cell selector to the top of any column in the database. When you're ready, select the /Database, Data Entry command and then select the option you want, Labels Only or Dates Only. Quattro Pro prompts you for a block to format.

Press End-↓. Quattro Pro highlights all the cells in the column. Press Enter to confirm your selection and complete the command.

To reset a column to accepting general entries again, select /Database, Data Entry and then select General. When Quattro Pro prompts you for a cell block, highlight the appropriate block of cells and press Enter.

Figure 10.2 shows how you might use the /Database, Data Entry command to format the fields in the EMPDATA.WQ1 database. In particular, notice that columns A through C are formatted as Labels Only and column D is formatted as Dates Only.

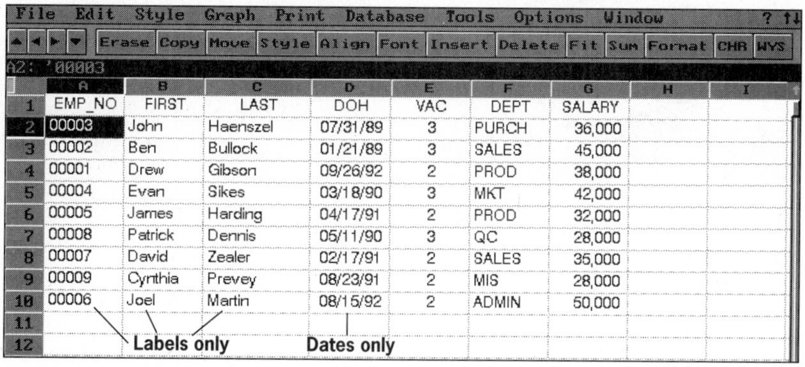

	A	B	C	D	E	F	G	H	I
1	EMP_NO	FIRST	LAST	DOH	VAC	DEPT	SALARY		
2	00003	John	Haenszel	07/31/89	3	PURCH	36,000		
3	00002	Ben	Bullock	01/21/89	3	SALES	45,000		
4	00001	Drew	Gibson	09/26/92	2	PROD	38,000		
5	00004	Evan	Sikes	03/18/90	3	MKT	42,000		
6	00005	James	Harding	04/17/91	2	PROD	32,000		
7	00008	Patrick	Dennis	05/11/90	3	QC	28,000		
8	00007	David	Zealer	02/17/91	2	SALES	35,000		
9	00009	Cynthia	Prevey	08/23/91	2	MIS	28,000		
10	00006	Joel	Martin	08/15/92	2	ADMIN	50,000		

Figure 10.2 Using the /Database, Data Entry command

Sorting the Database

Once you enter the records for your database, you can use the /Database, Sort command to sort it in various ways. You can sort some or all of the records in either ascending or descending order. The order of the sort is based on the contents of one or more fields in the database. For example, imagine you want to sort the records in Figure 10.2 by last name in ascending order (from A to Z). The next section shows you how to do just that.

NOTE. *The sections that follow describe how you can use the /Database, Sort command in the context of sorting the records in a Quattro Pro database. However, you can also use this command to sort one or more columns of data located anywhere in your spreadsheet.*

Sorting on a Single Field

As mentioned, the /Database, Sort command sorts the records in a database according to the contents of one or more of its fields. For example, imagine you want to sort the database in Figure 10.2 in ascending order by last name. To do this, perform the following steps:

1. Move the cell selector to cell A2 and select the /Database, Sort command. Quattro Pro displays the Sort menu shown in Figure 10.3.

Figure 10.3

The Sort menu

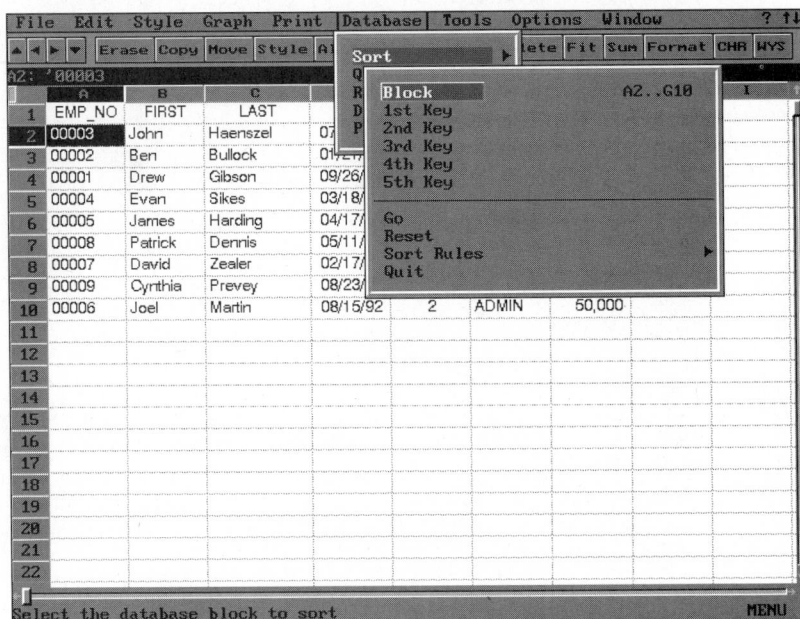

2. Select the Block option from the Sort menu. Quattro Pro prompts you for a block of data to sort.

3. Specify the block A2..G10, which includes all of the records in the database (or specify its block name). Do *not* include the field names at the top of the database. If you do, they may be sorted into the body of the database when you later execute the sort. To confirm your selection of a sort block, press Enter. Quattro Pro returns you to the /Database, Sort menu, and your selection is recorded next to the Block option.

4. Select the 1st Key option. Quattro Pro prompts you to specify a field on which to sort the database.

5. Move the cell pointer to any cell within column C and press Enter. (Alternatively, you can specify a block name of a cell in column C.) Quattro Pro prompts you to specify the order of the sort. The options are D for

descending (the default), meaning labels are sorted *Z* to *A* and numbers are sorted highest to lowest, or A for ascending, meaning labels are sorted from *A* to *Z* and numbers are sorted lowest to highest.

6. Type **A** and press Enter to specify an ascending sort. Quattro Pro returns you to the Sort menu.

7. Select Go to perform the sort. Quattro Pro sorts all of the records in the block in ascending order using the contents of column C (the LAST field) as a guide. When the sort is complete, your screen looks like Figure 10.4. Notice that the records are now in alphabetical order by last name.

Figure 10.4

The employee database sorted by last name

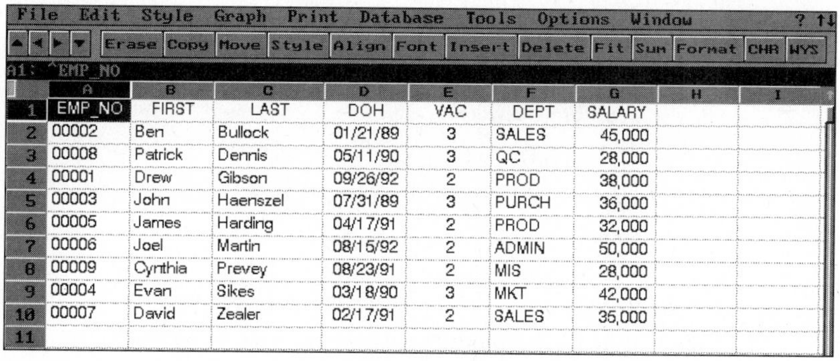

File	Edit	Style	Graph	Print	Database	Tools	Options	Window		? ↑↓

| ▲ ◄ ► ▼ | Erase | Copy | Move | Style | Align | Font | Insert | Delete | Fit | Sum | Format | CHR | WYS |

A1: 'EMP_NO

	A	B	C	D	E	F	G	H	I
1	EMP_NO	FIRST	LAST	DOH	VAC	DEPT	SALARY		
2	00002	Ben	Bullock	01/21/89	3	SALES	45,000		
3	00008	Patrick	Dennis	05/11/90	3	QC	28,000		
4	00001	Drew	Gibson	09/26/92	2	PROD	38,000		
5	00003	John	Haenszel	07/31/89	3	PURCH	36,000		
6	00005	James	Harding	04/17/91	2	PROD	32,000		
7	00006	Joel	Martin	08/15/92	2	ADMIN	50,000		
8	00009	Cynthia	Prevey	08/23/91	2	MIS	28,000		
9	00004	Evan	Sikes	03/18/90	3	MKT	42,000		
10	00007	David	Zealer	02/17/91	2	SALES	35,000		
11									

When you specify settings for the /Database, Sort command, Quattro Pro remembers them for the remainder of the current session. The next time you select the /Database, Sort command, Quattro Pro will show you those same settings. In addition, when you save the current spreadsheet, your /Database, Sort settings are saved along with it. That way, when you later load the same spreadsheet into memory, you can immediately select the /Database, Sort, Go command to sort the database using your old settings. If you want to clear all of the current settings for the /Database, Sort command, select the Reset option from the /Database, Sort menu.

A common trap is failing to sort all the fields in a database. For example, imagine that rather than specify a sort block of **A2..G10** in Figure 10.4, you specify a sort block of **A2..F10**, leaving out column G, the SALARY field. When the sort is performed, the result is something of a mess; that is, a mismatching of fields occurs among records. Reconstructing the database manually can be tedious at best and virtually impossible if the database is quite large. However, there are several techniques you can use to fix a sort gone awry. See "Fixing a Bad Sort" later for more details on this.

When you add records to the end of a database, Quattro Pro does not update your setting for the /Database, Sort, Block command accordingly. Therefore, before you sort the database the next time, you must reselect the /Database, Sort, Block command and specify a sort block that includes the new records you've added.

In the example in Figure 10.4, you sorted the database using the contents of a field containing labels. You can also sort the database using the contents of a numeric field—for example, the SALARY field (column G). However, if you are sorting numbers of varying lengths that have been entered as labels, you will have difficulty sorting them reliably. For example, you'll notice in column A of Figure 10.4 that the EMP_NO field (column A) has numbers entered as labels. These numbers are padded with leading zeros to make them the same length. Therefore, you can sort the database on the EMP_NO field and get the results you expect. On the other hand, if you are working with street addresses, which often begin with numbers of varying lengths, you may have to pad some of those addresses with leading zeros to get the results you want.

Sorting on More Than One Field

You can also sort a database on more than one field. In fact, you can specify as many as five different fields on which to sort a database. For example, imagine you want to sort the database in Figure 10.4 by department (column F) and then by last name (column C) within those departments. That way, the database would appear as shown in Figure 10.5. To sort the database in this way, you must specify both a *primary* and a *secondary* key field for the sort. You can do this by performing the following steps:

1. Select the /Database, Sort command to display the Sort menu.

2. Select the Block option, specify the block **A2..G10** if you haven't already, and press Enter. Quattro Pro returns you to the Sort menu. (You'll notice that the block you've just selected includes all the records in the database, but not the field names.)

3. Select the 1st Key option. Quattro Pro prompts you for a primary field on which to sort the database. The field you subsequently select will receive the first order of precedence when the sort is eventually performed. (If you previously selected a block for this option, Quattro Pro places the cell selector on that block.)

4. Move the cell selector to any cell in column F (the DEPT field) and press Enter. Quattro Pro displays a prompt box asking you to specify D for a descending sort or A for an ascending sort. (If you've previously specified a setting here, Quattro Pro shows you that same setting again.)

5. Type **A** for an ascending sort and press Enter to return to the Sort menu.

6. Select the 2nd Key option from the Sort menu. Quattro Pro prompts you for a second sort field. The field you subsequently select will receive the second order of precedence when the database is sorted.

Figure 10.5

The employee database sorted by both department and last name

File	Edit	Style	Graph	Print	Database	Tools	Options	Window	? ↑↓

| ▲ ◀ ▶ ▼ | Erase | Copy | Move | Style | Align | Font | Insert | Delete | Fit | Sum | Format | CHR | WYS |

A1: ^EMP_NO

	A	B	C	D	E	F	G	H	I
1	EMP_NO	FIRST	LAST	DOH	VAC	DEPT	SALARY		
2	00006	Joel	Martin	08/15/92	2	ADMIN	50,000		
3	00009	Cynthia	Prevey	08/23/91	2	MIS	28,000		
4	00004	Evan	Sikes	03/18/90	3	MKT	42,000		
5	00001	Drew	Gibson	09/26/92	2	PROD	38,000		
6	00005	James	Harding	04/17/91	2	PROD	32,000		
7	00003	John	Haenszel	07/31/89	3	PURCH	36,000		
8	00008	Patrick	Dennis	05/11/90	3	QC	28,000		
9	00002	Ben	Bullock	01/21/89	3	SALES	45,000		
10	00007	David	Zealer	02/17/91	2	SALES	35,000		
11									

7. Move the cell selector to any cell in column C (the LAST field) and press Enter. Quattro Pro displays a prompt box asking you to specify a descending or ascending sort for this field.

8. Type **A** to specify an ascending sort, and press Enter. Quattro Pro returns you to the Sort menu.

9. Select Go to perform the sort. Quattro Pro sorts the database in ascending order based on the contents of column F (the DEPT field). The database is then further sorted using the contents of column C (the LAST field). When the sort is completed, the database appears as shown in Figure 10.5.

The example just outlined shows you how to sort a database by using the contents of two fields. However, as mentioned, you can sort a database by using up to five of its fields. To specify the third, fourth, and fifth sort fields, you use the 3rd Key, 4th Key, and 5th Key options on the Sort menu. As you might imagine, each of these options has a lower precedence than the previous one when the sort is performed.

You can easily reassign any sort key whenever you want. To do this, simply select the appropriate Key option from the Sort menu. Quattro Pro will show the block or field to which that Key option is presently assigned. Use the arrow keys or your mouse to select any cell from another field (column) in the database. When prompted, specify an ascending or descending sort order for that field. If you have multiple Key options to reassign, you may find it easier to simply clear the settings for the /Database, Sort command and start over. You can do this by selecting the Reset option from the Sort menu.

Fixing a Bad Sort

Occasionally, even the most skilled spreadsheet user will perform a bad sort. For this reason it's always a good idea to save the current spreadsheet before using the /Database, Sort command. That way, if things go wrong, you can use the /File, Retrieve command to reload the file into the current window and try the sort again. However, if you've neglected to do this, and a great deal of work hangs in the balance, there are several options you can try.

If the Undo feature is enabled, you can immediately select /Edit, Undo (or press Alt-F5) to undo the last command. (The Undo feature is discussed in detail in Chapter 1.) Quattro Pro will restore your spreadsheet to the way it was before you used the /Database, Sort command.

On the other hand, if the Undo feature is disabled, or if you've entered several commands after the /Database, Sort command, you can use the Transcript facility. This facility lets you play back the commands you have entered since opening the current spreadsheet. Essentially, it allows you to rebuild all or part of a spreadsheet. You'll find a detailed discussion of how to use the Transcript facility in Chapter 1.

If you don't want to rely on either the Undo feature or the Transcript facility to restore your spreadsheet after a bad sort, there is yet another technique you can try. This technique involves adding a new field to the end of the database, containing a sequential number for each record in the database. That way, if things go awry, you can restore the database to its former order by sorting it on this *original-record* field.

To create an original-record field, move the cell selector to the column just beyond the rightmost field in the database. When you are ready,

Note. You must create this original-record field before you sort the database.

1. Select the /Edit, Fill command. Quattro Pro prompts you for a block to fill with sequential values.

2. Specify a block of sufficient size in the current column such that it spans all the records in the database.

3. Press Enter to confirm your selection. Quattro Pro prompts you for a start value.

4. Type **1**. Quattro Pro prompts you for a step value and recommends 1.

5. Press Enter to accept this value. Quattro Pro prompts you for a stop value and recommends 8,192.

6. Press Enter to accept this value.

Quattro Pro fills the current column with sequential values, one for each record in the database. You can now sort the database by using the /Database, Sort command. If things go wrong, you can use your original-record field to restore the database to its former order.

Changing the Sorting Sequence

You can use the /Database, Sort, Sort Rules command to change the sorting sequence used by Quattro Pro. When you select this command, Quattro Pro 4.0 displays a menu with three options, Numbers before Labels, Label Order, and Sort Rows/Columns (explained in the next section). If you select Numbers before Labels, Quattro Pro displays yet another submenu with No and Yes. The No setting is the default. With this setting, Quattro Pro sorts your data in the following order when you specify an ascending sort:

1. Blank cells

2. Labels beginning with numbers (in numeric order)

3. Labels beginning with letters

4. Values in numeric order

If you select the /Database, Sort, Sort Rules, Numbers before Labels, Yes command, Quattro Pro sorts your data in the following order when you specify an ascending sort:

1. Blank cells

2. Labels beginning with letters

3. Labels beginning with numbers (in numeric order)

4. Values in numeric order

You can use the /Database, Sort, Sort Rules, Label Order command to specify how Quattro Pro sorts your labels. When you select this command, Quattro Pro displays a menu with two options, ASCII (the default) and Dictionary. These options have the following effect:

■ *ASCII*   Specifies an ASCII sort order for labels, to sort labels alphabetically based on the ASCII code value of each letter in the label. Because uppercase letters have higher ASCII values than do lowercase letters, though, Quattro Pro will sort all labels that begin with an uppercase letter before those that begin with a lowercase letter. Therefore *Garfield* would be sorted before *chambers*.

■ *Dictionary*   Specifies that labels be sorted purely alphabetically, regardless of case, just as they would appear in the dictionary. Therefore, *chambers* is sorted in front of *Garfield*.

Sorting by Columns Rather than Rows

Quattro Pro sorts your data by rows as the default. In Quattro Pro 4.0, however, you can also sort by columns. This feature can be useful when you are working with a database in which the records are arranged in columns rather than in rows. For example, suppose you were to flip the employee database on its side, counterclockwise. The field names would appear in column A, each row would become a field, and each column would contain a record.

To sort by columns, select the /Database, Sort, Sort Rules, Sort Rows/Columns command and then select Columns. Finally, select Quit to return to the Sort menu. Quattro Pro will then sort by columns rather than by rows.

The procedure for sorting by columns is basically the same as sorting by rows. The only difference is specifying your sort keys. Instead of specifying a column as a sort key, you must specify a row. When you select Go to begin sorting, Quattro Pro will sort the data within the sort range by columns, using the contents of the key row as a guide.

Querying the Database

In addition to sorting a database, you can also *query* it—that is, search for records that meet a specified set of conditions. Once you locate the records you want, Quattro Pro lets you perform various actions on those records. For example, you can simply view and edit those records one at a time. Alternatively, you can copy all or some of the fields in each of those records to another part of the spreadsheet. That way, you can view the records and manipulate the data they contain independently of the database. For example, you might create a graph from the copied records. Finally, Quattro Pro lets you maintain your database by deleting records that you no longer need.

Overview

To query a database, you use the /Database, Query command. When you select this command, Quattro Pro displays the submenu of options shown in Figure 10.6. As you'll notice, this menu is divided into three sections. The top portion of this menu lets you define the block in your spreadsheet where the database resides. It also lets you define the block containing the *criteria* you wish to use to locate a specific set of records in the database. Finally, this section lets you specify an optional output block where you want to copy the records that are selected from the database.

Figure 10.6

The Database
Query menu

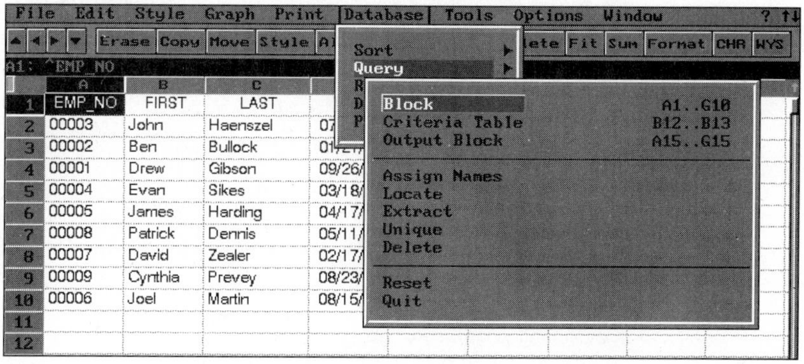

The second section of the Database Query menu lets you define the type of operation you want to perform. You can locate records and view them one by one, copy them to another area of the spreadsheet, or delete them. Finally, the bottom section of the menu lets you either clear the settings you've made for the /Database, Query command, or quit and return to the current spreadsheet.

Extracting Data: An Example

Perhaps the best way to show how to query a database is through an example. Along the way, you'll encounter a few new commands and procedures, but don't worry about this for now. You'll find each of these commands and procedures discussed in detail in the pages that follow.

The following example will show you how to locate specific records in the employee database shown again in Figure 10.7, and copy them to another area of the spreadsheet. The records you'll locate and copy will have a value greater than $40,000 in the SALARY field (column G of Figure 10.7). When you're done, your screen will look like Figure 10.8.

Perform the following steps:

1. Make sure the employee database is displayed on your screen as shown in Figure 10.7. Move the cell selector to cell G1.

2. Select the /Edit, Copy command and copy the field name *SALARY* from cell G1 to cell B12 as it appears in Figure 10.8.

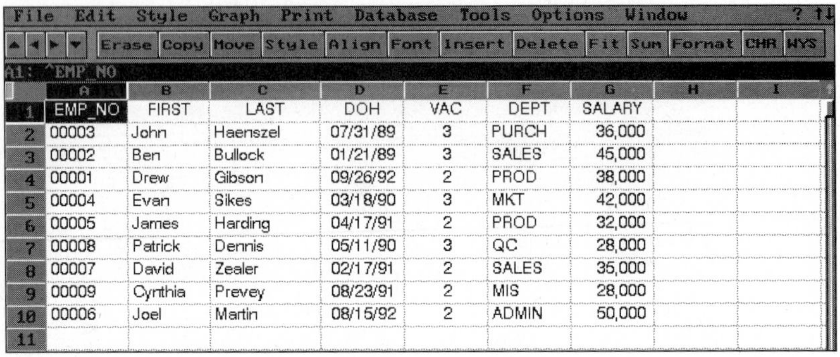

Figure 10.7

The employee
database

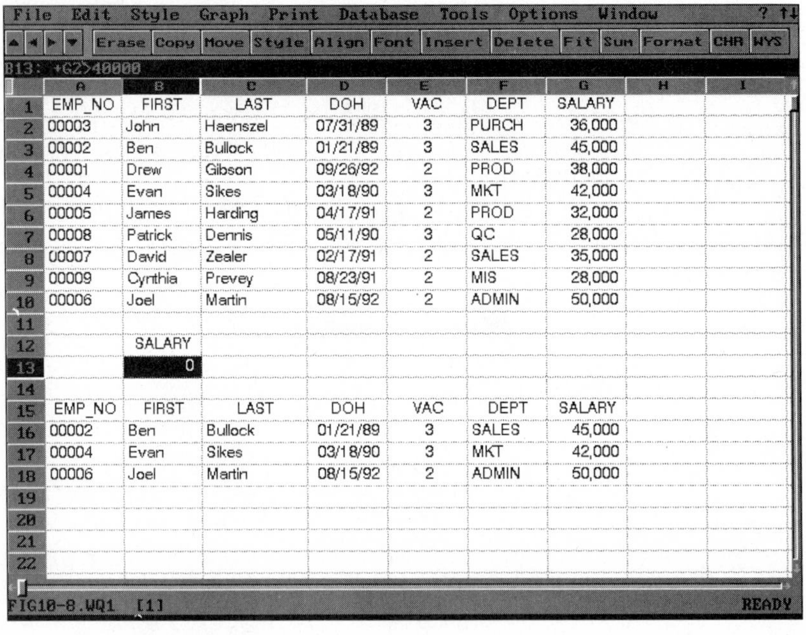

| File | Edit | Style | Graph | Print | Database | Tools | Options | Window | ? ↑↓ |

| ▲ ◄ ► ▼ | Erase | Copy | Move | Style | Align | Font | Insert | Delete | Fit | Sum | Format | CHR | WYS |

A1: 'EMP_NO

	A	B	C	D	E	F	G	H	I
1	EMP_NO	FIRST	LAST	DOH	VAC	DEPT	SALARY		
2	00003	John	Haenszel	07/31/89	3	PURCH	36,000		
3	00002	Ben	Bullock	01/21/89	3	SALES	45,000		
4	00001	Drew	Gibson	09/26/92	2	PROD	38,000		
5	00004	Evan	Sikes	03/18/90	3	MKT	42,000		
6	00005	James	Harding	04/17/91	2	PROD	32,000		
7	00008	Patrick	Dennis	05/11/90	3	QC	28,000		
8	00007	David	Zealer	02/17/91	2	SALES	35,000		
9	00009	Cynthia	Prevey	08/23/92	2	MIS	28,000		
10	00006	Joel	Martin	08/15/92	2	ADMIN	50,000		
11									

Figure 10.8

Using /Database,
Query, Extract to
copy records

| File | Edit | Style | Graph | Print | Database | Tools | Options | Window | ? ↑↓ |

| ▲ ◄ ► ▼ | Erase | Copy | Move | Style | Align | Font | Insert | Delete | Fit | Sum | Format | CHR | WYS |

B13: +G2>40000

	A	B	C	D	E	F	G	H	I
1	EMP_NO	FIRST	LAST	DOH	VAC	DEPT	SALARY		
2	00003	John	Haenszel	07/31/89	3	PURCH	36,000		
3	00002	Ben	Bullock	01/21/89	3	SALES	45,000		
4	00001	Drew	Gibson	09/26/92	2	PROD	38,000		
5	00004	Evan	Sikes	03/18/90	3	MKT	42,000		
6	00005	James	Harding	04/17/91	2	PROD	32,000		
7	00008	Patrick	Dennis	05/11/90	3	QC	28,000		
8	00007	David	Zealer	02/17/91	2	SALES	35,000		
9	00009	Cynthia	Prevey	08/23/91	2	MIS	28,000		
10	00006	Joel	Martin	08/15/92	2	ADMIN	50,000		
11									
12		SALARY							
13		0							
14									
15	EMP_NO	FIRST	LAST	DOH	VAC	DEPT	SALARY		
16	00002	Ben	Bullock	01/21/89	3	SALES	45,000		
17	00004	Evan	Sikes	03/18/90	3	MKT	42,000		
18	00006	Joel	Martin	08/15/92	2	ADMIN	50,000		
19									
20									
21									
22									

FIG10-8.WQ1   [1]   READY

3. Press Home to move the cell selector to cell A1.

4. Select the /Edit, Copy command and press End-→ to highlight the first row of field names in the employee database. Press Enter to confirm this block. Next, move the cell selector to cell A15 and press Enter. Quattro Pro copies the row of field names from row 1 to row 15.

5. Move the cell selector to cell B13 and enter the formula **+G2>40000**. You've just entered the criteria that will be used to search the database.

6. Select the /Database, Query command. Quattro Pro opens the Database Query menu.

7. Select the Block option. Quattro Pro prompts you to specify the block that contains the database.

8. Press Home to move the cell selector to cell A1, and then press **.** (period) to anchor it. Next, press End-→ followed by End-↓ to highlight the block A1..G10. (You'll notice this block includes all the records in the database as well as its field names.) Press Enter to confirm your selection and return to the Database Query menu.

9. Select the Criteria Table option. Quattro Pro prompts you for a *criterion block* (the block that contains the criteria that will be used to search the database).

10. Move the cell selector to cell B12 (which contains the field name *SALARY*) and type **.** (period) to anchor it. Next, press ↓ to expand the highlight to include the block B12..B13, and press Enter to confirm your selection and return to the Database Query menu. You've just selected your first *criteria table*. Notice that this block includes both the *SALARY* field name and the formula beneath it. Later, when this query is executed, Quattro Pro will search the SALARY field in the employee database for those records that have a value greater than 40,000.

11. Select the Output Block option from the Database Query menu. Quattro Pro prompts you for an *output block* (the block to which selected records will be copied).

12. Move the cell selector to cell A15 and type **.** (period) to anchor it. Then press End-→ to highlight the block A15..G15, which contains all the field names in row 15. Press Enter to confirm your selection and return to the Database Query menu.

13. Execute the query by selecting the Extract option from the Database Query menu. Quattro Pro hesitates for a moment and then repaints your screen. When the dust settles, your screen appears as shown in Figure 10.8.

Okay, so what just happened? Well, you have performed the three basic steps in executing a database query. These are:

■ Set up the query in advance, which means setting up your criteria table and your output range (should you decide to use one) in the spreadsheet.

- Select the /Database, Query command and define the database block, the criteria table block, and an optional output block.

- Select the type of query you want to execute.

In determining which records to select from the database, Quattro Pro relies upon the search criteria you defined in the criteria table block. As you may recall, the criteria block in Figure 10.8 is B12..B13, which contains a field name with a formula beneath it. The field name tells Quattro Pro which field in the database to search (in this case, the SALARY field). The formula beneath the field name tells Quattro Pro what to search for in that field (in this case, a value greater than 40,000). See "About the Criteria Table" and "Defining Criteria" later for additional information on how to define criteria for searching a database.

When the query is finally executed, Quattro Pro begins by locating those records in the database block that meet the criteria defined in the criteria table. In the previous example, the selected records are copied to an output block. As you can see in Figure 10.8, only three records in the employee database meet the search criteria (that is, have a value greater than 40,000 in the SALARY field). These records belong to employees Bullock, Sikes, and Martin.

Quattro Pro retains the settings you make for the /Database, Query command. The next time you enter the command, Quattro Pro will show you those same settings. In addition, when you save the current spreadsheet, the settings for the /Database, Query command are saved along with it.

TIP. *Because Quattro Pro retains the settings you make for the /Database, Query command, you can repeat the most recent /Database, Query command whenever you want. To do this, simply press the Query key (F7). Quattro Pro executes the last /Database, Query command you entered, using the settings you've previously established.*

About the Database Block

As mentioned, you select the database block (the block containing the database you want to search) by using the /Database, Query, Block command. In the example just presented (Figure 10.8), you defined the block A1..G10 as a database block, which included all of the records in the database *and* its field names. This is very important. If you fail to include the field names in the database block, Quattro Pro won't execute the query properly.

You don't have to include all the records in the database within your database block; you can include just the top part of the database. Quattro Pro will still perform the query properly, searching just the records you've selected.

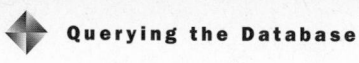

When you add records to the bottom of a database, Quattro Pro does not update your /Database, Query, Block setting accordingly. Instead, you'll have to do this yourself before querying the database the next time. When you select the command, Quattro Pro shows you the database block you've previously defined. Use the arrow keys to expand the block you've previously defined and press Enter to record the new setting.

Your database block does not have to be in the same spreadsheet as your criteria table and output blocks. For example, your database block might be in SHEET1.WQ1 and your criteria table and output blocks might be in SHEET2.WQ1. With this type of configuration, however, you'll have to use linking syntax to identify the location of the output block. For example, imagine that SHEET2.WQ1, which contains the criteria table and output blocks, is the current spreadsheet (that is, it contains the cell selector). To reference the database located in block A1..G10 of SHEET1.WQ1, select the /Database, Query, Block command and specify

```
[SHEET1.WQ1]A1..G10
```

As you might imagine, the SHEET1.WQ1 file must be open on the desktop both for the /Database, Query, Block command and for the execution of the actual query. For more on using linking syntax in commands and formulas, see Chapter 2.

About the Criteria Table

As mentioned, the criteria table holds the information that will be used to search the database and select records from it. You must set up the criteria table before you query the database. Once you've set up the criteria table, you can tell Quattro Pro where it is located by using the /Database, Query, Criteria Table command and pointing to the appropriate block.

At a minimum, the criteria table block is composed of two vertically adjacent cells. The top cell contains a field name from the database, entered as a label. This label tells Quattro Pro which field in the database to search. Although the case and alignment of this label are not important, the spelling is. The name *must* be spelled exactly the same as its corresponding field name in the database. Otherwise, Quattro Pro won't execute the query properly. For this reason, it is a common practice to copy field names from the database to the first row of the criteria table block.

Beneath the field name in the criteria table block, you can enter a number, label, or formula that defines the information you want Quattro Pro to search for in that field. For example, as you may recall from the example in

Figure 10.8, the criteria table block is B12..B13, and it contains the following entries:

B12	SALARY
B13	+G2>40000

This set of criteria tells Quattro Pro to search the SALARY field in the database and locate all records with a value greater than 40,000 in that field.

The criteria table in Figure 10.8 is relatively simple. You can define far more complex criteria if you so desire. In fact, Quattro Pro will accept up to 256 field names in the first row of the criteria table with a label, number, or formula search argument beneath each one of them. Each field name you include in the first row of the criteria table will be searched to find records that satisfy the search arguments in the row below each field name. What's more, the criteria table can be multiple rows deep with search arguments in each row.

It is critically important to define your search criteria properly. In fact, it is of such importance, you'll find two sections later in this chapter, "Defining Criteria" and "Defining Multiple Criteria," that are devoted solely to this topic.

You can locate the criteria table anywhere you want, including in another spreadsheet. It does not have to be in the same spreadsheet as the database itself. However, if you decide to locate the criteria table in another spreadsheet, make sure that spreadsheet is open on the desktop when you query the database.

CAUTION! *It is important that you enter a valid search argument in the criteria table. If you leave the criteria table blank, or if you enter an invalid search argument, Quattro Pro will select all the records in the database. This may or may not be what you want. For example, later, under "Deleting Records," you'll learn about the /Database, Query, Delete command, which lets you delete those records that match the selection criteria in the criteria table. If the criteria table is left blank for this command, or if it does not contain at least one valid search argument, Quattro Pro will delete all of the records in your database.*

If you frequently perform different queries on a specific database, you may want to set up various criteria tables for it. Once the criteria tables are set up, you can use the /Edit, Names, Create command to assign a block name to each of them. That way, you can select the /Database, Query, Criteria Table command and press Choices (F3) to have Quattro Pro show you a list of block names in the current spreadsheet. You can then select the name of a particular criteria table. This technique lets you quickly switch from one criteria table to another as you query the database.

About the Output Block

As mentioned, you can define an output block by using the /Database, Query, Output Block command. Specifying an output block is optional. You should only specify an output block when you intend to copy selected records from the database to another location in the spreadsheet. You can copy records from the database by using the /Database, Query, Extract and Unique commands. You'll find these commands discussed later under "Extracting Records" and "Extracting Unique Records."

You must prepare the output block before you query the database. Once the output block has been prepared, you can tell Quattro Pro where it is located by using the /Database, Query, Output Block command. For example, as you may recall, the output block in the example in Figure 10.8 is A15..G15, which contains the field names from the employee database.

Quattro Pro uses the field names in the first row of the output block to determine which fields of information to copy from the database. You can include all or just some of the field names from the database in the output block, and you can place them in any order you want. For example, Figure 10.9 shows the same query previously shown in Figure 10.8. However, only four field names have been included in the output block (A15..D15) and their order has been changed. Notice that only the fields referenced in the output block have been copied from the database and that the order of the information displayed is controlled by the order of the field names in the output block.

Although the capitalization and alignment of the field names are of no importance, the spelling is critical. The spelling of each field name in the output block must exactly match the spelling of its corresponding field name in the database. Otherwise, Quattro Pro will not perform the query properly.

You can define a single-row output block or a multiple-row output block. A single-row output block includes just the field names in the first row. When Quattro Pro copies records to a single-row output block, it uses as many rows as needed beneath the first row of field names to copy all of the records selected from the database. In addition, after all selected records have been copied, Quattro Pro will erase all cells beneath the output block, down to the bottom of the spreadsheet. Therefore, if you have any important data located beneath a single-row output block, make sure you copy or move that data elsewhere before executing a /Database, Query, Extract or Unique command.

A multiple-row output block includes the initial row of field names plus any additional rows below this that you may feel are needed. When you specify a multiple-row output block, Quattro Pro still attempts to copy all of the selected records from the database. However, if there are not sufficient rows available in the output block, Quattro Pro will copy as many records as it can and then issue an error message. Any data located beneath the output block is not affected.

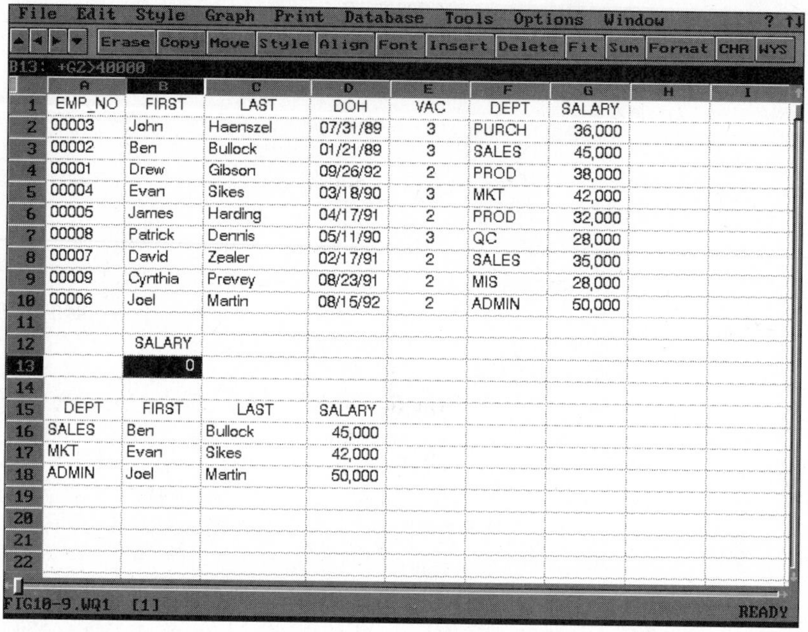

Figure 10.9

An output block
using just some of
the field names
from the database

	A	B	C	D	E	F	G	H	I
	File Edit Style Graph Print Database Tools Options Window							? ↑↓		
	▲ ◀ ▼ Erase Copy Move Style Align Font Insert Delete Fit Sum Format CHR WYS									
B13:	+G2>40000								
1	EMP_NO	FIRST	LAST	DOH	VAC	DEPT	SALARY		
2	00003	John	Haenszel	07/31/89	3	PURCH	36,000		
3	00002	Ben	Bullock	01/21/89	3	SALES	45,000		
4	00001	Drew	Gibson	09/26/92	2	PROD	38,000		
5	00004	Evan	Sikes	03/18/90	3	MKT	42,000		
6	00005	James	Harding	04/17/91	2	PROD	32,000		
7	00008	Patrick	Dennis	05/11/90	3	QC	28,000		
8	00007	David	Zealer	02/17/91	2	SALES	35,000		
9	00009	Cynthia	Prevey	08/23/91	2	MIS	28,000		
10	00006	Joel	Martin	08/15/92	2	ADMIN	50,000		
11									
12		SALARY							
13		0							
14									
15	DEPT	FIRST	LAST	SALARY					
16	SALES	Ben	Bullock	45,000					
17	MKT	Evan	Sikes	42,000					
18	ADMIN	Joel	Martin	50,000					
19									
20									
21									
22									

FIG10-9.WQ1 [1]   READY

You can locate the output block anywhere you want, including in another spreadsheet. Like the criteria table block, the output database does not have to be located in the same spreadsheet as the database. However, if you decide to locate the output block outside the current spreadsheet, that spreadsheet must be open when you perform the query.

As you know, if you've used the /Options, Recalculation, Mode, Manual command, you must press the Calc key (F9) to have Quattro Pro recalculate the spreadsheet. However, if recalculation is set to manual, you may have difficulties with the /Database, Query command. Quattro Pro needs to recalculate the spreadsheet after a /Database, Query, Extract or /Database, Query, Unique command. Therefore, you should leave recalculation set to Background (the default) for these commands.

Defining Criteria

Properly setting up the criteria table is the key to querying a database successfully. This section shows the various types of search arguments you can define in the criteria table to locate specific records in a database. "Defining Multiple Criteria" later shows you how to build a criteria table that contains multiple search arguments to further refine the search.

The upcoming sections contain numerous examples of how to build criteria tables for the /Database, Query commands. The /Database, Query commands themselves are discussed immediately afterward under "Using the /Database, Query Commands." If you find that you are getting the gist of how to build a criteria table, and you want to try it out on a database, feel free to jump forward to "Using the /Database, Query Commands" at any time.

Using Labels

Figure 10.10 shows an example of how you might use a label as a search argument in the criteria table. In this case, the criteria table is located in the block B12..B13. Cell B12 contains the field name *LAST*, which corresponds to the LAST field (column C) in the employee database (A1..G10). Beneath this field name in cell B13 is the label *Gibson*. When this query is executed, Quattro Pro will search the LAST field in the employee database and select those records with the label *Gibson* in the LAST field. As you can see in the output block (A15..G15 of Figure 10.10), only one record in the employee database meets this criterion.

Figure 10.10

Using a label in the criteria table

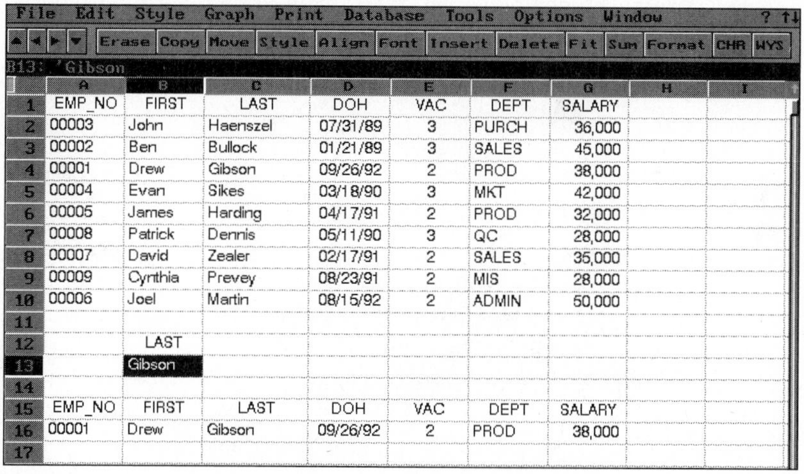

To execute this query yourself, begin by setting up the criteria table as you see it in Figure 10.10. Next, set up the output block as shown in that same figure. When you're ready, select the /Database, Query command and specify the block settings:

Block	A1..G10
Criteria Table	B12..B13
Output Block	A15..G15

To execute the query, select /Database, Query, Extract command. Quattro Pro searches the LAST field in the employee database to find all records with the label *Gibson* in that field. The records it finds are then copied to the output block, as shown in Figure 10.10.

Normally, when you use a label as a search argument, Quattro Pro does not conduct a case-sensitive search. For example, the search label *Gibson* will find records with *GIBSON*, *gibson*, *Gibson*, *GIBson*, and so on. However, if you need to conduct a case-sensitive search, you can use the @EXACT function in your criteria table. (This function is discussed in detail in Chapter 7.) This function evaluates the contents of a cell versus a label you supply. If the match is exact, the function returns 1; otherwise, a value of 0 is returned. For example, imagine you want to locate those records with *Gibson* (not *gibson* or *GIBSON*) in the LAST field of the employee database in Figure 10.10. To do this, you can enter the following formula in cell B13 of the criteria table in the figure:

```
@EXACT(C2,"Gibson")
```

Using Wildcard Characters

You can supplement label search arguments in the criteria table with *wildcard* characters. Wildcard characters serve as substitutes for one or more characters in a label. You can use these characters when you need to find groups of records containing labels that have something in common or when you're not sure of the correct spelling of a label.

Quattro Pro supports the following wildcard characters:

* (asterisk)	Represents any group of characters
? (question mark)	Represents any one character
~ (tilde)	Negates a character

Figure 10.11 shows an example of how you might use the * (asterisk) wildcard character in the criteria table (B12..B13) to find the records of those employees whose last name begins with H. Notice that cell B12 contains the

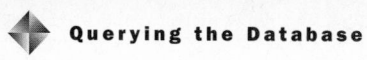

label *LAST*, referring to the LAST field (column C) in the employee database. Beneath this, cell B13 contains the label *H**. When this query is executed, Quattro Pro will search the LAST field in the employee database to find all labels that begin with *H* followed by any combination of characters. The results of this query are shown in the output block (A15..G17) of Figure 10.11. Notice that only two records meet this criterion.

Figure 10.11

Using a wildcard character to search a database

File	Edit	Style	Graph	Print	Database	Tools	Options	Window		? ↑↓

▲ ◄ ► ▼	Erase	Copy	Move	Style	Align	Font	Insert	Delete	Fit	Sum	Format	CHR	WYS

B13: 'H*

	A	B	C	D	E	F	G	H	I
1	EMP_NO	FIRST	LAST	DOH	VAC	DEPT	SALARY		
2	00003	John	Haenszel	07/31/89	3	PURCH	36,000		
3	00002	Ben	Bullock	01/21/89	3	SALES	45,000		
4	00001	Drew	Gibson	09/26/92	2	PROD	38,000		
5	00004	Evan	Sikes	03/18/90	3	MKT	42,000		
6	00005	James	Harding	04/17/91	2	PROD	32,000		
7	00008	Patrick	Dennis	05/11/90	3	QC	28,000		
8	00007	David	Zealer	02/17/91	2	SALES	35,000		
9	00009	Cynthia	Prevey	08/23/91	2	MIS	28,000		
10	00006	Joel	Martin	08/15/92	2	ADMIN	50,000		
11									
12		LAST							
13		H*							
14									
15	EMP_NO	FIRST	LAST	DOH	VAC	DEPT	SALARY		
16	00004	John	Haenszel	07/31/89	3	PURCH	36,000		
17	00005	James	Harding	04/17/91	2	PROD	32,000		
18									
19									
20									
21									
22									

FIG10-11.WQ1 [1]   READY

The ? (question mark) wildcard symbol, on the other hand, can be used as a substitute for any one character. You might use this wildcard symbol when you're not sure of the spelling of a label. For example, imagine you want to find the record of an employee named Haenszel. However, you can't remember if the appropriate spelling is *Haenszel* or *Heanszel*. To find this label, you can use the search argument *H??nszel*, which will find the occurrence of either label.

To exclude labels from a database search, use the ~ (tilde) wildcard symbol followed by the label you want to exclude. For example, imagine you want to locate the records of all employees, except those who work in the sales department. To do this, you might enter the following information in the criteria table (B12..B13) of Figure 10.11:

```
DEPT
~SALES
```

When this query is executed, Quattro Pro will search the DEPT field in the employee database, and select all records except those that contain the label *SALES* in the DEPT field.

You can even combine the wildcard symbols to build a search label. For example, imagine you want to locate all records in the employee database except those that have a department beginning with the letter *M* (MKT and MIS). To do this, you can use a search argument label like ~*M** beneath the field name *DEPT* in the criteria table block.

Using Values

Figure 10.12 shows an example of how you might use a value in the criteria table to search a database. In this case the criteria table block is B12..B13. In the first row of the table appears the label *SALARY*, referring to the SALARY field (a numeric field) in the employee database. Beneath this, in cell B13, appears the value 28000. When this query is executed, Quattro Pro will search the SALARY field in the employee database to find those records that have the value 28,000 in that field. As you can see in the output range (A15..G17) of Figure 10.12, two records meet this criteria.

Using Logical Formulas

A criteria table can include logical formulas to select database records that fall within a given category. For example, you might want to locate all records in the employee database with a value greater than 40,000 in the SALARY field.

Logical formulas in a criteria table are composed of the following three elements:

- A reference to the first cell in a field of the database—for example, +G2

- A logical operator: =, <, <=, >, >=, or <>

- A value for comparison

Figure 10.13 shows an example of a logical formula in the criteria table B12..B13. The label *SALARY* appears in the first row of the table (cell B12), referring to the SALARY field in the employee database (column G). Beneath this, in cell B13, appears the following formula:

```
+G2>=40000
```

Breaking this formula down, +G2 is a reference to the first cell in the SAL-ARY field (column G) of the database block (A1..G10). >= is the logical operator, greater than or equal to, and 40000 is simply a value for comparison. When this query is executed, Quattro Pro will select all the records with a value greater than or equal to 40,000 in the salary field. As you can see in the output block (A15..G18) of Figure 10.13, three of the records in the employee database qualify in this category.

Figure 10.12

Using a value as a selection criterion

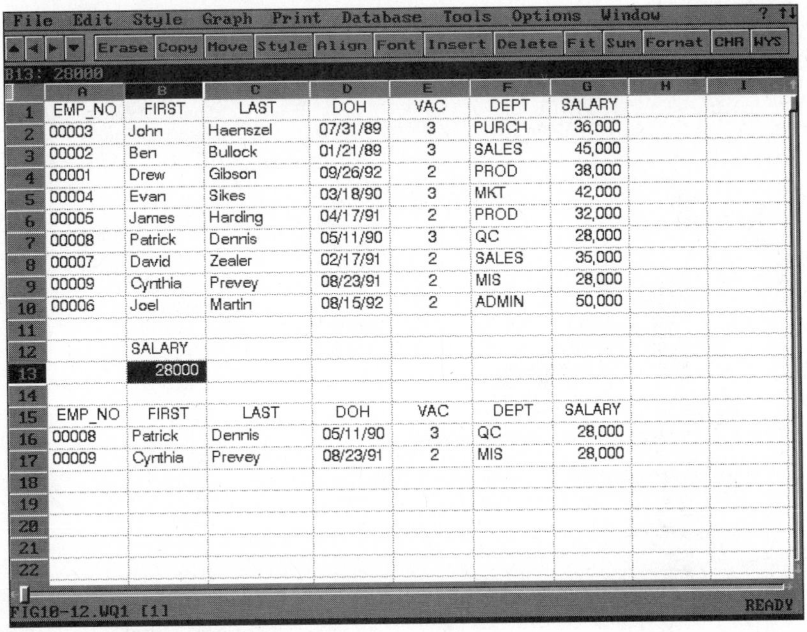

	EMP_NO	FIRST	LAST	DOH	VAC	DEPT	SALARY		
1	EMP_NO	FIRST	LAST	DOH	VAC	DEPT	SALARY		
2	00003	John	Haenszel	07/31/89	3	PURCH	36,000		
3	00002	Ben	Bullock	01/21/89	3	SALES	45,000		
4	00001	Drew	Gibson	09/26/92	2	PROD	38,000		
5	00004	Evan	Sikes	03/18/90	3	MKT	42,000		
6	00005	James	Harding	04/17/91	2	PROD	32,000		
7	00008	Patrick	Dennis	05/11/90	3	QC	28,000		
8	00007	David	Zealer	02/17/91	2	SALES	35,000		
9	00009	Cynthia	Prevey	08/23/91	2	MIS	28,000		
10	00006	Joel	Martin	08/15/92	2	ADMIN	50,000		
11									
12		SALARY							
13		28000							
14									
15	EMP_NO	FIRST	LAST	DOH	VAC	DEPT	SALARY		
16	00008	Patrick	Dennis	05/11/90	3	QC	28,000		
17	00009	Cynthia	Prevey	08/23/91	2	MIS	28,000		
18									

Logical formulas perform true/false tests—that is, the condition they define is either true or it is not. If the condition is true, Quattro Pro displays 1 in the cell containing the logical formula, and if it's false, 0 is displayed. This has no impact on the success of the current query. For example, notice in cell B13 of Figure 10.13 that 0 is displayed, indicating that the logical formula in that cell is false. (Cell G2 does not contain a value greater than or equal to 40,000.) However, the query still yields successful results.

You can also use logical formulas to search for labels in a database. Simply enclose the label you want to locate in quotes. For example, as you may recall from earlier in this chapter, the numbers in the EMP_NO (employee number) field (column A) of the employee database are entered as labels.

Therefore, to find the record that corresponds to employee number 00001, you can use the logical formula

```
+A2="00001"
```

in cell B13 of the criteria table in Figure 10.13. You'll find this same technique useful when searching for zip codes in a mailing list. These are often entered as labels to accommodate zip codes that begin with zero.

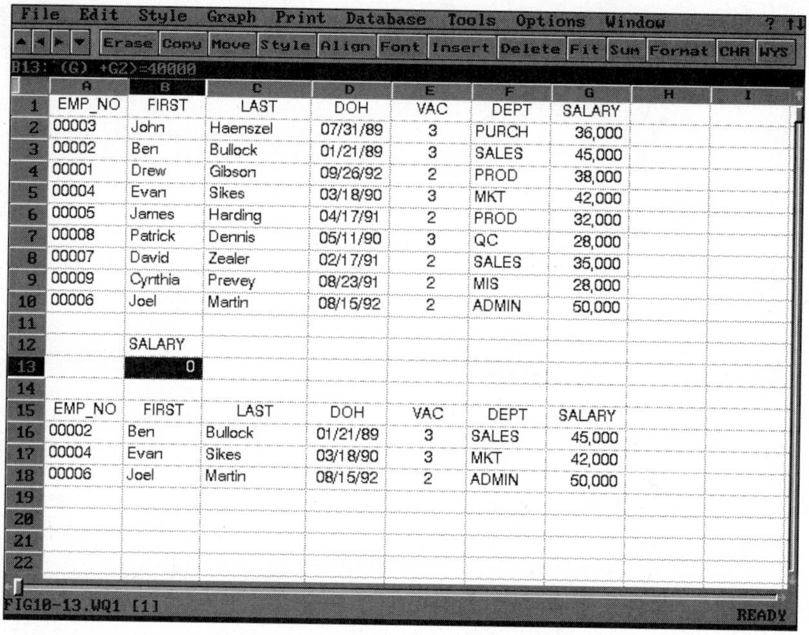

Figure 10.13

Using a logical formula in the criteria table

```
File   Edit   Style   Graph   Print   Database   Tools   Options   Window        ? ↑↓
▲ ◄ ► ▼  Erase Copy Move Style Align Font Insert Delete Fit Sum Format CHR WYS
B13:  (G)  +G2>=40000
```

	A	B	C	D	E	F	G	H	I
1	EMP_NO	FIRST	LAST	DOH	VAC	DEPT	SALARY		
2	00003	John	Haenszel	07/31/89	3	PURCH	36,000		
3	00002	Ben	Bullock	01/21/89	3	SALES	45,000		
4	00001	Drew	Gibson	09/26/92	2	PROD	38,000		
5	00004	Evan	Sikes	03/18/90	3	MKT	42,000		
6	00005	James	Harding	04/17/91	2	PROD	32,000		
7	00008	Patrick	Dennis	05/11/90	3	QC	28,000		
8	00007	David	Zealer	02/17/91	2	SALES	35,000		
9	00009	Cynthia	Prevey	08/23/91	2	MIS	28,000		
10	00006	Joel	Martin	08/15/92	2	ADMIN	50,000		
11									
12		SALARY							
13		0							
14									
15	EMP_NO	FIRST	LAST	DOH	VAC	DEPT	SALARY		
16	00002	Ben	Bullock	01/21/89	3	SALES	45,000		
17	00004	Evan	Sikes	03/18/90	3	MKT	42,000		
18	00006	Joel	Martin	08/15/92	2	ADMIN	50,000		
19									
20									
21									
22									

```
FIG10-13.WQ1 [1]                                                        READY
```

Because logical formulas must contain a reference to the first cell in a field of the database, you can locate them under any field name. For example, you can change the field name in cell B12 of Figure 10.13 and the query will still be successful.

You can make your logical formulas more intelligible by naming the first cell of each field of your database. In fact, Quattro Pro offers a special command, /Database, Query, Assign Names, for just this purpose. When you select this command, Quattro Pro uses the field names in the top row of the database to name the cells immediately below (similar to the /Edit, Name, Labels, Down command, but with a lot less work). Once the first cell in each field is named, you can use those names in your criteria table formulas. For example, rather than the formula +G2>=40000 in cell B13 of Figure 10.13,

you can use the formula +SALARY>=40000, which is easier to read and
understand.

Defining Multiple Criteria

As mentioned, you can also define multiple criteria with which to search a
database. For example, suppose you want to search the employee database
for those records that meet two conditions. Both conditions must be met for
a record to be selected. For example, you might want to find the records of
those employees who make more than $40,000 *and* who were hired after a
certain date.

Or, suppose you want to select a record from the database when any one
of several search conditions is true. For example, suppose you want to search
the employee database to find the records of those employees who work in either the sales department *or* in the production department. In this case, you
want a record selected when either one *or* the other of these conditions is met.

The And Query

When two or more search arguments appear in the same row of the criteria
table, all of them must be met before a record will be selected from the database. Essentially, the two search arguments have an implied "and" relationship between them.

Figure 10.14 shows an example of two search arguments in the same
row of the criteria table C12..D13. The top row of the table contains two
field names, SALARY and DOH, referring to the SALARY and DOH
(Date of Hire) fields in the employee database (A1..G10). Beneath these
two field names are two search arguments in cells C13 and D13, respectively. Cell C13 contains the formula +G2>=40000 and cell D13 contains
the formula +D2>@DATE(90,1,1). When this query is executed, Quattro
Pro will search the SALARY field of the employee database (column G)
for values greater than 40,000. At the same time, Quattro Pro will search
the DOH field (column D) for date values greater than 01/01/90. Only if
both of these conditions are true for a given record will that record be selected from the database.

You can also use the #AND# logical operator to combine two or more
search arguments. Once again, all search arguments must be met before a
record will be selected from the database. For example, you could perform
the same query shown in Figure 10.14 by using the following formula beneath any field name in the second row of the criteria table (C12..C13):

```
+G2>=40000#AND#D2>@DATE(90,1,1)
```

If your database contains a date field, you can use the #AND# logical operator to select records between two dates. For example, notice that the employee database in Figure 10.14 contains a date field, DOH (column D). To

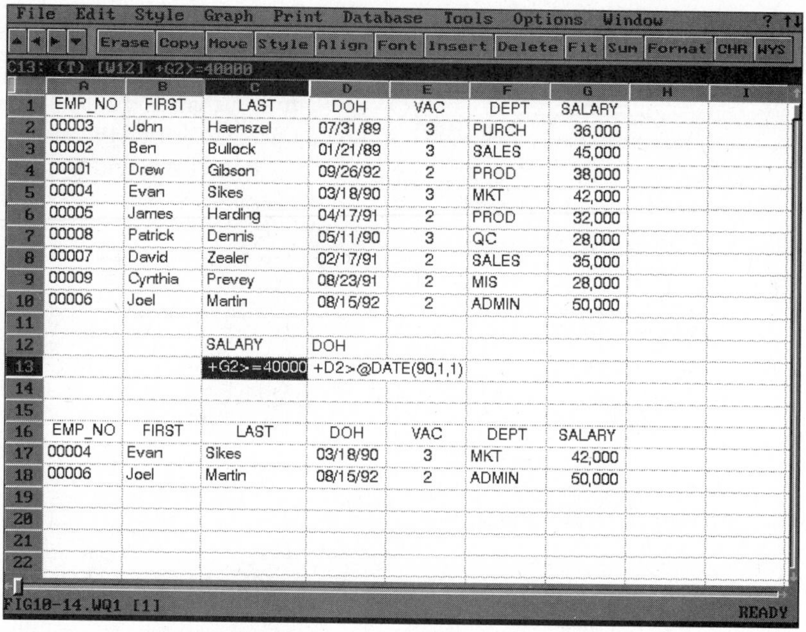

Figure 10.14

Performing an And query

| File | Edit | Style | Graph | Print | Database | Tools | Options | Window | ? ↑↓ |

| ▲ ◀ ▶ ▼ | Erase | Copy | Move | Style | Align | Font | Insert | Delete | Fit | Sum | Format | CHR | WYS |

C13: (T) [W12] +G2>=40000

	A	B	C	D	E	F	G	H	I
1	EMP_NO	FIRST	LAST	DOH	VAC	DEPT	SALARY		
2	00003	John	Haenszel	07/31/89	3	PURCH	36,000		
3	00002	Ben	Bullock	01/21/89	3	SALES	45,000		
4	00001	Drew	Gibson	09/26/92	2	PROD	38,000		
5	00004	Evan	Sikes	03/18/90	3	MKT	42,000		
6	00005	James	Harding	04/17/91	2	PROD	32,000		
7	00008	Patrick	Dennis	05/11/90	3	QC	28,000		
8	00007	David	Zealer	02/17/91	2	SALES	35,000		
9	00009	Cynthia	Prevey	08/23/91	2	MIS	28,000		
10	00006	Joel	Martin	08/15/92	2	ADMIN	50,000		
11									
12			SALARY	DOH					
13			+G2>=40000	+D2>@DATE(90,1,1)					
14									
15									
16	EMP_NO	FIRST	LAST	DOH	VAC	DEPT	SALARY		
17	00004	Evan	Sikes	03/18/90	3	MKT	42,000		
18	00006	Joel	Martin	08/15/92	2	ADMIN	50,000		
19									
20									
21									
22									

FIG10-14.WQ1 [1]   READY

select all records from this database between 01/01/90 and 12/31/90, for example, you can use the following formula in the criteria table:

```
+D2>=@DATE(90,1,1)#AND#D2<=@DATE(90,12,31)
```

The Or Query

When two search arguments appear in different rows of the criteria table, Quattro Pro will select records that meet either of the search arguments. In essence, there is an implied "or" relationship between the two arguments.

Figure 10.15 shows an example of two search arguments located in different rows of the criteria table C12..C14. In the first row of the table (cell C12) appears the field name DEPT, referring to the DEPT (Department) field (column F) in the employee database (A1..G10). Beneath this field name, the label "SALES" appears in cell C13 and the label "PROD" appears in C14. When this query is executed, Quattro Pro will search the employee database for those records with either the label "SALES" *or* the label "PROD" in the DEPT field. The results of this query are shown in the output block A16..G20 of Figure 10.15.

You can also use the #OR# logical operator to combine two or more search arguments in a single cell and create an implied "or" relationship between them. If any of the search arguments is met for a given record, that record will be selected from the database. For example, you could write the same query shown in Figure 10.15 by using the following formula beneath the DEPT field name in the criteria table:

```
+F2="SALES"#OR#F2="PROD"
```

NOTE. *Avoid leaving a blank row between search arguments in a multiple-row criteria table. Otherwise, Quattro Pro will select all the records in the database.*

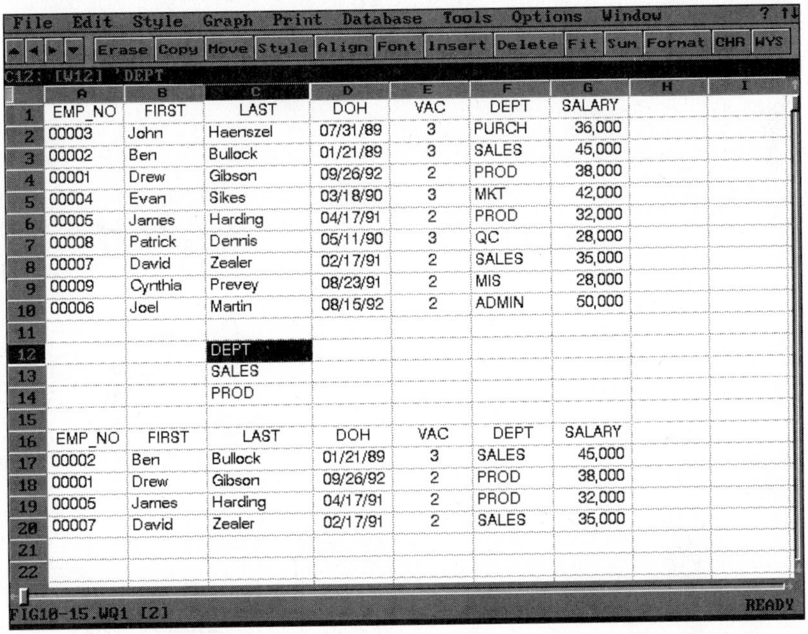

Figure 10.15
Performing an Or query

The Not Query

You can use the #NOT# logical operator in a multiple-criteria query to exclude records from being selected. For example, suppose you want to see the records of those employees in the employee database who make between $30,000 and $40,000, but who don't work in the sales department. To do this, you could use the following formula beneath any field name in the criteria table block:

```
+SALARY>30000#AND#SALARY<40000#AND##NOT#DEPT="SALES"
```

The first part of this formula, +SALARY>30000#AND#SALARY<40000, will cause Quattro Pro to select all records from the database with a value between 30,000 and 40,000 in the SALARY field (column G). (This assumes that cell G2 of the employee database has been named SALARY.) However, the latter part of this formula, #AND##NOT#DEPT="SALES", adds the condition that the DEPT (Department) field (column F) may not contain the label "SALES". (Once again, this assumes that cell F2 in the employee database has been assigned the block name DEPT.)

Combining And and Or Queries

You can mix and match And and Or queries in the criteria table to further refine which records are selected from the database. For instance, Figure 10.16 shows an example criteria table in the block C12..D14. You'll notice that beneath the field names there are two rows of criteria with two search arguments in each row.

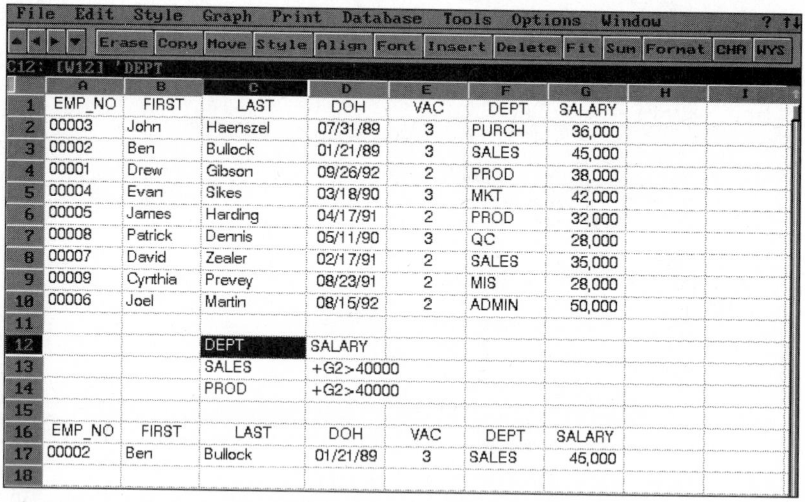

Figure 10.16

Combining And and Or selection criteria in the criteria table

The two field names in the top row of the table, DEPT and SALARY, refer to the DEPT (Department) and SALARY (Gross Salary) fields in the employee database (columns F and G). Beneath the DEPT field name are two labels, "SALES" and "PROD", which appear in rows 13 and 14, respectively. Moreover, beneath the SALARY field name, the formula, +G2>40000, appears in both rows 13 and 14. When this query is executed, Quattro Pro will select those records with the label "SALES" in the DEPT field and a value greater than 40,000 in the SALARY field. It will also select those with

"PROD" in the DEPT field and a value greater than 40,000 in the SALARY field. The results of this query appear in the output block (A16..G17) of Figure 10.16. As you can see, only a single record was selected. That record belongs to an employee in the sales department. Obviously, nobody in production makes $40,000 or more.

You can use the #AND# and #OR# logical operators to build a single search argument that will yield the same result as shown in Figure 10.16. To do this, type the following formula beneath any field name in the criteria table block:

```
+F2="DEPT"#AND#G2>40000#OR#+F2="SALES"#AND#G2>40000
```

Using the /Database, Query Commands

As mentioned, you can use /Database, Query to search a database for those records that meet the criteria in the criteria table. Once those records are found, you can either display them for editing, copy them to an output block located in another area of the spreadsheet, or delete them.

The sections that follow assume you know how to prepare a criteria table block and an output block for the /Database, Query commands. If you are not familiar with these features, take a moment to scan the information in the beginning of this section ("Querying the Database").

Displaying and Editing Records

To locate specific records and display them for viewing and editing, use the /Database, Query, Locate command. Before you use this command, however, you must first define a database block and a criteria block. You do not have to define an output block.

For example, suppose once more that you are working with the employee database in Figure 10.17. You want to locate and edit the records of those employees who work in the sales department. Begin by defining the criteria table that will be used to search the database. For example, referring to Figure 10.17, move the cell selector to cell B12 and enter the label **DEPT**. This refers to the DEPT field name (column F) in the employee database. Press ↓ to move to cell B13 and enter the label **SALES**. (See "Defining Criteria" for details on how this criteria is used to search the database.) When you are ready, perform the following steps:

1. Select the /Database, Query command. Quattro Pro displays the Database Query menu.

2. Select the Block option. Quattro Pro prompts you for a database block. Highlight the block A1..G10, which includes the employee database and

its field names, and press Enter. Quattro Pro returns you to the Database Query menu.

Figure 10.17

Using the /Database, Query, Locate command to locate records and display them for editing

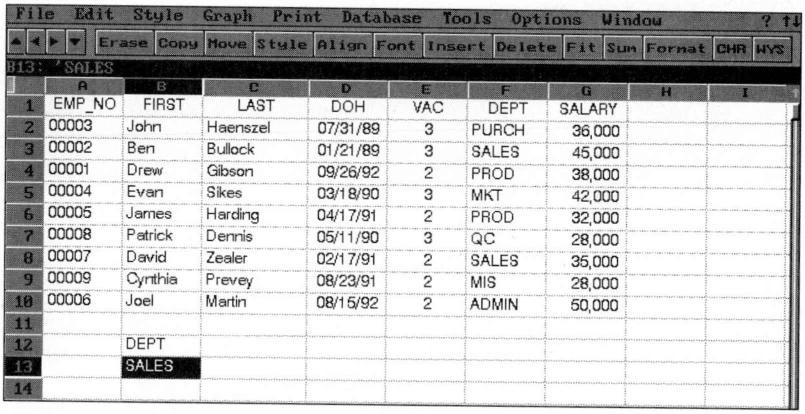

	A	B	C	D	E	F	G	H	I
	File Edit Style Graph Print Database Tools Options Window ? ↑↓
	▲ ◄ ► ▼ Erase Copy Move Style Align Font Insert Delete Fit Sum Format CHR WYS
	B13: 'SALES
1	EMP_NO	FIRST	LAST	DOH	VAC	DEPT	SALARY		
2	00003	John	Haenszel	07/31/89	3	PURCH	36,000		
3	00002	Ben	Bullock	01/21/89	3	SALES	45,000		
4	00001	Drew	Gibson	09/26/92	2	PROD	38,000		
5	00004	Evan	Sikes	03/18/90	3	MKT	42,000		
6	00005	James	Harding	04/17/91	2	PROD	32,000		
7	00008	Patrick	Dennis	05/11/90	3	QC	28,000		
8	00007	David	Zealer	02/17/91	2	SALES	35,000		
9	00009	Cynthia	Prevey	08/23/91	2	MIS	28,000		
10	00006	Joel	Martin	08/15/92	2	ADMIN	50,000		
11									
12		DEPT							
13		SALES							
14									

3. Select the Criteria Table option. Quattro Pro prompts you for the location of the criteria table. Highlight the block B12..B13 and press Enter. Quattro Pro returns you to the Database Query menu.

4. Select the Locate option. Quattro Pro displays a FIND indicator in the Status bar, and moves the cell selector to the first field in the first record that has the label "SALES" in the DEPT (Department) field (column F).

5. To edit any of the fields in the current record, press → to get to the field you want, then press Edit (F2) to display the contents of that cell in the Input Line. When you're done editing, press Enter to confirm your edit.

6. To move to the next record that meets the criteria in the criteria table, press ↓. Quattro Pro moves the cell selector to that record (row 8 in Figure 10.17).

7. To move to the first or last records of the database, whether they meet the current search criteria or not, press Home or End.

8. To end the /Database, Query, Locate command, press Esc or Enter. Quattro Pro returns you to the Database Query menu. Select Quit to return to the spreadsheet in Ready mode.

Extracting Records

You can copy specific records from a database to another area of the spreadsheet by using the /Database, Query, Extract command. This command selects

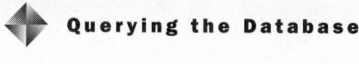

those records that meet the criteria defined in the criteria table and copies them to a predefined output block. Therefore, before you use this command, you must set up both a criteria table and an output block.

Suppose you want to locate the records of those employees in the employee database who have three weeks of vacation and copy them to an output block, as shown in Figure 10.18. To do this, prepare the criteria table first. For example, move the cell selector to cell B12, or another cell of your choice and enter the label **VAC**. Next, press ↓ to move to cell B13 and enter the number 3. That way, Quattro Pro will search the employee database for those records with the number 3 in the VAC (Vacation) field (column E). To prepare the output block, use the /Edit, Copy command to copy the field names in row 1 of Figure 10.18 to row 15. Now that both the criteria table and output blocks are prepared, perform the following steps:

1. Select the /Database, Query command. Quattro Pro displays the Database Query menu.

2. Select the Block option. Quattro Pro prompts you for a database block. Highlight the block A1..G10, which includes the employee database and its field names, and press Enter. Quattro Pro returns you to the Database Query menu.

3. Select the Criteria Table option. Quattro Pro prompts you for the location of the criteria table. Highlight the block B12..B13 and press Enter. Quattro Pro returns you to the Database Query menu.

4. Select the Output Block option. Quattro Pro asks you for the location of the output block. Highlight the block A15..G15 and press Enter. Quattro Pro returns you to the Database Query menu.

5. Select the Extract option. Quattro Pro copies those records in the employee database that meet the criteria in the criteria table to the output block, as shown in Figure 10.18. As you can see, four employees in the employee database are entitled to three weeks of vacation.

Extracting Unique Records

You can use the /Database, Query, Unique command to copy only unique records from a database to another area of the spreadsheet. This command works exactly like the /Database, Query, Extract command. However, if you have duplicate records in the database, only one record (the first one) is copied to the output block. Once again, since you will be copying records from the database, you'll need to prepare both a criteria table and an output block before using this command.

Figure 10.18

Using the /Database, Query, Extract command to copy selected records to an output block

| File | Edit | Style | Graph | Print | Database | Tools | Options | Window | ? ↑↓ |

| ▲ ◄ ► ▼ | Erase | Copy | Move | Style | Align | Font | Insert | Delete | Fit | Sum | Format | CHR | WYS |

A2: '00003

	A	B	C	D	E	F	G	H	I
1	EMP_NO	FIRST	LAST	DOH	VAC	DEPT	SALARY		
2	00003	John	Haenszel	07/31/89	3	PURCH	36,000		
3	00002	Ben	Bullock	01/21/89	3	SALES	45,000		
4	00001	Drew	Gibson	09/26/92	2	PROD	38,000		
5	00004	Evan	Sikes	03/18/90	3	MKT	42,000		
6	00005	James	Harding	04/17/91	2	PROD	32,000		
7	00008	Patrick	Dennis	05/11/90	3	QC	28,000		
8	00007	David	Zealer	02/17/91	2	SALES	35,000		
9	00009	Cynthia	Prevey	08/23/91	2	MIS	28,000		
10	00006	Joel	Martin	08/15/92	2	ADMIN	50,000		
11									
12		VAC							
13		3							
14									
15	EMP_NO	FIRST	LAST	DOH	VAC	DEPT	SALARY		
16	00003	John	Haenszel	07/31/89	3	PURCH	36,000		
17	00002	Ben	Bullock	01/21/89	3	SALES	45,000		
18	00004	Evan	Sikes	03/18/90	3	MKT	42,000		
19	00008	Patrick	Dennis	05/11/90	3	QC	28,000		
20									
21									
22									

FIG10-18.WQ1 [2]   READY

You might want to use the /Database, Query, Unique command when you know that there are duplicate records in a database. For example, suppose you are preparing a mailing list from a database containing orders. You happen to know that the names and addresses of some of your larger customers are repeated multiple times. In this case, you can use the /Database, Query, Unique command to copy a single name and address for each customer to another area of the spreadsheet.

The uniqueness of records in a database is determined by the fields you include in the output block for the /Database, Query, Unique command. For example, suppose you are working with the employee database shown in Figure 10.19. As you scan the records in that database, you can see that each record is unique. Although some of the fields in each record contain the same entries, at least one field in each record contains a unique entry, making that record unlike any of the others. However, you can still use the /Database, Query, Unique command with this database. For example, suppose you want to create a list of the departments included in the employee database. To do this, you'll use the contents of the DEPT (Department) field (column F). As you can see, the names of several departments appear duplicated in that field.

To perform this query, you'll need to set up the criteria table and output blocks in advance. To set up the criteria table, move the cell selector anywhere outside the database block—for example, cell B12—and enter the label **DEPT**, referring to the DEPT field name in the employee database. Don't put any search argument beneath this field name. As you may recall, when you leave the criteria table blank, Quattro Pro automatically selects all the records in the database. That's exactly what you want here. To set up the output block, enter the label **DEPT** in cell B15, just as you see it in Figure 10.19. When you're ready, perform the following steps:

1. Select the /Database, Query command to open the Database Query menu.

2. Select the Block option. Quattro Pro prompts you for a database block. Highlight the block A1..G10 and press Enter. Quattro Pro returns you to the Database Query menu.

3. Select the Criteria Table option. Quattro Pro prompts you for the location of the criteria table. Highlight the block B12..B13 and press Enter. Quattro Pro returns you to the Database Query menu.

4. Select the Output Block option. Quattro Pro asks you for the location of the output block. Highlight the block B15 and press Enter. Quattro Pro returns you to the Database Query menu.

5. Select the Unique option. Quattro Pro locates those records in the employee database that both meet the criteria in the criteria table and are unique (as defined by the field names included in the output block). All duplicates are eliminated and a single record is copied to the output block. In this case, a single instance of each department name in the employee database is copied to the output block.

Deleting Records

You delete specific records in a database by using the /Database, Query, Delete command. This command will delete those records in the database block that meet the criteria in the criteria table. Because this command does not copy records from the database, you don't need to create an output block in advance, only a criteria table.

When you delete records with the /Database, Query, Delete command, Quattro Pro erases them from the database and closes up the space they previously occupied. The deletion takes place based on the selection criteria in the criteria table. As you might imagine, if the selection criteria in the criteria table are wrong, invalid, or the criteria table is left blank, the effects of this command can be devastating.

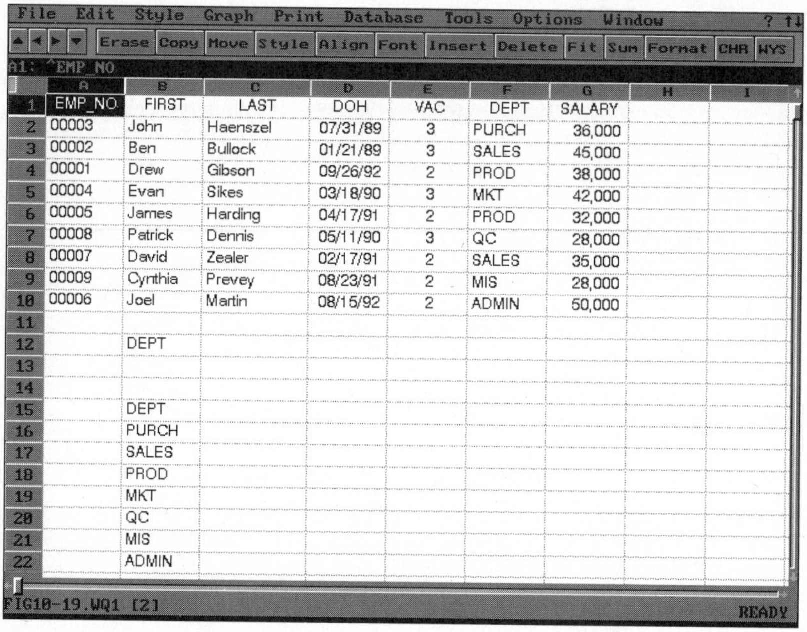

Figure 10.19

Using the /Database, Query, Unique command to copy unique information from a database to another area of the spreadsheet

| File | Edit | Style | Graph | Print | Database | Tools | Options | Window | ? ↑↓ |

| ▲ ◀ ▶ ▼ | Erase | Copy | Move | Style | Align | Font | Insert | Delete | Fit | Sum | Format | CHR | WYS |

A1: 'EMP_NO

	A	B	C	D	E	F	G	H	I
1	EMP_NO	FIRST	LAST	DOH	VAC	DEPT	SALARY		
2	00003	John	Haenszel	07/31/89	3	PURCH	36,000		
3	00002	Ben	Bullock	01/21/89	3	SALES	45,000		
4	00001	Drew	Gibson	09/26/92	2	PROD	38,000		
5	00004	Evan	Sikes	03/18/90	3	MKT	42,000		
6	00005	James	Harding	04/17/91	2	PROD	32,000		
7	00008	Patrick	Dennis	05/11/90	3	QC	28,000		
8	00007	David	Zealer	02/17/91	2	SALES	35,000		
9	00009	Cynthia	Prevey	08/23/91	2	MIS	28,000		
10	00006	Joel	Martin	08/15/92	2	ADMIN	50,000		
11									
12		DEPT							
13									
14									
15		DEPT							
16		PURCH							
17		SALES							
18		PROD							
19		MKT							
20		QC							
21		MIS							
22		ADMIN							

FIG10-19.WQ1 [2]   READY

You can, of course, undo the /Database, Query, Delete command by selecting /Edit, Undo (or pressing Alt-F5) immediately afterward. Or, if the undo feature is disabled (the default), you can rebuild the spreadsheet through the use of the Transcript facility. (Both of these options are covered in Chapter 1). To avoid having to rely on either of these data-recovery options, though, you can test the selection criteria in the criteria table before using the /Database, Query, Delete command. To do this, simply use the /Database, Query, Locate command discussed earlier and note the records that are selected. If you want to save a copy of the deleted records, you can also use the /Database, Query, Extract command beforehand.

Suppose you want to delete the record of a specific employee from the employee database shown earlier in Figure 10.19. The record you want to delete is employee 00007, David Zealer. To do this, move the cell selector anywhere outside the database block—for example, cell B12—and type the field name **EMP_NO**, referring to the EMP_NO (Employee Number) field in the employee database. Beneath this, type the label **'00007**. When you're ready, perform the following steps:

1. Select the /Database, Query command to open the Database Query menu.

2. Select the Block option. Quattro Pro prompts you for a database block. Highlight the block A1..G10 and press Enter. Quattro Pro returns you to the Database Query menu.

3. Select the Criteria Table option. Quattro Pro prompts you for the location of the criteria table. Highlight the block B12..B13 and press Enter. Quattro Pro returns you to the Database Query menu.

4. Select the Delete option. Quattro Pro deletes the record for employee 00007, David Zealer, from the database.

Querying an External Database

You can query an external database by using Quattro Pro's /Database, Query, Extract command. An *external database* is one that has been created with a software program other than Quattro Pro—for example, Paradox. When you query an external database, the results of that query are displayed in your Quattro Pro spreadsheet. That way, you can use Quattro Pro's formatting, analytical, and graphing tools to work with the data. Quattro Pro lets you query external databases that have been created with any of the following software programs: Paradox and Reflex from Borland, and dBASE II, III, III Plus, or IV from Ashton-Tate.

Querying an external database with /Database, Query, Extract is very similar to querying a database that is located in a Quattro Pro spreadsheet. (See the discussion on extracting records, "Using the /Database, Query Commands," for details on how to use this command.) However, unlike a Quattro Pro spreadsheet database, an external database does not have to be open in memory. Instead, the database remains closed on disk.

In preparation for extracting records from an external database, you must use the /Database, Query, Block, Criteria Table, and Output Block commands to specify the database block, the criteria table block, and an output block. However, instead of specifying a block address or name for the /Database, Query, Block command, you must enter a special form of linking formula that refers to the external database by using its file name. This linking formula takes the following form:

```
[Database-filename]A1..A2
```

The block address reference (A1..A2) is there only to conform to Quattro Pro's link-formula syntax; it serves no other purpose. You can use any valid address in the current spreadsheet that includes at least two rows. The [*Database-filename*] reference, on the other hand, is what provides a link between your spreadsheet and the external database. To create a link to an external database, simply enclose its file name in square brackets. If the database is located outside the current directory, make sure you precede the file name with the appropriate path. For example, suppose you want to query a Paradox database named EMPLOYEE.DB located in your E:\PDOX35\SAMPLE directory. (This database is displayed in Figure 10.20, shown open on the Paradox desktop.) To do this, select the /Database, Query, Block command, and type the following:

```
[E:\PDOX35\SAMPLE\EMPLOYEE.DB]A1..A2
```

You use a similar form of linking syntax to specify search arguments in the criteria table for the query. Once again, the file name for the database is enclosed in square brackets—for example [EMPLOYEE.DB]. However, instead of following this reference with a fake block address, you follow it with a logical formula that contains an actual field name from the external database. For example, Figure 10.21 shows a sample criteria table set up in the block A1..A2. Notice that at the top of this table the field name SALARY appears in cell A1. This is an actual field name from the EMPLOYEE.DB database in Figure 10.20. Beneath this, in cell A2, appears the following formula:

```
[\PDOX35\SAMPLE\EMPLOYEE.DB]SALARY>=15000
```

Figure 10.20

A sample Paradox database

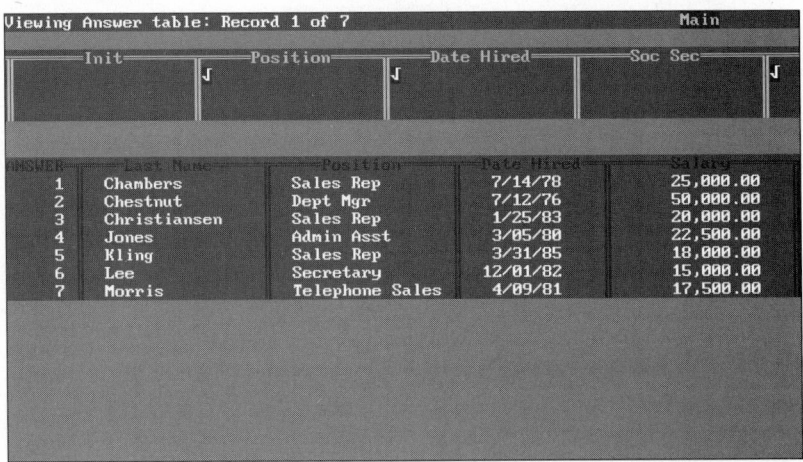

As you can see, the first part of this search argument is simply the full path and file name of the external database enclosed in square brackets. The second part, SALARY>=15000, is a logical formula composed of a field name from the external database (SALARY) followed by a logical operator (>=) and value for comparison. When this query is executed, Quattro Pro will select those records from the EMPLOYEE.DB database, with a value that is greater than or equal to $15,000 in the SALARY field. Once your criteria table has been properly set up, you can inform Quattro Pro of its location by selecting the /Database, Query, Criteria Table command and specifying the block address A1..A2.

Setting up your output block is perhaps the easiest step of all. Simply enter the actual field names from the external database in any row of your spreadsheet. The field names you enter will determine both which fields are copied from the external database and their order. You can use all the field names from the external database or just some of them. For example, Figure 10.21 shows a sample output block (A4..D4) that includes only four field names from the EMPLOYEE.DB database. When this query is executed, only information from those four fields will be copied to the spreadsheet. To inform Quattro Pro of the location of the output block, select the /Database, Query, Output, Block command and specify the block A4..D4.

Figure 10.21

A sample query using data from an external database

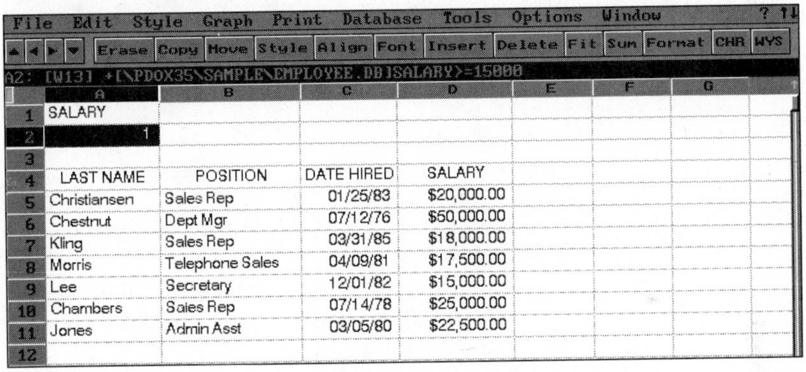

To execute the query, select the /Database, Query, Extract command. Quattro Pro searches the EMPLOYEE.DB database on disk to find those records that meet the criteria in the criteria table (A1..A2 of Figure 10.21). It then copies the information in those fields referenced in the output block (A4..D4) from the external database to the spreadsheet, as shown in Figure 10.21. You can now work with the data just as you would any other data in your Quattro Pro spreadsheet.

Using Quattro Pro's Paradox Access Feature

Quattro Pro takes the process of working with information in external databases a step further through its Paradox Access feature. If you own Paradox version 3.5 or later, you can run both Quattro Pro and Paradox at the same time and switch back and forth between them. And, after performing a query on a database in Paradox, you can switch to Quattro Pro and "dump" the results of that query directly into your Quattro Pro spreadsheet. That way, you can use Quattro Pro's commands to work with that data, just as you would any other data in your spreadsheet.

The sections that follow assume you are familiar with commands and procedures in Paradox. If you aren't, take a moment to review the manual labeled "Introduction" that came with your copy of Paradox.

Setting Up for Paradox Access

To use the Paradox Access feature you'll need the following:

- A copy of Quattro Pro 2.0 or later.

- A copy of Paradox 3.5 or later.

- An 80286/AT-style or faster computer.

- At least 2Mb of RAM configured as extended memory. (If you intend to work with very large spreadsheets in Quattro Pro, you may also need additional expanded memory.)

Before you're ready to use the Paradox Access feature, you must configure Quattro Pro accordingly. Here are the steps you'll need to take:

1. Make sure the Files= statement in your CONFIG.SYS file is set to at least Files=40. As you know, this file is located on the root directory of your hard disk and can be edited by any word processor that reads and writes ASCII files.

2. The DOS file SHARE.EXE must be located in a directory that is included in the PATH statement in your AUTOEXEC.BAT file. The SHARE.EXE file comes with your copy of DOS. See your DOS manual for instructions on copying this file to your hard disk.

3. Both Quattro Pro and Paradox must be properly installed in different directories and both of those directories must be included in the PATH statement in your AUTOEXEC.BAT file.

4. Check to make sure that your Paradox working directory is different from your private directory. (If you are running Paradox on a network, this shouldn't be a problem.) If they are the same, run the Custom Configuration Program and use the Options SetDirectory command to change the location of your Paradox working directory.

5. From within Quattro Pro, select the /Options, Other, Paradox, Directory command and specify one of two settings. If you are working on a

stand-alone computer that is not connected to a network, specify the root drive of your computer—for example **C:**. If you are working on a network, specify the path to the directory that contains your PARA-DOX.NET file.

6. From within Quattro Pro, select the /Options, Other, Paradox, Network Type command and specify one of two settings. If you are working on a stand-alone machine that is not connected to a network, choose Dis-abled (or Other if you're running Quatro Pro 3.0). If you are working on a network, choose the type of network for which Paradox is currently in-stalled from the list provided.

To use the Paradox Access feature you must start Paradox first. To do this, you'll use the PXACCESS.BAT file that comes with your copy of Quat-tro Pro. This file is automatically copied to your Quattro Pro directory when you install Quattro Pro. You can run this file by simply typing **PXACCESS** at the DOS prompt. When you run the PXACCESS.BAT file, you'll see the following parameters appear on your screen:

```
SHARE
PARADOX -qpro -leaveK 512 -emk 0
```

The first line, SHARE, runs the DOS SHARE.EXE program. The second starts Paradox with the -qpro option and allocates sufficient expanded mem-ory for Quattro Pro to run. A short time later Paradox appears on your screen. (See "About the PXACCESS.BAT File" later for additional details on the PXACCESS.BAT file parameters.)

Once Paradox is displayed on your screen, you can switch to Quattro Pro at any time by pressing Ctrl-F10. When you press this key sequence, your screen will go blank for a moment. The Quattro Pro banner screen will then appear, followed by the main Quattro Pro screen. You can switch back to Paradox at any time by pressing Ctrl-F10 again. Alternatively, you can se-lect Quattro Pro's /Database, Paradox, Access, Go command to switch back to Paradox.

As mentioned, Quattro Pro's Paradox Access feature lets you capture the results of a Paradox database query in your Quattro Pro spreadsheet. In order to understand how this is done, however, you'll need to understand a little about how Paradox handles and stores the results of its queries.

To process its queries, as well as perform other operations, Paradox uses a series of 12 temporary tables, called *Answer tables*. These temporary tables are just that, temporary—that is, they are only stored in memory while they are needed. When you leave Paradox, they are deleted from memory. Further-more, Paradox's Answer tables are constantly subject to change. When new information becomes available for a specific table, the old version of the table is overwritten with a new version containing the most recent information.

You can use the Paradox Access feature to gain access to information in any of the following Answer tables:

Table	Information
Answer	Results of the most recent query
Changed	Old copies of changed records
Crosstab	Results of a crosstab operation
Deleted	Old copies of deleted records
Entry	Copies of new records for a table
Family	Reports and forms for a table
Inserted	Records that have been inserted into a table
Keyviol	Records with duplicate key values
List	Tables, scripts, files, network users, or locks
Password	List of auxiliary passwords
Problems	Unconverted records
Struct	Shows database structure (fields and data types)

Perhaps the most commonly used Answer table is Answer (ANSWER.DB), which contains the results of the most recent Paradox query. It is through this table that Quattro Pro can gain access to the most recent Paradox query. In fact, the first time you press Ctrl-F10 to switch from Paradox to Quattro Pro, Quattro Pro will attempt to load the ANSWER.DB file into the current spreadsheet, provided, of course, that ANSWER.DB exists.

Configuring Quattro Pro

To configure Quattro Pro for Paradox Access, you use the /Database, Paradox Access command. When you select this command, Quattro Pro displays a submenu with the Go, Load File, and Autoload options. These options perform the following functions:

- *Go* switches from Quattro Pro to Paradox. As mentioned, the short-cut key for this command is Ctrl-F10.

- *Load File* lets you specify the name of a Paradox Answer table that will be automatically loaded when you switch from Paradox to Quattro Pro. The default setting here is ANSWER.DB, which contains the results of the most recent Paradox query. However, you can also specify the name of another Paradox Answer table or the name of a Quattro Pro spreadsheet file. This option is directly related to the Autoload option.

- *Autoload* lets you specify whether the file associated with the Load File option is automatically loaded into the Quattro Pro spreadsheet whenever you switch from Paradox to Quattro Pro. When you select this option, Quattro Pro displays a submenu with two options, Yes and No. Yes, the default, specifies that the file named by the Load File option will be loaded automatically each time you switch to Quattro Pro. (With this setting, any autoloading file you've specified with the /Options, Startup, Autoload File command is ignored.) Select No to turn this feature off.

A Sample Paradox Access Session

To take advantage of Paradox Access, begin by starting Paradox with the PXACCESS.BAT file located in your Quattro Pro program directory. Assuming your Quattro Pro directory is in your path, you can do this by typing **PXACCESS** at the DOS prompt.

Once Paradox is up and running, perform a query using the database table of your choice. For example, Figure 10.22 shows what the Paradox screen looks like after using the Query By Example (QBE) feature to query a database table called EMPLOYEE.DB. (This database table is one of the sample tables that comes with Paradox 3.5.) This query selects information from four fields in the EMPLOYEE.DB table. As you can see, the results of this query are displayed in an on-screen table labeled ANSWER (ANSWER.DB).

Figure 10.22

A sample query in Paradox

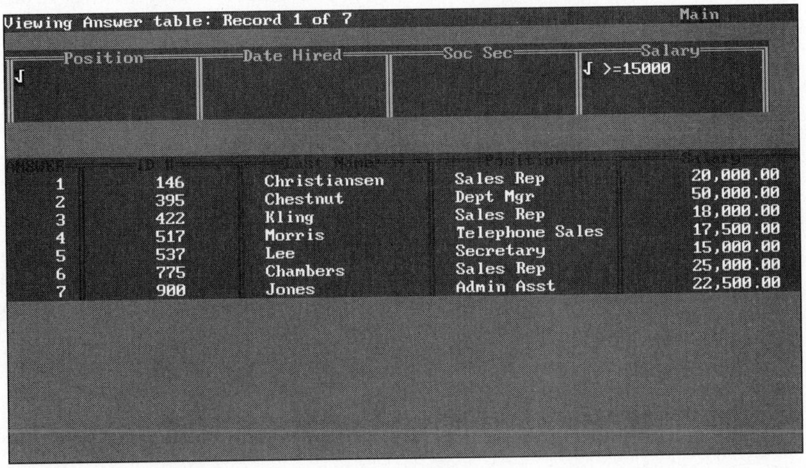

Once the results of your query are displayed in the ANSWER.DB table, select Ctrl-F10 to switch to Quattro Pro. Your screen goes blank for a moment, then the Quattro Pro banner screen appears. A moment later, the usual spreadsheet window is opened and the results of the most recent Paradox query are loaded into the spreadsheet, starting in cell A1. Your screen looks like Figure 10.23 (after a little column widening, of course). You can now refer to that data in commands and formulas, just as you would any other data in your Quattro Pro spreadsheet.

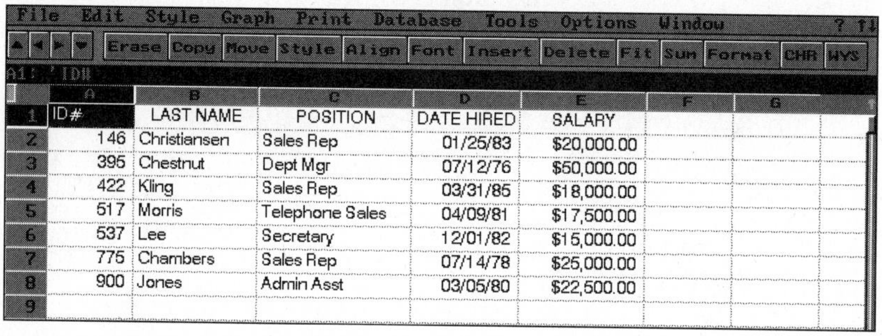

ID#	LAST NAME	POSITION	DATE HIRED	SALARY
146	Christiansen	Sales Rep	01/25/83	$20,000.00
395	Chestnut	Dept Mgr	07/12/76	$50,000.00
422	Kling	Sales Rep	03/31/85	$18,000.00
517	Morris	Telephone Sales	04/09/81	$17,500.00
537	Lee	Secretary	12/01/82	$15,000.00
775	Chambers	Sales Rep	07/14/78	$25,000.00
900	Jones	Admin Asst	03/05/80	$22,500.00

Figure 10.23 The results of a Paradox query displayed in a Quattro Pro spreadsheet via the Paradox Access feature

To get back to Paradox, press Ctrl-F10 (or select /Database, Paradox Access, Go). You are returned to Paradox in the same state in which you left it. In the meantime, your Quattro Pro session has been suspended, but remains unchanged. You can return to that session whenever you want by pressing Ctrl-F10.

Each time you switch from Paradox to Quattro Pro, Quattro Pro attempts to load the most recent version of the ANSWER.DB table. This may, or may not, be what you want. To turn off this autoloading feature, select Quattro Pro's /Database, Paradox Access, Autoload, No command.

Of Macros and Scripts

In recognition of the Paradox Access feature, Quattro Pro provides the command {/ Paradox;SwitchGo}. This command lets you switch back to Paradox from within a macro. On the other side of the coin, Paradox 3.5 includes the script command TOQPRO. This command passes control to Quattro Pro, just as though you pressed Ctrl-F10. You might want to include this command in your INIT.SC file to pass control to Quattro Pro on Paradox startup.

About the PXACCESS.BAT File

The PXACCESS.BAT file is used to start Paradox and activate the Paradox Access feature. This .BAT file contains the following command lines:

```
SHARE
PARADOX -qpro -leaveK 512 -emk 0
```

The command line SHARE runs the DOS SHARE.EXE file. The second command line starts Paradox with the appropriate parameters. Briefly, these parameters perform the following functions:

- The -qpro parameter configures Paradox for Quattro Pro's Paradox Access feature. It also allocates sufficient memory for Quattro Pro.

- The -leaveK 512 parameter reserves an additional 512k of extended memory (if it is available) that Paradox cannot use. That memory is allocated to Quattro Pro for storage of the VROOMM object cache. Quattro Pro uses this cache to store segments of its executable program objects, rather than having to read them from disk. This can result in a noticeable improvement in performance. See Chapter 15 for further details on how the VROOMM memory manager works and how the VROOMM object cache is used. To take advantage of this extended memory, though, the next option must also be included in the PXACCESS.BAT file.

- The -emk 0 parameter stops Paradox from using any expanded memory, thereby reserving it for use by Quattro Pro.

In most cases, you won't need to change the contents of the PXAC-CESS.BAT file. However, you can if you need to by using any word processor capable of reading and writing ASCII files.

Using the Database @Functions

The database @functions let you statistically analyze the contents of a field in the database. All of these functions begin with the symbol @, followed by a D, and a name that is descriptive of what they do—for example, @DAVG, @DCOUNT, or @DSUM.

The unique aspect of the database @functions is that they accept a criteria table argument. Therefore, they act only on specific records in the database that you define. For example, you could use the @DCOUNT function to count the total number of employees in the employee database that work in the production department.

One advantage to using the database @functions is that they are dynamic. Whenever the information in the database or the criteria table changes, the database @function is automatically updated for the change.

Database @Function Syntax

All of the database @functions use the following syntax:

```
@Dfunction(Database-block,Offset,Criteria-table-block)
```

@Dfunction is the name of the particular database @function you want to use—for example, @DAVG, @DCOUNT, @DSUM, @DMIN, @DMAX, @DSTD, @DVAR, @DSTDS, or @DVARS.

Database-block is the block address or block name that identifies the location of the records in the database and its field names—for example, A1..G10 or EMPLOYEE.

Offset is a number that identifies the field in the database you want to analyze. Each field in a database is assigned a sequential number, working from left to right. The first field is given the value 0, the second field a value of 1, the third field a value of 2, and so on.

Criteria-table-block is the block address or block name that identifies the location of the criteria table. The conventions for defining selection criteria in the criteria table for the database @functions are exactly the same as the conventions used for the /Database, Query commands. See "Defining Criteria" earlier in this chapter for a detailed description of how to define selection criteria in a criteria table.

Calculating Averages with @DAVG

The @DAVG function lets you calculate an average for a numeric field in a database. However, the average yielded applies only to those records selected from the database by using the selection criteria in the criteria table. Figure 10.24 shows an example of the @DAVG function in cell E17. (The formula in cell E17 also appears as a label starting in cell B17.) As you can see, this formula reads

```
@DAVG(A1..G10,6,B12..B13)
```

The first argument for this function, A1..G10, identifies the database block that contains all the records in the employee database and its field names. The second argument, 6, is an offset value that refers to the SALARY field in the employee database (seventh column from the left). The third argument, B12..B13, identifies the location of the criteria table that will be used to select records from the database. As you can see in Figure 10.24, this block contains the SALARY field name with the formula +G2>=35000 beneath it. Therefore, only records with a value that is greater than or equal to 35,000 in the SALARY field will be selected from the employee database. These criteria apply to six of the records in the database. Therefore, the @DAVG function in cell E17 applies only to those six records.

Figure 10.24

Using the database @functions

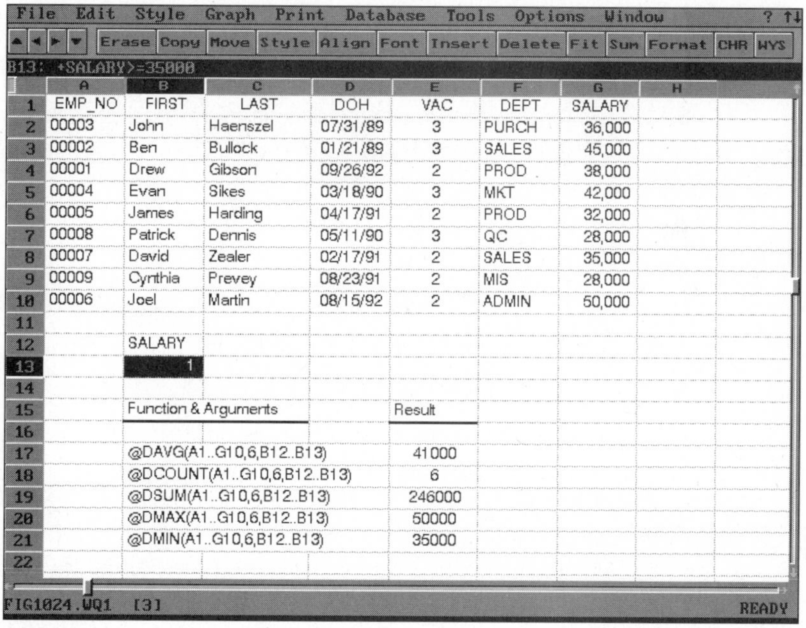

File	Edit	Style	Graph	Print	Database	Tools	Options	Window	? ↑↓

| ▲ ◀ ▶ ▼ | Erase | Copy | Move | Style | Align | Font | Insert | Delete | Fit | Sum | Format | CHR | WYS |

B13: +SALARY>=35000

	A	B	C	D	E	F	G	H
1	EMP_NO	FIRST	LAST	DOH	VAC	DEPT	SALARY	
2	00003	John	Haenszel	07/31/89	3	PURCH	36,000	
3	00002	Ben	Bullock	01/21/89	3	SALES	45,000	
4	00001	Drew	Gibson	09/26/92	2	PROD	38,000	
5	00004	Evan	Sikes	03/18/90	3	MKT	42,000	
6	00005	James	Harding	04/17/91	2	PROD	32,000	
7	00008	Patrick	Dennis	05/11/90	3	QC	28,000	
8	00007	David	Zealer	02/17/91	2	SALES	35,000	
9	00009	Cynthia	Prevey	08/23/91	2	MIS	28,000	
10	00006	Joel	Martin	08/15/92	2	ADMIN	50,000	
11								
12		SALARY						
13		1						
14								
15		Function & Arguments			Result			
16								
17		@DAVG(A1..G10,6,B12..B13)			41000			
18		@DCOUNT(A1..G10,6,B12..B13)			6			
19		@DSUM(A1..G10,6,B12..B13)			246000			
20		@DMAX(A1..G10,6,B12..B13)			50000			
21		@DMIN(A1..G10,6,B12..B13)			35000			
22								

FIG1024.WQ1 [3] READY

The @DAVG function calculates its average using standard mathematical rules. In this case, it adds up the values for the SALARY field of the employee database for each record selected from that database. It then divides by the total number of records selected. The result is a simple average of the field values for the selected records.

Using @DCOUNT to Count Values and Labels

The @DCOUNT function lets you count the values or labels in a specific field of a database. Typical of the database @functions, however, the count applies only to the records selected from the database by using the selection criteria in the criteria table.

Figure 10.24 shows an example of the @DCOUNT function in cell E18. The function reads

```
@DCOUNT(A1..G10,6,B12..B13)
```

The first argument, A1..G10, defines the location of all the records in the employee database as well as its field names. The second argument, 6, is an offset value referring to the SALARY field in the database (the seventh field from the left). The third argument, B12..B13, defines the location of the criteria table for the function. As you may recall, the selection criteria in this table selects all records with a value greater than or equal to $35,000 in the SALARY field of the employee database. The function returns a value of 6, indicating that six records in the employee database fall into this category.

Adding Values with @DSUM

The @DSUM function lets you add the values in a given numeric field for a specific set of records in a database. An example of this function appears in cell E19 of Figure 10.24. The function reads

```
@DSUM(A1..G10,6,B12..B13)
```

where A1..G10 identifies the location of all the records in the employee database and its field names, 6 is an offset value referring to the seventh field in the database (SALARY), and B12..B13 identifies the location of the criteria table for the database @function.

Like all the database @functions, the result of the @DSUM function applies only to those records in the database that meet the selection criteria in the criteria table. As you may recall, the criteria table block in Figure 10.24 is B12..B13, and it will select those records in the employee database with a value that is greater than or equal to $35,000 in the SALARY field (column G). These criteria apply to six records in the employee database. Therefore, the result of the @DSUM function in cell E19 shows a total of the contents of the SALARY field for those records selected of $246,000.

Finding the Highest Value with @DMAX

As you might have gathered from its name, the @DMAX function returns the highest value in a field of a database for a selected group of records. Once again, the set of records analyzed is determined by the selection criteria in the criteria table for the function. Figure 10.24 shows an example of this function in cell E20, which reads

```
@DMAX(A1..G10,6,B12..B13)
```

The first argument in this function, A1..G10, identifies the location of the employee database. Notice that both the records in the database and its field names have been included. The second argument, 6, is an offset value referring to the seventh field from the left in the database (the SALARY field, column G). This is the field that will be analyzed by the function. The third argument, B12..B13, identifies the location of the criteria table for the function. As you may recall, the selection criteria in this table selects those records from the employee database with values greater than or equal to $35,000 in the SALARY field. These criteria select six records from the database. The @DMAX function in cell E20 indicates that from among these six records, the highest value in the SALARY field is $50,000.

Using @DMIN to Find the Lowest Value

The @DMIN function returns the lowest value in a field of a database for a selected group of records; it works exactly like the @DMAX function. An example of @DMIN is shown in cell E21 of Figure 10.24. The function has been entered as follows:

```
@DMIN(A1..G10,6,B12..B13)
```

The first argument in this function, A1..G10, identifies the block containing the employee database along with its field names. The second argument, 6, is an offset value that identifies the field in the database that will be searched. In this case, it refers to the seventh field from the left in the database (the SALARY field, column G). The third argument, B12..B13, identifies the block containing the criteria table for the function. These criteria select six records from the employee database. From among those six records, the lowest value in the SALARY field is $35,000.

Calculating Standard Deviation and Variance

Quattro Pro provides four database @functions for calculating standard deviation and variance—@DSTD, @DVAR, @DSTDS, and @DVARS. The first two are used when you are evaluating an entire population, and the last two are used when the population you are evaluating represents only a sample of the entire population. All four functions work in the same way and take the same arguments.

If you are familiar with statistics, you'll recall that the *standard deviation* is a measure of the degree to which the values in a population vary from the mean (average) for the population. The smaller the standard deviation, the closer values are clustered about the mean. In a normally distributed population, roughly 68% of the values in the population will fall within plus or minus one standard deviation of the mean, and 95% will fall within two standard deviations. The standard deviation is calculated by taking the square root of the variance.

The *variance* is a measure of the amount of dispersion in your population. That is, it measures the amount of variation of all the values in a population from the mean (average). The lower the value of the variance, the less the individual values in the population vary from the mean, and the more reliable the mean (average) is as an expression of a trend for the population. A variance of 0 means that all of the values in the population are equal to the mean.

@DSTD and @DVAR

The @DSTD and @DVAR functions let you calculate the standard deviation and variance, respectively, for the values in a numeric field of a database. The values to be analyzed are selected based on the selection criteria you've defined in the criteria table for the @DSTD or @DVAR function.

Both of the @DSTD and @DVAR functions return population (n, or biased) statistics as opposed to sample ($n-1$, unbiased) statistics. That is, both functions assume you are measuring the entire population of all available values. To calculate the standard deviation and variance for a population by using the sample ($n-1$, unbiased) method, you'll need to use the @DSTDS and @DVARS functions discussed in the next section.

Figure 10.25 shows an example of the @DSTD function in cell E17 and the @DVAR function in cell E18. Both functions evaluate the contents of the SALARY field (column G) in the employee database and both have the same arguments:

```
@DSTD(A1..G10,6,B12..B13)
@DVAR(A1..G10,6,B12..B13)
```

The first argument, A1..G10, defines the block containing the records in the employee database along with its field names. The second argument, 6, is an offset value that defines the field in the database whose contents will be evaluated. In this case, the field to be evaluated is the seventh field from the left (the SALARY field, column G). The final argument, B12..B13, defines the block containing the criteria table for the function. As you can see, this block contains the field name SALARY with nothing beneath it. Therefore Quattro Pro will automatically select all the records in the database.

Let's take a look at the results of the @DSTD and @DVAR functions in cells E17 and E18 of Figure 10.25. The @DSTD function returns a value of 7,078. Thus, if the contents of the SALARY field of the employee database were normally distributed about the mean (cell E21), 68% of the values in the population would fall between $33,033 and $44,189. On the other hand, the @DVAR function in cell E18 returns 50,098,765. If you take the square root of this value, you get 7,078, the standard deviation.

@DSTDS and @DVARS

Note. @DSTDS and @DVARS are not supported by versions of Lotus 1-2-3 prior to Release 3.0. Therefore, if you intend to use the current Quattro Pro spreadsheet with a version of Lotus 1-2-3 prior to Release 3.0, you'll have to use the @DSTD and @DVAR functions.

The @DSTDS and @DVARS functions let you calculate the standard deviation and variance for the values in a numeric field of a database. Unlike @DSTD and @DVAR, however, these functions are useful when the population you are evaluating represents only a sample of the entire population.

Because these functions use the sample (n–1, unbiased) method of calculating the standard deviation and variance, they tend to return slightly higher results than @DSTD and @DVAR. This tends to offset any errors that may occur in the sampling process as the result of evaluating a sample of the population rather than the entire population. For example, Figure 10.25 shows examples of the @DSTDS and @DVARS functions in cells E19 and E20. The functions were entered using the same block arguments as the @DSTD and @DVAR functions above (cells E17 and E18). However, notice that these functions return slightly higher values for the same population of values.

Figure 10.25
Calculating standard deviation and variance with the database @functions

| File | Edit | Style | Graph | Print | Database | Tools | Options | Window | ? ↑↓ |

| ◆ ◀ ▶ ▼ | Erase | Copy | Move | Style | Align | Font | Insert | Delete | Fit | Sum | Format | CHR | WYS |

B17: (,0) [W10] @DSTD(A1..G10,6,B12..B13)

	A	B	C	D	E	F	G	H
1	EMP_NO	FIRST	LAST	DOH	VAC	DEPT	SALARY	
2	00003	John	Haenszel	07/31/89	3	PURCH	36,000	
3	00002	Ben	Bullock	01/21/89	3	SALES	45,000	
4	00001	Drew	Gibson	09/26/92	2	PROD	38,000	
5	00004	Evan	Sikes	03/18/90	3	MKT	42,000	
6	00005	James	Harding	04/17/91	2	PROD	32,000	
7	00008	Patrick	Dennis	05/11/90	3	QC	28,000	
8	00007	David	Zealer	02/17/91	2	SALES	35,000	
9	00009	Cynthia	Prevey	08/23/91	2	MIS	28,000	
10	00006	Joel	Martin	08/15/92	2	ADMIN	50,000	
11								
12		SALARY						
13								
14								
15		Function & Arguments			Result			
16								
17		@DSTD(A1..G10,6,B12..B13)			7,078			
18		@DVAR(A1..G10,6,B12..B13)			50,098,765			
19		@DSTDS(A1..G10,6,B12..B13)			7,507			
20		@DVARS(A1..G10,6,B12..B13)			56,361,111			
21		@DAVG(A1..G10,6,B12..B13)			37,111			
22								

FIG10-25.WQ1 [3]   READY

Creating a Custom Data-Entry Form

You can specify the location of a custom data-entry form by using the /Database, Restrict Input command. This command is often used in conjunction with an interactive macro to add records to a database.

You must prepare your data-entry form before using the /Database, Restrict Input command. For example, Figure 10.26 shows an example data-entry form in the block J1..M12. Notice that lines have been drawn around the outside of the form, causing it to stand out. You could also include some shading or some different fonts to make the form more attractive. See Chapter 3 for details on how you can create special display effects in your Quattro Pro spreadsheet.

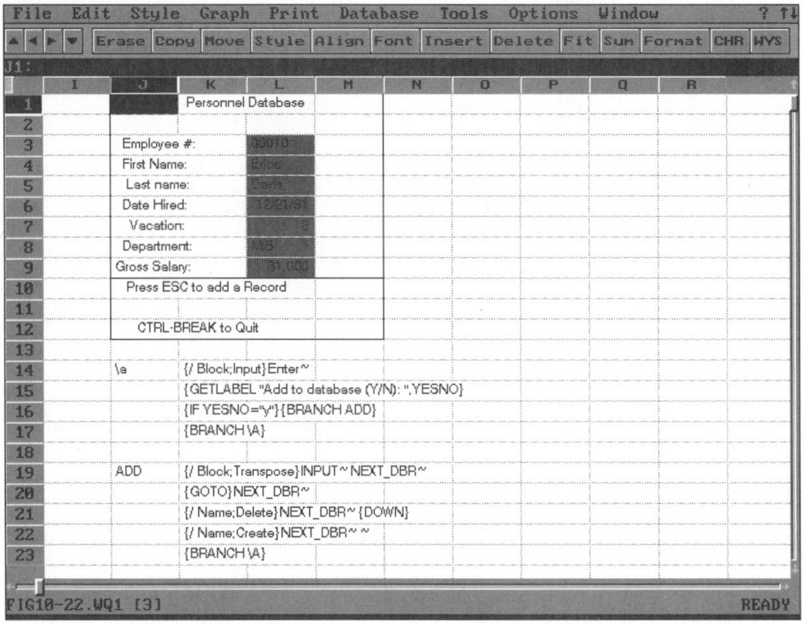

Figure 10.26

A custom data-entry form prepared for the /Database, Restrict Input command

Note. See Chapter 2 for additional details on how you can use the /Style, Protection command to protect and unprotect cells.

Once you've created your data-entry form, you are ready to define the cells within that form in which you will allow data entry. To do this, you must unprotect those cells with the /Style, Protection, Unprotect command. For example, in the data-entry form in Figure 10.26, you might want to unprotect the cells in the block L3..L9. When your data-entry form is displayed, Quattro Pro will allow entries only in these cells and no others.

To display the custom form, select the /Database, Restrict Input command. Quattro Pro prompts you for the block that contains the data-entry form. Highlight that block (J1..M12 in Figure 10.26) and press Enter. Alternatively, you can specify the block name of the data-entry form and press Enter. Either way, Quattro Pro moves the data-entry form to the upper-left corner of the current spreadsheet window. The cell selector is then located in the first unprotected cell within the form. At that point, you can begin typing the contents of each field for the new record. To confirm each entry, press Enter or ↓. You can edit an entry by using standard text editing keys. However, if you try to move the cell selector outside the block of unprotected cells, Quattro Pro won't let you. Further, if you attempt to enter a command, Quattro Pro simply ignores it. To exit the data-entry form, press Esc.

As mentioned, the /Database, Restrict Input command is usually called from a macro. Figure 10.26 shows a sample data-entry macro starting in cell K14. (Normally this macro would be safely tucked away where the user can't see it.) The first command in the macro is the macro command-language equivalent for the /Database, Restrict Input command. Once this command is in force, Quattro Pro suspends further execution of the macro until you press Esc. Once Esc is pressed, the macro continues. To tell you exactly how the macro in Figure 10.26 actually works would be to steal thunder from Chapter 12 and Chapter 13. These chapters tell you how you can use Quattro Pro's macro programming language to create your own sophisticated applications.

11

Analyzing Data

Creating a Frequency
Distribution Table

Using a Frequency
Distribution Table in
an Analysis

Performing
Regression Analysis

Manipulating Matrices

What-If Analysis
Using Data Tables

Solving a Formula
Backwards

Obtaining the Optimal
Solution in Quattro
Pro 3.0

Obtaining the Optimal
Solution in Quattro
Pro 4.0

Auditing Your
Spreadsheets in
Quattro Pro 4.0

QUATTRO PRO PROVIDES A VARIETY OF COMMANDS, ACCESSED through the /Tools menu, that perform sophisticated data analysis. For example, you can perform statistical analysis, manipulate matrices to solve for a unique solution, and perform different types of sensitivity analysis.

Although many of the commands and techniques you use are the same for both Quattro Pro 3.0 and 4.0, there are two differences. First, the Optimizer, which solves for the optimal solution to a problem with multiple variables and solutions, is different in version 3.0 and 4.0. For this reason, the Optimizer in each version will be discussed separately in this chapter.

Second, version 4.0 includes the new /Tools, Audit command, which allows you to analyze the data in your spreadsheet. You can trace cell dependencies, find circular references, locate formulas that refer to blank cells or label references, examine formulas that contain external links, and find cells that return ERR.

Creating a Frequency Distribution Table

A *frequency distribution table* categorizes information for use in analysis. To create this table for a block of values, you first divide the data into a limited number of categories (*intervals*). Then you record the number of times (*frequency*) the values in the block occur in each category.

Instead of manually counting each occurrence, and then categorizing the information in a frequency distribution table, you can use the /Tools, Frequency command to perform these calculations.

For example, imagine that you are a washing machine manufacturer. Your quality control department has been monitoring a sample of 15 machines. In Figure 11.1, the block B4..B18 contains the number of years each machine has been in operation without needing a repair. You can create a frequency distribution table that categorizes the number of years of repair-free service.

Entering the Values to Be Categorized (Value Block)

Before you use the /Tools, Frequency command, you must enter the data you want categorized, such as the number of repair-free years entered in the block B4..B18. Quattro Pro calls these values the *Value block*, which can be entered in a column, row, or block.

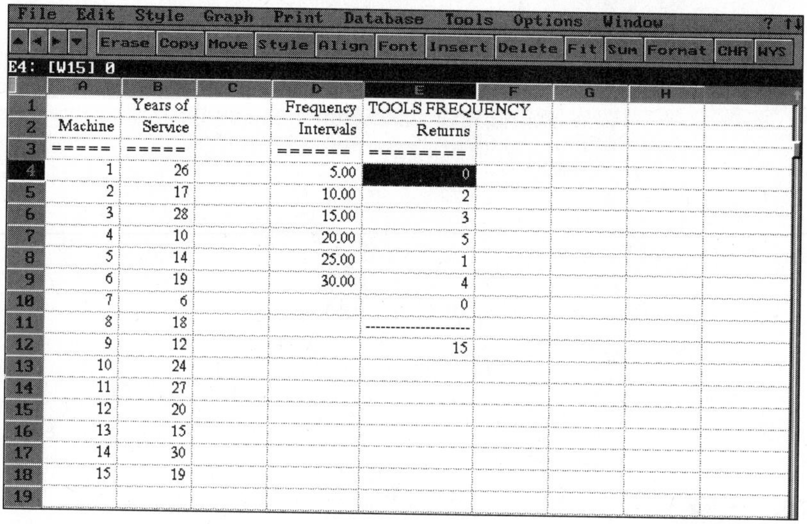

Figure 11.1

A frequency
distribution table

	A	B	C	D	E	F	G	H
	File Edit Style Graph Print Database Tools Options Window ? ↑↓							
	Erase Copy Move Style Align Font Insert Delete Fit Sum Format CHR NYS							
E4: [W15] 0								
1		Years of		Frequency	TOOLS FREQUENCY			
2	Machine	Service		Intervals	Returns			
3	=====	=====		======	=========			
4	1	26		5.00	0			
5	2	17		10.00	2			
6	3	28		15.00	3			
7	4	10		20.00	5			
8	5	14		25.00	1			
9	6	19		30.00	4			
10	7	6			0			
11	8	18			-------------			
12	9	12			15			
13	10	24						
14	11	27						
15	12	20						
16	13	15						
17	14	30						
18	15	19						
19								

Determining and Entering Frequency Intervals (Bin Block)

Determine the frequency intervals—called the *Bin block*—of your value categories using the following rules:

- In general, each category should have the same *interval* (value span).

- Intervals should be defined so that no single observation can fall into multiple categories.

- The combined range of frequency intervals should encompass the entire range of values in the block. For example, if your sample values range from 0 to 30, then your frequency intervals in total should span the interval 0 to 30.

- Specify intervals that are meaningful and provide information to you. Make intervals small enough so that the midpoint of an interval is representative of the values that fall into that category. For this reason, you will normally use between 6 and 20 intervals.

Let's return to the quality control analysis example in Figure 11.1. Using the foregoing criteria, reasonable frequency intervals occur at five-year increments, such as 0 to 5 years, 5.01 to 10 years, and so on, up to the highest interval of 25.01 to 30 years.

The next step is to enter your frequency intervals (Bin block) in the spreadsheet, using the following guidelines:

- Enter all categories in *ascending* order in a column. Otherwise, Quattro Pro incorrectly calculates the frequency distribution table.

- Enter only the highest value in a category.

- Enter each frequency interval as a number or a formula. To efficiently create a Bin block containing equally spaced intervals, you can use the /Edit, Fill command. (See Chapter 10 for more information.)

- Make sure that the cells E4..E10 in Figure 11.1 in the column directly to the right of the Bin block are empty. Quattro Pro writes over any existing information in these cells when it creates the frequency distribution table.

In Figure 11.1, the frequency intervals are entered in the block D4..D9. For the category 0 to 5 years, 5 is entered in cell D4; for the next category, 10 is entered in cell D5. Quattro Pro evaluates the first interval as any value equal to or less than 5 (including negative values), and the second interval as any value greater than 5 (the previous category) but less than or equal to 10, and so on. The highest interval is evaluated as any value greater than 25 but less than or equal to 30. (Quattro Pro always automatically includes one *additional* frequency interval in the frequency distribution table, which in this example is evaluated as values greater than 30.)

Using the /Tools, Frequency Command

Now you're ready to create the frequency distribution table. Select /Tools, Frequency and specify the Value block as **B4..B18** and the Bin block as the frequency intervals block, **D4..D9**.

CAUTION! *Frequency interval counts can be corrupted if any cells in your Value block contain the special values ERR and NA. Quattro Pro includes any NA values in your lowest interval, but assigns any ERR values to your highest interval. However, any blank cells or labels in your Value block are not counted.*

Take a look at the frequency distribution table Quattro Pro creates in the block E4..E10. In the Value block (B4..B18), Quattro Pro counts two values that are greater than 5 but less than or equal to 10, three values greater than 10 but less than or equal to 15, and so on. Notice the extra frequency value, 0 in cell E10, representing the number of values in the block that exceed 30, your highest frequency interval. In cell E12, the formula @SUM(E4..E10) has been used to confirm that all 15 values in the Value block have been assigned to a frequency interval.

NOTE. *Quattro Pro does not automatically update the values in a frequency distribution table, even if you recalculate your spreadsheet. So if you change any values in the Value and Bin blocks, you must reuse the /Tools, Frequency command.*

Using a Frequency Distribution Table in an Analysis

Here's one way to use the output of a frequency distribution table in an analysis. Suppose that for marketing purposes, your company wants to institute a warranty program under which you will repair, free of charge, any malfunctioning machines. But how many years of service should this warranty cover? If the sample is normally distributed, your quality control group can use information returned by the /Tools, Frequency command in a statistical analysis to determine a reasonable warranty period.

A *normally distributed sample* looks like a bell-shaped curve. Approximately 68.3% of the values are within ±1 standard deviation (Std Dev) of the mean (average); 95.4% are within ±2 Std Dev; and 99.7% are within ±3 Std Dev of the mean. As you know, a frequency distribution table provides the number of values within a frequency interval. Therefore, if you specify the intervals in your Bin block as these standard deviation ranges, the /Tools, Frequency command will count the number of values within these ranges.

For example, in Figure 11.2, the mean (average) of the sample is calculated in cell D16 with @AVG(B4..B18). In cell D17, the sample standard deviation is calculated using @STDS(B4..B18). (See "Statistical Functions" in Chapter 7 for a discussion of the @AVG and @STDS functions.) Then, in cell D5, the first frequency category in the Bin block is calculated as +D16–1*D17, or +Mean–3*Std Dev. All other categories in the Bin block are similarly computed.

After these calculations are made, and you use /Tools, Frequency to specify your Value block as B4..B18 and your Bin block as D5..D10, Quattro Pro creates the frequency distribution table shown in E5..E11 of Figure 11.2. For example, two values in the sample are greater than 4.03 (Mean–2 Std Dev) but less than or equal to 11.68 (Mean–1 Std Dev).

You can use these counts to verify that your sample data is in fact normally distributed, based on the following:

■ In column F, the total number of values between Mean±1 Std Dev is ten, or 66.7% of the total number of values in the sample—the same as the count for the 26.98 (Mean+1 Std Dev) interval, since the bottom of this interval is Mean–1 Std Dev (11.68).

■ In column G, the number of values within ±2 Std Dev of the mean is 14, or 93.3% of the sample—the total count for the 11.68 interval (greater than Mean–2 Std Dev, but less than or equal to Mean–1 Std Dev), plus the 26.98 interval (Mean ±1 Std Dev), plus the 34.63 interval (greater than Mean+1 Std Dev, but less than or equal to Mean+2 Std Dev).

Figure 11.2

Verifying a normal distribution using /Tools, Frequency

File	Edit	Style	Graph	Print	Database	Tools	Options	Window		? ↑↓

Erase Copy Move Style Align Font Insert Delete Fit Sum Format CHR WYS

D8: (F2) [W12] +D$16+(1*D$17)

	A	B	C	D	E	F	G	H
1		Years of				TOOLS	STD	STD	STD
2	Machine	Service		Frequency	FREQUENCY	DEV	DEV	DEV
3	=====	=====		Intervals	Returns	+-1	+-2	+-3
4	1	26		======	========	=====	=====	=====
5	2	17	Mean-3*STD DEV	-3.62	0			
6	3	28	Mean-2*STD DEV	4.03	0			0
7	4	10	Mean-1*STD DEV	11.68	2		2	2
8	5	14	Mean+1*STD DEV		10	10	10	10
9	6	19	Mean+2*STD DEV	34.63	2		2	2
10	7	6	Mean+3*STD DEV	42.28	1			1
11	8	18			0			
12	9	12			========	=====	=====	=====
13	10	24	Total within Range		15	10	14	15
14	11	27	Percent within Range			66.67%	93.33%	100.00%
15	12	20						
16	13	15	MEAN (AVG)	19.33				
17	14	35	STD DEVIATION	7.65				
18	15	19						
19								

- In column H, all 15, or 100% of the sample fall within ±3 Std Dev of the mean. This count includes all the intervals *except* the lowest interval of –3.62 (less than or equal to Mean–3 Std Dev), and the highest interval (greater than Mean+3 Std Dev) that Quattro Pro includes in cell E10.

Now, knowing that your sample is normally distributed, you can do further analysis and make an informed decision. For example, in column E the frequency distribution table shows that no machines fall into the first two intervals, which have a maximum value of 4.03 years. Therefore, if you institute a free-service warranty program that covers all repairs in the first 4 years, it clearly can be maintained at minimal cost. On the other hand, a warranty program that covers the first 11.68 years of service will most likely require you to service, free of charge, approximately 13.33% (2/15) of the machines you sell.

Performing Regression Analysis

Regression analysis allows you to analyze trends in data, such as sales in relation to advertising expenditures, or labor efficiency in relation to production hours. In other words, regression analysis allows you to analyze relationships between *variables*. You might use regression analysis to determine, for example, if a consistent relationship exists between housing starts and interest rates. Mathematically, you want to verify, using historical data, that the number of housing starts is *dependent* on interest rates. In this instance, you are using regression analysis in a *descriptive* way, to determine if there is a mathematical formula that describes the relationship between housing starts and interest rates.

You can also use regression analysis as a *predictive* tool. For example, suppose you have used regression analysis to determine that a linear relationship (formula) exists between housing starts and interest rates for the last ten years. You can then enter a specific interest rate into this formula and predict next year's housing starts.

Typically, regression analysis entails an immense amount of data manipulation. However, you can use the /Tools, Advanced Math, Regression command to perform this number crunching for you. This section introduces you to the fundamentals of regression analysis, shows how you can graph regression results for a visual representation of your analysis, and presents two examples of how regression analysis can be used.

Regression Analysis Basics

The goal of regression analysis is to determine if a variable, such as housing starts, can be described mathematically by another variable, such as interest rates. In this case, interest rates is the *independent variable*, and housing starts is the *dependent variable*, because the value of housing starts depends on the interest rate value. The dependent variable, housing starts, is the value you want to be able to predict.

Simple Linear Regression

The most basic form of regression analysis is *simple linear regression*—a mathematical method of determining the "best" line through a series of data points. Using a linear formula, simple linear regression relates one dependent variable, such as housing starts, to a single independent variable, such as interest rates.

In regression analysis, it is typically uneconomical or impossible to evaluate an entire population of data; therefore, a sample of that population is usually used. For instance, you might perform a regression analysis of housing starts and interest rates using quarterly values (the sample) instead of daily values (the population). A *simple linear regression line* for a sample is expressed mathematically as

$$\bar{y} = C + bx$$

where $\bar{y}$ is a sample mean value (average) of the dependent variable; C is the y-intercept of the x-axis; b is the slope of the regression line; and x is the independent variable. This directly translates into a *simple linear regression model* for a sample, expressed mathematically as

$$\bar{y} = C + bx + e$$

where e (often called "residuals") is the sample regression error caused by the difference between the mean value $\bar{y}$ and the actual value of y. Both C and b are known as *regression coefficients*.

Here's a quick explanation of how linear regression works and how Quattro Pro performs a regression analysis. The Regression command uses the *least squares method* to determine a regression line; this is a process of finding the regression coefficients C and b. The least squares method minimizes the sum of squared deviations (e^2), or *squared errors*, which are the vertical deviations of the sample points from the regression line. Looking at the sample linear regression model above, this means when y equals $\bar{y}$ (mean), and x equals $\bar{x}$ (mean), then the error e equals 0. This method assumes that error terms for a population (estimated by the sample error term e) are independent of x, normally distributed, have a mean value of 0, are independent of one another, and have a finite variance that is constant.

Multiple Linear Regression

You can also use Quattro Pro to perform *multiple linear regression*. Multiple linear regression relates one dependent variable, such as housing starts, to multiple independent variables, such as interest rates, number of baby boomers, and number of building permits issued.

A *multiple linear regression model* for a sample is expressed mathematically as

$$\bar{y} = C + b_1 x_1 + b_2 x_2 + b_3 x_3 + \ldots + b_n x_n + e$$

This formula is similar to the simple linear regression model, except that it includes multiple independent x variables, and corresponding b coefficients for each x.

TIP. *In many cases you can perform a linear regression analysis on a nonlinear relationship by first manipulating the data. For example, the data for a learning curve (where the independent variable is cumulative production hours, and the dependent variable is cumulative units produced) actually fits an exponential relationship of the form* y=Cx^b*. However, if you take the natural log of all data points, the data can be used in a linear regression analysis and approximates the linear equation* Lny = LnC + bLnx*. See a statistics text for more detail.*

Error Analysis Basics

When you perform a linear regression, the following questions need to be answered:

- Is a straight-line approximation of the data reasonable?

- How much unexplainable error exists (not explained by the regression line)?

The higher the proportion of unexplained error (*deviation*), the less reliable the linear equation is in describing the relationship between variables, and in predicting other values of the dependent variable *y*. In a regression model, the total deviation is defined as

$$Total\ Deviation\ =\ Unexplained\ Deviation\ +\ \begin{array}{l}Explained\ Deviation\\Accounted\ for\\by\ Regression\ Line\end{array}$$

or, in other terms,

$$SST\qquad\qquad = SSE\qquad\qquad + SSR$$
(Sum of squares total) *(Sum of squares error)* *(Sum of squares regression)*

This concept is the underlying basis for error analysis in any linear regression.

Quattro Pro's Regression Output Table

When you perform a regression analysis, Quattro Pro displays a Regression Output table that enables you to create a "best fit" linear equation, based on your data, and to analyze the reliability of this linear equation.

- *Constant (C)* is the y-intercept of the x-axis. The value 0 is RETURNED if you force this intercept to 0 during the Regression command; otherwise, Quattro Pro computes the value.

- *X Coefficient(s)* is calculated for each independent *x* variable that you include in the Regression Independent block.

In the Regression Output table, Quattro Pro also provides the following information for error and reliability analysis:

- *Number of Observations* is the total number of *y* values included in the Regression Dependent block.

- *Degrees of Freedom* is calculated in one of two ways. If the y-intercept (C) is forced to 0, then degrees of freedom is calculated as the number of observations less the number of independent (x) variables. However, if the y-intercept (C) is computed, then degrees of freedom is calculated as this value less 1. If the degrees of freedom is negative, the error message "Overflow occurred" is displayed.

- *Standard Error of Y Estimate* (also known as S_e) calculates the standard deviation of the sample points about the sample regression line. In other words, it measures the variability of the sample points about the regression line, and is a measure of goodness of fit of the regression line to the sample data. Mathematically, it is expressed as

$$S_e = \sqrt{(SSE)\,/\,No.\ of\ degrees\ of\ freedom}$$

The value of S_e can be interpreted in a manner similar to a sample standard deviation. Approximately 99.7% of the observations in the sample data fall within $\pm 3S_e$, 95.4% within $\pm 2S_e$, and 68.3% within $\pm 1S_e$. For example, $\pm 3S_e$ gives a good estimate of the magnitude of potential error when a regression model is used for predicting a *y* value.

- *Standard Error of X Coefficient(s)* (also known as S_b) measures the amount an independent variable *x* influences the dependent variable *y*. For a multiple regression model, Quattro Pro provides an S_b value for each independent *x* variable. In other words, S_b evaluates the amount of error in the regression model caused by an independent *x* variable. Mathematically, it is expressed as

$$S_b = \sqrt{S_e\,(1/\,(x_1 - \bar{x}^2))}$$

S_b is typically used in the t-test, $t=X/S_b$, to determine whether the *x* variable (as measured by the *X* Coefficient) has an important influence on the dependent *y* variable—even after accounting for the influence of all other independent variables included in a multiple regression model. The higher the *t* value, the more influential an independent variable is in determining the dependent *y* variable. Typically, if S_b is less than 50% of *X*, there does exist a relationship between *x* and *y*. Conversely, the larger S_b is in relation to *X* (*x* coefficient), the less reliable the prediction.

- *R Squared* (also known as the Coefficient of Determination, or R^2) measures the goodness of fit of the sample points to the regression line; it is an indication of the strength of the linear relationship. R^2 is equal to SSR/SST (see "Error Analysis Basics"), so it measures the proportion of the total variation explained by the regression line. (If the y-intercept is forced to 0, Quattro Pro computes R^2 as 1–SSE/SST.) For example, if R^2 equals 0.6, then 60% of the variation in the sample y values to the regression line is explained by x. If the regression line is a perfect fit to the data, then SSE=0, and R^2=1.

For a specific dependent y variable, R^2 can also be used to determine the best regression model between different models you have created. Given that each model has the same number of independent variables, the regression line with the highest R^2 is the best fit.

A Simple Linear Regression Example

Suppose you want to analyze what factors determine a person's weight. In Figure 11.3, the weight of 15 people has been entered in column A, and the daily calories consumed by that person in column B. Weight is the dependent variable y, and Daily Calories Consumed is the independent variable x. Notice that the x and y data are entered in adjacent columns, such as x_1 in cell A5, and y_1 in cell B5, with an equal number of x and y entries. If you enter your data points in rowwise fashion, Quattro Pro displays the error message "Too few observations" when you attempt to carry out the regression.

Figure 11.3

Performing a simple linear regression

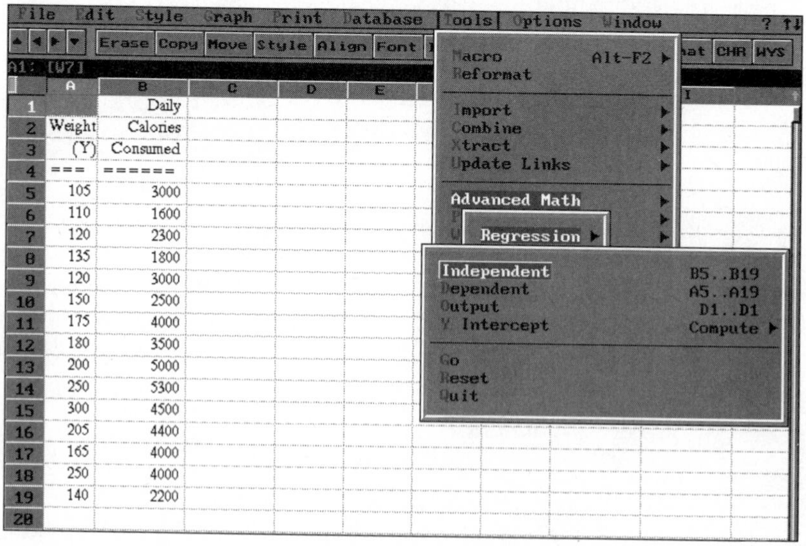

Try a simple linear regression on Quattro Pro by following this procedure:

1. Select the /Tools, Advanced Math, Regression command. Quattro Pro displays the Regression menu shown in Figure 11.3.

2. Specify Independent as the independent *x* values in **B5..B19**.

3. Specify Dependent as the dependent *y* values in **A5..A19**.

4. Specify Output as the upper-left cell of the spreadsheet location for the regression output, D1 in this case. (For simple linear regression, the output table is nine rows deep and four columns wide.)

5. Since you want to compute the y-intercept, and the Y Intercept default is Compute, you need not select this command. (To force the y-intercept to 0, select Y Intercept, Zero.)

6. Select Go.

As shown in Figure 11.4, Quattro performs the regression analysis and builds a Regression Output table beginning in cell D1. You can now use Quattro Pro's calculated regression coefficients to determine the linear equation between weight and daily calories consumed. You can also use the other information in the table to analyze the strength and relative reliability of this relationship.

Figure 11.4

A Regression
Output table

File	Edit	Style	Graph	Print	Database	Tools	Options	Window	? ↑↓

▲ ◄ ► ▼ | Erase | Copy | Move | Style | Align | Font | Insert | Delete | Fit | Sum | Format | CHR | WYS

B5: [W12] 3000

	A	B	C	D	E	F	G	H	I
1		Daily		Regression Output:					
2	Weight	Calories		Constant			40.32215		
3	(Y)	Consumed		Std Err of Y Est			37.14585		
4	===	======		R Squared			0.619348		
5	105	3000		No. of Observations			15		
6	110	1600		Degrees of Freedom			13		
7	120	2300							
8	135	1800		X Coefficient(s)		0.039142			
9	120	3000		Std Err of Coef.		0.008511			
10	150	2500							
11	175	4000							
12	180	3500							
13	200	5000							
14	250	5300							
15	300	4500							
16	205	4400							
17	165	4000							
18	250	4000							
19	140	2200							
20									

First, let's develop the linear equation. In Figure 11.5, the Regression Output table includes the Constant value 40.32, and the X Coefficient value 0.039. Therefore, the regression linear equation is

$$y = 40.32 + 0.039x$$

But how well does this linear equation fit the data points? You can analyze its validity using the other values in the output table.

Figure 11.5

Developing the linear equation from the Regression Output table

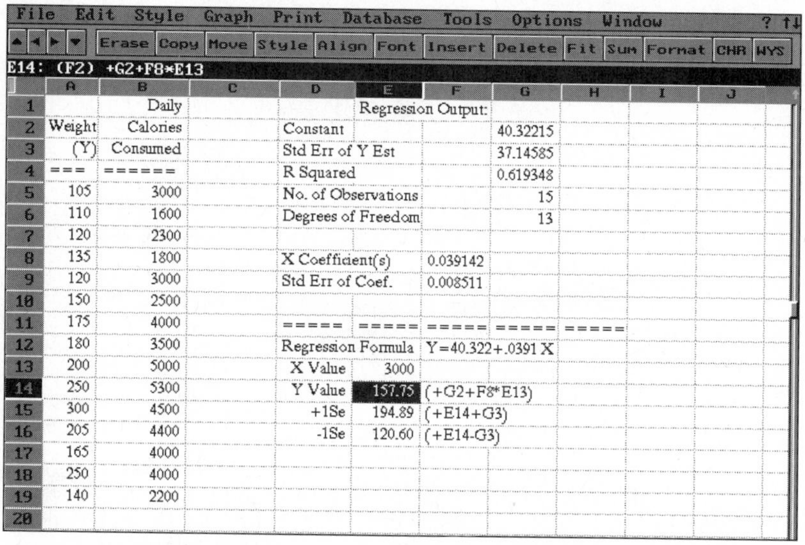

Since 1 is the optimal R^2 value, and R^2 is 0.619, then in the sample approximately 62% of a person's weight is explained by the regression line, or by the number of calories consumed. Secondly, the Standard Error of the X Coefficient (S_b) is 0.0085. The t value, calculated as X/S_b is 0.039/0.0085, or 4.6. Since S_b is approximately 22% of the X coefficient, there exists a strong relationship between weight and daily calories consumed. All in all, these error analysis values confirm that this linear equation provides a moderately good "fit" to the data points.

It is also reasonable to use this linear equation to predict the weight of a person (y), given the daily calories consumed (x). Since Quattro Pro actually enters the regression output into cells in your output block, you can reference these cells in a formula. For example, suppose you enter the x value **3000** (calories) in cell E13. Then enter the regression line formula **+G2+F8*E13** in cell E14.

Tip. Before you perform a new analysis, you should clear any old settings, using Regression, Reset.

The regression line equation calculates that a person who consumes 3,000 calories a day weighs 157.75 pounds. However, because the Standard Error of the Y Estimate, S_e, is 37.15, there is a 68.3% chance that this y value is really between 194.89 pounds ($y+1S_e$) and 120.6 pounds ($y-1S_e$). Because this is a relatively high range of error, you may want to determine if there is another independent x variable that, when combined in a *multiple* linear regression equation with daily calories consumed, returns a better fit to the data points.

Before doing this, let's first graph these data points and the linear regression line for a visual representation of the regression analysis.

NOTE. *If you change any values in your x and y blocks, Quattro Pro does not automatically update the values returned in a regression analysis, even when you recalculate your spreadsheet. So if you change any values in your Dependent or Independent blocks, you must reuse /Tools, Advanced Math, Regression. Because this command remembers your last settings, you can simply select Go from the Regression menu to update your current analysis.*

Graphing Data Points and the Regression Line

Once you have performed a regression analysis, you can use Quattro Pro's /Graph command to graph both your data points and your linear regression line on the same graph, by

1. Sorting the x and y values in ascending order, using the /Database, Sort command.

2. Using the regression equation to calculate y values for the x values in your block.

3. Using the /Graph command to create the graph of your data points and the linear regression line.

Here's how to specifically apply these steps to create a graph of the example in Figure 11.4. First you need to sort the values in ascending order, using the /Database, Sort command to the y (Dependent) values in **A5..B19** as the Block to be sorted; the 1st Key block as the x (Independent) values in **B5..B19;** and an Ascending sort order. When you select Go, Quattro Pro sorts these data points by independent x values in ascending order as shown in Figure 11.6. (See Chapter 10 for further discussion of /Database, Sort.)

Next, for each x value in your block, use the regression equation to calculate a corresponding y value. By including these values in your graph, Quattro Pro can graph the regression line through these points. In column C of Figure 11.6, a CALCULATED Y VALUES column has been created by entering the linear regression formula **–G\$2+F\$8*B5** in cell C5, then copying this formula to **C6..C19.** (The mixed addresses G\$2 and F\$8 are included to keep these cell references fixed during the following copy operation.)

Figure 11.6
Sorting data points before graphing

File Edit Style Graph Print Database Tools Options Window

Erase Copy Move Style Align Font Insert Delete Fit Sum Format CHR WYS

C5: (F0) [W16] +G$2+F$8*B5

	A	B	C	D	E	F	G	H
1		Daily			Regression Output:			
2	Weight	Calories	CALCULATED	Constant			40.32214601	
3	(Y)	Consumed	Y VALUES	Std Err of Y Est			37.14584974	
4	===	======	=========	R Squared			0.61934815	
5	110	1600	103	No. of Observations			15	
6	135	1800	111	Degrees of Freedom			13	
7	140	2200	126					
8	120	2300	130	X Coefficient(s)		0.039142227		
9	150	2500	138	Std Err of Coef.		0.0085108		
10	105	3000	158	========	===	======		
11	120	3000	158					
12	180	3500	177	Regr Formula	Y = 40.322 + .0391 X			
13	165	4000	197					
14	250	4000	197					
15	175	4000	197					
16	205	4400	213					
17	300	4500	216					
18	200	5000	236					
19	250	5300	248					
20								

You can now use the /Graph command to graph these points by specifying an XY Graph Type; the *y* block **A5..A19** as the 1st Series; the CALCULATED Y VALUES block **C5..C19** as the 2nd Series; and the *x* block **B5..B19** as the X-Axis Series. (See Chapter 8 for further discussion of XY graphs.)

Because you want only the regression line to show in the graph, and not the line through the *y* data points, you need to customize this graph using Customize Series, Markers & Lines, Formats, 1st Series, Symbols and 2nd Series, Lines. The graph created in Figure 11.7 displays the regression line through the calculated *y* values, along with the actual sample *x* and *y* data points.

NOTE. *Quattro Pro 4.0 users can use the new /Graph, Series Analyze, Linear Fit command to create a graphed regression line without even performing the linear regression. See Chapter 8.*

A Multiple Linear Regression Example

You can use multiple linear regression to relate a dependent *y* variable to multiple independent *x* variables in a single linear equation.

Let's return to the example in Figure 11.4. As shown in Figure 11.8, a second independent *x* variable is now included in column C—daily calories expended through exercise. By using the Regression command you can see if multiple linear regression creates a better fit between a person's weight and *two* independent *x* variables (daily calories consumed and daily exercise calories).

Figure 11.7

Graphing data points and the regression line on one graph

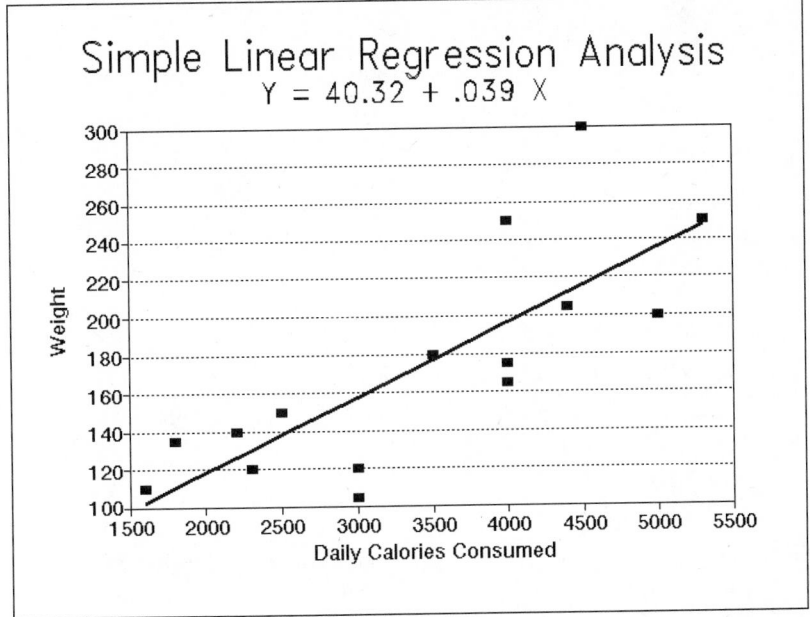

To do this, select /Tools, Advanced Math, Regression and specify Independent as the two independent *x* variables in the block **B5..C19**, Dependent as the dependent (*y*) variable block **A5..A19**, and Output as **D1**, the upper-left corner of the block where you want the Regression Output table to appear. (For multiple linear regression, the output table is nine rows deep and two columns wider than the number of columns in the Independent block. In this case, then, the table will be four columns wide.)

When you select Go, Quattro Pro performs the regression analysis and builds a Regression Output table, beginning in cell D1. This table includes an X Coefficient and a Standard Error of the Coefficient for each independent *x* variable.

Using the information in the Regression Output table, the multiple linear regression equation is

$$y = 72.36 + 0.039x_1 - 0.071x_2$$

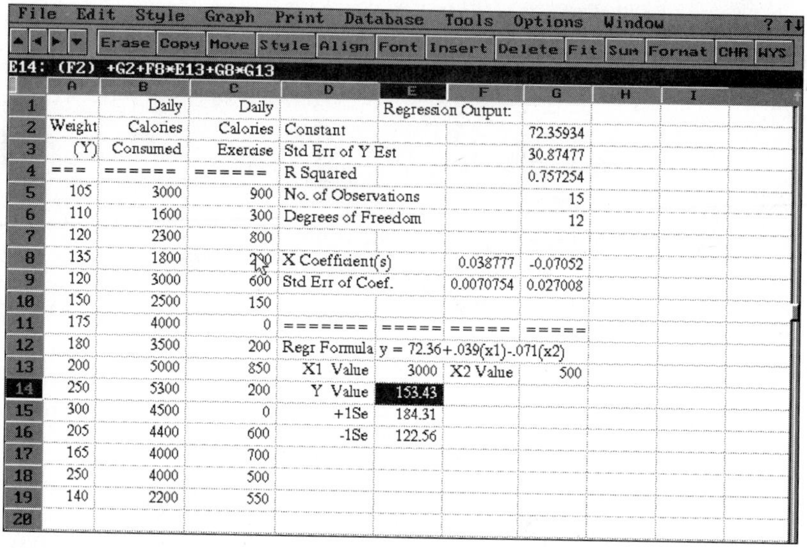

Figure 11.8
Using multiple
linear regression

File Edit Style Graph Print Database Tools Options Window	? ↑↓
� ◀ ▶ ▼   Erase Copy Move Style Align Font Insert Delete Fit Sum Format CHR WYS

E14: (F2) +G2+F8*E13+G8*G13

	A	B	C	D	E	F	G	H	I
1		Daily	Daily		Regression Output:				
2	Weight	Calories	Calories	Constant			72.35934		
3	(Y)	Consumed	Exercise	Std Err of Y Est			30.87477		
4	===	======	======	R Squared			0.757254		
5	105	3000	900	No. of Observations			15		
6	110	1600	300	Degrees of Freedom			12		
7	120	2300	800						
8	135	1800	200	X Coefficient(s)		0.038777	-0.07052		
9	120	3000	600	Std Err of Coef.		0.0070754	0.027008		
10	150	2500	150						
11	175	4000	0	======	=====	=====	=====		
12	180	3500	200	Regr Formula y = 72.36+.039(x1)-.071(x2)					
13	200	5000	850	X1 Value	3000	X2 Value	500		
14	250	5300	200	Y Value	153.43				
15	300	4500	0	+1Se	184.31				
16	205	4400	600	-1Se	122.56				
17	165	4000	700						
18	250	4000	500						
19	140	2200	550						
20									

Notice that x_2, exercise calories, has a *negative* coefficient, offsetting the positive coefficient of x_1, calories consumed. Since R^2 is 0.757, this multiple linear equation fits the data points better than the simple linear equation in Figure 11.7, which has an R^2 of 0.619. Therefore, approximately 76% of the people's weight in the sample is explained by the regression line, or by the daily number of calories consumed *and* the calories expended in exercise. You can also use data in the Regression Output table to analyze the strength of each independent x variable.

- For x_1, the Standard Error of the X Coefficient (S_b) is 0.0071; and the t value, calculated as x_1/S_b, is 0.0039/0.0071, or 5.48. Since S_b is approximately 18% of x_1, there exists a very strong relationship between weight and daily calories consumed.

- For x_2, the exercise calories x variable, S_b, is 0.027. Therefore t equals –0.071/0.027, or –2.61. Because S_b is approximately –38% of x_2, there exists a strong *inverse* relationship between weight (y) and exercise calories (x_2).

Now let's use this multiple regression equation to predict the weight of a person (y), given an x_1 and an x_2 value. For example, suppose you enter the x_1 value **3000** (calories consumed) in cell E13, and the x_2 value **500** (exercise calories) in cell G13. Then in cell E14, enter the regression line formula

`+G2+F8*E13+G8*G13`

This regression line equation calculates that a person who consumes 3,000 calories a day and uses up 500 calories in exercise weighs 153.43 pounds. However, the Standard Error of the Y Estimate, S_e, is 30.8. So there is a 68.3% chance that this y value is really between 184.3 pounds ($y+1S_e$) and 122.6 pounds ($y-1S_e$). Because this is a lower error range than for the simple linear regression equation in Figure 11.5, the multiple linear regression equation in Figure 11.8 is a better fit to the data points, and will also "predict" more accurate y values. However, since R^2 is 0.757 and not 1, there are obviously other factors that affect a person's weight (such as heredity), which are not included in this multiple regression model.

Manipulating Matrices

Quattro Pro's /Tools, Advanced Math, Multiply and Invert commands manipulate matrices. The next sections explain how you can use these commands to

- Solve simultaneous linear equations for a unique solution

- Calculate values that would otherwise require lengthy multiplication formulas

Solving Simultaneous Linear Equations

You must use the /Tools, Advanced Math, Multiply and Invert commands to solve simultaneous linear equations. For instance, suppose you have the following equations:

$$4x + 5y + 6z = 100$$

$$7x + 10y + 0z = 100$$

$$5x + 0y + 20z = 300$$

A *matrix*—a rectangular table of values—is a shorthand method of expressing these equations. You can represent these simultaneous linear equations in matrix form as

Matrix of Coefficients × **Variables** = **Matrix of Constants**

$$\begin{vmatrix} 4 & 5 & 6 \\ 7 & 10 & 0 \\ 5 & 0 & 20 \end{vmatrix} \times \begin{vmatrix} x \\ y \\ z \end{vmatrix} = \begin{vmatrix} 100 \\ 200 \\ 300 \end{vmatrix}$$

If there is a single unique solution to all of these linear equations, it can be calculated by first determining the inverse matrix of the Matrix of Coefficients, then multiplying this inverse matrix by the Matrix of Constants.

Inverting a Matrix

The *inverse* of a matrix is a new matrix that, when multiplied by the first matrix, results in an *identity matrix* (a matrix containing 0's and 1's, for which the determinant is equal to 1).

If a Matrix of Coefficients can be successfully inverted, then there is a unique solution to the simultaneous linear equations. Conversely, if a matrix cannot be inverted, the simultaneous linear equations either have no solution or have infinite solutions.

A Matrix of Coefficients can only be inverted if

- It is a square matrix (an equal number of columns and rows).

- The columns of the matrix are linearly independent.

- The determinant of the matrix is *not* equal to zero.

Additionally, a matrix cannot be inverted if it includes redundancies or inconsistencies. A *redundancy* occurs when one equation is a multiple of another equation, or is the result of the addition of two equations. For instance, the equations x+y=1 and 2x+2y=2 are redundant. On the other hand, an *inconsistency* occurs when two essentially identical equations give conflicting results, such as x+y=500 and x+y=3000.

If you specify a nonsquare matrix, Quattro Pro displays the error message "Not a square matrix." However, if you specify a matrix that includes any redundancies or inconsistencies, you see the error message "Matrix is singular."

In Figure 11.9, the Matrix of Coefficients for the simultaneous linear equations resides in the block A3..C5. To invert this Matrix of Coefficients, select the /Tools, Advanced Math, Invert command, and specify the source block **A3..C5**. Then specify the upper-left corner of the block where you want the inverted matrix to appear. In this case, **A9**.

As shown in Figure 11.9, Quattro Pro successfully inverts this Matrix of Coefficients and displays the inverted matrix in the block beginning in cell A9. Because the matrix was inverted, you know there is a unique solution to these simultaneous linear equations, which can be found by multiplying the inverse matrix by the Matrix of Constants.

Tip. If you can't invert a matrix because multiple solutions exist for the simultaneous linear equations, you can still return the optimal solution using Quattro Pro's Optimizer, discussed later in this chapter.

NOTE. *If you specify the same source and destination blocks, Quattro Pro writes over the matrix with its inverse. To undo this and restore your original matrix, select Edit Undo (Alt-F5) immediately after the completion of the /Tools, Advanced Math, Inverse command.*

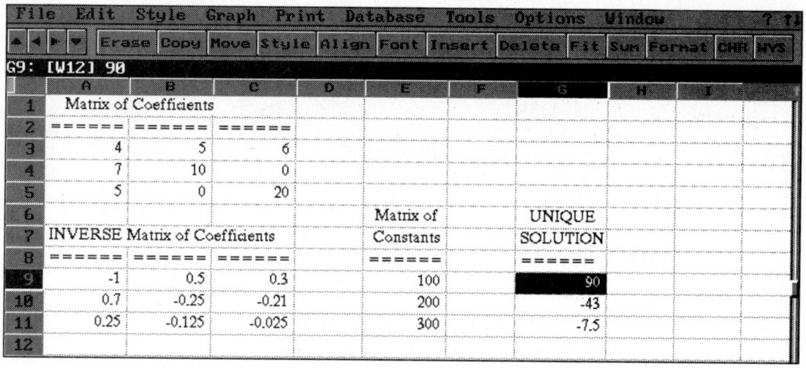

Figure 11.9
Solving
simultaneous linear
equations

```
 File   Edit   Style   Graph   Print   Database   Tools   Options   Window          ? t‖
 ▲ ◄ ► ▼  Erase Copy Move Style Align Font Insert Delete Fit Sum Format CHR NYS
 G9: [W12] 90
```

	A	B	C	D	E	F	G	H	I
1	Matrix of Coefficients								
2	=====	=====	=====						
3	4	5	6						
4	7	10	0						
5	5	0	20						
6					Matrix of		UNIQUE		
7	INVERSE Matrix of Coefficients				Constants		SOLUTION		
8	=====	=====	=====		=====		=====		
9	-1	0.5	0.3		100		90		
10	0.7	-0.25	-0.21		200		-43		
11	0.25	-0.125	-0.025		300		-7.5		
12									

Speeding Up Matrix Inversion   The time required by Quattro Pro to invert a matrix is determined by both the matrix size and the speed of your personal computer. On a 286-based PC running at 12 MHz, Quattro Pro takes approximately five seconds to invert a 21-by-21 matrix, but approximately five minutes to invert a 90-by-90 matrix (the largest size matrix Quattro Pro can invert). Furthermore, the 90-by-90 matrix requires expanded memory. If you plan to use Quattro Pro frequently to invert matrices, you might want to consider adding both a coprocessor and expanded memory to your PC.

Multiplying Matrices

Using matrix multiplication rules, the /Tools, Advanced Math, Multiply command multiplies the values in two matrices and returns a resulting matrix. For a successful multiplication to occur, however, the number of columns in the first matrix must equal the number of rows in the second matrix. (Otherwise, you'll get the error message "Matrices incompatible for multiplication.") The result is a new matrix containing the same number of rows as the first matrix, and the same number of columns as the second. Quattro Pro can multiply two matrices if each is 100-by-100 or smaller. (For large matrices, your PC may need expanded memory.)

Let's return to the example in Figure 11.9, and use /Tools, Advanced Math, Multiply to solve for the unique solution to the simultaneous linear equations by multiplying the inverse matrix by the Matrix of Constants. Simply select /Tools, Advanced Math, Multiply, and specify the 1st matrix as the inverted matrix in block **A9..C11**, the 2nd matrix as the Matrix of Constants in the block **E9..E11**. Then specify the destination as the upper-left corner of the block where you want the resulting matrix to appear, in this case, **G9**.

Quattro Pro multiplies the two matrices and displays the result in a new matrix beginning in cell G9. In our example, Quattro Pro has calculated the resulting value 90 in cell G9 as

```
+A9*E9+B9*E10+C9*E11
```

or

```
-1*100+0.5*200+0.3*300
```

The three values in the resulting matrix, 90, –43, and –7.5, are the *only* values for *x*, *y*, and *z* that make the simultaneous equations true.

Calculating Values More Efficiently

You can also use /Tools, Advanced Math, Multiply in nonmatrix applications, like value calculations that would otherwise require lengthy multiplication formulas. Suppose you create a spreadsheet with sales information like that in Figure 11.10. The block B6..E9 contains the 1991 historical product sales for each salesperson, and the block B16..B19 displays the projected 1992 gross profit percentage for each product.

Now imagine that you want to calculate the *total* gross profit that each salesperson is projected to contribute to the company in 1992. For instance, in cell E16, M. Hall's projected 1992 total gross profit, $52,300, could be calculated by entering either

```
+B6*B16+C6*B17+D6*B18+E6*B19
```

or

```
$50,000*0.20+$100,000*0.40+$20,000*0.05+$2,000*.65
```

However, instead of entering formulas, you can use /Tools, Advanced Math, Multiply with matrix multiplication to calculate these totals for you by specifying **B6..E9** as the first matrix, **B16..B19** as the second matrix, and **E16** as the destination. Quattro Pro multiplies the two matrices and displays the resulting values in a new matrix in the block E16..E19. For instance, cell E16 now contains the $52,300 projected gross profit for M. Hall.

NOTE. *If you change any values in your matrices, Quattro Pro does not automatically update the resulting matrix when you recalculate your spreadsheet. So don't forget to reuse the /Tools, Advanced Math, Multiply command.*

Figure 11.10

Calculating values using /Tools, Advanced Math, Multiply

| File | Edit | Style | Graph | Print | Database | Tools | Options | Window | ? ↑↓ |

| ▲ ◄ ► ▼ | Erase | Copy | Move | Style | Align | Font | Insert | Delete | Fit | Sum | Format | CHR | WYS |

E16: (C0) [W16] 52300

	A	B	C	D	E	F	G
2		1991 Sales Per Salesperson					
3		---------------	---------------	---------------	---------------		
4	Salesperson	Prod 1	Prod 2	Prod 3	Prod 4		
5	---------------	---------------	---------------	---------------	---------------		
6	M. Hall	$50,000	$100,000	$20,000	$2,000		
7	T. Smith	$30,000	$100,000	$250,000	$75,000		
8	N. Kramer	$150,000	$5,000	$50,000	$600,000		
9	T. Bill	$75,000	$25,000	$200,000	$10,000		
10							
11					1992		
12		Projected			Projected		
13		1992 Unit			Gross Profit Per		
14		Gross Profit		Salesperson	Salesperson		
15		---------------		---------------	---------------		
16	Prod 1	20.00%		M. Hall	$52,300		
17	Prod 2	40.00%		T. Smith	$107,250		
18	Prod 3	5.00%		N. Kramer	$424,500		
19	Prod 4	65.00%		T. Bill	$41,500		
20							

What-If Analysis Using Data Tables

/Tools, What-If is a powerful command in Quattro Pro's sensitivity analysis arsenal, and is used to perform repetitive what-if calculations. /Tools, What-If creates a *data table*, separate from the rest of the information in your spreadsheet, that displays the result of your sensitivity analysis. You can generate a *one-way data table* that analyzes the effect of changing one variable in one or more formulas. Or you can create a *two-way data table* that displays the effect of changing two variables in a single formula.

Since a data table is a convenient method of creating and storing related information, the /Tools, What-If command lends itself to a variety of applications. For instance, you can create a lookup table for related information. Or, instead of using /Edit, Copy with relative cell addressing to create a block of values, you can generate the same information in a data table. Using a data table in place of formulas is helpful in a large spreadsheet when memory becomes a consideration. Finally, one of the most powerful applications of /Tools, What-If is creating a data table that accesses and evaluates database information without corrupting the database.

Creating a One-Way Data Table

A one-way data table like the one in Figure 11.11 displays the results for one formula when the value of a single variable is changed and all else is held constant. Let's say you're considering purchasing a house and incurring a $100,000, 30-year, 10% fixed-rate mortgage. Because you can prepay this mortgage, you want to calculate and compare the monthly payments for each 5-year decrease in the mortgage term.

Figure 11.11

A one-way data table

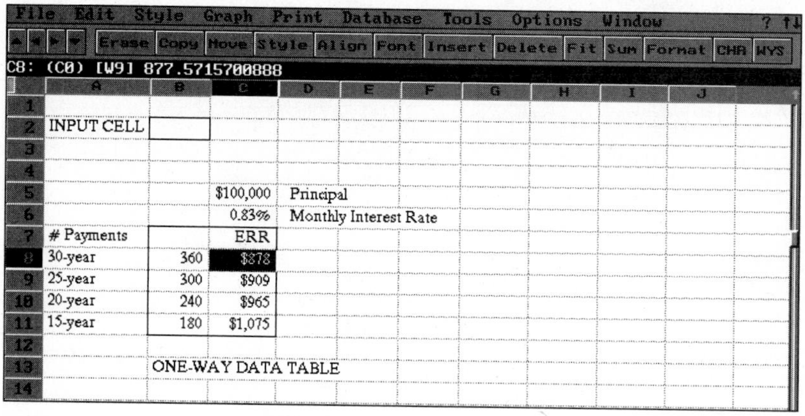

In essence, you want to change one variable in a formula—the total number of payments—and then display the resulting monthly payments for the different mortgage terms. You can use the /Tools, What-If, 1 Variable command to create a one-way data table summarizing this information. Before you can use this command, you must set up the framework of the one-way data table by entering substitution values, a data table formula, and an input cell.

Substitution Values

Substitution values are the values that you want Quattro Pro to substitute in a formula, then display the results for, in a data table. In the current example, the substitution values are the different total numbers of mortgage payments.

You must enter substitution values in a column that represents the leftmost edge of the one-way data table. In Figure 11.11, the total number of monthly payments for mortgages of 30, 25, 20, and 15 years are entered in the block B8..B11. (Don't enter your substitution values in a row, or Quattro Pro will incorrectly calculate the data table results and simply copy the substitution values to the row below these values.)

You can enter substitution values as either numbers or the results of formulas. For substitution values that are equally spaced numbers, consider entering them using the /Edit, Fill command (see Chapter 4).

The Input Cell

The /Tools, Frequency command uses an *input cell* to enter each substitution value into a formula. An input cell must be located outside the data table block, such as cell B2 in Figure 11.11. In a one-way data table, you can also specify the input cell as the upper-left cell of the data table, B7 in Figure 11.11.

The Data Table Formula

The *data table formula* creates the relationship that you want to analyze. In our mortgage example, you need a formula that calculates the monthly payments using your variables: principal amount, interest rate, and number of payments. Therefore, you can use the @PMT(*principal,interest rate,number of payments*) function, which calculates a fixed mortgage payment. Because you are calculating a monthly payment, *interest rate* must be a monthly interest rate, and *number of payments* must represent the total number of monthly payments. (See "Financial Functions" in Chapter 7 for more details.)

A data table formula can reference information anywhere in your spreadsheet, *except* the information in the data table block. For example, in Figure 11.11 you could enter the principal amount ($100,000) in cell C5, and make +C5 the *principal* argument in the @PMT function. In this example, however, the *principal* value is entered directly into the @PMT function, which you can see in the input line in Figure 11.11.

To calculate the monthly mortgage payment for different mortgage terms, you must tell Quattro Pro to enter your substitution values into the *number of payments* argument in your @PMT formula. In the /Tools, What-If command, the input cell performs this function. So the input cell B2 must be the *number of payments* argument in the @PMT function.

In a one-way data table, you enter the data table formula one row above and one column to the right of the first substitution value. So in cell C7, enter the formula **@PMT(100000,.1/12,B2)**. Don't worry that Quattro Pro returns ERR for this formula; it occurs because the *number of payments* argument is referencing the blank input cell B2.

Using /Tools, What-If, 1 Variable

Note. Since /Tools, What-If remembers your last settings, you should clear any old settings using /Tools, What-If, Reset before you specify a new analysis.

You can now create the one-way data table by selecting the /Tools, What-If, 1 Variable command and specifying the block that includes the substitution values and data table formula, B7..C11, and then the Input Cell as B2. Select Quit to return to the spreadsheet.

In Figure 11.11, Quattro Pro filled in the block C8..C11 in the one-way data table by first calculating the value in cell C8. It enters the first substitution value, 360, in the input cell B2. Then it solves your test formula in C7 and enters the result, $878, in C8. Moving down column C, this process is reiterated for each substitution value in the table.

CAUTION! *Be very careful when you specify your data table block and input cell. If you incorrectly specify either one, Quattro Pro runs the what-if analysis and erases the information in the data table block you specified.*

This one-way data table tells you that you must make a monthly payment of $878 to retire a $100,000, 10% mortgage in 30 years, although you can repay this mortgage in 15 years by making monthly payments of $1,075.

NOTE. *Quattro Pro enters the data table results as values, not as formulas. Therefore, if you change any information relating to a data table, the table's results are not updated even when you recalculate the spreadsheet. Update your data table either by reusing the /Tools, What-If command, or, since Quattro Pro remembers your last What-If settings, by pressing F8 (Table).*

Using Two Formulas in a One-Way Data Table

You can also create a one-way data table that analyzes, side by side, the results of different formulas that use the same substitution values. Building on the previous example, suppose that the owner of the house you are purchasing has offered you a $110,000, 30-year, 8% mortgage, provided that you pay $10,000 more for the house. You can also prepay this mortgage.

You can easily create a one-way data table that displays the resulting monthly payments for both the $100,000, 10% mortgage and the $110,000, 8% mortgage. As shown in Figure 11.12, you include a second formula for the $110,000 mortgage in the data table, **@PMT(110000,.08/12,B2)** in cell D7. Since both data table formulas must use the same substitution values, they must also use the same input cell. Quattro Pro also returns ERR for this function.

Now when you select /Tools, What-If, specify the data table block as **B7..D11** and input cell **B2**. Figure 11.12 illustrates how Quattro Pro fills in block C8..D11 for both mortgages.

Note. In theory, you can use Quattro Pro's /Tools, What-If command to create a data table that is as large as your spreadsheet. However, the size of a data table is actually limited by the amount of your PC's memory.

Creating a Two-Way Data Table

A two-way data table displays the effect of changing the values of *two* variables in a single formula. To see this, let's stay with our mortgage example. Suppose the current house owner decides that the $110,000, 30-year, 8% mortgage will have a variable interest rate that can increase to a maximum 12%. Obviously, before you agree to these terms, you'll want to evaluate your monthly payments as both the number of payments and the interest rate change.

You'll need to analyze two variables in the @PMT function—*number of payments* and the *interest rate*. You can use the /Tools, What-If, 2 Variables command to create a two-way data table displaying the different results returned by the @PMT function. Since a two-way table analyzes the effect of changing two variables in a formula, the table framework differs slightly from that of a one-way table.

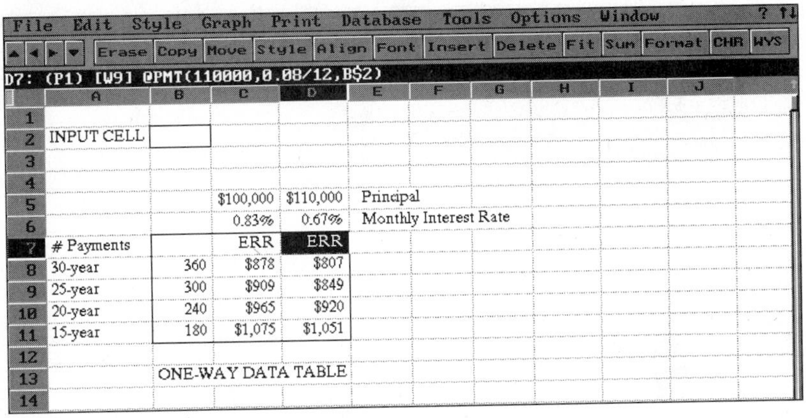

Figure 11.12

Using two formulas in a one-way data table

Substitution Values

As its name implies, a two-way data table uses two blocks of substitution values, one for each variable being analyzed. As shown in Figure 11.13, block B8..B11 still contains the four substitution values for the *number of payments* argument. However, in a two-way data table, the top line of the table contains a second set of substitution values entered in rowwise fashion. In Figure 11.13, five monthly *interest rate* substitution values are entered in block C7..G7. For instance, .08/12 is entered in C7 to produce the 0.7% monthly interest rate, .09/12 is entered in D7, and so on.

The Input Cells

Naturally, a two-way data table has two input cells for the two variables being analyzed. In Figure 11.13, B2 is the input cell for the *number of payments* substitution values, and B4 is the input cell for the *interest rate* substitution values. Both input cells must be located outside the data table block. Don't locate either input cell inside the data table, or Quattro Pro will incorrectly calculate the results for the column that holds the input cell.

The Data Table Formula

Because you are now analyzing two variables, the data table formula @PMT(110000,B4,B2) must reference both the input cells. In a two-way data table, you must enter this function in the upper-left corner of the data table (cell B7 in this case). Quattro Pro once again returns ERR for this formula, because the *number of payments* and *interest rate* arguments are referencing blank input cells.

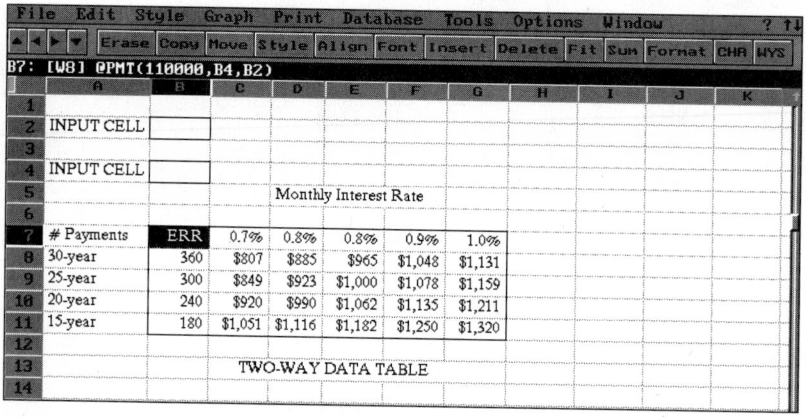

Figure 11.13

A two-way data table

Using /Tools, What-If, 2 Variables

Now you're ready to create a two-way data table.

1. Select the /Tools, What-If, 2 Variables command, and specify the data table block **B7..G11**.

2. In response to the "Input Cell from column:" prompt, select **B2** as the input cell for the *number of payments* argument.

3. In response to the "Input Cell from top row:" prompt, select cell **B4** as the input cell for the *interest rate* argument.

4. Select Quit to return to the spreadsheet.

In Figure 11.13, Quattro Pro fills in C8..G11 in the two-way data table. Beginning in cell C8, Quattro Pro uses the first *number of payments* substitution value, 360, in the input cell B2, and the first *interest rate* substitution value, 0.7% (.08/12) in the input cell B4 to solve the @PMT formula in B7, and return the result, $807, in C8. In column C, this process is reiterated for each *number of payments* substitution value in the table. In column D, 0.8% (.09/12) *interest rate* substitution value from cell D8 is used. Quattro Pro continues to work its way down column D, and then columns E, F, and G, entering the corresponding *number of payments* and *interest rate* substitution values in the input cells, recalculating the formula in cell B7, and entering each result in the data table.

This two-way data table tells you that for a 30-year mortgage, your monthly mortgage payment is $807 (cell C8) when the annual interest rate is 8%, but $1,131 (cell G8) if the interest rate increases to 12%. Moreover, if the interest rate remains at 8%, you can repay your mortgage in 15 years with monthly payments of $1,051, but it will take $1,320 a month (cell G11) to repay the mortgage in 15 years at the 12% annual rate.

Creating a Data Table for a Database

One of the most powerful applications of the /Tools, What-If command is to create a data table for a database. When you use a database function in a data table, this combination allows you to create a one-way or a two-way data table that accesses, manipulates, and evaluates information in the data table fields without affecting your database.

A One-Way Data Table for a Database

Suppose you are a hotel manager. The database in Figure 11.14 represents the guests that will be arriving tomorrow. For scheduling purposes, you need to calculate the number of rooms needed for each room preference. Furthermore, you always calculate the average days' stay for each type of room. By creating a one-way data table you can search the database, and then calculate and display the information you need. The test formulas, substitution values, and input cells used in a data table, however, are modified for database applications.

Figure 11.14

A one-way data table for a database

File	Edit	Style	Graph	Print	Database	Tools	Options	Window	?

| ▲ ◄ ► ▼ | Erase | Copy | Move | Style | Align | Font | Insert | Delete | Fit | Sum | Format | CHR | WYS |

B12: (F1) [W14] @DCOUNT(A1..D10,2,E10..E11)

	A	B	C	D	E	F	G	H
1	NAME	LAST VISIT	PREFERENCE	DAYS STAY				
2	L. Bachta	Feb-92	Suite	2				
3	C. LeBlond	Dec-84	Single	1				
4	K. Watson	Jun-91	Economy	3				
5	G. Raffe	Aug-91	Single	3				
6	M. Erickson	Nov-90	Double	5				
7	J. Naylor	Mar-92	Suite	1				
8	L. Kleinman	May-86	Double	4				
9	D. Waller	Feb-90	Economy	2				
10	F. Chayes	Jan-92	Double	1	PREFERENCE			
11		# Rooms	Avg Stay	INPUT CELL				
12		9.0	2.4					
13	Single	2.0	2.0	@DAVG(A1..D10,3,E10..E11)			
14	Double	3.0	3.3					
15	Economy	2.0	2.5	@DCOUNT(A1..D10,2,E10..E11)			
16	Suite	2.0	1.5					
17		ONE-WAY DATA TABLE						
18								

Substitution Values   When you create a data table for a database, the substitution values are the labels or values in the database field you want to search. For example, in Figure 11.14, the substitution values in A13..A16 are the categories in the PREFERENCE field.

Input Cell   Like other data tables, the input cell must be located outside the data table block, for example, cell E11 in Figure 11.14. However, for a database, the input cell is included in the *criteria block* argument (explained below) of a database function.

Data Table Formula   In many cases when you use /Tools, What-If to access database information, a database function is used as the data table formula. A database function uses the following syntax:

`@DFUNCTION(input block,offset value,criteria block)`

Let's take a look at each of the arguments in a database function:

Note. See Chapter 10 for a further discussion of database functions.

- When you use a database function in a data table, the *input block* argument is the database you want to search, for example, the database block A1..D10 in Figure 11.14.

- The *offset value* argument is the field you want to evaluate, that is, the field for which that you want Quattro Pro to display results in the data table. In Figure 11.14, to evaluate the PREFERENCE field, use an *offset value* of 2. To return information for the DAYS STAY field, use an *offset value* of 3.

- The *criteria block* argument is a block that contains both the name of the field you want to search, and a blank cell. In Figure 11.14, the *criteria block* is E10..E11. Cell E10 contains the name of the field you will search, PREFERENCE; directly below it, cell E11 is the input cell.

Now enter your formulas as you would for any other one-way data table. For each room category, @DCOUNT(A1..D10,2,E10..E11) in cell B12 will return the number of rooms in the PREFERENCE field. Using @DAVG(A1..D10,3,E10..E11) in cell C12 will calculate the average days' stay in the DAYS STAY field for each category in the PREFERENCE field.

Creating the Data Table   To create the one-way data table, select /Tools, What-If, 1 Variable and specify the data table block **A12..C16** and the input cell **E11**. In Figure 11.14, Quattro Pro creates the table by entering the first substitution label, "Single," in the input cell E11. Then, using the @DCOUNT function in cell B12, it searches the PREFERENCE field, counts two occurrences of this category, and enters this result in cell B13. Quattro Pro moves down column B, reiterating this process for each substitution label in your table. The data table shows that you need two each of suites, single, and economy rooms, but three double rooms.

Next, Quattro Pro moves to the top of column C and enters the first substitution label, "Single," into the input cell E11, which is evaluated by the @DAVG function in cell C12. Using the *offset value* argument of 3 and the *criteria block* containing PREFERENCE, the average days' stay in the DAYS STAY field for all occurrences of Single in the PREFERENCE field, 2.0 days, is entered in cell C13. Quattro Pro then moves down column C, calculating the average days' stay for each substitution label in your data table. As you can see in Figure 11.14, people who stay in a double room tend to stay the longest, at 3.3 days.

A Two-Way Data Table for a Database

Now suppose that you want to query your database for each PREFERENCE field category, and return the number of stays between 0 and 3 days, and those between 3 and 6 days, in the DAYS STAY field. You can use the /Tools, What-If, 2 Variables command to create a two-way data table that uses the @DCOUNT function to select this information in your database. First, however, you must enter the framework of a two-way data table in your spreadsheet.

Substitution Values   As shown in Figure 11.15, column A still contains the substitution values for the categories of the PREFERENCE field. In addition, at the topmost edge (block B12..C12) of this two-way table, the substitution values for your second search criteria are entered: the upper limits of the DAYS STAY categories, 3 and 6.

Input Cells   Like other two-way data tables, a two-way table for a database requires two input cells, both located outside the data table block.

Furthermore, since you are querying a database, both input cells are included in the criteria block argument E10..F11 of the @DCOUNT function.

Let's stop and look at this analysis for a minute. When /Tools, What-If substitutes the DAYS STAY substitution values in the input cell F11, it will return the number of occurrences for that particular value only. In this case, only the occurrences of the first substitution value, 3, will be evaluated. To return the count for *each* range of values, 0 to 3 days and 3 to 6 days, you *must add a second input* cell for DAYS STAY. In Figure 11.15, cell D11 is designated as the second DAYS STAY input cell.

Now, in your *first* input cell for DAYS STAY, cell F11, enter the formula

```
+D2>$D$11-3#AND#+D2<=$D$11
```

When the substitution value in cell D11 is 3, this formula returns the range 0 to 3; when it is 6, the formula returns the range 3.01 to 6. You must enter your second input cell for DAYS STAY, $D$11, as an absolute address.

File	Edit	Style	Graph	Print	Database	Tools	Options	Window	? ↑↓

| ▲ ◄ ► ▼ | Erase | Copy | Move | Style | Align | Font | Insert | Delete | Fit | Sum | Format | CHR | WYS |

F11: [W9] +D2>$D$11-3#AND#+D2<=$D$11

	A	B	C	D	E	F	G
1	NAME	LAST VISIT	PREFERENCE	DAYS STAY			
2	L. Bachta	Feb-92	Suite	2			
3	C. LeBlond	Dec-84	Single	1			
4	K. Watson	Jun-91	Economy	3			
5	G. Raffe	Aug-91	Single	3			
6	M. Erickson	Nov-90	Double	5			
7	J. Naylor	Mar-92	Suite	1			
8	L. Kleinman	May-86	Double	4			
9	D. Waller	Feb-90	Economy	2			
10	F. Chayes	Jan-92	Double	1	PREFERENCE	DAYS STAY	
11						$0	
12	0	3	6	SECOND	INPUT CELL	INPUT CELL	
13	Single	2.0	0.0	INPUT CELL	COLUMNS	ROWS	
14	Double	1.0	2.0	ROWS			
15	Economy	2.0	0.0				
16	Suite	2.0	0.0				
17		TWO-WAY DATA TABLE					
18							

Data Table Formula In Figure 11.15, the @DCOUNT function is used to count the occurrences in the DAYS STAY field, from 0 to 3 and from 3.01 to 6, for each PREFERENCE category. Once again, the *input block* A1..D10 is the database you want to search. The *offset value* argument is the field for which you want Quattro Pro to display results in the data table. Since you are evaluating information in the DAYS STAY field, use an *offset value* of 3.

The *criteria block* argument must contain the field name of each field you want to search, and an input cell for *each* set of substitution values. In Figure 11.17, this *criteria block* is E10..F11. Cell E10 contains the field name for the PREFERENCE substitution labels; directly below it, cell E11 is the input cell. Likewise, cell F10 contains the field name for the DAYS STAY substitution values, and cell F11 is its input cell. The data table formula

```
@DCOUNT(A1..D10,3,E10..F11)
```

is entered in the upper-left cell of the table, cell A12.

Creating the Data Table To create the two-way data table, select /Tools, What-If, 2 Variables and specify the data table block, **A12..C16**. For the "Input cell from column:" prompt, specify **E11**. However, in response to the "Input cell from top row:" prompt, specify the *second* DAYS STAY input cell, **D11**.

During the /Tools, What-If operation, Quattro Pro begins calculating in cell B13. It enters the first substitution label, "Single," in the input cell E11, and the first substitution value, 3, in the *second* DAYS STAY *input cell*, D11. Now cell F11, the first input cell for the DAYS STAY field, comes into play. Cell F11 contains the comparison formula +D2>$D$11–3#AND#+D2<=$D$11. Because the first DAYS STAY substitution value (3) is in cell D11, in cell F11 this comparison formula evaluates to the range 0 to 3. So the @DCOUNT function in cell A12 counts the number of Single entries between 0 and 3 in the DAYS STAY field. Quattro Pro enters this result, 2, in cell B13.

In column B, you see that in all rooms except double rooms, two guests will stay fewer than 3 days. Likewise, the results in column C indicate that only guests in double rooms stay longer than 3 days.

Solving a Formula Backwards

Quattro Pro first introduced a new sensitivity analysis command, /Tools, Solve For, in version 2.0. This command performs goal seeking by solving a formula backwards.

/Tools, Solve For begins with a specific target, such as a gross profit objective. Then, using a formula that you supply to calculate gross profit, Quattro Pro uses an iterative process to compute the value of another variable in this formula, such as sales, that forces the formula to return the gross profit target value.

Using /Tools, Solve For in a Simple Analysis

Suppose you have developed the simple relationship between sales and gross profit shown in Figure 11.16. Direct material is calculated as 20% of sales, direct labor is 30% of sales, and overhead costs are fixed at $100,000. Gross profit is computed using the general formula SALES–(0.2+0.3)*SALES–$100,000. Break-even sales of $200,000 generate the $0 gross profit in cell C7, which is computed using the formula +C2–@SUM(C3..C5).

Imagine that your division is expected to contribute $100,000 gross profit to the corporation; you need to determine the level of sales that will achieve this profit objective. Beginning with the *result* of your equation, $100,000 gross profit, you can use /Tools, Solve For to perform this goal-seeking operation by defining a target value, a formula that solves for this value, and another variable in this formula that can be changed to achieve the target value.

Target Value
In the /Tools, Solve For command, the *target value* is simply the objective you want to achieve. In the spreadsheet shown in Figure 11.17, cell C9

contains the $100,000 gross profit target value. /Tools, Solve For only accepts a specific target value. If you enter a conditional target value, such as >=100,000, Quattro Pro returns the error message "Invalid number" during the command operation.

Figure 11.16
A sales vs. gross profit relationship

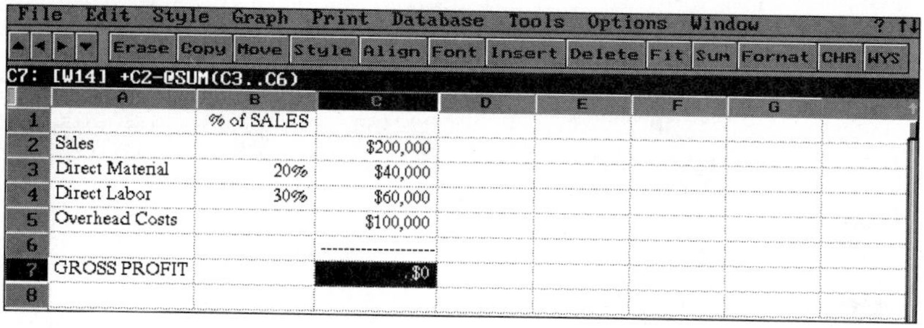

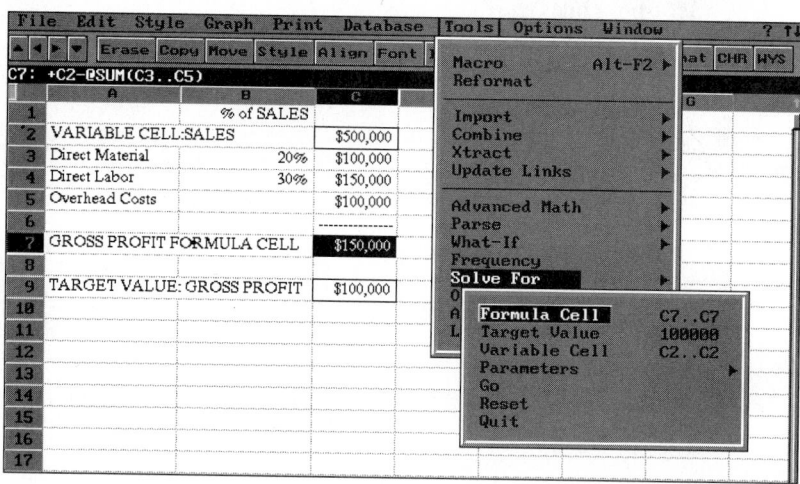

Figure 11.17
Setting up the /Tools, Solve For analysis

You can enter the target value either in your spreadsheet or directly into the /Tools, Solve For command. In Figure 11.17, for example, the target value can be specified as the formula +C9. Although you can also enter the target value into the /Tools, Solve For command as either a number or a formula, when you enter it as a formula, /Tools, Solve For converts it into a value. Therefore, if the target value changes, remember to specify this new value in the /Tools, Solve For command.

Variable Cell

/Tools, Solve For uses another variable to force your formula to return the target value. Because gross profit is calculated as a function of sales, sales is the variable that you want Quattro Pro to calculate. You must supply Quattro Pro with an initial estimate for this variable using these guidelines:

- Enter the estimated variable as a value only. If you enter this value using a formula, a label, or a date, Quattro Pro returns the error message "Invalid Value in Variable Cell" during the /Tools, Solve For operation.

- Use a realistic estimate. /Tools, Solve For performs five iterations (the default) to calculate this variable result. If you use a value that is too far from the actual value, Quattro Pro cannot calculate the result and returns the error message "Maximum iterations reached." To overcome this problem, you can also use /Tools, Solve For, Parameters, Max Iterations to increase the number of iterations up to a maximum of 99.

In Figure 11.17, a $500,000 estimated sales value is entered in the variable cell C2.

CAUTION! *The /Tools, Solve For command returns its solution in the variable cell, writing over your estimate in the process. Any formulas in the spreadsheet that reference the variable cell will use this calculated value. To undo a completed /Tools, Solve For operation, use /Edit, Undo (Alt-F5) immediately after /Tools, Solve For.*

Formula Cell

In a goal-seeking analysis, a formula links the target value and estimated variable. For example, if the target value is gross profit and the variable is sales, then the formula must calculate gross profit as a function of sales.

In Figure 11.17, the *formula cell* C7 contains the formula that calculates gross profit. Since this formula references the $500,000 sales estimate in cell C2, the result is a $150,000 gross profit.

Here are the rules for creating a /Tools, Solve For formula.

- The formula must reference the variable cell; otherwise, Quattro Pro can't solve for your target value. (In Figure 11.17, all sales components in the formula reference cell C2.)

- The formula cannot contain any strings or functions that evaluate to strings.

Performing the Goal Seeking

Once you have determined the target value and created the variable and formula cells, here's how you can solve your formula backwards.

Note. Since /Tools, Solve For remembers your last settings, you'll need to clear old settings using /Tools, Solve For, Reset before you specify a new analysis.

1. Select the /Tools, Solve For command. Quattro Pro displays the Solve For menu shown in Figure 11.17.

2. Specify Formula Cell as cell **C7**, which contains your formula.

3. Specify Target Value as a formula referencing the location of your target value, **+C9**. As shown in the figure, Quattro Pro converts this formula to the value 100000. (If you want, you can just enter **100000** in the Target Value prompt box.)

4. Specify Variable Cell as **C2**, which contains your sales variable estimate.

5. Select Go, and then Quit.

Quattro Pro solves for the sales value that makes your formula return the $100,000 gross profit target value. Since the /Tools, Solve For, Parameters default values were used, this result is calculated within an accuracy of 0.005 in five or fewer iterations. Quattro Pro enters this calculated sales value in the variable cell C2, overwriting your sales estimate in the process.

As shown in Figure 11.18, the /Tools, Solve For command returns $400,000 in cell C2. In cell C7, the formula uses this $400,000 value and calculates the $100,000 gross profit objective.

NOTE. *Quattro Pro does not automatically update the result returned by /Tools, Solve For, even when the spreadsheet is recalculated. Therefore, if any information referenced by your formula changes, or if you change your target value or estimated variable, then you must reuse /Tools, Solve For.*

Using /Tools, Solve For with a Conditional Formula

Even when multiple conditions exist, you can still use the /Tools, Solve For command. Building on the previous example, suppose two relationships exist between sales and gross profit. As shown in Figure 11.19, for sales less than or equal to $200,000, the relationship established in the previous example still applies. However, for sales above $200,000, the economies of scale resulting from the increased volume decrease direct material costs to 15% of sales, and direct labor costs to 25% of gross sales. Therefore, in the /Tools, Solve For command, you need to use a conditional formula that includes both these relationships.

In this case, the $100,000 gross profit target value is entered in cell C11. The variable cell, C12, contains a $400,000 estimated sales value. The following conditional formula resides in the formula cell, C13:

```
@IF(C12<=C2,C12-(B3+B4)*C12-C5,C12-(D3+D4)*C12-E5)
```

If sales are less than or equal to $200,000, this @IF function calculates gross profit using the direct material and labor percentages in cells B3 and B4. Otherwise, gross profit is computed using the second set of percentages in cells D3 and D4. By creating formula and variable cells separate from your model, you are able to keep your model's logic intact.

Figure 11.18

The /Tools, Solve For solution

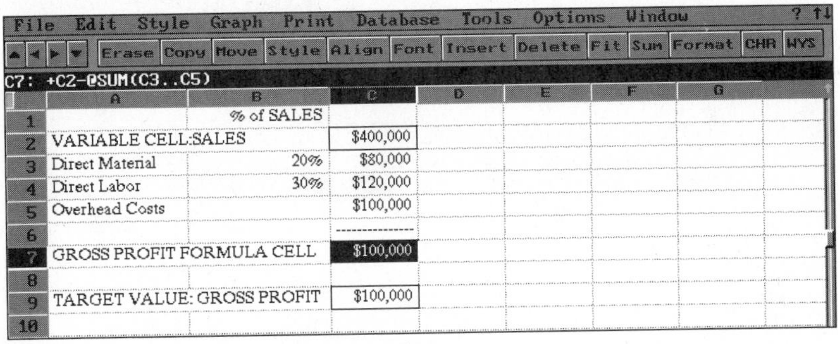

Figure 11.19

Using /Tools, Solve For with a conditional formula

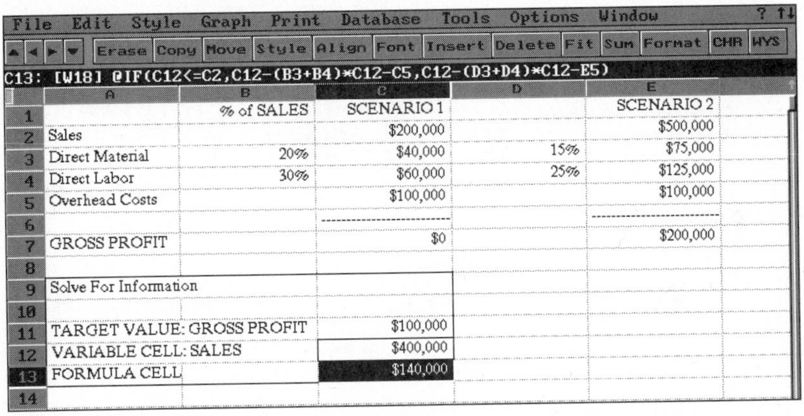

When you select /Tools, Solve For, specify the target value as the formula **+C11**, the variable cell as **C12**, and the formula cell as **C13**, as shown in Figure 11.20, Quattro Pro returns sales of $333,333 in cell C12. Using this calculated sales value, the formula in cell C13 returns the $100,000 gross profit objective. The analysis indicates that, because of the economies of scale enjoyed at this sales level, you need only generate $333,333 in sales to achieve your $100,000 gross profit objective.

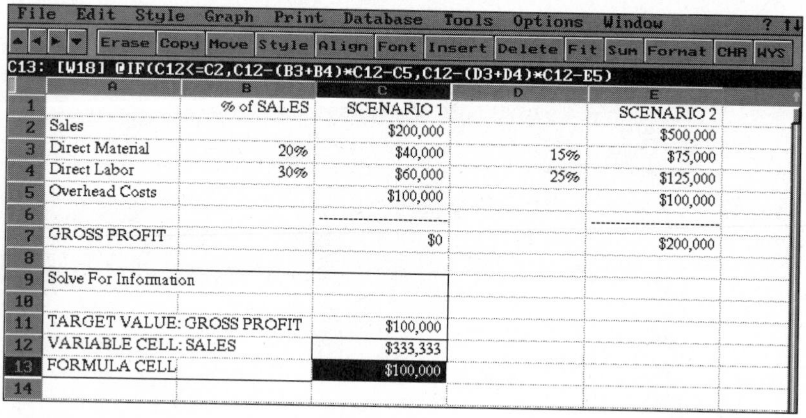

Figure 11.20

The /Tools, Solve For solution using multiple conditions

By modifying your model's logic, you can perform a goal-seeking analysis without creating such a complex formula. Simply enter the $400,000 sales estimate in the variable cell (C2). In cell C3, calculate direct material using the logical formula

```
@IF(C2<=200000,B3*C2,D3*C2)
```

And calculate direct labor in cell C4 using

```
@IF(C2<=200000,B4*C2,D4*C2)
```

Then the gross profit formula in cell C7 still applies, and can be designated as the formula cell.

Using @Functions with the /Tools, Solve For Command

You can use the /Tools, Solve For command in conjunction with many of Quattro Pro's @functions to "backsolve" (solve backwards) a complicated relationship. /Tools, Solve For forces a function to return your target value by varying one of the function's arguments.

For example, imagine that your startup company has taken out a $200,000, 12% fixed-rate, 10-year note. The company has become successful and is beginning to generate excess cash, so you want to prepay the note in five years. To determine the monthly payment that accomplishes this, you can use the @NPER function, which calculates a loan term (number of payments) in /Tools, Solve For.

In this case, the formula is the @NPER function, the target value is the reduced loan term, and the variable is the *payment* argument of the @NPER function. So in Figure 11.21, the target term of 60 (12*5) monthly payments is entered in cell C9. In the variable cell (C10), the variable estimate is the current monthly payment ($2,841) entered as a value. Finally, the formula cell (C11) contains the function @NPER(C1,C10,C2,C3,C4), which uses the variable cell reference C10 as the *payment* argument. Since monthly payments are made, a monthly interest rate is used, and this @NPER function calculates the loan term in months. Therefore, cell C12 contains the formula +C11/12 to convert this result to years.

Figure 11.21

Using @NPER with /Tools, Solve For

File	Edit	Style	Graph	Print	Database	Tools	Options	Window	? ↑↓

▲ ◄ ► ▼	Erase	Copy	Move	Style	Align	Font	Insert	Delete	Fit	Sum	Format	CHR	WYS

C11: (F2) [W14] @NPER(C1,C10,C2,C3,C4)

	A	B	C	D	E	F
1	MONTHLY INTEREST RATE		1.0%			
2	PRESENT VALUE		($200,000)			
3	ENDING FUTURE VALUE		$0			
4	TYPE OF CASH FLOW	End of Month	1			
5	CURRENT MONTHLY PAYMENT		$2,841			
6						
7	Solve For Information					
8						
9	TARGET VALUE: TERM OF NOTE		60			
10	VARIABLE CELL: MONTHLY PAYMENT		$2,841			
11	FORMULA CELL: NUMBER OF PAYMENTS		120.00			
12	NUMBER OF YEARS		10.00			
13						

When you enter the /Tools, Solve For command, specify the target value as **+C9**, the variable cell as **C10**, and the formula cell as **C11**. Because the @NPER function calculates a complicated relationship between multiple variables, select Parameters, Max Iterations, and enter **20** (iterations). (Otherwise, Quattro Pro returns the error message "Maximum iterations reached.") To complete the command, select Go, and then Quit.

In cell C10 of Figure 11.22, /Tools, Solve For returns a monthly payment of $4,405. The @NPER function references this payment and returns a loan term of 60 months, or 5 years, in cell C11.

Limitations of /Tools, Solve For

Although the /Tools, Solve For command is a useful addition to Quattro Pro, it performs only limited sensitivity analysis. /Tools, Solve For's limitations occur for the following reasons:

- Multiple variables cannot be simultaneously changed. Thus you cannot solve for the values of two variables, such as material and labor.

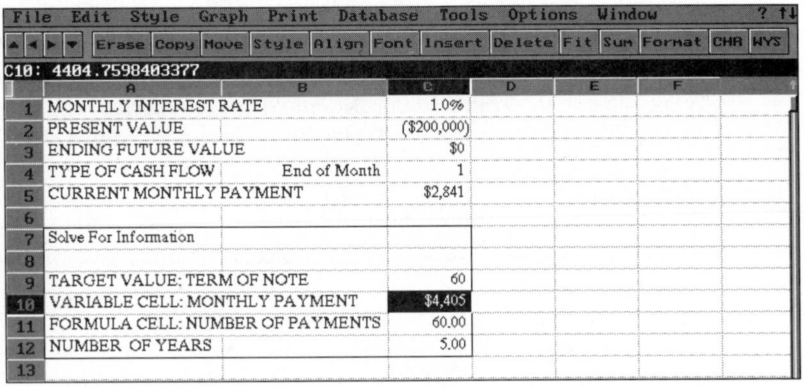

Figure 11.22

The /Tools, Solve For solution using @NPER

	A	B	C	D	E	F
			1.0%			
1	MONTHLY INTEREST RATE		1.0%			
2	PRESENT VALUE		($200,000)			
3	ENDING FUTURE VALUE		$0			
4	TYPE OF CASH FLOW	End of Month	1			
5	CURRENT MONTHLY PAYMENT		$2,841			
6						
7	Solve For Information					
8						
9	TARGET VALUE: TERM OF NOTE		60			
10	VARIABLE CELL: MONTHLY PAYMENT		$4,405			
11	FORMULA CELL: NUMBER OF PAYMENTS		60.00			
12	NUMBER OF YEARS		5.00			
13						

C10: 4404.7598403377

File Edit Style Graph Print Database Tools Options Window   ? ↑↓
Erase Copy Move Style Align Font Insert Delete Fit Sum Format CHR WYS

- You must specify a particular target value. Frequently you will be more interested in a target range; in these cases you must reuse the /Tools, Solve For command for the different values in your target range.

- /Tools, Solve For works best when you calculate the dominant variable in a formula. If you compute a secondary variable, you must freeze the dominant variable, which is usually an unrealistic assumption. For example, sales, calculated by

    # units sold * unit price

  is the dominant variable in most calculations for gross profit. Direct labor, calculated by

    hourly wage * # units sold / # manufactured per hour

  is a secondary variable. So, to solve for direct labor, you must hold # units sold, or sales, constant.

  Luckily, Quattro Pro provides another sensitivity analysis tool that overcomes many of these limitations: the Optimizer.

Obtaining the Optimal Solution in Quattro Pro 3.0

The /Tools, Advanced Math, Optimization command in Quattro Pro 3.0 is its most powerful sensitivity analysis tool. It is extremely useful whenever you need to analyze a problem that involves multiple variables, or may have multiple solutions.

For example, imagine that you manufacture five products in one plant. You can use /Tools, Advanced Math, Optimization to calculate the production level for each product that *maximizes* your gross profit. You can also compute the production levels that *minimize* your total labor cost. The /Tools, Advanced Math, Optimization command analyzes all of your information as a linear model. Quattro Pro then uses linear programming to solve the simultaneous linear equations in the model, returning the best or *optimal* solution.

/Tools, Advanced Math, Optimization requires significant user input and a thorough understanding of the problem you are modeling. You must be able to debug an analysis and to determine if the optimal solution returned is a reasonable one for your analysis. If you're a beginning user, you may find it slow going until you become familiar with the command's input format. However, once you become comfortable with this command, you will find it a powerful sensitivity analysis tool.

Optimization Basics

A *linear equation* expresses a relationship using one or more variables. In Table 11.1, each equation is expressed as a function of at least one of the variables A, B, C, and D. All of the equations in this table are *linear* because each variable is independent of the other variables.

A *nonlinear* equation includes two codependent variables, indicated by a term like $2*A*B$, or a nonlinear term like C^2. Nonlinear relationships cannot be solved using linear programming, or by Quattro Pro 3.0's /Tools, Advanced Math, Optimization command.

NOTE. *The Optimizer in Quattro Pro 4.0 can solve nonlinear models. See "Obtaining the Optimal Solution in Quattro Pro 4.0," later in this chapter.*

Table 11.1   Simultaneous Linear Equations

Ice Hockey		Basketball		Concerts		Mud Wrestling			Total Tickets
$75,000*A$	+	$75,000*B$	+	$75,000*C$	+	$75,000*D$	<=		600,000
$20,000*A$	+	$20,000*B$	+	$20,000*C$	+	$20,000*D$	>=		160,000
$40,000*A$	+	$30,000*B$	+	$50,000*C$	+	$75,000*D$	>=		390,000
$0*A$	+	$30,000*B$	+	$50,000*C$	+	$75,000*D$	>=		410,000

You can represent a real-life situation mathematically using a *linear model*, which is composed of a group of *simultaneous linear equations* like those in Table 11.1. These equations are simultaneously true and use the same independent variables. Simultaneous linear equations actually represent *constraints*, or limitations placed on the variables A, B, C, and D.

Linear programming is a mathematical method of solving a system of linear equations. Sometimes there exists only one unique solution for a set of simultaneous linear equations. (See "Manipulating Matrices" in this chapter for further discussion.) In other cases there is no solution that makes all of these equations simultaneously true. However, in most cases multiple solutions exist—especially when there are more variables than equations. While linear programming finds all solutions that exist for a system of linear equations, Quattro Pro 3.0's /Tools, Advanced Math, Optimization command returns the best answer from this solution set.

In order to solve such a complex analysis as a linear model, the /Tools, Advanced Math, Optimization command requires constraints (simultaneous linear equations), bounds, and an optimization formula.

Creating Simultaneous Linear Equations (Constraints)

Suppose you are a sports arena promoter. You have eight open dates left for the 1992 winter season, and four different types of events to choose from: ice hockey, basketball, concerts, and mud wrestling. Obviously, you want to maximize your gross ticket sales for these eight dates.

You have gathered the following information to help you make your decision. First, the maximum seating capacity of each event is 75,000, or 600,000 for eight events. Second, any event is cancelable if 20,000 tickets are not sold in advance. You can express this information mathematically using the following linear equations:

Ice Hockey		Basketball		Concerts		Mud Wrestling		Total Tickets
$75{,}000*A$	$+$	$75{,}000*B$	$+$	$75{,}000*C$	$+$	$75{,}000*D$	$<=$	$600{,}000$
$20{,}000*A$	$+$	$20{,}000*B$	$+$	$20{,}000*C$	$+$	$20{,}000*D$	$>=$	$160{,}000$

Since you are trying to calculate the mix of events that maximizes your ticket sale revenue, your variables are simply the number of occurrences of each type of event. Therefore, variable A represents the number of ice hockey events, B the number of basketball events, C the number of concert events, and D the number of mud wrestling events.

You also know that a mud wrestling event is usually a sellout, a concert typically draws 50,000 people, and an ice hockey game draws 40,000 fans. Since your city's basketball team has been in last place for years, you can expect only 30,000 diehards to appear for those games. Furthermore, on two dates, concerts and ice hockey games coincide, so you must choose between those events.

All this information can be used to develop two more linear equations:

Ice Hockey		Basketball		Concerts		Mud Wrestling			Total Tickets
40,000*A	+	30,000*B	+	50,000*C	+	75,000*D	>=		390,000
0*A		+ 30,000*B	+	50,000*C	+	75,000*D	>=		410,000

The first equation in this table expresses mathematically that for two events each of ice hockey, basketball, concerts, and mud wrestling, you expect to sell at least 390,000 tickets. The last equation in the foregoing table represents that you expect to sell at least 410,000 tickets when the eight events include no hockey games but four concerts. (You could also express this fourth equation as 50,000*C >= 200,000.)

These four equations (constraints) are all simultaneously true, and all use the same variables, A, B, C, and D. Even though the fourth equation excludes the variable A, it is still a valid part of this group of simultaneous linear equations.

NOTE. *In this simple scheduling example, all equations relate to total tickets sold (the right-hand side of the equation). You will see in later examples, however, that each constraint in a system of simultaneous linear equations can solve for a different constant term, such as direct labor or direct material.*

Inequality and Equality Constraints

The simultaneous linear equations, which represent variable constraints, are also designated as either equality constraints or inequality constraints. An *equality constraint* is simply a linear equation that equates both sides of an equation, using an equal sign (=). On the other hand, an *inequality constraint* relates both sides of an equation using one of the simple logical operators in Table 11.2. You cannot use complex logical operators, however, such as #AND#, #OR#, and #NOT#; instead, you must create two linear equations to represent such relationships.

Table 11.2   Optimization Inequality Constraints

Inequality Constraint	Description
<	Less than
<=	Less than or equal to
>	Greater than
>=	Greater than or equal to

In Quattro Pro 3.0, the set of simultaneous linear equations can be a mixture of equality and inequality constraints. For example, Table 11.1 includes equations with different inequality constraints.

Determining the Appropriate Constraint   It is *very* important to use the correct inequality constraint in a linear equation. If you use an incorrect constraint, the Optimization command may not be able to solve your analysis, and will return the error message "Problem is infeasible." Or, the program may return an incorrect optimum value.

In many cases it can be difficult to determine the correct inequality constraint. For example, consider the third formula in Table 11.1:

```
40,000*A+30,000*B+50,000*C+75,000*D>=390,000
```

This formula represents that for two dates of each event you expect to sell *at least* 390,000 tickets. The formula uses the expected number of tickets sold as the *minimum* sold for an event, such as 40,000 for an ice hockey game. This interpretation of the information is conveyed by the >= (greater than or equal to) constraint.

On the other hand, you could also assume that these expected values are *maximum* values, and use a <= (less than or equal to) constraint in the formula. But if you do so, the Optimization command returns either an incorrect optimum value, or the *opposite* of your objective—a value that minimizes your constraints when you are attempting to maximize them.

When you are unsure which inequality constraint is appropriate, just use this rule of thumb: *If you are solving for the maximum optimum value, use a >= constraint; if you are solving for the minimum value, use a <= constraint.* Since in this example you want to maximize your ticket sales, the third and fourth equations in Table 11.1 use a >= constraint.

Constraints in Matrix Form

You can use matrices as a shorthand method of expressing a system of simultaneous linear equations. The equations in Table 11.1, for instance, can be expressed in the matrix form shown in Table 11.3. (See "Manipulating Matrices" earlier in this chapter.)

Table 11.3   **Simultaneous Linear Equations in Matrix Form**

Linear Constraints Coefficient Matrix					Variable Matrix	Inequality Relations Matrix	Constant Constraints Matrix
75,000	75,000	75,000	75,000		A	<=	600,000
20,000	20,000	20,000	20,000	×	B	>=	160,000
40,000	30,000	50,000	75,000		C	>=	390,000
0	30,000	50,000	75,000		D	>=	410,000

In Table 11.3 the Linear Constraints Coefficient Matrix contains the variable coefficients for each equation. This matrix must contain a row for each linear equation, and a column for each variable. Since you are analyzing four equations using four different variables in this instance, you use a 4-by-4 matrix. Use the following rules to create a Linear Constraints Coefficients Matrix:

- Enter the coefficients for your first equation in row 1, those for the second equation in row 2, and so on.

- For all equations, enter the coefficients for a particular variable in the same column. For example, enter all *A* coefficients in the first column.

- For each equation, enter a coefficient for each variable. If a variable is not represented in an equation, enter 0 in the correct cell in the matrix. In Table 11.3, a 0 value is entered for the *A* coefficient in the fourth equation.

The inequality constraints also are expressed in matrix form in Table 11.3. Placement of these constraints corresponds to the row placement of the equations in the Linear Constraints Coefficient Matrix. For example, because the first equation in Table 11.1 is entered in the first row of the Linear Constraints Coefficient Matrix of Table 11.3, the equation's corresponding inequality constraint is entered in the first row of the *Inequality Relations* Matrix column.

The *Constant Constraints Matrix* column contains values that correspond to the right-hand side of each linear equation. If an equation does not use this format—constant value on the right, and all variables on the left—you must rearrange the formula to conform to this convention. Once again, the placement of these values corresponds to the row placement of the equations in the Linear Constraints Coefficient Matrix.

When you use Quattro Pro 3.0's /Tools, Advanced Math, Optimization command, you can specify your simultaneous linear equations in matrix form, as demonstrated in Figure 11.23. In this example, the Linear Constraints Coefficient Matrix is entered in the block A3..D6. The inequality coefficients are entered as labels in matrix form in the block E3..E6. Finally, the Constant Constraints Matrix is entered in the block F3..F6.

Figure 11.23
Using matrices in an optimization analysis in Quattro Pro 3.0

File Edit Style Graph Print Database Tools Options Window							
E11: (,0) [W14]							
	A	B	C	D	E	F	G	H
1	LINEAR CONSTRAINTS COEFFICIENT MATRIX				INEQUALITY	CONSTANT		
2	A	B	C	D	RELATIONS	COEFFICIENTS		
3	75,000	75,000	75,000	75,000	<=	600,000		
4	20,000	20,000	20,000	20,000	>=	160,000		
5	40,000	30,000	50,000	75,000	>=	390,000		
6	0	30,000	50,000	75,000	>=	410,000		
7	BOUNDS FOR VARIABLE COEFFICIENTS							
8	0	0	0	0	Lower bounds			
9	2	2	4	2	Upper bounds			
10	OBJECTIVE FUNCTION COEFFICIENTS				OPTIMAL SOLUTION			
11	$800,000	$750,000	$1,000,000	$1,125,000				
12					VARIABLES			
13								

Notice that the information in the *Variable Matrix* column of Table 11.3 is implicit in the Linear Constraints Coefficient Matrix, and need not be entered in the spreadsheet.

One of the nice features of Quattro Pro 3.0's Optimization command is that the information in your matrices can reference other information in these same matrices and in other areas of your spreadsheet. For example, cell D6 contains the formula +D3. And in cell F5, the constant value 390,000 is calculated as 2*@SUM(A5..D5), because this equation assumes two dates for each type of event.

Tip. If all of your equations use equality constraints (= signs), you need not enter an Equality Relations Matrix in your spreadsheet. When this matrix is absent, the Optimization command assumes an equality matrix (the default).

Constraints as Non-Negative Formulas
In some instances, you can use the /Tools, Advanced Math, Optimization, Formula constraints option to express constraints as formulas rather than in matrix form. In order to use this option, however, each simultaneous linear equation must equate to a non-negative formula (>= 0). Because of this limitation, you will find that you can rarely use this method when Quattro Pro calculates an optimal solution that maximizes your analysis.

For example, you can rearrange the simultaneous linear equations in Table 11.1 to the formulas in Table 11.4. (Because these formulas are rearranged so that the right-hand side is equal to 0, the inequality signs change direction.) Unluckily, in this example three of the formulas now equate to <= 0. So you cannot use this formula method; if you do, Quattro Pro mistakenly evaluates these equations as >= 0, and returns an optimal solution that *minimizes* these constraints. Instead, you must enter all of these equations in matrix form.

Table 11.4   **Simultaneous Linear Equations as Formulas**

$$600{,}000 \; - \; (75{,}000*A \; + \; 75{,}000*B \; + \; 75{,}000*C \; + \; 75{,}000*D) \;\; \geq \;\; 0$$

$$160{,}000 \; - \; (20{,}000*A \; + \; 20{,}000*B \; + \; 20{,}000*C \; + \; 20{,}000*D) \;\; \leq \;\; 0$$

$$390{,}000 \; - \; (40{,}000*A \; + \; 30{,}000*B \; + \; 50{,}000*C \; + \; 75{,}000*D) \;\; \leq \;\; 0$$

$$410{,}000 \; - \; (\quad\; 0*A \; + \; 30{,}000*B \; + \; 50{,}000*C \; + \; 75{,}000*D) \;\; \leq \;\; 0$$

You will most often be able to use the Optimization, Formula constraints option when you calculate the optimal solution that *minimizes* a problem, because the constraints will usually be non-negative formulas and evaluate to >=0. Additionally, you must define any minimum capacity constraints in the bound block, so that you do not include a constraint that evaluates to <=0.

If you're lucky enough to have a set of simultaneous linear equations that conform to the non-negative formula format, you only need to enter the left-hand side of each equation in your spreadsheet. The Optimization command then assumes that the remaining portion of your equation is >=0.

When you use the Optimization, Formula constraints option, you must enter all of your constraint formulas together in a block of cells, one formula to a cell. You can enter the entire formula in a cell, or you can build it as a formula that references coefficient and constant values in other cells.

Unlike the matrix format, this non-negative formula format *includes* the variables A, B, C, and D. You specify these variables in each formula by referencing the appropriate blank cells in the *variable block*. The variable block is a solution block, where Quattro Pro 3.0 returns the variable value that it uses to calculate the optimal solution. A variable block *must* conform to the variable placement in the Linear Constraints Coefficient Matrix. For instance, in the empty variable block A12..D12 in Figure 11.23, cell A12 represents variable A, cell B12 variable B, and so on. So if *all* of your equations are non-negative formulas, you can enter the first equation in Table 11.4 as

```
600000-(75000*A12+75000*B12+75000*C12+75000*D12)
```

CAUTION! *When you use the Formula constraints option, be careful to verify that Quattro Pro 3.0 is returning the true optimal solution for your problem. Should you inadvertently forget to include a variable in one of your constraints, or include one equation that is not a non-negative formula, Quattro Pro 3.0 will incorrectly evaluate your constraints when you use the Formula constraints option. The program may indeed return a solution, but it will be an optimal solution for a problem different from the one you are analyzing.*

Working with Variable Bounds

The variables in your simultaneous linear equations may also be subject to their own constraints, or *bounds*. A *lower bound* limits the minimum value of a variable, and an *upper bound* limits its maximum value. Bounds not only limit a variable to an appropriate range of values; they also limit the number of solutions for a set of constraints.

In a system of simultaneous linear equations, each variable may be unbounded, bounded in both directions, restricted by an upper bound but no lower bound, or restricted by a lower bound but no upper bound. So, in an analysis, some variables may not be bounded, while others may be partially or fully bounded.

Let's return to the previous scheduling example, and suppose that ice hockey is scheduled for no events or up to two events. Thus Variable A (ice hockey) has a lower bound of 0 and an upper bound of 2. Likewise, variable C (concerts) has a lower bound of 2 and an upper bound of 4. Both basketball and mud wrestling are scheduled for two dates, however, so the variables B and D have a lower bound *and* an upper bound of 2. This tells Quattro Pro 3.0 not to calculate more or less than two dates for these events.

In Figure 11.23, the bounds are entered in the block A8..D9—lower bounds in the first row, and upper bounds in the second row. Notice that the bounds values must correspond to the placement of the variable coefficients in the Linear Constraints Coefficient Matrix. For example, since the first column in this matrix contains A coefficients, you also enter the A variable bounds in the first column of the Bounds block.

In the /Tools, Advanced Math, Optimization command, however, you do not have to bound any of your variables. If no bounds are specified, Quattro Pro 3.0 restricts your variables to non-negative real numbers ($>=0$). Thus for each variable, the default lower bound is 0, but no upper bound exists. Nevertheless, if just one variable has one bound, you must create a bound block, with corresponding upper and lower bounds cells for each variable. Then, for those variables with no bounds, leave the corresponding cells blank.

Determining the Objective Function

The goal of any optimization analysis is to find the best solution for a set of constraints. In many cases, however, multiple solutions exist. To arrive at an optimal solution, then, Quattro Pro 3.0 optimizes one equation that you specify, the *objective function*. In other words, the Optimization command calculates the best solution for the objective function, given your other constraints.

In the current example, you want to optimize your total ticket sales revenues. You know that ice hockey and concert tickets sell for $20 each, basketball tickets for $25, and mud wrestling tickets for $15. Furthermore, ice hockey games draw 40,000 fans, basketball games 30,000, a concert 50,000; and a mud wrestling event always attracts a sellout crowd of 75,000. So, total ticket revenues can be calculated like this:

```
20*40,000*A+25*30,000*B+20*50,000*C+
15*75,000*D=Total Ticket Revenues
```

You can convert this formula to an objective function, using the following rules. An objective function

- Must be a linear equation that uses an equality constraint (= sign)

- Must include on one side of the equation all of the variables that are used in the other simultaneous linear equations of the Linear Constraints Coefficient Matrix

- Must solve for the optimal solution on the other side of the equation

- Must be entered in your spreadsheet separately from the other simultaneous linear equations (constraints)

Using these rules, you can convert the Total Ticket Revenues formula into an objective function using the matrix form shown in Table 11.5. Using this format, the left-hand side of this objective function is entered in Figure 11.23 in the block A11..D11. Since Quattro Pro 3.0 assumes that the coefficients correspond to the placement of the variable coefficients in the Linear Constraints Coefficient Matrix, you must enter the objective function in row-wise fashion, using the same variable placement. In Figure 11.23, the first column in the Linear Constraints Coefficient Matrix contains *A* coefficients, so the first column in the objective function block, cell A11, must contain the *A* coefficient, 800,000. Remember: Because Quattro Pro 3.0 implicitly understands the variable placement, you don't need to enter the Variable Matrix in Table 11.5 in your spreadsheet. And because Quattro Pro 3.0 requires that an objective function use an equality constraint, you do not need to enter the Equality Relation in Table 11.5 in your spreadsheet.

Table 11.5   **Objective Function in Matrix Form**

Optimal Coefficients Matrix	Variable Matrix	Equality Relation	Optimal Solution
20*40,000 25*30,000 20*50,000 15*75,000	A	=	Optimal Solution
	B		
	C		
	D		

The /Tools, Advanced Math, Optimization command calculates the best so-lution for the objective function. In other words, it returns the optimal value for the right-hand side of the equation. Therefore, simply designate a blank cell—such as E11 in Figure 11.23—as the optimal solution cell in your spreadsheet. The Optimization command calculates the best solution for the objective func-tion in block A11..D11, and places the optimal value in the solution cell, E11.

Using @SUMPRODUCT for the Objective Function

You can also use Quattro Pro's @SUMPRODUCT function to enter your ob-jective function directly in the optimal solution cell. For example, suppose you have entered the information in Figure 11.23 in your spreadsheet. Row 11 contains the coefficients for the objective function formula. Row 12 is blank, and will receive the optimal values that Quattro Pro 3.0 calculates for the A, B, C, and D variables. You can specify the objective function in the op-timal solution cell E11, using this function:

```
@SUMPRODUCT(Objective Function Row, Variables Row)
```

Thus in cell E11, you can enter the formula

```
@SUMPRODUCT(A11..D11,A12..D12)
```

This will initially return ERR, because of the blank cells in the variable block A12..D12.

With this formula in E11, you need not specify an objective function when you use the Optimization command.

Calculating the Optimal Solution

The heart of any optimization analysis is expressing the problem in mathe-matical terms. So, once you have established the constraints (linear equa-tions), bounds, and objective function for an analysis like the one in Figure

Tip. Before you specify a new analysis, use the Optimization, Reset command to clear any old settings.

11.23, it is a simple procedure to use the Optimization command to calculate the optimal solution to the problem:

1. Select the /Tools, Advanced Math, Optimization command. Quattro Pro 3.0 displays the Optimization menu shown in Figure 11.24.

Figure 11.24

The /Tools, Advanced Math, Optimization menu in Quattro Pro 3.0

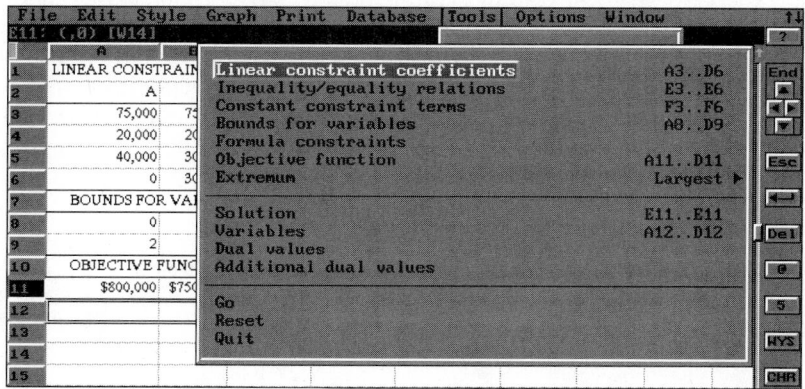

2. Select the Linear constraint coefficients option and specify the block **A3..D6**, which contains the Linear Constraints Coefficient Matrix in Figure 11.23.

3. Select the Inequality/equality relations option and specify the block **E3..E6**, which contains the Inequality Relations matrix.

4. Select the Constant constraint terms option and specify the Constant Coefficients matrix in the block **F3..F6**.

NOTE. *If you specify your constraints as non-negative formulas, disregard steps 2 through 4. Instead, select the Formula constraints option and in response to the "Block of formulas constrained to be >= 0:" prompt, specify the block that contains your constraint formulas. Then continue at step 5.*

5. Select the Bounds for variables option and specify the bounds for the variables in **A8..D9**.

6. Select Objective function option and specify the Objective function coefficients in **A11..D11**.

7. Select Extremum. Since you want to calculate the optimal value that *maximizes* your objective function, select Largest. (To calculate the optimal value that *minimizes* the objective function, select Smallest.)

Tip. The /Tools, Advanced Math, Optimization settings are automatically adjusted if you move any of your selections to another location in the spreadsheet.

8. Select Solution and specify cell **E11** as the location for Quattro Pro to return the optimal value.

9. Select Variables and specify the location for Quattro Pro 3.0 to return the values of the variables *A*, *B*, *C*, and *D* that result in the optimal solution as either the block A12..D12 or just the first cell of this row, A12.

10. To complete this command and return to the spreadsheet, select Go.

As shown in Figure 11.25, Quattro Pro 3.0 computes $7,750,000 as the maximum ticket revenue you can obtain given your constraints. Quattro Pro 3.0 calculates this optimal value using the variable values, also returned for you in the block A12..D12. These variable values conform to the variable placement in the Linear Constraints Coefficient Matrix.

Figure 11.25

Optimal solution returned by the Optimization command in Quattro Pro 3.0

File Edit Style Graph Print Database Tools Options Window								
E11: (C0) [W14] 7750000								?
	A	B	C	D	E	F	G	H
1	LINEAR CONSTRAINTS COEFFICIENT MATRIX				INEQUALITY	CONSTANT		
2	A	B	C	D	RELATIONS	COEFFICIENTS		
3	75,000	75,000	75,000	75,000	< =	600,000		
4	20,000	20,000	20,000	20,000	> =	160,000		
5	40,000	30,000	50,000	75,000	> =	390,000		
6	0	30,000	50,000	75,000	> =	410,000		
7	BOUNDS FOR VARIABLE COEFFICIENTS							
8	0	2	2	2	Lower bounds			
9	2	2	4	2	Upper bounds			
10	OBJECTIVE FUNCTION COEFFICIENTS				OPTIMAL SOLUTION			
11	$800,000	$750,000	$1,000,000	$1,125,000	$7,750,000			
12	0	2	4	2	VARIABLES			
13								

The results say that to realize this optimal ticket revenue, you should schedule no *A* events (ice hockey), two *B* events (basketball), four *C* events (concerts), and two *D* events (mud wrestling). Notice that these variable values, when multiplied by the following respective objective function coefficients,

```
0*$800,000+2*$750,000+4*$1,000,000+2*$1,125,000
```

return the optimal solution value, $7,750,000.

NOTE. *Any results returned by the Optimization command are not updated, even when the spreadsheet is recalculated. So if you change any constraint, bounds, or objective information, remember to reuse the Optimization command to get the new results. Since your last settings are retained, just reselect /Tools, Advanced Math, Optimization, Go.*

Optimization Sensitivity Analysis

The /Tools, Advanced Math, Optimization command also provides two other options, Dual values and Additional dual values, that allow you to analyze the relationships between the optimal solution value and your constraints, variables, and variable bounds.

A *dual value* measures the strength of the relationship between the constant coefficient of a constraint and the calculated optimal solution. An *additional dual value* indicates the strength of the relationship between the optimal value and a set of variable bounds, and thus indirectly between the optimal solution and a variable.

You can choose to calculate only the dual values, only the additional dual values, or both these sets of sensitivity analysis information. In Figure 11.24, for example, suppose you select /Tools, Advanced Math, Optimization, Dual values, and designate the location for the constant coefficient (constraint) dual values, **G3..G6**. Then select Additional dual values and indicate the location for the dual values for the variable bounds, **A13..D13**. When you select Go and then Quit to complete the command and return to the spreadsheet, Quattro Pro 3.0 calculates the dual values in G3..G6 of Figure 11.26 for each constant coefficient (constraint) in F3..F6. In A13..D13 it returns additional dual values for each set of variable bounds in A8..D9.

Interpreting Dual Values for Constant Coefficients

As shown in Figure 11.26, Quattro Pro 3.0 calculates a dual value in G3..G6 for each constant coefficient in F3..F6. These dual values conform to the variable placement in the Constant Coefficients Matrix. For example, the first constant coefficient in cell F3 (or the first constraint in row 3), has a dual value of 10.7.

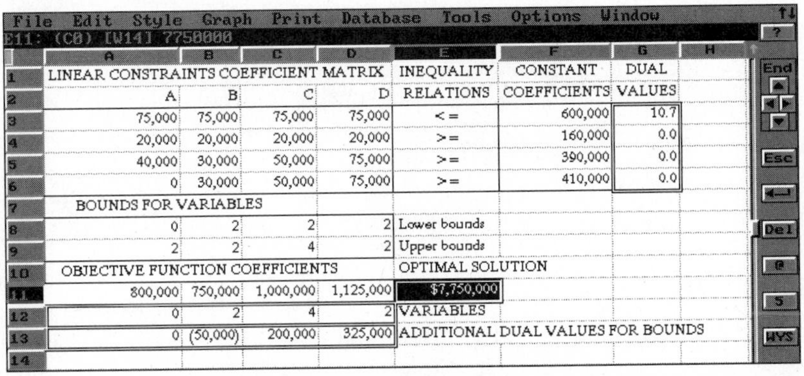

Figure 11.26

Calculating dual values for constraints and bounds in Quattro Pro 3.0

	A	B	C	D	E	F	G	H
	LINEAR CONSTRAINTS COEFFICIENT MATRIX				INEQUALITY	CONSTANT	DUAL	
2	A	B	C	D	RELATIONS	COEFFICIENTS	VALUES	
3	75,000	75,000	75,000	75,000	<=	600,000	10.7	
4	20,000	20,000	20,000	20,000	>=	160,000	0.0	
5	40,000	30,000	50,000	75,000	>=	390,000	0.0	
6	0	30,000	50,000	75,000	>=	410,000	0.0	
7	BOUNDS FOR VARIABLES							
8	0	2	2	2	Lower bounds			
9	2	2	4	2	Upper bounds			
10	OBJECTIVE FUNCTION COEFFICIENTS				OPTIMAL SOLUTION			
11	800,000	750,000	1,000,000	1,125,000	$7,750,000			
12	0	2	4	2	VARIABLES			
13	0	(50,000)	200,000	325,000	ADDITIONAL DUAL VALUES FOR BOUNDS			
14								

File   Edit   Style   Graph   Print   Database   Tools   Options   Window
B11: (C0) [W14] 7750000

You can interpret a dual value as follows:

- A *positive* dual value indicates the *incremental* amount that the optimal value (cell E11) will *increase* if the constant coefficient value of a constraint increases by 1 unit.

- A *negative* dual value indicates the *decremental* amount the optimal value will *decrease* if a constraint coefficient value decreases by 1 unit.

- A 0 dual value indicates that a small change in the constant coefficient will cause no change in the optimal value. Therefore, the constraint has little or no *incremental* effect on the optimal value.

Notice that Quattro Pro 3.0 has calculated a 0 dual value for the last three constraints. Changing the constant coefficient values of these equations would have no additional maximizing effect on the optimal solution value, $7,750,000, in cell E11.

Quattro Pro 3.0 has returned a positive dual value of 10.7 for the first linear equation, which calculates maximum seating capacity. Therefore, if you increase the constant coefficient in cell F3 by 1, to 600,001 (total seating capacity for all eight events), and then reuse the Optimization command, total optimal ticket revenue will increase by $10.70, and Quattro Pro 3.0 will return a new optimal solution of $7,750,011 in cell E11.

Interpreting Additional Dual Values for Bounds

As you know, an additional dual value measures the strength of the relationship between the optimal value and a set of variable bounds. Quattro Pro 3.0 only returns one additional dual value for each set of lower and upper variable bounds. As shown in Figure 11.26, Quattro Pro 3.0 calculates additional dual values in the block A13..D13 that relate to the variable bounds. These dual values conform to the variable placement in the Bounds block A8..D9.

When you *maximize* a solution, use these general guidelines to interpret additional dual values:

- A positive additional dual value indicates that the variable value is equal to its *upper* bound. Therefore, this bound is limiting the optimal variable value, and thus the optimal solution. A positive additional dual value then represents the *incremental increase* in the optimal solution value if you *increase* the upper bound by one unit.

- A negative additional dual value indicates that the variable value is equal to its *lower* bound, and that this bound is limiting the optimal value. A negative additional dual value then represents the *incremental decrease* in the optimal solution value if you *increase* the lower bound by one unit.

■ A 0 additional dual value can indicate that an optimal variable value is not equal to its upper or lower bound, so changing a bound will have no effect on the optimal variable value and thus the optimal solution. On the other hand, if one of the variable bounds is 0, then a 0 dual value indicates that changing that bound will have no effect on the optimal solution value.

For example, in cell A13, Quattro Pro 3.0 has returned a 0 additional dual value for the *A* bounds in the block A8..A9, even though both the lower bound and the computed *A* value is 0. Therefore, even if you increase the *A* bounds in either direction, it will have no effect on the *A* value in cell A12 or on the optimal solution value in cell E11.

In cell C13, Quattro Pro 3.0 has computed a 200,000 additional dual value for the *C* bounds. Since this value is not equal to 0, you know that the computed *C* value in C12, 4, is either an upper or lower bound. As you can see in Figure 11.26, 4 is the upper *C* bound in C9. So the upper *C* bound is *active*, and you can interpret the dual value in the appropriate manner. If you increase the upper *C* bound (and thus the *C* variable) by 1, the optimal solution value will increase by 200,000. In other words, if you add one additional concert to your schedule, you can increase your ticket revenues by $200,000.

It takes a little work to see why revenues would increase only $200,000. First, the optimal *B* and *D* variables, 2 and 2, are both equal to their upper bounds in cells B9 and D9. So, given the current constraints and bounds, Quattro Pro 3.0 cannot increase the number of basketball games or mud wrestling events. Therefore, if you only increase the *C* upper bound by one, the Optimization command can theoretically add only one *A* event (ice hockey), or one *C* event (a concert). Increase the upper *C* bound to 5, however, and the *incremental* increase in ticket revenues is the difference between a concert and an ice hockey game ($1,000,000–$800,000), $200,000.

Tip. If you are not sure which bound is active, just change either the upper or lower bound by one unit, and then reuse the Optimization command. The bound that causes the additional dual value to be 0 is the active bound.

It is somewhat more difficult to interpret the additional dual value for the *B* bounds, because the *B* upper and lower bounds are both specified as 2. Therefore, in cell B11 Quattro Pro returned the optimal *B* value of two basketball games. Because the –50,000 *B* dual value is negative, the *lower* bound is active. So if you increase the lower bound by one (the upper bound, too, in this example), your optimal ticket revenues will decrease by $50,000. Since the optimal *C* and *D* variables are equal to their upper bounds, if you increase the *B* lower bound to 3, Quattro Pro 3.0 will *theoretically* substitute a *B* event for an *A* event. Under this scenario, the incremental *decrease* in ticket revenues would be $750,000–$800,000, or –$50,000.

Interpreting the *D* bound's additional dual value is similar to interpreting the *B* additional dual value, because the *D* upper and lower bounds are also both specified as 2, and in cell D12 Quattro Pro returns the optimal *D* value of two mud wrestling events. However, since the *D* additional dual value (325,000) is positive, then the upper *D* bound is active. So if you add one additional mud wrestling event, you can increase total ticket revenues by $325,000. This incremental increase in the optimal solution is equal to the incremental revenue difference between one mud wrestling event and one ice hockey game ($1,125,000–$800,000 = $325,000).

You can glean even more information from these additional dual values. First, as long as just one variable generates a positive dual value, you can increase the optimal solution if you can increase its active bound. Second, since the *D* additional dual value (325,000) is the largest for all variables, the easiest way to maximize total ticket revenues is to schedule as many mud wrestling events as possible.

NOTE. *When you* minimize *an optimal solution, a* negative *additional dual value represents the amount the optimal solution will* decrease *if you* increase the upper *bound. However, a* positive *additional dual value represents the amount the optimal solution will* increase *if you* decrease the lower *bound. Therefore, when you minimize a solution, you are interested in the* upper *bounds that generate a* negative *additional dual value.*

For another discussion of dual and additional dual values, read the next section.

Optimizing a Startup Company's Profits: An Example

Suppose your startup company has finally taken off. You can now sell as many of the four products shown in Figure 11.27 as you can produce. However, your growing company is short of cash. This cash crunch results in constraints on your resources, limiting the amount of people you can employ, as well as your credit lines with suppliers.

Given these constraints, you want to calculate a product mix that maximizes your gross profit. You can use /Tools, Advanced Math, Optimization to find this optimal solution, using a three-step process: defining the problem mathematically, calculating the optimal solution, and finally analyzing the results returned by the Optimization command.

Defining the Problem Mathematically

First you must create a synopsis of the relevant information, like the one in Figure 11.27. Product A, which you sell for $17 each, is manufactured using a 24-hour continuous process overseen by a small number of personnel. Although each unit of Product A consumes $2.50 in material, the per-unit labor cost is only $0.50. Furthermore, the maximum capacity of this process is 300,000 units, but it is costly to shut down. You therefore require a minimum production level of 50,000 units to keep the process running at a break-even level.

Production of this product is currently limited by the $300,000 credit line imposed by your material supplier, which equates to material for 120,000 units.

Figure 11.27

Setting up an analysis in Quattro Pro 3.0

File Edit Style Graph Print Database Tools Options Window									↑↓
E19: (C2) [W9] +E4-E9-E17									?
	A	B	C	D	E	F	G	H	I
1		Continuous	Assembly	Scrap	Imported	Total			
2	PRODUCT	A	B	C	D				
3									
4	Price/Unit	$17.00	$15.00	$6.00	$15.00				
5									
6	MAX Capacity	300,000	250,000	200,000	0	750,000			
7	MIN Capacity	50,000	70,000	50,000	0	170,000			
8									
9	Material/Unit	$2.50	$1.50	$0.00	$3.50				
10	Credit Limit	$300,000	$150,000	$0	$350,000	$800,000			
11	Units	120,000	100,000	0	100,000	320,000			
12									
13	Direct Labor:workers					25			
14	Units/Hour	16	5	16	80	50,000			
15	Unit Labor	0.06	0.20	0.06	0.013				
16	Hourly wage	$8	$8	$8	$8				
17	Unit Cost	$0.50	$1.60	$0.50	$0.10				
18									
19	Unit Profit	$14.00	$11.90	$5.50	$11.40				
20	========	=====	=====	====	=====				
21									
22									
23									

OPTIM6.WQ1   [1]   READY

Product B, which you assemble, test, and then sell for $13 each, is subject to numerous constraints. First, the product uses parts from a supplier who limits your credit to $150,000. Thus, your outstanding orders are restricted to 100,000 units, because the unit material cost is $1.50. In addition, the assembly and test equipment limits Product B's production to 250,000 units. More importantly, this labor-intensive process is a drain on a limited resource—your work force—because a worker can only assemble and test five units per hour ($1.60 per-unit labor cost). Therefore, Product B production (or that of Products A, C, and D) is limited by your labor shortage. However, a 70,000 minimum production level for Product B is required to honor a long-term government contract you have recently won.

Discarded Product B scrap metal is melted and recast into Product C, using induction heating equipment with a maximum production capacity of 200,000 units. Since the minimum Product B production level generates enough scrap for 100,000 units, Product C's direct material cost is assumed to be $0. However, your induction heating system is not profitable unless you manufacture 70,000 units during one manufacturing run. Furthermore, the

$0.50 per-unit labor cost represents that one person can oversee production of 20 units per hour. Since you can sell Product C for $6 each, this is a profitable product line which does not tax your credit limit and labor constraints.

Finally, Product D is a Korean product that you import prepackaged and ready to go. This product benefits you strategically because it uses minimal labor and has no maximum manufacturing capacity. You only inventory and ship this product, so your labor cost is only $0.10 per unit. However, you must use a letter of credit to purchase this product overseas, or essentially prepay for this material. When you order at least 100,000 units, you can buy each unit for $3.50, including freight-in. At this direct material price, you can sell Product D in the United States quite profitably for $15 each. Therefore, Product D is limited by a 100,000-unit economical order size, and the resulting $350,000 letter of credit.

As shown in column F of Figure 11.27, the constraints for these four products also translate into total constraints, such as a 170,000-unit minimum production capacity and a 750,000-unit maximum production capacity. Furthermore, total credit is restricted to $800,000, and direct labor is limited to 50,000 man-hours (a 25-person work force working 40 hours a week). As shown in row 19, you can also use this information to compute the per-unit gross profit contribution for each product (Price/Unit–Material Unit–Unit labor cost).

Calculating the Optimal Solution

Now that you have determined the relevant information in your analysis, you must enter this information in a spreadsheet using a format compatible with /Tools, Advanced Math, Optimization. The information in Figure 11.27 is used to develop four constraints. Each of these constraints uses the same four variables—A, B, C, and D, representing the number of units produced for Products A, B, C, and D. The constraints are as follows:

- The 750,000 production unit MAX Capacity in cell F6 is used to create $1*A+1*B+1*C+0*D<=750,000$.

- The 170,000 production unit MIN Capacity in cell F7 is used to create $1*A+1*B+1*C+0*D>=170,000$.

- The Material/Unit values in row 9 and the $800,000 Credit Limit in cell F10 are used to create $2.50*A+1.50*B+0.00*C+3.50*D<=800,000$.

- The Direct Labor Units/Hour values in row 15 and the 50,000 total man-hour constraint in cell F14 are used to create $.06*A+.20*B+.06*C+.013*D<=50,000$.

These constraints are then entered in matrix form in the block B3..G6 in Figure 11.28.

Figure 11.28

Using the Optimization command to maximize an optimal solution in Quattro Pro 3.0

File	Edit	Style	Graph	Print	Database	Tools	Options	Window			↑↓
G10: (C0) [W12] [F5] 5956923.0769231											?

	A	B	C	D	E	F	G	H	I	J	
1		Linear Constraints Coefficient Matrix				Inequal.	Constant	DUAL			End
2	PRODUCT	A	B	C	D	Relation	Coeff.	VALUES			
3	Max Units	1.0	1.0	1.0	0.0	< =	750,000	$0.0			
4	Min Unit	1.0	1.0	1.0	0.0	> =	170,000	$0.0			
5	Credit	2.5	1.5	0.0	3.5	< =	600,000	$5.1			
6	Labor hours	0.06	0.20	0.06	0.01	< =	50,000	$21.5			Esc
7	Lower bound	50,000	70,000	50,000	0						
8	Upper bound	300,000	250,000	200,000	100,000						
9		OBJECTIVE FUNCTION					SOLUTION				
10	PROFIT	$14.00	$11.90	$5.50	$11.40		$5,956,923				
11	UNITS	255,385	107,692	200,000	0	VARIABLES SOLUTION					Del
12		$0.00	$0.00	$4.15	($6.58)	ADD'I DUAL VALUES FOR BOUNDS					
13											

The variables A, B, C, and D are further limited by minimum and maximum production capacity bounds. The lower and upper bounds, entered in the block B7..E8 in Figure 11.28, are derived from the MIN and MAX Capacity production units in rows 7 and 8 of Figure 11.27.

Finally, because you want to maximize gross profit, you need to create an objective function that calculates the gross profit for each variable. Thus, the Unit Profit values in row 19 in Figure 11.27 are used to create

$14.00*A+11.90*B+5.50*C+11.40*D=$Optimal solution

The left side of this equation, in matrix form, is then entered as the Objective Function in the block B10..E10 in Figure 11.28. The right side of this equation is the solution that Quattro Pro 3.0 will calculate and enter in the Solution cell G10.

You can now use all this information to calculate an optimal solution for your startup company. Select /Tools, Advanced Math, Optimization. Specify the linear constraint coefficients block as **B3..E6**, the inequality/equality relations block as **F3..F6**, the constant constraint terms block as **G3..G6**, the bounds for variables block as **B7..E8**, and the objective function block as **B10..E10**. Then choose Extremum Largest to maximize this information. Next, specify the solution cell as **G10**, the variables block as **B11..E11**, the dual values block as **H3..H6**, and the additional dual values block as **B12..E12**. Finally, choose Go and then Quit to complete the command and return to the spreadsheet.

Evaluating the Results

As shown in Figure 11.28, Quattro Pro 3.0 returns $5,956,923 as the optimal gross profit in cell G10. In block B11..E11, Quattro Pro also returns the A, B, C, and D variable values that it uses in the objective function to calculate this optimal solution. Therefore, you need to manufacture 255,385 A units,

107,692 B units, 200,000 C units, and no D units to achieve this optimal gross profit level.

In column H, Quattro Pro 3.0 returns a 0 dual value for both the Min Unit and Max Unit capacity constraints; these constraints are not currently limiting your gross profit. However, the dual value for the Credit constraint indicates that for each $1.00 you can raise your credit limit, you can increase your gross profit by $5.10. Even more intriguing is the Labor hours constraint dual value, which signifies that your gross profit increases $21.50 for each additional one *hour* of labor you can pay for.

As the variable values in row 11 indicate, Quattro Pro 3.0 is calculating the optimal solution largely as a function of your credit and labor restrictions. Optimizing the product mix as a function of the highest gross profit contribution is only a secondary consideration. For example, the C value, 200,000, is the only variable equal to its upper bound (capacity constraint), even though this product contributes the lowest per-unit gross profit of all of these products.

In row 12, Quattro Pro 3.0 returns a 0 additional dual value for the A and B variables. Thus, neither of these variables is equal to its upper or lower bound. However, Quattro Pro 3.0 calculates a positive $4.15 additional dual value for the variable C bounds; so the 200,000 unit C value in cell C11 is equal to its upper bound. Therefore, for every unit increase to your C production capacity, you can increase your optimal gross profit by $4.15. However, Quattro Pro 3.0 returns a –$6.58 dual value for the D variable bounds—indicating that the lower D bound, 0, is active. If you enter 1 in cell E7, and then reuse the Optimization command, Quattro Pro 3.0 *decreases* the optimal solution by $6.58. (This is the net effect of increasing both D and B by one unit, and decreasing A by two units.) In other words, for every D unit you import, you consume credit almost equivalent to that used for two units of A.

Suppose this analysis attracts an investor to your company. You gain the financial resources to double both your work force and your credit lines; this is reflected in the Credit and Labor hours constant coefficients in Figure 11.29. Now when you use the Optimization command to calculate the optimal gross profit solution, you get substantially different results.

- By easing your credit and labor restrictions, you can increase your gross profit to $9,415,000.

- The only positive dual value in column H, $5.50, indicates that you are now restricted by your Max Units capacity constraint. (This is also indicated by the positive additional dual values for variables A, C, and D, which signify that each of these variable values is equal to its upper bound, or maximum capacity constraint.)

Figure 11.29

The effects of relaxing credit and labor constraints in Quattro Pro 3.0

File	Edit	Style	Graph	Print	Database		Tools	Options	Window		↑↓

G10: (C0) [W12] [F5] 9415000

	A	B	C	D	E	F	G	H	I	J
1		Linear Constraints Coefficient Matrix				Inequal.	Constant	DUAL		
2	PRODUCT	A	B	C	D	Relation	Coeff.	VALUES		
3	Max Units	1.0	1.0	1.0	0.0	< =	750,000	$5.5		
4	Min Unit	1.0	1.0	1.0	0.0	> =	170,000	$0.0		
5	Credit	2.5	1.5	0.0	3.5	< =	1,600,000	$0.0		
6	Labor hours	0.08	0.20	0.08	0.01	< =	100,000	$0.0		
7	Lower bound	50,000	70,000	50,000	0					
8	Upper bound	300,000	250,000	200,000	100,000					
9		OBJECTIVE FUNCTION					SOLUTION			
10	PROFIT	$14.00	$11.90	$5.50	$11.40		$9,415,000			
11	UNITS	300,000	250,000	200,000	100,000	VARIABLES SOLUTION				
12		$8.50	$8.40	$0.00	$11.40	ADD'L DUAL VALUES FOR BOUNDS				
13										

- More importantly, Quattro Pro 3.0 now optimizes the production levels as a function of the highest gross profit contribution. For this reason, Product *C*, which generates the smallest gross profit contribution, is the only product for which the optimal value is less than its maximum production capacity.

- Since you can still maximize your gross profit even further by increasing the production capacity of products *A*, *B*, and *D*, this analysis indicates that you and your new partner now need to expand your production facilities.

Debugging an Analysis

When you perform an analysis using the /Tools, Advanced Math, Optimization command, here are the most common reasons why Quattro Pro 3.0 returns an error message:

Caution! If you have entered your constraints, bounds, and an objective function that incorrectly model your problem, Quattro Pro may still be able to return a solution for the data you enter. Therefore, always check to make sure that the solution you get is reasonable for your particular problem.

- You mathematically expressed an analysis incorrectly, and Quattro Pro 3.0 can't calculate a solution. For example, you may have included conflicting constraints, constraints that conflict with bounds, or inequality relations that are inconsistent with your Extremum selection (Largest or Smallest), which maximizes or minimizes the analysis.

- You did not use the format required by the Optimization command when you entered your information in the spreadsheet.

- You specified an input incorrectly during the Optimization command operation, such as the size or location of a block.

Unfortunately, the Optimization command does not help you identify the type of error you have made. In fact, when you use this command, you may encounter a few obscure error messages. This makes it especially difficult to debug an optimization analysis. Table 11.6, which lists some of the reasons why certain error messages are displayed, has been accumulated from the authors' experience.

Table 11.6   **Error Messages Returned by /Tools, Advanced Math, Optimization**

Error Message	Reason
"Formula not linear"	A term in a formula constraint is not linear, such as A*B or D^2.
"Formulas are too complicated"	In a formula constraint, a term references or creates a circular reference.
	Optimization formula constraints depend on too many cells. Simplify optimization.
	Constant coefficient block larger than 90×254.
"Invalid cell or block address"	In a formula constraint, you entered variables as letters, rather than referencing cells in variable block.
"Invalid constraint coefficients"	Linear constraint coefficients block includes a blank cell, or is not specified.
	In a formula constraint, variables do not reference cells in variable block.
"Invalid constraint constants"	Constant coefficients block not specified or incorrectly specified. Must be one column and same number of rows as linear constraint coefficients block.
"Invalid constraint relations"	Inequality relations block incorrectly specified. Must be one column and same number of rows as linear constraint coefficients block.
"Invalid objective function"	Linear constraint coefficients block includes ERR, NA, a blank cell, or is incorrectly specified in relation to other blocks.
	Objective block includes ERR, NA, a blank cell, or is incorrectly specified. Must be one row and same number of columns as linear constraint coefficients block.
"Invalid output block"	No variable block specified.
	No solution cell specified.
"Invalid variable bounds"	Bounds block incorrectly specified. Must be two rows: first row lower bounds, second row upper bounds, with same number of columns as linear constraint coefficients block.

Table 11.6	**(Continued)**

Error Message	Reason
"Matrix is singular"	Bounds block includes ERR or NA.
	Inequality/equality relations block not specified.
"Overflow occurred"	Constant coefficients block includes a blank cell, ERR, or NA.
"Problem is infeasible"	Inequality relations block includes an incorrect inequality constraint which conflicts with other constraints.
	Blank cell in inequality relations block treated as equality constraint, which conflicts with other constraints.
	Inequality relations block includes other than simple logical operators (labels, numbers, or complex logical operators).
	No solution exists.
	Constraints are conflicting and no solution can be found.
	Constraints and bounds are conflicting and no solution can be found.
"Problem is unbounded"	No constraints or bounds limit optimal solution, so infinite solutions exist.
"Too many constraints"	Many more constraints listed than variables, so variables are "overdetermined" and optimization is not possible.
"Too many iterations"	Contact Borland if you get this message. Optimization command execution is terminated if Quattro Pro performs a very large number of iterations to solve a problem.
	Constraints do not limit optimal solution, so infinite solutions exist.

Limitations of the Optimization Command

Although /Tools, Advanced Math, Optimization is a powerful sensitivity analysis tool, you should be aware of its limitations.

- Quattro Pro 3.0 only returns one solution. Therefore, you cannot easily determine if it is a unique solution, or if it is the optimal solution chosen from multiple solutions. Furthermore, you cannot easily analyze the other solutions from which the program selected the optimal solution. This prevents you from gaining additional insight into your problem.

■ If the constraints, bounds, and objective function incorrectly model your problem, Quattro Pro 3.0 may still be able to return an optimal solution for the data you entered. Therefore, you must be able to determine if the solution returned by the program is a reasonable optimal solution for your particular analysis.

■ If you use any incorrect inequality constraints, Quattro Pro 3.0 may return the solution that minimizes your model, although you chose to maximize it. Conversely, the program may also return the solution that maximizes your problem when you want to minimize it. Here, also, you must be able to detect this error by analyzing Quattro Pro 3.0's solution.

■ It is difficult to debug an optimization analysis. See the previous section, "Debugging an Analysis," for further discussion.

TIP. *The new Optimizer in Quattro Pro 4.0 has addressed many of these limitations. See "Obtaining the Optimal Solution in Quattro Pro 4.0," later in this chapter.*

Obtaining the Optimal Solution in Quattro Pro 4.0

In Quattro Pro 4.0, the /Tools, Optimizer command allows you to perform what-if or sensitivity analysis for a problem with multiple variables and multiple solutions. Quattro Pro 4.0 then solves for the best or optimal solution.

If you're upgrading from Quattro Pro 2.0 or 3.0, you're going to find the Optimizer considerably different, and in some areas much improved. First, the Optimizer now uses nonlinear programming, so it's capable of solving more complex problems than before. Second, the way you define a problem is much easier and more logical. And finally, you can use the Optimizer to generate reports that can help you analyze the results returned.

However, you may also encounter significant problems in the new Optimizer. By far the most crucial one is the difficulty in determining whether the Optimizer did in fact return the optimal answer for a problem. Because of this, the following discussion concentrates on helping you define your model and Optimizer settings so that you do get a true optimal answer. A second problem, falling into the irritating category, is the amount of memory the Optimizer requires.

Memory Considerations and the Optimizer

The Optimizer is an EMS memory hog. For example, if you're running Quattro Pro 4.0 in DOS without any EMS memory, you might not be able to solve the small example we've used in the following sections. A good solution is to run Quattro Pro 4.0 under Windows in 386 Enhanced mode. However, you may still encounter memory limitations, such as not being able to show iteration results in your spreadsheet, unless you increase the EMS memory settings in Quattro Pro 4.0's PIF (program information file). You can usually make available up to 8 megabytes of EMS memory, provided, of course, that you have sufficient RAM. See Chapter 15 for more about running Quattro Pro 4.0 under Windows.

Defining the Problem

Tip. Quattro Pro 4.0 includes a sample Optimizer problem, OPTIMIZER.WQ1, located in the QPRO directory.

The Optimizer is simply a tool that efficiently performs what-if analysis on a particular problem or model. How well you set up your problem determines the quality of the results you'll get. You must define a problem so that it reflects the real-world situation you are modeling in a format compatible with the way in which the Optimizer performs its mathematical calculations.

Figure 11.30 shows a typical situation where the Optimizer can help perform sensitivity analysis. Here, the goal is to maximize Total Gross Profit in cell H11, given the company's cost and price structure. For example, the data in column B represents the per-unit data for Product A in column E. Only the 500,000 units in cell E3 is entered as a value; all other Product A values are calculated as a function of units and the per-unit values. For instance, the $20,000,000 Product A Sales in cell E4 is computed as the 40.0 unit sales price in cell B4 times the 500,000 units in cell E3. The totals in column H are summations of the Product A, B, and C values.

Figure 11.30

Setting up the model

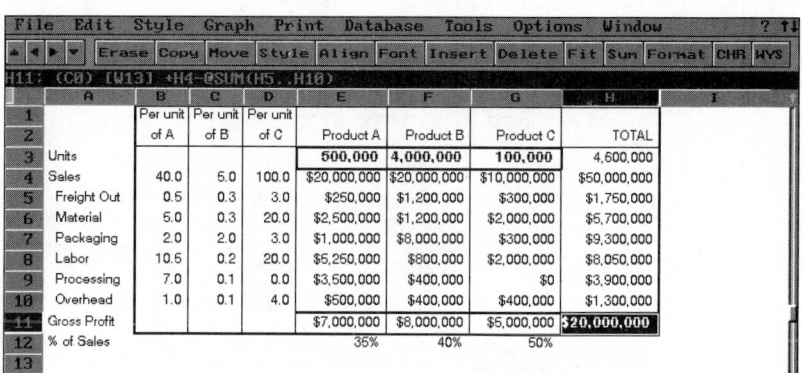

TIP. *Because many of Quattro Pro's functions, such as financial functions, are nonlinear, including a lot of them in a model increases the complexity of the problem. You should limit your use of them when possible. Not only can they increase the time it takes the Optimizer to solve the problem, but they can also contribute to a nonoptimal answer.*

To define this problem in a format compatible with the Optimizer, you'll need to assign:

- Variable cells—the variables that can be changed.

- An optional solution cell—the variable to be optimized.

- Constraints—logical formulas that reflect real-world limitations and limit the number of possible solutions.

Variable Cells

Note. To optimize a variable, make it the solution cell, discussed next.

Naturally, to perform what-if analysis, a model must contain variables that can be changed. In the Optimizer, each variable is designated as a *variable cell*.

In Figure 11.30, everything depends on the number of units for each product. In effect, units drive this model. For this reason, the Units values in E3, F3, and G3 are designated as variable cells in Figure 11.31.

Figure 11.31

Setting up the problem in Optimizer's format

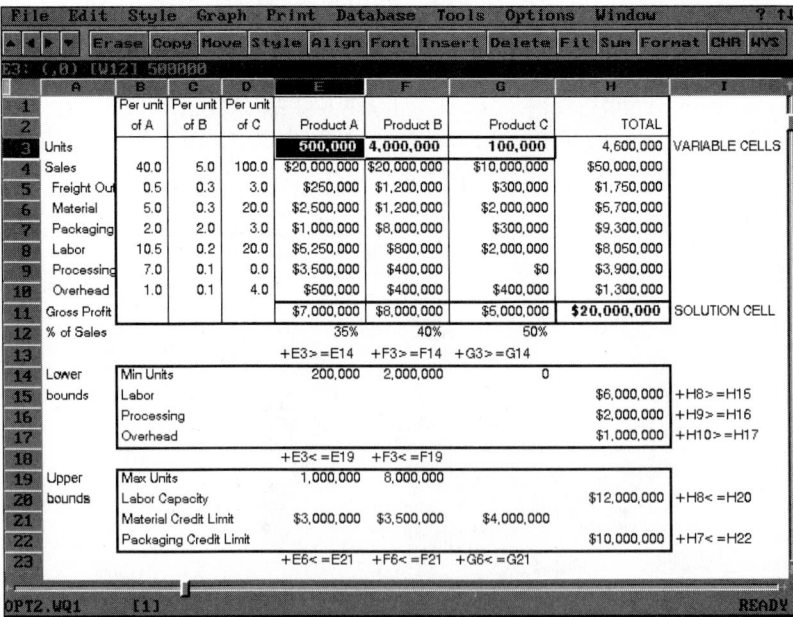

A variable cell, such as E3, should contain a value. When you use the Optimizer, it enters the results for each variable cell in that cell; if a variable cell contains a formula, it will be overwritten. Obviously, when you must use a formula to refer to other information, don't assign its location as a variable cell. Instead, designate the values the formula refers to as variable cells.

Because variable cells must be located in a contiguous block of cells, you may find that you have to adjust the layout of your model to be compatible with the Optimizer. (If the block includes blank cells, you'll see the error message "Inconsistent problem data set.") In Figure 11.31, the per-unit data would normally be next to the corresponding product information; for example, the per-unit data for Product A would be positioned next to the Product A information. In this case, the model had to be rearranged so that the variable cells were located in one contiguous block, E3..G3.

As a general rule, you should limit the number of variable cells to those that are really driving the model. Although you can specify up to 200 variable cells, a large number increases the number of possible solutions, which increases the time it takes the Optimizer to solve the problem and the likelihood that the Optimizer may return a suspect answer. Even more important, the amount of variable cells directly impacts the amount of EMS memory the Optimizer needs.

After you decide on the variable cells, you must set constraints on them. Besides limiting the range of values allowed in each variable cell to a real-world level, constraints also limit the number of possible solutions. (See "Constraints" later.)

Solution Cell

If you want, you can appoint one variable as the *solution cell*, which Quattro Pro 4.0 optimizes (maximizes or minimizes) over all other variables designated as variable cells. If you specify Total Gross Profit in cell H11 of Figure 11.31 as the solution cell, for instance, the Optimizer will try to optimize gross profit, given the other variables and constraints in the problem. A solution cell provides an additional benefit: It further limits the number of possible solutions and makes it easier for the Optimizer to solve the problem.

Note. A solution cell can contain a value if you also specify it as a variable cell.

A solution cell must contain a formula that directly or indirectly depends on at least one variable cell. The H11 solution cell in Figure 11.31, for instance, calculates Total Gross Profit as +H4–@SUM(H5..H10), which indirectly depends on each of the Units variable cells.

Constraints must be directly or indirectly imposed on a solution cell so that the Optimizer can solve the problem. In fact, out of all the constraints you specify, those limiting the solution cell ensure that there aren't infinite solutions. See "Constraints," next.

TIP. *One of the major reasons why you should include a solution cell is what happens if you don't. When you fail to specify a solution cell, the Optimizer doesn't have a single target to converge on. Instead, the Optimizer begins with the values in the variable cells, and then performs a number of repetitive iterations within the time specified, essentially meandering in any direction it chooses. (See "Evaluating the Optimizer's Answer," later.) Only the constraints you specify provide any direction to the solving process. The end result is that the answer may not be the optimal answer to the problem.*

Constraints

A *constraint* is a logical formula that limits the problem being solved. In the Optimizer, constraints are used to directly or indirectly impose boundaries on the variable cells and solution cell. You can specify up to 100 constraints.

Constraints are important for a variety of reasons. First, they allow you to limit the possible solutions to real-world ones. Second, well-designed, stringent constraints can steer the Optimizer in the right direction during the iterative solution process so that it does return the optimal solution. And finally, because constraints limit the number of possible solutions, they can decrease the time it takes for the Optimizer to solve the problem.

A constraint is a logical formula that usually takes this form:

Cell-Being-Constrained   Operator   Constraint-Value

For example, +E2<=20000 is a valid constraint that limits the value in cell E2 to less than or equal to 20,000. So is +E2<=Z100, when cell Z100 contains 20000. Valid operators are <=, = , and >=. The Optimizer doesn't support < and >. The complex logical operators #AND#, #OR#, and #NOT# aren't supported either, specify multiple constraints instead.

To limit the number of possible solutions, you must create constraints that directly or indirectly limit the variable and solution cells in the correct direction. If you are trying to maximize a variable, such as sales or profit, then you need an upper bound constraint (<=) limiting the maximum value. By contrast, if you're minimizing a variable, such as taxes, then you need a lower bound constraint (>=) limiting the minimum value. In some instances, a variable is fully bounded by both upper and lower bound constraints. The trick is to impose constraints that limit the possible solutions without *overdetermining* the problem—imposing so many constraints that you don't give the Optimizer enough room to maneuver.

NOTE. *The constraint formulas shown in Figure 11.31 are for discussion purposes only. You actually specify constraints in the /Tools, Optimizer command; you don't create the formulas in the spreadsheet. If you want, though, you can set up the constraint values in the spreadsheet, such as the constraint value 200,000 in cell E14. See "Specifying the Problem in the Optimizer," next.*

In Figure 11.31, for instance, gross profit will be maximized. To limit the possible solution set, then, *upper bound* constraints are needed. Here, upper bounds represent limitations restricting growth—credit limits at suppliers, for example. In row 23, the credit limit at the material supplier for Product A is portrayed by +E6<=E21, which limits Product A's material cost in E6 to $3,000,000. In column I, the upper bound constraint +H7<=H22 limits the Total Packaging cost in cell H7 to $10,000,000—the credit limit at the sole packaging supplier. All of these constraints indirectly limit the maximum Units values in the variable cells and therefore the maximum Gross Profit value in the solution cell.

Lower bound constraints are also used in Figure 11.31 to limit the possible solutions to a real-world level. In column I, three lower bounds represent minimum production levels to keep the plant running; +H8>=H15 says that minimum labor costs are $6,000,000; +H9>=H16 reflects the minimum $2,000,000 operating cost of keeping the continuous manufacturing process on-line; +H10>=H17 reflects the minimum $1,000,000 overhead level.

CAUTION! *Mistakenly using an incorrect logical operator in a constraint is one of the most common reasons why Optimizer may return an answer that appears to be incorrect.*

The variable cells E3 and F3—units of A and B—are *fully bounded* by the lower bound Min Units constraints and the upper bound Max Units constraints. In row 13, Product A's lower bound of +E3>=E14 represents a 200,000 unit contract; in row 18, its Max Units upper bound +E3<=E19 is a production capacity constraint limiting units produced to 1,000,000. Product B's lower bound of +F3>=F14 represents current backorders of 2,000,000 units; its capacity upper bound, +F3<=F19, constrains production to 8,000,000 units.

By including a lower bound constraint like +G3>=G14 in Figure 11.31, you can limit the possible solutions to real-world levels by prohibiting the Optimizer from returning unrealistic negative values. For example, +G3>=G14 limits units of Product C in cell G3 to at least 0.

Specifying the Problem in the Optimizer

Once you've correctly set up the problem in a format acceptable to the Optimizer, using the /Tools, Optimizer command is simply procedural. For example, here's how you specify the problem in Figure 11.31:

1. Select /Tools, Optimizer to access the dialog box shown in Figure 11.32.

2. Choose Solution Cell, and in the menu shown second from the front in Figure 11.33, specify cell H11. Then tell the Optimizer to maximize the Solution Cell by choosing Maximize. (Choose Minimize if you want to

minimize the Solution Cell.) The default None setting works like Equal, and would cause the Optimizer to ignore the Solution Cell.

Figure 11.32

Defining the problem in the /Tools, Optimizer format

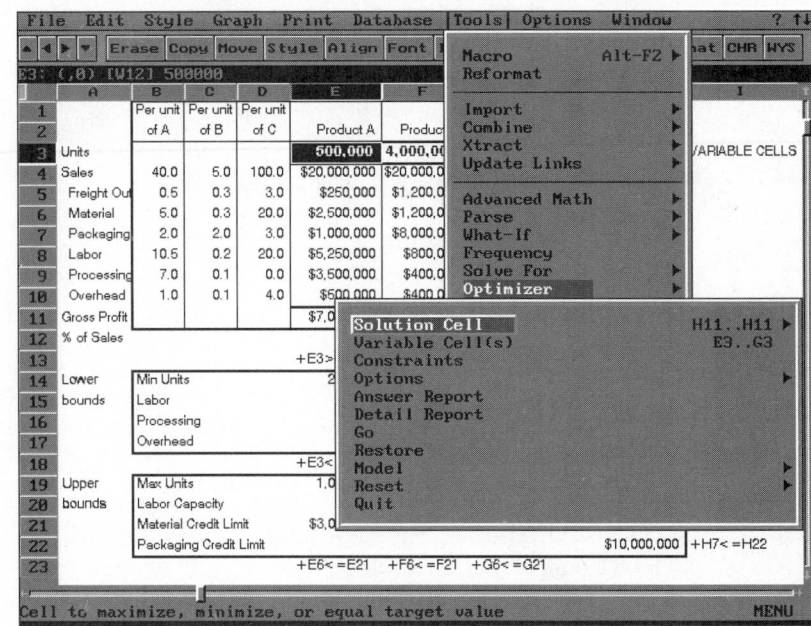

3. Specify the Variable Cells(s) block E3..G3.

4. To specify the bounds, select Constraints. You'll see a dialog box like the one in Figure 11.34. To add a constraint, such as the first one shown, E3>=E14, choose <Add New Constraint>. Specify the cell being constrained, E3. You'll see the menu in Figure 11.35 listing the acceptable operators: =, <=, and >=. Because this constraint is a lower bound, choose >=. You can specify the constraint value either as a value, 2000000 in this case, or as the cell address E14. Repeat this procedure so that all 13 constraints shown in Figure 11.31 are specified.

Note. If some constraints have the same operator and constraint value, you can specify them all at once as a block, as in D20..D23<=100.

NOTE. *To change a constraint, simply choose it in the Constraints menu, and then specify it as if it were a new constraint. To delete one or more constraints, see "Saving and Loading Optimizer Settings," later. To delete all constraints, see "Clearing Optimizer Settings," later.*

5. Select Go to have the Optimizer start trying to solve the problem.

Figure 11.33
Specifying Solution
Cell settings

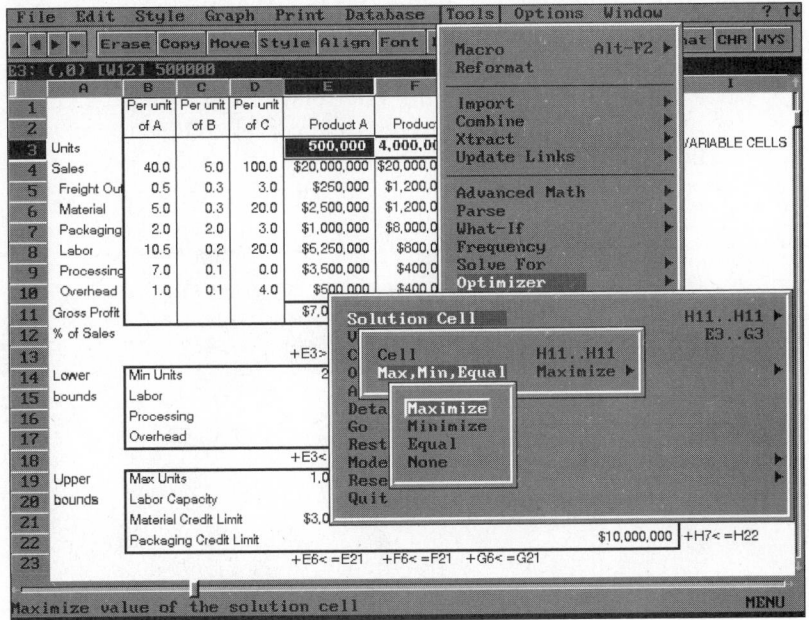

To stop the solution process at any time, press Ctrl-Break. To save your Optimizer settings so you can specify new ones, see "Saving and Loading Optimizer Settings," later.

How the Optimizer Solves a Problem

Note. See
"Changing How the
Optimizer Solves a
Problem," later in
this section, for
ways to change the
Optimizer's Options
settings.

Many of the /Tools, Optimizer, Options settings shown in Figure 11.36 control how the Optimizer tries to solve a problem. That is, it attempts within 100 seconds (Max Time) and/or up to 100 iterations (Max Iterations) to return an answer within 0.0005 places (Precision) using nonlinear programming (Linear or Nonlinear). Because Show Iterations Results is set to No, Quattro Pro 4.0 only returns the best or optimal answer, if it finds one.

TIP. *Creating a detail report is the best way to see the interim answers Quattro Pro 4.0 returns. See "Generating Reports," later.*

When the Optimizer Can't or Won't Solve a Problem

Typically, the Optimizer won't try to solve a problem when you haven't specified, or haven't properly specified, variable cells, at least one constraint, or at least one constraint that limits the solution cell. In fact, Quattro Pro 4.0, in a considerable improvement over Quattro Pro 3.0, now provides understandable messages that will help you if you haven't specified the minimum Optimizer requirements. For example, if you don't specify any constraints, you'll see "Solution cell or at least one constraint not selected." If you haven't directly or indirectly limited the solution cell in the proper direction—an upper bound constraint if you're maximizing, or a lower bound constraint if you're minimizing—you'll see "An unbounded solution cell."

Figure 11.34
Adding a constraint

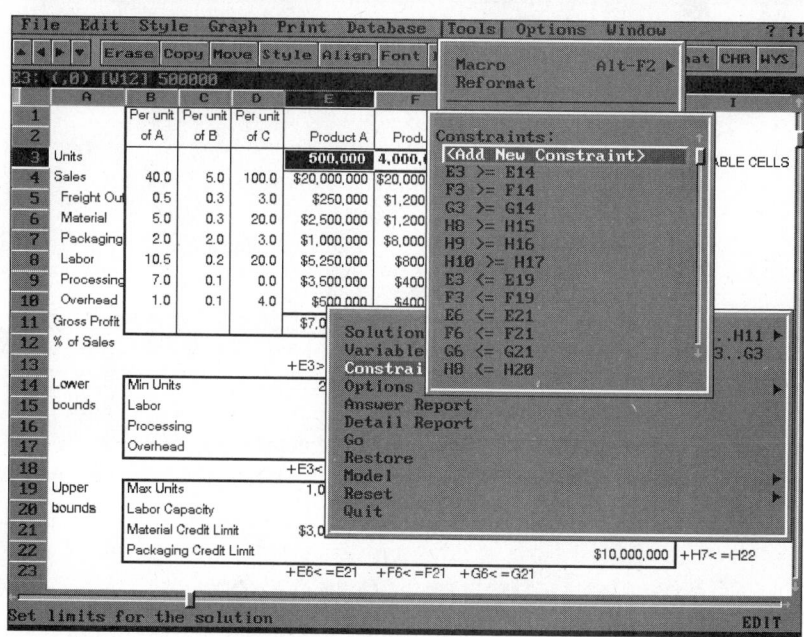

However, some of the error messages you'll see don't indicate the true problem. By far the most frustrating message is "Problem is infeasible," which covers a variety of ills. For instance, sometimes you'll see this message if you've specified conflicting constraints, or specified the wrong variable cells or solution cell. Another cause of this message is when the constraints don't sufficiently limit the problem. On the other hand, for these same problems, Quattro Pro 4.0 sometimes returns an answer instead.

For a complex or large problem, Quattro Pro may display an error message saying that there isn't enough memory for the Optimizer to complete an operation, such as the solving process. If this happens, try increasing the amount of EMS memory available to Quattro Pro. (See Chapter 15.) In fact, by running Quattro Pro 4.0 in 386 Enhanced mode Windows, you can have Windows automatically provide EMS for you.

Figure 11.35

Specifying the operator for a constraint

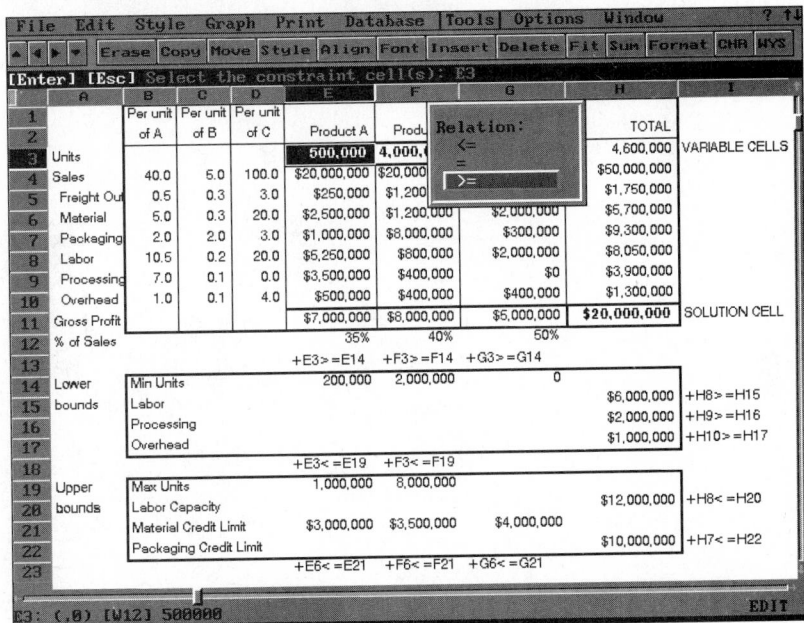

TIP. *Take the error message "Objective function changing too slowly" as a solid hint that Quattro Pro is having trouble solving the problem. Even if you modify the model or the Optimizer settings so that you do get an answer, be sure to check it. (Sometimes, changing the Options, Search setting to Conjugate helps.)*

When the Optimizer Returns an Answer

If the Optimizer can find a solution to the problem, the answer is returned in the spreadsheet. For example, Figure 11.37 shows the optimal answer Quattro Pro 4.0 returns. Here, Quattro Pro enters the variable cell values that maximize the solution cell value. For example, it enters 600,000 in cell E3; 4,100,000 in cell F3; and 200,000 in cell G3. Therefore, selling and producing 600,000 units of Product A, 4,100,000 units of Product B, and 200,000 units of Product C will optimize gross profit at $26,600,000 in cell H11, given the constraints. Quattro Pro 4.0 doesn't enter this solution cell value in the spreadsheet; because the solution cell uses a formula that indirectly refers to the variable cells, the optimal variable cell values produce this optimal gross profit value.

Figure 11.36

The /Tools, Optimizer, Options settings Quattro Pro 4.0 uses to solve a problem

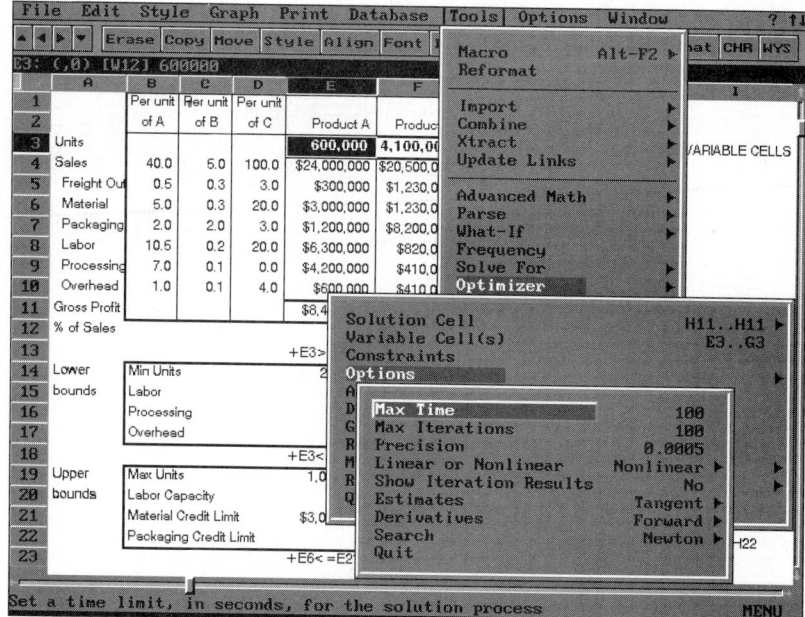

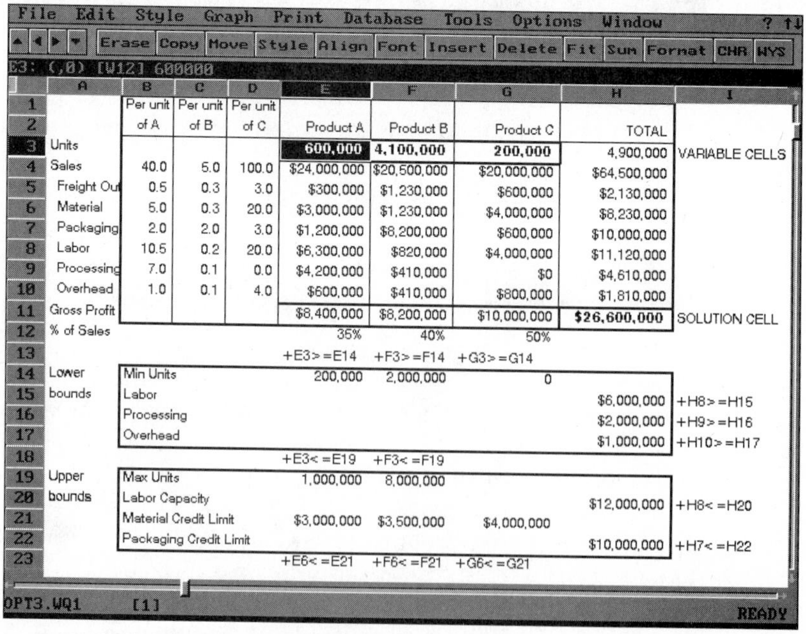

Figure 11.37

The optimal answer Quattro Pro 4.0 returns

If you don't want to save this answer in the spreadsheet, select Restore in the Optimizer menu. This restores the spreadsheet to the state it was in immediately before you selected Go. Be aware, however, that Quattro Pro 4.0 won't save the answer it found when you save the file, although it does remember your /Tools, Optimizer settings.

TIP. *To save both the answer returned and the original values, create an answer report. See "Generating Reports," later.*

Evaluating the Optimizer's Answer

Unfortunately, one of the most difficult things to determine is whether the answer returned by the Optimizer is in fact the optimal answer. Because of the "black box" nature of the Optimizer—it sends your Optimizer settings into the netherworld of EMS memory, and then spits out a result—you may rightly feel hesitant about relying on the answer returned. In our own quest to feel comfortable about the accuracy of the Optimizer, we spent quite a bit of time talking to Borland and FrontLine Systems (the developer of the Optimizer engine).

Here's the conclusion we reached. If you properly model and define a problem in the Optimizer, the answer you get is most likely the optimal answer. If you're a linear programmer with a sound understanding of the mathematical process Quattro Pro 4.0 uses, you should be able to assess the information returned by the Optimizer and achieve a comfort level you're happy with. But if you're a general business user, even with a strong mathematical bent, you're probably going to have some lingering doubts about whether you should rely on the Optimizer's result. All we can suggest is that you define your problem, especially the constraints, so that you can perform enough what-if scenarios to decide for yourself what you think the optimal answer should be.

The best way to determine whether Quattro Pro 4.0 returned a valid optimal answer is to examine the answer in relation to

- The underlying assumptions driving the model

- The way Quattro Pro solved the problem as seen through answer and detail reports (see the next section)

For example, the strongest argument for the answer in Figure 11.37 comes from looking at the model. If there were no limiting constraints, only units of Product C, with a 50% return on sales, should be produced. But because the constraint imposed by the supplier (G6<=G21) limits Product C material to $4,000,000, other products are produced. Nevertheless, it's obvious that the Optimizer tried to maximize gross profit. The answer and detail reports can also provide additional insights.

Generating Reports

The Optimizer in Quattro Pro 4.0 allows you to create two types of reports: an answer report and a detail report. An *answer report* provides information about the results you receive—for example, what constraints are limiting the optimal answer. A *detail report* summarizes how Quattro Pro 4.0 arrived at its answer by showing the interim results at each iteration.

Note. Some of the empty rows in the answer and detail reports in Figures 11.38 and 11.39 have been deleted, and the headings realigned.

You need to create an answer or detail report at the same time the Optimizer solves a problem. For example, to generate an answer report, choose this selection in the Optimizer menu shown in Figure 11.32, and then specify the upper-left cell where you want the table to begin. Figure 11.38, for instance, shows the answer report, beginning in cell A25, created for the problem in Figure 11.31 and the answer in Figure 11.37. Figure 11.39 shows a detail report for this problem, beginning in cell A58. Note that Quattro Pro automatically adjusts column widths to display the values in an answer or detail report.

Figure 11.38

An answer report for the problem in Figure 11.31 and the answer in Figure 11.37

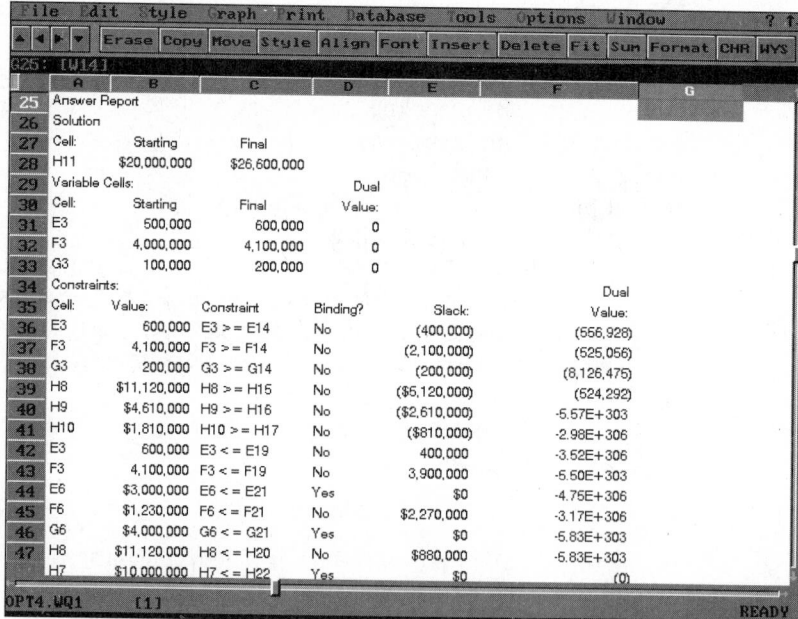

Evaluating an Answer Report

The answer report in Figure 11.38 indicates that the answer in Figure 11.37 is probably an optimal answer. As you can see, it's reasonable that three of the constraints are *binding*, or limiting the optimal solution. The first binding constraint, E6<=E21, is the credit limit imposed by the supplier for the material used to produce Product A. The Value, $3,000,000, indicates that the answer hits the limit imposed by this constraint. (You can also see in Figure 11.37 that cell E6 contains $3,000,000.) Likewise, the second binding constraint, G6<=G21, represents the credit limit of $4,000,000 imposed by the supplier for the material used to produce Product C. The third binding constraint, H7<=H22, represents the $10,000,000 credit limit at the packaging supplier.

Figure 11.39

A detail report for the problem in Figure 11.31 and the answer in Figure 11.37

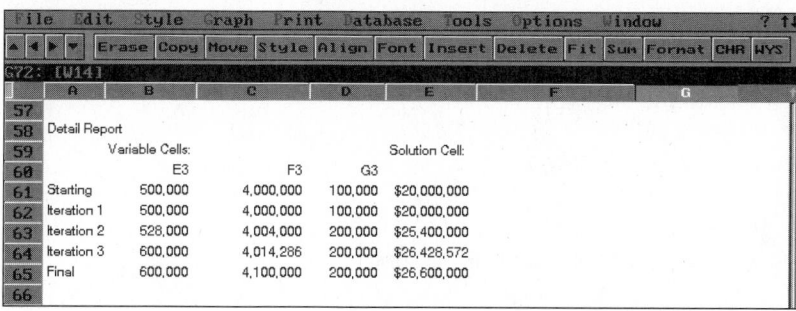

In an answer report, the Slack and Dual Value amounts provide additional sensitivity analysis information. If a constraint isn't binding, the Slack represents the amount you can change that constraint and not change the answer, when all else in the problem remains the same. For example, the first constraint in Figure 11.38, E3>=E14, limits Product A units to at least 200,000. Because this results in a 600,000 Value, the (400,000) Slack says that you can increase this constraint by 400,000 units and not change the answer. As an alternative, you can decrease Product A units by 400,000 before this particular constraint becomes a limiting factor. Likewise, the 400,000 slack in the constraint E3<=E19 (limiting Product A units to 1,000,000 units) says that you can decrease this constraint by 400,000 units and not change the answer, or increase the answer by 400,000 units before the constraint becomes a consideration.

For a constraint, the Dual Value (also known as the Lagrange Multiplier) represents the amount the solution cell will change if you relax the constraint by one unit—increase an upper bound constraint by one or decrease a lower bound constraint by one. For a variable cell, the Dual Value (also known as the reduced gradient) represents how a one-unit change in the variable cell answer will change the solution cell answer. A positive Dual Value indicates the amount the solution cell answer will increase; a negative Dual Value indicates the amount the solution cell answer will decrease.

For example, when you maximize a solution cell, a positive Dual Value indicates that the variable is equal to its upper bound, and represents how much the optimal answer in the solution cell will increase if you increase the limit on this variable cell by one unit. A negative Dual Value means that the variable is equal to its lower bound, and represents how much the optimal answer will decrease if you increase the variable limit by one unit. (You can see examples by looking ahead to Figure 11.41.) A 0 Dual Value indicates that changing a bound for that variable will have no effect on the solution cell answer.

CAUTION! *At the time this book was written, it appears that the Dual Values Quattro Pro returns are inconsistent and probably shouldn't be relied on. Sometimes you may get different Dual Values for the same problem. Other times, you may get Dual Values that are definitely suspect. In Figure 11.38 for instance, the majority of the constraint dual values represent negative infinity. At other times, 0 and positive infinity values were returned instead.*

Evaluating a Detail Report

At first glance, the detail report in Figure 11.39, which shows each iteration Quattro Pro performed, appears to provide insights about how Quattro Pro reached its answer. Although to a linear programmer it may provide valuable information, to a general business user, the information in this report can be misleading. If you're a general business user, a detail report generates just enough information to raise doubts about the answer returned and add uncertainty to the decision-making process.

Here's a simplistic explanation of how the Optimizer performs the calculations represented in a detail report. At the beginning of each iteration, Quattro Pro creates initial estimates or starting points (first-order derivatives) that are used as the basis for the calculation performed during that iteration. These estimates, however, aren't based solely on the last iteration, but are based on all the information the Optimizer has gathered in all the prior iterations. For example, the direction during iteration 4 may be the result of information generated during iterations 1, 2 and 3. What this means is that you can't take a logical, step-by-step approach to the detail report and determine whether the Optimizer headed in the right direction.

In Figure 11.39, for instance, taking a step-by-step analysis of the iterations can raise doubts about the answer returned. Here, the second iteration seems reasonable because units of C, which has the highest gross profit margin (50%), are maximized until the material constraint G6<=G21 is reached. The third iteration primarily concentrates on Product A; its maximum units are reached in the fourth and final iteration. But because Product A has the lowest gross profit margin, 35%, you might find it worrisome that it was optimized over Product B. This worry might be reinforced by the fact that the

Optimizer is also concentrating on minimizing packaging costs—the packaging constraint starts becoming a limiting factor during this iteration—since both Product A and Product B use $2 worth of packaging per unit. What *isn't* apparent is that Quattro Pro used decisions during iteration 1, not just iteration 2, to make the "logical leap" in iteration 3.

The point here is that, for the general business user, a detail report normally doesn't provide any useful information. In fact, evaluated incorrectly, a detail report can lead to incorrect conclusions concerning the validity of an answer.

Changing How the Optimizer Solves a Problem

The Options choices shown in Figure 11.40 provide a way to customize the way in which the Optimizer tries to solve a problem. They also provide alternative methods to try when the Optimizer can't solve a problem, or is having a difficult time of it.

Note. The default Options settings are discussed in "How the Optimizer Solves a Problem," earlier.

Max Time and Max Iterations
The Max Time and Max Iteration settings specify a limit on how long the Optimizer will spend trying to solve a problem. The default is 100 seconds or 100 iterations, whichever is reached first. You can specify up to 1000 seconds and 1000 iterations.

The length of the solving process depends primarily on the number of variable cells and constraints, the nonlinearity of a problem, and the complexity of a problem. Obviously, if you see the error messages "Maximum time exceeded" or "Maximum iterations reached," try changing these settings.

Precision
The Precision setting, 0.0005 by default, controls the accuracy level at which Quattro Pro tries to return an answer. You can specify a value from 0 to 1. When you see the error message "Objective function changing too slowly" or "Problem is infeasible," increasing the precision may make it easier for Quattro Pro to solve the problem. The tradeoff, however, is that the accuracy of the result will decrease.

Linear or Nonlinear
By default, the Optimizer uses nonlinear programming to solve a problem. How Quattro Pro tries to find an answer when NonLinear is specified is controlled by the Estimates, Derivatives, and Search settings, discussed later.

Usually, you'll want to keep this option set to Nonlinear, although changing to Linear can decrease the solving time if a problem is linear. If you specify Linear when the problem isn't, you'll see the error message "Linear model is not a valid assumption." If your model incorporates Quattro Pro functions, remember that many of them, such as the financial functions, are nonlinear.

Figure 11.40

The Optimizer's Option settings

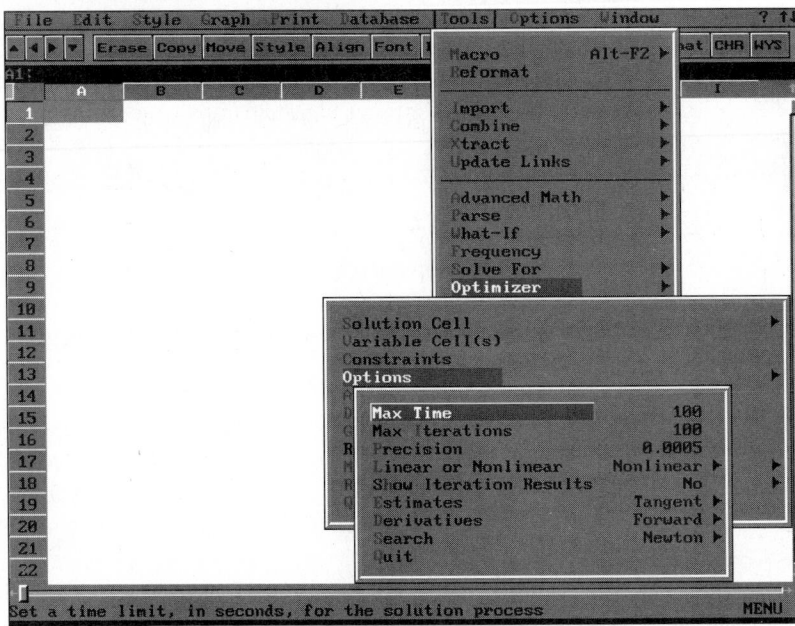

Figure 11.40

The Optimizer's Option settings

Show Iteration Results

The Show Iteration Results default, No, specifies that only the final answer is returned in the spreadsheet. Specify Yes to have Quattro Pro show the result after each iteration. (Press Esc to resume the solving process; press Ctrl-Break to abort.) Another way to see the answer at each iteration is to create a detail report. (See "Generating Reports," earlier.)

TIP. *Many times when you specify Yes, you'll see the error message "Not enough memory to show iteration results." If this happens to you, try increasing the amount of EMS memory available to Quattro Pro. (See Chapter 15.) In fact, when running Quattro Pro 4.0 under Windows in 386 Enhanced mode, Windows will automatically provide EMS provided you've increased the EMS memory setting in Quatro Pro 4.0's PIF file.*

Estimates

The Estimates setting controls the method Quattro Pro uses to obtain the initial variable values (estimates) it uses during each iteration. The default, Tangent, specifies linear extrapolation from a tangent vector. Consider using

Quadratic, which specifies quadratic extrapolation, for a highly nonlinear problem—one containing many nonlinear functions, for instance.

Derivatives

The Derivatives setting controls the differencing method Quattro Pro uses for its estimates of partial derivatives. The default is Forward. Because Central differencing uses more iterations, specifying this setting may help when you get the error message "All remedies failed to find a better point."

Search

The Search setting controls the search method Quattro Pro uses during the iteration process. The default, Newton, is actually a quasi-Newton method usually faster than the other choice, Conjugate. Try Conjugate when you're not sure that Quattro Pro returned the true optimal answer, or when you see the message "Objective function changing too slowly."

Clearing Optimizer Settings

One of the nice features of the Optimizer in Quattro Pro 4.0 is that it lets you clear all or just some of the settings you specified. Here's what the options in the Reset menu shown in Figure 11.41 do:

- *Solution Cell* clears the cell reference and sets the optimization to None.

- *Variable Cell(s)* clears the variable cell block.

- *Constraints* clears all of the constraints specified. (To clear just one constraint, see "Saving and Loading Optimizer settings," next.)

- *Options* resets all Options settings to the defaults shown in Figure 11.36.

- *Answer Report* clears the upper-left cell reference of the answer report location so that an answer report isn't created.

- *Detail Report* clears the upper-left cell reference of the detail report location so that a detail report isn't created.

- *All* clears all cell reference settings and constraints, and returns the Options settings to the defaults.

Saving and Loading Optimizer Settings

Rather than clearing all the /Tools, Optimizer settings when you want to modify or change a problem, you can use the Optimizer's Model option to save the settings in the spreadsheet and then reload them later. For instance, for the model in Figure 11.31, Figure 11.42 shows how the Optimizer settings are entered into the spreadsheet when you choose Model Save and specify J1 as the upper-left cell of the destination. (Don't be concerned that the @COUNT function is incorporated into the left side of each constraint.) These settings are retained in the Optimizer until you select Reset All.

Figure 11.41

Clearing some or all of the Optimizer settings

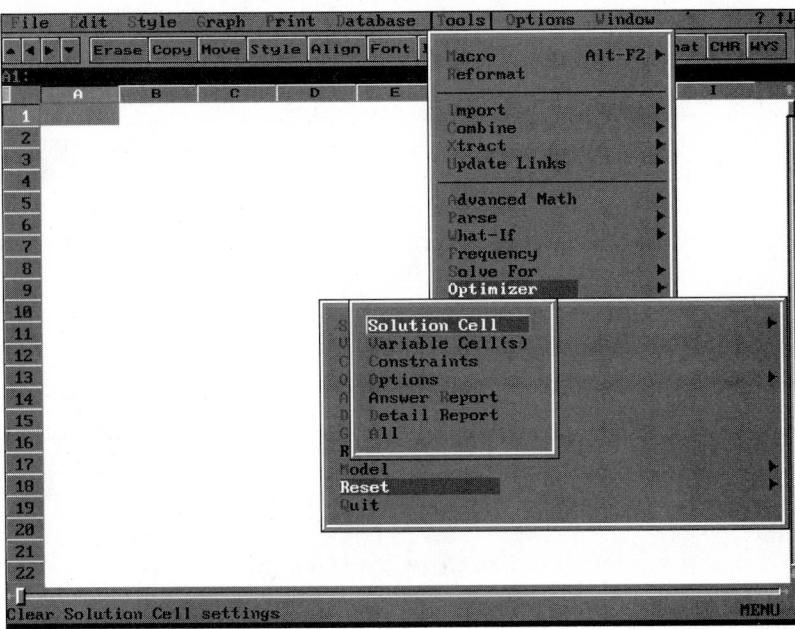

To reuse the settings from Figure 11.42 in the Optimizer, use Model Load, and then specify the entire block J1..L18. Another alternative is to name this block (see Chapter 1), and then refer to it by name.

TIP. *You can use the Model option to delete one or two constraints from a problem. First, use Model Save to display the Optimizer settings in the spreadsheet. Next, delete the constraints you don't want, and then adjust the block so there aren't any blank rows. When you use Model Load and specify the entire block, Quattro Pro will insert the revised settings into the Optimizer.*

Auditing Your Spreadsheets in Quattro Pro 4.0

Since version 2.0, Quattro Pro has offered the /Window, Options, Map View command, which gives you something akin to an aerial view of your spreadsheet, with each cell appearing one character wide and showing the type of data that resides there (see Chapter 2). Although this feature is helpful for getting an overall picture of your spreadsheet, it isn't sufficient alone to be a meaningful auditing tool.

Figure 11.42

Saving Optimizer settings in a spreadsheet

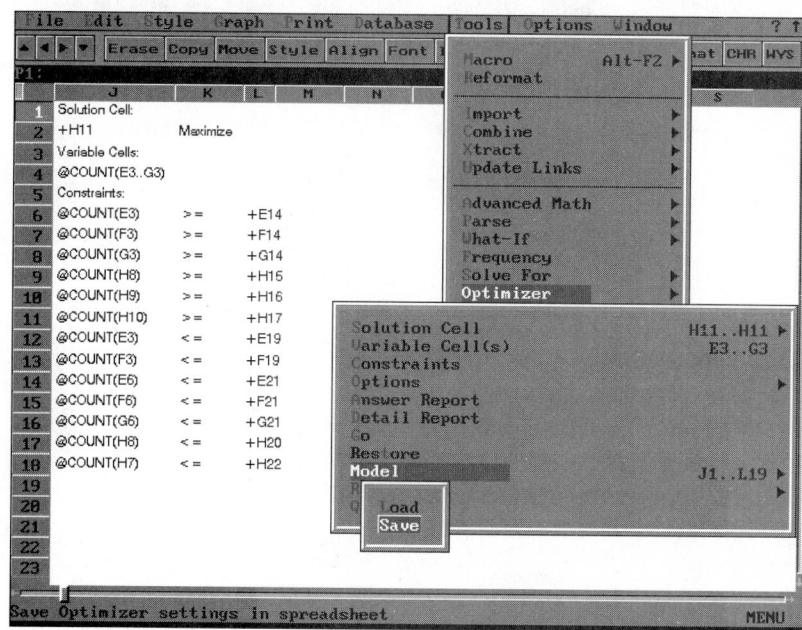

In version 4.0, Borland has beefed up Quattro Pro's spreadsheet auditing capabilities by adding a full suite of troubleshooting features, all available from the /Tools, Audit menu. Here are some of the types of auditing you can perform with these new features:

- Checking cell dependencies by viewing a tree diagram.

- Finding and eliminating circular references.

- Finding formulas that refer to blank cells or label references.

- Finding cells that return ERR.

- Examining formulas that contain external links.

The sections that follow describe each of these auditing capabilities in more detail.

Checking Cell Dependencies

With the /Tools, Audit, Dependency command, you can see a tree diagram of the relationships in your spreadsheet. This can be helpful when you want to determine the effect that changing the value in one cell will have on other related cells. An easy way to get a feel for how this command works is to open the file SAMPLE.WQ1, found in the Quattro Pro directory. Figure 11.43 shows a view of this file with all its important formulas enumerated.

Figure 11.43
The formulas used in SAMPLE.WQ1

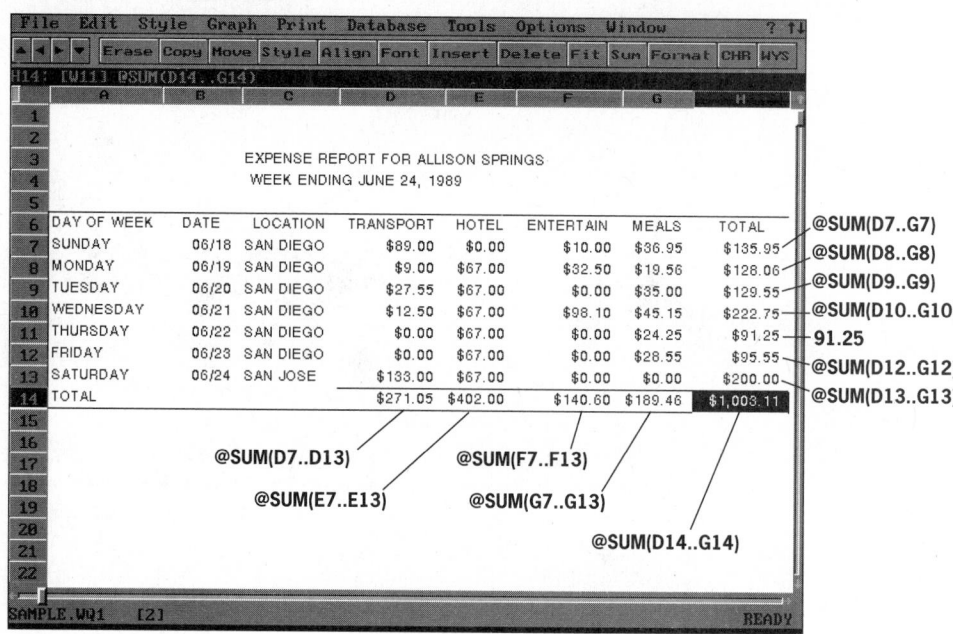

To audit this spreadsheet, select /Tools, Audit, Dependency and specify the block D7..H14. Figure 11.44 shows the dependency screen that appears. Here's a breakdown of the screen elements:

■ The *audit status line* tells you how many cells are in the audit block ("Number of references found") and the number of the reference currently displayed ("Current reference"), which in the current example is 1.

■ The *input line* shows the address of the cell that is being audited, cell D7 in this example.

■ Below the input line are the worksheet *filename* (in this case, SAMPLE) and *cell address* (again, cell D7).

Figure 11.44

The dependency screen for SAMPLE.WQ1

Audit status line

Input line

Filename and audited cell address

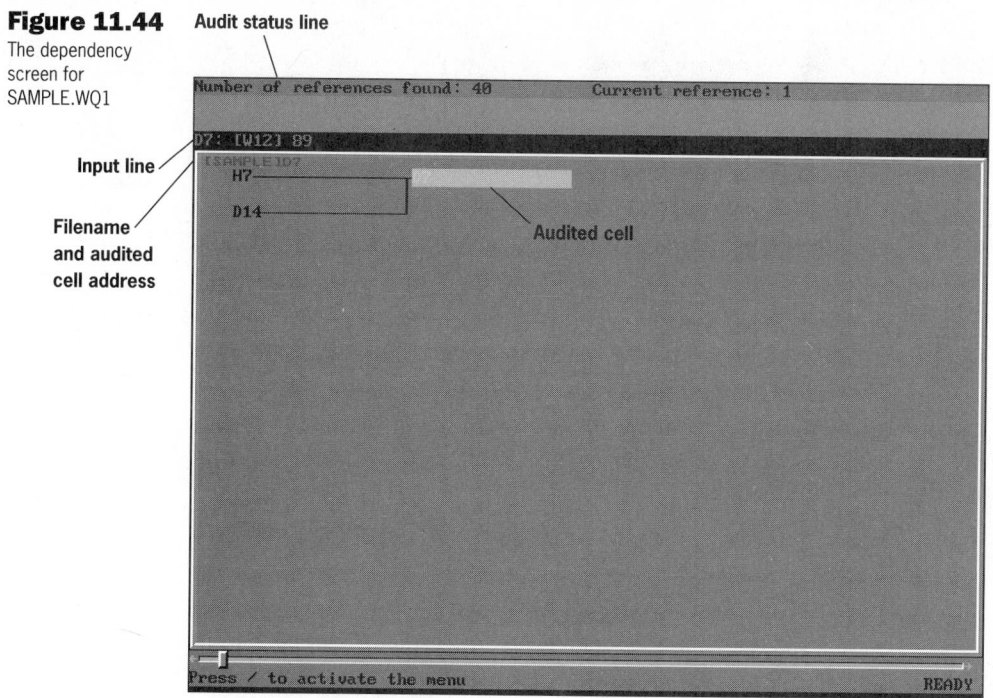

Audited cell

- The *audited cell* always appears near the center of the screen. Cells to the left of center are dependent on the audited cell for their values (cells H7 and D14 in the current example); cells to the right of center (none in the current example) are those that the audited cell depends on for its value.

When you activate the dependency screen, the first cell in the selected block is the focus of attention. You can navigate around the tree to see the relationships of other cells in the block. For example, if you press ← to move the highlight to H7 and select the /Begin command (or its shortcut, Enter), that cell becomes the audited cell, as shown in Figure 11.45. You can use the arrow keys and the /Begin command to view the relationships of any cell in the selected block. Here are some other helpful commands and keys:

- */Next (or PgDn)*   Shows the relationships of the next cell in the selected block.

- */Previous (or PgUp)*   Shows the relationships of the previous cell in the selected block.

Figure 11.45

After moving to
another cell and
pressing Enter

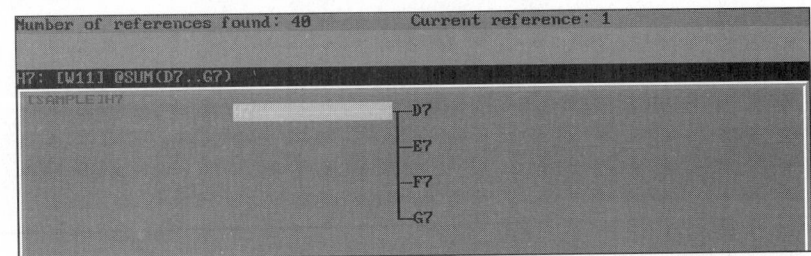

- *■ /GoTo (or F5)*   Lets you jump to the selected cell in the spreadsheet. (The dependency screen disappears.)

- *■ /Quit*   Returns you to the Audit menu.

To leave the dependency screen and return to the spreadsheet, press Ctrl-Break.

Eliminating Circular References

When a cell formula references itself, usually by way of other cell formulas, you have a circular reference. When a circular reference is unintentional, as they usually are, the results can be quite detrimental to your spreadsheet. Even with the help of Quattro Pro's /Options, Recalculation command, which shows you one cell involved in the circular reference, eliminating the circular logic can be quite difficult, especially when you're dealing with a complex spreadsheet.

With Quattro Pro 4.0's new /Tools, Audit, Circular command, you can now see all the cells that are involved in a circular reference, making the job of eliminating any circular logic significantly easier. The screen that appears when you select this command is similar to the dependency screen just discussed, and all the same keys and menu commands apply. For example, Figure 11.46 shows a circular reference screen for the simple case where cells A1 and B1 refer to one another. Notice that a CIRC appears at the end of the branch, indicating that a circular reference exists between the two cells.

Figure 11.46

The circular
reference screen

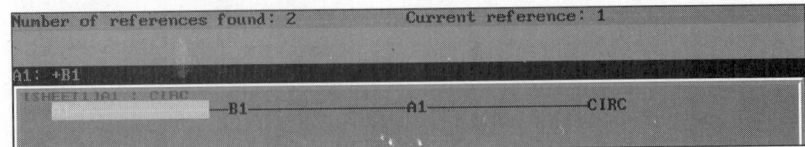

Finding Blank Cells and Label References

Two of the most common reasons for incorrect spreadsheet results are

- Having "hard" numbers where formulas belong, preventing the spreadsheet from recalculating properly when values changed.

- Referencing labels or blank cells unintentionally. Because labels and blank cells are treated as zero values, calculations that involve these cells often produce incorrect results.

To diagnose the first problem, you can use the /Tools, Audit, Dependency command discussed earlier (see "Checking Cell Dependencies"). To diagnose the second, Quattro Pro 4.0's new /Tools, Audit, Label References and Blank References commands are most useful. As an example, Figure 11.47 shows the screen that appears when you use the Label References command. Although it's difficult to tell from the "Label In" reference, the problem cell in this example is C11; it contains a label where a number belongs. As this example shows, when the problem cell is part of a block reference, you'll need to do some further investigating on your own to find it.

Figure 11.47
The label reference screen

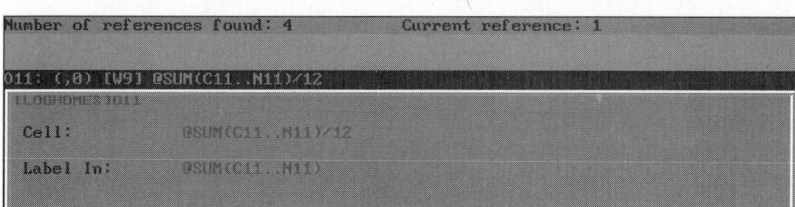

If you look at the status line at the top of the figure, you'll see that there are actually four label references in this spreadsheet. By using the /Next (PgDn) and /Previous (PgUp) commands, you can cycle through these references and diagnose the problem cells.

Finding Cells that Return ERR

When a formula returns ERR, any cells that reference it also return ERR. In this way, ERR values can quickly proliferate throughout your spreadsheet. If this should happen to you, an easy way to find the source of the original ERR value is to use Quattro Pro 4.0's new /Tools, Audit, ERR command. The ERR screen behaves like the label references screen, including all commands and keystrokes for navigating between references.

One problem with the ERR screen is that it does not let you navigate all the way back to the original source of the ERR value. It does, however, show you the next cell that is dependent on that value, allowing you to move the problem cell on your own.

Examining External Links

When a spreadsheet contains external links and you rename or delete files that are named by those links, errors can arise. If you suspect that your link references have become invalid, or if you just want to inspect them, you can use Quattro Pro 4.0's /Tools, Audit, External Links command. The External Links screen behaves like the label references screen in all respects.

12

Creating Macros

MACROS LET YOU SAVE KEYSTROKES AND COMMANDS AND THEN have Quattro Pro "play" them back automatically. Simple macros take the form of actual keystrokes stored as labels in the spreadsheet. For instance, when you run the macro represented by the label /fs, it "presses" the / (slash) key, which invokes the main menu. Next, it presses the F key, invoking the File menu. Finally, it presses the S key, invoking the Save command and saving the spreadsheet.

Macros are a useful and powerful feature of Quattro Pro, because they perform tedious and repetitive spreadsheet tasks for you automatically. Moreover, many spreadsheet tasks benefit from the speed and accuracy gained through the automation that macros provide. Although *you* might forget a critical step in preparing a complex printed report, with a macro you know the same commands will be executed every time—at computer speed, rather than your typing speed.

Quattro Pro's comprehensive macro facility includes these features:

- *Macro libraries*   Normally, a macro can only be executed in the spreadsheet in which it is defined. By placing a macro in a macro library, however, any open spreadsheet can execute it. With this feature you can develop a suite of commonly used macros and give all of your spreadsheets access to them.

- *Macro Debugger*   This powerful tool allows you to execute a macro one command at a time, while you watch.

- *Macro command list*   The Macros key (Shift-F3) gives you a complete list of Quattro Pro's macro commands. You can enter macro commands from this list and, in conjunction with the Help system (F1), determine the syntax for any particular macro command.

- *Menu-equivalent commands*   These are easy-to-read alternatives to keystroke macros. You can run them independent of the menu tree.

In this chapter, you'll learn about creating and running macros, how to record a macro, and the best way to debug macros. The next chapter will explore Quattro Pro's special macro programming commands. You can use these commands to prompt the user for input, display messages, create custom menus, and read and write external files. By the time you've mastered these concepts and commands, you'll have all the tools you need to build dedicated spreadsheet applications.

Creating a Simple Macro: An Example

One of the easiest ways to learn about Quattro Pro's macro facility is to create a simple macro. The example you'll see here automatically enters the days of the week in a spreadsheet; it reduces to a single step the 56 key-strokes required for this task. This macro saves you time because you can enter the data in the spreadsheet more quickly, and also more accurately. The macro inserts the labels Monday, Tuesday, and so on through Sunday in seven consecutive cells, starting at the current cell selector position.

Building the Macro

Macros are entered in the spreadsheet as labels in consecutive columnar cells. In this example, the macro starts in cell B3, but you can place a macro anywhere in the spreadsheet. (For hints on the best location for your macros, see "Placing Macros in Your Spreadsheet" later in this chapter.)

Enter the following labels exactly as shown in the spreadsheet of Figure 12.1. Type them in just as you would any label.

Figure 12.1

A simple macro that enters the days of the week in a column

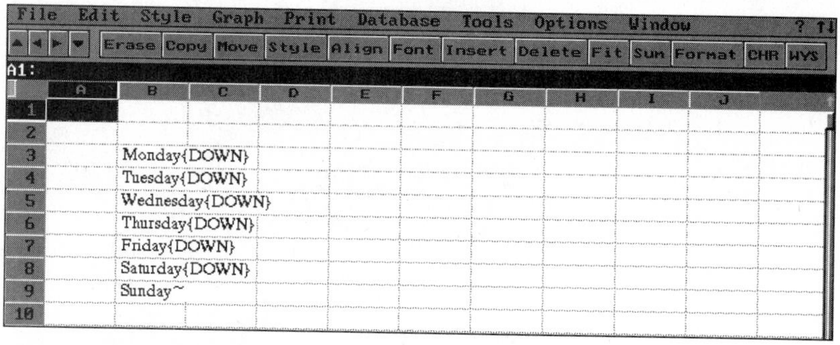

Cell	Label
B3	Monday{DOWN}
B4	Tuesday{DOWN}
B5	Wednesday{DOWN}
B5	Thursday{DOWN}
B6	Friday{DOWN}
B7	Saturday{DOWN}
B8	Sunday~

Naming the Macro

Now that you have entered the macro labels, you want to name the macro so that you can invoke the macro instructions contained in the labels with a single keystroke combination. If you name the first cell of the block that contains the macro instructions (cell B3) with a backslash-letter combination, for example, \A, Quattro Pro will execute the macro whenever you press the Alt key together with the letter (in this case, Alt-A). This type of macro is called an *instant macro.*

To name the macro,

1. Select the /Edit, Names, Create command.

2. When Quattro Pro prompts you for the name of the macro, type **\A** and press Enter.

3. When prompted for the block location, type **B3** and press Enter.

Running the Macro

Before starting the macro, make sure that no spreadsheet data will be overwritten by the labels when they are entered by the macro. Position the cell selector at cell E1, and press Alt-A to invoke the macro. The MACRO indicator appears on the status line for a brief second, and the labels are entered in E1..E7. Your spreadsheet now looks like Figure 12.2.

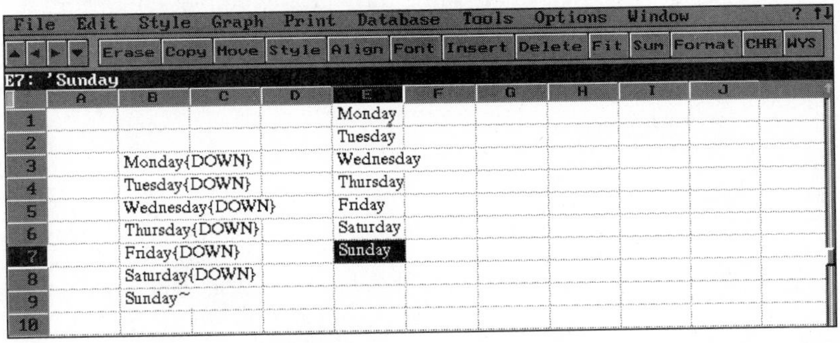

Figure 12.2

The spreadsheet after executing the \A macro

How the Macro Works

Here is what actually happens when you press Alt-A to start the macro. Quattro Pro searches the spreadsheet for the block named \A. When it finds the block, it starts interpreting the labels in the block a character at a time, starting in the first cell of the block—in this case, cell B3. (If Quattro Pro cannot find the named block, it beeps.)

Each character that Quattro Pro encounters in the macro is interpreted as a keystroke you've pressed. For instance, when Quattro Pro encounters the *M* in the word Monday, it places an M on the edit line—just as if you had pressed *M* yourself. The same thing happens for the *o*, *n*, and all the remaining characters in Monday. Quattro Pro interprets all alphanumeric characters this way, except those delimited (surrounded) by the { and } characters. When Quattro Pro sees these, it expects a special macro command. In our example, {DOWN} is such a command. It tells Quattro Pro to end the current cell entry and move the cell selector down one cell.

When Quattro Pro reaches the end of each label, it moves down to the next cell and begins interpreting and executing the characters in that cell's label. In the current example, it repeats this process in B4, B5, and so on, down to B9.

In cell B9, the ~ (tilde) character after Sunday is another special macro command. It tells Quattro Pro to press the Enter key.

Quattro Pro stops macro execution when it reaches a blank cell (or a cell containing a value). In this example, because cell B10 is blank, macro execution stops, and the MACRO indicator disappears from the status line.

Tip. You also can create simple keystroke macros, such as the one in Figure 12.1, by using the Macro Record mode described later in this chapter.

Macro Basics

Now that you know how to create and run a simple macro, you'll need to learn some macro fundamentals—for example, the different ways to build macros, macro syntax, how to enter macros in a spreadsheet, and how to represent special keys. You'll also learn how to name, document, run, and save macros.

Macro Syntax

Quattro Pro macro commands can be created in three ways, with

- *Keystroke instructions* that mimic your own keypresses—the simplest form of macro instruction

- *Menu-equivalent commands*, one of which is associated with each menu action

- *Special macro commands* that control the program flow of macros, keyboard input, screen appearance, user interaction, data entry into spreadsheet cells, and the reading and writing of external files

Macro keystroke instructions and menu-equivalent commands are described in this section. Special macro commands are covered in Chapter 13.

Macro Keystroke Instructions

You can use two types of keystroke instructions in Quattro Pro macros.

- Single-character keypresses, such as /, F, and S.

- Keyboard commands that represent nonalphanumeric keystrokes, such as function keys, cursor movement keys, and editing keys. Examples are {GOTO}, {UP}, and {CLEAR}. Table 12.1 lists these keyboard commands.

Press the Macros key (Shift-F3), and Quattro Pro lists all of its macro commands. The Macros key not only lists macro commands, but also provides an easy (and error-free) way to enter macro commands into your spreadsheets. To enter a command from the list, simply press Shift-F3, navigate among the menus to get to the category of commands you want, highlight the macro command name, and press Enter. Quattro Pro enters the macro command on the edit line. Press Enter again, and you can enter the command into the spreadsheet at the current cell selector location.

At any time while the macro command list is present, you can also press Help (F1) to see the syntax for a particular macro command.

Keys That Cannot Be Represented in Macros

Although Quattro Pro gives you a macro representation for almost every keystroke, there are two keys that do not have macro commands associated with them: Print Screen (PrtSc) and Shift. A macro command for PrtSc is unnecessary, because spreadsheet printing is conventionally done through Quattro Pro's Print commands. As for Shift, you can include this keypress in a macro by toggling Caps Lock on and off, using the {CAPON} and {CAPOFF} commands (see Table 12.1).

Keystroke Abbreviations

As shown in Table 12.1, Quattro Pro includes abbreviated forms of the cursor movement and editing keys. For example, {U} is the equivalent of {UP}. Experienced macro writers appreciate this feature, because it reduces the number of keystrokes necessary to write a macro.

Table 12.1   Keyboard Commands in Macros

Category	Quattro Pro Key	Macro Instruction
Cursor Movement		
←		{LEFT} or {L}
→		{RIGHT} or {R}
↑		{UP} or {U}
↓		{DOWN} or {D}
Ctrl-←		{BIGLEFT}
Tab		{TAB}
Ctrl-→		{BIGRIGHT}
Shift-Tab		{BACKTAB}
Home		{HOME}
End		{END}
PgUp		{PGUP}
PgDn		{PGDN}
Function Keys		
Edit	F2	{EDIT}
Name	F3	{NAME}
ABS	F4	{ABS}
GoTo	F5	{GOTO}
Window	F6	{WINDOW}
Query	F7	{QUERY}
Table	F8	{TABLE}
Calc	F9	{CALC}
Graph	F10	{GRAPH}
Debug	Shift-F2	{DEBUG}
Macros	Shift-F3	{MACROS}
Choose	Shift-F5	{CHOOSE}
NextWin	Shift-F6	{NEXTWIN}
* Mark	Shift-F7	{MARK}
† Move	Shift-F8	{MOVE}
† Copy	Shift-F9	{COPY}
† Paste	Shift-F10	{PASTE}
† PdxGo	Ctrl-F10	{PDXGO}
Functions	Alt-F3	{FUNCTIONS}
Undo	Alt-F5	{UNDO}
Zoom	Alt-F6	{ZOOM}
† MarkAll	Alt-F7	{MARKALL}

Table 12.1 **(Continued)**

Category	Quattro Pro Key	Macro Instruction
Window Keys		
Choose	(Alt-0)	{CHOOSE}
Window1	(Alt-1)	{WINDOW1}
Window2	(Alt-2)	{WINDOW2}
Window3	(Alt-3)	{WINDOW3}
Window4	(Alt-4)	{WINDOW4}
Window5	(Alt-5)	{WINDOW5}
Window6	(Alt-6)	{WINDOW6}
Window7	(Alt-7)	{WINDOW7}
Window8	(Alt-8)	{WINDOW8}
Window9	(Alt-9)	{WINDOW9}
Editing Keys		
Backspace		{BACKSPACE} or {BS}
Del		{DELETE} or {DEL}
Ctrl-\		{DELEOL}
Ctrl-Backspace		{CLEAR}
Insert		{INS} or {INSERT}
Others		
Caps Lock Off		{CAPOFF}
Caps Lock On		{CAPON}
Insert Off		{INSOFF}
Insert On		{INSON}
Num Lock Off		{NUMOFF}
Num Lock On		{NUMON}
Scroll Lock Off		{SCROLLOFF}
Scroll Lock On		{SCROLLON}
Ctrl-D		{DATE}
Esc		{ESC}
Ctrl-Break		{BREAK}
~ (tilde)		{~} or {CR}
{ (open brace)		{{}
} (close brace)		}
/		{MENU}

* Invokes Extend Block mode in spreadsheet; marks current file in File Manager.

† Used exclusively in File Manager

‡ Switches from Paradox to Quattro Pro (in Paradox Access)

Repeating Keystrokes

Often, you will want to repeat a keystroke command in a macro. For instance, the following commands move the cell selector down three cells:

{DOWN}{DOWN}{DOWN}

These three commands can be represented more efficiently as

{DOWN 3}

Here the macro command is followed by a space and the number of times the command is to be repeated (the *repetition argument*). This convenient technique speeds up the writing and modification of macros. All macro keystroke commands can accept repetition arguments.

You can also use cell references and formulas to represent the number of times a macro command is to be repeated. For instance, if you have the value 3 in a cell named NUMBER, the command {UP NUMBER} will move the cell selector up three cells from its current position. The macros {UP NUMBER/2}, {UP SALES}, and {UP +B11} are other examples of entering a macro with a repetition argument.

Menu-Equivalent Commands

Note. All menu equivalent commands require a space following the "{/". If you omit this space, Quattro Pro won't execute the command.

As you know, every menu command in Quattro Pro effects some sort of action. Choosing the /File, Save command, for instance, saves the current file. Each menu item also has a *menu-equivalent command* associated with it. For example, the menu-equivalent command associated with /File, Save is {/ File; SaveNow}. If you wish, you can use these menu-equivalent commands in place of keystroke commands in your macros. For example, the macro commands /fsr (/File, Save, Replace) can be replaced with the menu-equivalent commands {/ File;SaveNow}r.

There are advantages to using menu-equivalent rather than keystroke commands. First, menu-equivalent commands are much easier to read. Compare the two functionally equivalent macros, \A and \B, in Figure 12.3. Clearly, it's much easier to see that the \B macro opens Quattro Pro's File Manager.

The second advantage is that macro keystroke instructions are dependent on the menu tree for which they are written, but menu-equivalent commands are not. For example, the \A macro in Figure 12.3 executes /File, Utilities, File Manager with the QUATTRO menu tree (QUATTRO.MU). However, if the Q1 menu tree (Q1.MU) is loaded, the \A macro will bring up the /File, Update Links menu. (You can change the menu tree using the /Options, Startup, Menu Tree command.) If you use a customized menu tree (customized with the Menu Builder), the results of the \A macro are unpredictable. On the other hand, the \B macro in Figure 12.3 will always open a File Manager window, regardless of which menu tree is loaded.

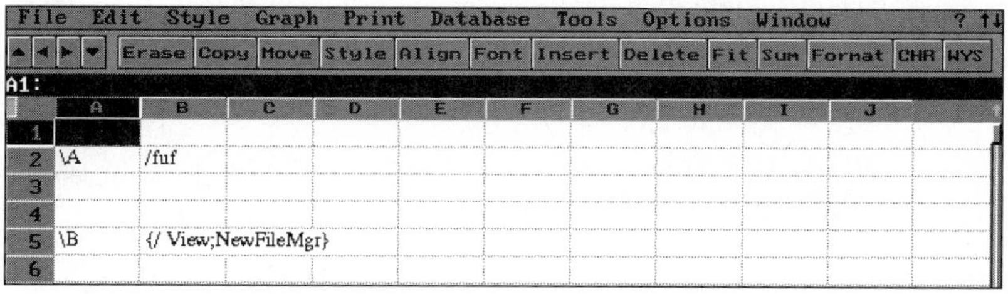

Figure 12.3

Comparing a keystroke macro and a menu-equivalent command macro

File	Edit	Style	Graph	Print	Database	Tools	Options	Window	? ↑↓

| ▲ ◄ ► ▼ | Erase | Copy | Move | Style | Align | Font | Insert | Delete | Fit | Sum | Format | CHR | WYS |

A1:

	A	B	C	D	E	F	G	H	I	J
1										
2	\A	/fuf								
3										
4										
5	\B	{/ View;NewFileMgr}								
6										

You will find a list of the menu-equivalent commands in the back of the Quattro Pro *@Functions and Macros* booklet.

Using Capitalization in Macro Commands

Quattro Pro accepts macro commands (and menu-equivalent commands) written in any combination of upper- and lowercase letters. For example, the macro commands {BEEP} and {beep} are equivalent, as are /faWEST~r and /FAwest~R. Nevertheless, you may want to use the following guidelines to make your macros easier to read:

- Use all uppercase for macro commands in braces, as in {BEEP}.

- Use all uppercase for block names, as in WEST.

- Use all lowercase for keystroke instructions, as in /fsr.

- Use mixed case for menu-equivalent commands, as in {/ GraphPrint; DestIsPreview}.

These suggestions are only guidelines, and your own style of writing macros may be different. What is important is that you are consistent with whatever style you choose.

Using Label Prefixes in Macros

When Quattro Pro interprets macros, it ignores the label prefix character that it adds automatically to the beginning of every label as you enter it into the spreadsheet. When a macro is played back, only the keystrokes you entered are played back—not the extra character added by Quattro Pro.

The way that Quattro Pro ignores label prefixes comes in handy when you want your macro to enter values. For example, the macro '34000 will be entered as the value 34000; the label prefix character is ignored. There are, however, two cases where you want Quattro Pro to enter a label prefix character: when you're entering numbers as labels, and when you're specifying the alignment of data being entered. In these two cases, you must enter the prefix character explicitly into your macro.

Take another look at the macro in Figure 12.1, and suppose you want to center-align each day of the week as it is entered. To make this happen, the caret label prefix character (^) must occur between each default label prefix and the rest of the label. For example, you need to change the label 'Monday to '^Monday. Figure 12.4 shows the sample macro edited to enter each label centered. When you press Alt-A to run this edited macro, your spreadsheet will look like Figure 12.5.

Figure 12.4

The macro from Figure 12.1 modified to center-align the days of the week in the cells

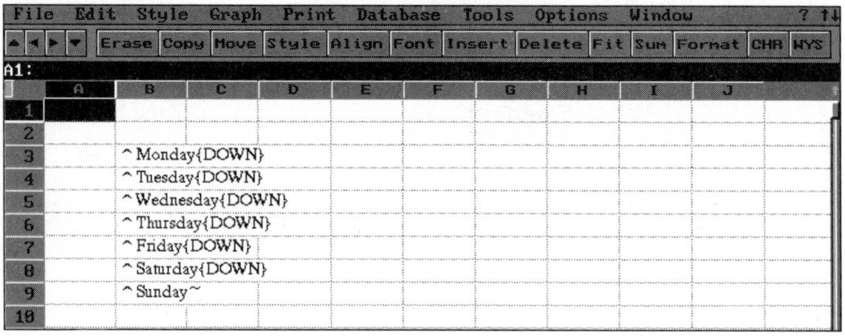

Figure 12.5

Results of the macro in Figure 12.4

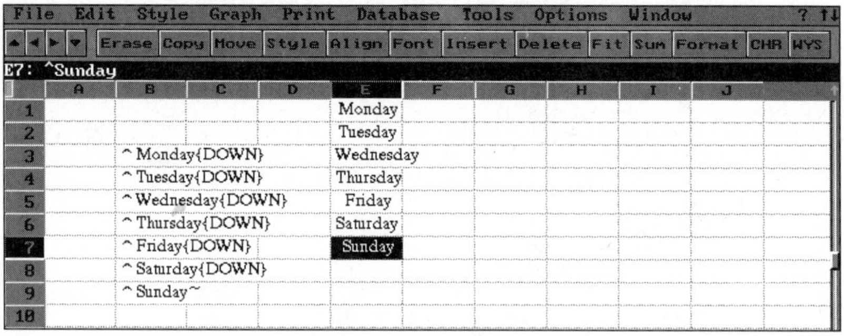

As you know, when entering numbers like addresses or telephone numbers as labels in a spreadsheet, you must precede the number with a label prefix character. Otherwise, Quattro Pro mistakenly assumes you are entering a number. Your macros must therefore include *two* label prefix characters, because Quattro Pro ignores the first one. For instance, to enter the label 1800 Green Hills Road in a macro, you would type

```
''1800 Green Hills Road
```

When you run this macro, the first label prefix character is ignored, and the left-alignment prefix character (') is entered on the edit line, followed by the remainder of the label.

Building Efficient Macros

When you built the macro in Figure 12.1, you entered a day of the week into each cell, followed by a keystroke macro command. You might have built the macro with fewer commands per cell, as shown in Figure 12.6.

Figure 12.6

The macro from Figure 12.1 rewritten with one command per cell

File	Edit	Style	Graph	Print	Database	Tools	Options	Window	? ↑↓

| ▲ ◄ ► ▼ | Erase | Copy | Move | Style | Align | Font | Insert | Delete | Fit | Sum | Format | CHR | WYS |

A1:

	A	B	C	D	E	F	G	H	I	J
1										
2										
3		Monday								
4		{DOWN}								
5		Tuesday								
6		{DOWN}								
7		Wednesday								
8		{DOWN}								
9		Thursday								
10		{DOWN}								
11		Friday								
12		{DOWN}								
13		Saturday								
14		{DOWN}								
15		Sunday								
16		~								
17										

Although the macro in Figure 12.6 is easier to read and functionally identical to the one in Figure 12.1, it takes up more space and memory. Additionally, you may not be able to view all of this macro within one screen, should you decide to add to it. For readability, it helps to keep macros within one screen—but this isn't always possible.

When writing macros, try to balance the efficient use of screen space against readability. In Figure 12.7, for example, space is efficiently used, but the macro is difficult to read. (This macro is also functionally the same as the one in Figure 12.1.) In fact, you can combine macro commands within one cell up to the maximum allowable string length—254 characters. Though this does conserve spreadsheet cells (and memory), it also makes the macro difficult to read. In addition, consider that this rewrite would make editing the macro more difficult, due to the extra cursor movement required to reach a particular section of the macro.

Figure 12.7

The macro from
Figure 12.1
rewritten with many
commands per cell

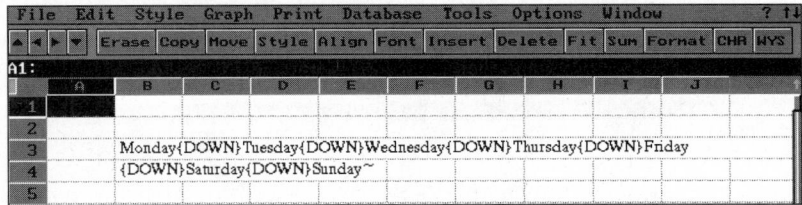

Of all the versions of the example macro, then, the one in Figure 12.1 is
built with the best balance between space and readability.

Placing Macros in Your Spreadsheet

The location of your macros is important to ensure the integrity of both your
data and your macros. You will want to place your macros so that when you
edit them, the added or deleted rows do not interfere with data in other
areas of the spreadsheet. By the same token, you don't want your editing of
the spreadsheet data areas to affect your macros. For example, if you delete
a column or row in a projection, you don't want to lose any macro instructions that exist in the projection spreadsheet.

Since many macros you write will be specific to a particular spreadsheet,
it will make sense to store those with the spreadsheet. However, when macros can be used by several spreadsheets, consider storing them in a *macro library*. (See "Designating Macro Libraries" in this chapter.)

The location of your macros in the spreadsheet will depend on what
your macro does. In most cases, you can place your macros one or two
screens below the active portion of the spreadsheet. That way, pressing
Home gets you to the active portion of the spreadsheet, and pressing PgDn
gets you to the macros area. This lets you easily edit both your macros and
the data area, without interfering with either area.

Bear in mind that this guideline for macro placement does not work if
your macro appends information to a list that is in the active portion of the
spreadsheet, as shown in Figure 12.8. In this case, it's better to place your
macros one screen to the right of the active portion of the spreadsheet. Thus,
pressing Home gets you to the data area, and pressing Tab gets you to the
macros area. The disadvantage to this placement is that you cannot insert or
delete rows in the macro area without disturbing the data in the active portion of the spreadsheet.

Tip. The cleanest
way to separate
your macros from
your data is to
place them in a
macro library. See
"Designating Macro
Libraries" for
details.

Figure 12.8

Spreadsheet with macros placed to right of active data area

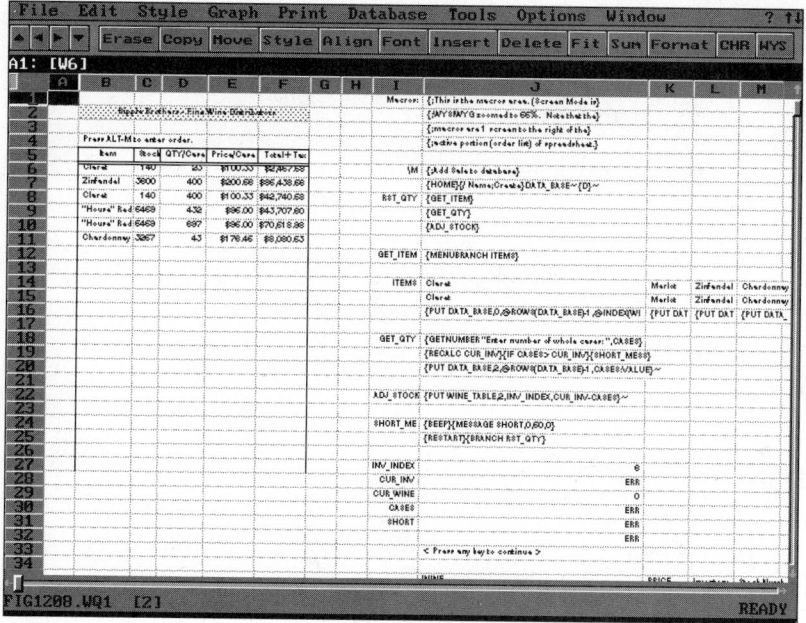

The safest area for your macros is to the right *and* below the active portion of the spreadsheet. By starting the macro section at cell AA4000, for example, you can be fairly confident that your macros and data will not interfere with one another. Unfortunately, this approach does make your macros harder to find. To get around this inconvenience, you can use the /Edit, Names, Create command to give cell AA4000 the name MACROS. Then, to easily find your macros, you can press GoTo (F5), then Name (F3), select MACROS from the list, and press Enter.

Naming Macros

You should name your macros for two reasons. First, as mentioned in the earlier days-of-the-week example, by naming an instant macro with a backslash and an alpha character (\A), you can invoke the macro easily using the Alt key in combination with the alpha character macro name. In Figure 12.9, you can invoke the \A macro that begins in cell B1 by pressing Alt-A. By the way, when you give a macro an instant macro name, it's a good idea to use a letter that reminds you of the macro's purpose. For instance, a macro that formats a date in a cell might be named \D.

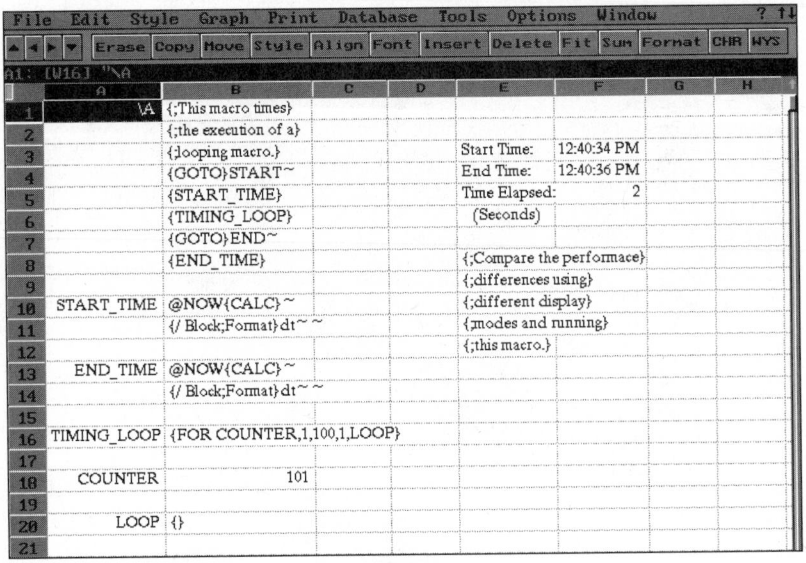

Figure 12.9

An instant macro
(\A) that uses
subroutines

	A	B	C	D	E	F	G	H
		A1: [W16] '\A						
1	\A	{;This macro times}						
2		{;the execution of a}						
3		{;looping macro.}			Start Time:	12:40:34 PM		
4		{GOTO}START~			End Time:	12:40:36 PM		
5		{START_TIME}			Time Elapsed:	2		
6		{TIMING_LOOP}			(Seconds)			
7		{GOTO}END~						
8		{END_TIME}			{;Compare the performace}			
9					{;differences using}			
10	START_TIME	@NOW{CALC}~			{;different display}			
11		{/ Block;Format}dt~ ~			{;modes and running}			
12					{;this macro.}			
13	END_TIME	@NOW{CALC}~						
14		{/ Block;Format}dt~ ~						
15								
16	TIMING_LOOP	{FOR COUNTER,1,100,1,LOOP}						
17								
18	COUNTER	101						
19								
20	LOOP	{}						
21								

The second reason to name macros is so that you can invoke them from within other macros. A macro invoked by another macro is known as a *subroutine*. If you want a macro to invoke a subroutine, you must name the subroutine and refer to that name in the main macro. Figure 12.9 shows that the macro \A uses the subroutines START_TIME, END_TIME, TIMING_LOOP, and LOOP. (See Chapter 13 for more on subroutines.)

As with block names, macro names allow you to associate an easy-to-remember, descriptive phrase with each macro. These names also allow you to easily locate your macros using GoTo (F5) and Name (F3), and to run the macros using the /Tools, Macro, Execute command. See the next section, "Starting a Macro," for details on using this command.

To name a macro, use the /Edit, Names, Create command, just as you would to name a block. (You can also use the equivalent /Tools, Macro, Name, Create command.) Macro names can be either upper- or lowercase. For example, to name a macro TOTAL,

1. Move the cell selector to the first cell of the macro.

2. Select the /Edit, Names, Create command.

3. Type **TOTAL** and press Enter.

4. Press Enter again to confirm the address.

It's easier to distinguish block names from macro names when you begin every macro name with a unique identifier, such as an exclamation point (!) or an M_ character sequence. This way, all your macro names will be grouped together when you use the /Tools, Macro, Execute command–or Macros (Alt-F2) Execute—and then press Name (F3) to select from a list of macro names. Likewise, they will also be grouped when you press GoTo (F5) and Name (F3).

Be careful not to use cell addresses (such as A1 or E2..F9) or macro commands (such as BEEP and LOOK) for macro names. Although you can successfully assign these names, Quattro Pro doesn't handle them properly. It ignores macros named with cell addresses, and overrides the reserved definition for a macro command with your macro.

Using /Edit, Names, Labels, Right to Name Macros

An easy way to name a macro and, at the same time, keep track of its name is to place the name to the left of the macro's starting cell, and use the /Edit, Names, Labels, Right command.

Suppose you want to assign the name START_TIME to the macro that begins in cell B10 of Figure 12.9. To do this, you would place the label START_TIME in cell A10, as shown. Next, with the cell selector still in A10, you would choose /Edit, Names, Labels, Right and press Enter.

Starting a Macro

Quattro Pro's macro facility lets you invoke a macro stored in your spreadsheet by using any of these seven techniques:

- An Alt-key combination

- An Execute command

- A startup macro

- Graph buttons

- A DOS command line entry

- The mouse palette

- A spreadsheet menu

Instant Macros

You have already learned that instant macros are those named with a backslash and an alpha character. Instant macros have the advantage of being the easiest to start—you need only press the Alt key in combination with the alpha character.

The Execute Command

Another way to invoke a macro is by using /Tools, Macro, Execute or Macros (Alt-F2) Execute, and then entering either the macro name, or the cell address where you want execution to begin. For example, you can invoke the \A macro in Figure 12.9 in any of the following ways:

- Select /Tools, Macro, Execute, type **\A** (the macro name), and press Enter.

- Select /Tools, Macro, Execute, press Name (F3), highlight **\A** in the list, and press Enter.

- Select /Tools, Macro, Execute, type **B1** (the macro address), and press Enter.

NOTE. *If you use the macro address, the macro does not have to be named in order to be executed. What's more, you can start macro execution anywhere, not necessarily in the first cell of a macro. This feature has significant benefits when you are debugging macros (details are in the section "Debugging Macros").*

Startup Macros

A macro can be automatically invoked when the spreadsheet containing it is retrieved. This is called a *startup macro*. Every time you retrieve a spreadsheet, Quattro Pro searches it for the macro you have specified as the startup macro. (To specify the startup macro, you use the /Options, Startup, Startup Macro command, as shown in Figure 12.10.)

The default startup macro name is \0, but you can use any macro name you like. If Quattro Pro finds this macro, it automatically executes it.

If you do name the startup macro using \0, be aware that you cannot re-execute this macro using the Alt-0 key sequence, because that sequence is assigned as a shortcut for the /Window, Pane command. You can, however, run the startup macro again by assigning it another name, such as \A, and then pressing the associated Alt-key sequence. Of course, to avoid the trouble of assigning another startup macro name, just use /Tools, Macro, Execute to re-execute it.

To make sure that the startup macro runs without interruption, always begin it with the {ESC} command. This cancels the Spreadsheet Link prompt if the spreadsheet is linked to another. You can then use the /Tools, Update Links, Load Supporting or Refresh command in your startup macro to bring the spreadsheet up to date before proceeding.

Graph Buttons

One of Quattro Pro's most exciting new features is that it lets you attach macros to graph buttons. A *graph button* is a special text box that you add to a

graph using the Annotator (see Chapter 9). These techniques are discussed in "Using Graph Buttons to Start Macros" later in this chapter.

Figure 12.10

Designating a startup macro with /Options, Startup, Startup Macro

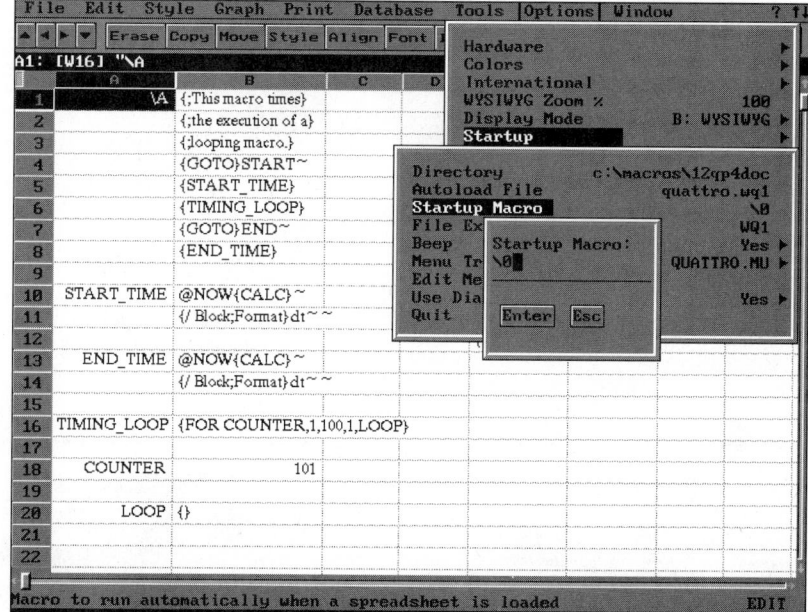

Starting Macros from DOS

Another way to automatically execute a macro when you start up Quattro Pro is by entering the macro's name as a DOS command line argument with the Quattro Pro startup command. For example, the following command entered at the DOS prompt starts Quattro Pro, loads the spreadsheet with the file name APRIL, and runs the macro named \A:

```
Q APRIL \A
```

SpeedBar Buttons in Quattro Pro 4.0

If you're using a mouse with Quattro Pro 4.0, you undoubtedly are already acquainted with the SpeedBar at the top of your screen. All the SpeedBar buttons except the arrow buttons can be customized to execute any macro or spreadsheet command (see Figure 12.11). You can also assign up to ten letters of text to each of these buttons in WYSIWYG mode and up to three letters in Character mode.

Figure 12.11

Quattro Pro 4.0's customizable SpeedBar buttons

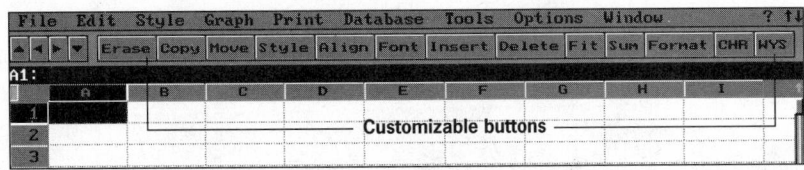

To attach a macro command to a Ready mode SpeedBar button, you use the /Options, SpeedBar, READY mode SpeedBar command and select from the options A Button through O Button, as illustrated in Figure 12.12. You then use the Macro option to enter the name of the related macro, subroutine, or menu-equivalent command. In the example in Figure 12.12, the C button has the menu-equivalent commands {BREAK}{/ Block;Move} associated with it. Thus you can move data by clicking the mouse on the C button, the third button to the right of the arrow buttons.

Figure 12.12

Assigning a macro to a customizable SpeedBar button

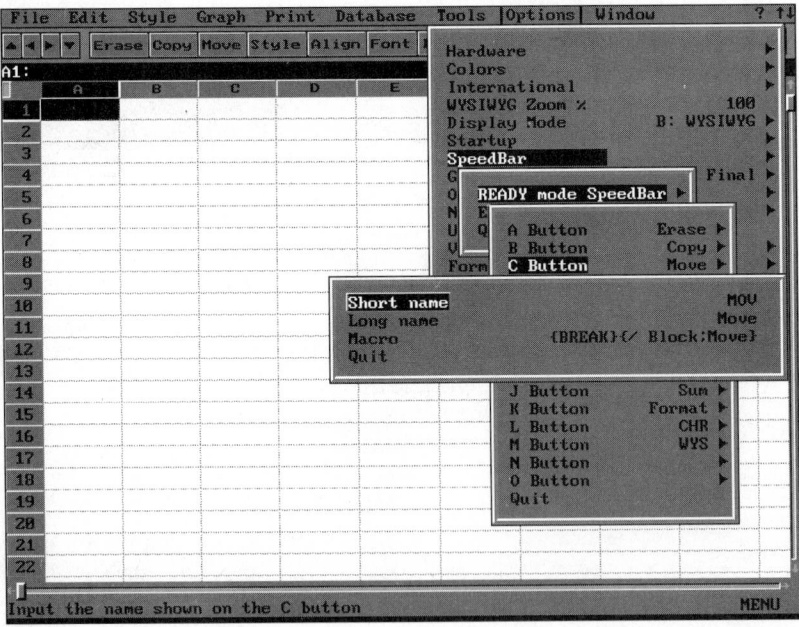

You can also change the labels that appear on each button with the /Options, SpeedBar, READY mode SpeedBar, A Button through O Button

commands. To change the labels that appear in WYSIWYG mode, select Long name and enter up to ten characters (letters, numbers, or even graphics characters) to describe the macro associated with the button. To change the labels that appear in Character mode, select Short name and enter up to three characters.

When you make changes to the SpeedBar, they are in effect only until the end of the current Quattro Pro session. To make your changes permanent, use /Options, Update.

Mouse Palette Buttons in Quattro Pro 3.0

To attach a macro command to a mouse palette button in Quattro Pro 3.0 (Figure 12.13), use /Options, Mouse Palette, and select from the options 1st Button through 7th Button. Then select Macro and assign a macro, subroutine, or menu-equivalent command. To change the button labels, use /Options, Mouse Palette, 1st through 7th Button, Text command. Then enter up to three characters, numbers, or graphics characters that describe the macro attached to the button. To save these changes for future Quattro Pro 3.0 sessions, use /Options, Update.

Figure 12.13

Quattro Pro 3.0's customizable buttons

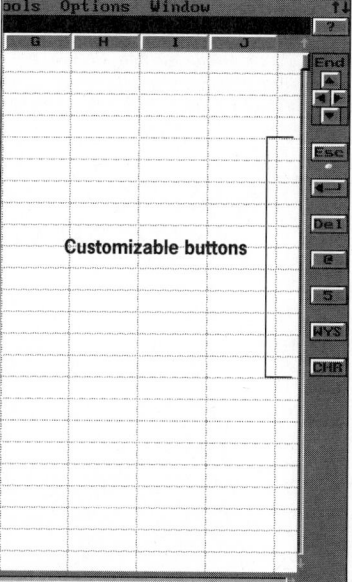

Executing Macros from Spreadsheet Menus

Another way to execute a macro is to include it on a spreadsheet menu. You can then access the macro as you would any Quattro Pro menu command. See "Attaching Macros to Quattro Pro Menus" later in the chapter.

Documenting Macros

If you don't use a macro for a while, you may not remember later how the macro works—especially if the macro is lengthy or complicated. Therefore, it's wise to document your macros, to remind yourself (and explain to others) what each macro does. Documenting macros also lets you describe the assumptions under which you are operating a macro.

Here are some convenient ways to document your macros.

- Some spreadsheet programs (such as 1-2-3) encourage you to document your macros by placing labels in the cells to the right of the macro commands. Quattro Pro's {;} macro command, however, provides a better way to add comments to your macros. Simply insert your comments to the right of the semicolon, as shown in cells B1..B3 of Figure 12.10. When Quattro Pro encounters a {;} command, it ignores it. By documenting your macros in this way, you can clearly associate your comments with a particular macro. Using the {;} command for comments also distinguishes macro comments from spreadsheet data.

- To label a macro, insert the macro's name to the left of the macro's starting cell (see the earlier section "Naming Macros").

- Use menu-equivalent commands whenever possible to make your macros easier to understand.

Stopping a Macro

To stop a macro while it is running, use Ctrl-Break. The macro stops execution at the current command, a beep sounds, and an error message is displayed telling you the location (spreadsheet and address) of the last macro command executed.

CAUTION! *Ctrl-Break will not work if it has been disabled by the {BREAK-OFF} macro command. Use {BREAKOFF} with caution in your macros, and only after you are sure that the routine is working satisfactorily.*

In Debug mode, the /Abort command also stops macro execution, even if a {BREAKOFF} command has been processed. See "Managing Ctrl-Break" in Chapter 13 for more on the {BREAKOFF} command, and "Debugging Macros" later in this chapter.

You can also use the Pause key (a grey key located to the right of the function keys on most 101-key keyboards) to temporarily suspend macro execution (or any other process). Press any other key to continue execution of the macro.

Attaching Macros to Quattro Pro Menus

Note. For a detailed discussion of Menu Builder, see Chapter 15.

You can use the Menu Builder feature to attach a macro to a spreadsheet menu, from which you can then access the macro as you would any menu command. There are four steps for creating a menu tree option that invokes a macro.

1. Load the Menu Builder.

2. Add the menu option.

3. Attach the macro to the menu option.

4. Save the menu tree.

Suppose you want to add a time-stamp feature to your Quattro Pro main menu, such as a Now command that invokes the macro {NOW}. This macro, shown in Figure 12.14, enters the current time where the cell selector is located and displays it in the D7 (HH:MM AM/PM) format. When you add a menu option that invokes a macro, you can create the macro either before or after you customize the menu. In this example, you create the macro after customizing the menu. The sections that follow show you how to add this new menu option and attach the macro to it.

Figure 12.14
Macro to be invoked by customized menu

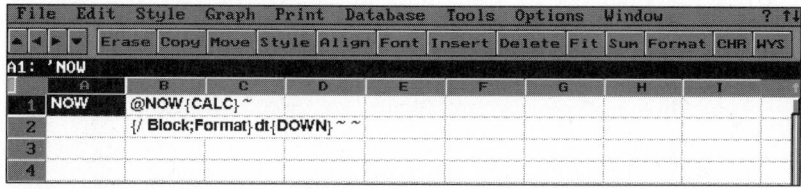

Loading the Menu Builder

The first step in adding a menu option is to load the Menu Builder. Select /Options, Startup, Edit Menus. After a healthy pause while Quattro Pro loads the current menu, your screen will look like Figure 12.15.

Figure 12.15

The Menu Builder screen

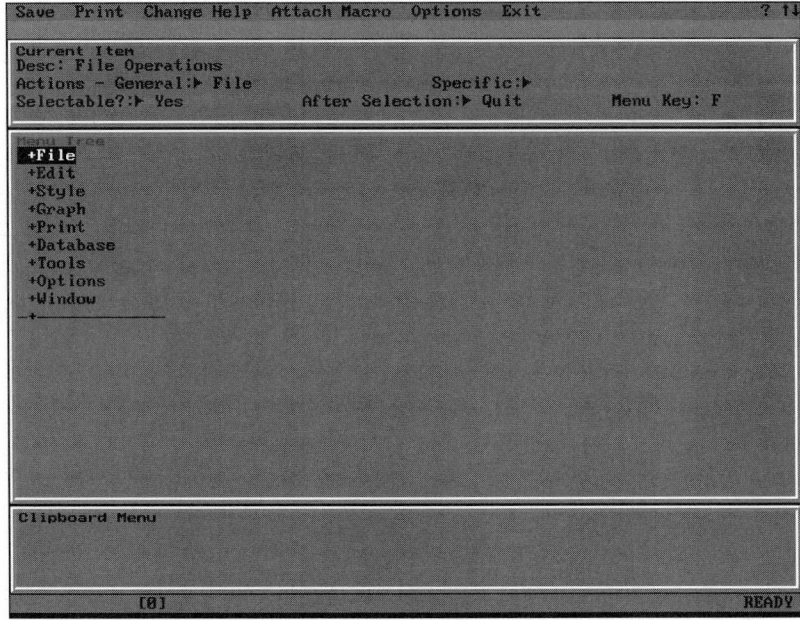

Adding a Menu Option to a Menu

The Now menu option, when added, will appear at the far right of the main menu bar, to the right of the Window option. To add this new option, use the following steps.

1. Press the ↓ key until the Window menu option is highlighted.

2. Press Enter to insert a blank menu option.

3. Type **Now** and press Enter to append the Now menu option.

Attaching a Macro to a Customized Menu Option

Next you will attach the {NOW} macro to the customized menu option. To attach the macro to the new Now menu option,

1. Press Pane (F6) to change to the current item pane.

2. In the Desc (description) field, enter the hint that you want to appear when the cursor is highlighting this menu option. Type

```
Time-stamp a spreadsheet
```

and press Enter.

Note. The /Attach Macro command *must* be preceded by a / or it won't work.

3. Attach the macro to this menu option by selecting the /Attach Macro command. At the prompt, enter the name of the macro, including the curly braces. For our example, enter

{NOW}

and press Enter. Note that Quattro Pro inserts "Name" in the Actions-General field and "Attach" in the Actions-Specific field of the Menu Builder screen. Together these commands cause Quattro Pro to use the menu-equivalent command {/ Name;Attach} when you select the Now menu option. This command then passes the {NOW} command to Quattro Pro.

Saving the Menu Tree

Now that you have attached the macro to a customized menu option, you need to save the menu tree you have just modified. To do this, use the following steps. Remember to type a slash in front of all the Menu Builder's commands.

1. Select /Save from Menu Builder's command menu.

2. Enter the new name for the menu. You can use any file name except the name of the currently loaded menu tree. If you attempt to overwrite the current menu tree, Quattro Pro generates an error and requests another file name. For this example, type **NOW** and press Enter. Quattro Pro saves your menu to the NOW.MU file on disk.

3. Select /Exit to leave the Menu Builder.

Using the Customized Menu Tree

To use the new customized menu tree, you must replace the one currently loaded, as follows:

Note. If you use the macro commands {?}, {STEP}, {STEPON}, and {STEPOFF} in a macro that is invoked from a customized menu, Quattro Pro will ignore them.

1. Select /Options, Startup, Menu Tree.

2. Select the menu tree you want to load by pressing the ↑ or ↓ key until the NOW menu is highlighted.

3. Press Enter to load the NOW menu tree. Your screen will look like Figure 12.16.

To use your new Now menu command, you must have a macro called NOW in the active spreadsheet or in a spreadsheet designated as a macro library. If you haven't already, create the macro (as shown in Figure 12.14), and name it NOW. You can now enter the current time where the cell selector is located using the new /Now command.

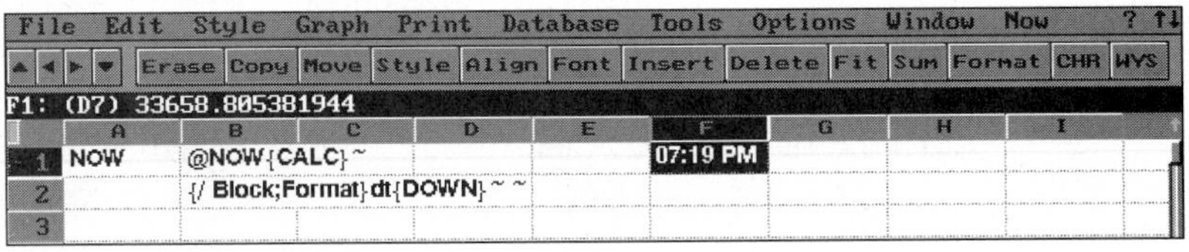

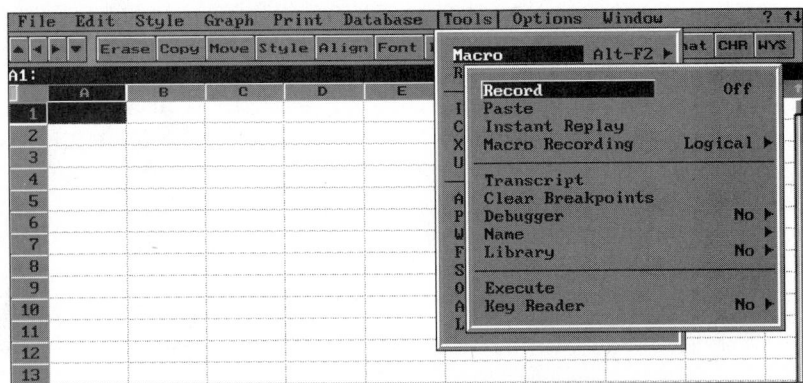

Figure 12.16

Customized menu tree with Add option and NOW macro

Writing Macros with Macro Record

Quattro Pro's Macro Record feature is an easy way to write macros. You simply paste into your spreadsheet the keystrokes that you have recorded. The top part of the /Tools, Macro menu is dedicated to the Macro Record mode, as shown in Figure 12.17.

Figure 12.17

The /Tools, Macro menu

Recording and Playing Back Keystrokes

There are two main steps to using Macro Record mode: recording the macro and playing it back. Try this example.

1. Select /Tools, Macro (Alt-F2), and then select Record. Note the REC indicator on the status line. Now, every keystroke you type will be recorded.

2. Select the /Style, Column Width command, type **15**, and press Enter.

3. Again select /Tools, Macro (Alt-F2), and Record—this time to turn recording off. You have just recorded a macro that sets the current column width to 15.

To play back this macro,

4. Place the cell selector in the column to be set to a width of 15.

5. Select /Tools, Macro (Alt-F2), and Instant Replay.

The keystrokes you recorded are played back. As you can see, Instant Replay replays the last recorded macro.

Note. When you select Paste or Instant Replay while in Macro Record mode, Quattro Pro first turns off the Recorder before pasting or playing back the recorded macro.

Pasting a Recorded Macro

To save a recorded macro in your spreadsheet, you need to paste it into the spreadsheet.

1. Select /Tools, Macro (Alt-F2), Paste.

2. Enter a name for the macro. Type **\A** and press Enter.

Quattro Pro always prompts you for a name for the macro. If you don't want to name the macro, and block names already exist in your spreadsheet, simply press Esc at the macro name prompt. However, if no block names exist, press Enter to proceed.

3. Point to the location in the spreadsheet where you want to place the macro. For our example, point to cell A1 and press Enter. Your spreadsheet will now look like Figure 12.18.

Figure 12.18

Macro pasted from Macro Record

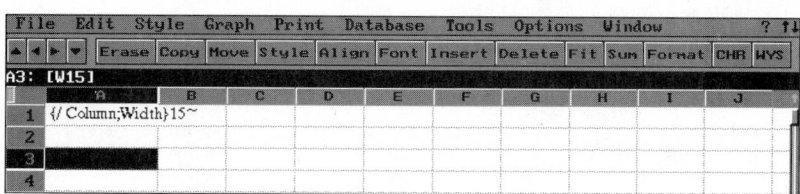

Before you paste your recorded macro into the spreadsheet, position the cell selector first, in the location where you want pasting to begin. Then you can simply press Enter when prompted for the macro's cell address. If you change your mind about the location for pasting the macro, press Esc at the prompt for the cell address, and then point to (or type) the block name or cell address.

You can specify one cell or a multicell block as the paste location. When you specify one cell, Quattro Pro will start pasting at this cell and continue pasting into the cells below it until all of the macro has been pasted. When you use a multicell block, on the other hand, such as A15..A20, Quattro Pro attempts to paste all of the macro into this block. If the block is too small, the program will paste in what it can and then issue the error message "Macro block is full."

CAUTION! *When you use a single-cell location for the paste location, make sure there is no data in the cells immediately below the target cell. If any data is present, it may be overwritten when the macro is pasted into the spreadsheet.*

Pasting Macros into Other Spreadsheets

To paste a recorded macro into another open spreadsheet, such as a macro library, use Quattro Pro linking syntax when specifying the paste block. For instance, to paste a macro into cell A1 of the spreadsheet MACROLIB.WQ1, select /Tools, Macro (Alt-F2), Paste. In response to the macro name prompt, type \A and press Enter. Then type **[MACROLIB]A1** and press Enter. Alternatively, you can use Next Window (Shift-F6), Pick Window (Shift-F5), or Alt-0 to switch to the MACROLIB.WQ1 spreadsheet and then point to cell A1. The macro will then be pasted into the MACROLIB.WQ1 spreadsheet starting at cell A1.

Note that the macro name in the above example is located in the spreadsheet that is the source of the pasted macro—not in the spreadsheet MACROLIB.WQ1. Also, notice that the source spreadsheet is now linked to the spreadsheet MACROLIB.WQ1 by the address of the block name.

The Two Macro Recording Methods: Logical and Keystroke

With the Macro Record feature, there are two ways you can record your macros: the *logical* method or the *keystroke* method.

■ The *logical method* (the Quattro Pro default) records your macros using menu-equivalent commands. Every action invoked through the menus has a menu-equivalent command associated with it. The logical method records menu equivalents instead of the actual keystrokes you press when you record your macro. As explained earlier in this chapter, this method of macro construction has decided advantages.

- The *keystroke method* records the actual keystrokes you press. You may want to use the keystroke method if you are going to use your recorded macros in Lotus 1-2-3.

To switch between the two macro recording methods, use the /Tools, Macro (Alt-F2), Macro Recording command (see Figure 12.17).

A Helpful Recording Technique   When recording your macros, take care to explicitly enter all commands and cell addresses rather than accepting the current settings. For instance, if you are recording a printing macro, it's wise to specify the print block by first pressing Esc (or Ctrl-Backspace) to remove an existing setting and then explicitly type in or point to the print block coordinates—even if this block setting is already the current print block. If you simply press Enter to accept the existing print block, your macro when run will print whatever is defined as the print block; this may not be what you had in mind when you recorded your macro.

Using Menu Commands in Macros

Most of the macros discussed up to this point have been simple macros that have entered text into cells and moved the cell selector. Let's now explore how to access Quattro Pro's menus with macro commands.

A Simple Command Macro Example

Formatting numeric values to currency is a common spreadsheet task. In this next example, you will use Macro Record to create a macro that will perform this formatting. First you'll need to create the simple spreadsheet shown in Figure 12.19, and position the cell selector in a cell containing numeric values, such as D8.

1. Select /Tools, Macro (Alt-F2), Record to enable Macro Record mode.

2. Choose the /Style, Numeric Format, Currency command and press Enter twice.

3. Again select /Tools, Macro (Alt-F2), Record to disable Macro Record mode.

4. Now paste the macro into the spreadsheet you just created. First move the cell selector to an empty cell (A1, for example).

5. Select /Tools, Macro (Alt-F2), Record, Paste.

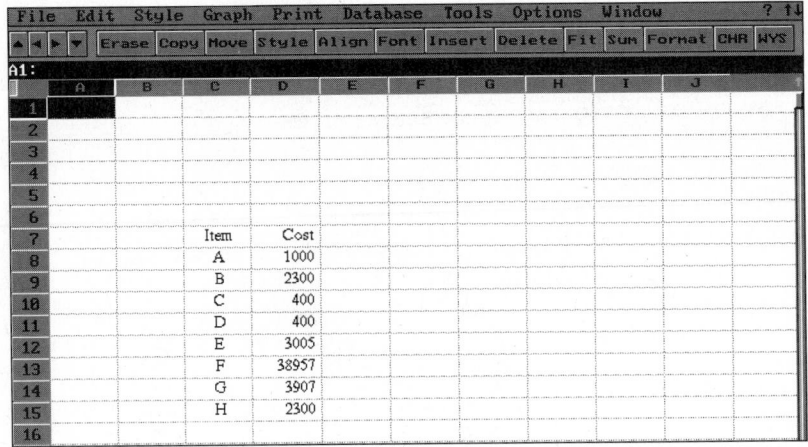

Figure 12.19

Cell contents to be formatted as currency values

6. For the macro name, type \C and press Enter.

7. Press Enter again to confirm the current cell address. Your spreadsheet will now look like Figure 12.20.

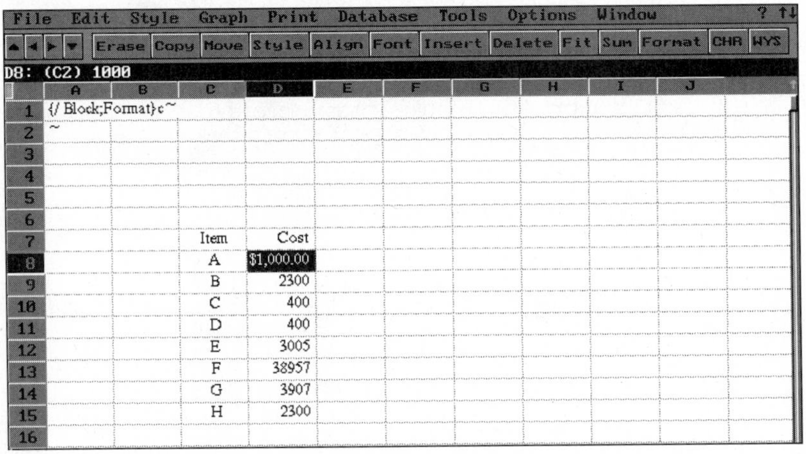

Figure 12.20

A currency-formatting macro pasted into the spreadsheet

Now, if you position the cell selector on cell D8 and press Alt-C, the instant macro you just recorded formats cell D8 to the currency format. (The column width may have to be adjusted to properly accept the formatted values.)

Use Block Names Rather than Cell Addresses

In macros that operate on blocks of data, it is good practice to name these blocks and then refer to the block names, rather than their addresses, in your macros. This is important in case the block is moved or resized.

For instance, imagine you've written the macro

```
{/ Block;Erase}A1..A10~
```

that erases some sales numbers in the block A1..A10. Later on, you enter a new set of numbers in the block, and then insert a new row in the middle. When you run the macro again, you want it to erase all the numbers in the enlarged block A1..A11. However, it only erases block A1..A10, as specified in the macro.

A better form of this macro would be

```
{/ Block;Erase}SALES_S~
```

where SALES_S is the name of the block A1..A10. This way, Quattro Pro automatically updates the block when you insert a row, and you don't have to change your macro every time your block of data changes.

Spreadsheet Linking and Its Effect on Macros

Spreadsheet linking literally adds another dimension to your macros. By using spreadsheet linking in the commands within a macro, you can access data in different spreadsheets, execute macros in other open spreadsheets, and store user input in other files.

The linking syntax you use for the commands stored in a macro is the same as it is when you use those commands on their own. For example, in the macro

```
{/ Block;Format}c~[SALES]TOTAL~
```

[SALES] refers to the open spreadsheet SALES.WQ1. If a spreadsheet is stored in a different directory and/or drive, you can specify either or both within the brackets. This macro will format the block TOTAL in the spreadsheet SALES.WQ1.

Using Undo with Macros

Undo is useful for reversing any undesirable effects your macro may have had on your spreadsheet. This reversal may be somewhat limited with long macros, because Undo only restores the last reversible operation. For instance, in a macro that enters data into five cells, only the entry in the fifth cell can be undone. See Chapter 1 for a detailed description of Undo.

Including the {UNDO} command in your macro applications allows users to reverse operations such as sorting a database or deleting block names. For example, the macro in Figure 12.21 sorts a database. The last portion of the macro presents the user with a menu that offers the choice of undoing the last sort performed. (See Chapter 13 for more on the {MENUBRANCH} command.) When the user selects the "Undo last sort" option, the {UNDO} macro command executes, and the database is returned to its previous state.

Figure 12.21

Macro that includes the {UNDO} command

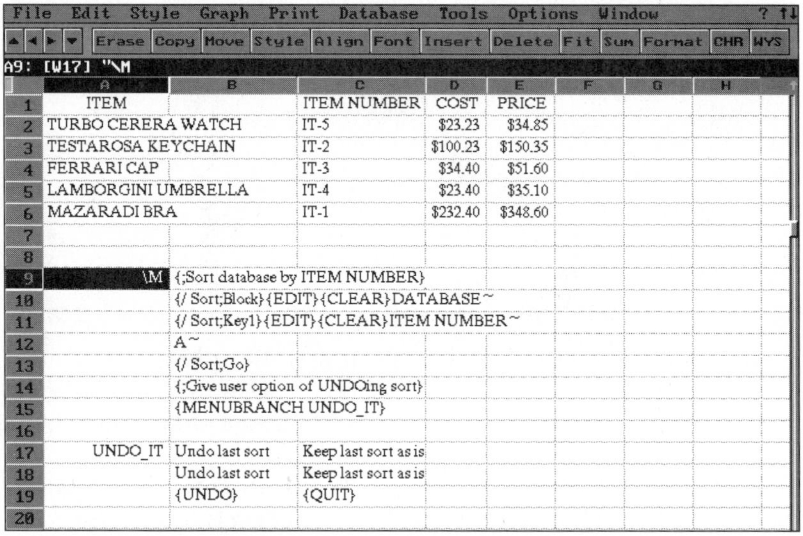

Debugging Macros

Quattro Pro's Macro Debugger is a unique and powerful tool that lets you execute a macro one command at a time, while you view the commands being executed. This helps you quickly isolate and fix any errors in your macros.

Working in Debug Mode

To start the Macro Debugger and enter Debug mode, select /Tools, Macro (Alt-F2), Debugger, Yes (Shift-F2). Notice the DEBUG indicator on the status line. Now, whenever a macro is executed, it will pause before the first command is processed and display the Macro Debugger window.

Unlike other Quattro Pro main menu commands, the Macro Debugger can be toggled on or off at any time, even when you're in the middle of a menu. For example, you will often want to first turn on Debug mode before using /Tools, Macro (Alt-F2), Execute to start a macro. This can be done at any point during the Execute command operation—while in the menu system, while pointing to the macro, or while selecting its name.

Here is a list of the Macro Debugger key assignments.

- *Enter* executes the macro at full speed until a breakpoint is reached.

- *F1* brings up Help on the Macro Debugger.

- *F3* and **/** bring up the Macro Debugger menu (Figure 12.22).

Figure 12.22
The Macro
Debugger menu

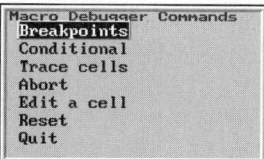

- *Esc* turns off the Macro Debugger Window. This temporarily removes the window so that you can view the spreadsheet unobstructed. The window is turned on again with the next keystroke.

- *Shift-F2* toggles the Macro Debugger on and off.

- *Mouse clicks and all other keystrokes,* including the spacebar, execute the next command of the macro you are debugging and then return to the Macro Debugger Window.

The Macro Debugger Window (see Figure 12.23) is divided into two panes. The top portion, called the Debug Window, displays the current macro command being executed, including its spreadsheet and cell address location. The command executed prior to the current command is displayed on the row above the current command. The next command to be executed is displayed below the current command. The bottom portion is called the Trace Window. It displays the content and location of up to four trace cells.

Stepping Through Macros One Command at a Time

Executing your macros one command at a time (or *stepping through* them) is an effective means of pinpointing errors and problem areas in your macro code. Quattro Pro calls this Step mode.

Figure 12.23

The Macro
Debugger Window

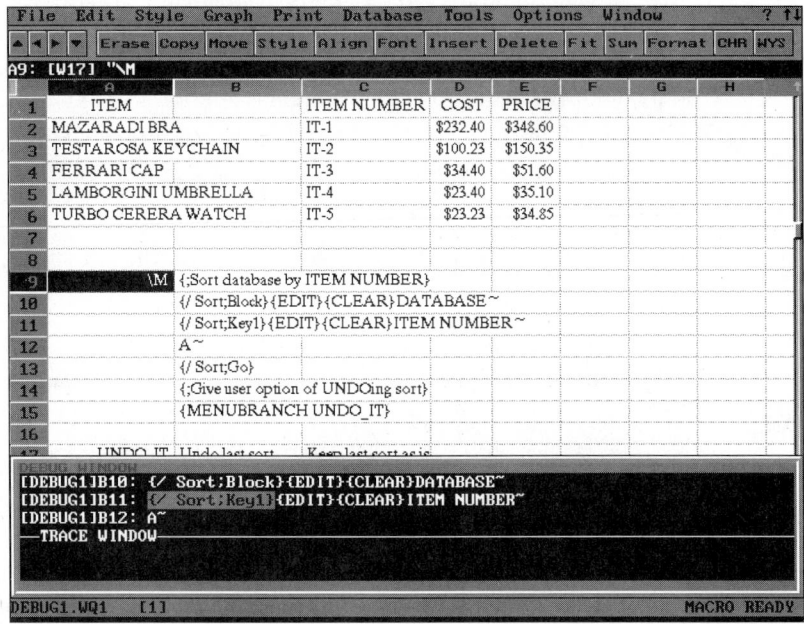

To step through a macro,

1. Press Shift-F2 to turn on the Macro Debugger.

2. Invoke the macro.

3. To step through your macro a command at a time, press the spacebar until you've reached the problem area of your macro. Press Enter at any time to continue with your macro at full speed.

For example, suppose you have the print macro in Figure 12.24, which contains an error, and you want to debug it by stepping through it a command at a time. Figure 12.24 shows how your screen appears after you have turned on the Macro Debugger and invoked the macro. Notice in the Debug Window that the initial lines of the macro appear, and the first macro instruction, /, is highlighted.

When you press the spacebar for the first time, Quattro Pro executes the / instruction, which accesses the main menu (File in the menu tree is highlighted). In the Debug Window, the next macro instruction, p, is highlighted, as shown in Figure 12.25. Press the spacebar a second time, and Quattro Pro executes this instruction and displays the Print menu.

Debugging Macros 887

Figure 12.24
Debugging a
simple print macro

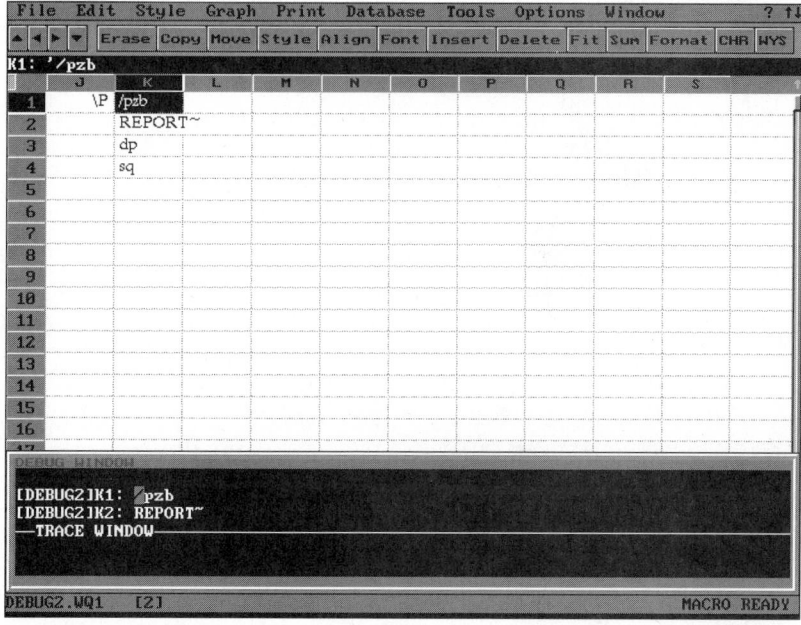

Figure 12.25
Debug Window
after pressing the
spacebar

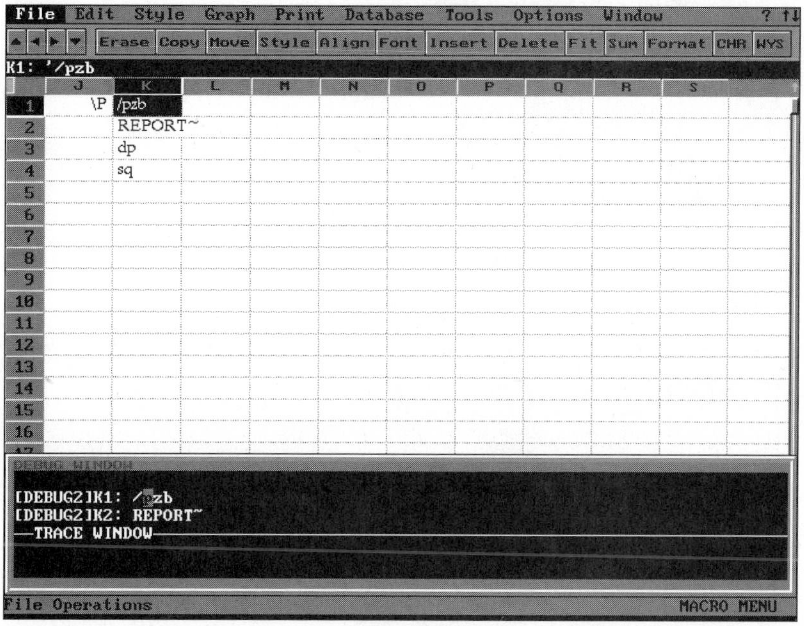

When you press the spacebar a third time, Quattro Pro beeps because the z instruction is invalid; it does not correspond to an option on the /Print menu. At this point, you can press Ctrl-Break to stop the macro, followed by Esc or Enter to clear the error message that appears. You can then edit the first line of the macro to correct the errant z instruction there.

Setting Breakpoints

Stepping through each command in a long macro can be tedious. Frequently you will want to skip directly to a suspected problem area of your macro. You can start macro execution at the suspect area of your macro by using /Tools, Macro, Execute and specifying the address where the command starts. Sometimes, however, this isn't practical, because one portion of the macro may depend on a previous portion. *Breakpoints* solve this problem by letting you specify the cell (breakpoint) where you want macro execution to stop, so that you can debug the macro from there.

Quattro Pro's Macro Debugger supports two types of breakpoints: standard and conditional. With standard breakpoints, your macro returns control to the Debugger when it reaches an instruction located in a cell you specify. Conditional breakpoints, on the other hand, return control to the Macro Debugger when a logical formula in a specified cell evaluates to true.

Setting Standard Breakpoints

You can set up to four standard breakpoints during any given macro debugging session. To specify a breakpoint, follow these steps:

1. Turn on the Macro Debugger with /Tools, Macros, Debug, Yes, or press Shift-F2.

2. Invoke the macro you want to debug.

3. Select the /Breakpoints command from the Macro Debugger menu, and specify which breakpoint to set, 1 through 4. Quattro Pro displays the menu in Figure 12.26.

Figure 12.26

The /Breakpoints menu

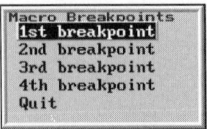

```
Macro Breakpoints
1st breakpoint
2nd breakpoint
3rd breakpoint
4th breakpoint
Quit
```

4. Select Block and choose the breakpoint cell (the cell where you want the Debugger to stop).

5. If you wish, you can use the /Pass Count option to enter a *pass count*, which is the number of times you want the Debugger to pass a breakpoint before stopping the macro and entering Step mode. You can specify up to 240 passes, but usually you will want to use the default value of 0. This tells the Macro Debugger to stop every time it comes to this breakpoint.

6. Select /Quit three times to remove the Macro Debugger menu.

Suppose you have the \L macro in Figure 12.27, which tests the speed of the cell selector in different display modes. The first command in the macro, {BLANK COUNT}, deletes the contents of COUNT (cell B9). The next command, {LET COUNT,COUNT+1}, increases COUNT by 1. The macro then calls a subroutine, {SCREEN}, which begins in B13 and moves the cell selector around the screen. When the subroutine is completed (when Quattro Pro encounters a blank cell, B17), control returns to the command that follows the subroutine call—the {BRANCH CONTINUE} command. This command transfers control back to CONTINUE (cell B5), which repeats the macro. (See Chapter 13 for more on these special macro programming commands.)

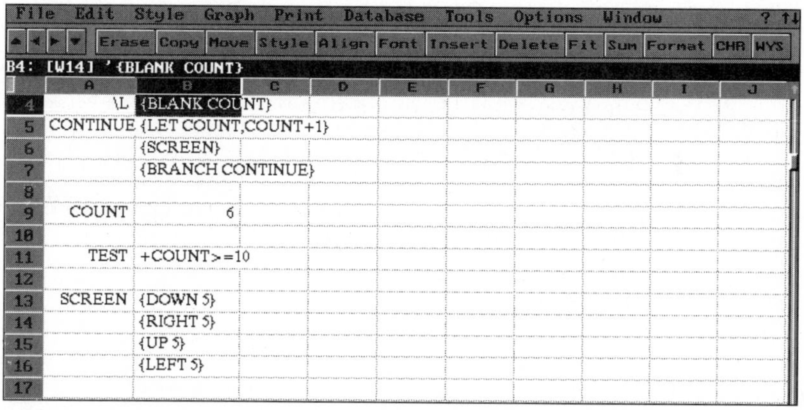

Figure 12.27

An example macro for debugging

To debug this macro, set the cell named CONTINUE (B5) as the first breakpoint. The Debugger will then stop every time it reaches this cell, and display the Debugger Window. Press Enter and the macro will continue until it again reaches the cell CONTINUE. In this example, if the pass count were set to 10, you would see that COUNT (B9) had increased by 10 with each iteration.

Setting Conditional Breakpoints

Conditional breakpoints are similar to standard breakpoints, except that they stop the macro when a given condition is met instead of at a specific cell. In addition to four standard breakpoints, you can set up to four conditional breakpoints during any macro debugging session.

To specify a conditional breakpoint, you must first enter a conditional expression into the spreadsheet. A conditional expression is a formula that uses a logical operator (=, < , >, or <>) to compare two values. For example, the formula

    +COUNT>=1Ø

returns 1 if the cell count contains a value greater than or equal to 10; otherwise, it returns 0. You can enter the conditional expression in any cell in the spreadsheet, though it is wise to choose a cell near the macro you are debugging, so that the expression is visible on the screen.

After entering a conditional expression in the spreadsheet, you can set up a conditional breakpoint, as follows:

1. Press Shift-F2 to enter Debug mode.

2. Invoke the macro to be debugged.

3. Select /Conditional from the Macro Debugger menu, and choose which breakpoint to set, 1 through 4.

4. Select the cell that contains the conditional expression.

5. Select /Quit twice to return to the Debug Window.

Take another look at Figure 12.27. The cell named TEST (B11), which is formatted to display a formula instead of a value (with /Style, Numeric Format, Text), is set as the first conditional breakpoint. After you press Enter, the macro will stop only when the conditional expression evaluates to true—that is, when COUNT (B9) has reached the value of 10.

Using Trace Cells

Trace cells are useful for examining the contents of cells during macro debugging. Quattro Pro shows the contents of trace cells in the Trace Window panel of the Macro Debugger Window. The main reason for using trace cells is that they let you view the contents of cells that you otherwise could not see while your macro is running. By viewing the contents of a trace cell, you can determine whether your macro is updating the cell properly. You can specify up to four trace cells for any given macro debugging session.

Here are the steps to set up a trace cell:

1. Press Shift-F2 to enter Debug mode.

2. Invoke the macro to be debugged.

3. Select /Trace cells from the Macro Debugger menu, and specify which trace cell to set, 1 through 4.

4. Specify the address of the trace cell (the cell you wish to watch during your debugging session).

5. Select /Quit twice to leave the Macro Debugger menu.

From this point on, you can observe the contents of the trace cells in the Trace Window panel.

Removing Breakpoints and Trace Cells

Breakpoints and trace cells remain set until you quit Quattro Pro, even when you are not in Debug mode. To remove them, use the /Reset command in the Macro Debugger menu. This removes *all* breakpoints and trace cells, so use /Reset with discretion.

Breakpoints and trace cells cannot be saved with a spreadsheet; nor is there a way to set default breakpoints or trace cells.

Correcting Macro Errors

To edit a cell during a macro debugging session, use the /Edit a cell command from the Macro Debugger menu. When you select the cell to be edited and press Enter, the content of that cell appears on the edit line for your alteration. Complete your editing, and press Enter or any cursor movement key to leave Edit mode. Next, select /Quit to remove the Macro Debugger menu.

CAUTION! *Do not use this command to edit the macro command that is currently being executed.*

Tips for Debugging Macros

- Use the macro commands {STEP}, {STEPON}, and {STEPOFF} to "hard code" macro breakpoints into your macros. The {STEP} command toggles the Macro Debugger on *and* off; {STEPON} and {STEPOFF} turn the Macro Debugger on and off respectively, regardless of its current state.

- At times during a debugging session, you may wish to temporarily skip suspected "buggy" macro routines. You can "comment out" a given macro command or routine by adding the {; character sequence to the beginning of the macro. For instance, to skip the routine {TOTAL}, edit the label to read {;{TOTAL}. To use this routine again later, simply remove the {; characters.

- During normal macro execution, the screen is not updated until the macro has terminated, or until a specific screen refresh command, such as {WINDOWSON}, has been processed. During a macro debugging session, however, the screen is updated after every command. The moral of this story is don't expect the cell selector position or the contents of the screen during normal execution to appear as they are during a macro debugging session.

Designating Macro Libraries

Normally, macros can only be executed within the spreadsheet in which they reside. By designating a separate spreadsheet as a *macro library,* you can select macros from that library to execute in any open spreadsheet.

To designate a spreadsheet as a macro library, use the /Tools, Macro (Alt-F2), Macro Library, Yes command. You can make this setting permanent for the library spreadsheet by simply saving the spreadsheet. To remove the macro library status from a spreadsheet, use Macro Library, No.

Figure 12.28 is a macro library spreadsheet. It includes some common macros for everyday spreadsheet operations. When this spreadsheet is open on the desktop, any of its macros can be executed from other spreadsheets.

If you want a macro to branch out from the macro library to the active spreadsheet, use linking syntax with empty braces. This causes the macro to branch to the block specified in the active spreadsheet. For instance, the macro command

```
{BRANCH []\A}
```

when placed in a library macro will cause the macro to branch to the macro named \A in the active spreadsheet, rather than look for the library macro named \A.

When you start a macro, Quattro Pro first searches the active spreadsheet for the macro name. If a macro in the active spreadsheet and one in the library have the same name, the spreadsheet macro is the one that is executed. If the macro name cannot be found in the active spreadsheet, all open macro libraries are searched. It's good practice, then, to have only one macro library open at a time; if more than one library is open and they contain some of the same macro names, you cannot control which macro will be executed.

Figure 12.28

A macro library containing common spreadsheet macros

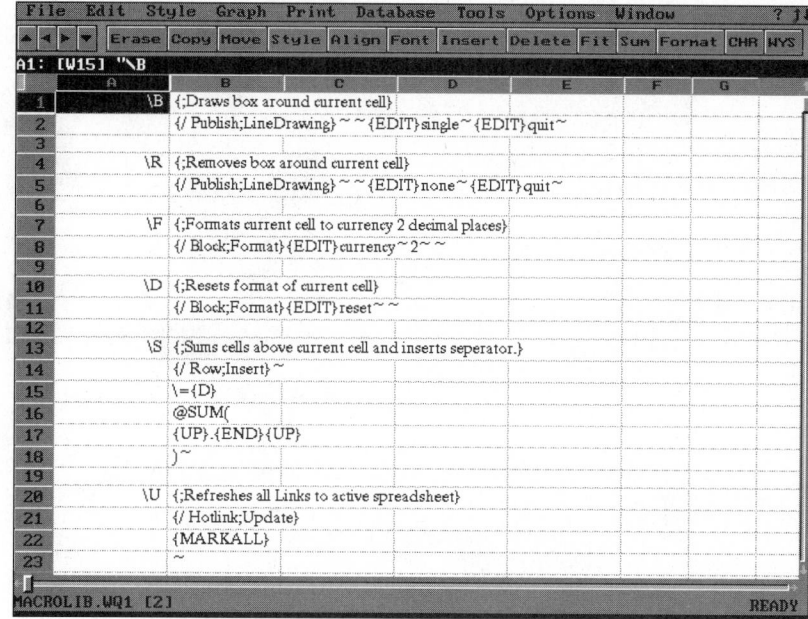

TIP. *To have your macro library automatically loaded at startup, use /Options, Startup, Autoload File and enter the name of your library spreadsheet as the name of the Autoload File. An example of this is shown in Figure 12.29. To save this as a permanent setting, use /Options, Update.*

Using Transcript to Create Macros

As soon as you start Quattro Pro, its Transcript utility begins recording every keystroke you make during a Quattro Pro session. Transcript does its recording quietly in the background, without effort on your part. You can easily create macros from previous keystrokes by copying keystrokes out of Transcript's log file and inserting them into your spreadsheet. This section shows how you can apply the Transcript utility to writing macros.

To view Transcript's log file, select /Tools, Macro (Alt-F2), Transcript. Then press the / (slash) key to bring up the Transcript menu; your screen will look something like Figure 12.30. The vertical bar in the left margin of the Transcript log window tells you which keystrokes were saved by Transcript since the file was last retrieved.

Figure 12.29

Designating a
macro library as
the Autoload File

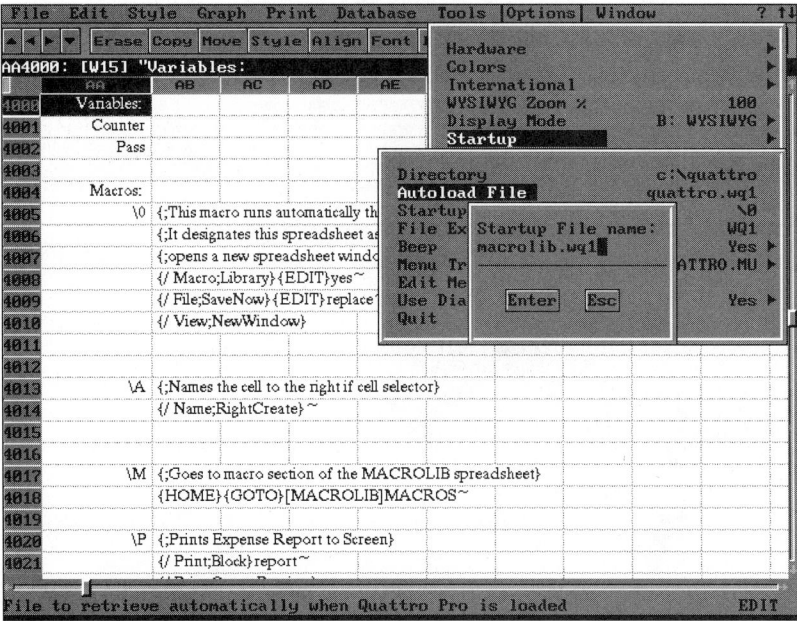

Figure 12.30

Transcript log and
menu

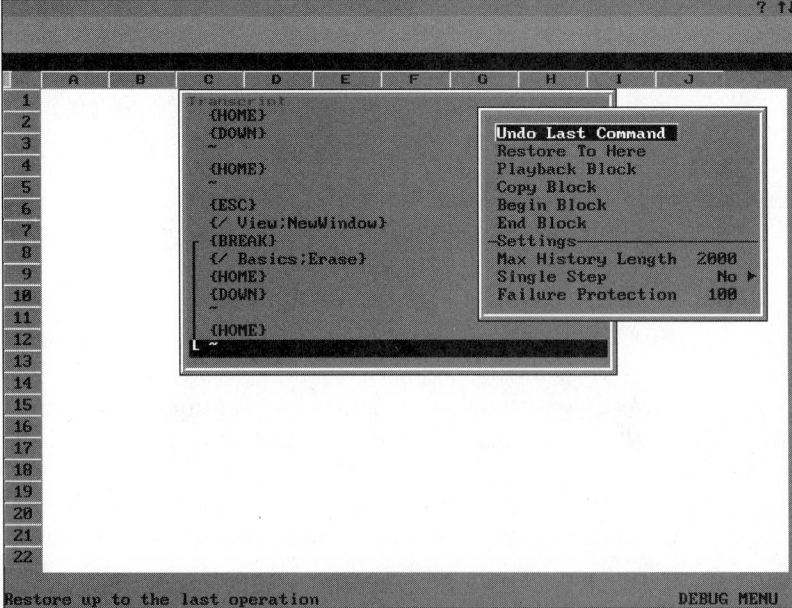

Imagine that you have just formatted a cell for currency, and you want to create an instant macro from these keystrokes, so that you can use Alt-F to format other cells. Here is how to paste the recorded keystrokes into your spreadsheet from the Transcript log file.

1. Invoke Transcript by pressing Alt-F2 and typing **T** (for the Transcript menu option). Your spreadsheet will look like Figure 12.31.

Figure 12.31

Quattro Pro's
Transcript window

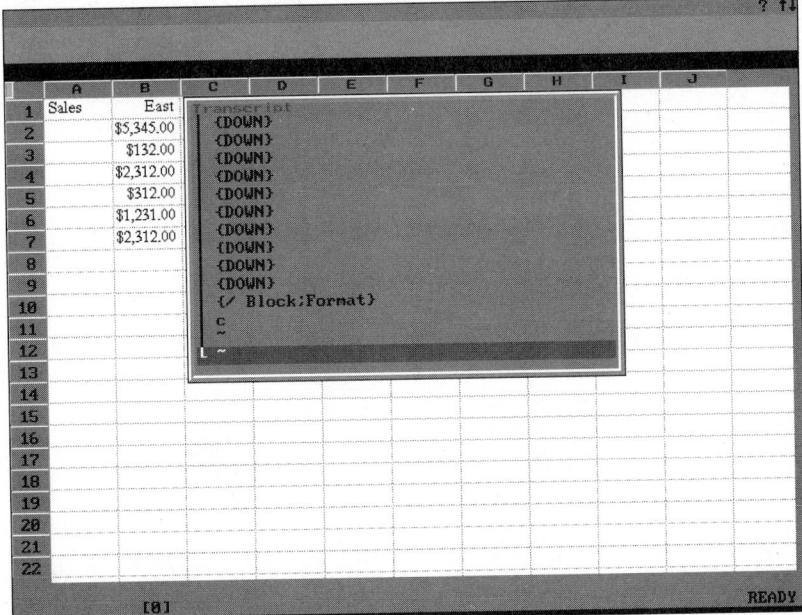

2. Using the Transcript menu's /Begin Block command, mark the beginning of the block of commands you wish to paste into the spreadsheet. In our example, you will first move the cursor (with the ↑ key) to highlight the {/ Block;Format} command. Then press **/** to invoke the Transcript menu, and type **B** for the Begin Block menu option.

3. With the /End Block command, mark the end of the block of commands you wish to paste. First move the cursor (with the ↓ key) to highlight the second ~ (tilde) command. Then press **/** and **E**.

4. Using the /Copy Block command, copy the block to your spreadsheet. When copying the block to your spreadsheet, Quattro Pro always prompts you for a name. If you don't want to give the macro a name,

and block names already exist in the spreadsheet, press Esc at the macro name prompt; if no block names exist, press Enter to proceed. For this example, select /Copy Block by pressing **/** and **C**. At the Block Name prompt, type **\F** and press Enter. At the Block address prompt, type **A10** and press Enter.

Your spreadsheet will now look like Figure 12.32.

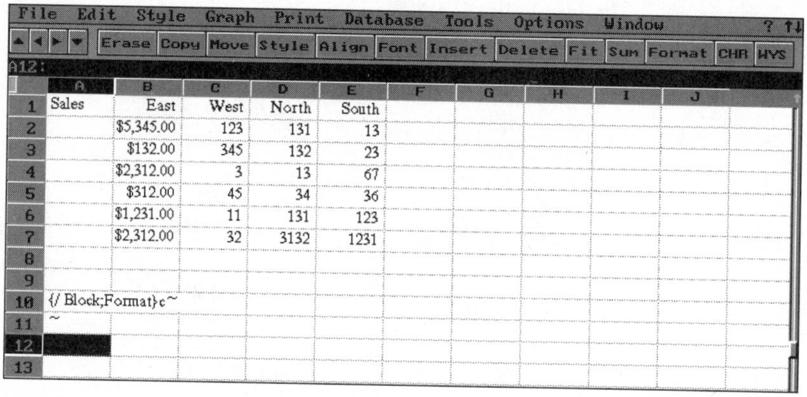

Figure 12.32

Spreadsheet after commands from Transcript log are pasted in

CAUTION! *See the section "Pasting a Recorded Macro" earlier in this chapter for limitations and caveats on pasting (copying) macros into your spreadsheet.*

Running 1-2-3–Compatible Macros with Key Reader

Quattro Pro's Key Reader feature lets you run Lotus 1-2-3–compatible macros without changing menu trees. To run a Quattro Pro macro that is compatible with 1-2-3, use the /Tools, Macro (Alt-F2), Key Reader, Yes command. Then all keystroke macros, such as /wc, will be interpreted as if they are being run under the 1-2-3–compatible menu tree.

Key Reader can be designated as a spreadsheet default with the /Options, Update command.

TIP. *To run a macro written in 1-2-3 without loading the 123.MU menu tree, change the macro so that it begins with this menu-equivalent command:*

```
{/ Macro;Reader}{EDIT}YES~
```

Using Graph Buttons to Start Macros

As mentioned earlier, you can invoke macros with Quattro Pro's graph buttons. A *graph button* is a special graph text box that you add to a graph with the Annotator. (Chapter 9 tells all about the Annotator.)

Creating a Graph Button

Creating a graph button is easy, as described in the following steps.

1. Enter the Annotator with the /Graph, Annotate command.

2. To enter a text box, just start typing text—for example, **Access Paradox**. Press Enter to complete the text box.

3. Quit the Annotator with the /Quit command.

4. Save the graph with the /Graph, Name, Create command. Enter a name for the graph, such as **BUTTONS**.

   In Figure 12.33, there are four graph buttons defined, corresponding to the four rounded rectangles.

Figure 12.33
Graph with four
graph buttons

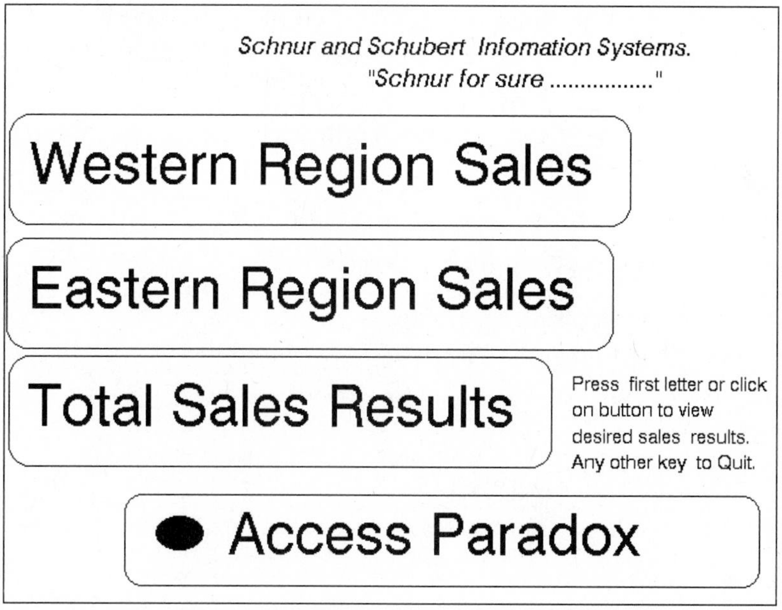

Schnur and Schubert Infomation Systems.
"Schnur for sure ...."

Western Region Sales

Eastern Region Sales

Total Sales Results

Press first letter or click
on button to view
desired sales results.
Any other key to Quit.

● Access Paradox

Attaching Macros to Graph Buttons

Once you have created your text box, the next step is to assign a macro to that text box, thereby creating a graph button. Here are the steps to follow.

1. Enter the Annotator with the /Graph, Annotate command.

2. Using the Tab key, select the button to which you want to attach the macro.

3. Attach the macro to the graph button by pressing F3. This activates the Property Sheet. Choose the Graph Button command, and Quattro Pro displays a list of available graph names.

4. At the "Enter graph name:" prompt, type the name of the macro, with curly braces on either side, to attach to this button—for instance, **{PAR-ADOX_ACCESS}**—and press Enter.

5. Quit the Annotator with the /Quit command.

6. Save the graph again with /Graph, Name, Create.

A Tip for Entering Graph Names

In macros that are invoked from graph buttons, Quattro Pro ignores the macro commands {?}, {STEP}, {STEPON}, and {STEPOFF}. If you have a macro that includes one of these commands, however, there is a way to get around this limitation. Simply follow these guidelines when entering the macro name for the graph button:

- Precede the macro name with the menu-equivalent command {/ Name; Execute}.

- Do not enclose the macro name in braces.

- End the macro with a ~ (tilde).

For example, to attach the macro named \A to a graph button, at the "Enter graph name:" prompt enter

```
{/ Name;Execute}\A~
```

By doing this, you will ensure that the above-mentioned unique commands will work as you expect.

Invoking a Macro with a Graph Button

To invoke a macro with a graph button, the graph must be viewed "full screen." That is, you cannot use a graph button while you're in the Annotator or in an inserted graph. To invoke a macro with a graph button,

1. Choose the /Graph, Name, Display command, and select the graph to view.

2. Invoke the macro by pressing the first letter of the text in the text box, or by clicking the mouse on the appropriate graph button.

For example, in Figure 12.33, typing **W** for Western Region Sales invokes the macro {WEST} attached to this graph button. Clicking the mouse on the box does the same thing.

Figure 12.34 shows the macros that are linked to the graph buttons in Figure 12.33. This table will help you decipher each macro.

Button	Macro Name and Location
Western Region Sales	WEST (cell B7)
Eastern Region Sales	EAST (cell B4)
Total Sales Results	TOTAL (cell B10)
Access Paradox	PARADOX_GO (cell B1)

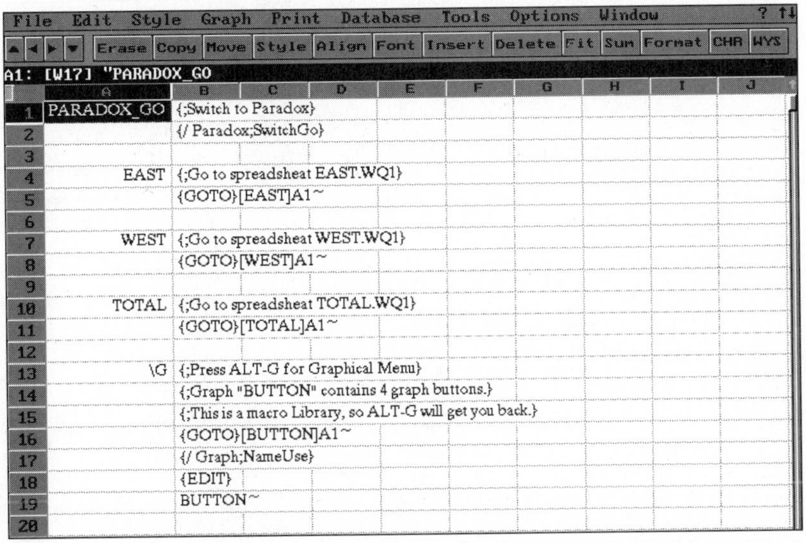

Figure 12.34

Graph button macro

13

Programming
with Macros

*Quattro Pro's Macro
Programming
Commands*

The /X Commands

*Programming
Command Syntax*

Getting User Input

Manipulating Data

*Stopping and
Suspending
Macro Execution*

*Decision-Making
Commands*

Branching

Subroutines

*Error Trapping
with {ONERROR}*

Building Menus

Managing the Screen

*Controlling
Recalculation*

*Reading and Writing
ASCII Files*

Advanced Techniques

■N CHAPTER 12, YOU LEARNED HOW TO CREATE SIMPLE MACROS THAT entered data into cells and invoked Quattro Pro menu commands. For the most part, these macros provide a quick and error-free way of entering keystrokes that you would otherwise have to type yourself. Although simple keystroke macros are certainly useful, they are also somewhat limited. To get at the real power of Quattro Pro's macro facility, you must use the macro programming commands. With these commands, you can

- Prompt for user input

- Design custom menus

- Modify the contents of spreadsheet cells

- Provide messages and error handling

- Control the appearance of the screen

- Perform conditional branching and looping

- Execute subroutines

- Read and write ASCII text files

Quattro Pro's Macro Programming Commands

Table 13.1 lists Quattro Pro's macro programming commands in alphabetical order. Each of these commands is described in this chapter.

TIP. *The {} command is known as the "do nothing" command. It acts as bridge or placeholder between rows of macro commands.*

The /X Commands

In 1-2-3 Release 1A, Lotus Development Corporation included eight simple programming commands, collectively called the /X ("slash X") commands. Because these commands are so rarely used today, you may never run across them. Nevertheless, to provide compatibility with 1-2-3, Quattro Pro also includes these commands. They are listed in Table 13.2 with their Quattro Pro equivalents.

Table 13.1 **Quattro Pro's Macro Programming Commands**

Command	Description
{?}	Pauses macro execution for user input until Enter is pressed.
{BEEP [*tone-number*]}	Sounds computer's speaker.
{BLANK *location*}	Erases contents of cell or block specified by *location*.
{BRANCH *location*}	Continues macro execution at *location*.
{BREAKOFF}	Disables Ctrl-Break keyboard sequence used to interrupt macro execution. Usually used in conjunction with {BREAKON} command.
{BREAKON}	Enables Ctrl-Break keyboard sequence.
{CLOSE}	Closes an open ASCII text file.
{CONTENTS *destination, source,*[*width*] [*format*]}	Copies contents of *source* location to *destination* location as a label.
{DEFINE *location1* [:string/value], *location2* [:string/value],...}	Used with a subroutine to specify location and type of arguments to be passed to the subroutine.
{DISPATCH *location*}	Performs indirect branch to cell whose name is specified as a label in *location*.
{FILESIZE *location*}	Enters file size (in bytes) of an open ASCII text file in *location*.
{FOR *counter,start-number,stop-number,start,step-number,subroutine*}	Executes *subroutine* while *start-number* + *counter* is less than *stop-number*. Each time *subroutine* is executed, *counter* is incremented by *step-number*.
{FORBREAK}	Stops current {FOR} command and passes control to command immediately following {FOR} command.
{GET *location*}	Waits for keypress and stores keypress at *location* as a label.
{GETLABEL *prompt,location*}	Displays *prompt* on input line, and allows data entry until Enter is pressed. Stores input in *location* as a label.
{GETNUMBER *prompt,location*}	Displays *prompt* on input line, and allows data entry until Enter is pressed. Stores input in *location* as a value.
{GETPOS *location*}	Determines position of file pointer in the open ASCII text file. Stores position in *location* as a value.

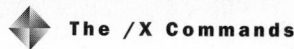

Table 13.1 (Continued)

Command	Description
{GRAPHCHAR *location*}	Stores key pressed while graph or {MESSAGE} is displayed in *location*.
{IF *logical-expression*}	Evaluates *logical-expression* to determine if true or false. If true, macro execution continues in same cell. If false, macro execution skips to next cell below.
{IFKEY *string*}	Evaluates *string* and determines whether it is keystroke representation. If it is, macro execution continues in same cell. If not, macro execution skips to next cell.
{INDICATE *string*}	Changes mode indicator (in status line) to *string*.
{LET *location,data*}	Places *data* (value, string, or result of expression) in *location*.
{LOOK *location*}	Places first keystroke pressed while macro is running into *location*.
{MENUBRANCH *location*}	Displays custom menu defined at *location*, waits for a selection, and branches to commands for that selection.
{MENUCALL *location*}	Displays custom menu defined at *location*, waits for a selection, and performs subroutine call to commands for that selection.
{MESSAGE *location, left, top, time*}	Displays label in *location* in a bordered box, beginning at screen column *left* and screen row *top*. Box remains until current time is equal to *time*.
{ONERROR *branch-location*, [*message-location*], [*error-location*]}	Provides error handling in macros. Branches to *branch-location* when error occurs. Optionally, error message returned by Quattro Pro is stored at *message-location*, and address of offending macro command is stored at [*error-location*].
{OPEN *filename, access-mode*}	Opens an ASCII file for reading, writing, modifying, or appending.
{PANELOFF}	Suppresses display of menus and prompts during macro execution.
{PANELON}	Cancels previously set {PANELOFF} command, allowing display of menus and prompts.
{PLAY *filename*}	Plays a digitized sound (.SND) file.

Table 13.1   (Continued)

Command	Description
{PUT *block*, *column-offset*, *row-offset*,*data*}	Enters *data* (value, string, or result of expression) into *block* at *column-offset* and *row-offset*.
{QUIT}	Stops macro execution.
{READ *byte-count*, *location*}	Reads *byte-count* bytes from the open ASCII file and enters them in *location*.
{READLN *location*}	Reads a line from the open ASCII file and enters it in *location*.
{RECALC *location*, [*condition*], [*iterations*]}	Recalculates *location* in row-by-row fashion until *condition* is met, or for number of *iterations* specified.
{RECALCCOL *location* [*condition*], [*iterations*]}	Recalculates *location* in column-by-column fashion until *condition* is met, or for number of *iterations* specified.
{RESTART}	Clears the subroutine stack (next command in current subroutine is treated as beginning of a new macro).
{RETURN}	Used in subroutines; returns control to the command following {*subroutine*} call.
{SETPOS *position*}	Moves position of file pointer in the open ASCII file to value specified by *position*.
{WAIT *time-number*}	Suspends macro execution until current time is equal to *time-number*.
{WINDOWSOFF}	Suppresses normal screen updating.
{WINDOWSON}	Resumes normal screen updating.
{WRITE *string*}	Copies *string* to the open ASCII file.
{WRITELN *string*}	Copies *string*, followed by a carriage-return, line-feed character sequence, to the open ASCII file.

As the syntax shows, the /X command arguments appear directly after the command itself. In addition, the tildes (~) represent the Enter key. For example, the command

```
/XLWhat is your first name? ~FIRST~
```

displays the prompt "What is your first name?" on the input line, and suspends macro execution while waiting for your response. When you type it and press Enter, Quattro Pro stores your response as a label in the range FIRST.

Table 13.2   **Lotus 1-2-3 /X Commands and Their Quattro Pro Equivalents**

/X Command	Description	Quattro Pro Equivalent
/XC*location*~	Calls a subroutine at *location*.	{*subroutine*}
/XG*location*~	Branches to *location*.	{BRANCH *location*}
/XI*condition*~	If *condition* is true, then next instruction is executed; otherwise, skips to next cell.	{IF *condition*}
/XL*prompt*~[*location*]~	Displays *prompt* in control panel, and enters your response as a label in *location*.	{GETLABEL *prompt,location*}
/XM*location*~	Activates a macro menu stored at *location*.	{MENUBRANCH *location*}
/XN*prompt*~[*location*]~	Displays *prompt* in control panel, and enters your response as a number in *location*.	{GETNUMBER *prompt, location*}
/XQ	Terminates the macro.	{QUIT}
/XR	Returns control from the current subroutine to a main macro. Used in conjunction with /XC.	{RETURN}

Programming Command Syntax

In Chapter 12 you learned some of the basic rules of macro syntax. For example, you know that macro keystroke instructions and menu-equivalent commands must appear within braces, as in {UP 5} and {/ File;SaveAll}, and that you cannot split these instructions onto more than one line. The same general rules apply to macro programming commands, along with some additional syntax rules. These rules are illustrated in Figure 13.1, and explained in the paragraphs that follow.

Figure 13.1

Macro
programming
command syntax

{KEYWORD arg1, arg2,...,arg3}

The command *keyword* immediately follows the left (opening) brace. The keyword identifies the action the command is to perform.

An *argument list* usually follows the keyword, with a space between the keyword and list. The arguments within the argument list provide the information necessary to carry out the command, and are separated by commas or semicolons. Arguments can be labels, values, addresses, block names, or logical expressions. A right (closing) brace always completes the command.

Conventions Used in This Chapter

In this chapter, all macro programming commands appear in uppercase. (Remember, though, that macro commands are not case sensitive.) Arguments appear in italic. If an argument is optional, it is enclosed in brackets, as in {BEEP [*tone-value*]}; this means that the {BEEP} command will work with or without a *tone-value* argument. If an argument is required, it appears without brackets, as in {GRAPHCHAR *location*}; in this case, you must specify a *location* argument for the {GRAPHCHAR} command.

Getting User Input

The Quattro Pro macro language provides six commands for getting user input: {?}, {GET}, {GETLABEL}, {GETNUMBER}, {LOOK}, and {GRAPHCHAR}. You can use these commands to solicit values, labels, menu selections, and keystrokes.

The {?} Command

{?} pauses macro execution until you press the Enter key. While the macro is suspended, you can position the cell selector, edit a cell entry, point to a block, or even select a menu command.

The simple macro in Figure 13.2 demonstrates one use of the {?} command. First the {/ Print;Block} menu-equivalent command prompts you for a block to print. The {?} then pauses the macro, allowing you to select the print block as you normally would—by entering a block address (or name), or by pointing to a block of cells. Note that when you press Enter to confirm your selection, Quattro Pro interprets this as a signal to continue on with the macro;

contrary to what you might expect, it does not treat your keypress as a confirmation response. Therefore, the macro includes a ~ (tilde) following the {?} to provide the confirmation. Without it, the macro does not work as intended.

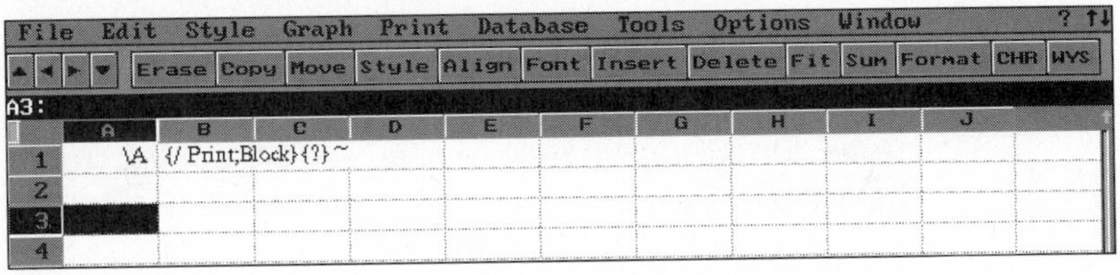

Figure 13.2

Example macro using the {?} command

As another example, suppose you want to use a macro to save the current spreadsheet.

You could use the following commands:

```
{/ File;Save}{?}~
```

When you run this macro, Quattro Pro presents you with a dialog box that contains the current name of the spreadsheet. You can accept the name as is or change it to whatever you like. When you press Enter to confirm your entry, Quattro Pro resumes macro execution with the ~ command, which saves the spreadsheet.

You can also use the {?} command as a debugging tool. Simply insert it where you want your macro to pause. While the macro is suspended, you can inspect various areas of the spreadsheet to verify your macro's operation. When you are finished, press Enter to continue with the macro. However, there is one caveat: Be careful when using {?} with macros that are dependent on the position of the cell selector; if you press Enter without first returning the cell selector to the appropriate cell, your macro will not work properly.

The {GET} Command

{GET} is useful for capturing single keystrokes. The syntax of the command is

```
{GET location}
```

This command halts macro execution until you press a key. Quattro Pro then stores the key as a left-aligned label in *location*. You can specify either a cell or a block for *location*. If you use a block, the keystroke is stored in the first cell of the block.

How your keystroke is represented in the left-aligned label depends on the key you press. For instance, if you press a standard letter or number key,

Quattro Pro uses that letter or number in the label—for example, pressing **1** produces the label '1. If there is a keystroke instruction associated with the key, however, Quattro Pro uses that instruction instead—for instance, pressing the → key produces the label '{RIGHT}. (See Table 12.1 in Chapter 12 for a list of keyboard commands in macros.)

The only keystrokes that cannot be captured with {GET} are Help (F1), which cannot be accessed from within a macro, and Ctrl-Break, which interrupts the current macro (provided {BREAKOFF} is not in effect).

Figure 13.3 demonstrates use of the {GET} command. The first line of the macro displays the prompt "Do you want to continue (Y/N)?" on the edit line. To speed updating of the screen, Quattro Pro always turns off the panel display (the edit line and menus). Therefore, the next command in this macro, {PANELON}, turns the panel display back on so that you can see the new prompt on the edit line. (If you do not include this command, the prompt will not appear. See "Managing the Screen" later for more on {PANELON}.) The {GET KEY} command waits for a keypress and enters that keypress into the cell KEY (B8). {ESC} then removes the prompt from the edit line. {IF} tests whether you press N or n. If you press either one, the macro continues executing the instructions to the right of the {IF} command, where {HOME} places the cell selector at cell A1 and {QUIT} terminates the macro. If you press any other key, the macro simply starts at the beginning again, repeating indefinitely until you press N or n in response to the prompt.

Figure 13.3

A macro using the {GET} command

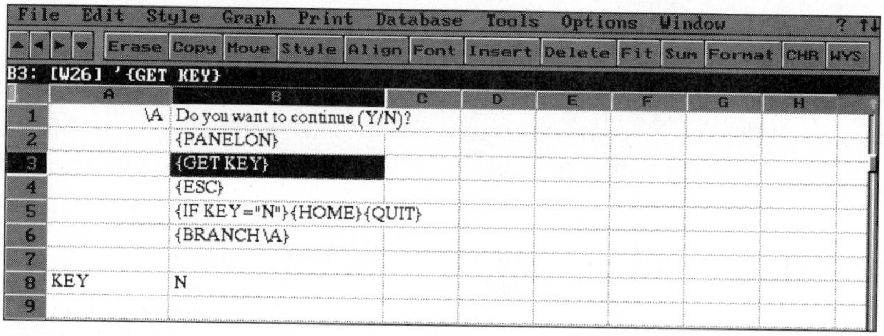

The {GETLABEL} Command

{GETLABEL} is useful for getting label input. This command takes the form

```
{GETLABEL prompt,location}
```

When Quattro Pro executes this command, it displays the first argument, *prompt*, in the input line and waits for your response. You can use any literal

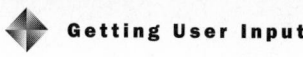

string for *prompt*. If the prompt string contains any commas, colons, or semi-colons, it must be enclosed in quotes. Note that because the prompt argument is processed literally, you cannot use a cell address or block name. The prompt string can be as many characters as will fit within the input line. If the prompt is longer, Quattro Pro wraps the prompt onto the next line.

Once you type a response and press Enter, {GETLABEL} stores your response as a left-aligned label in the cell address or block name specified by *location*. Like the {GET} command, if you specify a block for *location*, the keystroke is stored in the first cell of the block. If you press Enter without typing a response, Quattro Pro stores a ' label prefix in *location*.

The macro in Figure 13.4 uses the {GETLABEL} command to prompt you for address information, and stores that information in the spreadsheet. The macro starts by displaying the prompt "Please enter your name:" on the input line. After you type your name and press Enter, Quattro Pro stores your response in the block NAME (B8). Similar {GETLABEL} commands are used in each subsequent line of the macro. Notice that when you enter numbers in response to {GETLABEL}, they are stored as labels. For instance, the zip code 80213 is entered as '80213 in ZIP (B12).

Figure 13.4

A macro with several {GETLABEL} commands

	File	Edit	Style	Graph	Print	Database	Tools	Options	Window		? ↑↓
	▲ ◄ ► ▼	Erase	Copy	Move	Style	Align	Font	Insert	Delete	Fit	Sum	Format	CHR	WYS

A1: [W15] "\A

	A	B	C	D	E	F	G	H	I	J
1	\A	{GETLABEL "Please enter your name:",NAME}								
2		{GETLABEL "Please enter your address:",ADDRESS}								
3		{GETLABEL "Please enter the city you reside in:",CITY}								
4		{GETLABEL "Please enter the state you reside in:",STATE}								
5		{GETLABEL "Please enter your Zip code:",ZIP}								
6										
7										
8	NAME	Grizzly Adams								
9	ADDRESS	4433 Pine Cone Path								
10	CITY	Rocky Moutains								
11	STATE	CO								
12	ZIP	80213								
13										

The {GETNUMBER} Command

The {GETNUMBER} command is similar to {GETLABEL}, except that you use {GETNUMBER} to get numeric input.

The syntax is as follows:

```
{GETNUMBER prompt,location}
```

For an explanation of the arguments, see {GETLABEL}.

The response to the {GETNUMBER} prompt must be a number, a numeric formula, or a cell address or block name of a number or numeric formula. If you enter a label, a string formula, or a reference to a cell containing a label or string formula, Quattro Pro stores ERR in *location*. Likewise, if you press Enter without typing a response, Quattro Pro stores ERR in *location*.

The macro in Figure 13.5 uses the {GETNUMBER} command to prompt you for your age and stores it in AGE (B4). For example, if you type **34** in response to the prompt and press Enter, Quattro Pro places that value in B4. Suppose you want to enter your age in months. If you run the macro again and type the formula **12*34**, Quattro Pro stores the number 408 in B4.

Figure 13.5

The {GETNUMBER} command

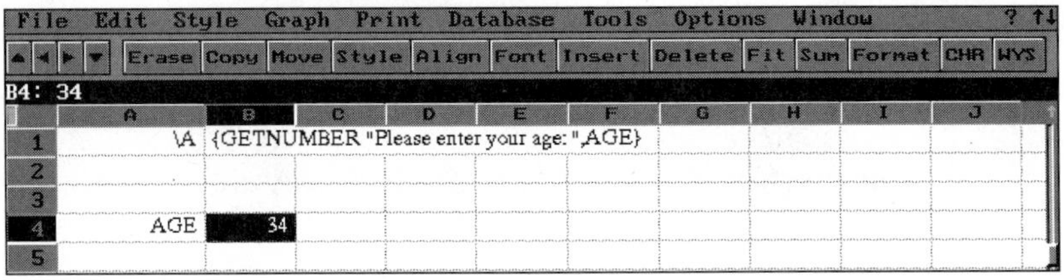

The {LOOK} Command

{LOOK} is used for monitoring the keyboard buffer while a macro is running. If you type keystrokes while a macro is not receiving user input, Quattro Pro stores them in an area of RAM called the *keyboard buffer*. It then uses the stored keystrokes the next time the macro pauses for input (or when the macro terminates).

The syntax of this command is

```
{LOOK location}
```

where *location* is the address or name of a cell in which you want Quattro Pro to store the first keystroke from the keyboard buffer. As with the {GET} command, the keystroke is stored as a left-aligned label. If a keystroke is not found in the keyboard buffer, Quattro Pro enters a ' label prefix in *location*.

The macro in Figure 13.6 uses the {LOOK} command to monitor the keyboard while a print macro is executing. First the {GETNUMBER} command is used to prompt you for the number of lines to advance the printer. The value you enter is stored in the cell named LINES (B19) and is used as the iteration count for the {FOR} command (see "Decision-Making Commands" later). The {FOR} command processes the subroutine ADVANCE (beginning in cell B4) for the number of times specified in LINES.

Figure 13.6
The {LOOK}
command

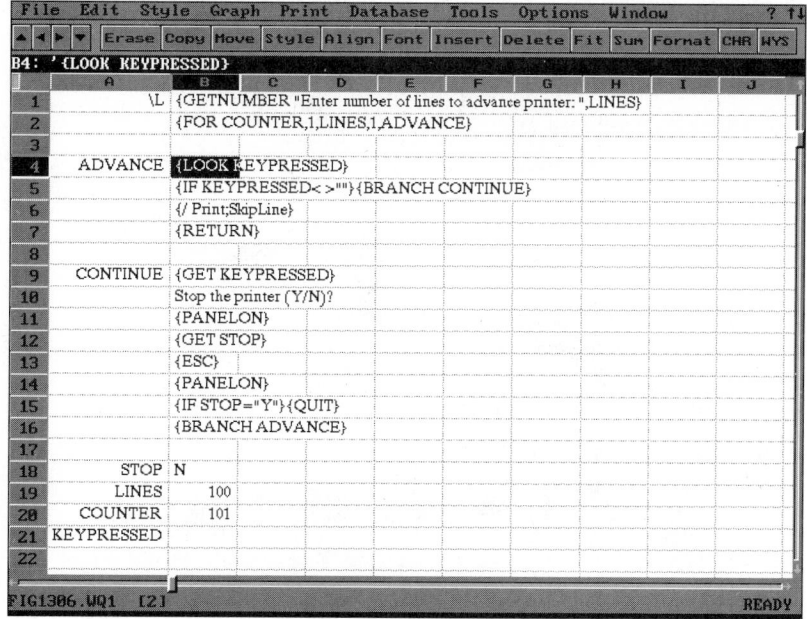

Note. {LOOK} does not remove the keystroke from the keyboard buffer—it merely examines it. If you want to retrieve the keystroke from the buffer, you'll need to use the {GET} command.

The first line of the ADVANCE subroutine uses {LOOK} to write the first keystroke in the keystroke buffer to the cell named KEYPRESSED (B21). The {IF} command in the second line then tests the contents of KEY-PRESSED. If KEYPRESSED contains a label—that is, you pressed a key to interrupt the macro—the macro branches to CONTINUE (cell B9). Otherwise, it processes the {/ Print;SkipLine} menu-equivalent command to advance the printer by one line, executes the {RETURN} command (which completes the subroutine), and returns control to the {FOR} command for the next iteration.

The {GET KEYPRESSED} command in the first line of the CONTINUE routine is necessary to cast away the keystroke you entered to interrupt the macro. Without this command, the keystroke remains in the keyboard buffer and might interfere with the {GET STOP} that follows. After {GET KEY-PRESSED}, the remaining commands in the CONTINUE routine are nearly identical to those for the macro in Figure 13.3. The macro displays the prompt "Stop the printer (Y/N)?" in the input line. If you press n or N, the macro terminates; if you press any other key, the macro branches back to the AD-VANCE subroutine and continues.

The {GRAPHCHAR} Command

{GRAPHCHAR} lets you capture the keystroke that was entered to leave a graph or to clear a message box. (To produce a message box, you use the {MESSAGE} command. See "Managing the Screen" later in this chapter.) The syntax for {GRAPHCHAR} is

{GRAPHCHAR *location*}

where *location* is the cell address or block name where {GRAPHCHAR} stores the keystroke as a left-aligned label.

You can use {GRAPHCHAR} together with {MESSAGE} to create interactive messages. For example, the macro in Figure 13.7 uses these commands to present the user with a menu of printing options.

Figure 13.7

A macro using the {GRAPHCHAR} command

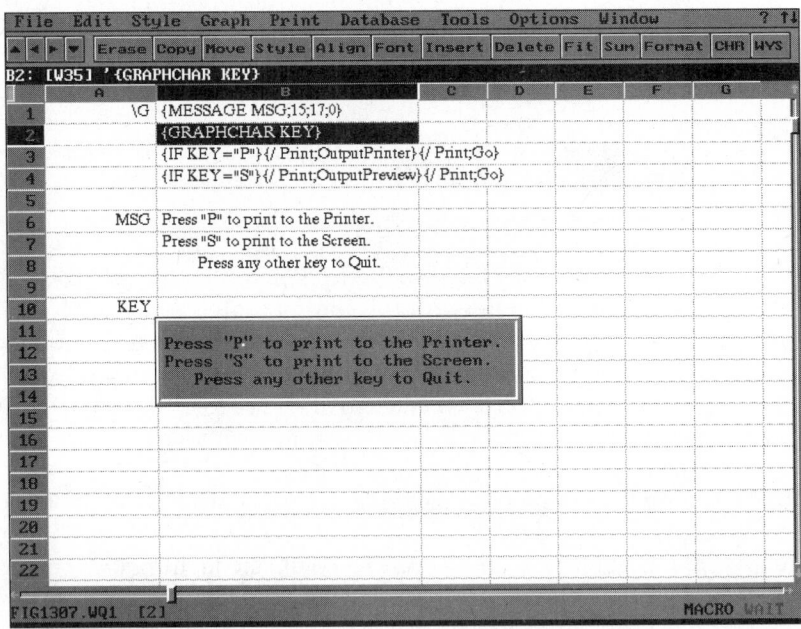

Note. The {GRAPHCHAR} command can only by used with a {MESSAGE} command that has a time argument of 0.

The {MESSAGE} command in the first line of the macro displays the message defined in the MSG block (B6..B8). Because {MESSAGE} has a *time* argument of 0, the message remains on the screen until you press a key. At that point the message is read by {GRAPHCHAR}, which stores the keypress in KEY (B10). The subsequent {IF} commands test the contents of KEY. The first {IF} tests whether KEY is equal to P (that is, you pressed p or

P in response to the message box). If it is, the macro uses the {/ Print;Output-Printer} and {/ Print;Go} commands to direct your output to the printer. On the other hand, if KEY is equal to S (you pressed s or S in response to the message box), the commands {/ Print;OutputPreview} and {/ Print;Go} are executed to direct your output to the screen.

Manipulating Data

Quattro Pro provides four macro commands for manipulating spreadsheet data. These commands are similar to the /Edit, Erase Block, /Edit, Values, and /Edit, Copy menu commands, but are more powerful.

The {BLANK} Command

{BLANK} erases the contents of a cell or block of cells. The syntax for the command is

```
{BLANK location}
```

where *location* is a cell or block. For example, the command {BLANK A1} erases the contents of cell A1. Likewise, {BLANK ZEBRA} erases the contents of the block named ZEBRA.

Like the /Edit, Erase Block command, {BLANK} does not remove cell formatting. This macro command is useful for initializing cells that your macro may later use.

The {CONTENTS} Command

{CONTENTS} copies the contents of a cell to another cell as a label. The label that Quattro Pro produces resembles the contents of the original cell as displayed on the screen. This command is most helpful for converting a numeric or date value to a label for use in a string formula.

The syntax of the command is

```
{CONTENTS destination,source,[width],[format]}
```

where *destination* is the cell to which you want the string written, and *source* is the cell containing the data to be copied. *Width* is an optional argument specifying the width of the *destination* string. The *format* argument, also optional, specifies the numeric format of the *destination* string.

If you don't specify a *width* argument, Quattro Pro uses the width of the *source* cell (not the width of the *destination* cell) to determine the length of the destination string. Quattro Pro accepts any number or expression in the range 0 to 254 for the *width* argument. The *width* argument is especially useful when your *source* value is displayed as a series of asterisks (******), indicating that the column it resides in is too narrow for the value. By using a *width* argument that is sufficiently large, you can be sure that the *destination* string will appear in the proper numeric format.

As shown in the input line in Figure 13.8, the value stored in B3 (SALES) is 120.34. But because this value is formatted as Currency, 2 places, and the column is only six characters wide, the value is displayed as asterisks. The macro in B1 uses the {CONTENTS} command to copy the contents of SALES as displayed in that cell, to OUTPUT (B4). To allow the *destination* string to appear as ' $120.34 , rather than all asterisks, {CONTENTS} includes a *width* argument of 9. In this case, there is one blank space preceding the $ and another following the 4. In fact, this is how the value in cell B3 would appear on the screen if the width of column A were set to 9.

Figure 13.8

The {CONTENTS} command using the *width* argument

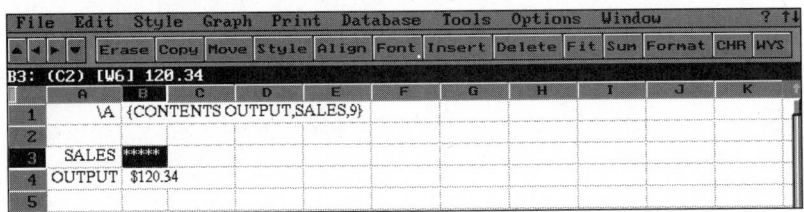

Notice that no *format* argument is used in the previous example. When the *format* argument is absent, the format of the *destination* string is the same as the *source* value. If you want to change the format of the *destination* string, you can use one of the special format codes in Table 13.3.

Figure 13.9 shows the *format* argument used with the {CONTENTS} command to change the format of the *destination* string. In this example, cell B3 (CLOSE) contains the date value 33969 and is formatted using the Long International format. To change the format of the *destination* string to Date 1 (DD-MMM-YY), a *format* argument of 114 is used.

Figure 13.9

Using a *format* argument with the {CONTENTS} command to change the format of the *destination* string

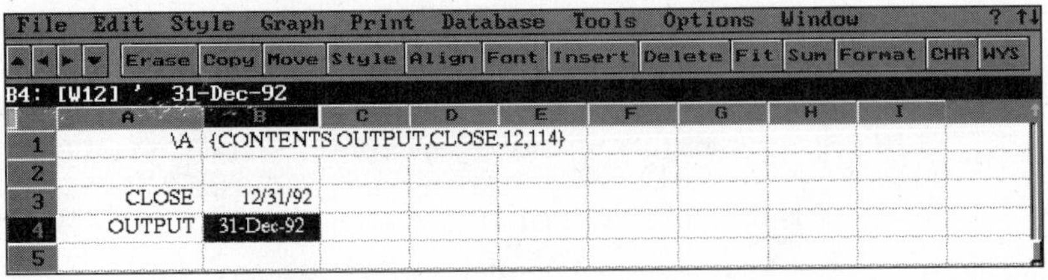

Table 13.3 **Numeric Format Codes for the {CONTENTS} Command**

Code Number	Resulting Cell Format
0 to 15	Fixed, 0 to 15 decimals
16 to 31	Scientific, 0 to 15 decimals
32 to 47	Currency, 0 to 15 decimals
48 to 63	% (Percent), 0 to 15 decimals
64 to 79	, (Comma), 0 to 15 decimals
112	+/– (Bar Graph)
113	General
114	Date [1] (DD-MMM-YY)
115	Date [2] (DD-MMM)
116	Date [3] (MMM-YY)
117	Text
118	Hidden
119	Time [1] (HH:MM:SS AM/PM)
120	Time [2] (HH:MM AM/PM)
121	Date [4] (Long International)
122	Date [5] (Short International)
123	Time [3] (Long International)
124	Time [4] (Short International)
127	Default (set with /Options, Formats, Numeric Format)

The {LET} Command

{LET} is used to copy label or numeric data from one cell to another.
Though there are other Quattro Pro commands that perform this same function—for example, /Edit, Copy—{LET} is the only one that does not change,
nor is it sensitive to, the position of the cell selector. Nor does the {LET}
command copy format information.

The syntax of {LET} is

```
{LET location,data}
```

where *location* can be a cell or block. If *location* is a block, Quattro Pro will use the first cell in the block. *Data* can be any string, number, formula, or block name. If you use a formula for *data*, Quattro Pro evaluates the formula and stores the result in *location*.

For example, suppose you want to include in your macro a counter that is incremented by one each time the macro is run. Figure 13.10 shows such a macro. Here the {LET} command simply adds one to the current value of COUNT (cell B3) and stores it back into COUNT. Every time you run this macro, COUNT will be incremented by one.

Figure 13.10
The {LET} command

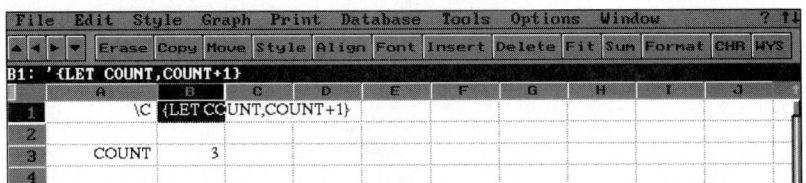

As you use the {LET} command, be aware that if the block named in the *data* argument contains more than one cell, then the block name itself is treated as the data to be copied. For instance, with the command {LET A1,TOTAL}, if TOTAL is a one-cell block, then Quattro Pro copies the contents of TOTAL to cell A1. If TOTAL contains more than one cell, however, then the label 'TOTAL is copied to cell A1.

The :string and :value Suffixes

Note. The :string and :value suffixes are also an important ingredient of the {DEFINE} command, because they let you control the input to a subroutine.

You can use a :string or :value suffix to control how Quattro Pro treats the *data* argument in the {LET} command. A :string suffix following the *data* argument, tells Quattro Pro to handle the argument as a string and place it in the spreadsheet as is. If you use the :value suffix, however, Quattro Pro evaluates the argument first before placing it in the spreadsheet.

For instance, if cell A2 contains the value 10, and cell A3 contains the value 20, the command {LET A1,+A2+A3:value} stores the value 30 in cell A1. On the other hand, the command {LET A1,+A2+A3:string} stores the string '+A2+A3 in cell A1.

The {PUT} Command

Like the {LET} command, {PUT} copies a value or string from one cell to another. Instead of storing the value in an explicit location, however, {PUT} uses row and column offsets within a cell block to determine where to store the data.

The syntax of the command is

```
{PUT location,column,row,data}
```

where *location* is a two-dimensional block of any size, and *row* and *column* are zero-based offsets within that block.

The *column* and *row* arguments are handled much the same as the offsets you use for the @HLOOKUP and @VLOOKUP functions discussed in Chapter 7. The first column (or row) in the block is offset 0, the second column (or row) is offset 1, and so on. If you want to address the cell that is in column 4 and row 6 of *location*, for example, you would use a *column* argument of 3 and a *row* argument of 5.

As with the {LET} command, the *data* argument for {PUT} can be any string, number, formula, or block name, and you can use a :string or :value suffix to control how the *data* argument is treated.

Suppose you need a macro that will enter amounts into a matrix whose columns represent years and rows represent months, as in the example macro in Figure 13.11. The first three lines of the macro use {GETNUMBER} to prompt you for the year, month (as a number), and amount. The {PUT} command in the fourth line uses the @MOD function to determine in what column and row within the LOCATION block (B11..F13) the amount should be stored. Let's say you enter 1992 for the year, 3 (March) for the month, and 3000 for the amount. The {PUT} command determines the *column* and *row* arguments as follows: *column* resolves to 4, because it is the remainder (or *modula*) of 1992 divided by 1988; *row* resolves to 2, because it is the modula of 3+2 divided by 3. Therefore, the value 3000 is stored in the lower-right corner of the matrix, or where the year 1992 and the month of March intersect.

Stopping and Suspending Macro Execution

Quattro Pro provides two commands for stopping and suspending macro execution—{QUIT} and {WAIT}. The {QUIT} command stops a macro entirely. When you need to pause or suspend your macro for a period of time, however, you can use the {WAIT} command.

Figure 13.11

A macro using the
{PUT} command

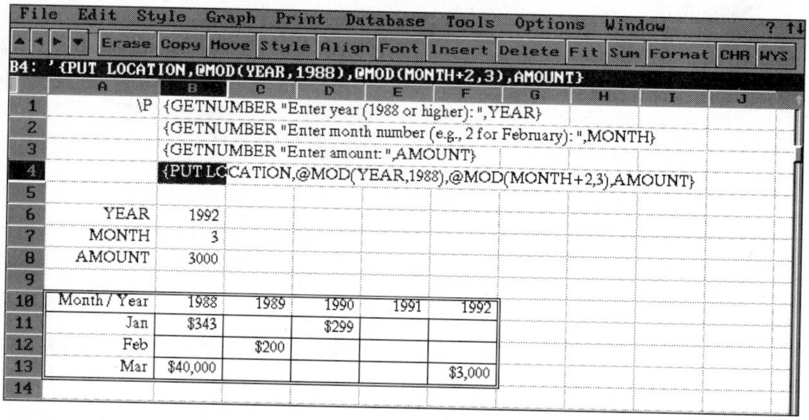

The {QUIT} Command

You will recall from Chapter 12 that Quattro Pro stops macro execution when
it encounters an empty cell. Another way of stopping macro execution is by
using the {QUIT} command. The advantage of using {QUIT} is that you can
place it anywhere in a macro, either in the main macro routine or a subroutine.

{QUIT} is particularly useful for stopping a macro when a certain condition is met. For example, the following macro code uses {QUIT} in combination with {IF} to stop the macro when a certain value is reached:

```
{IF COUNT=10}{QUIT}
```

This code assumes that you have another macro statement that is increment-
ing COUNT, such as {LET COUNT,COUNT+1}. When COUNT is equal to
10, Quattro Pro processes the {QUIT} command following the {IF}, terminating the macro.

The {WAIT} Command

{WAIT} pauses a macro until a specified time. The syntax of the command is

```
{WAIT date-time-number}
```

where *date-time-number* is a future point in time, and may be a literal date
number, a date formula, or a cell reference to either one of these. A formula is commonly used as the *date-time-number* argument. For example,
the command

```
{WAIT @NOW+@TIME(0,0,10)}
```

changes the status line indicator to WAIT, and pauses the macro until your system time is equal to the current time plus 10 seconds. It's important that *date-time-number* is a future point in time; otherwise, your macro will not pause at all.

If you find that you are waiting "forever" for the {WAIT} command to end, you can use Ctrl-Break, as always, to interrupt the macro. Of course, the exception to this is when you have a {BREAKOFF} in effect. Then your only recourse is to reboot.

Managing Ctrl-Break

As you know, you can press Ctrl-Break at any time while a macro is running, to stop its execution. If your macro is to be used by others, however, you may want to prevent them from using Ctrl-Break during certain critical macro tasks, such as when the macro is writing to a file. Quattro Pro provides two macro commands for managing Ctrl-Break: {BREAKOFF} and {BREAKON}. {BREAKOFF} disables the Ctrl-Break sequence, and {BREAKON} reactivates it.

The following commands demonstrate how you can use {BREAKOFF} and {BREAKON} to manage Ctrl-Break:

```
{BREAKOFF}
{PRINT_IT}
{BREAKON}
```

Here {BREAKOFF} disables Ctrl-Break before a printing subroutine commences. When the {PRINT_IT} subroutine has finished, the {BREAKON} command gets processed, restoring the validity of Ctrl-Break.

Besides protecting critical macro tasks from being interrupted, another reason to disable Ctrl-Break is to prevent users from inadvertently overwriting your macro instructions. Suppressing Ctrl-Break also ensures that your macro will be executed as you intended, from start to finish.

The disadvantage to disabling Ctrl-Break is that it prevents the user from aborting a macro that was started inadvertently. Moreover, it precludes the user from stopping a macro that is looping or waiting endlessly. The only recourse under these circumstances is to reboot the computer. Therefore, it's wise to fully debug a macro before adding a {BREAKOFF} command to it.

{BREAK} has the same effect as pressing Ctrl-Break. That is, it returns the spreadsheet to Ready mode from any other current mode. For instance, pressing Ctrl-Break when editing a cell (Edit mode) or when selecting a print block (Point mode) aborts the current operation and returns Quattro Pro to Ready mode. Note that the {BREAK} command is not at all related to {BREAKOFF} and {BREAKON}.

Decision-Making Commands

Much of the power of Quattro Pro's macro language comes from its decision-making commands—in particular, the ones that provide conditional processing and looping. *Conditional processing* refers to a program's ability to change its execution path based on a condition. The {IF} and {IFKEY} commands are used for conditional processing. *Looping*, on the other hand, means repeating a command until a condition is met. {FOR} and {FORBREAK} are the macro commands used to implement looping.

The {IF} Command

The {IF} command performs the simplest kind of conditional processing in Quattro Pro. You use it to make a decision when there are two alternative outcomes. The syntax for the command is

```
{IF condition}
```

where *condition* is a logical expression—a formula that compares values or strings, using a conditional operator, and resolves to either true or false. *Condition* is false if it resolves to zero. All other values for *condition* are true. *Condition* can also be the address of a cell that contains a label, value, or logical expression.

When *condition* resolves to true, macro execution continues with the commands in the same cell that follow the {IF}. When *condition* resolves to false, Quattro Pro skips to the cell directly beneath the {IF} command and begins executing the commands in that cell. {IF} commands cannot be nested.

Figure 13.12 demonstrates some typical {IF} commands. The first example uses a straightforward numeric comparison. In this case, if the value in INVOICE_AMOUNT is greater than 5000, the macro branches to the subroutine CALC_DISCOUNT. Otherwise, the macro branches to NO_DISCOUNT.

The second {IF} command performs a simple string comparison. Like the @IF function, the comparison is not case sensitive. In other words, the strings "Donald Trump" and "DONALD TRUMP" are treated as equal.

When Quattro Pro compares a string to a value, however, the string is assigned a value of zero. Unfortunately, this is the same value assigned to a blank cell. For instance, if A1 is blank, the formula +A1="Quattro Pro" returns true (1). You can get around this undesirable behavior by using two {IF} statements in succession; the first one tests for a blank cell, and the second performs the string comparison. For example, in B10 of Figure 13.12, both {IF} commands are necessary to handle the case when CUSTOMER is blank.

Figure 13.12

Typical {IF} command applications

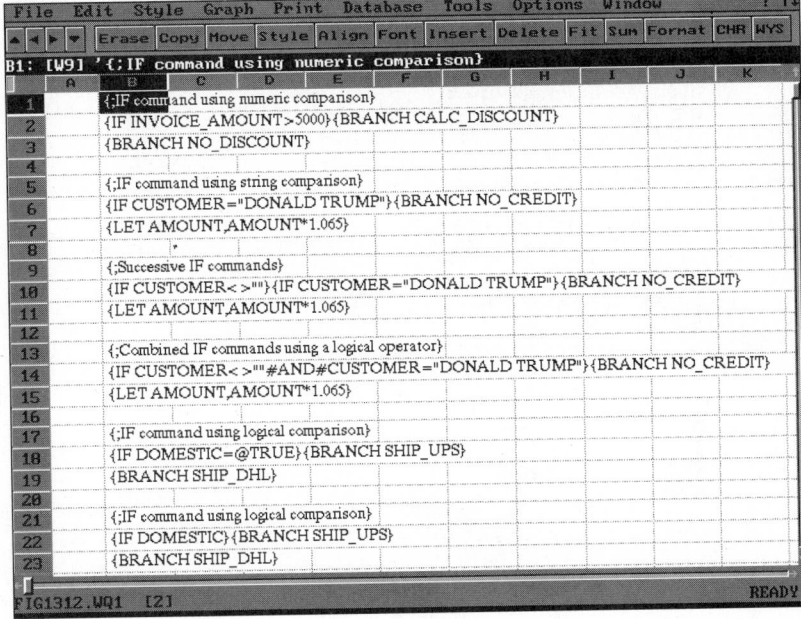

```
 File  Edit  Style  Graph  Print  Database  Tools  Options  Window    ? ↑↓
 ◄ ◄ ► ▼  Erase Copy Move Style Align Font Insert Delete Fit Sum Format CHR WYS
B1: [W9] '{;IF command using numeric comparison}
      A       B        C        D       E       F       G       H       I       J       K
 1         {;IF command using numeric comparison}
 2         {IF INVOICE_AMOUNT>5000}{BRANCH CALC_DISCOUNT}
 3         {BRANCH NO_DISCOUNT}
 4
 5         {;IF command using string comparison}
 6         {IF CUSTOMER="DONALD TRUMP"}{BRANCH NO_CREDIT}
 7         {LET AMOUNT,AMOUNT*1.065}
 8
 9         {;Successive IF commands}
10         {IF CUSTOMER<>""}{IF CUSTOMER="DONALD TRUMP"}{BRANCH NO_CREDIT}
11         {LET AMOUNT,AMOUNT*1.065}
12
13         {;Combined IF commands using a logical operator}
14         {IF CUSTOMER<>""#AND#CUSTOMER="DONALD TRUMP"}{BRANCH NO_CREDIT}
15         {LET AMOUNT,AMOUNT*1.065}
16
17         {;IF command using logical comparison}
18         {IF DOMESTIC=@TRUE}{BRANCH SHIP_UPS}
19         {BRANCH SHIP_DHL}
20
21         {;IF command using logical comparison}
22         {IF DOMESTIC}{BRANCH SHIP_UPS}
23         {BRANCH SHIP_DHL}
FIG1312.WQ1  [2]                                                      READY
```

The fourth example in Figure 13.12 demonstrates how you can combine two {IF} statements into one by using compound logical *conditions*. In this case, the two *conditions* are joined with the #AND# logical operator. This macro command is functionally equivalent to the two successive {IF}s in the previous example.

The fifth example in Figure 13.12 shows how you can use a logical comparison in an {IF} command. It evaluates to true if the cell DOMESTIC is nonzero. The sixth {IF} command is functionally equivalent to the fifth one.

The {IFKEY} Command

{IFKEY} performs another type of conditional processing. It returns true if the keystroke string passed to it is associated with a macro keystroke representation. This command is useful for checking what type of key the user has pressed. (See Table 12.1 for a list of macro keystroke instructions.)

The syntax for this command is

```
{IFKEY string}
```

If you want to use a cell reference or block name to reference a string, the *string* argument must be preceded by a plus (+) symbol. For example, {IFKEY +A1} evaluates the string in cell A1.

Suppose you want to allow the user to move about the spreadsheet from within a macro, but only by pressing cursor movement keys. The macro in Figure 13.13 demonstrates how to do this.

Figure 13.13

An {IFKEY} macro

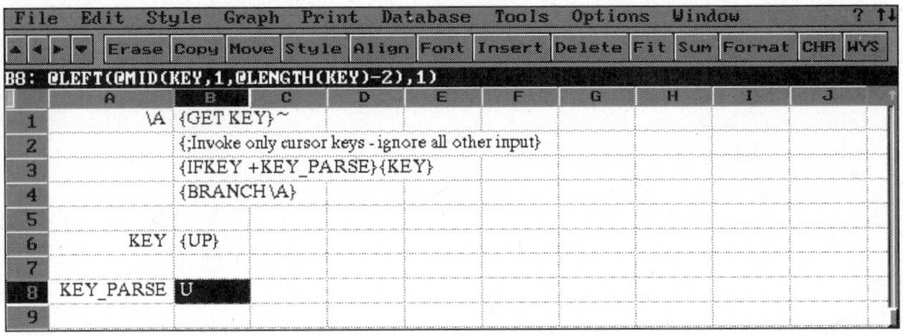

	File Edit Style Graph Print Database Tools Options Window								? ↑↓
▲ ◄ ► ▼	Erase	Copy	Move	Style	Align	Font	Insert	Delete	Fit	Sum	Format	CHR	WYS

B8: @LEFT(@MID(KEY,1,@LENGTH(KEY)-2),1)

	A	B	C	D	E	F	G	H	I	J
1		\A	{GET KEY}~							
2			{;Invoke only cursor keys - ignore all other input}							
3			{IFKEY +KEY_PARSE}{KEY}							
4			{BRANCH \A}							
5										
6		KEY	{UP}							
7										
8	KEY_PARSE	U								
9										

The first line of the macro uses {GET} to get a single keystroke from the user and then store it in KEY (cell B6). The tilde (~) following {GET} is necessary to update any cells that depend on the KEY cell, in this case KEY_PARSE (B8). To evaluate the input keystroke string properly, {IFKEY} must look at the string without the braces. Therefore, cell KEY_PARSE uses the following formula:

```
@LEFT(@MID(KEY,1,@LENGTH(KEY)-2),1)
```

The @MID(KEY,1,@LENGTH(KEY)–2) portion of this formula strips the braces from the input string—for example, {DOWN} becomes DOWN. Because you want to limit the user's keystrokes to only cursor keys, the @LEFT function strips all characters from the keystroke string except the first—for example, DOWN becomes D. You'll see the importance of these gymnastics in a minute.

The second line of the macro uses {IFKEY} to determine whether the string in the KEY_PARSE cell is one of the macro keystroke commands. Because {IFKEY} is looking at only one character of the keystroke string (by virtue of the @LEFT function in the KEY_PARSE formula), the only keystroke strings that evaluate to true are U, D, L, and R (the macro keystroke abbreviations for the cursor keys {U}, {D}, {L}, and {R}, without the curly braces). When KEY_PARSE evaluates to one of these strings, macro execution continues in the same cell, invoking the {KEY} subroutine, which contains the cursor key that was pressed. This results in the accordant movement of the cell selector. If any other keystrokes are entered, they are simply ignored.

The {FOR} Command

{FOR} is used to repeatedly call a subroutine. It is the {FOR} command that gives Quattro Pro's macro language its looping capability. Here is the syntax for the command, followed by definitions of its arguments.

```
{FOR counter,start-number,stop-number,step-number,location}
```

- *Counter* is a spreadsheet cell to which the value of *start-number* is set when the {FOR} command begins. Each time the macro at *location* is executed, the number stored in *counter* is incremented by *step-number*.

- *Start-number* is the number to which *counter* is set when the {FOR} command begins.

- *Stop-number* is the number that determines when Quattro Pro stops looping. When the *counter* is equal to or greater than *stop-number*, the {FOR} command is terminated and control is passed to the next macro command.

- *Step-number* is the number by which *counter* is incremented each time through the loop.

- *Location* is an address or block name identifying the starting cell of the subroutine to be executed.

Note. Because Quattro Pro stores the *start-*, *stop-*, and *step-number* values internally, there is no way to modify them while the {FOR} command is executing.

Figure 13.14 shows how you might use {FOR} to enter a series of values starting at the current cell selector location, and format them as currency. The first two lines of the macro use {GETNUMBER} to prompt you for the number of values to enter and the starting value of the series. Next, the macro executes the {FOR} command in cell B3. This command sets up the *counter* argument as COUNTER (B5). The *start-number* argument is 1; the *stop-number* argument is NUMBER (cell B6, where Quattro Pro stores your response for the number of values to enter); and the *step-number* argument is 1.

When the {FOR} command begins, *start-number* is copied to COUNTER (B5), and the LOOP subroutine is executed. This subroutine uses a {LET} command to add the START and COUNTER values and place the result at the current cell selector location. (It is important to start this macro in a column of empty cells; otherwise, data will be overwritten.) The cell is then formatted to Currency, 2 places, and the last command of the LOOP subroutine moves the cell selector down one cell. Then control returns to the {FOR} command. COUNTER is incremented by one, and COUNTER and NUMBER are compared. The LOOP macro is then processed repeatedly until COUNTER is greater than or equal to NUMBER.

See Figure 13.6 for another example of the {FOR} command.

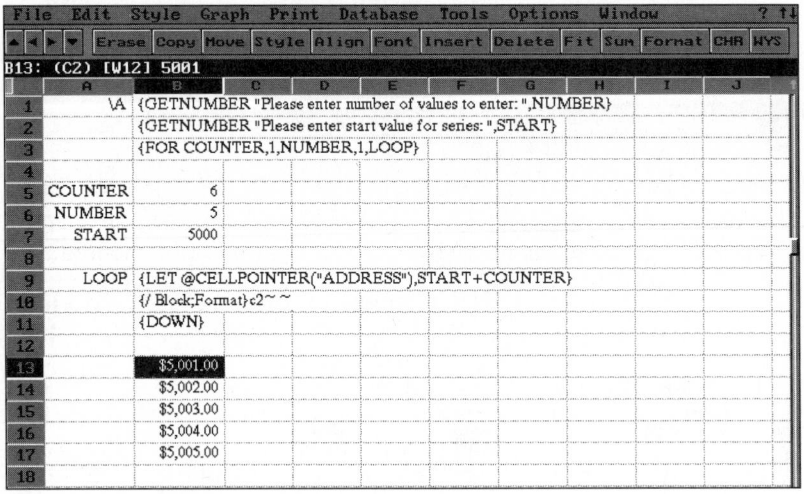

Figure 13.14

Using the {FOR} command in a macro

	File	Edit	Style	Graph	Print	Database	Tools	Options	Window	? ↑↓

| ▲ ◄ ► ▼ | Erase | Copy | Move | Style | Align | Font | Insert | Delete | Fit | Sum | Format | CHR | WYS |

B13: (C2) [W12] 5001

	A	B	C	D	E	F	G	H	I	J
1	\A	{GETNUMBER "Please enter number of values to enter: ",NUMBER}								
2		{GETNUMBER "Please enter start value for series: ",START}								
3		{FOR COUNTER,1,NUMBER,1,LOOP}								
4										
5	COUNTER	6								
6	NUMBER	5								
7	START	5000								
8										
9	LOOP	{LET @CELLPOINTER("ADDRESS"),START+COUNTER}								
10		{/ Block;Format}c2~ ~								
11		{DOWN}								
12										
13		$5,001.00								
14		$5,002.00								
15		$5,003.00								
16		$5,004.00								
17		$5,005.00								
18										

The {FORBREAK} Command

{FORBREAK} lets you cancel the execution of a {FOR} loop before its natural completion. When a macro encounters a {FORBREAK} command, it immediately returns execution to the cell below the one containing the {FOR} command. The {FORBREAK} command requires no arguments.

Figure 13.15 shows an example of the {FORBREAK} command. This macro prints ten copies of the current graph, but stops if a key is pressed. When you press a key during the {FOR} loop, the {FORBREAK} command is processed, thus passing control to the {/ Print;FormFeed} menu-equivalent command in the cell below the {FOR} command.

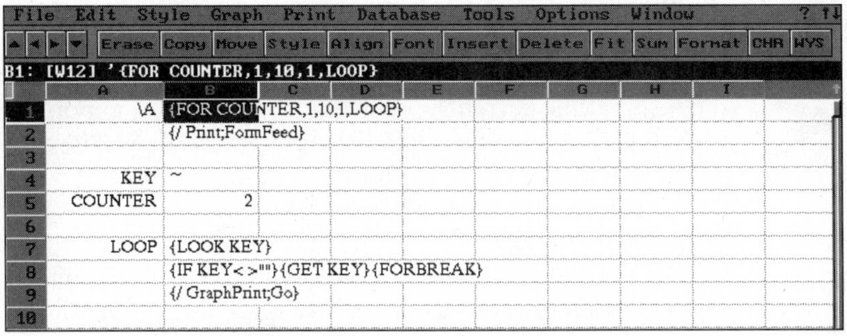

Figure 13.15

A macro using the {FORBREAK} command

	File	Edit	Style	Graph	Print	Database	Tools	Options	Window	? ↑↓

| ▲ ◄ ► ▼ | Erase | Copy | Move | Style | Align | Font | Insert | Delete | Fit | Sum | Format | CHR | WYS |

B1: [W12] '{FOR COUNTER,1,10,1,LOOP}

	A	B	C	D	E	F	G	H	I
1	\A	{FOR COUNTER,1,10,1,LOOP}							
2		{/ Print;FormFeed}							
3									
4	KEY	~							
5	COUNTER	2							
6									
7	LOOP	{LOOK KEY}							
8		{IF KEY<>""}{GET KEY}{FORBREAK}							
9		{/ GraphPrint;Go}							
10									

Branching

As you know, Quattro Pro processes your macro commands one at a time, proceeding down the column of macro labels until it encounters a blank cell or a {QUIT} command. With the {BRANCH} and {DISPATCH} commands, however, you can explicitly define the location at which Quattro Pro processes the next command.

The {BRANCH} Command

You can use {BRANCH} to transfer macro processing to another location in the spreadsheet. The syntax of the command is

```
{BRANCH location}
```

where *location* is the cell containing the command you want Quattro Pro to execute next. *Location* can be a cell address, a block reference, or a block name.

The {BRANCH} command is most often used with {IF}, as in the following macro line:

```
{IF COUNTER<100}{BRANCH NEXT}
```

The {IF} command performs a logical test. Here it tests whether the value in the cell named COUNTER is less than 100. If the test is true, Quattro Pro executes the {BRANCH} command following the {IF}, which transfers control to the cell named NEXT.

Suppose you want to create a macro to verify that the user has entered a value within a specified range. The macro in Figure 13.16 begins by prompting you to enter a month number from 1 to 12. If you enter a value outside this range, the logical test within {IF} resolves to true, and {BEEP} is processed, followed by {BRANCH}. {BRANCH} then transfers macro processing back to \A (cell A1, the beginning of the macro). This macro will repeat indefinitely until you enter a valid month number.

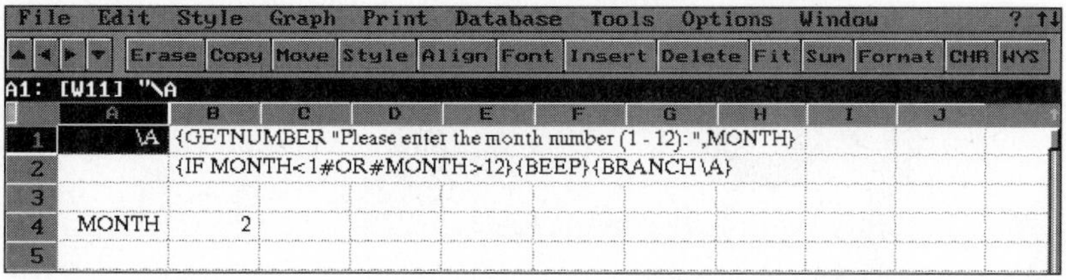

Figure 13.16

A macro using the {BRANCH} command

	A	B	C	D	E	F	G	H	I	J
1	\A	{GETNUMBER "Please enter the month number (1 - 12): ",MONTH}								
2		{IF MONTH<1#OR#MONTH>12}{BEEP}{BRANCH \A}								
3										
4	MONTH	2								
5										

A1: [W11] '\A

You can perform three types of branching with the {BRANCH} command, as follows:

■ *Branching within the active spreadsheet*   For example, the command {BRANCH \A} branches to the macro named \A in the active spreadsheet. If the name is not found in the active spreadsheet, Quattro Pro branches to the \A macro in a macro library, provided a macro library is open.

■ *Branching to another active spreadsheet*   For example, the command {BRANCH [SALES]\A} branches to the macro named \A in the SALES.WQ1 worksheet, provided the worksheet is active. If this \A macro is not found, Quattro Pro returns the error "Invalid cell or block address." Macro libraries are not searched.

■ *Branching from a macro library to the active spreadsheet*   For example, the macro {BRANCH []\A}, when placed in a macro library, branches to the macro named \A in the active spreadsheet.

The {DISPATCH} Command

{DISPATCH} works similarly to {BRANCH}, except that {DISPATCH} is used to perform indirect branching, where the argument you provide serves as a pointer to another cell. The syntax of the command is

```
{DISPATCH location}
```

where *location* is the cell address or block name of a cell containing another cell address or block name. The latter serves as the location to which Quattro Pro transfers macro processing.

For example, the {DISPATCH REFERENCE} command in Figure 13.17 does not cause Quattro Pro to branch to the cell named REFERENCE (B3). Rather, it branches to the block name DO_BEEP, as specified in the cell REFERENCE, and processes the {BEEP} command.

Figure 13.17

The {DISPATCH} command

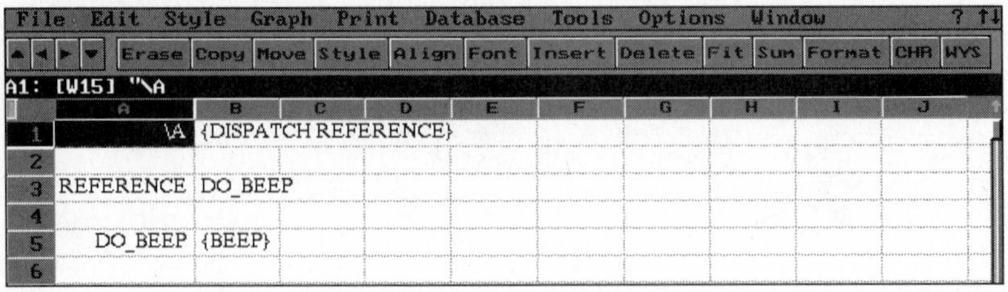

Subroutines

A subroutine is simply a macro invoked from another macro. The one special characteristic of a subroutine is that after Quattro Pro has finished processing it, control is returned back to the calling macro. A subroutine command takes the form

    {subroutine}

where *subroutine* is the cell address or block name where the subroutine begins. For example, the command {A1} tells Quattro Pro to process the series of commands starting in cell A1. Likewise, {DO_LAYOUT} tells Quattro Pro to process the commands beginning at the cell named DO_LAYOUT. Using subroutines, you can, in effect, create your own advanced macro commands.

You can nest subroutines—that is, one subroutine can call another subroutine—up to 32 levels.

Be careful not to use Quattro Pro macro names when assigning names to your subroutines. If your subroutine's name is the same as one of Quattro Pro's reserved macro commands, the Quattro Pro command will be executed, not your subroutine.

Suppose you want to write a macro that prompts you for a block name, enters that name as an uppercase label in the current cell, and then automatically uses the label to assign a block name to the cell immediately to the right. The macro in Figure 13.18 accomplishes these steps using a subroutine to perform the majority of the work. In the first line of the macro, a {GET-LABEL} command prompts you for the name of the block. The second line of the macro invokes the {NAME_CREATE} subroutine. When this subroutine has completed processing (Quattro Pro encounters a blank cell), control is returned to the cell following the {NAME_CREATE} subroutine call.

The {RETURN} Command

{RETURN} allows you to pass control back to the calling macro before a subroutine has completed.

The {PRINT_IT} subroutine in Figure 13.19 shows how you might use the {RETURN} command to exit a subroutine—without having to execute all the commands within it. In this example, if you type n or N in response to the "Print label?" prompt, Quattro Pro executes the {RETURN} command, ending the subroutine. The printing portion of the subroutine is never executed.

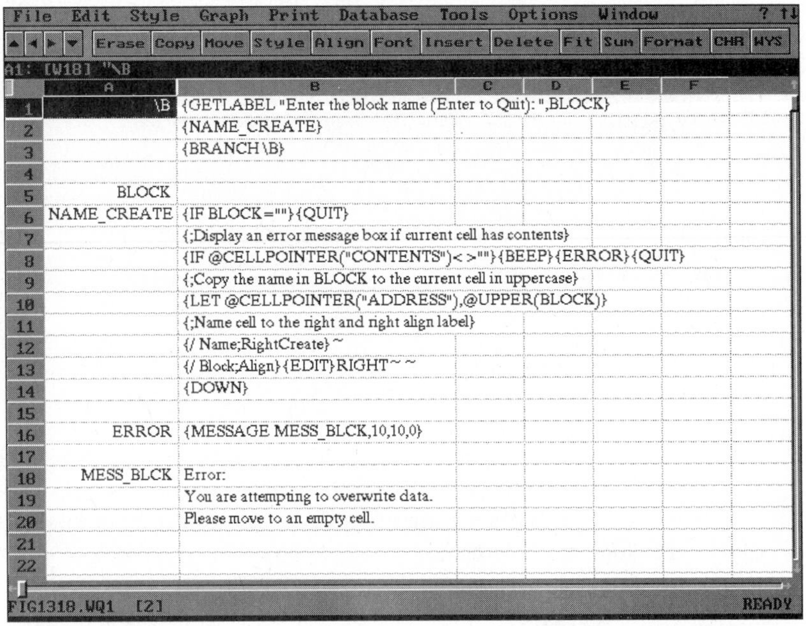

Figure 13.18

A macro that contains a {subroutine} command

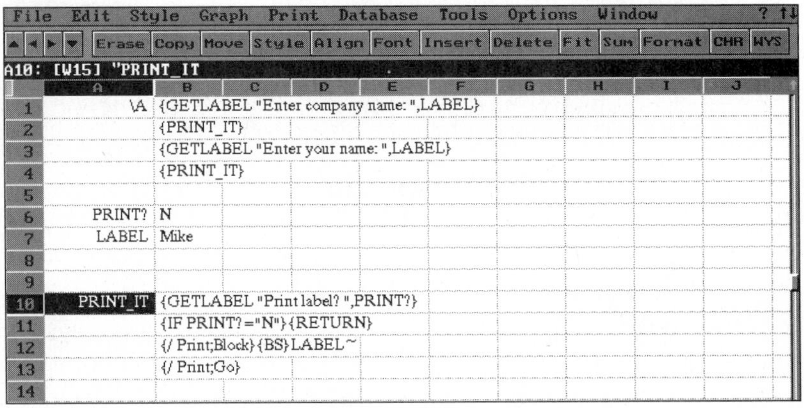

	File Edit Style Graph Print Database Tools Options Window	? ↑↓
	Erase Copy Move Style Align Font Insert Delete Fit Sum Format CHR WYS	

A1: [W18] '\B

	A	B	C	D	E	F
1	\B	{GETLABEL "Enter the block name (Enter to Quit): ",BLOCK}				
2		{NAME_CREATE}				
3		{BRANCH \B}				
4						
5	BLOCK					
6	NAME_CREATE	{IF BLOCK=""}{QUIT}				
7		{;Display an error message box if current cell has contents}				
8		{IF @CELLPOINTER("CONTENTS")< >""}{BEEP}{ERROR}{QUIT}				
9		{;Copy the name in BLOCK to the current cell in uppercase}				
10		{LET @CELLPOINTER("ADDRESS"),@UPPER(BLOCK)}				
11		{;Name cell to the right and right align label}				
12		{/ Name;RightCreate} ~				
13		{/ Block;Align}{EDIT}RIGHT~ ~				
14		{DOWN}				
15						
16	ERROR	{MESSAGE MESS_BLCK,10,10,0}				
17						
18	MESS_BLCK	Error:				
19		You are attempting to overwrite data.				
20		Please move to an empty cell.				
21						
22						

FIG1318.WQ1 [2]   READY

Figure 13.19

Using the {RETURN} command in a subroutine

	File Edit Style Graph Print Database Tools Options Window	? ↑↓
	Erase Copy Move Style Align Font Insert Delete Fit Sum Format CHR WYS	

A10: [W15] "PRINT_IT

	A	B	C	D	E	F	G	H	I	J
1	\A	{GETLABEL "Enter company name: ",LABEL}								
2		{PRINT_IT}								
3		{GETLABEL "Enter your name: ",LABEL}								
4		{PRINT_IT}								
5										
6	PRINT?	N								
7	LABEL	Mike								
8										
9										
10	PRINT_IT	{GETLABEL "Print label? ",PRINT?}								
11		{IF PRINT?="N"}{RETURN}								
12		{/ Print;Block}{BS}LABEL~								
13		{/ Print;Go}								
14										

Passing Arguments to Subroutines

The ability to pass arguments to subroutines is a significant feature of Quattro Pro's macro language. By passing arguments, you can explicitly control the set of information your subroutine will process. The syntax for using arguments with a subroutine is

```
{subroutine [argument1],[argument2],...,[argumentN]}
```

When you pass arguments to a subroutine, it must contain a {DEFINE} command that tells the subroutine what to do with the arguments.

The {DEFINE} Command

The {DEFINE} command receives the arguments passed to a subroutine. The syntax for this command is

```
{DEFINE location1[:string/value],location2[:string/value],...}
```

where each *location* argument specifies the storage location (a cell address or block reference) for each argument in the {*subroutine*} command. The optional :string and :value suffixes tell Quattro Pro to treat the argument passed to the subroutine as either a value or string (see the earlier section, "The :string and :value Suffixes").

Each argument of the calling subroutine corresponds by position with the *location* arguments in the {DEFINE} command. If more arguments are passed from the subroutine than there are *locations*, the extra arguments are ignored, and Quattro Pro terminates the macro with an error message.

Suppose you need a macro that can print multiple copies of either spreadsheet or graph data. Figure 13.20 shows such a macro. When you execute the \A macro beginning in cell B1, it calls the {PRINT_LOOP} subroutine and passes to it the following arguments:

S, telling it to print spreadsheet data

BLOCK1, the name of the print block to print

2, the number of copies to print

The {DEFINE TYPE:s,BLOCK:s,COPIES:v} command in cell B9 then evaluates and stores the passed arguments. Note that each argument is stored in an intermediate cell that is assigned a block name—TYPE (cell B4), BLOCK (cell B5), and COPIES (cell B6); without this step, the subroutine does not work as intended. Because the TYPE and BLOCK arguments in the {DEFINE} command include an :s suffix, the macro stores the data passed to them as strings. The data passed to the COPIES argument, however, is stored as a value, because of the :v suffix.

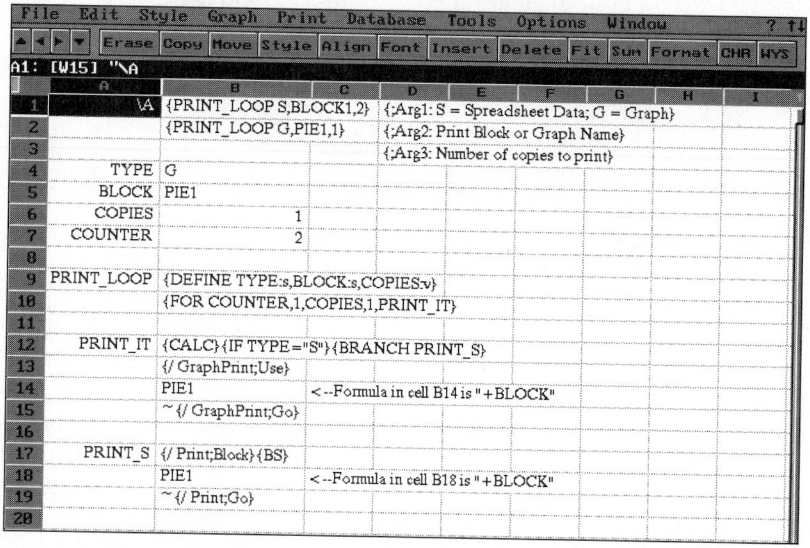

Figure 13.20

The {DEFINE} command in a subroutine

	A	B	C	D	E	F	G	H	I
	File	Edit	Style	Graph	Print	Database	Tools	Options	Window	? ↑↓

```
A1: [W15] "\A
```

	A	B	C	D	E	F	G	H	I
1	\A	{PRINT_LOOP S,BLOCK1,2}	{;Arg1: S = Spreadsheet Data; G = Graph}					
2		{PRINT_LOOP G,PIE1,1}	{;Arg2: Print Block or Graph Name}					
3			{;Arg3: Number of copies to print}					
4	TYPE	G						
5	BLOCK	PIE1						
6	COPIES	1						
7	COUNTER	2						
8								
9	PRINT_LOOP	{DEFINE TYPE:s,BLOCK:s,COPIES:v}						
10		{FOR COUNTER,1,COPIES,1,PRINT_IT}						
11								
12	PRINT_IT	{CALC}{IF TYPE="S"}{BRANCH PRINT_S}						
13		{/ GraphPrint;Use}						
14		PIE1	<--Formula in cell B14 is "+BLOCK"					
15		~{/ GraphPrint;Go}						
16								
17	PRINT_S	{/ Print;Block}{BS}						
18		PIE1	<--Formula in cell B18 is "+BLOCK"					
19		~{/ Print;Go}						
20								

After {DEFINE} stores the passed data, the {FOR} command is processed. This command calls the {PRINT_IT} subroutine as many times as specified by the COPIES argument. Each time {PRINT_IT} is called, it uses an {IF} to evaluate the TYPE argument. If TYPE is equal to S (for spreadsheet data), Quattro Pro branches to the {PRINT_S} subroutine, where the spreadsheet block specified by the BLOCK argument is printed. If TYPE is not equal to S, the macro assumes you want to print a graph, and prints the graph specified by the BLOCK argument.

The {RESTART} Command

As you know, when a subroutine has completed its execution, control is passed back to the calling macro. Quattro Pro keeps track of the flow of control in its *subroutine stack*, which holds up to 32 levels of subroutine calls. The {RESTART} command clears the subroutine stack so that the current subroutine does not return to the macro that called it. Instead, the current subroutine is treated as the start of a new macro. {RESTART} is often used in error-handling subroutines where you need to branch to a routine without returning to the calling macro.

Consider the \A macro in Figure 13.21. In this example, when you execute the \A macro, the {MESSAGE} command displays a message box that shows the name of the current routine (\A). Next, the {SUB1} subroutine is invoked, placing the \A routine on the subroutine stack. Like the previous routine (\A), the name of the {SUB1} routine is also displayed by a {MESSAGE} command. Next, the {SUB2} subroutine is invoked, placing the {SUB1} routine on the subroutine stack. Now the stack has two subroutines on it—{SUB1} and {SUB2}. However, because of the {RESTART} command at the end of the macro, {SUB2} does not return control to the subroutine that called it—{SUB1}—and macro execution stops when {SUB2} has completed.

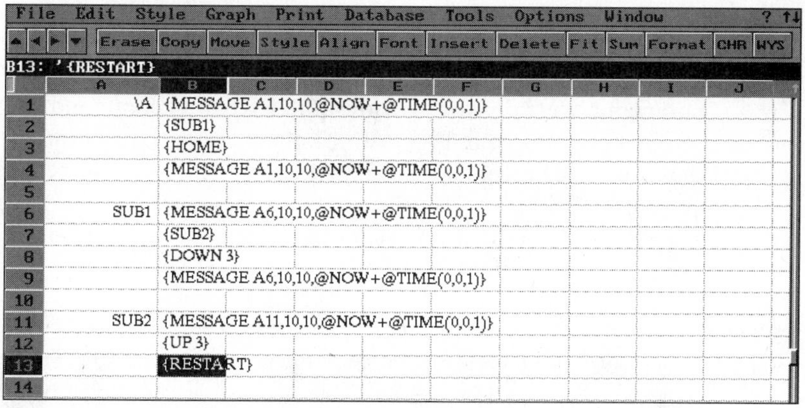

Figure 13.21

Using the {RESTART} command to clear the subroutine stack

	File Edit Style Graph Print Database Tools Options Window ? ↑↓
	▲ ◀ ▶ ▼ Erase Copy Move Style Align Font Insert Delete Fit Sum Format CHR WYS
	B13: ' {RESTART}

	A	B	C	D	E	F	G	H	I	J
1	\A	{MESSAGE A1,10,10,@NOW+@TIME(0,0,1)}								
2		{SUB1}								
3		{HOME}								
4		{MESSAGE A1,10,10,@NOW+@TIME(0,0,1)}								
5										
6	SUB1	{MESSAGE A6,10,10,@NOW+@TIME(0,0,1)}								
7		{SUB2}								
8		{DOWN 3}								
9		{MESSAGE A6,10,10,@NOW+@TIME(0,0,1)}								
10										
11	SUB2	{MESSAGE A11,10,10,@NOW+@TIME(0,0,1)}								
12		{UP 3}								
13		{RESTART}								
14										

 If you remove the {RESTART} command and run the macro again, you get entirely different results. This time, when {SUB2} is completed, control returns to the subroutine that called it. Likewise, the {SUB1} subroutine returns control to the \A routine. Along the way, the {MESSAGE} commands show the active routine.

Error Trapping with {ONERROR}

Normally, when an error occurs during a Quattro Pro session, the program suspends the current action, sounds a beep, and displays an error message. When a macro triggers an error, however, Quattro Pro terminates the macro. You can prevent Quattro Pro from terminating your macro and provide your own error handling by using the {ONERROR} command.

Note. The {ONERROR} command cannot trap macro command syntax errors. Nor can it trap many programming errors, such as attempting to call a subroutine that does not exist.

{ONERROR} lets you trap errors during macro execution and have Quattro Pro branch to appropriate error-handling routines. The syntax for this command is

```
{ONERROR branch-location,[message-location],[error-location]}
```

where *branch-location* is the cell address or block name of the macro to which you want to branch when an error occurs. If you include the optional *message-location* argument, you can store the error message in the spreadsheet; Quattro Pro stores the message as a left-aligned label in the specified location. You can also opt to store the address of the offending macro command at *error-location*.

When an error occurs, macro control is transferred to *branch-location*, and the {ONERROR} command is no longer in effect. That is, to reestablish error trapping, the {ONERROR} command must be invoked again. Only one {ONERROR} command can be in effect at a time. Each {ONERROR} command overrides the previous {ONERROR} command.

In the example in Figure 13.22, the macro prompts you for a file name and saves the current spreadsheet to drive A. The {ONERROR} command traps the "Drive not ready" error, allowing you to correct the error by inserting a floppy into the drive. Without the {ONERROR}, the macro would abort without giving you the chance to correct the problem.

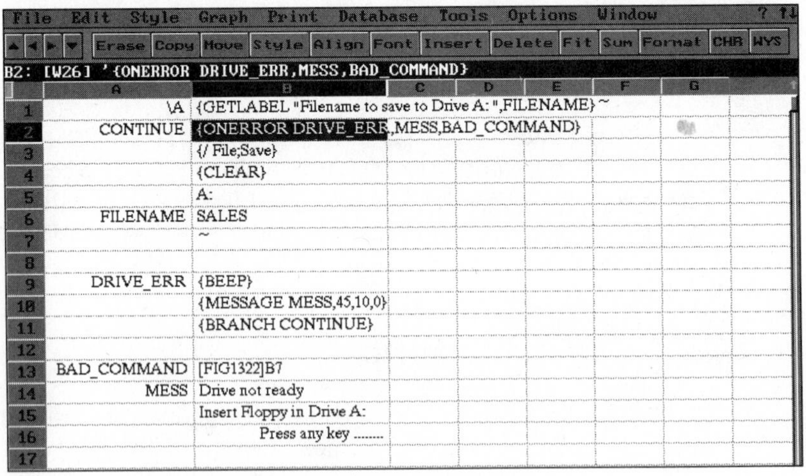

Figure 13.22

Using the {ONERROR} command

Building Menus

One of the most beneficial applications of Quattro Pro's macro facility is in building your own custom menus. The menus you design will look and operate like a Quattro Pro pull-down menu, complete with command highlight and command descriptions.

Quattro Pro provides two commands, {MENUBRANCH} and {MENUCALL}, for building custom menus. The difference between the two commands is the same as the difference between the {BRANCH} and {subroutine} commands. With {MENUBRANCH}, control transfers to the commands associated with a menu item; the commands following {MENUBRANCH} in the original macro routine are not executed, unless you press Esc while the menu is displayed. With {MENUCALL}, however, control returns to the original routine, and execution begins again with the command following {MENUCALL}.

Following the next two sections, which describe {MENUBRANCH} and {MENUCALL} in more detail, you'll find an example showing how to build a custom menu.

The {MENUBRANCH} Command

{MENUBRANCH} passes control to a menu routine, waits for you to select an option, and branches to the macro commands associated with that option. This command takes the form

```
{MENUBRANCH location}
```

where *location* is the cell that stores the string for the first menu item.

For example, Figure 13.23 shows a {MENUBRANCH} command in cell B5, and the pull-down menu the command creates. The *location* argument for {MENUBRANCH} is MENU, the name assigned to B8. Note that this cell contains the label 'Enter Invoice, which is the first option in the pull-down menu that the {MENUBRANCH} command creates.

If you select the Enter Invoice command from the menu, the macro executes the {INVOICE} command, which makes a call to the INVOICE subroutine. When the INVOICE subroutine is completed, the macro ends because of the blank cell in B11. Control never returns to the \M routine from which the {MENUBRANCH} command originates, so {BEEP} is never executed. If you press Esc while the menu is on the screen, however, the {MENUBRANCH} command is aborted. In this macro, the {BEEP} following {MENUBRANCH} is then executed.

Figure 13.23

Using the {MENUBRANCH} command to display a pull-down menu

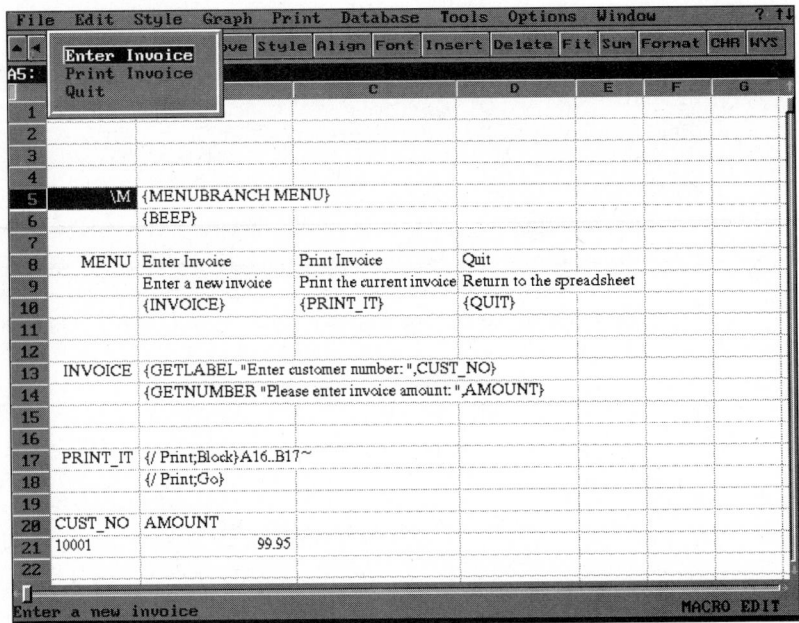

The {MENUCALL} Command

{MENUCALL} differs from {MENUBRANCH} only in that it performs a subroutine call to menu instructions. The syntax for {MENUCALL} is the same as for {MENUBRANCH}

```
{MENUCALL location}
```

{MENUCALL} displays a pull-down menu referenced by the *location* argument and waits for you to choose an option. After the instructions for the chosen option are completed, control returns to the command following the {MENUCALL} command, and the subsequent commands are executed.

Let's say you change the {MENUBRANCH} command in cell B5 of Figure 13.23 to a {MENUCALL}. If you then select the Enter Invoice option, Quattro Pro executes the {INVOICE} subroutine, and returns control to the command following {MENUCALL}. In this macro, the {BEEP} command in B6 is always executed.

A Sample Menu

Each option in the sample menu in Figure 13.24 performs a simple Quattro Pro function related to changing the display screen. The Split option, for instance, splits the window vertically; the Unsplit option clears the split window. Use the following steps to create this simple utility menu:

1. In a fresh spreadsheet, select cell A5 and enter the label **'\U** in the cell.

Figure 13.24

A sample utility menu

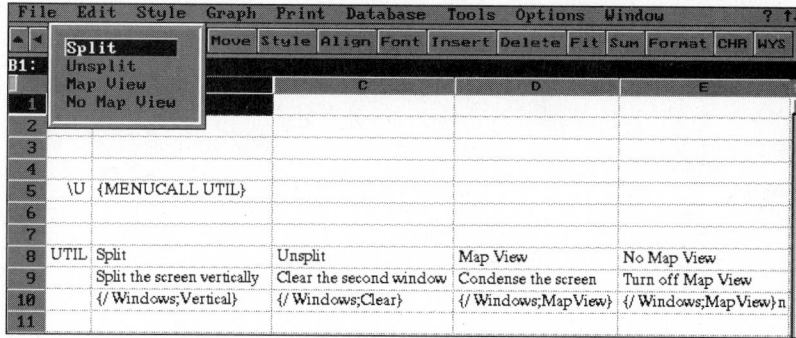

2. Use the /Edit, Names, Labels, Right command to assign the name \U to cell B5. In B5 enter **{MENUCALL UTIL}**.

3. Enter the label **UTIL** in cell A8. This is the name you will assign to your menu instructions.

4. Use /Edit, Names, Labels, Right to assign the name UTIL to cell B8.

5. Beginning with the cell selector in cell B8, enter the following menu options across row 8. Use Figure 13.24 as a guide.

Cell	Contents
B8	'Split
C8	'Unsplit
D8	'Map View
E8	'No Map View

6. Beginning with the cell selector in cell B9, enter the following command descriptions:

Cell	Description
B9	'Split the screen vertically
C9	'Clear the second window
D9	'Condense the screen
E9	'Turn off Map View

7. Enter the macro instruction associated with each menu item in the third row of the menu (screen row 10), as follows:

Cell	Command
B10	'{/ Windows;Vertical}
C10	'{/ Windows;Clear}
D10	'{/ Windows;MapView}y
E10	'{/ Windows;MapView}n

Now you are ready to try your menu. Since you named the macro \U, press Alt-U. The menu is displayed, waiting for you to select an option.

Guidelines for Building a Menu

Here are some guidelines for entering menu options when you are building a custom menu.

- A custom menu can contain up to 256 menu options (the width of the spreadsheet). When your menu exceeds 17 options, Quattro Pro adds a scroll bar at the right side of the menu box to allow mouse access to all of the menu commands.

- Options can be entered as labels or string formulas, but not values. If you want to use numbers as menu options, enter them as labels.

- Menu options can be up to 254 characters long (the maximum length of a cell entry). As a general rule, though, it is wise to keep your menu options short and plan to use command descriptions for explaining each option when it is highlighted.

- Start each menu item with a different letter or number. Then you'll be able to select from your menu by pressing the first character of an option. Consider, for example, a menu that has Edit and Exit as two options. If you press E on this menu, Quattro Pro selects the first option that starts with the character E—in this case, Edit. You can still select the Exit option with the mouse, however, or by highlighting it and pressing Enter.

- Avoid leaving blank cells between menu items. Quattro Pro interprets a blank cell as the end of your menu, and any items you have entered to the right of the blank cell won't display when you invoke your menu.

- The width of the columns in which you place your menu items has no effect on how Quattro Pro displays the items. Nevertheless, you may find it helpful to widen the columns to make the menu options easier to read and edit in the spreadsheet.

Managing the Screen

Quattro Pro's macro facility provides commands that allow you to control the appearance of the screen. With these commands, you can suppress the redrawing of the spreadsheet area of the screen, control the redrawing of the menus, customize the mode indicators, and sound the computer's speaker.

The {INDICATE} Command

{INDICATE} lets you change the mode indicator to any five-character string. Changing the mode indicator is useful when you want to display the status of your macro. The syntax of this command is

```
{INDICATE [string]}
```

where *string* is the string (or cell address or block name of the string) you wish to display as the indicator. Note that if you use a cell address or block name for *string*, you must precede it with the + symbol; otherwise, Quattro Pro uses the cell address or block name itself as the indicator. Likewise, if the referenced cell contains a value, then the cell reference itself is displayed as the argument. For example, if cell A1 contains the label 'Split, then the command {INDICATE +A1} sets the mode indicator to Split. If you omit the plus sign preceding the *string* argument, however—as in {INDICATE A1}—Quattro Pro sets the mode indicator to A1.

Unlike other macro commands that change the screen display, {INDICATE}'s effect on the screen remains after your macro has completed execution. Therefore, unless your macro resets the mode indicator, Quattro

Pro will continue to display the custom indicator even when your macro has finished.

To reset the indicator, use {INDICATE}, without an argument. Another option is to exit and retrieve the spreadsheet again.

If you use this command with a null string argument—for example, {INDICATE " "}—no indicator at all is displayed.

The {MESSAGE} Command

{MESSAGE} lets you display a message box for a specified amount of time, or until a key is pressed. You can define where on the screen the message box should be displayed and for how long. Here are the syntax of the command and definitions of its arguments.

```
{MESSAGE block,left,top,time}
```

Block is the block name or cell address where the text to be displayed is stored. *Left* is the screen column number (counting by characters) where the upper-left corner of the message box will appear. *Right* is the screen line number where the upper border of the message box will appear. *Time* is a future point in time when the box should be removed from the screen. If the *time* argument is set to zero, the message box remains on the screen until a key is pressed.

The dimensions of the message box are determined by the width and height of *block*, counting its width in standard screen characters and its height in standard screen lines. For example, if *block* is defined as A1..A2 and column A is nine characters wide, then the interior of the message box will be nine characters wide and two lines high.

Figure 13.25 demonstrates a macro that displays a message box showing the current time. The {MESSAGE} command in cell B1 displays the text stored in the block MSG_TEXT (B5..B7). Notice that the width of column B has been adjusted to 27 characters; setting it any narrower would cause the text to appear truncated (especially in the second {MESSAGE} command in B2). The upper-left corner of the message box begins in column 40 and row 10, as defined by the *left* and *top* arguments. A *time* argument of 0 causes the message to be displayed until a key is pressed.

The second {MESSAGE} command uses the formula

```
@NOW+@TIME(0,0,5)
```

to display the message "Thank you for your support!" (stored in MSG_END; cell B9) for five seconds. Note that when a time argument is specified, pressing a key does not remove the message.

To calculate the *left* and *top* arguments that will center the message box on the screen, the formulas in COLUMN (cell B15) and ROW (cell B16) are used. (These formulas assume 29 screen lines and 80 screen columns—settings that are appropriate only for WYSIWYG display mode on a standard VGA screen. If you are using Quattro Pro with a different screen type or display mode, you'll need to adjust the formulas.)

Figure 13.25

Using the {MESSAGE} command to display a message box

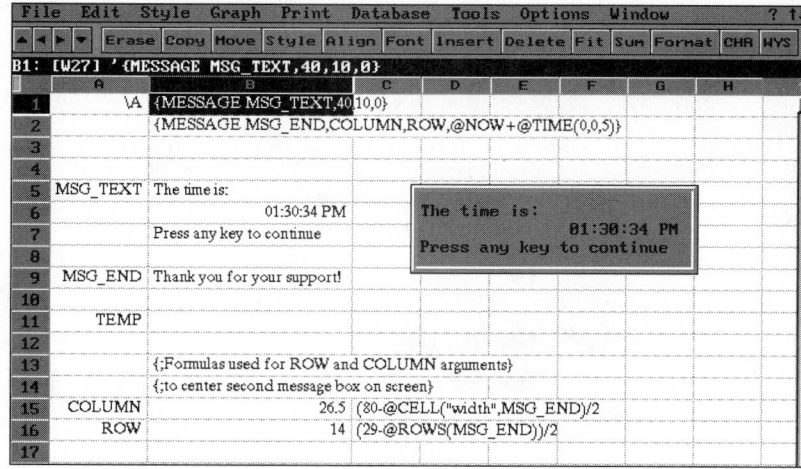

Here are some things to keep in mind as you use the {MESSAGE} command:

- The maximum width and height of a message box depends on the graphics display mode. In Character mode, for example, the maximum width of a message box is 74 characters and the maximum height is 20 lines. In WYSIWYG mode on a standard VGA monitor, however, the maximum width and height increases to approximately 84 characters by 29 lines. In other display modes, such as VGA: 80x50, Quattro Pro will display even more lines.

- When displaying a message, Quattro Pro does not use the fonts you've assigned to the cells in *block*. Rather, it uses the standard screen font; this is the same font it uses for menus, and for column and row text. Therefore, when estimating the size of a message box, base your calculations on the font you see in the menus, not the fonts you see in the spreadsheet cells.

- If you want to capture the keystroke that was typed to exit a message box, you can use the {GRAPHCHAR} command as described earlier in the chapter.

The {BEEP} Command

{BEEP} sounds your computer's speaker. This is helpful when you need to get the user's attention—for example, to signal that an error has occurred or a process has completed.

The syntax of this command is

```
{BEEP [tone-number]}
```

Note. {BEEP} will sound the computer's speaker even if the speaker is disabled with the /Options, Startup, Beep, No command.

where *tone-number* is an optional argument controlling the tone of the beep. There are four possible tones: 1, 2, 3, and 4. If you use a number other than these, Quattro Pro determines the number to use by dividing your *tone-number* value by 4 and using the remainder. For example, if *tone-number* is equal to 5, the result of 5 divided by 4 is 1 with a remainder of 1; thus {BEEP 5} is equivalent to {BEEP 1}. {BEEP} without an argument is equivalent to {BEEP 1}.

The {PLAY} Command

The {PLAY} command lets you add sound effects to your macros. The syntax of this command is

```
{PLAY filename}
```

Note. If you use Quattro Pro within Windows 3.0, Quattro Pro's sound effect files may not work properly. Avoid using this command when your macro will be used by others.

where *filename* is one of the digitized sound (.SND) files that comes with Quattro Pro. (If you do not specify a path, Quattro Pro will look in the Quattro Pro program directory for the sound file.) For example, the command

```
{PLAY FANFARE.SND}
```

causes Quattro Pro to play the FANFARE.SND file located in the Quattro Pro program directory. If Quattro Pro cannot find the sound file specified, it will issue an error and the macro will abort.

The {PANELOFF} and {PANELON} Commands

When Quattro Pro runs your macros, menus and prompts are suppressed. This increases the speed of your macros, because Quattro Pro does not have to pause and update the first few lines of the screen. The same is not true of 1-2-3, however. It updates the first few lines of the screen repeatedly as it runs your macros, creating a kind of flashing effect. To suppress this screen updating, 1-2-3 provides the {PANELOFF} command and the {PANELON} command to reinstate the updating.

For compatibility with 1-2-3, Quattro Pro, too, offers the {PANELOFF} and {PANELON} commands. The only time you will want to use them, however, is when you have deliberately set Quattro Pro to update the menus and prompts during macro execution; you can do this with the /Options, Other, Macro, None command. {PANELOFF} suppresses the updating of the menus and edit line, and {PANELON} reinstates it.

The {WINDOWSOFF} and {WINDOWSON} Commands

{WINDOWSOFF} and {WINDOWSON} are used to control the redrawing of the spreadsheet area during macro execution. Like {PANELOFF} and {PANELON}, these commands are offered to provide 1-2-3 macro compatibility, since Quattro Pro normally suppresses redrawing of the spreadsheet area for performance reasons.

If you want Quattro Pro to update the spreadsheet area during macro execution, use /Options, Other, Macro, None. You can then include the {WINDOWSOFF} command in your Quattro Pro macro to selectively suppress updating of the spreadsheet area, and {WINDOWSON} to restore screen updating.

TIP. *If you are running macros written in 1-2-3, you should use /Options, Other, Macro, None to emulate 1-2-3's method of screen updating—that is, complete redrawing of both the spreadsheet area and first few lines of the screen. This way, your macros using the {WINDOWSON}, {WINDOWS-OFF}, {PANELON}, and {PANELOFF} commands will run properly.*

Controlling Recalculation

Quattro Pro's background recalculation method is a welcome feature, because it allows Quattro Pro to recalculate your formulas in between keystrokes. This feature does have its limitations in macros, however, when commands within those macros depend on certain spreadsheet values. Since macros work so fast, the values that a macro references may not be up to date, because Quattro Pro is still calculating them. This is especially true when a macro is located in a large spreadsheet that contains many formulas. To solve this problem, you can have Quattro Pro recalculate only specific areas of the spreadsheet as needed.

The {RECALC} and {RECALCCOL} Commands

With {RECALC} and {RECALCCOL} you can limit recalculation to specific areas of the spreadsheet. {RECALC} calculates the specified area row by row; {RECALCCOL} calculates it column by column.

These commands have the following syntax and argument definitions:

```
{RECALC location,[condition],[iterations]}
{RECALCCOL location,[condition],[iterations]}
```

- *Location* is the cell or block you want to recalculate.

- *Condition* is an optional argument; you can use it to specify a condition that must be met before Quattro Pro stops recalculating. For instance, the macro command {RECALC B1,B1=100} tells Quattro Pro to recalculate cell B1 until it is equal to 100.

- *Iterations* is an optional argument that lets you specify the maximum number of times Quattro Pro recalculates *location* in order to meet *condition*. For example, the command

```
{RECALC TOTAL,TOTAL>30,25}
```

attempts to recalculate the cell TOTAL a maximum of 25 times, until it is greater than 30.

Figure 13.26 provides a simple demonstration of these two commands. The \A macro totals the sales for each tire model and then prints a report. Here the {RECALC TOTAL} command causes Quattro Pro to recalculate the Grand Total in cell C8 prior to printing. Without this command, zero will be printed for the Grand Total, because Quattro Pro does not have enough time to recalculate the spreadsheet.

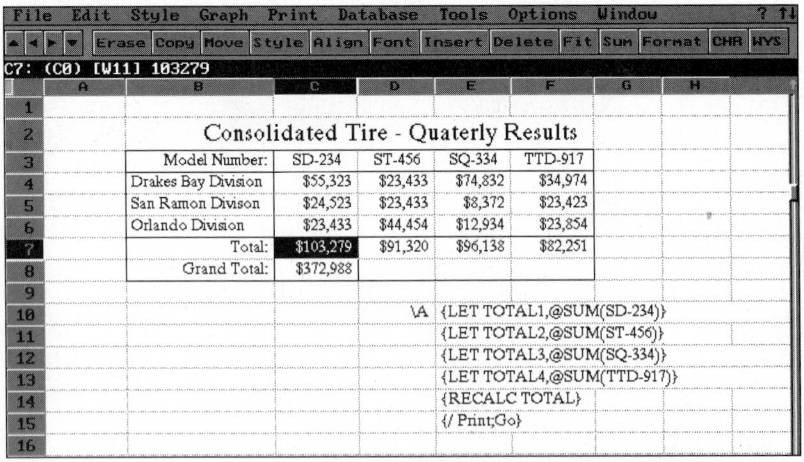

Figure 13.26

A macro using the {RECALC} command

Note that you could use the {CALC} command in place of {RECALC} in Figure 13.26 and still get the correct result. However, if this spreadsheet contained many formulas, the macro would have to wait until Quattro Pro had recalculated all of them before it continued on and printed the report. With the {RECALC TOTAL} command, only the value you need for the report, TOTAL, is recalculated.

Reading and Writing ASCII Files

As you probably know, ASCII text files are the least common denominator for sharing data between programs on the IBM PC. Most applications do store data in their own file format (like Quattro Pro's own .WQ1 file format), but most also have the ability to read and write ASCII files.

To read an ASCII file into Quattro Pro, you use the /Tools, Import, ASCII Text File command. Conversely, to write a spreadsheet block to an ASCII file on disk, you print the block to a file in draft mode. By using these techniques, you can read and write large portions of files to and from disk.

Quattro Pro's macro facility, too, provides commands for reading and writing ASCII files. These commands let you work with ASCII files on a detailed level—for instance, to modify statements in your CONFIG.SYS and AUTOEXEC.BAT files, or to manipulate data downloaded from a mainframe computer or on-line service (such as CompuServe or Prodigy) on a byte-by-byte basis.

Processing an ASCII text file in a Quattro Pro macro is a three-step process. First, you must open the file with the {OPEN} command. Once the file is open, you can either read from it (with {READ} or {READLN}) or write to it (with {WRITE} or {WRITELN}). Finally, when you have finished with the file, you must close it with the {CLOSE} command.

To read or write information starting at a specific location in a file, you can use the {SETPOS} command. This command lets you position the DOS file pointer to an exact location in a file before reading and/or writing. The {GETPOS} and {FILESIZE} commands are adjuncts of {SETPOS}. {GETPOS} lets you determine the current position of the DOS file pointer, and {FILESIZE} tells you the size of the current file in bytes.

The sections that follow describe each of these commands in more detail. Following these descriptions are two examples that show you first how to read from a file, and then how to write to a file using the DOS file pointer.

Opening a File with {OPEN}

The {OPEN} command is the first step required for processing an ASCII text file. With this command, access to the file is requested from DOS. If the file exists and access is granted, Quattro Pro opens the file for reading, writing, or both. The syntax for this command is

```
{OPEN filename,access-mode}
```

where *filename* is the string or cell reference in the cell containing the name of the file to open. The *access-mode* tells Quattro Pro what type of file operation you will perform on the file, as defined in the following list:

Access-Mode	Description
R	Read-only; the file can be read from but not written to.
W	Write; opens a new file with the given name. If a file already exists, it is overwritten. You can read from and write to the new file.
M	Modify; opens an existing file for modification. The file can be written to or read from.
A	Append; opens an existing file for modification. File can only be written to, starting at the end of the file.

If the file named in the command cannot be opened, either because it does not exist or DOS is denying you access to it, the {OPEN} command fails and the commands to the right of the {OPEN} command are processed. If the {OPEN} command is successful, however, the macro skips to the row below, ignoring the commands to the right of the {OPEN} command.

NOTE. *All the other file-handling commands—{READ}, {READLN}, {WRITE}, {WRITELN}, {SETPOS}, {GETPOS}, and {FILESIZE}—behave in the same way as {OPEN}. That is, the macro skips to the next line when the command is successful.*

Reading from a File

Quattro Pro has two commands for reading data from an ASCII text file: {READLN} and {READ}. These commands read data from the file that is opened with {OPEN}, and store it into a spreadsheet cell as a left-aligned label. The {READLN} command reads an entire line of data from a file. The {READ} command, on the other hand, lets you read a specified number of bytes. In order to read from a file, you must open it with the R (Read-only), W (Write), or M (Modify) option.

The {READLN} Command

{READLN} reads characters from an ASCII file until a carriage return/line feed combination is encountered. The syntax for this command is

```
{READLN location}
```

where *location* is the cell that will store the data. The {READLN} command begins reading at the current file pointer position and continues reading until it reaches a carriage return/line feed pair. The characters that are read prior to the carriage return character are written to the *location* cell. The carriage return and line feed characters are not read into the cell. If 254 characters are read before reaching a carriage return/line feed, the read operation is terminated.

The {READ} Command

{READ} is very similar to {READLN}, except that {READ} lets you read a specified number of bytes (characters) from an ASCII file. The syntax for this command is

```
{READ byte-count,location}
```

where *byte-count* is the number of bytes to be read from the currently open file. Quattro Pro begins reading at the current file pointer position. The *location* argument is the cell address or block name of the cell where the data is to be stored. Quattro Pro can read 254 characters at a time (the maximum number of characters allowed in a cell). When the {READ} command is completed, the file pointer moves one character beyond the last character read.

Note that unlike {READLN}, the {READ} command does not discard carriage return and line feed characters, but rather reads them into the cell as it does any other character.

Writing to a File

When you've opened a file using the W (Write), M (Modify), or A (Append) option, you can then write information from the spreadsheet to that file. To do so, you use the {WRITE} and {WRITELN} commands.

The {WRITELN} Command

{WRITELN} lets you write to a file beginning at the current file pointer location. It always adds a carriage return/line feed pair to the end of each text line. The syntax for this command is

```
{WRITELN string}
```

where *string* can be a literal string, a string formula, or a reference to a cell that contains a string or string formula. If you attempt to write a numeric value, Quattro Pro will generate an error. After Quattro Pro completes writing the line to the file, the file pointer advances one character beyond the last character written (the line feed character).

TIP. *To use {WRITE} or {WRITELN} to write a number to a text file, you can use the @STRING function to convert the number to a string. For example, here's a typical command: {WRITE @STRING(TOTAL,2)}.*

The {WRITE} Command

{WRITE} is nearly identical to {WRITELN}, except that {WRITE} does not add a carriage return/line feed pair to the end of the line. The syntax for this command is

```
{WRITE string}
```

where *string* can be a literal string, a string formula, or a reference to a cell that contains a string or string formula. After Quattro Pro finishes writing to the file, the file pointer advances one character beyond the last character written.

If you use two {WRITE} commands in succession, the second command picks up where the previous one ended. For example, the following commands will write the characters *WillSikes* to an open file:

```
WRITE("Will")
WRITE("Sikes")
```

Closing a File with {CLOSE}

When Quattro Pro executes a {WRITE} or {WRITELN} command, data isn't necessarily written to disk. To optimize performance, Quattro Pro writes data to RAM, because it's faster to write to RAM than to disk. To avoid losing the data in an ASCII file in the case of a power failure, you need to use the {CLOSE} command in your macros. This forces Quattro Pro to write any data associated with the currently open ASCII file from RAM to disk.

As a rule, it is wise to always use the {CLOSE} command to close the open file. However, Quattro Pro automatically closes a file under the following circumstances:

- When another {OPEN} command is processed, because only one ASCII file can be open at a time

- When you quit the program

Moving the File Pointer

Quattro Pro uses a *file pointer* to keep track of where it is reading from or writing to in the open ASCII file. The file pointer is always located in the position where it will next read or write a character. Many times you will need to move about in the open file and begin reading or writing at a point somewhere in the middle of the file. The {SETPOS}, {GETPOS}, and {FILESIZE} commands provide this capability by allowing you to modify the position of the file pointer.

When you use either the W (Write), M (Modify), or R (Read) option with the {OPEN} command, the file pointer is automatically positioned at the beginning of the newly opened file. On the other hand, if you use the A (Append) option with {OPEN}, the file pointer is automatically positioned at the end of the file.

The {SETPOS} Command

{SETPOS} moves the file pointer to a specified character position in the open ASCII file. The first character in the file is given the number 0, the second character the number 1, the third character the number 2, and so on. The command takes the form

```
{SETPOS position}
```

where *position* is the number of the byte position within the file. The *position* argument can be a number, numeric formula, or a reference to a cell containing either of these. If you specify a number that exceeds the number of bytes in the file, the file pointer moves one character beyond the last character in the file. When Quattro Pro completes processing the {SETPOS} command, it skips immediately to the next line of the macro; the commands in the same cell as {SETPOS} are ignored.

The {GETPOS} Command

{GETPOS} lets you determine the current position of the file pointer in the open ASCII file. The syntax of the command is

```
{GETPOS location}
```

where *location* is a cell address or block name. When Quattro Pro executes this command, it copies to *location* a number that represents the character position of the file pointer in the open ASCII file, where 0 is the first position in the file, 1 is the second position, 2 is the third position, and so on.

The {FILESIZE} Command

{FILESIZE} lets you determine the size (in bytes) of the currently open ASCII file. It takes the form

```
{FILESIZE location}
```

where *location* is a cell address or block name. To this cell address or range name, Quattro Pro copies the total byte count of the open ASCII file.

Read/Write Macro Examples

Suppose you would like to read the contents of the PATH statement in your AUTOEXEC.BAT file using Quattro Pro macro commands. The macro in Figure 13.27 illustrates how you might go about doing this. When the \A macro is invoked, the

```
{OPEN "C:\AUTOEXEC.BAT",r}
```

command is processed. If DOS grants access to the file, it is opened for reading, as specified by the *access-mode* argument, r; any attempts to write to the file, however, will fail. If DOS won't grant access to the file—for example, if it cannot find the file or another program is using the file—the {OPEN} command fails and the {BEEP} and {QUIT} commands are then processed.

Once the file has been successfully opened, the macro executes the {FIND_PATH} routine, where a {FOR} command calls the {LOOP} subroutine repetitively. In the first line of {LOOP} (B11), the {READLN} command reads a line from the AUTOEXEC.BAT file into TEXT (B9). Next, the {IF} command tests whether the line contains the string "PATH". (The @ISERR function is helpful here because the @FIND function returns ERR when "PATH" is not found within TEXT.) If "PATH" is not found, the {RETURN} command ends the subroutine, and control is returned to {FOR} so that it can read the next line in the file. If "PATH" is found, however, the macro displays a message telling you the line number within AUTOEXEC.BAT. When you press a key to clear the message box, {FORBREAK} causes Quattro Pro to return control all the way back to the main routine, where the {CLOSE} command closes the AUTOEXEC.BAT file.

In another example, Figure 13.28 shows a simple macro that writes long labels from the block A1..A4 to the file CLIENT.PRN in the current directory. The macro begins in B6 by moving the cell selector to A1. Next, the {OPEN} command opens the CLIENT.PRN file for writing. (Each time you run this macro, it will overwrite the CLIENT.PRN file.) If Quattro Pro cannot successfully open the file, the macro branches to OPEN_ERR, where a message is displayed to that effect.

Figure 13.27
A macro that reads
the PATH statement
in C:\AUTOEXEC.BAT

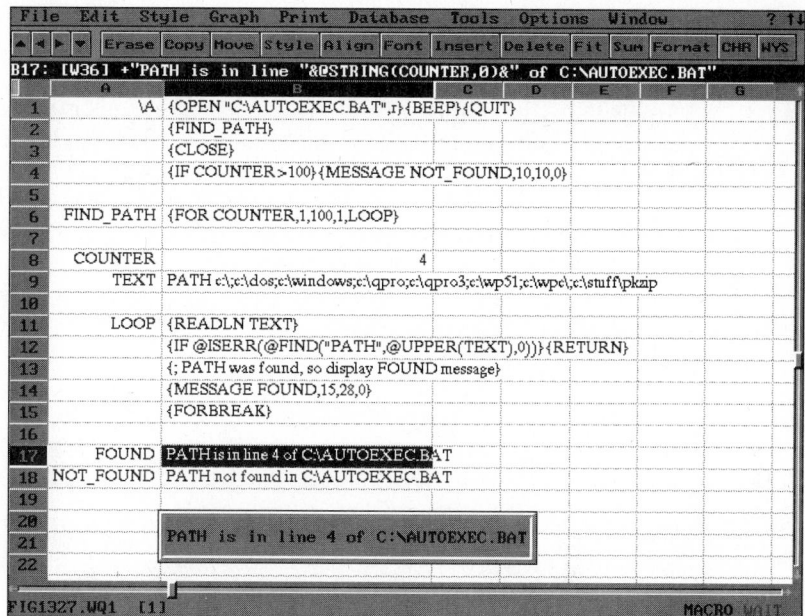

Figure 13.28
A macro that writes
a simple ASCII file

After the file is successfully opened, the {FOR} command calls the {WRITE_IT} subroutine four times. Each time {WRITE_IT} executes, it uses the {WRITELN @CELLPOINTER("contents")} command to write data from the current cell selector location to CLIENT.PRN. The next command, {DOWN}, moves the cell selector down a cell. After all four records have been written to the file, the {CLOSE} command closes the file.

For the final example, the macro in Figure 13.29 reads a line from the CLIENT.PRN file created in the previous example (Figure 13.28). Here the macro uses the {SETPOS} command to position the file pointer to read the third line in the file. Although you can't easily tell from Figure 13.28, each label written to CLIENT.PRN is 34 characters long. When Quattro Pro adds a carriage return/line feed pair to each file, the resulting line length is 36 characters. Thus, with a *position* argument of 72, {SETPOS} locates the file pointer at character 73, the start of the third line. {READLN} then reads from that position to the next carriage return/line feed and saves the data in GET_IT (B6).

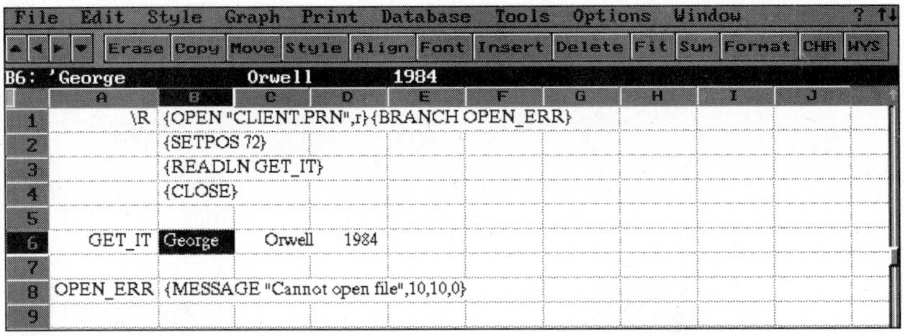

Figure 13.29

A macro using {SETPOS} to read a specific line from an ASCII file

As you can see, the label

```
'George          Orwell          1984
```

already resides in the cell.

Advanced Techniques

As you become more expert in programming macros, you will find yourself searching for ways to make your macros more flexible—that is, to have them work in a variety of circumstances without having to modify them. There are a number of techniques available for making your macros more flexible. We'll look at two of the most common ones here. First, Quattro Pro lets you

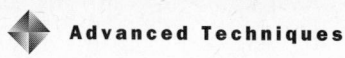

use formulas and @functions as arguments in macro commands. Second, you can create self-modifying macros that change the content of their own instructions as they execute. With these advanced techniques, you'll find that you can get more done with fewer macro commands.

Using Formulas and @Functions in Macros

One of the easiest ways to make your macros more flexible is to use @functions and formulas as arguments in your macro commands. For example, rather than use cell addresses for the *location* and *data* arguments in the {LET} command, you can use @functions, like this:

```
{LET @CELLPOINTER("address"),@TODAY}
{/ Block;Format}D4~
```

The formula @CELLPOINTER("address") returns the address of the current cell and provides the *location* argument for {LET}. Likewise, the @TODAY function, which returns a date number representing the current date, serves as the *data* argument. (The second line of the macro merely assigns the Long International date format to the current cell.)

You can also use other types of formulas as arguments to your macros. The only thing to watch out for is making sure the formula provides the proper type of argument. For example, the macro in Figure 13.30 shows how you can use a string formula to create the prompt for a {GETNUMBER} command. In this example, the command

```
{GETNUMBER +"Customer is "&A1&". Please enter amount: ",A2}
```

uses the customer name, Autorella Auto Body, stored in cell A1 to produce the prompt

```
Customer is Autorella Auto Body. Please enter amount:
```

Figure 13.30

Using a formula to create the prompt for a {GETNUMBER} command

File	Edit	Style	Graph	Print	Database	Tools	Options	Window	? ↑↓

▲ ◀ ▶ ▼	Erase	Copy	Move	Style	Align	Font	Insert	Delete	Fit	Sum	Format	CHR	WYS

[Enter] [Esc] Customer is Autorella Auto Body. Please enter amount:

	A	B	C	D	E	F	G	H	I	J
1	Autorella Auto Body									
2										
3										
4										
5	\G	{GETLABEL "Please enter customer name: ",A1}								
6		{GETNUMBER +"Customer is "&A1&". Please enter amount: ",A2}								
7										

Self-Modifying Macros

Self-modifying macros provide another important way to increase the flexibility of your macros, by using string formulas stored in the spreadsheet to change the actual macro commands themselves as data in the spreadsheet changes. For example, in Figure 13.31, the {GETLABEL} command in B2 is derived from a string formula, as shown in the edit line. The content of the command varies with the value the user enters in response to the preceding {GETNUMBER} prompt.

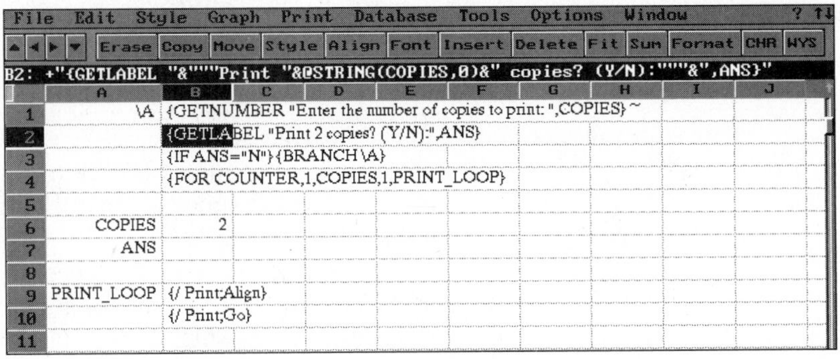

Figure 13.31

A simple self-modifying macro

File	Edit	Style	Graph	Print	Database	Tools	Options	Window	? ↑↓

▲ ◀ ▶ ▼	Erase	Copy	Move	Style	Align	Font	Insert	Delete	Fit	Sum	Format	CHR	WYS

B2: +"{GETLABEL "&""""Print "&@STRING(COPIES,0)&" copies? (Y/N):"""&",ANS}"

	A	B	C	D	E	F	G	H	I	J
1		\A	{GETNUMBER "Enter the number of copies to print: ",COPIES} ~							
2		{GETLABEL "Print 2 copies? (Y/N):",ANS}								
3		{IF ANS="N"}{BRANCH \A}								
4		{FOR COUNTER,1,COPIES,1,PRINT_LOOP}								
5										
6	COPIES	2								
7	ANS									
8										
9	PRINT_LOOP	{/ Print;Align}								
10		{/ Print;Go}								
11										

14

Networking
Quattro Pro

L OCAL-AREA NETWORKS, OR LANS, ARE BECOMING MORE WIDELY ACCEP-
ted all the time. They provide a cost-effective way for multiple users
to share limited resources. With a network, applications and data
files are centrally stored on a dedicated high-performance computer
known as a *server*. Each user's individual PC is connected to that server.
Often, individual computers connected to the server are referred to as *workstations*. Through his or her workstation, each user has access to the applications and data files that are stored on the server. In addition, each user has
access to the peripheral devices (printers, modems, and so on) that are connected to the server.

Quattro Pro has been networkable since the introduction of version 1.0.
However, with version 2.0, Quattro Pro's network architecture was dramatically enhanced. As you might imagine, those enhancements have been carried forward to versions 3.0 and 4.0. Now, multiple users with different
hardware configurations can simultaneously use a single copy of Quattro Pro
located on the network server and access spreadsheet files located in shared
directories.

This chapter brings you up to date on all the network features that Quattro Pro has to offer. It begins with an overview of the various network configurations for Quattro Pro along with hardware and software requirements.
This section should be of interest to both users and network administrators.
You'll then learn how to install Quattro Pro on the network server. The chapter concludes with an overview of commands and techniques for using Quattro Pro to access spreadsheet files in shared directories on the network.

This chapter assumes you have a basic familiarity with your particular
network. For example, it assumes that you know how to link your PC to
shared directories on the server.

A Networking Overview

You don't have to install Quattro Pro on the network server to access spreadsheet files in shared network directories. In fact, you can use a local (worksta-
tion-based) copy of Quattro Pro to retrieve and save spreadsheet files stored
on the network server. This section explains the various network configurations you can set up for Quattro Pro. Table 14.1 summarizes the three data
access possibilities for different configurations of Quattro Pro.

In the most basic case, Quattro Pro can be installed on a local hard disk
without a network connection. Obviously, you don't have access to files on
the network with this configuration. What's more, Quattro Pro's files consume approximately 4Mb of valuable hard-disk space, plus any additional
space required to store fonts.

In the second scenario, Quattro Pro is installed on a local hard disk with
a network connection. In this case, you have access to all the data files on

your local disk as well as data files stored on the network. (See "File Sharing with Quattro Pro" for details on how you can access data files on the network server.) This configuration also consumes about 4Mb of disk space on your local hard drive. Also, any fonts you generate are stored locally, requiring even more disk space.

Table 14.1   Quattro Pro Data Access

Type of Installation	Access Data on Local Disk	Access Data on Network	Local Disk Space Consumed
Local, no network connection	Yes	No	Approx. 4Mb plus space for fonts, using version 3.0; 5Mb using Quattro Pro 4.0
Local, connected to network	Yes	Yes	Approx. 4Mb plus space for fonts, using version 3.0; 5Mb using Quattro Pro 4.0
Quattro Pro, installed on network	Yes	Yes	0

In the third case, Quattro Pro is installed on a network server. As in the second scenario, you have access to data on your local disk as well as on the network. However, the big advantage here is that Quattro Pro doesn't take up any local disk space. Instead, all program files reside on the network server. All Quattro Pro users are serviced by one set of files. Further, with this configuration, you can run Quattro Pro from a workstation that doesn't have a hard or floppy disk—often called a *diskless* workstation.

The Network Version of Quattro Pro

When you purchase the single-user version of Quattro Pro, you automatically get the network version along with it. In fact, it's ready to install on a LAN. (See "Installing Quattro Pro on a Network.") However, after you install the software on the network server, only one user can actually load and use Quattro Pro. To grant access to additional users, you must purchase Quattro Pro LAN Packs. (These are less expensive than the single-user version.)

You should purchase enough LAN Packs to handle all the users that you anticipate will be *concurrently* using Quattro Pro. Each Quattro Pro LAN Pack includes a serial number that lets you add one user. For example, suppose you have 12 workstations on your network. However, you anticipate that only ten of those users will be concurrently using Quattro Pro. To handle this load, you should purchase nine LAN Packs. (You already have one license by virtue of purchasing the single-user version of Quattro Pro.) However, if an 11th user attempts to use Quattro Pro, access will be denied. (Hopefully, this 11th user won't be your boss.) See "Adding Other Users" for details on how to install Quattro Pro LAN Packs.

NOTE. *If you already have registered copies of the single-user version of Quattro Pro in use on individual workstations, you can use the serial numbers from those copies to add users for the network version of the software. However, you must then remove those locally installed copies of Quattro Pro from your workstations.*

Shared Fonts

When Quattro Pro is installed on a network, all users share the same fonts. For example, suppose you have two users, both of whom are using a 12-point Swiss font in their spreadsheet. Instead of Quattro Pro creating a set of fonts for each user, only a single font set is created for the first user. This set is then available for use by the second user. However, be aware that Quattro Pro can build only one font at a time. This may cause some delays. For example, if Quattro Pro is busy building a font for one user, a second user requesting a different font will have to wait until Quattro Pro is finished building the font requested by the first user.

What You Need

Quattro Pro will not run on all networks. In fact, only the following networks are supported:

- Novell Advanced NetWare version 2.0A or higher

- 3Com 3+Share version 1.0 or higher

- Any other network that is 100 percent compatible with one of the networks above and compatible with DOS version 3.1 or higher

You will need approximately 4Mb of free disk space on the server to install Quattro Pro. You will also need at least one personal computer to serve as a workstation. Moreover, all workstations on which Quattro Pro will be used must meet the following specifications:

- IBM PC or 100 percent compatible

- At least 640k of RAM memory

- Using DOS 3.1 or higher

Quattro Pro's Network Strategy

Quattro Pro's network strategy is to allow multiple users to simultaneously load Quattro Pro and share program and font files. However, each user will most likely have a slightly different hardware configuration. In addition, each user will undoubtedly have different preferences (settings, menus, and so on) for how he or she prefers to use Quattro Pro.

To compensate for these differences in hardware and preferences, Quattro Pro allows you to set up a private directory for each user on the network. These private directories can be located on either the server itself or on each user's workstation.

These private directories contain the default configuration files for each workstation. It is through these directories that each user can customize their particular invocation of Quattro Pro. For example, each user can specify such default settings as the default start-up directory, the display mode, and the printer to use for their particular invocation of Quattro Pro.

Unlike the single-user version of Quattro Pro, the network version cannot be loaded from the directory in which the program files exist. Instead, Quattro Pro must be invoked through the PATH statement in each user's AUTOEXEC.BAT file. The PATH statement must reference both the location of the user's private directory and the location of the Quattro Pro program files on the network server. (See "Updating AUTOEXEC.BAT Files.")

There are two types of default configuration files that must be installed in each user's private directory—system defaults and menu preferences. The Quattro Pro system default settings, such as display mode and printer selection, are stored in the file called RSC.RF. Default settings that are specific to menu selections, such as menu trees, shortcut keys, and mouse palette settings, are stored in Menu Preference (.MP) files.

You create Menu Preference (.MP) files with the MPMAKE utility. The use of this utility is described later under "Creating Menu Preference (.MP) Files." You must use MPMAKE to create a separate .MP file for each menu tree a user wants to access. In most cases, you will only need to create a single QUATTRO.MP file, which gives you access to the Quattro Pro menu tree. However, you can also create a 123.MP file for those users that prefer the Lotus 1-2-3–style menu or a Q1.MP file for those users who prefer the Quattro Pro version 1.0 style menu.

Installing Quattro Pro on a Network

Installing Quattro Pro on a network is much like installing the single-user version of Quattro Pro. In fact, you'll use the same program, INSTALL.EXE, to perform the installation. However, there are a few important differences in the placement of program files.

As you can see in Figure 14.1, you'll need to create several directories to contain the necessary Quattro Pro program files. The role of each of these directories is explained in the sections that follow. Briefly, the \QPRONET directory contains the QPRO.NET utility, which keeps track of how many users have accessed Quattro Pro. The \QPRO directory contains the main Quattro Pro program files. (The \QPRO\FONTS subdirectory contains the fonts for Quattro Pro and will be created for you during installation.) Finally, the \PRIV directory contains the private directories for each user that will access Quattro Pro. These directories contain the RSC.RF and Menu Preference (.MP) files for each user. As you may recall, these files are used to specify Quattro Pro's default settings for each user. In Figure 14.1, these private directories are shown as being located on the server. However, you can also place them on each individual's workstation.

Figure 14.1
Suggested network directory structure for Quattro Pro

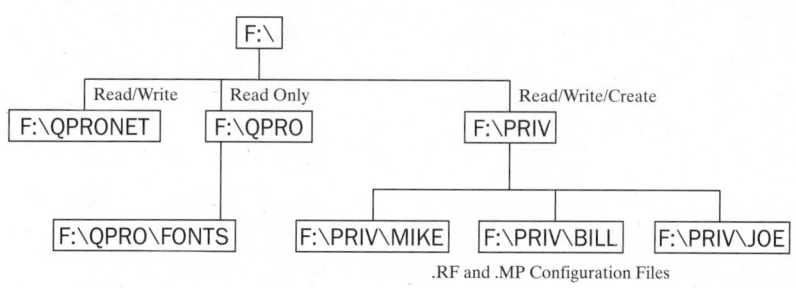

Creating the Required Directories

Before installing Quattro Pro on a network, you need to create two of the directories shown in Figure 14.1 (\QPRONET and \QPRO). To do this, log on to the network from a workstation. Make sure you have read, write, and create rights to the area on the server in which you are planning to install Quattro Pro.

First, create the \QPRONET directory that will contain the QPRO.NET file. During installation, you will be given an opportunity to reference this directory. Quattro Pro will then create the QPRO.NET file and store it in the directory you specify. This file keeps track of the number of times Q.EXE has been invoked. We recommend you name this directory QPRONET and place it off of the root directory, as shown in Figure 14.1.

Next, create a private directory, \PRIV, for each Quattro Pro user. These directories can exist on the server, as shown in Figure 14.1, or you can create a private directory on each user's local hard disk.

Note. You do not need to create the \QPRO or \QPRO fonts directories in advance. The INSTALL.EXE program will do this for you automatically.

Using INSTALL.EXE

After you have created the \QPRONET and \PRIV directories, run the IN-STALL.EXE program from the Quattro Pro single-user disk set (not a LAN Pack). The use of this program is fairly straightforward. During installation, you will be prompted for the following information:

1. *Source drive*   Enter the letter of the drive that will be used to read the Quattro Pro program disks, for example **A**.

2. *Quattro Pro directory*   Enter the directory on the server in which the Quattro Pro program will be installed, for example **F:\QPRO**.

3. *Company name and user name*   Enter this information carefully, as these settings are permanent.

4. *Serial Number*   Enter the serial number from the label on Disk 1.

5. *Are you installing Quattro Pro on a Network Server?*   Answer Yes.

6. *Path to QPRO.NET*   Enter **F:\QPRONET**, where F: is the network drive on which you are installing Quattro Pro, and QPRONET is the directory you created before running the Install program.

7. *Printer*   Press Esc to skip the printer selection section. This can be customized at each workstation later. (See "Printing on a Network.")

8. *Fonts*   If you are installing Quattro Pro 3.0 and you wish to build fonts, select the set of fonts you wish to create from the list. You'll probably want to create a full set of fonts. This will save time later on.

Adding Other Users

After the Install program has completed its operations, you are ready to enter the serial numbers of any additional copies of Quattro Pro. As you may recall, you must do this if you want more than one user to be able to use Quattro Pro. To add these serial numbers, you'll use the QPUPDATE.EXE file as follows:

1. Change to the QPRO directory on the server.

2. Type **QPUPDATE** and press Enter. The QPUPDATE.EXE file is loaded.

3. Press Enter followed by F2 to display the serial number screen shown in Figure 14.2.

4. Use the ↓ key to move to the first empty field in the Serial Number column. Enter the serial number from the first Quattro Pro LAN Pack disk.

(You can also enter the serial number from a single-user version of Quattro Pro that is different from the single-user version you just installed.) Press Enter to complete your entry.

Figure 14.2
QPUPDATE serial
number screen

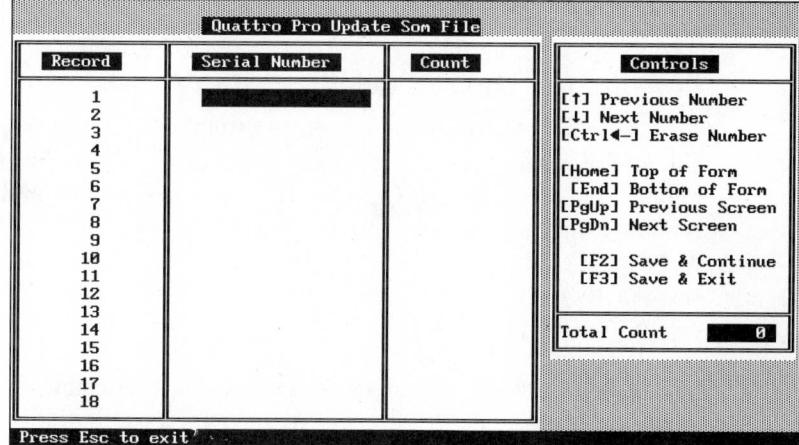

```
┌─────────────────────────────────────────────────────────────────────┐
│                     Quattro Pro Update Som File                       │
│ ┌────────────┬──────────────────┬──────────┐  ┌────────────────────┐ │
│ │   Record   │  Serial Number   │  Count   │  │      Controls      │ │
│ │     1      │ ███████████████  │          │  │ [↑] Previous Number│ │
│ │     2      │                  │          │  │ [↓] Next Number    │ │
│ │     3      │                  │          │  │ [Ctrl◄─] Erase Number│ │
│ │     4      │                  │          │  │                    │ │
│ │     5      │                  │          │  │ [Home] Top of Form │ │
│ │     6      │                  │          │  │  [End] Bottom of Form│ │
│ │     7      │                  │          │  │ [PgUp] Previous Screen│ │
│ │     8      │                  │          │  │ [PgDn] Next Screen │ │
│ │     9      │                  │          │  │                    │ │
│ │    10      │                  │          │  │  [F2] Save & Continue│ │
│ │    11      │                  │          │  │  [F3] Save & Exit  │ │
│ │    12      │                  │          │  │                    │ │
│ │    13      │                  │          │  ├────────────────────┤ │
│ │    14      │                  │          │  │Total Count    │  0 ││ │
│ │    15      │                  │          │  └────────────────────┘ │
│ │    16      │                  │          │                         │
│ │    17      │                  │          │                         │
│ │    18      │                  │          │                         │
│ └────────────┴──────────────────┴──────────┘                         │
│ Press Esc to exit                                                     │
└─────────────────────────────────────────────────────────────────────┘
```

5. Enter the serial numbers for the rest of your Quattro Pro LAN Packs.

6. Press F3 to save the serial numbers you've added and return to DOS.

When you complete these steps, QPUPDATE modifies the QPRO.SOM file, which keeps track of your Quattro Pro serial numbers. Quattro Pro reads this file at start-up to determine the maximum number of concurrent users that are allowed to access Quattro Pro.

Creating Menu Preferences (.MP) Files

As part of the installation process, you'll also need to create an .MP file for each user by using the MPMAKE utility. A separate .MP file needs to be created for each menu tree the user wishes to use. In most cases, however, you will only need to create a single .MP file using the QUATTRO.MU file. This file contains the settings for the standard Quattro Pro menu tree.

You must create the .MP file in the user's private directory. This private directory can be located on either the user's local hard disk or on the network server. For example, suppose the private directory \QPRO is located on a user's local disk drive C. To create an .MP file in this directory, log on to the network from that user's workstation, then perform the following steps:

1. Change to the network drive (F:, for example).

Note. If the user prefers the Lotus 1-2-3 style interface, you would type **MPMAKE 123.MU C:\QPRO** in step 3.

2. Change to the directory in which you installed Quattro Pro—for example, type **CD \QPRO**.

3. Now enter **MPMAKE QUATTRO.MU C:\QPRO** to create a QUATTRO.MP file in the C:\QPRO directory.

That user will now have access to Quattro Pro's standard menu tree.

Copying the Default Configuration File

Once you have created the appropriate .MP file in each user's private directory, you are ready to copy the Quattro Pro default configuration file, RSC.RF, to that same directory. If the private directories are located on the server, this is a simple matter. Just log on to the server and copy the RSC.RF file to each user's private directory. On the other hand, if each user's private directory is located on their workstation, you'll have to log on to each workstation individually to copy the file.

After you copy the RSC.RF file to each user's private directory, you must delete this file from the directory in which you installed Quattro Pro. If you don't do this, Quattro Pro will get its default configuration settings from the RSC.RF file in the main /QPRO directory on the server, and each user's default preference settings will be ignored.

TIP. *You may want to create a master resource directory containing the needed .MP and .RF files. That way, when you add a new user, you need only copy the needed .MP and .RF files to the user's private directory.*

Protecting the Quattro Pro Directory

Now that the needed files have been copied from the Quattro Pro program directory on the server to each user's private directory, you are ready to protect the Quattro Pro files. To do this, make the directory on the server that contains these files a read-only directory. One way to do this is with the DOS ATTRIB command. To use this command, make the Quattro Pro program directory on the server current and type **ATTRIB+R*.***. That way, users will be able to read and search the files in the Quattro Pro directory, but they will not be able to overwrite them or delete them.

Updating AUTOEXEC.BAT Files

Each Quattro Pro user on the network will need to have the AUTOEXEC-.BAT file for his or her workstation modified as follows:

1. Add the command SHARE to each user's AUTOEXEC.BAT file. This statement runs the SHARE.EXE program that comes with each user's

copy of DOS. Include a path to this file, if necessary. For example, if SHARE.EXE is located in a directory called \DOS off of the root directory on the user's machine, you would add the line C:\DOS\SHARE to AUTOEXEC.BAT.

SHARE.EXE is a memory-resident utility program. It provides file sharing and locking on a network. See "File Sharing with Quattro Pro" for an example of the effects this file has in a network environment.

2. Add the path to the user's private directory, as well as to the Quattro Pro program. For example, if the user's private directory is C:\QPRO and the Quattro Pro program files are stored in F:\QPRO, you would update the PATH statement as follows:

```
PATH=C:\QPRO;F:\QPRO;<rest of path>
```

Most networks allow you to create a log-in script that connects logical drives on a user's workstation to network drives on the server. However, as part of this log-in script, some networks also modify or override the path parameters for the workstation. If you have such a network, make sure any changes to path parameters do not interfere with the reference to both the Quattro Pro directory on the network and the user's private default directory for Quattro Pro. Otherwise, you may not get the results you expect.

File Sharing with Quattro Pro

The network version of Quattro Pro allows multiple users to access the same spreadsheet files stored in shared directories on the server. However, because of Quattro Pro's built-in file-locking capability, only the first user to access a spreadsheet file can save the file under the same name. Other users can, of course, open the same file, view it, and even edit it, but they cannot save it using the same file name. In this way, Quattro Pro prevents users from destroying each other's work.

For example, suppose you used the /File, Retrieve command to load the file BUDGET.WQ1 from a shared directory located on the network. A short time later, another user, say Charlie in Engineering, retrieves that same file. However, when Charlie opens the BUDGET.WQ1 file, a prompt box is displayed that says "Open file for read only?" along with Yes and No menu options. If Charlie selects Yes, Quattro Pro will bring the file into memory as a read-only file. That is, Charlie can look at the file and he can edit it, but he can't save it under the same name. If Charlie attempts to save the file under the same name in the same directory, he will get the error message "Sharing Violation." He can, however, press Esc to clear this message and save the file under a different name. In this way, two network users can access the same data file without overwriting each other's changes.

Charlie can eventually get access to your version of the BUDGET.WQ1 file, however. Suppose you are finished editing the BUDGET.WQ1 file. You then save the file to disk and clear it from memory. At that point, Charlie can open the file without getting the read-only message. When the file is opened on Charlie's workstation, your changes to the file are displayed.

Printing on a Network

If you are using a network version of Quattro Pro, you don't have to do anything special to print to a printer that is connected to your computer. However, printing to a network printer is a different matter.

If you wish to print to a network printer, you must use the appropriate network utility for redirecting the output of your local printer port to the network printer. In addition, this network utility will need to be set to handle graphic images generated by Quattro Pro in WYSIWYG mode, rather than text.

For example, if you are printing to a network printer on a Novell Net-Ware network you would use the CAPTURE command to redirect the output of your LPT1 port on your local workstation to the network printer as follows:

```
CAPTURE TI=50 NB S=HARVEY Q=LASERJETIII L=1
```

This command directs the data sent to your local LPT1 port to the server HARVEY with the following parameters:

- Sets the timeout option to 50 (TI=50)

- Suppresses the banner page (NB)

- Sends the data to the print queue for the LaserJet III printer (P=LASER-JETIII)

The extended timeout value of 50 gives the printer more time to process the data sent to it from the network. This is necessary when printing graphic images. The banner is turned off, since printing the text banner confuses the network software into thinking that it is printing text data.

Once you are properly connected to the network printer, you can print from Quattro Pro by using the /Print command. Your data will be sent to the network printer you specified.

Many networks support the use of a log-in script. This script runs automatically when you log on to the network. The purpose of this script is to connect your workstation to directories on the network server and to shared devices, such as printers. Therefore, if you know that you are automatically connected to a network printer when you log on to the network, you do not need to connect to the network printer. Quattro Pro will recognize the connection automatically. You can simply print from Quattro Pro in the usual way.

Support for Novell Networks

Quattro Pro 4.0 includes some additional support for Novell NetWare. If you are running Novell NetWare 286 2.15C or higher or NetWare 386 3.1 or higher, you can do the following without having to leave Quattro Pro:

- Map to shared directories on the network server

- Log on to a server to which you have access

- Monitor the status of the network print queues

- Control selected printing options

These capabilities are only available if you are running on NetWare. If you try these operations with another type of network, Quattro Pro will display a "Network shell not loaded" error message.

You can configure most of Quattro Pro's "hooks" into Novell NetWare by using the /Options, Network menu displayed in Figure 14.3. Among other things, this menu lets you create drive mappings to shared directories on the NetWare server and to control various printing features. Each of the options in this menu will be discussed in the sections that follow.

NOTE. *The sections that follow assume you that you have logged on to the network before starting Quattro Pro. That way, the program will come up recognizing your connections to the network automatically. See "Logging On to a Network Server" later to learn how to access files on the network server if you start Quattro Pro before logging on to the network.*

Defining a Default User Name

To get started, we recommend you set up a default user name. As you'll soon see, Quattro Pro requires this name in several of its network-related commands. If you establish a default user name now, Quattro Pro will provide it for you automatically when it is required. This will save you the trouble of having to type it over and over again.

To specify a default user name, select the User Name option from the /Options, Network menu. Quattro Pro will prompt you for a user name. Type the name of your choice and press Enter. Although you can provide any name you want, we recommend you use your NetWare login name here.

Figure 14.3

The /Options,
Network menu

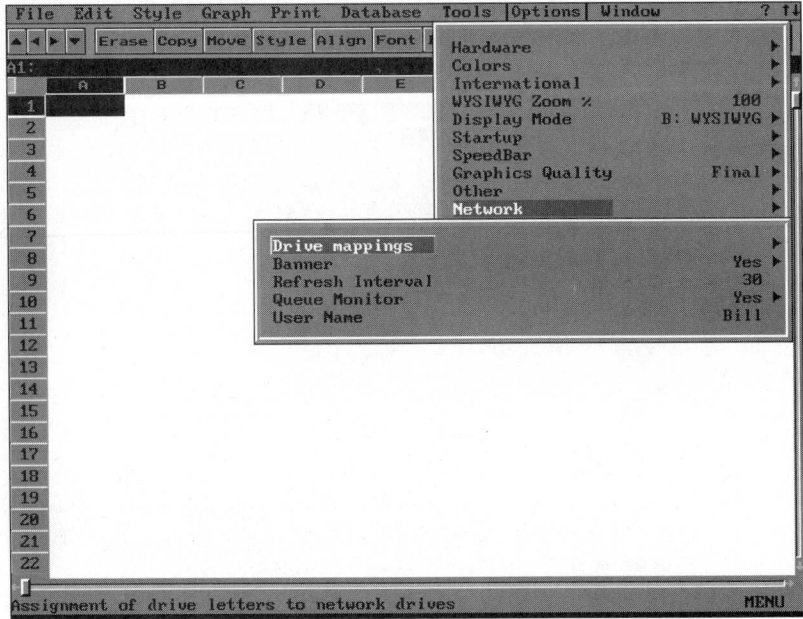

Mapping to Network Directories with /Options, Network, Drive Mappings

As you know, you can access data in shared directories on the network
server from within Quattro Pro. To make accessing files just that much easier, Quattro Pro 4.0 lets you take advantage of NetWare drive mappings, too.

NetWare drive mappings let you link a logical drive letter on your PC to
a shared directory on the network server. For example, you might link your
drive G to the F:\DATA\BUDGETS directory on the server. Once this drive
mapping is set up, you can use it with Quattro Pro commands. For example,
if you select the /File, Open or /File, Retrieve command and select the DRV
button, drive G will appear in the list of available drives. When you select
drive G, the files and subdirectories of the F:\DATA\BUDGETS directory
will appear in the files dialog box for your selection.

To create NetWare drive mappings from within Quattro Pro, select the
/Options, Network, Drive mappings command. Quattro Pro displays the
Drive mappings dialog box shown in Figure 14.4. Initially, this dialog box

contains eight empty slots. To add your first drive mapping to this dialog box, perform the following steps:

1. With the highlight resting on the first empty slot (1), press Enter. Quattro Pro prompts you for a logical drive letter.

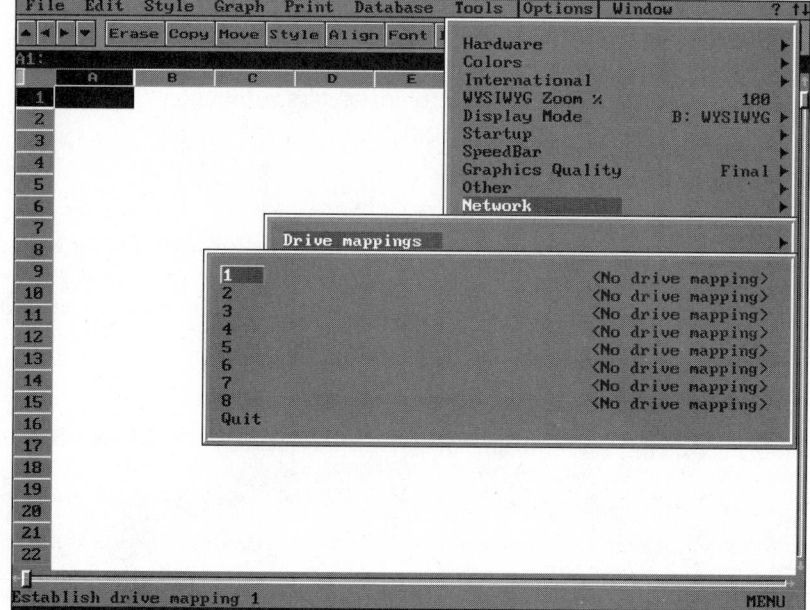

Figure 14.4

The Drive mappings dialog box with eight empty slots

2. Specify your next available logical drive letter. Press Enter to confirm your entry. If you are connected to the network, Quattro Pro displays a list of server names. Normally, DOS reserves the letters A through E for local drives. In addition, NetWare usually reserves drive F as its login drive. Therefore, you'll want to specify a drive letter between G and Z here. (If you specify a drive letter that is already in use, Quattro Pro will allow you to set up the drive mapping, but will ignore it.)

3. Select the server you want from the list that is provided and press Enter. Quattro Pro will prompt you for a volume name. If the server you want is not listed, select <Other> and type a server name. If you are not connected to the network, a dialog box is displayed, prompting you for a server name. Type the name of a server and press Enter.

4. Select a volume name from the list provided and press Enter. If the volume name you want is not listed, select <Other>, type the desired volume name, and press Enter. Either way, Quattro Pro will prompt you for a directory name. If you are not connected to the network, or if you typed a server name in the previous step, a dialog box will be displayed here, prompting you to provide a volume name. Type an appropriate volume name and press Enter.

5. Type the directory name you want to map to—for example, **\data\budgets**. Press Enter to confirm your entry. Quattro Pro will prompt you for a user name. If you do not specify a directory here—that is, if you leave this text box blank—the drive letter you specified in step 2 will be mapped to the root of the server volume.

6. Specify a user name. If you've previously specified a user name with /Options, Network, User Name, that name will appear, and you can simply select it and press Enter. Otherwise you must type it and press Enter. Either way, Quattro Pro records your new drive mapping and displays it in the Drive mappings dialog box as shown in Figure 14.5.

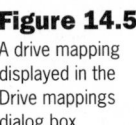

Figure 14.5

A drive mapping displayed in the Drive mappings dialog box

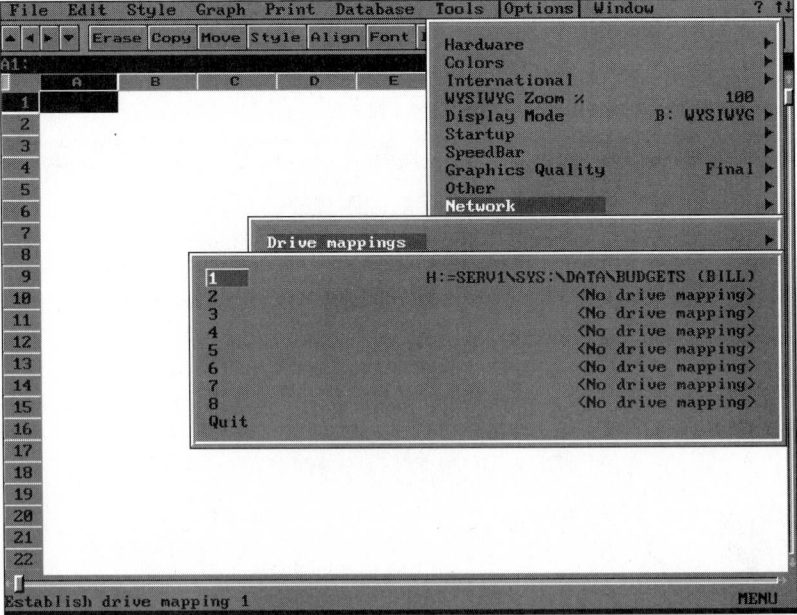

At this point, you can specify additional drive mappings (up to seven of them) using the procedure outlined above. Or, you can select Quit to return to the /Options menu. To save your new drive mapping for future Quattro Pro sessions, take a moment to select Update from the /Options menu. That way, your new drive mappings will be available the next time you start Quattro Pro.

Quattro Pro's drive mapping are not cast in stone. In fact, you can change them quite easily. To do this, select the /Options, Network, Drive mappings command to display the Drive mappings dialog box in Figure 14.5. Highlight the drive mapping you want to change and press Enter. Quattro Pro will take you through the steps outlined above, showing you the existing values at each stage of the process. You can change any part of the drive mapping at any stage.

You can also delete a drive mapping. To do this, select the drive mapping you want to delete and press Enter. When Quattro Pro prompts you for a drive letter, enter a space, and then press Enter at each subsequent prompt. When you confirm the last prompt, Quattro Pro will display <No drive mapping> in the current slot.

Mapping to Network Directories with the NET Button

You can also set up NetWare drive mappings for Quattro Pro without using the /Options, Network, Drive mappings command. To do this, select the NET button that is displayed in the files list dialog box for the /File Open, /File Retrieve, or /File Save As command. When you select this button, Quattro Pro will display the Drive mappings dialog box as shown in Figure 14.6. You can then use the techniques described above under "Mapping to Network Directories" to create or modify a NetWare drive mapping.

Using Your Quattro Pro Drive Mappings

Once a drive mapping is set up for Quattro Pro, you can use it in various ways. You'll find that mapped drives can be used with the following commands and operations:

- /File commands that lead to a files dialog box—for example, /File, Open; /File, Retrieve; /File, Save As; /File, Workspace, Restore; or /File, Workspace, Save.

- Commands in File Manager.

- The Clipboard, Paste From command in Annotator.

- Printing to a file.

- Setting default directories with /File, Directory; /Options Startup, Directory; or /Options, Other, Paradox, Directory.

Figure 14.6

Using the NET button in the files dialog box to create a NetWare drive mapping

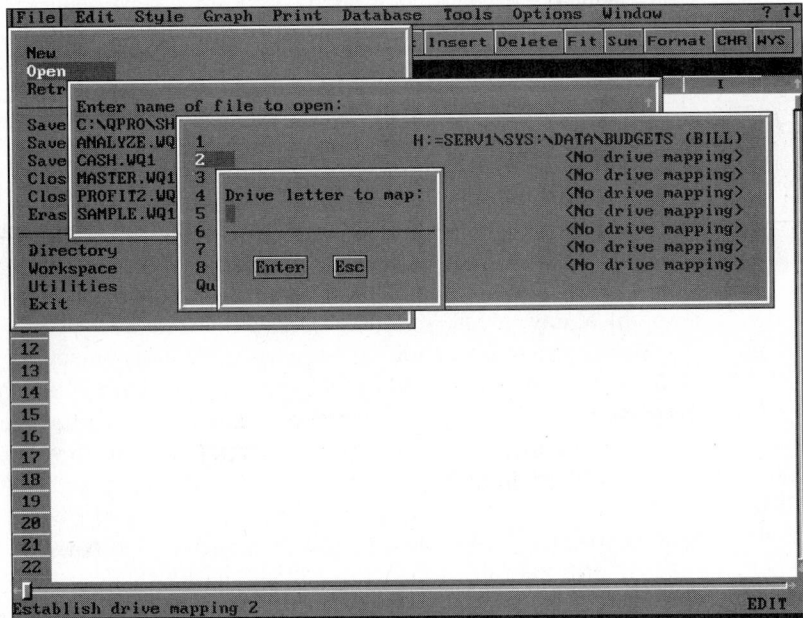

Quattro Pro's Drive Mappings and the Network

The drive mappings you create within Quattro Pro are only intended for use by Quattro Pro. When you leave the program, your drive mappings are returned to the way they were before you started Quattro Pro.

Do not attempt to create a drive mapping for a logical drive letter that was already in use before you started Quattro Pro. Although you are allowed to create such a drive mapping, Quattro Pro will ignore it. In short, Quattro Pro will not allow you to override the NetWare drive mappings that were in effect before you started the program.

If you've just installed Quattro Pro and you don't know which logical drive letters are already in use, you can easily check without leaving Quattro Pro. To do this, select either the /File, Open, or /File, Retrieve command and then select the DRV button. Quattro Pro will show you a list of both the local and remote drives to which you are connected. Once you set up additional drive mappings from within Quattro Pro, however, this method will no longer be reliable. Your new Quattro Pro drive mappings will appear in the DRV list along with those established by NetWare before you started Quattro Pro. In this case, the most reliable means of checking your existing drive mappings before starting Quattro Pro is to simply use NetWare's MAP

command. To do this, type **MAP** at the DOS prompt and press Enter. Net-Ware will show you a complete list of all your drive mappings.

Logging On to a Network Server

In most cases you'll probably log on to the network before you start Quattro Pro. That way, it comes up recognizing your connection to the network automatically. You can then use the /File, Open; /File, Retrieve; and /File, Save As commands to manage files on network drives. If you are not logged onto the network, however, you can still access files on the network server without leaving Quattro Pro. To do this, perform the following steps:

1. Select the /File, Open command to have Quattro Pro display the files dialog box.

2. Specify a network drive letter. You can specify a network drive letter by selecting the DRV button and then selecting a network drive letter you've previously set up with /Options, Network, Drive mappings. Alternatively, you can press Esc twice, type a network drive letter—for example, G:—and then press Enter. Either way, Quattro Pro will display the dialog box in Figure 14.7, prompting you to log on to the network.

3. If a password is required to log on to the network, type the password at the prompt and press Enter. (Quattro Pro will display bullets in place of the letters as you type.) If a password is not required, simply press Enter. Either way, Quattro Pro will log you on to the network and display the files on the drive you specified in the files dialog box. You can then select the one you want.

Connecting to Print Queues

As mentioned earlier in this chapter, you can use NetWare's CAPTURE command to redirect one of your PC's local parallel (LPT) ports to a network print queue. You can then start Quattro Pro and use the /Options, Hardware, Printers 1st (or 2nd) Printer, Device command to select the port referenced by the CAPTURE command. When you print from Quattro Pro, your output is automatically sent to the print queue you specified with CAPTURE.

Although this method will work just fine, it is somewhat static—that is, you cannot direct your output to another network print queue without leaving Quattro Pro. In addition, you must remember to use the CAPTURE command before starting Quattro Pro.

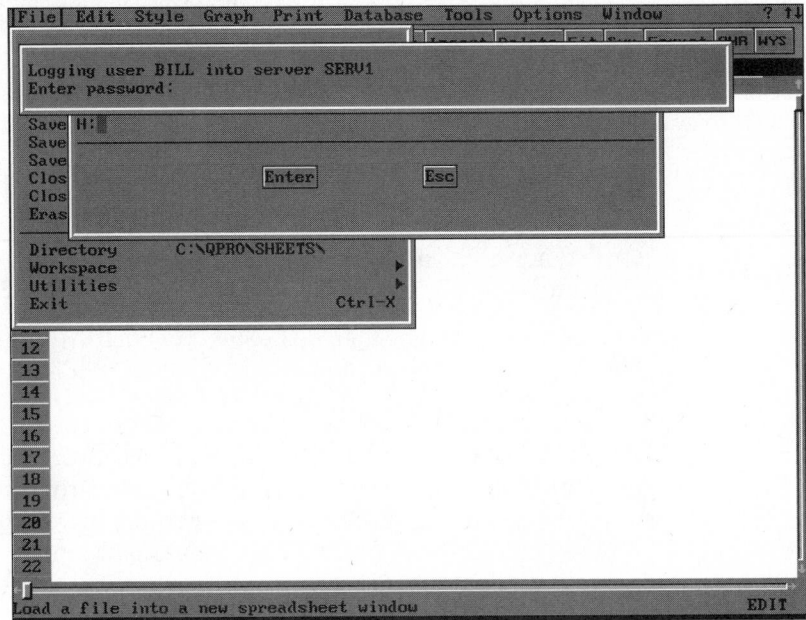

Figure 14.7

Prompt to log on to the network

Fortunately, there is a better way. Quattro Pro 4.0 lets you connect to different network print queues from within the program. To do this, perform the following steps:

1. Select the /Options, Hardware, Printers, 1st (or 2nd) Printer, Device command. Quattro Pro displays a menu of port connections as shown in Figure 14.8.

2. Select Network Queue. Quattro Pro prompts you for a server name.

3. Select a server name from the list displayed or choose <Other> and type a server name. Quattro Pro prompts you for a user name.

4. Type your user name and press Enter. Quattro Pro displays a list of available print queues.

5. Select the name of the print queue you want to use or select <Other> and type the name of the print queue. When you make a selection, Quattro Pro records it on the Device line in the Type of Printer dialog box.

6. Select Quit twice to return to the /Options menu. To save the setting for future Quattro Pro sessions, select Update, Quit.

Once you have established a connection to a network print queue, you can begin using it immediately. Just use the /Print command to print as you normally would.

Figure 14.8

Choosing Network Queue to connect to a network print queue

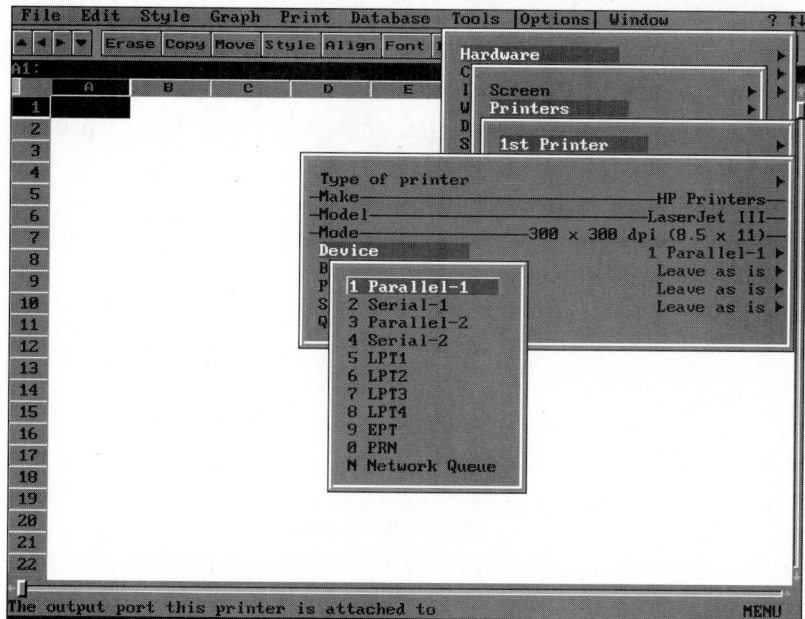

Quattro Pro also lets you print a banner page immediately before your print job. A banner page can help to separate one print job from another as they come out on the network printer. To have a banner page printed, use the /Options, Network, Banner command and select Yes. To suppress the banner page, select No. Suppressing the banner page saves paper and may be necessary if you are using a PostScript printer.

Monitoring Print Queues

Quattro Pro 4.0 provides two ways for you to monitor the status of the network print queues. The one you choose depends on how much information you need. If you want complete information, you can use Print Manager. If all you need is a rough indicator of where your own print jobs stand in relation to others in the queue, you can use Queue Monitor. Both methods are discussed in the sections that follow.

Using Print Manager

You can use Print Manager to monitor the status of the network print queues. Like NetWare's PCONSOLE utility, Print Manager lets you see what print jobs are in the queue, who sent them, and how large they are. You'll find Print Manager discussed in Chapter 6; this section focuses on using it to view the network print queue.

To view a network print queue using Print Manager, perform the following steps:

1. Select the /Print, Print Manager command to open a Print Manager window.

2. Select the /Queue, Network command from Print Manager's menu. Print Manager prompts you for a server name.

3. Select a server name from the list provided, or choose <Other>, type a server name, and press Enter. Quattro Pro prompts you for a user name.

4. Type your user name in the box provided and press Enter. (If you've previously defined a user name with /Options, Network, User Name, a user name is provided for you automatically.) Quattro Pro displays a list of print queue names for your selection.

5. Select a print queue name from the list provided, or choose <Other>, type a print queue name, and press Enter. Quattro Pro shows you a list of print jobs in the queue you've selected, as shown in Figure 14.9.

In Chapter 6, you'll find a complete description of the contents of Print Manager's window and instructions on how to use its menus to manage print jobs in the print queue. For example, you'll learn how to delete a print job or place one on hold. Be aware, however, that you cannot delete a print job in a network print queue unless you have the appropriate rights.

To keep you posted on the status of the network print queue, Print Manager's window must be updated periodically. You can control how frequently this window is updated by using /Options, Network, Refresh Interval command and specifying the number of seconds between updates. The default value is 30 seconds. Be aware that decreasing this value will give you more frequent updates, but may also slow down the operation of Quattro Pro.

You can also monitor more than one network print queue at the same time. In fact, you can use the /Print, Print Manager command to open up eight different Print Manager windows, each showing a different network print queue.

Figure 14.9
Using Print
Manager to view
the network print
queue

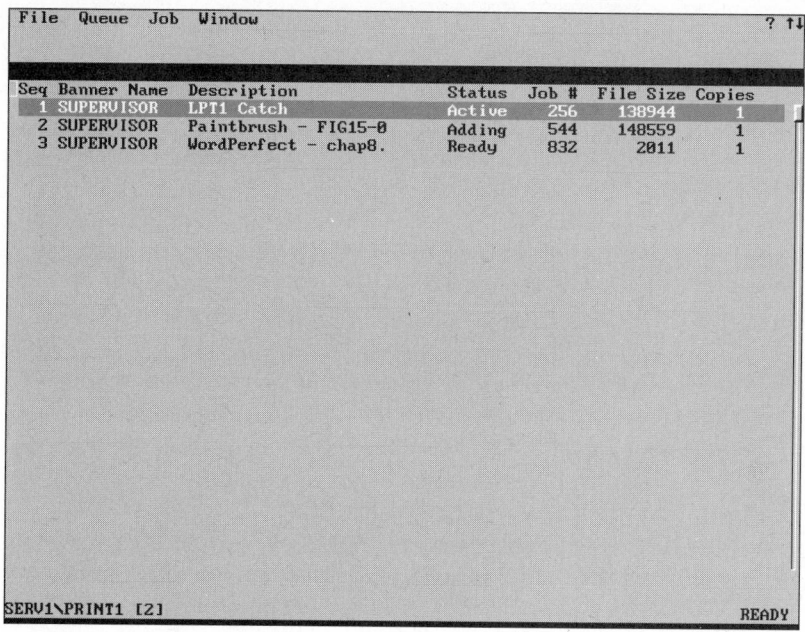

```
File   Queue  Job  Window                                           ? ↑↓

Seq Banner Name  Description              Status  Job #  File Size Copies
  1 SUPERVISOR   LPT1 Catch               Active    256   138944     1
  2 SUPERVISOR   Paintbrush - FIG15-8     Adding    544   148559     1
  3 SUPERVISOR   WordPerfect - chap8.     Ready     832     2011     1


















SERV1\PRINT1 [2]                                                    READY
```

Using Queue Monitor

In order to use the Queue Monitor to monitor a network print queue, you must load the Borland Print Spooler (BPS). The procedure for loading this utility is described in Chapter 6. In addition, you must use the /Options, Hardware, Printers, 1st (or 2nd) Printer, Device, Network Queue command to specify a network print queue. Finally, /Options, Network, Queue Monitor must be set to Yes.

When the Queue Monitor is active, Quattro Pro shows you the status of your own print jobs in the Status line at the bottom of your screen. (This information replaces the date and clock display.)

The following information is available from the Queue Monitor:

■ How many of your print jobs are not yet printed

■ How many print jobs are ahead of the first one you sent

■ The status of your first uncompleted print job

For example, if you initiated three print jobs from Quattro Pro, and there are seven jobs ahead of these, and first job you sent is ready to print, Quattro Pro displays the following:

```
3jobs|7ahead|Actv
```

When all of your print jobs have been completed, Quattro Pro briefly displays the following in the Status line:

```
0jobs|Complete
```

Configuring Paradox Network Access

To access Paradox tables stored on a network, you must tell Quattro Pro where to find the PARADOX.NET file. This is necessary because Quattro Pro respects the Paradox file-locking mechanism used when a table is being accessed by more than one user. For details on the Paradox locking mechanism, see your Paradox documentation. If you don't know the location of the directory containing the PARADOX.NET file, ask your system administrator. Once you know the correct directory, use the /Options, Other, Paradox, Directory command and specify the directory where the PARADOX.NET file is stored. Next, select the /Options, Other, Paradox, Network command and choose the type of network you are on from the list that is provided.

15

Customizing Quattro Pro

*Your Default
System Settings*

*Configuring Quattro
Pro for Your Hardware*

*Changing Quattro
Pro's Colors*

*Specifying International
Option Settings*

*Setting Startup
Parameters*

Customizing Menus

*Suppressing the Display
During Macro Execution*

*Changing the
Clock Display*

Memory Management

*Running Quattro Pro
Under Windows 3.x*

U NLIKE SOME SPREADSHEET PROGRAMS, YOU DON'T HAVE TO RUN A separate setup program to customize the operation of Quattro Pro. Instead, through its menu system, Quattro Pro lets you change many of its default settings from within the program itself. In fact, Quattro Pro provides more ways to customize its operation than any other spreadsheet program.

This chapter tells you all about how to customize Quattro Pro to suit your particular equipment and computing environment. Here are some of the topics covered:

- Configuring your screen display

- Setting the display mode

- Setting up your printer

- Changing display colors

- Setting startup parameters

- Using custom menus

- Configuring expanded memory

- Setting startup switches to limit Quattro Pro's use of expanded memory or to place the VROOMM object cache in extended memory

- Running Quattro Pro under Windows 3.x

Your Default System Settings

You customize the operation of Quattro Pro through the /Options menu. This menu offers an extensive set of options that let you change the program's default settings, and is the primary focus of this chapter.

Changes you make with the /Options menu apply only to the current Quattro Pro session, unless you specify otherwise. To save the changes you've made for use in future Quattro Pro sessions, you must use the /Options, Update command. This command saves the current default settings to a file named RSC.RF, which Quattro Pro reads each time you start the program.

The /Options menu is actually divided into two sections. In Quattro Pro 4.0, this division is marked by the Values option in the /Options menu; in Quattro Pro 3.0, this division is marked by a line. The settings changes you make using any one of the options above the Values option apply to all your spreadsheets, as well as to the operation of Quattro Pro itself. These are often referred to as the *default system settings*. These are the settings that are saved when you select /Options, Update. The options including and below the Values option in the /Options menu apply only to the current spreadsheet.

You can determine the current default system settings for Quattro Pro by using the /Options, Values command to display a settings sheet like the one in Figure 15.1. This sheet gives you a complete rundown of the current default system settings for Quattro Pro. The sections that follow discuss these settings and how you can change them to customize the operation of Quattro Pro to suit your particular needs.

Figure 15.1

The /Options, Values settings sheet

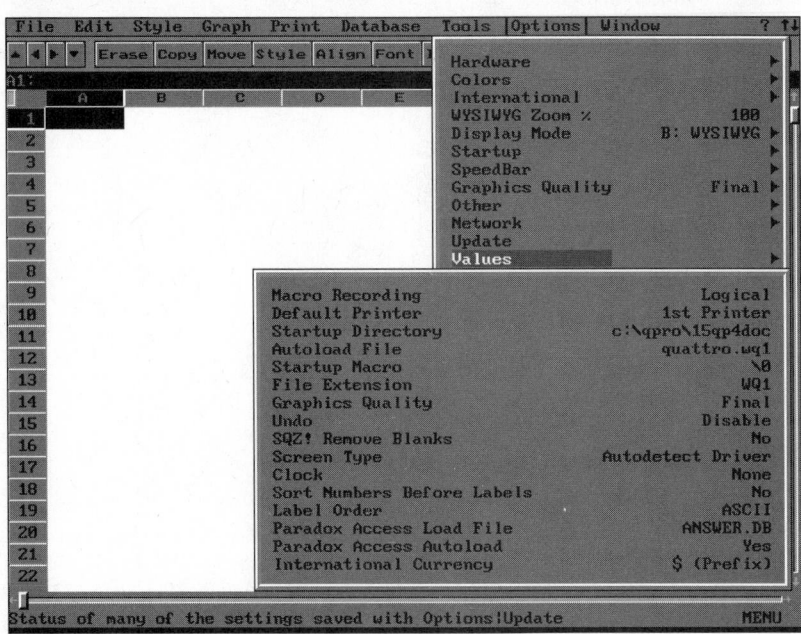

Configuring Quattro Pro for Your Hardware

With some spreadsheet programs, you must go to great effort to tell the program all about the hardware you are using. With Lotus 1-2-3, for example, you must carefully identify your display and printer hardware and save those settings in a driver set file. Without this step, the program may not run, and it will never display graphs.

Quattro Pro, on the other hand, is more accommodating. You can almost always get it to work without having to identify your hardware. Of course, if you want to print, you must specify the type of printer you are using. But Quattro Pro automatically determines the rest, detecting the type of hardware you are using and customizing itself accordingly.

You may find, however, that you want to override the program's automatic settings. For example, you may want to show more (or less) information on the screen, or change some aspect of the way graphs are displayed. You may also need to tell the program more about your printer—for example, what port the printer is connected to and, if it is a serial port, the speed at which to send the data. This section explains the customization of Quattro Pro's various hardware settings.

Configuring Your Screen Display

When you first install Quattro Pro, it performs some tests on your system's ROM and screen memory to detect the type of display hardware you are using. The program then automatically configures itself accordingly. You can override these screen display settings in any of the following ways:

- Choose a different screen type

- Change the resolution it uses to display graphs

- Change the aspect ratio to make pie charts and circles appear rounded

Choosing a Screen Type

If you need to override the screen type that Quattro Pro automatically uses, use the /Options, Hardware, Screen, Screen Type command. When you select this command, you see a list like the one in Figure 15.2.

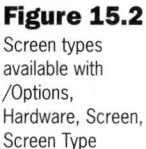

Figure 15.2
Screen types available with /Options, Hardware, Screen, Screen Type

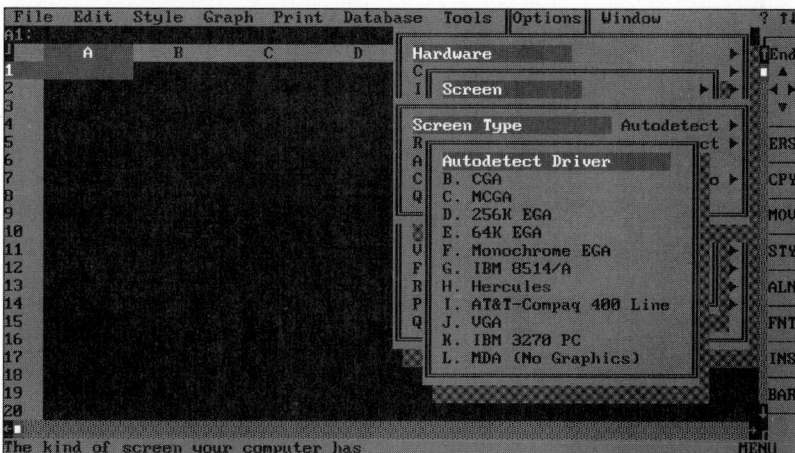

Quattro Pro's default screen type is Autodetect Driver. To select and use another driver type—CGA, for example—simply choose that option from the list. As soon as you leave the menu, Quattro Pro begins using the new driver. To save the setting for future sessions, use /Options, Update.

Note that if you are running Quattro Pro in WYSIWYG display mode, you cannot override the installed screen settings with /Options, Hardware, Screen, Screen Type. To do this, you must first switch to another display mode—for example, 80x25 text mode. See the section "Changing the Display Mode" later in this chapter.

Changing the Screen Resolution

Note. If you have a CGA monitor, Quattro Pro displays your graphs in black and white, to attain the highest possible resolution. Therefore, you cannot display your graphs in color with a CGA.

Normally, when Quattro Pro displays your graphs, it uses the highest resolution available for your screen type. If you have a color monitor, however, you can change the resolution used for displaying graphs with the /Options, Hardware, Screen, Resolution command. When you select this command, Quattro Pro displays a menu of the available resolutions for your particular screen type. For example, here are the choices for a VGA display:

640x200 EGA

640x350 EGA

640x480 VGA

(If you do not have a color monitor, no options are listed.) After you've selected a resolution from the menu, Quattro Pro will use it for the remainder of the current session. If you want to use the new resolution in future sessions, choose /Options, Update.

Note that you cannot use /Options, Hardware, Screen, Resolution when you are running in WYSIWYG display mode. Switch to another display mode—for example, 80x25 text mode—and then try the command.

Controlling the Aspect Ratio

If you find that your pie charts appear egg-shaped on the screen, you can adjust the screen's aspect ratio—the ratio of the screen's width to its height—with the /Options, Hardware, Screen, Aspect Ratio command. When you select this command, Quattro Pro displays a circle on your screen. Use the ↑ and ↓ keys to increase or decrease the circle's height until it is rounded to your satisfaction. Then press Enter. Quattro Pro then uses the new aspect ratio setting the next time it displays a pie chart or a circle in the Annotator. After adjusting the aspect ratio, you can choose the /Options, Update command to save the setting for future sessions. For more on creating pie charts with Quattro Pro, see Chapter 8.

Changing the Display Mode

Besides changing the screen driver, you can also change the display mode that Quattro Pro uses. Normally, Quattro Pro uses 80x25 Character (text) mode to display your spreadsheets. If you have an EGA or VGA card, Quattro Pro also offers WYSIWYG (What You See Is What You Get) display mode. In WYSIWYG mode, Quattro Pro shows the following on-screen features:

- Actual font types and sizes are displayed.

- The mouse pointer appears as an arrowhead rather than a rectangle.

- When you insert a graph in your spreadsheet (see Chapter 8), it appears as a graph rather than as a shaded area.

- The /Graph, Graph Type menu appears as a pictorial gallery.

Character and WYSIWYG are but two of the display modes Quattro Pro offers. You can also choose other display modes for specific graphics cards. For example, if you have a VGA card, you can choose VGA: 80x50 mode, which displays 80 characters across and 50 characters down (about 45 lines of spreadsheet data). There is also a 132-column display if you have a VGA card that supports extended text. Here are some of the VGA cards that support this format, for which Quattro Pro has special drivers:

Ahead Systems VGA Wizard
ATI VGA Wonder
Compaq integrated (132-column) VGS
Everex Viewpoint VGA/EV-673 VGA
Genoa Systems Super VGA
Orchid ProDesigner VGA
Paradise EGA 480/VGA 1024
Sigma VGA Legend/HP16
STB PowerGraph VGA
Video-7 VRAM VGA

To change the display mode,

1. Choose /Options, Display Mode. Quattro Pro displays a list of different screen modes.

2. Choose the display mode you want to use from the list.

3. If you want to save the new display mode for future sessions, choose /Options, Update to store the setting.

Setting Up Your Printer

Tip. If Quattro Pro is unable to print a complete page on your laser printer, chances are you don't have sufficient memory in your printer. Select a printer mode that requires fewer dots per inch.

When you first installed Quattro Pro, you were given the chance to select your printer make and model. If you opted not to install a printer at that time, you can install it at any later time with the /Options, Hardware, Printers command. You also use this command when you want to change the settings for an existing printer or to install a second printer.

Installing a Printer

To install a printer or change a printer's mode (the resolution in dots per inch for a given page size), follow these steps:

1. Choose the /Options, Hardware, Printers, 1st Printer or 2nd Printer command. Figure 15.3 shows the menu that appears.

Figure 15.3

The /Options, Hardware, Printers, 1st Printer or 2nd Printer menu

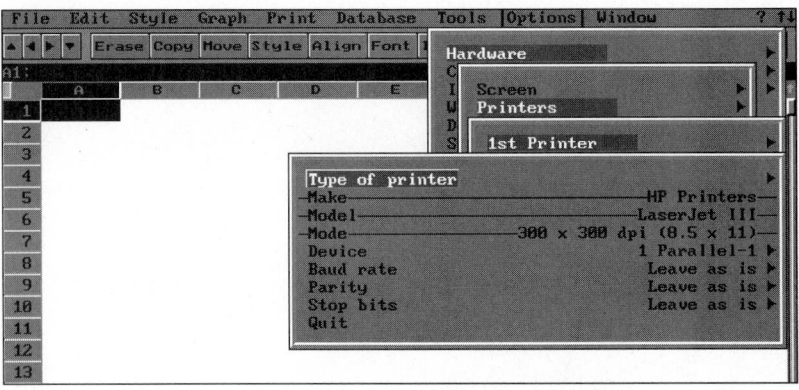

2. Select the Type of printer option, and then the printer make, model, and mode from the lists that subsequently appear.

3. Choose the Device option, and specify the type of printer port (see the section just below).

4. If you've chosen a serial port, you can adjust the baud rate, parity, and stop bit settings using appropriate options on this menu.

5. Select Quit twice and then Update from the /Options menu to save the settings you have chosen.

As you can see in Figure 15.3, /Options, Hardware, Printer, 1st Printer lets you select the type of printer you want to install, as well as configure various hardware options for its operation. The 2nd Printer command offers the same options, allowing you to set up a second printer for use with Quattro Pro. If you decide to install a second printer, and you want Quattro Pro to use it instead of the first printer, you must establish it as the default printer. See "Changing the Default Printer" later in this chapter.

Changing the Port Settings

When you install a printer, Quattro Pro automatically assigns it to Parallel 1, the first parallel port. If you want to use another port, follow these steps:

1. Select the /Options, Hardware, Printers, 1st Printer or 2nd Printer command (Figure 15.3).

2. Select the Device option, and you'll see the following menu options:

Note. The EPT option in the Device menu is for printing to the IBM Personal Pageprinter. EPT refers to the specific adapter the printer uses.

1 Parallel-1

2 Serial-1

3 Parallel-2

4 Serial-2

5 LPT1

6 LPT2

7 LPT3

8 LPT4

9 EPT

0 PRN

N Network Queue (version 4.0 only)

3. Select a printer connection from the list.

4. If you choose a serial port, set the baud rate, parity, and stop bits (as explained in the next section).

5. Select Quit twice, and then choose Update from the /Options menu.

Setting Baud Rate, Parity, and Stop Bits

When you select a serial port for your printer, Quattro Pro normally uses the setup established by DOS for the baud rate, parity, and stop bits. Therefore, if you've already used the MODE command from DOS to initiate the settings for the device, you don't have to worry about them—just leave them as they are. If you haven't used MODE, however, you may need to change these settings to get your printer to function properly.

Follow these steps:

1. If you haven't done so already, select the /Options, Hardware, Printers, 1st Printer or 2nd Printer command.

2. Select the Baud rate option, and choose a rate from 110 to 19200. (The Leave as is option uses the baud rate set by the DOS MODE command.)

3. Select the Parity option, and select Odd, Even, None, or Leave as is. (The default, Leave as is, uses the parity set by the DOS MODE command.)

4. Select the Stop bits option (this controls the number of bits sent at the end of each transmitted byte), and select 1 bit, 2 bits, or Leave as is. (The default, Leave as is, uses the number of stop bits set by the DOS MODE command.)

5. Select Quit twice, and choose Update from the /Options menu.

Turning Off Automatic Linefeed

Normally, Quattro Pro issues a carriage return and a line feed after each printed line. With some printers, however, the line feed is not necessary because the printer itself automatically issues one after a carriage return. (You'll know when your printer has this automatic line feed because all of your printed output will appear double-spaced.) To tell Quattro Pro that your printer has automatic line feed, select /Options, Hardware, Printers, Auto LF, Yes. If your printed output currently appears single-spaced, as it should, you can leave the Auto LF setting at No (the default).

Using Printer-Specific Fonts

When you install an HP LaserJet or PostScript-compatible printer, Quattro Pro automatically provides additional printer-specific fonts for your selection. For PostScript-compatible printers, Quattro Pro supports the 35 most popular fonts available on most PostScript printers. For LaserJet printers, Quattro Pro supports the fonts that are internal to the printer itself (burned into its ROM), as well as any cartridge fonts supplied by cartridges that plug into the printer. These fonts are available via the /Style, Fonts menu, and can be used to format the appearance of your data on screen as well as when you print.

Quattro Pro does not automatically recognize cartridge fonts for HP Laserjet-compatible printers. Instead, you must instruct Quattro Pro to add cartridge fonts for an HP LaserJet. For example, suppose you have a 92286B Tms Proportional 1 font cartridge for your HP LaserJet Series II printer. To have Quattro Pro recognize this cartridge, select the /Options, Hardware, Printers, Fonts command. Quattro Pro displays a menu with Cartridge Fonts and Autoscale Fonts; select Cartridge Fonts. The next menu offers Left Cartridge, Right Cartridge, and Shading Level. Select either Left Cartridge or Right Cartridge to indicate the printer slot where the cartridge currently resides. Quattro Pro displays a list of 24 cartridges it supports for the HP Laser-Jet family of printers. Select B-TmsRmn Proportional.

Once your printer-specific fonts are properly installed, you can use them to format the appearance of your data. For example, to select a printer-specific font as the default for the current spreadsheet, you can select /Style, FontTable, Edit Fonts, Font 1, Typeface. Quattro Pro will then display a list of fonts available for your selection, as shown in Figure 15.4. This list includes the standard Bitstream and Hershey bitmap fonts that come with Quattro Pro, followed by any fonts specific to your printer. Select the printer-specific font you want, and Quattro Pro will then build that font for the screen display. When you eventually print the data, Quattro Pro will use either the fonts that are resident to the printer, or those supplied by a cartridge.

Figure 15.4

Selecting printer-specific fonts

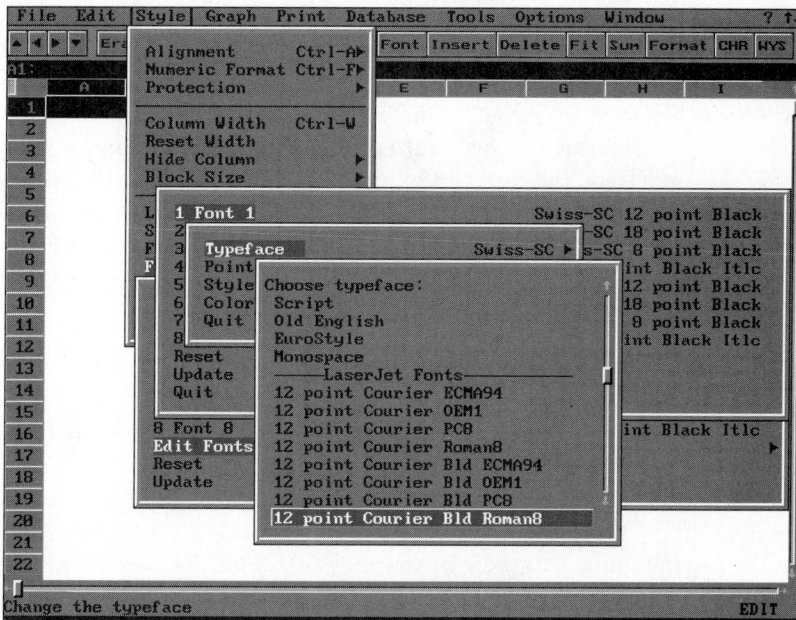

If you elect to use a printer-specific font, keep the following in mind:

- You cannot change the style or the point size for a printer-specific font.

■ You must print in graphics mode to see your printer-specific fonts. That is, you must select the /Print, Destination command and choose Graphics Printer.

See Chapter 3 for more on using printer-specific fonts to format your screen data. Also, see Chapter 6 for more on printing with printer-specific fonts.

NOTE. *If you specify a font cartridge that you do not have, Quattro Pro will display the fonts for that cartridge on the /Style, Fonts, Edit Fonts, Font 1, Typeface menu. What's more, it builds the appropriate fonts and uses them for screen display. However, when you print, Quattro Pro will not print that exact font. Instead, it substitutes the closest available font that is directly available from the printer.*

Autoscaling of Fonts

By default, Quattro Pro autoscales the fonts that appear in your graphs when you display and print them. The size of the fonts used depends upon the height of the graph. For example, suppose you use /Print, Graph Print, Layout to specify the height and width of a graph when printed. When you select Go to begin printing, Quattro Pro will adjust the size of the fonts in the graph as needed to maintain a pleasing, balanced appearance.

You can, however, turn off the autoscaling of fonts in graphs if you so desire. To do this, select /Options, Hardware, Printers, Fonts, Autoscale Fonts. Quattro Pro then displays a Yes/No menu. If you select Yes (the default), Quattro Pro adjusts the font's point size to fit the dimensions of the displayed or printed graph. Select No, and Quattro Pro uses the exact point size, regardless of graph size.

Installing Additional Bitstream Fonts

Note. Quattro Pro 4.0 supports the newer Bitstream scalable (Speedo) fonts. The installation program for these fonts is SPDINST.EXE.

You can install additional Bitstream fonts for Quattro Pro by using the BINST.EXE program. This program converts Bitstream fonts you've purchased separately to a format that Quattro Pro can use. You must run this program from the DOS prompt. First, make your Quattro Pro program directory current by using the DOS CD command. Next, insert in drive A the disk containing your new Bitstream (.BCO) font files. Finally, type **BINST** and press Enter. The BINST.EXE program copies all the font files on the disk in drive A to your Quattro Pro program directory, and converts them to a format usable by Quattro Pro. When this process is completed, the BINST.EXE program asks if you want to convert additional font files. You can type **Y** to continue, or **N** to quit. The next time you start Quattro Pro, the new fonts will be available for your selection.

Adjusting Shading on an HP LaserJet

You can set an overall grey-shading level for your LaserJet printer by using the /Options, Hardware, Printers, Fonts, Cartridge Fonts, Shading Level command. Quattro Pro displays a prompt box that lets you set the shading level to any whole number between 0% and 100% (the default is 30%). The lower the number, the lighter the shading. Specifying a value of 100% is equivalent to using the /Style, Shading, Black command.

The following eight levels of shading are available for an HP LaserJet.

Percent	LaserJet Shading level
1 to 2%	1
3 to 10%	2
11 to 20%	3
21 to 35%	4
36 to 55%	5
56 to 80%	6
81 to 99%	7
100%	8 (black)

Because there are only seven shades of gray on a LaserJet, don't expect them to closely conform to standard typographic shading percentages.

Choosing Draft Versus Presentation Quality

Quattro Pro 3.0 relies upon raster font (.FON) files to display various text fonts in your spreadsheets, graphs, and printed output. When you define a font for the first time, the program pauses for a moment to build the appropriate font file. Once the needed font file has been built, though, you can use that same font again in future sessions and Quattro Pro will respond almost immediately.

Quattro Pro 4.0 can also make use of raster font files. In this respect, it functions much like Quattro Pro 3.0. Normally, however, Quattro Pro 4.0 uses scalable fonts (Swiss-SC, Courier-SC, and Dutch-SC) for screen display. Because these fonts can be built rather quickly, you won't see the program pause the first time one of these fonts is defined. You will, however, get a "Building Fonts" message when you print these fonts. In order to print, Quattro Pro 4.0 must build .FN2 (raster) font files for these fonts in your \QPRO\FONTS directory. The fonts are then downloaded to your printer.

You may want to specify that Quattro Pro not build font files by using the /Options, Graphics Quality command. This command has two settings, Draft and Final (the default). If you select Draft, Quattro Pro does not pause to create new raster fonts as you request them with /Style, Font. Instead, Quattro Pro substitutes its closest available Hershey font; thus you can continue working without interruption.

You might use the Draft setting when you are creating a spreadsheet for your personal use, and speed rather than appearance is the important issue. If you want to publish the spreadsheet later for general viewing, select /Options, Graphics Quality, Final to reenable font building. Use the /Style, Fonts command as needed to format specific areas of your spreadsheet, and Quattro Pro will then build the appropriate font files—at your convenience rather than its own.

Changing the Default Printer

In the earlier section, "Installing a Printer," you learned to use the /Options, Hardware, Printers, 2nd Printer command to set up a second printer for use with Quattro Pro, including selection of the various hardware options for the second printer's operation.

If you've installed both a first and second printer, you can choose which one will be used as the default printer. To do this, select /Options, Hardware, Printers, Default Printer. On the menu that next appears, choose 1st Printer or 2nd Printer as the default printer you want Quattro Pro to use. If you want to make this setting the new default for future sessions, select Quit to return to the /Options menu, and then select Update.

Quattro Pro will use the default printer you specify for all its printing operations. For example, all output sent to a file on disk, to a graphics printer, or to Screen Preview will be generated using the settings for the default printer.

Using a Mouse

Using a mouse with Quattro Pro is optional, but it can enhance your efficiency with the product. For example, the Graph Annotator and the new /File dialog box buttons in Quattro Pro 4.0 are easier to use with a mouse. In addition, some features—for instance, graph zoom and pan—only work with a mouse.

Quattro Pro supports both Microsoft- and Logitech-compatible mice. In order to use these mice with Quattro Pro, a mouse-driver program must be loaded into memory before Quattro Pro is started. Upon startup, Quattro Pro will detect the presence of the mouse driver in memory, and will recognize your mouse automatically. To indicate this, the mouse pointer is displayed as a small arrow (in WYSIWYG mode) or as a small block (in Character mode). In addition, if you are running in Character mode, the mouse palette is displayed on the right side of your screen.

Most mice come with two driver files, usually named MOUSE.COM and MOUSE.SYS, that allow your computer to recognize the particular make and model of your mouse. (This is true of both serial mice, which plug into a COM port at the back of your computer, and bus mice, which come with a separate card that you plug into a slot inside your computer.) You must use either one or the other of these drivers; you don't need both.

The most efficient way to load MOUSE.COM is to add an entry such as mouse, or mouse/C2 (serial mouse on COM2) to your AUTOEXEC.BAT file. That way, the mouse driver will be loaded into memory automatically when you boot your machine. (The installation programs for some mice will do this for you.)

MOUSE.SYS, on the other hand, must be loaded by placing the an entry in your CONFIG.SYS file (usually, DEVICE=MOUSE.SYS). The mouse driver is then installed in memory when you start your computer. For more information about the appropriate settings for your mouse, see your mouse user's guide.

Some mouse drivers won't work with all of Quattro Pro's EGA and VGA graphics display modes. Specifically, some older mouse drivers won't support a display mode of more than 80 columns by 24 lines. To support Quattro Pro's EGA 80x43, VGA 80x50, or EGA/VGA graphics display modes, you'll need one of these mouse drivers:

Logitech	4.0 and higher
Microsoft	6.11 and higher
Mouse Systems	6.01 and higher
PC Mouse	6.01 and higher

Although it is rare , you may encounter cursor display problems when using Microsoft mouse driver version 7.04—usually, with Video 7-compatible display adapters. You can eliminate these problems by changing the DE-VICE=MOUSE.SYS statement in your CONFIG.SYS file to read DEVICE=MOUSE.SYS /Y.

Changing the Active Mouse Button

Normally, Quattro Pro recognizes the left mouse button as the active button. If you're left-handed, however, swapping the two buttons may allow you to work more efficiently. To make the right mouse button the active button, select the /Options, Hardware, Mouse, Right command. Select /Options, Update to make this setting permanent.

Changing Quattro Pro's Colors

Quattro Pro's default color scheme provides exceptional contrast and readability on a typical color monitor. However, because not all users have color monitors, and because color preferences often vary, Quattro Pro lets you change the color of its screen elements with the /Options, Colors command.

The /Options, Colors command lets you change the color options for the system; that is, when you change the color of a screen element, that color will be used whenever that element appears. For example, change the color of the cell selector, and it will retain that color for every spreadsheet. When you make a change with the /Options, Colors command, that change applies only to the current session. To save the setting as the new default for future sessions, you must use the /Options, Update command.

Sometimes changing Quattro Pro's colors is as much a matter of necessity as it is preference. For example, if you are using an EGA or VGA (color) graphics card with a black-and-white screen, you may find that the standard Quattro Pro colors are hard to see. In this case, you might want to use /Options, Colors, Palettes, Black and White to access Quattro Pro's standard black-and-white color scheme and bring more focus and clarity to your display.

In other cases, changing a color display element can help to improve your work efficiency. For example, Quattro Pro lets you add special shading to cells with negative numbers, making them easier to spot. Or, you can differentiate cells with labels and cells with values by displaying them in two different shades. You can even use a different color for values that fall outside a given range; this allows you to easily spot problem areas.

Working with Monochrome Versus Color Screens

The option of changing the color of Quattro Pro's screen elements is not limited to color monitors. Even if you have a monochrome monitor, you can still modify the shading of any of Quattro Pro's display elements. In fact, the program offers you five different shading attributes: Normal, Bold, Underline, Inverse, and Empty (no display element).

A color monitor can be converted to a monochrome display. In fact, through its /Options, Colors, Palettes command, Quattro Pro lets you choose from its default Black and White, Monochrome, or Grey Scale color schemes. Quattro Pro 4.0 also adds the Version 3 color option, which displays a color scheme that is consistent with Quattro Pro 3.0. These schemes can be useful if you are using screen-capture software to capture images of the Quattro Pro screen. You'll find you get a more consistent look when the image is reproduced on your printer.

Using the /Options, Colors, Menu

Note. You can also change Quattro Pro's default color scheme from within File Manager. In fact, the /Options, Colors menu is precisely replicated in File Manager.

To change the existing color of a display element, select the /Options, Colors command, and you'll see the menu of screen element categories shown in Figure 15.5. Each category displays its own list of screen elements. When you select a specific screen element, Quattro Pro displays a palette of colors for your selection. For example, if you are using a color display, Quattro Pro displays the palette of colors demonstrated in Figure 15.6, where you can choose from any combination of eight background colors and fifteen foreground colors. The current color for the element you've selected is marked by a rotating cursor. To select a new color combination, click on it with your mouse, or use the arrow keys to move the rotating cursor and then press Enter. Quattro Pro implements your color selection and returns you to the /Options, Colors menu.

Figure 15.5
The /Options, Colors menu

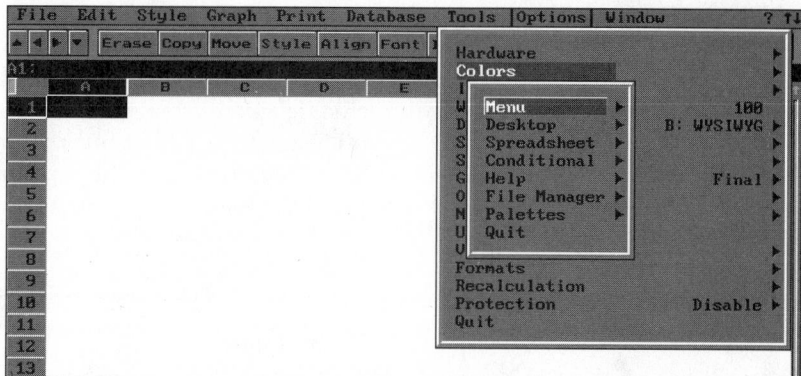

Figure 15.6
Choosing from the palette of colors for a screen element

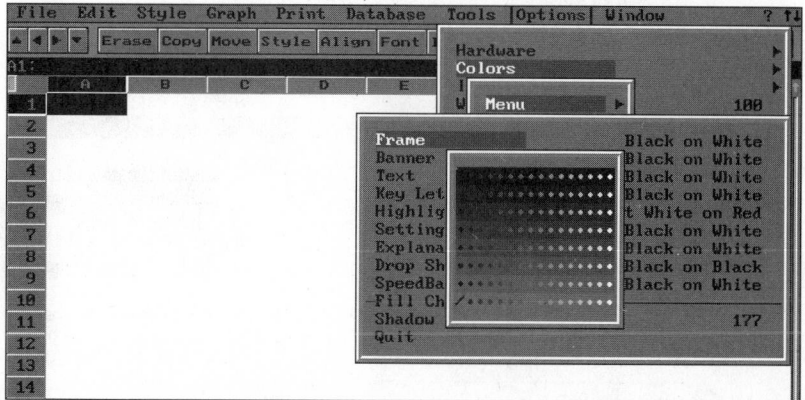

If you don't like your new color choice, you can always change it. Simply repeat the appropriate /Options, Colors command sequence, and select a new color. If you can't find the color combination you want, or you want to start over, just select /Options, Colors, Palettes again to restore Quattro Pro's original default color scheme.

On a monochrome display, Quattro Pro does not display the color palette in Figure 15.6. Instead, when you select a screen element, a menu of display attributes appears. You can choose a Normal, Bold, Underline, Inverse, or Empty display, in most cases. Empty means no screen attribute is applied.

TIP. *Color contrast is the key to character legibility. Don't use the same background and foreground colors for a display element unless you want to hide that element. Similarly, avoid choosing the same background colors for screen elements that physically border on each other, unless you want to obscure the border.*

Changing the Menu Colors

As mentioned, when you select /Options, Colors, Quattro Pro displays a list of screen element categories. The first option on that list is Menu, which lets you change the color of the screen elements that make up Quattro Pro's pop-up and pull-down menus. The ten screen elements that make up its menus are illustrated in Figure 15.7. Simply select Menu, then the element whose color you want to change, and then the appropriate color from the color palette.

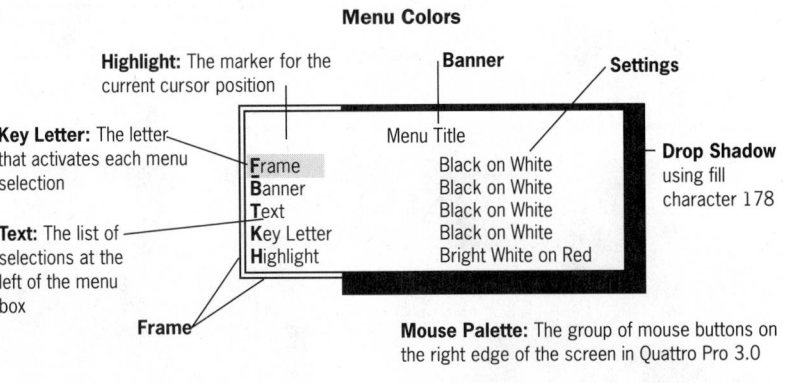

Figure 15.7

The screen elements that make up a Quattro Pro menu

Changing the Desktop Colors

The next option on the /Options, Colors menu is Desktop, which includes the elements in the display area that are not covered by the following option, Spreadsheet. These elements are portrayed by the diagram in Figure 15.8.

- *Status*   Color of the status line at the bottom of your screen

- *Highlight Status*   Color of the status and mode indicators on the Status line

- *Errors*   Color of the error messages displayed on the screen

- *Background*   Color of the background area beneath spreadsheet windows

- *Fill Character*   The ASCII character Quattro Pro uses to fill in the screen background and for shading when you are in Character mode (by default, ASCII character 178)

Changing Spreadsheet Colors

The Spreadsheet option in the /Options, Colors menu lets you change the colors of screen elements that occur within the spreadsheet area. These elements are summarized in Figure 15.9. The first 12 selections apply to Character mode only. When you select an element, Quattro Pro displays the color palette, and you can select the color you want for that element.

Figure 15.8

Desktop screen elements whose colors you can change

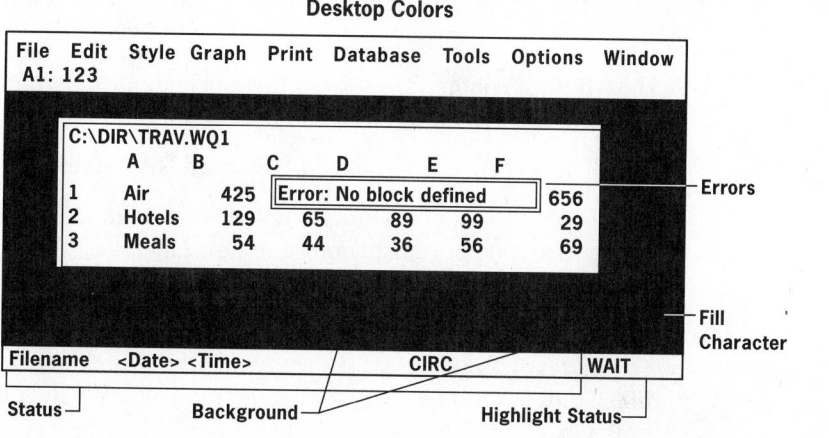

Desktop Colors

On the /Options, Colors, Spreadsheets menu you'll also find a WYSI-WYG Colors option. This option opens up a separate menu of spreadsheet elements that apply strictly to WYSIWYG mode. See "Changing Quattro Pro's WYSIWYG Colors" later for details on using this menu.

Figure 15.9

Spreadsheet elements whose colors you can change

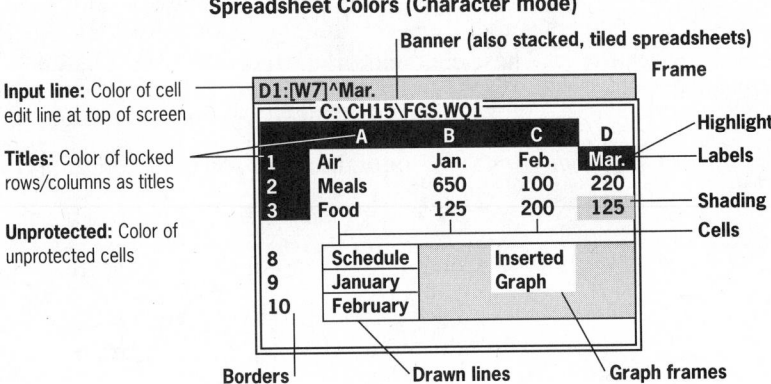

Spreadsheet Colors (Character mode)

Banner (also stacked, tiled spreadsheets)

Frame

Input line: Color of cell edit line at top of screen

Titles: Color of locked rows/columns as titles

Unprotected: Color of unprotected cells

Highlight

Labels

Shading

Cells

Borders

Drawn lines

Graph frames

Changing Conditional Colors

The /Options, Colors, Conditional command is one of the more useful and unique colorization tools Quattro Pro has to offer. It lets you choose a color for a spreadsheet entry based on a given condition. For example, you might display negative values in red, and values greater than 10,000 in green. You can also apply colors to ERR and NA values. As you might imagine, this feature is useful for emphasizing unusual or potential problem entries in your spreadsheet. Selecting the /Options, Colors, Conditional command displays a menu with the following choices:

- *On/Off* turns conditional color settings on and off. When you select this option, Quattro Pro displays a menu with Enable and Disable (the default).

- *ERR* lets you choose a color for ERR and NA values.

- *Smallest Normal Value* works in conjunction with Greatest Normal Value to let you establish a range of normal values. When you select this option, Quattro Pro prompts you for a value. To apply a color to below-normal values, use the Below Normal Value option.

- *Greatest Normal Value* works with Smallest Normal Value to let you define a range of values that you consider normal. When you select this option, Quattro Pro prompts you for a value. To apply a color to above-normal values, use the Above Normal Color option.

- *Below Normal Color* lets you specify a color for all values below the Smallest Normal Value.

- *Normal Cell Color* lets you specify a color for values within the normal limits you have defined.

- *Above Normal Color* lets you specify a color for values that are above the Greatest Normal Value.

NOTE. *Make sure you remember to turn the Conditional colors setting off. Leaving it turned on can consume memory and possibly slow down the operation of Quattro Pro.*

Changing Help Colors

You can change the colors of Quattro Pro's help screens by using /Options, Colors, Help. When you select this command, Quattro Pro displays a menu with the following help screen elements:

- *Frame*   The color of boxes around help text

- *Banner*   The color of the headings for help screens

- *Text*   The color of the actual text displayed in help screens

- *Keywords*   The color of words used to index and direct you to further help screens

- *Highlight*   The color of the cursor you use to select keywords in help.

Changing File Manager's Colors

The /Options, Colors, File Manager command lets you change the colors of the eight screen elements that make up the File Manager window. These elements are summarized in Figure 15.10. When you select an element, Quattro Pro displays the color palette from which you can choose the color you want.

Figure 15.10

File Manager screen elements whose colors you can change

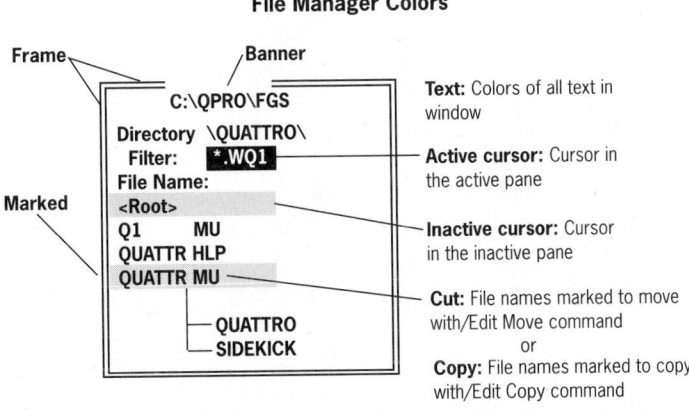

File Manager Colors

You can also change Quattro Pro's colors from within File Manager's window. In fact, you'll find that the File Manager's menu contains an /Options, Colors command whose options precisely mirror those presented by this command when invoked from the spreadsheet menu bar.

Restoring the Default Colors

Quattro Pro 4.0 comes with five default color schemes, or palettes. You can choose a palette by using the /Options, Colors, Palettes command. This command is particularly useful when you've changed the color of one or more of Quattro Pro's screen elements, and you want to restore them to their original Quattro Pro default values. The /Options, Colors, Palettes menu offers the following choices:

- *Color* restores original default colors for color screens (EGA and VGA).

- *Monochrome* restores original default colors for monochrome screens.

- *Black and White* restores original default colors for black-and-white (CGA) screens.

- *Gray Scale* restores original default color scheme for gray scale.

- *Version 3 Color* restores the Quattro Pro version 3 color scheme.

Changing Quattro Pro's WYSIWYG Colors

It is important to note that Quattro Pro makes a distinction between WYSIWYG and Character modes where colors are concerned. In fact, Quattro Pro includes a separate menu—/Options, Colors, Spreadsheet, WYSIWYG Colors—that lets you change display colors for screen elements that are within the physical boundaries of the WYSIWYG spreadsheet. You'll no doubt notice some duplication on this menu of screen elements that appear in Character mode. However, when you make a color change using the WYSIWYG Colors menu, that change applies only while Quattro Pro is in WYSIWYG mode.

You can use the /Options, Colors, Spreadsheet, WYSIWYG Colors command to change the color of the following screen elements displayed only in WYSIWYG mode:

- *Background*   Background of the cells (default: Bright White).

- *Cursor*   The cell selector (default: Black).

- *Grid Lines*   WYSIWYG Grid Lines (default: Gray).

- *Unprotected*   Unprotected cells (default: Cyan).

- *Drawn Lines*   Lines you draw around cells with /Style, Line Drawing (default: Black).

- *Shaded Cells*   Shaded cells (default: Gray).

- *Locked Titles Text*   Text in locked titles (default: Bright White).

- *Titles Background*   Background in locked titles (default: White).

- *Row and Column Labels*   The elements that make up row and column labels (the boxes along the left and top edges of the spreadsheet that identify each row and column). You can change the color of the Highlight (the left and top edges of column and row headings), the Shadow (the right and bottom edges of columns and row headings), the Face (the front of the boxes), and the Text (the row and column title text).

When you select a WYSIWYG element you want to change, Quattro Pro displays a special WYSIWYG color palette, as shown in Figure 15.11. To choose a color from this palette, use the arrow keys to move to the color and press Enter, or click on the color with your mouse. Either way, Quattro Pro updates the screen to reflect your choice.

Figure 15.11

The /Options, Colors, Spreadsheet, WYSIWYG Colors menu and palette

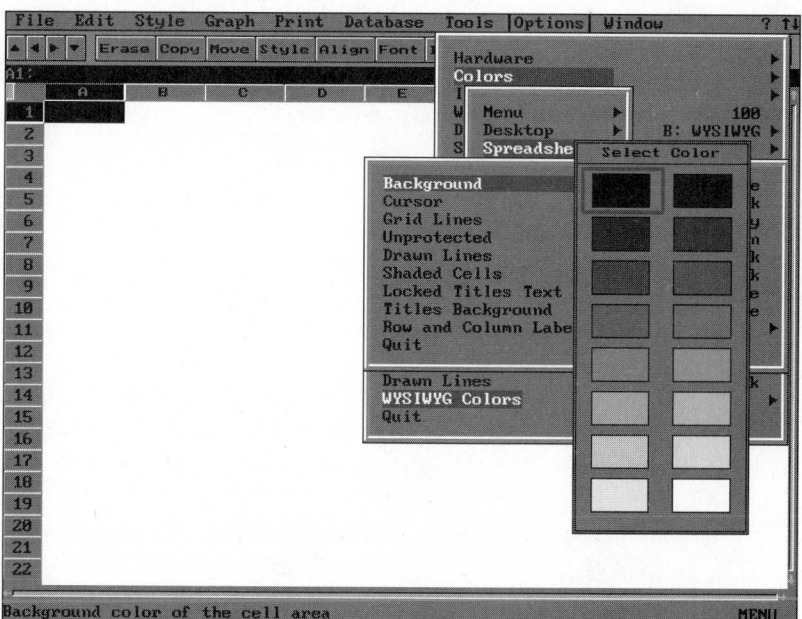

Specifying International Option Settings

The /Options, International command lets you customize Quattro Pro according to the language, currency, date, and time conventions of the country in which you are currently working. When you select this command, Quattro Pro displays the menu in Figure 15.12. The changes you make apply only to the current session. To save your settings for future sessions, select the /Options, Update command.

You'll see the effects of the /Options, International settings when you format data in your spreadsheet. The changes you make with this command affect the /Style, Numeric Format, Currency, Date or Time commands. As explained in Chapter 3, these commands are used to format blocks of data. The /Options, International settings also affect the /Options, Formats, Numeric Format, Currency, Date or Time commands, which are used to set global formatting options for the entire spreadsheet.

Figure 15.12

The /Options, International menu

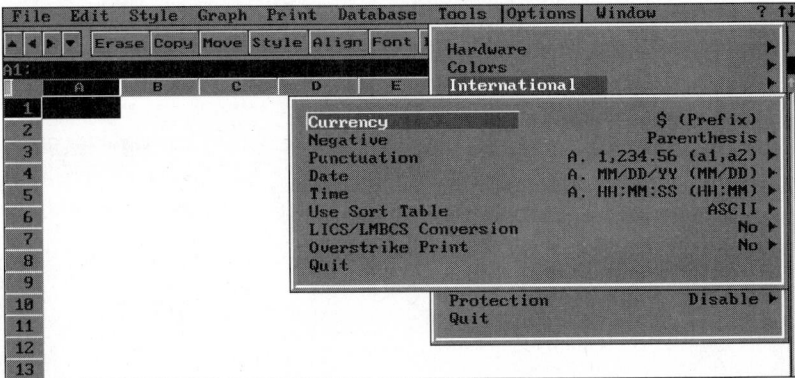

Currency Settings

The /Options, International, Currency command lets you specify the characters Quattro Pro uses to indicate currency. You can change the default dollar sign ($) to any other ASCII character.

When you select this command, Quattro Pro prompts you for a currency symbol. You can type any character you want, including special characters produced with the Alt key and the numeric keypad. For example, you might hold down the Alt key and type **156** to produce the British pound symbol, or **157** to produce the Japanese yen symbol. To confirm your entry, press Enter. When you do, Quattro Pro asks you if you want the currency symbol to appear as a prefix or suffix to currency values; choose the positioning you want. Your new currency symbol will then be used whenever you select /Options, Numeric Format, Currency or when you select /Style, Numeric Format, Currency.

Punctuation Settings

You can use the /Options, International, Punctuation command to specify punctuation settings for Quattro Pro. Punctuation settings determine the characters used to display the decimal point in numbers, to separate the arguments in @functions and macros, and to separate the thousands in numbers. The default characters are the comma as a thousands separator, the period as a decimal point, and the comma (or semicolon) for @function and macro argument separators.

When you select the /Options, International, Punctuation command, Quattro Pro displays a menu with eight punctuation combination choices. Each choice offers a different combination of thousands, decimal, and argument separator symbols.

Date Display

Use the /Options, International, Date command to change the display of Long and Short International date formats. As explained in Chapter 3, when you select /Style, Numeric Format, Date or /Options, Formats, Numeric Format, Date, Quattro Pro gives you five possible date format choices. Two of these choices are labeled Long intl. and Short intl. You can change the Long International format setting from the default MM/DD/YY to either DD/MM/YY, DD.MM.YY, or YY-MM-DD. You can change the Short International setting from the default MM/DD to either DD/MM, DD.MM, or MM-DD.

Time Display

Use the /Options, International, Time command to change the Long and Short International time formats. Your settings affect both the /Style, Numeric Format, Date, Time command and the /Options, Formats, Numeric Format, Date, Time command. As explained in Chapter 3, the default settings for these commands are HH:MM:SS (Long International) and HH:MM (Short International). However, /Options, International, Time lets you choose from any one of four different international time formats.

Sorting Sequence

The /Options, International, Use Sort Table command lets you change the sorting sequence used by Quattro Pro to sort information in databases. By default, Quattro Pro uses an ASCII sorting sequence that sorts all words beginning with uppercase letters before words beginning with lowercase letters.

If you want, you can change the default sorting sequence to conform to international sorting rules that are not case sensitive, by selecting the INTL.SOR option. If you are sorting a database in Norway or Denmark, you can select the Norwegian/Danish (NORDEN.SOR) option and use international rules adapted to those countries. A Swedish/Finnish (SWEDFIN.SOR) option is also available.

LICS/LMBCS Conversion in Quattro Pro 4.0

When you select /Options, International, LICS/LMBCS Conversion, Yes, Quattro Pro automatically converts Lotus International Character Set (LICS) characters and Lotus MultiByte Character Set (LMBCS) characters in any 123.WK1 or 123.WK3 spreadsheet files you retrieve into standard ASCII characters. Quattro Pro also converts the ASCII characters back to LICS or LMBCS when you save the file in Lotus 1-2-3 (.WK1 or .WK3) format. LMBCS conversion is not provided in Quattro Pro 3.0.

Overstrike Print

The /Options, International, Overstrike Print command is specifically provided for Quattro Pro users who have a 7-bit printer, and want to print diacritical marks, such as the French accent acute (´), grave (`), or circumflex (^). If you select the Yes option, Quattro Pro tells your printer to print a letter, such as an e, and then backspace and print the diacritic over the top of the letter.

Setting Startup Parameters

The /Options, Startup command lets you specify various parameters that Quattro Pro will use at startup. When you select this command, Quattro Pro displays the menu shown in Figure 15.13. The options on this menu perform the following functions:

- *Directory* lets you define the default directory in which Quattro Pro will search for and save its files. This option is discussed at length in Chapter 5, under "Changing Directories."

- *Autoload File* lets you specify a spreadsheet file to be loaded automatically when you start Quattro Pro. This option is also discussed in Chapter 5, under "Autoloading Spreadsheets."

- *Startup Macro* lets you specify the name of a macro that will be run automatically when you load a spreadsheet file into memory. The default startup macro name is \0, but you can change this name if you want. See "Startup Macros" in Chapter 12 for additional details.

Figure 15.13

The /Options, Startup menu

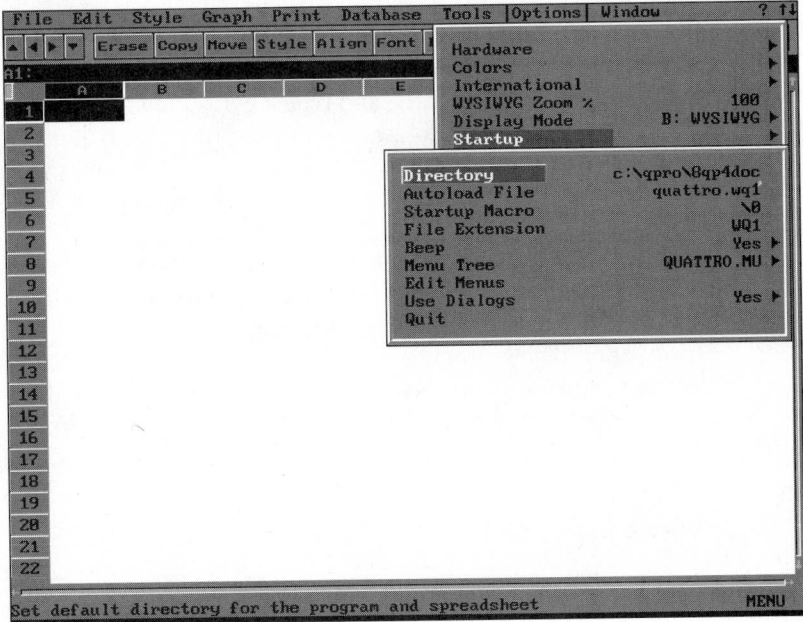

- *File Extension* lets you change the default file extension used by Quattro Pro for spreadsheet files. This option is discussed later in this section.

- *Beep* lets you turn Quattro Pro's warning beep off and on. This option is discussed later in this section.

- *Menu Tree* lets you select a different default menu tree for Quattro Pro. See the next section, "Customizing Menus," for details.

- *Edit Menus* lets you edit the current default menu tree. See "Customizing Menus" for details on this option, as well.

- In Quattro Pro 4.0, *Use Dialogs* lets you replace the following submenus with corresponding dialog boxes: /Graph, Customize; /Graph, X-Axis; /Graph, Y-Axis; /Graph, Overall; and /Print, Layout.

Setting the Default File Name Extension

As you know, the default extension used by Quattro Pro for spreadsheet file names is .WQ1. However, you can change this default with the /Options, Startup, File Extension command. This command lets you define the three-letter file name extension that Quattro Pro will use when saving and retrieving your files.

To change the extension, select /Options, Startup, File Extension. Quattro Pro displays a prompt box showing the current default extension, .WQ1. Press Esc to clear this entry, and type a period followed by the new three-letter extension you want to use. When you press Enter, Quattro Pro adopts your new extension as the default for all spreadsheet files you create in the remainder of the current session. To save this setting for future sessions, you must select the /Options, Update command.

If you change the default file name extension to one used by another spreadsheet or database program, Quattro Pro may translate the files you save into a format compatible with that program. (See Table 5.3 in Chapter 5 for a list of file name extensions used by other popular software.) Quattro Pro is capable of saving your files in different formats used by various popular business software packages. See "Translating to and from Other File Formats" in Chapter 5 for details on this.

Turning Off the Beep

You may have heard the warning beep that Quattro Pro sounds when you attempt to perform an unsupported operation. If this sound bothers you, you can turn it off by using the /Options, Startup, Beep, No command. This command affects only the remainder of the current Quattro Pro session; of course, you can turn the beep back on by selecting /Options, Startup, Beep, Yes. To save the setting for future sessions, use /Options, Update.

Customizing Menus

Perhaps one of the more unique features of Quattro Pro is its ability to let you customize menus; in fact, Quattro Pro 4.0 comes with two different *menu trees* from which you can choose. For example, in addition to the standard Quattro Pro menu, you can opt for a menu in the Lotus 1-2-3 style. (In Quattro Pro 3.0, you can also choose the version 1.0 Quattro Pro menu.) Moreover, Quattro Pro lets you customize any of these menus to suit your particular needs, by changing command names, moving them from one menu to another, or creating an entirely new menu item that runs one of your macros. To customize menu trees, you use Quattro Pro's Menu Builder feature, as discussed later in this section.

A menu tree is a hierarchical layout of menu commands. Quattro Pro stores its menu trees in files with an .MU extension, located in your Quattro Pro program directory. The standard Quattro Pro menu is QUATTRO.MU and the Lotus 1-2-3 equivalent menu is stored as 123.MU.

Choosing a Different Menu Tree

You can change to a new menu tree by using the /Options, Startup, Menu Tree command, which displays a submenu containing the names of menu files, less their .MU extensions. Initially, only two options, 123 and Quattro, apppear on this menu, but when you create new menu trees and save them under different .MU file names, they will be added to the list.

When you select a menu file, Quattro Pro replaces the current menu tree with the one you've selected, and you can use it for the remainder of the current session. To save this setting for future Quattro Pro sessions, select the /Options, Update command.

Creating a Custom Menu

To create a custom menu tree, you use the Menu Builder to modify one of Quattro Pro's standard menu trees, and then save it under a different .MU file name. Therefore, to begin, make a specific menu tree current by using the /Options, Startup, Menu Tree command. Then you're ready to open the Menu Builder window. To do this, use the /Options, Startup, Edit Menus command. Quattro Pro opens the Menu Builder window and reads the .MU file for the current menu tree into memory. When this process is complete, your screen will look similar to Figure 15.14.

The Menu Builder Window

When you open the Menu Builder window, you'll notice it is divided into three panes. At the top, the Current Item pane is used to assign actions to menu items. The middle Menu Tree pane lets you add new items to a menu and modify existing ones. The bottom pane, the Clipboard Menu pane, shows the names of menu items that have either been deleted or that you are in the process of moving from one location to another. To move between panes in the Menu Builder window, you use the Pane (F6) key.

The Menu Tree Pane

When you first open the Menu Builder window, the Menu Tree pane is active (contains the highlight). This pane displays the main menu commands for the current menu tree. Menu commands that have child menus (submenus) are marked by a + (plus) before the command name. To display the child menu for a parent menu item in the Menu Tree pane, use the arrow keys to highlight it and press the gray + key on the numeric keypad. To hide a child menu again, press the gray – (minus) key.

You can use either the arrow keys or the spacebar to move the highlight from one menu command to the next in the Menu Tree pane. The object here is to highlight the command you want to modify, move, or eliminate.

Figure 15.14

The Menu Builder window

```
 Save  Print  Change Help  Attach Macro  Options  Exit                    ? ↑↓
┌──────────────────────────────────────────────────────────────────────────┐
│ Current Item                                                               │
│ Desc: Numbers and labels centered within the cell width                    │
│ Actions – General:▶ Publish              Specific:▶ AlignCenter            │
│ Selectable?:▶ Yes            After Selection:▶ Quit      Menu Key: C       │
└──────────────────────────────────────────────────────────────────────────┘
┌─Menu Tree─────────────────────────────────────────────────────────────────┐
│  +File                                                                      │
│  +Edit                                                                      │
│  +Style                                                                     │
│       +Alignment                                                            │
│            General                                                          │
│            Left                                                             │
│            Right                                                            │
│            Center                                                           │
│       Numeric Format                                                        │
│       +Protection                                                           │
│                                                                             │
│       Column Width                                                          │
│       Reset Width                                                           │
│       +Hide Column                                                          │
│       +Block Size                                                           │
│                                                                             │
│       Line Drawing                                                          │
│       +Shading                                                              │
│       Font                                                                  │
└─────────────────────────────────────────────────────────────────────────┘
┌─Clipboard Menu────────────────────────────────────────────────────────────┐
│                                                                            │
│                                                                            │
│                                                                            │
│                                                                            │
└────────────────────────────────────────────────────────────────────────────┘
            [0]                                                      READY
```

The Current Item Pane

As mentioned, the Current Item pane lets you apply actions to menu items. Here Quattro Pro displays six fields of information that define the functions of a command. You can use these fields to define or redefine any command currently highlighted in the Menu Tree pane.

The first field, *Desc*, stores a description of the current menu item. This is the description that appears in the status line when you are using a menu item. To accept an existing command description, press Enter. Or you can modify the description by highlighting the Desc field, pressing F2 (Edit), and then typing your edit. To replace the entire command description or insert a new one, simply type it in and then press Enter. Next, you can specify the action you want applied to the menu item.

There are two forms of *Actions* for each menu item, General and Specific. Menu items that do not invoke a specific operation, but instead lead to another command menu, are General actions. Specific action items do just that—immediately result in a specific action. Both General and Specific actions correspond to the menu equivalents for Quattro Pro commands. You'll find a list of these menu equivalents in the @Functions and Macros handbook that came with your Quattro Pro package.

Each menu-equivalent command is composed of a General action and a Specific action. The General action describes the basic category of the command, and the Specific action indicates exactly what the command does. For example, Publish is a General action that corresponds to the /Style command, and AlignCenter is a Specific action that centers the contents of a cell, and corresponds to the Alignment, Center option in the /Style menu. Together, the menu-equivalent keywords Publish, AlignCenter define both General and Specific actions that correspond to the /Style, Alignment, Center command.

To change a General action field, first make the Current Item pane active by pressing Pane (F6) to move to it. Press Tab to highlight the General field, and press Enter or the spacebar to display a list of available actions in the General category. Select the one you want. Once the General action has been defined, press Tab to highlight the Specific action field. Press Enter, and Quattro Pro displays a list of Specific actions that are available for the General action you've selected. Choose the Specific action you want.

Once you have designated a General and Specific action for the menu item, press Tab to move the highlight to the *Selectable?* field in the Current Item pane. Here, you indicate that you want to be able to select the command from a menu, or that the item will be used only to display status information. Most menu items are selectable; for these, type **Y** for Yes. Otherwise, Type **N** for No.

Normally, after you select an item from a menu, Quattro Pro either leaves the menu displayed, returns you to the parent menu, or exits the menu altogether. You must define one of these actions for your custom menu items, using the After Selection field in the Current Item pane. To do this, press Tab to move to the *After Selection* field. Press Enter and you'll see a menu with three choices—Stay, Go to Parent, and Quit. Stay keeps the same command highlighted after it is executed. Go to Parent returns you to the previous menu, and Quit returns you to the spreadsheet. Choose the option you want.

The last field in the Current Item pane is the *Menu Key* field, in which you designate a key the user must press to select the command that is highlighted in the Menu Tree pane. You can type in any letter that is part of the command name. The first letter is a common choice; however, make sure the letter is not the same as other key letters in the current menu. Otherwise, you will have a conflict with another menu item.

The Clipboard Menu Pane

Below the Menu Tree pane, in the Clipboard Menu pane, you will temporarily store and display menu commands that you have deleted, or that you are in the process of moving. As you'll soon see, you can cut a menu item from the current Menu Tree window by highlighting it and pressing the Del key. (See "Deleting a Menu Item.") This action moves the menu item to the Clipboard Menu pane, from which you can paste the menu item to another menu.

Saving the Current Menu

When you make a change to a menu, you can save that menu under the same current .MU filename, or you can specify a different name. To save the current menu, press F10 or / (slash) to activate the Menu Builder's main menu; then select the Save option. You'll see a prompt box listing the names of .MU files in the Quattro Pro program directory. If you are replacing an existing .MU file, highlight its name and press Enter. On the Cancel, Replace, Backup menu that then appears, select Replace to replace the menu file, or Backup to rename the file on disk with a .BAK extension and then save the file in memory with the .MU extension. To save the file under a new name, type a name of eight characters or less and press Enter. Quattro Pro saves the menu file under the name you've specified, and adds the .MU extension. You can now use the /Options, Startup, Menu Tree command to make the new menu current.

Editing a Command Name

You can edit the name of a command in the Menu Tree pane by highlighting the name, and either typing a new name, or pressing Edit (F2) and editing the existing name. To confirm your edit, press Enter.

Adding a Command Name

You can insert a new command anywhere you want in the menu tree. To do this, begin by highlighting the command immediately above where the new item will be added in the Menu Tree pane. Press Enter to have Quattro Pro insert a blank line in the menu tree. Now move to the blank line, and type the name for the new command. Then you can move to the Current Item pane and define the General and Specific actions for the menu item.

When you also need to create a new child menu item for a command, you must first highlight the affected parent command, and then insert the command you want to have in the related child menu. To do this, first open the parent menu, by pressing the + (plus) key on the numeric keypad. Once the parent menu is open, use the arrow keys to move down the existing child menu items until you get to the appropriate spot. Press Enter to insert a blank line in the Menu Tree pane, and then you can type the name for the new child menu item. Press Enter a second time to highlight it. You can then move to the Current Item pane by pressing Pane (F6), and define the General and Specific actions for the new child menu option.

Deleting a Menu Item

It's easy to delete any parent or child menu item; just highlight it in the Menu Tree pane, and press the Del key. When you delete a menu item, Quattro Pro doesn't discard it. Instead, that menu item and its properties are transferred to the Clipboard Menu pane. If you leave the Menu Builder window at this

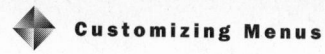
point, Quattro Pro prompts you to save the current menu. If you save the current menu with either a new or existing name, Quattro Pro will save the menu without the item you've deleted.

Deleted menu items that Quattro Pro has placed in the Menu Builder clipboard are not lost. In fact, you can paste these items into another menu, if you so desire, as explained next.

Moving a Menu Item

There are three steps to moving a menu item: First, delete it from the current menu tree by using the Del key, thus placing it in the Clipboard Menu pane. Second, choose the new position for the item in the Menu Tree pane. Finally, paste the menu item from the clipboard into the menu tree, by using the Ins key. Quattro Pro moves the command out of the Clipboard Menu pane, and into the Menu Tree location you've selected.

Perhaps the best way to learn how to move a menu item is through an example. Suppose you want to move the /Style, Alignment, Center child menu command and make it a main menu command, called /Center, between the /Tools and /Options commands. This will give you a main menu bar command for aligning blocks of data in your spreadsheet. To do this, first open the Menu Builder by choosing /Options, Startup, Edit Menus. When you're ready, perform the following steps:

1. When you enter the Menu Builder, Quattro Pro automatically places the highlight in the Menu Tree. Press the → key six times to move the highlight from the /File command through the main menu commands to the /Tools command, and press Enter. This creates a blank space between /Tools and /Options, which is available for pasting in a new menu option.

2. Move the highlight to the /Style, Alignment, Center command in the Menu Tree window. To do this, press ← four times to move back up the list of commands to /Style.

3. Expand the /Style menu to display its child menus by pressing the + key on the numeric keypad.

4. Press → once to move to the Alignment child menu, and press + again to expand Alignment.

5. Press → four more times to highlight the Center option.

6. Press the Del key to remove the highlighted Center option from the current menu and temporarily place it in the Clipboard Menu pane.

7. Move the highlight back to the blank line you created between /Tools and /Options, and press the Ins key. Quattro Pro pastes the /Style, Alignment, Center command, now called Center, in that location.

8. Save the current menu tree by using the /Save command and exit the Menu Builder window with /Exit. Finally, use the /Options, Startup, Menu Tree command to activate your new custom menu tree and test your new menu item.

Attaching a Macro to a Menu

You can also attach an executable macro to a menu command with the Menu Builder's /Attach Macro command. You can add a macro to the main menu, or to one of the child menus (submenus). To do so, however, a spreadsheet file containing the macro must be open on the desktop. For example, suppose you want to attach the \A data-entry macro shown in Figure 15.15 to your /Database menu. (This macro is used to add records to a database of clients.)

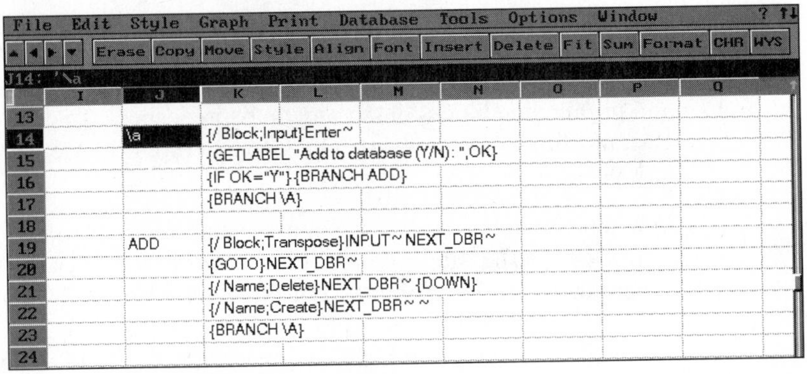

Figure 15.15

A sample data-entry macro named \A

	File	Edit	Style	Graph	Print	Database	Tools	Options	Window		? ↑↓
▲ ◄ ► ▼	Erase	Copy	Move	Style	Align	Font	Insert	Delete	Fit	Sum	Format	CHR	WYS

J14: '\a

	I	J	K	L	M	N	O	P	Q
13									
14		\a	{/ Block;Input}Enter~						
15			{GETLABEL "Add to database (Y/N): ",OK}						
16			{IF OK="Y"}{BRANCH ADD}						
17			{BRANCH \A}						
18									
19		ADD	{/ Block;Transpose}INPUT~ NEXT_DBR~						
20			{GOTO}NEXT_DBR~						
21			{/ Name;Delete}NEXT_DBR~ {DOWN}						
22			{/ Name;Create}NEXT_DBR~ ~						
23			{BRANCH \A}						
24									

Here are the steps:

1. Open the Menu Builder with the /Options, Startup, Edit Menus command.

2. Use the ↓ key to highlight the /Database command in the Menu Tree pane.

3. Press the + key on the numeric keypad to display the /Database child menu, and press → then ↓ four times until you reach the Paradox Access option. Then press Enter to create a blank line after that option.

4. Move to the blank line and type **Add Record**. This will be the name of your new command option.

5. Press Pane (F6) to move to the Current Item window.

6. In the Desc field, type **Adds client's name to custom database**.

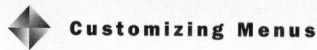
7. Press Tab to move to the General Action field, and press Enter to display the list of General actions. From that list, select Name.

8. Press Tab to move to the Specific Action field, and press Enter to display the list of Specific actions. From that list, select Attach.

9. Tab to the Selectable? field and type Yes (**Y**), if it isn't already selected.

10. Tab to the After Selection field and Enter Stay (**S**), if it isn't already selected.

11. Tab to the Menu Key field and type **A**, if it isn't already there. This will let you type A to access this menu item.

12. Press Pane (F6) to move back into the Menu Tree pane; then select the /Attach Macro command from Menu Builder's menu. Quattro Pro prompts you for the macro name.

13. Type the name of the macro, enclosed in curly braces—in this case **{\A}**—and press Enter.

14. Select /Save from Menu Builder's menu. Quattro Pro prompts you for the name for the new menu file. Type **ADD** and press Enter, to name the menu file ADD.MU.

15. Select /Exit from Menu Builder's menu. Quattro Pro closes the Menu Builder window and returns you to the spreadsheet.

16. Select /Options, Startup, Menu Tree and choose **ADD**. Your new menu item now appears in the menu, as shown in Figure 15.16.

Other Menu Builder Commands

The /Print, /Change Help, and /Options items on the Menu Builder menu let you print the current menu tree, change Quattro Pro's help screens, and set various options for a menu item, as explained in the paragraphs that follow.

The Menu Builder /Print Command

The /Print command on the Menu Builder performs a very simple function: it prints the contents of the Menu Tree pane to your printer, or to a file as ASCII text. When you select the /Print command, Quattro Pro displays a two-option menu with Printer and File. Select Printer to send the data to the current default printer. If you select File, Quattro Pro prompts you for the name of a file. Type the file name of your choice, press Enter, and Quattro Pro prints the contents of the Menu Tree pane to a file with the name you specified, plus an .MNU extension.

Figure 15.16

A menu item added to the /Database menu, to run the \A macro from Figure 15.15

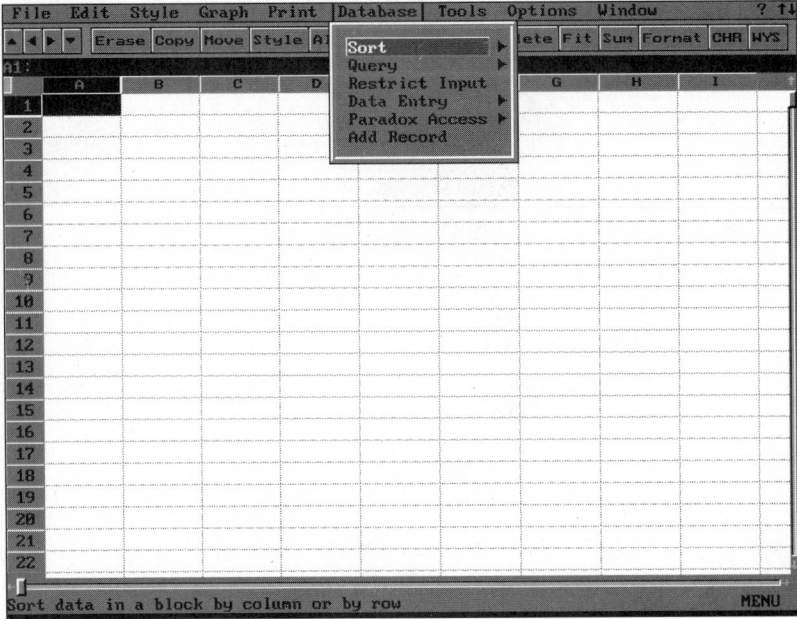

The Menu Builder /Change Help Command

The /Change Help command lets you assign a different help screen to the command currently highlighted in the Menu Tree pane. In preparation for this command, highlight the name of the command whose assigned help screen you want to change. Select the /Change Help command, and Quattro Pro shows you the help screen that is currently assigned to that menu item. Use the keywords from the help index to move to the screen you want. When you are ready, press Esc. Quattro Pro asks you if you want to attach the current help screen to the current menu item. To attach the screen, select Yes; to cancel the operation, select Cancel.

The Menu Builder /Options Command

The /Options menu lets you set the following options to make the current menu compatible with other software programs, such as Lotus 1-2-3:

- *Autoload File* lets you specify the name of a spreadsheet file to be loaded automatically when you start Quattro Pro.

- *File Extension* lets you specify the default file extension Quattro Pro uses for all its spreadsheet files. You might specify .WK1 (or .WK3 in Quattro Pro 4.0) here if you want to maintain compatibility with 1-2-3.

- *Macro Recording* changes between menu-equivalent and keystroke-equivalent macro recording modes. If you don't expect to use your Quattro Pro macros with 1-2-3, it's best to leave Macro Recording set to Logical (the default). Macros will then be recorded using menu-equivalent commands. That way, your macros can be read by any Quattro Pro menu tree.

- *Use Menu Bar* defines whether Quattro Pro displays menus using a horizontal menu bar at the top of the screen (the default), or a system of pop-up menus that disappear whenever you're not using them. The default is to use the menu bar for both the standard Quattro Pro and 1-2-3 menus.

- *Borland Style* designates when and how confirmation and warning prompts are displayed. If you're using the standard Quattro Pro menus, the default setting is Yes. With this setting, a confirmation menu appears whenever you are about to perform an operation that may cause data loss. If you're using 1-2-3 menus, this option is set to No. This means that Quattro Pro uses 1-2-3's standards for confirmation prompts. You may want to use the No option if you want to record macros that are 1-2-3-compatible.

- *During Macros* indicates whether Quattro Pro displays menus while a macro is executing. The default for Quattro Pro and 1-2-3 menus is Yes, which requires that you confirm menus as necessary while a macro is running.

Suppressing the Display During Macro Execution

Normally, Quattro Pro suppresses the redrawing of your screen while a macro is executing. This allows most macros to run much faster, because Quattro Pro is not kept busy redrawing unnecessary screen elements. When the macro is finished running, the screen is updated to reflect any changes brought about by the macro. That way, your screen is refreshed only once instead of multiple times.

You can control the redrawing of your screen during macro execution, using the /Options, Other, Macro command. When you select this command, Quattro Pro displays a menu with the following options:

- *Both* suppresses menu/prompt displays, as well as spreadsheet redrawing (the default).

- *Panel* suppresses menu/prompt displays only.

- *Window* suppresses spreadsheet redrawing only.

- *None* enables both spreadsheet redrawing and menu/prompt displays.

The effects of the /Options, Other, Macro command are directly related to the {PANELON}, {PANELOFF}, {WINDOWSON}, and {WINDOW-SOFF} advanced macro commands (discussed at length in Chapter 13). These commands are provided solely for compatibility with Lotus 1-2-3. Briefly, {PANELON} and {PANELOFF} turn the display of menus and prompts on and off during macro execution. {WINDOWSON} and {WIN-DOWSOFF} turn redrawing of the spreadsheet window on and off.

When /Options, Other, Macro is set to None, the {WINDOWSOFF} and {PANELOFF} commands will have the intended effect—that is, they will act as they do in the 1-2-3 environment. You might want to use /Options, Other, Macro, None when you are running a 1-2-3 macro that contains {PANELON}, {PANELOFF}, {WINDOWSON}, or {WINDOWSOFF} commands, or when you are preparing a macro in Quattro Pro for use in 1-2-3.

Changing the Clock Display

Normally Quattro Pro displays file information at the left side of the status line. You can, however, replace this information with the current date and time. Select the /Options, Other, Clock command, and Quattro Pro displays a menu with the following options:

- *None* displays no clock (the default).

- *Standard* displays the date and time in standard format—for dates, DD-MMM-YY, and for times, HH:MM AM/PM.

- *International* displays date and time in the formats indicated by the /Options, International, Date and Time settings, discussed earlier in the chapter.

When you make a selection, Quattro Pro displays the date and time in your chosen format for the remainder of the current session. To save the clock settings for future sessions, select /Options, Update.

Quattro Pro obtains its date and time displays from your computer's internal clock. If the display is incorrect, you can change the date and time settings by using the /File, Utilities, DOS Shell command, and using either the DOS Time or Date command.

Memory Management

Both Quattro Pro 3.0 and Quattro Pro 4.0 support the VROOMM memory manager, which makes it possible to store larger and more complex spreadsheets than could be stored in previous versions of Quattro Pro. VROOMM stands for Virtual Runtime Object-Oriented Memory Manager. See "Placing the VROOMM Object Cache in Extended Memory" later for details on how VROOMM works.

Like previous versions, versions 3.0 and 4.0 are capable of using both conventional memory (sometimes called standard, system, or normal memory) and expanded memory to store your spreadsheets. Conventional memory is defined as the first 640K of RAM (random access memory) that is directly addressable by DOS.

Expanded memory, on the other hand, can come from either an expanded memory card, or an expanded memory manager (EMM)—for example, QEMM from Quarter Deck. In the case of an expanded memory card, Quattro Pro automatically recognizes whatever expanded memory the card has. On the other hand, an EMM is capable of *emulating* expanded memory by using extended memory. Extended memory is only available on machines with one full megabyte of memory or more.

Quattro Pro supports the LIM (Lotus-Intel-Microsoft) 4.0 expanded memory specification, which allows Quattro Pro to access up to 8Mb of expanded (EMS) memory. Therefore, if you are considering purchase of an expanded memory card for your machine, make sure it conforms to the LIM 4.0 specification (most do). Quattro Pro also supports the LIM 3.2 standard, allowing it to access up to 4Mb of extended memory.

Note. Quattro Pro is also capable of using extended memory to store part of its program code. See "Placing the VROOMM Object Cache in Extended Memory" later for details.

Checking Available Memory

The /Options, Hardware command menu makes it easy to check how much memory is available to Quattro Pro. As shown in Figure 15.17, the bottom two-thirds of this menu reports information about conventional memory and expanded (EMS) memory. Both sections show memory in bytes, including available memory, total memory, and the percent of total memory that is still available for use.

Configuring Expanded Memory

If you have expanded memory, Quattro Pro automatically recognizes it, and uses it to store your spreadsheet data. Often, having expanded memory available allows you to create larger and more complex spreadsheets.

Quattro Pro uses expanded memory to store spreadsheet values, labels, and formulas, as well as pointers to labels and formulas. Quattro Pro can also store formatting information in expanded memory. As a result, more conventional memory is made available for the operation of Quattro Pro itself. This both improves the overall performance of Quattro Pro and lets you load larger and more complex spreadsheets.

Figure 15.17

The /Options, Hardware menu's data on available memory

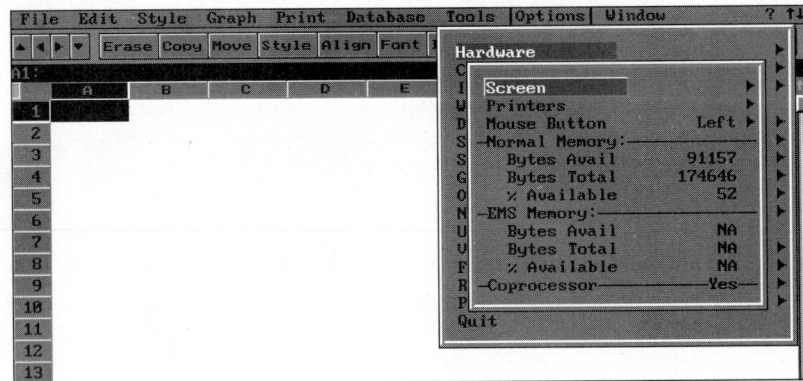

When you want to work with your data, Quattro Pro must move that data out of expanded memory and into conventional memory. This is a time-consuming process that can noticeably slow down Quattro Pro's operation. For this reason, only part of your spreadsheet information (its data) is stored in expanded memory. All formatting information is stored in conventional memory, along with most of Quattro Pro's program code. In this way, Quattro Pro attempts to strike a balance between data storage and performance issues. The trade-off is that you may run out of conventional memory if you are working with exceptionally large or multiple spreadsheets that have lots of formatting, though you may have a substantial amount of expanded memory available.

If a shortage of conventional memory becomes a problem for you, you might consider changing the way that Quattro Pro uses expanded memory. To do this, use the /Options, Other, Expanded Memory command. When you select this command, Quattro Pro displays a menu with the following options:

- *Both* stores both spreadsheet data and cell formatting in expanded memory.

- *Spreadsheet Data* stores spreadsheet cell data (values, labels, and formulas) in expanded memory.

- *Format* stores cell formatting in expanded memory.

- *None* eliminates the use of expanded memory by Quattro Pro.

The Both option may provide the solution you are looking for, but it may cause a decline in Quattro Pro's performance.

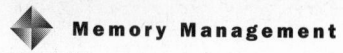

When you make a change with the /Options, Other, Expanded Memory command, you must close all open spreadsheet windows and then reopen them for your change to take effect.

Tips on Saving Memory

Here are some tips you may find useful when memory gets tight.

- Build several smaller spreadsheets and link them together with link formulas, rather than building one large spreadsheet.

- Use Hershey instead of Bitstream fonts to format your data. (Quattro Pro needs 125K of free memory to create a new Bitstream font.)

- Formulas require more memory than values. If you have formulas whose values you are sure will not change, use the /Edit, Values command to convert them to their current values.

- Preformatting large areas of a spreadsheet can consume extensive memory. It's better to format only small areas of the spreadsheet as needed. An even better solution is to set a global format for the spreadsheet by using /Options, Formats.

- Try to design your spreadsheet so that its information is as close to the left edge of the spreadsheet as possible. Quattro Pro uses less memory to store information in rows than it does in columns.

- Use @SUM to add columns or rows of values. Avoid using the plus (+) symbol together with cell references.

- If you have expanded memory, use the /Options, Other, Expanded Memory, Both command to have Quattro Pro store both cell contents and cell formatting in expanded memory.

Startup Techniques

As you learned in Chapter 5, if you provide a spreadsheet or workspace file name on the DOS command line when you start Quattro Pro, it will automatically load the file you specify. For example, to load the file BUDGET.WQ1 at startup, you might enter **Q BUDGET**.

There are a number of other parameters that you can use from the DOS command line to configure various startup options for Quattro Pro. To do this, use a command line that takes the following form:

```
Q filename macroname /options
```

The *filename* argument is the name of a spreadsheet file you want Quattro Pro to load automatically. If the file is located in a directory other than the current one, make sure you precede the file name with the appropriate path. This file specification will override the current /Options, Startup, Autoload File setting.

The *macroname* argument is the block name of a macro you want Quattro Pro to run automatically. This argument can be used together with the [*filename*] argument to load a specific spreadsheet and also start a specific macro. This macro name specification overrides the current /Options, Startup, Startup Macro setting.

The */options* argument designates one or more startup switches, preceded by a / (slash), that configure the operation of Quattro Pro. For example, you might specify a default configuration file other than RSC.RF. Or, you might configure the amount of expanded memory available to Quattro Pro. All the startup switches are explained in the remaining paragraphs of this section.

Suppose you want to start Quattro Pro, load a file named CUST.WQ1 in the C:\QPRO\SHEETS directory, and run a macro named DENTER in that file. You can specify all these items in the DOS command line, as follows:

```
Q C:\QPRO\SHEETS\CUST DENTER
```

Loading an Alternate Configuration File

As explained earlier in this chapter under "Your Default System Settings," Quattro Pro gets its default settings from a file named RSC.RF. This is the file that is updated when you select the /Options, Update command to save the current default system settings, including any changes you have made. Quattro Pro reads this file each time you start the program.

There is nothing magic about the RSC.RF file name. In fact, you can create several different default configuration files for Quattro Pro, under different file names, and specify at startup the one you want. To do this, first configure the appropriate options on Quattro Pro's /Options menu. Then use /Options, Update to update the RSC.RF file. Next, leave Quattro Pro, and use the DOS COPY command to copy the RSC.RF file to another name of your choosing—for example, CFG1.RF. (The new file name must have an .RF extension.) You can then start Quattro Pro and use the settings in your new configuration file by using the /D switch at the DOS command line, for example:

```
Q/DCFG1.RF
```

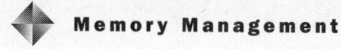
Loading Quattro Pro with the Autodetect Screen Driver

You can use the /I switch to start Quattro Pro with the Autodetect screen hardware feature enabled. Using this switch at the DOS prompt is equivalent to entering the /Options, Hardware, Screen, Screen Type, Autodetect Driver command from within Quattro Pro. With this driver selected, Quattro Pro will at startup check your machine's BIOS and determine the type of video display driver (EGA, VGA, and so on) that you are currently using. To use this switch, type **Q/I** at the DOS prompt to start Quattro Pro.

Choosing a Default Color Palette

You can also add arguments to the /I switch to automatically load a specific color palette at startup. The following three options are available:

- /IC loads Quattro Pro with a color palette.

- /IM loads Quattro Pro with a monochrome palette.

- /IB loads Quattro Pro with a black-and-white palette.

Using these /I switch arguments is equivalent to using the /Options, Colors, Palettes command from within Quattro Pro.

Limiting Quattro Pro's Use of Expanded Memory

You can limit the amount of expanded memory used by Quattro Pro by starting the program with the /E switch. This switch takes a numeric argument, from 0 to 63555, that lets you allocate expanded memory for Quattro Pro's exclusive use in 16K pages. You might want to use this option to make more expanded memory available for TSR (terminate-and-stay-resident) programs that use expanded memory.

For example, to have Quattro Pro not use any expanded memory at all, you can start the program with **Q/E0** at the DOS prompt. On the other hand, if you want to limit Quattro Pro's use of expanded memory to eight 16K pages (128K), enter **Q/E8**.

To determine the number of expanded memory pages you have to work with, select the /Options, Hardware command; note the value for EMS Memory, Bytes Total, and divide this by 16K (16,000). If you use the /E switch to allocate more expanded memory pages than are physically available, Quattro Pro will simply use all the expanded memory that is available.

Placing the VROOMM Object Cache in Extended Memory

Along with Quattro Pro, you automatically get the VROOMM memory management technology (Virtual Real-time Object-Oriented Memory Manager), which allows you to create larger spreadsheet applications.

Unlike some spreadsheet programs that load a few large overlay files into memory as needed, Quattro Pro is composed of hundreds of smaller object modules. The various operations of Quattro Pro require different executable object modules. The VROOMM memory manager loads only those object modules that are required to support those operations currently under way in the spreadsheets you have open. What's more, when an object module is no longer required, the VROOMM memory manager discards it from memory. The result is that only the minimum amount of Quattro Pro's program code is resident in memory at any given time, leaving the maximum amount of memory available for your spreadsheet data.

If you have extended memory, you can enhance program operation by creating a VROOMM Object Cache. This cache allows VROOMM to store its executable object modules in memory, rather than loading them from disk. The result is a noticeable improvement in performance. However, this option is available only if your computer has one full megabyte of memory or more.

To take advantage of the VROOMM Object Cache, use the /X switch when you start Quattro Pro. This switch lets Quattro Pro use up to 512K of extended memory to store its executable object modules. At the DOS prompt, type **Q/X**.

Another advanced feature of the VROOMM memory manager is its ability to intelligently store recurring formulas and labels that have the same structure. It does this by maintaining pointers to the original formula or label, rather than creating separate formulas or labels and storing them in memory individually. The pointers require less memory. For example, suppose you have a formula that adds the values in a row of a spreadsheet. You copy that formula down the column, replicating it ten times. Rather than storing ten new formulas, Quattro Pro creates ten pointers to the original formula.

Using DOS Batch Files

Typing startup switch parameters at the DOS prompt each time you want to start Quattro Pro can be a tedious process. It's much easier to create a DOS batch (.BAT) file that contains the appropriate command line entries, and then run that .BAT file to start Quattro Pro.

You can create a DOS .BAT file by using the COPY CON command (see your DOS manual) or by using any word processor capable of reading and writing ASCII files—for example, WordPerfect. However, make sure you save the file with a .BAT extension.

Consider, for example, a DOS batch file that contains the following statement:

```
Q %1 /X
```

The Q starts Quattro Pro. Following this, the %1 allows you to pass a parameter to the batch file (in this case, the file name of a spreadsheet you want loaded automatically). Finally, the /X switch takes advantage of the VROOMM Object Cache. Once these command lines have been typed, save the file as an ASCII file with a .BAT extension in a directory that is included in your PATH statement. For example, you might assign the name 1.BAT to this file.

Once the .BAT file has been created, you can now run this batch file from the DOS prompt, by typing **1** followed by a space and the name of a spreadsheet or workspace file you want loaded automatically. For example,

```
1 MYFILE
```

starts Quattro Pro, loads the file MYFILE.WQ1, and sets up the VROOMM Object Cache.

Running Quattro Pro Under Windows 3.x

In recognition of the commercial success of Windows 3.x, Borland has made several provisions for running Quattro Pro under Windows. This section introduces those provisions, and offers tips and techniques for running Quattro Pro under Windows 3.0 and higher.

During Installation

When you install Quattro Pro 3.0, you are asked if you want to install for Windows. If you elect to do so, Quattro Pro copies the appropriate files to your Quattro Pro program directory. You are then asked for the path to your Windows directory. At that point, Quattro Pro's Install program searches your Windows program directory to find the WIN.INI configuration file. Install then modifies the RUN= statement in this file to reference a special Windows program called SETUP.EXE in your QPRO directory, for example, RUN=C:\QPRO\SETUP.EXE. That way, the next time you start Windows, the SETUP.EXE program will be run automatically.

Quattro Pro's SETUP.EXE program is actually a Windows application that performs several functions. First, it creates a Program Manager group window entitled QPRO. Next, it places an icon for Quattro Pro in that group window. Finally, it restores the RUN= statement in your WIN.INI file to its original form, eliminating the reference to the SETUP.EXE program. When this process is complete, a small dialog box appears; select OK to clear it. You can now run Quattro Pro under Windows by double-clicking on its icon in the QPRO group window.

About the Quattro Pro Icon

The Quattro Pro icon is displayed by using a file called Q.ICO that resides in your Quattro Pro program directory. In fact, if you use Program Manager's File Properties command and select the Change Icon button, you'll see a reference to the Q.ICO file—for example C:\QPRO\Q.ICO. Keep this in mind if you accidentally or intentionally delete the Quattro Pro icon and need to set it up again. (If you're running Windows 3.1, the Quattro Pro icon in MORICONS.DLL is used.)

Recommended .PIF File Settings

Quattro Pro comes with its own .PIF (Program Information File) named Q.PIF. This file resides in your Quattro Pro program directory. In Windows, .PIF files tell Windows how to best allocate resources to a DOS application such as Quattro Pro.

When you start Quattro Pro from within Windows by using the Quattro Pro icon, the Q.PIF file is run automatically. In fact, if you select Program Manager's File Properties command to display the Program Item Properties dialog box for the Quattro Pro icon, you'll see a reference to the Q.PIF file in the Command Line Text box—for example C:\QPRO\Q.PIF.

Generally speaking, you should run Quattro Pro under Windows by using the Q.PIF file. Borland has made a special effort to set up this file appropriately. If you don't run Quattro Pro by using Q.PIF, you may experience reduced performance, especially in WYSIWYG mode.

Figures 15.18 and 15.19 show the default settings for the Q.PIF file. These illustrations are actually pictures of the Windows 3.1 PIF Editor in 386 Enhanced mode. (To look at these settings yourself, simply double-click on the PIF Editor icon in the Accessories group window, and use File Open to open the Q.PIF file located in your QPRO directory.)

If you are running Windows in 386 Enhanced mode, there is one minor memory use change you may want to make to the Q.PIF file. (In addition, you may have needs of your own.) For this reason, here is an overview of the settings in the Q.PIF file.

- *Program Filename* The default entry is Q.EXE, which starts Quattro Pro. You shouldn't need to change this entry.

- *Start-up Directory* The default entry is a reference to your Quattro Pro program directory, for example, C:\QPRO. Thus your Quattro Pro program directory is the default working directory for the application. You don't need to change this. You can easily override this setting by using the /File, Directory or /Options, Startup, Startup Directory command from within Quattro Pro.

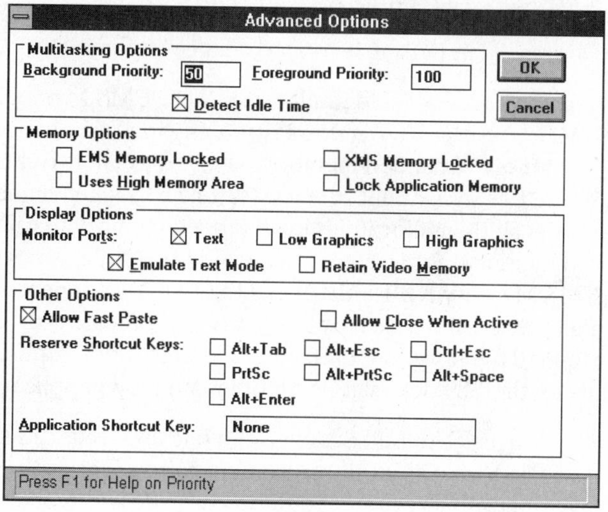

Figure 15.18

The advanced options for the Q.PIF file under Windows 3.1

Figure 15.19

The Windows 3.1 PIF Editor window with Q.PIF loaded (386 Enhanced mode)

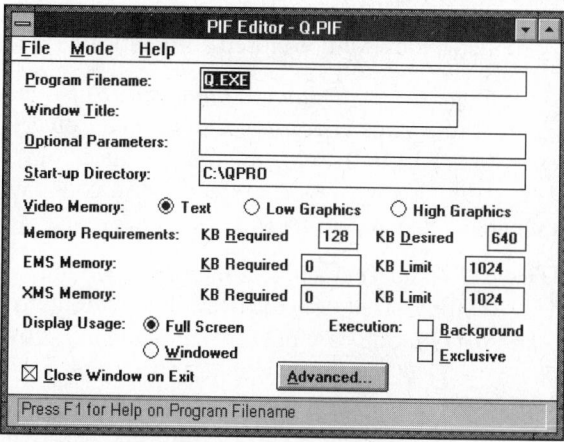

- *Video Memory*   The Text radio button is selected here. This setting should be appropriate in most instances. However, if you are running Quattro Pro in WYSIWYG mode and you experience screen-redraw problems when you switch away from Quattro Pro and then switch back, you may want to try the High Graphics radio button. In addition, you may want to select the Retain Video Memory check box in the Advanced Options dialog box (Figure 15.19).

- *KB Required*   The setting is 128; no change needed.

- *KB Desired*   The setting is 640; no change needed.

- *Memory Required*   The default settings are EMS Memory 1024 and XMS Memory 1024. If Windows is running in 386 Enhanced mode, and you want more expanded memory allocated to Quattro Pro, you can increase the EMS KB Limit Memory setting to a value higher than 1024. Windows will then allocate more extended memory to Quattro Pro as expanded memory, if it is available. In addition, you may want to change the XMS Memory KB Limit setting to 0. This is not necessary—in fact, a setting other than 0 here may inadvertently allocate a significant chunk of extended memory to Quattro Pro (though it doesn't use extended memory), thereby depriving your other Windows applications.

- *Display Usage*   The Full Screen radio button is selected here, causing Quattro Pro to run as a full-screen application. This is the appropriate setting, especially if you intend to use WYSIWYG mode. You'll learn why later, under "Problems When Running Quattro Pro in a Window Under Windows 3.0."

- *Close Window on Exit*   This box is checked, so that when you leave Quattro Pro, its window will be closed automatically.

- *Multitasking Options* (*386 Enhanced mode only*)   Notice in Figure 15.19 that the Detect Idle Time check box is selected. (You can access the dialog boxes in Figure 15.19 by selecting the Advanced button in Figure 15.18.) This setting is very important; without it, you may notice a slowdown in Quattro Pro's performance.

- *Display Options*   The Text and Emulate Text Mode check boxes are selected. These settings are fine. However, if you intend to run Quattro Pro in WYSIWYG mode, you may notice a slight improvement in performance if you select the High Graphics check box as well.

Tip. If you have a large spreadsheet and are using a substantial amount of expanded memory, turn on the Locked check box in the EMS Memory section. Otherwise, Windows may page your expanded memory out to disk.

Problems When Running Quattro Pro in a Window Under Windows 3.0

To run in WYSIWYG mode, Quattro Pro must use high-resolution graphics. Therefore, you will have some problems running Quattro Pro in a window under Windows 3.0. (This problem has been solved under Windows 3.1.) You can display Quattro Pro in a window, but you can't invoke any commands or enter any data. For example, suppose you currently have Quattro Pro running in WYSIWYG mode as a full-screen display in 386 Enhanced mode under Windows 3.0. Let's say you press Alt-Enter to switch to a windowed display. Everything goes well until you press the / key to select a menu item, or press a keyboard key to enter data. At that point, Windows displays an error message informing you that the current application is using high-resolution graphics and that it will be suspended until you return to a full-screen display. When you clear the message and press Alt-Enter to return to a full-screen display, Quattro Pro again runs just fine.

To solve this problem, simply run Quattro Pro in Character mode, rather than WYSIWYG. When you press Alt-Enter to switch to a windowed display, Quattro Pro will appear in its own window, and you can then work with the program as you normally do. Although Windows will monitor Quattro Pro's operation it will not interfere with it.

Using Expanded Memory Under Windows

In addition to conventional memory, Quattro Pro can use expanded memory, allowing you to build larger and more complex spreadsheets. Here are techniques you can use to make expanded memory available when running Quattro Pro under Windows.

386 Enhanced Mode

In 386 Enhanced mode, Windows can use extended memory to emulate expanded memory, and allocate that memory to DOS applications, such as Quattro Pro, that request it (assuming that sufficient extended memory is available). To have Quattro Pro request expanded memory from Windows, you must make the appropriate setting in the .PIF file for the application. The Q.PIF file that comes with Quattro Pro already contains a setting that should be appropriate in most instances. See the earlier section, "Recommended .PIF File Settings."

Standard Mode

If you are running Windows in Standard mode, there is no provision for allocating expanded memory to Quattro Pro. Instead, you must rely on other means. For example, if you have an expanded memory board properly installed, Quattro Pro will recognize that board automatically. Or you can install some memory management software, such as QEMM from Quarter Deck, which is capable of using extended memory to emulate expanded memory. Quattro Pro will also recognize that memory automatically.

Windows 3.0 Real Mode

If you are running Windows 3.0 in Real mode, you can still make expanded memory available to Quattro Pro. On a 286 computer with an expanded memory board properly installed, Quattro Pro will recognize that memory automatically. For a 386 computer with one megabyte of memory or more, you can use the EMM386.SYS device driver that comes with Windows. Once again, this software is capable of using extended memory to emulate expanded memory, and Quattro Pro will use it automatically.

INDEX

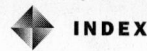

F

for headers and footers, 383

Hershey, 196–197

libraries of, 197–198, 200–202

and page length settings, 372–374

printer-specific, 196, 197, 357, 367, 986–988

for printing, 365–368

proportionally spaced, 194–195, 378–379

raster, 193

and row heights, 206–208

scalable outline, 193–194

shared on networks, 957

soft, 196

for spreadsheet publishing, 193–206

footers. *See* headers and footers

{FOR} macro programming command, 902, 923–924

{FORBREAK} macro programming command, 902, 924

foreground recalculation, 90

form feeds, 348–349

Format (SpeedBar icon), 14, 162

FORMAT CODES, 177

format lines, 330, 331–333

formatting, 151. *See also* numeric formatting

by aligning data, 154–159

with bulleted lists, 214–216

of columns, 182–192

example of spreadsheet publishing, 216–220

and fonts, 193–208

globally or by blocks, 151–154

with lines and boxes, 210–214

with named styles in version 4.0, 220–225

of numeric data, 159–175

of numeric data with user-defined formats, 176–182

and shading effects, 208–210

forms, customizing for database data entry, 764–765

formula cell, 799

Formula contains hot links (message), 145

formulas. *See also* link formulas; recalculation

adding notes to, 50

block insertion/deletion with version 4.0, 87, 89

block selection with, 55–56

with circular references, 94–97

of constraints (simultaneous linear equations), 810–812

copying, 249, 252–260

copying to disk files, 324–326

copying as values, 263–266

data table, 789, 790, 791–792, 794, 796

displaying in text form, 172–173

entering in cells, 40–42

error values, 48

with forward reference, 94

functions, 47–48

logical, 46–47

in macros, 951–952

moving between files, 241–242

moving within files, 236–239

numeric, 42–46

order of precedence, 48–50

as query criteria, 736–739

referencing cells in, 43–46

with relative/absolute/mixed references, 252–258

row/column insertion or deletion, 84–86

row/column transpositions, 268–269

search and replace operations on, 64–67

solving backwards for data analysis, 797–804

string, 46, 233

forward reference, 94

free cell, 54

frequency distribution, 767–771

FRMT indicator, 5

full view, 307

function keys. *See also* F2 *etc.*

for cell selector movement, 17

tasks assigned to, 8–10

functions

add-in, 458–459, 515–516

arguments used in, 416–417

date, 436–444

depreciation, 505–509

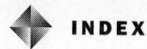

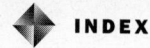

typestyles. *See* fonts

U

U, as protection status indicator, 3, 146

underlining, 36, 195–196

underscore, in block names, 58

Undo (Alt-F5), 64, 73

Undo feature, 72–74

@UPPER FU, 469–470

user input, getting for macros, 902, 907–908

user-defined numeric formats, 176–182

users, adding to networks, 960–961

V

Value block, for frequency distribution
    analysis, 767–769

@VALUE function, 477–478

VALUE indicator, 6, 30, 37

:value suffix, for macro programming
    commands, 916

values. *See also* formulas; recalculation

    absolute, 418

    adding in database fields, 760

    adding numerically from other
        spreadsheets, 321–322

    as arguments for functions, 416

    calculating maximum and minimum,
        432–433

    calculating with /Tools, Advanced Math,
        Multiply command, 786–787

    concatenating with labels, 476–477

    converting from strings, 477–478

    converting to strings, 476–477

    copying formulas as, 263–266

    copying to disk files, 324–326

    counting in database fields, 759–760

    defined, 30, 37

    entering in cells, 37–38

    entering sequential with /Edit, Fill,
        227–230

    evaluating with @IF function, 450

    finding highest and lowest in database
        records, 760–761

    graph data series as, 528

as query criteria, 736

random number generation, 421

returning last acted upon, 514

search and replace operations on, 67–69

specifying for storage in compressed files,
    288–289

substitution, 788, 791, 794, 795

subtracting numerically from other
    spreadsheets, 322–323

testing for, 457–458

for time calculations, 444–445

@VAR function, 433–434

variable cells, 799–800, 830–831

variables

    dependent and independent, 772

    relationships between (regression
        analysis), 772

variance, 433

    for database fields, 761–763

@VARS function, 434–435

version 3.0

    assigning new fonts in, 202–205

    Character display mode in, 7

    circular references as problems in, 95

    default font as Swiss 12-point, 85

    default fonts available with, 197

    mouse palette feature, 2, 12, 13

    print layout options in, 350

    question mark for help feature, 11

version 4.0

    alphabetical list of help topics, 11

    analytical graphing in, 621–630

    assigning new fonts in, 202–205

    block insertion and deletion in, 87–90

    bubble graphs new to, 530

    Character display mode in, 7

    customizable functions in, 415

    default fonts available with, 197

    using dialog boxes in, 30

    display of named block notes in, 60

    display of print blocks in, 357

    /Edit, Copy Special command, 227,
        250–251

    file handling enhancements in, 271

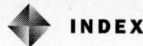